Lecture Notes in Computer Science   12550

More information about this subseries at http://www.springer.com/series/7410

Rafael Pass · Krzysztof Pietrzak (Eds.)

Theory of Cryptography

18th International Conference, TCC 2020
Durham, NC, USA, November 16–19, 2020
Proceedings, Part I

 Springer

Editors
Rafael Pass
Cornell Tech
New York, NY, USA

Krzysztof Pietrzak
Institute of Science and Technology Austria
Klosterneuburg, Austria

ISSN 0302-9743 ISSN 1611-3349 (electronic)
Lecture Notes in Computer Science
ISBN 978-3-030-64374-4 ISBN 978-3-030-64375-1 (eBook)
https://doi.org/10.1007/978-3-030-64375-1

LNCS Sublibrary: SL4 – Security and Cryptology

This Springer imprint is published by the registered company Springer Nature Switzerland AG
The registered company address is: Gewerbestrasse 11, 6330 Cham, Switzerland

Preface

The 18th Theory of Cryptography Conference (TCC 2020) was held virtually during November 16–19, 2020. It was sponsored by the International Association for Cryptologic Research (IACR). The general chair of the conference was Alessandra Scafuro.

TCC 2020 was originally planned to be co-located with FOCS 2020 in Durham, North Carolina, USA. Due to the COVID-19 pandemic both events were converted into virtual events, and were held on the same day at the same time. The authors uploaded videos of roughly 20 minutes prior to the conference, and at the conference had a 10-minute window to present a summary of their work and answer questions. The virtual event would not have been possible without the generous help of Kevin and Kay McCurley, and we would like to thank them wholeheartedly.

The conference received 167 submissions, of which the Program Committee (PC) selected 71 for presentation. Each submission was reviewed by at least four PC members. The 39 PC members (including PC chairs), all top researchers in the field, were helped by 226 external reviewers, who were consulted when appropriate. These proceedings consist of the revised version of the 71 accepted papers. The revisions were not reviewed, and the authors bear full responsibility for the content of their papers.

As in previous years, we used Shai Halevi's excellent Web-review software, and are extremely grateful to him for writing it, and for providing fast and reliable technical support whenever we had any questions.

This was the 7th year that TCC presented the Test of Time Award to an outstanding paper that was published at TCC at least eight years ago, making a significant contribution to the theory of cryptography, preferably with influence also in other areas of cryptography, theory, and beyond. This year the Test of Time Award Committee selected the following paper, published at TCC 2008: "Perfectly-Secure MPC with Linear Communication Complexity" by Zuzana Trubini and Martin Hirt. The Award Committee recognized this paper "for introducing hyper-invertible matrices to perfectly secure multiparty computation, thus enabling significant efficiency improvements and, eventually, constructions with minimal communication complexity."

We are greatly indebted to many people who were involved in making TCC 2020 a success. A big thanks to the authors who submitted their papers and to the PC members and external reviewers for their hard work, dedication, and diligence in reviewing the papers, verifying the correctness, and in-depth discussions. A special thanks goes to the general chair Alessandra Scafuro and the TCC Steering Committee.

October 2020

Rafael Pass
Krzysztof Pietrzak

Organization

General Chair

Alessandra Scafuro   North Carolina State University, USA

Program Chairs

Rafael Pass   Cornell Tech, USA
Krzysztof Pietrzak   IST Austria, Austria

Program Committee

Prabhanjan Ananth	University of California, Santa Barbara, USA
Marshall Ball	Columbia University, USA
Sonia Belaïd	CryptoExperts, France
Jeremiah Blocki	Purdue University, USA
Andrej Bogdanov	The Chinese University of Hong Kong, Hong Kong
Chris Brzuszka	Aalto University, Finland
Ignacio Cascudo	IMDEA Software Institute, Spain
Kai-Min Chung	Academia Sinica, Taiwan
Aloni Cohen	Boston University, USA
Ran Cohen	Northeastern University, USA
Nico Dottling	CISPA - Helmholtz Center for Information Security, Germany
Stefan Dziembowski	University of Warsaw, Poland
Oriol Farràs	Universitat Rovira i Virgili, Spain
Georg Fuchsbauer	TU Wien, Austria
Niv Gilboa	Ben-Gurion University of the Negev, Israel
Vipul Goyal	Carnegie Mellon University, USA
Mohammad Hajiabadi	University of California, Berkeley, USA
Justin Holmgren	NTT Research, USA
Zahra Jafargholi	Aarhus University, Denmark
Yael Tauman Kalai	Microsoft Research and MIT, USA
Seny Kamara	Brown University, USA
Dakshita Khurana	University of Illinois Urbana-Champaign, USA
Markulf Kohlweiss	The University of Edinburgh, UK
Ilan Komargodski	NTT Research, USA
Huijia Lin	University of Washington, USA
Mohammad Mahmoody	University of Virginia, USA
Jesper Buus Nielsen	Aarhus University, Denmark
Emmanuela Orsini	KU Leuven, Belgium
Sunoo Park	MIT and Harvard University, USA

Anat Paskin-Cherniavsky	Ariel University, Israel
Oxana Poburinnaya	Simons Institute for the Theory of Computing, USA
Silas Richelson	University of California, Riverside, USA
Alon Rosen	IDC Herzliya, Israel
Abhi Shelat	Northeastern University, USA
Nicholas Spooner	University of California, Berkeley, USA
Uri Stemmer	Ben-Gurion University of the Negev, Israel
Justin Thaler	Georgetown University, USA
Daniel Wichs	Northeastern University and NTT Research, USA
Eylon Yogev	Boston University, USA, and Tel Aviv University, Israel

External Reviewers

Hamza Abusalah	Yilei Chen	Rex Fernando
Amit Agarwal	Ilaria Chillotti	Ben Fisch
Archita Agarwal	Arka Rai Choudhuri	Cody Freitag
Divesh Aggarwal	Hao Chung	Shiuan Fu
Navid Alamati	Michele Ciampi	Tommaso Gagliardoni
Younes Talibi Alaoui	Katriel Cohn-Gordon	Chaya Ganesh
Bar Alon	Sandro Coretti	Sanjam Garg
Joel Alwen	Sandro Coretti-Drayton	Romain Gay
Joël Alwen	Henry Corrigan-Gibbs	Marilyn George
Miguel Ambrona	Geoffroy Couteau	Marios Georgiou
Ghous Amjad	Dana Dachman-Soled	Essam Ghadafi
Christian Badertscher	Hila Dahari	Alexandru Gheorghiu
Saikrishna	Jost Daniel	Satrajit Ghosh
Badrinarayanan	Pratish Datta	Aarushi Goel
James Bartusek	Bernardo David	Sasha Golovnev
Balthazar Bauer	Bernardo Machado David	Junqing Gong
Carsten Baum	Gareth Davies	Rishab Goyal
Alex Block	Akshay Degwekar	Daniel Grier
Alexander Block	Jack Doerner	Alex Grilo
Jonathan Bootle	Rafael Dowsley	Siyao Guo
Adam Bouland	Betul Durak	Iftach Haitner
Elette Boyle	Betül Durak	Britta Hale
Zvika Brakerski	Naomi Ephraim	Ariel Hamlin
Pedro Branco	Daniel Escudero	Adam Blatchley Hansen
Benedikt Bünz	Grzegorz Fabianski	Alexander Hartl
Alper Cakan	Islam Faisal	Carmit Hazay
Matteo Campanelli	Xiong Fan	Javier Herranz
Wouter Castryck	Song Fang	Kyle Hogan
Hubert Chan	Antonio Faonio	Thibaut Horel
Lijie Chen	Prastudy Fauzi	Yao-Ching Hsieh
Yanlin Chen	Serge Fehr	James Hulett

Contents – Part I

Lossiness and Entropic Hardness for Ring-LWE 1
  Zvika Brakerski and Nico Döttling

Multi-key Fully-Homomorphic Encryption in the Plain Model 28
  Prabhanjan Ananth, Abhishek Jain, Zhengzhong Jin,
  and Giulio Malavolta

Constant Ciphertext-Rate Non-committing Encryption from Standard
Assumptions 58
  Zvika Brakerski, Pedro Branco, Nico Döttling, Sanjam Garg,
  and Giulio Malavolta

Efficient Range-Trapdoor Functions and Applications: Rate-1 OT
and More 88
  Sanjam Garg, Mohammad Hajiabadi, and Rafail Ostrovsky

CP-ABE for Circuits (and More) in the Symmetric Key Setting 117
  Shweta Agrawal and Shota Yamada

Optimal Broadcast Encryption from LWE and Pairings in the Standard
Model 149
  Shweta Agrawal, Daniel Wichs, and Shota Yamada

Equipping Public-Key Cryptographic Primitives with Watermarking
(or: A Hole Is to Watermark) 179
  Ryo Nishimaki

Functional Encryption for Quadratic Functions from k-Lin, Revisited 210
  Hoeteck Wee

On Perfect Correctness in (Lockable) Obfuscation 229
  Rishab Goyal, Venkata Koppula, Satyanarayana Vusirikala,
  and Brent Waters

Can a Public Blockchain Keep a Secret? 260
  Fabrice Benhamouda, Craig Gentry, Sergey Gorbunov, Shai Halevi,
  Hugo Krawczyk, Chengyu Lin, Tal Rabin, and Leonid Reyzin

Blockchains from Non-idealized Hash Functions 291
  Juan A. Garay, Aggelos Kiayias, and Giorgos Panagiotakos

Ledger Combiners for Fast Settlement 322
  Matthias Fitzi, Peter Gaži, Aggelos Kiayias, and Alexander Russell

Asynchronous Byzantine Agreement with Subquadratic Communication   353
   Erica Blum, Jonathan Katz, Chen-Da Liu-Zhang, and Julian Loss

Expected Constant Round Byzantine Broadcast Under Dishonest Majority . . .   381
   Jun Wan, Hanshen Xiao, Elaine Shi, and Srinivas Devadas

Round-Efficient Byzantine Broadcast Under Strongly Adaptive
and Majority Corruptions.   412
   Jun Wan, Hanshen Xiao, Srinivas Devadas, and Elaine Shi

A Lower Bound for One-Round Oblivious RAM   457
   David Cash, Andrew Drucker, and Alexander Hoover

Lower Bounds for Multi-server Oblivious RAMs   486
   Kasper Green Larsen, Mark Simkin, and Kevin Yeo

On Computational Shortcuts for Information-Theoretic PIR   504
   Matthew M. Hong, Yuval Ishai, Victor I. Kolobov, and Russell W. F. Lai

Characterizing Deterministic-Prover Zero Knowledge   535
   Nir Bitansky and Arka Rai Choudhuri

NIZK from SNARG   567
   Fuyuki Kitagawa, Takahiro Matsuda, and Takashi Yamakawa

Weakly Extractable One-Way Functions   596
   Nir Bitansky, Noa Eizenstadt, and Omer Paneth

Towards Non-interactive Witness Hiding.   627
   Benjamin Kuykendall and Mark Zhandry

FHE-Based Bootstrapping of Designated-Prover NIZK   657
   Zvika Brakerski, Sanjam Garg, and Rotem Tsabary

Perfect Zero Knowledge: New Upperbounds and Relativized Separations. . . .   684
   Peter Dixon, Sutanu Gayen, A. Pavan, and N. V. Vinodchandran

Author Index   705

Contents – Part II

Recursive Proof Composition from Accumulation Schemes   1
  Benedikt Bünz, Alessandro Chiesa, Pratyush Mishra,
  and Nicholas Spooner

Linear-Time Arguments with Sublinear Verification from Tensor Codes   19
  Jonathan Bootle, Alessandro Chiesa, and Jens Groth

Barriers for Succinct Arguments in the Random Oracle Model   47
  Alessandro Chiesa and Eylon Yogev

Accumulators in (and Beyond) Generic Groups: Non-trivial Batch
Verification Requires Interaction   77
  Gili Schul-Ganz and Gil Segev

Batch Verification and Proofs of Proximity with Polylog Overhead 108
  Guy N. Rothblum and Ron D. Rothblum

Batch Verification for Statistical Zero Knowledge Proofs 139
  Inbar Kaslasi, Guy N. Rothblum, Ron D. Rothblum, Adam Sealfon,
  and Prashant Nalini Vasudevan

Public-Coin Zero-Knowledge Arguments with (almost) Minimal Time
and Space Overheads 168
  Alexander R. Block, Justin Holmgren, Alon Rosen, Ron D. Rothblum,
  and Pratik Soni

On the Price of Concurrency in Group Ratcheting Protocols 198
  Alexander Bienstock, Yevgeniy Dodis, and Paul Rösler

Stronger Security and Constructions of Multi-designated Verifier
Signatures 229
  Ivan Damgård, Helene Haagh, Rebekah Mercer, Anca Nitulescu,
  Claudio Orlandi, and Sophia Yakoubov

Continuous Group Key Agreement with Active Security 261
  Joël Alwen, Sandro Coretti, Daniel Jost, and Marta Mularczyk

Round Optimal Secure Multiparty Computation
from Minimal Assumptions 291
  Arka Rai Choudhuri, Michele Ciampi, Vipul Goyal,
  Abhishek Jain, and Rafail Ostrovsky

Reusable Two-Round MPC from DDH 320
  James Bartusek, Sanjam Garg, Daniel Masny, and Pratyay Mukherjee

Mr NISC: Multiparty Reusable Non-Interactive Secure Computation 349
  Fabrice Benhamouda and Huijia Lin

Secure Massively Parallel Computation for Dishonest Majority 379
  Rex Fernando, Ilan Komargodski, Yanyi Liu, and Elaine Shi

Towards Multiparty Computation Withstanding Coercion of All Parties 410
  Ran Canetti and Oxana Poburinnaya

Synchronous Constructive Cryptography 439
  Chen-Da Liu-Zhang and Ueli Maurer

Topology-Hiding Communication from Minimal Assumptions 473
  *Marshall Ball, Elette Boyle, Ran Cohen, Lisa Kohl, Tal Malkin,
  Pierre Meyer, and Tal Moran*

Information-Theoretic 2-Round MPC Without Round Collapsing: Adaptive
Security, and More 502
  Huijia Lin, Tianren Liu, and Hoeteck Wee

On Statistical Security in Two-Party Computation 532
  Dakshita Khurana and Muhammad Haris Mughees

The Resiliency of MPC with Low Interaction: The Benefit of Making
Errors (Extended Abstract) 562
  Benny Applebaum, Eliran Kachlon, and Arpita Patra

Revisiting Fairness in MPC: Polynomial Number of Parties and General
Adversarial Structures 595
  Dana Dachman-Soled

On the Power of an Honest Majority in Three-Party Computation
Without Broadcast... 621
  Bar Alon, Ran Cohen, Eran Omri, and Tom Suad

A Secret-Sharing Based MPC Protocol for Boolean Circuits with Good
Amortized Complexity...................................... 652
  Ignacio Cascudo and Jaron Skovsted Gundersen

On the Round Complexity of the Shuffle Model..................... 683
  Amos Beimel, Iftach Haitner, Kobbi Nissim, and Uri Stemmer

Author Index 713

Contents – Part III

Universal Composition with Global Subroutines: Capturing Global Setup
Within Plain UC.. 1
   Christian Badertscher, Ran Canetti, Julia Hesse, Björn Tackmann,
   and Vassilis Zikas

Security Analysis of *SPAKE2+* 31
   Victor Shoup

Schrödinger's Pirate: How to Trace a Quantum Decoder 61
   Mark Zhandry

Quantum Encryption with Certified Deletion 92
   Anne Broadbent and Rabib Islam

Secure Quantum Extraction Protocols 123
   Prabhanjan Ananth and Rolando L. La Placa

Non-interactive Classical Verification of Quantum Computation 153
   Gorjan Alagic, Andrew M. Childs, Alex B. Grilo, and Shih-Han Hung

Classical Verification of Quantum Computations with Efficient Verifier..... 181
   Nai-Hui Chia, Kai-Min Chung, and Takashi Yamakawa

Coupling of Random Systems.................................. 207
   David Lanzenberger and Ueli Maurer

Towards Defeating Backdoored Random Oracles: Indifferentiability
with Bounded Adaptivity..................................... 241
   Yevgeniy Dodis, Pooya Farshim, Sogol Mazaheri, and Stefano Tessaro

Zero-Communication Reductions............................... 274
   Varun Narayanan, Manoj Prabhakaran, and Vinod M. Prabhakaran

Lower Bounds on the Time/Memory Tradeoff of Function Inversion....... 305
   Dror Chawin, Iftach Haitner, and Noam Mazor

Super-Linear Time-Memory Trade-Offs for Symmetric Encryption 335
   Wei Dai, Stefano Tessaro, and Xihu Zhang

Algebraic Distinguishers: From Discrete Logarithms to Decisional
Uber Assumptions.. 366
   Lior Rotem and Gil Segev

On the Security of Time-Lock Puzzles and Timed Commitments   390
  Jonathan Katz, Julian Loss, and Jiayu Xu

Expected-Time Cryptography: Generic Techniques and Applications
to Concrete Soundness.   414
  Joseph Jaeger and Stefano Tessaro

On the Complexity of Arithmetic Secret Sharing.   444
  Ronald Cramer, Chaoping Xing, and Chen Yuan

Robust Secret Sharing with Almost Optimal Share Size and Security
Against Rushing Adversaries   470
  Serge Fehr and Chen Yuan

The Share Size of Secret-Sharing Schemes for Almost All Access
Structures and Graphs   499
  Amos Beimel and Oriol Farràs

Transparent Error Correcting in a Computationally Bounded World.   530
  Ofer Grossman, Justin Holmgren, and Eylon Yogev

New Techniques in Replica Encodings with Client Setup.   550
  Rachit Garg, George Lu, and Brent Waters

Non-malleable Codes, Extractors and Secret Sharing for Interleaved
Tampering and Composition of Tampering.   584
  Eshan Chattopadhyay and Xin Li

On Average-Case Hardness in TFNP from One-Way Functions   614
  Pavel Hubáček, Chethan Kamath, Karel Král, and Veronika Slívová

On Pseudorandom Encodings   639
  Thomas Agrikola, Geoffroy Couteau, Yuval Ishai, Stanisław Jarecki,
  and Amit Sahai

Author Index   671

Lossiness and Entropic Hardness
for Ring-LWE

Zvika Brakerski[1] and Nico Döttling[2]($^{(\boxtimes)}$)

[1] Weizmann Institute of Science, Rehovot, Israel
[2] CISPA Helmholtz Center for Information Security, Saarbrücken, Germany
nico.doettling@gmail.com

Abstract. The hardness of the Ring Learning with Errors problem (RLWE) is a central building block for efficiency-oriented lattice-based cryptography. Many applications use an "entropic" variant of the problem where the so-called "secret" is not distributed uniformly as prescribed but instead comes from some distribution with sufficient min-entropy. However, the hardness of the entropic variant has not been substantiated thus far.

For standard LWE (not over rings) entropic results are known, using a "lossiness approach" but it was not known how to adapt this approach to the ring setting. In this work we present the first such results, where entropic security is established either under RLWE or under the Decisional Small Polynomial Ratio (DSPR) assumption which is a mild variant of the NTRU assumption.

In the context of general entropic distributions, our results in the ring setting essentially match the known lower bounds (Bolboceanu et al., Asiacrypt 2019; Brakerski and Döttling, Eurocrypt 2020).

1 Introduction

Lyubashevsky, Peikert and Regev [16,17] introduced the Ring Learning with Errors (RLWE) problem as a structured variant of the celebrated LWE problem [24]. RLWE (and similar variants such as ideal/polynomial LWE [28]) are by now an indispensable tool for constructing efficient lattice-based cryptographic primitives, such as public-key encryption, key agreement and signatures. It is appealing to use RLWE-based cryptographic primitives since they are usually more succinct and efficient than their non-ring counterparts. Translating a cryptographic construction from LWE to RLWE is often straightforward, and indeed many LWE based constructions have RLWE counterparts that enjoy a higher level of efficiency (at the cost of only enjoying hardness respective to a special class of lattices instead of all lattices as in LWE).

Z. Brakerski—Supported by the Binational Science Foundation (Grant No. 2016726), and by the European Union Horizon 2020 Research and Innovation Program via ERC Project REACT (Grant 756482) and via Project PROMETHEUS (Grant 780701).
N. Döttling—This work is partially funded by the Helmholtz Association within the project "Trustworthy Federated Data Analytics" (TFDA) (funding number ZT-I-OO1 4).

R. Pass and K. Pietrzak (Eds.): TCC 2020, LNCS 12550, pp. 1–27, 2020.
https://doi.org/10.1007/978-3-030-64375-1_1

The focus of this work is *entropic hardness*, which is an important property of LWE-based cryptography [2,4,6,8,18] that so far resisted translation to the RLWE regime. Entropic hardness is the property of the LWE problem (and hopefully also RLWE) to remain hard even when the so called "LWE secret" is not sampled from the prescribed distribution, but instead is sampled from some distribution with sufficient min-entropy. This is relevant in the context of key-leakage (see e.g. [12] for a survey), and in a number of other applications which use RLWE with a key that is not sampled according to the prescribed distribution. These include implementations of fully homomorphic encryption such as [5,9,10,25] and even some of the candidates in the NIST post-quantum cryptography contest [19].

The question of entropic security for RLWE is therefore highly motivated. Nevertheless, very little was known about its security prior to this work. The only work we are aware of in this context is by Bolboceanu et al. [3], which introduced a non-standard assumption that they call HLBDD. They prove the hardness of entropic RLWE for a class of distributions that they call k-wise independent, based on the hardness of HLBDD and standard RLWE. This solution has a number of drawbacks in not addressing general entropic distributions, being applicable only in certain rings (it requires that the ring has CRT representation) and making a new assumption.

One would have hoped that it would be possible to use similar methods to those used in the context of LWE also for RLWE. After all, the structure of the problems is very similar. However, the same barrier seemed to have stopped all prior attempts. In a nutshell, it is the failure to find a proper analog *lossiness argument* in the ring setting. This term refers to a family of proof techniques that underlie all known entropic hardness results [2,4,6,8,18]. We explain this barrier in more detail below.

We recall that in standard LWE, an instance is composed of a random matrix $\mathbf{A} \in \mathbb{Z}_q^{n \times N}$ with $N \gg n$, and a vector $\mathbf{y} = \mathbf{sA} + \mathbf{e}$, where $\mathbf{s}$ is the "LWE secret" and $\mathbf{e}$ is a noise vector (usually sampled from a Gaussian). The goal is to find the vector $\mathbf{s}$, or in the *decisional* version of the problem to distinguish $(\mathbf{A}, \mathbf{y})$ from uniform. The RLWE problem is a structured variant of the above, usually defined using elements from the ring of integers of an algebraic number field (and its dual). For the purpose of this work, it will be instructive to consider an equivalent (and in fact more general) formulation of RLWE that does not refer to algebraic number theory at all and takes great resemblance to the above LWE description. Let us rewrite the above LWE instance as follows, consider the case where $N = n \cdot m$. We can break the matrix $\mathbf{A}$ into square blocks s.t. $\mathbf{A} = [\mathbf{A}_1, \ldots, \mathbf{A}_m]$ and consider the LWE instance as a sequence of blocks of the form $\{(\mathbf{A}_i, \mathbf{y}_i = \mathbf{sA}_i + \mathbf{e}_i)\}_{i=1}^m$. RLWE instances can be presented in the same way, except the matrices $\mathbf{A}_i$ are no longer uniform, but instead are drawn from a distribution over *structured* matrices.[1] Throughout this work we will attempt to state our results and techniques in terms of this *Structured LWE*

---

[1] Essentially this structure represents the multiplication of an element a from the (dual) of a ring of integers by an element from the ring of integers.

formulation as much as possible, without specifying the exact structure of the matrices $\mathbf{A}_i$, and the instantiations to the special case of number fields will follow as straightforward corollaries.

A lossiness argument for LWE hinges on the observation that the entropic LWE distribution is computationally indistinguishable from one where the matrices $\mathbf{A}_i$ are not uniform, but instead are distributed as $\mathbf{A}_i = \mathbf{B} \cdot \mathbf{C}_i + \mathbf{F}_i$, where $\mathbf{B} \in \mathbb{Z}_q^{n \times k}$ (note that the same $\mathbf{B}$ is used for all i) for $k \ll n$, $\mathbf{C}_i \in \mathbb{Z}_q^{k \times n}$, and $\mathbf{F}_i$ is small noise. Indistinguishability is established by decisional LWE. This step makes the matrices $\mathbf{A}_i$ "close to low-rank". Furthermore, now $\mathbf{y}_i = \mathbf{s}\mathbf{A}_i = \mathbf{s}\mathbf{B}\mathbf{C}_i + \mathbf{s}\mathbf{F}_i + \mathbf{e}_i$. From this point the methods diverge somewhat, let us stick to the approach of [2,4] that we follow in this paper. In these works, it is shown that *even information theoretically* $\mathbf{s}$ cannot be recovered, essentially because the adversary only has access to $\mathbf{s}\mathbf{B}$, which has dimension k and therefore does not contain much information, and to the terms $\mathbf{s}\mathbf{F}_i + \mathbf{e}_i$, where it is shown that the entropy in $\mathbf{e}_i$ masks the information about $\mathbf{s}$.

Trying to apply this argument in the structured LWE setting runs into a problem. The matrices $\mathbf{A}_i$ are no longer uniform but instead have some (efficiently verifiable) structure. Therefore, we need to find a distribution that is both indistinguishable from the structured $\mathbf{A}_i$ distribution, and has lossiness properties as above. In the context of the structure that is imposed by RLWE, this seems hopeless since the structure imposed by the ring does not allow the $\mathbf{A}_i$ matrices to be close to low-rank for general rings.[2] In this work we overcome this barrier.

1.1 Our Results

We present a new approach to achieve lossiness that generalizes the "closeness to low-rank" approach, but that can be applied for general RLWE (and possibly other structured LWE variants). Concretely, we observe that it suffices to replace $\mathbf{A}_i$ with a matrix whose span contains short vectors. That is, we will set $\mathbf{A}_i = \mathbf{H} \cdot \mathbf{Z}_i$, where $\mathbf{H}$ is an invertible matrix that is sampled once and used for all i, and the $\mathbf{Z}_i$ come from a distribution over low-norm matrices. The exact norm that we use depends on the underlying ring, but for the purposes of this overview, it suffices to think of $\mathbf{Z}_i$ as a matrix where all entries are shorter than some bound $\ll q$. We observe that the matrices $\mathbf{H} \cdot \mathbf{Z}_i$ are neither low rank nor close to low-rank, however they become close to low rank under a (common) *basis-change* corresponding to the matrix $\mathbf{H}$.[3] The level of lossiness will be dictated by the properties of $\mathbf{Z}_i$: the lower the norm of $\mathbf{Z}_i$, the more lossiness is obtained. We note that we can assume that $\mathbf{H}$ itself has a short inverse, that we denote by $\mathbf{Z}_0$

---

[2] The work of [3] can be viewed as targeting a special case where this is possible, the case where the ring decomposes into a "CRT representation". This requires making a non-standard assumption like their HLBDD assumption which only applies to that special setting.

[3] In fact, under this basis change the matrices are even close to the 0 matrix, which has the lowest possible rank.

(we explain below that this does not actually impose an additional restriction). We show that this notion is both sufficient for proving entropic security, and that there exist such lossy distributions that are indistinguishable from uniform under standard assumptions.

The DSPR and NTRU Assumptions. We notice that the assumption as described above closely resembles the Decisional Small Polynomial Ratio (DSPR) [15] and NTRU assumptions [11]. Both assumptions are defined over polynomial rings and have very similar syntax. Both essentially assert that over some polynomial ring, there is a distribution over ring elements s.t. when sampling $f, g_1, \ldots, g_m$ from this distribution, it holds that $g_1/f, \ldots, g_m/f$ are jointly indistinguishable from a set of uniformly random ring elements. The NTRU cryptosystem uses a specific and very short distributions for f, g_i (over polynomials with $\{-1, 0, +1\}$ coefficients) and DSPR considers a Gaussian distribution (say with some Gaussian parameter γ) which will be easier to use.[4] The assumption becomes weaker as γ increases. As observed by Stehlé and Steinfeld [27], when the distributions become wide enough ($\gamma \gtrsim \sqrt{q}$), this assumption is actually implied by RLWE. For other parameter regimes, however, DSPR appears to provide a lower level of security compared to RLWE, at least with respect to state of the art attacks [13]. Translating the above into the structured LWE terminology, we can define $\mathbf{Z}_0$ as the matrix that corresponds to the operator of multiplying by f, and $\mathbf{Z}_i$ as the matrix that corresponds to multiplying by g_i. Intuitively the parameter γ can be thought of as a measure for the smallness of the elements in the $\mathbf{Z}_i$ matrices. We note that since the polynomial rings are commutative, the matrices $\mathbf{H}, \mathbf{Z}_0, \mathbf{Z}_i$ all commute with each other in the actual instantiation. However, we will not require this property.

Lastly, we point out that while RLWE enjoys a worst-case to average-case hardness reduction [16,23], such reduction is not known for NTRU/DSPR with small γ. Hence there is a tradeoff between the quality of the result obtained and the hardness of the assumption that we need to make.

Noise Lossiness and Entropic Security Under DSPR. We follow the approach of [4] and consider the notion of *noise lossiness* of a distribution of secrets $\mathcal{S}$, which is defined to be the conditional smooth min-entropy of a sample from $\mathcal{S}$ conditioned on learning its perturbation by Gaussian noise. Formally:

$$\nu_\sigma(\mathcal{S}) = \tilde{H}_\infty(\mathbf{s}|\mathbf{s} + \mathbf{e}), \tag{1}$$

where $\mathbf{e}$ is Gaussian with parameter σ. We also recall that [4] show a general relation between noise lossiness and entropy

$$\nu_\sigma(\mathcal{S}) \gtrsim \tilde{H}_\infty(\mathcal{S}) - n\log(q/\sigma). \tag{2}$$

We show that similarly to LWE, the hardness of entropic RLWE on a given secret distribution $\mathcal{S}$ is also related to its noise lossiness. We present our result

---

[4] We will consider Gaussians over the *canonical embedding* of ring elements into Euclidean space.

in the context of RLWE in power-of-2 cyclotomic number fields, but the result is modular and applies to RLWE on any ring that has reasonable regularity condition. See also discussion below.

Theorem 1.1 (Informal). *Assume DSPR with parameter γ. Let $\mathcal{S}$ be a distribution s.t. for some σ' it holds that $\nu_{\sigma'}(\mathcal{S}) \gtrsim n \log(\gamma\mathsf{poly}(n)) + \omega(\log \lambda)$. Then Entropic RLWE in a power-of-2 cyclotomic with secret distribution $\mathcal{S}$ and Gaussian noise parameter $\sigma \approx \sigma' \cdot \mathsf{poly}(n) \cdot \sqrt{m}$ is hard.*

Plugging in Eq. (2), we get that for general entropic distributions we require average min-entropy of roughly $\tilde{H}_\infty(\mathcal{S}) \gtrsim n \log(q/\sigma) + O(n \log(nm\gamma)) + \omega(\log \lambda)$ in order to achieve entropic hardness. We note that better bounds on noise lossiness are known for "short" distributions, where the entropy requirement can go almost all the way down to $n \log \gamma$, which allows to show entropic hardness for many low-norm distributions but unfortunately is still insufficient for the widely used setting where the secret is chosen as a ring element with binary coefficients. Indeed, even in our results, we need to make stronger DSPR assumptions as we wish to deal with secrets of lower entropy. We believe that there is an inherent difficulty for proving hardness of such distributions without making extreme hardness assumptions.

Our results are stated in a rather general form. We present a notion of "structured LWE" problem, which captures standard LWE, RLWE and potentially other problems, and present lossiness results based on a "matrix DSPR" assumption, assuming that the matrix distributions in the DSPR instance satisfy some (mild) non-degeneracy conditions. Proving that the non-degeneracy conditions indeed hold is the only place where the specifics of the number field are required. The aforementioned [27] fortunately implies these required conditions for power-of-2 cyclotomic number fields. We believe that the proof can be generalized to other number fields (especially cyclotomics) but this would require essentially repeating the [27] proofs in more generality which we feel is tangent to the purpose of this work.

Since our paper is written in a modular manner, it suffices to simply prove the non-degeneracy conditions in Sect. 6 in order to obtain entropic hardness results for other variants of structured LWE, be it RLWE in other number fields (or a different embedding) or other forms of the problem completely.

To conclude, let us discuss the applicability of our techniques to the so called "module LWE" problem [1,5,14,22]. Module-LWE interpolates between LWE and ring-LWE and is appealing in the practical context as it may offer superior security benefits over RLWE with minimal additional computational cost. Viewed as a structured LWE problem, in module-LWE the matrix $\mathbf{A}$ is simply a block matrix, where each block is an independent RLWE matrix. Our methods apply to such matrices as well, under a matrix DSPR assumption. We can instantiate matrix DSPR under RLWE-like assumptions, but we do not know of variants of this assumption that rely on module-LWE-like structures. A complete module LWE analog of our result would require introducing such an analog.

1.2 Our Techniques

As explained above, in order to prove security for entropic structured LWE, we rely on the assumption that we can replace the uniform $\mathbf{A}_i$ with $\mathbf{A}_i = \mathbf{H} \cdot \mathbf{Z}_i$, where $\mathbf{Z}_i$ are short, and there exists $\mathbf{Z}_0$ (also short) s.t. $\mathbf{HZ}_0 = \mathbf{I} \pmod{q}$. We note that a survey by Peikert [21] uses a similar method when sketching a proof that the hardness of NTRU implies that of RLWE. Namely, replacing the a_i elements in RLWE samples with NTRU values, and arguing that the RLWE secret should become information-theoretically irrecoverable. One can view our method as putting together a rigorous variant of Peikert's arguments, and showing that it is possible to obtain lossiness for various entropic distributions.

We start by examining the distribution of the $\mathbf{y}_i$ values after substituting $\mathbf{A}_i = \mathbf{H} \cdot \mathbf{Z}_i$. We have

$$\mathbf{y}_i = \mathbf{sA}_i + \mathbf{e}_i = \mathbf{sH} \cdot \mathbf{Z}_i + \mathbf{e}_i.$$

We now take the approach of "flooding at the source" [4]. The idea is to "bring the noise closer to the secret" and show that all structured LWE blocks in fact depend on a noisy version of the secret, which allows to apply noise lossiness. Specifically, the technique that is used is Gaussian decomposition. Using Gaussian decomposition it is possible to show that if the $\mathbf{e}_i$ Gaussians are wide enough relative to the norm of the $\mathbf{Z}_i$ matrices, it is possible to find $\mathbf{e}$ s.t. for all i, $\mathbf{e}_i = \mathbf{eZ}_i + \mathbf{e}'_i$, where $\mathbf{e}$ and all $\mathbf{e}'_i$ are independent. This essentially follows from the covariance-additivity of Gaussian vectors, which can be carried over to discrete Gaussians as well.

Plugging this decomposed Gaussian into the equation for $\mathbf{y}_i$, we get

$$\mathbf{sH} \cdot \mathbf{Z}_i + \mathbf{eZ}_i + \mathbf{e}'_i = (\mathbf{sH} + \mathbf{e})\mathbf{Z}_i + \mathbf{e}'_i.$$

This implies that all information about $\mathbf{s}$ is captured in the term $\mathbf{sH} + \mathbf{e} \pmod{q}$.

We now note that already at this point we can derive a non-trivial entropic result. Let us denote $\mathbf{s}' = \mathbf{sH}$, and notice that since $\mathbf{H}$ is invertible, the entropy of $\mathbf{s}'$ is the same as that of $\mathbf{s}$ and recovering $\mathbf{s}$ is information-theoretically equivalent to recovering $\mathbf{s}'$. Now, essentially by definition, the probability of recovering $\mathbf{s}'$ is exactly captured by its noise lossiness. Specifically, if the noise lossiness is super-logarithmic then $\mathbf{s}'$ is not recoverable. Since we can relate noise lossiness to entropy (recall Eq. (2)) we have

$$\nu_\sigma(\mathbf{s}') \gtrsim \tilde{H}_\infty(\mathbf{s}') - n\log(q/\sigma) = \tilde{H}_\infty(\mathbf{s}) - n\log(q/\sigma),$$

where σ is the Gaussian parameter of $\mathbf{e}$. Therefore, so long as it holds that $\tilde{H}_\infty(\mathbf{s}) \gtrsim n\log(q/\sigma) + \omega(\lambda)$, then we have entropic security for RLWE with secret coming from the distribution of $\mathbf{s}$. This is indeed a non-trivial bound which may be useful in certain settings (e.g. when we only know the entropy of the distribution of $\mathbf{s}$ but do not know any other properties), but in many cases we would like to take into account additional properties of the distribution that reduce the large gap of $n\log(q/\sigma)$ between noise lossiness and entropy. However, in the current analysis we can say very little about the distribution of $\mathbf{s}'$ given the distribution of $\mathbf{s}$ (other than the entropy being preserved). We therefore proceed to show a connection that directly relates to the noise lossiness of $\mathbf{s}$ itself.

Recall that we deduced that all information about $\mathbf{s}$ is captured in the term $\mathbf{sH} + \mathbf{e} \pmod{q}$. Since $\mathbf{H}$ is invertible, we can multiply the equation by its inverse $\mathbf{Z}_0$ (on the right) to obtain $\mathbf{s} + \mathbf{eZ}_0 \pmod{q}$. We conclude that even information theoretically, an attacker can only recover $\mathbf{s} + \mathbf{eZ}_0 \pmod{q}$, where $\mathbf{e}$ is Gaussian and $\mathbf{Z}_0$ is a low-norm matrix which is known to the attacker.

We wish to show that $\mathbf{s} + \mathbf{eZ}_0 \pmod{q}$ does not leak much information about $\mathbf{s}$. We can see that some information can in fact be leaked. For example, if $\mathbf{s}$ is short, then the reduction modulo q does not have any effect, and the adversary can learn $\mathbf{s} + \mathbf{eZ}_0$ (as a value over the integers), this in particular allows to learn the coset of $\mathbf{s}$ relative to the lattice spanned by the rows of $\mathbf{Z}_0$ (henceforth we refer to it as the "$\mathbf{Z}_0$ lattice"). This is essentially the reason why our techniques don't carry over to the setting of very low norm $\mathbf{s}$ – this would require sampling $\mathbf{Z}_0$ from a very narrow distribution that would imply very strong and unrealistic parameters for our DSPR assumption.

Instead, we show that essentially all the entropy that can be gained by the adversary, beyond the "usual" noise lossiness, is indeed proportional to learning a coset of the $\mathbf{Z}_0$ lattice. The number of such cosets is $\approx \gamma^n$, and thus the loss in entropy of $n \log \gamma$ in Theorem 1.1.

To see this, we consider the distribution: $(\mathbf{Z}_0, \mathbf{s} + \tilde{\mathbf{e}}, c)$, where $\tilde{\mathbf{e}}$ is a spherical discrete Gaussian over the integers, and c indicates a coset of $\tilde{\mathbf{e}}$ with respect to the $\mathbf{Z}_0$ lattice. We show that there is a (randomized) process that takes this distribution as input, and outputs $(\mathbf{Z}_0, \mathbf{s} + \mathbf{eZ}_0)$. This means that the adversary cannot learn about $\mathbf{s}$ from $(\mathbf{Z}_0, \mathbf{s} + \mathbf{eZ}_0)$ more than it can from $(\mathbf{Z}_0, \mathbf{s} + \tilde{\mathbf{e}}, c)$. The latter, just by definition, translates to the noise lossiness of $\mathbf{s}$ (with respect to the Gaussian parameter of $\tilde{\mathbf{e}}$), minus the "leakage" that is imposed by providing the adversary the value c. Since this value is a coset indicator, this leakage is bounded.

To generate $(\mathbf{Z}_0, \mathbf{s} + \mathbf{eZ}_0)$ from $(\mathbf{Z}_0, \mathbf{s} + \tilde{\mathbf{e}}, c)$, we use the Gaussian convolution theorem of Peikert [20]. This theorem shows that it is possible to sample the term $\mathbf{eZ}_0$, which is just a (non spherical) discrete Gaussian over the $\mathbf{Z}_0$ lattice, in two steps: first sampling from a Gaussian over the integer lattice, and then "rounding" the sample into the $\mathbf{Z}_0$ lattice. The rounding step only requires to know the coset of the first step (in order to cancel it out). Setting the parameters appropriately, the theorem can be used and the result follows.

In order to be able to apply Gaussian decomposition and also the Gaussian convolution theorem, we rely on probabilistic properties of the $\mathbf{Z}$ matrices, in particular their minimal and maximal singular values. The properties required in order for our method to go through turn out not to hold with high probability, but rather only with some fixed inverse-polynomial probability. We thus introduce a notion of "sometimes lossiness" and show that it suffices for proving entropic hardness. In Sect. 5 we show how to obtain entropic hardness based on probabilistic properties of the $\mathbf{Z}$ matrices. Then in Sect. 6 we show that these properties hold for RLWE over power-of-two cyclotomics, using properties proved in [27].

1.3 Paper Organization

We try to keep the discussion abstract and use the notion of "structured LWE" as much as we can. Eventually we state our result in terms of properties that need to hold for the structured LWE problem at hand, and show that the RLWE/DSPR instantiation indeed possesses these properties. Standard preliminaries in information theory, lattices and algebraic number theory are provided in Sect. 2. Section 3 introduces the entropic structured LWE (entSLWE) problem and shows that mild form of (entropic) hardness for entSLWE with relatively few samples implies full-fledged (entropic) hardness. Section 4 presents a notion of lossiness that we call "sometimes lossiness" and shows how it is used to prove (entropic) hardness, then a sometimes lossy distribution is constructed in Sect. 5 based on an abstract problem we call Decisional Small Ratio (DSR) problem. Finally Sect. 6 shows how to instantiate all required building blocks in the RLWE setting.

2 Notation and Definitions

We will denote the security parameter by λ. We say a function $\nu(\lambda)$ is negligible if $\nu(\lambda) \in \lambda^{-\omega(1)}$. We will generally denote row vectors by $\mathbf{x}$ and column vectors by $\mathbf{x}^\top$. We will denote the L_2 norm of a vector $\mathbf{x}$ by $\|\mathbf{x}\| = \sqrt{\sum_i x_i^2}$ and the L_∞ norm by $\|\mathbf{x}\|_\infty = \max_i |x_i|$.

Let X, Y be two discrete random variables defined on a common support $\mathcal{X}$. We define the statistical distance between X and Y as

$$\Delta(X, Y) = \frac{1}{2} \sum_{x \in \mathcal{X}} |\Pr[X = x] - \Pr[Y = x]|.$$

Consider a real valued matrix $\mathbf{A} \in \mathbb{R}^{n \times m}$, assume for convenience that $m \geq n$. The singular values of $\mathbf{A}$ are the square roots of the eigenvalues of the positive semidefinite (PSD) matrix $\mathbf{A}\mathbf{A}^\top$. We will denote the largest singular value of $\mathbf{A}$ by $\sigma_{max}(\mathbf{A})$. The *spectral norm* of $\mathbf{A}$ is $\sigma_{max}(\mathbf{A})$. It holds that

$$\sigma_{max}(\mathbf{A}) = \max_{\mathbf{x} \in \mathbb{R}^m \setminus \{\mathbf{0}\}} \frac{\|\mathbf{A}\mathbf{x}\|}{\|\mathbf{x}\|}.$$

2.1 Min-Entropy

Let $\mathbf{x}$ be a discrete random variable supported on a set X and $\mathbf{z}$ be a possibly (continuous) random variable supported on a (measurable) set Z. The conditional min-entropy $\tilde{H}_\infty(\mathbf{x}|\mathbf{z})$ of $\mathbf{x}$ given $\mathbf{z}$ is defined by

$$\tilde{H}_\infty(\mathbf{x}|\mathbf{z}) = -\log\left(\mathsf{E}_{\mathbf{z}'}\left[\max_{\mathbf{x}' \in X} \Pr[\mathbf{x} = \mathbf{x}'|\mathbf{z} = \mathbf{z}']\right]\right).$$

In the case that $\mathbf{z}$ is continuous, this becomes

$$\tilde{H}_\infty(\mathbf{x}|\mathbf{z}) = -\log\left(\int_{\mathbf{z}'} p_{\mathbf{z}}(\mathbf{z}') \max_{\mathbf{x}'\in X} \Pr[\mathbf{x} = \mathbf{x}'|\mathbf{z} = \mathbf{z}']\right),$$

where $p_{\mathbf{z}}(\cdot)$ is the probability density of $\mathbf{z}$.

For an $\epsilon > 0$ we define the ϵ-smooth min-entropy $\tilde{H}_\infty^\epsilon(\mathbf{x}|\mathbf{z})$ as the maximum over all $\tilde{H}_\infty^\epsilon(\mathbf{x}'|\mathbf{z}')$ for which $(\mathbf{x}', \mathbf{z}')$ is ϵ-close to $(\mathbf{x}, \mathbf{z})$ in statistical distance.

2.2   Leftover Hashing

We recall a version of the generalized leftover hash lemma [7,24].

Lemma 2.1. *Let $\mathbb{G}$ be a finite Abelian group, and $\mathcal{Y}$ be a finite set. Let $\ell \geq \log(|\mathbb{G}|) + \log(|\mathcal{Y}|) + \omega(\log(\lambda))$ be an integer. Let $g_1, \ldots, g_\ell \leftarrow_\$ \mathbb{G}$ be chosen uniformly at random. Further let $\mathbf{x} \leftarrow_\$ \{0,1\}^\ell$ be chosen uniformly at random. Let Y be a random variable supported on $\mathcal{Y}$ which is possibly correlated with $\mathbf{x}$ but independent of the g_i. Then it holds that $(g_1, \ldots, g_\ell, \sum_i x_i g_i, Y)$ is statistically close to $(g_1, \ldots, g_\ell, u, Y)$, where $u \leftarrow_\$ \mathbb{G}$ is chosen uniformly at random.*

2.3   Lattices and Gaussians

Lattices. We recall the standard facts about lattices. A lattice $\Lambda \subseteq \mathbb{R}^m$ is the set of all integer-linear combinations of a set of linearly independent basis-vectors, i.e. for every lattice Λ there exists a full-rank matrix $\mathbf{B} \in \mathbb{R}^{k\times m}$ such that $\Lambda = \Lambda(\mathbf{B}) = \{\mathbf{z}\cdot\mathbf{B} \mid \mathbf{z}\in\mathbb{Z}^k\}$. We call k the rank of Λ and $\mathbf{B}$ a basis of Λ, and we say that Λ is full-rank if $k = m$. For a lattice $\Lambda \subseteq \mathbb{R}^m$, the dual lattice Λ^* is defined by $\Lambda^* = \{\mathbf{x}\in\mathsf{Span}(\Lambda) \mid \forall\mathbf{z}\in\Lambda : \langle\mathbf{z},\mathbf{x}\rangle\in\mathbb{Z}\}$.

We say that a lattice is q-ary if $(q\mathbb{Z})^m \subseteq \Lambda \subseteq \mathbb{Z}^m$. In particular, for every q-ary lattice Λ there exists a matrix $\mathbf{A} \in \mathbb{Z}_q^{k\times m}$ such that $\Lambda = \Lambda_q(\mathbf{A}) = \{\mathbf{y}\in\mathbb{Z}^m \mid \exists\mathbf{x}\in\mathbb{Z}_q^k : \mathbf{y} = \mathbf{x}\cdot\mathbf{A}\bmod q\}$. We also define the lattice $\Lambda_q^\perp(\mathbf{A}) = \{\mathbf{y}\in\mathbb{Z}^m \mid \mathbf{A}\cdot\mathbf{y} = 0\bmod q\}$.

Gaussians. The Gaussian function $\rho_\sigma : \mathbb{R}^n \to \mathbb{R}$ is defined by

$$\rho_\sigma(\mathbf{x}) = e^{-\pi\cdot\frac{\|\mathbf{x}\|^2}{\sigma^2}}.$$

For a a non-singular matrix $\mathbf{B}$ we define $\rho_{\mathbf{B}}(\mathbf{x}) = \rho(\mathbf{x}\mathbf{B}^{-1})$.

The continuous gaussian distribution $D_{\mathbf{B}}$ on $\mathbb{R}^n$ has the probability density function $\rho_{\mathbf{B}}(\mathbf{x})/\rho_{\mathbf{B}}(\mathbb{R}^n)$. We call $\mathbf{\Sigma} = \mathbf{B}^\top\mathbf{B}$ the covariance matrix of the gaussian $D_{\mathbf{B}}$. For a lattice Λ, the discrete gaussian distribution $D_{\Lambda,\mathbf{B}}$ supported on Λ has the probability mass function $\rho_{\mathbf{B}}(\mathbf{x})/\rho_{\mathbf{B}}(\Lambda)$.

For a lattice Λ and a positive real $\epsilon > 0$, the *smoothing parameter* $\eta_\epsilon(\Lambda)$ is defined to be the smallest real number s for which $\rho_{1/s}(\Lambda^*\backslash\{0\}) \leq \epsilon$. For a matrix $\mathbf{B}$ we write $\mathbf{B} \geq \eta_\epsilon(\Lambda)$ if $\eta_\epsilon(\Lambda\mathbf{B}^{-1}) \leq 1$.

The following claim follows routinely from the definition of the smoothing parameter.

Claim. Let $\Lambda \subseteq \mathbb{R}^n$ and $\mathbf{V} \in \mathbb{R}^{n \times n}$ be a matrix with largest singular value $\sigma_{max}(\mathbf{V})$. It holds that $\eta_\epsilon(\Lambda \cdot \mathbf{V}) \leq \sigma_{max}(\mathbf{V}) \cdot \eta_\epsilon(\Lambda)$.

The following proposition allows us to decompose spherical gaussians with respect to a matrix $\mathbf{F}$.

Proposition 2.2 ([4], **Proposition 3.2**). *Let $\mathbf{F} \in \mathbb{R}^{n \times m}$ be an arbitrary matrix with spectral norm σ_F. Let $\sigma, \sigma_1 > 0$ be s.t. $\sigma > \sigma_1 \cdot \sigma_F$. Let $\mathbf{e}_1 \sim D_{\sigma_1}^n$ and let $\mathbf{e}_2 \sim D_{\sqrt{\Sigma}}$ for $\Sigma = \sigma^2 \mathbf{I} - \sigma_1^2 \mathbf{F}^\top \mathbf{F}$. Then the random variable $\mathbf{e} = \mathbf{e}_1 \mathbf{F} + \mathbf{e}_2$ is distributed according to D_σ^m.*

2.4 Noise Lossiness

The noise lossiness of a distribution $\mathcal{S}$ measures how much information is lost about a sample of $\mathcal{S}$ when adding gaussian noise. Another way to think about noise lossiness is as a measure of how bad $\mathcal{S}$ performs as a Euclidean error-correcting code. The following definition of noise lossiness slightly deviates from the definition given in [4] by considering potentially non-spherical gaussians.

Definition 2.3 (Noise Lossiness). *Fix a matrix $\mathbf{B} \in \mathbb{R}^{n \times n}$. Let $\mathcal{S} \subseteq \mathbb{Z}_q^n$ be a distribution of secrets and let $\sigma > 0$ be a gaussian parameter. We define the noise-lossiness $\nu_{\sigma\mathbf{B}}(\mathcal{S})$ by*

$$\nu_{\sigma\mathbf{B}}(\mathcal{S}) = \tilde{H}_\infty(\mathbf{s}|\mathbf{s} + \mathbf{e})$$

where $\mathbf{s} \leftarrow_\$ \mathcal{S}$ and $\mathbf{e} \leftarrow_\$ D_{\sigma\mathbf{B}}$.

In [4] the following bounds for the noise lossiness of distributions were provided.

Lemma 2.4 (Noise-Lossiness for General Entropic Distributions). *Let $0 < \sigma \leq q\sqrt{\pi/\ln(4n)}$ be a gaussian parameter and let $\mathcal{S}$ be any distribution on $\mathbb{Z}_q^n$. Then it holds that*

$$\nu_\sigma(\mathcal{S}) \geq \tilde{H}_\infty(\mathcal{S}) - n \cdot \log(q/\sigma) - 1$$

Lemma 2.5 (Noise-Lossiness for Short Distributions). *Let $\sigma > 0$ be a gaussian parameter and let $\mathcal{S}$ be a r-bounded distribution on $\mathbb{Z}_q^n$. Then it holds that*

$$\nu_\sigma(\mathcal{S}) \geq \tilde{H}_\infty(\mathcal{S}) - \sqrt{2\pi n}\log(e) \cdot \frac{r}{\sigma}.$$

2.5 Algebraic Number Fields

We will briefly reiterate some basics about algebraic number fields and the Learning with Errors Problem over Rings. See e.g., [16,17] for more details.

An algebraic number field K is a finite extension of the rationals $\mathbb{Q}$, every number field can be constructed via $\mathbb{Q}(\xi) = \mathbb{Q}[X]/(f(X))$ where $f \in \mathbb{Q}[X]$ is a monic irreducible polynomial and ξ is a root of f. The degree n of K is defined to be the degree of f and K can be seen as an n-dimensional $\mathbb{Q}$-vectorspace.

The number fields most relevant to us are power-of-two cyclotomics. For this instantiation the polynomial f is of the form $f = X^n + 1$ where n is a power of two.

A number field K of degree n has n embeddings, that is injective ring homomorphisms into the complex numbers $\mathbb{C}$, usually denoted by $\sigma_i : \mathsf{K} \to \mathbb{C}$. Each σ_i is defined by sending ξ to one of the roots of f in $\mathbb{C}$.

The embeddings σ_i come in conjugate pairs, there are s_1 real embeddings and $2s_2$ complex conjugate embeddings with $n = s_1 + 2s_2$. We can define the space $H \subseteq \mathbb{R}^{s_1} \times \mathbb{C}^{2s_2}$ by

$$H = \{(x_1, \ldots, x_n) \in \mathbb{R}^{s_1} \times \mathbb{C}^{2s_2} \mid \forall j \in [s_2] : x_{s_1 + s_2 + j} = \overline{x_{s_1 + j}}\}.$$

It can be shown that the space H is isomorphic to $\mathbb{R}^n$ as an inner product space. Let $\Theta : H \to \mathbb{R}^n$ be this isomorphism. Moreover, the space H is isomorphic as a ring to the field tensor product $\mathsf{K}_{\mathbb{R}} = \mathsf{K} \otimes_{\mathbb{Q}} \mathbb{R}$. Let $\bar{\Theta} : \mathsf{K}_{\mathbb{R}} \to \mathbb{R}^n$ be the metric isomorphism which takes $\mathsf{K}_{\mathbb{R}}$ to $\mathbb{R}^n$, i.e. $\bar{\Theta}$ is just the concatenation of σ and Θ.

The *canonical embedding* $\sigma : \mathsf{K} \to H$ is given by $\sigma(x) = (\sigma_1(x), \ldots, \sigma_n(x))$. It can be shown that σ is a ring-homomorphism, where both addition and multiplication on $\mathbb{C}^n$ are defined component-wise. The canonical embedding induces a geometry on K, that is we can define a eucilidean norm on K via the euclidean norm on $\mathbb{C}^n$, concretely for $x \in \mathsf{K}$ we define $\|x\| = \|\sigma(x)\|$. Note that $\|\sigma(x)\| = \|\Theta(\sigma(x))\|$.

While $\| \cdot \|$ immediately satisfies the triangle inequality, in the canonical embedding also the following multiplicative inequality holds: For all $x, y \in \mathsf{K}_{\mathbb{R}}$ it holds that $\|x \cdot y\| \leq \|x\|_\infty \cdot \|y\|$. Here, $\| \cdot \|_\infty$ is the L_∞ norm defined by $\|x\|_\infty = \max_i |\sigma_i(x)|$. We will also use the inequality $\|x \cdot y\|_\infty \leq \|x\|_\infty \cdot \|y\|_\infty$.

We can define a gaussian distribution $D_{\mathsf{K}_{\mathbb{R}}, \sqrt{\Sigma}}$ via the gaussian distribution $D_{\sqrt{\Sigma}}$ on $\mathbb{R}^n$, i.e. we set $D_{\mathsf{K}_{\mathbb{R}}, \sqrt{\Sigma}} = \bar{\Theta}^{-1}(D_{\sqrt{\Sigma}})$.

A element $x \in \mathsf{K}$ is called *algebraic integer*, if the minimal polynomial of x has integer coefficients. For a number field K we denote by $\mathsf{R} \subseteq \mathsf{K}$ the set of all algebraic integers in K, which can be shown to be a sub-ring of K. For the special case that K is a cyclotomic, it holds that $\mathsf{R} = \mathbb{Z}[\xi]$.

Since R is a finitely generated $\mathbb{Z}$-module, it holds that $\Lambda = \bar{\Theta}(\mathsf{R}) \subseteq \mathbb{R}^n$ is a lattice. We let $\mathbf{L}$ denote some basis for this lattice and we denote $\mathbf{B} = \mathbf{L}^{-1}$. In this notation, multiplication by the matrix $\mathbf{B}$ maps a $\mathbf{x} \in \lambda$ to an integer vector, i.e. $\mathbf{x}\mathbf{B} \in \mathbb{Z}^n$, which is exactly the coefficient vector of the ring element with respect to the basis $\mathbf{L}$. We define the smoothing parameter $\eta_\epsilon(\mathsf{R})$ of R to be $\eta_\epsilon(\Lambda)$.

Gaussian distributions over K, or more precisely over $\mathsf{K}_{\mathbb{R}}$ are defined as follows. Given a Gaussian distribution $D_{\sqrt{\Sigma}}$ over $\mathbb{R}^n$, we map it to $\mathsf{K}_{\mathbb{R}}$ via $\bar{\Theta}^{-1}$. The resulting distribution is the Gaussian with parameter $\sqrt{\Sigma}$ over $\mathsf{K}_{\mathbb{R}}$.

2.6   Ring-LWE

Let q be a modulus and R be a ring of integers of a number field K. We will briefly define the (non-dual) decisional Ring Learning with Errors (Ring-LWE) problem in Hermite form for an error-distribution χ supported on R is defined as follows. We discuss other versions of the Ring LWE problem in Sect. 3. We use a definition provided by Peikert [21, Section 4.4.1] which is slightly different from the one in [16] but easier to work with. See discussion in [21, Section 4.4.1] for details.

Definition 2.6 (Decisional Ring-LWE (Hermite Form)). *Let* $\mathsf{s} \leftarrow_{\$} \chi$. *Given* m *samples* $(\mathbf{a}_i, \mathbf{b}_i) \in \mathsf{R}_q \times \mathsf{R}_q$, *the task is to decide whether the* $\mathbf{b}_i$ *are of the form* $\mathbf{b}_i = \mathbf{a}_i \mathsf{s} + \mathbf{e}_i$ *for errors* $\mathbf{e}_i \leftarrow_{\$} \chi$ *or if the* $\mathbf{b}_i$ *are chosen uniformly at random from* R_q.

Lyubashevsky, Peikert and Regev [16] provided a worst-to-average case reduction for the Ring LWE problem relative to worst-case problems in ideal lattices. In particular, they show that if the error distribution χ is an appropriate gaussian, then the Ring LWE search problem is as hard as the approximate shortest vector problem in worst case ideal lattices. Furthermore, [16] provide a search-to-decision reduction which bases the hardness of decisional Ring LWE on the search variant.

3   (Entropic) Structured LWE

In this section, we define a version of LWE which we call *structured LWE*. Structured LWE generalizes both standard and ring-LWE.

We will only consider the search version of structured LWE in this work.

Definition 3.1 (Entropic Structured Learning with Errors). *Let* q *be a modulus and* n, k *be integers. Let* $\mathcal{M}$ *be a distribution of matrices on* $\mathbb{Z}_q^{n \times n}$ *and* Υ *be a distribution of error-distributions on* $\mathbb{R}^n$. *Furthermore, let* $\mathcal{S}$ *be a distribution on* $\mathbb{Z}_q^n$. *The goal of the* $\mathsf{entSLWE}(q, k, \mathcal{M}, \Upsilon, \mathcal{S})$ *problem is to find a secret* $\mathbf{s} \leftarrow_{\$} \mathcal{S}$ *given* k *samples* $((\mathbf{A}_1, \mathbf{y}_1), \ldots, (\mathbf{A}_k, \mathbf{y}_k))$, *where* $\chi \leftarrow_{\$} \Upsilon$ *is an error distribution and for all* $i \in [k]$ *we have* $\mathbf{A}_i \leftarrow_{\$} \mathcal{M}$, $\mathbf{e}_i \leftarrow_{\$} \chi$ *and* $\mathbf{y}_i \leftarrow \mathbf{s}\mathbf{A}_i + \mathbf{e}_i$.

If $\mathbf{A} = (\mathbf{A}_1, \ldots, \mathbf{A}_k)$, $\mathbf{e} = (\mathbf{e}_1, \ldots, \mathbf{e}_k)$ and $\mathbf{y} = (\mathbf{y}_1, \ldots, \mathbf{y}_k)$ where $\mathbf{y}_i = \mathbf{s}\mathbf{A}_i + \mathbf{e}_i$, we will use the shorthand $\mathbf{y} = \mathbf{s}\mathbf{A} + \mathbf{e}$. This in fact corresponds to the standard matrix multiplication and vector addition if we identify $\mathbf{A}$ with to be the horizontal concatenation of all $\mathbf{A}_i$ and $\mathbf{e}$ the horizontal concatenation of all $\mathbf{e}_i$. If an unbounded number of samples are given (via an oracle), then we will omit the parameter k. We note that Regev's LWE is obtained when $\mathcal{M}, \mathcal{S}$ are uniform and Υ is Gaussian. The Ring-LWE instantiation is discussed in Sect. 3.2 below.

We will consider two different hardness notions for $\mathsf{entSLWE}$. In the standard notion, we require that no PPT adversary find the secret $\mathbf{s}$ with non-negligible probability.

Definition 3.2 (Standard Hardness). *Let q, n, k, $\mathcal{M}$, Υ and $\mathcal{S}$ be as above. We say that the* $\mathsf{entSLWE}(q, k, \mathcal{M}, \Upsilon, \mathcal{S})$ *problem is (standard-) hard, if it holds for every PPT adversary $\mathcal{A}$ that*

$$\Pr[\mathcal{A}(\mathbf{A}, \mathbf{sA} + \mathbf{e}) = \mathbf{s}] < \mathsf{negl}(\lambda),$$

where $\chi \leftarrow_\$ \Upsilon$, $\mathbf{A} \leftarrow_\$ \mathcal{M}^k$, $\mathbf{s} \leftarrow_\$ \mathcal{S}$ and $\mathbf{e} \leftarrow_\$ \chi^k$.

We call the second notion mild hardness. In essence, the success probability of an adversary which breaks mild hardness only depends on the choice of $\mathbf{s}$ and $\mathbf{e}$, but not on the choice of $\mathbf{A}$.

Definition 3.3 (Mild Hardness). *Let q, n, k, $\mathcal{M}$, Υ and $\mathcal{S}$ be as above. We say that the problem* $\mathsf{entSLWE}(q, k, \mathcal{M}, \Upsilon, \mathcal{S})$ *is mildly hard, if for every PPT adversary $\mathcal{A}$ and every negligible function ν it holds that*

$$\Pr_{\mathbf{s}, \mathbf{e}, \chi}[\Pr_{\mathbf{A}}[\mathcal{A}(\mathbf{A}, \mathbf{sA} + \mathbf{e}) = \mathbf{s}] > 1 - \nu] < \mathsf{negl}(\lambda).$$

In this work we will focus on the notion of mild hardness. While this seems like a restriction at first glance, it follows by a routine amplification argument that, given an unbounded number of samples, mild hardness implies standard hardness.

Lemma 3.4. *Let q, n, $\mathcal{M}$ and $\mathcal{S}$ be as above and let Υ be a distribution of error-distributions. If* $\mathsf{entSLWE}(q, \mathcal{M}, \Upsilon, \mathcal{S})$ *is mildly hard, then it is also standard hard.*

Proof. Assume towards contradiction there was a PPT search adversary $\mathcal{A}$ with non-negligible success probability ϵ' against standard hardness of the problem $\mathsf{entSLWE}(q, \mathcal{M}, \Upsilon, \mathcal{S})$. For notational convenience, the adversary $\mathcal{A}$ obtains its samples via an oracle $\mathcal{O}_{\mathbf{s}, \chi}$, which has $\mathbf{s}$ and χ hardwired. When queried, $\mathcal{O}_{\mathbf{s}, \chi}$ chooses $\mathbf{A} \leftarrow_\$ \mathcal{M}$ and $\mathbf{e} \leftarrow_\$ \chi$ and outputs a sample $(\mathbf{A}, \mathbf{sA} + \mathbf{e})$. Let $\epsilon = 1/\mathsf{poly}(\lambda)$ be such that $\epsilon(\lambda) = \epsilon'(\lambda)$ infinitely often. We will construct an adversary $\mathcal{B}$ against the mild hardness of $\mathsf{entSLWE}(q, \mathcal{M}, \Upsilon, \mathcal{S})$ as follows.

Algorithm $\mathcal{B}^{\mathcal{O}_{\mathbf{s}, \chi}}$
- For $i = 1, \ldots, 2\lambda/\epsilon$:
    - Compute $\mathbf{s}_i \leftarrow \mathcal{A}^{\mathcal{O}_{\mathbf{s}, \chi}}(1^\lambda)$.
    - Query λ additional samples and test whether $\mathbf{s}_i$ is a valid solution, if so output $\mathbf{s} \leftarrow \mathbf{s}_i$
- If none of the $\mathbf{s}_i$ passed the check, output $\perp$.

Assume that $\mathbf{y}_i = \mathbf{sA}_i + \mathbf{e}_i$ for all $i \in [k]$. We will now analyze the success probability of $\mathcal{B}$. Say that a pair $(\mathbf{s}, \chi)$ is *good*, if it holds that

$$\Pr[\mathcal{A}^{\mathcal{O}_{\mathbf{s}, \chi}}(1^\lambda) = \mathbf{s}] \geq \epsilon/2,$$

where the probability is taken over the remaining random choices of $\mathcal{O}$ and the random coins of $\mathcal{A}$. By a Markov inequality, it holds that

$$\Pr_{\mathbf{s}, \chi}[(\mathbf{s}, \chi) \text{ good}] = \Pr_{\mathbf{s}, \chi}[\Pr[\mathcal{A}^{\mathcal{O}_{\mathbf{s}, \chi}(\cdot)}(1^\lambda) = \mathbf{s}] \geq \epsilon/2] \geq \epsilon/2.$$

Now, fix a good $(\mathbf{s}, \chi)$. We will bound the probability that all iterations of $\mathcal{B}$ fail to compute $\mathbf{s}$. Once we have fixed $\mathbf{s}$ and χ, all iterations use independent random coins, and thus their outcomes are independent. Consequently, it holds that

$$\Pr[\forall i \in [2\lambda/\epsilon] : \mathcal{A}^{\mathcal{O}_{\mathbf{s},\chi}(\cdot)}(1^\lambda) \neq \mathbf{s}] = \prod_{i=1}^{2\lambda/\epsilon} \Pr[\mathcal{A}^{\mathcal{O}_{\mathbf{s},\chi}(\cdot)}(1^\lambda) \neq \mathbf{s}]$$
$$\leq (1 - \epsilon/2)^{2\lambda/\epsilon}$$
$$\leq \exp(-\epsilon/2 \cdot 2\lambda/\epsilon)$$
$$= \exp(-\lambda),$$

which is negligible. We can conclude that

$$\Pr_{\mathbf{s}}[\Pr[\mathcal{B}((\mathbf{A}_i, \mathbf{s}\mathbf{A}_i + \mathbf{e}_i)_{i\in[k]}) = \mathbf{s}] > 1 - \exp(-\lambda)] \geq \epsilon/2,$$

which means that $\mathcal{B}$ breaks the mild hardness of $\mathsf{entSLWE}(q, \mathcal{M}, \Upsilon, \mathcal{S})$.

3.1   Rerandomization

Lemma 3.4 holds given an unbounded number of samples. We will now consider statistical rerandomization procedures which allow to generate an unbounded number of samples $(\mathbf{A}_i, \mathbf{s}\mathbf{A}_i + \mathbf{e}_i)$ from a fixed number of samples. A typical artifact of statistical re-randomization is that if one starts with a bounded number of samples for a fixed error distribution χ, then the rerandomized samples will have an error that comes from a distribution of error distributions. We provide a simple rerandomization procedure which takes random subset sums over the input samples. While the norm of errors in the output distribution will be bounded, these errors will not follow a *nice* distribution.

Lemma 3.5. *Let $k \geq \log(|\mathbb{G}|) + n\log(q) + \omega(\log(\lambda))$, let Φ be an error distribution on $\mathbb{Z}^n$. The distribution of error-distributions $\Upsilon_{\Phi,bin}$ is defined as follows: A distribution $\chi \leftarrow_\$ \Upsilon_{\Phi,bin}$ is determined by k elements $\mathbf{e}_1, \ldots, \mathbf{e}_k \in \mathbb{Z}^n$ chosen from Φ. To sample from the distribution χ, choose a $\mathbf{x} \leftarrow_\$ \{0,1\}^k$ uniformly at random and output $\sum_i x_i \mathbf{e}_i$.*

If $\mathsf{entSLWE}(q, k, \mathcal{M}, \Phi, \mathcal{S})$ is mildly hard, then $\mathsf{entSLWE}(q, \mathcal{M}, \Upsilon_{\Phi,bin}, \mathcal{S})$ is also mildly hard.

Note that if the distribution Φ is B-bounded, then $\Upsilon_{\Phi,bin}$ is kB-bounded.

Proof. The reduction proceeds via statistical rerandomization. Let $\mathcal{A}$ be an adversary against the mild hardness of $\mathsf{entSLWE}(q, \mathcal{M}, \Upsilon_{\Phi,bin}, \mathcal{S})$. We will construct an adversary $\mathcal{B}$ against the mild hardness of $\mathsf{entSLWE}(q, k, \mathcal{M}, \Phi, \mathcal{S})$. More concretely, assume there is a negligible function ν and a non-negligible function ϵ such that

$$\Pr_{\mathbf{s},\mathbf{e},\chi}[\Pr_{\mathbf{A}}[\mathcal{A}(\mathbf{A}, \mathbf{s}\mathbf{A} + \mathbf{e}) = \mathbf{s}] > 1 - \nu] > \epsilon.$$

The adversary $\mathcal{B}$ proceeds as follows.

Algorithm $\mathcal{B}$
- Input: k samples $(\mathbf{A}_1, \mathbf{y}_1), \ldots, (\mathbf{A}_k, \mathbf{y}_k)$.
- Setup an oracle $\mathcal{O}$, which when queried chooses a uniformly random $\mathbf{x} \in \{0,1\}^k$ and outputs $(\sum_i \mathbf{x}_i \mathbf{A}_i, \sum_i \mathbf{x}_i \mathbf{y}_i)$.
- Compute and output $\mathbf{s} \leftarrow \mathcal{A}^{\mathcal{O}(\cdot)}(1^\lambda)$

We will now show that $\mathcal{B}$ faithfully simulates the oracle $\mathcal{O}$ of the problem entSLWE$(q, \mathcal{M}, \Upsilon_{\Phi,\text{bin}}, \mathcal{S})$. Assume that $\mathbf{y}_i = \mathbf{s}\mathbf{A}_i + \mathbf{e}_i$. Then the rerandomized sample

$$\left(\sum_i \mathbf{x}_i \mathbf{A}_i, \sum_i \mathbf{x}_i \mathbf{y}_i = \mathbf{s}\left(\sum_i \mathbf{x}_i \mathbf{A}_i\right) + \sum_i \mathbf{x}_i \mathbf{e}_i\right)$$

has an error term $\mathbf{e}^* = \sum_i \mathbf{x}_i \mathbf{e}_i$ which follows a distribution χ of $\Upsilon_{\Phi,\text{bin}}$, where χ is defined by $\mathbf{e}_1, \ldots, \mathbf{e}_k \in \mathbb{Z}^n$. Note that $\mathbf{e}^*$ is supported on $\mathbb{Z}_q^n$. Thus, by the leftover hash lemma (Lemma 2.1), the distribution of $\sum_i \mathbf{x}_i \mathbf{A}_i$ is statistically close to uniform in $\mathbb{G}$ given the $\mathbf{e}^*$ and we conclude that the distribution of the samples generated by $\mathcal{O}$ is statistically close to the correct distribution, which concludes the proof.

3.2   Ring-LWE as Structured LWE

Recall the conventions and properties from algebraic number theory as described in Sect. 2.5, and the definition of RLWE from Sect. 2.6 (note that we use the simpler definition that does not use the so-called dual-ring). In particular recall that the ring of integers R of the number field K is a finitely generated $\mathbb{Z}$-module. Since the number field K is mapped into $\mathbb{R}^n$ via the mapping $\bar{\Theta}$, this mapping allows to cast R as a lattice Λ. We denote the basis of this lattice by $\mathbf{L}$ and its inverse by $\mathbf{B} = \mathbf{L}^{-1}$. The mapping $\mathbf{B} \circ \bar{\Theta}$ therefore maps from K to $\mathbb{R}^n$ such that the image of R is $\mathbb{Z}^n$.

Let $a \in \mathsf{R}$. Since multiplication with a is a linear function, there exists a matrix $\mathbf{A}_a \in \mathbb{Z}^{n \times n}$, such that for all $s \in \mathsf{R}$, if $\mathbf{s} \in \mathbb{Z}^n$ is the vector representation of s according to the aforementioned mapping, then $\mathbf{A}_a \mathbf{s}$ is the vector representation of $a \cdot s \in \mathsf{R}$ according to the above mapping. A Gaussian distribution with parameter $\sqrt{\Sigma}$ over the field is mapped by $\mathbf{B} \circ \bar{\Theta}$ to a Gaussian over $\mathbb{R}^n$ with parameter $\sigma\mathbf{B}$.

Therefore, a Ring-LWE equation of the form $as + e$, with $a, s \in \mathsf{R}_q = \mathsf{R}/q\mathsf{R}$ is translated by the mapping $\mathbf{B} \circ \bar{\Theta}$ (which is efficiently computable and efficiently invertible given $\mathbf{B}$) into the linear equation $\mathbf{A}_a \mathbf{s} + \mathbf{e} \pmod{q}$, where $\mathbf{A}_a \in \mathbb{Z}_q^{n \times n}$, $\mathbf{s} \in \mathbb{Z}_q^n$ and e is sampled from the distribution $\chi = D_{\sigma\mathbf{B}}$.

Therefore given a Ring-LWE instance, we can convert it into a structured LWE instance with the aforementioned parameters, so that solving the structured-LWE instance will also imply a solution to the original Ring-LWE instance. The "quality" of the translation relies on the properties of the matrix $\mathbf{B}$, i.e. on how good of a basis for R we can obtain. We discuss the properties of $\mathbf{B}$ in the case of power-of-two cyclotomic number fields in Sect. 6.

4   Sometimes Lossiness and Hardness of Entropic Structured LWE

We will first define a new lossiness notion which we call *Sometimes Lossiness*. This notion will serve as our main tool to establish hardness of entropic generalized LWE problems. Recall the definitions of smooth min-entropy (see Sect. 2.1).

Definition 4.1. *Let q, n, k be integers. Let $\mathcal{X}$ be a distribution on $(\mathbb{Z}_q^{n \times n})^k$, $\mathcal{S}$ be a distribution on $\mathbb{Z}_q^n$ and χ be an error-distribution on $\mathbb{Z}_q^n$. We say that $\mathcal{X}$ is a sometimes lossy pseudorandom distribution for $\mathcal{S}$ and χ if there exists negligible function ϵ, a $\kappa = \omega(\log(\lambda))$ and a $\delta \geq 1/\mathsf{poly}(\lambda)$ such that the following properties hold.*

- *Pseudorandomness:* $\mathcal{X}$ *is computationally indistinguishable from* $\mathcal{M}^k$.
- *Sometimes Lossiness:* *It holds that*

$$\Pr_{\mathbf{A} \leftarrow_\$ \mathcal{X}}[\tilde{H}_\infty^\epsilon(\mathbf{s} | \mathbf{A}, \mathbf{sA} + \mathbf{e}) \geq \kappa] \geq \delta,$$

where $\mathbf{s} \leftarrow_\$ \mathcal{S}$ *and* $\mathbf{e} \leftarrow_\$ \chi^k$.

4.1   From Sometimes Lossiness to the Hardness of Entropic Structured LWE

We will now show that a sometimes lossy pseudorandom distribution $\mathcal{X}$ for a distribution of secrets $\mathcal{S}$ and an error distribution χ implies that hardness of $\mathsf{entSLWE}(q, k, \mathcal{M}, \chi, \mathcal{S})$.

Theorem 4.2. *Let $\mathcal{S}$ be a distribution of secrets and let χ be an error distribution. Assume there exists a sometimes lossy pseudorandom distribution $\mathcal{X}$ on $(\mathbb{Z}_q^{n \times n})^k$. Then $\mathsf{entSLWE}(q, k, \mathcal{M}, \chi, \mathcal{S})$ is mildly hard.*

Proof. Let $\delta = 1/\mathsf{poly}(\lambda)$ be as in Definition 4.1. Set $\ell = \lambda/\delta = \mathsf{poly}(\lambda)$. By a standard hybrid argument, it holds that

$$(\mathbf{A}^{(1)}, \dots, \mathbf{A}^{(\ell)}) \approx_c (\mathbf{U}^{(1)}, \dots, \mathbf{U}^\ell),$$

where $\mathbf{A}^{(i)} \leftarrow_\$ \mathcal{X}$ and $\mathbf{U}^{(i)} \leftarrow_\$ \mathcal{M}^k$ for all $i = 1, \dots, \ell$. Our argument will make use of the fact that by our choice of ℓ, *some* of the $\mathbf{A}^{(i)}$ must be lossy, except with some negligible probability.

Assume towards contradiction that $\mathsf{entSLWE}(q, k, \mathcal{M}, \chi, \mathcal{S})$ is not mildly hard, i.e. there exists a PPT adversary $\mathcal{A}$ against $\mathsf{entSLWE}(q, k, \mathcal{M}, \chi, \mathcal{S})$ such that

$$\Pr_{\mathbf{s}, \mathbf{e}}[\Pr_{\mathbf{A}}[\mathcal{A}(\mathbf{A}, \mathbf{sA} + \mathbf{e}) = \mathbf{s}] > 1 - \nu] > \epsilon,$$

where $\mathbf{s} \leftarrow_\$ \mathcal{S}$, $\mathbf{A} \leftarrow_\$ \mathcal{X}$, $\mathbf{e} \leftarrow_\$ \chi$, $\nu = \nu(\lambda)$ is negligible and $\epsilon \geq 1/\mathsf{poly}(\lambda)$.

We will use $\mathcal{A}$ to construct a distinguisher $\mathcal{D}$ which distinguishes the random variables $(\mathbf{A}^{(1)}, \dots, \mathbf{A}^{(\ell)})$ and $(\mathbf{U}^{(1)}, \dots, \mathbf{U}^{(\ell)})$ with non-negligible advantage. Let $N = \lambda/\epsilon = \mathsf{poly}(\lambda)$. The distinguisher $\mathcal{D}$ is given as follows.

$\mathcal{D}(\mathbf{A}_1, \ldots, \mathbf{A}_\ell)$:
For $i = 1, \ldots, \ell$:
- For $j = 1, \ldots, N$:
  - Choose $\mathbf{s}_{i,j} \leftarrow_\$ \mathcal{S}$ and $\mathbf{e}_{i,j} \leftarrow_\$ \chi^k$
  - Compute $\mathbf{s}'_{i,j} \leftarrow \mathcal{A}(\mathbf{A}^{(i)}, \mathbf{s}_{i,j}\mathbf{A}^{(i)} + \mathbf{e}_{i,j})$
- If for all $j \in [N]$ it holds that $\mathbf{s}'_{i,j} \neq \mathbf{s}_{i,j}$, abort and output 1.
Output 0.

We will now analyze the distinguishing advantage of $\mathcal{D}$.

1. First assume that $\mathcal{A}$'s input is $(\mathbf{A}^{(1)}, \ldots, \mathbf{A}^{(\ell)})$, where each $\mathbf{A}^{(i)}$ is chosen from $\mathcal{X}$. Since the $\mathbf{A}^{(i)}$ are all independent and $\mathcal{X}$ is sometimes lossy for $\mathcal{S}$ and χ, recalling that $\ell = \lambda/\epsilon$ it holds that

$$\Pr_{\mathbf{A}^{(1)}, \ldots, \mathbf{A}^{(\ell)}}[\forall i \in [\ell] : \tilde{H}_\infty(\mathbf{s}|\mathbf{s}\mathbf{A}^{(i)} + \mathbf{e}) < \kappa] = \prod_{i=1}^{\ell} \Pr_{\mathbf{A}^{(i)}}[\tilde{H}_\infty(\mathbf{s}|\mathbf{s}\mathbf{A}^{(i)} + \mathbf{e}) < \kappa]$$
$$\leq (1 - \epsilon)^\ell \leq e^{-\epsilon\ell} = e^{-\lambda},$$

which is negligible. Consequently, there exists an index $i \in [\ell]$ such that $\tilde{H}_\infty(\mathbf{s}|\mathbf{s}\mathbf{A}^{(i)} + \mathbf{e}) \geq k$, except with negligible probability over the choice of the $\mathbf{A}^{(1)}, \ldots, \mathbf{A}^{(\ell)}$. Thus, fix $\mathbf{A}^{(1)}, \ldots, \mathbf{A}^{(\ell)}$ for which there exists an index $i^* \in [\ell]$ with $\tilde{H}_\infty(\mathbf{s}|\mathbf{s}\mathbf{A}^{(i^*)} + \mathbf{e}) \geq k$. Now, since $\mathbf{s}_{i^*,1}, \ldots, \mathbf{s}_{i^*,N} \leftarrow_\$ \mathcal{S}$, it holds by a union-bound that

$$\Pr[\exists j \in [N] : \mathcal{A}(\mathbf{A}^{(i^*)}, \mathbf{s}_{i^*,j}\mathbf{A}^{(i^*)} + \mathbf{e}_{i^*,j}) = \mathbf{s}_{i^*,j}]$$
$$\leq N \cdot \Pr[\mathcal{A}(\mathbf{A}^{(i^*)}, \mathbf{s}\mathbf{A}^{(i^*)} + \mathbf{e}) = \mathbf{s}]$$
$$\leq N \cdot 2^{-\tilde{H}_\infty(\mathbf{s}|\mathbf{A}^{(i^*)}, \mathbf{s}\mathbf{A}^{(i^*)} + \mathbf{e})}$$
$$\leq N \cdot 2^{-\kappa},$$

where $\mathbf{s} \leftarrow_\$ \mathcal{S}$ and $\mathbf{e} \leftarrow_\$ \chi$. The term $N \cdot 2^{-\kappa}$ is negligible as $N = \mathsf{poly}(\lambda)$ and $\kappa = \omega(\log(\lambda))$. Consequently, it follows that in the computation of $\mathcal{D}(\mathbf{A}^{(1)}, \ldots, \mathbf{A}^{(\ell)})$ in the i^*-th iteration of the outer loop it will hold that $\mathbf{s}'_{i^*,j} \neq \mathbf{s}_{i^*,j}$ for all $j \in [N]$, except with negligible probability over the choice of $\mathbf{s}_{i^*,1}, \ldots, \mathbf{s}_{i^*,N}$ and $\mathbf{e}_{i^*,1}, \ldots, \mathbf{e}_{i^*,N}$. This will cause $\mathcal{D}(\mathbf{A}^{(1)}, \ldots, \mathbf{A}^{(\ell)})$ to output 1.
   All together, we conclude that in case $(\mathbf{A}^{(1)}, \ldots, \mathbf{A}^{(\ell)})$ is chosen from $\mathcal{X}^\ell$, it holds that $\mathcal{D}(\mathbf{A}^{(1)}, \ldots, \mathbf{A}^{(\ell)}) = 1$, except with negligible probability over the choice of $(\mathbf{A}^{(1)}, \ldots, \mathbf{A}^{(\ell)})$ and the random coins of $\mathcal{D}$.
2. Now assume that $\mathcal{A}$'s input is $(\mathbf{U}^{(1)}, \ldots, \mathbf{U}^{(\ell)})$, where each $\mathbf{U}_i$ is chosen from $\mathcal{M}^k$. We will show that with high probability over the choice of the $(\mathbf{U}^{(1)}, \ldots, \mathbf{U}^{(\ell)})$ and the random coins of $\mathcal{D}$, for every iteration i there will be an index j such that $\mathbf{s}'_{i,j} = \mathbf{s}_{i,j}$, which will cause $\mathcal{D}(\mathbf{U}^{(1)}, \ldots, \mathbf{U}^{(\ell)})$ to output 0.
   Now fix an $i^* \in [\ell]$. Define the event $\mathsf{BAD}(\mathbf{s}, \mathbf{e})$ by

$$\mathsf{BAD}(\mathbf{s}, \mathbf{e}) :\Leftrightarrow \Pr_{\mathbf{U}}[\mathcal{A}(\mathbf{U}, \mathbf{s}\mathbf{U} + \mathbf{e}) = \mathbf{s}] \leq 1 - \nu,$$

where $\mathbf{U} \leftarrow_\$ \mathcal{M}$. Recall that since we assume that $\mathcal{A}$ breaks mild hardness it holds that $\Pr_{\mathbf{s},\mathbf{e}}[\mathsf{BAD}(\mathbf{s},\mathbf{e})] \leq 1 - \epsilon$. We will now bound the probability that all $(\mathbf{s}_{i^*,1}, \mathbf{e}_{i^*,1}), \ldots, (\mathbf{s}_{i^*,N}, i^*, N)$ are bad. Since all the pairs $(\mathbf{s}_{i^*,1}, \mathbf{e}_{i^*,1}), \ldots, (\mathbf{s}_{i^*,N}, i^*, N)$ are independent, it holds that

$$\Pr[\forall j \in [N] : \mathsf{BAD}(\mathbf{s}_{i^*,j}, \mathbf{e}_{i^*,j})] = \prod_{j \in [N]} \Pr[\mathsf{BAD}(\mathbf{s}_{i^*,j}, \mathbf{e}_{i^*,j})]$$

$$\leq (1 - \epsilon)^N \leq \exp(-\epsilon \cdot N) = \exp(-\lambda),$$

where we have used that $N = \lambda/\epsilon$. Consequently, it holds with overwhelming probability $1 - \exp(-\lambda)$ that at least one $\mathbf{s}_{i^*,j}$ is not bad. Thus, fix $(\mathbf{s}_{i^*,1}, \mathbf{e}_{i^*,1}), \ldots, (\mathbf{s}_{i^*,N}, i^*, N)$ such that there is an index j^* such that the pair $(\mathbf{s}_{i^*,j^*}, \mathbf{e}_{i^*,j^*})$ is not bad, i.e. $\Pr_{\mathbf{U}}[\mathcal{A}(\mathbf{U}, \mathbf{s}_{i^*,j^*}\mathbf{U} + \mathbf{e}_{i^*,j^*}) = \mathbf{s}_{i^*,j^*}] > 1 - \nu$. It follows that

$$\Pr_{\mathbf{U}^{(i^*)}}[\exists j \in [N] : \mathcal{A}(\mathbf{U}^{(i^*)}, \mathbf{s}_{i^*,j}\mathbf{U}^{(i^*)} + \mathbf{e}_{i^*,j}) = \mathbf{s}_{i^*,j}]$$

$$\geq \Pr_{\mathbf{U}^{(i^*)}}[\mathcal{A}(\mathbf{U}^{(i^*)}, \mathbf{s}_{i^*,j^*}\mathbf{U}^{(i^*)} + \mathbf{e}_{i^*,j^*}) = \mathbf{s}_{i^*,j^*}]$$

$$\geq 1 - \nu,$$

which is overwhelming. We can conclude that, it happens with at most negligible probability over the choice of the $\mathbf{s}_{i^*,1}, \ldots, \mathbf{s}_{i^*,N}$, $\mathbf{e}_{i^*,1}, \ldots, \mathbf{e}_{i^*,N}$ and $\mathbf{U}^{(i^*)}$ that the i^*-th iteration of the outer loop *does not* results in an abort with output 1.

A union-bound over all $i^* \in [\ell]$ yields that with at most negligible probability over the choice of the $\mathbf{U}^{(1)}, \ldots, \mathbf{U}^{(\ell)}$ and the random coins of $\mathcal{D}$ that in the computation of $\mathcal{D}(\mathbf{U}^{(1)}, \ldots, \mathbf{U}^{(\ell)})$ any of the ℓ iterations of the outer loop results in an abort with output 1. By construction of $\mathcal{D}$, this means that $\mathcal{D}(\mathbf{U}^{(1)}, \ldots, \mathbf{U}^{(\ell)}) = 0$ with overwhelming probability.

Putting everything together, we conclude that

$$\Pr[\mathcal{D}(\mathbf{A}^{(1)}, \ldots, \mathbf{A}^{(\ell)}) = 1] - \Pr[\mathcal{D}(\mathbf{U}^{(1)}, \ldots, \mathbf{U}^{(\ell)}) = 1]$$

$$= \Pr[\mathcal{D}(\mathbf{A}^{(1)}, \ldots, \mathbf{A}^{(\ell)}) = 1] + \Pr[\mathcal{D}(\mathbf{U}^{(1)}, \ldots, \mathbf{U}^{(\ell)}) = 0] - 1$$

$$= 1 - \mathsf{negl}(\lambda),$$

Thus, $\mathcal{D}$ distinguishes $\mathcal{X}$ and $\mathcal{M}^k$ with advantage close to 1, which contradicts the assumption that $\mathcal{X}$ and $\mathcal{M}$ are computationally indistinguishable. This concludes the proof.

5   Construction of Sometimes Lossy Distributions

In this section we will construct sometimes lossy distributions from a somewhat general problem we call Decisional Small Ratio (DSR) problem. In Sect. 6 we will show that DSR can be instantiated with by the Decisional Small Polynomial Ratio (DSPR) assumption (which is related to the NTRU problem) or the standard RLWE assumption, leading to sometimes lossy distributions with different parameters.

Definition 5.1 (Decisional Small Ratio (DSR) Assumption). *Let q be a modulus and k, n be integers and let $\mathcal{M}$ be a distribution of matrices on $\mathbb{Z}_q^{n \times n}$. Let Ψ be a distribution on $(\mathbb{Z}_q^{n \times n})^{\times} \times \mathbb{Z}_q^{n \times nk}$. The DSR assumption for q, n, k, $\mathcal{M}$ and Ψ postulates that*

$$\mathbf{H} \cdot \mathbf{Z} \approx_c \mathbf{U},$$

where $(\mathbf{Z}_0, \mathbf{Z}) \leftarrow_\$ \Psi$, $\mathbf{H}$ is the $\mathbb{Z}_q$-inverse of $\mathbf{Z}_0 \mod q$ and $\mathbf{U} \leftarrow_\$ \mathcal{M}^k$.

The DSR assumption generalizes the Decisional Small Polynomial Ration (DSPR) assumption [15], which itself is a generalization of the decisional NTRU assumption. We will show that under certain conditions the DSR assumption implies a sometimes lossy mode for LWE.

In our analysis, we will make use of the following smoothing lemma and convolution theorem.

Lemma 5.2 ([24, Claim 3.9]). *Let $\Lambda \subseteq \mathbb{R}^n$ be a lattice and let $\sigma \geq \sqrt{2}\eta_\epsilon(\Lambda)$. Let $\mathbf{e} \sim D_{\Lambda,\sigma}$ be a discrete gaussian and $\mathbf{e}' \sim D_{\mathbb{R}^n,\sigma}$ be a continuous gaussian. Then $\mathbf{e} + vce'$ is 4ϵ close to $D_{\mathbb{R}^n,\sqrt{2}\sigma}$.*

Theorem 5.3 ([20, Thm 3.1]). *Let $\Sigma_1, \Sigma_2 > 0$ be two positive definite matrices such that $\Sigma = \Sigma_1 + \Sigma_2 > 0$ and $\Sigma_1^{-1} + \Sigma_2^{-1} > 0$. Let Λ_1, Λ_2 be two lattices such that $\sqrt{\Sigma_1} \geq \eta_\epsilon(\Lambda_1)$ and $\sqrt{\Lambda_2} \geq \eta_\epsilon(\Lambda_2)$ for some $\epsilon > 0$. Let $\mathbf{c}_1, \mathbf{c}_2 \in \mathbb{R}^n$ be arbitrary. Consider the following sampling procedure for $\mathbf{x} \in \Lambda_2 + \mathbf{c}_2$.*

- *Choose $\mathbf{x}_1 \leftarrow_\$ D_{\Lambda_1 + \mathbf{c}_1, \sqrt{\Sigma_1}}$.*
- *Choose $\mathbf{x} \leftarrow_\$ \mathbf{x}_1 + D_{\Lambda_2 + \mathbf{c}_2 - \mathbf{x}_1, \sqrt{\Sigma_2}}$.*

Then it holds that the marginal distribution of $\mathbf{x}$ is within statistical distance 8ϵ to $D_{\Lambda_2 + \mathbf{c}_2}$.

Lemmas 5.4, 5.5 and 5.6 will be used to prove Theorem 5.7, the main technical result of this section.

Convention: In the following lemmas, always assume the following: q is a modulus, n is an integer and $\mathbf{B} \in \mathbb{R}^{n \times n}$. Moreover let $\Lambda = \Lambda(\mathbf{B}^{-1})$ and set $s = \eta_\epsilon(\Lambda)$.

Lemma 5.4 (Blockwise Gaussian Decomposition). *Let $\mathbf{F} = (\mathbf{F}_1, \ldots, \mathbf{F}_k)$ $\in \mathbb{R}^{n \times nk}$, where for all i $\mathbf{F}_i \in \mathbb{R}^{n \times n}$ and set $\mathbf{F}' = (\mathbf{B}\mathbf{F}_1\mathbf{B}^{-1}, \ldots, \mathbf{B}\mathbf{F}_k\mathbf{B}^{-1})$. Assume that the largest singular value of $\mathbf{F}'$ is $\sigma_{\mathbf{F}'}$. Let $\sigma, \sigma_1 > 0$ be such that $\sigma \geq \sigma_{\mathbf{F}'} \cdot \sigma_1$. There exists a distribution Ψ on $\mathbb{R}^{nk}$, such that if $\mathbf{e}' \sim D_{\sigma_1 \cdot \mathbf{B}}$ and $\mathbf{e}'' \sim \Psi$ are independent, then $\mathbf{e} = \mathbf{e}'\mathbf{F} + \mathbf{e}''$ is distributed according to $D_{\sigma\mathbf{B}}^k$.*

Proof. Let $\Sigma = \sigma^2 \mathbf{I} - \sigma_1^2 \mathbf{F}'^{\top} \mathbf{F}'$. Let $\mathbf{f}' \sim D_{\sigma_1 \mathbf{I}} = D_{\sigma_1}^n$ and $\mathbf{f}'' \sim D_{\sqrt{\Sigma}}$. By Proposition 2.2 it holds that $\mathbf{f} = \mathbf{f}'\mathbf{F}' + \mathbf{f}''$ is distributed according to $D_\sigma^{nk} = D_{\sigma\mathbf{I}}^k$.

Write $\mathbf{f} = (\mathbf{f}_1, \ldots, \mathbf{f}_k)$ and $\mathbf{f}'' = (\mathbf{f}_1'', \ldots, \mathbf{f}_k'')$. Then it holds for all i

$$\mathbf{f}_i = \mathbf{f}' \cdot \mathbf{F}_i' + \mathbf{f}'' = \mathbf{f}'\mathbf{BF}_i\mathbf{B}^{-1} + \mathbf{f}_i''.$$

Multiplying both sides with $\mathbf{B}$ yields

$$\mathbf{f}_i\mathbf{B} = \mathbf{f}'\mathbf{BF} + \mathbf{f}_i''\mathbf{B}.$$

Now notice that $\mathbf{f}'\mathbf{B}$ is distributed according to $D_{\sigma_1\mathbf{B}}$ and for all $i \in [k]$ it holds that $\mathbf{f}_i\mathbf{B}$ is distributed according to $D_{\sigma\mathbf{B}}$. Note that $\mathbf{e}'$ and $\mathbf{f}'\mathbf{B}$ are identically distributed, and also $\mathbf{e}_i$ and $\mathbf{f}_i\mathbf{B}$ are identically distributed for all $i \in [k]$. Setting Ψ to be the distribution of the $\mathbf{f}''\mathbf{B}$ the result follows.

Lemma 5.5 (Continuous to Discrete). *Let $\mathbf{Z}_0 \in \mathbb{Z}^{n \times n}$. Let τ_2 be the largest singular value of $\mathbf{Z}_0' = \mathbf{BZ}_0\mathbf{B}^{-1}$. Assume that $\sigma > \sqrt{2}\tau_2\eta_\epsilon(\mathbf{B}^{-1})$. Let $\mathbf{f} \sim D_{\sqrt{2}\sigma\mathbf{B}}$ and $\mathbf{e} \sim D_{\Lambda(\mathbf{Z}_0),\sigma\cdot\mathbf{B}}$. Let S be a random variable supported on $\mathbb{Z}_q^n$. Then it holds that*

$$\tilde{H}_\infty^{4\epsilon}(\mathbf{s}|\mathbf{s} + \mathbf{fZ}_0^{-1}) \geq \tilde{H}_\infty(\mathbf{s}|\mathbf{s} + \mathbf{eZ}_0^{-1}).$$

Proof. Let $\tilde{\mathbf{e}}' \sim D_{\sigma\mathbf{I}}$ be a spherical continuous gaussian and let $\tilde{\mathbf{e}}$ be distributed according to $D_{\Lambda(\mathbf{B}^{-1}\mathbf{Z}_0'),\sigma\mathbf{I}}$. By Claim 2.3 we have that $\tau_1 \cdot \eta_\epsilon(\mathbf{B}^{-1}) \geq \sigma_{max}(\mathbf{Z}_0') \cdot \eta_\epsilon(\Lambda(\mathbf{B}^{-1})) \geq \eta_\epsilon(\Lambda(\mathbf{B}^{-1} \cdot \mathbf{Z}_0'))$. Now let $\tilde{\mathbf{f}} \sim D_{\sqrt{2}\sigma\mathbf{I}}$. Then it holds by Lemma 5.2 that $\tilde{\mathbf{f}}$ and $\tilde{\mathbf{e}} + \tilde{\mathbf{e}}'$ are 4ϵ close.

Now note that by the definition of $\mathbf{e}$ we have that $\mathbf{e}$ and $\tilde{\mathbf{e}} \cdot \mathbf{B}$ are identically distributed, also $\mathbf{f}$ and $\tilde{\mathbf{f}} \cdot \mathbf{B}$ are identically distributed. Setting $\mathbf{e}' = \tilde{\mathbf{e}}'\mathbf{B}$, we obtain that $\mathbf{fZ}_0^{-1}$ and $\mathbf{eZ}_0^{-1} + \mathbf{e}'\mathbf{Z}_0^{-1}$ are 4ϵ-close. We can conclude that

$$\tilde{H}_\infty(\mathbf{s}|\mathbf{s}+\mathbf{eZ}_0^{-1}) = \tilde{H}_\infty(\mathbf{s}|\mathbf{s}+\mathbf{eZ}_0^{-1},\mathbf{e}') \leq \tilde{H}_\infty(\mathbf{s}|\mathbf{s}+\mathbf{eZ}_0^{-1}+\mathbf{e}'\mathbf{Z}_0^{-1}) \leq \tilde{H}_\infty^{4\epsilon}(\mathbf{s}|\mathbf{s}+\mathbf{fZ}_0^{-1}).$$

Lemma 5.6 (Discrete to Continuous). *Let $\mathbf{f} \leftarrow_\$ D_{\mathbb{Z}^n,\sqrt{2}\sigma\cdot\mathbf{B}}$ and $\mathbf{e} \leftarrow_\$ D_{\sigma\mathbf{B}}$, then it holds that*

$$\tilde{H}_\infty^{8\epsilon}(\mathbf{s}|\mathbf{s} + \mathbf{f}) \geq \tilde{H}_\infty(\mathbf{s}|\mathbf{s} + \mathbf{e}).$$

Proof Let $\mathbf{e}'$ be distributed according to $D_{\mathbb{Z}^n-\mathbf{e},\sigma\mathbf{B}}$. Then it holds by Theorem 5.3 that the statistical distance between $\mathbf{e} + \mathbf{e}'$ and $\mathbf{f}$ is smaller than 8ϵ.

Theorem 5.7. *Let $\mathbf{Z}_0 \in \mathbb{Z}^{n \times n}$ and for $i \in [k]$ $\mathbf{Z}_i \in \mathbb{Z}^{n \times n}$ be matrices and let $\mathbf{Z} = (\mathbf{Z}_1, \ldots, \mathbf{Z}_k) \in \mathbb{Z}_q^{n \times nk}$ be the matrix obtained by concatenating the $\mathbf{Z}_i$. Further let $\mathbf{Z}_0^{-1} \in \mathbb{Q}^{n \times n}$ be the rational inverse of $\mathbf{Z}_0$ and $\mathbf{H} \in \mathbb{Z}_q^{n \times n}$ be the $\mathbb{Z}_q$-inverse of $\mathbf{Z}_0$ mod q.*

Define the matrix $\mathbf{Z}_0' = \mathbf{BZ}_0\mathbf{B}^{-1}$ and $\mathbf{Z}' = (\mathbf{BZ}_1\mathbf{B}^{-1}, \ldots, \mathbf{BZ}_k\mathbf{B}^{-1})$. Let τ_1 be the largest singular value of $\mathbf{Z}_0'^{-1}\mathbf{Z}'$ and τ_2 be the largest singular value of $\mathbf{Z}_0'$. For a $\sigma > \tau_2\eta_\epsilon(\Lambda(\mathbf{B}^{-1}))$ let $\sigma_0 \geq 2^{3/2}\sigma \cdot \tau_1$. Then it holds that

$$\tilde{H}_\infty^{20\epsilon}(\mathbf{s}|\mathbf{sHZ} + \mathbf{e}_0) \geq \tilde{H}_\infty(\mathbf{s}|\mathbf{s} + \mathbf{e}) - n\log(\tau_2),$$

where $\mathbf{e}_0 \leftarrow_\$ D_{\sigma_0\mathbf{B}}^k$ and $\mathbf{e} \leftarrow_\$ D_{\sigma\mathbf{B}}$.

Proof. Fix a distribution of secrets $\mathcal{S}$ and let $\mathbf{s} \leftarrow_\$ \mathcal{S}$. Let $\sigma_1 = \sigma_0/\tau_1 \geq 2^{3/2}\sigma$

Since the largest singular value of $\mathbf{Z}_0'^{-1}\mathbf{Z}'$ is τ_1, by Lemma 5.4 there exists a distribution Ψ over $\mathbb{R}^{nk}$ such that we can equivalently sample $\mathbf{e}_0$ by $\mathbf{e}_0 = \mathbf{e}_1\mathbf{Z}_0^{-1}\mathbf{Z} + \mathbf{e}_1'$, where $\mathbf{e}_1 \sim D_{\sigma_1\mathbf{B}}$ and $\mathbf{e}_1' \sim \Psi$. Consequently, we can write

$$\mathbf{y} = \mathbf{sHZ} + \mathbf{e}_0 = \mathbf{sHZ} + \mathbf{e}_1\mathbf{Z}_0^{-1}\mathbf{Z} + \mathbf{e}_1' = (\mathbf{sH} + \mathbf{e}_1\mathbf{Z}_0^{-1})\mathbf{Z} + \mathbf{e}_1'.$$

Thus, since $\mathbf{y}$ can be computed from $\mathbf{sH} + \mathbf{e}_1\mathbf{Z}_0^{-1}$ and $\mathbf{e}_1'$ it follows that

$$\tilde{H}_\infty(\mathbf{s}|\mathbf{sHZ} + \mathbf{e}_0) = \tilde{H}_\infty(\mathbf{s}|\mathbf{sH} + \mathbf{e}_1\mathbf{Z}_0^{-1}, \mathbf{e}_1') = \tilde{H}_\infty(\mathbf{s}|\mathbf{sH} + \mathbf{e}_1\mathbf{Z}_0^{-1}),$$

where the second equality follows as $\mathbf{e}_1'$ is independent from $\mathbf{s}$ and $\mathbf{e}_1$.

Now let $\sigma_2 = \sigma_1/\sqrt{2} \geq 2\sigma$ and let $\mathbf{e}_2 \sim D_{\Lambda(\mathbf{Z}_0),\sigma_2\mathbf{B}}$ be a discrete gaussian. By Lemma 5.5 it holds that

$$\tilde{H}_\infty^{4\epsilon}(\mathbf{s}|\mathbf{s} + \mathbf{e}_1\mathbf{Z}_0^{-1}) \geq \tilde{H}_\infty(\mathbf{s}|\mathbf{s} + \mathbf{e}_2\mathbf{Z}_0^{-1}).$$

Now, since $\mathbf{H}$ is the $\mathbb{Z}_q$-inverse of $\mathbf{Z}_0 \mod q$, multiplying $\mathbf{sH} + \mathbf{e}_2\mathbf{Z}_0^{-1}$ by $\mathbf{Z}_0$ yields

$$\tilde{H}_\infty(\mathbf{s}|\mathbf{sH} + \mathbf{e}_2\mathbf{Z}_0^{-1}) = \tilde{H}_\infty(\mathbf{s}|\mathbf{s} + \mathbf{e}_2).$$

Now let $\sigma_3 = \sigma_2/\sqrt{2} \geq \sqrt{2}\sigma$, $\mathbf{e}_3 \sim D_{\mathbb{Z}^n,\sigma_3\mathbf{B}}$ and $\mathbf{e}_3' \sim D_{\Lambda(\mathbf{Z}_0)-\mathbf{e}_3,\sigma_3\mathbf{B}}$. Setting $\Lambda_2 = \mathbb{Z}^n$ and $\Lambda_1 = \Lambda(\mathbf{Z}_0)$ in Theorem 5.3 and noting that $\sigma_3 > \sigma > \eta_\epsilon(\Lambda(\mathbf{B}^{-1}))$ we obtain that the statistical distance between $\mathbf{e}_2$ and $\mathbf{e}_3 + \mathbf{e}_3'$ is at most 8ϵ.

It follows that

$$\tilde{H}_\infty^{8\epsilon}(\mathbf{s}|\mathbf{s} + \mathbf{e}_2) \geq \tilde{H}_\infty(\mathbf{s}|\mathbf{s} + \mathbf{e}_3 + \mathbf{e}_3') \geq \tilde{H}_\infty(\mathbf{s}|\mathbf{s} + \mathbf{e}_3, \mathbf{e}_3').$$

Since $\mathbf{e}_3'$ is distributed according to $D_{\Lambda(\mathbf{Z}_0)-\mathbf{e}_3,\sigma_3}$, it only depends on $\mathbf{e}_3 \mod \Lambda(\mathbf{Z}_0)$. Thus

$$\begin{aligned}
\tilde{H}_\infty(\mathbf{s}|\mathbf{s} + \mathbf{e}_3, \mathbf{e}_3') &\geq \tilde{H}_\infty(\mathbf{s}|\mathbf{s} + \mathbf{e}_3) - H_0(\mathbf{e}_3') \\
&\geq \tilde{H}_\infty(\mathbf{s}|\mathbf{s} + \mathbf{e}_3) - \log(\det(\mathbf{Z}_0)) \\
&\geq \tilde{H}_\infty(\mathbf{s}|\mathbf{s} + \mathbf{e}_3) - n \cdot \log(\tau_2),
\end{aligned}$$

as $|\mathbb{Z}^n/\Lambda(\mathbf{Z}_0)| = \det(\mathbf{Z}_0) = \det(\mathbf{Z}_0') \leq n \cdot \log(\tau)$ (as the largest singular value of $\mathbf{Z}_0'$ is τ_2).

Finally as $\sigma_3/\sqrt{2} = \sigma > \eta_\epsilon(\mathbf{B}^{-1})$, by Lemma 5.5 we can bound

$$\tilde{H}_\infty^{8\epsilon}(\mathbf{s}|\mathbf{s} + \mathbf{e}_3) \geq \tilde{H}_\infty(\mathbf{s}|\mathbf{s} + \mathbf{e}),$$

where $\mathbf{e} \leftarrow_\$ D_{\sigma\mathbf{B}}$. Putting everything together, we obtain that

$$\tilde{H}_\infty^{20\epsilon}(\mathbf{s}|\mathbf{sHZ} + \mathbf{e}_0) \geq \tilde{H}_\infty(\mathbf{s}|\mathbf{s} + \mathbf{e}) - n \cdot \log(\tau_2).$$

We can now summarize the results of this section in the following theorem.

Theorem 5.8. *Let $\tau_1, \tau_2 > 0$. Let Ψ be a distribution on $(\mathbb{Z}^{n \times n})^\times \times \mathbb{Z}^{n \times nk}$ and assume the Decisional Small Ratio assumption holds for Ψ. Assume further that if $(\mathbf{Z}_0, \mathbf{Z}) \leftarrow_\$ \Psi$ then*

– $\sigma_{max}(\mathbf{B}\mathbf{Z}_0^{-1}\mathbf{Z}\mathbf{B}^{-1}) \leq \tau_1$ where $\mathbf{Z}_0^{-1}$ is the rational inverse of $\mathbf{Z}_0$.
– $\sigma_{max}(\mathbf{B}\mathbf{Z}_0\mathbf{B}^{-1}) \leq \tau_2$

with probability at least δ over the choice of $(\mathbf{Z}_0, \mathbf{Z})$. Define the distribution $\mathcal{X}$ on $\mathbb{Z}_q^{n \times m}$ by $\mathbf{H}\mathbf{Z}$, where $(\mathbf{Z}_0, \mathbf{Z}) \leftarrow_\$ \Psi$ and $\mathbf{H} \in \mathbb{Z}^{n \times n}$ is the $\mathbb{Z}_q$-inverse of $\mathbf{Z}_0$. Let $\sigma > \tau_2 \eta_\epsilon(\Lambda(\mathbf{B}^{-1}))$ and $\sigma_0 > 2^{3/2}\tau_1\sigma$. Now let $\chi = D_{\sigma_0\mathbf{B}}$. Further assume that $\nu_{\sigma\mathbf{B}}(\mathcal{S}) \geq n\log(\tau_2) + \omega(\log(\lambda))$.

Then $\mathcal{X}$ is a sometimes lossy pseudorandom distribution for $\mathcal{S}$ and error distribution χ.

By combining Theorems 5.8 and 4.2 we obtain the following corollary.

Corollary 5.9. *Assume that the conditions of Theorem 5.8 are satisfied. Then* entSLWE$(q, k, \mathcal{M}, D_{\sigma_0\mathbf{B}}, \mathcal{S})$ *is mildly hard.*

6   Instantiation for RLWE over Power-of-Two Cyclotomics

In this Section, we will instantiate the results of Sect. 5 for Ring LWE over power-of-two cyclotomics. That is, we will construct a sometimes lossy pseudorandom distribution in this setting.

Throughout this section let $\mathbf{B} \in \mathbb{R}^{n \times n}$ be a basis-change matrix as described in Sect. 3.2.

First recall the Decisional Small Polynomial Ratio (DSPR) problem, as defined by Lopez-Alt et al. [15]. The DSPR problem is in fact a generalization of the NTRU problem.

Definition 6.1 (Decisional Small Polynomial Ratio problem (DSPR)). *Let* R *be a ring of integers of a number field* K *and let* q *be a modulus. Let* $\gamma > 0$. *Let* $\mathbf{g} \leftarrow_\$ D_{\mathsf{R},\gamma}$ *and* $\mathbf{f} \leftarrow_\$ D_{\mathsf{R},\gamma}$ *conditioned on* $\mathbf{f} \mod q \in \mathsf{R}_q^\times$. *Let* $\mathbf{h}$ *be the* R_q-*inverse of* $\mathbf{f}$. *The DSPR problem for distribution* $D_{\mathsf{R},\gamma}$ *asks to distinguish* $\mathbf{h}\mathbf{g} \in \mathsf{R}_q$ *from a uniformly random* $\mathbf{a} \leftarrow_\$ \mathsf{R}_q$.

We will make use of the following Lemmas and Theorems of Stehlé and Steinfeld [27].

Theorem 6.2 shows that if the a gaussian χ is sufficiently wide, then ring elements $\mathbf{h}\mathbf{g}$ are actually statistically close to a uniform $\mathbf{a} \leftarrow_\$ \mathsf{R}_q$.

Theorem 6.2 ([27, Theorem 3.2 restated]). *Let* $n \geq 8$ *be a power of 2 such that* $\Phi = X^n + 1$ *splits into* n *linear factors modulo a prime* $q \geq 5$. *Let* $0 < \alpha < 1/3$ *and assume that* $\gamma \geq n \cdot \sqrt{\ln(8nq)} \cdot q^{1/2 + \alpha}$ *and that* $\mathbf{f}, \mathbf{g} \leftarrow_\$ D_{\mathsf{R}_q^\times, \gamma}$. *Let* $\mathbf{h}$ *be the* R_q-*inverse of* $\mathbf{f}$. *Then it holds that* $\mathbf{h}\mathbf{g}$ *is within statistical distance* $2^{10n} \cdot q^{-\alpha n}$ *of the uniform distribution on* $\mathsf{R}_q^\times$.

Lemma 6.3 ([27, Lemma 3.5 restated]). *Let* $n \geq 8$ *be a power of 2 such that* $\Phi = X^n + 1$ *splits into* n *linear factors modulo* $q \geq 5$. *Let* $\gamma \geq \sqrt{n \cdot \ln(2n(1 + n^2))/\pi} \cdot q^{1/n}$. *Then it holds that*

$$\Pr_{\mathbf{f} \leftarrow_\$ D_{\mathsf{R},\gamma}} [\mathbf{f} \notin \mathsf{R}_q^\times] \leq n(1/q + 2/n^2).$$

Lemma 6.4 ([27, Lemma 2.8 restated]). *Let* R *be a ring of integers. Then it holds for any* $\gamma \geq \eta_\epsilon(\mathsf{R})$ *that*

$$\Pr_{\mathbf{f} \leftarrow_\$ D_{\mathsf{R},\gamma}} [\|\mathbf{f}\| \geq \gamma \log(n)\sqrt{n}] \leq \mathsf{negl}(\lambda)$$

Lemma 6.5 ([27, Lemma 4.1 restated]). *Let* $n \geq 8$ *be a power of 2,* $\Phi = X^n + 1$ *and* $\mathsf{R} = \mathbb{Z}[X]/(\Phi)$. *For any* $\gamma \geq 8n\eta_\epsilon(\mathsf{R})$ *it holds that*

$$\Pr_{\mathbf{f} \leftarrow_\$ D_{\mathsf{R},\gamma}} \left[\|\mathbf{f}^{-1}\| \geq \frac{24\sqrt{n}}{\gamma} \right] \leq 1/2$$

We will now establish the hardness of an instance of the DSR problem, assuming RLWE and either the DSPR problem or Theorem 6.2. Let χ be a B-bounded error distribution on R and let $\gamma > 0$ be a gaussian parameter. Define the distribution Ψ as follows:

– Choose $\mathbf{f}, \mathbf{g} \leftarrow_\$ D_{\mathsf{R},\gamma}$ such that $\mathbf{f} \bmod q \in \mathsf{R}_q^\times$.
– Choose $\mathbf{e}_1, \ldots, \mathbf{e}_k \leftarrow_\$ \chi$ and $\mathbf{e}'_1, \ldots, \mathbf{e}'_k \leftarrow_\$ \chi$
– For all $i \in [k]$ set $\mathbf{z}_i = \mathbf{g} \cdot \mathbf{e}_i + \mathbf{f} \cdot \mathbf{e}'_i$.
– Let $\mathbf{Z}_0$ be the multiplication matrix of $\mathbf{f}$ and for all $i \in [k]$ let $\mathbf{Z}_i$ be the multiplication matrix of $\mathbf{z}_i$
– Set $\mathbf{Z} = (\mathbf{Z}_1, \ldots, \mathbf{Z}_k)$
– Output $(\mathbf{Z}_0, \mathbf{Z})$

We will now show that the distribution Ψ is a sometimes lossy pseudorandom distribution. Recall that by Theorem 5.8 it is sufficient to bound the maximal singular values of $\mathbf{B}\mathbf{Z}_0\mathbf{B}^{-1}$, $\mathbf{B}\mathbf{Z}_0^{-1}\mathbf{Z}\mathbf{B}^{-1}$ and establish that the DSR assumption for Ψ holds. We will start by showing that if the Ring LWE assumption for error distribution χ and the DSPR assumptions hold, then the DSR assumption holds for Ψ.

Lemma 6.6. *Assuming both DSPR for distribution* $D_{\mathsf{R},\gamma}$ *and RLWE for error-distribution* χ, *it follows that DSR for distribution* Ψ *is hard. Moreover, if* $\chi = D_{\mathsf{R}_q^\times,\gamma}$ *and the conditions of Theorem 6.2 are met, then the DSPR assumption is not necessary.*

Proof. Let $\mathbf{h}$ be the R_q-inverse of $\mathbf{f}$. Observe that $\mathbf{y}_i = \mathbf{h}\mathbf{z}_i = \mathbf{h}\mathbf{g} \cdot \mathbf{e}_i + \mathbf{e}'_i$. Under the DSPR assumption we can replace $\mathbf{h}\mathbf{g}$ by a uniformly random $\mathbf{a} \in \mathsf{R}_q$. It then follows by a simple hybrid argument that for all i $\mathbf{y}_i = \mathbf{a}\mathbf{e}_i + \mathbf{e}'_i$ is indistinguishable from a uniformly random $\mathbf{u}_i$ under Hermite RLWE for error distribution χ'.

Likewise, if the conditions of Theorem 6.2 are met, $\mathbf{h}\mathbf{g}$ is statistically close to a uniformly random $\mathbf{a} \in \mathsf{R}_q^\times$. It follows again via a hybrid argument that for all i $\mathbf{y}_i = \mathbf{a}\mathbf{e}_i + \mathbf{e}'_i$ is indistinguishable from a uniformly random $\mathbf{u}_i$ under Hermite RLWE for error distribution χ'. Note that RLWE also holds if we condition on $\mathbf{a} \in \mathsf{R}_q^\times$, as this event happens with significant probability.

The following technical lemma lets us bound the maximal singular value of a matrix $\mathbf{Z}'$ by bounding the singular values of *blocks* of $\mathbf{Z}'$.

Lemma 6.7. *Let* $\mathbf{Z}' = (\mathbf{Z}_1'|\ldots|\mathbf{Z}_m') \in \mathbb{R}^{n \times n \cdot k}$ *be a block matrix where each* $\mathbf{Z}_i' \in \mathbb{R}^{n \times n}$. *Assume that it holds for all i that* $\sigma_{max}(\mathbf{Z}_i') \le \gamma$. *Then it holds that* $\sigma_{max}(\mathbf{Z}') \le \sqrt{k} \cdot \gamma$.

Proof. Fix any vector $\mathbf{x} = (\mathbf{x}_1, \ldots, \mathbf{x}_k) \in \mathbb{R}^{nk}$, where the $\mathbf{x}_i \in \mathbb{R}^n$. Then it holds that

$$\|\mathbf{Z}'\mathbf{x}\| = \|\sum_{i=1}^{k} \mathbf{Z}_i'\mathbf{x}_i\| \le \sum_{i=1}^{k} \|\mathbf{Z}_i'\mathbf{x}_i\| \le \sum_{i=1}^{k} \gamma\|\mathbf{x}_i\| \le \gamma\sqrt{k} \cdot \sqrt{\sum_{i=1}^{k} \|\mathbf{x}_i\|^2} = \gamma\sqrt{k} \cdot \|\mathbf{x}\|,$$

where the last inequality follows from the relationship between the L_1 and L_2 norms. It follows that $\sigma_{max}(\mathbf{Z}') \le \sqrt{k} \cdot \gamma$

Lemma 6.8 bounds the maximal singular values of $\mathbf{BZ}_0\mathbf{B}^{-1}$ and $\mathbf{BZ}_0^{-1}\mathbf{ZB}^{-1}$

Lemma 6.8. *Let* $\gamma > \max\{\sqrt{n \cdot \ln(2n(1+n^2))/\pi} \cdot q^{1/n}, 8n\eta_\epsilon(\mathsf{R})\}$ *and assume that χ is B-bounded. Let* $(\mathbf{Z}_0, \mathbf{Z}) \leftarrow_\$ \Psi$. *It holds that*

- $\mathbf{Z}_0$ *is invertible in* $\mathbb{Z}_q^{n \times n}$
- $\sigma_{max}(\mathbf{BZ}_0\mathbf{B}^{-1}) \le O(\gamma \log(n)\sqrt{n})$
- $\sigma_{max}(\mathbf{BZ}_0^{-1}\mathbf{ZB}^{-1}) \le O(n \log(n)\sqrt{k}B)$

except with probability $1/2 + o(1)$ *over the choice of* $(\mathbf{Z}_0, \mathbf{Z})$.

Proof. We will bound the maximal singular value of $\mathbf{BZ}_0\mathbf{B}^{-1}$ by $\|\sigma(\mathbf{f})\|_\infty$. Likewise, we will bound the maximal singular values of the $\mathbf{BZ}_0^{-1}\mathbf{Z}_i\mathbf{B}^{-1}$ via $\|\sigma(\mathbf{f}^{-1}\mathbf{z}_i)\|_\infty$. The bound on the maximal singular value of $\mathbf{BZB}^{-1}$ will follow by Lemma 6.7.

Note that

- It holds by Lemma 6.3 that $\mathbf{f}$ in invertible in $\mathsf{R}_q^\times$, except with probability $n/q + 2/n = O(1/n)$.
- It holds by Lemma 6.4 and a union bound that $\|\sigma(\mathbf{f})\| \le \gamma \log(n)\sqrt{n}$ and $\|\sigma(\mathbf{z}_i)\| \le \gamma \log(n)\sqrt{n}$ for all $i \in [k]$, except with negligible probability.
- By Lemma 6.5 we have that $\|\sigma(\mathbf{f}^{-1})\| \le 24\sqrt{n}/\gamma$, except with probability $\le 1/2$.

Consequently, all 3 items hold, except with probability $1/2 + o(1)$. Moreover, since the $\mathbf{e}_i$ and $\mathbf{e}_i'$ are distributed according to χ and χ is B-bounded, it holds that for all $i \in [k]$ that $\|\sigma(\mathbf{e}_i)\| \le B$ and $\|\sigma(\mathbf{e}_i')\| \le B$.

Thus, we have that

$$\sigma_{max}(\mathbf{BZ}_0\mathbf{B}^{-1}) \le \|\sigma(\mathbf{f})\|_\infty \le \|\sigma(\mathbf{f})\| \le \gamma \log(n)\sqrt{n} = O(\gamma \log(n)\sqrt{n}).$$

Moreover, it holds for all i that

$$
\begin{aligned}
\sigma_{max}(\mathbf{BZ}_0^{-1}\mathbf{Z}_i\mathbf{B}^{-1}) &\leq \|\sigma(\mathbf{f}^{-1}\mathbf{z}_i)\|_\infty \\
&= \|\sigma(\mathbf{f}^{-1}\mathbf{ge}_i + \mathbf{e}_i')\|_\infty \\
&\leq \|\sigma(\mathbf{f}^{-1})\|_\infty \cdot \|\sigma(\mathbf{g})\|_\infty \cdot \|\sigma(\mathbf{e}_i)\|_\infty + \|\sigma(\mathbf{e}_i')\|_\infty \\
&\leq \|\sigma(\mathbf{f}^{-1})\| \cdot \|\sigma(\mathbf{g})\| \cdot \|\sigma(\mathbf{e}_i)\| + \|\sigma(\mathbf{e}_i')\| \\
&\leq 24n\log(n) \cdot B = O(n\log(n)B)
\end{aligned}
$$

By Lemma 6.7 we conclude that $\sigma_{max}(\mathbf{BZB}^{-1}) \leq O(n\log(n)\sqrt{k}B)$.

We can now summarize the results of this section in our main theorem by combining Lemma 6.8 with Corollary 5.9.

Theorem 6.9. *Assume that DSPR with parameter γ and Ring LWE with a B-bounded noise distribution χ holds. Let $\mathcal{S}$ be a distribution s.t. for some σ it holds that $\nu_\sigma(\mathcal{S}) \geq n\log(\gamma \cdot \log(n)\sqrt{n}) + \omega(\log\lambda)$. Then Entropic Ring LWE for power-of-two cyclotomics with k samples, secret distribution $\mathcal{S}$ and Gaussian noise parameter $\sigma_0 \geq O(\sigma n\log(n)B\sqrt{k})$ is mildly hard.*

By Theorem 6.2 we know that we can drop the DSPR assumption provided that $\gamma \geq \mathsf{poly}(n)q^{1/2+\alpha}$ for an arbitrarily small constant α. This translates to the stronger requirement that $\nu_\sigma(\mathcal{S}) \geq (1/2 + \alpha)n\log(q) + O(n\log(n))$. Thus, the distribution $\mathcal{S}$ must have at more than $(1/2 + \alpha)n\log(q) + O(n\log(n))$ min-entropy to begin with. However, note that if $\mathcal{S}$ is an r-bounded distribution, where $r \geq \mathsf{poly}(n)q^{1/2+\alpha}$, then Lemma 2.5 tells us if σ is a $\mathsf{poly}(n)$ factor larger than r, we have essentially $\nu_\sigma(\mathcal{S}) \approx \tilde{H}_\infty(\mathcal{S})$ and the requirements can be met.

References

1. Albrecht, M.R., Deo, A.: Large modulus ring-LWE $\geq$ module-LWE. In: Takagi, T., Peyrin, T. (eds.) ASIACRYPT 2017. LNCS, vol. 10624, pp. 267–296. Springer, Cham (2017). https://doi.org/10.1007/978-3-319-70694-8_10
2. Alwen, J., Krenn, S., Pietrzak, K., Wichs, D.: Learning with rounding, revisited-new reduction, properties and applications. In: Canetti, R., Garay, J.A. (eds.) CRYPTO 2013. LNCS, vol. 8042, pp. 57–74. Springer, Heidelberg (2013). https://doi.org/10.1007/978-3-642-40041-4_4
3. Bolboceanu, M., Brakerski, Z., Perlman, R., Sharma, D.: Order-LWE and the hardness of ring-LWE with entropic secrets. In: Asiacrypt (2019). https://eprint.iacr.org/2018/494
4. Brakerski, Z., Döttling, N.: Hardness of LWE on general entropic distributions. In: Canteaut, A., Ishai, Y. (eds.) EUROCRYPT 2020. LNCS, vol. 12106, pp. 551–575. Springer, Cham (2020). https://doi.org/10.1007/978-3-030-45724-2_19
5. Brakerski, Z., Gentry, C., Vaikuntanathan, V.: (Leveled) fully homomorphic encryption without bootstrapping. In: Goldwasser, S. (ed.) ITCS 2012: 3rd Innovations in Theoretical Computer Science, pp. 309–325. Association for Computing Machinery, Cambridge, 8–10 January 2012

6. Brakerski, Z., Langlois, A., Peikert, C., Regev, O., Stehlé, D.: Classical hardness of learning with errors. In: Boneh, D., Roughgarden, T., Feigenbaum, J. (eds.) 45th Annual ACM Symposium on Theory of Computing, pp. 575–584. ACM Press, Palo Alto, 1–4 June 2013
7. Dodis, Y., Ostrovsky, R., Reyzin, L., Smith, A.D.: Fuzzy extractors: how to generate strong keys from biometrics and other noisy data. SIAM J. Comput. **38**(1), 97–139 (2008)
8. Goldwasser, S., Kalai, Y.T., Peikert, C., Vaikuntanathan, V.: Robustness of the learning with errors assumption. In: Yao, A.C.C. (ed.) ICS 2010: 1st Innovations in Computer Science, pp. 230–240. Tsinghua University Press, Tsinghua University, Beijing, 5–7 January 2010
9. Halevi, S., Shoup, V.: Algorithms in HElib. In: Garay, J.A., Gennaro, R. (eds.) CRYPTO 2014. LNCS, vol. 8616, pp. 554–571. Springer, Heidelberg (2014). https://doi.org/10.1007/978-3-662-44371-2_31
10. Halevi, S., Shoup, V.: Bootstrapping for HElib. In: Oswald, E., Fischlin, M. (eds.) EUROCRYPT 2015. LNCS, vol. 9056, pp. 641–670. Springer, Heidelberg (2015). https://doi.org/10.1007/978-3-662-46800-5_25
11. Hoffstein, J., Pipher, J., Silverman, J.H.: NTRU: a ring-based public key cryptosystem. In: Buhler, J.P. (ed.) ANTS 1998. LNCS, vol. 1423, pp. 267–288. Springer, Heidelberg (1998). https://doi.org/10.1007/BFb0054868
12. Kalai, Y.T., Reyzin, L.: A survey of leakage-resilient cryptography. IACR Cryptol. ePrint Arch. **2019**, 302 (2019)
13. Kirchner, P., Fouque, P.-A.: Revisiting lattice attacks on overstretched NTRU parameters. In: Coron, J.-S., Nielsen, J.B. (eds.) EUROCRYPT 2017. LNCS, vol. 10210, pp. 3–26. Springer, Cham (2017). https://doi.org/10.1007/978-3-319-56620-7_1
14. Langlois, A., Stehlé, D.: Worst-case to average-case reductions for module lattices. Des. Codes Cryptogr. **75**(3), 565–599 (2015)
15. López-Alt, A., Tromer, E., Vaikuntanathan, V.: On-the-fly multiparty computation on the cloud via multikey fully homomorphic encryption. In: Karloff, H.J., Pitassi, T. (eds.) 44th Annual ACM Symposium on Theory of Computing, pp. 1219–1234. ACM Press, New York, 19–22 May 2012
16. Lyubashevsky, V., Peikert, C., Regev, O.: On ideal lattices and learning with errors over rings. In: Gilbert, H. (ed.) EUROCRYPT 2010. LNCS, vol. 6110, pp. 1–23. Springer, Heidelberg (2010). https://doi.org/10.1007/978-3-642-13190-5_1
17. Lyubashevsky, V., Peikert, C., Regev, O.: A toolkit for ring-LWE cryptography. In: Johansson, T., Nguyen, P.Q. (eds.) EUROCRYPT 2013. LNCS, vol. 7881, pp. 35–54. Springer, Heidelberg (2013). https://doi.org/10.1007/978-3-642-38348-9_3
18. Micciancio, D.: On the hardness of learning with errors with binary secrets. Theory Comput. **14**(1), 1–17 (2018)
19. NIST: Post-quantum cryptography standardization. https://csrc.nist.gov/Projects/Post-Quantum-Cryptography
20. Peikert, C.: An efficient and parallel gaussian sampler for lattices. In: Rabin, T. (ed.) CRYPTO 2010. LNCS, vol. 6223, pp. 80–97. Springer, Heidelberg (2010). https://doi.org/10.1007/978-3-642-14623-7_5
21. Peikert, C.: A decade of lattice cryptography. Found. Trends Theor. Comput. Sci. **10**(4). 283–424 (2016). https://doi.org/10.1561/0400000074, Specific references are to the ePrint version https://eprint.iacr.org/2015/939
22. Peikert, C., Pepin, Z.: Algebraically structured LWE, revisited. In: Hofheinz, D., Rosen, A. (eds.) TCC 2019. LNCS, vol. 11891, pp. 1–23. Springer, Cham (2019). https://doi.org/10.1007/978-3-030-36030-6_1

23. Peikert, C., Regev, O., Stephens-Davidowitz, N.: Pseudorandomness of ring-LWE for any ring and modulus. In: Hatami, H., McKenzie, P., King, V. (eds.) Proceedings of the 49th Annual ACM SIGACT Symposium on Theory of Computing, STOC 2017, Montreal, QC, Canada, 19–23 June 2017, pp. 461–473. ACM (2017). https://doi.org/10.1145/3055399.3055489

24. Regev, O.: On lattices, learning with errors, random linear codes, and cryptography. In: Gabow, H.N., Fagin, R. (eds.) 37th Annual ACM Symposium on Theory of Computing, pp. 84–93. ACM Press, Baltimore, 22–24 May 2005

25. Microsoft SEAL. microsoft Research, Redmond, October 2018. http://sealcrypto.org

26. Stehlé, D., Steinfeld, R.: Making NTRU as secure as worst-case problems over ideal lattices. In: Paterson, K.G. (ed.) EUROCRYPT 2011. LNCS, vol. 6632, pp. 27–47. Springer, Heidelberg (2011). https://doi.org/10.1007/978-3-642-20465-4_4

27. Stehlé, D., Steinfeld, R.: Making NTRUEncrypt and NTRUsign as secure as standard worst-case problems over ideal lattices. IACR Cryptol. ePrintArch. **2013**, p. 4 (2013). http://eprint.iacr.org/2013/004, preliminary version in [26]

28. Stehlé, D., Steinfeld, R., Tanaka, K., Xagawa, K.: Efficient public key encryption based on ideal lattices. In: Matsui, M. (ed.) ASIACRYPT 2009. LNCS, vol. 5912, pp. 617–635. Springer, Heidelberg (2009). https://doi.org/10.1007/978-3-642-10366-7_36

Multi-key Fully-Homomorphic Encryption in the Plain Model

Prabhanjan Ananth[1($\boxtimes$)], Abhishek Jain[2], Zhengzhong Jin[2],
and Giulio Malavolta[3]

[1] University of California Santa Barbara, Santa Barbara, CA, USA
`prabhanjan@cs.ucsb.edu`
[2] Johns Hopkins University, Baltimore, MD, USA
`{abhishek,zzjin}@cs.jhu.edu`
[3] Max Planck Institute for Security and Privacy, Bochum, Germany
`giulio.malavolta@hotmail.it`

Abstract. The notion of multi-key fully homomorphic encryption (multi-key FHE) [López-Alt, Tromer, Vaikuntanathan, STOC'12] was proposed as a generalization of fully homomorphic encryption to the multiparty setting. In a multi-key FHE scheme for n parties, each party can individually choose a key pair and use it to encrypt its own private input. Given n ciphertexts computed in this manner, the parties can homomorphically evaluate a circuit C over them to obtain a new ciphertext containing the output of C, which can then be decrypted via a decryption protocol. The key efficiency property is that the size of the (evaluated) ciphertext is independent of the size of the circuit.

Multi-key FHE with *one-round* decryption [Mukherjee and Wichs, Eurocrypt'16], has found several powerful applications in cryptography over the past few years. However, an important drawback of all such known schemes is that they require a *trusted setup*.

In this work, we address the problem of constructing multi-key FHE in the plain model. We obtain the following results:
- A multi-key FHE scheme with one-round decryption based on the hardness of learning with errors (LWE), ring LWE, and decisional small polynomial ratio (DSPR) problems.
- A variant of multi-key FHE where we relax the decryption algorithm to be non-compact – i.e., where the decryption complexity can depend on the size of C – based on the hardness of LWE. We call this variant *multi-homomorphic encryption* (MHE). We observe that MHE is already sufficient for some of the applications of multi-key FHE.

1 Introduction

Fully-homomorphic encryption [21] (FHE) allows one to compute on encrypted data. An important limitation of FHE is that it requires all of the data to be

R. Pass and K. Pietrzak (Eds.): TCC 2020, LNCS 12550, pp. 28–57, 2020.
https://doi.org/10.1007/978-3-030-64375-1_2

encrypted under the same public key in order to perform homomorphic evaluations. To circumvent this shortcoming, López-Alt et al. [29] proposed a multiparty extension of FHE, namely, *multi-key FHE*, where each party can sample a key pair $(\mathsf{sk}_i, \mathsf{pk}_i)$ locally and encrypt its message under its own public key. Then one can publicly evaluate any (polynomially computable) circuit over the resulting ciphertexts $c_i = \mathsf{Enc}(\mathsf{pk}_i, m_i)$, each encrypted under an independently sampled public key. Naturally, decrypting the resulting multi-key ciphertext requires one to know *all* the secret keys for the parties involved.

In this work we are interested in multi-key FHE schemes with a one-round decryption protocol: Given a multi-key ciphertext $c = \mathsf{Enc}((\mathsf{pk}_1, \ldots, \mathsf{pk}_N), C(m_1, \ldots, m_N))$, the decryption consists of (i) a local phase, where each party independently computes a decryption share p_i using its secret key sk_i, and a (ii) public phase, where the plaintext m can be publicly recovered from the decryption shares $(p_1, \ldots, p_N)$.

Other than being an interesting primitive on its own, multi-key FHE with one-round (also referred to as "non-interactive") decryption implies a natural solution for secure multi-party computation (MPC) with *optimal* round complexity and communication complexity *independent* of the size of the circuit being computed [31]. Additionally, multi-key FHE with one-round decryption has proven to be a versatile tool to construct powerful cryptographic primitives, such as spooky encryption [18], homomorphic secret sharing [11,12], obfuscation and functional encryption combiners [4,5], multiparty obfuscation [25], homomorphic time-lock puzzles [14,30], and ad-hoc multi-input functional encryption [1].

To the best of our knowledge, all known multi-key FHE schemes with one-round decryption assume a trusted setup [16,17,31,32] or require non-standard assumptions, such as the existence of sub-exponentially secure general-purpose obfuscation [18]. A major open question in this area (stated in [16,31]) is whether it is possible to avoid the use of a common setup and obtain a solution in the *plain model*.

1.1 Our Results

We present the first construction of a multi-key FHE with one-round decryption in the plain model, i.e. without a trusted setup, from standard assumptions over lattices. Specifically, we prove the following main theorem:

Theorem 1 (Informal). *Assuming,*

- *Two-round semi-malicious oblivious transfer in the plain model,*
- *Multi-key FHE with trusted setup and one-round decryption and,*
- *Multi-key FHE in the plain model but with arbitrary round decryption,*

there exists multi-key FHE in the plain model with one-round decryption.

A multi-key FHE with one-round decryption in the common reference string (CRS) model can be constructed assuming the hardness of the standard learning with errors (LWE) problem [17,31]. Similarly, two-round semi-malicious oblivious transfer can also be instantiated assuming learning with errors [13]. On the other hand, a multi-key FHE scheme without setup, but with complex decryption, was proposed in [29] assuming the hardness of the Ring LWE and the decisional small polynomial ratio (DSPR) problems,[1] Thus, we obtain the following implication:

Theorem 2 (Informal). *Assuming that the LWE, Ring LWE, and DSPR problems are hard, there exists a leveled multi-key FHE scheme in the plain model with one-round decryption. Additionally assuming circular security of our scheme, there exists multi-key FHE in the plain model with one-round decryption.*

We remark that our compiler is completely generic in the choice of the scheme and thus can benefit from future development in the realm of multi-key FHE with multi-round decryption. We also point out that our construction achieves a relaxed security notion where, among other differences, we require computational indistinguishability of simulated decryption shares, whereas the works of [16,31, 32] achieved statistical indistinguishability (see Sect. 4 for a precise statement). To the best of our knowledge, this definition suffices for known applications of multi-key FHE.

Multiparty Homomorphic Encryption. As a stepping stone towards our main result, we introduce the notion of *multiparty homomorphic encryption* (MHE). MHE is a variant of multi-key FHE that retains its key virtue of communication efficiency but sacrifices on the efficiency of final output computation step. Specifically, the reconstruction of the message from the decryption shares is "non-compact", i.e. its computational complexity might depend on the size of the evaluated circuit. Crucially, we still require that the size of the (evaluated) ciphertexts is independent of size of the circuit. As we discuss below, MHE suffices for some applications of multi-key FHE, including a two-round MPC protocol where the first message depends only on the input of each party and can be reused for arbitrarily many evaluations of different circuits.

Note that unlike the case of (single-key) FHE, allowing for non-compact output computation does *not* trivialize the notion of MHE. Indeed, in the case of FHE, a trivial scheme with non-compact output computation can be obtained via any public-key encryption scheme by simply considering a decryption process that first recovers the plaintext and then evaluates the circuit to compute the output. Such an approach, however, does not extend to the multiparty setting since it would violate the security requirement of MHE (defined similarly to that of multi-key FHE).

We prove the following theorem:

---

[1] These assumptions have been cryptanalyzed in [2,27], which affects the concrete choice of the parameters of the scheme. However, all known attacks (including these works) run in sub-exponential time. We refer the reader to [26] for recommendations on the parameter choices for conjectured λ-bits of security.

Theorem 3 (Informal). *Assuming the hardness of the LWE problem (with sub-exponential modulus-to-noise ratio), there exists an MHE scheme in the plain model.*

At a technical level, we develop a recursive *self-synthesis* transformation that lifts any one-time MHE scheme (i.e. where the first message can be securely used only for the evaluation of a single circuit) to an unbounded MHE. Our approach bears resemblance to and builds upon several seemingly unrelated works dating as far back as the construction of pseudorandom functions from pseudorandom generators [23], as well as recent constructions of indistinguishability obfuscation from functional encryption [6,9] (and even more recently, constructions of identity-based encryption [15,20]).

Reusable MPC. A direct application of MHE is a two-round (semi-honest) MPC protocol in the plain model with the following two salient properties:

- The first round of the protocol, which only depends on the inputs of the parties, can be *reused* for an arbitrary number of computations. That is, after the completion of the first round, the parties can execute the second round multiple times, each time with a different circuit C_ℓ of their choice, to learn the output of C_ℓ over their fixed inputs.
- The communication complexity of the protocol is independent of the circuit size (and only depends on the circuit depth).

Alternately, we can use our multi-key FHE to achieve the same result with communication complexity *independent* of the circuit size, albeit based on stronger assumptions.

Previously, such a protocol – obtained via multi-key FHE – was only known in the CRS model [31]. Benhamouda and Lin [8] recently investigated the problem of two-round reusable MPC (with circuit-size dependent communication) and give a construction for the same, in the plain model, based on bilinear maps.[2] Our construction is based on a different assumption, namely, LWE, and therefore can be conjectured to satisfy post-quantum security.

Concurrent Work on Reusable MPC. The work of Bartusek et al. [7] investigate the question of two-round MPC with reusable first message. They propose schemes assuming the hardness of the DDH assumption over traditional groups. In contrast with our work, the resulting MPC is non-compact, i.e. the communication complexity is proportional to the size of the circuit. Moreover, unlike [7], our scheme can be conjectured to be secure against quantum adversaries.

1.2 Open Problems

Our work leaves open some interesting directions for future research. The most compelling problem is to construct a multi-key FHE with one-round decryption

---

[2] The authors communicated their result statement privately to us. A public version of their paper was not available at the time of first writing of this paper, but can now be found in [8].

assuming only the hardness of the (plain) LWE problem. Another relevant direction is to improve the practical efficiency of our proposal and to obtain a more "direct" construction of multi-key FHE from lattice assumptions.

2   Technical Overview

Towards constructing both multi-key FHE and MHE, we first consider a relaxed notion of MHE where the evaluation algorithm is allowed to be *private*; we call this notion pMHE.

MHE with Private Evaluation (pMHE). An MHE scheme with private evaluation, associated with n parties, consists of the following algorithms:

- **Encryption**: The ith party, for $i \in [n]$, on input x_i produces a ciphertext ct_i and secret key sk_i.
- **Evaluation**: The ith party on input all the ciphertexts $\mathsf{ct}_1, \ldots, \mathsf{ct}_N$, secret key sk_i, and circuit C, it evaluates the ciphertexts to obtain a partial decrypted value p_i. We emphasize that the ith party requires sk_i for its evaluation and thus is not a public operation.
- **Final Decryption**: Given all the partial decrypted values $(p_1, \ldots, p_N)$ and the circuit C, reconstruct the output $C(x_1, \ldots, x_N)$.

Towards obtaining our main results, we will also sometimes consider a version of pMHE in the CRS model, where the encryption, evaluation and the final decryption algorithms additionally take as input a CRS, generated by a trusted setup. Furthermore, we will also consider pMHE schemes with an efficiency property that we refer to as *ciphertext succinctness*. We postpone defining this property to later in this section.

Roadmap of our Approach. Using the abstraction of pMHE, we achieve both of our results as illustrated in Fig. 1:

- The starting point of our approach is a one-time pMHE, namely, a pMHE scheme where the initial ciphertexts, i.e., encryptions of x_i for every $i \in [n]$, can be evaluated upon only once. The first step in our approach, involving the technical bulk of our work, is a *reusability transformation* that takes a one-time pMHE in the CRS model and converts it into a pMHE scheme (in the plain model), that allows for (unbounded) polynomially-many homomorphic evaluations (of different circuits) over the initial ciphertexts. We outline this in Sect. 2.1.
- We next describe two different transformations: The first transformation converts a pMHE scheme to multi-key FHE (Sect. 2.2) and the second transformation converts it to an MHE scheme (Sect. 2.3).
- Finally, in Sect. 2.4, we discuss instantiation of one-time pMHE.

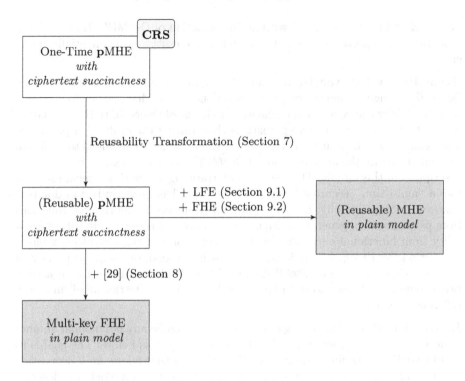

Fig. 1. Our approach

2.1   Reusability Transformation

We now proceed to describe our reusability transformation from a one-time pMHE scheme in the CRS model to a (reusable) pMHE scheme in the plain model. We will in fact first consider the simpler problem of obtaining a pMHE scheme in the CRS model. Later, we show how we can modify the transformation to get rid of the CRS.

Reusability: Naive Attempt. Let OneMHE denote a one-time pMHE scheme. Using two instantiations of OneMHE that we call $OneMHE_0$ and $OneMHE_1$, we first attempt to build an pMHE scheme for a circuit class $\mathcal{C} = \{C_0, C_1\}$ that allows for only *two* decryption queries, denoted by TwoMHE.

- The ith party, for $i \in [N]$, on input x_i, produces two ciphertexts ct_0^i and ct_1^i, where ct_0^i is computed by encrypting x_i using $OneMHE_0$ and ct_1 is computed by encrypting x_i using $OneMHE_1$.
- To evaluate a circuit C_b, for $b \in \{0,1\}$, run the evaluation procedure of $OneMHE_b$ to obtain the partial decrypted values.
- The final decryption on input C_b and partial decrypted values produces the output.

It is easy to see that the above scheme supports two decryption queries. While the above template can be generalized if $\mathcal{C}$ consists of polynomially many circuits;

every circuit in $\mathcal{C}$ is associated with an instantiation of OneMHE. However, it is clear that this approach does not scale when $\mathcal{C}$ consists of exponentially many circuits.

Recursive Self-synthesis. Instead of generating all the instantiations of OneMHE during the encryption phase, as is done in TwoMHE, our main insight is to instead defer the generation of the instantiations of OneMHE to the evaluation phase. The advantage of this approach is that, during the evaluation phase, we know exactly which circuit is being evaluated and thus we can afford to be frugal and only generate the instantiations of OneMHE that are necessary, based on the description of this circuit. The idea of bootstrapping a"one-time" secure scheme into a "multi-time" secure scheme is not new and has been studied in different contexts in cryptography; be it the classical result on pseudorandom functions from pseudorandom generators [24] or the more recent results on indistinguishability from functional encryption [6,10,28] and constructions of identity-based encryption [15,19,20]. In particular, as we will see soon, our implementation of deferring the executions of OneMHE and only invoke the instantiations as needed bears some resemblance to techniques developed in these works, albeit in a very different context.

Illustration. Before explaining our approach to handle any polynomial number of decryption queries, we start with the same example as before: The goal is to build pMHE scheme for a circuit class $\mathcal{C} = \{C_0, C_1\}$ that allows for 2 decryption queries. The difference, however, is, unlike before, the approach we describe below will scale to exponentially many circuits.

We employ a tree-based approach to solve this problem. The tree associated with this scheme consists of three nodes: a root and two leaves. The first leaf is associated with the circuit C_0 and the second leaf is associated with the circuit C_1. Every node is associated with an instantiation of the one-time pMHE scheme. Denote the one-time pMHE scheme associated with the root to be $\mathsf{OneMHE}_\perp$, with the left leaf to be OneMHE_0 and the right leaf node to be OneMHE_1.

Armed with the above notation, we now present an overview of construction of a pMHE scheme for $\mathcal{C} = \{C_0, C_1\}$ allowing for 2 decryption queries as follows:

- The ith party, for $i \in [N]$, on input x_i, produces the ciphertext $\mathsf{ct}_\perp^i$, where $\mathsf{ct}_\perp^i$ is computed by encrypting x_i using $\mathsf{OneMHE}_\perp$.
- To evaluate a circuit C_b, for $b \in \{0, 1\}$, the ith party does the following:
    - First run the evaluation procedure of $\mathsf{OneMHE}_\perp$ on input circuit $C_\perp$ (defined below) to obtain the ith partial decrypted value associated with $\mathsf{OneMHE}_\perp$.
      Denote $C_\perp$ to be the circuit[3] that takes as input $(x_1, \ldots, x_N)$ and produces: (i) $GC_{i,0}$ wire labels for OneMHE_0 ciphertext of x_i under the ith party's secret key, for every i, and, (ii) $GC_{i,1}$ wire labels for OneMHE_1 ciphertext of x_i under the ith party's secret key, for every i.

---

[3] We consider the setting where the circuit is randomized; this is without loss of generality since we can assume that the randomness for this circuit is supplied by the parties.

- It computes a garbled circuit $GC_{i,b}$ defined below.

  Denote $GC_{i,b}$ to be the garbling of a circuit that takes as input OneMHE_b ciphertexts of $x_1, \ldots, x_N$, performs evaluation of C_b using the ith secret key associated with OneMHE_b and outputs the OneMHE_b partial decryption values.

  Output the ith partial decrypted value of $\mathsf{OneMHE}_\perp$ and the garbled circuit $GC_{i,b}$.

- The final decryption algorithm takes as input the $\mathsf{OneMHE}_\perp$ partial decryption values from all the parties, garbled circuits $GC_{1,b}, \ldots, GC_{N,b}$, circuit C_b (to be evaluated) and performs the following operations:
  - It first runs the final decryption procedure of $\mathsf{OneMHE}_\perp$ to obtain the wire labels corresponding to all the garbled circuits $GC_{1,b}, \ldots, GC_{N,b}$.
  - It then evaluates all the garbled circuits to obtain the OneMHE_b partial decryption values.
  - Using the OneMHE_b partial decryption values, compute the final decryption procedure of OneMHE_b to obtain $C_b(x_1, \ldots, x_N)$.

Full-Fledged Tree-Based Approach. We can generalize the above approach to construct a pMHE scheme for any circuit class and that handles any polynomially many queries. If s is the maximum size of the circuit in the class of circuits, we consider a binary tree of depth s.

- Every edge in the tree is labeled. If an edge e is incident from the parent to its left child then label it with 0 and if e is incident from the parent to its right child then label it with 1.
- Every node in the tree is labeled. The label is the concatenation of all the edge labels on the path from the root to the node.
- Every leaf is associated with a circuit of size s.

With each node v, associate with v a new instantiation of a one-time pMHE scheme, that we denote by $\mathsf{OneMHE}_{l(v)}$, where $l(v)$ is the label associated with node v. If v is the root node $l(v) = \perp$.

Informally, the encryption algorithm of pMHE generates $\mathsf{OneMHE}_\perp$ encryption of x_i under the ith secret key. During the evaluation procedure, on input C, each party generates s garbled circuits, one for every node on the path from the root to the leaf labeled with C. The role of these garbled circuits is to delegate the computation of the partial decrypted values to the final decryption phase. In more detail, the garbled circuit associated with the node v computes the partial decrypted values associated with $\mathsf{OneMHE}_{l(v)}$. The partial decryption values will be generated by homomorphically evaluating the following circuit: (i) the wire labels, associated with $\mathsf{OneMHE}_{lv||0}$ encryptions of $x_1, \ldots, x_N$, of all the N garbled circuits associated with the node $v||0$ and, (ii) the wire labels, associated with $\mathsf{OneMHE}_{lv||1}$ encryptions of $x_1, \ldots, x_N$, of all the N garbled circuits associated with the node $v||1$. Note that the homomorphic evaluation is performed inside the garbled circuit.

During the final decryption, starting from the root node, each garbled circuit (of every party) is evaluated to obtain wire labels of the garbled circuit associated with the child node on the path from the root to the leaf labelled with C. Finally, the garbled circuit associated with the leaf labelled with C is then evaluated to obtain the OneMHE_C partial decrypted values. These partial decrypted values are then decoded to recover the final output $C(x_1, \ldots, x_N)$.

We give an overview of the final decryption process in Fig. 2.

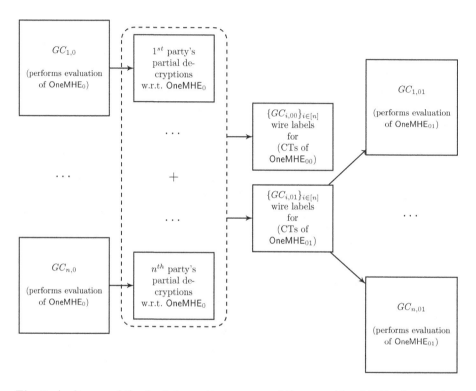

Fig. 2. A glimpse of the final decryption process of the reusable pMHE scheme when evaluated upon the circuit with the boolean representation $C = 01 \cdots$. During the evaluation process, the ith party generates the garbled circuits $GC_{i,0}, GC_{i,01}, \cdots, GC_{i,C}$ as part of the partial decrypted values. The garbled circuit $GC_{i,\mathbf{l}(v)}$, associated with the prefix $\mathbf{l}(v)$ of C, computes the evaluation procedure of $\mathsf{OneMHE}_{\mathbf{l}(v)}$. The output of final decryption of $\mathsf{OneMHE}_{\mathbf{l}(v)}$ are (i) the wire labels of $GC_{i,\mathbf{l}(v)||0}$, for every $i \in [n]$, of the encryptions of all the inputs of the parties, $x_1, \ldots, x_N$ generated with respect to $\mathsf{OneMHE}_{\mathbf{l}(v)||0}$ and, (ii) the wire labels of $GC_{i,\mathbf{l}(v)||1}$, for every $i \in [n]$, for the encryptions of all the inputs of the parties, $x_1, \ldots, x_N$ generated with respect to $\mathsf{OneMHE}_{\mathbf{l}(v)||1}$.

Efficiency Challenges. To argue that the above scheme is a pMHE scheme, we should at the very least argue that the encryption, evaluation and final decryption algorithms can be executed in polynomial time. Let us first argue that all the garbled circuits can be computed in polynomial time by the ith party. The time to compute the garbled circuit associated with the root node is polynomial in the time to compute OneMHE_0 and OneMHE_1 ciphertexts. Even if the time to compute OneMHE_0 and OneMHE_1 ciphertexts only grows proportional to the depth of the circuits being evaluated, the recursion would already blow up the size of the first garbled circuit to be *exponential* in s! This suggests that we need to define a suitable succinctness property on OneMHE in order to make the above transformation work.

Identifying the Necessary Efficiency for Recursion. To make the above recursion idea work, we impose a stringent efficiency constraint on the encryption complexity of OneMHE. In particular, we require two properties to hold:

1. The *size* of the encryption circuit is a polynomial in the security parameter λ, the number of parties, the input length, and the depth of the circuit.
2. The *depth* of the encryption circuit OneMHE grows polynomially in λ, the number of parties and and the input length.

Put together, we refer to the above efficiency properties as *ciphertext succinctness*. It turns out that *if* we have an OneMHE scheme with ciphertext succinctness, then the resulting reusable pMHE scheme has polynomial efficiency and moreover, the ciphertext sizes in the resulting scheme are polynomial in the security parameter alone.[4]

Removing the CRS. Note that if we start with OneMHE in the CRS model, we end up with reusable pMHE scheme still in the CRS model. However, our goal was to construct a pMHE in the plain model. To fix this, we revisit the tree-based approach to construct pMHE and make two important changes.

The first change is the following: Instead of instantiating the root node with a OneMHE scheme satisfying ciphertext succinctness, we instantiate it by a OneMHE scheme that need not satisfy any succinctness property (and thus can be instantiated by *any* semi-malicious MPC in the plain model); if we work out the recursion analysis carefully it turns out that its not necessary that the OneMHE scheme associated with the root node satisfy ciphertext succinctness. The intermediate nodes, however, still need to satisfy ciphertext succinctness and thus need to be instantiated using OneMHE in the CRS model.

Since the intermediate nodes still require a CRS, we make the parent node generate the CRS for its children. That is, upon evaluating the partial decryption values output by a garbled circuit associated with node v (see Fig. 2 for reference), we obtain: (i) wire labels for $\mathsf{crs}_{1v||0}$ and the $\mathsf{OneMHE}_{1(v)||0}$ ciphertexts computed with respect to the common reference string $\mathsf{crs}_{1(v)||0}$ and, (ii)

---

[4] An informed reader may wish to draw an analogy to recent works that devise recursive strategies to build indistinguishability obfuscation from functional encryption [6,10,28]. These works show that a functional encryption scheme with a sufficiently compact encryption procedure (roughly, where the complexity of encryption is sublinear in the size of the circuit) can be used to build an indistinguishability obfuscation scheme. In a similar vein, ciphertext succinctness can be seen as the necessary efficiency notion for driving the recursion in our setting without blowing up efficiency.

wire labels for $\mathsf{crs}_{\mathsf{l}v\|1}$ and $\mathsf{OneMHE}_{\mathsf{l}(v)\|1}$ ciphertexts computed with respect to the common reference string $\mathsf{crs}_{\mathsf{l}(v)\|1}$. That is, the circuit being homomorphically evaluated by $\mathsf{OneMHE}_{\mathsf{l}(v)}$ first generates $\mathsf{crs}_{\mathsf{l}(v)\|0}, \mathsf{crs}_{\mathsf{l}(v)\|1}$, then generates the $\mathsf{OneMHE}_{\mathsf{l}(v)\|0}, \mathsf{OneMHE}_{\mathsf{l}(v)\|1}$ ciphertexts followed by generating wire labels for these ciphertexts. This is the reason why we require the root node to be associated with a OneMHE scheme in the plain model; if not, its unclear how we would be able to generate the CRS for the root node.

2.2   From pMHE to Multi-key FHE

Once we obtain a reusable pMHE in the plain model, our main result follows from a simple bootstrapping procedure. Our transformation lifts a multi-key FHE scheme in the plain model with "complex" (i.e. not one-round) decryption to a multi-key FHE in the plain model with one-round decryption, by additionally assuming the existence of a reusable pMHE. Plugging the scheme from [29] into our compiler yields our main result.

The high-level idea of our transformation is to use the pMHE scheme to securely evaluate the decryption circuit (no matter how complex is) of input the multi-key FHE. This allows us to combine the *compactness* of the multi-key FHE and the *one-round decryption* of the pMHE into a single scheme that inherits the best of both worlds. More concretely, our compiled scheme looks as follows.

-   **Key Generation**: The i-th party runs the key generation algorithm of the underlying multi-key FHE to obtain a key pair $(\mathsf{pk}_i, \mathsf{sk}_i)$, then computes the pMHE encryption of sk_i to obtain a ciphertext $\tilde{\mathsf{ct}}_i$ and an secret evaluation key $\tilde{\mathsf{sk}}_i$. The public key is set to $(\mathsf{pk}_i, \tilde{\mathsf{ct}}_i)$.
-   **Encryption**: To encrypt a message m_i, the i-th party simply runs the encryption algorithm of the multi-key FHE scheme to obtain a ciphertext ct_i.
-   **Evaluation**: On input the ciphertexts $\mathsf{ct}_1, \ldots, \mathsf{ct}_N$ and a circuit C, the i-th party runs the (deterministic) multi-key evaluation algorithm to obtain an evaluated ciphertext ct. Then each party runs the evaluation algorithm of the pMHE scheme for the circuit

$$\Gamma(\mathsf{sk}_1, \ldots, \mathsf{sk}_N) = \mathsf{Dec}((\mathsf{sk}_i, \ldots, \mathsf{sk}_N), \mathsf{ct})$$

over the pMHE ciphertexts $\tilde{\mathsf{ct}}_1, \ldots, \tilde{\mathsf{ct}}_N$, where the value ct is hardwired in the circuit. The i-th party returns the corresponding output p_i.
-   **Final Decryption**: Given the description of the circuit Γ (which is known to all parties) and the decryption shares $(p_1, \ldots, p_N)$, reconstruct the output using the final decryption algorithm of pMHE.

We stress that, in order to achieve the functionality of a multi-key FHE scheme, it is imperative that the underlying pMHE scheme has reusable ciphertexts, which was indeed the main challenge for our construction. It is important to observe that even thought the pMHE scheme does *not* have a compact decryption algorithm, this does not affect the compactness of the complied scheme. This is because the size of the circuit Γ is *independent* of the size of the evaluated circuit C, by the compactness of the underlying multi-key FHE scheme.

2.3 From pMHE to MHE

Equipped with pMHE, we discuss how to construct a full-fledged MHE scheme. There are two hurdles we need to cross to obtain this application. The first being the fact that pMHE only supports private evaluation and the second being that pMHE only satisfies ciphertext succinctness and in particular, could have large partial decryption values.

We address the second problem by applying a compiler that generically transforms a pMHE scheme with large partial decryption values into a scheme with succinct partial decryption values; that is, one that only grows proportional to the input, output lengths and the depth of the circuit being evaluated. Such compilers, that we refer to as *low communication* compilers were recently studied in the context of two-round secure MPC protocols [3,33] and we adapt them to our setting. Once we apply such a compiler, we achieve our desired pMHE scheme that satisfies the required efficiency property.

To achieve an MHE scheme with public evaluation, we use a (single-key) leveled FHE scheme. Each party encrypts its secret key using FHE, that is, the ith party generates an FHE key pair $(\mathsf{pk}_i, \mathsf{sk}_i)$ and encrypts the ith secret key of pMHE under pk_i; we denote the resulting ciphertext as $\mathsf{FHE.ct}_i$. The ith party ciphertext of the MHE scheme $(\mathsf{MHE.ct}_i)$ now consists of the ith party ciphertext of the pMHE scheme $(\mathsf{pMHE.ct}_i)$ along with $\mathsf{FHE.ct}_i$. The public evaluation of MHE now consists of homomorphically evaluating the pMHE private evaluation circuit, with $(C, \mathsf{pMHE.ct}_1, \ldots, \mathsf{pMHE.ct}_N)$ hardwired, on the ciphertext $\mathsf{FHE.ct}_i$. Since this is performed for each party, there are N resulting FHE ciphertexts $(\widehat{\mathsf{FHE.ct}_1}, \ldots, \widehat{\mathsf{FHE.ct}_N})$. During the partial decryption phase, the ith party decrypts $\widehat{\mathsf{FHE.ct}_i}$ using sk_i to obtain the partial decryption value corresponds to the pMHE scheme. The final decryption of MHE is the same as the final decryption of pMHE.

2.4 Instantiating One-Time pMHE in the CRS Model

So far we have shown that one-time pMHE suffices to achieve both of our results. All that remains is to instantiate the one-time pMHE in the CRS model. We instantiate this using the multi-key FHE scheme with one-round decryption in the CRS model. A sequence of works [16,17,31] have presented a construction of such a scheme based on the LWE problem.

3 Preliminaries

We denote the security parameter by λ. We focus only on boolean circuits in this work. For any circuit C, let $C.\mathsf{in}, C.\mathsf{out}, C.\mathsf{depth}$ be the input length, output length and depth of the circuit C, respectively. Denote $C.\mathsf{params} = (C.\mathsf{in}, C.\mathsf{out}, C.\mathsf{depth})$.

For any totally ordered sets $S_1, S_2, \ldots, S_n$, and any tuple $(i_1^*, i_2^*, \ldots, i_n^*) \in S_1 \times S_2 \times \cdots \times S_n$, we use the notation $(i_1^*, i_2^*, \ldots, i_n^*) + 1$ (resp. $(i_1^*, i_2^*, \ldots, i_n^*) - 1$)

to denote the lexicographical smallest (resp. biggest) element in $S_1 \times S_2 \times \cdots \times S_n$ that is lexicographical greater (resp. less) than $(i_1^*, i_2^*, \ldots, i_n^*)$.

Pseudorandom Generators. We recall the definition of pseudorandom generators. A function $\mathsf{PRG}_\lambda : \{0,1\}^{\mathsf{PRG.in}_\lambda} \to \{0,1\}^{\mathsf{PRG.out}_\lambda}$ is a pseduorandom generator, if for any PPT distinguisher $\mathcal{D}$, there exits a negligible function $\nu(\lambda)$ such that

$$\left| \Pr\left[s \leftarrow \{0,1\}^{\mathsf{PRG.in}_\lambda} : \mathcal{D}(1^\lambda, \mathsf{PRG}_\lambda(s)) = 1\right] - \right.$$

$$\left. \Pr\left[u \leftarrow \{0,1\}^{\mathsf{PRG.out}_\lambda} : \mathcal{D}(1^\lambda, u) = 1\right] \right| < \nu(\lambda).$$

Learning with Errors. We recall the learning with errors (LWE) distribution.

Definition 1 (LWE distribution). *For a positive integer dimension n and modulo q, the LWE distribution $A_{\mathbf{s},\chi}$ is obtained by sampling $\mathbf{a} \leftarrow \mathbb{Z}_q^n$, and an error $e \leftarrow \chi$, then outputting $(\mathbf{a}, b = \mathbf{s}^T \cdot \mathbf{a} + e) \in \mathbb{Z}_q^n \times \mathbb{Z}_q$.*

Definition 2 (LWE problem). *The decisional $\mathsf{LWE}_{n,m,q,\chi}$ problem is to distinguish the uniform distribution from the distribution $A_{\mathbf{s},\chi}$, where $\mathbf{s} \leftarrow \mathbb{Z}_q^n$, and the distinguisher is given m samples.*

Standard instantiation of LWE takes χ to be a *discrete Gaussian* distribution.

Definition 3 (LWE assumption). *Let $n = n(\lambda), m = m(\lambda), q = q(\lambda)$ and $\chi = \chi(\lambda)$. The Learning with Error (LWE) assumption states that for any PPT distinguisher $\mathcal{D}$, there exits a negligible function $\nu(\lambda)$ such that*

$$| \Pr[\mathcal{D}(1^\lambda, (\mathbf{A}, \mathbf{s}^T\mathbf{A} + \mathbf{e})) = 1] - \Pr[\mathcal{D}(1^\lambda, (\mathbf{A}, \mathbf{u})) = 1]| < \nu(\lambda)$$

where $\mathbf{A} \leftarrow \mathbb{Z}_q^{n\times m}, \mathbf{s} \leftarrow \mathbb{Z}_q^n, \mathbf{u} \leftarrow \mathbb{Z}_q^m, \mathbf{e} \leftarrow \chi^m$.

3.1 Garbling Schemes

A garbling scheme [34] is a tuple of algorithms $(\mathsf{GC.Garble}, \mathsf{GC.Eval})$ defined as follows.

$\mathsf{GC.Garble}(1^\lambda, C, \mathsf{lab})$ On input the security parameter, a circuit C, and a set of labels $\mathsf{lab} = \{\mathsf{lab}_{i,b}\}_{i\in[C.\mathsf{in}], b\in\{0,1\}}$, where $\mathsf{lab}_{i,b} \in \{0,1\}^\lambda$, it outputs a garbled circuit $\widetilde{C}$.

$\mathsf{GC.Eval}(\widetilde{C}, \mathsf{lab})$ On input a garbled circuit $\widetilde{C}$ and a set of labels $\mathsf{lab} = \{\mathsf{lab}_i\}_{i\in[C.\mathsf{in}]}$, it outputs a value y.

We require the garbling scheme to satisfy the following properties.

Correctness. For any circuit C, and any input $x \in \{0,1\}^{C.\mathsf{in}}$,

$$\Pr\left[\substack{\mathsf{lab}=\{\mathsf{lab}_{i,b}\}_{(i,b)\in[C.\mathsf{in}]\times\{0,1\}} \leftarrow \{0,1\}^{2\lambda C.\mathsf{in}}, \\ \widetilde{C}\leftarrow\mathsf{GC.Garble}(1^\lambda,C,\mathsf{lab}), y\leftarrow\mathsf{GC.Eval}(\widetilde{C},(\mathsf{lab}_{i,x_i})_{i\in[C.\mathsf{in}]})} : y = C(x) \right] = 1.$$

Simulation Security. There exits a simulator $\mathsf{Sim} = (\mathsf{Sim}_1, \mathsf{Sim}_2)$ such that, for any input x, any circuit C, and any non-uniform PPT distinguisher $\mathcal{D}$, we have

$$\left| \Pr\left[\mathsf{lab} \leftarrow \{0,1\}^{2\lambda C.\mathsf{in}}, \widetilde{C} \leftarrow \mathsf{GC.Garble}(1^\lambda, C, \mathsf{lab}) : \mathcal{D}(1^\lambda, \mathsf{lab}_x, \widetilde{C}) = 1 \right] - \right.$$

$$\left. \Pr\left[(\mathsf{st}_S, \widetilde{\mathsf{lab}}) \leftarrow \mathsf{Sim}_1(1^\lambda, C.\mathsf{params}), \widetilde{C} \leftarrow \mathsf{Sim}_2(\mathsf{st}_S, C(x)) : \mathcal{D}(1^\lambda, \widetilde{\mathsf{lab}}, \widetilde{C}) = 1 \right] \right| < \nu(\lambda).$$

Theorem 4 ([34]). *There exists a garbling scheme for all poly-sized circuits from one-way functions.*

Remark 1. For the ease of representation, for any labels $\mathsf{lab} = \{\mathsf{lab}_{i,b}\}_{i \in [n], b \in \{0,1\}}$, and any input $x \in \{0,1\}^n$, we denote $\mathsf{lab}_x = \{\mathsf{lab}_{i,x_i}\}_{i \in [n]}$.

3.2 Laconic Function Evaluation

A laconic function evaluation (LFE) scheme [33] for a class of poly-sized circuits consists of four PPT algorithms $\mathsf{crsGen}, \mathsf{Compress}, \mathsf{Enc}, \mathsf{Dec}$ described below.

$\mathsf{crsGen}(1^\lambda, \mathsf{params})$ It takes as input the security parameter λ, circuit parameters params and outputs a uniformly random common string crs.

$\mathsf{Compress}(\mathsf{crs}, C)$ It takes as input the common random string crs, poly-sized circuit C and outputs a digest digest_C. This is a deterministic algorithm.

$\mathsf{Enc}(\mathsf{crs}, \mathsf{digest}_C, x)$ It takes as input the common random string crs, a digest digest_C, a message x and outputs a ciphertext ct.

$\mathsf{Dec}(\mathsf{crs}, C, \mathsf{ct})$ It takes as input the common random string crs, circuit C, ciphertext ct and outputs a message y.

Correctness. We require the following to hold:

$$\Pr\left[\begin{array}{c} \mathsf{crs} \leftarrow \mathsf{crsGen}(1^\lambda, \mathsf{params}) \\ \mathsf{digest}_C \leftarrow \mathsf{Compress}(\mathsf{crs}, C) \\ \mathsf{ct} \leftarrow \mathsf{Enc}(\mathsf{crs}, \mathsf{digest}_C, x) \\ y \leftarrow \mathsf{Dec}(\mathsf{crs}, C, \mathsf{ct}) \end{array} : y = C(x) \right] = 1.$$

Efficiency. The size of CRS should be polynomial in λ, the input, output lengths and the depth of C. The size of digest, namely digest_C, should be polynomial in λ, the input, output lengths and the depth of C. The size of the output of $\mathsf{Enc}(\mathsf{crs}, \mathsf{digest}_C)$ should be polynomial in λ, the input, output lengths and the depth of C.

Security. For every PPT adversary $\mathcal{A}$, input x, circuit C, there exists a PPT simulator Sim such that for every PPT distinguisher $\mathcal{D}$, there exists a negligible function $\nu(\lambda)$ such that

$$\left| \Pr_{\substack{\mathsf{crs} \leftarrow \mathsf{crsGen}(1^\lambda, \mathsf{params}) \\ \mathsf{digest}_C \leftarrow \mathsf{Compress}(\mathsf{crs}, C)}} \left[1 \leftarrow \mathcal{D}\left(1^\lambda, \mathsf{crs}, \mathsf{digest}_C, \mathsf{Enc}(\mathsf{crs}, \mathsf{digest}_C, x) \right) \right] - \right.$$

$$\left. \Pr_{\substack{\mathsf{crs} \leftarrow \mathsf{crsGen}(1^\lambda, \mathsf{params}) \\ \mathsf{digest}_C \leftarrow \mathsf{Compress}(\mathsf{crs}, C)}} \left[1 \leftarrow \mathcal{D}\left(1^\lambda, \mathsf{crs}, \mathsf{digest}_C, \mathsf{Sim}(\mathsf{crs}, \mathsf{digest}_C, C(x)) \right) \right] \right| < \nu(\lambda).$$

Remark 2. A strong version of security, termed as adaptive security, was defined in [33]; for our construction, selective security suffices.

Theorem 5 ([33]). *Assuming the hardness of learning with errors, there exists a laconic function evaluation protocol.*

4   Multi-key Fully Homomorphic Encryption

A multi-key FHE [29] allows one to compute functions over ciphertexts encrypted under different and independently sampled keys. One can then decrypt the result of the computation by gathering together the corresponding secret keys and run a decryption algorithm. In this work we explicitly distinguish between two families of schemes, depending on structural properties of the decryption algorithm.

- **One-Round Decryption:** The decryption algorithm consists of two subroutines (i) a local phase (PartDec) where each party computes a decryption share of the ciphertext based only on its secret key and (ii) a public phase (FinDec) where the plaintext can be publicly reconstructed from the decryption shares. This variant is the focus of our work.
- **Unstructured Decryption:** The decryption is a (possibly interactive) protocol that takes as input a ciphertext and all secret keys and returns the underlying plaintext. No special structural requirements are imposed.

In this work we are interested in constructing the former. However, the latter is going to be a useful building block in our transformation. More formally, a multi-key FHE is a tuple of algorithms MKFHE = (KeyGen, Enc, Eval, Dec) defined as follows.

KeyGen($1^\lambda, i$) On input the security parameter λ, and an index $i \in [N]$, it outputs a public-key secret-key pair $(\mathsf{pk}_i, \mathsf{sk}_i)$ for the i-th party.

Enc(pk_i, x_i) On input a public key pk_i of the i-th party, and a message x_i, it outputs a ciphertext ct_i.

Eval($C, (\mathsf{ct}_j)_{j \in [N]}$) On input the circuit C of size polynomial in λ and the ciphertexts $(\mathsf{ct}_j)_{j \in [N]}$, it outputs the evaluated ciphertext $\widehat{\mathsf{ct}}$.

Dec($(\mathsf{sk}_j)_{j \in [N]}, \widehat{\mathsf{ct}}$) On input a set of keys $\mathsf{sk}_1, \ldots, \mathsf{sk}_N$ and the evaluated ciphertext $\widehat{\mathsf{ct}}$, it outputs a value $y \in \{0, 1\}^{C.\mathsf{out}}$. We say that a multi-key FHE has a *one-round decryption* if the decryption protocol consists of the algorithms PartDec and FinDec with the following syntax.

PartDec($\mathsf{sk}_i, i, \widehat{\mathsf{ct}}$) On input the secret key sk_i of ith party, the index i, and the evaluated ciphertext $\widehat{\mathsf{ct}}$, it outputs the partial decryption p_i of the ith party.

FinDec($C, (p_j)_{j \in [N]}$) On input all the partial decryptions $(p_j)_{j \in [N]}$, it outputs a value $y \in \{0, 1\}^{C.\mathsf{out}}$.

We say that the scheme is *fully* homomorphic if it is homomorphic for P/poly.

Trusted Setup. We also consider multi-key FHE schemes in the presence of a trusted setup, in which case we also include an algorithm Setup that, on input the security parameter 1^λ, outputs a common reference string crs that is given as input to all algorithms.

Correctness. We define correctness for multi-key FHE with one-round decryption, the more general notion can be obtained by modifying our definition in a natural way. Note that we only define correctness for a single application (single-hop) of the homomorphic evaluation procedure. It is well known that (multi-key) FHE schemes can be generically converted to satisfy the more general notion of multi-hop correctness [22].

Definition 4 (Correctness). *A scheme* MKFHE = (KeyGen, Enc, Eval, PartDec, FinDec) *is said to satisfy the correctness of an MHE scheme if for any inputs* $(x_i)_{i\in[N]}$, *and circuit* C, *the following holds:*

$$\Pr\left[\begin{array}{l}\forall i\in[N],(\mathsf{pk}_i,\mathsf{sk}_i)\leftarrow\mathsf{KeyGen}(1^\lambda,i)\\ \quad\mathsf{ct}_i\leftarrow\mathsf{Enc}(\mathsf{pk}_i,x_i)\\ \widehat{\mathsf{ct}}\leftarrow\mathsf{Eval}(C,(\mathsf{ct}_j)_{j\in[N]})\\ \quad p_i\leftarrow\mathsf{PartDec}(\mathsf{sk}_i,i,\widehat{\mathsf{ct}})\\ \quad y\leftarrow\mathsf{FinDec}((p_j)_{j\in[N]})\end{array}: y=C(x_1,\ldots,x_N)\right]=1.$$

Compactness. We say that a scheme is compact if the size of the evaluated ciphertexts does not depend on the size of the circuit C and only grows with the security parameter (and possibly the number of keys N). Furthermore, we require that the runtime of the decryption algorithm (and of its subroutines PartDec and FinDec) is independent of the size of the circuit C.

Reusable Semi-malicious Security. We define the notion of reusable security for multi-key FHE with one-round decryption. Intuitively, this notion says that the decryption share do not reveal anything beyond the plaintext that they reconstruct to. In this work we present a unified notion that combines semantic security and *computational* indistingushability of partial decryption shares. This is a weakening of the definition given in [31], where the simulated decryption shares were required to be *statistically* close to the honestly compute ones. To the best of our knowledge, this weaker notion is sufficient for all applications of multi-key FHE. Note that by default we consider a *semi-malicious* adversary, that is allowed to choose the random coins of the corrupted parties arbitrarily.

We define security in the real/ideal world framework. The experiments are parameterized by adversary $\mathcal{A} = (\mathcal{A}_1, \mathcal{A}_2)$, a PPT simulator Sim implemented as algorithms $(\mathsf{Sim}_1, \mathsf{Sim}_2)$, the subset of honest parties $H \subseteq [N]$, and their input $(x_i)_{i\in H}$. For the simplicity, we denote $\bar{H} = [N] \setminus H$.

$\underline{\mathsf{Real}^{\mathcal{A}}(1^\lambda, H, (x_i)_{i \in H})}$

for $i \in H$,

    $(\mathsf{pk}_i, \mathsf{sk}_i) \leftarrow \mathsf{KeyGen}(1^\lambda, i)$

    $\mathsf{ct}_i \leftarrow \mathsf{Enc}(\mathsf{pk}_i, x_i)$

endfor

$(\mathsf{st}_{\mathcal{A}}, (x_i, r_i, r_i')_{i \in \bar{H}}) \leftarrow \mathcal{A}_1(1^\lambda, (\mathsf{pk}_i, \mathsf{ct}_i)_{i \in H})$

for $i \in \bar{H}$,

    $(\mathsf{pk}_i, \mathsf{sk}_i) = \mathsf{KeyGen}(1^\lambda, i; r_i)$

    $\mathsf{ct}_i = \mathsf{Enc}(\mathsf{pk}_i, x_i; r_i')$

endfor

$\mathcal{A}_2^{\mathcal{O}(1^\lambda, \cdot)}(\mathsf{st}_{\mathcal{A}})$

return $\mathsf{View}_{\mathcal{A}}$

$\underline{\mathsf{Ideal}^{\mathcal{A}}(1^\lambda, H, (x_i)_{i \in H})}$

$(\mathsf{st}_S, (\mathsf{pk}_i, \mathsf{ct}_i)_{i \in H}) \leftarrow \mathsf{Sim}_1(1^\lambda, H)$

$(\mathsf{st}_{\mathcal{A}}, (x_i, r_i, r_i')_{i \in \bar{H}}) \leftarrow \mathcal{A}_1(1^\lambda, (\mathsf{pk}_i, \mathsf{ct}_i)_{i \in H})$

$\mathcal{A}_2^{\mathcal{O}'(1^\lambda, \cdot)}(\mathsf{st}_{\mathcal{A}})$

return $\mathsf{View}_{\mathcal{A}}$

$\underline{\mathcal{O}(1^\lambda, C)}$

$\widehat{\mathsf{ct}} \leftarrow \mathsf{Eval}(C, (\mathsf{ct}_j)_{j \in [N]})$

for $i \in H, p_i \leftarrow \mathsf{PartDec}(\mathsf{sk}_i, i, \widehat{\mathsf{ct}})$

return $(p_i)_{i \in H}$

$\underline{\mathcal{O}'(1^\lambda, C)}$

$(\mathsf{st}_S', (p_i)_{i \in H}) \leftarrow \mathsf{Sim}_2(\mathsf{st}_S, C, C((x_i)_{i \in [N]}), (x_i, r_i, r_i')_{i \in \bar{H}})$

Update $\mathsf{st}_S = \mathsf{st}_S'$

return $(p_i)_{i \in H}$

Definition 5. *A scheme* $\mathsf{MKFHE} = (\mathsf{KeyGen}, \mathsf{Enc}, \mathsf{Eval}, \mathsf{PartDec}, \mathsf{FinDec})$ *is said to satisfy the reusable semi-malicious security if the following holds: there exists a simulator* $\mathsf{Sim} = (\mathsf{Sim}_1, \mathsf{Sim}_2)$ *such that for any PPT adversary* $\mathcal{A}$*, for any set of honest parties* $H \subseteq [N]$*, any n.u. PPT distinguisher* $\mathcal{D}$*, and any messages* $(x_i)_{i \in H}$*, there exists a negligible function* $\nu(\lambda)$ *such that*

$$\left| \Pr\left[\mathcal{D}\left(1^\lambda, \mathsf{Real}^{\mathcal{A}}(1^\lambda, H, (x_i)_{i \in H})\right) = 1 \right] - \right.$$
$$\left. \Pr\left[\mathcal{D}\left(1^\lambda, \mathsf{Ideal}^{\mathcal{A}}(1^\lambda, H, (x_i)_{i \in H})\right) = 1 \right] \right| < \nu(\lambda).$$

5   Multiparty Homomorphic Encryption

We define the notion of multiparty homomorphic encryption (MHE) in this section. As mentioned earlier, this notion can be seen as a variant of multi-key FHE [17,31]; unlike multi-key FHE, this notion does not require a trusted setup, however, the final decryption phase needs to take as input the circuit being evaluated as input.

5.1   Definition

A multiparty homomorphic encryption is a tuple of algorithms $\mathsf{MHE} = (\mathsf{KeyGen}, \mathsf{Enc}, \mathsf{Eval}, \mathsf{PartDec}, \mathsf{FinDec})$, which are defined as follows.

$\mathsf{KeyGen}(1^\lambda, i)$ On input the security parameter λ, and an index $i \in [N]$, it outputs a public-key secret-key pair $(\mathsf{pk}_i, \mathsf{sk}_i)$ for the i-th party.

$\mathsf{Enc}(\mathsf{pk}_i, x_i)$ On input a public key pk_i of the i-th party, and a message x_i, it outputs a ciphertext ct_i.

$\mathsf{Eval}(C, (\mathsf{ct}_j)_{j \in [N]})$ On input the circuit C of size polynomial in λ and the ciphertexts $(\mathsf{ct}_j)_{j \in [N]}$, it outputs the evaluated ciphertext $\widehat{\mathsf{ct}}$.

$\mathsf{PartDec}(\mathsf{sk}_i, i, \widehat{\mathsf{ct}})$ On input the secret key sk_i of ith party, the index i, and the evaluated ciphertext $\widehat{\mathsf{ct}}$, it outputs the partial decryption p_i of the ith party.

$\mathsf{FinDec}(C, (p_j)_{j \in [N]})$ On input the circuit C, and all the partial decryptions $(p_j)_{j \in [N]}$, it outputs a value $y \in \{0, 1\}^{C.\mathsf{out}}$.

We require that a MHE scheme satisfies the properties of correctness, succinctness and reusable simulation security.

Correctness. We require the following definition to hold.

Definition 6 (Correctness). *A scheme* $\mathsf{MHE} = (\mathsf{KeyGen}, \mathsf{Enc}, \mathsf{Eval}, \mathsf{PartDec}, \mathsf{FinDec})$ *is said to satisfy the correctness of an MHE scheme if for any inputs* $(x_i)_{i \in [N]}$, *and circuit* C, *the following holds:*

$$\Pr\left[\begin{array}{l} \forall i \in [N], (\mathsf{pk}_i, \mathsf{sk}_i) \leftarrow \mathsf{KeyGen}(1^\lambda, i) \\ \mathsf{ct}_i \leftarrow \mathsf{Enc}(\mathsf{pk}_i, x_i) \\ \widehat{\mathsf{ct}} \leftarrow \mathsf{Eval}(C, (\mathsf{ct}_j)_{j \in [N]}) \\ p_i \leftarrow \mathsf{PartDec}(\mathsf{sk}_i, i, \widehat{\mathsf{ct}}) \\ y \leftarrow \mathsf{FinDec}(C, (p_j)_{j \in [N]}) \end{array} : y = C(x_1, \ldots, x_N) \right] = 1.$$

Succinctness. We require that the size of the ciphertexts and the partial decrypted values to be independent of the size of the circuit being evaluated. More formally,

Definition 7 (Succinctness). *A scheme* $\mathsf{MHE} = (\mathsf{KeyGen}, \mathsf{Enc}, \mathsf{Eval}, \mathsf{PartDec}, \mathsf{FinDec})$ *is said to satisfy the succinctness property of an MHE scheme if for any inputs* $(x_i)_{i \in [N]}$, *and circuit* C, *the following holds: for any inputs* $(x_i)_{i \in [N]}$, *and circuit* C,

- Succinctness of Ciphertext: *for* $j \in [N]$, $|\mathsf{ct}_j| = \mathsf{poly}(\lambda, |x_j|)$.
- Succinctness of Partial Decryptions: *for* $j \in [N]$, $|p_j| = \mathsf{poly}(\lambda, N, C.\mathsf{in}, C.\mathsf{out}, C.\mathsf{depth})$, *where* N *is the number of parties,* $C.\mathsf{in}$ *is the input length of the circuit being evaluated,* $C.\mathsf{out}$ *is the output length and* $C.\mathsf{depth}$ *is the depth of the circuit.*

where, for every $i \in [N]$, *(i)* $(\mathsf{pk}_i, \mathsf{sk}_i) \leftarrow \mathsf{KeyGen}(1^\lambda, i)$, *(ii)* $\mathsf{ct}_i \leftarrow \mathsf{Enc}(\mathsf{pk}_i, x_i)$, *(iii)* $\widehat{\mathsf{ct}} \leftarrow \mathsf{Eval}(C, (\mathsf{ct}_j)_{j \in [N]})$ *and, (iv)* $p_i \leftarrow \mathsf{PartDec}(\mathsf{sk}_i, i, \widehat{\mathsf{ct}})$.

Remark 3. En route to constructing MHE schemes satisfying the above succinctness properties, we also consider MHE schemes that satisfy the correctness and security (stated next) properties but fail to satisfy the above succinctness definition. We refer to such schemes as non-succinct MHE schemes.

5.2 Security

We define the security of MHE by real world-ideal world paradigm. We only consider the semi-honest security notion.

In the real world, the adversary is given the public key pk_i and ciphertext ct_i for the honest parties, and also the uniform randomness coins r_i, r_i' for the dishonest parties, where r_i is used for the key generation, and r_i' is used for the encryption. In addition, the adversary is given access to an oracle $\mathcal{O}$. Each time, the adversary can query $\mathcal{O}$ with a circuit C. The oracle $\mathcal{O}$ firstly evaluates C homomorphically over the ciphertexts $(\mathsf{ct}_i)_{i \in [N]}$, and obtains an evaluated ciphertext $\widehat{\mathsf{ct}}$. Then it outputs the partial decryption of $\widehat{\mathsf{ct}}$ of the honest parties.

In the ideal world, a simulator Sim_1 generates the pk_i and ct_i of honest parties, and also the random coins $(r_i, r_i')_{i \in \bar{H}}$ of dishonest parties, and sends them the the adversary. Then, the adversary is given access to an oracle $\mathcal{O}'$. For each query C made by the adversary, the oracle $\mathcal{O}'$ executes the *stateful* simulator Sim_2 to obtain the simulating partial decryption messages $(p_i)_{i \in H}$ of honest parties. Then the oracle $\mathcal{O}'$ outputs $(p_i)_{i \in H}$.

Reusable Semi-honest Security. We define the real and ideal experiments below. The experiments are parameterized by adversary $\mathcal{A}$, a PPT simulator Sim implemented as algorithms $(\mathsf{Sim}_1, \mathsf{Sim}_2)$, the subset of honest parties $H \subseteq [N]$, and the input $(x_i)_{i \in [N]}$. For the simplicity, we denote $\bar{H} = [N] \setminus H$.

$\underline{\mathsf{Real}^{\mathcal{A}}(1^\lambda, H, (x_i)_{i \in H})}$

for $i \in [N]$,

   $r_i, r_i' \leftarrow \{0,1\}^*$

   $(\mathsf{pk}_i, \mathsf{sk}_i) = \mathsf{KeyGen}(1^\lambda, i; r_i)$

   $\mathsf{ct}_i = \mathsf{Enc}(\mathsf{pk}_i, x_i; r_i')$

endfor

$\mathcal{A}^{\mathcal{O}(1^\lambda, \cdot)}(1^\lambda, (\mathsf{pk}_i, \mathsf{ct}_i)_{i \in H}, (r_i, r_i')_{i \in \bar{H}})$

return $\mathsf{View}_{\mathcal{A}}$

$\underline{\mathsf{Ideal}^{\mathcal{A}}(1^\lambda, H, (x_i)_{i \in H})}$

$(\mathsf{st}_S, (\mathsf{pk}_i, \mathsf{ct}_i)_{i \in H}, (r_i, r_i')_{i \in \bar{H}}) \leftarrow \mathsf{Sim}_1(1^\lambda, H, (x_i)_{i \in H})$

$\mathcal{A}_2^{\mathcal{O}'(1^\lambda, \cdot)}(1^\lambda, (\mathsf{pk}_i, \mathsf{ct}_i)_{i \in H}, (r_i, r_i')_{i \in \bar{H}})$

return $\mathsf{View}_{\mathcal{A}}$

$\underline{\mathcal{O}(1^\lambda, C)}$

$\widehat{\mathsf{ct}} \leftarrow \mathsf{Eval}(C, (\mathsf{ct}_j)_{j \in [N]})$

for $i \in H, p_i \leftarrow \mathsf{PartDec}(\mathsf{sk}_i, i, \widehat{\mathsf{ct}})$

return $(p_i)_{i \in H}$

$\underline{\mathcal{O}'(1^\lambda, C)}$

$(\mathsf{st}_S', (p_i)_{i \in H}) \leftarrow \mathsf{Sim}_2(\mathsf{st}_S, C, C((x_i)_{i \in [N]}))$

Update $\mathsf{st}_S = \mathsf{st}_S'$

return $(p_i)_{i \in H}$

Definition 8. *A scheme* (MHE.KeyGen, MHE.Enc, MHE.Eval, MHE.PartDec, MHE.FinDec) *is said to satisfy the reusable semi-honest security if the following holds: there exists a simulator* MHE.Sim = (MHE.Sim$_1$, MHE.Sim$_2$) *such that for any PPT adversary* $\mathcal{A}$, *for any set of honest parties* $H \subseteq [N]$, *any n.u. PPT distinguisher* $\mathcal{D}$, *and any messages* $(x_i)_{i \in [H]}$, *there exists a negligible function* $\nu(\lambda)$ *such that*

$$\left| \Pr\left[\mathcal{D}\left(1^\lambda, \mathsf{Real}^{\mathcal{A}}(1^\lambda, H, (x_i)_{i\in[N]})\right) = 1 \right] - \right.$$

$$\left. \Pr\left[\mathcal{D}\left(1^\lambda, \mathsf{Ideal}^{\mathcal{A}}(1^\lambda, H, (x_i)_{i\in[N]})\right) = 1 \right] \right| < \nu(\lambda).$$

Remark. Definition 8 directly captures the reusability property implied by the definition of [31]. However, our definition is somewhat incomparable to [31] due to the following reasons: [31] give a one-time (semi-malicious) statistical simulation security definition for threshold decryption, which implies multi-use security via a standard hybrid argument. In contrast, Definition 8, which guarantees (semi-honest) computational security, is given directly for the multi-use setting. Second, [31] define security of threshold decryption only for $n-1$ corruptions[5] whereas our definition captures any dishonest majority.

6 Intermediate Notion: MHE with Private Evaluation (pMHE)

Towards achieving MHE, we first consider a relaxation of the notion of MHE where we allow the evaluation algorithm to be a private-key procedure. We call this notion *MHE with private evaluation*, denoted by pMHE.

A multiparty homomorphic encryption with private evaluation (pMHE) is a tuple of algorithms (Enc, PrivEval, FinDec), which are defined as follows.

$\mathsf{Enc}(1^\lambda, C.\mathsf{params}, i, x_i)$ On input the security parameter λ, the parameters of a circuit C, $C.\mathsf{params} = (C.\mathsf{in}, C.\mathsf{out}, C.\mathsf{depth})$, an index i, and an input x_i, it outputs a ciphertext ct_i, and a partial decryption key sk_i.

$\mathsf{PrivEval}(\mathsf{sk}_i, C, (\mathsf{ct}_j)_{j\in[N]})$[6] On input the partial decryption key sk_i, a circuit C, and the ciphertexts $(\mathsf{ct}_j)_{j\in[N]}$, it outputs a partial decryption message p_i.

$\mathsf{FinDec}(C, (p_j)_{j\in[N]})$ On input the circuit C and the partial decryptions $(p_j)_{j\in[N]}$, it outputs $y \in \{0,1\}^{C.\mathsf{out}}$.

Correctness. For any input $(x_i)_{i\in[N]}$, and any circuit C, we have

$$\Pr\left[\begin{array}{l} \forall i\ (\mathsf{ct}_i,\mathsf{sk}_i)\leftarrow\mathsf{Enc}(1^\lambda,C.\mathsf{params},i,x_i) \\ \forall i\ p_i\leftarrow\mathsf{PrivEval}(\mathsf{sk}_i,C,(\mathsf{ct}_j)_{j\in[N]}) \\ y\leftarrow\mathsf{FinDec}(C,(p_j)_{j\in[N]}) \end{array} : y = C((x_i)_{i\in[N]}) \right] = 1.$$

Reusable Semi-malicious Security. The experiments are parameterized by the adversary $\mathcal{A} = (\mathcal{A}_1, \mathcal{A}_2)$, the subset of honest parties $H \subseteq [N]$, the inputs $(x_i)_{i\in H}$, and the PPT simulator Sim implemented as algorithms $(\mathsf{Sim}_1, \mathsf{Sim}_2)$. Denote $\bar{H} = [N] \setminus H$.

---

[5] As such, counter-intuitively, additional work is required when using it in applications such as MPC, when less than $n-1$ parties may be corrupted. We refer the reader to [31] for details.

[6] In fact, PrivEval is a combination of private evaluation and partial decryption.

$\underline{\text{Real}^{\mathcal{A}}(1^{\lambda}, H, (x_i)_{i \in H})}$

for $i \in H, (\text{ct}_i, \text{sk}_i) \leftarrow \text{Enc}(1^{\lambda}, C.\text{params}, i, x_i)$
$(\text{st}_{\mathcal{A}}, (x_i, r_i)_{i \in \bar{H}}) \leftarrow \mathcal{A}_1(1^{\lambda}, (\text{ct}_i)_{i \in H})$
for $i \in \bar{H}, (\text{ct}_i, \text{sk}_i) = \text{Enc}(1^{\lambda}, C.\text{params}, i, x_i; r_i)$
$\mathcal{A}_2^{\mathcal{O}(1^{\lambda}, \cdot)}(\text{st}_{\mathcal{A}})$
return $\text{View}_{\mathcal{A}}$

$\underline{\mathcal{O}(1^{\lambda}, C)}$

for $i \in H, p_i \leftarrow \text{PrivEval}(\text{sk}_i, C, (\text{ct}_j)_{j \in [N]})$
return $(p_i)_{i \in H}$

$\underline{\text{Ideal}^{\mathcal{A}}(1^{\lambda}, H, (x_i)_{i \in H})}$

$(\text{st}_S, (\text{ct}_i)_{i \in H}) \leftarrow \text{Sim}_1(1^{\lambda}, H, C.\text{params})$
$(\text{st}_{\mathcal{A}}, (x_i, r_i)_{i \in \bar{H}}) \leftarrow \mathcal{A}_1(1^{\lambda}, (\text{ct}_i)_{i \in H})$
$\mathcal{A}_2^{\mathcal{O}'(1^{\lambda}, \cdot)}(\text{st}_{\mathcal{A}})$
return $\text{View}_{\mathcal{A}}$

$\underline{\mathcal{O}'(1^{\lambda}, C)}$

$(\text{st}'_S, (p_i)_{i \in H}) \leftarrow \text{Sim}_2(\text{st}_S, C, C((x_i)_{i \in [N]}), (x_i, r_i)_{i \in \bar{H}})$
Update $\text{st}_S = \text{st}'_S$
return $(p_i)_{i \in H}$

Definition 9. *A scheme* pMHE = (Enc, PrivEval, FinDec) *is said to satisfy the reusable semi-malicious security if the following holds: there exists a simulator* Sim = (Sim$_1$, Sim$_2$) *such that for any PPT adversary* $\mathcal{A}$, *for any set of honest parties* $H \subseteq [N]$, *PPT distinguisher* $\mathcal{D}$, *and any messages* $(x_i)_{i \in H}$, *there exists a negligible function* $\nu(\lambda)$ *such that*

$$\left| \Pr\left[\mathcal{D}\left(1^{\lambda}, \text{Real}^{\mathcal{A}}(1^{\lambda}, H, (x_i)_{i \in H})\right) = 1\right] - \right.$$
$$\left. \Pr\left[\mathcal{D}\left(1^{\lambda}, \text{Ideal}^{\mathcal{A}}(1^{\lambda}, H, (x_i)_{i \in H})\right) = 1\right] \right| < \nu(\lambda).$$

6.1 CRS Model

A pMHE in the common random/reference string model is a tuple of algorithms pMHE = (Setup, Enc, PrivEval, FinDec), where the PrivEval, FinDec works the same way as in the plain model, while Setup, Enc are defined as follows.

Setup(1^{λ}) On input the security parameter, it outputs a common reference string crs.

Enc(crs, $C.\text{params}, i, x_i$) On input the common reference string crs, the parameters of C, an index i, and an input x_i, it output a ciphertext ct_i, and a partial decryption key sk_i.

6.2 One-Time pMHE

We consider a weak version of pMHE scheme called one-time pMHE.

Definition 10. *A pMHE scheme is a* one-time *pMHE scheme, if the security holds for all n.u. PPT adversary* $\mathcal{A}$ *that only query the oracle* $\mathcal{O}$ *at most once.*

We will use a one-time pMHE scheme as a starting point in the reusability transformation.

Remark 4. In this setting, without loss of generality, we assume that the private evaluation algorithm PrivEval is deterministic, and the secret key is the randomness used by Enc.

6.3   Ciphertext Succinctness

We define the notion of ciphertext succinctness associated with a pMHE scheme. Roughly, we require the size of the encryption circuit to only grow with the depth of the circuits being homomorphically evaluated. We additionally require the depth of the encryption circuit to be only poly-logarithmically in the depth. We allow the depth of the encryption circuit to, however, grow polynomially in the number of parties and input lengths. We impose similar efficiency requirements on the setup procedure as well.

Note that this is an incomparable to the traditional succinctness property we defined for an MHE scheme; on one hand, ciphertext succinctness imposes an additional requirement on the encryption circuit whereas it doesn't say anything about the size of the partial decryption values. The succinctness property of MHE is about the size of the ciphertexts whereas the ciphertext succinctness property is about the complexity of the encryption circuit.

Definition 11 (Ciphertext Succinctness). *A pMHE scheme with a setup* pMHE $=$ (Setup, Enc, PrivEval, FinDec) *is said to satisfy strong ciphertext succinctness property if it satisfies the correctness, strong semi-honest security, and in addition, satisfies the following properties:*

- *The size of the* Setup *circuit is* $\mathrm{poly}(\lambda, N, C.\mathsf{depth})$.
- *The depth of the* Setup *circuit is* $\mathrm{poly}(\lambda, N, \log(C.\mathsf{depth}))$.
- *The size of the* Enc *circuit is* $\mathrm{poly}(\lambda, N, C.\mathsf{in}, C.\mathsf{depth})$.
- *The depth of the* Enc *circuit is* $\mathrm{poly}(\lambda, N, C.\mathsf{in}, \log(C.\mathsf{depth}))$.

where N is the number of parties, and $(C.\mathsf{in}, C.\mathsf{out}, C.\mathsf{depth})$ are the parameters associated with the circuits being evaluated.

Remark 5. The ciphertext succinctness property is incomparable with the succinctness property of an MHE scheme; while there is no requirement on the size of the partial decryptions in the above definitions, there is a strict requirement on the complexity of the encryption procedure in the above definition as against a requirement on just the size of the ciphertexts as specified in the succinctness definition of MHE.

6.4   Instantiation

We can instantiate any one-time pMHE scheme satisfying ciphertext sucinctness in the CRS model from any multi-key FHE in the CRS model. Thus, have the following:

Theorem 6 (Ciphertext-Succinct One-Time pMHE with CRS from LWE). *Assuming learning with errors, there exists a one-time pMHE scheme in the CRS model satisfying ciphertext succinctness property.*

We defer the proof to the full version.

7   Main Step: One-Time pMHE in CRS $\Longrightarrow$ Reusable pMHE

In this section, we show how to bootstrap from a one-time pMHE with ciphertext succinctness property into a (possibly non-succinct) reusable pMHE scheme.

Lemma 1 (Bootstrap from One-Time Ciphertext Succinctness Scheme to Reusable Scheme). *From the following primitives,*

- pMHE$'$ = (pMHE$'$.Setup, pMHE$'$.Enc, pMHE$'$.PrivEval, pMHE$'$.FinDec): *a one-time ciphertext succinct pMHE scheme in the CRS model.*
- pMHE$_0$ = (pMHE$_0$.Enc, pMHE$_0$.PrivEval, pMHE$_0$.FinDec): *a one-time delayed-function semi-malicious pMHE scheme without setup. (Note: this pMHE scheme need not satisfy any succinctness property)*
- PRG : $\{0,1\}^{\mathsf{PRG.in}} \to \{0,1\}^{\mathsf{PRG.out}}$, *a pseudorandom generator, where* PRG.out = poly(PRG.in) *for some large polynomial* poly. *Moreover, we require the depth of* PRG *to be* poly(λ, log(PRG.out)) *for some fixed* poly *independent of* PRG.out.

we can build a reusable semi-malicious pMHE scheme pMHE = (pMHE.Enc, pMHE.PrivEval, pMHE.FinDec) *without the trusted setup.*

Construction. We present the construction below.

In our construction, each party generates a PRG seed k_i, then in on the t-th level of the tree, the i-th party uses k_i to generate a pseudorandom string, which is divided into the following 5 parts.

1. $(\mathsf{lab}^{i,t+1,b})_{b \in \{0,1\}}$ is used as the labels of the children nodes.
2. $(k_{i,b}^{t+1})_{b \in \{0,1\}}$ are the PRG seeds for the children nodes.
3. $(r_{i,1,b}^{t+1})_{b \in \{0,1\}}$ is the randomness used to generate the two new ciphertexts for the children nodes.
4. $(r_{i,2,b}^{t+1})_{b \in \{0,1\}}$ is the randomness used to generate the garbled circuits for the children nodes.
5. $(r_{i,3,b}^{t+1})_{b \in \{0,1\}}$ is the randomness used to generate the CRS of the children nodes. We will xor the $r_{i,3,b}$ for all the parties to achieve semi-malicious security.

pMHE.Enc($1^\lambda, C.$params$, i, x_i$):
- Randomly sample $k_i \leftarrow \{0,1\}^{\mathsf{PRG.in}}$, and random coins r_i.
- $(\mathsf{ct}_i', \mathsf{sk}_i') \leftarrow$ pMHE$_0$.Enc($1^\lambda,$ NewEnc^1.params$, i, (x_i, k_i)$), where NewEnc^1 is defined in Fig. 3.
- Let $\mathsf{ct}_i = \mathsf{ct}_i'$ and $\mathsf{sk}_i = (\mathsf{sk}_i', (k_i, r_i))$.
Output $(\mathsf{ct}_i, \mathsf{sk}_i)$.

pMHE.PrivEval($\mathsf{sk}_i, C, (\mathsf{ct}_j)_{j \in [N]}$):
- Parse sk_i as $(\mathsf{sk}_i', (k_i, r_i))$.
- Let id be the binary representation of the circuit C. Denote $n = |\mathsf{id}|$.

$$\underline{\mathsf{NewEnc}^t\left((x_j, k_j)_{j \in [N]}\right)}$$

- For any $j \in [N]$, parse $\mathsf{PRG}(k_j)$ as $(\mathsf{lab}^{j,t,b}, k_{j,b}^t, r_{j,1,b}^t, r_{j,2,b}^t, r_{j,3,b}^t)_{b \in \{0,1\}}$.
- For any $b \in \{0,1\}$, $\mathsf{crs}_b = \mathsf{pMHE}'.\mathsf{Setup}(1^\lambda; \bigoplus_{j \in [N]} r_{j,3,b}^t)$
- For any $j \in [N], b \in \{0,1\}$,

$$(\mathsf{ct}_{j,b}, \mathsf{sk}_{j,b}) = \mathsf{pMHE}'.\mathsf{Enc}(\mathsf{crs}_b, \mathsf{NewEnc}^{t+1}.\mathsf{params}, j, (x_j, k_{j,b}^t); r_{j,1,b}^t)$$

- For any $b \in \{0,1\}$, let $\mathsf{ct}_b = (\mathsf{ct}_{j,b})_{j \in [N]}$.
- Output $(\mathsf{lab}_{\mathsf{ct}_0}^{i,t,0}, \mathsf{lab}_{\mathsf{ct}_1}^{i,t,1})_{i \in [N]}$.

Fig. 3. Description of NewEnc^t, for $t \in [n]$.

- For $t \in [n]$, Boot^t is defined as follows.
    $\mathsf{Boot}_{[\mathsf{sk}_i^t]}^t(\mathsf{ct}^t)$
    • Let $p_i^t = \mathsf{pMHE}'.\mathsf{PrivEval}(\mathsf{sk}_i^t, \mathsf{NewEnc}^{t+1}, \mathsf{ct}^t)$, where NewEnc is defined in Figs. 3 and 4.
    • Output p_i^t.
- Let $p_i^0 = \mathsf{pMHE}'.\mathsf{PrivEval}(\mathsf{sk}_i', \mathsf{NewEnc}^1, (\mathsf{ct}_j)_{j \in [N]}; r_i)$, $k_i^0 = k_i$.
- For each $t = 1, 2, \ldots, n$,
    Let $b = \mathsf{id}[t]$. Parse $\mathsf{PRG}(k_i^{t-1})$ as $(\mathsf{lab}^{i,t,b'}, k_{i,b'}^t, r_{i,1,b'}^t, r_{i,2,b'}^t, r_{i,3,b'}^t)_{b' \in \{0,1\}}$
    Let $\mathsf{sk}_i^t = r_{i,1,b}^t$, $\widetilde{\mathsf{Boot}_i^t} \leftarrow \mathsf{GC}.\mathsf{Garble}(1^\lambda, \mathsf{Boot}_{[\mathsf{sk}_i^t]}^t, \mathsf{lab}^{i,t,b}; r_{i,2,b}^t)$.
    Let $k_i^t = k_{i,b}^t$.
- Let $p_i = (p_i^0, (\widetilde{\mathsf{Boot}_i^t})_{t \in [n]}, \mathsf{ct}_i)$.
- Output p_i.

$$\underline{\mathsf{NewEnc}^{n+1}\left((x_j, k_j)_{j \in [N]}\right)}$$

- Let $y = C((x_j)_{j \in [N]})$.
- Output y.

Fig. 4. Description of NewEnc^{n+1}.

$\mathsf{pMHE.FinDec}(C, (p_i)_{i \in [N]})$:

- Let id be the binary representation of C. Parse p_i as $(p_i^0, (\widetilde{\mathsf{Boot}_i^t})_{t \in [n]}, \mathsf{ct}_i)$.
- For each $t = 1, 2, \ldots, n$,

  Let $b = \mathsf{id}[t]$.

  If $t = 1$, $(\mathsf{lab}'^{i,t,0}, \mathsf{lab}'^{i,t,1})_{i \in [N]} \leftarrow \mathsf{pMHE}_0.\mathsf{FinDec}(\mathsf{NewEnc}^t, (p_i^{t-1})_{i \in [N]})$.

  Otherwise, $(\mathsf{lab}'^{i,t,0}, \mathsf{lab}'^{i,t,1})_{i \in [N]} \leftarrow \mathsf{pMHE}'.\mathsf{FinDec}(\mathsf{NewEnc}^t, (p_i^{t-1})_{i \in [N]})$.

  For each $i \in [N]$, execute $p_i^t \leftarrow \mathsf{GC.Eval}(1^\lambda, \widetilde{\mathsf{Boot}_i^t}, \mathsf{lab}'^{i,t,b})$.
- Let $y \leftarrow \mathsf{pMHE}'.\mathsf{FinDec}(\mathsf{NewEnc}^{n+1}, (p_i^n)_{i \in [N]})$.
- Output y.

7.1 Correctness

Lemma 2 (Correctness). *The construction of* pMHE *is correct.*

We defer the proof to the full version.

7.2 Security

Lemma 3 (Reusable Semi-malicious Security). *The construction of* pMHE *is reusable semi-malicious secure.*

We defer the proof to the full version.

7.3 Instantiation

We can instantiate pMHE_0 based on any two-round semi-malicious MPC in the plain model and this in turn can be based on any two-round semi-malicious oblivious transfer (OT); we crucially use the fact that pMHE_0 need not satisfy any succinctness property for this implication. Furthermore, we can instantiate the two-round semi-malicious OT from learning with errors [13]. Similarly, we can also instantiate one-time pMHE in the CRS model with ciphertext succcintness from learning with errors (Theorem 6) and finally, the pseudorandom generator mentioned above any pseudorandom function which in turn can be based on one-way functions. Thus, we have the following theorem.

Theorem 7. *Assuming LWE, there exists a (non-succinct) reusable pMHE scheme in the plain model.*

8 Result #1: Construction of Multi-key FHE

In the following we show how to combine a multi-key FHE with unstructured decryption with a reusable pMHE without trusted setup to obtain a multi-key FHE scheme in the plain model with one-round decryption.

Theorem 8 (Multi-key FHE in the Plain Model). *If there exists a semantically secure multi-key FHE scheme* $\mathsf{MKFHE}' = (\mathsf{MKFHE}'.\mathsf{KeyGen}, \mathsf{MKFHE}'.\mathsf{Enc},$ $\mathsf{MKFHE}'.\mathsf{Eval}, \mathsf{MKFHE}'.\mathsf{Dec})$ *without trusted setup and with unstructured decryption, and a reusable semi-malicious pMHE scheme* $\mathsf{pMHE} = (\mathsf{pMHE}.\mathsf{Enc},$ $\mathsf{pMHE}.\mathsf{PrivEval}, \mathsf{pMHE}.\mathsf{FinDec})$ *without trusted setup, then there exists a semimalicious multi-key FHE scheme* $\mathsf{MKFHE} = (\mathsf{MKFHE}.\mathsf{KeyGen}, \mathsf{MKFHE}.\mathsf{Enc},$ $\mathsf{MKFHE}.\mathsf{Eval}, \mathsf{MKFHE}.\mathsf{PartDec}, \mathsf{MKFHE}.\mathsf{FinDec})$ *without trusted setup.*

Construction. Let $\Gamma.\mathsf{params}$ be the input, output size, and depth of the decryption circuit of the multi-key FHE scheme MKFHE'. The construction is described below.

$\mathsf{MKFHE}.\mathsf{KeyGen}(1^\lambda, i)$:

> Let $(\mathsf{MKFHE}'.\mathsf{pk}_i, \mathsf{MKFHE}'.\mathsf{sk}_i) \leftarrow \mathsf{MKFHE}'.\mathsf{KeyGen}(1^\lambda, i)$.
> Let $(\mathsf{pMHE}.\mathsf{ct}_i, \mathsf{pMHE}.\mathsf{sk}_i) \leftarrow \mathsf{pMHE}.\mathsf{Enc}(1^\lambda, \Gamma.\mathsf{params}, i, \mathsf{MKFHE}'.\mathsf{sk}_i)$
> Let $\mathsf{pk}_i = (\mathsf{MKFHE}'.\mathsf{pk}_i, \mathsf{pMHE}.\mathsf{ct}_i)$, and $\mathsf{sk}_i = (\mathsf{MKFHE}'.\mathsf{sk}_i, \mathsf{pMHE}.\mathsf{sk}_i)$.
> Output $(\mathsf{pk}_i, \mathsf{sk}_i)$.

$\mathsf{MKFHE}.\mathsf{Enc}(\mathsf{pk}_i, x_i)$:

> Parse pk_i as $(\mathsf{MKFHE}'.\mathsf{pk}_i, \mathsf{pMHE}.\mathsf{ct}_i)$.
> Let $\mathsf{MKFHE}'.\mathsf{ct}_i \leftarrow \mathsf{MKFHE}'.\mathsf{Enc}(\mathsf{MKFHE}'.\mathsf{pk}_i, x_i)$.
> Let $\mathsf{ct}_i = (\mathsf{MKFHE}'.\mathsf{ct}_i, \mathsf{pMHE}.\mathsf{ct}_i)$.
> Output ct_i.

$\mathsf{MKFHE}.\mathsf{Eval}(C, (\mathsf{ct}_j)_{j \in [N]})$:

> For all $j \in [N]$ parse ct_j as $(\mathsf{MKFHE}'.\mathsf{ct}_j, \mathsf{pMHE}.\mathsf{ct}_j)$.
> Compute $\mathsf{MKFHE}'.\widehat{\mathsf{ct}} \leftarrow \mathsf{MKFHE}'.\mathsf{Eval}(C, (\mathsf{ct}_j)_{j \in [N]})$.
> Let $\widehat{\mathsf{ct}} = (\mathsf{MKFHE}'.\widehat{\mathsf{ct}}, (\mathsf{pMHE}.\mathsf{ct}_j)_{j \in [N]})$.
> Output $\widehat{\mathsf{ct}}$.

$\mathsf{MKFHE}.\mathsf{PartDec}(\mathsf{sk}_i, i, \widehat{\mathsf{ct}})$:

> Parse $\widehat{\mathsf{ct}}$ as $(\mathsf{MKFHE}'.\widehat{\mathsf{ct}}, (\mathsf{pMHE}.\mathsf{ct}_j)_{j \in [N]})$.
> Parse sk_i as $(\mathsf{MKFHE}'.\mathsf{sk}_i, \mathsf{pMHE}.\mathsf{sk}_i)$.
> Define $\Gamma((s_j)_{j \in [N]}) = \mathsf{MKFHE}'.\mathsf{Dec}((s_j)_{j \in [N]}, \widehat{\mathsf{ct}})$.
> Let $\mathsf{pMHE}.p_i \leftarrow \mathsf{pMHE}.\mathsf{PrivEval}(\mathsf{pMHE}.\mathsf{sk}_i, \Gamma, (\mathsf{pMHE}.\mathsf{ct}_j)_{j \in [N]})$.
> Let $p_i = (\mathsf{pMHE}.p_i, \widehat{\mathsf{ct}})$
> Output p_i.

$\mathsf{MKFHE}.\mathsf{FinDec}((p_j)_{j \in [N]})$:

> For all $j \in [N]$ parse p_j as $(\mathsf{pMHE}.p_j, \widehat{\mathsf{ct}})$.
> Define $\Gamma((s_j)_{j \in [N]}) = \mathsf{MKFHE}'.\mathsf{Dec}((s_j)_{j \in [N]}, \widehat{\mathsf{ct}})$.
> Let $y \leftarrow \mathsf{pMHE}.\mathsf{FinDec}(\Gamma, (\mathsf{pMHE}.p_j)_{j \in [N]})$.
> Output y.

We defer the proof to the full version.

8.1 Instantiation

By Theorem 7 we can instantiate the reusable semi-malicious pMHE scheme from the LWE problem (with sub-exponential modulus-to-noise ratio). For the multi-key FHE with unstructured decryption, we can use the scheme from [29], which is shown semantically secure against the Ring LWE and the DSPR problem. Thus we obtain the following implication.

Theorem 9. *Assuming LWE, Ring LWE, and DSPR, there exists a multi-key FHE scheme with one-round decryption in the plain model.*

9 Result #2: Construction of MHE

We now show how to construct an MHE scheme. In Sect. 7, we constructed a pMHE scheme satisfying ciphertext succinctness. To obtain an MHE scheme from pMHE with ciphertext succinctness, we perform the following two steps: (1) first, we transform the above pMHE scheme into another scheme satisfying succinctness (recall that succinctness is incomparable to ciphertext succinctness) and, (2) secondly, we show how to achieve public evaluation generically to obtain the MHE scheme.

9.1 Non-Succinct pMHE to Succinct pMHE

We now show how to generically transform a non-succinct pMHE scheme into a succinct pMHE scheme. Furthermore, the transformation preserves the number of queries the adversary can make to the decryption oracle. That is, if the underlying pMHE scheme is *reusable*, then so is the resulting scheme.

Theorem 10. *Assuming LWE, there exists a generic transformation from any non-succinct (Remark 3) semi-honest pMHE to a succinct (Definition 7) semi-honest pMHE scheme.*

We defer the proof to the full version.

9.2 pMHE to MHE: Private to Public Evaluation

We show how to construct an MHE scheme from pMHE and a leveled fully homomorphic encryption scheme.

Theorem 11 (From pMHE to MHE). *If there exits a reusable semi-honest secure pMHE scheme* pMHE *with succinctness property, and a (leveled) fully homomorphic encryption scheme* FHE = (FHE.KeyGen, FHE.Enc, FHE.Dec, FHE.Eval), *then there exits a reusable semi-honest secure MHE scheme* MHE *with succinctness property.*

We defer the proof to the full version.

Acknowledgments. The second and third author were supported in part by a DARPA/ARL Safeware Grant W911NF-15-C-0213, NSF CNS-1814919, NSF CAREER 1942789, Samsung Global Research Outreach award and Johns Hopkins University Catalyst award.

References

1. Agrawal, S., Clear, M., Frieder, O., Garg, S., O'Neill, A., Thaler, J.: Ad hoc multi-input functional encryption. In: Vidick, T. (ed.) ITCS 2020, vol. 151, pp. 40:1–40:41. LIPIcs, Seattle, WA, USA, 12–14 January 2020. https://doi.org/10.4230/LIPIcs.ITCS.2020.40
2. Albrecht, M., Bai, S., Ducas, L.: A subfield lattice attack on overstretched NTRU assumptions. In: Robshaw, M., Katz, J. (eds.) CRYPTO 2016, Part 1. LNCS, vol. 9814, pp. 153–178. Springer, Heidelberg (2016). https://doi.org/10.1007/978-3-662-53018-4_6
3. Ananth, P., Badrinarayanan, S., Jain, A., Manohar, N., Sahai, A.: From FE combiners to secure MPC and back. In: Hofheinz, D., Rosen, A. (eds.) TCC 2019. LNCS, vol. 11891, pp. 199–228. Springer, Cham (2019). https://doi.org/10.1007/978-3-030-36030-6_9
4. Ananth, P., Jain, A., Naor, M., Sahai, A., Yogev, E.: Universal constructions and robust combiners for indistinguishability obfuscation and witness encryption. In: Robshaw, M., Katz, J. (eds.) CRYPTO 2016, Part 2. LNCS, vol. 9815, pp. 491–520. Springer, Heidelberg (2016). https://doi.org/10.1007/978-3-662-53008-5_17
5. Ananth, P., Jain, A., Sahai, A.: Robust transforming combiners from indistinguishability obfuscation to functional encryption. In: Coron, J.-S., Nielsen, J.B. (eds.) EUROCRYPT 2017, Part 1. LNCS, vol. 10210, pp. 91–121. Springer, Cham (2017). https://doi.org/10.1007/978-3-319-56620-7_4
6. Ananth, P., Jain, A.: Indistinguishability obfuscation from compact functional encryption. In: Gennaro, R., Robshaw, M. (eds.) CRYPTO 2015, Part 1. LNCS, vol. 9215, pp. 308–326. Springer, Heidelberg (2015). https://doi.org/10.1007/978-3-662-47989-6_15
7. Bartusek, J., Garg, S., Masny, D., Mukherjee, P.: Reusable two-round MPC from DDH. Cryptology ePrint Archive, Report 2020/170 (2020). https://eprint.iacr.org/2020/170
8. Benhamouda, F., Lin, H.: Multiparty reusable non-interactive secure computation. Cryptology ePrint Archive, Report 2020/221 (2020). https://eprint.iacr.org/2020/221
9. Bitansky, N., Vaikuntanathan, V.: Indistinguishability obfuscation from functional encryption. In: Guruswami, V. (ed.) 56th FOCS. pp. 171–190. IEEE Computer Society Press, Berkeley, CA, USA, 17–20 Oct 2015. https://doi.org/10.1109/FOCS.2015.20
10. Bitansky, N., Vaikuntanathan, V.: Indistinguishability obfuscation from functional encryption. J. ACM (JACM) **65**(6), 39 (2018)
11. Boyle, E., Gilboa, N., Ishai, Y.: Breaking the circuit size barrier for secure computation under DDH. In: Robshaw, M., Katz, J. (eds.) CRYPTO 2016, Part 1. LNCS, vol. 9814, pp. 509–539. Springer, Heidelberg (2016). https://doi.org/10.1007/978-3-662-53018-4_19
12. Boyle, E., Gilboa, N., Ishai, Y.: Group-based secure computation: optimizing rounds, communication, and computation. In: Coron, J.-S., Nielsen, J.B. (eds.) EUROCRYPT 2017, Part 2. LNCS, vol. 10211, pp. 163–193. Springer, Cham (2017). https://doi.org/10.1007/978-3-319-56614-6_6
13. Brakerski, Z., Döttling, N.: Two-message statistically sender-private OT from LWE. In: Beimel, A., Dziembowski, S. (eds.) TCC 2018. LNCS, vol. 11240, pp. 370–390. Springer, Cham (2018). https://doi.org/10.1007/978-3-030-03810-6_14

14. Brakerski, Z., Döttling, N., Garg, S., Malavolta, G.: Leveraging linear decryption: rate-1 fully-homomorphic encryption and time-lock puzzles. In: Hofheinz, D., Rosen, A. (eds.) TCC 2019, Part 2. LNCS, vol. 11892, pp. 407–437. Springer, Cham (2019). https://doi.org/10.1007/978-3-030-36033-7_16

15. Brakerski, Z., Lombardi, A., Segev, G., Vaikuntanathan, V.: Anonymous IBE, leakage resilience and circular security from new assumptions. In: Nielsen, J.B., Rijmen, V. (eds.) EUROCRYPT 2018, Part 1. LNCS, vol. 10820, pp. 535–564. Springer, Cham (2018). https://doi.org/10.1007/978-3-319-78381-9_20

16. Brakerski, Z., Perlman, R.: Lattice-based fully dynamic multi-key FHE with short ciphertexts. In: Robshaw, M., Katz, J. (eds.) CRYPTO 2016, Part 1. LNCS, vol. 9814, pp. 190–213. Springer, Heidelberg (2016). https://doi.org/10.1007/978-3-662-53018-4_8

17. Clear, M., McGoldrick, C.: Multi-identity and multi-key leveled FHE from learning with errors. In: Gennaro, R., Robshaw, M. (eds.) CRYPTO 2015, Part 2. LNCS, vol. 9216, pp. 630–656. Springer, Heidelberg (2015). https://doi.org/10.1007/978-3-662-48000-7_31

18. Dodis, Y., Halevi, S., Rothblum, R.D., Wichs, D.: Spooky encryption and its applications. In: Robshaw, M., Katz, J. (eds.) CRYPTO 2016, Part 3. LNCS, vol. 9816, pp. 93–122. Springer, Heidelberg (2016). https://doi.org/10.1007/978-3-662-53015-3_4

19. Döttling, N., Garg, S.: From selective IBE to full IBE and selective HIBE. In: Kalai, Y., Reyzin, L. (eds.) TCC 2017, Part 1. LNCS, vol. 10677, pp. 372–408. Springer, Cham (2017). https://doi.org/10.1007/978-3-319-70500-2_13

20. Döttling, N., Garg, S.: Identity-based encryption from the Diffie-Hellman assumption. In: Katz, J., Shacham, H. (eds.) CRYPTO 2017, Part 1. LNCS, vol. 10401, pp. 537–569. Springer, Cham (2017). https://doi.org/10.1007/978-3-319-63688-7_18

21. Gentry, C.: Fully homomorphic encryption using ideal lattices. In: Mitzenmacher, M. (ed.) 41st ACM STOC. pp. 169–178. ACM Press, Bethesda, 31 May –2 Jun 2009. https://doi.org/10.1145/1536414.1536440

22. Gentry, C., Halevi, S., Vaikuntanathan, V.: i-hop homomorphic encryption and rerandomizable yao circuits. In: Rabin, T. (ed.) CRYPTO 2010. LNCS, vol. 6223, pp. 155–172. Springer, Heidelberg (2010). https://doi.org/10.1007/978-3-642-14623-7_9

23. Goldreich, O., Goldwasser, S., Micali, S.: How to construct random functions (extended abstract). In: 25th FOCS, pp. 464–479. IEEE Computer Society Press, Singer Island, 24–26 Oct 1984. https://doi.org/10.1109/SFCS.1984.715949

24. Goldreich, O., Goldwasser, S., Micali, S.: How to construct random functions. J. ACM (JACM) **33**(4), 792–807 (1986)

25. Halevi, S., Ishai, Y., Jain, A., Komargodski, I., Sahai, A., Yogev, E.: Non-interactive multiparty computation without correlated randomness. In: Takagi, T., Peyrin, T. (eds.) ASIACRYPT 2017, Part 3. LNCS, vol. 10626, pp. 181–211. Springer, Cham (2017). https://doi.org/10.1007/978-3-319-70700-6_7

26. Kirchner, P., Fouque, P.A.: Comparison between subfield and straightforward attacks on NTRU. IACR Cryptol. ePrint Arch. **2016**, 717 (2016)

27. Kirchner, P., Fouque, P.-A.: Revisiting lattice attacks on overstretched NTRU parameters. In: Coron, J.-S., Nielsen, J.B. (eds.) EUROCRYPT 2017, Part 1. LNCS, vol. 10210, pp. 3–26. Springer, Cham (2017). https://doi.org/10.1007/978-3-319-56620-7_1

28. Lin, H., Pass, R., Seth, K., Telang, S.: Output-compressing randomized encodings and applications. In: Kushilevitz, E., Malkin, T. (eds.) TCC 2016, Part 1. LNCS, vol. 9562, pp. 96–124. Springer, Heidelberg (2016). https://doi.org/10.1007/978-3-662-49096-9_5
29. López-Alt, A., Tromer, E., Vaikuntanathan, V.: On-the-fly multiparty computation on the cloud via multikey fully homomorphic encryption. In: Karloff, H.J., Pitassi, T. (eds.) 44th ACM STOC, pp. 1219–1234. ACM Press, New York, 19–22 May 2012. https://doi.org/10.1145/2213977.2214086
30. Malavolta, G., Thyagarajan, S.A.K.: Homomorphic time-lock puzzles and applications. In: Boldyreva, A., Micciancio, D. (eds.) CRYPTO 2019, Part 1. LNCS, vol. 11692, pp. 620–649. Springer, Cham (2019). https://doi.org/10.1007/978-3-030-26948-7_22
31. Mukherjee, P., Wichs, D.: Two round multiparty computation via multi-key FHE. In: Fischlin, M., Coron, J.-S. (eds.) EUROCRYPT 2016, Part 2. LNCS, vol. 9666, pp. 735–763. Springer, Heidelberg (2016). https://doi.org/10.1007/978-3-662-49896-5_26
32. Peikert, C., Shiehian, S.: Multi-key FHE from LWE, revisited. In: Hirt, M., Smith, A. (eds.) TCC 2016, Part 2. LNCS, vol. 9986, pp. 217–238. Springer, Heidelberg (2016). https://doi.org/10.1007/978-3-662-53644-5_9
33. Quach, W., Wee, H., Wichs, D.: Laconic function evaluation and applications. In: Thorup, M. (ed.) 59th FOCS, pp. 859–870. IEEE Computer Society Press, Paris, 7–9 October 2018. https://doi.org/10.1109/FOCS.2018.00086
34. Yao, A.C.C.: How to generate and exchange secrets (extended abstract). In: 27th FOCS, pp. 162–167. IEEE Computer Society Press, Toronto, Ontario, 27–29 October 1986. https://doi.org/10.1109/SFCS.1986.25

Constant Ciphertext-Rate Non-committing Encryption from Standard Assumptions

Zvika Brakerski[1], Pedro Branco[2(✉)], Nico Döttling[3], Sanjam Garg[4], and Giulio Malavolta[5]

[1] Weizmann Institute of Science, Rehovot, Israel
zvika.brakerski@weizmann.ac.il
[2] IT, IST - University of Lisbon, Lisbon, Portugal
pmbranco@math.tecnico.ulisboa.pt
[3] Helmholtz Center for Information Security (CISPA), Saarbrücken, Germany
doettling@cispa.saarland
[4] UC Berkeley, Berkeley, USA
sanjamg@berkeley.edu
[5] Max Planck Institute for Security and Privacy, Bochum, Germany
giulio.malavolta@hotmail.it

Abstract. Non-committing encryption (NCE) is a type of public key encryption which comes with the ability to equivocate ciphertexts to encryptions of arbitrary messages, i.e., it allows one to find coins for key generation and encryption which "explain" a given ciphertext as an encryption of any message. NCE is the cornerstone to construct adaptively secure multiparty computation [Canetti et al. STOC'96] and can be seen as the quintessential notion of security for public key encryption to realize ideal communication channels.

A large body of literature investigates what is the best message-to-ciphertext ratio (i.e., the rate) that one can hope to achieve for NCE. In this work we propose a near complete resolution to this question and we show how to construct NCE with constant rate in the plain model from a variety of assumptions, such as the hardness of the learning with errors (LWE), the decisional Diffie-Hellman (DDH), or the quadratic residuosity (QR) problem. Prior to our work, constructing NCE with constant rate required a trusted setup and indistinguishability obfuscation [Canetti et al. ASIACRYPT'17].

1 Introduction

Multiparty computation (MPC) considers the problem of mutually distrustful parties computing a function over their inputs, while revealing no information beyond the output of the function [13,22]. Traditionally, the security of MPC protocols is analyzed considering two different adversarial models: In the *static* settings, the adversary is required to announce the set of parties that he wants to corrupt prior to the execution of the protocol. On the other hand, in the

© International Association for Cryptologic Research 2020
R. Pass and K. Pietrzak (Eds.): TCC 2020, LNCS 12550, pp. 58–87, 2020.
https://doi.org/10.1007/978-3-030-64375-1_3

adaptive settings, the adversary can corrupt parties at any point in time of the execution, possibly depending on previously exchanged messages. Adaptive security is widely believed to be the correct notion of security to consider when analyzing the security of cryptographic protocols as we do not have any real-life justification for the static model (except that adaptive security is in general harder to achieve).

Non-Committing Encryption (NCE) was presented in [4] as the cornerstone to construct adaptively-secure MPC, both in the stand-alone model [4] and in the UC settings [5]. Loosely speaking, NCE incarnates the notion of an ideal private channel, which retains the security of its messages, even if it is corrupted at a later point in time. NCE is a public-key encryption (PKE) scheme for which there exists a simulator that is able to create a pair of public key pk and ciphertext ct, indistinguishable from a real pair public key/ciphertext. Given any message M at any later point in time, the simulator can craft random coins that explain the transcript (pk, ct) for M. A central efficiency measure for PKE is the rate of encryption, i.e., the asymptotic ratio between the size of the message and the size of the ciphertext. While we know how to construct high-rate PKE[1] from numerous hardness assumptions, the situation is less cheerful for NCE. The most efficient schemes from the literature in the plain model have ciphertext-rate polylogarithmic in the security parameter [16,23], whereas (asymptotically) matching the efficiency of PKE currently requires a trusted setup and indistinguishability obfuscation [6]. Motivated by the current state of affairs, we ask the following question:

Can we build NCE with ciphertext rate $\mathcal{O}(1)$ from standard assumptions?

1.1 Our Results

We present a nearly complete resolution of this question by constructing the first NCE schemes with constant ciphertext-rate from a new abstraction, which we call Packed Encryption with Partial Equivocality (PEPE). Then we show how to instantiate PEPE from several standard problems, such as learning with errors (LWE), decisional Diffie-Hellman (DDH), and quadratic residuosity (QR). Specifically, we prove the following main theorem.

Theorem 1 (Informal). *Assuming the hardness of the {LWE, DDH, QR} problem, there exists a non-committing encryption scheme with ciphertext rate $\mathcal{O}(1)$.*

We note that our PEPE schemes achieve rate 1. The rate of our NCE schemes is a small constant which is mostly determined by an information-theoretic technique in the construction of NCE from PEPE.

As a contribution of independent interest, we present a novel ciphertext-compression technique for packed ElGamal encryption schemes which preserves correctness perfectly. As a direct corollary, we obtain a linearly-homomorphic encryption scheme with rate 1 from the DDH assumption.

---

[1] Rate-1 PKE can be easily constructed using hybrid encryption.

Theorem 2 (Informal). *Assuming the hardness of the DDH problem, there exists a linearly homomorphic encryption scheme with rate* 1.

This result generalizes and improves the recent work of Döttling *et al.* [10], where they obtained a rate-1 oblivious transfer from DDH (trivially implied by rate-1 linearly-homomorphic encryption) with inverse polynomial correctness error. Their scheme could be lifted to achieve negligible decryption error at the cost of introducing error-correcting codes, thus losing the additive homomorphism. Among other things, our scheme implies simpler and more direct constructions of rate-1 private information retrieval and rate-1 lossy trapdoor functions (using the same compilers as described in [10]) from the DDH assumption, without error correcting codes.

1.2 Related Work

The study of the rate of NCE has been the subject of a large body of literature. In the following we briefly review prior progress on improving the rate of NCE. We only consider NCE schemes with optimal round complexity, i.e., two-round protocols. The first instantiation of NCE is due to Canetti *et al.* [4] and achieved quadratic ciphertext-rate $\mathcal{O}(\lambda^2)$ under the RSA or the Computational Diffie-Hellman (CDH) assumption. Some three-round protocols were proposed after that [1,8] (both achieving linear rate), but the only improvement in the two-round settings was only made several years later in [7], where an NCE with ciphertext-rate $\mathcal{O}(\lambda)$ was presented, assuming the hardness of factoring Blum integers.

The rate question for NCE has recently received renewed interest: In [17], a scheme based on the ϕ-hiding assumption and achieving polylogarithmic (in the length of the message) ciphertext-rate was presented. This result was improved in a subsequent work [16], where a scheme with polylogarithmic (in the security parameter) ciphertext-rate and based on the LWE assumption with superpolynomial modulus-to-noise ratio was proposed. Finally, a scheme with quasi-optimal (i.e., logarithmic) ciphertext-rate was presented in [23], assuming the hardness of the DDH problem. We also mention the work of Canetti *et al.* [6], which constructs NCE with optimal rate (i.e., $1 - o(1)$) but at the cost of assuming indistinguishability obfuscation (i$\mathcal{O}$) and a trusted setup. A comparison with our results is presented in Table 1.

1.3 Discussion and Open Problems

We stress that, as done in (most of) prior works improving the rate of NCE (e.g. [17,23]), we do not take the size of the public key into account when measuring the rate of the scheme. This is justified by the fact that (i) the public keys do not depend on the encrypted messages: In some scenarios it might be acceptable to have a more expensive "offline" communication while optimizing for an efficient "online" (i.e. message-dependent) phase. Furthermore, (ii) one can encrypt multiple messages under the same public key. That is, the size of

Table 1. Comparison with previous work. We focus only on constructions which have two rounds of communication. λ denotes the security parameter and ℓ denotes the length of the message to be encrypted.

	Ciphertext rate	Hardness assumption	Setup
[4]	$\mathcal{O}(\lambda^2)$	RSA, CDH	–
[7]	$\mathcal{O}(\lambda)$	Factoring Blum integers	–
[20]	$\mathcal{O}(\lambda)$	DDH, LWE, Factoring Blum integers	–
[17]	$\mathsf{poly}(\log \ell)$	ϕ-hiding	Oblivious sampling of RSA modulus
[16]	$\mathsf{poly}(\log \lambda)$	LWE	–
[6]	$1 - o(1)$	$i\mathcal{O}$	CRS
[23]	$\mathcal{O}(\log \lambda)$	DDH	–
Our result	$\mathcal{O}(1)$	LWE, DDH, QR	–

the public key grows linearly with the number of *equivocable* ciphertexts, as opposed to *all* ciphertexts.

Finally, our work still leaves open the question about the *true* rate of NCE: Is (round-optimal) NCE with (asymptotic) rate 1 possible from standard assumptions and in the plain model, or is a small constant rate, as achieved in this work, the best we can hope for?

2 Technical Overview

Before delving in the presentation of our scheme, we briefly recall the NCE scheme of [16], which is based on LWE with superpolynomial modulus-to-noise ratio. Let $M \in \{0, 1\}^\ell$ be a (long) message we want to encrypt. The public key of this scheme is essentially a *packed Regev* key, that is it consists of a matrix $\mathbf{A}$ and vectors $\mathbf{v}_1, \ldots, \mathbf{v}_\ell$. The matrix $\mathbf{A} \in \mathbb{Z}_q^{k \times n}$ is chosen uniformly random (where k, n are two polynomials in the security parameter λ) whereas the vectors $\mathbf{v}_i$ are chosen in two different modes. Let $I_R \subseteq [\ell]$ be a set of indices of size $\ell/8$ chosen at random by the key generator. We think of this set as part of the secret key.

- For all $i \in I_R$ the component public key $\mathbf{v}_i$ is computed by $\mathbf{v}_i = \mathbf{s}_i \mathbf{A} + \mathbf{e}_i$ where $\mathbf{s} \leftarrow_\$ \mathbb{Z}_q^k$ is the corresponding component secret key and $\mathbf{e}_i \leftarrow_\$ \chi^n$ is a noise term, chosen from an appropriate LWE error distribution χ.
- For all $i \notin I_R$ the component keys $\mathbf{v}_i \leftarrow_\$ \mathbb{Z}_q^n$ are chosen uniformly random.

To encrypt a message M, it is first encoded into a binary string $\mathbf{y} \in \{0,1\}^\ell$ using a suitable error-correcting code (ECC), the choice of which is rather delicate[2]. The encrypter then chooses a random subset $I_S \subseteq [\ell]$, also of size $\ell/8$. For all indices $i \in I_S$, we replace the i-th component of the string $\mathbf{y}$ by uniformly random bits.

The (modified) string $\mathbf{y}$ is then encrypted using a noisy version of the packed Regev scheme [21] in its gaussian variant. More precisely, one first samples a vector $\mathbf{r}$ from a suitable discrete gaussian over $\mathbb{Z}^n$ and computes

$$\mathbf{c}_1 = \mathbf{A}\mathbf{r}^T$$
$$\forall i \in [\ell] : w_i = \mathbf{v}_i \mathbf{r}^T + e_i^* + \mathbf{y}_i \cdot q/2,$$

where the *masking noise terms* e_i^* are chosen from an appropriate discrete gaussian. To decrypt a ciphertext $(\mathbf{c}_1, w_1, \ldots, w_\ell)$ one proceeds as follows. For all indices $i \in I_R$, the decrypter is in possession of a component secret key $\mathbf{s}_i$ which allows him to recover $\mathbf{y}_i$ by computing $w_i - \mathbf{s}_i \mathbf{c}_1 \approx \mathbf{y}_i \cdot q/2$ and rounding. All components with indices outside of I_R are effectively erased from the view of the receiver. However, by the above choice of parameters the receiver will be able to recover the message M with high probability using the efficient decoder of ECC. This establishes correctness of the scheme.

We will briefly discuss how we can equivocate messages if the system is set up in simulation mode. Instead of running honest key generation, the simulator chooses a set $I_b \subseteq [\ell]$ of size $\ell/4$. We call I_b the set of *bad* indices. Now, the simulator chooses the matrix $\mathbf{A}$ jointly with the $\mathbf{v}_i$ for $i \in I_b$ via a lattice trapdoor sampler. I.e., the simulator generates a matrix $\mathbf{B} \in \mathbb{Z}_q^{(k+\ell/4) \times n}$ with a lattice trapdoor $\mathsf{td}_\mathbf{B}$, then sets $\mathbf{A}$ to be the first k rows of $\mathbf{B}$ and uses the remaining $\ell/4$ rows for the vectors $\mathbf{v}_i$ with indices $i \in I_b$. The remaining $\mathbf{v}_i$ with indices in the good set $I_g = [\ell] \setminus I_b$ will be chosen as LWE samples, i.e. for these components the simulator will know a corresponding secret key $\mathbf{s}_i$.

To simulate a ciphertext, the simulator chooses a uniformly random bit string $\mathbf{y}'$ and encrypts it as before via noisy Regev encryption. We will briefly sketch the main ideas of how ciphertexts are equivoked. Given a message M, the simulator needs to compute random coins r_G which explain the public key pk and r_E which explain the ciphertext ct. Now, M is encoded into a binary string $\mathbf{y} \in \{0,1\}^\ell$ via ECC. Now, note since the string $\mathbf{y}'$ was chosen at random, it will agree with $\mathbf{y}$ in approximately 50% of the indices. For the remaining 50% of indices on which $\mathbf{y}'$ and $\mathbf{y}$ disagree, the simulator has two strategies at its disposal.

– For all indices $i \in I_b$ it will be able to resample the gaussian $\mathbf{r}$ via a gaussian sampler that uses the lattice trapdoor $\mathsf{td}_\mathbf{B}$. This effectively allows the simulator to *reprogram* all ciphertext components w_i with index $i \in I_b$ as encryptions of $\mathbf{y}_i$ (instead of $\mathbf{y}'_i$). This resampling procedure is the reason the masking noise terms e_i^* are needed. The resampling procedure creates small

---

[2] We need a code ECC which can efficiently decode from a $1/2 - \delta$ fraction of *random* errors.

artifacts in the ciphertext components with indices $i \in I_g$, and the masking noise terms are used to statistically drown these artifacts.
- For the remaining indices, it will claim they were in the set I_S by choosing this set appropriately.

A good deal of care has to be taken when opening the sets I_R and I_S in order to ensure that they have *the right statistics*. In order to ensure this, the simulator will make use of the fact that any component key in the set I_g can be claimed to be either from the set I_R or $[\ell] \setminus I_R$.

2.1 Packed Encryption with Equivocality

Our first contribution is an abstraction of the above framework into a generic construction of NCE using a novel primitive that we call Packed Encryption with Partial Equivocality (PEPE).[3] A PEPE is a cryptographic primitive that allows one to encrypt a message $M \in \{0,1\}^\ell$ into a ciphertext ct, using random coins r_E. Later, we can find random coins r'_E such that the encryption of $M' \neq M$ is exactly ct, conditioned on the fact that M' and M differ only on some predefined positions. More precisely, a PEPE consists of the following algorithms.

- **Key Generation:** Given a subset $I \subset [\ell]$ and a bit b, it outputs a pair of public and secret keys $(\mathsf{pk}, \mathsf{sk}) \leftarrow \mathsf{KG}(b, I; r_G)$ on either the real mode (if $b = 0$) or on the ideal mode (if $b = 1$), created using random coins r_G. Public keys created in different modes should be indistinguishable. A pair of keys created in the ideal mode will allow for equivocation of some of the positions of an encrypted message.
- **Encryption:** Given a message $M \in \{0,1\}^\ell$ and a public key pk, it outputs a ciphertext $\mathsf{ct} \leftarrow \mathsf{E}(\mathsf{pk}, M; r_E)$ encrypted using random coins r_E.
- **Decryption:** Given a secret key sk corresponding to the subset I, it outputs M_i for $i \in I$.

Additionally, a PEPE scheme is equipped with the algorithms EquivPK and EquivCT defined as follows.

- **Equivocation of public key randomness:** Given a subset $I' \subset I$ and the pair $(\mathsf{pk}, \mathsf{sk}) \leftarrow \mathsf{KG}(b, I; r_G)$, this algorithm outputs r'_G such that $(\mathsf{pk}, \mathsf{sk}') = \mathsf{KG}(0, I'; r'_G)$.
- **Equivocation of ciphertext randomness.** Given a message M' (that differs from M only in the indexes not in I) and random coins r_E, this algorithm outputs random coins r'_E such that $\mathsf{E}(\mathsf{pk}, M; r_E) = \mathsf{E}(\mathsf{pk}, M'; r'_E)$.

As security requirement, the random coins outputted by the algorithms described above should be indistinguishable from real random coins.

---

[3] A somewhat similar notion is the one of Somewhere Equivocal Encryption [15]. However, Somewhere Equivocal Encryption is a purely symmetric-key primitive and equivocation is performed by finding a new secret key. On the other hand, PEPE is a public-key primitive and equivocation is achieved by finding new random coins for the key generation and encryption algorithms.

NCE from PEPE. Our construction of NCE from PEPE closely follows the outline [16] as explained above, where we replace packed Regev encryption with a PEPE scheme. In the real mode, we also setup the PEPE scheme in real mode. In simulation mode, we setup keys in the appropriate simulation mode. The ciphertext randomness equivocation property of the PEPE scheme serves as a drop-in replacement for the gaussian sampling property of the packed Regev scheme in [16]. The remaining aspects are essentially identical to the [16] such as the use of error correcting codes and set partitions.

Assuming that we have a PEPE scheme which achieves constant rate, then the rate of this NCE construction is dominated by the rate penalty of the error correcting code ECC. Consequently, given that ECC has constant rate, this transformation results in an NCE scheme with constant rate.

In the remainder of this outline we briefly discuss constructing rate-1 PEPE schemes from LWE, DDH, and QR.

2.2   Construction from LWE

Before presenting our construction for PEPE from the LWE assumption, we recall a compression technique for Regev's scheme, recently introduced in [3]. Recall that in packed Regev encryption, a ciphertext is of the form

$$\mathsf{ct} = (\mathbf{c}_1, (w_1, \ldots, w_\ell)) \in \mathbb{Z}_q^n \times \mathbb{Z}_q^\ell$$

where $\mathbf{c}_1$ is a *ciphertext header* and $w_1, \ldots, w_\ell$ are the ciphertext payload components. As explained above, given a component secret key $\mathbf{s}_i$ a component w_i can be decrypted by computing $w_i - \mathbf{s}_i \cdot \mathbf{c}_1$ and rounding the result to either 0 or $q/2$. Given that the modulus q is sufficiently large, we can compress such a ciphertext by choosing an offset z such that for all indices i

$$w_i + z \notin [q/4 - B, q/4 + B] \cup [-q/4 - B, -q/4 + B],$$

where B is a bound on the decryption noise. Given that the modulus q is large enough, we can ensure that such an offset z always exists and can be found efficiently. Note that z is computed from the ciphertext only, i.e. without the knowledge of the corresponding plaintexts. Given such a z, we can compress the w_i into single bits by computing $c_i = \lfloor w_i + z \rceil_2$. The new compressed ciphertext is composed by $(\mathbf{c}_1, \{c_i\}_{i \in [\ell]}, z)$. To decrypt such a compressed ciphertext, we compute $c_i - \lfloor \mathbf{s}_i \mathbf{c}_1 + z \rceil_2$. A routine calculation shows that, given that z satisfies the constraints above, decryption is always correct.

PEPE from LWE. Recasting the construction of [16] in terms of PEPE, immediately gives us a PEPE scheme of polylogarithmic rate. Since the scheme obtained in this way is a packed Regev scheme, it is naturally compatible with the ciphertext compression technique provided above.

To see that the resulting scheme still supports public key and ciphertext equivocation, note first that we leave the public key unmodified. On the other hand, note that ciphertext compression is merely a public post-processing operation on a ciphertext. Consequently, to equivocate a compressed ciphertext, all we have to do is to equivocate the underlying uncompressed ciphertext. Thus, given that the message length ℓ is sufficiently large, we obtain a PEPE scheme with rate 1 under the same assumptions as above.

2.3 Construction from DDH

We will now outline our DDH-based construction, which follows the same blueprint as the LWE-based construction. We first construct a PEPE scheme with poor rate ($\mathcal{O}(\lambda)$), and then combine it with a public ciphertext compression technique.

We will first explain our novel ciphertext compression technique for the discrete logarithm settings. This algorithm, can be seen as the computational analog of the one described above and it is inspired by recent techniques developed in the domain of homomorphic secret sharing [2]. The scheme is perfectly correct, however the caveat is that the compression algorithm will run in *expected* polynomial time (or, alternatively, will introduce a decryption error with negligible probability). Let $\mathbb{G}$ be a prime order group with generator g and let

$$(h_1 = g^{s_1}, \ldots, h_\ell = g^{s_\ell})$$

be a set of public keys. The ciphertexts that we want to compress are of the form

$$(g^r, (h_1^r g^{M_1}, \ldots, h_\ell^r g^{M_\ell})) = (c_1, (w_1, \ldots, w_\ell)) \in \mathbb{G}^{\ell+1}$$

where $r \leftarrow_{\$} \mathbb{Z}_p$ and $M \in \{0,1\}^\ell$, which is an extended version of the El-Gamal scheme. Decryption is performed component-wise by computing $w_i/c_1^{s_i}$ and checking if the result is equal to 1 (in which case, $M_i = 0$) or g ($M_i = 1$).

Let T be a polynomial in the security parameter. Our compression algorithm uses a pseudorandom function $\mathsf{PRF} : \{0,1\}^\lambda \times \mathbb{G} \to \{0,1\}^\tau$. On input a ciphertext $(c_1, (w_1, \ldots, w_\ell))$, the compression algorithm samples a random key K for the PRF until the following two conditions are simultaneously satisfied: For all $i \in [\ell]$ it holds that

(1) $\mathsf{PRF}(K, w_i/g) \neq 0$.
(2) There exists a $\delta_i \in [T-1]$ such that $\mathsf{PRF}(K, w_i \cdot g^{\delta_i}) = 0$.

The compressed ciphertext ct is composed by $\mathsf{ct} = (K, c_1, \delta_1 \bmod 2, \ldots, \delta_\ell \bmod 2) \in \{0,1\}^\lambda \times \mathbb{G} \times \{0,1\}^\ell$ where δ_i is the smallest integer that satisfies condition (2). In order to decrypt, one needs to find, for every $i \in [\ell]$, the smallest γ_i such that $\mathsf{PRF}(K, c_1^{s_i} \cdot g^{\gamma_i}) = 0$ by exhaustive search. Finally it outputs $M_i = \delta_i \oplus \mathsf{LSB}(\gamma_i)$, where LSB denotes the least significant bit of an integer. Note that the scheme is correct with probability 1, since condition (1) ensures that there is no ambiguity in the decoding of the bit M_i. By setting the parameters appropriately, we can guarantee that K can always be found in polynomial time, except with negligible probability.

PEPE from DDH. We will now outline our uncompressed DDH-based PEPE construction, which shares some ideas with the LWE based construction above. Assume that the underlying group $\mathbb{G}$ supports oblivious sampling, i.e. we can sample uniformly random group elements without knowledge of any discrete logarithm relation. For a vector $\mathbf{a} \in \mathbb{Z}_p^n$ we will use the notation $[\mathbf{a}]$ to denote $g^{\mathbf{a}}$ (i.e. the component-wise exponentiation). In real mode, the public key $\mathsf{pk} = ([\mathbf{a}], \{[\mathbf{v}]\})$ of our DDH-based PEPE is chosen as follows. Choose the vector $[\mathbf{a}]$ and all $[\mathbf{v}_i]$ for $i \in [\ell] \setminus I$ obliviously. For all indices $i \in I$ choose a uniformly random $s_i \leftarrow_\$ \mathbb{Z}_p$ and set $[\mathbf{v}_i] = s_i \cdot [\mathbf{a}] = [s_i \cdot \mathbf{a}]$ (where we write exponentiation multiplicatively). The secret key consists of the component keys $\{s_i\}_{i \in I}$.

To encrypt a message $M \in \{0,1\}^\ell$, first choose a uniformly random $\mathbf{r} \leftarrow_\$ \mathbb{Z}_p^n$ and compute $[\mathbf{c}_1] = [\mathbf{a}] \cdot \mathbf{r} = [\mathbf{a} \cdot \mathbf{r}]$ and for all $i \in [\ell]$ $[w_i] = [\mathbf{v}_i] \cdot \mathbf{r} + [M_i]$. The vector $\mathbf{r} \in \mathbb{Z}_p^n$ constitute the random coins for encryption. To decrypt the i-th ciphertext component, compute $[w_i] - s_i \cdot [\mathbf{c}_1]$, output 0 if this equals 1 and 1 if it equals $g = [1]$.

We will now briefly outline how ciphertext equivocation works for this scheme. In the ideal mode, all elements of the public key are computed *non-obliviously* with respect to a single generator $g = [1]$. That is, we sample $[\mathbf{a}]$ by choosing a uniformly random $\mathbf{a}' \leftarrow_\$ \mathbb{Z}_p^n$ and setting $[\mathbf{a}] = \mathbf{a}' \cdot [1]$. For all $i \in I$ we choose a random $s_i \leftarrow_\$ \mathbb{Z}_p$ and set $[\mathbf{v}_i] = s_i \cdot \mathbf{a}' \cdot [1]$. For all $i \in [\ell] \setminus I$ we choose a uniformly random $\mathbf{v}'_i \leftarrow_\$ \mathbb{Z}_p^n$ and set $[\mathbf{v}_i] = \mathbf{v}'_i \cdot [1]$. The simulator will keep all non-obliviously sampled ring elements as equivocation trapdoor. Notice that obliviously sampled public keys and non-obliviously sampled public keys are identically distributed.

We will finally describe how ciphertexts are equivoked. For a given a ciphertext $\mathsf{ct} = ([\mathbf{c}_1], [w_1], \dots, [w_\ell])$ encrypting a message $M \in \{0,1\}^\ell$, the simulator knows the random coins $\mathbf{r}$ that were used to generate this ciphertext. I.e. it knows (in $\mathbb{Z}_p$) that

$$\mathbf{c}_1 = \mathbf{a} \cdot \mathbf{r}$$
$$w_1 = \mathbf{v}_1 \cdot \mathbf{r} + M_1$$
$$\vdots$$
$$w_\ell = \mathbf{v}_\ell \cdot \mathbf{r} + M_\ell$$

Now, given a message $M' \in \{0,1\}^\ell$ which agrees with M on the index set I we can equivoke the ciphertext ct as an encryption of M' by by uniformly choosing a solution $\bar{\mathbf{r}} \in \mathbb{Z}_p^n$ for the linear equation system

$$\mathbf{c}_1 = \mathbf{a} \cdot \bar{\mathbf{r}}$$
$$w_1 = \mathbf{v}_{i_1} \cdot \bar{\mathbf{r}} + M'_{i_1}$$
$$\vdots$$
$$w_{i_k} = \mathbf{v}_{i_k} \cdot \bar{\mathbf{r}} + M'_{i_k}$$

where $[\ell] \setminus I = \{i_1, \dots, i_k\}$. Notice that since for $i \in [\ell] \setminus I$ the $\mathbf{v}_i$ are chosen uniformly at random, given that $k + 1 \leq n$ this system has full rank with overwhelming probability. Consequently, we can sample a uniform solution $\bar{\mathbf{r}}$ via basic linear algebra. Finally, note that since for $i \in I$ the $\mathbf{v}_i$ are of the form $s_i \cdot \mathbf{a}$, it also holds that $w_i = \mathbf{v}_i \cdot \bar{\mathbf{r}} + M_i'$, as $\mathbf{ar} = \mathbf{c}_1 = \mathbf{a}\bar{\mathbf{r}}_1$ and $M_i = M_i'$. Thus this scheme has perfect ciphertext equivocality.

Finally, applying the oblivious ciphertext compression algorithm described above yields a PEPE scheme of rate 1.

2.4 Construction from QR

We conclude our overview by briefly sketching how to adapt the above developed techniques to construct PEPE from the QR assumption.[4] Similarly to the DDH case, the public is composed by

$$\mathsf{pk} = \big([\mathbf{a}], \{[\mathbf{v}_i]\}_{i \in [\ell]}\big)$$

where $[\mathbf{a}] \leftarrow_{\$} \mathbb{QR}_N^n$ and $[\mathbf{v}_i] = s_i[\mathbf{a}]$ for $i \in I$ and $[\mathbf{v}_i] \leftarrow_{\$} \mathbb{QR}_N^n$. To encrypt a message $M \in \{0,1\}^\ell$, we compute

$$\tilde{\mathsf{ct}} = ([\mathbf{ar}^T], ((-1)^{M_1} \cdot [\mathbf{v}_1\mathbf{r}^T], \ldots, (-1)^{M_\ell} \cdot [\mathbf{v}_\ell\mathbf{r}^T]) \in \mathbb{QR}_N{}^n \times \mathbb{G}^\ell$$

with a uniformly chosen $\mathbf{r} \leftarrow_{\$} \mathbb{Z}_{(N-1)/2}^n$, and compress it into $\mathsf{ct} = ([\mathbf{ar}^T], (b_1, \ldots, b_\ell)) \in \mathbb{QR}_N^n \times \{0,1\}^\ell$ via the compressing procedure of [10]. When generating a public key in the equivocal mode, the simulator keeps $\mathbf{a}$ and the vectors $\mathbf{v}_i$, for $i \notin I$, to himself. The vectors $\mathbf{a}$ and $\mathbf{v}_i$ will allow him to equivocate by solving a linear system of equations in a similar fashion as in the DDH case.

3 Preliminaries

Throughout this work, λ denotes the natural security parameter. By $\mathsf{negl}[\lambda]$, we denote a negligible function in λ, that is, a function that vanishes faster than any polynomial in λ.

Let $n \in \mathbb{N}$. Then, $[n]$ denotes the set $\{1, \ldots, n\}$. If $\mathcal{A}$ is an algorithm, we denote by $y \leftarrow \mathcal{A}(x)$ the output y after running $\mathcal{A}$ on input x. If S is a (finite) set, we denote by $x \leftarrow_{\$} S$ the experiment of sampling uniformly at random an element x from S. If D is a distribution over S, we denote by $x \leftarrow_{\$} D$ the element x sampled from S according to D. We say that D is B-bounded if for every $\mathbf{x} \leftarrow_{\$} D$, we have $\|\mathbf{x}\| < B$, except with negligible probability, and where $\|\mathbf{x}\|$ is the usual ℓ_2 norm. We will usually use bold upper-case letters (e.g., $\mathbf{M}$) to denote matrices and lower-case letters (e.g., $\mathbf{v}$) to denote vectors, unless explicitly state otherwise. Let $q \in \mathbb{N}$. We define the rounding function $\lfloor \cdot \rceil_2 : \mathbb{Z}_q \rightarrow \mathbb{Z}_2$ as $\lfloor x \rceil_2 = \lfloor x \cdot 2/q \rceil \mod 2$.

We say that two distributions are computationally indistinguishable if no probabilistic polynomial-time (PPT) adversary can distinguish them.

The following lemma will be useful and provides a tail bound for the hypergeometric distribution.

---

[4] The QR-based construction is presented in the full version of this paper.

Lemma 3. *Let* $H(a, b, n)$ *be a hypergeometric distribution, with* $a = \alpha n$ *and* $b = \beta n$, *and let* X *be a random variable sampled from* $H(a, b, n)$. *Then*

$$\Pr\left[X \leq (\alpha\beta - \varepsilon)n\right] \leq \mathsf{negl}[n]$$

for some constant $0 < \varepsilon < 1$.

3.1   Coding Theory

We present some basic coding theory definitions and results that will be useful for our work.

Definition 4 (Error-Correcting Code). *A (binary) Error-Correnting Code (ECC) consists of a pair of algorithms* $\mathsf{ECC}_{N,n} = (\mathsf{Encode}, \mathsf{Decode})$ *such that:*

- $\mathbf{c} \leftarrow \mathsf{Encode}(M \in \{0,1\}^n)$ *takes as input a message* $M \in \{0,1\}^n$ *to be encoded. It outputs a codeword* $\mathbf{c} \in \{0,1\}^N$.
- $M \leftarrow \mathsf{Decode}(\mathbf{c}')$ *takes as input a corrupted codeword* $\mathbf{c}' \in \{0,1\}^N$. *It outputs* M *if* $\mathbf{c}'$ *and* $\mathbf{c} \leftarrow \mathsf{Decode}(M)$ *differ in at most t positions.*

Let $\mathsf{ECC}_{N,n}$ be a ECC. We call $R = n/N$ the rate of a code C. The error rate is defined as $E = t/N$. A list-decoding ECC [14] is a ECC such that the Decode algorithm outputs a list S of polynomial size (in the security parameter), one of which is the correct original encoded message. Constructions for list-decoding ECC with constant rate and that correct a large amount of errors (say, $1/2 - \zeta$ for any constant $\zeta > 0$) are known to exist [14].

Lemma 5 [18]. *Let* C *be a list-decoding ECC with rate* R *and error rate* E. *Then, there exists a unique-decoding error correction code with rate* R *and error rate* E *given that One-Way Functions exist.*

In particular, there exists a code with constant rate R *and error rate of* $1/2 - \zeta$, *for any constant* $\zeta > 0$, *given that One-Way Functions exist.*

3.2   Hardness Assumptions

In the following, we present the hardness assumptions that we use in this work.

Learning with Errors. The Learning with Errors (LWE) problem was firstly presented in [21]. We now present the decisional version of the problem. In the following, let D_σ be a discrete Gaussian distribution with parameter σ.

Definition 6 (Learning with Errors). *Let* $k, q \in \mathbb{Z}$ *and let* D_σ *be an error distribution. The LWE assumption holds if for any PPT adversary*

$$\left|\Pr\left[1 \leftarrow \mathcal{A}(\mathbf{A}, \mathbf{s}\mathbf{A} + \mathbf{e})\right] - \Pr\left[1 \leftarrow \mathcal{A}(\mathbf{A}, \mathbf{u})\right]\right| \leq \mathsf{negl}[\lambda]$$

for all $n \in \mathbb{Z}$, *where* $\mathbf{A} \leftarrow_{\$} \mathbb{Z}_q^{k \times n}$, $\mathbf{s} \leftarrow_{\$} \mathbb{Z}_q^k$, $\mathbf{e} \leftarrow_{\$} D_\sigma^n$ *and* $\mathbf{u} \leftarrow_{\$} \mathbb{Z}_q^n$.

In this work, we assume the hardness of the LWE with superpolynomial modulus-to-noise ratio. That is, we assume that the problem remains hard even when $B/q = \mathsf{negl}[\lambda]$ where the error e comes from a B-bounded distribution.

The following lemma states that we can *drown* (i.e., statistically hide) an error vector with a much wider distribution.

Lemma 7. *Let* q, B, σ *such that* $q = \lambda^{\omega(1)}$ *and* $\sigma/B = \lambda^{\omega(1)}$. *Then the distributions* D_σ *and* $D_\sigma + e$ *are statistically close, where* e *is sampled from a B-bounded distribution.*

The following lemma states that there are matrices statistically close to uniform and for which we can sample low-norm pre-images with the help of a trapdoor [12,19].

Lemma 8 [19]. *There exists a pair of algorithms* (TrapGen, SampleD) *such that:*

- $(\mathbf{B}, \mathsf{td}) \leftarrow \mathsf{TrapGen}(1^\lambda, k, n, q)$ *takes as input the security parameter λ and* $n, k, q \in \mathbb{Z}$. *It outputs a matrix* $\mathbf{B} \in \mathbb{Z}_q^{k \times n}$ *and a trapdoor* td. *The matrix* $\mathbf{B}$ *is 2^{-k} close to uniform.*
- $\mathbf{r} \leftarrow \mathsf{SampleD}(\mathsf{td}, \mathbf{B}, \mathbf{y}, \sigma)$ *takes as input a trapdoor* td, *a matrix* $\mathbf{B}$ *and a vector* $\mathbf{y} \in \mathbb{Z}_q^k$. *It outputs* $\mathbf{r} \in \mathbb{Z}_q^n$ *such that* $\mathbf{r} \leftarrow_\$ D_{\Lambda_\mathbf{y}^\perp(\mathbf{B}),\sigma}$, *where* $D_{\Lambda_\mathbf{y}^\perp(\mathbf{B}),\sigma}$ *is the discrete Gaussian distribution with standard deviation σ over the lattice* $\Lambda_\mathbf{y}^\perp(\mathbf{B}) = \{\mathbf{r} \in \mathbb{Z}_q^n : \mathbf{Ar}^T = \mathbf{y}\}$.

Decisional Diffie-Hellman. A (prime-order) *group generator* is an algorithm $\mathcal{G}$ that takes as an input a security parameter 1^λ and outputs $(\mathbb{G}, p, g)$, where $\mathbb{G}$ is the description of a multiplicative cyclic group, p is the order of the group which is always a prime number unless differently specified, and g is a generator of the group. In the following we state the decisional version of the Diffie-Hellman (DDH) assumption [9].

Definition 9 (Decisional Diffie-Hellman Assumption). *A group generator algorithm $\mathcal{G}$ satisfies the DDH assumption (or is DDH-hard) if for any PPT adversary $\mathcal{A}$*

$$\left| \Pr[1 \leftarrow \mathcal{A}((\mathbb{G}, p, g), (g^a, g^b, g^{ab}))] - \Pr[1 \leftarrow \mathcal{A}((\mathbb{G}, p, g), (g^a, g^b, g^c))] \right| \leq \mathsf{negl}[\lambda]$$

where $(\mathbb{G}, p, g) \leftarrow_\$ \mathcal{G}(1^\lambda)$ *and* $(a, b, c) \leftarrow_\$ \mathbb{Z}_p$.

In this work, we use the matrix version of the DDH assumption, called the Matrix Decisional Diffie-Hellman Assumption (MDDH), which generalizes the DDH assumption (and other number-theoretic assumptions). Let $g \in \mathbb{G}$ and let $\mathbf{M} \in \mathbb{Z}_p^{k \times n}$. We denote by $[\mathbf{M}] \in \mathbb{G}^{k \times n}$ the matrix

$$g^\mathbf{M} = \begin{pmatrix} g^{\mathbf{M}_{1,1}} & \cdots & g^{\mathbf{M}_{1,n}} \\ \vdots & \ddots & \vdots \\ g^{\mathbf{M}_{k,1}} & \cdots & g^{\mathbf{M}_{k,n}} \end{pmatrix}.$$

Definition 10 (Matrix Decisional Diffie-Hellman Assumption [11]). *A group generator algorithm $\mathcal{G}$ satisfies the MDDH if for any PPT algorithm $\mathcal{A}$ such that*

$$|\Pr[1 \leftarrow \mathcal{A}((\mathbb{G}, p, g), ([\mathbf{A}], [\mathbf{wA}]))] - \Pr[1 \leftarrow \mathcal{A}((\mathbb{G}, p, g), ([\mathbf{A}], [\mathbf{u}]))]| \leq \mathsf{negl}[\lambda]$$

where $(\mathbb{G}, p, g) \leftarrow_\$ \mathcal{G}(1^\lambda)$, $k < n$, $\mathbf{A} \leftarrow_\$ \mathbb{Z}_p^{k \times n}$, $\mathbf{w} \leftarrow_\$ \mathbb{Z}_p^k$ and $\mathbf{u} \leftarrow_\$ \mathbb{Z}_p^n$.

Observe that anyone can compute $s[\mathbf{A}] = [s\mathbf{A}]$, $\mathbf{w}[\mathbf{A}] = [\mathbf{wA}]$ or $[\mathbf{A}]\mathbf{v}^T = [\mathbf{Av}^T]$ knowing $[\mathbf{A}]$, s, $\mathbf{w}$ and $\mathbf{v}$, for any $\mathbf{A} \in \mathbb{Z}_q^{k \times n}$, $s \in \mathbb{Z}_q$, $\mathbf{w} \in \mathbb{Z}_q^k$ and $\mathbf{v} \in \mathbb{Z}_q^n$.

Quadratic Residuosity. In this version, we omit the QR assumption description due to space restrictions.

3.3 Non-committing Encryption

The formal definition of Non-Committing Encryption, as well as its security requirements, are presented below.

Definition 11 (Non-committing Encryption). *A Non-Committing Encryption (NCE) scheme is composed by a tuple of algorithms $(\mathsf{Gen}, \mathsf{Enc}, \mathsf{Dec}, \mathsf{Sim}_1, \mathsf{Sim}_2)$ such that:*

- *$(\mathsf{pk}, \mathsf{sk}) \leftarrow \mathsf{Gen}(1^\lambda, r_G)$ takes as input a security parameter λ and some randomness r_G. It outputs a pair of public and secret keys $(\mathsf{pk}, \mathsf{sk})$.*
- *$c \leftarrow \mathsf{Enc}(\mathsf{pk}, M, r_E)$ takes as input a public key pk, a message M and randomness r_E. It outputs a ciphertext c.*
- *$M/\bot \leftarrow \mathsf{Dec}(\mathsf{sk}, c)$ takes as input a secret key sk and a ciphertext c. It outputs either a message M or an error message $\bot$.*
- *$(\mathsf{pk}, c, \mathsf{st}) \leftarrow \mathsf{Sim}_1(1^\lambda)$ takes as input a security parameter λ. It outputs a simulated public key pk, a ciphertext c and an internal state st.*
- *$(r_G, r_E) \leftarrow \mathsf{Sim}_2(M, \mathsf{st})$ takes as input a message M and an internal state st. It outputs a pair of randomness for key generation and for encryption (r_G, r_E).*

A NCE scheme should have the following properties:

- **Correctness.** A NCE scheme is said to be correct if

$$\Pr\left[M \leftarrow \mathsf{Dec}(\mathsf{sk}, c) : \begin{matrix} (\mathsf{pk}, \mathsf{sk}) \leftarrow \mathsf{Gen}(1^\lambda) \\ c \leftarrow \mathsf{Enc}(\mathsf{pk}, M) \end{matrix}\right] \geq 1 - \mathsf{negl}[\lambda].$$

- **Simulatability.** Let $\mathcal{A}$ be any PPT adversary. A NCE scheme is said to be simulatable if the distributions IDEAL and REAL are computationally indistinguishable to $\mathcal{A}$, where

$$\mathsf{IDEAL} = \left\{ (M, \mathsf{pk}, c, r_G, r_E) : \begin{matrix} (\mathsf{pk}, c, \mathsf{st}) \leftarrow \mathsf{Sim}_1(1^\lambda) \\ M \leftarrow \mathcal{A}(\mathsf{pk}) \\ (r_G, r_E) \leftarrow \mathsf{Sim}_2(M, \mathsf{st}) \end{matrix} \right\}$$

and

$$\text{REAL} = \left\{ (M, \mathsf{pk}, c, r_G, r_E) : \begin{array}{c} (\mathsf{pk}, \mathsf{sk}) \leftarrow \mathsf{Gen}(1^\lambda, r_G) \\ M \leftarrow \mathcal{A}(\mathsf{pk}) \\ c \leftarrow \mathsf{Enc}(\mathsf{pk}, M, r_E) \end{array} \right\}.$$

4 Ciphertext Shrinking Algorithms

In this section we discuss how we can shrink the ciphertext of certain cryptosystems based on LWE, DDH or QR. Every procedure presented in this section is a post-processing operation that is applied to a ciphertext in order to reduce its size.

4.1 Ciphertext Shrinking Algorithm for LWE-Based Encryption Schemes

The following technique to shrink ciphertexts of LWE-based PKE schemes was firstly introduced in [3]. This is a post-processing technique that can be applied to every decrypt-and-multiply PKE scheme (see [3] for details). In particular, it can be applied to the usual Regev's scheme [21] which we use to construct our NCE scheme.

Construction 1. *Consider a PKE scheme with ciphertexts of the form $(\mathbf{c}_1, (w_{2,1}, \ldots, w_{2,\ell})) \in \mathbb{Z}_q^n \times \mathbb{Z}_q^\ell$, secret key $\mathbf{S} \in \mathbb{Z}_q^{\ell \times n}$ and where decryption is computed by multiplying $\lfloor (w_{2,1}, \ldots, w_{2,\ell}) - \mathbf{S}\mathbf{c}_1^T \rceil_2 = \lfloor M + e \rceil_2$ where e is sampled from a B-bounded distribution. We describe the shrinking algorithms in detail:*

$\mathsf{Shrink}(\mathsf{pk}, (\mathbf{c}_1, (w_{2,1}, \ldots, w_{2,\ell})))$:

- *Choose $z \leftarrow_\$ \mathbb{Z}_q \setminus U$ where*

$$U = \bigcup_{i=1}^\ell \left(\left[-\frac{q}{4} - w_{2,i} - B, -\frac{q}{4} - w_{2,i} + B \right] \cup \left[\frac{q}{4} - w_{2,i} - B, \frac{q}{4} - w_{2,i} + B \right] \right).$$

- *Compute $c_{2,i} = \lfloor w_{2,i} + z \rceil_2 \in \mathbb{Z}_2$ for every $i \in [\ell]$.*
- *Output $\mathsf{ct} = (\mathbf{c}_1, (c_{2,1}, \ldots, c_{2,\ell}), z)$.*

$\mathsf{ShrinkDec}(\mathsf{sk} = \mathbf{S}, \mathsf{ct})$:

- *Parse ct as $(\mathbf{c}_1, (c_{2,1}, \ldots, c_{2,\ell}), z)$.*
- *Compute $M_i \leftarrow \left(c_{2,i} - \lfloor \mathbf{s}_i \mathbf{c}_1^T + z \rceil_2 \right) \mod 2$ where $\mathbf{s}_i$ is the i-th row of $\mathbf{S}$.*
- *Output $M = (M_1, \ldots, M_\ell)$.*

Note that each bit of M is independently recovered from the other ones. Hence, we can relax the definition of $\mathsf{ShrinkDec}$ in order to output only a partial decryption of M. More precisely, if a subset $I \subseteq [\ell]$ is given as input to $\mathsf{ShrinkDec}$, then it outputs $\{M_i\}_{i \in I}$.

The following lemma guarantees the correctness of the shrinking procedure presented above.

Lemma 12 [3]. *Let $B = B(\lambda)$ and $q > 4\ell B$. Then the shrinking algorithm described in Construction 1 is correct up to noise B.*

4.2   Ciphertext Shrinking Algorithm for DDH-Based Encryption Schemes

Before presenting the shrinking procedure compatible with DDH-based encryption schemes, recall the definition of Pseudorandom Functions (PRF).

Definition 13 (Pseudorandom Function). *Let $\alpha = \alpha(\lambda)$ and $\beta = \beta(\lambda)$. A Pseudorandom Function (PRF) is defined by a keyed function* $\mathsf{PRF} : \{0,1\}^\lambda \times \{0,1\}^\alpha \to \{0,1\}^\beta$ *such that, for any adversary $\mathcal{A}$*

$$|\Pr\left[1 \leftarrow \mathcal{A}(y,x) : y \leftarrow \mathsf{PRF}(K,x)\right] - \Pr\left[1 \leftarrow \mathcal{A}(y,x) : y \leftarrow f(x)\right]| \leq \mathsf{negl}[\lambda]$$

for any $x \in \{0,1\}^\alpha$, where $f : \{0,1\}^\alpha \to \{0,1\}^\beta$ is a uniformly chosen random function and the key K is sampled uniformly at random from $\{0,1\}^\lambda$.

We now explain how one can compress ciphertexts of ElGamal-based encryption schemes. The following technique is a variant of the compression technique introduced in [2,10]. However, in this variant we achieve perfect correctness.

Construction 2. *Below we show our DDH-based scheme, with message space $\mathbb{Z}_q^\ell$, for some polynomials $q = q(\lambda)$ and $\ell = \ell(\lambda)$. The scheme is parametrized by two polynomials $\tau = \tau(\lambda)$ and $T = T(\lambda)$ that influence the runtime of the evaluation algorithm, whose exact value will be fixed later. The scheme assumes the existence of a pseudorandom function $\mathsf{PRF} : \{0,1\}^\lambda \times \mathbb{G} \to \{0,1\}^\tau$. We also assume that we have ciphertexts of the form $(c_1, (w_{2,1}, \dots, w_{2,\ell})) \in \mathbb{G} \times \mathbb{G}^\ell$ and that the secret key is of the form $(x_1, \dots x_\ell) \in \mathbb{Z}_p^\ell$. Decryption is done by computing $w_{2,i}/c_1^{x_i} = g^{M_i}$ and recovering $M_i \in \mathbb{Z}_q$, for each $i \in [\ell]$.*

$\mathsf{Shrink}(\mathsf{pk}, (c_1, (w_{2,1}, \dots, w_{2,\ell})))$:

- *Set $d_0 = c_1$ and $d_i = w_{2,i}$, for all $i = 1, \dots, \ell$.*
- *Sample a uniform key $K \leftarrow_\$ \{0,1\}^\lambda$ such that the following conditions are simultaneously satisfied:*
  (1) For all $i = 1, \dots, \ell$ and for all $k = 1, \dots, (q-1)$ it holds that

$$\mathsf{PRF}(K, d_i/g^k) \neq 0^\tau.$$

  (2) For all $i = 1, \dots, \ell$ there exists some $k = 0, \dots, (T-1)$ such that $\mathsf{PRF}(K, d_i \cdot g^k) = 0^\tau$.
- *For all $i = 1, \dots, \ell$ let δ_i be the smallest non-negative integer such that $\mathsf{PRF}(K, d_i \cdot g^{\delta_i}) = 0^\tau$.*
- *Return $\mathsf{ct} = (K, d_0, \delta_1 \bmod q, \dots, \delta_\ell \bmod q)$.*

$\mathsf{ShrinkDec}(\mathsf{sk}, \mathsf{ct})$:

- *Parse sk as $(x_1, \dots, x_\ell)$ and ct as $(K, d_0, \delta_1 \bmod q, \dots, \delta_\ell \bmod q)$.*
- *Compute for all $i = 1, \dots, \ell$ the smallest non-negative integer γ_i such that $\mathsf{PRF}(K, d_0^{x_i} \cdot g^{\gamma_i}) = 0^\tau$*
- *Set $M_i = \delta_i - \gamma_i \bmod q$.*
- *Return $M = (M_1, \dots, M_\ell)$.*

Again, note that each element M_i can be independently decrypted. Thus, if the $\mathsf{ShrinkDec}$ algorithm receives as input a subset $I \subseteq [\ell]$, it outputs $\{M_i\}$ for $i \in I$.

Analysis. The more interesting aspects of this scheme concern its correctness and the runtime of the subroutines.

Lemma 14. *The scheme as described in Construction 2 is perfectly correct.*

Proof. We assume without loss of generality that the decryption algorithm takes as input an evaluated ciphertext $\mathsf{ct} = (K, d_0, \delta_1, \ldots, \delta_\ell)$. Recall that $d_0 = c_1 = g^r$ for a random $r \leftarrow_\$ \mathbb{Z}_p$. Furthermore, for all $i = 1, \ldots, \ell$ the term δ_i is defined to be the smallest non-negative integer (mod q) such that $\mathsf{PRF}(K, d_i \cdot g^{\delta_i}) = 0^\tau$, where

$$d_i = h_i^r g^{M_i} = g^{x_i r_i} g^{M_i} = d_0^{x_i} g^{M_i}$$

Recall that γ_i is defined to be the smallest non-negative integer such that $\mathsf{PRF}(K, d_0^{x_i} \cdot g^{\gamma_i}) = 0^\tau$. Note that the pair (δ_i, γ_i) is always well defined by condition (2). We claim that

$$d_i \cdot g^{\delta_i} = d_0^{x_i} \cdot g^{\gamma_i}$$

with probability 1. Assume that this is not the case, then we have that $M_i + \delta_i \neq \gamma_i$. We distinguish two cases:

(a) $M_i + \delta_i < \gamma_i$: This case cannot happen since we assumed that γ_i was the smallest non-negative integer such that $\mathsf{PRF}(K, d_0^{x_i} \cdot g^{\gamma_i}) = 0^\tau$.
(b) $M_i + \delta_i > \gamma_i$: This case implies that $\gamma_i < q$ since $M_i \leq q$ and δ_i is the smallest non-negative integer such that $\mathsf{PRF}(K, d_i \cdot g^{\delta_i}) = \mathsf{PRF}(K, d_0^{x_i} \cdot g^{M_i} \cdot g^{\delta_i}) = 0^\tau$. Consequently we have that $\mathsf{PRF}(K, d_i/g^{\gamma_i}) = 0^\tau$ where $\gamma_i < q$, which violates condition (2).

Therefore we have that

$$M_i = \gamma_i - \delta_i \bmod q$$

for all $i = 1, \ldots, \ell$. This concludes our proof.

By condition (2), the values of γ_i always lie within $T - 1$ steps from $d_0^{x_i}$ and therefore ShrinkDec runs in strict polynomial time. What is left to be shown is that Shrink runs in expected polynomial time.

Lemma 15. *Let* PRF *be a pseudorandom function, let* $\tau = \log_2(2(q-1)\ell)$ *and let* $T = 2^\tau \lambda \log_e(\ell) + (q-1)\ell$. *Then* Shrink *terminates within* λ *iterations except with negligible probability.*

Proof. Observe that all the subroutines of Shrink run in strict polynomial time, except for the sampling of K. It therefore suffices to bound the probability that some K satisfies conditions (1) and (2) simultaneously. Throughout the following analysis we treat $\mathsf{PRF}(K, \cdot)$ as a truly random function (indexed by K) and the same analysis holds true, up to a negligible amount, for the case that $\mathsf{PRF}(K, \cdot)$ is a pseudorandom function by a standard argument.

We first bound from below the probability that a uniform $K \leftarrow_\$ \{0,1\}^\lambda$ satisfies condition (1), that is,

$$\Pr\left[\forall i \in [\ell], \forall k \in [q-1] : \mathsf{PRF}(K, d_i/g^k) \neq 0^\tau\right] \geq \left(1 - \frac{1}{2^\tau}\right)^{(q-1)\ell}$$

$$\geq 1 - \frac{(q-1)\ell}{2^\tau} = 1 - \frac{(q-1)\ell}{2(q-1)\ell} = \frac{1}{2}$$

* where the probability is taken over the random choice of K. The first inequality comes from the fact that we assume that all points d_i/g^k are distinct (since it minimizes the probability) and therefore the outputs of $\mathsf{PRF}(K, \cdot)$ are uniformly and independently distributed over $\{0,1\}^\tau$. The second inequality is from Bernoulli. We now bound from above the probability that condition (2) is not satisfied, conditioned on the fact that condition (1) is met. Let us denote by $S \subseteq \{0,1\}^\lambda$ the set of all keys K that satisfy condition (1). Then we have

$$\Pr\left[\exists i \in [\ell] \text{ s.t. } \forall k = 0, \ldots, (T-1) : \mathsf{PRF}(K, d_i \cdot g^k) \neq 0^\tau \,\middle|\, K \in S\right]$$

$$\leq \sum_{i=1}^{\ell} \Pr\left[\forall k = 0, \ldots, (T-1) : \mathsf{PRF}(K, d_i \cdot g^k) \neq 0^\tau \,\middle|\, K \in S\right]$$

$$\leq \sum_{i=1}^{\ell} \left(1 - \frac{1}{2^\tau}\right)^{T-(q-1)\ell} \leq \sum_{i=1}^{\ell} e^{-\frac{T-(q-1)\ell}{2^\tau}} = \sum_{i=1}^{\ell} e^{-\lambda \log_e(\ell)} = e^{-\lambda}$$

where the probability is taken over the random choice of K. The first inequality comes from a union bound whereas the second inequality is derived by observing that the constraint $K \in S$ fixes the value of $\mathsf{PRF}(K, \cdot)$ on at most $(q-1)\ell$ points.

To conclude, the probability that condition (1) is not satisfied after λ uniform choices of K is at most $2^{-\lambda}$ and the probability that condition (2) is not satisfied constrained on meeting condition (1) is $e^{-\lambda}$. By a union bound, the probability that Shrink does not terminate after λ iterations is at most $2^{-\lambda} + e^{-\lambda}$.

Rate-1 Linearly Homomorphic Encryption from DDH. An interesting consequence of our algorithm is that it yields a linearly homomorphic encryption scheme with rate approaching 1 from the DDH assumption. To see why this is the case, we recall the packed version of ElGamal encryption: The public key of the scheme consists of the tuple $(g, h_1, \ldots, h_\ell) = (g, g^{x_1}, \ldots, g^{x_\ell})$, and a ciphertext for a message $(M_1, \ldots, M_\ell)$ is of the form

$$(g^r, h_1^r \cdot g^{M_1}, \ldots, h_\ell^r \cdot g^{M_\ell})$$

for some uniformly chosen $r \leftarrow_\$ \mathbb{Z}_p$. This scheme can be shown secure by ℓ invocations of the DDH assumption and satisfies the structural requirements to apply our shrinking algorithm as described above. Furthermore note that the scheme supports the homomorphic evaluation of linear functions $f : \mathbb{Z}_q^\ell \to \mathbb{Z}_q$. One caveat of this scheme is that the runtime of the shrinking algorithm is polynomial q and therefore the function f has a polynomial-size range (we stress that q

is a bound on the output size and not the order of the DDH-hard group p). Yet these homomorphic capabilities suffice for many interesting applications, such as constructing rate-1 oblivious transfer, or semi-compact homomorphic encryption for branching programs [10].

4.3 Ciphertext Shrinking Algorithm for QR-Based Encryption Schemes

The ciphertext shrinking algorithm for QR-based encryption schemes is the one presented in [10]. We omit it here due to space restrictions.

5 Packed Encryption with Partial Equivocality

We begin this section by presenting the formal definition of PEPE as well as its security properties. We then show how to construct this primitive under several hardness assumptions. Then, we present constructions of PEPE from LWE, DDH and QR assumptions.

Definition 16. *A Packed Encryption with Partial Equivocality (PEPE) scheme that encrypts messages in $\{0,1\}^\ell$ is composed by a tuple of algorithms* (KG, E, D, EquivPK, EquivCT) *where:*

- $(\mathsf{pk}, \mathsf{sk}) \leftarrow \mathsf{KG}(1^\lambda, b \in \{0,1\}, I, r)$ *takes as input a security parameter λ, a bit b, a set of indexes $I \in [\ell]$ and random coins r.[5] It outputs a pair of public and secret keys $(\mathsf{pk}, \mathsf{sk})$. When $b = 0$ we say that the keys were generated in the real mode. Otherwise, if $b = 1$, we say that the keys were generated in the ideal mode.*
- $\mathsf{ct} \leftarrow \mathsf{E}(\mathsf{pk}, M \in \{0,1\}^\ell, r)$ *takes as input a public key pk, a message M and random coins r, and outputs a ciphertext ct.*
- $(M_i)_{i \in I} \leftarrow \mathsf{D}(\mathsf{sk}, \mathsf{ct})$ *takes as input a secret key sk and a ciphertext ct. It outputs bits M_i, for $i \in I$.*
- $r' \leftarrow \mathsf{EquivPK}(\mathsf{sk}, b, (I, r), I')$ *takes as input a secret key sk, a bit b, subsets $I, I' \subseteq [\ell]$ and randomness r. It outputs randomness r'.*
- $r' \leftarrow \mathsf{EquivCT}(\mathsf{sk}, (M, r), \{M'_i\}_{i \notin I})$ *takes as input a secret key sk, a pair of message and randomness (M, r) and some bits $\{M'_i\}_{i \notin I}$ together with a subset $I \subseteq [\ell]$. It outputs random coins r'.*

A PEPE scheme should fulfill correctness for decryption and for equivocality. Also, the random coins used in the key generation and encryption algorithms should be indistinguishable from random coins outputted by the equivocality algorithms.

---

[5] When the random coins r are omitted, it means they are chosen uniformly at random during the execution of the algorithm. In this case, the algorithm also outputs r. The same happens for algorithm E.

- **Correctness.** For any message $M \in \{0,1\}^\ell$ and any subset $I \subset [\ell]$, we have that

$$\Pr \left[\{M_i\}_{i \in I} = \{M_i'\}_{i \in I} : \begin{array}{c} (\mathsf{pk}, \mathsf{sk}) \leftarrow \mathsf{KG}(1^\lambda, 0, I, r_G) \\ \mathsf{ct} \leftarrow \mathsf{E}(\mathsf{pk}, M, r_E) \\ \{M_i'\}_{i \in I} \leftarrow \mathsf{D}(\mathsf{sk}, \mathsf{ct}) \end{array} \right] \geq 1 - \mathsf{negl}[\lambda].$$

- **Public key randomness indistinguishability.** The random coins outputted by the algorithm EquivPK should be *computationally indistinguishable* from true random coins. That is, the distributions $\mathsf{IDEAL}_{\mathsf{pk}}$ and $\mathsf{REAL}_{\mathsf{pk}}$ should be computationally indistinguishable, where

$$\mathsf{IDEAL}_{\mathsf{pk}_b} = \left\{ r_G : \begin{array}{c} (\mathsf{pk}, \mathsf{sk}) \leftarrow \mathsf{KG}(1^\lambda, b, I', r_G') \\ r_G \leftarrow \mathsf{EquivPK}(\mathsf{sk}, b, (I', r_G'), I) \end{array} \right\}$$

and

$$\mathsf{REAL}_{\mathsf{pk}} = \left\{ r_G : (\mathsf{pk}, \mathsf{sk}) \leftarrow \mathsf{KG}(1^\lambda, 0, I, r_G) \right\}$$

for any subsets $I, I' \subset [\ell]$ such that $I \subset I'$ and any $b \in \{0,1\}$.
Note that this also ensures that no adversary can distinguish public keys created in the ideal mode or in the real mode as the distribution of both keys are indistinguishable.

- **Ciphertext randomness indistinguishability.** The random coins outputted by the algorithm EquivCT should be *statistically close* to true random coins. That is, for any subset $I \subset [\ell]$ and any message $M' \in \{0,1\}^\ell$, the distributions $\mathsf{IDEAL}_{\mathsf{ct}}$ and $\mathsf{REAL}_{\mathsf{ct}}$ should be statistically close, where

$$\mathsf{IDEAL}_{\mathsf{ct}} = \left\{ (\mathsf{pk}, M, r_E) : \begin{array}{c} (\mathsf{pk}, \mathsf{sk}) \leftarrow \mathsf{KG}(1^\lambda, 1, I, r_G') \\ \mathsf{ct} \leftarrow \mathsf{E}(\mathsf{pk}, M', r_E') \\ M \leftarrow \mathcal{A}(\mathsf{pk}) \\ r_E \leftarrow \mathsf{EquivCT}(\mathsf{sk}, (M', r_E'), \{M_i\}_{i \notin I}) \end{array} \right\}$$

and

$$\mathsf{REAL}_{\mathsf{ct}} = \left\{ (\mathsf{pk}, M, r_E) : \begin{array}{c} (\mathsf{pk}, \mathsf{sk}) \leftarrow \mathsf{KG}(1^\lambda, 0, I, r_G') \\ M \leftarrow \mathcal{A}(\mathsf{pk}) \\ \mathsf{ct} \leftarrow \mathsf{E}(\mathsf{pk}, M, r_E) \end{array} \right\}$$

where $\mathcal{A}$ is an unbounded adversary which outputs a message M such that $M_i = M_i'$ for $i \in I$.

5.1 Packed Encryption with Partial Equivocality from LWE

We now present a PEPE scheme from the LWE assumption. The construction is similar to the one in [16], except that we use the compression technique introduced in [3] to achieve better rate.

Construction 3. *Let* (TrapGen, SampleD) *be the pair of algorithms described in Lemma 8, let* (Shrink, ShrinkDec) *the pair of algorithms described in Construction 1 and let* $\sigma, \sigma' \in \mathbb{R}$ *such that* $\sigma/\sigma' = \mathsf{negl}[\lambda]$.

$\mathsf{KG}(1^\lambda, b \in \{0,1\}, I, r_G)$:

- *If $b = 0$, do the following:*
    - *Choose $\mathbf{A} \leftarrow_\$ \mathbb{Z}_q^{k \times n}$*
    - *For $i \in I$, set $\mathbf{v}_i = \mathbf{s}_i \mathbf{A} + \mathbf{e}_i$ where $\mathbf{s}_i \leftarrow_\$ \mathbb{Z}_q^k$ and $\mathbf{e}_i \leftarrow_\$ D_\sigma^n$.*
    - *For $i \notin I$, set $\mathbf{v}_i \leftarrow_\$ \mathbb{Z}_q^n$.*
    - *Set $\mathsf{pk} = (\mathbf{A}, \{\mathbf{v}_i\}_{i \in [\ell]})$ and $\mathsf{sk} = (I, \{\mathbf{s}_i\}_{i \in I})$*
    - *Set the random coins $r_G = \{\mathbf{e}_i\}_{i \in I}$.*
- *Else if $b = 1$, do the following:*
    - *Run $(\mathbf{B}, \mathsf{td_B}) \leftarrow \mathsf{TrapGen}(1^\lambda, k + \ell - |I|, n, q)$ and parse $\mathbf{B}$ as $\begin{pmatrix} \mathbf{A} \\ \mathbf{V} \end{pmatrix} \in$ $\mathbb{Z}_q^{(k+\ell-|I|) \times n}$.*
    - *For $i \in I$, set*
    $$\mathbf{v}_i = \mathbf{s}_i \mathbf{A} + \mathbf{e}_i$$
    where $\mathbf{s}_i \leftarrow_\$ \mathbb{Z}_q^k$ and $\mathbf{e}_i \leftarrow_\$ D_\sigma^n$.
    - *For $i \notin I$, set $\mathbf{v}_i = \mathbf{V}_i$, where $\mathbf{V}_i$ is the i-th row of $\mathbf{V}$.*
    - *Set $\mathsf{pk} = (\mathbf{A}, \{\mathbf{v}_i\}_{i \in [\ell]})$ and $\mathsf{sk} = (I, \{\mathbf{s}_i\}_{i \in I}, \mathsf{td_B})$.*
    - *Set the random coins $r_G = \{\mathbf{e}_i\}_{i \in I}$.*
- *Output $(\mathsf{pk}, \mathsf{sk})$*

$\mathsf{E}(\mathsf{pk}, M \in \{0,1\}^\ell, r_E)$:

- *Parse $\mathsf{pk} = (\mathbf{A}, \{\mathbf{v}_i\}_{i \in [\ell]})$.*
- *Sample $\mathbf{r} \leftarrow_\$ D_\sigma^n$.*
- *Compute $\mathbf{c}_1 \leftarrow \mathbf{A}\mathbf{r}^T$ and $w_{2,i} = \mathbf{v}_i \mathbf{r}^T + e_i + \lfloor q/2 \rfloor \cdot M_i \in \mathbb{Z}_q$, for every $i \in [\ell]$, where $e_i \leftarrow_\$ D_{\sigma'}$.*
- *Compress $(\mathbf{c}_1, (w_{2,1}, \ldots, w_{2,\ell}))$ into*
$$(\mathbf{c}_1, (c_{2,1}, \ldots, c_{2,\ell}), z) \leftarrow \mathsf{Shrink}(\mathbf{c}_1, (w_{2,1}, \ldots, w_{2,\ell})).$$
- *Set the random coins r_E to be $(\mathbf{r}, \{e_i\}_{i \in [\ell]})$.*
- *Output $\mathsf{ct} = (\mathbf{c}_1, (c_{2,1}, \ldots, c_{2,\ell}), z)$.*

$\mathsf{D}(\mathsf{sk}, \mathsf{ct})$:

- *Parse sk as $(I, \{\mathbf{s}_i\}_{i \in I})$ and ct as $(\mathbf{c}_1, (c_{2,1}, \ldots, c_{2,\ell}), z)$.*
- *Compute $\{M_i\}_{i \in I} \leftarrow \mathsf{ShrinkDec}(\mathsf{sk}, \mathsf{ct}, I)$.*
- *Output $\{M_i\}_{i \in I}$.*

$\mathsf{EquivPK}(\mathsf{sk}, b, (I, r), I')$:

- *If $I' \not\subseteq I$, then abort the protocol. Else, continue.*
- *Parse r as $\{\mathbf{e}_i\}_{i \in I}$.*
- *If $b = 0$, parse sk as $(I, \{\mathbf{s}_i\}_{i \in I})$. Else, parse $\mathsf{sk} = (I, \{\mathbf{s}_i\}_{i \in I}, \mathsf{td_B})$.*
- *Set $r' = \{\mathbf{e}_i\}_{i \in I'}$ and $\mathsf{sk} = (I', \{\mathbf{s}_i\}_{i \in I'})$*
- *Output (sk', r')*

$\mathsf{EquivCT}((\mathsf{sk}, r_G), (M, r), (M_i')_{i \notin I})$:

- *Parse sk as $(I, \{\mathbf{s}_i\}_{i \in I}, \mathsf{td_B})$ and $r_G = \{\mathbf{e}_i\}_{i \in I}$. Set $\mathsf{ct} = (\mathbf{c}_1, (c_{2,1}, \ldots, c_{2,\ell}), z)$ $\leftarrow \mathsf{E}(\mathsf{pk}, M, r)$ where $r = (\mathbf{r}, \{e_i^*\}_{i \in [\ell]})$.*
- *Sample $e_i' \leftarrow_\$ D_{\sigma'}$ for $i \notin I$, and $\bar{\mathbf{r}} \leftarrow \mathsf{SampleD}(\mathsf{td_B}, \mathbf{B}, \mathbf{y}, \sigma)$ where $\mathbf{y} = (\mathbf{c}_1, \{w_{2,i} - \lfloor q/2 \rfloor M_i - e_i'\}_{i \notin I})$*

– For $i \in I$, set $e'_i = e^*_i + \mathbf{e}_i(\mathbf{r} - \bar{\mathbf{r}})^T$.
– Output $r' = (\bar{\mathbf{r}}, \{e'_i\}_{i \in [\ell]})$.

Analysis. Correctness for decryption follows from the correctness of the usual Regev's scheme and from Lemma 12.

Lemma 17 (Public-key randomness indistinguishability). *The scheme in Construction 3 is public key randomness indistinguishable given that the LWE assumption holds.*

Proof. Assume that $b = 1$ in the experiment $\mathsf{IDEAL}_{\mathsf{pk}}$ (the case where $b = 0$ is just a particular case of this one). The proof follows from the following sequence of hybrids:

Hybrid $\mathcal{H}_0$. This is the experiment $\mathsf{IDEAL}_{\mathsf{pk}}$ between a challenger C and an adversary $\mathcal{A}$:

– $(\mathsf{pk}, \mathsf{sk}) \leftarrow \mathsf{KG}(1^\lambda, 1, I', r'_G)$ where $\mathsf{pk} = (\mathbf{A}, \{\mathbf{v}_i\}_{i \in [\ell]})$ and $\mathsf{sk} = (I', \{\mathbf{s}_i\}_{i \in I'}, \mathsf{td}_\mathbf{B})$.
– Run $r_G \leftarrow \mathsf{EquivPK}(\mathsf{sk}, 1, (I', r'_G), I)$.
– $b \leftarrow \mathcal{A}(r_G)$.

Hybrid $\mathcal{H}_1$. In this hybrid, we replace the matrix $\mathbf{A}$ and the vectors $\mathbf{v}_i$, when $i \notin I'$, for uniform ones.

– C chooses $\mathbf{A} \leftarrow \mathbb{Z}_q^{k \times n}$ and $\mathbf{v}_i \leftarrow_\$ \mathbb{Z}_q^n$ for $i \notin I'$. For $i \in I'$, it computes $\mathbf{v}_i \leftarrow \mathbf{s}_i\mathbf{A} + \mathbf{e}_i$. For $I \subset I'$, set $r_G = \{(\mathbf{s}_i, \mathbf{e}_i)\}_{i \in I}$. It sends r_G to $\mathcal{A}$.
– $b \leftarrow \mathcal{A}(r_G)$.

Claim. $|\Pr[1 \leftarrow \mathcal{A} : \mathcal{A} \text{ plays } \mathcal{H}_0] - \Pr[1 \leftarrow \mathcal{A} : \mathcal{A} \text{ plays } \mathcal{H}_1]| \leq \mathsf{negl}[\lambda]$.

By Lemma 8, $\mathbf{A}$ is statistically close to a uniform matrix. Using the same lemma, each $\mathbf{v}_i$, for $i \notin I'$, is also statistically close to a uniform vector. The claim follows.

Hybrid $\mathcal{H}_2$. In this hybrid, we replace each $\mathbf{v}_i$ for $i \in I' \setminus I$ by a uniform vector.

– C chooses $\mathbf{A} \leftarrow \mathbb{Z}_q^{k \times n}$ and $\mathbf{v}_i \leftarrow_\$ \mathbb{Z}_q^n$ for $i \notin I'$ and for $i \in I' \setminus I$. For $i \in I$, it computes $\mathbf{v}_i \leftarrow \mathbf{s}_i\mathbf{A} + \mathbf{e}_i$. For $I \subset I'$, it sets $r_G = \{\mathbf{s}_i, \mathbf{e}_i\}_{i \in I}$. It sends r_G to $\mathcal{A}$.
– $b \leftarrow \mathcal{A}(r_G)$.

Claim. Assume that the LWE assumption holds. Then

$$|\Pr[1 \leftarrow \mathcal{A} : \mathcal{A} \text{ plays } \mathcal{H}_1] - \Pr[1 \leftarrow \mathcal{A} : \mathcal{A} \text{ plays } \mathcal{H}_2]| \leq \mathsf{negl}[\lambda].$$

It is straightforward to build an algorithm that decides the LWE assumption given an adversary that is able to distinguish hybrids $\mathcal{H}_1$ and $\mathcal{H}_2$. The claim follows.

Finally, note that hybrid $\mathcal{H}_2$ is exactly the experiment $\mathsf{REAL}_{\mathsf{pk}}$. Hence, the distributions are computationally indistinguishability given that the LWE assumption holds.

Lemma 18 (Ciphertext randomness indistinguishability). *The scheme in Construction 3 is ciphertext randomness indistinguishable.*

Proof. Let $\mathsf{ct} = (\mathbf{c}_1, (c_{2,1}, \ldots, c_{2,\ell})) \leftarrow \mathsf{E}(\mathsf{pk}, M, r_E)$ for $(\mathsf{pk}, \mathsf{sk}) \leftarrow \mathsf{KG}(1^\lambda, 1, I, r_G)$ where $\mathsf{pk} = (\mathbf{A}, \{\mathbf{v}_i\}_{i \in [\ell]})$, $\mathsf{sk} = (I, \{\mathbf{s}_i\}_{i \in I}, \mathsf{td_B})$, and $r_E = (\mathbf{r}, \{e_i\}_{i \in [\ell]})$ is the randomness used in E to encrypt the message $M = (M_1, \ldots, M_\ell)$. Now let $M' = (M'_1, \ldots, M'_\ell)$ such that $M_i = M'_i$, for all $i \in I$, and $M_i \neq M'_i$ otherwise. After running $\mathsf{EquivCT}(\mathsf{sk}, (M, r_E), (M'_i)_{i \notin I})$ we obtain

$$r'_E = (\bar{\mathbf{r}}, \{e'_i\}_{i \notin I}).$$

Let $\mathsf{ct}' = (\mathbf{c}'_1, (c'_{2,1}, \ldots, c'_{2,\ell})) \leftarrow \mathsf{E}(\mathsf{pk}, M', r'_E)$. First, note that by definition of the algorithm $\mathsf{SampleD}$ (Lemma 8) we have that $\mathbf{A}\mathbf{r}^T = \mathbf{A}\bar{\mathbf{r}}^T$. Hence $\mathbf{c}_1 = \mathbf{c}'_1$.

For $i \in I$, we have that

$$\mathbf{v}_i \mathbf{r}^T + e_i^* + \left\lceil \frac{q}{2} \right\rceil M_i = \mathbf{v}_i \bar{\mathbf{r}}^T + e'_i + \left\lceil \frac{q}{2} \right\rceil M_i,$$

hence the rounded values are the same.

Finally, for $i \notin I$, by definition of $\mathsf{SampleD}$, we have that

$$\mathbf{v}_i \mathbf{r} + e_i + \left\lceil \frac{q}{2} \right\rceil M_i = \mathbf{v}_i \bar{\mathbf{r}} + e'_i + \lfloor q/2 \rceil M'_i.$$

Hence,

$$c_{2,i} = \lfloor \mathbf{v}_i \mathbf{r} + e_i + \lfloor q/2 \rceil M_i + z \rceil_2 = \lfloor \mathbf{v}_i \bar{\mathbf{r}} + e'_i + \lfloor q/2 \rceil M'_i + z \rceil_2 = c'_{2,i}.$$

We conclude that $\mathsf{ct} = \mathsf{ct}'$.

By Lemma 7, we have that $e'_i \leftarrow_\$ D_{\sigma'} + \mathbf{e}_i(\mathbf{r} - \bar{\mathbf{r}})^T$ and $e_i^* \leftarrow_\$ D_{\sigma'}$ are statistically close. $\qquad \blacksquare$

5.2 Packed Encryption with Partial Equivocality from DDH

The DDH-based construction for PEPE is presented below as well as the corresponding security proofs.

Construction 4. *Let $(\mathbb{G}, p, g) \leftarrow \mathcal{G}(1^\lambda)$, $n \in \mathbb{N}$ and $(\mathsf{Shrink}, \mathsf{ShrinkDec})$ be the algorithms from Construction 2. The DDH-based PEPE scheme is defined as follows:*

$\mathsf{KG}(1^\lambda, b \in \{0, 1\}, I, r_G)$:

– *If $b = 0$, do the following:*

- *Choose $[\mathbf{a}] = g^\mathbf{a}$ where $\mathbf{a} \leftarrow_\$ \mathbb{Z}_p^n$, (here $[\mathbf{a}]$ is chosen obliviously).*
- *For $i \in I$, set $[\mathbf{v}_i] = s_i[\mathbf{a}]$ where $s_i \leftarrow_\$ \mathbb{Z}_p$.*
- *For $i \notin I$, set $[\mathbf{v}_i] \leftarrow_\$ \mathbb{G}^n$.*
- *Set $\mathsf{pk} = ([\mathbf{a}], \{[\mathbf{v}_i]\}_{i \in [\ell]})$ and $\mathsf{sk} = (I, \{s_i\}_{i \in I})$.*

– *Else if $b = 1$, do the following:*
  - *Choose $\mathbf{a} \leftarrow_\$ \mathbb{Z}_p^n$ and compute $[\mathbf{a}] = g^{\mathbf{a}}$.*
  - *For $i \in I$, set $[\mathbf{v}_i] = s_i[\mathbf{a}]$ where $s_i \leftarrow_\$ \mathbb{Z}_p^k$.*
  - *For $i \notin I$, set $[\mathbf{v}_i] \leftarrow_\$ \mathbb{G}^n$.*
  - *Set $\mathsf{pk} = ([\mathbf{a}], \{[\mathbf{v}_i]\}_{i \in [\ell]})$ and $\mathsf{sk} = (I, \mathbf{a}, \{s_i\}_{i \in I}, \{\mathbf{v}_i\}_{i \notin I})$.*
– *Output $(\mathsf{pk}, \mathsf{sk})$*

$\mathsf{E}(\mathsf{pk}, M \in \{0,1\}^\ell, r_E)$:

– *Parse $\mathsf{pk} = ([\mathbf{a}], \{[\mathbf{v}_i]\}_{i \in [\ell]})$.*
– *Choose $\mathbf{r} \leftarrow_\$ \mathbb{Z}_p^n$.*
– *Compute $[c_1] = [\mathbf{a}\mathbf{r}^T]$ and $w_{2,i} = [\mathbf{v}_i\mathbf{r}^T] \cdot g^{M_i}$ for every $i \in [\ell]$.*
– *Compress $([c_1], (w_{2,1}, \ldots, w_{2,\ell}))$ into*

$$(K, [c_1], (c_{2,1}, \ldots, c_{2,\ell})) \leftarrow \mathsf{Shrink}([c_1], (w_{2,1}, \ldots, w_{2,\ell}))$$

  where $(c_{2,1}, \ldots, c_{2,\ell}) = (\delta_1 \bmod 2, \ldots, \delta_\ell \bmod 2)$.
– *Set the random coins r_E to be $\mathbf{r}$.*
– *Output $\mathsf{ct} = (K, [c_1], (c_{2,1}, \ldots, c_{2,\ell}))$.*

$\mathsf{D}(\mathsf{sk}, \mathsf{ct})$:

– *Parse sk as $(I, \{s_i\}_{i \in I})$ and ct as $(K, [c_1], (c_{2,1}, \ldots, c_{2,\ell}))$.*
– *Compute $\{M_i\}_{i \in I} \leftarrow \mathsf{ShrinkDec}(\mathsf{sk}, \mathsf{ct}, I)$.*
– *Output $\{M_i\}_{i \in I}$.*

$\mathsf{EquivPK}(\mathsf{sk}, b, (I, r), I')$:

– *If $I' \nsubseteq I$, then abort the protocol. Else, continue.*
– *If $b = 0$, parse sk as $(I, \{s_i\}_{i \in I})$. Else, parse sk as $(I, \mathbf{a}, \{s_i\}_{i \in I}, \{\mathbf{v}_i\}_{i \notin I})$.*
– *Set $\mathsf{sk}' = (I', \{s_i\}_{i \in I'})$*
– *Output sk'*

$\mathsf{EquivCT}(\mathsf{sk}, (M, r), \{M_i'\}_{i \notin I})$:

– *Parse sk as $(I, \mathbf{a}, \{s_i\}_{i \in I}, \{\mathbf{v}_i\}_{i \notin I})$ and $r = \mathbf{r} \in \mathbb{Z}_p^n$. Let $\{i_1, \ldots, i_\alpha\} = [\ell] \setminus I$*
– *Sample uniformly at random a solution $\bar{\mathbf{r}} \in \mathbb{Z}_p^n$ for*

$$\begin{pmatrix} \mathbf{a} & 0 \\ \mathbf{v}_{i_1} & M_{i_1}' \\ \vdots & \vdots \\ \mathbf{v}_{i_\alpha} & M_{i_\alpha}' \end{pmatrix} \begin{pmatrix} \bar{\mathbf{r}}^T \\ 1 \end{pmatrix} = \begin{pmatrix} \mathbf{a}\mathbf{r}^T \\ \mathbf{v}_{i_1}\mathbf{r}^T + M_{i_1} \\ \vdots \\ \mathbf{v}_{i_\alpha}\mathbf{r}^T + M_{i_\alpha} \end{pmatrix}.$$

– *Output $r_E = \bar{\mathbf{r}}$.*

Analysis. We now proceed to the analysis of the construction above.

Lemma 19. *The scheme in Construction 4 is correct.*

Correctness for decryption follows from the correctness of the matrix version of the El Gamal scheme and from Lemma 14.

Lemma 20 (Public-key randomness indistinguishability). *The scheme in Construction 4 is public key randomness indistinguishable given that the MDDH assumption holds.*

Proof. The proof follows from the following sequence of hybrids:

Hybrid $\mathcal{H}_0$. This is the experiment $\mathsf{IDEAL}_{\mathsf{pk}}$ between a challenger C and an adversary $\mathcal{A}$:

- $(\mathsf{pk}, \mathsf{sk}) \leftarrow \mathsf{KG}(1^\lambda, 1, I', r'_G)$ where $\mathsf{pk} = (\mathbf{a}, \{[\mathbf{v}_i]\}_{i \in [\ell]})$ and $\mathsf{sk} = (I', \{s_i\}_{i \in I'})$.
- Run $r_G \leftarrow \mathsf{EquivPK}(\mathsf{sk}, 1, (I', r'_G), I)$.
- $b \leftarrow \mathcal{A}(r_G)$.

Hybrid $\mathcal{H}_1$. In this hybrid, we replace the vectors $\mathbf{v}_i$, when $i \in I' \setminus I$, for uniform ones.

- C chooses $\mathbf{a} \leftarrow \mathbb{Z}_p^n$ and $\mathbf{v}_i \leftarrow_{\$} \mathbb{Z}_p^n$ for $i \notin I'$ and for $i \in I' \setminus I$. For $i \in I$, it computes $[\mathbf{v}_i] \leftarrow s_i[\mathbf{a}]$. For $I \subset I'$, set $r_G = \{s_i\}_{i \in I}$. It sends r_G to $\mathcal{A}$.
- $b \leftarrow \mathcal{A}(r_G)$.

Claim. $|\Pr[1 \leftarrow \mathcal{A} : \mathcal{A} \text{ plays } \mathcal{H}_0] - \Pr[1 \leftarrow \mathcal{A} : \mathcal{A} \text{ plays } \mathcal{H}_1]| \le \mathsf{negl}[\lambda]$.

It is straightforward to build a distinguisher for the MDDH assumption if we are given an algorithm $\mathcal{A}$ that can distinguish both hybrids.

Finally, note that hybrid $\mathcal{H}_1$ is exactly the experiment $\mathsf{REAL}_{\mathsf{pk}}$. Hence, the distributions are computationally indistinguishability given that the MDDH assumption holds.

Lemma 21 (Ciphertext randomness indistinguishability). *The scheme in Construction 4 is ciphertext randomness indistinguishable, if $1 + \alpha \le n$.*

Proof. Let $M, M' \in \{0,1\}^\ell$ be any two messages such that $M_i = M'_i$, for $i \in I$, and $M_i \ne M'_i$ otherwise. We prove that, if $1 + \alpha \le n$, then the equation

$$\begin{pmatrix} \mathbf{a} & 0 \\ \mathbf{v}_{i_1} & M'_{i_1} \\ \vdots & \vdots \\ \mathbf{v}_{i_\alpha} & M'_{i_\alpha} \end{pmatrix} \begin{pmatrix} \bar{\mathbf{r}}^T \\ 1 \end{pmatrix} = \begin{pmatrix} \mathbf{a}\mathbf{r}^T \\ \mathbf{v}_1\mathbf{r}^T + M_{i_1} \\ \vdots \\ \mathbf{v}_{i_\alpha}\mathbf{r}^T + M_{i_\alpha} \end{pmatrix} \tag{1}$$

has a solution $\bar{\mathbf{r}} \in \mathbb{Z}_p^n$, except with negligible probability.

First, note that the equation in 1 is equivalent to

$$
\begin{pmatrix} \mathbf{a} \\ \mathbf{v}_{i_1} \\ \vdots \\ \mathbf{v}_{i_\alpha} \end{pmatrix} (\bar{\mathbf{r}}^T) = \begin{pmatrix} \mathbf{a}\mathbf{r}^T \\ \mathbf{v}_1\mathbf{r}^T + M_{i_1} - M'_{i_1} \\ \vdots \\ \mathbf{v}_{i_\alpha}\mathbf{r}^T + M_{i_\alpha} - M'_{i_\alpha} \end{pmatrix}
$$

We now prove that the rank β of the matrix on the left side is maximal, that is, $\beta = 1 + \alpha$. Note that, every row of this matrix is uniformly chosen at random.

By a simple counting argument, we have that the rank of the matrix on the left side is maximal, except with probability $1/|\mathbb{G}|$. Since $|\mathbb{G}| \in \mathcal{O}(2^{\omega(\log \lambda)})$, then

$$
\Pr\left[\beta = 1 + \alpha\right] \geq 1 - \frac{1}{|\mathbb{G}|} \geq 1 - \mathsf{negl}[\lambda].
$$

If the rank of the matrix is equal to the rank of the augmented matrix, then the system of equations has solutions. Hence, we can find a solution $\bar{\mathbf{r}}$ for Eq. 1, except with negligible probability.

We now prove that, given $\bar{\mathbf{r}}$ satisfying Eq. 1, $\mathsf{ct} = \mathsf{ct}'$, where $\mathsf{ct} = (K, [c_1], (c_{2,1}, \ldots, c_{2,\ell})) \leftarrow \mathsf{E}(\mathsf{pk}, M, r_E)$ and $\mathsf{ct}' = (K, [c'_1], (c'_{2,1}, \ldots, c'_{2,\ell})) \leftarrow \mathsf{E}(\mathsf{pk}, M', r'_E)$ where M' is such that $M'_i = M_i$ for $i \in I$ and $r_E = \mathbf{r}$, $r'_E = \bar{\mathbf{r}}$.

First, note that by Eq. 1 we have that $\mathbf{a}\mathbf{r}^T = \mathbf{a}\bar{\mathbf{r}}^T$. Hence,

$$
\left[\mathbf{a}\mathbf{r}^T\right] = \left[\mathbf{a}\bar{\mathbf{r}}^T\right] \Leftrightarrow [c_1] = [c'_1]. \tag{2}
$$

A direct consequence of Eq. 2 is that

$$
s_i\mathbf{a}\mathbf{r}^T + M_i = s_i\mathbf{a}\bar{\mathbf{r}}^T + M_i \Leftrightarrow c_{2_i} = c'_{2,i}
$$

for $i \in I$. It remains to show that $c_{2,i} = c'_{2,i}$ for $i \notin I$. Observe that

$$
\mathbf{v}_i\mathbf{r}^T + M_i = \mathbf{v}_i\bar{\mathbf{r}}^T + M'_i
$$

for $i \notin I$, from Eq. 1. Hence, $c_{2,i} = c'_{2,i}$ for $i \notin I$.

Finally, the random coins r_E used in the encryption algorithm E (in the real mode) and the random coins r'_E outputted by the equivocation algorithm $\mathsf{EquivCT}$ have exactly the same distribution.

5.3 Packed Encryption with Partial Equivocality from QR

The construction of PEPE from QR is follows the same blueprint as the DDH construction. We omit the construction in this version.

6 From PEPE to Constant Ciphertext-Rate NCE

Finally, we present the generic construction for NCE from PEPE, which generalizes the construction of [16]. Then, we analyze the security and efficiency of the construction.

The following lemma is adapted from [16] and will help us to prove security for the construction.

Lemma 22 [16]. *Let* $\mathsf{ECC}_{\ell,\ell'} = (\mathsf{ECC.Encode}, \mathsf{ECC.Decode})$ *be an error-correcting code and let* $\mathsf{PEPE} = (\mathsf{PEPE.KG}, \mathsf{PEPE.E}, \mathsf{PEPE.D}, \mathsf{PEPE.Equiv})$ *be a PEPE scheme. There exists an algorithm* $\mathsf{F_{id}}$ *such that*

$$(I_R, I_S, \mathbf{z}') \leftarrow \mathsf{F_{id}}(I_g, \mathbf{y}, \mathbf{z})$$

where I_R, I_S, I_g *are subsets of* $[\ell]$ *and* $\mathbf{y}, \mathbf{z}, \mathbf{z}' \in \{0,1\}^\ell$. *Moreover, the distributions* $\mathsf{IDEAL_{sets}}$ *and* $\mathsf{REAL_{sets}}$ *are computationally indistinguishable given that the underlying PEPE scheme is public key randomness indistinguishable, where*

$$\mathsf{IDEAL_{sets}} = \left\{ (I_R, I_S, \mathbf{z}') : \begin{array}{c} I_g \leftarrow_\$ W_g \\ (\mathsf{pk}, \mathsf{sk}) \leftarrow \mathsf{PEPE.KG}(1^\lambda, 1, I_g, r_G) \\ \mathbf{z} \leftarrow_\$ \{0,1\}^\ell \\ M \leftarrow \mathcal{A}(\mathsf{pk}) \\ \mathbf{y} \leftarrow \mathsf{ECC.Encode}(M) \\ (I_R, I_S, \mathbf{z}') \leftarrow \mathsf{F_{id}}(I_g, \mathbf{y}, \mathbf{z}) \end{array} \right\},$$

and

$$\mathsf{REAL_{sets}} = \left\{ (I_R, I_S, \mathbf{z}') : \begin{array}{c} I_R \leftarrow_\$ W \\ (\mathsf{pk}, \mathsf{sk}) \leftarrow \mathsf{PEPE.KG}(1^\lambda, 0, I_R, r_G) \\ M \leftarrow \mathcal{A}(\mathsf{pk}) \\ \mathbf{y} \leftarrow \mathsf{ECC.Encode}(M) \\ I_S \leftarrow_\$ W \\ \mathbf{z}' \leftarrow f(\mathbf{y}, I_S) \end{array} \right\}$$

for any message M, *where* $W_g = \{I \subset [\ell] : |I| = 3\ell/4\}$, $W = \{I \subset [\ell] : |I| = \ell/8\}$, $I_R \subset I_g$, $\mathbf{y} = (y_1, \ldots, y_\ell)$ *and* f *is a function such that if* $\mathbf{z}' = (z_1', \ldots, z_\ell') \leftarrow f(\mathbf{y}, I_S)$ *then*

$$z_i' = \begin{cases} y_i, & \text{if } i \in I_S \\ z_i' \leftarrow_\$ \{0,1\}, & \text{otherwise} \end{cases}.$$

Construction 5. *Let* $\mathsf{ECC}_{\ell,\ell'} = (\mathsf{ECC.Encode}, \mathsf{ECC.Decode})$ *be a suitable error-correcting code with constant rate* $\mathcal{O}(1)$ *(Lemma 5) and* $\mathsf{PEPE} = (\mathsf{PEPE.KG}, \mathsf{PEPE.E}, \mathsf{PEPE.D}, \mathsf{PEPE.EquivPK}, \mathsf{PEPE.EquivCT})$ *be a PEPE scheme with message space* $\{0,1\}^{\ell'}$. $\mathsf{F_{id}}$ *is the algorithm of Lemma 22. We describe the NCE construction in full detail:*

KeyGen(1^λ):

- *Choose a random subset $I_R \subset [\ell]$ such that $|I_R| = \ell/8$.*
- *Compute $(\mathsf{pk}_{\mathsf{pepe}}, \mathsf{sk}_{\mathsf{pepe}}) \leftarrow \mathsf{PEPE.KG}(1^\lambda, 0, I_R, r_{G,\mathsf{pepe}})$, where $r_{G,\mathsf{pepe}}$ are the random coins.*
- *Output $\mathsf{pk} = \mathsf{pk}_{\mathsf{pepe}}$, $\mathsf{sk} = (\mathsf{sk}_{\mathsf{pepe}}, I_R)$ and $r_G = (r_{G,\mathsf{pepe}}, I_R)$.*

Enc(pk, M):

- *Parse pk as $\mathsf{pk}_{\mathsf{pepe}}$.*
- *Encode the message by computing $\mathbf{y} = (y_1, \ldots, y_\ell) \leftarrow \mathsf{ECC.Encode}(M)$.*
- *Choose a random subset $I_S \subset [\ell]$ such that $|I_S| = \ell/8$. For every $i \in [\ell]$, set*

$$z_i = \begin{cases} y_i, \text{ if } i \in I_S \\ z_i' \leftarrow_\$ \{0,1\}, \text{ otherwise} \end{cases}$$

for every $i \in [\ell]$ and $\mathbf{z} = (z_1, \ldots, z_\ell)$.
- *Compute $\mathsf{ct} \leftarrow \mathsf{PEPE.E}(\mathsf{pk}_{\mathsf{pepe}}, \mathbf{z}, r_{E,\mathsf{pepe}})$ where $r_{E,\mathsf{pepe}}$ are random coins*
- *Output ct and $r_E = (\mathbf{z}, r_{E,\mathsf{pepe}}, I_S)$.*

Dec(sk, ct):

- *Parse sk as $(\mathsf{sk}_{\mathsf{pepe}}, I_R)$.*
- *Compute $\{z_i\}_{i \in I_R} \leftarrow \mathsf{PEPE.D}(\mathsf{sk}_{\mathsf{pepe}}, \mathsf{ct})$.*
- *For $i \notin I_R$, set $z_i \leftarrow_\$ \{0,1\}$.*
- *Output $M \leftarrow \mathsf{ECC.Decode}(\mathbf{z})$ where $\mathbf{z} = (z_1, \ldots, z_\ell)$.*

$\mathsf{Sim}_1(1^\lambda)$:

- *Choose a random subset $I_g \subset [\ell]$ such that $|I_g| = 3\ell/4$.*
- *Compute $(\mathsf{pk}_{\mathsf{pepe}}, \mathsf{sk}_{\mathsf{pepe}}) \leftarrow \mathsf{PEPE.KG}(1^\lambda, 1, I_g, r_{G,\mathsf{pepe}})$, where $r_{G,\mathsf{pepe}}$ are the random coins.*
- *Choose a random encoding $\mathbf{z} \leftarrow_\$ \{0,1\}^\ell$ and encrypt it*

$$\mathsf{ct} \leftarrow \mathsf{PEPE.E}(\mathsf{pk}_{\mathsf{pepe}}, \mathbf{z}, r_{E,\mathsf{pepe}}).$$

- *Output $\mathsf{pk} = \mathsf{pk}_{\mathsf{pepe}}$, ct and $\mathsf{st} = (I_g, \mathbf{z}, r_{G,\mathsf{pepe}}, r_{E,\mathsf{pepe}})$.*

$\mathsf{Sim}_2(M, \mathsf{st})$:

- *Parse $\mathsf{st} = (\mathsf{pk}_{\mathsf{pepe}}, \mathsf{ct}, \mathsf{sk}_{\mathsf{pepe}}, I_g, \mathbf{z}, r_{G,\mathsf{pepe}}, r_{E,\mathsf{pepe}})$.*
- *Encode the message M into $\mathbf{y} \leftarrow \mathsf{ECC.Encode}(M)$.*
- *Compute $(I_R, I_S, \mathbf{z}') \leftarrow \mathsf{F}_{\mathsf{id}}(I_g, \mathbf{y}, \mathbf{z})$.*
- *Set $r_{G,\mathsf{pepe}}' \leftarrow \mathsf{PEPE.EquivPK}(\mathsf{sk}_{\mathsf{pepe}}, 1, (I_g, r_{G,\mathsf{pepe}}), I_R)$ to be the randomness according to I_R.*
- *Let $J = \{i \in [\ell] \setminus I_g : z_i \neq z_i'\}$. Compute*

$$r_{E,\mathsf{pepe}}' \leftarrow \mathsf{PEPE.EquivCT}(\mathsf{sk}_{\mathsf{pepe}}, (\mathbf{z}, r_{E,\mathsf{pepe}}), \{z_i\}_{i \in J}).$$

- *Set $r_G = (r_{G,\mathsf{pepe}}', I_R)$ and $r_E = (\mathbf{z}', r_{E,\mathsf{pepe}}', I_S)$. Output (r_G, r_E).*

Analysis. We now proceed to the analysis of the scheme described above.

Theorem 23 (Correctness). *Let* $\mathsf{ECC}_{\ell,\ell'} = (\mathsf{ECC.Encode}, \mathsf{ECC.Decode})$ *be an ECC with error-rate* $1/2 - \delta$ *for some constant* $\delta > 0$ *(Lemma 5) and* $\mathsf{PEPE} = (\mathsf{PEPE.KG}, \mathsf{PEPE.E}, \mathsf{PEPE.D}, \mathsf{PEPE.EquivPK}, \mathsf{PEPE.EquivCT})$ *be a PEPE scheme. Then the scheme described in Construction 5 is correct.*

Proof. The proof of correctness follows the proof of correctness presented in [16]. Let $\mathbf{z} = (z_1, \ldots, z_\ell)$ be the codeword obtained after running Dec. The key observation is that $|I_R \cap I_S| = \xi$ follows a hypergeometric distribution $\mathsf{H}(1/8, 1/8, \ell)$. Thus, we can bound the maximum value of ξ, using Lemma 3, except with negligible probability. On the other hand, all other positions of $\mathbf{z}$ are correct with probability $1/2$. Thus, we can estimate the number of errors γ of $\mathbf{z}$:

$$\gamma \leq \left(\frac{1}{2} + \varepsilon\right)(\ell - \xi) \leq \ell\left(\frac{1}{2} + \varepsilon\right)\left(1 + \varepsilon - \frac{1}{16\ell^2}\right) \leq \ell\left(\frac{1}{2} - \delta\right)$$

where the second inequality follows from Lemma 3, and the third one follows from considering an appropriate value for the constant $\varepsilon > 0$. ∎

Theorem 24 (Simulatability). *Let* PEPE *be a PEPE scheme. Then the scheme in Construction 5 is simulatable.*

The proof of the theorem above is presented in the full version of this paper.

Ciphertext-Rate of the NCE Scheme. Let $R = \ell'/\ell$ be the rate of the code used in Construction 5 and $M \in \{0,1\}^{\ell'}$. We now analyze the ciphertext-rate of the scheme for the LWE case when instantiated with the PEPE constructions of Sect. 5. The analysis for the DDH case follows the same reasoning.

The ciphertext is composed by $\mathsf{ct} = (\mathbf{c}_1, (c_{2,1}, \ldots, c_{2,\ell}), z) \in \mathbb{Z}_q^n \times \{0,1\}^\ell \times \mathbb{Z}_q$. Then, the ciphertext-rate is

$$\frac{(n+1)\log q + \ell}{\ell'} = \frac{(n+1)\log q}{\ell'} + R^{-1}.$$

The ciphertext-rate is equal to R^{-1} when ℓ' tends to infinity. When we use a code as in Lemma 5, then $R = \mathcal{O}(1)$, therefore the whole rate of the NCE scheme is $\mathcal{O}(1)$.

Acknowledgements. Z. Brakerski is supported by the Binational Science Foundation (Grant No. 2016726), and by the European Union Horizon 2020 Research and Innovation Program via ERC Project REACT (Grant 756482) and via Project PROMETHEUS (Grant 780701).

P. Branco thanks the support from DP-PMI and FCT (Portugal) through the grant PD/BD/135181/2017. This work is supported by Security and Quantum Information Group of Instituto de Telecomunicações, by the Fundação para a Ciência e a Tecnologia (FCT) through national funds, by FEDER, COMPETE 2020, and by Regional Operational Program of Lisbon, under UIDB/50008/2020.

N. Döttling: This work is partially funded by the Helmholtz Association within the project "Trustworthy Federated Data Analytics" (TFDA) (funding number ZT-I-OO1 4).

S. Garg supported in part from AFOSR Award FA9550-19-1-0200, NSF CNS Award 1936826, DARPA SIEVE Award, and research grants by the Sloan Foundation, Visa Inc., and Center for Long-Term Cybersecurity (CLTC, UC Berkeley). Any opinions, findings and conclusions or recommendations expressed in this material are those of the author(s) and do not necessarily reflect the views of the funding agencies.

References

1. Beaver, D.: Plug and play encryption. In: Kaliski, B.S. (ed.) CRYPTO 1997. LNCS, vol. 1294, pp. 75–89. Springer, Heidelberg (1997). https://doi.org/10.1007/BFb0052228
2. Boyle, E., Gilboa, N., Ishai, Y.: Breaking the circuit size barrier for secure computation under DDH. In: Robshaw, M., Katz, J. (eds.) CRYPTO 2016. LNCS, vol. 9814, pp. 509–539. Springer, Heidelberg (2016). https://doi.org/10.1007/978-3-662-53018-4_19
3. Brakerski, Z., Döttling, N., Garg, S., Malavolta, G.: Leveraging linear decryption: rate-1 fully-homomorphic encryption and time-lock puzzles. In: Hofheinz, D., Rosen, A. (eds.) TCC 2019. LNCS, vol. 11892, pp. 407–437. Springer, Cham (2019). https://doi.org/10.1007/978-3-030-36033-7_16
4. Canetti, R., Feige, U., Goldreich, O., Naor, M.: Adaptively secure multi-party computation. In: Proceedings of the Twenty-eighth Annual ACM Symposium on Theory of Computing, pp. 639–648. STOC 1996. ACM, New York (1996). http://doi.acm.org/10.1145/237814.238015
5. Canetti, R., Lindell, Y., Ostrovsky, R., Sahai, A.: Universally composable two-party and multi-party secure computation. In: Proceedings of the Thiry-Fourth Annual ACM Symposium on Theory of Computing, pp. 494–503. STOC 202, Association for Computing Machinery, New York (2002). https://doi.org/10.1145/509907.509980
6. Canetti, R., Poburinnaya, O., Raykova, M.: Optimal-rate non-committing encryption. In: Takagi, T., Peyrin, T. (eds.) ASIACRYPT 2017. LNCS, vol. 10626, pp. 212–241. Springer, Cham (2017). https://doi.org/10.1007/978-3-319-70700-6_8
7. Choi, S.G., Dachman-Soled, D., Malkin, T., Wee, H.: Improved non-committing encryption with applications to adaptively secure protocols. In: Matsui, M. (ed.) ASIACRYPT 2009. LNCS, vol. 5912, pp. 287–302. Springer, Heidelberg (2009). https://doi.org/10.1007/978-3-642-10366-7_17
8. Damgård, I., Nielsen, J.B.: Improved non-committing encryption schemes based on a general complexity assumption. In: Bellare, M. (ed.) CRYPTO 2000. LNCS, vol. 1880, pp. 432–450. Springer, Heidelberg (2000). https://doi.org/10.1007/3-540-44598-6_27
9. Diffie, W., Hellman, M.E.: New directions in cryptography. IEEE Trans. Inf. Theory **22**(6), 644–654 (1976)
10. Döttling, N., Garg, S., Ishai, Y., Malavolta, G., Mour, T., Ostrovsky, R.: Trapdoor hash functions and their applications. In: Boldyreva, A., Micciancio, D. (eds.) CRYPTO 2019. LNCS, vol. 11694, pp. 3–32. Springer, Cham (2019). https://doi.org/10.1007/978-3-030-26954-8_1

11. Escala, A., Herold, G., Kiltz, E., Ràfols, C., Villar, J.: An algebraic framework for Diffie-Hellman assumptions. In: Canetti, R., Garay, J.A. (eds.) CRYPTO 2013. LNCS, vol. 8043, pp. 129–147. Springer, Heidelberg (2013). https://doi.org/10.1007/978-3-642-40084-1_8

12. Gentry, C., Peikert, C., Vaikuntanathan, V.: Trapdoors for hard lattices and new cryptographic constructions. In: Proceedings of the Fortieth Annual ACM Symposium on Theory of Computing, pp. 197–206. STOC 2008, ACM, New York (2008). http://doi.acm.org/10.1145/1374376.1374407

13. Goldreich, O., Micali, S., Wigderson, A.: How to play any mental game. In: Proceedings of the Nineteenth Annual ACM Symposium on Theory of Computing, STOC 1987, pp. 218–229. Association for Computing Machinery, New York (1987). https://doi.org/10.1145/28395.28420

14. Guruswami, V., Sudan, M.: List decoding algorithms for certain concatenated codes. In: Proceedings of the Thirty-Second Annual ACM Symposium on Theory of Computing, STOC 2000, pp. 181–190. ACM, New York (2000). http://doi.acm.org/10.1145/335305.335327

15. Hemenway, B., Jafargholi, Z., Ostrovsky, R., Scafuro, A., Wichs, D.: Adaptively secure garbled circuits from one-way functions. In: Robshaw, M., Katz, J. (eds.) CRYPTO 2016, Part 3. LNCS, vol. 9816, pp. 149–178. Springer, Heidelberg (2016). https://doi.org/10.1007/978-3-662-53015-3_6

16. Hemenway, B., Ostrovsky, R., Richelson, S., Rosen, A.: Adaptive security with quasi-optimal rate. In: Kushilevitz, E., Malkin, T. (eds.) TCC 2016. LNCS, vol. 9562, pp. 525–541. Springer, Heidelberg (2016). https://doi.org/10.1007/978-3-662-49096-9_22

17. Hemenway, B., Ostrovsky, R., Rosen, A.: Non-committing encryption from ϕ-hiding. In: Dodis, Y., Nielsen, J.B. (eds.) TCC 2015. LNCS, vol. 9014, pp. 591–608. Springer, Heidelberg (2015). https://doi.org/10.1007/978-3-662-46494-6_24

18. Micali, S., Peikert, C., Sudan, M., Wilson, D.A.: Optimal error correction against computationally bounded noise. In: Kilian, J. (ed.) TCC 2005. LNCS, vol. 3378, pp. 1–16. Springer, Heidelberg (2005). https://doi.org/10.1007/978-3-540-30576-7_1

19. Micciancio, D., Peikert, C.: Trapdoors for lattices: simpler, tighter, faster, smaller. In: Pointcheval, D., Johansson, T. (eds.) EUROCRYPT 2012. LNCS, vol. 7237, pp. 700–718. Springer, Heidelberg (2012). https://doi.org/10.1007/978-3-642-29011-4_41

20. O'Neill, A., Peikert, C., Waters, B.: Bi-deniable public-key encryption. In: Rogaway, P. (ed.) CRYPTO 2011. LNCS, vol. 6841, pp. 525–542. Springer, Heidelberg (2011). https://doi.org/10.1007/978-3-642-22792-9_30

21. Regev, O.: On lattices, learning with errors, random linear codes, and cryptography. In: Proceedings of the Thirty-Seventh Annual ACM Symposium on Theory of Computing, STOC 2005, pp. 84–93. ACM, New York (2005). http://doi.acm.org/10.1145/1060590.1060603

22. Yao, A.C.: Protocols for secure computations. In: 23rd Annual Symposium on Foundations of Computer Science (sfcs 1982), pp. 160–164, November 1982

23. Yoshida, Y., Kitagawa, F., Tanaka, K.: Non-committing encryption with quasi-optimal ciphertext-rate based on the DDH problem. In: Galbraith, S.D., Moriai, S. (eds.) ASIACRYPT 2019. LNCS, vol. 11923, pp. 128–158. Springer, Cham (2019). https://doi.org/10.1007/978-3-030-34618-8_5

Efficient Range-Trapdoor Functions and Applications: Rate-1 OT and More

Sanjam Garg[1], Mohammad Hajiabadi[2(✉)], and Rafail Ostrovsky[3]

[1] University of California, Berkeley, USA
[2] Penn State University, State College, USA
mdhajiabadi@psu.edu
[3] UCLA, Los Angeles, USA

Abstract. Substantial work on trapdoor functions (TDFs) has led to many powerful notions and applications. However, despite tremendous work and progress, all known constructions have prohibitively large public keys.

In this work, we introduce new techniques for realizing so-called range-trapdoor hash functions with short public keys. This notion, introduced by Döttling et al. [Crypto 2019], allows for encoding a range of indices into a public key in a way that the public key leaks no information about the range, yet an associated trapdoor enables recovery of the corresponding input part.

We give constructions of range-trapdoor hash functions, where for a given range I the public key consists of $O(n)$ group elements, improving upon $O(n|I|)$ achieved by Döttling et al. Moreover, by designing our evaluation algorithm in a special way involving Toeplitz matrix multiplication and by showing how to perform fast-Fourier transforms in the exponent, we arrive at $O(n \log n)$ group operations for evaluation, improving upon $O(n^2)$, required of previous constructions. Our constructions rely on power-DDH assumptions in pairing-free groups.

As applications of our results we obtain

1. The first construction of (rate-1) lossy TDFs with public keys consisting of a linear number of group elements (without pairings).
2. Rate-1 string OT with receiver communication complexity of $O(n)$ group elements, where n is the sender's message size, improving upon $O(n^2)$ [Crypto 2019].
3. Two-round private-information retrieval protocols for one-bit records, where for a server of N bits, the client's message consists of $O(\lambda)\mathsf{polylog}(N)$ group elements, improving upon $O(\lambda^2)\mathsf{polylog}(N)$.

S. Garg—University of California, Berkeley. supported in part from DARPA/ARL SAFEWARE Award W911NF15C0210, AFOSR Award FA9550-15-1-0274, AFOSR Award FA9550-19-1-0200, AFOSR YIP Award, NSF CNS Award 1936826, DARPA and SPAWAR under contract N66001-15-C-4065, a Hellman Award and research grants by the Okawa Foundation, Visa Inc., and Center for Long-Term Cybersecurity (CLTC, UC Berkeley). The views expressed are those of the author and do not reflect the official policy or position of the funding agencies.
R. Ostrovsky—University of California, Los Angeles. Supported by DARPA SPAWAR contract N66001-15-C-4065.

© International Association for Cryptologic Research 2020
R. Pass and K. Pietrzak (Eds.): TCC 2020, LNCS 12550, pp. 88–116, 2020.
https://doi.org/10.1007/978-3-030-64375-1_4

4. Semi-compact homomorphic encryption for branching programs: A construction of homomorphic encryption for branching programs, with ciphertexts consisting of $O(\lambda nd^2)$ group elements, improving upon $O(\lambda^2 nd^3)$. Here λ denotes the security parameter, n the input size and d the depth of the program.

1   Introduction

Trapdoor cryptosystems are at the heart of modern cryptography. What is common among all these cryptosystems is the notion of a trapdoor key, which allows a certain computation to be inverted. The exact formulation of what inversion means specifies the strength of the notion.

For example, trapdoor functions (TDFs) extend the functionality of public-key encryption (PKE) by requiring the inversion algorithm to recover the entire input. This extension makes the notion relatively versatile, enabling applications (from variants of TDFs) including CCA2-secure PKE, selective-opening security and designated-verifier non-interactive (NIZK) [PW08, BFOR08, BHY09, LQR+19], which are currently out of reach of the basic PKE primitives.

Perhaps not surprisingly, trapdoor systems that demand a richer functionality are harder to realize, and in cases this is possible, the resulting realizations come with poor efficiency. For instance, while for PKE we have a plethora of instantiations with close to optimal public-key, secret-key and ciphertext sizes, the situation for TDFs is much different. Concretely, the public keys of all DDH-based TDFs consist of $O(n^2)$ group elements, where n is the input size, lagging behind their PKE counterparts, which consist of a constant number of group elements. Although recent works [GH18, GGH19, DGI+19, DGH+19] showed how to make the image size of TDFs almost the same as the input size, they too are stuck with the $O(n^2)$ group elements overhead for the public key. As we will see later, this is due to a lack of *batching techniques* for TDF keys. Our goal, in this work, is to develop techniques that help us mitigate this issue. We will do this in a way general enough to be applicable not just to TDFs, but also to more advanced primitives, such as lossy TDFs [PW08] and trapdoor hash functions [DGI+19].

Trapdoor Hash (TDH) Functions. Recently, Döttling, Garg, Ishai, Malavolta, Mour and Ostrovsky introduced a primitive, called trapdoor hash functions [DGI+19], and showed extensive applications of this notion, including lossy TDFs, rate-1 oblivious transfer (OT), private information retrieval (PIR) with low communication complexity and more. In its simplest form, a TDH scheme comes with a length-compressing hash function $H_{hk}: \{0,1\}^n \rightarrow \{0,1\}^\lambda$ and an evaluation algorithm E. The scheme allows one to generate an evaluation/trapdoor key (ik_i, tk_i) for any particular index $i \in [n]$ in such a way that (1) the output of $E(ik_i, x)$ is a single bit, (2) using tk_i, one may retrieve the value of x_i from $H(hk, x) \in \{0,1\}^\lambda$ and $E(ik_i, x) \in \{0,1\}$ and (3) ik_i hides the index i.

Usefulness of Trapdoor Hash. To show the utility of this notion, let us sketch a construction of lossy TDFs using this primitive, given by [DGI+19]. Consider a sequence of TDH-evaluation keys $\mathsf{ik}_1, \ldots, \mathsf{ik}_{n/2}$ generated for the range of indices $[1, n/2]$ and suppose we additionally include a message $\mathsf{x}^* \xleftarrow{\$} \{0,1\}^{n/2}$ as part of the public key. Assume the input x to the lossy TDF has $n/2$ bits. To evaluate x, form a bigger string $\mathsf{x}' := (\mathsf{x}||\mathsf{x}^*) \in \{0,1\}^n$ and return $(\mathsf{H}(\mathsf{hk}, \mathsf{x}'), \mathsf{E}(\mathsf{ik}_1, \mathsf{x}'), \ldots, \mathsf{E}(\mathsf{ik}_{n/2}, \mathsf{x}'))$.[1] Using the trapdoor keys of $\mathsf{ik}_1, \ldots, \mathsf{ik}_{n/2}$, we may recover x. Now if we switch the evaluation keys to $\mathsf{ik}_{n/2+1}, \ldots, \mathsf{ik}_n$ corresponding to the second-half range of indices, then we will statistically lose information about x. The reason is that $n/2 - \lambda$ bits of information are lost about x.

Rate-1 Two-Round Oblivious Transfer (OT): Another important application of trapdoor hash is in realizing rate-1 two-round OT protocols [DGI+19]. We say that an OT protocol achieves rate-1 if the ratio $|\mathsf{m}_0|/|\mathsf{ots}|$ asymptotically approaches one, where ots is the sender's protocol message on a pair of inputs $(\mathsf{m}_0 \in \{0,1\}^n, \mathsf{m}_1 \in \{0,1\}^n)$ and on the corresponding message otr of the receiver. As shown by Ishai and Paskin [IP07], rate-1 OT leads to constructions of semi-compact homomorphic encryption for branching programs (where the ciphertext size grows only with the depth as opposed to the size of the program) as well as communication-efficient private-information retrieval (PIR) protocols. All these applications rely on the rate-1 property of the OT in a crucial way, allowing one to sequentially pass ots as an input to a new OT-sender's message and pass the resulting ots to the next sender's message and so on; this can continue for a polynomial number of times without having an exponential-size blowup. Trapdoor hash schemes provide an elegant way for realizing rate-1 OT [DGI+19]. Specifically, if the size of each message of the sender is n, the receiver on an input bit b sends n evaluations key $\mathsf{ek}_1, \ldots, \mathsf{ek}_n$ corresponding to either indices in $[1, n]$ or $[n + 1, \ldots, 2n]$. The sender then returns $(\mathsf{H}(\mathsf{hk}, \mathsf{m}_0||\mathsf{m}_1)), \mathsf{E}(\mathsf{ek}_1, \mathsf{m}_0||\mathsf{m}_1), \ldots, \mathsf{E}(\mathsf{ek}_n, \mathsf{m}_0||\mathsf{m}_1)$. The receiver may then use his trapdoors to recover the corresponding message.[2] We have $|\mathsf{ots}| = n + \mathsf{poly}(\lambda)$, where poly is a fixed function, and hence the protocol has rate-1 (asymptotically). Döttling et al. [DGI+19] used the above protocol to get the first constructions of rate-1 OT from DDH, OR and LWE.

Lack of Batching Techniques for Evaluation Keys. In the examples above, the public key of the lossy TDF or the receiver's message in the OT protocol each consists of $O(n)$ TDH-evaluation keys. Under DDH instantiations of

---

[1] Here for simplicity we assume that E is deterministic and that each trapdoor enables perfect recovery of the underlying indexed bit. Under the actual definition, the function E should be randomized, so as to provide the desired privacy guarantees, needed by OT, etc applications. This issue can be handled by using a fixed randomness for the sketched construction.

[2] Again, we are giving an over-simplified construction, by assuming that decryption has perfect correctness. Moreover, in the actual construction, the function H should be randomized, so to provide sender privacy.

TDH [DGI+19], an evaluation key for any given index has $O(n)$ group elements, resulting in $O(n^2)$ group elements for the whole range, an overhead alluded to earlier. Moreover, lack of batching methods affects similarly the other applications: the ciphertext size in the case of homomorphic encryption for branching programs, and the client's message size in the case of PIR. While bilinear maps may open up venues for batching-style tricks [BW10,DGI+19], it is not clear how to do so without pairings. (See Sect. 1.3 for more details.)

Obtaining Linear-Sized Public Keys Asymptotically. We note that if one's goal is solely to obtain TDFs with public-key size linear in input size, that is easy to do by making the input larger; e.g., $\mathsf{TDF}(\mathsf{ik}, x_1 || \ldots || x_n) = \mathsf{TDF}(\mathsf{ik}, x_1) || \cdots || \mathsf{TDF}(\mathsf{ik}_n, x_n)$. Similarly, one may make the size of the receiver's message otr in an OT protocol almost the same as that of the sender's input, by making each of the sender's input consist of (sufficiently) many blocks of messages and re-using otr across each opposite pair of them. These results are only for the asymptotic case, falling short in concrete cases. For example, increasing the size of the sender's input messages (so to make the size of otr close to that of the sender's message) translates into larger homomorphically-evaluated ciphertexts for branching programs.

1.1 Our Results

In this work, we will mitigate the above-mentioned issue, through efficient realizations of a new notion of range-trapdoor hash, which we introduce next.

Range-Trapdoor Hash. We introduce a notion called range-trapdoor hash functions, which is an immediate generalization of TDH schemes for index functions. In particular, under range-trapdoor hash, one would issue evaluation keys ek_I (based on a public parameter) for a range of indices $I = [i+1, ..., i+s]$, in such a way that given ek_I's trapdoor key, one can recover $x[I] := (x_{i+1}, \ldots, x_{i+s})$ from $H(\mathsf{hk}, x)$ and $E(\mathsf{ek}_I, x)$. We require that ek_I should hide I (except for $|I|$) and that $|E(\mathsf{ek}_I, x)| = |I|$. Under Diffie-Hellman type assumptions, we seek realizations where ek_I consists only of $O(n)$ group elements, as opposed to $O(n|I|)$.

Our Construction. We give constructions of range-trapdoor hash schemes, where on inputs of length n, an encoding key for a given range $I \subseteq [n]$ consists of $O(n)$ group elements, irrespective of $|I|$. Our construction relies on the $2n$-power DDH assumption—namely, that the distribution $(g, g^a, g^{a^2}, \ldots, g^{a^{2n}})$ should be pseudorandom, where g is a random generator of the group and a is a uniformly-random exponent. This notion has been used in some previous works, e.g., [BB04,DY05,CNs07,AHI11,BMZ19], but for different purposes.

In addition to obtaining a smaller ek_I, we obtain efficiency improvements in the computation time of the evaluation algorithm. Specifically, while the evaluation algorithm of [DGI+19] requires $O(n|I|)$ group operations (among some other private-key operations), the number of public-key operations in our construction is only $O(n \log |I|)$. At a high level, we achieve this by designing our range-trapdoor hash scheme in a structured way, so that the evaluation involves multiplying a Toeplitz matrix (given in the exponent) with an input vector x^T. Since Toeplitz matrices are closely related to circulant matrices which are amenable to the fast-Fourier transform, we show how to do this matrix multiplication in a fast way using (inverse) discrete Fourier transform (IDFT/DFT) modulo $\mathbb{Z}_p$ in the exponent.

Applications: Rate-1 Two-Message String OT and More. Our techniques yield a construction of string OT with rate-1 from the power-DDH assumption with improved communication and computation. Specifically, in our two round protocol the communication from receiver to sender consists of a linear (in sender's message size) number of group elements. The previous work of [DGI+19] required a quadratic number of group elements by relying on DDH. Additionally, our construction also improves the computational cost of the sender—namely, our construction improves the computational effort of the sender from quadratic to quasi-linear. This allows us to obtain the following new results:

1. *Lossy Trapdoor Functions:* We obtain the first construction of lossy trapdoor functions [PW08], where on inputs of size n, the public key consists of $O(n)$ group elements. All previous (even non-lossy) TDF constructions from pairing-free groups had public keys with $O(n^2)$ group elements.
2. *Semi-Compact Homomorphic Encryption for Branching Programs:* A construction of public-key homomorphic encryption for branching programs, with ciphertexts consisting of $O(\lambda n d^2)$ group elements, improving upon $O(\lambda^2 n d^3)$ [DGI+19], where d denotes the depth of the program. We achieve this by plugging our rate-1 OT scheme into the homomorphic encryption construction of [IP07]. See Table 1.
3. *Private Information Retrieval:* For a database of N bits, we get a two-message PIR protocol with total communication complexity that grows only polylogarithmically with the database size, and with a client's message consisting of $O(\lambda)\mathsf{polylog}(N)$ group elements, improving upon $O(\lambda^2)\mathsf{polylog}(N)$, given by [DGI+19]. See Table 2.

Table 1. Bit complexity for branching programs. The size of public keys, secret keys and homomorphically-evaluated ciphertexts in both schemes are the same. Here $p = \Theta(2^\lambda)$ is the group order, n is the input size of the program and d is the depth of the branching program.

Work	Assumption	Ciphertext size
Ours	$O(\lambda d)$-power DDH	$\lambda n d^2 \log p$
[DGI+19]	DDH	$\lambda^2 n d^3 \log p$

Table 2. Bit complexity: $p = \Theta(2^\lambda)$ is the order of the group and n is the bit size of each of the sender's message (in the case of OT) and N is the database size (in the case of PIR).

Work	Assumption	Primitive	Receiver message	Sender message
Ours	$2n$-power DDH	OT	$\Theta(n \log p)$	$n + \log p$
[DGI+19]	DDH	OT	$\Theta(n^2 \log p)$	$n + \log p$
Ours	Power-DDH	PIR	$\Theta(\lambda^2)\mathsf{polylog}(N)$	$\log(N) \log p$
[DGI+19]	DDH	PIR	$\Theta(\lambda^3)\mathsf{polylog}(N)$	$\log(N) \log p$

1.2   Related Work and Open Problems

As mentioned above, Döttling et al. [DGI+19] introduced the notion of trapdoor hash, and used it to build several new primitives. Among others, they obtained the first DDH-based and QR-based constructions of PIR for one-bit records with a total communication complexity that grows polylogarithmically with the database size; i.e., it is $\mathsf{p}(\lambda)\mathsf{polylog}(N))$ for a fixed function p, where N is the database size and λ is the security parameter. Previously, such protocols were only known under DCR, LWE and Φ-hiding assumptions [CMS99, Cha04, Lip05, OS07].

A recent result by Brakerski, Koppula and Mour [BKM20] shows how to build correlation-intractable hash functions for constant-degree functions from trapdoor hash schemes. This result is used in conjunction with appropriate commitment schemes (which can in turn be built from LPN) in order to instantiate the Fiat-Shamir paradigm for obtaining NIZK for all NP.

The notion of trapdoor hash builds on tools that were developed in the context of trapdoor function constructions [GH18, GGH19], as well as those developed in the context of identity-based encryption (IBE) [DG17b, DG17a, BLSV18, DGHM18].

Variants of TDFs are typically used as CCA-enhancing tools [PW08, RS09, GH18, GGH19]. Koppula and Waters [KW19] showed that for CCA applications, full randomness recovery, a feature provided by TDF-based tools, is not necessary. They gave a generic transformation from CPA to CCA for PKE and attribute-based encryption (ABE) using hinting pseudorandom generators (PRGs). The notion of hinting PRGs was later used in subsequent works in contexts such as designated-verifier NIZK [LQR+19] and CCA key-dependent-message (KDM) security [KMT19]. Boyen and Waters show that in the bilinear setting one may shorten the public key of lossy-TDF construction from a quadratic number of group elements to linear [BW10].

Concurrent Work. In independent and concurrent work, Goyal, Vusirikala and Waters [GVW19] give constructions of primitives such as hinting PRGs [KW19] and one-way function with encryption (OWFE) [GH18] with short public-parameter and ciphertext sizes. In terms of Diffie-Hellman related assumptions, they give (1) a construction of hinting PRGs from power-DDH-related assumptions (without pairings) with public parameters of $O(n)$ group elements and (2) a construction of OWFE from pairing-based power-DDH-related assumptions with public parameters of $O(n)$ group elements and ciphertexts of one group element. Specifically, their result (2) also leads to a construction of TDFs (and deterministic encryption) with public keys of $O(n)$ group elements and images of $O(n)$ bits. In contrast, in our work we do not use pairings, but focus primitives such as lossy TDFs and range-trapdoor hash schemes, which have applications in constructing OT and PIR.

Open Problems. The main open problem is to achieve the same results from DDH, LWE or QR. Also, it would be interesting to see if one can strengthen DDH (along the generalization of power-DDH from plain-DDH) which would allow one to build trapdoor-hash schemes beyond constant-degree polynomials (even without the range-compactness property).

1.3   Technical Overview

It will be instructive to give an overview of our results in the context of lossy TDFs and then to adapt them to the trapdoor-hash setting. Let us review an optimized version of the DDH-based lossy TDF of [PW08], given by [FGK+10]. Recall that in a group with a generator g, if we have an encoding $[\mathbf{M}] = g^{\mathbf{M}}$ of an invertible matrix $\mathbf{M}$ of exponents, we may encode any column vector $\mathbf{X}$ of bits by computing $\mathbf{M} \cdot \mathbf{X}$ in the exponent. One may invert using $\mathbf{M}^{-1}$. Lossiness is argued by making the matrix $\mathbf{M}$ rank one. The downside of this scheme is that a public key and an image point consist of, respectively, n^2 and n group elements, which is rather large. Recent works [GH18,GGH19], which in turn inspired the notion of TDH, showed how to make the image size linear in input size, but they still leave us with public keys of $O(n^2)$ group elements.

Parallels from Ideal Lattices? To make the public keys smaller, one may be tempted to draw inspirations from ideal lattices [LPR10,LPR13], and especially the way ring-LWE is used to shorten public keys. Sample a vector $\mathbf{v} := (g_1, \ldots, g_n)$ and expand $\mathbf{v}$ into a "circulant-like" matrix

$$\mathbf{M} := \begin{pmatrix} g_1 & g_2 & \cdots & g_{n-1} & g_n \\ g_2 & g_3 & \cdots & g_n & g_1 \\ \vdots & \vdots & \vdots & \vdots & \vdots \\ g_n & g_1 & \cdots & g_{n-2} & g_{n-1} \end{pmatrix}, \tag{1}$$

and use $\mathbf{M}$ as the public key of the TDF given above. The problem with this approach is that we do not know how to prove one-wayness. Even if there is a clever way to prove one-wayness, this approach does not appear to scale to give us more advanced schemes such as lossy TDFs, (range) trapdoor hash schemes, or TDFs with linear-sized outputs.

Circulant Structure Using Power DDH. We show how to work out the above intuition by relying on the power DDH assumption. Specifically, we give a way of expanding two vectors ($\mathbf{v} \in \mathbb{G}^n, \mathbf{w} \in \mathbb{G}^{2n-1}$) into an $(n+1) \times n$ matrix, and two indistinguishable distributions over $(\mathbf{v}, \mathbf{w})$, where under one distribution we can invert, while under the other, we will lose information.

Given two vectors $\mathbf{v} = (v_1, \ldots, v_n) \in \mathbb{G}^n$ and $\mathbf{w} = (w_1, \ldots, w_{2n-1}) \in \mathbb{G}^{2n-1}$, we expand them into an $(n+1) \times n$ matrix $\mathbf{M} = \mathsf{Expand}(\mathbf{v}, \mathbf{w})$ as follows:

$$\mathbf{M} := \begin{pmatrix} \mathbf{m}_1 \\ \mathbf{m}_2 \\ \vdots \\ \mathbf{m}_{n+1} \end{pmatrix} := \begin{pmatrix} v_1 & v_2 & \cdots & v_n \\ w_n & w_{n+1} & \cdots & w_{2n-1} \\ w_{n-1} & w_n & \cdots & w_{2n-2} \\ \vdots & \vdots & \cdots & \vdots \\ w_1 & w_2 & \cdots & w_n \end{pmatrix} \in \mathbb{G}^{(n+1) \times n} \quad (2)$$

To evaluate an input $\mathsf{x} \in \{0,1\}^n$ using $\mathbf{M}$, return $(\mathsf{x} \cdot \mathbf{m}_1, \ldots, \mathsf{x} \cdot \mathbf{m}_{n+1})$, where $\mathsf{x} \cdot \mathbf{v} := \prod_{i=1}^n v_i^{x_i}$. Define the lossy distribution lossy as

$$\mathsf{lossy} \quad \mathbf{v} := (g^\alpha, g^{\alpha^2}, \ldots, g^{\alpha^n})$$
$$\mathbf{w} := (g^{r\alpha}, g^{r\alpha^2}, \ldots, g^{r\alpha^{2n-1}}).$$

If $(\mathbf{v}, \mathbf{w}) \xleftarrow{\$} \mathsf{lossy}$, then $\mathbf{M} := \mathsf{Expand}(\mathbf{v}, \mathbf{w})$ will be of rank one, statistically losing information about x. We set the real (i.e., injective) distribution by putting a *bump* g on the nth element of $\mathbf{w}$:

$$\mathsf{real} \quad \mathbf{v} := (g^\alpha, g^{\alpha^2}, \ldots, g^{\alpha^n}) \quad (3)$$
$$\mathbf{w} := (g^{r\alpha}, g^{r\alpha^2}, \ldots, g^{r\alpha^{n-1}}, gg^{r\alpha^n}, g^{r\alpha^{n+1}}, \ldots, g^{r\alpha^{2n-1}}). \quad (4)$$

To see how to invert in injective mode, notice that the matrix $\mathbf{M} := \mathsf{Expand}(\mathbf{v}, \mathbf{w})$ is

$$\mathbf{M} := \begin{pmatrix} \mathbf{m}_1 \\ \mathbf{m}_2 \\ \vdots \\ \mathbf{m}_{n+1} \end{pmatrix} = \begin{pmatrix} g^\alpha & g^{\alpha^2} & \cdots & g^{\alpha^{n-1}} & g^{\alpha^n} \\ gg^{r\alpha^n} & g^{r\alpha^{n+1}} & \cdots & g^{r\alpha^{2n-2}} & g^{r\alpha^{2n-1}} \\ g^{r\alpha^{n-1}} & gg^{r\alpha^n} & \cdots & g^{r\alpha^{2n-3}} & g^{r\alpha^{2n-2}} \\ \vdots & \vdots & \vdots & \vdots & \vdots \\ g^{r\alpha^2} & g^{r\alpha^3} & \cdots & gg^{r\alpha^n} & g^{r\alpha^{n+1}} \\ g^{r\alpha} & g^{r\alpha^2} & \cdots & g^{r\alpha^{n-1}} & gg^{r\alpha^n} \end{pmatrix} \in \mathbb{G}^{(n+1) \times n}, \quad (5)$$

where the bump g propagates as indicated. Using the trapdoor values α and r, we show how to recover the ith bit of x from the image $\mathsf{u} := (g_h, g_1, \ldots, g_n) := (\mathsf{x} \cdot \mathbf{m}_1, \ldots, \mathsf{x} \cdot \mathbf{m}_{n+1})$. To do this, notice that the bump that affects the ith bit of x occurs in row $i+1$ of matrix $\mathbf{M}$, which is off the first row by an exponent $r\alpha^{n-i}$ (excluding the bump). Thus, we may compute $g^{x_i} \in \{g^0, g^1\}$ as

$$g^{x_i} = \frac{g_i}{g_h^{r\alpha^{n-i}}} \in \{g^0, g^1\}. \quad (6)$$

Finally, the indistinguishability between lossy and real follows from $(2n-1)$-power DDH, which implies that the distribution $((g^{\alpha}, g^{\alpha^2}, \ldots, g^{\alpha^{2n-1}}), (g^{r\alpha}, g^{r\alpha^2}, \ldots, g^{r\alpha^{2n-1}}))$ is pseudorandom: the pseudorandom of the first vector comes from $2n-1$-power DDH and the pseudorandomness of the second one is implied by the fact that t-power (for $t \geq 3$) implies DDH (Lemma 1).

Source of Computational Efficiency. Excluding the first row of matrix **M**, the rest of the matrix is Toeplitz-like, which, if given in the clear as opposed to in the exponent, can be multiplied with any given vector in time $O(n \log n)$ using discrete FFT techniques. We observe that this computation may in fact be carried out in the exponent, enabling a relatively fast way of $O(n \log n)$ group exponentiations for evaluating an input. See Sect. 4 for more details.

Making the Image Shorter. The public key of the above lossy TDF has $O(n)$ group elements, a goal we had set before. The image, however, is quite large, consisting of $n+1$ group elements. We now show how to use image-shrinking techniques of Garg, Gay and Hajiabadi [GGH19] (later improved by Döttling et al. [DGI+19]) in order to make the image size linear in input size. Looking ahead, this will allow us to make $|\mathsf{E}(\mathsf{ek}_I, \mathsf{x})| = |I|$, where ek_I is the TDH-evaluation key for a range I. For concreteness, let us focus on how to recover the first bit x_1 from a succinct output. If the corresponding (long) image of x is $\mathsf{u} := (g_h, g_1, \ldots, g_n)$, then for recovering x_1 we have to look at g_h and g_1: we either have $g_1 = g_h^{r\alpha^{n-1}}$, in which case $\mathsf{x}_n = 0$, or $g_1 = gg_h^{r\alpha^{n-1}}$, in which case $\mathsf{x}_n = 1$ (or informally, x_n has hit the bump). Now instead of outputting one whole group element g_1, we output a single bit, corresponding to the output of a hint function $\Phi_k : \mathbb{G} \to \{0,1\}$ on g_1. This function guarantees that for any $g^* \in \mathbb{G}$, the probability that $\Phi_k(g^*) = \Phi_k(g^*g)$ (a.k.a., the *hung* probability) is very small, where k is chosen at random (and included in the public key). The inverter will then match $\Phi_k(g_1)$, comes as part of the image, against $\Phi_k(g_h^r)$ and $\Phi_k(g_h^r g)$, hence decoding x_1. Garg, Gay and Hajiabadi [GGH19] gave a function Φ which outputs a constant c number of bits (instead of a single bit) with hung probability being $\frac{1}{2^c}$. Later, Döttling et al. [DGI+19] substantially improved this by making Φ output a single bit with hung probability being at most $\frac{1}{n^c}$, for any desired constant c. They achieved this using a PRF-based distance-function technique from [BGI16]. Finally, since the inversion algorithm may fail (i.e., be hung) for some indices, we pre-process the TDF input using erasure-correcting codes, making the task of decoding easier.

Adaptation to the Trapdoor Hash Setting. The lossy TDF sketched above (without erasure-correcting codes) lends itself naturally into the range TDH setting. Recall that for range trapdoor hash, we encode an index range $I = [s+1, s+t]$ into an encoding key ek in such a way that (1) ek only reveals $|I|$ and (2) Using the associated trapdoors, one can recover each bit of $\mathsf{x}[I]$ with high probability from $\mathsf{H}(\mathsf{hk}, \mathsf{x})$ and $\mathsf{E}(\mathsf{ek}, \mathsf{x}) \in \{0,1\}^{|I|}$. Moreover, ek should only contain $O(n)$ group elements (as opposed to $O(n|I|)$).

We achieve range-trapdoor hash by carefully placing the bump in a coordinate which enables recovery of exactly $\mathsf{x}[I]$, but nothing more. First, let $\mathsf{hk} := \mathbf{v} := (g^\alpha, g^{\alpha^2}, \ldots, g^{\alpha^n})$ and define $\mathsf{H}(\mathsf{hk}, \mathsf{x}) = \mathsf{x} \cdot \mathbf{v}$. Assuming $I = [s+1, s+t]$ and noting that $|I| = t$, set $\mathsf{ek} := (\mathbf{w}, t)$, where

$$\mathbf{w} := (g^{r\alpha}, g^{r\alpha^2}, \ldots, g^{r\alpha^{s+t-1}}, gg^{r\alpha^{s+t}}, g^{r\alpha^{s+t+1}}, \ldots, g^{r\alpha^{2n-1}}), \tag{7}$$

obtained from hk by raising every element to the power of r and putting the bump g in the $(s+t)$'th coordinate. Now to evaluate x on $\mathsf{ek} := (\mathbf{w}, t+1)$, return

$$(\mathsf{x} \cdot \mathbf{w}[t, n+t-1], \mathsf{x} \cdot \mathbf{w}[t-1, n+t-2], \ldots, \mathsf{x} \cdot \mathbf{w}[1, n]) \in \mathbb{G}^n,$$

where $\mathbf{w}[i, j]$ denotes the elements of $\mathbf{w}$ which are in the range $\{i, i+1, \ldots, j\}$. Given α and r we may recover all the bits $\mathsf{x}[s, s+t]$. The only remaining thing is that the output of E consists of t group elements, as opposed to t bits. We make it consist of t bits by using image-shrinking techniques described above.

2   Preliminaries

Notation. We use λ for the security parameter. We use , to denote computational indistinguishability and use $\equiv$ to denote two distributions are identical. For a distribution $\mathcal{S}$ we use $x \xleftarrow{\$} \mathcal{S}$ to mean x is sampled according to $\mathcal{S}$ and use $y \in \mathcal{S}$ to mean $y \in \sup(\mathcal{S})$, where sup denotes the support of a distribution. For a set S we overload the notation to use $x \xleftarrow{\$} \mathsf{S}$ to indicate that x is chosen uniformly at random from S. If $\mathsf{A}(x_1, \ldots, x_n)$ is a randomized algorithm, then $\mathsf{A}(a_1, \ldots, a_n)$, for deterministic inputs $a_1, \ldots, a_n$, denotes the random variable obtained by sampling random coins r uniformly at random and returning $\mathsf{A}(a_1, \ldots, a_n; r)$. We use $[n] := \{1, \ldots, n\}$ and $[i, i+s] := \{i, i+1, \ldots, i+s\}$. For a vector $\mathbf{v} = (v_1, \ldots, v_n)$ we define $\mathbf{v}[i, i+s] := (v_i, v_{i+1}, \ldots, v_{i+s})$.

2.1   Standard Definitions and Lemmas

Definition 1 (Trapdoor functions (TDFs)). *Let $n = n(\lambda)$ be a polynomial. A family of trapdoor functions TDF with domain $\{0, 1\}^n$ consists of three PPT algorithms TDF.KG, TDF.F and TDF.F^{-1} with the following syntax and security properties.*

- *TDF.KG(1^λ): Takes 1^λ as input, and outputs a pair $(\mathsf{ik}, \mathsf{tk})$ of index/trapdoor keys.*
- *TDF.F$(\mathsf{ik}, \mathsf{x})$: Takes an index key ik and a domain element $\mathsf{x} \in \{0, 1\}^n$ and deterministically outputs an image element u.*
- *TDF.F$^{-1}(\mathsf{tk}, \mathsf{u})$: Takes a trapdoor key tk and an image element u and outputs a value $\mathsf{x} \in \{0, 1\}^n \cup \{\bot\}$.*

We require the following properties.

- **Correctness:** $\Pr[\exists x \in \{0,1\}^n \text{ s.t. } \mathsf{TDF.F}^{-1}(\mathsf{tk}, \mathsf{TDF.F}(\mathsf{ik}, x)) \neq x] = \mathsf{negl}(\lambda)$, *where the probability is taken over* $(\mathsf{ik}, \mathsf{tk}) \xleftarrow{\$} \mathsf{TDF.KG}(1^\lambda)$.
- **One-wayness:** *For any PPT adversary* $\mathcal{A}$: $\Pr[\mathcal{A}(\mathsf{ik}, \mathsf{u}) = x] = \mathsf{negl}(\lambda)$, *where* $(\mathsf{ik}, \mathsf{tk}) \xleftarrow{\$} \mathsf{TDF.KG}(1^\lambda)$, $x \xleftarrow{\$} \{0,1\}^n$ *and* $\mathsf{u} := \mathsf{TDF.F}(\mathsf{ik}, x)$.

Definition 2 (Lossy TDFs [PW08, PW11]). *An* (n, k)-*lossy TDF* $((n, k)$-*LTDF) is given by four PPT algorithms* $\mathsf{TDF.KG}$, $\mathsf{TDF.KG_{ls}}$, $\mathsf{TDF.F}$, $\mathsf{TDF.F}^{-1}$, *where* $\mathsf{TDF.KG_{ls}}(1^\lambda)$ *only outputs a single key (as opposed to a pair of keys), and where the following properties hold:*

- **Correctness in real mode.** *The TDF* $(\mathsf{TDF.KG}, \mathsf{TDF.F}, \mathsf{TDF.F}^{-1})$ *satisfies correctness in the sense of Definition 1.*
- k-**Lossiness.** *For all but negligible probability over the choice of* $\mathsf{ik_{ls}} \xleftarrow{\$} \mathsf{TDF.KG_{ls}}(1^\lambda)$, *we have* $|\mathsf{TDF.F}(\mathsf{ik_{ls}}, \{0,1\}^n)| \leq 2^k$, *where we use* $\mathsf{TDF.F}(\mathsf{ik_{ls}}, \{0,1\}^n)$ *to denote the set of all images of* $\mathsf{TDF.F}(\mathsf{ik_{ls}}, \cdot)$.
- **Indistinguishability of real and lossy modes.** *We have* $\mathsf{ik}, \mathsf{ik_{ls}}$, *where* $(\mathsf{ik}, *) \xleftarrow{\$} \mathsf{TDF.KG}(1^\lambda)$ *and* $\mathsf{ik_{ls}} \xleftarrow{\$} \mathsf{TDF.KG_{ls}}(1^\lambda)$.

Lossiness Rate. In the definition above, we refer to the fraction $1 - k/n$ as the *lossiness rate*, describing the fraction of the bits lost. Ideally, we want this fraction to be as close to 1 as possible, e.g., $1 - o(1)$.

Expansion Rate. In the definition above, we refer to $n/|\mathsf{u}|$ as the expansion rate, and say the scheme has *rate 1* if this fraction approaches one asymptotically.

2.2 Computational Assumptions

We review the power DDH assumption, used in our constructions. This notion is a variant of the t-Diffie-Hellman Inversion (t-DHI) problem [BB04]: given $(g, g^\alpha, \ldots, g^{\alpha^t})$ the adversary should distinguish $g^{1/\alpha}$ from random. Under our variant, we require the whole distribution $(g^{1/\alpha}, g, g^\alpha, \ldots, g^{\alpha^t})$ to be pseudorandom. We present this version, called power-DDH [CNs07], below.

Definition 3 (t-power DDH assumption [CNs07, AHI11]). *Let* G *be a group-generator scheme, which on input* 1^λ *outputs* $(\mathbb{G}, p, g)$, *where* $\mathbb{G}$ *is the description of a group,* p *is the order of the group which is always a prime number and* g *is a generator for the group. Let* $t := t(\lambda)$. *We say that* G *is* t-*DDH-hard if the distribution* $(g, g^\alpha, \ldots, g^{\alpha^t})$ *is pseudorandom, where* $(\mathbb{G}, p, g) \xleftarrow{\$} \mathsf{G}(1^\lambda)$ *and* $\alpha \xleftarrow{\$} \mathbb{Z}_p$.

Boneh and Boyen [BB04] show that t-DHI implies the so-called $(t + 1)$-generalized Diffie-Hellman ($(t + 1)$-generalized DH): given $(g, g^{a_1}, \ldots, g^{a_t})$ and an oracle that for any given *proper* subset $S \subset [t]$ returns $g^{\Pi_{i \in S} a_i}$, the adversary should distinguish $g^{a_1 \cdots a_t}$ from random. The following lemma gives an adaptation of this lemma to the power-DDH setting for a very simple case: namely that power-DDH hadrness implies DDH hardness.

Lemma 1. *Let* $\mathbb{G}$ *be t-power DDH hard. Then* $(g_1, g_1^{\alpha}, \ldots, g_1^{\alpha^t})$ *is pseudorandom, where* $(\mathbb{G}, p, g) \xleftarrow{\$} \mathsf{G}(1^{\lambda})$, $g_1 \xleftarrow{\$} \mathbb{G}$ *and* $\alpha \xleftarrow{\$} \mathbb{Z}_p$.[3] *Also, for any* $t \geq 3$, *if a group is t-power DDH hard, it is also DDH-hard.*

Proof. The first part of the lemma follows straightforwardly using random self reducibility. The second part follows immediately from techniques of [BB04], but we give the proof for completeness. Notice that if a group is $t + 1$-power DDH hard, then it is also t-power DDH hard. Thus, it suffices to show that 3-power DDH hardness implies DDH hardness. Suppose for a group $\mathbb{G}$ there is a DDH adversary $\mathcal{A}$ that can distinguish (g, g^a, g^b, g^{ab}) from random. We want to use $\mathcal{A}$ to distinguish $(g, g^{\alpha}, g^{\alpha^2}, g^{\alpha^3})$ from random, hence breaking 3-power DDH hardness. The problem is that $\mathcal{A}$ is only guaranteed to work as long as the two exponents a and b are chosen uniformly at random—while in the 3-power DDH case the two exponents α and α^2 are correlated.

To fix the above problem, we use the random-self reducibility of DDH [NR97]. That is, letting (g, g_1, g_2, g_3) be the challenge tuple, we sample $r_1, r_2 \xleftarrow{\$} \mathbb{Z}_p$ and call $\mathcal{A}$ on $(g, g_1^{r_1}, g_2^{r_2}, g_3^{r_1 r_2})$.

It is easy to see that the above transformation converts a 3-power DDH tuple into a random DDH tuple, and converts a random tuple into another random tuple. $\square$

2.3   Standard Lemmas

Lemma 2 (Chernoff inequality). *Let* X *be binomially distributed with parameters* $n \in \mathbb{N}$ *and* $p \in [0, 1]$. *Assuming* $p' > p$:

$$\Pr[X > 2p'n] < e^{-p'n/3}.$$

In some of our proofs, we need to use a version of Chernoff bounds involving Bernoulli variables which are not necessarily independent, but where each of them has a bounded probability of success, conditioned on any fixed sequence of outcomes of the others. We give such a version of the Chernoff inequality below, and prove it by relying on Lemma 2.

Lemma 3 (Chernoff inequality with bounded dependence). *Let* $X_1, \ldots, X_n$ *be Bernoulli variables (not necessarily independent), where for all* i, *and for all values* $b_1, \ldots, b_{i-1}, b_{i+1}, \ldots, b_n$:

$$\Pr[X_i = 1 \mid X_1 = b_1, \ldots, X_{i-1} = b_{i-1}, X_{i+1} = b_{i+1}, \ldots, X_n = b_n] \leq p. \quad (8)$$

Assuming $p' > p$:

$$\Pr[\sum_{i \in [n]} X_i > 2p'n] < e^{-p'n/3}.$$

---

[3] Notice that the only difference between this version and the standard t-power DDH assumption is that the element g_1 is now also chosen uniformly at random—as opposed to it being g, the fixed group generator.

Proof. We will define n random variables $X'_1, \ldots, X'_n$ and also n independent i.i.d. boolean random variables $Y_1, \ldots, Y_n$, where $\Pr[Y_1] = p$, and where

1. $(X'_1, \ldots, X'_n)$ is identically distributed as $(X_1, \ldots, X_n)$; and
2. for all $i \in [n]$, $X'_i \leq Y_i$.

Thus

$$\Pr_{(X_1,\ldots,X_n)}[\sum_{i\in[n]} X_i > 2p'n] = \Pr_{(X'_1,\ldots,X'_n)}[\sum_{i\in[n]} X'_i > 2p'n] \leq \Pr[\sum_{i\in[n]} Y_i > 2p'n] < e^{-p'n/3},$$

where the last inequality comes from Lemma 2.

To define Y_i, let U_i for $i \in [n]$ be i.i.d. real-valued random variables, each uniformly distributed over $[0,1]$. For $i \in [n]$ let Y_i be the Bernouli random variable where $Y_i = 1$ iff $U_i \leq p$.

For $b_1, \ldots, b_{i-1} \in \{0,1\}$ define $\mathcal{Z} = \Pr[X_1]$ and

$$\mathcal{Z}(b_1, \ldots, b_{i-1}) = \Pr[X_i = 1 | X_1 = b_1, \ldots, X_{i-1} = b_{i-1}].$$

We may now represent the joint distribution $(X_1, \ldots, X_n)$ as

$$(X'_1, \ldots, X'_n) := (U_1 \leq \mathcal{Z}, U_2 \leq \mathcal{Z}(X_1), \ldots, U_n \leq \mathcal{Z}(X_1, \ldots, X_{n-1})), \qquad (9)$$

where $A \leq B$ is the Bernoulli random variable which is one if and only if $A \leq B$.

We now show that whenever $U_i \leq \mathcal{Z}(X_1, \ldots, X_{i-1})$, we have $Y_i = 1$, as desired. To see this, recall that by Eq. 8 $\mathcal{Z}(X_1, \ldots, X_{i-1}) \leq p$. Thus, whenever $U_i \leq \mathcal{Z}(X_1, \ldots, X_{i-1})$, we have $U_i \leq p$, which means $Y_i = 1$. The proof is now complete. $\qquad \square$

2.4 Error Correcting Codes

Definition 4 ($(n, m, s)_2$-Codes). *We recall the notion of $(n, m, s)_2$ erasure-correcting codes. Such a code is given by efficiently computable functions* (Encode, Decode), *where* Encode $: \{0,1\}^n \to \{0,1\}^m$, *and where*

1. *Minimum distance. For any two distinct* $x_1, x_2 \in \{0,1\}^n$, H_{dst}(Encode(x_1), Encode(x_2)) $\geq s$, *where* H_{dst} *denotes the Hamming distance.*
2. *Erasure correction. For any* $x \in \{0,1\}^n$, *letting* $z :=$ Encode(x), *given any string* $z' \in \{0,1,\perp\}^m$, *which has at most* $s - 1$ $\perp$ *symbols, and whose all non-$\perp$ symbols agree with* z, *we have* Decode(z') $= x$.

We are interested in rate-1 codes (that is, n/m approaches 1 asymptotically) with fast encoding and decoding algorithms. If we are willing to settle for a constant rate (as opposed to rate 1), there are binary concatenated codes which are linear time for both encoding and decoding; see, e.g., [GI05], Theorem 6. For rate-1 binary codes, we use the following code from [CDD+16].

Theorem 1 ([CDD+16], Theorem 6). *Fix a finite field* $\mathbb{F}$ *of constant size. There exists a constant* $\upsilon > 0$ *and a family of $\mathbb{F}$-linear codes* $\mathsf{C} = \{\mathsf{C}_s\}_s$ *with codeword length* $O(s^2)$, *rate* $1 - \frac{1}{s^\upsilon}$ *and minimum distance at least* s. *Moreover,* C *admits a linear-time computable encoding algorithm* Encode.

3 Lossy TDFs with Short Public Keys from Power DDH

As a warm-up to our range-trapdoor hash construction, we first give a construction of rate-1 lossy TDFs from the $O(n)$-power DDH assumption, wherein a public key has only $O(n)$ group elements.

For our construction, we need a function $\Phi \colon \mathbb{G} \to \{0,1\}$ which has the property that for any group element h, $\Phi(h) \neq \Phi(hg)$ with high probability. The work of Boyle, Gilboa and Ishai [BGI16] gives such a function. Below we review an adaptation of this function to the binary output space, as done by [DGI+19]. In what follows, we use $\mathsf{LSB}(i)$ to denote the least significant bit of i.

Distance Function $\mathsf{Dist}_{\mathbb{G},g}(h, \delta, M, f)$ [BGI16]. Given a group $\mathbb{G}$ with a generator g, a group element h, a value $0 < \delta < 1$, integer $M \geq 1$ and a function $f : \mathbb{G} \to \{0,1\}^{\log(2M/\delta)}$, we define a function Dist as follows:

1. Let $T := \lceil 2M \log_e(2/\delta) \rceil / \delta$ and set $i := 0$.
2. While $i \leq T$:
   (a) if $f(hg^i) = 0^{\log(2M/\delta)}$, then output $\mathsf{LSB}(i)$, otherwise set $i = i + 1$.
3. Output $\mathsf{LSB}(i)$.

T-Close/Far Group Elements. For an integer T, we say two group elements g_1 and g_2 are *T-close* with respect to g if $g_2 \in \{g_1, g_1g, \ldots, g_1g^T\}$ or $g_1 \in \{g_2, g_2g, \ldots, g_2g^T\}$. We say g_1 and g_2 are at least $(T+1)$-*far* with respect to g if g_1 and g_2 are not T-close with respect to g. When g is clear from the context, we simply say g_1 and g_2 are T-far/T-close.

The following lemma is from [BGI16], giving a distance function, defined based on a randomly chosen function f, which serves a hint bit in our construction (i.e., the function Φ described above). We will later replace such a random function with a PRF.

Lemma 4 (Proposition 3.2 in [BGI16]). *Let $\mathbb{G}$ be a group of prime order p, $g \in \mathbb{G}$, $M \in \mathbb{N}$, $\delta > 0$ and assume $\lceil 2M \log_e (2/\delta) \rceil / \delta < p$. Let RF be the set of all functions $f : \mathbb{G} \to \{0,1\}^{\lceil \log(2M/\delta) \rceil}$. Then for any integer $x \leq M$ and $h \in \mathbb{G}$*

$$\Pr_{f \xleftarrow{\$} \mathsf{RF}} [\mathsf{Dist}_{\mathbb{G},g}(h, \delta, M, f) = \mathsf{LSB}(x) - \mathsf{Dist}_{\mathbb{G},g}(hg^x, \delta, M, f)] \geq 1 - \delta. \qquad (10)$$

Moreover, for any set of group elements $h_1, \ldots, h_m$ which are mutually at least $(T+2)$-far, the events $\mathsf{Success}_1, \ldots, \mathsf{Success}_m$ are independent, where $\mathsf{Success}_i$ is the event that $\mathsf{Dist}_{\mathbb{G},g}(h_i, \delta, M, f) = 1 - \mathsf{Dist}_{\mathbb{G},g}(h_ig, \delta, M, f)$.

Proof. The first part of the lemma was proved in [BGI16]. The second part follows because (1) f is chosen at random and (2) for any group element h, the outputs of $\mathsf{Dist}_{\mathbb{G},g}(h, \delta, M, f)$ and $\mathsf{Dist}_{\mathbb{G},g}(hg, \delta, M, f)$ only depend on the outputs of f on $\{h, hg, hg^2, \ldots, hg^{T+1}\}$. □

Notation. For $\mathsf{x} \in \{0,1\}^n$ and $\mathbf{v} := (g_1, \ldots, g_n) \in \mathbb{G}^n$ we define $\mathsf{x} \cdot \mathbf{v} := \prod_{i=1}^{n} g_i^{\mathsf{x}_i}$.

Construction 2 (Doubly-Linear lossy TDF). *Let* G *be a group scheme and let* $(\mathsf{Encode}, \mathsf{Decode})$ *for* $\mathsf{Encode} \colon \{0,1\}^n \to \{0,1\}^m$ *be an ECC code. Let* $\ell := \log(2/\delta)$ *and let* $\mathsf{PRF} \colon \mathbb{G} \to \{0,1\}^\ell$ *be a PRF with key space* $\{0,1\}^\lambda$. *We will instantiate the value of* δ *later.*

- $\mathsf{TDF.KG}(1^\lambda)$:

  1. *Sample* $(\mathbb{G}, p, g) \xleftarrow{\$} \mathsf{G}(1^\lambda)$. *Sample* $\alpha, r \xleftarrow{\$} \mathbb{Z}_p$ *and set*

$$\mathbf{v} := (g^\alpha, g^{\alpha^2}, \dots, g^{\alpha^m}) \tag{11}$$

$$\mathbf{w} := (g^{r\alpha}, g^{r\alpha^2}, \dots, g^{r\alpha^{m-1}}, gg^{r\alpha^m}, g^{r\alpha^{m+1}}, \dots, g^{r\alpha^{2m-1}}). \tag{12}$$

  2. *Sample a key* $K \xleftarrow{\$} \{0,1\}^\lambda$ *for* PRF.
  3. *Set* $\mathsf{ik} := (K, g, \mathbf{v}, \mathbf{w})$ *and* $\mathsf{tk} := (K, g, \alpha, r)$. *Return* $(\mathsf{ik}, \mathsf{tk})$.

- $\mathsf{TDF.KG}_{\mathrm{ls}}(1^\lambda)$: *Return* $\mathsf{ik}_{\mathrm{ls}} := (g, \mathbf{v}, \mathbf{w}')$, *where* $g, \mathbf{v}$ *are as above, and*

$$\mathbf{w}' := (g^{r\alpha}, g^{r\alpha^2}, \dots, g^{r\alpha^{2m-1}}). \tag{13}$$

- $\mathsf{TDF.F}(\mathsf{ik}, \mathbf{x} \in \{0,1\}^n)$: *Parse* $\mathsf{ik} := (g, \mathbf{v}, \mathbf{w})$ *and* $\mathbf{z} := \mathsf{Encode}(\mathbf{x})$. *For* $1 \le i \le m$

  1. *Let* $\mathbf{w}'_i = \mathbf{w}[m+1-i, 2m-i]$.
  2. *Let* $g_i = \mathbf{z} \cdot \mathbf{w}'_i$.
  3. *Let* $b_i := \mathsf{Dist}_{\mathbb{G},g}(g_i, \delta, 1, \mathsf{PRF}_K)$.
  Let $g_c := \mathbf{z} \cdot \mathbf{v}$ *and return*

$$\mathsf{u} := (g_c, b_1, \dots, b_m). \tag{14}$$

- $\mathsf{TDF.F}^{-1}(\mathsf{tk}, \mathsf{u})$: *Parse* $\mathsf{u} := (g_c, b_1, \dots, b_m)$. *Recover* $\mathbf{z}$ *bit-by-bit as follows. For* $i \in [m]$:

  1. *Let* $g_{i,0} = g_c^{r\alpha^{m-i}}$ *and* $g_{i,1} = g_{i,0}g$.
  2. *If*
     (a) $\mathsf{Dist}_{\mathbb{G},g}(g_{i,0}, \delta, 1, \mathsf{PRF}_K) = \mathsf{Dist}_{\mathbb{G},g}(g_{i,1}, \delta, 1, \mathsf{PRF}_K)$, *then set* $\mathbf{z}_i = \bot$;
     (b) *Else, let* b *the bit for which* $\mathsf{Dist}_{\mathbb{G},g}(g_{i,b}, \delta, 1, \mathsf{PRF}_K) = b_i$, *and set* $\mathbf{z}_i = b$.
  Return $\mathsf{Decode}(\mathbf{z})$.

We now prove all the required properties of the scheme.

Lemma 5 (Mode indistinguishability). *We have* $\mathsf{ik}, \mathsf{ik}_{\mathrm{ls}}$, *where* $\mathsf{ik} \xleftarrow{\$} \mathsf{TDF.KG}(1^\lambda)$ *and* $\mathsf{ik}_{\mathrm{ls}} \xleftarrow{\$} \mathsf{TDF.KG}_{\mathrm{ls}}$.

Proof. Follows immediately from $(2m-1)$-power DDH (Lemma 1). $\qquad\square$

Lemma 6 (Lossiness). *Assuming* p *is the oder of the group, for any* $\mathsf{ik}_{\mathrm{ls}} \in \mathsf{TDF.KG}_{\mathrm{ls}}(1^\lambda)$,

$$|\mathsf{TDF.F}(\mathsf{ik}_{\mathrm{ls}}, \{0,1\}^n)| \le p.$$

Proof. Parse $\mathsf{ik}_{\mathsf{ls}} := (g, \mathbf{v}, \mathbf{w}')$, where $\mathbf{v}$ is sampled as in Eq. 11 and $\mathbf{w}'$ is sampled as in Eq. 13. We claim the following: for any $\mathsf{x}', \mathsf{x}' \in \{0,1\}^n$, letting $\mathsf{z} := \mathsf{Encode}(\mathsf{x})$ and $\mathsf{z}' := \mathsf{Encode}(\mathsf{x}')$, if $\mathsf{z} \cdot \mathbf{v} = \mathsf{z}' \cdot \mathbf{v}$, then $\mathsf{TDF.F}(\mathsf{ik}_{\mathsf{ls}}, \mathsf{x}) = \mathsf{TDF.F}(\mathsf{ik}_{\mathsf{ls}}, \mathsf{x})$. Assuming the claim holds, the lemma follows immediately. This is because, under the lossy key $\mathsf{ik}_{\mathsf{ls}}$, once the first component g_c of the image $\mathbf{u} := (g_c, \dots)$ is determined, the rest of the output is uniquely determined. To prove the claim, suppose $g_c = \mathsf{z} \cdot \mathbf{v} = \mathsf{z}' \cdot \mathbf{v}$. Notice that the group element g_i computed in Line 2 of $\mathsf{TDF.F}$ is equal to the fixed element $g_c^{r \alpha^{m-i}}$, irrespective of whether the underlying input is x or x'. This follows from the way $\mathbf{w}'$ is formed (Eq. 13). The proof is now complete. $\qquad\square$

Lemma 7 (Correctness). *Let* $(\mathsf{Encode}, \mathsf{Decode})$ *be an* $(n, m, s)_2$ *code, where* $n = \lambda + \omega(\log \lambda)$. *Assuming* $\delta \le \frac{s-1}{2m}$ *and* $T := \lceil 2 \log_e(2/\delta) \rceil / \delta = \mathsf{poly}(\lambda)$, *for any input* x:

$$\beta(\lambda) := \Pr_{(\mathsf{ik},\mathsf{tk})} [\mathsf{TDF.F}^{-1}(\mathsf{tk}, \mathsf{TDF.F}(\mathsf{ik}, \mathsf{x})) \ne \mathsf{x}] \le \frac{1}{e^{\frac{s-1}{6}}} + \mathsf{negl}(\lambda), \qquad (15)$$

where the probability is taken over $(\mathsf{ik}, \mathsf{tk}) \xleftarrow{\$} \mathsf{TDF.KG}(1^\lambda)$. *In particular, by setting* $n = \lambda + \omega(\log \lambda)$, $s \in \omega(\log \lambda)$ *and* $\delta \le \frac{s-1}{2m}$, *we will have a negligible inversion error.*

Proof. Fix $\mathsf{x} \in \{0,1\}^n$ and let $\mathsf{z} := \mathsf{Encode}(\mathsf{x})$. Consider a variant of Construction 2, in which we replace the PRF PRF_K with a truly random function $f : \mathbb{G} \xleftarrow{\$} \{0,1\}^\ell$. (Recall that $\ell = \log(2/\delta)$.) That is, in this variant, calls of the form $\mathsf{Dist}_{\mathbb{G},g}(g_i, \delta, 1, K)$ are replaced with $\mathsf{Dist}_{\mathbb{G},g}(g_i, \delta, 1, f)$. Let β' be the probability that $\mathsf{TDF.F}^{-1}(\mathsf{tk}, \mathsf{TDF.F}(\mathsf{ik}, \mathsf{x})) \ne \mathsf{x}$ in this experiment. We will show $\beta' \le \frac{1}{e^{\frac{s-1}{6}}} + \mathsf{negl}(\lambda)$. By PRF security we have $\beta \le \beta' + \mathsf{negl}(\lambda)$, and thus Eq. 15 will follow. The reason that we can use PRF security here (despite the fact that K is given in the clear in ik) is that the procedure Dist may efficiently be computed via only blackbox access to PRF_K (resp., f alternatively) and that we evaluate PRF_K on inputs generated independently of K.

For an index $i \in [m]$, let $g_i = \mathsf{z} \cdot \mathbf{w}'_i$ be the group element computed in Line 2 of $\mathsf{TDF.F}$, and let $g_{i,0} = g_c^{r \alpha^{m-i}}$ and $g_{i,1} = g_{i,0} g$ be the two corresponding group elements computed during inversion. Notice that $g_i = g_{i,\mathsf{z}_i}$.

For $i \in [m]$, let the indicator variable

$$\mathsf{Fail}_i = 1 \Leftrightarrow \mathsf{Dist}_{\mathbb{G},g}(g_{i,0}, \delta, 1, f) = \mathsf{Dist}_{\mathbb{G},g}(g_{i,1}, \delta, 1, f).$$

Notice that $\mathsf{Fail}_i = 1$ iff we fail to recover z_i. For all i, by setting $M = 1$ in Lemma 4, $\Pr[\mathsf{Fail}_i] < \delta$, and hence $\Pr[\mathsf{Fail}_i] < p'$, where $p' = \frac{s-1}{2m}$.

Let $\mathsf{Fail} = \sum_{i \in [m]} \mathsf{Fail}_i$. Inversion fails if $\mathsf{Fail} > s - 1$. We may now be tempted to use Lemma 2 to bound the probability that $\mathsf{Fail} > s - 1$. The problem is that the events Fail_i's may not be independent. Thus, we define an event Bad which captures all the dependencies, and then we will argue that conditioned on $\overline{\mathsf{Bad}}$, the events $\{\mathsf{Fail}_i\}_{i \in [m]}$ are independent.

– Bad: there are two distinct indices $i, j \in [m]$ such that $g_{i,0}$ and $g_{j,0}$ are $(T+1)$-close, where $T := [2\log_e(2/\delta)]/\delta$.

By Lemma 4 we know that conditioned on $\overline{\mathsf{Bad}}$, the events Fail_i's are independent. Below we will show $\Pr[\mathsf{Bad}] = \mathsf{negl}(\lambda)$, but assuming this for now:

$$\Pr[\mathsf{Fail} > s - 1] \leq \Pr[\mathsf{Bad}] + \Pr[\mathsf{Fail} > 2p'm \mid \overline{\mathsf{Bad}}] <^* \mathsf{negl}(\lambda) + \frac{1}{e^{p'm/3}} = \mathsf{negl}(\lambda) + \frac{1}{e^{\frac{s-1}{6}}},$$

where the inequality marked with $*$ follows from Lemma 2, noting that conditioned on $\overline{\mathsf{Bad}}$, the events $\{\mathsf{Fail}_i\}_{i \in [m]}$ are independent.

We are now left to prove $\Pr[\mathsf{Bad}] = \mathsf{negl}(\lambda)$. Recall that $(g_{1,0}, \ldots, g_{m,0}) = (g_c^{r\alpha^{m-1}}, \ldots, g_c^{r\alpha^0})$. Notice that $g_c \neq 1$ except with negligible probability, and thus g_c^r is statistically close to a uniformly random group element. By Lemma 1

$$(g_{1,0}, \ldots, g_{m,0}) = (g_c^{r\alpha^{m-1}}, \ldots, g_c^{r\alpha^0}), (g_1', \ldots, g_m'),$$

where g_i''s are random group elements. When replacing $\{g_{i,0}\}_{i \in [m]}$ with $\{g_i'\}_{i \in [m]}$ the probability of the event Bad becomes negligible. (This is because $T = \mathsf{poly}(\lambda)$). Thus, the event Bad with $g_{i,0}$'s should also be negligible.   □

3.1   Running Time of Our Lossy TDFs

We count the number of public-key operations (i.e., group operations) involved in the computation of TDF.F. (The other operations involved in TDF.F are either private-key, i.e., PRF evaluations, or information theoretic; i.e., error correcting codes).[4] For TDF.F, in Line 2, one may compute the group elements $g_i = \mathbf{z} \cdot \mathbf{w}_i'$ one at a time, by using m group multiplications for each of them, hence $O(m^2)$ group multiplications in total. We observe that the computations of all g_i's together may be thought of as multiplying a Toeplitz matrix $g^{\mathbf{M}} \in \mathbb{G}^{m \times m}$, given in the exponent, with a given vector $\mathbf{z}^T$ of bits. It is known that one can compute $\mathbf{M} \times \mathbf{z}^T \pmod{p}$ in $O(m \log m)$ time using (inverse) discrete Fourier transform (IDFT/DFT) modulo p. In Sect. 4 we show how to carry out this computation in the exponent, at the cost of $O(m \log m)$ group exponentiations.

Comparison with the Trivial Approach. As mentioned above, the trivial computation takes $O(m^2)$ group multiplications. Our FFT-based approach takes $O(m \log m)$ group exponentiations, which translate into $O(m\lambda \log m)$ multiplications, assuming $|\mathbb{G}| = 2^\lambda$. Thus, we obtain improvements when $\lambda \log m \in \omega(m)$. We also note that the reason that the trivial approach takes $O(m \log m)$ multiplications (as opposed to exponentiations) is that we multiply with a bit vector, translating into multiplications. In applications where the entries of the given vector are integers modulo p, the trivial approach will take $O(m^2)$ exponentiations, while our FFT-based approach still takes $O(m \log m)$ exponentiations. This observation may be useful in future work.

---

[4] We only focus on TDF.F, because TDF.F^{-1} may be done using n group exponentiations, which seems hard to improve.

4   Fast Fourier Transform in the Exponent

In this section we show how to perform FFT in the exponent in order to have a fast algorithm for multiplying a circulant or a Toeplitz matrix, given in the exponent, with a vector of integers, with the result being computed in the exponent. We begin with some basic background.

For a vector $\mathbf{u}$ of integers and a group element g we use $g^{\mathbf{u}}$ to mean element-wise exponentiation.

Lemma 8 (Primitive nth root of unity mod p). *We say $w \in \mathbb{Z}_p$ is a primitive nth root of unity mod p if $w^n \equiv 1 \pmod{p}$ and for all $i \in [n-1]$, $w^i \not\equiv 1 \pmod{p}$. If p is prime, then $\mathbb{Z}_p$ has a primitive nth root of unity if and only if $p \equiv 1 \pmod{n}$.*

(Inverse) Discrete Fourier Modulo $\mathbb{Z}_p$. Let $w \in \mathbb{Z}_p$ be a primitive nth root of unity modulo p (Lemma 8). The discrete fourier transform (DFT) of $(y_0, \ldots, y_{n-1}) \in \mathbb{Z}_p^n$, denoted $\mathsf{DFT}(y_0, \ldots, y_{n-1})$, is $(d_0, \ldots, d_{n-1}) \in \mathbb{Z}_p^n$, where for $k \in \{0\} \cup [n-1]$:

$$d_k = \sum_{j=0}^{n-1} y_j w^{-jk} \pmod{p}. \tag{16}$$

The inverse discrete Fourier transform (IDFT) inverts the above process. For $(d_0, \ldots, d_{n-1}) \in \mathbb{Z}_p^n$, $\mathsf{IDFT}(d_0, \ldots, d_{n-1})$ is defined to be $(y_0, \ldots, y_{n-1})$, where for $k \in \{0\} \cup [n-1]$

$$y_k = n^{-1} \sum_{j=0}^{n-1} d_j w^{jk} \pmod{p}. \tag{17}$$

For all $(y_0, \ldots, y_{n-1}) \in \mathbb{Z}_p^n$, $\mathsf{IDFT}(\mathsf{DFT}(y_0, \ldots, y_{n-1})) = (y_0, \ldots, y_{n-1})$.

A major step in performing fast circulant matrix multiplication involves computing DFT and IDFT in a fast way.

Computing (I)DFT in the Exponent. For $\mathbf{y} := (y_0, \ldots, y_{n-1}) \in \mathbb{Z}_p^n$, we would like to compute $\mathsf{DFT}(\mathbf{y})$ in the exponent; i.e., to compute $g^{\mathsf{DFT}(\mathbf{Y})}$ from $g^{\mathbf{y}}$. Since $\mathsf{DFT}(\mathbf{y})$ is a linear function in the entries of $\mathbf{y}$ and w is a fixed integer, we may compute each component of $\mathsf{DFT}(\mathbf{y})$ using n exponentiations, resulting in a total of $O(n^2)$ exponentiations. There is, however, a faster, recursive way of doing this using $O(n \log n)$ exponentiations.

Let $f = w^{-1}$, and note that f is also a primitive nth root of unity. Computing $\mathsf{DFT}(\mathbf{y})$ amounts to evaluating a degree $n-1$ polynomial $p(x) = \sum_{j=0}^{n-1} y_j x^j$ at $(p(1), p(f), \ldots, p(f^{n-1}))$. We may now evaluate these n invocations in time $O(n \log n)$ using divide-and-conquer. Specifically, letting $n = 2t$, we can find two degree $t - 1 = n/2 - 1$ polynomials p_{even} and p_{odd} such that

(a) $p(f^{2k}) = p_{\mathsf{even}}(f^{2k})$ for $k \in \{0\} \cup [t-1]$; and
(b) $p(f^{2k+1}) = p_{\mathsf{odd}}(f^{2k})$ for $k \in \{0\} \cup [t-1]$.

Now since f^2 is a primitive t'th root of unity and since the degree of each of p_{even} and p_{odd} is $t - 1$, we can recursively continue this process. We now explain how to find p_{even} and p_{odd}.

Specifically, $p_{\text{even}}(x) := \sum_{j=0}^{t-1} \alpha_j x^j$ and $p_{\text{odd}}(x) := \sum_{j=0}^{t-1} \beta_j x^j$, where

$$\alpha_j := y_j + y_{j+t} \qquad\qquad \beta_j := (y_j - y_{j+t})f^j. \tag{18}$$

We now show why p_{even} and p_{odd} satisfy Items (a) and (b) above.

$$p(f^{2k}) = \sum_{j=0}^{t-1} y_j f^{2kj} + \sum_{j=t}^{n-1} y_j f^{2kj} = \sum_{j=0}^{t-1}(y_j f^{2kj} + y_{j+t}f^{2k(j+t)}) = \sum_{j=0}^{t-1}(y_j f^{2kj} + y_{j+t}f^{2kj}f^{kn})$$

$$= \sum_{j=0}^{t-1}(y_j + y_{j+t})f^{2kj} = p_{\text{even}}(f^{2k}). \tag{19}$$

$$p(f^{2k+1}) = \sum_{j=0}^{t-1}(y_j f^{(2k+1)j} + y_{j+t}f^{(2k+1)(j+t)}) = \sum_{j=0}^{t-1}(y_j f^j)f^{2kj} + (y_{j+t}f^j)f^{2kj}f^{kn+t}$$

$$=^* \sum_{j=0}^{t-1}(y_j f^j)f^{2kj} + (y_{j+t}f^j)f^{2kj}(-1) = \sum_{j=0}^{t-1}(y_j - y_{j+t})f^{(2k+1)j} = p_{\text{odd}}(f^{2k}), \tag{20}$$

where the equation marked with * follows from the fact that $f^t = f^{n/2} = -1$. Finally, notice that given $\mathbf{y} := (y_0, \ldots, y_{n-1})$ in the exponent (i.e., given $g^{\mathbf{y}}$), the coefficients of p_{even} and p_{odd} (Eq. 18) can also be computed in the exponent. Thus, we have the following lemma.

Lemma 9 (DFT/IDFT in the exponent). *Let n be a power of two, let p be a prime number satisfying $p \equiv 1 \pmod{n}$ and let $\mathbb{G}$ be group of order p with a generator g. Let $w \in \mathbb{Z}_p$ be a primitive nth root of unity modulo p (which exists by Lemma 8). For any $\mathbf{y} \in \mathbb{Z}_p^n$ we may compute $g^{\text{DFT}(\mathbf{y})}$ from $g^{\mathbf{y}}$ using $O(n \log n)$ group exponentiations. The same holds for computing $g^{\text{IDFT}(\mathbf{y})}$.*

Circulant Matrices. Let $\mathbf{v} = (v_0, \ldots, v_{n-1})$ be a vector of dimension n. The circulant matrix of $\mathbf{v}$, denoted $\text{Rot}(\mathbf{v})$, is

$$\text{Rot}(\mathbf{v}) := \begin{pmatrix} v_0 & v_{n-1} & v_{n-2} & \cdots & v_3 & v_2 & v_1 \\ v_1 & v_0 & v_{n-1} & \cdots & v_4 & v_3 & v_2 \\ v_2 & v_1 & v_0 & \cdots & v_5 & v_4 & v_3 \\ \vdots & \vdots & \vdots & \cdots & \vdots & \vdots & \vdots \\ v_{n-1} & v_{n-2} & v_{n-3} & \cdots & v_0 & v_{n-1} & v_{n-2} \\ v_{n-2} & v_{n-3} & v_{n-4} & \cdots & v_1 & v_0 & v_{n-1} \\ v_{n-1} & v_{n-2} & v_{n-3} & \cdots & v_2 & v_1 & v_0 \end{pmatrix} \tag{21}$$

Lemma 10 (Circulant matrix multiplication in the exponent). *Let n, p, $\mathbb{G}$ and w be as in Lemma 9. Let $\mathbf{u} := (u_0, \ldots, u_{n-1}) \in \mathbb{Z}_p^n$ and $\mathbf{v} := (v_0, \ldots, v_{n-1}) \in \mathbb{Z}_p^n$ and $\mathbf{M} := \text{Rot}(\mathbf{v})$. Then we can compute $g^{\mathbf{M}\mathbf{u}^{\mathsf{T}}}$ from $g^{\mathbf{v}}$ and $\mathbf{u}$ via $O(n \log n)$ group exponentiations.*

Proof. Throughout the proof, we may use negative indices, with the understanding the index is taken modulo n. For example, we may write u_{-1} for u_{n-1}. Given $g^{\mathbf{v}}$ and $\mathbf{u}$, for $k \in \{0\} \cup [n-1]$ we need to compute g^{h_k}, where

$$h_k = \sum_{i=0}^{n-1} v_j u_{k-j}. \tag{22}$$

Let $(a_0, \ldots, a_{n-1})$ and $(b_0, \ldots, b_{n-1})$ be the discrete fourier transform of the two sequences $(v_0, \ldots, v_{k-1})$ and $(u_0, \ldots, u_{k-1})$, respectively. That is, for $k \in \{0, \ldots, n-1\}$

$$a_k = \sum_{j=0}^{n-1} v_j w^{-jk} \pmod{p} \qquad b_k = \sum_{j=0}^{n-1} u_j w^{-jk} \pmod{p}.$$

It is well-known that the inverse fourier transform of $(a_0 b_0, \ldots, a_{n-1} b_{n-1})$ gives us the values $(h_0, \ldots, h_{n-1})$. That is, for $k \in \{0\} \cup [n-1]$

$$(h_0, \ldots, h_{n-1}) = \mathsf{IDFT}(a_0 b_0, \ldots, a_{n-1} b_{n-1}). \tag{23}$$

By Lemma 9 we can perform all the above steps via $O(n \log n)$ exponentiations. □

Fast Toeplitz Matrix Multiplication. We now show how to perform fast Topelitz matrix multiplication in the exponent, via a well-known conversion to circulant matrices. See [BDD+00] for further conversions. For $\mathbf{x} := (x_1, \ldots, x_{2n-1}) \in \mathbb{Z}_p^{2n-1}$ we define

$$\mathsf{Toep}(\mathbf{x}) := \begin{pmatrix} x_n & x_{n-1} & \cdots & x_1 \\ x_{n+1} & x_n & \cdots & x_2 \\ \vdots & \vdots & \cdots & \vdots \\ x_{2n-1} & x_{2n-2} & \cdots & x_n \end{pmatrix}. \tag{24}$$

Let $\mathbf{M} := \mathsf{Toep}(\mathbf{x})$ and $\mathbf{y} \in \mathbb{Z}_p^n$. We show how to compute $g^{\mathbf{My}}$ from $g^{\mathbf{M}}$ and $\mathbf{y}$. Toward this, define

$$\mathbf{S} := \begin{pmatrix} 0 & x_1 & x_2 & \cdots & x_{n-1} \\ x_{2n-1} & 0 & x_1 & \cdots & x_{n-2} \\ x_{2n-2} & x_{2n-1} & 0 & \cdots & x_{n-3} \\ \vdots & \vdots & & \cdots & \vdots \\ x_{n+1} & x_{n+2} & x_{n+3} & \cdots & 0 \end{pmatrix} \in \mathbb{Z}_p^{n \times n}. \tag{25}$$

Let $\mathbf{T} := \begin{pmatrix} \mathbf{M} & \mathbf{S} \\ \mathbf{S} & \mathbf{M} \end{pmatrix} \in \mathbb{Z}_p^{2n \times 2n}$. Note that $\mathbf{T}$ is a circulant matrix. We have

$\mathbf{M} \begin{pmatrix} \mathbf{y} \\ \mathbf{0}_{n \times 1} \end{pmatrix} = \begin{pmatrix} \mathbf{Ty} \\ \mathbf{Sy} \end{pmatrix}$. Thus, we may compute $\mathbf{My}$ in the exponent via $O(n \log n)$ group exponentiations. Thus, we have the following lemma.

Lemma 11 (Toeplitz matrix multiplication in the exponent). *Let n, p, $\mathbb{G}$ and w be as in Lemma 9. Let $\mathbf{u} := (u_0, \dots, u_{n-1}) \in \mathbb{Z}_p^n$ and $\mathbf{v} := (v_0, \dots, v_{n-1}) \in \mathbb{Z}_p^n$ and $\mathbf{M} := \mathsf{Toep}(\mathbf{v})$. Then we can compute $g^{\mathbf{M}\mathbf{u}^\top}$ from $g^{\mathbf{M}}$ and $\mathbf{u}$ using $O(n \log n)$ group exponentiations.*

5   Range-Trapdoor Hash Functions

In this section we define the notion of range-trapdoor hash functions and give a construction of this notion with short evaluation keys. This notion generalizes the notion of trapdoor hash functions for index keys [DGI+19]. We say that an index set I is a *range set* if $I = \{s+1, \dots, s+t\}$ for some integers s and t. We now give the definition of range-trapdoor hash for the special case where we output a single-bit hint for every index in the range set.

Definition 5 (Range Trapdoor Hash). *An n-bit input, range-trapdoor hash is a tuple of PPT algorithms $\mathcal{H} = (\mathsf{S}, \mathsf{KG}, \mathsf{H}, \mathsf{E}, \mathsf{D})$ with the following syntax, correctness and security properties.*

- *$\mathsf{S}(1^\lambda, n)$: Takes the security parameter 1^λ and input length n, and outputs a hashing key hk and a trapdoor key thk.*
- *$\mathsf{KG}(\mathsf{hk}, I)$: Takes hk and a range of indices $I = [s+1, \dots, s+t] \subseteq [n]$ as input, and outputs an evaluation key ek and a trapdoor key tk. We assume ek contains $|I|$; i.e., $\mathsf{ek} := (|I|, \dots)$, and also assume $\mathsf{tk} := (I, \dots)$.*
- *$\mathsf{H}(\mathsf{hk}, \mathsf{x}; \rho)$: Takes hk, a message $\mathsf{x} \in \{0,1\}^n$ and randomness ρ as input, and outputs a hash value h.*
- *$\mathsf{E}(\mathsf{ek}, \mathsf{x}; \rho)$: Takes an evaluation key ek, message x and randomness ρ as input, and outputs a hint value $\mathsf{e} \in \{0,1\}^{|I|}$.*
- *$\mathsf{D}(\mathsf{thk}, \mathsf{tk}, \mathsf{h}, \mathsf{e})$: Takes as input a hash-trapdoor key thk, a trapdoor key $\mathsf{tk} := (I, \dots)$, a hash value h and a hint value e, and deterministically outputs $|I|$ pairs of $0/1$-encodings $(\mathsf{e}_{i,0}, \mathsf{e}_{i,1}) \in \{0,1\} \times \{0,1\}$, for $i \in [|I|]$.*

We require the following properties.

- **Correctness:** *For $0 \le \epsilon < 1$ we say $\mathcal{H}$ is $1 - \epsilon$ correct (or has ϵ decryption error) if for any n, any range set $I := [s+1, s+t] \subseteq [n]$, both the following conditions hold:*
  1. *For any $i \in [t]$ and for any input $\mathsf{x} \in \{0,1\}^n$, $\Pr[\mathsf{e}_i = \mathsf{e}_{i,\mathsf{x}[s+i]}] = 1$; and*
  2. *For any input $\mathsf{x} \in \{0,1\}^n$, any $i \in [t]$ and any $b_j \in \{0,1\}$ for $j \in [t] \setminus \{i\}$:*

$$\Pr[\mathsf{Fail}_i = 1 \mid \mathsf{Fail}_j = b_j \text{ for } j \in [t]/\{i\}] \le \epsilon + \mathsf{negl}(\lambda), \qquad (26)$$

  where for $i \in [t]$, Fail_i is an indicator variable, defined as $\mathsf{Fail}_i = 1$ if $\mathsf{e}_i = \mathsf{e}_{i,1-\mathsf{x}[s+i]}$,
  where $(\mathsf{hk}, \mathsf{thk}) \xleftarrow{\$} \mathsf{S}(1^\lambda, n)$, $(\mathsf{ek}, \mathsf{tk}) \xleftarrow{\$} \mathsf{KG}(\mathsf{hk}, I)$, $\rho \xleftarrow{\$} \{0,1\}^*$, $\mathsf{h} := \mathsf{H}(\mathsf{hk}, \mathsf{x}; \rho)$, $\mathsf{e} := \mathsf{E}(\mathsf{ek}, \mathsf{x}; \rho)$, $(\mathsf{e}_{i,0}, \mathsf{e}_{i,1})_{i \in [t]} := \mathsf{D}(\mathsf{thk}, \mathsf{tk}, \mathsf{h}, \mathsf{e})$.

- **Range privacy:** *For any n and any two range sets $I, I' \subseteq [n]$ satisfying $|I| = |I'|$, $(\mathsf{hk}, \mathsf{ek}), (\mathsf{hk}', \mathsf{ek}')$, where $(\mathsf{hk}, *) \xleftarrow{\$} \mathsf{S}(1^\lambda, n)$, $(\mathsf{ek}, *) \xleftarrow{\$} \mathsf{KG}(\mathsf{hk}, I)$ and $(\mathsf{ek}', *) \xleftarrow{\$} \mathsf{KG}(\mathsf{hk}, I')$.*
- **Input privacy:** *Fix polynomial $n := n(\lambda)$. For any two inputs $\mathsf{x}, \mathsf{x}' \in \{0,1\}^n$, $(\mathsf{hk}, \mathsf{h}), (\mathsf{hk}, \mathsf{h}')$, where $(\mathsf{hk}, *) \xleftarrow{\$} \mathsf{S}(1^\lambda, n)$, $\mathsf{h} \xleftarrow{\$} \mathsf{H}(\mathsf{hk}, \mathsf{x})$ and $\mathsf{h}' \xleftarrow{\$} \mathsf{H}(\mathsf{hk}, \mathsf{x}')$.*
- **Compactness:** *There exists a polynomial $\mathsf{poly}(\lambda)$ such that for all $n := n(\lambda)$, $|\mathsf{H}(\mathsf{hk}, \mathsf{x})| \leq \mathsf{poly}(\lambda)$, where $(\mathsf{hk}, *) \xleftarrow{\$} \mathsf{S}(1^\lambda, n)$ and $\mathsf{x} \in \{0,1\}^n$.*

We note the following remark.

Remark 3. *For decryption we also require a trapdoor key* thk *associated with* hk. *This will be required in our construction. In contrast, the notion of trapdoor hash as defined in* [DGI+19] *does not require a trapdoor for the hash function in order to perform decryption. Nonetheless, all applications stated in* [DGI+19] *still hold with respect to our definition.*

Implicit in the work of [DGI+19] is the following construction of range-trapdoor hash.

Lemma 12 (Theorem 4.3 of [DGI+19]). *Assuming DDH, there exists a range-trapdoor hash scheme where for inputs of length n, an evaluation key for a range set I consists of $O(n|I|)$ group elements.*

We give the following corollary, which helps one in bounding the number of Fail_i's in situations where, e.g., we need to do error correction, such as the rate-1 OT application. We say $\epsilon > \mathsf{negl}(\lambda)$ if ϵ is not a negligible function.

Lemma 13. *Assuming a trapdoor hash scheme $\mathcal{H} = (\mathsf{S}, \mathsf{KG}, \mathsf{H}, \mathsf{E}, \mathsf{D})$ has decryption error ϵ, and that $\epsilon > \mathsf{negl}(\lambda)$, then for any constant $c > 1$:*

$$\Pr[\mathsf{Fail} > 2c\epsilon|I|] < e^{-c\epsilon|I|/3},$$

where $\mathsf{Fail} := \sum_{i=1}^{|I|} \mathsf{Fail}_i$ and Fail_i is defined in the correctness condition of Definition 5.

Proof. The proof follows immediately from the bounded-dependence version of the Chernoff bound (Lemma 3). □

We now show how to adapt our batching technique from Sect. 3 to obtain range-trapdoor hash schemes, where the evaluation key consists of $O(n)$ group elements, as opposed to $O(n|I|)$ group elements given by [DGI+19]. As we will see in Sect. 6, this size reduction results in a shorter receiver's message in rate-1 OT protocols and shorter ciphertexts in homomorphic encryption for branching programs.

5.1   Range-Trapdoor Hash with Linear-Sized Evaluation Keys

Construction 4. *Let $\epsilon \in [0, 1)$ be the decryption error we are wiling to tolerate. Let $\ell := \log(2/\epsilon)$, G be a group scheme and $\mathsf{PRF} : \mathbb{G} \to \{0,1\}^\ell$ a PRF with key space $\{0,1\}^\lambda$.*

- *$\mathsf{S}(1^\lambda, n)$: and $(\mathbb{G}, p, g) \overset{\$}{\leftarrow} \mathsf{G}(1^\lambda)$. Sample $\alpha \overset{\$}{\leftarrow} \mathbb{Z}_p$, set $\mathsf{thk} := \alpha$ and $\mathsf{hk} := (\mathbb{G}, p, g, \mathbf{v})$, where $\mathbf{v} := (g^\alpha, g^{\alpha^2}, \ldots, g^{\alpha^{2n}})$. Return $(\mathsf{hk}, \mathsf{thk})$.*
- *$\mathsf{KG}(\mathsf{hk}, I)$: Sample a key $K \overset{\$}{\leftarrow} \{0,1\}^\lambda$ for PRF. Let $I = [s+1, s+t]$. Parse $\mathsf{hk} := (\mathbb{G}, p, g, \mathbf{v})$, where $\mathbf{v} := (g_1, \ldots, g_{2n})$. Sample $r \overset{\$}{\leftarrow} \mathbb{Z}_p$ and let*

$$\mathbf{w} := (g_1^r, g_2^r, \ldots, g_{s+t-1}^r, gg_{s+t}^r, g_{s+t+1}^r, \ldots, g_{2n}^r).$$

  Set $\mathsf{ek} := (t, \mathbf{w}, K)$ and $\mathsf{tk} := (I, r, K)$.
- *$\mathsf{H}(\mathsf{hk}, \mathsf{x}; \rho)$: Parse $\mathsf{hk} := (\mathbb{G}, p, g, \mathbf{v})$, where $\mathbf{v} := (g_1, \ldots, g_{2n})$. Let $\mathbf{v}' := (g_1, \ldots, g_n)$, and return $(\mathsf{x} \cdot \mathbf{v}')g_1^\rho$.*
- *$\mathsf{E}(\mathsf{ek}, \mathsf{x}; \rho)$: Parse $\mathsf{ek} := (t, \mathbf{w}, K)$, where $t \in \mathbb{N}$ and $\mathbf{w} \in \mathbb{G}^{2n}$. Parse $\mathbf{w} := (w_1, \ldots, w_{2n})$. For $i \in [t]$:*
   1. *let $\mathbf{w}'_i = (w_{1+t-i}, \ldots, w_{n+t-i}) \in \mathbb{G}^n$;*
   2. *let $g'_i := (\mathsf{x} \cdot \mathbf{w}'_i)w_{1+t-i}^\rho$;*
   3. *let $b_i := \mathsf{Dist}_{\mathbb{G}, g}(g'_i, \epsilon, 1, \mathsf{PRF}_K)$.*

   Return $(b_t, \ldots, b_1)$.
- *$\mathsf{D}(\mathsf{thk}, \mathsf{tk}, \mathsf{h}, \mathsf{e})$: Parse $\mathsf{thk} := \alpha$, $\mathsf{tk} := (I, r, K)$ and $I := [s+1, s+t]$. For $i \in [t]$, set $\mathsf{e}_{i,0} := \mathsf{Dist}_{\mathbb{G}, g}(\mathsf{h}^{r\alpha^{t-i}}, \epsilon, 1, \mathsf{PRF}_K)$ and $\mathsf{e}_{i,1} := \mathsf{Dist}_{\mathbb{G}, g}(g\mathsf{h}^{r\alpha^{t-i}}, \epsilon, 1, \mathsf{PRF}_K)$. Return $((\mathsf{e}_{1,0}, \mathsf{e}_{1,1}), \ldots, (\mathsf{e}_{t,0}, \mathsf{e}_{t,1}))$.*

The compactness of the scheme is clear. Range privacy follows from $2n$-power DDH. We now prove the input privacy and correctness of the scheme.

Lemma 14 (Input privacy). *The scheme provides perfect input privacy: for any two inputs $\mathsf{x}, \mathsf{x}' \in \{0,1\}^n$, $(\mathsf{hk}, \mathsf{h}) \equiv (\mathsf{hk}, \mathsf{h}')$, where $(\mathsf{hk}, *) \overset{\$}{\leftarrow} \mathsf{S}(1^\lambda, n)$, $\mathsf{h} \overset{\$}{\leftarrow} \mathsf{H}(\mathsf{hk}, \mathsf{x})$ and $\mathsf{h}' \overset{\$}{\leftarrow} \mathsf{H}(\mathsf{hk}, \mathsf{x})$.*

Proof. We need to show $(\mathbf{v}, (\mathsf{x} \cdot \mathbf{v})g^{\alpha\rho})$ is independent of x, where $\mathbf{v} := (g^\alpha, g^{\alpha^2}, \ldots, g^{\alpha^{2n}})$ and $\rho \overset{\$}{\leftarrow} \mathbb{Z}_p$. This immediately follows from the presence of the masking exponent ρ. $\square$

Lemma 15 (Correctness). *Assuming $T := [2\log_e(2/\epsilon)]/\epsilon = \mathsf{poly}(\lambda)$ (which is satisfied if ϵ is an inverse polynomial), the range TDH scheme provides $(1-\epsilon)$ correctness.*

Proof. Fix n, I, $\mathsf{x} \in \{0,1\}^n$ and suppose $I = [s+1, s+t]$. We need to prove Conditions 1 and 2 of the correctness definition. For $i \in [t]$ let g'_i be computed as in E (Line 2 of E's procedure) and let $g_{i,0} = \mathsf{h}^{r\alpha^{t-i}}$ and $g_{i,1} = g\mathsf{h}^{r\alpha^{t-i}}$.

First, we claim $g'_i = g_{i,x[s+i]}$, which proves Condition 1 of the correctness definition. To see why this claim holds, recall that

$$\mathbf{v}' = (g^\alpha, g^{\alpha^2}, \dots, g^{\alpha^n})$$

$$w_{1+t-i} = g^{r\alpha^{1+t-i}}$$

$$\mathbf{w}'_i = (g^{r\alpha^{1+t-i}}, \dots, g^{r\alpha^{s+t-1}}, \underbrace{gg^{r\alpha^{s+t}}}_{coordinate:s+i}, g^{r\alpha^{s+t+1}}, \dots, g^{r\alpha^{n+t-i}}),$$

and that $\mathsf{h} = (\mathsf{x} \cdot \mathbf{v}')g^{\alpha\rho}$, $g'_i := (\mathsf{x} \cdot \mathbf{w}'_i)w^\rho_{1+t-i}$. Letting $b = \mathsf{x}[s+i]$:

$$g_{i,x[s+i]} = g^b \mathsf{h}^{r\alpha^{t-i}} = g^b((\mathsf{x} \cdot \mathbf{v}')g^{\alpha\rho})^{r\alpha^{t-i}} = g^b(\mathsf{x} \cdot \mathbf{v}')^{r\alpha^{t-i}}(g^{r\alpha^{t-i+1}})^\rho$$

$$= g^b(\mathsf{x} \cdot \mathbf{v}')^{r\alpha^{t-i}}w^\rho_{1+t-i} = (\mathsf{x} \cdot \mathbf{w}'_i)w^\rho_{1+t-i} = g'_i, \qquad (27)$$

as desired.

We now prove Condition 2 of the correctness definition. Fix $\mathsf{x} \in \{0,1\}^n$, $i \in [t]$ and $b_j \in \{0,1\}$ for $j \in [t] \setminus \{i\}$, and let

$$\beta := \Pr[\mathsf{Fail}_i = 1 \mid \mathsf{Fail}_j = b_j \text{ for } j \in [t]/\{i\}]. \qquad (28)$$

Consider a variant of Construction 4, in which we replace the PRF PRF_K with a truly random function $f : \mathbb{G} \xleftarrow{\$} \{0,1\}^\ell$. That is, in this variant, calls of the form $\mathsf{Dist}_{\mathbb{G},g}(g_i, \epsilon, 1, K)$ are replaced with $\mathsf{Dist}_{\mathbb{G},g}(g_i, \epsilon, 1, f)$. Let β' be the probability that

$$\Pr[\mathsf{Fail}_i = 1 \mid \mathsf{Fail}_j = b_j \text{ for } j \in [t]/\{i\}] \qquad (29)$$

in the experiment where we replace PRF_K with a random f. We will show $\beta' \le \epsilon + \mathsf{negl}(\lambda)$. By PRF security we have $\beta \le \beta' + \mathsf{negl}(\lambda)$, and thus Eq. 28 will follow. The reason that we can use PRF security here (despite the fact that K is given in the clear in ik) is that the procedure Dist may efficiently be computed via only blackbox access to PRF_K (resp., f alternatively) and that we evaluate PRF_K on inputs generated independently of K.

To bound the probability in Eq. 29 we first define an event Bad which captures all the dependencies. Then we will argue that conditioned on $\overline{\mathsf{Bad}}$, the events $\{\mathsf{Fail}_j\}_{j \in [t]}$ are independent. To give some intuition, first notice that Fail_j holds iff

$$\mathsf{Dist}_{\mathbb{G},g}(g_{j,0}, \epsilon, 1, f) = \mathsf{Dist}_{\mathbb{G},g}(g_{j,0}g, \epsilon, 1, f), \qquad (30)$$

where recall that $g_{j,0} = \mathsf{h}^{r\alpha^{t-j}}$. Also, by definition of Dist, the outputs of the two distance functions of Eq. 30 are only dependent on the outputs of f on group elements $\{g_{j,0}, g_{j,0}g, \dots, g_{j,0}g^{T+1}\}$, where $T := \lceil 2\log_e(2/\epsilon)\rceil/\epsilon$. Since f is chosen at random, we will have dependencies across Fail_j's only when the following event Bad holds:

- Bad: there are two distinct indices $j, h \in [t]$ such that $g_{j,0}$ and $g_{h,0}$ are $(T+1)$-close, where $T := \lceil 2\log_e(2/\epsilon)\rceil/\epsilon$.

By Lemma 4

$$\Pr[\mathsf{Fail}_i = 1 \mid \overline{\mathsf{Bad}} \wedge \mathsf{Fail}_j = b_j \text{ for } j \in [t]/\{i\}] = \Pr[\mathsf{Fail}_i = 1] \leq \epsilon. \tag{31}$$

Below we will show $\Pr[\mathsf{Bad}] = \mathsf{negl}(\lambda)$, and this will allow us to conclude

$$\Pr[\mathsf{Fail}_i = 1 \mid \mathsf{Fail}_j = b_j \text{ for } j \in [t]/\{i\}] \leq \Pr[\mathsf{Bad}] + \Pr[\mathsf{Fail}_i = 1 \wedge \overline{\mathsf{Bad}} \mid \mathsf{Fail}_j = b_j \text{ for } j \in [t]/\{i\}]$$
$$\leq \mathsf{negl}(\lambda) + \Pr[\mathsf{Fail}_i = 1 \mid \overline{\mathsf{Bad}} \wedge \mathsf{Fail}_j = b_j \text{ for } j \in [t]/\{i\}] = \epsilon + \mathsf{negl}(\lambda), \tag{32}$$

as desired. It only remains to show $\Pr[\mathsf{Bad}] = \mathsf{negl}(\lambda)$. Recall that $(g_{1,0}, g_{2,0}, \ldots, g_{t,0}) = (\mathsf{h}^r, \mathsf{h}^{r\alpha} \ldots, \mathsf{h}^{r\alpha^{t-1}})$. Notice that $\mathsf{h} \neq 1$ except with negligible probability, and thus h^r is statistically close to a uniformly random group element. By Lemma 1

$$(g_{1,0}, g_{2,0}, \ldots, g_{t,0}) = (\mathsf{h}^{r\alpha^{t-1}}, \mathsf{h}^{r\alpha^{t-2}}, \ldots, \mathsf{h}^r), (g_1', g_2', \ldots, g_t'),$$

where g_i''s are random group elements. When replacing $\{g_{i,0}\}_{i \in [t]}$ with $\{g_i'\}_{i \in [t]}$, the probability of the event Bad becomes negligible. (This is because $T = \mathsf{poly}(\lambda)$.) Thus, the event Bad with $g_{j,0}$'s should also be negligible.   □

Running Time: We specify the running time for tolerated error $\epsilon = \frac{1}{n^c}$. For E, we can compute all the values $\mathsf{x} \cdot \mathbf{w}'_i$ altogether with total $O(n \log |I|)$ exponentiations by Lemma 11. Also, we spend $|I|$ exponentiations for computing w_i^ρ for $i \in [I]$. Thus, the total number of group operations is $O(n \log |I|)$ exponentiations.

6   Applications of Range-Trapdoor Hash

In this section we review the applications of our range-trapdoor hash scheme.

A two-round OT protocol consists of three PPT algorithms $(\mathsf{OT}_1, \mathsf{OT}_2, \mathsf{OT}_3)$, where $(\mathsf{OT}_1, \mathsf{OT}_3)$ are the two-stage algorithms run by the receiver, and OT_2 is run by the sender. We will be concerned with honest-but-curious security (for both parties), and the corresponding definitions of security are standard. We use otr and ots to denote the receiver's and sender's message, respectively.

For an OT protocol OT where the size of each message of the sender is n, we call $\frac{|n|}{|\mathsf{ots}|}$ the *download rate* of the protocol. We say OT is *rate-1* if $\frac{|n|}{|\mathsf{ots}|}$ asymptotically approaches one.

As shown in [IP07], a rate-1 OT implies homomorphic encryption for branching programs with *semi-compactness*: the size of ciphertexts only grows with the depth of the program, as opposed to the size.

Let us first present the implication of our results with respect to rate-1 OTs. Implicit in the work of [DGI+19] is a construction of rate-1 OT from range trapdoor-hash schemes; see Constructions 5.1 and 5.2 of [DGI+19]. This result of [DGI+19], combined with Lemma 4, gives us the following.

Corollary 1 (Rate-1 OT with short receiver's message). *Let* G *be a group scheme, where the size of a group element is* $O(\lambda)$. *Fix a message-size function* $t(\lambda) \in \omega(\lambda)$. *Assuming 2t-power DDH, there is a rate-1 two-round honest-but-curios OT protocol with sender's input* $(\mathsf{m}_0, \mathsf{m}_1) \in (\{0,1\}^t, \{0,1\}^t)$ *and receiver's input* $b \in \{0,1\}$, *where the receiver's message* otr *consists of* $O(t)$ *group elements.*

Comparison to [DGI+19]. The work of [DGI+19] gives a DDH-based rate-1 OT, where in the parameter regime of Lemma 1, otr consists of $O(t^2)$ group elements. Our efficiency improvement stems from shorter evaluation keys: for a range set I, our scheme's evaluation key contains $O(n)$ group elements, as opposed to $O(n|I|)$ group elements given by [DGI+19]. See Lemma 12.

Improving Upload Rate. As noted in [DGI+19], asymptotically speaking, one may make the length of |otr| as close as possible to $|m_0|$ (i.e., achieving *upload rate* 1, defined as $|m_0|/|otr|$) by re-using otr and making the input size of the sender larger. For example, assuming $|m_0| = |m_1| = O(\lambda^2)$, one may give a two-round OT based on DDH with both download and upload rates being 1. However, in concrete applications (e.g., homomorphic encryption for branching programs), the OT ends up being applied on sender's messages of much smaller asymptotic size, and thus improving the efficiency for this smaller regime leads to efficiency improvements in those applications.

Homomorphic Encryption for Branching Programs with Shorter Ciphertexts. Ishai and Paskin [IP07] show how to build semi-compact homomorphic encryption for bounded-depth branching programs from rate-1 OT. Semi-compact means that the size of a ciphertexts grows only with the depth and the input size, and is independent of the program size otherwise. For the OT protocol, let $\text{size}_r(\lambda, n)$ denote the size of otr when the length of each of sender's message is n. Assuming the input size is n and the depth of the branching program is at most d, the size of a ciphertext is $nd \times \text{size}_r(\lambda, t)$, where $t \in O(\lambda d)$. The result of [DGI+19] gives a DDH-based semi-compact encryption for branching programs with ciphertexts consisting of $O(\lambda^2 n d^3)$ group elements. Applying Corollary 1, our ciphertexts will contain $O(\lambda n d^2)$ group elements.

Corollary 2. *Assuming t-power DDH, there exists a PKE scheme for branching programs of depth d and input size n, where a ciphertext consists of $O(\lambda n d)$ group elements.*

Private Information Retrieval (PIR) with Improved Communication. A PIR protocol involves a server, holding $N = 2^d$ blocks $(m_1, \ldots, m_N)$, each of length β, and a client, holding an index $i \in [N]$. The goal is to allow the client to retrieve m_i while keeping i hidden from the server. We would like to achieve this while minimizing communication complexity. Ishai and Paskin [IP07] gives a two-round block single-server PIR (one message from each side), achieving download rate 1, from rate-1 OT. The download rate of a PIR is defined as the ratio between the server's message and β. The size of the client's message is $O(\text{size}_r(\lambda, \beta) \log N)$, where $\beta \in O(\lambda \log N)$, and recall that size_r denotes the size parameter of the receiver's message in the underlying OT protocol. Thus, under DDH, the rate-1 OT of [DGI+19] gives rise to a PIR, where the client's message consists of $O(\lambda^2 \text{polylog}(N))$ group elements. Using Corollary 1 and under the power DDH assumption, the client's message will have $O(\lambda \text{polylog}(N))$ group elements.

References

[AHI11]   Applebaum, B., Harnik, D., Ishai, Y.: Semantic security under related-key attacks and applications. In: ICS 2011, pp. 45–60, Tsinghua University Press, Beijing, China, 7–9 January 2011

[BB04]   Boneh, D., Boyen, X.: Efficient selective-ID secure identity-based encryption without random oracles. In: Cachin, C., Camenisch, J.L. (eds.) EURO-CRYPT 2004. LNCS, vol. 3027, pp. 223–238. Springer, Heidelberg (2004). https://doi.org/10.1007/978-3-540-24676-3_14

[BDD+00] Bai, Z., Demmel, J., Dongarra, J., Ruhe, A., van der Vorst, H.: Templates for the Solution of Algebraic Eigenvalue Problems: A Practical Guide. SIAM (2000)

[BFOR08] Bellare, M., Fischlin, M., O'Neill, A., Ristenpart, T.: Deterministic encryption: definitional equivalences and constructions without random oracles. In: Wagner, D. (ed.) CRYPTO 2008. LNCS, vol. 5157, pp. 360–378. Springer, Heidelberg (2008). https://doi.org/10.1007/978-3-540-85174-5_20

[BGI16]   Boyle, E., Gilboa, N., Ishai, Y.: Breaking the circuit size barrier for secure computation under DDH. In: Robshaw, M., Katz, J. (eds.) CRYPTO 2016, Part I. LNCS, vol. 9814, pp. 509–539. Springer, Heidelberg (2016). https://doi.org/10.1007/978-3-662-53018-4_19

[BHY09]   Bellare, M., Hofheinz, D., Yilek, S.: Possibility and impossibility results for encryption and commitment secure under selective opening. In: Joux, A. (ed.) EUROCRYPT 2009. LNCS, vol. 5479, pp. 1–35. Springer, Heidelberg (2009). https://doi.org/10.1007/978-3-642-01001-9_1

[BKM20]   Brakerski, Z., Koppula, V., Mour, T.: NIZK from LPN and trapdoor hash via correlation intractability for approximable relations. Cryptology ePrint Archive, Report 2020/258 (2020). https://eprint.iacr.org/2020/258

[BLSV18] Brakerski, Z., Lombardi, A., Segev, G., Vaikuntanathan, V.: Anonymous IBE, leakage resilience and circular security from new assumptions. In: Nielsen, J.B., Rijmen, V. (eds.) EUROCRYPT 2018, Part I. LNCS, vol. 10820, pp. 535–564. Springer, Cham (2018). https://doi.org/10.1007/978-3-319-78381-9_20

[BMZ19]   Bartusek, J., Ma, F., Zhandry, M.: The distinction between fixed and random generators in group-based assumptions. In: Boldyreva, A., Micciancio, D. (eds.) CRYPTO 2019, Part II. LNCS, vol. 11693, pp. 801–830. Springer, Cham (2019). https://doi.org/10.1007/978-3-030-26951-7_27

[BW10]   Boyen, X., Waters, B.: Shrinking the keys of discrete-log-type lossy trapdoor functions. In: Zhou, J., Yung, M. (eds.) ACNS 2010. LNCS, vol. 6123, pp. 35–52. Springer, Heidelberg (2010). https://doi.org/10.1007/978-3-642-13708-2_3

[CDD+16] Cascudo, I., Damgård, I., David, B., Döttling, N., Nielsen, J.B.: Rate-1, linear time and additively homomorphic UC commitments. In: Robshaw, M., Katz, J. (eds.) CRYPTO 2016, Part III. LNCS, vol. 9816, pp. 179–207. Springer, Heidelberg (2016). https://doi.org/10.1007/978-3-662-53015-3_7

[Cha04]   Chang, Y.-C.: Single database private information retrieval with logarithmic communication. In: Wang, H., Pieprzyk, J., Varadharajan, V. (eds.) ACISP 2004. LNCS, vol. 3108, pp. 50–61. Springer, Heidelberg (2004). https://doi.org/10.1007/978-3-540-27800-9_5

[CMS99] Cachin, C., Micali, S., Stadler, M.: Computationally private information retrieval with polylogarithmic communication. In: Stern, J. (ed.) EURO-CRYPT 1999. LNCS, vol. 1592, pp. 402–414. Springer, Heidelberg (1999). https://doi.org/10.1007/3-540-48910-X_28

[CNs07] Camenisch, J., Neven, G., shelat, A.: Simulatable adaptive oblivious transfer. In: Naor, M. (ed.) EUROCRYPT 2007. LNCS, vol. 4515, pp. 573–590. Springer, Heidelberg (2007). https://doi.org/10.1007/978-3-540-72540-4_33

[DG17a] Döttling, N., Garg, S.: From selective IBE to full IBE and selective HIBE. In: Kalai, Y., Reyzin, L. (eds.) TCC 2017, Part I. LNCS, vol. 10677, pp. 372–408. Springer, Cham (2017). https://doi.org/10.1007/978-3-319-70500-2_13

[DG17b] Döttling, N., Garg, S.: Identity-based encryption from the Diffie-Hellman assumption. In: Katz, J., Shacham, H. (eds.) CRYPTO 2017, Part I. LNCS, vol. 10401, pp. 537–569. Springer, Cham (2017). https://doi.org/10.1007/978-3-319-63688-7_18

[DGH+19] Döttling, N., Garg, S., Hajiabadi, M., Liu, K., Malavolta, G.: Rate-1 trapdoor functions from the Diffie-Hellman problem. In: Galbraith, S.D., Moriai, S. (eds.) ASIACRYPT 2019, Part III. LNCS, vol. 11923, pp. 585–606. Springer, Cham (2019). https://doi.org/10.1007/978-3-030-34618-8_20

[DGHM18] Döttling, N., Garg, S., Hajiabadi, M., Masny, D.: New constructions of identity-based and key-dependent message secure encryption schemes. In: Abdalla, M., Dahab, R. (eds.) PKC 2018, Part I. LNCS, vol. 10769, pp. 3–31. Springer, Cham (2018). https://doi.org/10.1007/978-3-319-76578-5_1

[DGI+19] Döttling, N., Garg, S., Ishai, Y., Malavolta, G., Mour, T., Ostrovsky, R.: Trapdoor hash functions and their applications. In: Boldyreva, A., Micciancio, D. (eds.) CRYPTO 2019, Part III. LNCS, vol. 11694, pp. 3–32. Springer, Cham (2019). https://doi.org/10.1007/978-3-030-26954-8_1

[DY05] Dodis, Y., Yampolskiy, A.: A verifiable random function with short proofs and keys. In: Vaudenay, S. (ed.) PKC 2005. LNCS, vol. 3386, pp. 416–431. Springer, Heidelberg (2005). https://doi.org/10.1007/978-3-540-30580-4_28

[FGK+10] Freeman, D.M., Goldreich, O., Kiltz, E., Rosen, A., Segev, G.: More constructions of lossy and correlation-secure trapdoor functions. In: Nguyen, P.Q., Pointcheval, D. (eds.) PKC 2010. LNCS, vol. 6056, pp. 279–295. Springer, Heidelberg (2010). https://doi.org/10.1007/978-3-642-13013-7_17

[GGH19] Garg, S., Gay, R., Hajiabadi, M.: New techniques for efficient trapdoor functions and applications. In: Ishai, Y., Rijmen, V. (eds.) EUROCRYPT 2019, Part III. LNCS, vol. 11478, pp. 33–63. Springer, Cham (2019). https://doi.org/10.1007/978-3-030-17659-4_2

[GH18] Garg, S., Hajiabadi, M.: Trapdoor functions from the computational Diffie-Hellman assumption. In: Shacham, H., Boldyreva, A. (eds.) CRYPTO 2018, Part II. LNCS, vol. 10992, pp. 362–391. Springer, Cham (2018). https://doi.org/10.1007/978-3-319-96881-0_13

[GI05] Guruswami, V., Indyk, P.: Linear-time encodable/decodable codes with near-optimal rate. IEEE Trans. Inf. Theory 51(10), 3393–3400 (2005)

[GVW19] Goyal, R., Vusirikala, S., Waters, B.: New constructions of hinting PRGs, OWFs with encryption, and more. Cryptology ePrint Archive, Report 2019/962 (2019). https://eprint.iacr.org/2019/962

[IP07]   Ishai, Y., Paskin, A.: Evaluating branching programs on encrypted data. In: Vadhan, S.P. (ed.) TCC 2007. LNCS, vol. 4392, pp. 575–594. Springer, Heidelberg (2007). https://doi.org/10.1007/978-3-540-70936-7_31

[KMT19] Kitagawa, F., Matsuda, T., Tanaka, K.: CCA security and trapdoor functions via key-dependent-message security. In: Boldyreva, A., Micciancio, D. (eds.) CRYPTO 2019, Part III. LNCS, vol. 11694, pp. 33–64. Springer, Cham (2019). https://doi.org/10.1007/978-3-030-26954-8_2

[KW19]   Koppula, V., Waters, B.: Realizing chosen ciphertext security generically in attribute-based encryption and predicate encryption. In: Boldyreva, A., Micciancio, D. (eds.) CRYPTO 2019, Part II. LNCS, vol. 11693, pp. 671–700. Springer, Cham (2019). https://doi.org/10.1007/978-3-030-26951-7_23

[Lip05] Lipmaa, H.: An oblivious transfer protocol with log-squared communication. In: Zhou, J., Lopez, J., Deng, R.H., Bao, F. (eds.) ISC 2005. LNCS, vol. 3650, pp. 314–328. Springer, Heidelberg (2005). https://doi.org/10.1007/11556992_23

[LPR10] Lyubashevsky, V., Peikert, C., Regev, O.: On ideal lattices and learning with errors over rings. In: Gilbert, H. (ed.) EUROCRYPT 2010. LNCS, vol. 6110, pp. 1–23. Springer, Heidelberg (2010). https://doi.org/10.1007/978-3-642-13190-5_1

[LPR13] Lyubashevsky, V., Peikert, C., Regev, O.: A toolkit for ring-LWE cryptography. In: Johansson, T., Nguyen, P.Q. (eds.) EUROCRYPT 2013. LNCS, vol. 7881, pp. 35–54. Springer, Heidelberg (2013). https://doi.org/10.1007/978-3-642-38348-9_3

[LQR+19] Lombardi, A., Quach, W., Rothblum, R.D., Wichs, D., Wu, D.J.: New constructions of reusable designated-verifier NIZKs. In: Boldyreva, A., Micciancio, D. (eds.) CRYPTO 2019, Part III. LNCS, vol. 11694, pp. 670–700. Springer, Cham (2019). https://doi.org/10.1007/978-3-030-26954-8_22

[NR97]   Naor, M., Reingold, O.: Number-theoretic constructions of efficient pseudorandom functions. In: 38th FOCS, Miami Beach, Florida, 19–22 October 1997, pp. 458–467. IEEE Computer Society Press (1997)

[OS07]   Ostrovsky, R., Skeith, W.E.: A survey of single-database private information retrieval: techniques and applications. In: Okamoto, T., Wang, X. (eds.) PKC 2007. LNCS, vol. 4450, pp. 393–411. Springer, Heidelberg (2007). https://doi.org/10.1007/978-3-540-71677-8_26

[PW08]   Peikert, C., Waters, B.: Lossy trapdoor functions and their applications. In: 40th ACM STOC, Victoria, BC, Canada, 17–20 May 2008, pp. 187–196. ACM Press (2008)

[PW11]   Peikert, C., Waters, B.: Lossy trapdoor functions and their applications. SIAM J. Comput. 40(6), 1803–1844 (2011)

[RS09]   Rosen, A., Segev, G.: Chosen-ciphertext security via correlated products. In: Reingold, O. (ed.) TCC 2009. LNCS, vol. 5444, pp. 419–436. Springer, Heidelberg (2009). https://doi.org/10.1007/978-3-642-00457-5_25

CP-ABE for Circuits (and More) in the Symmetric Key Setting

Shweta Agrawal[1] and Shota Yamada[2(✉)]

[1] IIT Madras, Chennai, India
shweta.a@cse.iitm.ac.in
[2] National Institute of Advanced Industrial Science and Technology (AIST),
Koto City, Japan
yamada-shota@aist.go.jp

Abstract. The celebrated work of Gorbunov, Vaikuntanathan and Wee [GVW13] provided the first key policy attribute based encryption scheme (ABE) for circuits from the Learning With Errors (LWE) assumption. However, the arguably more natural *ciphertext policy* variant has remained elusive, and is a central primitive not yet known from LWE.

In this work, we construct the first *symmetric key* ciphertext policy attribute based encryption scheme (CP-ABE) for all polynomial sized circuits from the learning with errors (LWE) assumption. In more detail, the ciphertext for a message m is labelled with an access control policy f, secret keys are labelled with public attributes $\mathbf{x}$ from the domain of f and decryption succeeds to yield the hidden message m if and only if $f(\mathbf{x}) = 1$. The size of our public and secret key do not depend on the size of the circuits supported by the scheme – this enables our construction to support circuits of *unbounded size* (but bounded depth). Our construction is secure against collusions of unbounded size. We note that current best CP-ABE schemes [BSW07, Wat11, LOS+10, OT10, LW12, RW13, Att14, Wee14, AHY15, CGW15, AC17, KW19] rely on pairings and only support circuits in the class NC_1 (albeit in the public key setting).

We adapt our construction to the public key setting for the case of *bounded* size circuits. The size of the ciphertext and secret key as well as running time of encryption, key generation and decryption satisfy the efficiency properties desired from CP-ABE, assuming that all algorithms have RAM access to the public key. However, the running time of the setup algorithm and size of the public key depends on the circuit size bound, restricting the construction to support circuits of a-priori bounded size. We remark that the inefficiency of setup is somewhat mitigated by the fact that setup must only be run once.

We generalize our construction to consider attribute and function hiding. The compiler of lockable obfuscation upgrades any attribute based encryption scheme to predicate encryption, i.e. with attribute hiding [GKW17, WZ17]. Since lockable obfuscation can be constructed from LWE, we achieve ciphertext policy predicate encryption immediately. For function privacy, we show that the most natural notion of function hiding ABE for circuits, even in the symmetric key setting, is sufficient to

© International Association for Cryptologic Research 2020
R. Pass and K. Pietrzak (Eds.): TCC 2020, LNCS 12550, pp. 117–148, 2020.
https://doi.org/10.1007/978-3-030-64375-1_5

imply indistinguishability obfuscation. We define a suitable weakening of function hiding to sidestep the implication and provide a construction to achieve this notion for both the key policy and ciphertext policy case. Previously, the largest function class for which function private predicate encryption (supporting unbounded keys) could be achieved was inner product zero testing, by Shen, Shi and Waters [SSW09].

1   Introduction

Attribute based encryption (ABE) [SW05] is a generalization of public key encryption that enables fine grained access control on encrypted data. In attribute based encryption, a message m is encrypted so that decryption succeeds if and only if the secret key holder is authorized to learn the message. Here, authorization is enforced via an access control policy modelled as a Boolean circuit f, which is computed over some public attributes $\mathbf{x}$ associated with the data/user. The access control policy may be embedded either in the key or the ciphertext, yielding key-policy (KP-ABE) or ciphertext-policy (CP-ABE) respectively.

In more detail, in a CP-ABE scheme, a ciphertext for a message m is labelled with an access control policy f, and secret keys are labelled with public attributes $\mathbf{x}$ from the domain of f. Decryption succeeds to yield the hidden message m if and only if the attribute satisfies the function, namely $f(\mathbf{x}) = 1$. In a KP-ABE, the placement of f and $\mathbf{x}$ are swapped.

Ciphertext Policy ABE for Circuits. Both KP-ABE [SW05, GPSW06, BW07, KSW08, LOS+10, OT10, OT12, CW14, AFV11, LW11, LW12, Wat12, GVW13, Wee14, Att14, BGG+14, GVW15, GV15, BV16, AF18] and CP-ABE schemes have received a lot of attention [BSW07, Wat11, LOS+10, OT10, LW12, RW13, Att14, Wee14, AHY15, CGW15, AC17, KW19] in the literature. While KP-ABE for the richest class of functions rely on the Learning With Errors (LWE) assumption and can support all polynomial sized circuits, the most general CP-ABE rely on pairings and can only support circuits in NC_1 [BSW07, Wat11, LOS+10, OT10, LW12, RW13, Att14, Wee14, AHY15, CGW15, AC17, KW19].

Recently, Tsabary [Tsa19] provided a construction of (public key) CP-ABE from Learning With Errors (LWE) for the very restricted class of t-CNF formulae, where t is constant. However, for all polynomial sized circuits, any construction from standard assumptions[1] has remained elusive despite substantial research effort. Very recently, Brakerski and Vaikuntanathan do provide a construction of (public key) CP-ABE using lattice based techniques [BV20], but their construction lacks a security proof. Their work further highlights the technical barriers to providing a construction from LWE. Indeed, constructing CP-ABE for even

---

[1] We note that from strong assumptions such as the the existence of multilinear maps [GGH13a], witness encryption [GTKP+13a] or indistinguishability obfuscation [BGI+01, GGH+13b], attribute based encryption (indeed, even its generalization *functional encryption*) has been constructed for all circuits, but these are not considered standard assumptions.

NC_1 from LWE is widely acknowledged as a central problem in lattice based cryptography and would be considered a major breakthrough.

Function Hiding. An ABE scheme encodes an attribute vector **x** and a Boolean circuit f. Hiding the attribute in these constructions, à la *Predicate Encryption* (PE) has met with fantastic success – the celebrated work of Gorbunov, Vaikuntanathan and Wee [GVW15] constructed a predicate encryption system for all circuits from LWE. More recently, Goyal, Koppula and Waters [GKW17] as well as Wichs and Zirdelis [WZ17] provided a powerful compiler for upgrading any ABE to PE by assuming LWE. However, much less is known about function hiding for ABE. For restricted functionalities such as identity based encryption and subspace membership testing, function hiding has received attention [BRS13a,BRS13b] in the public key setting, but serious technical barriers present themselves for more general function classes. We refer the reader to [BRS13a,BRS13b] for a detailed discussion.

In the symmetric key setting, function hiding for the stronger notion of *functional encryption* has been studied extensively [GTKP+13b,BS15] – however, since functional encryption is known to imply indistinguishability obfuscation [AJ15,BV15,BNPW16,KNT18] even without function hiding, there is limited optimism about achieving this notion for all circuits from standard assumptions, given current state of art. On the other hand, for the restricted inner product functionality, function hiding functional encryption can be achieved from standard assumptions [BJK15,KLM+16]. For the related (but distinct) functionality of inner product zero testing, Shen, Shi and Waters [SSW09] provided a construction of function hiding, symmetric key predicate encryption from bilinear maps.

The above state of affairs is dissatisfying and reveals several gaps in our understanding. Concretely, for general circuits and from standard assumptions, can we achieve function hiding in the symmetric key setting? Note that while attribute based encryption [GVW13,BGG+14] and predicate encryption [GVW15] are achievable from standard assumptions for all circuits, the richest functionality for which function hiding predicate encryption has been achieved is the inner product zero testing functionality [SSW09]. We emphasize that this question is not just of theoretical interest – as noted by Shen et al. [SSW09], function private predicate encryption in the symmetric key setting has many compelling applications. As an example [SSW09], a user may wish to store encrypted files on an untrusted server, and later retrieve only files that satisfy a given predicate. It is a natural security requirement that the server must learn nothing more about the predicate than minimum possible. We refer the reader to [SSW09] for a detailed discussion.

1.1   Our Results

In this work, we make substantial progress on both questions discussed above. Our results are summarized as follows:

1. We construct the first *symmetric key* ciphertext policy attribute based encryption scheme (CP-ABE) for all polynomial sized circuits from the learning

with errors (LWE) assumption. The sizes of our public and secret key do not depend on the size of the circuits supported by the scheme – this enables our construction to support circuits of *unbounded size* (but bounded depth). Our construction is secure against collusions of unbounded size in the multi-challenge ciphertext setting.[2]

This is the first construction of CP-ABE for polynomial circuits of unbounded size, supporting unbounded collusions, from standard assumptions.

2. We adapt our construction to the public key setting for the case of *bounded* size circuits. The size of the ciphertext and secret key as well as the runtime of encryption, key generation and decryption satisfy the efficiency properties desired from CP-ABE. However, the running time of the setup algorithm and the size of the public key depend on the circuit size bound, restricting the construction to support circuits of a-priori bounded size. We remark that this inefficiency is mitigated by the fact that setup must only run once. We summarize our results in Table 1.

Table 1. $|f_{\max}|$ denotes the worst case size bound on circuit size, and $|f|$ denotes the input circuit size. All the entries hide $\mathrm{poly}(\lambda)$ and logarithmic factors in $|f_{\max}|$. Due to space constraints, we include only the most recent pairings based cpABE in the table.

Scheme	Assumption	PK/SK	Setup Time	$|PK|$	Enc Time	$|CT|$	KeyGen Time	$|SK|$	Dec Time	Circuit Class
Ideal	Standard	PK	1	1	$|f|$	$|f|$	$|\mathbf{x}|$	$|\mathbf{x}|$	$|f|$	P
Naive (using [BGG+14])	LWE	PK	$|f_{\max}|$	$|f_{\max}|$	$|f_{\max}|$	$|f_{\max}|$	$|f_{\max}|$	1	$|f_{\max}|$	P
Naive ([BGG+14] & [BV16])[a]	LWE	PK	1	1	$|f_{\max}|$	$|f_{\max}|$	$|f_{\max}|$	1	$|f_{\max}|$	P
Sect. 3	LWE	SK	1	1	$|f|$	$|f|$	$|\mathbf{x}|$	$|\mathbf{x}|$	$|f|$	P
Sect. 4	LWE	PK	$|f_{\max}|$	$|f_{\max}|$	$|f|$	$|f|$	$|\mathbf{x}|$	$|\mathbf{x}|$	$|f|$	P
[KW19]	Pairings	PK	1	1	$|f|$	$|f|$	$|\mathbf{x}|$	$|\mathbf{x}|$	$|f|$	NC_1

This construction can be further improved by combining this with the "powers of 2" trick where we run parallel instances of the scheme that can deal with circuits with size at most 2^i for $i = 1, 2, \ldots \log|f_{\max}|$ and use appropriate instance when encrypting a message depending on the size of the circuit. As a result, the encryption time, the ciphertext size, and the (RAM efficiency of the) decryption algorithm can be reduced to be $|f|$ from $|f_{\max}|$.

3. We study the notion of function hiding attribute based encryption for circuits, in the symmetric key setting. In Sect. 5.3, we show that the most natural notion of function hiding ABE, even in the symmetric key setting is sufficient to imply indistinguishability obfuscation. We define a suitable weakening of function hiding to sidestep the implication and provide a construction in Sect. 5 to achieve this notion for both key policy and ciphertext policy predicate encryption. We instantiate our compiler with known constructions of PE to obtain the following theorems:

---

[2] In the symmetric key setting, single-challenge ciphertext security and multi-challenge ciphertext security are not equivalent. In our paper, we adopt the latter as the default security notion for symmetric key ABE, since it is stronger and more natural.

Theorem 1.1 (*Informal*). *Assuming subexponential LWE, we have function hiding, semi-adaptively secure predicate encryption for all polynomial circuits.*

Theorem 1.2 (*Informal*). *Assuming subexponential LWE and DLIN, we have function hiding, adaptively secure predicate encryption for* NC_1 *circuits.*

Please see Sect. 5.1 for details.

1.2   Our Techniques

In this section, we provide an overview of our techniques.

CP-ABE for Circuits. For this construction, we leverage techniques developed recently by Agrawal, Maitra and Yamada [AMY19] to handle inputs of unbounded size in the context of ABE for finite automata. We notice that these techniques are quite a bit more general than discussed in that work and can be adapted to the setting of ciphertext policy ABE supporting unbounded collusions.

Folklore Approach. We begin with a folklore transformation of KP-ABE to CP-ABE – namely, via the universal circuit. In more detail, let $U(\cdot, \cdot)$ be the universal circuit such that $f(\mathbf{x}) = U(\mathbf{x}, f)$. Next, let $U[\mathbf{x}]$ be the universal circuit with the input $\mathbf{x}$ hard-wired. Then, we may construct a CP-ABE scheme, denoted by cpABE using a KP-ABE scheme, denoted by kpABE as follows: the cpABE encryptor, given a message m and circuit f may compute kpABE ciphertext for (m, f) where f is viewed as a bit string representing kpABE attributes. The cpABE key generator, given an attribute string $\mathbf{x}$, may compute a kpABE function key for the circuit $U[\mathbf{x}]$. Decryption is straightforward using kpABE decryption as $U[\mathbf{x}](f) = U(\mathbf{x}, f) = f(\mathbf{x})$.

The above generic compiler has the drawback that the input of circuit $U[\mathbf{x}]$ is the circuit f. This limits the construction to only support circuits of a-priori bounded size $|f_{\max}|$ (say) and forces the size of the public key, ciphertext as well as runtime of setup, key generation, encryption and decryption to grow with $|f_{\max}|$ (please see Table 1). We emphasize that even the encryption and decryption algorithms, which must take time proportional to circuit size, now degrade with the worst case bound $|f_{\max}|$, rather than with input circuit $|f|$. The hit taken by key generation is significantly worse[3].

Re-distributing Computation. Note that the only algorithms which are allowed to depend on the size of the circuit length are the encryption and decryption algorithms. Hence, inspired by [AMY19], we re-distribute the computation of kpABE.KeyGen($U[\mathbf{x}]$) between the key generator and the encryptor to ensure that each algorithm satisfies the efficiency requirements of CP-ABE.

In more detail, the key generator may depend on the size of $\mathbf{x}$ but not on the size of f, while the encryptor and decryptor may depend on the size of f. In

---

[3] Although using the scheme by [BGG+14] allows for a small function key size.

order to redistribute computation, we rely on single-key functional encryption (FE), which can be constructed based on the LWE assumption [GKP+13]. Now, the ciphertext of cpABE is kpABE.CT(f, m) where f is treated as the attribute string. Additionally, the ciphertext contains FE.KeyGen(C) where the circuit $C(\cdot) = $ kpABE.KeyGen($U(\cdot)$). The secret key of cpABE is FE.Enc($\mathbf{x}$). Decryption in the cpABE scheme proceeds by first computing FE decryption to obtain kpABE.SK($U[\mathbf{x}]$) and then computing kpABE decryption with kpABE.CT(f, m) to obtain m iff $f(\mathbf{x}) = 1$. Care must be taken that single key security of the underlying FE scheme is not violated. For this, we ensure that the function key is generated for the *same* circuit $C(\cdot) = $ kpABE.KeyGen($U(\cdot)$) and using the *same* randomness (as specified in the master secret key), across all invocations of FE key generation.

In order to argue that the key generation algorithm does not depend on $|f|$, we rely on special properties of the FE scheme. Recall that the FE scheme of Goldwasser et al. is *succinct* which means that the running time of the encryption algorithm depends on the depth and output length of the circuits supported by the scheme but is independent of their size. The depth of the circuits supported by our construction is bounded by assumption and the depth of the kpABE key generation circuit is at most a polynomial factor larger than the depth of the circuit it supports. Hence, it remains to argue that the output length may be similarly bounded. To see this, note that in our construction, the function key is generated for circuit $C(\cdot) = $ kpABE.KeyGen($U(\cdot)$), whose output length depends on the size of the underlying kpABE function key. Fortunately, by using the kpABE scheme of Boneh et al. [BGG+14], we may bound the size of the kpABE scheme by a fixed polynomial.

Supporting Circuits of Unbounded Size. A detail brushed under the carpet in the above description is that the kpABE scheme which is used to encrypt f as an attribute string must be initialized with the length of f during the setup phase. Moreover, this input length is passed to all other kpABE algorithms, notably the key generation algorithm. Since we wish to support f of unbounded size, this poses a dilemma. An immediate question that arises is which algorithm of cpABE should invoke the setup algorithm of kpABE? Evidently, the setup of cpABE does not have the size of f, so it must be the encrypt algorithm. Hence, the cpABE encrypt algorithm samples the kpABE scheme and provides an FE secret key for the circuit kpABE.KeyGen($U(\cdot)$). A subtlety is that the kpABE key generation algorithm must depend on the length of f as discussed above. Then, if f is of varying size across different ciphertexts, the description of kpABE.KeyGen($U(\cdot)$) and hence FE.SK varies with the size of f. This is problematic – since FE only satisfies single key security!

We resolve the above conundrum by running $\lambda + 1$ instances of FE and kpABE in parallel – each to support f of length 2^i where $i \in [0, \lambda]$. The circuit size is padded to the next power of two – a trick used in many works, beginning with [GTKP+13a] – so that we only need to deal with $\lambda + 1$ possible FE, each of which supports the issuing of a *single* secret key, which will compute the kpABE key generation circuit for inputs of length 2^i. The cpABE key generator does not know which instance of FE it must encrypt with, so it encrypts with all of them. For details, please see Sect. 3.

Security. Our cpABE scheme achieves selective, indistinguishability based security. At a high level, security relies on the security of the instances of the single key FE schemes and kpABE schemes. Similarly to [AMY19], we begin by showing that by security of FE adversary cannot get anything beyond $\{\mathsf{FE.Dec}(\mathsf{FE.sk}_i, \mathsf{FE.ct}_i) = \mathsf{kpABE.sk}_i\}$ for $i \in [0, \lambda]$. Next, we rely on the security of kpABE to argue that the message bit is not revealed. As discussed above, we need to ensure that only single FE secret key is revealed to the adversary for each instance of FE. Fortunately, this can be guaranteed by the fact that for a given instance of FE, we must only release a secret key (of the FE) for the key generation algorithm of the corresponding kpABE.

Public Key Setting. Next, we construct a public key ciphertext policy ABE scheme for bounded sized circuits, where $|f_{\max}|$ is set as an upper bound on circuit size. In our construction, the size of the secret key and ciphertext satisfy the efficiency properties desired from CP-ABE (Definition 2.4). Additionally, the running time of the keygen, encrypt and decrypt algorithms depend only on the size of the input circuit f and not on the worst case circuit size $|f_{\max}|$, assuming that they have RAM access to the public key. However, the running time of the setup algorithm and the size of PK grows with the size $|f_{\max}|$ of the circuits supported by the scheme. We note that this inefficiency is mitigated since it must be only run once.

The construction is similar to the secret key cpABE provided in Sect. 3 but has some important differences. Let us try to adapt the secret key construction of Sect. 3 to the public key setting. Since the construction makes modular use of single key succinct FE [GKP+13] and key policy ABE [BGG+14], and both these schemes can be instantiated in the public key setting from LWE, a first attempt would be to use public key versions of these building blocks and compile a public key version of the secret key cpABE scheme. However this naive approach runs into multiple difficulties. For the key generation algorithm to be independent of the circuit size, it may not compute the circuit $U[\mathbf{x}]$ – indeed, this would render the role of FE useless and collapse back into the naive transformation of a kpABE to cpABE scheme via universal circuits. To avoid the dependence of keygen on circuit size, it is necessary for the encrypt algorithm to compute the FE secret key for the kpABE key generation algorithm, which in turn requires that the encrypt algorithm possess the master secret key FE.msk.

However, a crucial and useful property of the construction is that it only uses FE for a single fixed circuit – hence, to remove the dependence of Enc on FE.msk, an idea is to let setup compute the FE function key itself and provide it as part of the public key. The cpABE public key can contain the public keys of FE as well as kpABE, along with the FE function key for the kpABE key generation algorithm. Now, the encryptor, given input circuit f and message μ, can use the kpABE public key to compute a kpABE ciphertext for (f, μ). The key generator can compute the FE ciphertext for $\mathbf{x}$ and the decryptor can decrypt as before, by performing FE decryption to recover the kpABE function key, followed by kpABE decryption.

An immediate drawback is that this approach forces the circuit size to be fixed at setup time. Additionally, even if we assume an upper bound $|f_{\max}|$ on the size of supported circuits, this approach has the significant disadvantage that the runtime of encryption and decryption as well as the size of the ciphertext to depend on the upper bound $|f_{\max}|$ rather than the actual size of the circuit. When the input circuit is much smaller, this is a significant price to pay in terms of both communication and computation. Another disadvantage is that the size of the public key now grows with the upper bound $|f_{\max}|$. To see this, note that the kpABE public key in general depends on the size of the inputs supported by the scheme, which in this case can be as large as $|f_{\max}|$. There do exist clever ideas to make the size of the kpABE public key independent of the input size [BV16, GKW16], but they do so, unfortunately, at the expense of making the function key depend linearly on input size $|f_{\max}|$. But if the kpABE function key is large, then the size of the FE ciphertext would degrade to support this, making the cpABE function key large, which is precisely what we are trying to avoid!

These issues may be overcome if we assume that every algorithm has RAM access to cpABE.mpk. For simplicity, let us assume that circuit sizes come in powers of 2 – this assumption can be easily removed by padding circuits appropriately. In this case, we run $\eta := \lceil \log |f_{\max}| \rceil$ instances of kpABE in parallel, and let the ith instance handle inputs of length 2^i, for $i \in [\eta]$. Now, we have η public keys for kpABE, each of length 2^i, which together (along with FE.mpk$_i$ and FE.sk$_i$) comprise the final public key. If every algorithm has RAM access to this public key, then it may choose the component according to the actual input length of the circuit, namely it may choose i^* such that $|f| = 2^{i^*}$ and access only the i^{*th} component of the public key. Then, the runtime of the encrypt and decrypt algorithm depend on $|f|$ rather than $|f_{\max}|$. For more details, please see Sect. 4.

Function Hiding Predicate Encryption. Next, we generalize our construction to consider attribute and function hiding. The compiler of lockable obfuscation upgrades any attribute based encryption scheme to predicate encryption, i.e. with attribute hiding [GKW17, WZ17]. Since lockable obfuscation can be constructed from LWE, we achieve ciphertext policy predicate encryption immediately. We then turn to the question of function hiding predicate encryption for circuits. Here, we show that the natural notion of function hiding predicate encryption, i.e. that considered by [SSW09], when applied to all polynomial sized circuits, is strong enough to imply indistinguishability obfuscation.

Consider a function private ciphertext-policy *attribute based* encryption scheme cpABE[4]. The ciphertext is associated with a circuit f and a message m and the key is associated with an attribute vector $\mathbf{x}$. Intuitively, since the scheme is function hiding, $\mathbf{x}$ is hidden. Note that the attribute f is not hidden, since this an ABE scheme. A natural game of function hiding would allow

---

[4] Note that we are starting with a weaker object – this only strengthens our result.

an adversary to output challenge key queries $(\mathbf{x}_{0i}, \mathbf{x}_{1i})$ and ciphertext queries (f_j, μ_j) so that $f_j(\mathbf{x}_{0i}) = f_j(\mathbf{x}_{1i})$ for all i, j. The challenger responds by choosing a random bit b and returning the corresponding secret keys for $\mathbf{x}_{bi}$, along with ciphertexts for (f_j, μ_j). The adversary wins if she guesses the bit correctly[5].

We now show a reduction from secret key *functional encryption* (FE) to function hiding cpABE. Recall that in functional encryption, the ciphertext is associated with a vector $\mathbf{x}$, the secret key is associated with a circuit f and decryption enables the decryptor to recover $f(\mathbf{x})$. In the security game, the adversary must distinguish between encryptions of $\mathbf{x}_0$ and $\mathbf{x}_1$ given an arbitrary number of secret keys for circuits f_i where $f_i(\mathbf{x}_0) = f_i(\mathbf{x}_1)$. In our reduction, if cpABE supports unbounded ciphertext queries, then FE supports unbounded key queries. Such a functional encryption scheme is known to imply indistinguishability obfuscation (iO) [AJ15,BV15,BNPW16,KNT18].

It remains to outline the reduction. The reduction is remarkably simple: suppose that FE.Enc$(\mathbf{x}, \mathsf{msk})$ = cpABE.KeyGen$(\mathbf{x}, \mathsf{msk})$ and that FE.KeyGen(f, msk) = $(m, \mathsf{cpABE.Enc}(f, m, \mathsf{msk}))$ where m is a random bit. FE.Dec computes cpABE.Dec and outputs 1 if it recovers m correctly. Now, when the FE adversary outputs $\mathbf{x}_0, \mathbf{x}_1$ as challenge messages, the reduction outputs outputs $\mathbf{x}_0, \mathbf{x}_1$ as challenge keys and obtains the cpABE key for $\mathbf{x}_b$. When the FE adversary makes a key request for f_i, the reduction obtains the cpABE ciphertext for (f_i, m_i) where m_i is randomly chosen, and uses these to respond to the FE adversary. It is evident that if the FE adversary is legitimate, then so is the cpABE function hiding adversary. Also, clearly if the cpABE adversary wins the game, this translates to a win for the FE adversary.

To avoid the implication to FE, we weaken the function hiding definition. We provide a restricted definition of function hiding (Definition 2.14), in which the adversary is disallowed from making queries for vectors $\mathbf{x}_0, \mathbf{x}_1$ such that $f_i(\mathbf{x}_0) = f_i(\mathbf{x}_1) = 1$ for any requested f_i. The definition insists that $f_i(\mathbf{x}_0) = f_i(\mathbf{x}_1) = 0$ for all requests. Note that an admissible FE adversary may request keys for any circuits f_i as long as $f_i(\mathbf{x}_0) = f_i(\mathbf{x}_1)$, regardless of whether this value is 0 or 1. However, with the restriction on the function hiding definition, the above reduction fails and we fall back into "one sided security" that characterizes PE and is known to be achievable from standard assumptions. Please see Sect. 5.3 for the detailed argument.

In Sect. 5, we provide a construction of predicate encryption for circuits which achieves the above notion of function hiding. Our compiler is analogous to the compiler of Goldwasser et al. [GKP+13], which converts succinct functional encryption to reusable garbled circuits. In more detail, we construct function hiding PE from PE and a symmetric key encryption scheme SKE. For simplicity, we consider the key-policy setting, we show how to extend the argument to the ciphertext-policy setting in Sect. 5.

Since we are in the symmetric key setting, the SKE secret key SK (say) is known both to the key generation and the encrypt algorithms. Now, the

---

[5] Note that (f_j, μ_j) are ciphertext queries, not challenge ciphertexts, so the adversary is allowed to have decrypting keys for these in a function hiding game.

encryptor uses PE to encrypt its message with attribute $(SK, \mathbf{x})$. The key generator, given input circuit f, computes the SKE encryption $\hat{f}$ of f provides a key for an augmented circuit $U_{\hat{f}}(\cdot)$, which given input $(SK, \mathbf{x})$, first decrypts $\hat{f}$ to obtain f and then computes $f(\mathbf{x})$. Intuitively, since PE is attribute hiding, SK remains hidden, and since the key only reveals the encryption $\hat{f}$, the circuit f remains hidden. The formal argument is provided in Sect. 5.

1.3 Perspective and Open Problems

CP-ABE from LWE, for all polynomial sized circuits (or even NC_1) is a long standing open problem. Our work settles the question in the symmetric key case, and makes significant progress in the public key case. Our constructions use prior constructions of KP-ABE [BGG+14] and FE [GTKP+13a] as building blocks and combine them carefully to obtain the desired efficiency for CP-ABE. These building blocks satisfy certain special properties such as succinctness of ciphertext [GTKP+13a] and short secret key [BGG+14]. By noticing that the efficiency properties of these schemes *compose* in a fortuitous way, we achieve the required efficiency of CP-ABE by doing very little work[6]! Similar tricks were used by [AMY19] in the context of constructing ABE for finite automata – indeed, our constructions are *simpler* than theirs.

An obvious open problem is to close the "efficiency" gap in setup time that remains open in our public key construction. The chief hurdle in doing so is that the computation of the FE secret key is a secret key operation but the only algorithms in the construction that are allowed the time required by this computation, namely encrypt and decrypt, are public key algorithms. An approach may be to delegate the FE secret key generation using garbled circuits, as in [DG17] but a natural implementation of this idea turns out to be insecure. We conjecture that new techniques may be required to overcome this hurdle. In the context of function privacy, we obtain the first attribute based encryption schemes for circuits with function hiding, in the symmetric key setting. A natural open question is to provide constructions in the public key setting. However, as observed by [BRS13a], function privacy in the public key setting is significantly more challenging, with even the right definition being unclear. We conjecture that this problem may require significantly new ideas to resolve.

2 Preliminaries

Notation. We begin by defining the notation that we will use throughout the paper. We use bold letters to denote vectors and the notation $[a, b]$ to denote the set of integers $\{k \in \mathbb{N} \mid a \leq k \leq b\}$. We use $[n]$ to denote the set $[1, n]$. Concatenation is denoted by the symbol $\|$. Vectors will be column vectors unless stated otherwise.

We say a function $f(n)$ is *negligible* if it is $O(n^{-c})$ for all $c > 0$, and we use $\text{negl}(n)$ to denote a negligible function of n. We say $f(n)$ is *polynomial* if it

---

[6] Beyond what is already done by the "heavy hammers" of [BGG+14, GTKP+13b].

is $O(n^c)$ for some constant $c > 0$, and we use poly(n) to denote a polynomial function of n. We use the abbreviation PPT for probabilistic polynomial-time. We say an event occurs with *overwhelming probability* if its probability is $1 -$ negl(n). The function $\log x$ is the base 2 logarithm of x. For any finite set S we denote $\mathcal{P}(S)$ to be the power set of S. For a circuit $C : \{0,1\}^{\ell_1+\ell_2} \to \{0,1\}$ and a string $\mathbf{x} \in \{0,1\}^{\ell_1}$, $C[\mathbf{x}] : \{0,1\}^{\ell_2} \to \{0,1\}$ denotes a circuit that takes $\mathbf{y}$ and outputs $C(\mathbf{x}, \mathbf{y})$. We construct $C[\mathbf{x}]$ in the following specified way. Namely, $C[\mathbf{x}]$ is the circuit that takes as input $\mathbf{y}$ and sets

$$z_i = \begin{cases} y_1 \wedge \neg y_1 & \text{if } x_i = 0 \\ y_1 \vee \neg y_1 & \text{if } x_i = 1 \end{cases}$$

and then computes $C(\mathbf{z}, \mathbf{y})$, where x_i, y_i, and z_i are the i-th bit of $\mathbf{x}$, $\mathbf{y}$, and $\mathbf{z}$, respectively. In the above, it is clear that $z_i = x_i$ and we have $C(\mathbf{z}, \mathbf{y}) = C(\mathbf{x}, \mathbf{y})$. Furthermore, it is also easy to see that $\mathsf{depth}(C[\mathbf{x}]) \leq \mathsf{depth}(C) + O(1)$ holds.

Circuit Classes of Interest. For $\lambda \in \mathbb{N}$, let $\mathcal{C}_{\mathsf{inp},\mathsf{d},\mathsf{s}}$ denote a family of circuits with inp bit inputs, bounded depth d, bounded size s and binary output. When the size s is unspecified, it means that the circuit family $\mathcal{C}_{\mathsf{inp},\mathsf{d}}$ can have unbounded size.

2.1 Attribute Based Encryption for Circuits

Attribute based encryption comes in two flavours: key policy or ciphertext policy, depending on where the policy (represented as a Boolean circuit) is embedded. We define these next.

Ciphertext Policy Attribute Based Encryption for Circuits. Let $\mathcal{C} = \{\mathcal{C}_{\mathsf{inp}(\lambda),\mathsf{d}(\lambda)}\}_{\lambda \in \mathbb{N}}$. A ciphertext policy attribute-based encryption (ABE) scheme cpABE for $\mathcal{C}$ over a message space $\mathcal{M} = \{\mathcal{M}_\lambda\}_{\lambda \in \mathbb{N}}$ consists of four algorithms:

- cpABE.Setup($1^\lambda, 1^{\mathsf{inp}}, 1^{\mathsf{d}}$) is a PPT algorithm takes as input the unary representation of the security parameter, the length inp = inp(λ) of the input, the depth d = d(λ) of the circuit family $\mathcal{C}$ to be supported. It outputs the master public key and the master secret key (cpABE.mpk, cpABE.msk).

- cpABE.Enc(cpABE.mpk, C, m) is a PPT algorithm that takes as input the master public key cpABE.mpk, circuit $C \in \mathcal{C}_{\mathsf{inp}(\lambda),\mathsf{d}(\lambda)}$ and a message $m \in \mathcal{M}$. It outputs a ciphertext cpABE.ct.

- cpABE.KeyGen(cpABE.mpk, cpABE.msk, $\mathbf{x}$) is a PPT algorithm that takes as input the master public key cpABE.mpk, the master secret key cpABE.msk, and a a string $\mathbf{x} \in \{0,1\}^{\mathsf{inp}}$ and outputs a corresponding secret key cpABE.sk$_\mathbf{x}$.

– cpABE.Dec(cpABE.mpk, cpABE.sk$_\mathbf{x}$, $\mathbf{x}$, cpABE.ct, C) is a deterministic algorithm that takes as input the secret key cpABE.sk$_\mathbf{x}$, its associated attribute string $\mathbf{x}$, a ciphertext cpABE.ct, and its associated circuit C and outputs either a message m' or $\perp$.

Definition 2.1 (Correctness). *A ciphertext policy ABE scheme for circuits* cpABE *is correct if for all* $\lambda \in \mathbb{N}$, *polynomially bounded* inp *and* d, *all circuits* $C \in \mathcal{C}_{\mathrm{inp}(\lambda),\mathrm{d}(\lambda)}$, *all* $\mathbf{x} \in \{0,1\}^{\mathrm{inp}}$ *such that* $C(\mathbf{x}) = 1$ *and for all messages* $m \in \mathcal{M}$,

$$\Pr \left[\begin{array}{l} (\mathsf{cpABE.mpk}, \mathsf{cpABE.msk}) \leftarrow \mathsf{cpABE.Setup}(1^\lambda, 1^{\mathrm{inp}}, 1^{\mathrm{d}}), \\ \mathsf{cpABE.sk}_\mathbf{x} \leftarrow \mathsf{cpABE.KeyGen}(\mathsf{cpABE.mpk}, \mathsf{cpABE.msk}, \mathbf{x}), \\ \mathsf{cpABE.ct} \leftarrow \mathsf{cpABE.Enc}(\mathsf{cpABE.mpk}, C, m): \\ \mathsf{cpABE.Dec}\Big(\mathsf{cpABE.mpk}, \mathsf{cpABE.sk}_\mathbf{x}, \mathbf{x}, \mathsf{cpABE.ct}, C\Big) \neq m \end{array} \right] = \mathrm{negl}(\lambda)$$

where the probability is taken over the coins of cpABE.Setup, cpABE.KeyGen, *and* cpABE.Enc.

Definition 2.2. *[Selective Security for* cpABE*] The ABE scheme* cpABE *for a circuit family* $\mathcal{C} = \{\mathcal{C}_{\mathrm{inp}(\lambda),\mathrm{d}(\lambda)}\}_{\lambda \in \mathbb{N}}$ *and a message space* $\{\mathcal{M}_\lambda\}_{\lambda \in \mathbb{N}}$ *is said to satisfy selective security if for any stateful PPT adversary* A, *there exists a negligible function* $\mathrm{negl}(\cdot)$ *such that*

$$\mathsf{Adv}_{\mathsf{cpABE},\mathsf{A}}(1^\lambda) = \left| \Pr[\mathsf{Exp}^{(0)}_{\mathsf{cpABE},\mathsf{A}}(1^\lambda) = 1] - \Pr[\mathsf{Exp}^{(1)}_{\mathsf{cpABE},\mathsf{A}}(1^\lambda) = 1] \right| \leq \mathrm{negl}(\lambda),$$

for all sufficiently large $\lambda \in \mathbb{N}$, *where for each* $b \in \{0,1\}$ *and* $\lambda \in \mathbb{N}$, *the experiment* $\mathsf{Exp}^{(b)}_{\mathsf{cpABE},\mathsf{A}}$, *modeled as a game between adversary* A *and a challenger, is defined as follows:*

1. **Setup phase:** *On input* 1^λ, A *submits* $(1^{\mathrm{inp}}, 1^{\mathrm{d}})$ *and the target circuit set* ChalC $\subset \mathcal{C}_{\mathrm{inp}(\lambda),\mathrm{d}(\lambda)}$ *(of possibly varying sizes), to the challenger. The challenger samples* $(\mathsf{cpABE.mpk}, \mathsf{cpABE.msk}) \leftarrow \mathsf{cpABE.Setup}(1^\lambda, 1^{\mathrm{inp}}, 1^{\mathrm{d}})$ *and replies to* A *with* cpABE.mpk.
2. **Query phase:** *During the game,* A *adaptively makes the following queries, in an arbitrary order and unbounded many times.*
   (a) **Key Queries:** A *chooses an attribute string* $\mathbf{x} \in \{0,1\}^{\mathrm{inp}}$ *that satisfies* $C(\mathbf{x}) = 0$ *for all* $C \in$ ChalC. *For each such query, the challenger replies with* $\mathsf{cpABE.sk}_\mathbf{x} \leftarrow \mathsf{cpABE.KeyGen}(\mathsf{cpABE.mpk}, \mathsf{cpABE.msk}, \mathbf{x})$.
   (b) **Challenge Queries:** A *submits a circuit* $C \in$ ChalC *and a pair of equal length messages* $(m_0, m_1) \in (\mathcal{M})^2$ *to the challenger. The challenger replies to* A *with* $\mathsf{cpABE.ct} \leftarrow \mathsf{cpABE.Enc}(\mathsf{cpABE.mpk}, C, m_b)$.
3. **Output phase:** A *outputs a guess bit* b' *as the output of the experiment.*

Remark 2.3. The above definition allows an adversary to make challenge queries multiple times. A more standard (equivalent) notion of the security for an ABE restricts the adversary to make only single challenge query. As in [AMY19], we adopt the above definition since it is convenient for our purpose.

Symmetric Key Setting. In the symmetric key setting, the encryption algorithm additionally takes the master secret key as input and the adversary is permitted to make encryption queries in the security game. As for the security definition, we modify the above game so that the adversary is allowed to make the following type of queries in the query phase:

> *(c)* **Encryption Queries:** A *submits a circuit* $C \in \mathcal{C}_{\mathsf{inp}(\lambda),\mathsf{d}(\lambda)}$ *and a pair of equal length messages* $m \in \mathcal{M}$ *to the challenger. The challenger replies to* A *with* cpABE.ct $\leftarrow$ cpABE.Enc(cpABE.msk, C, m).

Unlike challenge queries, there is no restriction on C and the returned ciphertext may be decryptable by the adversary. Note that we did not have to consider above type of queries in the public key setting since the adversary can encrypt any message by itself. We also note that in the symmetric key setting, single-challenge ciphertext security and multi-challenge ciphertext security are not equivalent. We adopt the latter definition as the default security notion since it is stronger and more natural.

Definition 2.4 (Efficiency). *For* $\lambda \in \mathbb{N}$, *let* $\mathcal{C}_{\mathsf{inp},\mathsf{d}}$ *denote a family of circuits with* inp *bit inputs, bounded depth* d *and binary output. Let* $\mathcal{C} = \{\mathcal{C}_{\mathsf{inp}(\lambda),\mathsf{d}(\lambda)}\}_{\lambda \in \mathbb{N}}$. *We say a ciphertext policy attribute based encryption scheme* cpABE *for circuit class* $\mathcal{C}$ *is efficient if:*

1. **Setup.** *The runtime of the setup algorithm, and the size of the public key depends only on the input length* inp *and depth bound* d *of the supported circuits.*
2. **Key Generation.** *For an attribute* **x**, *the runtime of the key generation and size of* SK *depends on the attribute size* |**x**| *and (possibly) on circuit depth* d.
3. **Encryption and Decryption.** *The runtime of the encrypt and decrypt algorithms, as well as the size of ciphertext depend on the size of the given input circuit* |C|.

Our scheme presented in Sect. 3 supports unbounded circuits with the above efficiency properties.

Relaxation for Bounded Circuits. We also define a relaxed variant of efficiency for circuits of *bounded* size. In more detail, for $\lambda \in \mathbb{N}$, let $\mathcal{C}_{\mathsf{inp},\mathsf{d},\mathsf{s}}$ denote a family of circuits with inp bit inputs, bounded depth d, bounded size s and binary output. Let $\mathcal{C} = \{\mathcal{C}_{\mathsf{inp}(\lambda),\mathsf{d}(\lambda),\mathsf{s}}\}_{\lambda \in \mathbb{N}}$. Then cpABE for circuit class $\mathcal{C}$ allows the setup algorithm to take circuit size bound 1^{s} as input and its runtime depends on this. However, the runtime of the key generation and size of SK depends on the attribute size |**x**| and (possibly) on circuit depth d but not circuit size bound s. Similarly, the runtime of the encrypt and decrypt algorithms, as well as the size of ciphertext depend on the size of the given input circuit |C|, and not on worst case size bound s. Our scheme presented in Sect. 4 supports bounded circuits with the aforementioned relaxation in the efficiency properties.

Key Policy Attribute Based Encryption for Circuits. The definition of key policy attribute based encryption (kpABE) is exactly as above, with the role of the circuit C and the attribute $\mathbf{x}$ switched. For completeness, we provide this definition below.

For $\lambda \in \mathbb{N}$, let $\mathcal{C}_{\mathsf{inp},\mathsf{d}}$ denote a family of circuits with inp bit inputs, an a-priori bounded depth d, and binary output and $\mathcal{C} = \{\mathcal{C}_{\mathsf{inp}(\lambda),\mathsf{d}(\lambda)}\}_{\lambda \in \mathbb{N}}$. An attribute-based encryption (ABE) scheme kpABE for $\mathcal{C}$ over a message space $\mathcal{M} = \{\mathcal{M}_\lambda\}_{\lambda \in \mathbb{N}}$ consists of four algorithms:

- kpABE.Setup($1^\lambda, 1^{\mathsf{inp}}, 1^{\mathsf{d}}$) is a PPT algorithm takes as input the unary representation of the security parameter, the length $\mathsf{inp} = \mathsf{inp}(\lambda)$ of the input and the depth $\mathsf{d} = \mathsf{d}(\lambda)$ of the circuit family $\mathcal{C}_{\mathsf{inp}(\lambda),\mathsf{d}(\lambda)}$ to be supported. It outputs the master public key and the master secret key (kpABE.mpk, kpABE.msk).
- kpABE.Enc(kpABE.mpk, $\mathbf{x}, m$) is a PPT algorithm that takes as input the master public key kpABE.mpk, a string $\mathbf{x} \in \{0,1\}^{\mathsf{inp}}$ and a message $m \in \mathcal{M}$. It outputs a ciphertext kpABE.ct.
- kpABE.KeyGen(kpABE.mpk, kpABE.msk, C) is a PPT algorithm that takes as input the master secret key kpABE.msk and a circuit $C \in \mathcal{C}_{\mathsf{inp}(\lambda),\mathsf{d}(\lambda)}$ and outputs a corresponding secret key kpABE.sk$_C$.
- kpABE.Dec(kpABE.mpk, kpABE.sk$_C$, C, kpABE.ct, $\mathbf{x}$) is a deterministic algorithm that takes as input the secret key kpABE.sk$_C$, its associated circuit C, a ciphertext kpABE.ct, and its associated string $\mathbf{x}$ and outputs either a message m' or $\perp$.

Definition 2.5 (Correctness). *An ABE scheme for circuits kpABE is correct if for all $\lambda \in \mathbb{N}$, polynomially bounded inp and d, all circuits $C \in \mathcal{C}_{\mathsf{inp}(\lambda),\mathsf{d}(\lambda)}$, all $\mathbf{x} \in \{0,1\}^{\mathsf{inp}}$ such that $C(\mathbf{x}) = 1$ and for all messages $m \in \mathcal{M}$,*

$$\Pr\left[\begin{array}{l}(\mathsf{kpABE.mpk}, \mathsf{kpABE.msk}) \leftarrow \mathsf{kpABE.Setup}(1^\lambda, 1^{\mathsf{inp}}, 1^{\mathsf{d}}), \\ \mathsf{kpABE.sk}_C \leftarrow \mathsf{kpABE.KeyGen}(\mathsf{kpABE.mpk}, \mathsf{kpABE.msk}, C), \\ \mathsf{kpABE.ct} \leftarrow \mathsf{kpABE.Enc}(\mathsf{kpABE.mpk}, \mathbf{x}, m) : \\ \mathsf{kpABE.Dec}\Big(\mathsf{kpABE.mpk}, \mathsf{kpABE.sk}_C, C, \mathsf{kpABE.ct}, \mathbf{x}\Big) \neq m\end{array}\right] = \mathrm{negl}(\lambda)$$

where the probability is taken over the coins of kpABE.Setup, kpABE.KeyGen, *and* kpABE.Enc.

Definition 2.6 (Selective Security for kpABE). *The ABE scheme kpABE for a circuit family $\mathcal{C} = \{\mathcal{C}_{\mathsf{inp}(\lambda),\mathsf{d}(\lambda)}\}_{\lambda \in \mathbb{N}}$ and a message space $\{\mathcal{M}_\lambda\}_{\lambda \in \mathbb{N}}$ is said to satisfy selective security if for any stateful PPT adversary A, there exists a negligible function $\mathrm{negl}(\cdot)$ such that*

$$\mathsf{Adv}_{\mathsf{kpABE},\mathsf{A}}(1^\lambda) = \left|\Pr[\mathsf{Exp}^{(0)}_{\mathsf{kpABE},\mathsf{A}}(1^\lambda) = 1] - \Pr[\mathsf{Exp}^{(1)}_{\mathsf{kpABE},\mathsf{A}}(1^\lambda) = 1]\right| \leq \mathrm{negl}(\lambda),$$

for all sufficiently large $\lambda \in \mathbb{N}$, where for each $b \in \{0,1\}$ and $\lambda \in \mathbb{N}$, the experiment $\mathsf{Exp}^{(b)}_{\mathsf{kpABE},\mathsf{A}}$, modeled as a game between adversary A and a challenger, is defined as follows:

1. **Setup phase:** *On input* 1^λ, A *submits* $(1^{\mathsf{inp}}, 1^{\mathsf{d}})$ *and the target* $X \subset \{0,1\}^{\mathsf{inp}}$, *which is a set of binary strings of length* inp, *to the challenger. The challenger samples* $(\mathsf{kpABE.mpk}, \mathsf{kpABE.msk}) \leftarrow \mathsf{kpABE.Setup}(1^\lambda, 1^{\mathsf{inp}}, 1^{\mathsf{d}})$ *and replies to* A *with* $\mathsf{kpABE.mpk}$.

2. **Query phase:** *During the game,* A *adaptively makes the following queries, in an arbitrary order and unbounded many times.*

   (a) **Key Queries:** A *chooses a circuit* $C \in \mathcal{C}_{\mathsf{inp,d}}$ *that satisfies* $C(\mathbf{x}) = 0$ *for all* $\mathbf{x} \in X$. *For each such query, the challenger replies with* $\mathsf{kpABE.sk}_C \leftarrow$ $\mathsf{kpABE.KeyGen}(\mathsf{kpABE.mpk}, \mathsf{kpABE.msk}, C)$.

   (b) **Challenge Queries:** A *submits a string* $\mathbf{x} \in X$ *and a pair of equal length messages* $(m_0, m_1) \in (\mathcal{M})^2$ *to the challenger. The challenger replies to* A *with* $\mathsf{kpABE.ct} \leftarrow \mathsf{kpABE.Enc}(\mathsf{kpABE.mpk}, \mathbf{x}, m_b)$.

3. **Output phase:** A *outputs a guess bit* b' *as the output of the experiment.*

Remark 2.7. The above definition allows an adversary to make challenge queries multiple times. More standard notion of the security for an ABE restricts the adversary to make only a single challenge query. It is well-known that they are actually equivalent, which is shown by a simple hybrid argument. We adopt the above definition since it is convenient for our purpose.

Boneh et al. [BGG+14] provided a construction of kpABE which we will use in our construction of cpABE. The following theorem, provided in [AMY19] summarizes the efficiency properties of their construction.

Theorem 2.8 (Adapted from [BGG+14]). *There exists a selectively secure ABE scheme* $\mathsf{kpABE} = (\mathsf{kpABE.Setup}, \mathsf{kpABE.KeyGen}, \mathsf{kpABE.Enc}, \mathsf{kpABE.Dec})$ *with the following properties under the LWE assumption.*

1. *The circuit* $\mathsf{kpABE.Setup}(\cdot, \cdot, \cdot; \cdot)$, *which takes as input* $1^\lambda, 1^{\mathsf{inp}}, 1^{\mathsf{d}}$, *and a randomness* r *and outputs* $\mathsf{kpABE.msk} = \mathsf{kpABE.Setup}(1^\lambda, 1^{\mathsf{inp}}, 1^{\mathsf{d}}; r)$, *can be implemented with depth* $\mathrm{poly}(\lambda, \mathsf{d})$. *In particular, the depth of the circuit is independent of* inp *and the length of the randomness* r.

2. *We have* $|\mathsf{kpABE.sk}_C| \leq \mathrm{poly}(\lambda, \mathsf{d})$ *for any* $C \in \mathcal{C}_{\mathsf{inp,d}}$, *where* $(\mathsf{kpABE.mpk}, \mathsf{kpABE.msk}) \leftarrow \mathsf{kpABE.Setup}(1^\lambda, 1^{\mathsf{inp}}, 1^{\mathsf{d}})$ *and* $\mathsf{kpABE.sk}_C \leftarrow \mathsf{kpABE.KeyGen}$ $(\mathsf{kpABE.mpk}, \mathsf{kpABE.msk}, C)$. *In particular, the length of the secret key is independent of the input length* inp *and the size of the circuit* C.

3. *Let* $C : \{0,1\}^{\mathsf{inp}+\ell} \to \{0,1\}$ *be a circuit such that we have* $C[v] \in \mathcal{C}_{\mathsf{inp,d}}$ *for any* $v \in \{0,1\}^\ell$. *Then, the circuit* $\mathsf{kpABE.KeyGen}(\cdot, \cdot, C[\cdot]; \cdot)$, *that takes as input* $\mathsf{kpABE.mpk}$, $\mathsf{kpABE.msk}$, v, *and randomness* $\widehat{\mathsf{R}}$ *and outputs* $\mathsf{kpABE.KeyGen}($ $\mathsf{kpABE.mpk}, \mathsf{kpABE.msk}, C[v]; \widehat{\mathsf{R}})$, *can be implemented with depth* $\mathrm{depth}(C) \cdot$ $\mathrm{poly}(\lambda, \mathsf{d})$.

2.2 Key Policy Functional Encryption for Circuits

For $\lambda \in \mathbb{N}$, let $\mathcal{C}_{\mathsf{inp,d,out}}$ denote a family of circuits with inp bit inputs, depth d, and output length out and $\mathcal{C} = \{\mathcal{C}_{\mathsf{inp}(\lambda), \mathsf{d}(\lambda), \mathsf{out}(\lambda)}\}_{\lambda \in \mathbb{N}}$. A functional encryption (FE) scheme $\mathsf{FE} = (\mathsf{FE.Setup}, \mathsf{FE.KeyGen}, \mathsf{FE.Enc}, \mathsf{FE.Dec})$ for $\mathcal{C}$ consists of four algorithms:

– FE.Setup($1^\lambda, 1^{\mathsf{inp}}, 1^{\mathsf{d}}, 1^{\mathsf{out}}$) is a PPT algorithm takes as input the unary representation of the security parameter, the length $\mathsf{inp} = \mathsf{inp}(\lambda)$ of the input, depth $\mathsf{d} = \mathsf{d}(\lambda)$, and the length of the output $\mathsf{out} = \mathsf{out}(\lambda)$ of the circuit family $\mathcal{C}_{\mathsf{inp}(\lambda),\mathsf{d}(\lambda),\mathsf{out}(\lambda)}$ to be supported. It outputs the master public key FE.mpk and the master secret key FE.msk.

– FE.KeyGen(FE.mpk, FE.msk, C) is a PPT algorithm that takes as input the master public key FE.mpk, master secret key FE.msk, and a circuit $C \in \mathcal{C}_{\mathsf{inp}(\lambda),\mathsf{d}(\lambda),\mathsf{out}(\lambda)}$ and outputs a corresponding secret key FE.sk$_C$. We assume that FE.sk$_C$ contains C and FE.mpk.

– FE.Enc(FE.mpk, $\mathbf{x}$) is a PPT algorithm that takes as input the master public key FE.mpk and an input message $\mathbf{x} \in \{0,1\}^{\mathsf{inp}(\lambda)}$ and outputs a ciphertext FE.ct.

– FE.Dec(FE.mpk, FE.sk$_C$, FE.ct) is a deterministic algorithm that takes as input the master public key FE.mpk, a secret key FE.sk$_C$ and a ciphertext FE.ct and outputs $C(\mathbf{x})$.

Definition 2.9 (Correctness). *A functional encryption scheme* FE *is correct if for all* $C \in \mathcal{C}_{\mathsf{inp}(\lambda),\mathsf{d}(\lambda),\mathsf{out}(\lambda)}$ *and all* $\mathbf{x} \in \{0,1\}^{\mathsf{inp}(\lambda)}$,

$$\Pr\left[\begin{array}{l} (\mathsf{FE.mpk}, \mathsf{FE.msk}) \leftarrow \mathsf{FE.Setup}(1^\lambda, 1^{\mathsf{inp}(\lambda)}, 1^{\mathsf{d}(\lambda)}, 1^{\mathsf{out}(\lambda)}); \\ \mathsf{ct} \leftarrow \mathsf{FE.Enc}(\mathsf{FE.mpk}, \mathbf{x}); \\ \mathsf{FE.Dec}\Big(\mathsf{FE.mpk}, \mathsf{FE.KeyGen}(\mathsf{FE.mpk}, \mathsf{FE.msk}, C), \mathsf{ct}\Big) \neq C(\mathbf{x}) \end{array} \right] = \mathrm{negl}(\lambda)$$

where the probability is taken over the coins of FE.Setup, FE.KeyGen, FE.Enc *and,* FE.Dec*).*

We then define full simulation based security for single key FE as in [GKP+13, Defn 2.13].

Definition 2.10 (FULL-SIM Security). *Let* FE *be a functional encryption scheme for a circuits. For a stateful PPT adversary* A *and a stateless PPT simulator* Sim, *consider the following two experiments:*

$\mathsf{Exp}^{\mathsf{real}}_{\mathsf{FE},\mathsf{A}}(1^\lambda)$:	$\mathsf{Exp}^{\mathsf{ideal}}_{\mathsf{FE},\mathrm{Sim}}(1^\lambda)$:
1: $(1^{\mathsf{inp}}, 1^{\mathsf{d}}, 1^{\mathsf{out}}) \leftarrow \mathsf{A}(1^\lambda)$	*1:* $(1^{\mathsf{inp}}, 1^{\mathsf{d}}, 1^{\mathsf{out}}) \leftarrow \mathsf{A}(1^\lambda)$
2: (FE.mpk, FE.msk)	*2:* (FE.mpk, FE.msk)
$\leftarrow \mathsf{FE.Setup}(1^\lambda, 1^{\mathsf{inp}}, 1^{\mathsf{d}}, 1^{\mathsf{out}})$	$\leftarrow \mathsf{FE.Setup}(1^\lambda, 1^{\mathsf{inp}}, 1^{\mathsf{d}}, 1^{\mathsf{out}})$
3: $C \leftarrow \mathsf{A}(\mathsf{FE.mpk})$	*3:* $C \leftarrow \mathsf{A}(\mathsf{FE.mpk})$
4: FE.sk$_C$	*4:* FE.sk$_C$
$\leftarrow \mathsf{FE.KeyGen}(\mathsf{FE.mpk}, \mathsf{FE.msk}, C)$	$\leftarrow \mathsf{FE.KeyGen}(\mathsf{FE.mpk}, \mathsf{FE.msk}, C)$
5: $\alpha \leftarrow \mathsf{A}^{\mathsf{FE.Enc}(\mathsf{FE.mpk},\cdot)}(\mathsf{FE.mpk}, \mathsf{FE.sk}_C)$	*5:* $\alpha \leftarrow \mathsf{A}^{\mathcal{O}(\cdot)}(\mathsf{FE.mpk}, \mathsf{FE.sk}_C)$

Here, $O(\cdot)$ *is an oracle that on input* $\mathbf{x}$ *from* A, *runs* Sim *with inputs* $(\mathsf{FE.mpk}, \mathsf{sk}_C, C, C(\mathbf{x}), 1^{\mathsf{inp}})$ *to obtain a ciphertext* $\mathsf{FE.ct}$ *and returns it to the adversary* A.

The functional encryption scheme FE *is then said to be single query* FULL-SIM *secure if there exists a PPT simulator* Sim *such that for every PPT adversary* A, *the following two distributions are computationally indistinguishable:*

$$\left\{ \mathsf{Exp}_{\mathsf{FE,A}}^{\mathsf{real}}(1^\lambda) \right\}_{\lambda \in \mathbb{N}} \overset{c}{\approx} \left\{ \mathsf{Exp}_{\mathsf{FE,Sim}}^{\mathsf{ideal}}(1^\lambda) \right\}_{\lambda \in \mathbb{N}}$$

Remark 2.11. Our definition of FULL-SIM *security game for FE differs from* [GKP+13] *in that we allow the adversary to access challenge oracle (either* $O(\cdot)$ *or* $\mathsf{FE.Enc}(\mathsf{FE.mpk}, \cdot)$*) as many times as it wants whereas they only allow one-time access. However, it can be seen that these definitions are equivalent by a simple hybrid argument because the simulation of* $\mathsf{FE.Enc}(\cdot)$ *and* $O(\cdot)$ *does not require any secret information.*

Gorbunov et al. [GKP+13] *provided a construction of single key functional encryption from the learning with errors assumption. The following theorem summarizes the efficiency properties of their construction.*

Theorem 2.12 ([GKP+13]). *There exists an FE scheme* FE = (FE.Setup, FE. KeyGen, FE.Enc, FE.Dec) *with the following properties.*

1. *For any polynomially bounded* $\mathsf{inp}(\lambda), \mathsf{d}(\lambda), \mathsf{out}(\lambda)$, *all the algorithms in* FE *run in polynomial time. Namely, the running time of* FE.Setup *and* FE.Enc *do not depend on the size of circuit description to be supported by the scheme.*
2. *Assuming the subexponential hardness of the LWE problem, the scheme satisfies full-simulation-based security.*

We note that the first property above is called succinctness or semi-compactness of FE. A stronger version of the efficiency property called compactness requires the running time of the encryption algorithm to be dependent only on the length of input message $\mathbf{x}$. *An FE with compactness is known to imply indistinguishability obfuscation* [AJ15, BV15].

IND Based Security for Unbounded Keys. *A functional encryption scheme* FE *for a function family* $\mathcal{C}$ *is secure in the adaptive indistinguishability game, denoted as* ind *secure, if for all probabilistic polynomial-time adversaries* Adv, *the advantage of* Adv *in the following experiment is negligible in the security parameter* λ:

1. **Public Key.** *Challenger* Ch *returns* FE.mpk *to* Adv.
2. **Pre-Challenge Key Queries.** Adv *may adaptively request keys for any circuits* $C_1, \ldots, C_\ell \in \mathcal{C}$. *In response,* Adv *is given the corresponding keys* $\mathsf{FE.sk}_{C_i}$.
3. **Challenge.** Adv *outputs the challenges* $(\mathbf{x}_0, \mathbf{x}_1)$ *to the challenger, subject to the restriction that* $C_i(\mathbf{x}_0) = C_i(\mathbf{x}_1)$ *for all* $i \in [\ell]$. *The challenger chooses a random bit* b, *and returns the ciphertext* $\mathsf{CT}_{\mathbf{x}_b}$.

4. **Post-Challenge Key Queries.** *The adversary may continue to request keys for additional functions C_i, subject to the restriction that $C_i(\mathbf{x}_0) = C_i(\mathbf{x}_1)$ for all i. In response,* Adv *is given the corresponding keys* FE.sk$_{C_i}$.
5. **Guess.** Adv *outputs a bit b', and succeeds if $b' = b$.*

The advantage of Adv *is the absolute value of the difference between its success probability and $1/2$. In the* selective *game, the adversary must announce the challenge in the first step, before receiving the public key. Note that without loss of generality, in the selective game, the challenge ciphertext can be returned along with the public key. In the* semi-adaptive *game, the adversary must announce the challenge after seeing the public key but before making any key requests.*

Symmetric Key Variant. The symmetric key variant of the above definition follows naturally by removing the public key FE.mpk from all the algorithms, and providing the encryptor the master secret key FE.msk. In the security definition, the adversary may request encryption queries in addition to the key queries.

2.3   Predicate Encryption for Circuits

A (Key-Policy) Predicate Encryption scheme PE for an attribute universe $\mathcal{X}$, a predicate universe $\mathcal{C}$, and a message space $\mathcal{M}$, consists of four algorithms (PE.Setup, PE.Enc, PE.KeyGen, PE.Dec):

PE.Setup$(1^\lambda, \mathcal{X}, \mathcal{C}, \mathcal{M}) \to$ (PE.mpk, PE.msk). The setup algorithm gets as input the security parameter λ and a description of $(\mathcal{X}, \mathcal{C}, \mathcal{M})$ and outputs the public parameter PE.mpk, and the master key PE.msk.

PE.Enc(PE.mpk, $\mathbf{x}, \mu) \to$ CT. The encryption algorithm gets as input PE.mpk, an attribute $\mathbf{x} \in \mathcal{X}$ and a message $\mu \in \mathcal{M}$. It outputs a ciphertext CT.

PE.KeyGen(PE.msk, $C) \to$ SK$_C$. The key generation algorithm gets as input PE.msk and a predicate $C \in \mathcal{C}$. It outputs a secret key SK$_C$.

PE.Dec((SK$_C, C)$, CT) $\to \mu \vee \perp$. The decryption algorithm gets as input the secret key SK$_C$, a predicate C, and a ciphertext CT. It outputs a message $\mu \in \mathcal{M}$ or $\perp$.

Correctness. We require that for all (PE.mpk, PE.msk) $\leftarrow$ PE.Setup$(1^\lambda, \mathcal{X}, \mathcal{C}, \mathcal{M})$, for all $(\mathbf{x}, C) \in \mathcal{X} \times \mathcal{C}$ and for all $\mu \in \mathcal{M}$,

- For 1-queries, namely $C(\mathbf{x}) = 1$, $\left[\text{PE.Dec}\big((\text{SK}_C, C), \text{CT}\big) = \mu\right] \geq 1 - \text{negl}(\lambda)$
- For 0-queries, namely $C(\mathbf{x}) = 0$, $\left[\text{PE.Dec}\big((\text{SK}_C, C), \text{CT}\big) = \perp\right] \geq 1 - \text{negl}(\lambda)$

Semi-Adaptive Simulation Security. Below, we define the SA-SIM security experiment for predicate encryption (PE) similarly to Gorbunov et al. [GVW15].

Definition 2.13 (SA-SIM Security). *Let* PE *be a predicate encryption scheme for a circuit family $\mathcal{C}$. For every stateful p.p.t. adversary* Adv *and a stateful p.p.t. simulator* Sim, *consider the following two experiments:*

$\mathsf{Exp}^{\mathsf{real}}_{\mathsf{PE},\mathsf{Adv}}(1^\lambda)\mathbf{:}$	$\mathsf{Exp}^{\mathsf{ideal}}_{\mathsf{PE},\mathsf{Sim}}(1^\lambda)\mathbf{:}$
1: $(\mathsf{PE.mpk}, \mathsf{PE.msk}) \leftarrow \mathsf{PE.Setup}(1^\lambda)$	*1:* $\mathsf{PE.mpk} \leftarrow \mathsf{Sim}(1^\lambda)$
2: $\mathbf{x} \leftarrow \mathsf{Adv}(\mathsf{PE.mpk})$	*2:* $\mathbf{x} \leftarrow \mathsf{Adv}(\mathsf{PE.mpk})$
3: $\mu \leftarrow \mathsf{Adv}^{\mathsf{PE.KeyGen}(\mathsf{PE.msk},\cdot)}(\mathsf{PE.mpk})$	*3:* $\mu \leftarrow \mathsf{Adv}^{\mathsf{Sim}}(\mathsf{PE.mpk})$
4: $\mathsf{CT} \leftarrow \mathsf{PE.Enc}\big(\mathsf{PE.mpk}, \mathbf{x}, \mu\big)$	*4:* $\mathsf{CT} \leftarrow \mathsf{Sim}\,(\mathsf{PE.mpk}, 1^{|\mathbf{x}|}, 1^{|\mu|})$
5: $\alpha \leftarrow \mathsf{Adv}^{\mathsf{PE.KeyGen}(\mathsf{PE.msk},\cdot)}(\mathsf{CT})$	*5:* $\alpha \leftarrow \mathsf{Adv}^{\mathsf{Sim}}(\mathsf{CT})$
6: *Output* $(\mathbf{x}, \mu, \alpha)$	*6:* *Output* $(\mathbf{x}, \mu, \alpha)$

We say an adversary Adv *is admissible if for all queries* C *that it makes, it holds that* $C(\mathbf{x}) = 0$.

The predicate encryption scheme PE *is said to be* SA-SIM-*attribute hiding if there exists a p.p.t. simulator* Sim *such that for every admissible p.p.t. adversary* Adv, *the following two distributions are computationally indistinguishable:*

$$\left\{ \mathsf{Exp}^{\mathsf{real}}_{\mathsf{PE},\mathsf{Adv}}(1^\lambda) \right\}_{\lambda \in \mathbb{N}} \overset{c}{\approx} \left\{ \mathsf{Exp}^{\mathsf{ideal}}_{\mathsf{PE},\mathsf{Sim}}(1^\lambda) \right\}_{\lambda \in \mathbb{N}}$$

Symmetric Key Variant. The symmetric key variant of the above definition follows naturally by removing the public key PE.mpk from all the algorithms, and providing the encryptor the master secret key PE.msk. In the security definition, the adversary is given access to the encryption oracle in addition to the key generation oracle.

Ciphertext Policy Variant. The ciphertext policy variant of the above definition reverses the role of the ciphertext and key. In more detail, the ciphertext encodes the circuit C along with message μ, and the secret key contains the attribute $\mathbf{x}$. We require that the running time of the key generation algorithm does not depend on the size of the circuit $|C|$ (but may depend on its depth).

2.4   Function Hiding Symmetric Key Predicate Encryption

A Function Hiding Symmetric Key Predicate Encryption scheme FHPE for an attribute universe $\mathcal{X}$, a predicate universe $\mathcal{C}$, and a message space $\mathcal{M}$, consists of four algorithms (FHPE.Setup, FHPE.Enc, FHPE.KeyGen, FHPE.Dec):

FHPE.Setup($1^\lambda, \mathcal{X}, \mathcal{C}, \mathcal{M}$) $\to$ FHPE.msk. The setup algorithm gets as input the security parameter λ and a description of $(\mathcal{X}, \mathcal{C}, \mathcal{M})$ and outputs the master key FHPE.msk.

FHPE.Enc(FHPE.msk, $\mathbf{x}, \mu$) $\to$ CT. The encryption algorithm gets as input FHPE.msk, an attribute $\mathbf{x} \in \mathcal{X}$ and a message $\mu \in \mathcal{M}$. It outputs a ciphertext CT.

FHPE.KeyGen(FHPE.msk, C) $\to$ SK_C. The key generation algorithm gets as input FHPE.msk and a predicate $C \in \mathcal{C}$. It outputs a secret key SK_C.

FHPE.Dec(SK_C, CT) $\to \mu \vee \perp$. The decryption algorithm gets as input the secret key SK_C and a ciphertext CT. It outputs a message $\mu \in \mathcal{M}$ or $\perp$.

Correctness. We require that for all (FHPE.msk) ← FHPE.Setup($1^\lambda, \mathcal{X}, \mathcal{C}, \mathcal{M}$), for all $(\mathbf{x}, C) \in \mathcal{X} \times \mathcal{C}$ and for all $\mu \in \mathcal{M}$,

- For 1-queries, namely $C(\mathbf{x}) = 1$, $\Pr\left[\mathsf{PE.Dec}(\mathsf{SK}_C, \mathsf{CT}) = \mu\right] \geq 1 - \mathrm{negl}(\lambda)$
- For 0-queries, namely $C(\mathbf{x}) = 0$, $\Pr\left[\mathsf{PE.Dec}(\mathsf{SK}_C, \mathsf{CT}) = \bot\right] \geq 1 - \mathrm{negl}(\lambda)$

Function Hiding IND Security. The standard function hiding indistinguishability game for secret key predicate encryption may be defined as follows.

Definition 2.14 (Function hiding IND Security). *A symmetric key predicate encryption scheme* PE *is function-hiding, if every admissible PPT adversary* Adv *has negligible advantage in the following game:*

1. *Key Generation. The challenger* Ch *samples* msk ← FHPE.Setup(1^λ).
2. *The challenger* Ch *chooses a random bit b and repeats the following with* Adv *for an arbitrary number of times determined by* Adv:
   - *Function Queries. Upon* Adv *choosing a pair of functions* (C_0, C_1), Ch *sends* Adv *a function key* SK ← FHPE.KeyGen(msk, C_b).
   - *Message Queries. Upon* Adv *choosing a pair of attribute vectors* $(\mathbf{x}_0, \mathbf{x}_1)$ *and a message* μ, Ch *sends* Adv *a ciphertext* CT ← FHPE.Enc(msk, $\mathbf{x}_b, \mu$).
3. *The adversary outputs a guess b' for the bit b and wins if b = b'.*

We say an adversary is admissible if for all function and message queries, it holds that $C_0(\mathbf{x}_0) = C_1(\mathbf{x}_1) = 0$.

On Ciphertext Queries. A natural game would also allow the adversary to request ciphertexts for attribute vectors $\mathbf{x}_0, \mathbf{x}_1$ and message $\mu_0 = \mu_1 = \mu$ such that $C_0(\mathbf{x}_0) = C_1(\mathbf{x}_1) = 1$, enabling the adversary to recover μ. However, as we show in Sect. 5.3, such a game renders the primitive strong enough to imply symmetric key functional encryption, which in turn is sufficient to imply iO [BNPW16].

Function Hiding SIM Security. Below, we define attribute and function hiding SA-SIM security for predicate encryption (FHPE).

Definition 2.15 (Function Hiding SA-SIM Security). *Let* FHPE *be a function hiding, symmetric key predicate encryption scheme for a circuit family $\mathcal{C}$. For every stateful p.p.t. adversary* Adv *and a stateful p.p.t. simulator* Sim, *consider the following two experiments:*

$\mathsf{Exp}^{\mathrm{real}}_{\mathsf{PE},\mathsf{Adv}}(1^\lambda)$:	$\mathsf{Exp}^{\mathrm{ideal}}_{\mathsf{PE},\mathsf{Sim}}(1^\lambda)$:
1: FHPE.msk ← FHPE.Setup(1^λ)	
2: $\{\mathbf{x}^*_i\}_{i \in \mathrm{poly}} \leftarrow \mathsf{Adv}(1^\lambda)$	1: $\{\mathbf{x}^*_i\}_{i \in \mathrm{poly}} \leftarrow \mathsf{Adv}(1^\lambda)$
3: $\{\mu^*_i\}_{i \in \mathrm{poly}}, \{C^*_i\}_{i \in \mathrm{poly}} \leftarrow \mathsf{Adv}^{\mathcal{O}(\mathsf{msk}, \cdot)}$	2: $\{\mu^*_i\}_{i \in \mathrm{poly}}, \{C^*_i\}_{i \in \mathrm{poly}} \leftarrow \mathsf{Adv}^{\mathrm{Sim}}$
4: $\{\mathsf{CT}_i \leftarrow \mathsf{FHPE.Enc}(\mathsf{msk}, \mathbf{x}_i, \mu^*_i)\}_i$	3: $\{\mathsf{CT}_i\}, \{\mathsf{SK}_{C^*_i}\}_i$
5: $\{\mathsf{SK}_{C^*_i} \leftarrow \mathsf{FHPE.KeyGen}(\mathsf{msk}, C^*_i)\}_i$	$\leftarrow \mathsf{Sim}\left(\{1^{\|\mathbf{x}^*_i\|}, 1^{\|\mu^*_i\|}\}_i, \{1^{\|C^*_i\|}\}_i\right)$
6: $\alpha \leftarrow \mathsf{Adv}^{\mathcal{O}(\mathsf{msk}, \cdot)}(\{\mathsf{CT}_i\}, \{\mathsf{SK}_{C^*_i}\}_i)$	4: $\alpha \leftarrow \mathsf{Adv}^{\mathrm{Sim}}(\{\mathsf{CT}_i\}_i, \{\mathsf{SK}_{C^*_i}\}_i)$
7: *Output* $(\{\mathbf{x}^*_i, \mu^*_i\}_i, \{C^*_i\}_i, \alpha)$	5: *Output* $(\{\mathbf{x}^*_i, \mu_i\}_i, \{C^*_i\}_i, \alpha)$

Above, $\mathcal{O}$ is an oracle that upon receiving attribute and circuit queries from the adversary, returns ciphertexts and keys by running FHPE.Enc *and* FHPE.KeyGen *respectively.*

We say an adversary Adv *is admissible if for all circuit queries C_i and challenge circuits C_i^*, and for all attribute queries $\mathbf{x}_j$ and challenge attributes $\mathbf{x}_j^*$, it holds that $C_i(\mathbf{x}_j) = C_i^*(\mathbf{x}_j) = C_i(\mathbf{x}_j^*) = C_i^*(\mathbf{x}_j^*) = 0$.*

The symmetric key predicate encryption scheme PE *is said to be* SA-SIM *secure with attribute and function hiding if there exists a p.p.t. simulator* Sim *such that for every admissible p.p.t. adversary* Adv*, the following two distributions are computationally indistinguishable:*

$$\left\{ \mathsf{Exp}^{real}_{\mathsf{PE},\mathsf{Adv}}(1^\lambda) \right\}_{\lambda \in \mathbb{N}} \stackrel{c}{\approx} \left\{ \mathsf{Exp}^{ideal}_{\mathsf{PE},\mathrm{Sim}}(1^\lambda) \right\}_{\lambda \in \mathbb{N}}$$

Adaptive Variant of Security. We can consider stronger variant of the above security definition where the adversary interleaves the challenge queries $\mathbf{x}_i^*$ and C_i^* in an arbitrary order instead of submitting them at the beginning of the game. We call this security notion adaptive simulation function hiding security.

On Ciphertext Queries. We note that the above definition restricts the adversary in its encryption queries. A more natural game would allow an adversary to request a key for a circuit C and encryption for pair $(\mathbf{x}, \mu)$ such that $C(\mathbf{x}) = 1$. This enables the adversary to recover μ but intuitively does not violate security since μ was picked by the adversary. However, as discussed in the case of IND based function hiding, such a game renders the primitive strong enough to imply symmetric key functional encryption, which in turn is sufficient to imply iO [BNPW16].

3   Secret Key CP-ABE for Unbounded Circuits

We construct a secret key ciphertext policy ABE scheme for a family of circuits $\mathcal{C}_{\mathsf{n},\mathsf{d}}$ with n bit inputs, an a-priori bounded depth d, and binary output. Our scheme is denoted by cpABE = (cpABE.Setup, cpABE.KeyGen, cpABE.Enc, cpABE.Dec) and is constructed using the following ingredients:

1. PRF = (PRF.Setup, PRF.Eval): a pseudorandom function, where a PRF key $\mathsf{K} \leftarrow \mathsf{PRF.Setup}(1^\lambda)$ defines a function $\mathsf{PRF.Eval}(\mathsf{K}, \cdot) : \{0,1\}^\lambda \to \{0,1\}$. We denote the length of K by $|\mathsf{K}|$.
2. FE = (FE.Setup, FE.KeyGen, FE.Enc, FE.Dec): a functional encryption scheme for circuit with the efficiency property described in Item 1 of Theorem 2.12. We can instantiate FE with the scheme proposed by Goldwasser et al. [GKP+13].
3. kpABE = (kpABE.Setup, kpABE.KeyGen, kpABE.Enc, kpABE.Dec): An ABE scheme that satisfies the efficiency properties described in Theorem 2.8. We can instantiate kpABE with the scheme proposed by Boneh et al. [BGG+14].

4. $U(\cdot, \cdot)$: a universal circuit [CH85] that takes as input a circuit C of fixed depth and size and an input $\mathbf{x}$ to the circuit and outputs $C(\mathbf{x})$. We will denote by $U_y(\cdot, \cdot)$ the above circuit when the size of the first input C is y. We denote by $U_y[\mathbf{x}](\cdot) = U(\cdot, \mathbf{x})$ the above circuit with the second input $\mathbf{x}$ being hardwired. By the construction of universal circuit [CH85], we have $\mathsf{depth}(U) \leq O(\mathsf{depth}(C))$.

Below we provide our construction for secret key CP-ABE for circuits. Below, we overload notation and denote the randomness used in a PPT algorithm by a key K of a pseudorandom function PRF. Namely, for a PPT algorithm (or circuit) A that takes as input x and a randomness $r \in \{0,1\}^\ell$ and outputs y, $\mathsf{A}(x; \mathsf{K})$ denotes an algorithm that computes $r := \mathsf{PRF.Eval}(\mathsf{K}, 1) \| \mathsf{PRF.Eval}(\mathsf{K}, 2) \| \cdots \| \mathsf{PRF.Eval}(\mathsf{K}, \ell)$ and runs $\mathsf{A}(x; r)$.

$\mathsf{cpABE.Setup}(1^\lambda, 1^n, 1^d)$: On input the security parameter 1^λ and the input length n and depth d of the circuit family, do the following:

1. For all $j \in [0, \lambda]$, sample PRF keys $\widehat{\mathsf{K}}_j, \mathsf{R}_j \leftarrow \mathsf{PRF.Setup}(1^\lambda)$.
2. For all $j \in [0, \lambda]$, sample $(\mathsf{FE.mpk}_j, \mathsf{FE.msk}_j) \leftarrow \mathsf{FE.Setup}(1^\lambda, 1^{\mathsf{inp}(\lambda)}, 1^{\mathsf{out}(\lambda)}, 1^{d(\lambda)})$.

   Here, we generate $\lambda + 1$ instances of FE. Note that all instances support a circuit class with input length $\mathsf{inp}(\lambda) = n + 2|\mathsf{K}|$, output length $\mathsf{out}(\lambda)$, and depth $d(\lambda)$, where $\mathsf{out}(\lambda)$ and $d(\lambda)$ are polynomials in the security parameter that will be specified later.
3. Output $\mathsf{cpABE.msk} = (\{\widehat{\mathsf{K}}_j, \mathsf{R}_j, \mathsf{FE.mpk}_j, \mathsf{FE.msk}_j\}_{j \in [0,\lambda]})$.

$\mathsf{cpABE.Enc}(\mathsf{cpABE.msk}, C, m)$: On input the master secret key $\mathsf{cpABE.msk}$, a circuit $C \in \mathcal{C}_{n,d}$, and a message $m \in \mathcal{M}$, do the following:

1. Parse the master secret key as $\mathsf{cpABE.msk} \rightarrow (\{\widehat{\mathsf{K}}_j, \mathsf{R}_j, \mathsf{FE.mpk}_j, \mathsf{FE.msk}_j\}_{j \in [0,\lambda]})$.
2. Pad the circuit length to the next power of two: Let $\ell = |C|$ and $i = \lceil \log \ell \rceil$. Set $\hat{C} = C \| \perp^{2^i - \ell}$.
3. Sample a fresh kpABE scheme to support inputs of size $|\hat{C}|$: Compute a kpABE key pair

$$(\mathsf{kpABE.mpk}_i, \mathsf{kpABE.msk}_i) = \mathsf{kpABE.Setup}(1^\lambda, 1^{2^i}, 1^{\hat{d}}; \widehat{\mathsf{K}}_i)$$

   Here $\widehat{\mathsf{K}}_i$ is the randomness and $\hat{d}$ is a parameter chosen later.
4. Compute $\mathsf{kpABE.ct} \leftarrow \mathsf{kpABE.Enc}(\mathsf{kpABE.mpk}_i, \hat{C}, m)$ as an kpABE ciphertext for the message m under attribute $\hat{C}$.
5. Obtain $\mathsf{FE.sk}_i = \mathsf{FE.KeyGen}(\mathsf{FE.mpk}_i, \mathsf{FE.msk}_i, F_{n,2^i}; \mathsf{R}_i)$, where $F_{n,2^i}$ is a circuit described in Fig. 1.
6. Output $\mathsf{cpABE.ct} = (\mathsf{FE.sk}_i, \mathsf{kpABE.mpk}_i, \mathsf{kpABE.ct})$.

Function $F_{n,2^i}$

1. Parse the input $\mathbf{w} = (\mathbf{x}, \widehat{K}, \widehat{R})$, where $\mathbf{x}$ is an input string of length n and $\widehat{K}$ and $\widehat{R}$ are PRF keys.
2. Compute $(\mathsf{kpABE.mpk}, \mathsf{kpABE.msk}) = \mathsf{kpABE.Setup}(1^\lambda, 1^{2^i}, 1^{\widehat{d}}; \widehat{K})$.
3. Compute and output

$$\mathsf{kpABE.sk}_{U_{2^i}[\mathbf{x}]} = \mathsf{kpABE.KeyGen}(\mathsf{kpABE.mpk}, \mathsf{kpABE.msk}, U_{2^i}[\mathbf{x}]; \widehat{R})$$

Fig. 1. The definition of $F_{n,2^i}$

$\mathsf{cpABE.KeyGen}(\mathsf{cpABE.msk}, \mathbf{x})$: On input the master secret key $\mathsf{cpABE.msk}$ and the attribute vector $\mathbf{x}$, do the following:

1. Parse the master secret key as $\mathsf{cpABE.msk} \rightarrow (\{\widehat{K}_j, R_j, \mathsf{FE.mpk}_j, \mathsf{FE.msk}_j\}_{j \in [0,\lambda]})$.
2. Sample $\widetilde{R}_j \leftarrow \mathsf{PRF.Setup}(1^\lambda)$ for all $j \in [0, \lambda]$.
3. Compute $\mathsf{FE.ct}_j = \mathsf{FE.Enc}(\mathsf{FE.mpk}_j, (\mathbf{x}, \widehat{K}_j, \widehat{R}_j))$ for all $j \in [0, \lambda]$.
4. Output $\mathsf{cpABE.sk}_{\mathbf{x}} = \{\mathsf{FE.ct}_j\}_{j \in [0,\lambda]}$.

$\mathsf{cpABE.Dec}(\mathsf{cpABE.sk}_{\mathbf{x}}, \mathbf{x}, \mathsf{cpABE.ct}, C)$: On input a secret key for attribute vector $\mathbf{x}$ and a ciphertext encoded for circuit C, do the following:

1. Parse the secret key as $\mathsf{cpABE.sk}_{\mathbf{x}} = \{\mathsf{FE.ct}_j\}_{j \in [0,\lambda]}$ and the ciphertext as $\mathsf{cpABE.ct} = (\mathsf{FE.sk}_i, \mathsf{kpABE.mpk}_i, \mathsf{kpABE.ct})$.
2. Set $\ell = |C|$ and choose $\mathsf{FE.ct}_i$ from $\mathsf{cpABE.sk}_{\mathbf{x}} = \{\mathsf{FE.ct}_j\}_{j \in [0,\lambda]}$ such that $i = \lceil \log \ell \rceil < \lambda$.
3. Compute $y = \mathsf{FE.Dec}(\mathsf{FE.mpk}_i, \mathsf{FE.sk}_i, \mathsf{FE.ct}_i)$.
4. Compute and output $z = \mathsf{kpABE.Dec}(\mathsf{kpABE.mpk}_i, y, U_{2^i}[\mathbf{x}], \mathsf{kpABE.ct}_i, \widehat{C})$, where we interpret y as an ABE secret key and $\widehat{C} = C \| \perp^{2^i - \ell}$.

Efficiency. The following theorem asserts that our scheme is efficient.

Theorem 3.1. *For appropriately chosen $\widehat{\mathsf{d}}(\lambda)$, $\mathsf{out}(\lambda)$, and $\mathsf{d}(\lambda)$, each algorithm of our scheme* cpABE *runs in polynomial time of input length.*

Correctness. Intuitively, correctness follows directly from the correctness of kpABE and FE. The following theorem shows that our scheme is correct.

Theorem 3.2. *For appropriately chosen $\widehat{\mathsf{d}}(\lambda)$, $\mathsf{out}(\lambda)$, and $\mathsf{d}(\lambda)$, our scheme* cpABE *is correct for any polynomially bounded $\mathsf{n}(\lambda)$.*

Security. We can prove that if FE and kpABE are secure then so is the cpABE defined above. Formally, we have the following theorem.

Theorem 3.3. *Assume that FE satisfies full simulation based security, kpABE is selectively secure, and that PRF is a secure pseudorandom function. Then,* cpABE *satisfies selective security.*

The proof of the above theorems will appear in the full version.

4   Public Key CP-ABE for Bounded Circuits

In this section, we construct a public key ciphertext policy ABE scheme for bounded sized circuits $\mathcal{C}_{n,d,s}$, where n is the input length, d is the depth and s is the upper bound of the size . In our construction, the size of the secret key and ciphertext satisfy the efficiency properties desired from CP-ABE (Definition 2.4). Additionally, the running time of the encrypt and decrypt algorithms depend only on the size of the circuit C and not on the worst case circuit size s. However, the running time of the setup algorithm grows with the size s of the circuits supported by the scheme. We note that the inefficiency of setup is mitigated since it is only run once.

We provide the construction next.

cpABE.Setup($1^\lambda, 1^n, 1^d, 1^s$): On input the security parameter λ and the input length n, depth d and the upper bound of the size s of the circuit family, set $\eta := \lceil \log s \rceil$ and do the following:

1. For all $j \in [0, \eta]$, sample PRF keys $\widehat{K}_j, R_j \leftarrow$ PRF.Setup(1^λ).
2. For all $j \in [0, \eta]$, sample (kpABE.mpk$_j$, kpABE.msk$_j$) = kpABE.Setup $(1^\lambda, 1^{2^j}, 1^{\hat{d}}; \widehat{K}_j)$. Here, $\hat{d}$ is the depth of the universal circuit $U(\cdot, \cdot)$ for circuits of size $s \geq 2^j$ and depth d.
3. For all $j \in [0, \eta]$, sample (FE.mpk$_j$, FE.msk$_j$) $\leftarrow$ FE.Setup($1^\lambda, 1^{\mathsf{inp}(\lambda)}, 1^{\mathsf{out}(\lambda)}$, $1^{\mathsf{d}(\lambda)}$). Here, input length inp $= n + 2|K|$, output length out is the length of the kpABE secret key, and depth $\tilde{d}$ is the depth of the kpABE.KeyGen algorithm.
4. For all $j \in [0, \eta]$, obtain FE.sk$_j$ = FE.KeyGen(FE.mpk$_j$, FE.msk$_j$, $F_{n,2^j}$; R_j), where $F_{n,2^j}$ is a circuit described in Fig. 2.
5. Output cpABE.mpk = ({FE.mpk$_j$, kpABE.mpk$_j$, FE.sk$_j$}$_{j \in [0,\eta]}$) and cpABE. msk = ({$\widehat{K}_j$}$_{j \in [0,\eta]}$).

cpABE.Enc(cpABE.mpk, C, m): On input the master public key cpABE.mpk, a circuit C of size $|C| = \ell$, and a message $m \in \mathcal{M}$, do the following:

1. Parse the master public key as cpABE.mpk $\rightarrow$ ({FE.mpk$_j$, kpABE.mpk$_j$, FE.sk$_j$}$_{j \in [0,\eta]}$).
2. Pad the circuit length to the next power of two: Set $i = \lceil \log \ell \rceil$ and $\hat{C} = C \| \perp^{2^i - \ell}$.
3. Compute kpABE.ct $\leftarrow$ kpABE.Enc(kpABE.mpk$_i$, $\hat{C}, m$) as an kpABE ciphertext for the message m under attribute $\hat{C}$.
4. Output cpABE.ct = kpABE.ct.

Function $F_{n,2^i}$

(a) Parse the input $\mathbf{w} = (\mathbf{x}, \widehat{K}, \widehat{R})$, where $\mathbf{x}$ is an input string of length n and $\widehat{K}$ and $\widehat{R}$ are PRF keys.

(b) Compute $(\mathsf{kpABE.mpk}, \mathsf{kpABE.msk}) = \mathsf{kpABE.Setup}(1^\lambda, 1^{2^i}, 1^d; \widehat{K})$.

(c) Compute and output

$$\mathsf{kpABE.sk}_{U_{2^i}[\mathbf{x}]} = \mathsf{kpABE.KeyGen}(\mathsf{kpABE.mpk}, \mathsf{kpABE.msk}, U_{2^i}[\mathbf{x}]; \widehat{R})$$

Fig. 2. The definition of $F_{n,2^i}$

$\mathsf{cpABE.KeyGen}(\mathsf{cpABE.mpk}, \mathsf{cpABE.msk}, \mathbf{x})$: On input the master secret key $\mathsf{cpABE.msk}$ and the attribute vector $\mathbf{x}$, do the following:

1. Parse the master public key as $\mathsf{cpABE.mpk} \rightarrow (\{\mathsf{FE.mpk}_j, \mathsf{kpABE.mpk}_j, \mathsf{FE.sk}_j\}_{j\in[0,\eta]})$ and the master secret key as $\mathsf{cpABE.msk} \rightarrow (\{\widehat{K}_j\}_{j\in[0,\eta]})$.
2. Sample $\widehat{R}_j \leftarrow \mathsf{PRF.Setup}(1^\lambda)$ for all $j \in [0,\eta]$.
3. Compute $\mathsf{FE.ct}_j = \mathsf{FE.Enc}(\mathsf{FE.mpk}_j, (\mathbf{x}, \widehat{K}_j, \widehat{R}_j))$ for all $j \in [0,\eta]$.
4. Output $\mathsf{cpABE.sk}_{\mathbf{x}} = \{\mathsf{FE.ct}_j\}_{j\in[0,\eta]}$.

$\mathsf{cpABE.Dec}(\mathsf{cpABE.mpk}, \mathsf{cpABE.sk}_{\mathbf{x}}, \mathbf{x}, \mathsf{cpABE.ct}, C)$: On input a secret key for attribute vector $\mathbf{x}$ and a ciphertext encoded for circuit C, do the following:

1. Parse the secret key as $\mathsf{cpABE.sk}_{\mathbf{x}} = \{\mathsf{FE.ct}_j\}_{j\in[0,\lambda]}$ and the ciphertext as $\mathsf{cpABE.ct} = \mathsf{kpABE.ct}$.
2. Compute $y = \mathsf{FE.Dec}(\mathsf{FE.mpk}_i, \mathsf{FE.sk}_i, \mathsf{FE.ct}_i)$.
3. Compute and output $z = \mathsf{kpABE.Dec}(\mathsf{kpABE.mpk}_i, y, U_{2^i}[\mathbf{x}], \mathsf{kpABE.ct}, C)$, where we interpret y as an ABE secret key.

Correctness and Efficiency. Correctness is evident from correctness of FE and kpABE. By correctness of FE, we get that $y = \mathsf{kpABE.sk}_{U_{2^i}[\mathbf{x}]}$. By correctness of kpABE we get that $z = m$ iff $U_{2^i}[\mathbf{x}](C) = C(\mathbf{x}) = 1$.

Next, we discuss the efficiency of the above scheme. We assume that each algorithm has RAM access to $\mathsf{cpABE.mpk}$. Note that the encryption algorithm runs in time that depends only on the size of the input circuit $|C|$ and not on s. The key generation algorithm runs in polynomial time in $|\mathbf{x}|$ and λ, and the decryption algorithm runs in polynomial time in $|C|$, $|\mathbf{x}|$, and λ. Thus, the above scheme satisfies the relaxed efficiency of Definition 2.4. Note that this efficiency property does not hold if we remove the assumption that each algorithm has RAM access to $\mathsf{cpABE.mpk}$, since the length of $\mathsf{cpABE.mpk}$, which is input to these algorithms, is polynomially dependent on s.

Security. The proof of security directly follows from the secret key case (Sect. 3). In more detail, we have the following theorem. The proof of the theorem will appear in the full version.

Theorem 4.1. *Assume that* FE *satisfies full simulation based security (Definition 2.10),* kpABE *satisfies selectively security (Definition 2.6), and that* PRF *is a secure pseudorandom function. Then, the public key* cpABE *described above satisfies selective security (Definition 2.2).*

5 Function Hiding Predicate Encryption for Circuits

In this section, we provide a construction for function hiding predicate encryption in the symmetric key setting. Let the attribute universe be $\mathcal{X}$, the predicate universe be $\mathcal{C}$, the message space be $\mathcal{M}$. Then, we construct the algorithms (FHPE.Setup, FHPE.Enc, FHPE.KeyGen, FHPE.Dec) as follows:

FHPE.Setup($1^\lambda, \mathcal{X}, \mathcal{C}, \mathcal{M}$): The setup algorithm gets as input the security parameter λ and a description of $(\mathcal{X}, \mathcal{C}, \mathcal{M})$ and does the following:

1. Sample a symmetric key encryption scheme SKE. Let SKE.SK $\leftarrow$ SKE.Setup(1^λ).
2. Sample a symmetric key predicate encryption scheme PE without function hiding. Let PE.msk $\leftarrow$ PE.Setup(1^λ).
3. Output FHPE.msk $=$ (PE.msk, SKE.SK).

FHPE.Enc(FHPE.msk, $\mathbf{x}, \mu$): The encryption algorithm gets as input FHPE.msk, an attribute $\mathbf{x} \in \mathcal{X}$, a message $\mu \in \mathcal{M}$, and does the following:

1. Interpret FHPE.msk $=$ (PE.msk, SKE.SK).
2. Define $\mathbf{a} = (\mathbf{x}, \text{SKE.SK})$ and compute CT $\leftarrow$ PE.Enc(PE.msk, $\mathbf{a}, \mu$).
3. Output CT.

FHPE.KeyGen(FHPE.msk, C): The key generation algorithm gets as input FHPE.msk, a predicate $C \in \mathcal{C}$ and does the following:

1. Let $\hat{C} = $ SKE.Enc(SKE.SK, C).
2. Define the circuit $U_{\hat{C}}(\cdot)$ as in Fig. 3.
3. Compute $SK_C = $ PE.KeyGen(PE.msk, $U_{\hat{C}}$) and output it.

Function $U_{\hat{C}}$

(a) Parse the input $\mathbf{a} = (\mathbf{x}, \mathbf{k})$, where $\mathbf{x} \in \mathcal{X}$ is an input string and $\mathbf{k}$ is an SKE secret key of length λ.
(b) Compute $C = $ SKE.Dec($\hat{C}, \mathbf{k}$)
(c) Compute and output $C(\mathbf{x})$

Fig. 3. The definition of $U_{\hat{C}}$

FHPE.Dec(SK_C, CT): The decryption algorithm gets as input the secret key SK_C and a ciphertext CT, runs PE.Dec(SK_C, CT) and outputs it.

Correctness. Correctness follows directly from the correctness of PE and SKE. Note that, by correctness of PE we have that $\mathsf{PE.Dec}(\mathsf{SK}_C, \mathsf{CT}) = U_{\hat{C}}(\mathbf{x}, \mathsf{SKE.SK})$. Next, by correctness of SKE we have $\mathsf{SKE.Dec}(\hat{C}, \mathsf{SKE.SK}) = C$. Hence decryption outputs μ if and only if $U_{\hat{C}}(\mathbf{x}, \mathsf{SKE.SK}) = C(\mathbf{x}) = 1$.

Security. Next, we prove that the above construction satisfies function hiding as defined in Sect. 2.4. In more detail, we have:

Theorem 5.1. *Suppose that* PE *is a symmetric key predicate encryption scheme satisfying* SA-SIM[7] *attribute hiding (Definition 2.13) and* SKE *is a semantically secure symmetric key encryption scheme. Then the function hiding predicate encryption scheme* FHPE *described above satisfies* SA-SIM *attribute and function hiding (Definition 2.15).*

The proof of the theorem will appear in the full version.

5.1 Instantiating Function Hiding PE from Concrete Assumptions

In this section, we provide instantiations of function hiding predicate encryption from concrete assumptions.

Semi-adaptively Secure Constructions for Circuits from LWE. Here, we explain that we can construct adaptively secure function hiding PE scheme for circuits from LWE. To do so, we start with semi-adaptively secure ABE for circuits [BV16, GKW16]. This construction can be upgraded to be PE by using lockable obfuscation [GKW17, WZ17]. Plugging the obtained PE scheme into our construction, we obtain the following theorem:

Theorem 5.2. *Assuming LWE, we have function hiding* SA-SIM *secure predicate encryption for all polynomial sized circuits.*

Adaptive Simulation Secure Constructions for NC_1 *Circuits from Bilinear Maps and LWE.* The above construction only achieves selective security. Here, we explain that we can construct adaptive simulation secure function hiding PE scheme for NC_1 circuits by additionally using bilinear maps. To do so, we start with adaptively secure KP-ABE scheme for NC_1 circuits [CGW15, KW19] from the decisional linear (DLIN) assumption on bilinear groups. By applying the ABE-to-PE conversion using lockable obfuscation [GKW17, WZ17], we obtain an adaptively secure (key-policy) PE scheme for NC_1 circuits from the DLIN assumption and the LWE assumption. We can further upgrade its security to adaptive simulation security by the conversion shown by [GKW17, Appendix F]. We then instantiate our construction with this PE scheme. To do so, we need that $U_{\hat{C}}$ is implementable by an NC_1 circuit. It suffices to show that we can implement Step 2a and 2c of $U_{\hat{C}}$ by an NC_1 circuit. The former is possible by instantiating the underlying SKE scheme with the secret key version of the

---

[7] We note that for PE, IND based security can be bootstrapped into SIM based security as shown by [GKW17, Appendix F].

Regev encryption scheme [Reg09], which has NC_1 decryption circuit. The latter is also possible by using the depth-preserving universal circuit [CH85] that takes as input C and x and outputs $C(x)$ and whose depth is only constant time deeper than the depth of C. Summarizing the above discussion, we have the following theorem.

Theorem 5.3. *Assuming LWE assumption and DLIN, we have function hiding adaptive simulation secure predicate encryption for* NC_1 *circuits.*

5.2   Ciphertext Policy Predicate Encryption with Function Hiding

Above, we presented a construction for function hiding predicate encryption in the key policy setting. Now, we leverage this to provide a construction for function hiding predicate encryption in the ciphertext policy setting. Note that the construction for cpABE presented in Sect. 3 constructions uses a single key functional encryption scheme (FE) along with a key policy attribute based encryption scheme (kpABE) in a modular way. We claim that if we replace the kpABE scheme with a function hiding predicate encryption scheme constructed above, then the resultant scheme achieves attribute and function hiding as well. We refer the reader to the full version for more details.

5.3   Strong Function Hiding Implies iO

The function hiding predicate encryption scheme we constructed above achieves the weaker notion of security of Definition 2.14. As discussed in Sect. 1, if we have a scheme that satisfies a stronger, more natural version of the security, we can construct an iO from this scheme. We refer the reader to the full version for more details.

Acknowledgements. We would like to thank the anonymous reviewers of TCC 2020 for helpful comments. We would also like to thank the Simons Institute for the Theory of Computing, for hosting both authors during the program entitled "'Lattices: Algorithms, Complexity, and Cryptography". Dr. Agrawal is supported by the DST "Swarnajayanti" fellowship, an Indo-French CEFIPRA project and an "Indo-Israel" ISF-UGC project. The first author thanks Zvika Brakerski for suggesting that CP-ABE is interesting even for the case of bounded sized circuits which led to the construction of Sect. 4. The second author is supported by JST CREST Grant Number JPMJCR19F6 and JSPS KAKENHI Grant Number 19H01109.

References

[AC17]   Agrawal, S., Chase, M.: Simplifying design and analysis of complex predicate encryption schemes. In: Coron, J.-S., Nielsen, J.B. (eds.) EUROCRYPT 2017. LNCS, vol. 10210, pp. 627–656. Springer, Cham (2017). https://doi.org/10.1007/978-3-319-56620-7_22

[AF18] Ananth, P., Fan, X.: Attribute based encryption with sublinear decryption from LWE. Cryptology ePrint Archive, Report 2018/273 (2018). https://eprint.iacr.org/2018/273

[AFV11] Agrawal, S., Freeman, D.M., Vaikuntanathan, V.: Functional encryption for inner product predicates from learning with errors. In: Lee, D.H., Wang, X. (eds.) ASIACRYPT 2011. LNCS, vol. 7073, pp. 21–40. Springer, Heidelberg (2011). https://doi.org/10.1007/978-3-642-25385-0_2

[AHY15] Attrapadung, N., Hanaoka, G., Yamada, S.: Conversions among several classes of predicate encryption and applications to ABE with various compactness tradeoffs. In: Iwata, T., Cheon, J.H. (eds.) ASIACRYPT 2015. LNCS, vol. 9452, pp. 575–601. Springer, Heidelberg (2015). https://doi.org/10.1007/978-3-662-48797-6_24

[AJ15] Ananth, P., Jain, A.: Indistinguishability obfuscation from compact functional encryption. In: Gennaro, R., Robshaw, M. (eds.) CRYPTO 2015, Part I. LNCS, vol. 9215, pp. 308–326. Springer, Heidelberg (2015). https://doi.org/10.1007/978-3-662-47989-6_15

[AMY19] Agrawal, S., Maitra, M., Yamada, S.: Attribute based encryption (and more) for nondeterministic finite automata from LWE. In: Boldyreva, A., Micciancio, D. (eds.) CRYPTO 2019. LNCS, vol. 11693, pp. 765–797. Springer, Cham (2019). https://doi.org/10.1007/978-3-030-26951-7_26

[Att14] Attrapadung, N.: Dual system encryption via doubly selective security: framework, fully secure functional encryption for regular languages, and more. In: Nguyen, P.Q., Oswald, E. (eds.) EUROCRYPT 2014. LNCS, vol. 8441, pp. 557–577. Springer, Heidelberg (2014). https://doi.org/10.1007/978-3-642-55220-5_31

[BGG+14] Boneh, D., et al.: Fully key-homomorphic encryption, arithmetic circuit ABE and compact garbled circuits. In: Nguyen, P.Q., Oswald, E. (eds.) EUROCRYPT 2014. LNCS, vol. 8441, pp. 533–556. Springer, Heidelberg (2014). https://doi.org/10.1007/978-3-642-55220-5_30

[BGI+01] Barak, B., et al.: On the (im)possibility of obfuscating programs. In: Kilian, J. (ed.) CRYPTO 2001. LNCS, vol. 2139, pp. 1–18. Springer, Heidelberg (2001). https://doi.org/10.1007/3-540-44647-8_1

[BJK15] Bishop, A., Jain, A., Kowalczyk, L.: Function-hiding inner product encryption. In: Iwata, T., Cheon, J.H. (eds.) ASIACRYPT 2015. LNCS, vol. 9452, pp. 470–491. Springer, Heidelberg (2015). https://doi.org/10.1007/978-3-662-48797-6_20

[BNPW16] Bitansky, N., Nishimaki, R., Passelègue, A., Wichs, D.: From cryptomania to obfustopia through secret-key functional encryption. In: Hirt, M., Smith, A. (eds.) TCC 2016, Part II. LNCS, vol. 9986, pp. 391–418. Springer, Heidelberg (2016). https://doi.org/10.1007/978-3-662-53644-5_15

[BRS13a] Boneh, D., Raghunathan, A., Segev, G.: Function-private identity-based encryption: hiding the function in functional encryption. In: Canetti, R., Garay, J.A. (eds.) CRYPTO 2013. LNCS, vol. 8043, pp. 461–478. Springer, Heidelberg (2013). https://doi.org/10.1007/978-3-642-40084-1_26

[BRS13b] Boneh, D., Raghunathan, A., Segev, G.: Function-private subspace-membership encryption and its applications. In: Sako, K., Sarkar, P. (eds.) ASIACRYPT 2013. LNCS, vol. 8269, pp. 255–275. Springer, Heidelberg (2013). https://doi.org/10.1007/978-3-642-42033-7_14

[BS15] Brakerski, Z., Segev, G.: Function-private functional encryption in the private-key setting. In: Dodis, Y., Nielsen, J.B. (eds.) TCC 2015. LNCS, vol. 9015, pp. 306–324. Springer, Heidelberg (2015). https://doi.org/10.1007/978-3-662-46497-7_12

[BSW07] Bethencourt, J., Sahai, A., Waters, B.: Ciphertext-policy attribute-based encryption. In: IEEE Symposium on Security and Privacy, pp. 321–334 (2007)

[BV15] Bitansky, N., Vaikuntanathan, V.: Indistinguishability obfuscation from functional encryption. In: FOCS 2015, p. 163 (2015)

[BV16] Brakerski, Z., Vaikuntanathan, V.: Circuit-ABE from LWE: unbounded attributes and semi-adaptive security. In: Robshaw, M., Katz, J. (eds.) CRYPTO 2016. LNCS, vol. 9816, pp. 363–384. Springer, Heidelberg (2016). https://doi.org/10.1007/978-3-662-53015-3_13

[BV20] Brakerski, Z., Vaikuntanathan, V.: Lattice-inspired broadcast encryption and succinct ciphertext-policy ABE. Cryptology ePrint Archive, Report 2020/191 (2020). https://eprint.iacr.org/2020/191

[BW07] Boneh, D., Waters, B.: Conjunctive, subset, and range queries on encrypted data. In: Vadhan, S.P. (ed.) TCC 2007. LNCS, vol. 4392, pp. 535–554. Springer, Heidelberg (2007). https://doi.org/10.1007/978-3-540-70936-7_29

[CGW15] Chen, J., Gay, R., Wee, H.: Improved dual system ABE in prime-order groups via predicate encodings. In: Oswald, E., Fischlin, M. (eds.) EUROCRYPT 2015. LNCS, vol. 9057, pp. 595–624. Springer, Heidelberg (2015). https://doi.org/10.1007/978-3-662-46803-6_20

[CH85] Cook, S.A., Hoover, H.J.: A depth-universal circuit. SIAM J. Comput. 14(4), 833–839 (1985)

[CW14] Chen, J., Wee, H.: Semi-adaptive attribute-based encryption and improved delegation for boolean formula. In: Abdalla, M., De Prisco, R. (eds.) SCN 2014. LNCS, vol. 8642, pp. 277–297. Springer, Cham (2014). https://doi.org/10.1007/978-3-319-10879-7_16

[DG17] Döttling, N., Garg, S.: Identity-based encryption from the Diffie-Hellman assumption. In: Katz, J., Shacham, H. (eds.) CRYPTO 2017. LNCS, vol. 10401, pp. 537–569. Springer, Cham (2017). https://doi.org/10.1007/978-3-319-63688-7_18

[GGH13a] Garg, S., Gentry, C., Halevi, S.: Candidate multilinear maps from ideal lattices. In: Johansson, T., Nguyen, P.Q. (eds.) EUROCRYPT 2013. LNCS, vol. 7881, pp. 1–17. Springer, Heidelberg (2013). https://doi.org/10.1007/978-3-642-38348-9_1

[GGH+13b] Garg, S., Gentry, C., Halevi, S., Raykova, M., Sahai, A., Waters, B.: Candidate indistinguishability obfuscation and functional encryption for all circuits. In: FOCS (2013). http://eprint.iacr.org/

[GKP+13] Goldwasser, S., Kalai, Y.T., Popa, R.A., Vaikuntanathan, V., Zeldovich, N.: Reusable garbled circuits and succinct functional encryption. In: STOC, pp. 555–564 (2013)

[GKW16] Goyal, R., Koppula, V., Waters, B.: Semi-adaptive security and bundling functionalities made generic and easy. In: Hirt, M., Smith, A. (eds.) TCC 2016. LNCS, vol. 9986, pp. 361–388. Springer, Heidelberg (2016). https://doi.org/10.1007/978-3-662-53644-5_14

[GKW17] Goyal, R., Koppula, V., Waters, B.: Lockable obfuscation. In: FOCS (2017)

[GPSW06] Goyal, V., Pandey, O., Sahai, A., Waters, B.: Attribute-based encryption for fine-grained access control of encrypted data. In: ACM Conference on Computer and Communications Security, pp. 89–98 (2006)

[GTKP+13a] Goldwasser, S., Kalai, Y.T., Popa, R.A., Vaikuntanathan, V., Zeldovich, N.: How to run turing machines on encrypted data. In: Canetti, R., Garay, J.A. (eds.) CRYPTO 2013. LNCS, vol. 8043, pp. 536–553. Springer, Heidelberg (2013). https://doi.org/10.1007/978-3-642-40084-1_30

[GTKP+13b] Goldwasser, S., Tauman Kalai, Y., Popa, R., Vaikuntanathan, V., Zeldovich, N.: Reusable garbled circuits and succinct functional encryption. In: Proceedings of STOC, pp. 555–564. ACM Press (2013)

[GV15] Gorbunov, S., Vinayagamurthy, D.: Riding on asymmetry: efficient ABE for branching programs. In: Iwata, T., Cheon, J.H. (eds.) ASIACRYPT 2015. LNCS, vol. 9452, pp. 550–574. Springer, Heidelberg (2015). https://doi.org/10.1007/978-3-662-48797-6_23

[GVW13] Gorbunov, S., Vaikuntanathan, V., Wee, H.: Attribute based encryption for circuits. In: STOC (2013)

[GVW15] Gorbunov, S., Vaikuntanathan, V., Wee, H.: Predicate encryption for circuits from LWE. In: Gennaro, R., Robshaw, M. (eds.) CRYPTO 2015. LNCS, vol. 9216, pp. 503–523. Springer, Heidelberg (2015). https://doi.org/10.1007/978-3-662-48000-7_25

[KLM+16] Kim, S., Lewi, K., Mandal, A., Montgomery, H., Roy, A., Wu, D.J.: Function-hiding inner product encryption is practical. In: Catalano, D., De Prisco, R. (eds.) SCN 2018. LNCS, vol. 11035, pp. 544–562. Springer, Cham (2018). https://doi.org/10.1007/978-3-319-98113-0_29

[KNT18] Kitagawa, F., Nishimaki, R., Tanaka, K.: Obfustopia built on secret-key functional encryption. In: Nielsen, J.B., Rijmen, V. (eds.) EUROCRYPT 2018, Part II. LNCS, vol. 10821, pp. 603–648. Springer, Cham (2018). https://doi.org/10.1007/978-3-319-78375-8_20

[KSW08] Katz, J., Sahai, A., Waters, B.: Predicate encryption supporting disjunctions, polynomial equations, and inner products. In: Smart, N. (ed.) EUROCRYPT 2008. LNCS, vol. 4965, pp. 146–162. Springer, Heidelberg (2008). https://doi.org/10.1007/978-3-540-78967-3_9

[KW19] Kowalczyk, L., Wee, H.: Compact adaptively secure ABE for NC^1 from k-Lin. In: Ishai, Y., Rijmen, V. (eds.) EUROCRYPT 2019. LNCS, vol. 11476, pp. 3–33. Springer, Cham (2019). https://doi.org/10.1007/978-3-030-17653-2_1

[LOS+10] Lewko, A., Okamoto, T., Sahai, A., Takashima, K., Waters, B.: Fully Secure Functional Encryption: Attribute-Based Encryption and (Hierarchical) Inner Product Encryption. In: Gilbert, H. (ed.) EUROCRYPT 2010. LNCS, vol. 6110, pp. 62–91. Springer, Heidelberg (2010). https://doi.org/10.1007/978-3-642-13190-5_4

[LW11] Lewko, A., Waters, B.: Unbounded HIBE and attribute-based encryption. In: Paterson, K.G. (ed.) EUROCRYPT 2011. LNCS, vol. 6632, pp. 547–567. Springer, Heidelberg (2011). https://doi.org/10.1007/978-3-642-20465-4_30

[LW12] Lewko, A., Waters, B.: New proof methods for attribute-based encryption: achieving full security through selective techniques. In: Safavi-Naini, R., Canetti, R. (eds.) CRYPTO 2012. LNCS, vol. 7417, pp. 180–198. Springer, Heidelberg (2012). https://doi.org/10.1007/978-3-642-32009-5_12

[OT10] Okamoto, T., Takashima, K.: Fully secure functional encryption with general relations from the decisional linear assumption. In: Rabin, T. (ed.) CRYPTO 2010. LNCS, vol. 6223, pp. 191–208. Springer, Heidelberg (2010). https://doi.org/10.1007/978-3-642-14623-7_11

[OT12] Okamoto, T., Takashima, K.: Adaptively attribute-hiding (hierarchical) inner product encryption. In: Pointcheval, D., Johansson, T. (eds.) EUROCRYPT 2012. LNCS, vol. 7237, pp. 591–608. Springer, Heidelberg (2012). https://doi.org/10.1007/978-3-642-29011-4_35. Full version available at http://eprint.iacr.org/2011/543

[Reg09] Regev, O.: On lattices, learning with errors, random linear codes, and cryptography. J. ACM **56**(6), 1–40 (2009). Extended abstract in STOC 2005

[RW13] Rouselakis, Y., Waters, B.: Practical constructions and new proof methods for large universe attribute-based encryption. In: 2013 ACM SIGSAC Conference on Computer and Communications Security, CCS 2013, Berlin, Germany, 4–8 November 2013, pp. 463–474 (2013)

[SSW09] Shen, E., Shi, E., Waters, B.: Predicate privacy in encryption systems. In: Reingold, O. (ed.) TCC 2009. LNCS, vol. 5444, pp. 457–473. Springer, Heidelberg (2009). https://doi.org/10.1007/978-3-642-00457-5_27

[SW05] Sahai, A., Waters, B.: Fuzzy identity-based encryption. In: Cramer, R. (ed.) EUROCRYPT 2005. LNCS, vol. 3494, pp. 457–473. Springer, Heidelberg (2005). https://doi.org/10.1007/11426639_27

[Tsa19] Tsabary, R.: Fully Secure attribute-based encryption for t-CNF from LWE. In: Boldyreva, A., Micciancio, D. (eds.) CRYPTO 2019, Part I. LNCS, vol. 11692, pp. 62–85. Springer, Cham (2019). https://doi.org/10.1007/978-3-030-26948-7_3

[Wat11] Waters, B.: Ciphertext-policy attribute-based encryption: an expressive, efficient, and provably secure realization. In: Catalano, D., Fazio, N., Gennaro, R., Nicolosi, A. (eds.) PKC 2011. LNCS, vol. 6571, pp. 53–70. Springer, Heidelberg (2011). https://doi.org/10.1007/978-3-642-19379-8_4

[Wat12] Waters, B.: Functional encryption for regular languages. In: Safavi-Naini, R., Canetti, R. (eds.) CRYPTO 2012. LNCS, vol. 7417, pp. 218–235. Springer, Heidelberg (2012). https://doi.org/10.1007/978-3-642-32009-5_14

[Wee14] Wee, H.: Dual system encryption via predicate encodings. In: Lindell, Y. (ed.) TCC 2014. LNCS, vol. 8349, pp. 616–637. Springer, Heidelberg (2014). https://doi.org/10.1007/978-3-642-54242-8_26

[WZ17] Wichs, D., Zirdelis, G.: Obfuscating compute-and-compare programs under LWE. In: FOCS (2017)

Optimal Broadcast Encryption from LWE and Pairings in the Standard Model

Shweta Agrawal[1], Daniel Wichs[2], and Shota Yamada[3(✉)]

[1] IIT Madras, Chennai, India
shweta.a@cse.iitm.ac.in
[2] Northeastern University and NTT Resarch Inc., Boston, USA
wichs@ccs.neu.edu
[3] National Institute of Advanced Industrial Science and Technology (AIST),
Tokyo, Japan
yamada-shota@aist.go.jp

Abstract. Broadcast Encryption with optimal parameters was a long-standing problem, whose first solution was provided in an elegant work by Boneh, Waters and Zhandry [BWZ14]. However, this work relied on multilinear maps of logarithmic degree, which is not considered a standard assumption. Recently, Agrawal and Yamada [AY20] improved this state of affairs by providing the first construction of optimal broadcast encryption from Bilinear Maps and Learning With Errors (LWE). However, their proof of security was in the generic bilinear group model. In this work, we improve upon their result by providing a new construction and proof in the standard model. In more detail, we rely on the Learning With Errors (LWE) assumption and the Knowledge of OrthogonALity Assumption (KOALA) [BW19] on bilinear groups.

Our construction combines three building blocks: a (computational) nearly linear secret sharing scheme with compact shares which we construct from LWE, an inner-product functional encryption scheme with special properties which is constructed from the bilinear Matrix Decision Diffie Hellman (MDDH) assumption, and a certain form of hyperplane obfuscation, which is constructed using the KOALA assumption. While similar to that of Agrawal and Yamada, our construction provides a new understanding of how to decompose the construction into simpler, modular building blocks with concrete and easy-to-understand security requirements for each one. We believe this sheds new light on the requirements for optimal broadcast encryption, which may lead to new constructions in the future.

1 Introduction

Broadcast encryption [FN94] (BE) is a novel form of encryption that enables a sender to transmit a single ciphertext over a broadcast channel so that only an authorized subset S of total N users can decrypt and recover the message. Security requires that no collusion of unauthorized users can learn anything about the

© International Association for Cryptologic Research 2020
R. Pass and K. Pietrzak (Eds.): TCC 2020, LNCS 12550, pp. 149–178, 2020.
https://doi.org/10.1007/978-3-030-64375-1_6

encrypted message with non-negligible advantage. Evidently, broadcast encryption is implied by public key encryption if no restriction is placed on the size of the ciphertext. However, the size of the ciphertext in broadcast encryption is of paramount importance, and is quantified in terms of ciphertext *overhead*, namely, the size of the ciphertext not counting the description of the recipient set S. Thus, in an optimal solution, the ciphertext overhead would be of size proportional to a symmetric encryption of the plaintext message (upto constant factors), aside from the description of S which is provided in the clear.

In a celebrated work, Boneh, Gentry and Waters [BGW05] provided the first construction of broadcast encryption which achieved both optimal (constant) ciphertext overhead and short secret keys, but suffered from large public parameters, namely, linear in the number of users N. A series of elegant works provided improvements to this scheme [GW09, DPP07, Del07, SF, AL10, HWL+16, BZ17] achieving many interesting new features such as anonymity, adaptive security and such others, but failed to improve the size of the public parameters. In 2014, Boneh, Waters and Zhandry [BWZ14] provided the first solution to the long standing problem of BE with optimal parameters, but their construction relied on the existence of multilinear maps of degree $\log N$, which is not considered a standard assumption. Recently, Agrawal and Yamada [AY20] improved the state of affairs by achieving the same parameters from the learning with errors assumption (LWE) along with assumptions on bilinear maps. However, this construction [AY20] could only be proven secure in the generic bilinear group model. Independently, Brakerski and Vaikuntanathan [BV20] also provided a construction of BE with optimal parameters from new assumptions on lattices, but they were unable to provide a proof of security for their scheme.

While encouraging, this state of affairs nevertheless leaves much to be desired. It is evident that for a primitive as important as broadcast encryption, we would like to have a proof from well-studied standard assumptions, and in the standard model. However, so far such a construction has been elusive.

Our Results. In this work, we make further progress towards this goal and provide the first construction for broadcast encryption with optimal parameters, from Learning with Errors (LWE) [Reg09] and the Knowledge of OrthogonALity Assumption (KOALA) [BW19] in the standard model. While similar to that of Agrawal and Yamada, our construction provides a new understanding of how to decompose the construction into simpler, modular building blocks with concrete and easy-to-understand security requirements for each one. We believe this sheds new light on the requirements for optimal broadcast encryption, which may lead to new constructions in the future.

In more detail, as in [AY20], we provide a construction for ciphertext-policy attribute based encryption (cpABE) for NC_1 circuits, such that its ciphertext size, secret key size, and public key size are all independent of the *size* of the circuits supported by the scheme, and depend only on their input length and depth. Recall that in a cpABE scheme, a ciphertext for a message m is associated with a function (policy) f, and secret keys are associated with public attributes $\mathbf{x}$ from the domain of f. Decryption succeeds to yield the hidden message m if and only if the attribute satisfies the policy, namely $f(\mathbf{x}) = 1$. To see BE as a special case of cpABE, note that the circuit embedded in the ciphertext (F_S, say) can check for membership of a given user index in a set of authorised recipients S, and the attributes $\mathbf{x}$ may encode a user's index in the set N. Thus, a user i holds a secret key for attributes i and can decrypt a ciphertext associated with S if and only if i is a member of S. As observed in [AY20], the depth and input length of the circuit F_S are logarithmic in N, so it suffices to construct cpABE with parameters independent of the *width* of F_S, which is linear in N.

Building upon the construction of [AY20], we provide a new cpABE for NC_1 from the Learning with Errors (LWE) [Reg09] and the Knowledge of Orthogo-nALity Assumption (KOALA) [BW19]. The LWE assumption introduced in the seminal work of Regev [Reg09] enjoys worst case to average case hardness guarantees and is widely considered a standard assumption in the literature. The KOALA assumption introduced by Beullens and Wee [BW19] (also implicitly present in prior work such as [CRV10]) may be viewed as a decisional analogue of the algebraic group model [FKL18], which posits that the only way an adversary can compute a new group element is to take a linear combination of group elements already provided. More specifically, the KOALA assumption asserts that any adversary that can distinguish $g^{\mathbf{Mr}}$ from $g^{\mathbf{v}}$ for some matrix $\mathbf{M}$ and random vectors $\mathbf{r}, \mathbf{v}$, must know some nontrivial vector $\mathbf{z} \neq 0$ such that $\mathbf{z} \mathbf{M} = 0$. Beullens and Wee provided a proof of the KOALA assumption in the generic group model. While KOALA is a "knowledge assumption" and therefore not considered a standard assumption, we believe it is a significant improvement over [AY20] to rely on the hardness of a specific assumption in the standard model, than to rely on the the generic group model for the security of the entire scheme.

Technical Overview. We proceed to outline the main ideas of our construction. As discussed above, we construct a *ciphertext-policy attribute-based encryption* (cpABE) for NC_1 circuits. The cpABE is *compact*, meaning that the size of the ciphertexts and keys are all small, proportional only to the length of the inputs and the depth of the supported circuits, but independent of the circuit size. Our construction combines three building blocks: a (computational) *nearly linear secret sharing* scheme with compact shares, which we construct from Learning With Errors (LWE), a certain form of *inner-product functional encryption* (IPFE) [ABCP15,ALS16,LV16,Lin17,LL20], constructed from the bilinear Matrix Decision Diffie Hellman (MDDH) assumption, and a certain form of *hyperplane obfuscation* [CRV10], constructed using the KOALA assumption. Next, we describe each of these primitives individually and outline how they are combined to construct our cpABE.

Nearly Linear Secret Sharing. Our main building block is a new type of secret sharing scheme. Given a message $\mu \in \{0, 1\}$ and a circuit C with ℓ-bit input, the scheme outputs 2ℓ shares $\{\mathsf{share}_{i,b}\}_{i \in [\ell], b \in \{0,1\}}$. Each $\mathsf{share}_{i,b}$ is a vector over $\mathbb{Z}_p$. For any $x \in \{0,1\}^\ell$, let $\mathsf{share}_x = \{\mathsf{share}_{i,x_i}\}$, which we think of as a long vector produced by concatenating of all the component shares. If $C(x) = 0$ then share_x computationally hides the message μ, and moreover, share_x is even indistinguishable from a uniformly random vector. On the other hand, if $C(x) = 1$ then there is an efficient method to reconstruct the message μ from share_x. Moreover, this reconstruction procedure is "nearly linear" in the sense that given C, x, one can efficiently determine some linear function f such that $f(\mathsf{share}_x) = \mu \cdot \lceil p/2 \rceil + e$, where $|e| \ll p/2$ is some small polynomially bounded error.

We use LWE to construct this type of nearly linear secret sharing for all NC_1 circuits, where the size of the shares only depends on the security parameter and the depth of the circuit, but is independent of the circuit size. The construction closely follows the ideas behind the ABE scheme of [BGG+14] and the laconic function evaluation of [QWW18]. As in [AY20], we are restricted to NC_1 because we require the magnitude of the error e to be polynomially bounded. The construction additionally relies on some uniformly random public parameters pp, which we will ignore throughout the introduction.

Towards cpABE *from Secret Sharing.* In our cpABE construction, to encrypt a message μ under a given policy specified by an NC_1 circuit C, the encryptor creates a "nearly linear secret sharing" of the message resulting in shares $\{\mathsf{share}_{i,b}\}_{i \in [\ell], b \in \{0,1\}}$. At a high level, the encryptor then encrypts these shares using some form of *functional encryption* (FE) and outputs the FE ciphertext. Let us examine what kind of functional encryption would be helpful in this setting.

As a starting point, assume the shares are encrypted via an FE scheme such that a decryptor with a secret key for x only learns the subset $\mathsf{share}_x = \{\mathsf{share}_{i,x_i}\}$. Such an FE scheme is easy to construct by encrypting each of the 2ℓ shares under a different public key of a standard public-key encryption scheme and giving the decryptor the ℓ secret keys corresponding to the choice of x [SS10]. This would already provide security in the non-colluding setting – if the adversary has a secret key for a single value x such that $C(x) = 0$, then she cannot learn anything about the message by getting share_x. However, if the adversary has secret keys for even just two different values x_0, x_1, such that $C(x_0) = C(x_1) = 0$, all bets are off; indeed, with our scheme, she could easily recover the message.

To fix the above problem, we rely on a more restricted form of FE where the decryptor with a secret key for a value x would not learn share_x in full, but rather only a *hyperplane obfuscation* of the vector share_x. A hyperplane obfuscation [CRV10] of a vector $\boldsymbol{v}$ allows one to test whether various affine functions h evaluate to $h(\boldsymbol{v}) = 0$, but should not reveal anything else about the obfuscated vector beyond having black-box access to such tests. When $C(x) = 1$, a hyperplane obfuscation of share_x is sufficient to decrypt the message μ, since we have a linear function f such that $f(\mathsf{share}_x) = \mu \cdot \lceil p/2 \rceil + e$ and therefore, by testing whether $f(\mathsf{share}_x) - e' = 0$ for all values e' in the polynomial range that e comes from, we can determine whether $\mu = 0$ or $\mu = 1$. For security, consider an adversary has secret keys for some q inputs $x^{(1)}, \ldots, x^{(q)}$ such that $C(x^{(i)}) = 0$ and learns the corresponding hyperplane obfuscations of the vectors $\mathsf{share}_{x^{(i)}}$. We know that each of the vectors $\mathsf{share}_{x^{(i)}}$ is individually computationally indistinguishable from uniform, but mutually the vectors have non-trivial correlations and can be used to recover μ. We wish to conclude that the hyperplane obfuscations of $\mathsf{share}_{x^{(i)}}$ are mutually indistinguishable from obfuscations of random and independent vectors. Indeed, this follows if we had a *composable* [CD08,BC10] virtual-black-box (VBB) hyperplane obfuscator since, given black box access to each of these vectors, an adversary will never be able to find an affine function evaluates to 0 on any of them. To make this approach work, we therefore need to instantiate an appropriate hyperplane obfuscator together with a matching FE scheme that outputs a hyperplane obfuscations of share_x.

Hyperplane Obfuscation. We rely on the extremely simple hyperplane obfuscator of [CRV10]. Let G be a cyclic group of order p with a generator g. To obfuscate a vector $\boldsymbol{v} \in \mathbb{Z}_p^n$, we choose a random $\gamma \leftarrow \mathbb{Z}_p$ and output $g^\gamma, g^{\gamma \cdot \boldsymbol{v}}$. This allows one to test if an affine function h evaluates to $h(\boldsymbol{v}) = 0$ by computing $\gamma \cdot h(\boldsymbol{v})$ in the exponent. The work of [CRV10] shows that this is a VBB hyperplane obfuscator under a new assumption that they proposed, which can in retrospect be seen as a variant of the KOALA assumption restricted to spaces of dimension 1. However, they did not prove that the obfuscator is composable. In our work, we do not directly prove that this obfuscator satisfies composable VBB security, but rather prove that it satisfies a specialized property that suffices for us. Namely, we show that under the KOALA assumption the following holds: for any set of vectors that are individually indistinguishable from uniform but can be mutually correlated, one cannot distinguish between being given the hyperplane obfuscations of all the vectors in the set versus hyperplane obfuscations of uniformly random and independent vectors.

Functional Encryption for Inner Products. As the last step, we need to provide an appropriate (public-key) functional encryption (FE) scheme. Such an FE should allow us to encrypt a set of shares $\{\mathsf{share}_{i,b}\}_{i \in [\ell], b \in \{0,1\}}$, and give out secret keys for value $x \in \{0,1\}^\ell$, so that such a ciphertext/key pair (only) reveals a fresh hyperplane obfuscation of share_x and nothing else. We can simplify this problem by relying on a simpler "component" FE scheme and then combining the component FEs to get what we need. The component FE should allow us to encrypt a scalar $s \in \mathbb{Z}_p$ and give out secret keys for values g^γ, so that such a ciphertext/key pair only reveals $g^{\gamma \cdot s}$ and nothing else. We want to component FE to satisfy unbounded-collusion simulation-based security. Given such a component FE scheme, we can instantiate a separate copy of it for each $i \in [\ell], b \in \{0,1\}$ and each position in the share vector. The encryptor then encrypts each position of each share vector $\mathsf{share}_{i,b}$ under the appropriate copy of the component scheme. To create a secret key for $x \in \{0,1\}^\ell$ we choose a fresh random $\gamma \leftarrow \mathbb{Z}_p$ and give out a secret key for g^γ for each of the component schemes in locations (i, x_i). This would ensure that, given an encryption of $\{\mathsf{share}_{i,b}\}_{i \in [\ell], b \in \{0,1\}}$, a secret key for a value $x \in \{0,1\}^\ell$ only allows one to recover the hyperplane obfuscation of share_x given by $(g^\gamma, g^{\gamma \cdot \mathsf{share}_x})$.

The above almost works, up to one subtlety. When we instantiate the component FE scheme, we do so using bilinear groups $(\mathbb{G}_1, \mathbb{G}_2, \mathbb{G}_T)$ of order p with corresponding generators (g_1, g_2, g_T) and a bilinear map $e : \mathbb{G}_1 \times \mathbb{G}_2 \rightarrow \mathbb{G}_T$. We can create an encryption of a scalar $s \in \mathbb{Z}_p$ and give out a secret key for

$g_2^\gamma \in \mathbb{G}_2$ so that the decryption of the ciphertext with the secret key reveals $g_T^{\gamma \cdot s}$. However, we can only guarantee simulation based security when the simulator is given $g_2^{\gamma \cdot s}$. In other words, there is a discrepancy between correctness (where the honest users decrypt the product in the exponent of g_T) and security (where the simulator needs to know the product in the exponent of g_2). It turns out that this suffices for us. For correctness, the decryptor gets a hyperplane obfuscation over $\mathbb{G}_T$, which suffices to recover the message. For security, we need to rely on the hyerplane obfuscation being secure even when given over $\mathbb{G}_2$, which just requires us to assume that KOALA holds over $\mathbb{G}_2$. We instantiate the above type of component FE in a black-box way using the recent primitive of "Slotted Inner Product Functional Encryption" [LV16, Lin17, LL20].[1]

2 Preliminaries

In this section, we define some notation and preliminaries that we require.

Notation. We use bold letters to denote vectors. We treat a vector as a row vector by default. The notation $[a, b]$ denotes the set of integers $\{k \in \mathbb{N} \mid a \leq k \leq b\}$. We use $[n]$ to denote the set $[1, n]$. Throughout the paper, we use λ to denote the security parameter. We say a function $f(\lambda)$ is *negligible* if it is $O(\lambda^{-c})$ for all $c > 0$, and we use $\text{negl}(\lambda)$ to denote a negligible function of λ. We say $f(\lambda)$ is *polynomial* if it is $O(\lambda^c)$ for some constant $c > 0$, and we use $\text{poly}(\lambda)$ to denote a polynomial function of λ. Throughout the paper, we consider non-uniform adversaries that are modeled as polynomial-size circuits $\mathcal{A} = \{\mathcal{A}_\lambda\}_\lambda$ indexed by the security parameter. We often drop the subscript when it is clear from the context.

2.1 Bilinear Map Preliminaries

Here, we introduce our notation for bilinear maps and the bilinear generic group model following Baltico et al. [BCFG17], who specializes the framework by Barthe [BFF+14] for defining generic k-linear groups to the bilinear group settings. The definition closely follows that of Maurer [Mau05], which is equivalent to the alternative formulation by Shoup [Sho97].

Notation on Bilinear Maps. A bilinear group generator GroupGen takes as input 1^λ and outputs a group description $\mathbb{G} = (p, \mathbb{G}_1, \mathbb{G}_2, \mathbb{G}_T, e, g_1, g_2)$, where p is a prime of $\Theta(\lambda)$ bits, $\mathbb{G}_1$, $\mathbb{G}_2$, and $\mathbb{G}_T$ are cyclic groups of order p, $e : \mathbb{G}_1 \times \mathbb{G}_2 \to \mathbb{G}_T$ is a non-degenerate bilinear map, and g_1 and g_2 are generators of $\mathbb{G}_1$ and $\mathbb{G}_2$, respectively. We require that the group operations in $\mathbb{G}_1$, $\mathbb{G}_2$, and $\mathbb{G}_T$ as well as the bilinear map e can be efficiently computed. We employ the implicit

---

[1] In the technical sections we use IPFE directly rather than first showing that it provides an FE scheme with the above discrepancy between correctness and security and then relying on such an FE. This is purely to avoid proliferation of additional definitions/abstractions.

representation of group elements: for a matrix $\mathbf{A}$ over $\mathbb{Z}_p$, we define $[\mathbf{A}]_1 := g_1^{\mathbf{A}}$, $[\mathbf{A}]_2 := g_2^{\mathbf{A}}$, $[\mathbf{A}]_T := g_T^{\mathbf{A}}$, where exponentiation is carried out component-wise. We will use similar notation for vectors.

Generic Bilinear Group Model. Let $\mathbb{G} = (p, \mathbb{G}_1, \mathbb{G}_2, \mathbb{G}_T, e, g_1, g_2)$ be a bilinear group setting, L_1, L_2, and L_T be lists of group elements in $\mathbb{G}_1$, $\mathbb{G}_2$, and $\mathbb{G}_T$ respectively, and let $\mathcal{D}$ be a distribution over L_1, L_2, and L_T. The generic group model for a bilinear group setting $\mathbb{G}$ and a distribution $\mathcal{D}$ is described in Fig. 1. In this model, the challenger first initializes the lists L_1, L_2, and L_T by sampling the group elements according to $\mathcal{D}$, and the adversary receives handles for the elements in the lists. For $s \in \{1, 2, T\}$, $L_s[h]$ denotes the h-th element in the list L_s. The handle to this element is simply the pair (s, h). An adversary running in the generic bilinear group model can apply group operations and bilinear maps to the elements in the lists. To do this, the adversary has to call the appropriate oracle specifying handles for the input elements. The challenger computes the result of a query, stores it in the corresponding list, and returns to the adversary its (newly created) handle. Handles are not unique (i.e., the same group element may appear more than once in a list under different handles).

We remark that we slightly simplify the generic group model of Baltico et al. [BCFG17]. Whereas they allow the adversary to access the equality test oracle, which is given two handles (s, h_1) and (s, h_2) and returns 1 if $L_s[h_1] = L_s[h_2]$ and 0 otherwise for all $s \in \{1, 2, T\}$, we replace this oracle with the zero-test oracle, which is given a handle (s, h) and returns 1 if $L_s[h] = 0$ and 0 otherwise only for the case of $s = T$. We claim that even with this modification, the model is equivalent to the original one. This is because we can perform the equality test for (s, h_1) and (s, h_2) using our restricted oracles as follows. Let us first consider the case of $s = T$. In this case, we can get the handle (T, h') corresponding to $L_T[h_1] - L_T[h_2]$ by calling neg_T (see Fig. 1). We then make a zero-test query for (T, h'). Clearly, we get 1 if $L_s[h_1] = L_s[h_2]$ and 0 otherwise. We next consider the case of $s \in \{1, 2\}$. This case can be reduced to the case of $s = T$ by lifting the group elements corresponding to h_1 and h_2 to the group elements in $\mathbb{G}_T$ by taking bilinear maps with an arbitrary non-unit group element in $\mathbb{G}_{3-s}$, which is possible by calling map_e.

Symbolic Group Model. The symbolic group model for a bilinear group setting $\mathbb{G}$ and a distribution $\mathcal{D}_P$ gives to the adversary the same interface as the corresponding generic group model, except that internally the challenger stores lists of elements in the field $\mathbb{Z}_p[X_1, \ldots, X_n]$ instead of lists of group elements. The oracles add_s, neg_s, map, and zt computes addition, negation, multiplication, and equality in the field.

2.2 Slotted Inner Product Functional Encryption

We need slotted Inner Product Functional Encryption (IPFE) due to Lin and Vaikuntanathan [LV16,Lin17,LL20]. Slotted IPFE is a hybrid between a secret-key function-hiding IPFE and a public-key IPFE. In this scheme, a vector $\mathbf{u} \in \mathbb{Z}_p^n$ is divided into a public and private part respectively $\mathbf{u} = (\mathbf{u}_{\mathsf{pub}}, \mathbf{u}_{\mathsf{priv}})$ such that

State: Lists L_1, L_2, L_T over $\mathbb{G}_1$, $\mathbb{G}_2$, $\mathbb{G}_T$ respectively.
Initializations: Lists L_1, L_2, L_T sampled according to distribution $\mathcal{D}$.
Oracles: The oracles provide black-box access to the group operations, the bilinear map, and equalities.
- For all $s \in \{1, 2, T\}$: $\mathsf{add}_s(h_1, h_2)$ appends $L_s[h_1] + L_s[h_2]$ to L_s and returns its handle $(s, |L_s|)$.
- For all $s \in \{1, 2, T\}$: $\mathsf{neg}_s(h_1, h_2)$ appends $L_s[h_1] - L_s[h_2]$ to L_s and returns its handle $(s, |L_s|)$.
- $\mathsf{map}_e(h_1, h_2)$ appends $e(L_1[h_1], L_2[h_2])$ to L_T and returns its handle $(T, |L_T|)$.
- $\mathsf{zt}_T(h)$ returns 1 if $L_T[h] = 0$ and 0 otherwise.

All oracles return $\bot$ when given invalid indices.

Fig. 1. Generic group model for bilinear group setting $\mathbb{G} = (p, \mathbb{G}_1, \mathbb{G}_2, \mathbb{G}_T, e, g_1, g_2)$ and distribution $\mathcal{D}$.

given the master secret key, the encryption algorithm can encrypt any vector $\mathbf{u}$ of its choice, but given only the public key, it can encrypt only to the public slot, i.e. $\mathbf{u}_{\mathsf{priv}} = 0$. Slotted IPFE can guarantee function hiding only with respect to the private slot. We provide the definitions from [LL20].

Let $\mathsf{GroupGen}$ be a group generator that outputs bilinear group $\mathbb{G} = (p, \mathbb{G}_1, \mathbb{G}_2, \mathbb{G}_T, e, [1]_1, [1]_2)$. A slotted inner-product functional encryption (IPFE) scheme based on $\mathbb{G}$ consists of 5 efficient algorithms:

$\mathsf{Setup}(1^\lambda, \mathfrak{s}_{\mathsf{pub}}, \mathfrak{s}_{\mathsf{pri}}) \to (\mathsf{mpk}, \mathsf{msk})$: The setup algorithm takes as input two disjoint index sets, the public slot $\mathfrak{s}_{\mathsf{pub}}$ and the private slot $\mathfrak{s}_{\mathsf{pri}}$, and outputs a pair of master public key and master secret key $(\mathsf{mpk}, \mathsf{msk})$. The whole index set $\mathfrak{s}$ is $\mathfrak{s}_{\mathsf{pub}} \cup \mathfrak{s}_{\mathsf{pri}}$.

$\mathsf{KeyGen}(\mathsf{msk}, [\mathbf{v}]_2) \to \mathsf{sk}_\mathbf{v}$: The key generation algorithm takes as input the master secret key and an encoding of a function vector $[\mathbf{v}]_2$, and outputs a secret key $\mathsf{sk}_\mathbf{v}$ for $\mathbf{v} \in \mathbb{Z}_p^\mathfrak{s}$.

$\mathsf{Enc}(\mathsf{msk}, [\mathbf{u}]_1) \to \mathsf{ct}_\mathbf{u}$: The encrypt algorithm takes input the master secret key and an encoding of a message vector $[\mathbf{u}]_1$ and outputs a ciphertext $\mathsf{ct}_\mathbf{u}$ for $\mathbf{u} \in \mathbb{Z}_p^\mathfrak{s}$.

$\mathsf{Dec}(\mathsf{sk}_\mathbf{v}, \mathsf{ct}_\mathbf{u}) \to T \vee \bot$: The decrypt algorithm takes as input a secret key $\mathsf{sk}_\mathbf{v}$ and a ciphertext $\mathsf{ct}_\mathbf{u}$, and outputs an element $T \in \mathbb{G}_T$ or $\bot$.

$\mathsf{SlotEnc}(\mathsf{mpk}, [\mathbf{u}_{\mathsf{pub}}]_1) \to \mathsf{ct}_\mathbf{u}$: The slot encryption algorithm takes as input the master public key and a vector $\mathbf{u}_{\mathsf{pub}} \in \mathbb{Z}_p^{\mathfrak{s}_{\mathsf{pub}}}$, sets $\mathbf{u} = (\mathbf{u}_{\mathsf{pub}}, \mathbf{0}) \in \mathbb{Z}_p^\mathfrak{s}$ and outputs a ciphertext $\mathsf{ct}_\mathbf{u}$.

Correctness. We say the slotted inner-product functional encryption scheme satisfies decryption correctness if for all $\lambda \in \mathbb{N}$, all index sets $\mathfrak{s}$ and all vectors $\mathbf{u}, \mathbf{v} \in \mathbb{Z}_p^\mathfrak{s}$,

$$\Pr\left[\left.\mathsf{Dec}(\mathsf{sk}_\mathbf{v},\mathsf{ct}_\mathbf{u}) = \langle \mathbf{u},\ \mathbf{v}\rangle \right| \begin{array}{l} \mathsf{msk} \leftarrow \mathsf{Setup}(\mathfrak{s}_{\mathsf{pub}},\mathfrak{s}_{\mathsf{pri}}) \\ \mathsf{sk}_\mathbf{v} \leftarrow \mathsf{KeyGen}(\mathsf{msk},[\mathbf{v}]_2) \\ \mathsf{ct}_\mathbf{u} \leftarrow \mathsf{Enc}(\mathsf{msk},[\mathbf{u}]_1) \end{array}\right] = 1.$$

We say the slotted inner-product functional encryption scheme satisfies slot-mode correctness if for all $\lambda \in \mathbb{N}$, all disjoint index sets $\mathfrak{s}_{\mathsf{pub}}, \mathfrak{s}_{\mathsf{pri}}$ and all vectors $\mathbf{u} \in \mathbb{Z}_p^{\mathfrak{s}_{\mathsf{pub}}}$, the following two distributions should be identical:

$$\left\{ (\mathsf{mpk},\mathsf{msk},\mathsf{ct}) \left| \begin{array}{l} (\mathsf{mpk},\mathsf{msk}) \leftarrow \mathsf{Setup}(1^\lambda,\mathfrak{s}_{\mathsf{pub}},\mathfrak{s}_{\mathsf{pri}}) \\ \mathsf{ct}_\mathbf{u} \leftarrow \mathsf{Enc}(\mathsf{msk},[\mathbf{u}\|\mathbf{0}]_1) \end{array}\right.\right\}$$

and

$$\left\{ (\mathsf{mpk},\mathsf{msk},\mathsf{ct}) \left| \begin{array}{l} (\mathsf{mpk},\mathsf{msk}) \leftarrow \mathsf{Setup}(1^\lambda,\mathfrak{s}_{\mathsf{pub}},\mathfrak{s}_{\mathsf{pri}}) \\ \mathsf{ct}_\mathbf{u} \leftarrow \mathsf{SlotEnc}(\mathsf{msk},[\mathbf{u}]_1) \end{array}\right.\right\}$$

Slotted IPFE generalizes both secret-key and public-key IPFEs: we may obtain the former by setting $\mathfrak{s} = \mathfrak{s}_{\mathsf{pri}}$ and the latter by setting $\mathfrak{s} = \mathfrak{s}_{\mathsf{pub}}$.

Next, we define the adaptive function hiding property.

Definition 2.1 (Function Hiding Slotted IPFE). *Let* (Setup, KeyGen, Enc, Dec, SlotEnc) *be a slotted IPFE scheme as defined above. The scheme is function hiding if* $\mathsf{Exp}_{\mathsf{FH}}^0$ *is indistinguishable from* $\mathsf{Exp}_{\mathsf{FH}}^1$ *for all efficient adversary* $\mathcal{A} = \{\mathcal{A}_\lambda\}_\lambda$ *where* $\mathsf{Exp}_{\mathsf{FH}}^b$ *for* $b \in \{0,1\}$ *is defined as follows:*

1. **Setup:** Run the adversary $\mathcal{A}_\lambda$ and obtain the disjoint index sets $\mathfrak{s}_{\mathsf{pub}}, \mathfrak{s}_{\mathsf{pri}}$ from $\mathcal{A}_\lambda$. Let $\mathfrak{s} = \mathfrak{s}_{\mathsf{pub}} \cup \mathfrak{s}_{\mathsf{pri}}$. Let $(\mathsf{mpk},\mathsf{msk}) \leftarrow \mathsf{Setup}(1^\lambda,\mathfrak{s}_{\mathsf{pub}},\mathfrak{s}_{\mathsf{pri}})$ and return mpk to $\mathcal{A}_\lambda$.
2. **Challenge:** Repeat the following for arbitrarily many rounds determined by $\mathcal{A}_\lambda$: In each round, $\mathcal{A}_\lambda$ has 2 options:
   - $\mathcal{A}_\lambda$ chooses $\mathbf{v}_j^0, \mathbf{v}_j^1 \in \mathbb{Z}_p^{\mathfrak{s}}$ and submits $[\mathbf{v}_j^0]_2, [\mathbf{v}_j^1]_2$ for a secret key. Upon receiving this, compute $\mathsf{sk}_j \leftarrow \mathsf{KeyGen}(\mathsf{msk},[\mathbf{v}_j^b]_2)$ and return this to $\mathcal{A}_\lambda$.
   - $\mathcal{A}_\lambda$ chooses $\mathbf{u}_i^0, \mathbf{u}_i^1 \in \mathbb{Z}_p^{\mathfrak{s}}$ and submits $[\mathbf{u}_i^0]_1, [\mathbf{u}_i^1]_1$ for a ciphertext. Upon receiving this, compute $\mathsf{ct}_i \leftarrow \mathsf{Enc}(\mathsf{msk},[\mathbf{u}_i^b]_1)$ and return this to $\mathcal{A}_\lambda$.
3. **Guess:** $\mathcal{A}_\lambda$ outputs its guess b'.

The outcome of the experiment is defined as b' if all the public components of the key queries are equal, i.e. $\mathbf{v}_j^0|_{\mathfrak{s}_{\mathsf{pub}}} = \mathbf{v}_j^1|_{\mathfrak{s}_{\mathsf{pub}}}$ for all j and $\langle \mathbf{u}_i^0,\ \mathbf{v}_j^0\rangle = \langle \mathbf{u}_i^1,\ \mathbf{v}_j^1\rangle$ for all i, j.

We will also require the following lemma by [ALS16, Wee17, LV16, Lin17, LL20]:

Lemma 2.2. *Let* GroupGen *be a group generator that outputs bilinear group* $\mathbb{G} = (p, \mathbb{G}_1, \mathbb{G}_2, \mathbb{G}_T, e, [1]_1, [1]_2)$ *and* $k \geq 1$ *an integer constant. If* MDDH_k *holds in both* $\mathbb{G}_1$ *and* $\mathbb{G}_2$*, then there is an (adaptively) function-hiding slotted IPFE scheme on* GroupGen.

Note that the MDDH_k assumption on $\mathbb{G}_s$ ($s \in \{1,2\}$) says that a random group element $[\mathbf{r}]_s$ is indistinguishable from $[\mathbf{sA}]_s$ given $[\mathbf{A}]$, where $\mathbf{A} \leftarrow \mathbb{Z}_p^{k \times (k+1)}$, $\mathbf{r} \in \mathbb{Z}_p^{k+1}$, and $\mathbf{s} \in \mathbb{Z}_p^k$. The assumption is implied by the standard k-LIN assumption, which becomes progressively weaker as k becomes larger.

2.3   Attribute Based Encryption

Let $R = \{R_\lambda : A_\lambda \times B_\lambda \to \{0,1\}\}_\lambda$ be a relation where A_λ and B_λ denote "ciphertext attribute" and "key attribute" spaces. An attribute-based encryption (ABE) scheme for R is defined by the following PPT algorithms:

$\mathsf{Setup}(1^\lambda) \to (\mathsf{mpk}, \mathsf{msk})$: The setup algorithm takes as input the unary representation of the security parameter λ and outputs a master public key mpk and a master secret key msk.

$\mathsf{Enc}(\mathsf{mpk}, X, \mu) \to \mathsf{ct}$: The encryption algorithm takes as input a master public key mpk, a ciphertext attribute $X \in A_\lambda$, and a message bit μ. It outputs a ciphertext ct.

$\mathsf{KeyGen}(\mathsf{mpk}, \mathsf{msk}, Y) \to \mathsf{sk}_Y$: The key generation algorithm takes as input the master public key mpk, the master secret key msk, and a key attribute $Y \in B_\lambda$. It outputs a private key sk_Y.

$\mathsf{Dec}(\mathsf{mpk}, \mathsf{ct}, X, \mathsf{sk}_Y, Y) \to \mu$ or $\bot$: The decryption algorithm takes as input the master public key mpk, a ciphertext ct, ciphertext attribute $X \in A_\lambda$, a private key sk_Y, and private key attribute $Y \in B_\lambda$. It outputs the message μ or $\bot$ which represents that the ciphertext is not in a valid form.

Definition 2.3 (Correctness). *An ABE scheme for relation family R is correct if for all $\lambda \in \mathbb{N}$, $X \in A_\lambda, Y \in B_\lambda$ such that $R(X,Y) = 1$, and for all messages $\mu \in \mathcal{M}$,*

$$\Pr\left[\begin{array}{l} (\mathsf{mpk}, \mathsf{msk}) \leftarrow \mathsf{Setup}(1^\lambda), \ \mathsf{sk}_Y \leftarrow \mathsf{KeyGen}(\mathsf{mpk}, \mathsf{msk}, Y), \\ \mathsf{ct} \leftarrow \mathsf{Enc}(\mathsf{mpk}, X, \mu) : \ \mathsf{Dec}\Big(\mathsf{mpk}, \mathsf{sk}_Y, Y, \mathsf{ct}, X\Big) \neq \mu \end{array} \right] = \mathrm{negl}(\lambda)$$

where the probability is taken over the coins of Setup, KeyGen, and Enc.

Definition 2.4 (Sel-IND security for ABE). *For an ABE scheme $\mathsf{ABE} = \{\mathsf{Setup}, \mathsf{Enc}, \mathsf{KeyGen}, \mathsf{Dec}\}$ for a relation family $R = \{R_\lambda : A_\lambda \times B_\lambda \to \{0,1\}\}_\lambda$ and a message space $\{\mathcal{M}_\lambda\}_{\lambda \in \mathbb{N}}$ and an efficient adversary $\mathcal{A} = \{\mathcal{A}_\lambda\}_\lambda$, let us define $\mathsf{Sel\text{-}IND}$ security game as follows.*

1. **Choosing the Target:** *At the beginning of the game, $\mathcal{A}_\lambda$ chooses its target $X^\star \in A_\lambda$ and sends to the challenger.*
2. **Setup phase:** *On input 1^λ, the challenger samples $(\mathsf{mpk}, \mathsf{msk}) \leftarrow \mathsf{Setup}(1^\lambda)$ and gives mpk to $\mathcal{A}_\lambda$.*
3. **Query phase:** *During the game, $\mathcal{A}_\lambda$ adaptively makes the following queries, in an arbitrary order. $\mathcal{A}_\lambda$ can make unbounded many key queries, but can make only single challenge query.*

(a) **Key Queries:** $\mathcal{A}_\lambda$ chooses an input $Y \in B_\lambda$. For each such query, the challenger replies with $\mathsf{sk}_Y \leftarrow \mathsf{KeyGen}(\mathsf{mpk}, \mathsf{msk}, Y)$.

(b) **Challenge Query:** At some point, $\mathcal{A}_\lambda$ submits a pair of equal length messages $(\mu_0, \mu_1) \in (\mathcal{M})^2$ to the challenger. The challenger samples a random bit $\beta \leftarrow \{0,1\}$ and replies to $\mathcal{A}_\lambda$ with $\mathsf{ct} \leftarrow \mathsf{Enc}(\mathsf{mpk}, X^\star, \mu_\beta)$.

We require that $R(X^\star, Y) = 0$ holds for any Y such that $\mathcal{A}_\lambda$ makes a key query for Y in order to avoid trivial attacks.

4. **Output phase:** $\mathcal{A}_\lambda$ outputs a guess bit β' as the output of the experiment.

We define the advantage $\mathsf{Adv}^{\mathsf{Sel\text{-}IND}}_{\mathsf{ABE},\mathcal{A}}(1^\lambda)$ of $\mathcal{A}$ in the above game as

$$\mathsf{Adv}^{\mathsf{Sel\text{-}IND}}_{\mathsf{ABE},\mathcal{A}}(1^\lambda) := |\Pr[\mathcal{A} \text{ outputs } 1|\beta = 0] - \Pr[\mathcal{A} \text{outputs} 1|\beta = 1]| .$$

The ABE scheme ABE is said to satisfy $\mathsf{Sel\text{-}IND}$ security (or simply selective security) if for any efficient and stateful adversary $\mathcal{A} = \{\mathcal{A}_\lambda\}_\lambda$, there exists a negligible function $\mathsf{negl}(\cdot)$ such that $\mathsf{Adv}^{\mathsf{Sel\text{-}IND}}_{\mathsf{ABE},\mathcal{A}}(1^\lambda) \neq \mathsf{negl}(\lambda)$.

We can consider the following stronger version of the security where we require the ciphertext to be pseudorandom.

Definition 2.5 ($\mathsf{Sel\text{-}INDr}$ security for ABE). *We define $\mathsf{Sel\text{-}INDr}$ security game similarly to $\mathsf{Sel\text{-}IND}$ security game except that the adversary $\mathcal{A}$ chooses single message μ instead of (μ_0, μ_1) at the challenge phase and the challenger returns $\mathsf{ct} \leftarrow \mathsf{Enc}(\mathsf{mpk}, X^\star, \mu)$ if $\beta = 0$ and a random ciphertext $\mathsf{ct} \leftarrow \mathcal{CT}$ from a ciphertext space $\mathcal{CT}$ if $\beta = 1$. We define the advantage $\mathsf{Adv}^{\mathsf{Sel\text{-}INDr}}_{\mathsf{ABE},\mathcal{A}}(1^\lambda)$ of the adversary $\mathcal{A}$ accordingly and say that the scheme satisfies $\mathsf{Sel\text{-}INDr}$ security if the quantity is negligible.*

We also consider (weaker) version of the above notions, where $\mathcal{A}$ specifies the set $\mathcal{Y}$ of attributes for which it makes key queries along with $X^\star$ at the beginning of the game.

Definition 2.6 ($\mathsf{VerSel\text{-}IND}$ security for ABE). *We define $\mathsf{VerSel\text{-}IND}$ security game as $\mathsf{Sel\text{-}IND}$ security game with the exception that the adversary $\mathcal{A}$ has to choose the set $\mathcal{Y} \subseteq B_\lambda$ for which it makes key queries along with the challenge ciphertext attribute $X^\star$ before the setup phase but the choice of (μ_0, μ_1) can still be adaptive. After that, $\mathcal{A}_\lambda$ can make key queries for $Y_1, Y_2, \ldots$ adaptively, but we need $Y_i \in \mathcal{Y}$ for all queries. We define the advantage $\mathsf{Adv}^{\mathsf{VerSel\text{-}IND}}_{\mathsf{ABE},\mathcal{A}}(1^\lambda)$ of the adversary $\mathcal{A}$ accordingly and say that the scheme satisfies $\mathsf{VerSel\text{-}IND}$ security (or simply very selective security) if the quantity is negligible.*

In the following, we define standard notions of ciphertext-policy attribute-based encryption (CP-ABE) and broadcast encryption (BE) by specifying the relation R.

CP-ABE for Circuits. We define CP-ABE for circuit class $\{\mathcal{C}_\lambda\}_\lambda$ by specifying the relation. Here, $\mathcal{C}_\lambda$ is a set of circuits with input length $\ell(\lambda)$ and binary output.

We define $A_\lambda^{\mathsf{CP}} = C_\lambda$ and $B_\lambda^{\mathsf{CP}} = \{0, 1\}^\ell$. Furthermore, we define the relation R_λ^{CP} as $R_\lambda^{\mathsf{CP}}(C, \mathbf{x}) = \neg C(\mathbf{x})$.[2]

BE. To define BE, we define $A_\lambda^{\mathsf{BE}} = 2^{[N(\lambda)]}$ and $B_\lambda^{\mathsf{BE}} = [N(\lambda)]$, where $N(\lambda) = \mathrm{poly}(\lambda)$ is the number of users in the system and $2^{[N(\lambda)]}$ denotes all subsets of $[N]$. We also define $R_\lambda^{\mathsf{BE}} : A_\lambda^{\mathsf{BE}} \times B_\lambda^{\mathsf{BE}} \to \{0, 1\}$ as $R_\lambda^{\mathsf{BE}}(S, i) = 1$ when $i \in S$ and $R_\lambda^{\mathsf{BE}}(S, i) = 0$ otherwise. For BE, we typically require that the ciphertext size should be $o(N) \cdot \mathrm{poly}(\lambda)$, since otherwise we have a trivial construction from plain public key encryption.

Remark 2.7. We note that very selective security and selective security are in fact equivalent in the case of BE since one can convert selective adversary into very selective adversary as follows. Namely, if the selective adversary chooses its target $S \subseteq [N]$, the very selective adversary chooses the same target S and specifies the set of user indices for which it makes key queries as $[N] \backslash S$. Then, the very selective adversary can simulate the game for the selective adversary using the secret keys given by the challenger.

3   Computational Secret Sharing Scheme with Short Shares

We will use secret sharing scheme with special properties that we are going to define here. Let $\mathcal{C} = \{\mathcal{C}_\lambda\}_\lambda$ be a circuit class. A secret sharing scheme for the circuit class $\mathcal{C}$ is defined by the following PPT algorithms:

SS.Setup$(1^\lambda, p) \to \mathsf{pp}$: The setup algorithm takes as input the unary representation of the security parameter λ and the modulus p and outputs public parameter pp.

SS.Share(pp, C, μ): The sharing algorithm takes as input the public parameter pp, a circuit $C \in \mathcal{C}_\lambda$ that specifies access policy, and a message $\mu \in \{0, 1\}$ to be shared and outputs a set of shares $\{\mathsf{share}_{i,b} \in \mathbb{Z}_p^m\}_{i \in [\ell], b \in \{0,1\}}$, where ℓ is the input length of C and m is a parameter specified by λ and p.

SS.Recon$(\mathsf{pp}, C, x, \{\mathsf{share}_{i,x_i}\}_{i \in [\ell]}) \to \mu$ or $\bot$: The reconstruction algorithm takes as input the public parameter pp, a circuit C, an input $x \in \{0, 1\}^\ell$ to the circuit, and shares $\{\mathsf{share}_{i,x_i}\}_{i \in [\ell]}$ and outputs message μ or $\bot$.

We require correctness and security for the secret sharing scheme as defined in the following.

Definition 3.1 (Correctness). *We say that a secret sharing scheme* SS $=$ (SS.Setup, SS.Share, SS.Recon) *for circuit class $\mathcal{C}$ has correctness if there exists a function $p_0(\lambda)$ specified by the circuit class $\mathcal{C}$ such that for any $p > p_0(\lambda)$, $C \in \mathcal{C}$ with input length ℓ, $x \in \{0, 1\}^\ell$ satisfying $C(x) = 1$, and $\mu \in \{0, 1\}$, we have*

$$\Pr \left[\begin{array}{l} \mathsf{pp} \leftarrow \mathsf{SS.Setup}(1^\lambda, p), \\ \{\mathsf{share}_{i,b}\}_{i \in [\ell], b \in \{0,1\}} \leftarrow \mathsf{SS.Share}(\mathsf{pp}, C, \mu), \\ \mathsf{SS.Recon}\Big(\mathsf{pp}, \{\mathsf{share}_{i,x_i}\}_{i \in [\ell]}\Big) = \mu \end{array} \right] = 1$$

---

[2] Here, we follow the standard convention in lattice-based cryptography where the decryption succeeds when $C(\mathbf{x}) = 0$ rather than $C(\mathbf{x}) = 1$.

Definition 3.2 (Security). *We say that a secret sharing scheme* SS = (SS.Setup, SS.Share, SS.Recon) *for circuit class* $\mathcal{C} = \{\mathcal{C}_\lambda\}_\lambda$ *is secure if for any* $C \in \mathcal{C}_\lambda$ *with input length* $\ell = \ell(\lambda)$, $x \in \{0,1\}^\ell$ *satisfying* $C(x) = 0$, $\mu \in \{0,1\}$, $p \in \mathbb{N}$, *and for any efficient adversary* $\mathcal{A} = \{\mathcal{A}_\lambda\}$, *we have*

$$\left| \Pr\left[\mathcal{A}_\lambda \left(\begin{array}{c} \mathsf{pp}, C, x, \\ \{\mathsf{share}_{i,x_i}\}_{i\in[\ell]} \end{array} \right) \to 1 \right] - \Pr\left[\mathcal{A}_\lambda \left(\begin{array}{c} \mathsf{pp}, C, x, \\ \{\mathbf{v}_i\}_{i\in[\ell]} \end{array} \right) \to 1 \right] \right| = \mathsf{negl}(\lambda)$$

where the probability is taken over the choice of $\mathsf{pp} \leftarrow \mathsf{SS.Setup}(1^\lambda, p)$, $\{\mathsf{share}_{i,b}\}_{i,b} \leftarrow \mathsf{SS.Share}(\mathsf{pp}, C, \mu)$, $\mathbf{v}_i \leftarrow \mathbb{Z}_p^m$ *for* $i \in [\ell]$, *and the internal coin of* $\mathcal{A}_\lambda$.

We note that in the above, we not only require that the shares do not reveal μ if $C(x) = 0$, but also require that they look random.

We furthermore require following structural properties for the construction. First, we require that pp is a random string.

Definition 3.3 (Random Public Parameters). *We require that* pp *output by* $\mathsf{SS.Setup}(1^\lambda, p)$ *is statistically close to uniformly random, where the length of the string is deterministically determined by* p.

Looking ahead, the above property is crucial when we prove the security of our ABE scheme. If the public parameter of the secret sharing scheme was chosen from a structured distribution, we would have to rely on the bilinear KOALA assumption (Definition 4.1) with auxiliary input chosen from the same distribution. However, we cannot hope the assumption to hold for auxiliary input with general distribution as we will discuss in Remark 4.3.

We also require that the reconstruction algorithm is structured as two steps: a function evaluation step that computes the circuit on the shares to yield the message along with noise, followed by a rounding step that removes the noise. We require that the first step is *linear*. We refer to such a reconstruction algorithm as being "almost linear", and define it formally next.

Definition 3.4 (Almost Linear Reconstruction). *We say that a secret sharing scheme* SS = (SS.Setup, SS.Share, SS.Recon) *has almost linear reconstruction if the reconstruction algorithm is divided into two steps:*

- *Step 1 takes as input the public parameter* pp, *the circuit* C, *and the input* x. *It outputs a set of coefficients* $\{a_{i,j} \in \mathbb{Z}_p\}_{i\in[\ell],j\in[m]}$. *We denote this step as an algorithm* $\mathsf{SS.FindCoef}(\mathsf{pp}, C, x)$.
- *Step 2 takes as input the set of shares* $\{\mathsf{share}_{i,x_i}\}_{i\in[\ell]}$ *that corresponds to* x *and a set of linear coefficients* $\{a_{i,j}\}_{i\in[\ell],j\in[m]}$ *and computes*

$$d := \sum_{i\in[\ell],j\in[m]} a_{i,j}\mathsf{share}_{i,x_i,j} \mod p$$

where $\mathsf{share}_{i,x_i,j} \in \mathbb{Z}_p$ *is the* j-th *entry of the vector* share_{i,x_i}. *It then outputs* 1 *if* d *is closer to* $p/2$ *and* 0 *otherwise.*

We require the following property, which implies the correctness: For any
$x \in \{0,1\}^\ell$ *and* $C \in \mathcal{C}$ *satisfying* $C(x) = 1$ *and* $p > p_0$, *if we have:*

$$\mathsf{pp} \leftarrow \mathsf{SS.Setup}(1^\lambda, p), \{\mathsf{share}_{i,b}\}_{i \in [\ell]} \leftarrow \mathsf{SS.Share}(\mathsf{pp}, C, \mu),$$
$$\{a_{i,j}\}_{i,j} \leftarrow \mathsf{SS.FindCoef}(\mathsf{pp}, C, x),$$

where $i \in [\ell], j \in [m]$, *then there exists* $e \in [-B, B]$ *such that*

$$\sum_{i \in [\ell], j \in [m]} a_{i,j}\mathsf{share}_{i,x_i,j} = \mu \cdot \lceil p/2 \rceil + e \mod p$$

where $B(\lambda)$ *is an integer specified by* $\mathcal{C}$.

The following theorem asserts that we can construct a secret sharing scheme
with the desired properties under the LWE assumption.

Theorem 3.5. *For circuit class* $\mathcal{C}_{\ell,d} = \{\mathcal{C}_{\lambda,\ell(\lambda),d(\lambda)}\}_{\lambda \in \mathbb{N}}$ *consisting of circuits*
whose input length is $\ell(\lambda) = \mathrm{poly}(\lambda)$ *and depth* $d(\lambda) = O(\log \lambda)$, *we have secret*
sharing scheme that satisfies almost linear reconstruction (Definition 3.4) for
$p_0 = \mathrm{poly}(\lambda, 2^d, \ell)$ *and has random public parameters (Definition 3.3). We can*
prove the security of the scheme (Definition 3.2) under the LWE assumption
with approximation factor $p^\epsilon \cdot \mathrm{poly}(\lambda)$ *for some constant* $\epsilon < 1$. *Furthermore, the*
size of the parameters in the construction is as follows:

$$|\mathsf{pp}|, |\mathsf{share}_{i,b}| \leq \mathrm{poly}(\lambda, d, \ell), \quad B(\lambda) \leq \mathrm{poly}(\lambda, 2^d). \tag{3.1}$$

In particular, $B(\lambda)$ *is bounded by a polynomial in* λ *since* $d = O(\log \lambda)$.

Proof. The construction is based on the ABE scheme for circuit class $\{\mathcal{C}_{\ell,d}\}$ by
[GV15]. Here, we first show a construction that almost works but has a problem.
We then fix the problem by slightly modifying the construction. In our first
construction, we put the master public key and a secret key for circuit C of the
ABE scheme into pp, where the former consists of set of random matrices $\mathbf{A}$ and
$\{\mathbf{B}_{i,b}\}_{i,b}$ along with a random vector $\mathbf{u}$. To generate $\{\mathsf{share}_{i,b}\}_{i,b}$, we generate
LWE samples using corresponding matrices in $\{\mathbf{B}_{i,b}\}_{i,b}$ with respect to the same
secret, so that $\{\mathsf{share}_{i,x_i}\}_i$ constitutes a valid ABE ciphertext for attribute x
and message μ to be shared.[3] Most of the properties we require for the secret
sharing scheme are directly implied by the corresponding properties of the ABE
scheme. The correctness (Definition 3.1) and the security (Definition 3.2) of the
secret sharing scheme are implied by the corresponding properties of the ABE
scheme, where for the latter we use Sel-INDr security of the ABE scheme. The
size requirements for the parameters (Eq. (3.1)) are satisfied by the efficiency of
the ABE scheme. The almost linear reconstruction property (Definition 3.4) is
also satisfied by the structure of the decryption algorithm of the ABE scheme.

---

[3] In fact, the ABE ciphertext also has to include the LWE samples with respect to
the matrix $\mathbf{A}$ and the vector $\mathbf{u}$, where the latter will be used to mask the message.
These LWE samples are put into both of $\mathsf{share}_{1,0}$ and $\mathsf{share}_{1,1}$.

However, the above construction does not have the property of random public parameters (Definition 3.3) and we have to change it slightly. In particular, in the above, pp is chosen as follows: We first sample random matrices $\mathbf{A}$ and $\{\mathbf{B}_{i,b}\}_{i,b}$ and a random vector $\mathbf{u}$, where $\mathbf{A}$ is chosen along with a trapdoor. We then compute a matrix $\mathbf{B}_C$ corresponding to the circuit C from the matrices $\{\mathbf{B}_{i,b}\}_{i,b}$ and then generate a vector $\mathbf{r}$ from a Gaussian distribution over the integer lattice with the restriction

$$[\mathbf{A}|\mathbf{B}_C]\mathbf{r} = \mathbf{u} \mod q$$

using the trapdoor. We then set pp $= (\mathbf{A}, \mathbf{B}, \mathbf{u}, \mathbf{r})$. Because of the above relation between $\mathbf{r}$ and $\mathbf{u}$, pp is not random.

To address this issue, we first remove $\mathbf{u}$ from pp. We now have that the distribution of $\mathbf{r}$ is statistically close to the Gaussian distribution over the integer lattice (without the restriction), since for a vector $\mathbf{r}$ chosen from (sufficiently wide) Gaussian distribution over the integer lattice, $\mathbf{u}$ defined as $\mathbf{u} = [\mathbf{A}|\mathbf{B}_C]\mathbf{r}$ mod q is statistically close to uniform. Now, such $\mathbf{r}$ can be chosen from randomness of fixed polynomial length, in particular, without a trapdoor. We then put the randomness R used for sampling $\mathbf{r}$ into pp instead of $\mathbf{r}$ itself. We now have that pp is statistically close to random as desired.

It is easy to see that this change does not affect the properties that we want from the secret sharing scheme. In particular, the correctness is not lost since $\mathbf{u}$ can be recovered from $\mathbf{r}$. We note that for the security to be preserved, we need an efficient reverse sampling algorithm that is given $\mathbf{r}$ and samples randomness R conditioned that the Gaussian sampler outputs $\mathbf{r}$ on input R. The reason why we need this property is that the reduction algorithm that breaks the ABE scheme using the adversary against the secret sharing scheme should simulate the randomness R for sampling $\mathbf{r}$ only given $\mathbf{r}$, which is the secret key of the ABE scheme.

This property is satisfied by efficient Gaussian samplers such as [GPV08]. To see this, let us recall the procedure of sampling Gaussian on integer lattice in [GPV08] (See Lemma 4.3 in the paper). Without loss of generality, we can consider one-dimensional case since multi-dimensional case can be handled by running the algorithm for one-dimensional case in parallel. The sampling algorithm by [GPV08] was based on rejection sampling. The algorithm first samples a candidate for the output uniformly at random and outputs it with certain probability. This step is repeated until it outputs something or the number of times it repeats the procedure exceeds predetermined number. The idea for the reverse sampling is to first run the algorithm until it outputs something and then replace the randomness that was used for the output with that which leads to the intended output. The former step can be done straightforwardly since it is exactly the same as the original sampling algorithm. The purpose of performing this step is to simulate the failure. The latter step can be performed efficiently as well, since the randomness that leads to the output consists of the output value itself along with the randomness that allows the sampler to accept and output the value (rather than to reject). It is easy to see that this algorithm indeed works. This completes the proof of Theorem 3.5.

The complete description of the secret sharing scheme will appear in the full version.

4   Our Security Assumptions

In this section, we will introduce the bilinear knowledge of orthogonality (KOALA) assumption, which is an analogue of the KOALA assumption introduced in [BW19]. Looking ahead, the assumption will be used to prove the security of our ABE scheme in Sect. 5.1. We then introduce weak KOALA assumption (wKOALA) and show that it is implied by the bilinear KOALA assumption. While the former assumption is implied by the latter, the former is handier to use and would be of independent interest.

4.1   Bilinear KOALA Assumption

Here, we introduce bilinear KOALA assumption, which is an analogue of the KOALA assumption introduced in [BW19].

Definition 4.1 (Bilinear KOALA Assumption). *Let* $\mathsf{Samp} = \{\mathsf{Samp}_\lambda\}_\lambda$ *be an efficient sampling algorithm that takes as input an integer p and a string* aux *and outputs a matrix* $\mathbf{V} \in \mathbb{Z}_p^{\ell_1 \times \ell_2}$ *with $\ell_1 < \ell_2$. For an efficient adversary* $\mathcal{A} = \{\mathcal{A}_\lambda\}$, *let us define*

$$\mathsf{Adv}_{\mathcal{A},\mathbb{G},\mathsf{Samp}}^{\mathsf{BKOALA,dist}}(\lambda) := |\Pr[\mathcal{A}_\lambda(\mathbb{G}, \mathsf{aux}, [\mathbf{sV}]_2) \to 1] - \Pr[\mathcal{A}_\lambda(\mathbb{G}, \mathsf{aux}, [\mathbf{r}]_2) \to 1]|.$$

where the probabilities are taken over the choice of uniformly random aux, $\mathbb{G} = (p, \mathbb{G}_1, \mathbb{G}_2, \mathbb{G}_T, e, [1]_1, [1]_2) \leftarrow \mathsf{GroupGen}(1^\lambda)$, $\mathbf{V} \leftarrow \mathsf{Samp}(p, \mathsf{aux})$, $\mathbf{s} \leftarrow \mathbb{Z}_p^{\ell_1}$, $\mathbf{r} \leftarrow \mathbb{Z}_p^{\ell_2}$, *and the coin of* $\mathcal{A}_\lambda$.

Furthermore, for an efficient adversary $\mathcal{B} = \{\mathcal{B}_\lambda\}_\lambda$, *we also define*

$$\mathsf{Adv}_{\mathcal{B},\mathbb{G},\mathsf{Samp}}^{\mathsf{BKOALA,find}}(\lambda) := \Pr[\mathcal{B}_\lambda(\mathbb{G}, \mathsf{aux}) \to \mathbf{x} \wedge \mathbf{xV}^\top = \mathbf{0} \wedge \mathbf{x} \neq \mathbf{0}]$$

where the probability is taken over the choice of uniformly random aux, $\mathbb{G} = (p, \mathbb{G}_1, \mathbb{G}_2, \mathbb{G}_T, e, [1]_1, [1]_2) \leftarrow \mathsf{GroupGen}(1^\lambda)$, $\mathbf{V} \leftarrow \mathsf{Samp}_\lambda(p, \mathsf{aux})$, *and the coin of* $\mathcal{B}_\lambda$.

We say that the bilinear KOALA assumption holds with respect to $\mathsf{GroupGen}$ *if for any efficient adversary* $\mathcal{A}$ *and efficient sampler* Samp, *there exists another efficient adversary* $\mathcal{B}$ *and a polynomial function* $Q(\lambda)$ *such that*

$$\mathsf{Adv}_{\mathcal{B},\mathbb{G},\mathsf{Samp}}^{\mathsf{BKOALA,find}}(\lambda) \geq \mathsf{Adv}_{\mathcal{A},\mathbb{G},\mathsf{Samp}}^{\mathsf{BKOALA,dist}}(\lambda)/Q(\lambda) - \mathsf{negl}(\lambda).$$

Remark 4.2. Our definition of the bilinear KOALA assumption differs from the original KOALA assumption defined by Beullens and Wee [BW19] in several points. First, we consider the assumption in groups equipped with bilinear maps whereas they consider the assumption in groups without bilinear maps.

Second, in our assumption, the adversary is given an auxiliary input aux and $\mathbf{V}$ is chosen from a distribution specified by Samp whereas there is no any auxiliary information and $\mathbf{V}$ is fixed in [BW19]. This change is necessary to prove the security of our ABE scheme in Sect. 5, since we will use an adversary $\mathcal{B}$ that is obtained from $\mathcal{A}$ to break a computational assumption, where we put the problem instance of the assumption into aux.

Remark 4.3. One could consider simpler and stronger variant of the above assumption where Samp chooses aux along with $\mathbf{V}$ instead of letting aux to be a random string that is not controlled by Samp. However, we cannot hope this variant of the assumption to hold for all efficient samplers. For example, let us consider a sampler that outputs random $\mathbf{V}$ along with auxiliary information aux $= \mathcal{O}(C_{\mathbf{V}})$, which is an obfuscation of circuit $C_{\mathbf{V}}$ that takes as input group description $\mathbb{G}$ and elements $[\mathbf{v}]_2$ and returns whether $\mathbf{v}$ is in the space spanned by the rows of $\mathbf{V}$ or not. Using $\mathcal{O}(C_{\mathbf{V}})$, one can easily distinguish $[\mathbf{sV}]_2$ from $[\mathbf{r}]_2$ with high probability. However, an efficient adversary may not be able to find a vector $\mathbf{x} \neq \mathbf{0}$ that satisfies $\mathbf{xV} = \mathbf{0}$ even given $\mathcal{O}(C_{\mathbf{V}})$, if we use sufficiently strong obfuscator to obfuscate the circuit $C_{\mathbf{V}}$. Our assumption above excludes this kind of attack by making aux to be public randomness that is not touched by the sampler. Our definition is inspired by that of public coin differing input obfuscation [IPS15], where the authors exclude similar kind of attacks [GGHW14] in the context of differing input obfuscations by restricting the distribution of auxiliary input to be random.

The following theorem justifies the bilinear KOALA assumption on the bilinear generic group model. The proof is almost the same as that for the KOALA assumption in [BW19], but we have to adjust it into the setting where the groups are equipped with bilinear maps and the adversary is given auxiliary input.

Theorem 4.4. *The bilinear KOALA assumption holds under the bilinear generic group model, where $\mathcal{A}$ has access to the generic group oracles but Samp does not.*

Proof. Let us fix PPT sampler Samp and an adversary $\mathcal{A}$. We also let $Q_{zt}(\lambda)$ be the upper bound on the number of zero test queries that $\mathcal{A}$ makes. To prove the theorem, we consider following sequence of games. Let us denote the event that $\mathcal{A}$ outputs 1 at the end of $\mathbf{Game}_x$ as E_x.

Game$_1$: In this game, Samp takes as input the order of groups p and a random string aux and outputs $\mathbf{V} \in \mathbb{Z}_p^{\ell_1 \times \ell_2}$. By assumption, Samp does not have access to the generic group oracles. Then, the adversary $\mathcal{A}$ is given aux, handles corresponding to the group elements $[\mathbf{r}]_2$, where $\mathbf{r} = (r_1, \ldots, r_{\ell_2}) \leftarrow \mathbb{Z}_p^{\ell_2}$, and access to the oracles in generic group model and outputs a bit at the end of the game.

Game$_2$: In this game, we switch to symbolic group model and replace $r_1, \ldots, r_{\ell_2} \in \mathbb{Z}_p$ with formal variables $R_1, \ldots, R_{\ell_2}$. Note that all handles given to $\mathcal{A}$ during the game refer to a group element that is represented as

$$x_0 + \sum_{j \in [\ell_2]} x_j R_j \in \mathbb{Z}_p[R_1, \ldots, R_{\ell_2}]$$

where the challenger computes coefficients $\{x_j \in \mathbb{Z}_p\}_{j\in[0,\ell_2]}$ by keeping track of the group operations performed by $\mathcal{A}$.

We observe that this game differs from the previous game only when $\mathcal{A}$ makes a zero test query for $x_0 + \sum_{j\in[\ell_2]} x_j R_j$ such that $x_0 + \sum_{j\in[\ell_2]} x_j R_j \neq 0$ but $x_0 + \sum_{j\in[\ell_2]} x_j r_j$. However, this occurs with probability at most $1/p$ since $\mathbf{r}$ is chosen uniformly at random independently from anything else. Therefore, we have

$$|\Pr[\mathsf{E}_2] - \Pr[\mathsf{E}_1]| = \mathrm{negl}(\lambda).$$

Game$_3$: In this game, we replace the formal variable R_j with

$$\sum_{i\in[\ell_1]} v_{i,j} S_i$$

for all $j \in [\ell_2]$, where $v_{i,j}$ is the (i,j)-th entry of $\mathbf{V}$ and $S_1, \ldots, S_{\ell_1}$ are set of formal variables.

Game$_4$: In this game, we switch back to the generic group model (rather than the symbolic group model) and provide the adversary with handles for $[\mathbf{sV}]_2$ as input.

By the same reason as the game hop from **Game$_1$** to **Game$_2$**, we have

$$|\Pr[\mathsf{E}_4] - \Pr[\mathsf{E}_3]| = \mathrm{negl}(\lambda).$$

By the definition of the games, we have $|\Pr[\mathsf{E}_4] - \Pr[\mathsf{E}_1]| = \mathsf{Adv}^{\mathsf{BKOALA,dist}}_{\mathcal{A},\mathbb{G},\mathsf{Samp}}(\lambda)$. Let us define $\epsilon := |\Pr[\mathsf{E}_2] - \Pr[\mathsf{E}_3]|$. By triangular inequality, we have

$$\epsilon \geq |\Pr[\mathsf{E}_4] - \Pr[\mathsf{E}_1]| - |\Pr[\mathsf{E}_1] - \Pr[\mathsf{E}_2]| - |\Pr[\mathsf{E}_3] - \Pr[\mathsf{E}_4]|$$
$$\geq \mathsf{Adv}^{\mathsf{BKOALA,dist}}_{\mathcal{A},\mathbb{G},\mathsf{Samp}}(\lambda) - \mathrm{negl}(\lambda).$$

Therefore, it suffices to prove the following lemma to finish the proof of Theorem 4.4.

Lemma 4.5. *There exists an efficient adversary $\mathcal{B}$ that has access to the bilinear generic group oracles and* $\mathsf{Adv}^{\mathsf{BKOALA,find}}_{\mathcal{B},\mathbb{G},\mathsf{Samp}}(\lambda) \geq \epsilon/Q_{\mathsf{zt}}$.

Proof. We first observe that the oracle response to $\mathcal{A}$ in **Game$_2$** and **Game$_3$** differs only when $\mathcal{A}$ makes a zero-test query for a handle that corresponds to $x_0 + \sum_{j\in[\ell_2]} x_j R_j$ such that $x_0 + \sum_{j\in[\ell_2]} x_j R_j \neq 0$ over $\mathbb{Z}_p[R_1, \ldots, R_{\ell_2}]$ and

$$x_0 + \sum_{j\in[\ell_2]} x_j \left(\sum_{i\in[\ell_1]} v_{i,j} S_i\right) = x_0 + \sum_{i\in[\ell_1]} \left(\sum_{j\in[\ell_2]} x_j v_{i,j}\right) S_i = 0$$

over $\mathbb{Z}_p[S_1, \ldots, S_{\ell_1}]$. We call such a query *bad* query. We can see that $\mathcal{A}$ makes a bad query with probability at least ϵ in **Game$_2$**. We observe that for a bad query, we have $x_0 = 0$, $\mathbf{xV}^\top = \mathbf{0}$, and $\mathbf{x} \neq \mathbf{0}$ for $\mathbf{x} = (x_1, \ldots, x_{\ell_2})$.

To prove the theorem, we further consider the following sequence of games. In the following, let us denote F_x the event that $\mathcal{A}$ makes a bad query and the challenger does not output $\perp$ in **Game$_{2,\mathsf{x}}$**.

Game$_{2,1}$: This is the same as **Game$_2$**. Without loss of generality, we assume that the challenger simulates the generic group oracles for $\mathcal{A}$. By definition, we have

$$\Pr[\mathsf{F}_1] \geq \epsilon.$$

Game$_{2,2}$: In this game, we change the previous game so that the challenger picks a random guess k^* for the first bad query as $k^* \leftarrow [Q_{\mathsf{zt}}]$ at the beginning of the game. Furthermore, we change the game so that the challenger outputs $\bot$ at the end of the game if the k^*-th zero-test query is not the first bad query. Since k^* is chosen uniformly at random and independent from the view of $\mathcal{A}$, the guess is correct with probability $1/Q_{\mathsf{zt}}$ conditioned on F_1. Therefore, we have

$$\Pr[\mathsf{F}_2] \geq \Pr[\mathsf{F}_1]/Q_{\mathsf{zt}}.$$

Game$_{2,3}$: This game is the same as the previous game except that the challenger aborts the game and outputs $\bot$ immediately after $\mathcal{A}$ makes the k^*-th zero-test query. Since whether F_2 occurs or not is irrelevant to how the game proceeds after the k^*-th zero-test query is made by $\mathcal{A}$, we clearly have

$$\Pr[\mathsf{F}_3] = \Pr[\mathsf{F}_2].$$

We then construct $\mathcal{B}$, which acts as the challenger in **Game$_{2,3}$** for $\mathcal{A}$ as follows.

$\mathcal{B}$ takes aux as input and then chooses random $k^* \leftarrow [Q_{\mathsf{zt}}]$. It then runs $\mathcal{A}$ on input aux and handles for symbols $R_1, \ldots, R_{\ell_2}$. $\mathcal{B}$ then answers generic oracle queries made by $\mathcal{A}$ honestly until the k^*-th zero test query. When $\mathcal{A}$ makes the k^*-th zero test query, $\mathcal{B}$ extracts $(x_0, x_1, \ldots, x_{\ell_2})$ such that the query corresponds to the handle of $x_0 + \sum_{j \in [\ell_2]} x_j R_j$. This is possible by keeping track of $\mathcal{A}$'s group operations while simulating the generic group oracles. If $x_0 \neq 0$, $\mathcal{B}$ aborts and outputs $\bot$. Otherwise, it outputs the vector $\mathbf{x} = (x_1, \ldots, x_{\ell_2})$.

Since $\mathcal{B}$ perfectly simulates **Game$_{2,3}$** and thus the probability that $\mathcal{B}$ outputs $\mathbf{x}$ such that $\mathbf{x}\mathbf{V}^\top = 0$ and $\mathbf{x} \neq \mathbf{0}$ is $\Pr[\mathsf{F}_3] = \epsilon/Q_{\mathsf{zt}}$. This completes the proof of Lemma 4.5.

This completes the proof of Theorem 4.4.

4.2   Our New Assumption wKOALA

Here, we introduce our new assumption that we call wKOALA (for "weak" KOALA) that will be used to prove the security of our ABE scheme in Sect. 5. The assumption essentially says that for a sampler that outputs a set of vectors such that the vectors are individually pseudorandom but mutually correlated, it holds that the vectors appear mutually pseudorandom when they are lifted to the exponent and randomized by vector-wise randomness. We require that this hold even in the presence of random auxiliary input as is assumed for the case of the bilinear KOALA assumption.

Definition 4.6. *Let* Samp $= \{\mathsf{Samp}_\lambda\}_\lambda$ *be an efficient sampling algorithm that takes as input an integer p and a string* aux *and outputs a set of vectors $\{\mathbf{u}^{(j)} \in \mathbb{Z}_p^m\}_{j \in [t]}$. For an efficient adversary $\mathcal{A} = \{\mathcal{A}_\lambda\}_\lambda$ and $i := i(\lambda) \in \mathbb{N}$, let us define*

$$\mathsf{Adv}^{\mathsf{wKOALA,single}}_{\mathcal{A},\mathbb{G},\mathsf{Samp},i}(\lambda) := |\Pr[\mathcal{A}_\lambda(\mathbb{G}, \mathsf{aux}, \mathbf{u}^{(i)}) \to 1] - \Pr[\mathcal{A}_\lambda(\mathbb{G}, \mathsf{aux}, \mathbf{v}) \to 1]|,$$
(4.1)

where the probabilities are taken over the choice of uniformly random aux, $\mathbb{G} = (p, \mathbb{G}_1, \mathbb{G}_2, \mathbb{G}_T, e, [1]_1, [1]_2) \leftarrow \mathsf{GroupGen}(1^\lambda)$, , $\{\mathbf{u}^{(j)}\}_{j \in [t]} \leftarrow \mathsf{Samp}_\lambda(p, \mathsf{aux})$, $\mathbf{v} \leftarrow \mathbb{Z}_p^m$, *and the coin of $\mathcal{A}_\lambda$. In the above, we set $\mathbf{u}^{(i)} := \mathbf{v}$ if $i > t$. Furthermore, for an efficient adversary $\mathcal{B} = \{\mathcal{B}_\lambda\}$, we define*

$$\mathsf{Adv}^{\mathsf{wKOALA,multi}}_{\mathcal{B},\mathbb{G},\mathsf{Samp}}(\lambda) :=$$

$$\left| \Pr\left[\mathcal{B}_\lambda \left(\begin{array}{c} \mathbb{G}, \mathsf{aux}, \\ \left\{ [\gamma^{(j)}]_2, [\gamma^{(j)}\mathbf{u}^{(j)}]_2 \right\}_{j \in [t]} \end{array} \right) \to 1 \right] - \Pr\left[\mathcal{B}_\lambda \left(\begin{array}{c} \mathbb{G}, \mathsf{aux}, \\ \left\{ [\gamma^{(j)}]_2, [\mathbf{v}^{(j)}]_2 \right\}_{j \in [t]} \end{array} \right) \to 1 \right] \right|,$$
(4.2)

where the probabilities are taken over the choice of uniformly random aux, $\mathbb{G}$, $\{\mathbf{u}^{(j)}\}_{j \in [t]} \leftarrow \mathsf{Samp}_\lambda(p, \mathsf{aux})$, $\gamma^{(j)} \leftarrow \mathbb{Z}_p$, $\mathbf{v}^{(j)} \leftarrow \mathbb{Z}_p^m$ *for $j \in [t]$, and the coin of $\mathcal{B}_\lambda$. We say that* wKOALA *holds with respect to* GroupGen *if for any efficient sampler* Samp *such that* $\mathsf{Adv}^{\mathsf{wKOALA,single}}_{\mathcal{A},\mathbb{G},\mathsf{Samp},i}(\lambda)$ *is negligible for any efficient adversary $\mathcal{A}$ and $i(\lambda)$,* $\mathsf{Adv}^{\mathsf{wKOALA,multi}}_{\mathcal{B},\mathbb{G},\mathsf{Samp}}(\lambda)$ *is also negligible for any efficient adversary $\mathcal{B}$.*

The following theorem shows that wKOALA is in fact implied by the bilinear KOALA assumption.

Theorem 4.7. *If the bilinear KOALA assumption holds with respect to* GroupGen, *so does* wKOALA.

Proof. For the sake of contradiction, let us assume that wKOALA does not hold with respect to GroupGen, but the bilinear KOALA assumption holds with respect to GroupGen. The former assumption implies that there exists an efficient sampler Samp such that $\mathsf{Adv}^{\mathsf{wKOALA,single}}_{\mathcal{A},\mathbb{G},\mathsf{Samp},i}(\lambda)$ is negligible for any efficient adversary $\mathcal{A}$ and $i = i(\lambda)$, but there exists an efficient adversary $\mathcal{B}$ such that $\epsilon(\lambda) := \mathsf{Adv}^{\mathsf{wKOALA,multi}}_{\mathcal{B},\mathbb{G},\mathsf{Samp}}(\lambda)$ is non-negligible.

We then consider another sampler Samp' that takes as input p and aux and outputs matrix $\mathbf{V}$ defined as

$$\mathbf{V} = \begin{bmatrix} 1 & \mathbf{u}^{(1)} & & & \\ & & 1 & \mathbf{u}^{(2)} & \\ & & & & \ddots \\ & & & & & 1 & \mathbf{u}^{(t)} \end{bmatrix} \in \mathbb{Z}_p^{t \times (1+m)t},$$

where $\{\mathbf{u}^{(j)}\}_{j \in [t]} \leftarrow \mathsf{Samp}(p, \mathsf{aux})$. For this sampler Samp', we have

$$\mathsf{Adv}^{\mathsf{BKOALA,dist}}_{\mathcal{B},\mathbb{G},\mathsf{Samp}'}(\lambda) = \mathsf{Adv}^{\mathsf{wKOALA,multi}}_{\mathcal{B},\mathbb{G},\mathsf{Samp}}(\lambda) = \epsilon(\lambda),$$

which follows from the definition of $\mathsf{Adv}^{\mathsf{BKOALA,dist}}_{\mathcal{B},\mathbb{G},\mathsf{Samp}'}(\lambda)$ (See Definition 4.1). This further implies that there exists another adversary $\mathcal{B}'$ and polynomial function $Q(\lambda)$ such that

$$\mathsf{Adv}^{\mathsf{BKOALA,find}}_{\mathcal{B}',\mathbb{G},\mathsf{Samp}'}(\lambda) \geq \epsilon(\lambda)/Q(\lambda) - \mathrm{negl}(\lambda)$$

from the bilinear KOALA assumption. By the definition, $\mathcal{B}'$ takes as input aux and $\mathbb{G}$ and outputs a vector $\mathbf{x} \in \mathbb{Z}_p^{(1+m)t}$ such that $\mathbf{x}\mathbf{V}^\top = \mathbf{0}$ and $\mathbf{x} \neq \mathbf{0}$ with probability $\epsilon'(\lambda); = \epsilon(\lambda)/Q(\lambda) - \mathrm{negl}(\lambda)$. Let us denote

$$\mathbf{x} = (x^{(1)}, \mathbf{x}^{(1)}, x^{(2)}, \mathbf{x}^{(2)}, \ldots, x^{(t)}, \mathbf{x}^{(t)})$$

where $x^{(i)} \in \mathbb{Z}_p$ and $\mathbf{x}^{(i)} \in \mathbb{Z}_p^m$ for $i \in [t]$. Then, for such vector $\mathbf{x}$, we have

$$x^{(i)} + \langle \mathbf{x}^{(i)}, \mathbf{u}^{(i)} \rangle = 0 \mod p \quad \text{and} \quad (x^{(i)}, \mathbf{x}^{(i)}) \neq \mathbf{0} \mod p$$

for some $i \in [t]$ by the structure of $\mathbf{V}$. This further implies that there exists fixed $i^* = i^*(\lambda)$ such that $x^{(i^*)} + \langle \mathbf{x}^{(i^*)}, \mathbf{u}^{(i^*)} \rangle = 0 \mod p$ and $(x^{(i^*)}, \mathbf{x}^{(i^*)}) \neq \mathbf{0} \mod p$ hold with probability at least ϵ'/t.

We then use $\mathcal{B}'$ to construct an adversary $\mathcal{A}$ such that $\mathsf{Adv}^{\mathsf{wKOALA,single}}_{\mathcal{A},\mathbb{G},\mathsf{Samp},i^*}(\lambda)$ is non-negligible, which contradicts our assumption. $\mathcal{A}$ takes as input the group description $\mathbb{G}$, auxiliary information aux and a vector $\mathbf{v}$, which is either $\mathbf{v} \leftarrow \mathbb{Z}_p^m$ or $\mathbf{v} = \mathbf{u}^{(i^*)}$ with $\{\mathbf{u}^{(j)}\}_{j \in [t]} \leftarrow \mathsf{Samp}(p, \mathsf{aux})$. Then, $\mathcal{A}$ runs $\mathcal{B}'$ on input aux and $\mathbb{G}$. If $\mathcal{B}'$ outputs something outside of $\mathbb{Z}_p^m$, $\mathcal{A}$ outputs 0. Otherwise, let $\mathbf{x} \in \mathbb{Z}_p^m$ be the output by $\mathcal{B}'$. If $(x^{(i^*)}, \mathbf{x}^{(i^*)}) = \mathbf{0}$, $\mathcal{A}$ outputs 0. Otherwise, $\mathcal{A}$ checks whether

$$x^{(i^*)} + \langle \mathbf{x}^{(i^*)}, \mathbf{v} \rangle \stackrel{?}{=} 0. \tag{4.3}$$

It outputs 1 if it holds and 0 otherwise.

We evaluate the probability that $\mathcal{A}$ outputs 1. There are two cases to consider.

- If $\mathbf{v} = \mathbf{u}^{(i^*)}$, $\mathcal{B}'$ outputs non-zero vector $(x^{(i^*)}, \mathbf{x}^{(i^*)})$ satisfying Eq. (4.3) with probability at least ϵ'/t. $\mathcal{A}$ outputs 1 with the same probability.
- If $\mathbf{v}$ is chosen uniformly at random from $\mathbb{Z}_p^m$, Eq. (4.3) holds for $(x^{(i^*)}, \mathbf{x}^{(i^*)})$ output by $\mathcal{B}'$ with probability at most $1/p$ unless $(x^{(i^*)}, \mathbf{x}^{(i^*)}) = \mathbf{0} \mod p$, since $\mathbf{v}$ is information theoretically hidden from $\mathcal{B}'$. Since $\mathcal{A}$ outputs 1 only when $(x^{(i^*)}, \mathbf{x}^{(i^*)}) \neq \mathbf{0}$ and Eq. (4.3) holds, the probability that $\mathcal{A}$ outputs 1 is at most $1/p$.

We finally observe that

$$\mathsf{Adv}^{\mathsf{wKOALA,single}}_{\mathcal{A},\mathbb{G},\mathsf{Samp},i^*}(\lambda) = |\Pr[\mathcal{A}(\mathbb{G}, \mathsf{aux}, \mathbf{u}^{(i^*)}) \to 1] - \Pr[\mathcal{A}(\mathbb{G}, \mathsf{aux}, \mathbf{v}) \to 1]|$$
$$\geq \epsilon'/t - 1/p$$
$$\geq \epsilon/tQ - \mathrm{negl},$$

where the probabilities are taken over the choice of $\mathbb{G} \leftarrow \mathsf{GroupGen}(1^\lambda)$, $\mathbf{v} \leftarrow \mathbb{Z}_p^n$, random aux, $\{\mathbf{u}^{(j)}\}_{j \in [t]} \leftarrow \mathsf{Samp}(p, \mathsf{aux})$ and the internal coin of $\mathcal{A}$. Since $\epsilon/tQ - \mathrm{negl}$ is non-negligible, this contradicts our initial assumption. This completes the proof of Theorem 4.2.

5   Our CP-ABE Scheme

In this section, we provide our construction of CP-ABE scheme for NC_1 whose sizes of the parameters are independent from the size of the circuits supported by the scheme and only dependent on the input length and depth of the circuits. This efficiency property is not satisfied by most of the existing schemes except for [AY20, BV20]. Unlike [AY20, BV20], we provide the security proof in the standard model. We then show that the CP-ABE scheme can be used to construct BE with optimal efficiency. This provides the first optimal BE scheme whose security is proven in the standard model.

5.1   Construction

Here, we provide our construction of CP-ABE scheme that supports the circuit class $\mathcal{C}_{\ell,d} = \{\mathcal{C}_{\lambda,\ell(\lambda),d(\lambda)}\}_\lambda$, which is a set of all circuits with input length $\ell(\lambda)$ and depth at most $d(\lambda)$ with arbitrary $\ell(\lambda) = \mathrm{poly}(\lambda)$ and $d(\lambda) = O(\log \lambda)$. For our construction, we will use public key slotted IPFE scheme $\mathsf{IPFE} = (\mathsf{IPFE.Setup}, \mathsf{IPFE.KeyGen}, \mathsf{IPFE.Enc}, \mathsf{IPFE.SlotEnc}, \mathsf{IPFE.Dec})$, which is proposed by Lin and Luo [LL20], which is secure under the MDDH assumption, and a secret sharing scheme $\mathsf{SS} = (\mathsf{SS.Setup}, \mathsf{SS.Share}, \mathsf{SS.Recon})$ for $\mathcal{C}_{\ell(\lambda),d(\lambda)}$ that is provided in Sect. 3.

$\mathsf{ABE.Setup}(1^\lambda)$: On input 1^λ, the setup algorithm proceeds as follows.

1. Run $\mathbb{G} = (p, \mathbb{G}_1, \mathbb{G}_2, \mathbb{G}_T, e, [1]_1, [1]_2) \leftarrow \mathsf{GroupGen}(1^\lambda)$. Note that p and λ specify the parameter $m := m(\lambda)$ (See syntax of secret sharing scheme in Sect. 3).
2. Run $\mathsf{pp} \leftarrow \mathsf{SS.Setup}(1^\lambda, p)$.
3. Run $(\mathsf{IPFE.mpk}_{i,b,j}, \mathsf{IPFE.msk}_{i,b,j}) \leftarrow \mathsf{IPFE.Setup}(1^\lambda, \{1\}, \{2\})$ for $i \in [\ell]$, $b \in \{0,1\}$, and $j \in [m]$. Note that here we generate slotted IPFE instances whose the first entry is for public slot and the second entry is for private slot.
4. Output $\mathsf{ABE.mpk} = (\mathbb{G}, \mathsf{pp}, \{\mathsf{IPFE.mpk}_{i,b,j}\}_{i\in[\ell],b\in\{0,1\},j\in[m]})$ and $\mathsf{ABE.msk} = \{\mathsf{IPFE.msk}_{i,b,j}\}_{i\in[\ell],b\in\{0,1\},j\in[m]}$.

$\mathsf{ABE.KeyGen}(\mathsf{ABE.mpk}, \mathsf{ABE.msk}, x)$: The key generation algorithm takes as input the master public key $\mathsf{ABE.mpk}$, the master secret key $\mathsf{ABE.msk}$, and an attribute $x \in \{0,1\}^\ell$ and proceeds as follows.

1. Let $x_1 \cdots x_\ell \in \{0,1\}^\ell$ be the binary representation of $x \in \{0,1\}^\ell$.
2. Pick $\gamma \leftarrow \mathbb{Z}_p$ and compute $[\gamma]_T$.
3. Sample $\mathsf{IPFE.sk}_{i,x_i,j} \leftarrow \mathsf{IPFE.KeyGen}(\mathsf{IPFE.msk}_{i,x_i,j}, [(\gamma, 0)]_2)$ for all $i \in [\ell]$ and $j \in [m]$.
4. Output $\mathsf{ABE.sk} = ([\gamma]_T, \{\mathsf{IPFE.sk}_{i,x_i,j}\}_{i\in[\ell],j\in[m]})$.

$\mathsf{ABE.Enc}(\mathsf{ABE.mpk}, C, \mu)$: The encryption algorithm takes as input the master public key $\mathsf{ABE.mpk}$, a circuit C, and the message μ and proceeds as follows.

1. Run $\{\mathsf{share}_{i,b}\}_{i\in[\ell],b\in\{0,1\}} \leftarrow \mathsf{SS.Share}(\mathsf{pp}, C, \mu)$.
2. Parse each $\mathsf{share}_{i,b}$ as $\mathsf{share}_{i,b} = \{\mathsf{share}_{i,b,j} \in \mathbb{Z}_p\}_{j\in[m]}$.

3. Run IPFE.ct$_{i,b,j}$ ← IPFE.SlotEnc(IPFE.mpk$_{i,b,j}$, [share$_{i,b,j}$]$_1$) for $i \in [\ell]$, $b \in \{0,1\}$, $j \in [m]$.
4. Output ABE.ct = {IPFE.ct$_{i,b,j}$}$_{i \in [\ell], b \in \{0,1\}, j \in [m]}$.

ABE.Dec(ABE.mpk, ABE.sk, x, ABE.ct, C): The decryption algorithm takes as input the master public key ABE.mpk, the secret key ABE.sk along with x, the ciphertext ABE.ct along with C and does the following:

1. Parse the ciphertext as ABE.ct → {IPFE.ct$_{i,b,j}$}$_{i \in [\ell], b \in \{0,1\}, j \in [m]}$ and the secret key as ABE.sk → ([γ]$_T$, {IPFE.sk$_{i,x_i,j}$}$_{i \in [\ell], j \in [m]}$).
2. Run IPFE.Dec(IPFE.sk$_{i,x_i,j}$, IPFE.ct$_{i,x_i,j}$) → [$d_{i,j}$]$_T$ for $i \in [\ell]$ and $j \in [m]$.
3. Run SS.FindCoef(pp, C, x) → {$a_{i,j} \in \mathbb{Z}_p$}$_{i \in [\ell], j \in [m]}$.
4. Compute [d']$_T$ = [$\sum_{i \in [\ell], j \in [m]} a_{i,j} d_{i,j}$]$_T$ from {[$d_{i,j}$]$_T$}$_{i,j}$ and {$a_{i,j}$}$_{i,j}$.
5. Find $e \in [-B, B]$ and $\mu \in \{0,1\}$ such that [d']$_T$ = [$\gamma(\mu\lceil p/2 \rceil + e)$]$_T$ by Brute-force search using [γ]$_T$. If such a pair does not exist, output ⊥. Otherwise, output μ.

Correctness. To show correctness of the scheme, we first observe that $d_{i,j} = \gamma \cdot$ share$_{i,x_i,j}$ by the correctness of IPFE. We then observe that $d' = \sum_{i \in [\ell], j \in [m]} \gamma a_{i,j}$share$_{i,x_i,j} = \gamma(\mu \cdot \lceil p/2 \rceil + e)$ for some $e \in [-B, B]$ by the almost linear reconstruction property (Definition 3.4) of ABE. Since B is polynomially bounded by Theorem 3.5, the last step in the decryption algorithm works in polynomial time and recovers the message μ.

Efficiency. The master public key of the ABE consists of $O(\ell m)$ master public keys of the IPFE and the public parameter pp of the secret sharing scheme. The ciphertext and secret key of the ABE contain $O(\ell m)$ ciphertexts and secret keys of the IPFE, respectively. By the efficiency of the secret sharing scheme, m and the size of pp are bounded by poly(λ). Furthermore, each instance of IPFE only deals with constant dimension of vectors, which means that sizes of all the parameters of each instance of the IPFE scheme are bounded by poly(λ). Therefore, we can see that sizes of all the parameters in the ABE scheme are bounded by poly(λ, ℓ).

5.2 Security Proof

Here, we prove the security of our ABE scheme in Sect. 5.1. Before doing so, we prove the following lemma.

Lemma 5.1. *Let* $C \in \mathcal{C}_{\lambda, \ell(\lambda), d(\lambda)}$ *be a circuit and* $X \subseteq \{0,1\}^{\ell(\lambda)}$ *be a set of strings that satisfies* $C(x) = 0$ *for all* $x \in X$*, and* SS = (SS.Setup, SS.Share, SS.Recon) *be a secure secret sharing scheme for this circuit class as per Definition 3.2. Then, for any efficient adversary* $\mathcal{A} = \{\mathcal{A}_\lambda\}$*, we have*

$$\Pr\left[\mathcal{A}_\lambda\left(\begin{array}{c} \mathbb{G}, \text{pp}, \\ \{[\gamma^{(x)}]_2, \{[\gamma^{(x)}\text{share}_{i,x_i}]_2\}_{i \in [\ell]}\}_{x \in X} \end{array}\right) \to 1\right]$$

$$- \Pr\left[\mathcal{A}_\lambda\left(\begin{array}{c} \mathbb{G}, \text{pp}, \\ \{[\gamma^{(x)}]_2, \{[\gamma^{(x)}\mathbf{w}_i^{(x)}]_2\}_{i \in [\ell]}\}_{x \in X} \end{array}\right) \to 1\right] = \text{negl}(\lambda), \qquad (5.1)$$

under the bilinear KOALA assumption, where the probabilities are taken over the choice of $\mathbb{G} = (p, \mathbb{G}_1, \mathbb{G}_2, \mathbb{G}_T, e, [1]_1, [1]_2) \leftarrow \mathsf{GroupGen}(1^\lambda)$, $\gamma^{(x)} \leftarrow \mathbb{Z}_p$ *and* $\mathbf{w}_i^{(x)} \leftarrow \mathbb{Z}_p^m$ *for* $x \in X$, $\mathsf{pp} \leftarrow \mathsf{SS.Setup}(1^\lambda, p)$, *and* $\{\mathsf{share}_{i,b}\}_{i \in [\ell], b \in \{0,1\}} \leftarrow \mathsf{SS.Share}(\mathsf{pp}, C, \mu)$.

Proof. To prove the theorem, we set Samp to be an algorithm that takes as input an integer p and a random string aux, sets $\mathsf{pp} := \mathsf{aux}$, runs $\{\mathsf{share}_{i,b}\}_{i \in [\ell], b \in \{0,1\}} \leftarrow \mathsf{SS.Share}(\mathsf{pp}, C, \mu)$, and outputs

$$\left\{ \{\mathsf{share}_{i,x_i}\}_{i \in [\ell]} \right\}_{x \in X}.$$

Then, we argue that $\mathsf{Adv}_{\mathcal{A}, \mathbb{G}, \mathsf{Samp}, i}^{\mathsf{wKOALA,single}}(\lambda)$ defined in Eq. (4.1) is negligible for any i and any efficient adversary $\mathcal{A}$. To show this, we first fix i and $\mathcal{A}$ and observe that the quantity is negligible if we replace aux that is input to $\mathcal{A}$ with pp output by $\mathsf{SS.Setup}(1^\lambda, p)$, which follows from the security of SS (Definition 3.2) and from the fact that $C(x) = 0$ holds for all $x \in X$. We then observe that the adversary will not notice even if we replace pp with aux since the distributions of them are statistically close by the random public parameter property (Definition 3.3) of SS. We therefore have $\mathsf{Adv}_{\mathcal{A}, \mathbb{G}, \mathsf{Samp}, i}^{\mathsf{wKOALA,single}}(\lambda) = \mathsf{negl}(\lambda)$. This implies that $\mathsf{Adv}_{\mathcal{B}, \mathbb{G}, \mathsf{Samp}}^{\mathsf{wKOALA,multi}}(\lambda)$ defined in Eq. (4.2) is negligible for any efficient adversary $\mathcal{B}$ by wKOALA, which is implied by the bilinear KOALA assumption. Finally, by replacing aux with pp output by $\mathsf{SS.Setup}(1^\lambda, p)$ in Eq. (4.2), we have that Eq. (5.1) is negligible for any efficient adversary as desired.

The next theorem establishes the security of our ABE scheme.

Theorem 5.2. *Our ABE scheme satisfies very selective security under the MDDH assumption, the bilinear KOALA assumption, and the LWE assumption.*

Proof. To prove the theorem, we fix a PPT adversary $\mathcal{A} = \{\mathcal{A}_\lambda\}$. Without loss of generality, we make some simplifying assumptions on $\mathcal{A}$. First, we assume that $\mathcal{A}$ always chooses $(\mu_0, \mu_1) = (0, 1)$ as its target message at the challenge phase. This can be assumed without loss of generality since our scheme is a single-bit scheme. Second, we assume that the adversary does not make key queries for the same attribute x twice. The adversary that makes key queries for the same attribute more than once can be dealt with by making the key generation algorithm deterministic by changing the scheme so that it derives randomness using a PRF, which can be instantiated from any one-way functions. Third, we assume that the adversary chooses fixed challenge attribute $C = \{C_\lambda\}$ and key queries $X = \{X_\lambda\}$. This can be assumed without loss of generality because they are chosen by the adversary at the beginning of the game only depending on the security parameter and we can derandomize $\mathcal{A}$ by choosing the best randomness that maximizes the advantage of $\mathcal{A}$.

In order to prove the security, we consider following sequence of games. Let us denote the event that $\mathcal{A}$ outputs correct guess for b at the end of **Game$_\mathsf{x}$** as $\mathsf{E_x}$.

Game₁: This is the real very selective security game. To fix the notation and for the sake of concreteness, we briefly describe the game here. At the beginning of the game, the adversary chooses C and $X \subseteq \{0,1\}^\ell$. Then, the challenger first chooses the master public key ABE.mpk and the master secret key ABE.msk of the ABE scheme. It then generates the challenge ciphertext as follows. It first chooses the message $\beta \leftarrow \{0,1\}$ and runs $\{\mathsf{share}_{i,b}\}_{i \in [\ell], b \in \{0,1\}} \leftarrow$ SS.Share(pp, C, β). It then runs

$$\mathsf{IPFE.ct}_{i,b,j} \leftarrow \mathsf{IPFE.SlotEnc}(\mathsf{IPFE.mpk}_{i,b,j}, [\mathsf{share}_{i,b,j}]_1)$$

for $i \in [\ell]$, $b \in \{0,1\}$, $j \in [m]$ and sets the challenge ciphertext to be ABE.ct $= \{\mathsf{IPFE.ct}_{i,b,j}\}_{i \in [\ell], b \in \{0,1\}, j \in [m]}$. It also generates secret key ABE.sk$_x$ for all $x \in X$ as follows. It first generates $\gamma^{(x)} \leftarrow \mathbb{Z}_p$ and

$$\mathsf{IPFE.sk}_{i,x_i,j} \leftarrow \mathsf{IPFE.KeyGen}(\mathsf{IPFE.msk}_{i,x_i,j}, [(\gamma^{(x)}, 0)]_2)$$

for all $i \in [\ell]$ and $j \in [m]$. It then sets ABE.sk$_x = ([\gamma]_T, \{\mathsf{IPFE.sk}_{i,x_i,j}\}_{i \in [\ell], j \in [m]})$. Finally, the challenger returns ABE.mpk, ABE.ct, and $\{\mathsf{ABE.sk}_x\}_{x \in X}$ to $\mathcal{A}$, which then outputs a bit $\widehat{\beta}$ as a guess for β. By definition, the advantage of $\mathcal{A}$ against the scheme is

$$\left| \Pr[\mathsf{E}_1] - \frac{1}{2} \right|.$$

Game₂: In this game, we change the game so that the challenger generates the challenge ciphertext as follows. It first chooses the message $\beta \leftarrow \{0,1\}$ and runs $\{\mathsf{share}_{i,b}\}_{i \in [\ell], b \in \{0,1\}} \leftarrow$ SS.Share(pp, C, β). It then generates

$$\mathsf{IPFE.ct}_{i,b,j} \leftarrow \mathsf{IPFE.Enc}(\mathsf{IPFE.msk}_{i,b,j}, [(\mathsf{share}_{i,b,j}, 0)]_1)$$

for $i \in [\ell]$, $b \in \{0,1\}$, $j \in [m]$ and sets the challenge ciphertext to be ABE.ct $= \{\mathsf{IPFE.ct}_{i,b,j}\}_{i \in [\ell], b \in \{0,1\}, j \in [m]}$. By the slot-mode correctness of the IPFE, we have

$$\Pr[\mathsf{E}_1] = \Pr[\mathsf{E}_2].$$

Game₃: In this game, we change the way the challenge ciphertext and the secret keys are generated. In this game, the challenger generates the challenge ciphertext as follows. It first chooses the message $\beta \leftarrow \{0,1\}$ and runs $\{\mathsf{share}_{i,b}\}_{i \in [\ell], b \in \{0,1\}} \leftarrow$ SS.Share(pp, C, β). However, it ignores theses values and generates

$$\mathsf{IPFE.ct}_{i,b,j} \leftarrow \mathsf{IPFE.Enc}(\mathsf{IPFE.msk}_{i,b,j}, [(0,1)]_1)$$

for $i \in [\ell]$, $b \in \{0,1\}$, $j \in [m]$ and sets the challenge ciphertext to be ABE.ct $= \{\mathsf{IPFE.ct}_{i,b,j}\}_{i \in [\ell], b \in \{0,1\}, j \in [m]}$. We also change the way the challenger generates the secret keys as follows. For $x \in X$, it first generates $\gamma^{(x)} \leftarrow \mathbb{Z}_p$ and

$$\mathsf{IPFE.sk}_{i,x_i,j} \leftarrow \mathsf{IPFE.KeyGen}(\mathsf{IPFE.msk}_{i,x_i,j}, [(\gamma^{(x)}, \gamma^{(x)}\mathsf{share}_{i,x_i,j})]_2)$$

for all $i \in [\ell]$ and $j \in [m]$, where we use $\mathsf{share}_{i,x_i,j}$ that is generated when creating the challenge ciphertext. It then sets $\mathsf{ABE.sk}_x = ([\gamma^{(x)}]_T, \{\mathsf{IPFE.sk}_{i,x_i,j}\}_{i \in [\ell], j \in [m]})$.

We can observe that for each instance of IPFE, the inner products between the vector that is encoded in the ciphertext and the vectors encoded in the secret keys are unchanged. Furthermore, the values in the public slots of the vectors encoded in the secret keys are unchanged. Therefore, this game is indistinguishable from the previous game for $\mathcal{A}$ by the security of the IPFE, which follows from the MDDH assumption. We therefore have

$$|\Pr[\mathsf{E}_2] - \Pr[\mathsf{E}_3]| = \mathrm{negl}(\lambda).$$

Game$_4$: In this game, we further change the way the secret keys are generated as follows. The challenger first generates $\gamma^{(x)} \leftarrow \mathbb{Z}_p$ and chooses $\mathbf{w}_i^{(x)} \leftarrow \mathbb{Z}_p^m$ for $i \in [\ell]$. It then generates

$$\mathsf{IPFE.sk}_{i,x_i,j} \leftarrow \mathsf{IPFE.KeyGen}(\mathsf{IPFE.msk}_{i,x_i,j}, [(\gamma^{(x)}, w_{i,j}^{(x)})]_2)$$

for all $i \in [\ell]$ and $j \in [m]$, where $w_{i,j}^{(x)}$ is the j-th entry of the vector $\mathbf{w}_i^{(x)}$, and sets $\mathsf{ABE.sk}_x = ([\gamma]_T, \{\mathsf{IPFE.sk}_{i,x_i,j}\}_{i \in [\ell], j \in [m]})$.

We claim that this game is indistinguishable from the above game. To see this, let us assume that $\mathcal{A}$ distinguishes the games with non-negligible advantage for the sake of contradiction. Then, for $C = \{C_\lambda\}$ and $X = \{X_\lambda\}$ chosen by $\mathcal{A}$, we can construct another adversary $\mathcal{B} = \{\mathcal{B}_\lambda\}$ that distinguishes two distributions in Eq. (5.1) with non-negligible advantage as follows.

$\mathcal{B}$ takes as input $\mathbb{G}$, pp, $\left\{[\gamma^{(x)}]_2, \{[\mathbf{w}_i^{(x)}]_2\}_{i \in [\ell]}\right\}_{x \in X}$, where $\mathbf{w}_i^{(x)}$ is either random or $\mathbf{w}_i^{(x)} = \gamma^{(x)}\mathsf{share}_{i,x_i}$. It chooses $(\mathsf{IPFE.mpk}_{i,b,j}, \mathsf{IPFE.msk}_{i,b,j}) \leftarrow \mathsf{IPFE.Setup}(1^\lambda, \{1\}, \{2\})$ for all i, b, and j and sets the ABE.mpk and ABE.msk accordingly. It generates the challenge ciphertext using ABE.msk. It also generates a secret key for x using $[\gamma^{(x)}]_2, \{[\mathbf{w}_i^{(x)}]_2\}_{i \in [\ell]}$ and ABE.msk. In particular, the syntax of the slotted IPFE allows us to generate the secret key for the vector $[(\gamma^{(x)}, w_{i,j}^{(x)})]_2$ without knowing the corresponding discrete logarithm, which $\mathcal{B}$ does not know. $\mathcal{B}$ then inputs ABE.mpk, ABE.ct, and $\{\mathsf{ABE.sk}_x\}$ to $\mathcal{A}$ and outputs what $\mathcal{A}$ outputs.

Clearly, $\mathcal{B}$ simulates **Game$_3$** for $\mathcal{A}$ if $\mathbf{w}_i^{(x)} = \gamma^{(x)}\mathsf{share}_{i,x_i}$ and **Game$_4$** if $\mathbf{w}_i^{(x)}$ is random. Thus, $\mathcal{B}$ can distinguish the two distributions with the same advantage as $\mathcal{A}$. This contradicts the bilinear KOALA assumption and the security of the secret sharing scheme by Lemma 5.1, where the latter follows from the LWE assumption by Theorem 3.5. Therefore, we have

$$|\Pr[\mathsf{E}_3] - \Pr[\mathsf{E}_4]| = \mathrm{negl}(\lambda).$$

We can easily observe that the view of $\mathcal{A}$ in **Game$_4$** is independent from β and $\Pr[\mathsf{E}_4] = 1/2$. Therefore, we have

$$\left| \Pr[\mathsf{E}_1] - \frac{1}{2} \right| \leq \sum_{i \in [3]} |\Pr[\mathsf{E}_i] - \Pr[\mathsf{E}_{i+1}]| + \left| \Pr[\mathsf{E}_4] - \frac{1}{2} \right| \leq \mathsf{negl}(\lambda)$$

as desired. This completes the proof of Theorem 5.2.

5.3   Implication to Broadcast Encryption

Here, we show that our CP-ABE scheme implies BE by restricting the circuit class of the scheme to be some specific one as was observed in [AY20, BV20]. Let us consider the following circuit class $\mathcal{F}_{\mathsf{BE}}$:

$$\mathcal{F}_{\mathsf{BE}} = \left\{ F_S : \{0,1\}^{\lceil \log N \rceil} \rightarrow \{0,1\} \right\}_{S \subseteq [N]} \quad \text{where} \quad F_S(i) = \begin{cases} 1 & \text{if } i \in S \\ 0 & \text{if } i \notin S \end{cases}.$$

Here, we identify a user index $i \in [N]$ and elements in S with binary strings in $\{0,1\}^{\lceil \log N \rceil}$ by a natural bijection map between $\{0,1\}^{\lceil \log N \rceil}$ and $[2^{\lceil \log N \rceil}] \supseteq [N]$. Since the depth of F_S affects the efficiency of the DBE scheme, we want F_S to be as shallow as possible. For this purpose, we compute F_S by first computing $b_j := (i \overset{?}{=} j)$ for all $j \in S$ *in parallel* and then computing $\vee_{j \in S} b_j$. The first step can be implemented with depth $O(\log \log N)$ and the second step with $O(\log N)$. This allows us to implement F_S with depth $O(\log |S|) \leq O(\log N)$. Therefore, our CP-ABE scheme indeed supports this circuit class. Furthermore, by the definition of F_S, one can see that this CP-ABE scheme implements the functionality of BE. The obtained BE scheme has optimal efficiency in the sense that the size of the master public key, secret key, and the ciphertext is bounded by $\mathsf{poly}(\lambda, \ell, d) = \mathsf{poly}(\log N, \lambda) = \mathsf{poly}(\lambda)$, which is independent of the number of users N in the system. The scheme satisfies very selective security since so is the underlying CP-ABE. We note that our scheme indeed satisfies selective security since very selective security is equivalent to selective security in the setting of BE (See Remark 2.7).

Acknowledgement. We thank the anonymous reviewers of TCC 2020 for their helpful comments. Dr. Agrawal is supported by the DST "Swarnajayanti" fellowship, an Indo-French CEFIPRA project and an "Indo-Israel" ISF-UGC project. Daniel Wichs is supported by NSF grants CNS-1314722, CNS-1413964, CNS-1750795, and the Alfred P. Sloan Research Fellowship. Shota Yamada is supported by JST CREST Grant Number JPMJCR19F6 and JSPS KAKENHI Grant Number 19H01109. This work was done in part while the first and the third authors were visiting the Simons Institute for the Theory of Computing.

References

[ABCP15] Abdalla, M., Bourse, F., De Caro, A., Pointcheval, D.: Simple functional encryption schemes for inner products. Cryptology ePrint Archive, Report 2015/017 (2015). http://eprint.iacr.org/. To appear in PKC 2015

[AL10]   Attrapadung, N., Libert, B.: Functional encryption for inner product: achieving constant-size ciphertexts with adaptive security or support for negation. In: Nguyen, P.Q., Pointcheval, D. (eds.) PKC 2010. LNCS, vol. 6056, pp. 384–402. Springer, Heidelberg (2010). https://doi.org/10.1007/978-3-642-13013-7_23

[ALS16]   Agrawal, S., Libert, B., Stehle, D.: Fully secure functional encryption for linear functions from standard assumptions, and applications. In: Crypto (2016)

[AY20]   Agrawal, S., Yamada, S.: Optimal broadcast encryption from pairings and LWE. In: Canteaut, A., Ishai, Y. (eds.) EUROCRYPT 2020, Part I. LNCS, vol. 12105, pp. 13–43. Springer, Cham (2020). https://doi.org/10.1007/978-3-030-45721-1_2

[BC10]   Bitansky, N., Canetti, R.: On strong simulation and composable point obfuscation. In: Rabin, T. (ed.) CRYPTO 2010. LNCS, vol. 6223, pp. 520–537. Springer, Heidelberg (2010). https://doi.org/10.1007/978-3-642-14623-7_28

[BCFG17]   Baltico, C.E.Z., Catalano, D., Fiore, D., Gay, R.: Practical functional encryption for quadratic functions with applications to predicate encryption. In: Katz, J., Shacham, H. (eds.) CRYPTO 2017. LNCS, vol. 10401, pp. 67–98. Springer, Cham (2017). https://doi.org/10.1007/978-3-319-63688-7_3

[BFF+14]   Barthe, G., Fagerholm, E., Fiore, D., Mitchell, J., Scedrov, A., Schmidt, B.: Automated analysis of cryptographic assumptions in generic group models. In: Garay, J.A., Gennaro, R. (eds.) CRYPTO 2014. LNCS, vol. 8616, pp. 95–112. Springer, Heidelberg (2014). https://doi.org/10.1007/978-3-662-44371-2_6

[BGG+14]   Boneh, D., et al.: Fully key-homomorphic encryption, arithmetic circuit ABE and compact garbled circuits. In: Nguyen, P.Q., Oswald, E. (eds.) EUROCRYPT 2014. LNCS, vol. 8441, pp. 533–556. Springer, Heidelberg (2014). https://doi.org/10.1007/978-3-642-55220-5_30

[BGW05]   Boneh, D., Gentry, C., Waters, B.: Collusion resistant broadcast encryption with short ciphertexts and private keys. In: Shoup, V. (ed.) CRYPTO 2005. LNCS, vol. 3621, pp. 258–275. Springer, Heidelberg (2005). https://doi.org/10.1007/11535218_16

[BV20]   Brakerski, Z., Vaikuntanathan, V.: Lattice-inspired broadcast encryption and succinct ciphertext-policy ABE. IACR Cryptol. ePrint Arch. 2020: 191 (2020)

[BW19]   Lin, H., Luo, J.: Compact adaptively secure ABE from k-Lin: beyond NC1 and towards NL. In: Canteaut, A., Ishai, Y. (eds.) EUROCRYPT 2020, Part III. LNCS, vol. 12107, pp. 247–277. Springer, Cham (2020). https://doi.org/10.1007/978-3-030-45727-3_9

[BWZ14]   Boneh, D., Waters, B., Zhandry, M.: Low overhead broadcast encryption from multilinear maps. In: Garay, J.A., Gennaro, R. (eds.) CRYPTO 2014. LNCS, vol. 8616, pp. 206–223. Springer, Heidelberg (2014). https://doi.org/10.1007/978-3-662-44371-2_12

[BZ17]   Boneh, D., Zhandry, M.: Multiparty key exchange, efficient traitor tracing, and more from indistinguishability obfuscation. Algorithmica **79**(4), 1233–1285 (2017)

[CD08]   Canetti, R., Dakdouk, R.R.: Obfuscating point functions with multibit output. In: Smart, N. (ed.) EUROCRYPT 2008. LNCS, vol. 4965, pp. 489–508. Springer, Heidelberg (2008). https://doi.org/10.1007/978-3-540-78967-3_28

[CRV10]   Canetti, R., Rothblum, G.N., Varia, M.: Obfuscation of hyperplane membership. In: Micciancio, D. (ed.) TCC 2010. LNCS, vol. 5978, pp. 72–89. Springer, Heidelberg (2010). https://doi.org/10.1007/978-3-642-11799-2_5

[Del07]   Delerablée, C.: Identity-based broadcast encryption with constant size ciphertexts and private keys. In: Kurosawa, K. (ed.) ASIACRYPT 2007. LNCS, vol. 4833, pp. 200–215. Springer, Heidelberg (2007). https://doi.org/10.1007/978-3-540-76900-2_12

[DPP07]   Delerablée, C., Paillier, P., Pointcheval, D.: Fully collusion secure dynamic broadcast encryption with constant-size ciphertexts or decryption keys. In: Takagi, T., Okamoto, E., Okamoto, T., Okamoto, T. (eds.) Pairing 2007. LNCS, vol. 4575, pp. 39–59. Springer, Heidelberg (2007). https://doi.org/10.1007/978-3-540-73489-5_4

[FKL18]   Fuchsbauer, G., Kiltz, E., Loss, J.: The algebraic group model and its applications. In: Shacham, H., Boldyreva, A. (eds.) CRYPTO 2018. LNCS, vol. 10992, pp. 33–62. Springer, Cham (2018). https://doi.org/10.1007/978-3-319-96881-0_2

[FN94]   Fiat, A., Naor, M.: Broadcast encryption. In: Stinson, D.R. (ed.) CRYPTO 1993. LNCS, vol. 773, pp. 480–491. Springer, Heidelberg (1994). https://doi.org/10.1007/3-540-48329-2_40

[GGHW14] Garg, S., Gentry, C., Halevi, S., Wichs, D.: On the implausibility of differing-inputs obfuscation and extractable witness encryption with auxiliary input. In: Garay, J.A., Gennaro, R. (eds.) CRYPTO 2014, Part I. LNCS, vol. 8616, pp. 518–535. Springer, Heidelberg (2014). https://doi.org/10.1007/978-3-662-44371-2_29

[GPV08]   Gentry, C., Peikert, C., Vaikuntanathan, V.: Trapdoors for hard lattices and new cryptographic constructions. In: STOC, pp. 197–206 (2008)

[GV15]   Gorbunov, S., Vinayagamurthy, D.: Riding on asymmetry: efficient ABE for branching programs. In: Iwata, T., Cheon, J.H. (eds.) ASIACRYPT 2015. LNCS, vol. 9452, pp. 550–574. Springer, Heidelberg (2015). https://doi.org/10.1007/978-3-662-48797-6_23

[GW09]   Gentry, C., Waters, B.: Adaptive security in broadcast encryption systems (with short ciphertexts). In: Joux, A. (ed.) EUROCRYPT 2009. LNCS, vol. 5479, pp. 171–188. Springer, Heidelberg (2009). https://doi.org/10.1007/978-3-642-01001-9_10

[HWL+16] He, K., Weng, J., Liu, J.-N., Liu, J.K., Liu, W., Deng, R.H.: Anonymous identity-based broadcast encryption with chosen-ciphertext security. In: Proceedings of the 11th ACM on Asia Conference on Computer and Communications Security, ASIA CCS 2016 (2016)

[IPS15]   Ishai, Y., Pandey, O., Sahai, A.: Public-coin differing-inputs obfuscation and its applications. In: Dodis, Y., Nielsen, J.B. (eds.) TCC 2015, Part II. LNCS, vol. 9015, pp. 668–697. Springer, Heidelberg (2015). https://doi.org/10.1007/978-3-662-46497-7_26

[Lin17]   Lin, H.: Indistinguishability obfuscation from SXDH on 5-linear maps and locality-5 PRGs. In: Katz, J., Shacham, H. (eds.) CRYPTO 2017. LNCS, vol. 10401, pp. 599–629. Springer, Cham (2017). https://doi.org/10.1007/978-3-319-63688-7_20

[LL20]   Lin, H., Luo, J.: Compact adaptively secure ABE from k-Lin: beyond NC^1 and towards NL. In: Canteaut, A., Ishai, Y. (eds.) EUROCRYPT 2020. LNCS, vol. 12107, pp. 247–277. Springer, Cham (2020). https://doi.org/10.1007/978-3-030-45727-3_9

[LV16]   Lin, H., Vaikuntanathan, V.: Indistinguishability obfuscation from DDH-like assumptions on constant-degree graded encodings. In: FOCS (2016)

[Mau05]   Maurer, U.: Abstract models of computation in cryptography. In: Smart, N.P. (ed.) Cryptography and Coding 2005. LNCS, vol. 3796, pp. 1–12. Springer, Heidelberg (2005). https://doi.org/10.1007/11586821_1

[QWW18]   Quach, W., Wee, H., Wichs, D.: Laconic function evaluation and applications. In: 2018 IEEE 59th Annual Symposium on Foundations of Computer Science (FOCS), pp. 859–870. IEEE (2018)

[Reg09]   Regev, O.: On lattices, learning with errors, random linear codes, and cryptography. J. ACM **56**(6), 1–40 (2009). Extended abstract in STOC 2005

[SF]   Sakai, R., Furukawa, J.: Identity-based broadcast encryption. IACR Cryptology ePrint Archive (2007)

[Sho97]   Shoup, V.: Lower bounds for discrete logarithms and related problems. In: Fumy, W. (ed.) EUROCRYPT 1997. LNCS, vol. 1233, pp. 256–266. Springer, Heidelberg (1997). https://doi.org/10.1007/3-540-69053-0_18

[SS10]   Sahai, A., Seyalioglu, H.: Worry-free encryption: Functional encryption with public keys. In: Proceedings of the 17th ACM Conference on Computer and Communications Security, CCS 2010 (2010)

[Wee17]   Wee, H.: Attribute-hiding predicate encryption in bilinear groups, revisited. In: Kalai, Y., Reyzin, L. (eds.) TCC 2017. LNCS, vol. 10677, pp. 206–233. Springer, Cham (2017). https://doi.org/10.1007/978-3-319-70500-2_8

Equipping Public-Key Cryptographic Primitives with Watermarking (or: A Hole Is to Watermark)

Ryo Nishimaki[✉]

NTT Secure Platform Laboratories, Tokyo, Japan
ryo.nishimaki.zk@hco.ntt.co.jp

Abstract. Program watermarking enables users to embed an arbitrary string called a mark into a program while preserving the functionality of the program. Adversaries cannot remove the mark without destroying the functionality. Although there exist generic constructions of watermarking schemes for public-key cryptographic (PKC) primitives, those schemes are constructed from scratch and not efficient.

In this work, we present a general framework to equip a broad class of PKC primitives with an efficient watermarking scheme. The class consists of PKC primitives that have a *canonical all-but-one (ABO) reduction*. Canonical ABO reductions are standard techniques to prove selective security of PKC primitives, where adversaries must commit a target attribute at the beginning of the security game. Thus, we can obtain watermarking schemes for many existing efficient PKC schemes from standard cryptographic assumptions via our framework. Most well-known selectively secure PKC schemes have canonical ABO reductions. Notably, we can achieve watermarking for public-key encryption whose ciphertexts and secret-keys are constant-size, and that is chosen-ciphertext secure.

Our approach accommodates the canonical ABO reduction technique to the puncturable pseudorandom function (PRF) technique, which is used to achieve watermarkable PRFs. We find that canonical ABO reductions are compatible with such puncturable PRF-based watermarking schemes.

Keywords: Watermarking · Public-key cryptography · All-but-one reduction

1 Introduction

1.1 Background

Watermarking. Watermarking enables us to embed an arbitrary string called a "mark" into a digital object such as images, videos, programs. While an embedded mark is extractable, a watermarked object should be almost functionally

R. Pass and K. Pietrzak (Eds.): TCC 2020, LNCS 12550, pp. 179–209, 2020.
https://doi.org/10.1007/978-3-030-64375-1_7

equivalent to the original one. Watermarking ensures that no one can remove an embedded mark without destroying the original functionality. Watermarking has two main applications. One is identifying ownership of an object. We can verify who is the original creator of objects by extracting an embedded mark that includes a unique identifier. The other is tracing malicious users that illegally copy objects. Therefore, watermarking deters unauthorized distribution.

Barak, Goldreich, Impagliazzo, Rudich, Sahai, Vadhan, and Yang initiated the study of program watermarking and gave rigorous definitions of cryptographic watermarking for programs [8]. They proved that program watermarking with perfect functionality-preserving property does not exist if there exists indistinguishability obfuscation (IO) [8]. Hopper, Molnar, and Wagner gave more definitions of cryptographic watermarking for perceptual objects and studied the relationships among them [28].

Earlier works presented watermarking schemes for specific classes of cryptographic functionalities [35, 36, 45]. However, those schemes are secure in restricted models where we limit adversary's strategies due to the impossibility results by Barak et al. [8]. That is, earlier works [35, 36, 45] do not consider arbitrary removal strategies. Cohen, Holmgren, Nishimaki, Vaikuntanathan, and Wichs presented the first watermarking scheme for pseudorandom functions (PRFs) against arbitrary removal strategies by introducing a relaxed functionality-preserving property [19]. In addition, they observed two facts: even if we relax the functionality-preserving property, (1) we need to pick a target circuit from a distribution with high min-entropy to avoid trivial attacks in the security game. (2) learnable circuit families are not watermarkable [19]. These two facts are the reasons why most studies on cryptographic watermarking [12, 19, 22, 32, 33, 38, 44] focus on cryptographic primitives rather than arbitrary circuits.

We focus on achieving secure watermarking for *public-key cryptographic primitives* against arbitrary removal strategies in this study since public-key primitives are more versatile than secret-key ones.

Why Watermarking Public-Key Primitives?: An Application. Cohen et al. [19] presented an application of watermarked PRFs to electronic locks for cars. A car contains a PRF F and can only be opened by running a typical challenge-response identification protocol. A car owner has a software key (e.g., a smartphone application) that includes a marked PRF. We can embed some identifying information to PRFs. No one can remove the owner's information without losing the ability to unlock the car. Therefore, we can identify the car owner even if the software key is copied and the car is stolen (license plates can be forged). However, an automobile manufacturer can know user keys in this scenario since they are hard-coded in cars.[1]

If we can independently generate a key pair (public and secret-keys) of a public-key primitive from the watermarking setup, then an automobile

---

[1] If a car owner can directly install a PRF key into a car, and a watermarking scheme is public marking type, then watermarkable PRFs work in this scenario. However, this situation is not preferable.

manufacturer installs the public key to a car and need not know the secret-key. Therefore, we can run a typical challenge-response protocol by watermarkable public-key encryption (PKE) or signature without revealing secret-keys to manufacturers.[2]

Watermarking from Scratch or Retrofit. Goyal, Kim, Manohar, Waters, and Wu [22] presented the first feasibility result of watermarkable public-key cryptographic primitives from standard assumptions. This is an excellent work on general constructions of watermarkable public-key cryptographic primitives. However, their constructions of cryptographic primitives are built from scratch. Many efficient public-key cryptographic schemes (without watermarking functionalities) have been already proposed. One natural question is whether we can equip *existing* public-key cryptographic schemes with watermarking functionalities. If it is possible, we can obtain many efficient watermarkable cryptographic primitives. Our main question in this study is as follows.

Is there any general framework to equip public-key cryptographic schemes with watermarking functionalities?

We affirmatively answer to this question in this paper.

1.2 Our Contribution

We present a general framework to equip a broad class of public-key primitives with watermarking functionalities. The features of our watermarking schemes are as follows. Our watermarking schemes:

- almost preserve the efficiency of the original public-key primitives.
- apply to various primitives such as signature, PKE, key encapsulation mechanism (KEM), identity-based encryption (IBE), attribute-based encryption (ABE), inner-product encryption (IPE), predicate encryption (PE).
- are secure under the same assumptions as ones used in the original public-key primitives (i.e., CDH, decisional linear (DLIN), DBDH, short integer solution (SIS), LWE assumptions, and more).
- are independent of the original public-key primitives. (We do not need watermarking parameters to setup public-key primitives.)
- use simulation algorithms in security reductions of the original primitives.

More details of our watermarking schemes are explained in Sect. 1.4. We will explain our technique in Sect. 1.3.

Our primary advantages are: (1) semi-general applicability, that is, we can use many existing public-key schemes almost as they are. We do not need to construct watermarkable public-key schemes from scratch. (2) achieving CCA security for PKE. (3) efficiency based on concrete cryptographic assumptions. (See the comparison in Table 1.) Those are obtained from our framework using simulation algorithms.

---

[2] If a watermarking scheme is secret marking type, then we run a secure two-party computation between a user and a manufacturer.

Using Proof Techniques as Real Algorithms. Our construction technique significantly deviates from those of previous works. The most notable feature of our result is that we present a general method to use simulation algorithms that appear in reduction-based proofs as real cryptographic algorithms. Although our study is not the first study that uses simulation algorithms to achieve new cryptographic functionalities [29,30,36],[3] we present the first systematic approach using simulation algorithms in real schemes. We abstract a commonly used proof technique and show that if a public-key cryptographic scheme is proven to be secure via the proof technique, we can use simulation algorithms in the reduction as watermarked cryptographic functionalities. See Sect. 1.3 for the detail. This approach enables us to equip existing schemes with watermarking functionalities.

Terminology. Before we give a technical overview, we more formally explain watermarking. A watermarking scheme consists of three algorithms called setup, marking, and extraction algorithms. A setup algorithm Setup generates a marking key wmk and extraction key wxk. A marking algorithm Mark takes as input wmk, a circuit C, and a message ω, and outputs a marked circuit $\widetilde{C}$. Here, $\widetilde{C}$ should output the same output by C for most inputs. An extraction algorithm Extract takes as input wxk and circuit C', and outputs a string ω or special message unmarked. This type of watermarking is called message-embedding. If Mark does not take ω as input and Extract outputs marked or unmarked, then we call message-less watermarking. The basic security notion is unremovability, which means no adversary can construct a circuit C^* such that the functionality of C^* is almost equivalent to that of $\widetilde{C}$, but Extract(wxk, C^*) outputs $\omega^* \neq \omega$. If we can/not publish wmk and wxk, then we call public/secret marking and public/secret extraction, respectively.

1.3   Technical Overview

We present how to equip public-key primitives that have *canonical all-but-one reductions*[4] with watermarking functionalities. All-but-one (ABO) reductions are standard proof techniques to prove selective security of public-key primitives [1,3,9,10,20,21,25,31,40]. Although our technique is not fully general, that is, we cannot apply our technique to *all* selectively secure public-key primitives, many well-known schemes fall into the class of canonical ABO reductions, where our technique applies. Roughly speaking, our watermarked cryptographic functionalities are simulation algorithms in ABO reductions. This technique is of independent interest because we can use simulators in security reductions as real algorithms for achieving new functionalities.

Our watermarking schemes based on canonical ABO reductions are message-less. To achieve message-embedding watermarking, we need to extend (canonical) ABO reductions to (canonical) all-but-N (ABN) reductions. However, ABO

---

[3] Katsumata et al. [29,30] use simulation algorithms of ABE schemes to achieve homomorphic signatures.

[4] See Sect. 4.2 for the formal definition and the meaning of "canonical".

reductions are simpler to explain and it is easy to upgrade ABO reductions to ABN reductions for pairing-based schemes.[5] Thus, we first explain ABO reductions.

All-but-one Reduction. An ABO reduction is a polynomial-time algorithm that solves a problem instance π of a hard problem Π by using an adversary $\mathcal{A}$ that breaks *selective security* of a cryptographic primitive Σ. To explain ABO reductions and selective security, we introduce oracles in security games.

Adversaries have access to oracles that receives queries from adversaries and returns answers in some security games. Adversaries also declare a target to attack Σ at some point in the security game of Σ. We prohibit adversaries from sending a special query (or queries) that satisfies some conditions related to the target to prevent trivial attacks. We call such a special query "query on the target". In selective security games, adversaries must declare the target at the very beginning of the game.[6]

When we prove that if Π is hard, then Σ is selectively secure, we construct the following reduction R. After an adversary declares a target at the beginning of a selective security game, R simulates a public parameter by using a problem instance of Π and the target and sends the public parameter to the adversary. Then, R simulates answers to all queries from the adversary *except the queries on the target* by using the problem instance (and the target). Note that R completes the simulation *without (master) secret-keys* of Σ. This type of reduction is called *all-but-one* reductions due to the simulation manner. In other words, if there exists an ABO reduction, then there exists an oracle simulation algorithm that works for all queries except the target.

We give an example. In the selective security game of signature, an adversary $\mathcal{A}$ declares a target message m^* at the beginning of the game. Then a challenger sends a public verification-key VK to $\mathcal{A}$. After that, $\mathcal{A}$ can send polynomially many queries (i.e., messages) and receives signatures corresponding to the queried messages (except m^*). At some point, $\mathcal{A}$ sends a challenge (m^*, σ^*).

A typical example of ABO reductions is the security reduction of the Boneh-Boyen signature scheme [9]. The reduction (or called simulator) R is given a CDH instance $\pi = (G, G^x, G^y)$ where G is a generator of a group $\mathbb{G}$. When the adversary $\mathcal{A}$ declares a target m^*, R simulates VK by using π and m^* (embedding π and m^* into VK). Next, R simulates signatures σ_{m} for queried message m from $\mathcal{A}$ except m^*. Here, R *implicitly* embeds G^{xy} into the signing key by setting parameters carefully (note that R does *not* have G^{xy}). Thus, if we assume $\mathcal{A}$ breaks the signature scheme, then R can extract G^{xy} from the forged signature σ^* output by $\mathcal{A}$.

Although R embeds m^* in VK, the distribution of VK by R is perfectly the same as the original distribution. In addition, R can perfectly simulate signatures

---

[5] There is no general conversion from ABO to ABN reductions, but upgrading is possible for many concrete schemes by using programmable hash. See Sect. 4.5 for more detail.

[6] In adaptive security games, adversaries can select the target at any time.

for messages *except for the target message* m* due to the embedding of m*. For notational convention, we separate this signature simulation algorithm part as $\mathsf{SimSign}_{\neq \mathsf{m}^*}$. That is, we can construct an algorithm $\mathsf{SimSign}_{\neq \mathsf{m}^*}$ from π and m* that outputs σ_m for input m except m*. This is not necessarily possible for all selectively secure schemes since R might use oracle answers for simulation. Thus, we say a reduction is "canonical" if $\mathsf{SimSign}_{\neq \mathsf{m}^*}$ does not rely on oracle answers and is described as a stateless randomized algorithm. This proof style is sometimes called *puncturing proof technique* [39] since m* is like a *hole* in the message space and the reduction has no way to generate σ_{m^*} for m*. The graphical explanation is described in Fig. 1.

Although the case of encryption is slightly different from that of signatures, we can consider similar simulation strategies for encryption. In the PKE case, there is no "attribute", but we can use a part of a ciphertext (sometimes called tag) as an attribute (in particular, in the CCA setting).

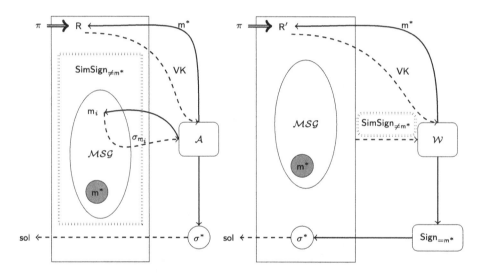

Fig. 1. Illustration of ABO reduction from the selective security of signature to Π. Solid lines denote outputs by the adversary $\mathcal{A}$ of signature. Dashed lines denote simulation by the reduction R. The grayed circle is the hole. Value sol denotes a solution to π.

Fig. 2. Illustration of reduction from the security of watermarking to π. Solid lines denote outputs by the adversary $\mathcal{W}$ of watermarking. Dashed lines denote simulation by reduction R'. The grayed circle is the hole. Value sol denotes a solution to π.

A Hole is to Watermark. We move to explain our unified framework to achieve watermarkable public-key primitives by using canonical ABO reductions. Roughly speaking, *a punctured hole in an ABO reduction works as a watermark because adversaries cannot fill the hole.* More concretely, we can consider the oracle simulation part $\mathsf{SimSign}_{\neq \mathsf{m}^*}$ of the canonical reduction R as a watermarked signature generation circuit in the signature case. In addition, no adversary can recover the ability to generate σ_{m^*} from $\mathsf{SimSign}_{\neq m^*}$ because otherwise, the adversary can break the security of the signature scheme. (The message m^* is the target.)

The ABO oracle simulation algorithm $\mathsf{SimSign}_{\neq m^*}$ preserves the functionality of the signature generation circuit except for an input m^*. To detect whether a circuit is watermarked or not, we check whether the circuit generates a correct output for the punctured input.[7] We can check whether a signature is valid for an message or not by using its verification algorithm. If a circuit does not generate a valid output for the punctured input (i.e., the hole), then we consider it as watermarked. In almost all ABO reductions, we have efficient algorithms that check the validity of answers from oracles.

The unremovability holds as follows. We construct a reduction R' that solves a problem instance π by using a watermarking adversary $\mathcal{W}$. R' can give $\mathsf{SimSign}_{\neq m^*}$ to $\mathcal{W}$ since R' has π and m^*.[8] Assume that $\mathcal{W}$ can remove the watermark. That is, we assume $\mathcal{W}$ is given $\mathsf{SimSign}_{\neq m^*}$ and generates a circuit $\mathsf{Sign}_{=m^*}$ that can generate a signature for the target m^* (i.e., filling *the hole*). Then, R' can break the security of signature. This is because $\mathsf{Sign}_{=m^*}$ yields a forgery σ^* for the target m^*. We can extract the solution for π from σ^* as the ABO reduction for Boneh-Boyen signature scheme.

Put it differently, the canonical ABO reduction $\mathsf{R}(\pi)$ works as well even if we replace the adversary $\mathcal{A}$ of a cryptographic scheme Σ with the adversary $\mathcal{W}$ for watermarking, which removes the watermark. The modified reduction $\mathsf{R}'(\pi)$ can solve π because the power of removing the watermark by $\mathcal{W}$ leads to breaking the security of Σ. Therefore, the watermarking scheme is secure if the underlying problem is hard. The graphical explanation is described as in Fig. 2.

There are a few issues in the overview above. One issue is giving the description of $\mathsf{SimSign}_{\neq m^*}$ to the adversary since it has only black-box access to the signature generation oracle in the security game. This issue is the reason why we use "canonical" ABO reductions. If ABO reductions satisfy the canonical property, then $\mathsf{SimSign}_{\neq m^*}$ does not need oracle answers from the hard problem Π to simulate the signature generation oracle and can be described as a stateless randomized algorithm.

Another issue is how to prepare a problem instance and randomness for simulating VK in an ABO reduction. To create an ABO reduction in the real world, we need a problem instance π. However, what we have in the real world is not a problem instance but a secret signing-key. It is easy to find that we can perfectly simulate a problem instance and randomness for reductions by using a secret key in the real world for most ABO reductions. In addition, although $\mathsf{SimSign}_{\neq m^*}$ includes randomness for simulating VK, this is not an issue thanks to the randomness of the problem instance π (i.e., secret-key in the real world). See Sects. 4 to 6 for details.

---

[7] A useless circuit that outputs $\perp$ for all inputs is watermarked by this detection. To prevent this, we test the functionalities of circuits. See Sect. 6 for details.

[8] We do not explain how to determine m^* here since it is not essential in this overview.

Although we gave only intuitions in this section, we formalize properties of canonical ABO reductions in Sect. 4 and prove that we can achieve watermarking from canonical ABO reductions in Sects. 5 and 6.

Extension to all-but-N Reduction. The watermarking based on ABO reductions above is message-less watermarking. To embed an arbitrary N-bit string, we need all-but-N reduction, which can simulate oracle answers except queries on N targets. Here, N is an a-priori bounded polynomial in the security parameter. We can easily extend known cryptographic primitives that have ABO reductions to ones that have all-but-N reductions by using the technique of programmable hash functions [27] for pairing-based cryptography. We also use the fully key-homomorphic technique [10] in the lattice setting or dynamic q-type assumptions [5] for the Boneh-Boyen IBE. See Sect. 4.4 for the detail.

First, we explain a reasonable but faulty idea to achieve message-embedding watermarking based on all-but-N reductions since it helps to understand our idea. We prepare N pairs of strings $\{t^*_{i,b}\}_{i \in [N], b \in \{0,1\}}$ as the public parameter of watermarking. To embed a message $\omega = (\omega_1, \ldots, \omega_N) \in \{0,1\}^N$, we consider an oracle simulation algorithm that can generate answers for queries except N points in $P := \{t^*_{1,\omega_1}, \ldots, t^*_{N,\omega_N}\}$. Concretely, in the case of signature, a signature oracle simulation algorithm $\mathsf{SimSign}_{\notin P}$ outputs a signature σ_{m} for a message m such that $\mathsf{m} \notin P$.[9] To extract an embedded message from a circuit C', we run the answer checking algorithm as in the message-less scheme for each $i \in [N]$ and $b \in \{0,1\}$. If C' outputs a valid $\sigma_{t^*_{i,1}}$ for input $t^*_{i,1}$ and does not output a valid $\sigma_{t^*_{i,0}}$ for input $t^*_{i,0}$, then we set the i-th bit of a message to 0 and vice versa.

This construction achieves the functionality of message-embedding watermarking. However, it is not secure because the adversary knows which points should not be punctured. That is, the points in $\overline{P} := \{t^*_{1,1-\omega_1}, \ldots, t^*_{N,1-\omega_N}\}$ (and P) are publicly available information. We call $\overline{P}$ the negation of punctured points P in this section. As already observed in some watermarkable PRFs [19,32,38], public punctured points could hurt watermarking security. In our case, adversary can easily destroy the functionality of cryptographic primitive at any point. More concretely, the adversary can easily modify a watermarked circuit where t^*_{i,ω_i} is punctured but $t^*_{i,1-\omega_i}$ is not punctured into a circuit that does not work for point $t^*_{i,1-\omega_i}$ too. Then, the extraction algorithm above outputs $\perp$ for the malformed circuit since the circuit outputs $\perp$ both for $t^*_{i,0}$ and $t^*_{i,1}$.

To solve the issue, we generate punctured points P and its negation $\overline{P}$ by using PRFs and hide them instead of using publicly known punctured points and its negation. This technique is commonly used in watermarkable PRFs [19,32,38]. We pseudo-randomly determine punctured points and its negation based on an embedded mark and the public parameter of the target master secret-key to be watermarked. Then, the adversary has no idea about the

---

[9] All-but-N reductions should be able to generate N simulated challenge ciphertexts in the encryption case. This simulation is easy to achieve by using random self-reducibility of underlying hard problems for the discrete-logarithm-based case. In the LWE case, polynomially many (so, N) problem instances can be given.

negation of punctured points $\overline{P}$ (and P). Therefore, it is hard for the adversary to intentionally modify a watermarked circuit into a circuit that does not work for points in $\overline{P}$. In fact, we must prepare many punctured points $p_i := (t_{i,\omega_i}^{(1)}, \ldots, t_{i,\omega_i}^{(T)})$ and its negation $\overline{p}_i := (t_{i,1-\omega_i}^{(1)}, \ldots, t_{i,1-\omega_i}^{(T)})$ for each bit position i and check all points to extract i-th bit of an embedded message, where T is a polynomial in the security parameter. If a circuit output $\perp$ for all points in p_i and *a correct value for at least one point in* $\overline{p}_i$, we extract ω_i as the i-th bit. To change the i-th bit of the embedded message without recovering the original functionality, adversaries must destroy the functionality of a circuit for all points in $\overline{p}_i$. Advesaries can indiscriminately destroy the functionality without knowing points $(p_i, \overline{p}_i)$. However, if the adversary makes a circuit that does not work for a $1/2$ plus a non-negligible fraction of inputs, then we can check that the circuit is not functionally similar to the original watermarked circuit. To make a circuit that is functionally similar to the watermarked circuit, but the extraction algorithm does not output ω_i from, all the adversary can do is recovering the functionality of the watermarked circuit at punctured points P (p_i). This event contradicts to all-but-N reductions as the case of the message-less scheme. Thus, we can achieve unremovability.

Although the message-embedding scheme above is secret marking and secret extraction, it is secure even if the adversary has the oracle access to the marking and extraction oracles. See Sect. 6 for the detail.

1.4 Comparison and Related Work

In this section, we review previous works on watermarking.[10] First, we compare our watermarking schemes with the schemes by Goyal et al. [22].

Efficient Direct Constructions and Generic Constructions. Goyal et al. [22] constructed a secret marking and secret extraction watermarking scheme for ABE (GKM+ABE) from mixed functional encryption (FE) and delegatable ABE, which can be instantiated only by the LWE assumption. They also constructed a public marking and public extraction watermarking scheme for PE (GKM+PE) from (bounded collusion-resistant) hierarchical FE, which can be instantiated by any PKE. Although the LWE assumption instantiates the schemes, the constructions are inefficient since they rely on heavy tools like mixed FE and hierarchical FE *even for watermarkable PKE*. In particular, in their watermarkable encryption schemes, not only the public key length but also the ciphertext length depend on the length of embedded massages (and the number of collusions in the GKM+PE case). The ciphertext size of GKM+ABE and GKM+PE is huge (See Table 1). They constructed a public marking and public extraction watermarking scheme for signature (GKM+SIG) from a prefix-constrained signature, which is instantiated with OWFs. GKM+SIG scheme is relatively efficient if it is instantiated with a signature scheme based on the symmetric external

---

[10] We do not consider constructions from strong assumptions such as IO in this study.

Table 1. Efficiency Comparison of Message-Embedding Watermarking (Advanced) Public-Key Encryption and Signature. We ignore MPK part in MSK. In "Assumption" column, we put references for concrete instantiations. Parameters λ and ℓ are the security parameter and the length of marks, respectively. In general, $|\mathbb{G}| = c\lambda$ and $|\mathbb{G}_T| = c_T\lambda$ for some small constant c and c_T (depends on pairing groups). We do not put Ours2 in this table since it is message-less type.

	|MPK|	|MSK|	|SK| or |σ|	|CT|	Assumption
GKM+ABE	$\mathrm{poly}(\lambda, \ell)$	$\mathrm{poly}(\lambda)$	$\mathrm{poly}(\lambda)$	$\mathrm{poly}(\lambda, \ell)^c$	LWE [23]
GKM+PE	$Q \cdot \mathrm{poly}(\lambda, \ell)$	$Q \cdot \mathrm{poly}(\lambda)$	$\mathrm{poly}(\lambda, \ell)$	$Q \cdot \mathrm{poly}(\lambda, \ell)^d$	PKE
Ours1 PKE[a]	$(2\ell\lambda + 5)\|\mathbb{G}\|$	$(2\ell\lambda + 2)\|\mathbb{Z}_p\|$	N/A	$6\|\mathbb{G}\|$	DLIN [31]
Ours1 KEM[b]	$(\ell\lambda + 4)\|\mathbb{G}\| + \|\mathsf{hk}\|$	$(\ell\lambda + 3)\|\mathbb{Z}_p\|$	N/A	$2\|\mathbb{G}\| + \|r\|$	DBDH [13]
Ours1 KEM[b]	$4\|\mathbb{G}\| + \|\mathsf{hk}\|$	$3\|\mathbb{Z}_p\|$	N/A	$2\|\mathbb{G}\| + \|r\|$	q-type [5]
Ours1 IBE	$(\ell\lambda + 4)\|\mathbb{G}\|$	$(\ell\lambda + 3)\|\mathbb{Z}_p\|$	$2\|\mathbb{G}\|$	$2\|\mathbb{G}\| + \|\mathbb{G}_T\|$	DBDH [9]
Ours1 IBE	$4\|\mathbb{G}\|$	$3\|\mathbb{Z}_p\|$	$2\|\mathbb{G}\|$	$2\|\mathbb{G}\| + \|\mathbb{G}_T\|$	q-type [5]
Ours1 IBE	$\ell\mathrm{poly}(\lambda)$	$\mathrm{poly}(\lambda)$	$\mathrm{poly}(\lambda)$	$\mathrm{poly}(\lambda)^e$	LWE [10]
GKM+SIG	$(\ell + 3)\|\mathbb{G}\|$	$\|\mathbb{Z}_p\|$	$(\ell + 7)\|\mathbb{G}\|$	N/A	CDH [42]
GKM+SIG	$8\|\mathbb{G}\| + \|\mathbb{G}_T\|$	$8\|\mathbb{Z}_p\|$	$16\|\mathbb{G}\| + \|\mathbb{G}_T\|$	N/A	SXDH [16]
Ours3 SIG	$(\ell\lambda + 4)\|\mathbb{G}\|$	$(\ell\lambda + 3)\|\mathbb{Z}_p\|$	$2\|\mathbb{G}\|$	N/A	CDH [9]
Ours3 SIG	$4\|\mathbb{G}\|$	$3\|\mathbb{Z}_p\|$	$2\|\mathbb{G}\|$	N/A	q-type [5]
Ours3 SIG	$\ell\mathrm{poly}(\lambda)$	$\mathrm{poly}(\lambda)$	$\mathrm{poly}(\lambda)$	N/A	LWE [10]

[a]Tag-based encryption.
[b]Value hk and r are a hash key and randomness of a chameleon hash function.
[c]At least $\ell^7\lambda^7$.
[d]At least $\ell^2\lambda^2$ if instantiated with FE by Ananth and Vaikuntanathan [4].
[e]At most $O(\lambda^3 \log^2 \lambda)$.

Diffie-Hellman (SXDH) assumption [16] since the transformation does not incur significant overhead.[11]

Our watermarking schemes can generally equip public-key primitives with watermarking functionalities if the primitives satisfy some conditions. The equipping procedure incurs only a little overhead. Although we need to modify public-key schemes so that they have $O(\ell\lambda)$-size master public parameters to achieve message-embedding watermarking where ℓ is the mark length and λ is the security parameter, the size of signatures/secret-keys/ciphertexts does not change. The signatures/secret-keys/ciphertexts consist of only a few group elements if we use group-based schemes. In addition, if we use a q-type assumption, we can use the original Boneh-Boyen scheme as it is (even the master public key is constant-size). Thus, our watermarkable public-key primitives are as efficient as known efficient public-key primitives such as Boneh-Boyen IBE scheme [9]. Therefore, in the case of encryption, our schemes are more efficient than those of Goyal et al. in the asymptotic sense. See Table 1 for the efficiency comparison.

---

[11] We focus on constructions in the standard model in this paper. If we instantiate a signature scheme with Schnorr signature scheme [41], GKM+SIG would be more efficient.

Functionalities of Watermarking. In GKM+PE, GKM+SIG, and our schemes, the watermarking setup algorithms are completely separated from the key generation algorithm of public-key primitives. However, in GKM+ABE, we need the public parameter of the watermarking scheme to generate keys of public-key primitives.

Although our message-embedding scheme is secret marking and secret extraction, it is secure even if adversaries have access to marking and extraction oracles, which answer a marked circuit and an embedded mark for queried circuits, respectively. GKM+ABE is also secret marking and secret extraction and secure under the marking and extraction oracles, but the number of extraction queries is a-priori bounded. On the other hand, GKM+PE and GKM+SIG are public marking and public extraction.

Our schemes for signature/TBE/KEM/IBE and all GKM+ schemes are message-embedding watermarking, but our schemes for ABE/PE are message-less watermarking.

Watermarking User Secret-Keys v.s. Master Secret-Keys. In GKM+ABE and GKM+PE, we can watermark user secret-keys such as secret-keys for identities (resp. policies) in IBE (resp. ABE). On the other hand, in our schemes, we can watermark master secret-keys of tag-based encryption (TBE), KEM, IBE, ABE, and PE. TBE is a variant of PKE. For signature/KEM/PKE cases, there is no difference since master secret-keys are user secret-keys in these cases.

Security Level. There are several security measures. (1) Ours for TBE/KEM achieves CCA-security, but GKM+ABE and GKM+PE for PKE do not. (2) GKM+PE and GKM+SIG are adaptively secure, but GKM+ABE and ours are selectively secure in terms of public-key primitives. In terms of embedded messages, GKM+ schemes are adaptively secure, but ours are selectively secure. See Sect. 3 for selective security of watermarking. (3) All schemes are secure even if the authority of watermarking setup is corrupted. (4) Regarding the parameter on how much adversaries should preserve functionalities to succeed attacks, GKM+ schemes are better than ours. (GKM+ is $1/\mathrm{poly}(\lambda)$ while ours is $1/2 + 1/\mathrm{poly}(\lambda)$.) (5) We can consider three types of collusion-resistance in this study.

Collusion-resistance w.r.t. cryptographic primitives: In security games of cryptographic primitives, adversaries are often allowed to send queries to master secret-key based oracles that gives additional information such as signatures in the signature case and secret-keys for identities in the IBE case. We say collusion-resistant w.r.t. cryptographic primitives if cryptographic schemes are secure even in such a setting. Both GKM+SIG and our watermarking schemes for signatures are collusion-resistant w.r.t. cryptographic primitives. GKM+ABE and our watermarking schemes for encryption (IBE, ABE, and PE) are collusion-resistant w.r.t. cryptographic primitives. On the other hand, GKM+PE is *bounded* collusion-resistant w.r.t. cryptographic primitives, where the number of queries is a-priori bounded.

Collusion-resistance w.r.t. watermarkable cryptographic primitives:
We say that a watermarking scheme is collusion-resistant w.r.t. watermarkable cryptographic primitives if it is unremovable even if adversaries have access to the master secret-key based oracle explained above in security games of watermarking for public-key primitives. Both GKM+SIG and our schemes for signature are collusion-resistant w.r.t. watermarkable cryptographic primitives. Our watermarking schemes for encryption (IBE, ABE, and PE) are collusion-resistant w.r.t. watermarkable cryptographic primitives, but GKM+ABE and GKM+PE schemes are not.

Collusion-resistance w.r.t. watermarking: We say that a watermarking scheme is collusion-resistant w.r.t. watermarking (collusion-resistant watermarking) if it is unremovable even if adversaries are given many watermarked keys for the same original key. GKM+ABE, GKM+PE, and GKM+SIG are collusion-resistant watermarking, but ours are not.

We emphasize that even if watermarking schemes do not satisfy collusion-resistance w.r.t. watermarking, they have an application to *ownership identification*. This is because each user can use *different keys* in some settings, as we can see in the application to electronic car-lock in Sect. 1.1. Moreover, collusion-resistant watermarkable encryption is essentially the same as traitor tracing (the definition by Goyal [22] for PKE implies traitor tracing).[12] In some scenarios (ownership identification), traitor tracing (and collusion-resistant watermarking) is over-engineered. Thus, watermarking without collusion-resistance w.r.t. watermarking is meaningful enough. Moreover, if we would like to use collusion-resistant watermarkable PKE, we already have traitor tracing schemes [14,24]. If we want to trace users in public-key primitives, we can directly consider traceable primitives rather than collusion-resistant watermarkable public-key primitives.

The construction technique by Goyal et al. relies on that of traitor tracing [17,37] to achieve collusion-resistance w.r.t. watermarking.

Summary of Comparison. We summarize watermarkable public-key primitives by Goyal et al. [22] and ours in Tables 1 and 2. PE and ABE include PKE/IBE/IPE as special cases. Notably, ours achieves CCA security for PKE. In addition, our message-embedding scheme (Ours1 in Table 2) is much more efficient than GKM+ABE and GKM+PE as we see in Table 1. In particular, the size of secret-keys and ciphertexts in our scheme does not depend on ℓ. If we use q-type assumption, then even the size of master public key does not depend on ℓ.

The disadvantages of Ours1 and Ours3 are (1) not collusion-resistant (2) secret marking/extraction (3) selective security (4) watermarking for master secret-keys (this is not a disadvantage for PKE and signature) (5) not supporting functionalities beyond IBE. We do not have a useful application of watermarking for master secret-keys in IBE/ABE/PE cases. On the other hand, all GKM+ constructions achieve collusion-resistance, watermarking for user secret keys, and

---

[12] Collusion-resistant watermarkable signatures may have an application to group signatures. However, the application is non-trivial since we should be able to trace users from signatures (not from signing keys) in the group signature setting.

Table 2. Comparison of Watermarking (Advanced) Public-Key Encryption. WM, CR, prim., auth., $\mathcal{MO}$, and $\mathcal{XO}$ stands for watermarking (or watermarkable), collusion-resistance, primitive, authority, marking oracle, and extraction oracle, respectively.

	GKM+ABE	Ours1	Ours2	GKM+PE	GKM+SIG	Ours3
Primitive	ABE	PKE^a/IBE	ABE/IPE/PE	PE	SIG	SIG
Assumption	LWE	DBDH/DLIN/LWE		PKE	OWF	CDH/SIS
Message-embedding	✓	✓	✗	✓	✓	✓
Public mark	✗	✗	✓	✓	✓	✗
Against $\mathcal{MO}$ attack	✓	✓	✓	✓	✓	✓
Public extraction	✗	✗	✓	✓	✓	✗
Against $\mathcal{XO}$ attack	bounded	✓	✓	✓	✓	✓
Separated setup	✗	✓	✓	✓	✓	✓
Marking MSK	✗	✓	✓	✗	N/A	N/A
Marking SK	✓	✗	✗	✓	✓	✓
CCA-secure PKE	✗	✓^{a}	✓^{a}	✗	N/A	N/A
CR w.r.t. prim.	✓	✓	✓	bounded	✓	✓
CR w.r.t. WM prim.	✗	✓	✓	✗	✓	✓
CR w.r.t. WM	✓	✗	N/A	bounded	✓	✗
Selective/Adaptive	selective	selective	selective	adaptive	adaptive	selective
Sec. against auth.	✓	✓	✓	✓	✓	✓

^{a}TBE and KEM.

support functionalities beyond IBE. GKM+PE and GKM+SIG achieve adaptive security. Although Ours2 is public marking/extraction and supports functionalities beyond IBE, it is message-less type and watermarking for master secret-keys. Therefore, GKM+ constructions and ours are incomparable.

More on Related Work. Cohen et al. gave the first positive result on program watermarking by introducing the statistical functionality-preserving property [19]. They presented public extraction message-embedding watermarkable PRFs based on IO. Subsequently, Kim and Wu [32,33] (KW17 and KW19) and Quach, Wichs, and Zirdelis [38] (QWZ18) presented secret extraction message-embedding watermarkable PRFs based on the LWE assumption. The KW19 and QWZ18 schemes are secure against extraction oracle attacks. In addition, QWZ18 scheme is public marking. Regarding message-embedding watermarkable PRFs, KW17, KW19, and QWZ18 schemes are relatively efficient since they are based on the LWE assumption.

Baldimtsi, Kiayias, and Samari presented watermarking schemes for public-key primitives in a relaxed model, where a trusted watermarking authority generates not only watermarked keys but also unmarked keys and algorithms are stateful [7]. We do not compare their scheme because this is a weaker model.

Goyal et al. presented not only constructions but also rigorous definitions of watermarkable public-key primitives and a relaxed functionality-preserving property for watermarkable public-key primitives [22].[13]

---

[13] Cohen et al. [18] considered watermarkable public-key primitives before Goyal et al., but even if a scheme satisfies their definitions, there exists simple attacks as observed by Goyal et al. [22].

Organization. In Sect. 2, we provide basic notions. Section 3 introduces the syntax and security definitions of watermarking. Section 4 defines canonical ABO reductions and gives examples of them. In Sect. 5, we present our message-less watermarking scheme. In Sect. 6, we present our message-embedding watermarking scheme and prove its security. Due to space limitations, we omitted many contents.

2   Preliminaries

We define some notations and introduce cryptographic notions in this section.

Notations and Basic Concepts. If $\mathcal{X}^{(b)} = \{X_\lambda^{(b)}\}_{\lambda \in \mathbb{N}}$ for $b \in \{0, 1\}$ are two ensembles of random variables indexed by $\lambda \in \mathbb{N}$, we say that $\mathcal{X}^{(0)}$ and $\mathcal{X}^{(1)}$ are computationally indistinguishable if for any PPT distinguisher $\mathcal{D}$, there exists a negligible function $\mathsf{negl}(\lambda)$, such that

$$\Delta := |\Pr[\mathcal{D}(X_\lambda^{(0)}) = 1] - \Pr[\mathcal{D}(X_\lambda^{(1)}) = 1]| \leq \mathsf{negl}(\lambda).$$

We write $\mathcal{X}^{(0)} \overset{c}{\approx} \mathcal{X}^{(1)}$ to denote that the advantage Δ is negligible.

The statistical distance between $\mathcal{X}^{(0)}$ and $\mathcal{X}^{(1)}$ over a countable set S is defined as $\Delta_{\mathsf{s}}(\mathcal{X}^{(0)}, \mathcal{X}^{(1)}) := \frac{1}{2} \sum_{\alpha \in S} |\Pr[X_\lambda^{(0)} = \alpha] - \Pr[X_\lambda^{(1)} = \alpha]|$. We say that $\mathcal{X}^{(0)}$ and $\mathcal{X}^{(1)}$ are statistically/perfectly indistinguishable (denoted by $\mathcal{X}^{(0)} \overset{s}{\approx} \mathcal{X}^{(1)}/\mathcal{X}^{(0)} \overset{p}{\approx} \mathcal{X}^{(1)}$) if $\Delta_{\mathsf{s}}(\mathcal{X}^{(0)}, \mathcal{X}^{(1)}) \leq \mathsf{negl}(\lambda)$ and $\Delta_{\mathsf{s}}(\mathcal{X}^{(0)}, \mathcal{X}^{(1)}) = 0$, respectively. We also say that $\mathcal{X}^{(0)}$ is ϵ-close to $\mathcal{X}^{(1)}$ if $\Delta_{\mathsf{s}}(\mathcal{X}^{(0)}, \mathcal{X}^{(1)}) = \epsilon$.

Definition 2.1 (Circuit similarity). *Let $\mathcal{C}$ be a circuit class whose input space is $\{0, 1\}^\ell$. For two circuits $C, C' \in \mathcal{C}$ and a non-decreasing function $\epsilon : \mathbb{N} \to \mathbb{N}$, we say that C is ϵ-close to C' if it holds that*

$$\Pr[C(x) \neq C'(x) \mid x \leftarrow \{0, 1\}^\ell] \leq \epsilon. \text{ (denoted by } C \cong_\epsilon C')$$

Similarly, we say that C is ϵ-far to C' if it holds that

$$\Pr[C(x) \neq C'(x) \mid x \leftarrow \{0, 1\}^\ell] > \epsilon. \text{ (denoted by } C \not\cong_\epsilon C')$$

3   Definitions of Watermarking for Cryptographic Primitives

In this section, we introduce the definitions of watermarking for cryptographic primitives. Although our definitions basically follow those of Goyal et al. [22], there are several differences.

We focus on cryptographic primitives that have a master parameter generation algorithm PGen and a master secret-key based algorithm MSKAlg in this study. For example, in IBE/ABE/IPE, PGen is a setup algorithm Setup and MSKAlg is a key generation algorithm for identity/attribute/policy KeyGen. In TBE/KEM/signature, PGen is a key generation algorithm Gen and MSKAlg is a decryption/signing algorithm Dec/Sign. Hereafter, we do not explicitly treat KEM, but it is easy to adapt all definitions to the KEM setting. We formalize the notion of master secret-key based cryptographic schemes as follows.

Definition 3.1 (Master secret-key based cryptographic scheme). *A master secret-key based cryptographic scheme Σ with spaces $(\mathcal{T}, \mathcal{Q}, \mathcal{P}, \mathcal{R}_{\mathsf{mka}})$ has at least two algorithms* PGen *and* MSKAlg.

Master parameter generation: PGen(1^λ) *takes as input the security parameter and outputs a master public parameter* PP $\in \mathcal{PP}$ *and a master secret key* MSK $\in \mathcal{MSK}$. *We often omit spaces $\mathcal{PP}$ and $\mathcal{MSK}$ from Σ.*

Master secret-key based algorithm: MSKAlg(MSK, X) *takes* MSK *and an input $X \in \mathcal{Q}$ and outputs $Y \in \mathcal{P}$. The randomness space of* MSKAlg *is $\mathcal{R}_{\mathsf{mka}}$.*

We assume that MSK *includes* PP. *$\Sigma = ($PGen, MSKAlg, $\ldots)$ has additional algorithm other than* PGen *and* MSKAlg. *The space $\mathcal{T}$ is used in the security game defined later (Definition 4.2).*[14]

Remark 3.1. In Definition 3.1, an output by MSKAlg is typically a secret key for an identity/policy X, signature for a message X. In the TBE case, X consists of a tag and ciphertext, and Y is a plaintext. We can consider encryption, decryption, and verification algorithms as additional algorithms. Definition 3.1 captures most popular cryptographic schemes such as PKE, TBE, IBE, ABE, IPE, PE, FE, signature, constrained signature.

Table 3. Concrete spaces and algorithms of master secret-key based cryptographic scheme.

	tag-based PKE	IBE	SIG
$\mathcal{T}$	tag space $\mathcal{TAG}$	identity space $\mathcal{ID}$	message space $\mathcal{MSG}$
$\mathcal{Q}$	tag and ciphertext space $\mathcal{TAG} \times \mathcal{CT}$	$\mathcal{ID}$	$\mathcal{MSG}$
$\mathcal{P}$	plaintext space $\mathcal{PT} \cup \{\bot\}$	secret key space $\mathcal{SK}$	signature space $\mathcal{SIG}$
MSKAlg(MSK, ·)	Dec(sk, ·)	KeyGen(MSK, ·)	Sign(sk, ·)

Definition 3.2 (Validity check algorithm for master secret-key based cryptographic scheme). *A master secret-key based cryptographic scheme Σ with spaces $(\mathcal{T}, \mathcal{Q}, \mathcal{P}, \mathcal{R}_{\mathsf{mka}})$ can have an optional algorithm* Valid-Out *that takes as inputs* PP, $X \in \mathcal{Q}$, *and $Y \in \mathcal{P}$ and outputs $\top/\bot$. For all* (PP, MSK) $\leftarrow$ PGen(1^λ) *and all $X \in \mathcal{Q}$,* Valid-Out(PP, X, Y) *outputs $\top$ if and only if $Y \leftarrow$* MSKAlg(MSK, X).

Remark 3.2. Although we do not explicitly consider validity check algorithms in signature and advanced encryption schemes, we can implement validity check algorithms in most schemes (and all schemes in this paper). See examples in Sects. 4.3 and 4.5. Note that Y is not necessarily unique since MSKAlg might be a randomized algorithm.

---

[14] Jumping ahead, $\mathcal{T}$ is a space where adversaries select targets at the beginning of security games.

Definition 3.3 (Watermarkable Public-Key Scheme). *A watermarking scheme with mark space $\mathcal{M}_w$ for master secret-key based cryptographic scheme Σ with spaces $(\mathcal{T}, \mathcal{Q}, \mathcal{P}, \mathcal{R}_{mka})$ is a tuple of algorithms* (WMSetup, Mark, Extract) *with the following properties:*

Setup: WMSetup(1^λ) *takes as input the security parameter and outputs a watermarking public parameter* wpp, *a marking key* wmk, *and an extraction key* wxk.

Mark: Mark(wpp, wmk, MSK, ω) *takes as input* wpp, wmk, *the master secret key* MSK $\in \mathcal{MSK}$ *of Σ, and a mark $\omega \in \mathcal{M}_w$ and outputs a deterministic circuit $\widetilde{C} : \mathcal{Q} \times \mathcal{R}_{mka} \to \mathcal{P}$. Note that $\widetilde{C}$ explicitly takes the randomness of* MSKAlg.

Extract: Extract(wpp, wxk, PP, C') *takes as input* wpp, wxk, *the public parameter* PP $\in \mathcal{PP}$ *of Σ, and a circuit $C' : \mathcal{Q} \times \mathcal{R}_{mka} \to \mathcal{P}$ and outputs a mark $\omega' \in \mathcal{M}_w$ or a special symbol* unmarked.

Remark 3.3. We can separately treat watermarking schemes and cryptographic primitives in our definition while in the definition of Goyal et al. [22], key generation algorithms of cryptographic primitives need public parameters of watermarking. The separated definition is preferable and the same definition as that of Cohen et al. [19].

Hereafter, we set wsk := wmk = wxk since we consider only two cases. One is the public marking and extraction case (wmk = wxk = $\perp$) and the other is the secret marking and extraction case (wsk = wmk = wxk) in this paper.

Hereafter, we focus on advanced encryption (IBE, IPE, ABE, PE) rather than TBE and signature for readability. Due to space limitations, we omit the definitions for TBE and signature.

Definition 3.4 (Correctness (Advanced encryption)). *Let* WM$_\Sigma$ = (WMSetup, Mark, Extract) *be a watermarking scheme for advanced encryption scheme Σ =* (Setup, KeyGen, Enc, Dec) *with spaces $(\mathcal{T}, \mathcal{Q}, \mathcal{P}, \mathcal{R}_{mka})$. In this case, $\mathcal{T} = \mathcal{ATT}$, $\mathcal{Q} = \mathcal{POL}$, $\mathcal{P} = \mathcal{SK}$, where $\mathcal{ATT}$ and $\mathcal{POL}$ is an attribute and policy space, respectively. We say that* WM$_\Sigma$ *is correct if it satisfies the following.*

Extraction correctness: *For all* (wpp, wsk) $\leftarrow$ WMSetup(1^λ), *all marks $\omega \in \mathcal{M}_w$,*

$$\Pr \left[\text{Extract}(\text{wpp}, \text{wsk}, \text{PP}, \widetilde{C}) \neq \omega \;\middle|\; \begin{array}{l} (\text{PP}, \text{MSK}) \leftarrow \text{Setup}(1^\lambda) \\ \widetilde{C} \leftarrow \text{Mark}(\text{wpp}, \text{wsk}, \text{MSK}, \omega) \end{array} \right] \leq \text{negl}(\lambda).$$

Meaningfulness: *There are two variants of meaningfulness.*

    Strong meaningfulness. *For all fixed circuits $C : \mathcal{POL} \times \mathcal{R}_{mka} \to \mathcal{SK}$,*

$$\Pr \left[\begin{array}{l} \text{Extract}(\text{wpp}, \text{wsk}, \text{PP}, C) \\ = \text{unmarked} \end{array} \;\middle|\; \begin{array}{l} (\text{wpp}, \text{wsk}) \leftarrow \text{WMSetup}(1^\lambda) \\ (\text{PP}, \text{MSK}) \leftarrow \text{Setup}(1^\lambda) \end{array} \right] > 1 - \text{negl}(\lambda).$$

    Weak meaningfulness. *For all* (wpp, wsk) $\leftarrow$ WMSetup(1^λ),

$$\Pr \left[\begin{array}{l} \text{Extract}(\text{wpp}, \text{wsk}, \text{PP}, \text{KeyGen}(\text{MSK}, \cdot)) \\ = \text{unmarked} \end{array} \;\middle|\; (\text{PP}, \text{MSK}) \leftarrow \text{Setup}(1^\lambda) \right] > 1 - \text{negl}(\lambda).$$

Functionality-preserving: *For all* (wpp, wsk) $\leftarrow$ WMSetup(1^λ), *for all* (PP, MSK) $\leftarrow$ Setup(1^λ), *all marks* $\omega \in \mathcal{M}_w$, *there exists* $\mathcal{PS} \subset \mathcal{ATT}$ *such that* $N := |\mathcal{PS}| \leq \text{poly}(\lambda)$, *for all* $\rho_{\text{mka}} \in \mathcal{R}_{\text{mka}}$, *all attributes* $x \in \mathcal{ATT} \setminus \mathcal{PS}$ *and all policy* $\mathsf{P} \in \mathcal{POL}$ *such that* $\mathsf{P}(x) = \top$, *we have that*

$$\Pr[\widetilde{C}(\mathsf{P}, \rho_{\text{mka}}) \overset{\mathsf{p}}{\approx} \text{KeyGen}(\text{MSK}, \mathsf{P}) \mid \widetilde{C} \leftarrow \text{Mark}(\text{wpp}, \text{wsk}, \text{MSK}, \omega)] > 1 - \text{negl}(\lambda).$$

Here, $\mathcal{PS}$ *stands for a "punctured set" since* $\widetilde{C}$ *does not work for policy* P *such that* $x \in \mathcal{PS}$ *and* $\mathsf{P}(x) = \bot$.

Condition $\mathsf{P}(x) = \bot$ *means attribute* x *is not qualified to policy* P.

In the IBE case, $\mathcal{T} = \mathcal{Q} = \mathcal{ID}$ (identity space), $\mathsf{P} = \text{id}_i$, $x = \text{id}$, and $\mathsf{P}(x) = \bot$ means $\text{id}_i \neq \text{id}$.

Remark 3.4. Although our definition has a few differences from the standard functionality preserving in the cryptographic watermarking context [19,32] on the surface, ours is basically the same as the standard one. We select the definition above to emphasize that there exists a punctured set $\mathcal{PS}$, and the set is explicitly used in the security definition.

In addition, this functionality-preserving is stronger than that by Goyal et al. [22] since the output distribution of marked circuits is perfectly the same as that of the original circuit on almost all inputs.

Definition 3.5 (Selective-Mark ϵ-Unremovability for Advanced Encryption). *For every PPT* $\mathcal{A}$, *we have*

$$\Pr[\text{Exp}_{\mathcal{A}, \text{WM}_\Sigma}^{\text{urmv-enc}}(\lambda, \epsilon) = 1] \leq \text{negl}(\lambda),$$

where ϵ *is a parameter of the scheme called the* approximation factor *and* $\text{Exp}_{\mathcal{A}, \text{WM}_\Sigma}^{\text{urmv-enc}}(\lambda, \epsilon)$ *is the game defined as follows.*

1. *The adversary* $\mathcal{A}$ *declares a target mark* $\omega^* \in \mathcal{M}_w$.
2. *The challenger generates* (PP, MSK) $\leftarrow$ Setup(1^λ), (wpp, wsk) $\leftarrow$ WMSetup(1^λ), *and* $\widetilde{C} \leftarrow$ Mark(wpp, wsk, MSK, ω^*), *and gives* (PP, wpp, $\widetilde{C}$) *to* $\mathcal{A}$. *At this point, a set* $\mathcal{PS} \subset \mathcal{T}$ *such that* $|\mathcal{PS}| = \text{poly}(\lambda)$ *is uniquely determined by* (wpp, wsk, PP, ω^*).
3. $\mathcal{A}$ *has oracle access to the key generation oracle* $\mathcal{KO}$. *If* $\mathcal{KO}$ *is queried with a policy* $\mathsf{P} \in \mathcal{POL}$ *such that* $\mathsf{P}(t_i^*) = \bot$ *for all* $t_i^* \in \mathcal{PS}$, *then* $\mathcal{KO}$ *answers with* KeyGen(MSK, P). *Otherwise, it answers* $\bot$. *Condition* $\mathsf{P}(x) = \bot$ *means attribute* x *is not qualified to policy* P.
4. $\mathcal{A}$ *has oracle access to the marking oracle* $\mathcal{MO}$. *If* $\mathcal{MO}$ *is queried with a master secret key* $\text{MSK}' \in \mathcal{MSK}$ *and a mark* $\omega' \in \mathcal{M}_w$, *then does the following. If the corresponding master public parameter* PP' *is equal to* PP, *then outputs* $\bot$. *Otherwise, answers with* Mark(wpp, wsk, MSK', ω').
5. $\mathcal{A}$ *has oracle access to the extraction oracle* $\mathcal{XO}$. *If* $\mathcal{XO}$ *is queried with a* PP' *and circuit* C', *then* $\mathcal{XO}$ *answers with* Extract(wpp, wsk, PP', C').

6. *Finally, $\mathcal{A}$ outputs a circuit C^*. If $\mathcal{A}$ is admissible (defined below) and* Extract(wpp, wsk, PP, C^*) $\neq \omega^*$ *then the experiment outputs 1, otherwise 0.*

We say that $\mathcal{A}$ is ϵ-admissible if C^* output by $\mathcal{A}$ in the experiment above satisfies

$$\Pr\left[\mathsf{Valid\text{-}Out}(\mathsf{PP},\mathsf{P},C^*(\mathsf{P},\rho_{\mathsf{mka}})) = \top \;\middle|\; \begin{matrix} \mathsf{P} \leftarrow \mathcal{POL} \\ \rho_{\mathsf{mka}} \leftarrow \mathcal{R}_{\mathsf{mka}} \end{matrix}\right] \geq \epsilon.$$

See Definition 3.2 for Valid-Out.

The admissibility requires the adversary to output C^* that agrees on an ϵ fraction of inputs with C. This formalizes that C^* should be similar to the original circuit C.

Remark 3.5. Our definition is the same as that of Goyal et al. [22] except for that

1. $\mathcal{A}$ must declare the target mark ω at the beginning of the game.
2. $\mathcal{A}$ does not receives answers for inputs in $\mathcal{PS}$ from the key generation oracle.
3. we do not consider collusion-resistance w.r.t. watermarking. That is, $\mathcal{A}$ is given only one target circuit $\widetilde{C}$.
4. we consider the oracles $\mathcal{KO}$ in the unremovability game while Goyal et al. do not.
5. we consider watermarking for *master secret-keys*. Thus, the admissible condition for advanced encryption (i.e., beyond PKE or TBE) is in terms of Valid-Out.

Unforgeability. We can consider another security notion for watermarking, called unforgeability [12,19,32], in the secret marking setting. Unforgeability says that adversaries cannot generate a marked circuit with sufficiently different functionality from that of given marked circuits without a marking key.

We do not formally define unforgeability in this work as Goyal et al. did not. However, we can achieve unforgeability by embedding not only a mark but also a signature for the embedded mark and master public key as Goyal et al. observed [22].[15]

On Security Against Malicious Authority. Our watermarkable public-key primitives are trivially secure against authorities of watermarking schemes if the underlying public-key primitives are secure since parameter generation algorithms PGen are independent of watermarking setup algorithms WMSetup. Thus, we omit the definition of security against malicious authority.

4   All-But-One Reductions

In this section, we formalize a class of security reductions, called canonical all-but-one (ABO) reductions. Canonical ABO reductions are often used to prove the hardness of breaking many cryptographic primitives. A typical example is the security reduction of Boneh-Boyen IBE based on the decisional bilinear Diffie-Hellman assumption [9].

---

[15] ePrint archive report 2019/628, Section 3.4 and C.4 (version 20190908).

4.1 Assumptions and Security Games

We need to define cryptographic assumptions and security games before we formalize canonical ABO reductions. The types of reductions depend on whether security games and underlying cryptographic assumptions are computational or decisional. Therefore, we consider two types of assumptions and games. However, we focus on the decisional case in the main body for readability. See the full version for the computational case.

Definition 4.1 (Decisional assumption). *A decisional assumption* DA *for problem Π is formalized by a game between the challenger $\mathcal{E}$ and the adversary $\mathcal{A}$. The problem Π consists of an efficient problem sampling algorithm* $\mathsf{PSample}_b$ *for $b \in \{0,1\}$. The game* $\mathsf{Expt}^{\mathsf{DA}}_{\Pi,\mathcal{E}\leftrightarrow\mathcal{A}}(\lambda, b)$ *is formalized as follows.*

- *On input security parameter λ, $\mathcal{E}$ samples a problem instance $\pi_b \leftarrow$ $\mathsf{PSample}_b(1^\lambda)$.*
- *$\mathcal{E}$ sends π_b to $\mathcal{A}$ and may interact with $\mathcal{A}(1^\lambda, \pi_b)$.*
- *At some point, $\mathcal{A}$ outputs a guess* coin* *and the game outputs* coin*.

We say a decisional assumption holds (or problem Π is hard) if it holds

$$\mathsf{Adv}^{\mathsf{DA}}_{\Pi,\mathcal{E}\leftrightarrow\mathcal{A}}(\lambda) := |\Pr[\mathsf{Expt}^{\mathsf{DA}}_{\Pi,\mathcal{E}\leftrightarrow\mathcal{A}}(\lambda, 0) = 1] - \Pr[\mathsf{Expt}^{\mathsf{DA}}_{\Pi,\mathcal{E}\leftrightarrow\mathcal{A}}(\lambda, 1) = 1]| \leq \mathsf{negl}(\lambda).$$

This definition captures the well-known DDH, DBDH, k-Lin, matrix-DDH, quadratic residuosity, LWE, decisional q-type assumptions (and more). Note that the assumption above also captures interactive oracle assumptions since $\mathcal{A}$ may interact with the challenger that plays the role of oracles.

Definition 4.2 (Selective Security Game (Decisional Case)). *We define selective security games (decisional case) between a challenger $\mathcal{C}$ and an adversary $\mathcal{A}$ for a master secret-key based scheme Σ with spaces $(\mathcal{T}, \mathcal{Q}, \mathcal{P}, \mathcal{R}_{\mathsf{mka}})$ associated with challenge space $\mathcal{H}$, challenge answer space $\mathcal{I}$, and admissible condition* Adml. *(See Table 4 for concrete examples.) The admissible condition* Adml *outputs $\top$ or $\bot$ depending on whether a query is allowed or not.*

We define the experiment $\mathsf{Exp}^{\mathsf{d\text{-}goal\text{-}atk}}_{\mathcal{A},\Sigma}(\lambda, \mathsf{coin})$ *between an adversary $\mathcal{A}$ and a challenger as follows.*

1. *$\mathcal{A}$ submits a target $t^* \in \mathcal{T}$ to the challenger.*
2. *The challenger runs* $(\mathsf{PP}, \mathsf{MSK}) \leftarrow \mathsf{PGen}(1^\lambda)$*, and gives* PP *to $\mathcal{A}$.*
3. *$\mathcal{A}$ sends a query* query $\in \mathcal{Q}$ *to the challenger. If* $\mathsf{Adml}(t^*, \mathsf{query}) = \top$*, the challenger sends an answer* answer $\leftarrow \mathsf{MSKAlg}(\mathsf{MSK}, \mathsf{query})$ *to $\mathcal{A}$. On the other hand, if* $\mathsf{Adml}(t^*, \mathsf{query}) = \bot$*, the challenger outputs $\bot$. ($\mathcal{A}$ can send polynomially many queries.)*
4. *At some point, $\mathcal{A}$ sends a challenge* challenge $\in \mathcal{H}$ *to the challenger. The challenger generates a challenge answer* c-ans* $\in \mathcal{I}$ *by using $(t^*, \mathsf{PP}, \mathsf{challenge}, \mathsf{coin})$ (denoted by $\mathcal{C}_\mathsf{a}(t^*, \mathsf{PP}, \mathsf{challenge}, \mathsf{coin})$) and sends* c-ans* *to $\mathcal{A}$.*
5. *Again, $\mathcal{A}$ is allowed to query (polynomially many)* query $\in \mathcal{Q}$ *such that* $\mathsf{Adml}(t^*, \mathsf{query}) = \top$*.*
6. *$\mathcal{A}$ outputs a guess* coin* *for* coin. *The experiment outputs* coin*.

We say that Σ is secure if for all $\mathcal{A}$, it holds that

$$\mathsf{Adv}_{\mathcal{A},\Sigma}^{\mathsf{d\text{-}goal\text{-}atk}}(\lambda) := |\Pr[\mathsf{Exp}_{\mathcal{A},\Sigma}^{\mathsf{d\text{-}goal\text{-}atk}}(\lambda, 0) = 1] - \Pr[\mathsf{Exp}_{\mathcal{A},\Sigma}^{\mathsf{d\text{-}goal\text{-}atk}}(\lambda, 1) = 1]| \le \mathsf{negl}(\lambda).$$

We say an adversary is successful if the advantage is non-negligible. We can consider the multi-challenge case, where the targets are $\boldsymbol{t}^* \in \mathcal{T}^N$ instead of the single t^*.

A concrete example of $\mathsf{Adml}(t^*, \mathsf{query})$ is $\mathsf{Adml}(t^*, \mathsf{query}) = \top$ if and only if $t^* \ne t$ where $\mathsf{query} = t$ in the signature/TBE/IBE cases (t is a message/tag/identity).

Although we can consider a stronger variant, called adaptive security games, we consider only selective security games since ABO reductions are basically applicable in the selective setting.

4.2   Abstraction of All-But-One Reductions for Decisional Case

Now, we are ready to define ABO reductions for the decisional case. We put red underlines on the parts related to "canonical" parts.

First, we present a simplified definition that does not capture the TBE/KEM case for readability.

Definition 4.3 (Canonical All-But-One Reduction for Decisional Case (Simplified)). *Let Σ be a master secret-key based scheme with $(\mathcal{T}, \mathcal{Q}, \mathcal{P}, \mathcal{R}_{\mathsf{mka}})$ associated with challenge space $\mathcal{H}$, challenge answer space $\mathcal{I}$, and admissible condition Adml. (See Table 4 for concrete examples.) A security reduction algorithm R from Σ to a hard problem Π is a canonical all-but-one reduction (or Σ has a canonical all-but-one reduction to Π) if it satisfies the following properties.*

Oracle access: *$\mathcal{A}$ has oracle access to $\mathcal{O}_{\mathsf{MSK}} : \mathcal{Q} \to \mathcal{P}$ in the security game $\mathsf{Exp}_{\mathcal{A},\Sigma}^{\mathsf{d\text{-}goal\text{-}atk}}$. This oracle receives a query $\mathsf{query} \in \mathcal{Q}$ and does the following. If $\mathsf{Adml}(t^*, \mathsf{query}) = \top$, where t^* is defined below, it sends an answer $\mathsf{answer} \leftarrow \mathsf{MSKAlg}(\mathsf{MSK}, \mathsf{query})$ to $\mathcal{A}$. On the other hand, if $\mathsf{Adml}(t^*, \mathsf{query}) = \bot$, it outputs $\bot$.*

Selective reduction: *R simulates the security game $\mathsf{Exp}_{\mathcal{A},\Sigma}^{\mathsf{d\text{-}goal\text{-}atk}}$ of Σ between the challenger $\mathcal{C}$ and the adversary $\mathcal{A}$ to win the game $\mathsf{Expt}_{\Pi,\mathcal{E}\leftrightarrow\mathsf{R}}^{\mathsf{DA}}$. That is, R plays the role of the challenger $\mathcal{C}$ in $\mathsf{Exp}_{\mathcal{A},\Sigma}^{\mathsf{d\text{-}goal\text{-}atk}}$ and that of the adversary in $\mathsf{Expt}_{\Pi,\mathcal{E}\leftrightarrow\mathsf{R}}^{\mathsf{DA}}$.*

1. *$\mathcal{A}$ declares an arbitrary string $t^* \in \mathcal{T}$ at the very begining of the game and send t^* to R. (We can allow R to determine t^* in some security games.)*
2. *R is given a problem instance π of the hard problem Π.*
3. *R simulates public parameters PP of Σ by using π and t^* and sends PP to $\mathcal{A}$.*
4. *R simulates an oracle $\mathcal{O}_{\mathsf{MSK}}$ of the security game of Σ when $\mathcal{A}$ sends oracle queries. That is, when $\mathcal{A}$ sends a query $\mathsf{query} \in \mathcal{Q}$, R simulates the value $\mathcal{O}_{\mathsf{MSK}}(\mathsf{query})$ and returns a simulated value $\mathsf{answer} \in \mathcal{P}$ to $\mathcal{A}$. If $\mathsf{Adml}(t^*, \mathsf{query}) = \bot$, then R outputs $\bot$.*
   At the oracle simulation phase, R never interacts with $\mathcal{E}$.

5. *At some point, $\mathcal{A}$ sends a challenge query* challenge $\in \mathcal{H}$ *to* R.
6. R *chooses* coin $\leftarrow \{0,1\}$ *and simulates a challenge answer* c-ans* $\in \mathcal{I}$ *of* $\mathcal{C}_{\mathsf{a}}(\mathsf{PP}, t^*, \mathsf{challenge}, b)$ *by using* $(\pi, \mathsf{PP}, t^*, \mathsf{challenge}, \mathsf{coin})$. *It sends* c-ans* *to* $\mathcal{A}$. R *is allowed to interact with* $\mathcal{E}$ *at this phase.*
7. *We can allow* $\mathcal{A}$ *to send queries to* $\mathcal{O}_{\mathsf{MSK}}$ *again. At some point,* $\mathcal{A}$ *outputs* coin*.
8. *Finally,* R *outputs a bit* sol $:= 0$ *if* coin $=$ coin*. *Otherwise (*coin $\neq$ coin**), outputs* sol $:= 1$.

R *consists of three algorithms* (PSim, OSim, CSim) *introduced below.*

All-but-one oracle simulation: R *can perfectly simulate the public parameter of* Σ *and the oracle* $\mathcal{O}_{\mathsf{MSK}}$. *That is, there exist parameter and oracle simulation algorithms* PSim *and* OSim *such that for all* $(\mathsf{PP}, \mathsf{MSK}) \leftarrow \mathsf{PGen}(1^\lambda)$, $b \in \{0,1\}$, $\pi \leftarrow \mathsf{PSample}_b(1^\lambda)$, $t^* \in \mathcal{T}$, *and* query $\in \mathcal{Q}$ *where* $\mathsf{Adml}(t^*, \mathsf{query}) = \top$, *it holds that*

$$\mathsf{PSim}(\pi, t^*; \rho) \overset{\mathsf{p}}{\approx} \mathsf{PP},$$

$$\mathsf{OSim}(\pi, \rho, t^*, \mathsf{query}) \overset{\mathsf{p}}{\approx} \mathcal{O}_{\mathsf{MSK}}(\mathsf{query}),$$

where ρ *is the randomness of* PSim. *Note that a query* query *such that* $\mathsf{Adml}(t^*, \mathsf{query}) = \bot$ *is not allowed in the selective security game of* Σ. *In particular,* OSim

  – *is described as a stateless randomized algorithm.*
  – *does not have any oracle access.*

Challenge simulation *Let* ρ *be the randomness used by* PSim. R *does all the steps from (1) to (5) in the selective reduction above and can simulate the challenge answer for the challenge query from* $\mathcal{A}$. *That is, there exists a challenge simulation algorithm* CSim *such that in the selective game above, if* $\pi_0 \leftarrow \mathsf{PSample}_0(1^\lambda)$, *then* R *perfectly simulates* $\mathsf{Exp}_{\mathcal{A},\Sigma}^{\mathsf{d\text{-}goal\text{-}atk}}(\lambda, \mathsf{coin})$ *and it holds that*

$$\mathsf{CSim}(\pi_0, \rho, t^*, \mathsf{challenge}, \mathsf{coin}) \overset{\mathsf{p}}{\approx} \mathcal{C}_{\mathsf{a}}(\mathsf{PP}, t^*, \mathsf{challenge}, \mathsf{coin}).$$

In addition, if $\pi_1 \leftarrow \mathsf{PSample}_1(1^\lambda)$, *then the output of* $\mathsf{CSim}(\pi_1, \rho, t^*, \mathsf{challenge}, \mathsf{coin})$ *is a valid challenge answer, but independent of* coin *and* $\Pr[\mathsf{coin} = \mathsf{coin}^*] = \frac{1}{2}$. *This property immediately implies*

$$\mathsf{Adv}_{\Pi,\mathcal{E}\leftrightarrow\mathsf{R}}^{\mathsf{DA}}(\lambda) \geq \frac{1}{2}\mathsf{Adv}_{\mathcal{A},\Sigma}^{\mathsf{d\text{-}goal\text{-}atk}}(\lambda).$$

Due to space limitations, we omit the proof.

Answer checkability: *There exists an efficient validity check algorithm* Valid *for* $\mathcal{Q}$ *such that for all* $(\mathsf{PP}, \mathsf{MSK}) \leftarrow \mathsf{PGen}(1^\lambda)$, query $\leftarrow \mathcal{Q}$, answer $\leftarrow \mathcal{O}_{\mathsf{MSK}}(\mathsf{query})$,

$$\Pr[\mathsf{Valid}(\mathsf{PP}, \mathsf{query}, \mathsf{answer}) = \top] = 1 - \mathsf{negl}(\lambda).$$

On the other hand, for all $b \in \{0,1\}$, $\pi \leftarrow \mathsf{PSample}_b(1^\lambda)$, $t^* \in \mathcal{T}$, $\mathsf{PP} \leftarrow \mathsf{PSim}(\pi, t^*; \rho)$, query *such that* $\mathsf{Adml}(t^*, \mathsf{query}) = \bot$,

$$\Pr[\mathsf{Valid}(\mathsf{PP}, \mathsf{query}, \mathsf{OSim}(\pi, \rho, t^*, \mathsf{query})) = \top] \leq \mathsf{negl}(\lambda).$$

Attack substitution: R *can solve a problem* π *if we have a valid answer* answer* $\in \mathcal{P}$ *for* query* $\in \mathcal{Q}$ *such that* $\mathsf{Adml}(t^*, \mathsf{query}^*) = \bot$ *(i.e., inadmissible query) instead of a successful adversary* $\mathcal{A}$ *in the selective reduction. That is, there exists an efficient algorithm* Solve *such that for all* $b \in \{0,1\}$, $\pi \leftarrow \mathsf{PSample}_b(1^\lambda)$, $t^* \in \mathcal{T}$, query* $\in \mathcal{Q}$, answer* $\in \mathcal{P}$ *such that* $\mathsf{Valid}(\mathsf{PP}, \mathsf{query}^*, \mathsf{answer}^*) = \top$ *and* $\mathsf{Adml}(t^*, \mathsf{query}^*) = \bot$, *we have that* $\mathsf{Solve}(\pi, \rho, t^*, \mathsf{query}^*, \mathsf{answer}^*)$ *outputs* sol *for* π *and*

$$\mathsf{Adv}^{\mathsf{DA}}_{\Pi, \mathcal{E} \leftrightarrow \mathsf{R}}(\lambda) > \mathsf{negl}(\lambda),$$

where ρ *is the randomnesses to sample* PP *in the selective reduction.*

Problem instance simulation: *We can perfectly simulate a problem instance and randomness used to generate* PP *in* PSim *if we have a master secret key of* Σ. *That is, there exists an efficient algorithm* MSKtoP *such that for all* $(\mathsf{PP}, \mathsf{MSK}) \leftarrow \mathsf{PGen}(1^\lambda)$, $\pi \leftarrow \mathsf{PSample}_0(1^\lambda)$, *all* $\rho \leftarrow \mathcal{R}_{\mathsf{PSim}}$, *and all* $t^* \in \mathcal{T}$,

$$(\pi', \rho', \mathsf{PP}) \overset{\mathsf{p}}{\approx} (\pi, \rho, \mathsf{PP}'),$$

where $(\pi', \rho') \leftarrow \mathsf{MSKtoP}(1^\lambda, \mathsf{MSK}, t^*)$, $\mathsf{PP}' = \mathsf{PSim}(\pi, t^*; \rho)$, ρ' *is a randomness to simulate* PP *via* PSim, *and* $\mathcal{R}_{\mathsf{PSim}}$ *is the randomness space of* PSim. *We can relax this condition to statistical indistinguishability for uniformly random* t^* *(instead of all* $t^* \in \mathcal{T}$*).*

On Canonical Property. As we can see in concrete examples (not only) in Sects. 4.3 and 4.5 (but also in many works), well-known selectively secure schemes have canonical ABO reductions. If a scheme has a reduction that must interact with the challenger in an assumption to simulate $\mathcal{O}_{\mathsf{MSK}}$, then the reduction is not canonical. Interestingly, even if a reduction is allowed to interact with the challenger, the reduction could be canonical *as long as the reduction does not need the interaction for* simulating $\mathcal{O}_{\mathsf{MSK}}$. More specifically, a canonical reduction is allowed to interact with the challenger in the assumption to *simulate a challenge answer*. See the full version for such an example.

Due to space limitations, we omit the general definition of canonical ABO reductions that also captures the TBE case.

Table 4 shows concrete example of spaces and oracles for various cryptographic primitives.

On Validity Check Algorithm. The validity check algorithm in Definition 4.3 verifies that a value in $\mathcal{P}$ is a correct value for input query $\in \mathcal{Q}$. Let $\rho_{\mathsf{mka}} \leftarrow \mathcal{R}_{\mathsf{mka}}$ and answer $= C(\mathsf{query}, \rho_{\mathsf{mka}})$. Then, Valid is described as follows.

$$\mathsf{Valid}(\mathsf{PP}, \mathsf{query}, \rho_q, \mathsf{answer}) := \mathsf{Valid\text{-}Out}(\mathsf{PP}, \mathsf{str}, C(\mathsf{str}, \rho_{\mathsf{mka}})) \quad \mathsf{SIG}/\mathsf{IBE}/\mathsf{ABE}$$

4.3 Concrete Examples

First, we list the references of well-known schemes that fall into the class of canonical ABO reductions [2,3,6,9–11,13,15,20,21,25,31,34,40,43]. Note that this is not the exhaustive list.

Table 4. Concrete sets, oracle, and admissible condition of ABO reductions for encryption.

ABO reduction	tag-based PKE	IBE	KP-ABE
$\mathcal{T}$	tag space $\mathcal{TAG}$	identity space $\mathcal{ID}$	attribute space $\mathcal{ATT}$
$\mathcal{Q}$	tag space $\mathcal{TAG}$	identity space $\mathcal{ID}$	policy space $\mathcal{POL}$
$\mathcal{P}$	plaintext space $\mathcal{PT} \cup \{\bot\}$	secret key space $\mathcal{SK}$	secret key space $\mathcal{SK}$
$\mathcal{H}$	plaintext space $\mathcal{PT}^2$	plaintext space $\mathcal{PT}^2$	plaintext space $\mathcal{PT}^2$
$\mathcal{I}$	$\mathcal{TAG} \times \mathcal{CT}$	$\mathcal{CT}$	$\mathcal{CT}$
$\mathcal{O}_{\mathsf{MSK}}$	dec oracle $\mathsf{Dec}(dk, \cdot)$	key oracle $\mathsf{KeyGen}(\mathsf{MSK}, \cdot)$	key oracle $\mathsf{KeyGen}(\mathsf{MSK}, \cdot)$
$\mathsf{Adml}(\cdot, \cdot) = \top$	$t^* \neq t$	$t^* \neq \mathsf{id}$	$\mathsf{P}(t^*) = \bot$

Next, we present concrete examples by picking up well-known selectively secure schemes. We often omit parameters if it is clear from the context.

Example 4.1 (Boneh-Boyen IBE). The Boneh-Boyen IBE scheme BB consists of the following algorithms.

$\mathsf{Setup}(1^\lambda)$:
- Generate params $:= (p, \mathbb{G}, \mathbb{G}_T, e, G) \leftarrow \mathcal{G}_{\mathsf{bmp}}(1^\lambda)$.
- Choose $x, y \leftarrow \mathbb{Z}_p$ and $h \leftarrow \mathbb{Z}_p$ and set $G_1 := G^x, G_2 := G^y, H := G^h$.
- Output $\mathsf{MPK} := (\mathsf{params}, G, G_1, G_2, H)$ and $\mathsf{MSK} := (\mathsf{MPK}, x, y, h)$.

$\mathsf{KeyGen}(\mathsf{MSK}, \mathsf{id})$:
- For $\mathsf{id} \in \mathbb{Z}_p$, choose $r \leftarrow \mathbb{Z}_p$ and output $\mathsf{SK}_{\mathsf{id}} := (G_2^x(G_1^{\mathsf{id}} \cdot H)^r, G^r)$.

$\mathsf{Enc}(\mathsf{MPK}, m)$:
- For $M \in \mathbb{G}_T$, choose $s \leftarrow \mathbb{Z}_p$ and output $\mathsf{CT} := (e(G_1, G_2)^s \cdot M, G^s, (G_1^{\mathsf{id}} \cdot H)^s)$.

$\mathsf{Dec}(\mathsf{SK}_{\mathsf{id}}, \mathsf{CT})$:
- Parse $\mathsf{sk}_{\mathsf{id}} = (D_1, D_2)$ and $\mathsf{CT} = (C_0, C_1, C_2)$, output $C_0 \cdot e(C_2, D_2) \cdot e(C_1, D_1)^{-1}$.

The reduction algorithm R of BB IBE scheme consists of three algorithms $(\mathsf{PSim}, \mathsf{OSim}, \mathsf{CSim})$. Below, we let $\pi := (G, G^x, G^y, G^z, T)$, $t^* := \mathsf{id}^*$, query $:= \mathsf{id}_i$, $\overline{\mathsf{query}} := \bot$, $\rho_{\mathsf{q}} := \bot$, challenge $:= (M_0, M_1)$, be a DBDH instance, the target identity, a query to the key generation oracle, a sub-query, the randomness to sample $\overline{\mathsf{query}} \in \overline{\mathcal{Q}}_{\mathsf{aux}}$, the challenge messages, respectively.

$\mathsf{PSim}(\pi, t^*)$: This algorithm is given a DBDH instance π and a target identity $t^* = \mathsf{id}^*$ and simulate MPK. It chooses $\beta \leftarrow \mathbb{Z}_p$, sets $G_1 := G^x$, $G_2 := G^y$, and $H := G_1^{-\mathsf{id}^*} \cdot G^\beta$, and outputs $\mathsf{MPK} := (G, G_1, G_2, H)$. The randomness ρ of this algorithm is $\rho := \beta$

$\mathsf{OSim}(\pi, \rho, t^*, \mathsf{query})$: This algorithms simulate secret keys for identity query $= \mathsf{id}_i \in \mathbb{Z}_p$ such that $\mathsf{id}_i \neq \mathsf{id}^* = t^*$. It parses $\rho = \beta$, chooses $r \leftarrow \mathbb{Z}_p$ and outputs $\mathsf{SK}_{\mathsf{id}_i} = (D_1, D_2)$ where

$$D_1 := G_2^{\frac{-\beta}{\mathsf{id}_i - \mathsf{id}^*}}(G_1^{\mathsf{id}_i} H)^r, \quad D_2 := G_2^{\frac{-1}{\mathsf{id}_i - \mathsf{id}^*}} G^r.$$

The randomness ρ_{o} of this algorithm is $\rho_{\mathsf{o}} = r$.

CSim$(\pi, \rho, t^*, \mathsf{challenge}, \mathsf{coin})$: This algorithms simulate a challenge ciphertext for challenge $= (M_0, M_1)$ under identity $t^* = \mathsf{id}^*$. It parses $\rho = \beta$ and outputs

$$\mathsf{CT}^* := (M_{\mathsf{coin}} \cdot T, G^z, (G^z)^{\beta}).$$

The auxiliary ABO reduction algorithms of BB IBE scheme consists of three algorithms (Valid, Solve, MSKtoP).

Valid$(\mathsf{MPK}, \mathsf{query}, \rho_{\mathsf{q}}, \mathsf{answer})$: This algorithm parses $\mathsf{MPK} = (G, G_1, G_2, H)$, query $= (\mathsf{id}, \bot)$, $\rho_{\mathsf{q}} = \bot$, and answer $= (D_1, D_2)$ (this is secret key $\mathsf{SK}_{\mathsf{id}}$ for identity id) and checks

$$e(G, D_1) = e(G_1, G_2) \cdot e(G_1^{\mathsf{id}} H, D_2). \tag{1}$$

If it holds, then output $\top$. Otherwise, outputs $\bot$.

Solve$(\pi, \rho, t^*, \mathsf{query}^*, \rho_{\mathsf{q}}, \mathsf{answer}^*)$: First, this algorithm parses $\mathsf{id}^* = t^*$, query$^* = (\mathsf{id}^*, \bot)$, $\rho = \beta$, and $\rho_{\mathsf{q}} = \bot$. It chooses M_0, M_1 and coin $\leftarrow \{0, 1\}$ and computes

$$\mathsf{CT}^* := (M_{\mathsf{coin}} \cdot T, G^z, (G^z)^{\beta}).$$

(this is the same as the output of CSim$(\pi, \rho, t^*, \mathsf{challenge}, \mathsf{coin})$). Then, it parses answer$^* = (G_2^x (G_1^{\mathsf{id}^*} H)^r, G^r)$ and decrypts CT^* by using $(G_2^x (G_1^{\mathsf{id}^*} H)^r, G^r)$. If it obtains M_{coin}, then outputs 0, otherwise 1.

MSKtoP$(1^\lambda, \mathsf{MSK}, t^*)$: First, this algorithms parses $\mathsf{MSK} = (\mathsf{MPK}, x, y, h)$, chooses $z \leftarrow \mathbb{Z}_p$, and computes $\beta := x \cdot \mathsf{id}^* + h$. Then, it outputs $\pi := (G, G^x, G^y, G^z, e(G, G)^{xyz})$ and $\rho' := \beta = x \cdot \mathsf{id}^* + h$.

Theorem 4.1. *Boneh-Boyen IBE scheme has a canocanil ABO reduction to the DBDH problem.*

Due to space limitations, we omit the proof.

4.4   All-But-N Reductions

We can extend canonical ABO reductions to canonical all-but-N (ABN) reductions. Here, N is an a-priori bounded/unbounded polynomial of the security parameter. Roughly speaking, a canonical ABN reduction punctures N points $t^* = (t_1^*, \dots, t_N^*) \in \mathcal{T}^N$ in a master secret-key based algorithm MSKAlg instead of a single point t^*.

We omit the definition due to space limitations. Basically, we simply replace a single point t^* with N points $t^* = (t_1^*, \dots, t_N^*)$ and require Adml$(t_i^*, \mathsf{query}) = \top$ for all $i \in [N]$ for admissible queries. See the full version for details.

4.5   Concrete Examples of Canonical ABN Reductions

It is easy to extend ABO reductions to ABN reductions for pairing-based schemes by using (weak) programmable hash functions [26, 27]. Due to space limitations, we omit details. We can obtain the modified Boneh-Boyen IBE scheme, which has a canonical all-but-N reduction, by using programmable hash $H_w(X) := \prod_{i=0}^{n} H_i^{X^i}$ where the hash key is $(H_0, H_1, \ldots, H_N)$ instead of the Boneh-Boyen hash function $H_{BB}(X) := G_1^X H$ where the hash key is (G_1, H).

The rough idea is as follows. The ABN reduction is given a DBDH instance $\pi = (G, G^x, G^y, G^z, T)$ and target identities $t^* = id^* = (id_1^*, \ldots, id_N^*)$, and simulates MPK. It chooses $id_0^* \leftarrow \mathbb{Z}_p$ and $(\beta_0, \ldots, \beta_N) \leftarrow \mathbb{Z}_p^{N+1}$, and computes $(\alpha_0, \ldots, \alpha_N)$ such that $\sum_{i=0}^{N} \alpha_i \cdot t^i = \prod_{i=0}^{N}(t - id_i^*) \in \mathbb{Z}_p[t]$. Then, it sets $G_1 := G^x$, $G_2 := G^y$, and $H_i := G_1^{\alpha_i} \cdot G^{\beta_i}$, and outputs MPK $:= (G, G^x, G_2, H_0, \ldots, H_N)$. By this parameter setting, we can implement canonical ABN reductions in a similar way to the ABO reduction of Boneh-Boyen IBE. See the full version for detail.

5 Message-Less Watermarking via Canonical ABO-reductions

In this section, we present a message-less watermarking scheme from all-but-one reductions. We focus on using canonical ABO reductions for the decisional case. It is easy to adapt that for the computational case, so we omit it.

First, we present our watermarking scheme $WM_\Sigma = (WMSetup, Mark, Extract)$ for Σ. Let MSK be a master secret-key generated by the setup algorithm of Σ. WM_Σ is a public mark and public extraction scheme. Thus, we do not need watermarking secret-key wsk.

WMSetup(1^λ):
  – Choose $t^* \leftarrow \mathcal{T}$ and output wpp $:= t^*$.
Mark(wpp, MSK):
  – Read MSK and generate $(\pi', \rho') \leftarrow MSKtoP(1^\lambda, MSK, t^*)$.
  – Generate a circuit $\widetilde{f_\Sigma}[\pi', \rho', t^*]$ described in Fig. 3.
Extract(wpp, PP, C'):
  – Choose query $\leftarrow \mathcal{Q}$ such that $Adml(t^*, query) = \top$.
  – Sample $\rho_o \leftarrow \mathcal{R}_{mka}$ and compute answer $\leftarrow C'(query, \rho_o)$.
  – Check $Valid(PP, query, answer) \stackrel{?}{=} \top$. If the equation holds, then output unmarked. Otherwise, marked.

Marked master secret-key $\widetilde{f_\Sigma}[\pi', \rho', t^*]$

Hardwired: π', ρ', t^*.
Input: An input query $\in \mathcal{Q}$ to MSKAlg and randomness $\rho_o \in \mathcal{R}_{mka}$.
Procedure: Compute and output answer $\leftarrow OSim(\pi', \rho', t^*, query; \rho_o)$.

Fig. 3. The description of $\widetilde{f_\Sigma}$

Remark 5.1. Even a useless circuit that outputs $\perp$ for all inputs is marked in the watermarking scheme above since $\mathsf{Valid}(\mathsf{PP}, \mathsf{query}, \rho_\mathsf{q}, \perp) = \perp$ for any PP, query, and ρ_q. To prevent this trivial watermarking, we need to check whether a circuit is similar to a master secret-key based algorithm whose corresponding master public parameter is PP. Although we omit this checking procedure for simplicity here (our final goal is achieving message-embedding schemes), we present test algorithms for this check in Sect. 6.

Theorem 5.1. *Let Σ be a master secret-key based scheme with $(\mathcal{T}, \mathcal{Q}, \mathcal{P}, \mathcal{R}_\mathsf{mka})$ associated with sub-query space $\mathcal{Q}_\mathsf{t}$, aux-query space $\mathcal{Q}_\mathsf{aux}$, challenge space $\mathcal{H}$, challenge answer space $\mathcal{I}$, and admissible condition AdmI. If Σ has a canonical all-but-one reduction to a hard problem Π, then there exists a message-less watermarking scheme WM_Σ for master secret-keys of Σ and WM satisfies Definition 3.5 with parameter $\epsilon = 1/\mathrm{poly}(\lambda)$ under the assumption that Π is hard.*

The intuition of security is that adversaries cannot recover the functionality of $\mathsf{MSKAlg}(\mathsf{MSK}, \cdot)$ for input t^* from the oracle simulation algorithm OSim since OSim is punctured at t^* (explained in Sect. 1.3). Due to space limitations, we omit the proof.

6   Message-Embedding Watermarking via Canonical ABN-reductions

In this section, we present a message-embedding watermarking scheme from canonical all-but-N reductions.

6.1   How to Test Circuit Similarity

Before we describe our message-embedding watermarking scheme, we present how to test a circuit is similar to the original circuit to be watermarked.

Test Circuits by Master Public Parameters. We define test algorithms Test described in Fig. 4 to verify that a circuit C' is close to a master secret-key based algorithm whose master secret key is MSK that corresponds to a master public parameter PP. We have two versions of Test since there are a few differences between one for signature/IBE/ABE/IPE/PE and one for TBE. However, we omit that of TBE due to space limitations. We set parameters $0 < \epsilon_1 < \epsilon_2 < 1/2$ where $\epsilon_2 - \epsilon_1 > 1/\mathrm{poly}(\lambda)$.

Theorem 6.1. *Assume that $0 < \epsilon_1 < \epsilon_2 < 1/2$ where $\epsilon_2 - \epsilon_1 > 1/\mathrm{poly}(\lambda)$. For all $(\mathsf{PP}, \mathsf{MSK}) \leftarrow \mathsf{PGen}(1^\lambda)$,*

- *For all $C'(\cdot, \cdot) \cong_{\epsilon_1} \mathsf{MSKAlg}(\mathsf{MSK}, \cdot; \cdot)$, $\Pr[\mathsf{Test}(\mathsf{PP}, C') = \top] \geq 1 - \mathsf{negl}(\lambda)$.*
- *For all $C'(\cdot, \cdot) \ncong_{\epsilon_2} \mathsf{MSKAlg}(\mathsf{MSK}, \cdot; \cdot)$, $\Pr[\mathsf{Test}(\mathsf{PP}, C') = \top] \leq \mathsf{negl}(\lambda)$.*

We omit the proof due to space limitations.

By the theorem, we can verify whether $C'(\cdot, \cdot) \cong_{\epsilon_1} \mathsf{MSKAlg}(\mathsf{MSK}, \cdot; \cdot)$ or not if $\epsilon_1 = 1/2 - 1/\mathrm{poly}(\lambda)$. That is, if the adversary $\mathcal{A}$ in ϵ-unremovability game is ϵ-admissible where $\epsilon = 1/2 + 1/\mathrm{poly}(\lambda)$, then the circuit C^* output by $\mathcal{A}$ passes the test.

> **Inputs:** A public parameter PP and a circuit C'.
> **Parameters:** $\delta := (\epsilon_2 - \epsilon_1)/2$, $S := \lambda/\delta^2$, $\epsilon := (\epsilon_1 + \epsilon_2)/2$.
>
> Set $\mathsf{cnt} := 0$. For $i = 1, \ldots, S$, do
>
> 1. Choose $z_i \leftarrow \mathcal{Q}$ and $\rho_i \leftarrow \mathcal{R}_{\mathsf{mka}}$.
> 2. If $\mathsf{Valid\text{-}Out}(\mathsf{PP}, z_i, C'(z_i, \rho_i)) = \bot$, then sets $\mathsf{cnt} := \mathsf{cnt} + 1$.
>
> If $\mathsf{cnt} \leq \epsilon S$, then output $\top$. Otherwise $\bot$.

Fig. 4. Test algorithm Test for IBE or signature

6.2 Message-Embedding Scheme

We present our message-embedding watermarking scheme $\mathsf{msWM}_\Sigma = (\mathsf{WMSetup}, \mathsf{Mark}, \mathsf{Extract})$ for Σ. We consider none of ABE, IPE, and PE for the message-embedding scheme since we do not have (canonical) ABN reductions of them. Thus, $\mathcal{T} = \mathcal{Q}_t$ in the rest of this section. Note that we implicitly assume that the master secret key MSK of Σ includes the corresponding public parameter PP. We use a PRF $(\mathsf{PRF.Gen}, \mathsf{PRF.Eval})$ such that $\mathsf{PRF.Eval}(\mathsf{K}, \cdot) : \{0,1\}^{|\mathsf{PP}|} \times [\ell] \times \{0,1\} \to \mathcal{T}^T$. We show only for the decisional case, but it is easy to adapt to the computational case.

$\mathsf{WMSetup}(1^\lambda)$:
  - Let $T := \lambda$.
  - Generate $\mathsf{K} \leftarrow \mathsf{PRF.Gen}(1^\lambda)$ and set $\mathsf{wpp} := \bot$ and $\mathsf{wsk} := \mathsf{K}$. We omit wpp hereafter since it is $\bot$.

$\mathsf{Mark}(\mathsf{wsk}, \mathsf{MSK}, \omega)$:
  - Compute $\boldsymbol{t}_i = (t_i^{(1)}, \ldots, t_i^{(T)}) \leftarrow \mathsf{PRF.Eval}(\mathsf{K}, (\mathsf{PP}, i, \omega_i))$ for $i \in [\ell]$ and set $\boldsymbol{t}_\omega := \{\boldsymbol{t}_i\}_{i \in [\ell]}$.
  - Read MSK and generate $(\pi', \rho') \leftarrow \mathsf{MSKtoP}(1^\lambda, \mathsf{MSK}, \boldsymbol{t}_\omega)$.
  - Generate a circuit $\widetilde{f_\Sigma}[\pi', \rho', \boldsymbol{t}_\omega]$ described in Fig. 5.

$\mathsf{Extract}(\mathsf{wsk}, \mathsf{PP}, C')$:
  - Compute $b_{\mathsf{PP}} \leftarrow \mathsf{Test}(\mathsf{PP}, C')$. If $b_{\mathsf{PP}} = \bot$, then output $\mathtt{Invalid\text{-}Key}$ and halt. Otherwise, do the following steps.
  - Compute $\widetilde{\boldsymbol{t}}_{i,b} = (\widetilde{t}_{i,b}^{(1)}, \ldots, \widetilde{t}_{i,b}^{(T)}) \leftarrow \mathsf{PRF.Eval}(\mathsf{K}, (\mathsf{PP}, i, b))$ for $i \in [\ell]$ and $b \in \{0,1\}$.
  - For $i \in [\ell]$, $b \in \{0,1\}$, set $\mathsf{query}_{i,b}^{(j)} := \widetilde{t}_{i,b}^{(j)}$, compute $\mathsf{answer}_{i,b}^{(j)} \leftarrow C'(\mathsf{query}_{i,b}^{(j)}, \rho_{\mathsf{o},j})$. Let $\widehat{N}_{i,b}$ be the number of indices $j \in [T]$ such that $\mathsf{Valid}(\mathsf{PP}, \mathsf{query}_{i,b}^{(j)}, \mathsf{answer}_{i,b}^{(j)}) = \bot$.
    - If there exists an index $i \in [\ell]$ where $\widehat{N}_{i,0}, \widehat{N}_{i,1} < T$ or $\widehat{N}_{i,0} = \widehat{N}_{i,1} = T$, then output $\bot$.
    - Otherwise, for each $i \in [\ell]$, let $\omega_i' \in \{0,1\}$ be the unique bit where $\widehat{N}_{i,\omega_i'} = T \wedge \widehat{N}_{i,1-\omega_i'} < T$ and output $\omega' := \omega_1' \ldots \omega_\ell'$.

Marked master secret-key $\widetilde{f}_\Sigma[\pi', \rho', t_\omega]$

Hardwired: π', ρ', t_ω.

Input: An input query $\in \mathcal{Q}$ to MSKAlg and randomness $\rho_o \in \mathcal{R}_{\mathsf{mka}}$.

Procedure: Compute and output answer $\leftarrow$ OSim(π', ρ', t_ω, query; ρ_o).

Fig. 5. The description of $\widetilde{f}_\Sigma$

Theorem 6.2. *Let Σ be a master secret-key based scheme with $(\mathcal{T}, \mathcal{Q}, \mathcal{P}, \mathcal{R}_{\mathsf{mka}})$ associated with challenge space $\mathcal{H}$, challenge answer space $\mathcal{I}$, and admissible condition AdmI. If Σ has a canonical all-but-N reduction to a hard problem Π and PRF is a PRF where $N = \ell\lambda$, then there exists a message-embedding watermarking scheme msWM_Σ for master secret keys of Σ and msWM_Σ satisfies Definition 3.5 with parameter $\epsilon = 1/2 + 1/\mathrm{poly}(\lambda)$ under the assumption that Π is hard.*

Due to space limitations, we omit the proof.

Acknowledgments. The author would like to thank Fuyuki Kitagawa for valuable discussion and insightful comments on watermarking. The author also thanks Shuichi Katsumata and Shota Yamada for answering questions about lattices and programmable hash functions, and TCC 2020 reviewers for very constructive comments on the presentation.

References

1. Agrawal, S., Boneh, D., Boyen, X.: Efficient lattice (H)IBE in the standard model. In: Gilbert, H. (ed.) EUROCRYPT 2010. LNCS, vol. 6110, pp. 553–572. Springer, Heidelberg (2010). https://doi.org/10.1007/978-3-642-13190-5_28
2. Agrawal, S., Boyen, X., Vaikuntanathan, V., Voulgaris, P., Wee, H.: Functional encryption for threshold functions (or Fuzzy IBE) from lattices. In: Fischlin, M., Buchmann, J., Manulis, M. (eds.) PKC 2012. LNCS, vol. 7293, pp. 280–297. Springer, Heidelberg (2012). https://doi.org/10.1007/978-3-642-30057-8_17
3. Agrawal, S., Freeman, D.M., Vaikuntanathan, V.: Functional encryption for inner product predicates from learning with errors. In: Lee, D.H., Wang, X. (eds.) ASIACRYPT 2011. LNCS, vol. 7073, pp. 21–40. Springer, Heidelberg (2011). https://doi.org/10.1007/978-3-642-25385-0_2
4. Ananth, P., Vaikuntanathan, V.: Optimal bounded-collusion secure functional encryption. In: Hofheinz, D., Rosen, A. (eds.) TCC 2019, Part I. LNCS, vol. 11891, pp. 174–198. Springer, Cham (2019). https://doi.org/10.1007/978-3-030-36030-6_8
5. Attrapadung, N., Hanaoka, G., Yamada, S.: New security proof for the Boneh-Boyen IBE: tight reduction in unbounded multi-challenge security. In: Hui, L.C.K., Qing, S.H., Shi, E., Yiu, S.M. (eds.) ICICS 2014. LNCS, vol. 8958, pp. 176–190. Springer, Cham (2015). https://doi.org/10.1007/978-3-319-21966-0_13

6. Attrapadung, N., Libert, B.: Functional encryption for inner product: achieving constant-size ciphertexts with adaptive security or support for negation. In: Nguyen, P.Q., Pointcheval, D. (eds.) PKC 2010. LNCS, vol. 6056, pp. 384–402. Springer, Heidelberg (2010). https://doi.org/10.1007/978-3-642-13013-7_23

7. Baldimtsi, F., Kiayias, A., Samari, K.: Watermarking public-key cryptographic functionalities and implementations. In: Nguyen, P., Zhou, J. (eds.) ISC 2017. LNCS, vol. 10599, pp. 173–191. Springer, Cham (2017). https://doi.org/10.1007/978-3-319-69659-1_10

8. Barak, B., et al.: On the (im)possibility of obfuscating programs. J. ACM 59(2), 6 (2012)

9. Boneh, D., Boyen, X.: Efficient selective identity-based encryption without random oracles. J. Cryptol. 24(4), 659–693 (2011). https://doi.org/10.1007/s00145-010-9078-6

10. Boneh, D., et al.: Fully key-homomorphic encryption, arithmetic circuit ABE and compact garbled circuits. In: Nguyen, P.Q., Oswald, E. (eds.) EUROCRYPT 2014. LNCS, vol. 8441, pp. 533–556. Springer, Heidelberg (2014). https://doi.org/10.1007/978-3-642-55220-5_30

11. Boneh, D., Hamburg, M.: Generalized identity based and broadcast encryption schemes. In: Pieprzyk, J. (ed.) ASIACRYPT 2008. LNCS, vol. 5350, pp. 455–470. Springer, Heidelberg (2008). https://doi.org/10.1007/978-3-540-89255-7_28

12. Boneh, D., Lewi, K., Wu, D.J.: Constraining pseudorandom functions privately. In: Fehr, S. (ed.) PKC 2017. LNCS, vol. 10175, pp. 494–524. Springer, Heidelberg (2017). https://doi.org/10.1007/978-3-662-54388-7_17

13. Boyen, X., Mei, Q., Waters, B.: Direct chosen ciphertext security from identity-based techniques. In: ACM CCS (2005)

14. Boneh, D., Sahai, A., Waters, B.: Fully collusion resistant traitor tracing with short ciphertexts and private keys. In: Vaudenay, S. (ed.) EUROCRYPT 2006. LNCS, vol. 4004, pp. 573–592. Springer, Heidelberg (2006). https://doi.org/10.1007/11761679_34

15. Cash, D., Hofheinz, D., Kiltz, E., Peikert, C.: Bonsai trees, or how to delegate a lattice basis. J. Cryptol. 25(4), 601–639 (2012). https://doi.org/10.1007/s00145-011-9105-2

16. Chen, J., Lim, H., Ling, S., Wang, H., Wee, H.: Shorter identity-based encryption via asymmetric pairings. Des. Codes Cryptogr. 73(3), 911–947 (2014). https://doi.org/10.1007/s10623-013-9834-3

17. Chor, B., Fiat, A., Naor, M.: Tracing traitors. In: Desmedt, Y.G. (ed.) CRYPTO 1994. LNCS, vol. 839, pp. 257–270. Springer, Heidelberg (1994). https://doi.org/10.1007/3-540-48658-5_25

18. Cohen, A., Holmgren, J., Nishimaki, R., Vaikuntanathan, V., Wichs, D.: Watermarking cryptographic capabilities. Cryptology ePrint Archive, Report 2015/1096

19. Cohen, A., Holmgren, J., Nishimaki, R., Vaikuntanathan, V., Wichs, D.: Watermarking cryptographic capabilities. SIAM J. Comput. 47(6), 2157–2202 (2018)

20. Gorbunov, S., Vaikuntanathan, V., Wee, H.: Attribute-based encryption for circuits. J. ACM 62(6), 45:1–45:33 (2015)

21. Gorbunov, S., Vaikuntanathan, V., Wee, H.: Predicate encryption for circuits from LWE. In: Gennaro, R., Robshaw, M. (eds.) CRYPTO 2015. LNCS, vol. 9216, pp. 503–523. Springer, Heidelberg (2015). https://doi.org/10.1007/978-3-662-48000-7_25

22. Goyal, R., Kim, S., Manohar, N., Waters, B., Wu, D.J.: Watermarking public-key cryptographic primitives. In: Boldyreva, A., Micciancio, D. (eds.) CRYPTO 2019.

LNCS, vol. 11694, pp. 367–398. Springer, Cham (2019). https://doi.org/10.1007/978-3-030-26954-8_12

23. Goyal, R., Koppula, V., Waters, B.: Collusion resistant traitor tracing from learning with errors. In:50th ACM STOC (2018)

24. Goyal, R., Koppula, V., Waters, B.: New approaches to traitor tracing with embedded identities. In: Hofheinz, D., Rosen, A. (eds.) TCC 2019. LNCS, vol. 11892, pp. 149–179. Springer, Cham (2019). https://doi.org/10.1007/978-3-030-36033-7_6

25. Goyal, V., Pandey, O., Sahai, A., Waters, B.: Attribute-based encryption for fine-grained access control of encrypted data. In: ACM CCS (2006)

26. Hofheinz, D., Jager, T., Kiltz, E.: Short signatures from weaker assumptions. In: Lee, D.H., Wang, X. (eds.) ASIACRYPT 2011. LNCS, vol. 7073, pp. 647–666. Springer, Heidelberg (2011). https://doi.org/10.1007/978-3-642-25385-0_35

27. Hofheinz, D., Kiltz, E.: Programmable hash functions and their applications. J. Cryptol. **25**(3), 484–527 (2012). https://doi.org/10.1007/s00145-011-9102-5

28. Hopper, N., Molnar, D., Wagner, D.: From weak to strong watermarking. In: Vadhan, S.P. (ed.) TCC 2007. LNCS, vol. 4392, pp. 362–382. Springer, Heidelberg (2007). https://doi.org/10.1007/978-3-540-70936-7_20

29. Katsumata, S., Nishimaki, R., Yamada, S., Yamakawa, T.: Designated verifier/prover and preprocessing NIZKs from Diffie-Hellman assumptions. In: Ishai, Y., Rijmen, V. (eds.) EUROCRYPT 2019. LNCS, vol. 11477, pp. 622–651. Springer, Cham (2019). https://doi.org/10.1007/978-3-030-17656-3_22

30. Katsumata, S., Nishimaki, R., Yamada, S., Yamakawa, T.: Exploring constructions of compact NIZKs from various assumptions. In: Boldyreva, A., Micciancio, D. (eds.) CRYPTO 2019. LNCS, vol. 11694, pp. 639–669. Springer, Cham (2019). https://doi.org/10.1007/978-3-030-26954-8_21

31. Kiltz, E.: Chosen-ciphertext security from tag-based encryption. In: Halevi, S., Rabin, T. (eds.) TCC 2006. LNCS, vol. 3876, pp. 581–600. Springer, Heidelberg (2006). https://doi.org/10.1007/11681878_30

32. Kim, S., Wu, D.J.: Watermarking cryptographic functionalities from standard lattice assumptions. In: Katz, J., Shacham, H. (eds.) CRYPTO 2017. LNCS, vol. 10401, pp. 503–536. Springer, Cham (2017). https://doi.org/10.1007/978-3-319-63688-7_17

33. Kim, S., Wu, D.J.: Watermarking PRFs from lattices: stronger security via extractable PRFs. In: Boldyreva, A., Micciancio, D. (eds.) CRYPTO 2019. LNCS, vol. 11694, pp. 335–366. Springer, Cham (2019). https://doi.org/10.1007/978-3-030-26954-8_11

34. Kurosawa, K., Trieu Phong, L.: Leakage resilient IBE and IPE under the DLIN assumption. In: Jacobson, M., Locasto, M., Mohassel, P., Safavi-Naini, R. (eds.) ACNS 2013. LNCS, vol. 7954, pp. 487–501. Springer, Heidelberg (2013). https://doi.org/10.1007/978-3-642-38980-1_31

35. Naccache, D., Shamir, A., Stern, J.P.: How to copyright a function? In: Imai, H., Zheng, Y. (eds.) PKC 1999. LNCS, vol. 1560, pp. 188–196. Springer, Heidelberg (1999). https://doi.org/10.1007/3-540-49162-7_14

36. Nishimaki, R.: How to watermark cryptographic functions by bilinear maps. IEICE Trans. **102–A**(1), 99–113 (2019)

37. Nishimaki, R., Wichs, D., Zhandry, M.: Anonymous traitor tracing: how to embed arbitrary information in a Key. In: Fischlin, M., Coron, J.-S. (eds.) EUROCRYPT 2016. LNCS, vol. 9666, pp. 388–419. Springer, Heidelberg (2016). https://doi.org/10.1007/978-3-662-49896-5_14

38. Quach, W., Wichs, D., Zirdelis, G.: Watermarking PRFs under standard assumptions: public marking and security with extraction queries. In: Beimel, A., Dziembowski, S. (eds.) TCC 2018. LNCS, vol. 11240, pp. 669–698. Springer, Cham (2018). https://doi.org/10.1007/978-3-030-03810-6_24

39. Sahai, A., Waters, B.: How to use indistinguishability obfuscation: deniable encryption, and more. In: 46th ACM STOC (2014)

40. Sahai, A., Waters, B.: Fuzzy identity-based encryption. In: Cramer, R. (ed.) EUROCRYPT 2005. LNCS, vol. 3494, pp. 457–473. Springer, Heidelberg (2005). https://doi.org/10.1007/11426639_27

41. Schnorr, C.: Efficient signature generation by smart cards. J. Cryptol. 4(3), 161–174 (1991). https://doi.org/10.1007/BF00196725

42. Waters, B.: Efficient identity-based encryption without random oracles. In: Cramer, R. (ed.) EUROCRYPT 2005. LNCS, vol. 3494, pp. 114–127. Springer, Heidelberg (2005). https://doi.org/10.1007/11426639_7

43. Waters, B.: Ciphertext-policy attribute-based encryption: an expressive, efficient, and provably secure realization. In: Catalano, D., Fazio, N., Gennaro, R., Nicolosi, A. (eds.) PKC 2011. LNCS, vol. 6571, pp. 53–70. Springer, Heidelberg (2011). https://doi.org/10.1007/978-3-642-19379-8_4

44. Yang, R., Au, M.H., Lai, J., Xu, Q., Yu, Z.: Collusion resistant watermarking schemes for cryptographic functionalities. In: Galbraith, S.D., Moriai, S. (eds.) ASIACRYPT 2019. LNCS, vol. 11921, pp. 371–398. Springer, Cham (2019). https://doi.org/10.1007/978-3-030-34578-5_14

45. Yoshida, M., Fujiwara, T.: Toward digital watermarking for cryptographic data. IEICE Trans. 94–A(1), 270–272 (2011)

Functional Encryption for Quadratic Functions from k-Lin, Revisited

Hoeteck Wee[(✉)]

NTT Research, California, USA
wee@di.ens.fr

Abstract. We present simple and improved constructions of public-key functional encryption (FE) schemes for quadratic functions. Our main results are:
- an FE scheme for quadratic functions with constant-size keys as well as shorter ciphertexts than all prior schemes based on static assumptions;
- a public-key partially-hiding FE that supports NC1 computation on public attributes and quadratic computation on the private message, with ciphertext size independent of the length of the public attribute.

Both constructions achieve selective, simulation-based security against unbounded collusions, and rely on the (bilateral) k-linear assumption in prime-order bilinear groups. At the core of these constructions is a new reduction from FE for quadratic functions to FE for linear functions.

1 Introduction

In this work, we study functional encryption for quadratic functions. That is, we would like to encrypt a message $\mathbf{z}$ to produce a ciphertext ct, and generate secret keys sk_f for quadratic functions f, so that decrypting ct with sk_f returns $f(\mathbf{z})$ while leaking no additional information about $\mathbf{z}$. In addition, we want (i) short ciphertexts that grow linearly with the length of $\mathbf{z}$, as well as (ii) simulation-based security against collusions, so that an adversary holding ct and secret keys for different functions $f_1, f_2, \ldots$ learns nothing about $\mathbf{z}$ beyond the outputs of these functions. Functional encryption for quadratic functions have a number of applications, including traitor-tracing schemes whose ciphertext size is sublinear in the total number of users [5,6,8,11,16]; obfuscation from simple assumptions [4,13,18,19]; as well as privacy-preserving machine learning for neural networks with quadratic activation functions [21].

1.1 Our Results

We present new pairing-based public-key functional encryption (FE) schemes for quadratic functions, improving upon the recent constructions in [5,12,19,20]. Our main results are:

- A FE scheme for quadratic functions with constant-size keys, whose ciphertext size is shorter than those of all prior public-key schemes based on static assumptions [5,12]; moreover, when instantiated over the BLS12-381 curve where $|\mathbb{G}_2| = 2|\mathbb{G}_1|$,

© International Association for Cryptologic Research 2020
R. Pass and K. Pietrzak (Eds.): TCC 2020, LNCS 12550, pp. 210–228, 2020.
https://doi.org/10.1007/978-3-030-64375-1_8

Scheme	|ct|	|sk|	Assumption	Security
BCFG17 [5]	$(6n_1 + 1)\|\mathbb{G}_1\| + (6n_2 + 1)\|\mathbb{G}_2\|$	$\|\mathbb{G}_1\| + \|\mathbb{G}_2\|$	SXDH, 3-PDDH	SEL-IND
RDGBP19 [21]	$(2n_1 + 1)\|\mathbb{G}_1\| + 2n_2\|\mathbb{G}_2\|$	$\|\mathbb{G}_2\|$	GGM	AD-IND
G20 [12]	$(4n_1 + 2n_2 + 2)\|\mathbb{G}_1\| + n_2\|\mathbb{G}_2\|$	$(3n_1 + 2n_2 + 2)\|\mathbb{G}_2\|$	SXDH, bi-2-Lin	SA-SIM
GQ20 [14]	$(2n_1 + 5)\|\mathbb{G}_1\| + (2n_2 + 5)\|\mathbb{G}_2\|$	$5\|\mathbb{G}_1\| + 5\|\mathbb{G}_2\|$	SXDH, bi-2-Lin	SA-SIM
this work	$((k+1)n_1 + kn_2 + k + 1)\|\mathbb{G}_1\| + n_2\|\mathbb{G}_2\|$	$(k+1)\|\mathbb{G}_2\|$	bi-k-Lin, $k > 1$	SA-SIM
	$(2n_1 + 2n_2 + 2)\|\mathbb{G}_1\| + n_2\|\mathbb{G}_2\|$	$2\|\mathbb{G}_2\|$	SXDH, bi-2-Lin	SA-SIM

Fig. 1. Comparison with prior public-key functional encryption schemes for quadratic functions $f : \mathbb{Z}_p^{n_1} \times \mathbb{Z}_p^{n_2} \to \mathbb{Z}_p$, as well as a concurrent work [14]. Note that $\|\mathsf{sk}\|$ ignores the contribution from the function f, which is "public". Here, SXDH = 1-Lin, and bi-k-Lin (bilateral k-Lin) is a strengthening of k-Lin. 3-PDDH asserts that $[abc]_2$ is pseudorandom given $[a]_1, [b]_2, [c]_1, [c]_2$. In bilinear groups where $\|\mathbb{G}\|_2 = 2\|\mathbb{G}_1\|$, we achieve $\|\mathsf{ct}\| = (2n_1 + 4n_2 + 2)\|\mathbb{G}_1\|$ under SXDH, bi 2-Lin, almost matching $\|\mathsf{ct}\| = (2n_1 + 4n_2 + 1)\|\mathbb{G}_1\|$ in RDGBP19.

our ciphertext size basically matches that of the most efficient scheme in the generic group model [21] (see Fig. 1).

- A partially-hiding FE that supports NC1 computation on public attributes $\mathbf{x}$ and quadratic computation on the private message $\mathbf{z}$; moreover, the ciphertext size grows linearly with $\mathbf{z}$ and independent of $\mathbf{x}$. The previous constructions in [13,19] have ciphertext sizes that grow linearly with both $\mathbf{z}$ and $\mathbf{x}$.

Both constructions achieve selective[1], simulation-based security against unbounded collusions, and rely on the bilateral k-linear assumption in prime-order bilinear groups.

At the core of these constructions is a new reduction from public-key FE for quadratic functions to that for linear functions. The reduction relies on the (bilateral) k-Lin assumption, and blows up the input size by a factor k. Note that the trivial reduction blows up the input size by $\|\mathbf{z}\|$. Our reduction is simpler and more direct than the previous reductions due to Lin [20] and Gay [12]: (i) we do not require function-hiding FE for linear functions, and (ii) our reduction works directly in the public-key setting. Thanks to (i), we can also decrease the secret key size from linear to constant.

1.2 Technical Overview

We proceed to provide an overview of our constructions. We rely on an asymmetric bilinear group $(\mathbb{G}_1, \mathbb{G}_2, \mathbb{G}_T, e)$ of prime order p where $e : \mathbb{G}_1 \times \mathbb{G}_2 \to \mathbb{G}_T$. We use $[\cdot]_1, [\cdot]_2, [\cdot]_T$ to denote component-wise exponentiations in respective groups $\mathbb{G}_1, \mathbb{G}_2, \mathbb{G}_T$ [10]. We use bold-face lower case to denote row vectors. The k-Lin assumption in $\mathbb{G}_b$ asserts that

$$([\mathbf{A}]_b, [\mathbf{sA}]_b) \approx_c ([\mathbf{A}]_b, [\mathbf{u}]_b), \quad \mathbf{s} \leftarrow \mathbb{Z}_p^k, \mathbf{A} \leftarrow \mathbb{Z}_p^{k \times \ell}, \mathbf{u} \leftarrow \mathbb{Z}_p^\ell, \ell > k$$

The bilateral k-Lin assumption is a strengthening of k-Lin, and asserts that

$$([\mathbf{A}]_1, [\mathbf{sA}]_1, [\mathbf{A}]_2, [\mathbf{sA}]_2) \approx_c ([\mathbf{A}]_1, [\mathbf{u}]_1, [\mathbf{A}]_2, [\mathbf{u}]_2)$$

---

[1] We actually achieve semi-adaptive security [9], a slight strengthening of selective security.

Note that bilateral 1-Lin is false, for the same reason DDH is false in symmetric bilinear groups.

FE for Quadratic Functions. Consider the class of quadratic functions over $\mathbb{Z}_p^n \times \mathbb{Z}_p^n$ given by

$$(\mathbf{z}_1, \mathbf{z}_2) \mapsto (\mathbf{z}_1 \otimes \mathbf{z}_2) \mathbf{f}^\top$$

where $\mathbf{f} \in \mathbb{Z}_p^{n^2}$ is the coefficient vector. We will first mask $\mathbf{z}_1, \mathbf{z}_2$ in the ciphertext using:

$$[\mathbf{s}_1 \mathbf{A}_1 + \mathbf{z}_1]_1, [\mathbf{s}_2 \mathbf{A}_2 + \mathbf{z}_2]_2$$

where the matrices

$$[\mathbf{A}_1]_1, [\mathbf{A}_2]_2, \mathbf{A}_1, \mathbf{A}_2 \leftarrow \mathbb{Z}_p^{k \times n}$$

are specified in the master public key. Next, observe that

$$((\mathbf{s}_1 \mathbf{A}_1 + \mathbf{z}_1) \otimes (\mathbf{s}_2 \mathbf{A}_2 + \mathbf{z}_2)) \cdot \mathbf{f}^\top = (\mathbf{z}_1 \otimes \mathbf{z}_2) \mathbf{f}^\top + \text{cross terms} \qquad (1)$$

Following [12,20], we will express the cross terms as a linear function evaluated on inputs of length $O(kn)$; the key difference in this work is that the linear function can be derived from the master public key and $\mathbf{f}$.

More precisely, we write

$$\underbrace{(\mathbf{s}_1 \mathbf{A}_1 + \mathbf{z}_1)}_{\mathbf{y}_1} \otimes \underbrace{(\mathbf{s}_2 \mathbf{A}_2 + \mathbf{z}_2)}_{\mathbf{y}_2} = (\mathbf{z}_1 \otimes \mathbf{z}_2) + \mathbf{s}_1 \mathbf{A}_1 \otimes \mathbf{z}_2 \qquad\qquad\qquad + \mathbf{y}_1 \otimes \mathbf{s}_2 \mathbf{A}_2$$

$$= (\mathbf{z}_1 \otimes \mathbf{z}_2) + (\mathbf{s}_1 \otimes \mathbf{z}_2) \cdot (\mathbf{A}_1 \otimes \mathbf{I}_n) \qquad + (\mathbf{y}_1 \otimes \mathbf{s}_2) \cdot (\mathbf{I}_n \otimes \mathbf{A}_2)$$

$$= (\mathbf{z}_1 \otimes \mathbf{z}_2) + (\mathbf{s}_1 \otimes \mathbf{z}_2 \| \mathbf{y}_1 \otimes \mathbf{s}_2) \begin{pmatrix} \mathbf{A}_1 \otimes \mathbf{I}_n \\ \mathbf{I}_n \otimes \mathbf{A}_2 \end{pmatrix}$$

where the second equality uses the mixed-product property of the tensor product, which tells us that $(\mathbf{M}_1 \otimes \mathbf{M}_2)(\mathbf{M}_3 \otimes \mathbf{M}_4) = (\mathbf{M}_1 \mathbf{M}_3) \otimes (\mathbf{M}_2 \mathbf{M}_4)$, and $\|$ denotes row vector concatenation. Multiplying both sides on the right by $\mathbf{f}^\top$ and rearranging the terms yields:

$$(\mathbf{z}_1 \otimes \mathbf{z}_2) \mathbf{f}^\top = (\mathbf{y}_1 \otimes \mathbf{y}_2) \mathbf{f}^\top - \boxed{(\mathbf{s}_1 \otimes \mathbf{z}_2 \| \mathbf{y}_1 \otimes \mathbf{s}_2) \mathbf{M} \mathbf{f}^\top} \qquad (2)$$

where $\mathbf{M} := \begin{pmatrix} \mathbf{A}_1 \otimes \mathbf{I}_n \\ \mathbf{I}_n \otimes \mathbf{A}_2 \end{pmatrix}$. As we mentioned earlier, the boxed term (= cross terms in (1))

$$(\mathbf{s}_1 \otimes \mathbf{z}_2 \| \mathbf{y}_1 \otimes \mathbf{s}_2) \cdot \mathbf{M} \mathbf{f}^\top \qquad (3)$$

corresponds to a linear computation where

- the input $(\mathbf{s}_1 \otimes \mathbf{z}_2 \| \mathbf{y}_1 \otimes \mathbf{s}_2)$ has length $O(kn)$;
- the linear function $\mathbf{M} \mathbf{f}^\top$ can be computed given $\mathbf{f}$ and the matrices $\mathbf{A}_1, \mathbf{A}_2$ in the public key.

The latter property pertaining to $\mathbf{M} \mathbf{f}^\top$ is what allows us to significantly simplify the previous reductions in [12,20], since there is nothing "secret" about the linear function $\mathbf{M} \mathbf{f}^\top$. In the prior works, the linear function leaks information about the master secret key beyond what can be computed from the master public key.

In particular, we can use a public-key FE for linear functions (linear FE for short) [1,3,22] to compute (3). That is, we encrypt $[\mathbf{s}_1 \otimes \mathbf{z}_2 \| \mathbf{y}_1 \otimes \mathbf{s}_2]_1$, and generate a secret key for $[\mathbf{M}\mathbf{f}^\top]_2$. The linear FE schemes in [3,22] extend readily to this setting where both the input and function are specified "in the exponent"; moreover, these schemes achieve selective, simulation-based security under the k-Lin assumption, with constant-size secret keys. The linear FE ciphertext would lie in $\mathbb{G}_1$, whereas both $\mathbf{M}$ and the secret key would lie in $\mathbb{G}_2$. Note that in order to compute $[\mathbf{M}]_2$, we would also publish $[\mathbf{A}_1]_2$ in the public key. We present a self-contained description of our quadratic FE in Sect. A.

Security Overview. Security, intuitively, is fairly straight-forward:

- First, observe that $[\mathbf{y}_1]_1, [\mathbf{y}_2]$ leaks no information about $\mathbf{z}_1, \mathbf{z}_2$, thanks to the k-Lin assumption;
- Next, we can simulate the ciphertext and secret key for the linear FE given $(\mathbf{s}_1 \otimes \mathbf{z}_2 \| \mathbf{y}_1 \otimes \mathbf{s}_2)\mathbf{M}\mathbf{f}^\top$, which we can rewrite as $(\mathbf{z}_1 \otimes \mathbf{z}_2)\mathbf{f}^\top - (\mathbf{y}_1 \otimes \mathbf{y}_2)\mathbf{f}^\top$. We can in turn compute the latter given just $\mathbf{y}_1, \mathbf{y}_2$ and the output of the ideal functionality and therefore the linear FE ciphertext-key pair leaks no additional information about $\mathbf{z}_1, \mathbf{z}_2$.

In the reduction, we would need to compute $[\mathbf{y}_1 \otimes \mathbf{y}_2]_2$ in order to simulate the secret key for the linear FE. This is something we can compute given either $\mathbf{y}_1, [\mathbf{y}_2]_2$ or $[\mathbf{y}_1]_2, \mathbf{y}_2$. The latter along with publishing $[\mathbf{A}_1]_2$ in the public key is why we require the bilateral k-Lin assumption. For the most efficient concrete instantiation, we will use the bilateral 2-Lin assumption together with SXDH (i.e., 1-Lin), where we sample $\mathbf{A}_1 \leftarrow \mathbb{Z}_p^{2 \times n}, \mathbf{A}_2 \leftarrow \mathbb{Z}_p^{1 \times n}$. We leave the question of basing quadratic FE solely on the standard k-Lin assumption as an open problem.

Extension to Partially Hiding FE. Our approach extends readily to partially hiding FE (PHFE) for the class

$$(\overbrace{\mathbf{x}}^{\text{public}}, \overbrace{(\mathbf{z}_1, \mathbf{z}_2)}^{\text{private}}) \mapsto (\mathbf{z}_1 \otimes \mathbf{z}_2)f(\mathbf{x})^\top$$

where f captures NC1 –more generally, any arithmetic branching program– computation on the public attribute $\mathbf{x}$ and outputs a vector in $\mathbb{Z}_p^{n^2}$. Note that FE for quadratic functions corresponds to the special case where f is a constant function (independent of $\mathbf{x}$). The idea behind the extension to PHFE is to replace $\mathbf{f}^\top$ in (2) with $f(\mathbf{x})$ (the decryptor can compute $f(\mathbf{x})$ since $\mathbf{x}$ is public), which yields:

$$(\mathbf{z}_1 \otimes \mathbf{z}_2)f(\mathbf{x})^\top = (\mathbf{y}_1 \otimes \mathbf{y}_2)f(\mathbf{x})^\top - \boxed{(\mathbf{s}_1 \otimes \mathbf{z}_2 \| \mathbf{y}_1 \otimes \mathbf{s}_2)\mathbf{M}f(\mathbf{x})^\top}$$

To compute the new boxed term, we will rely on the partially-hiding linear FE scheme in [2] for the class

$$(\overbrace{\mathbf{x}}^{\text{public}}, \overbrace{\mathbf{z}}^{\text{private}}) \mapsto \mathbf{z}f(\mathbf{x})^\top$$

We can augment the construction to take into account the matrix $\mathbf{M}$; some care is needed as the decryption algorithm only gets $[\mathbf{M}]_2$ and not $\mathbf{M}$. In the ensuing scheme as with [2], the ciphertext size grows linearly with the message and independent of $\mathbf{x}$, which we then inherit in our partially-hiding quadratic FE.

2 Preliminaries

Notations. We denote by $s \leftarrow S$ the fact that s is picked uniformly at random from a finite set S. We use $\approx_s$ to denote two distributions being statistically indistinguishable, and $\approx_c$ to denote two distributions being computationally indistinguishable. We use lower case boldface to denote *row* vectors and upper case boldcase to denote matrices. We use $\mathbf{e}_i$ to denote the i'th elementary row vector (with 1 at the i'th position and 0 elsewhere, and the total length of the vector specified by the context). For any positive integer N, we use $[N]$ to denote $\{1, 2, \ldots, N\}$.

The tensor product (Kronecker product) for matrices $\mathbf{A} = (a_{i,j}) \in \mathbb{Z}^{\ell \times m}$, $\mathbf{B} \in \mathbb{Z}^{n \times p}$ is defined as

$$
\mathbf{A} \otimes \mathbf{B} = \begin{bmatrix} a_{1,1}\mathbf{B}, \ldots, a_{1,m}\mathbf{B} \\ \ldots, \ldots, \ldots \\ a_{\ell,1}\mathbf{B}, \ldots, a_{\ell,m}\mathbf{B} \end{bmatrix} \in \mathbb{Z}^{\ell n \times mp}.
$$

The mixed-product property for tensor product says that

$$
(\mathbf{A} \otimes \mathbf{B})(\mathbf{C} \otimes \mathbf{D}) = (\mathbf{AC}) \otimes (\mathbf{BD})
$$

Arithmetic Branching Programs. A branching program is defined by a directed acyclic graph (V, E), two special vertices $v_0, v_1 \in V$ and a labeling function ϕ. An arithmetic branching program (ABP), where p is a prime, computes a function $f : \mathbb{Z}_p^n \rightarrow \mathbb{Z}_p$. Here, ϕ assigns to each edge in E an affine function in some input variable or a constant, and $f(x)$ is the sum over all v_0-v_1 paths of the product of all the values along the path. We refer to $|V| + |E|$ as the size of f. The definition extends in a coordinate-wise manner to functions $f : \mathbb{Z}_p^n \rightarrow \mathbb{Z}_p^{n'}$. Henceforth, we use $\mathcal{F}_{\mathsf{ABP},n,n'}$ to denote the class of ABP $f : \mathbb{Z}_p^n \rightarrow \mathbb{Z}_p^{n'}$.

We note that there is a linear-time algorithm that converts any boolean formula, boolean branching program or arithmetic formula to an arithmetic branching program with a constant blow-up in the representation size. Thus, ABPs can be viewed as a stronger computational model than all of the above. Recall also that branching programs and boolean formulas correspond to the complexity classes **LOGSPACE** and **NC1** respectively.

2.1 Prime-Order Bilinear Groups

A generator $\mathcal{G}$ takes as input a security parameter 1^λ and outputs a description $\mathbb{G} := (p, \mathbb{G}_1, \mathbb{G}_2, \mathbb{G}_T, e)$, where p is a prime of $\Theta(\lambda)$ bits, $\mathbb{G}_1, \mathbb{G}_2$ and $\mathbb{G}_T$ are cyclic groups of order p, and $e : \mathbb{G}_1 \times \mathbb{G}_2 \rightarrow \mathbb{G}_T$ is a non-degenerate bilinear map. We require that the group operations in $\mathbb{G}_1$, $\mathbb{G}_2$, $\mathbb{G}_T$ and the bilinear map e are computable in deterministic polynomial time in λ. Let $g_1 \in \mathbb{G}_1$, $g_2 \in \mathbb{G}_2$ and $g_T = e(g_1, g_2) \in \mathbb{G}_T$ be the respective generators. We employ the *implicit representation* of group elements: for a matrix $\mathbf{M}$ over $\mathbb{Z}_p$, we define $[\mathbf{M}]_1 := g_1^{\mathbf{M}}, [\mathbf{M}]_2 := g_2^{\mathbf{M}}, [\mathbf{M}]_T := g_T^{\mathbf{M}}$, where exponentiation is carried out component-wise. Also, given $[\mathbf{A}]_1, [\mathbf{B}]_2$, we let $e([\mathbf{A}]_1, [\mathbf{B}]_2) = [\mathbf{AB}]_T$. We recall the matrix Diffie-Hellman (MDDH) assumption on $\mathbb{G}_1$ [10]:

Assumption 1 ($\mathrm{MDDH}^d_{k,k'}$ **Assumption**). *Let $k, \ell, d \in \mathbb{N}$. We say that the $\mathrm{MDDH}^d_{k,\ell}$ assumption holds if for all PPT adversaries $\mathcal{A}$, the following advantage function is negligible in λ.*

$$\mathsf{Adv}^{\mathrm{MDDH}^d_{k,\ell}}_{\mathcal{A}}(\lambda) := \Big| \Pr[\mathcal{A}(\mathbb{G}, [\mathbf{M}]_1, \boxed{[\mathbf{MS}]_1}) = 1] - \Pr[\mathcal{A}(\mathbb{G}, [\mathbf{M}]_1, \boxed{[\mathbf{U}]_1}) = 1] \Big|$$

where $\mathbb{G} := (p, \mathbb{G}_1, \mathbb{G}_2, \mathbb{G}_T, e) \leftarrow \mathcal{G}(1^\lambda)$, $\mathbf{M} \leftarrow \mathbb{Z}_p^{\ell \times k}$, $\mathbf{S} \leftarrow \mathbb{Z}_p^{k \times d}$ and $\mathbf{U} \leftarrow \mathbb{Z}_p^{\ell \times d}$.

The MDDH assumption on $\mathbb{G}_2$ can be defined in an analogous way. Escala *et al.* [10] showed that

$$k\text{-Lin} \Rightarrow \mathrm{MDDH}^1_{k,k+1} \Rightarrow \mathrm{MDDH}^d_{k,\ell} \; \forall \, k, d \geq 1, \ell > k$$

with a tight security reduction. (In the setting where $\ell \leq k$, the $\mathrm{MDDH}^d_{k,\ell}$ assumption holds unconditionally.)

The bilateral MDDH assumption is defined analogously with the advantage function:

$$\Big| \Pr[\mathcal{A}(\mathbb{G}, [\mathbf{M}]_1, \boxed{[\mathbf{MS}]_1}, [\mathbf{M}]_2, \boxed{[\mathbf{MS}]_1}) = 2] - \Pr[\mathcal{A}(\mathbb{G}, [\mathbf{M}]_1, \boxed{[\mathbf{U}]_1}, [\mathbf{M}]_2, \boxed{[\mathbf{U}]_2}) = 1] \Big|$$

2.2 Partially-Hiding Functional Encryption (PHFE)

We recall the notion of partially-hiding functional encryption [4, 7, 15, 22] for the function class

$$(\mathbf{x}, \mathbf{z}) \in \mathbb{Z}_p^n \times \mathbb{Z}_p^{n'} \mapsto h(\mathbf{z}) f(\mathbf{x})^\top$$

where $h : \mathbb{Z}_p^{n'} \to \mathbb{Z}_p^{n''}$ is fixed and $f \in \mathcal{F}_{\mathrm{ABP}, n, n''}$ is specified by the secret key. We will be primarily interested in the settings $h(\mathbf{z}) = \mathbf{z}$ and $h(\mathbf{z}_1, \mathbf{z}_2) = \mathbf{z}_1 \otimes \mathbf{z}_2$, which generalize FE for linear functions and quadratic functions respectively.

Syntax. A *partially-hiding functional encryption scheme* (PHFE) consists of four algorithms:

Setup$(1^\lambda, 1^n, 1^{n'}, h)$: The setup algorithm gets as input the security parameter 1^λ and function parameters $1^n, 1^{n'}$ and $h : \mathbb{Z}_p^{n'} \to \mathbb{Z}_p^{n''}$. It outputs the master public key mpk and the master secret key msk.

Enc$(\mathsf{mpk}, \mathbf{x}, \mathbf{z})$: The encryption algorithm gets as input mpk and message $\mathbf{x}, \mathbf{z} \in \mathbb{Z}_p^n \times \mathbb{Z}_p^{n'}$. It outputs a ciphertext $\mathsf{ct}_{(\mathbf{x}, \mathbf{z})}$ with $\mathbf{x}$ being public.

KeyGen(msk, f) : The key generation algorithm gets as input msk and a function $f \in \mathcal{F}_{\mathrm{ABP}, n, n''}$. It outputs a secret key sk_f with f being public.

Dec$((\mathsf{sk}_f, f), (\mathsf{ct}_{(\mathbf{x}, \mathbf{z})}, \mathbf{x}))$: The decryption algorithm gets as input sk_f and $\mathsf{ct}_{(\mathbf{x}, \mathbf{z})}$ along with f and $\mathbf{x}$. It outputs a value in $\mathbb{Z}_p$.

Correctness. For all $(\mathbf{x}, \mathbf{z}) \in \mathbb{Z}_p^n \times \mathbb{Z}_p^{n'}$ and $f \in \mathcal{F}_{\mathsf{ABP},n,n''}$, we require

$$\Pr\left[\mathsf{Dec}((\mathsf{ct}_{(\mathbf{x},\mathbf{z})}, \mathbf{x}, (\mathsf{sk}_f, f)) = h(\mathbf{z})f(\mathbf{x})^\top : \begin{array}{l} (\mathsf{mpk}, \mathsf{msk}) \leftarrow \mathsf{Setup}(1^\lambda, 1^n, 1^{n'}, h) \\ \mathsf{sk}_f \leftarrow \mathsf{KeyGen}(\mathsf{msk}, f) \\ \mathsf{ct}_{(\mathbf{x},\mathbf{z})} \leftarrow \mathsf{Enc}(\mathsf{mpk}, \mathbf{x}, \mathbf{z}) \end{array} \right] = 1.$$

Remark 1 (Relaxation of correctness.). Our scheme only achieves a relaxation of correctness where the decryption algorithm takes an additional bound 1^B (and runs in time polynomial in B) and outputs $h(\mathbf{z})f(\mathbf{x})^\top$ if the value is bounded by B. This limitation is also present in prior works on (IP)FE from DDH and bilinear groups [1,3,5,20], due to the reliance on brute-force discrete log to recover the answer "from the exponent". We stress that the relaxation only refers to functionality and does not affect security.

Security Definition. We consider semi-adaptive [9] (strengthening of selective), simulation-based security, which stipulates that there exists a randomized simulator $(\mathsf{Setup}^*, \mathsf{Enc}^*, \mathsf{KeyGen}^*)$ such that for every efficient stateful adversary $\mathcal{A}$,

$$\left[\begin{array}{l} (\mathsf{mpk}, \mathsf{msk}) \leftarrow \mathsf{Setup}(1^\lambda, 1^n, 1^{n'}, h); \\ (\mathbf{x}^*, \mathbf{z}^*) \leftarrow \mathcal{A}(\mathsf{mpk}); \\ \mathsf{ct}^* \leftarrow \mathsf{Enc}(\mathsf{mpk}, (\mathbf{x}^*, \mathbf{z}^*)); \\ \text{output } \mathcal{A}^{\mathsf{KeyGen}(\mathsf{msk}, \cdot)}(\mathsf{mpk}, \mathsf{ct}^*) \end{array} \right] \approx_c \left[\begin{array}{l} (\mathsf{mpk}, \mathsf{msk}^*) \leftarrow \mathsf{Setup}^*(1^\lambda, 1^n, 1^{n'}, h); \\ (\mathbf{x}^*, \mathbf{z}^*) \leftarrow \mathcal{A}(\mathsf{mpk}); \\ \mathsf{ct}^* \leftarrow \mathsf{Enc}^*(\mathsf{msk}^*, \mathbf{x}^*); \\ \text{output } \mathcal{A}^{\mathsf{KeyGen}^*(\mathsf{msk}^*, \mathbf{x}^*, \cdot, \cdot)}(\mathsf{mpk}, \mathsf{ct}^*) \end{array} \right]$$

such that whenever $\mathcal{A}$ makes a query f to KeyGen, the simulator KeyGen^* gets f along with $h(\mathbf{z}^*)f(\mathbf{x}^*)^\top$. We use $\mathsf{Adv}_{\mathcal{A}}^{\mathsf{FE}}(\lambda)$ to denote the advantage in distinguishing the real and ideal games.

3   Main Construction

In this section, we present our PHFE scheme for the class

$$(\overbrace{\mathbf{x}}^{\text{public}}, \overbrace{(\mathbf{z}_1, \mathbf{z}_2)}^{\text{private}}) \in \mathbb{Z}_p^n \times \mathbb{Z}_p^{n_1' + n_2'} \mapsto (\mathbf{z}_1 \otimes \mathbf{z}_2)f(\mathbf{x})^\top, \quad f \in \mathcal{F}_{\mathsf{ABP},n,n_1'n_2'}$$

The scheme is SA-SIM-secure under the bilateral k-Lin assumption and the k'-Lin assumption in $\mathbb{G}_1, \mathbb{G}_2$ (for the most efficient concrete instantiation, we set $k = 2, k' = 1$). In our scheme, decryption actually computes $[(\mathbf{z}_1 \otimes \mathbf{z}_2)f(\mathbf{x})^\top]_T$, whereas the simulator only needs to get $[(\mathbf{z}_1 \otimes \mathbf{z}_2)f(\mathbf{x})^\top]_2$. Note that FE for quadratic functions is a special case of our PHFE (where f has the quadratic function hard-wired into it). We present a self-contained description of our quadratic FE in Sect. A.

As a building block, we rely on a SA-SIM-secure PHFE scheme $(\mathsf{Setup}_0, \mathsf{Enc}_0, \mathsf{KeyGen}_0, \mathsf{Dec}_0)$ for the class

$$(\overbrace{\mathbf{x}}^{\text{public}}, \overbrace{\mathbf{z}}^{\text{private}}) \in \mathbb{Z}_p^n \times \mathbb{Z}_p^{k'n_1' + kn_2'} \mapsto [\mathbf{z}\mathbf{M}f(\mathbf{x})^\top]_T, \quad f \in \mathcal{F}_{\mathsf{ABP},n,n_1'n_2'}$$

parameterized by a matrix $[\mathbf{M}]_2 \in \mathbb{G}_1^{(k'n_1' + kn_2') \times n_1'n_2'}$, where encryption gets $[\mathbf{z}]_1$ and the simulator gets $[\mathbf{z}\mathbf{M}f(\mathbf{x})^\top]_2$. We instantiate the building block in Sect. 4.

3.1 Our Scheme

- Setup($p, 1^n, 1^{n_1'}, 1^{n_2'}$): Run $\mathbb{G} = (\mathbb{G}_1, \mathbb{G}_2, \mathbb{G}_T, e) \leftarrow \mathcal{G}(p)$. Sample

$$\mathbf{A}_1 \leftarrow \mathbb{Z}_p^{k \times n_1'}, \mathbf{A}_2 \leftarrow \mathbb{Z}_p^{k' \times n_2'}, (\mathsf{mpk}_0, \mathsf{msk}_0) \leftarrow \mathsf{Setup}_0(p, 1^n, 1^{k'n_1' + kn_2'}, [\mathbf{M}]_2)$$

where

$$\mathbf{M} := \begin{pmatrix} \mathbf{A}_1 \otimes \mathbf{I}_{n_2'} \\ \mathbf{I}_{n_1'} \otimes \mathbf{A}_2 \end{pmatrix} \in \mathbb{Z}_p^{(k'n_1' + kn_2') \times n_1' n_2'}$$

and output

$$\mathsf{mpk} = \big(\, \mathbb{G}, [\mathbf{A}_1]_1, [\mathbf{A}_1]_2, [\mathbf{A}_2]_2, \mathsf{mpk}_0 \,\big) \quad \text{and} \quad \mathsf{msk} = \mathsf{msk}_0$$

Observe that given mpk, we can compute $[\mathbf{M}]_2$.

- Enc(mpk, $\mathbf{x}, (\mathbf{z}_1, \mathbf{z}_2)$): Sample

$$\mathbf{s}_1 \leftarrow \mathbb{Z}_p^k, \mathbf{s}_0, \mathbf{s}_2 \leftarrow \mathbb{Z}_p^{k'}, \quad \mathsf{ct}_0 \leftarrow \mathsf{Enc}_0\big(\mathsf{mpk}_0, \mathbf{x}, [\mathbf{s}_1 \otimes \mathbf{z}_2 \| \underbrace{(\mathbf{s}_1 \mathbf{A}_1 + \mathbf{z}_1)}_{\mathbf{y}_1} \otimes \mathbf{s}_2]_1\big)$$

and output

$$\mathsf{ct} = \big(\, [\underbrace{\mathbf{s}_1 \mathbf{A}_1 + \mathbf{z}_1}_{\mathbf{y}_1}]_1, [\underbrace{\mathbf{s}_2 \mathbf{A}_2 + \mathbf{z}_2}_{\mathbf{y}_2}]_2, \mathsf{ct}_0 \,\big)$$

- KeyGen(msk, f): Output

$$\mathsf{sk}_f \leftarrow \mathsf{KeyGen}_0(\mathsf{msk}_0, f)$$

- Dec($\mathsf{sk}_f, f, \mathsf{ct}, \mathbf{x}$): Output

$$[(\mathbf{y}_1 \otimes \mathbf{y}_2) \cdot f(\mathbf{x})^\top]_T \cdot \Big(\mathsf{Dec}_0(\mathsf{sk}_f, (f, [\mathbf{M}]_2), \mathsf{ct}_0, \mathbf{x}) \Big)^{-1}$$

Correctness. First, observe that we have

$$(\underbrace{\mathbf{s}_1 \mathbf{A}_1 + \mathbf{z}_1}_{\mathbf{y}_1}) \otimes (\underbrace{\mathbf{s}_2 \mathbf{A}_2 + \mathbf{z}_2}_{\mathbf{y}_2}) = (\mathbf{z}_1 \otimes \mathbf{z}_2) + \mathbf{s}_1 \mathbf{A}_1 \otimes \mathbf{z}_2 + \mathbf{y}_1 \otimes \mathbf{s}_2 \mathbf{A}_2$$

$$= (\mathbf{z}_1 \otimes \mathbf{z}_2) + (\mathbf{s}_1 \otimes \mathbf{z}_2) \cdot (\mathbf{A}_1 \otimes \mathbf{I}_{n_2'}) \quad + (\mathbf{y}_1 \otimes \mathbf{s}_2) \cdot (\mathbf{I}_{n_1'} \otimes \mathbf{A}_2)$$

$$= (\mathbf{z}_1 \otimes \mathbf{z}_2) + (\mathbf{s}_1 \otimes \mathbf{z}_2 \| \mathbf{y}_1 \otimes \mathbf{s}_2)\mathbf{M} \tag{4}$$

where the second equality uses the mixed-product property of the tensor product. Multiplying both sides of (4) by $f(\mathbf{x})^\top$ and rearranging the terms yields:

$$(\mathbf{z}_1 \otimes \mathbf{z}_2)f(\mathbf{x})^\top = (\mathbf{y}_1 \otimes \mathbf{y}_2)f(\mathbf{x})^\top - (\mathbf{s}_1 \otimes \mathbf{z}_2 \| \mathbf{y}_1 \otimes \mathbf{s}_2)\mathbf{M}f(\mathbf{x})^\top \tag{5}$$

Next, correctness of the underlying scheme tells us that

$$\mathsf{Dec}_0(\mathsf{sk}_f, (f, [\mathbf{M}]_2), \mathsf{ct}_0, \mathbf{x}) = (\mathbf{s}_1 \otimes \mathbf{z}_2 \| \mathbf{y}_1 \otimes \mathbf{s}_2)\mathbf{M}f(\mathbf{x})^\top$$

Correctness then follows readily.

3.2   Simulator

We start by describing the simulator.

- Setup$^*(p, 1^n, 1^{n_1'}, 1^{n_2'})$: Run $\mathbb{G} = (\mathbb{G}_1, \mathbb{G}_2, \mathbb{G}_T, e) \leftarrow \mathcal{G}(p)$. Sample

$$\mathbf{A}_1 \leftarrow \mathbb{Z}_p^{k \times n_1'}, \mathbf{A}_2 \leftarrow \mathbb{Z}_p^{k' \times n_2'}, (\mathsf{mpk}_0^*, \mathsf{msk}_0^*) \leftarrow \mathsf{Setup}_0^*(p, 1^n, 1^{k'n_1 + kn_2})$$

and output

$$\mathsf{mpk}^* = \big(\mathbb{G}, [\mathbf{A}_1]_1, [\mathbf{A}_1]_2, [\mathbf{A}_2]_2, \mathsf{mpk}_0^* \big) \quad \text{and} \quad \mathsf{msk}^* = \mathsf{msk}_0^*$$

- Enc$^*(\mathsf{msk}_0^*, \mathbf{x}^*)$: Sample

$$\mathbf{y}_1 \leftarrow \mathbb{Z}_p^{n_1'}, \mathbf{y}_2 \leftarrow \mathbb{Z}_p^{n_2'}, \mathsf{ct}_0^* \leftarrow \mathsf{Enc}_0^*(\mathsf{msk}_0^*, \mathbf{x}^*)$$

and output

$$\mathsf{ct}^* = \big([\mathbf{y}_1]_1, [\mathbf{y}_2]_1, \mathsf{ct}_0^* \big)$$

- KeyGen$^*(\mathsf{msk}^*, \mathbf{x}^*, f, [\mu]_2)$: Output

$$\mathsf{sk}_f \leftarrow \mathsf{KeyGen}_0^*(\mathsf{msk}_0^*, \mathbf{x}^*, f, [(\mathbf{y}_1 \otimes \mathbf{y}_2) f(\mathbf{x}^*)]_T \cdot [\mu]_2^{-1})$$

3.3   Proof of Security

We proceed via a series of games and we use Adv_i to denote the advantage of $\mathcal{A}$ in Game i. Let $\mathbf{x}^*, (\mathbf{z}_1^*, \mathbf{z}_2^*)$ denote the semi-adaptive challenge.

Game 0. Real game.

Game 1. Replace $(\mathsf{Setup}_0, \mathsf{Enc}_0, \mathsf{KeyGen}_0)$ in Game_0 with $(\mathsf{Setup}_0^*, \mathsf{Enc}_0^*, \mathsf{KeyGen}_0^*)$ where

$$\mathsf{ct}^* = ([\mathbf{y}_1]_1, [\mathbf{y}_2]_2, \mathsf{Enc}_0(\mathsf{msk}^*, \mathbf{x}^*)), \ \mathbf{y}_1 = \mathbf{s}_1 \mathbf{A}_1 + \mathbf{z}_1^*, \mathbf{y}_2 = \mathbf{s}_2 \mathbf{A}_2 + \mathbf{z}_2^*$$

$$\mathsf{sk}_f \leftarrow \mathsf{KeyGen}_0^*(\mathsf{msk}_0^*, \mathbf{x}^*, f, \boxed{[(\mathbf{s}_1 \otimes \mathbf{z}_2^* \| \mathbf{y}_1 \otimes \mathbf{s}_2) \mathbf{M} f(\mathbf{x}^*)^\top]_2})$$

We have $\mathsf{Game}_1 \approx_c \mathsf{Game}_0$, by security of the underlying PHFE scheme. The reduction samples

$$\mathbf{A}_1 \leftarrow \mathbb{Z}_p^{k \times n_1'}, \mathbf{A}_2 \leftarrow \mathbb{Z}_p^{k' \times n_2'}, \mathbf{s}_1 \leftarrow \mathbb{Z}_p^k, \mathbf{s}_0, \mathbf{s}_2 \leftarrow \mathbb{Z}_p^{k'},$$

and upon receiving $\mathbf{x}^*, (\mathbf{z}_1^*, \mathbf{z}_2^*)$ from $\mathcal{A}$, sends

$$\mathbf{x}^*, \mathbf{s}_1 \otimes \mathbf{z}_2^* \| (\mathbf{s}_1 \mathbf{A}_1 + \mathbf{z}_1^*) \otimes \mathbf{s}_2$$

as the semi-adaptive challenge.

Game 2. Replace sk_f in Game 1 with

$$\mathsf{sk}_f \leftarrow \mathsf{KeyGen}_0^*(\mathsf{msk}_0^*, \mathbf{x}^*, f, \boxed{[(\mathbf{y}_1 \otimes \mathbf{y}_2) f(\mathbf{x}^*)^\top]_2 \cdot [(\mathbf{z}_1^* \otimes \mathbf{z}_2^*) f(\mathbf{x}^*)^\top]_2^{-1}})$$

Here, we have $\mathsf{Game}_2 \equiv \mathsf{Game}_1$, thanks to (5), which tells us that

$$[(\mathbf{y}_1 \otimes \mathbf{y}_2)f(\mathbf{x}^*)^\top]_2 \cdot [(\mathbf{z}_1^* \otimes \mathbf{z}_2^*)f(\mathbf{x}^*)^\top]_2^{-1} = [(\mathbf{s}_1 \otimes \mathbf{z}_2^* \| \mathbf{y}_1 \otimes \mathbf{s}_2)\mathbf{M}f(\mathbf{x}^*)^\top]_2$$

Game 3. We replace $\boxed{[\mathbf{s}_1\mathbf{A}_1 + \mathbf{z}_1^*]_1}$ in ct* in Game_2 with $\boxed{[\mathbf{y}_1]_1}$ where $\boxed{\mathbf{y}_1 \leftarrow \mathbb{Z}_q^{n_1'}}$.
Then, we have $\mathsf{Game}_3 \approx_c \mathsf{Game}_2$ via the bi-lateral k-Lin assumption. The assumption
tells us that for all $\mathbf{z}_1^*$,

$$([\mathbf{A}_1]_1, [\mathbf{A}_1]_2, [\mathbf{s}^\top\mathbf{A}_1 + \mathbf{z}_1^*]_1, [\mathbf{s}^\top\mathbf{A}_1 + \mathbf{z}_1^*]_2) \approx_c ([\mathbf{A}_1]_1, [\mathbf{A}_1]_2, [\mathbf{y}_1]_1, [\mathbf{y}_1]_2)$$

where $\mathbf{s} \leftarrow \mathbb{Z}_p^k, \mathbf{y}_1 \leftarrow \mathbb{Z}_p^{n_1'}$. Note that this holds even if $\mathbf{z}_1^*$ is adaptively chosen after
seeing $[\mathbf{A}_1]_1, [\mathbf{A}_1]_2$. The reduction then samples

$$\mathbf{A}_2 \leftarrow \mathbb{Z}_p^{k' \times n_2'}, \quad \mathbf{s}_2 \leftarrow \mathbb{Z}_p^{k'}, \quad (\mathsf{mpk}_0^*, \mathsf{msk}_0^*) \leftarrow \mathsf{Setup}_0^*(p, 1^n, 1^{k'n_1 + kn_2})$$

sets $\mathbf{y}_2 := \mathbf{s}_2\mathbf{A}_2 + \mathbf{z}_2^*$, and uses the fact that in Games 2 and 3,

- it can compute $\mathsf{mpk}^*, \mathsf{ct}^*$ given $[\mathbf{A}_1]_1, [\mathbf{A}_1]_2, [\mathbf{y}_1]_1$ respectively;
- it can sample sk_f by using $[\mathbf{y}_1]_2, \mathbf{y}_2$ to compute $[\mathbf{y}_1 \otimes \mathbf{y}_2]_2$.

Game 4. We replace $\boxed{[\mathbf{s}_2\mathbf{A}_2 + \mathbf{z}_2^*]_1}$ in ct* in Game_3 with $\boxed{[\mathbf{y}_2]_1}$ where $\boxed{\mathbf{y}_2 \leftarrow \mathbb{Z}_q^{n_2'}}$.
Then, we have $\mathsf{Game}_4 \approx_c \mathsf{Game}_3$ via the k'-Lin assumption in $\mathbb{G}_2$. Here, we use the
fact that we can sample sk_f in Games 3 and 4 using $\mathbf{y}_1, [\mathbf{y}_2]_2$ to compute $[\mathbf{y}_1 \otimes \mathbf{y}_2]_2$.

Finally, note that Game_4 is exactly the output of the simulator.

4 Partially-Hiding FE for Linear Functions

In this section, we present our PHFE scheme for the class

$$(\overbrace{\mathbf{x}}^{\text{public}}, \overbrace{\mathbf{z}}^{\text{private}}) \mapsto [\mathbf{z}\mathbf{M}f(\mathbf{x})^\top]_T$$

parameterized by a matrix $[\mathbf{M}]_2$, where encryption gets $[\mathbf{z}]_1$, and the simulator gets
$[\mathbf{z}\mathbf{M}f(\mathbf{x})^\top]_2$. In fact, we present a scheme for a more general setting where the matrix
$[\mathbf{M}]_2$ is specified by the function corresponding to the secret key (that is, we allow a
different $[\mathbf{M}]_2$ for each secret key, rather than the same matrix for all keys). The scheme
is a somewhat straight-forward modification of that in [2]; some care is needed as the
decryption algorithm only gets $[\mathbf{M}]_2$ and not $\mathbf{M}$. This scheme achieves simulation-
based semi-adaptive security under k-Lin. Most of the text in this section is copied
verbatim from [2], with minor adaptations to account for $\mathbf{M}$.

4.1 Partial Garbling Scheme

The partial garbling scheme [2, 17, 22] for $\mathbf{z}f(\mathbf{x})^\top$ with $f \in \mathcal{F}_{\mathsf{ABP},n,n'}$ is a randomized algorithm that on input f outputs an affine function in $\mathbf{x}, \mathbf{z}$ of the form:

$$\mathbf{p}_{f,\mathbf{x},\mathbf{z}} = \big(\mathbf{z} - \underline{\mathbf{t}} \| \mathbf{t}(\mathbf{L}_1(\mathbf{x}^\top \otimes \mathbf{I}_m) + \mathbf{L}_0) \big)$$

where $\mathbf{L}_0 \in \mathbb{Z}_p^{t \times mn}, \mathbf{L}_1 \in \mathbb{Z}_p^{t \times m}$ depends only on f; $\mathbf{t} \leftarrow \mathbb{Z}_p^t$ is the random coin and $\underline{\mathbf{t}}$ consists of the last n' entries in $\mathbf{t}$, such that given $(\mathbf{p}_{f,\mathbf{x},\mathbf{z}}, f, \mathbf{x})$, we can recover $\mathbf{z}f(\mathbf{x})^\top$, while learning nothing else about $\mathbf{z}$.

Lemma 1 (partial garbling [2,17,22]**).** *There exists four efficient algorithms* (lgen, pgb, rec, pgb*) *with the following properties:*

- *syntax: on input* $f \in \mathcal{F}_{\mathsf{ABP},n,n'}$, $\mathsf{lgen}(f)$ *outputs* $\mathbf{L}_0 \in \mathbb{Z}_p^{t \times mn}, \mathbf{L}_1 \in \mathbb{Z}_p^{t \times m}$, *and*

$$\begin{aligned} \mathsf{pgb}(f, \mathbf{x}, \mathbf{z}; \mathbf{t}) &= \big(\mathbf{z} - \underline{\mathbf{t}}, \mathbf{t}(\mathbf{L}_1(\mathbf{x}^\top \otimes \mathbf{I}_m) + \mathbf{L}_0) \big) \\ \mathsf{pgb}^*(f, \mathbf{x}, \mu; \mathbf{t}) &= \big(\quad -\underline{\mathbf{t}}, \mathbf{t}(\mathbf{L}_1(\mathbf{x}^\top \otimes \mathbf{I}_m) + \mathbf{L}_0) + \mu \cdot \mathbf{e}_1 \big) \end{aligned}$$

  where $\mathbf{t} \in \mathbb{Z}_p^t$ *and* $\underline{\mathbf{t}}$ *consists of the last* n' *entries in* $\mathbf{t}$ *and* m, t *are linear in the size of* f.
- *reconstruction:* $\mathsf{rec}(f, \mathbf{x})$ *outputs* $\mathbf{d}_{f,\mathbf{x}}^\top \in \mathbb{Z}_p^{n'+m}$ *such that for all* $f, \mathbf{x}, \mathbf{z}, \mathbf{t}$, *we have* $\mathbf{p}_{f,\mathbf{x},\mathbf{z}}\mathbf{d}_{f,\mathbf{x}}^\top = \mathbf{z}f(\mathbf{x})^\top$ *where* $\mathbf{p}_{f,\mathbf{x},\mathbf{z}} = \mathsf{pgb}(f, \mathbf{x}, \mathbf{z}; \mathbf{t})$.
- *privacy: for all* $f, \mathbf{x}, \mathbf{z}$, *we have* $\mathsf{pgb}(f, \mathbf{x}, \mathbf{z}; \mathbf{t}) \approx_s \mathsf{pgb}^*(f, \mathbf{x}, \mathbf{z}f(\mathbf{x})^\top; \mathbf{t})$ *where the randomness is over* $\mathbf{t} \leftarrow \mathbb{Z}_p^t$.

4.2 Construction

Our scheme Π is similar to Π_{one} in [2], with the modifications marked using boxed terms. We rely on partial garbling to compute $\mathsf{pgb}(f, \mathbf{x}, \boxed{\mathbf{zM}}; \mathbf{t})$ instead of $\mathsf{pgb}(f, \mathbf{x}, \mathbf{z}; \mathbf{t})$ "in the exponent" over $\mathbb{G}_T$; applying the reconstruction algorithm (which requires knowing $f, \mathbf{x}$ but not $\mathbf{M}$) then returns $[\boxed{\mathbf{zM}}f(\mathbf{x})^\top]_T$.

- Setup$(1^\lambda, 1^n, 1^{n'})$: Run $\mathbb{G} = (p, \mathbb{G}_1, \mathbb{G}_2, \mathbb{G}_T, e) \leftarrow \mathcal{G}(1^\lambda)$. Sample

$$\mathbf{A} \leftarrow \mathbb{Z}_p^{k \times (k+1)} \quad \text{and} \quad \mathbf{W} \leftarrow \mathbb{Z}_p^{(k+1) \times n'}, \mathbf{U} \leftarrow \mathbb{Z}_p^{(k+1) \times kn}, \mathbf{V} \leftarrow \mathbb{Z}_p^{(k+1) \times k}$$

  and output

$$\mathsf{mpk} = \big(\mathbb{G}, [\mathbf{A}]_1, [\mathbf{AW}]_1, [\mathbf{AU}]_1, [\mathbf{AV}]_1 \big) \quad \text{and} \quad \mathsf{msk} = \big(\mathbf{W}, \mathbf{U}, \mathbf{V} \big).$$

- Enc$(\mathsf{mpk}, (\mathbf{x}, \mathbf{z}))$: Sample $\mathbf{s} \leftarrow \mathbb{Z}_p^k$ and output

$$\mathsf{ct}_{\mathbf{x},\mathbf{z}} = \big([\mathbf{sA}]_1, [\mathbf{z} + \mathbf{sAW}]_1, [\mathbf{sAU}(\mathbf{x}^\top \otimes \mathbf{I}_k) + \mathbf{sAV}]_1 \big) \quad \text{and} \quad \mathbf{x}.$$

  Note that it is sufficient for Enc to get $[\mathbf{z}]_1$.

- KeyGen(msk, $(f, [\mathbf{M}]_2)$): Run $(\mathbf{L}_1, \mathbf{L}_0) \leftarrow \mathsf{lgen}(f)$ where $\mathbf{L}_1 \in \mathbb{Z}_p^{t \times mn}, \mathbf{L}_0 \in \mathbb{Z}_p^{t \times m}$ (cf. Sect. 4.1). Sample $\mathbf{T} \leftarrow \mathbb{Z}_p^{(k+1) \times t}$ and $\mathbf{R} \leftarrow \mathbb{Z}_p^{k \times m}$ and output

$$\mathsf{sk}_{f,\mathbf{M}} = \left([\underline{\mathbf{T}} + \boxed{\mathbf{WM}}]_2, \; [\mathbf{TL}_1 + \mathbf{U}(\mathbf{I}_n \otimes \mathbf{R})]_2, \; [\mathbf{TL}_0 + \mathbf{VR}]_2, \; [\mathbf{R}]_2 \right) \quad \text{and} \quad (f, [\mathbf{M}]_2).$$

where $\underline{\mathbf{T}}$ refers to the matrix composed of the right most n' columns of $\mathbf{T}$.

- Dec$((\mathsf{sk}_{f,\mathbf{M}}, (f, [\mathbf{M}]_2)), (\mathsf{ct}_{\mathbf{x},\mathbf{z}}, \mathbf{x}))$: On input key:

$$\mathsf{sk}_{f,\mathbf{M}} = \left([\mathbf{K}_1]_2, [\mathbf{K}_2]_2, [\mathbf{K}_3]_2, [\mathbf{R}]_2 \right) \quad \text{and} \quad (f, [\mathbf{M}]_2)$$

and ciphertext:

$$\mathsf{ct}_{\mathbf{x},\mathbf{z}} = \left([\mathbf{c}_0]_1, [\mathbf{c}_1]_1, [\mathbf{c}_2]_1 \right) \quad \text{and} \quad \mathbf{x}$$

the decryption works as follows:

1. compute

$$[\mathbf{p}_1]_T = e([\mathbf{c}_1]_1, \boxed{[\mathbf{M}]_2}) \cdot e([\mathbf{c}_0]_1, [-\mathbf{K}_1]_2) \tag{6}$$

2. compute

$$[\mathbf{p}_2]_T = e([\mathbf{c}_0]_1, [\mathbf{K}_2(\mathbf{x}^\top \otimes \mathbf{I}_m) + \mathbf{K}_3]_2) \cdot e([-\mathbf{c}_2]_1, [\mathbf{R}]_2) \tag{7}$$

3. run $\mathbf{d}_{f,\mathbf{x}} \leftarrow \mathsf{rec}(f, \mathbf{x})$ (cf. Sect. 4.1), compute

$$[D]_T = [(\mathbf{p}_1 \| \mathbf{p}_2)\mathbf{d}_{f,\mathbf{x}}^\top]_T \tag{8}$$

Correctness. For $\mathsf{ct}_{\mathbf{x},\mathbf{z}}$ and $\mathsf{sk}_{f,\mathbf{M}}$, we have

$$\mathbf{p}_1 = \mathbf{zM} - \mathbf{sA}\underline{\mathbf{T}} \tag{9}$$
$$\mathbf{p}_2 = \mathbf{sATL}_1(\mathbf{x}^\top \otimes \mathbf{I}_m) + \mathbf{sATL}_0 \tag{10}$$
$$(\mathbf{p}_1 \| \mathbf{p}_2)\mathbf{d}_{f,\mathbf{x}}^\top = \mathbf{zM}f(\mathbf{x}) \tag{11}$$

Here (11) follows from the fact that

$$(\mathbf{p}_1 \| \mathbf{p}_2) = \mathsf{pgb}(f, \mathbf{x}, \mathbf{zM}; (\mathbf{sAT})) \quad \text{and} \quad \mathbf{d}_{f,\mathbf{x}} = \mathsf{rec}(f, \mathbf{x})$$

and reconstruction of the partial garbling in (6); the remaining two equalities follow from:

(9) $\quad \mathbf{z} - \mathbf{sA}\underline{\mathbf{T}} = (\mathbf{z} + \mathbf{sAW}) \cdot \mathbf{I}_{n'} - \mathbf{sA} \cdot (\underline{\mathbf{T}} + \mathbf{W})$

(10) $\mathbf{sATL}_1(\mathbf{x}^\top \otimes \mathbf{I}_m) + \mathbf{sATL}_0 = \mathbf{sA} \cdot ((\mathbf{TL}_1 + \mathbf{U}(\mathbf{I}_n \otimes \mathbf{R}))(\mathbf{x}^\top \otimes \mathbf{I}_m) + (\mathbf{TL}_0 + \mathbf{VR}))$
$$- (\mathbf{sAU}(\mathbf{x}^\top \otimes \mathbf{I}_k) + \mathbf{sAV}) \cdot \mathbf{R}$$

in which we use the equality $(\mathbf{I}_n \otimes \mathbf{R})(\mathbf{x}^\top \otimes \mathbf{I}_m) = (\mathbf{x}^\top \otimes \mathbf{I}_k)\mathbf{R}$. This readily proves the correctness.

Simulator. We describe the simulator. We defer the analysis to Sect. B.

- Setup$^*(1^\lambda, 1^n, 1^{n'})$: Run $\mathbb{G} = (p, \mathbb{G}_1, \mathbb{G}_2, \mathbb{G}_T, e) \leftarrow \mathcal{G}(1^\lambda)$. Sample

$$\mathbf{A} \leftarrow \mathbb{Z}_p^{(k+1) \times k} \quad \text{and} \quad \mathbf{W} \leftarrow \mathbb{Z}_p^{(k+1) \times n'}, \mathbf{U} \leftarrow \mathbb{Z}_p^{(k+1) \times kn}, \mathbf{V} \leftarrow \mathbb{Z}_p^{(k+1) \times k}$$
$$\mathbf{c} \leftarrow \mathbb{Z}_p^{k+1} \qquad\qquad\quad \widetilde{\mathbf{w}} \leftarrow \mathbb{Z}_p^{n'}, \qquad\qquad\qquad\qquad \widetilde{\mathbf{v}} \leftarrow \mathbb{Z}_p^{k}$$

and output

$$\mathsf{mpk} = \big(\, \mathbb{G}, [\mathbf{A}^\top]_1, [\mathbf{A}^\top \mathbf{W}]_1, [\mathbf{A}^\top \mathbf{U}]_1, [\mathbf{A}^\top \mathbf{V}]_1 \,\big)$$
$$\mathsf{msk}^* = \big(\, \mathbf{W}, \mathbf{U}, \mathbf{V}, \widetilde{\mathbf{w}}, \widetilde{\mathbf{v}}, \mathbf{c}, \mathbf{C}^\perp, \mathbf{A}, \mathbf{a}^\perp \,\big)$$

where $(\mathbf{A}|\mathbf{c})^\top (\mathbf{C}^\perp|\mathbf{a}^\perp) = \mathbf{I}_{k+1}$. Here we assume that $(\mathbf{A}|\mathbf{c})$ has full rank, which happens with probability $1 - 1/p$.

- Enc$^*(\mathsf{msk}^*, \mathbf{x}^*)$: Output

$$\mathsf{ct}^* = \big(\, [\mathbf{c}^\top]_1, [\widetilde{\mathbf{w}}]_1, [\widetilde{\mathbf{v}}]_1 \,\big) \quad \text{and} \quad \mathbf{x}^*.$$

- KeyGen$^*(\mathsf{msk}^*, \mathbf{x}^*, (f, [\mathbf{M}]_2), [\mu]_2)$: Run

$$(\mathbf{L}_1, \mathbf{L}_0) \leftarrow \mathsf{lgen}(f) \quad \text{and} \quad ([\mathbf{p}_1^*]_2, [\mathbf{p}_2^*]_2) \leftarrow \mathsf{pgb}^*(f, \mathbf{x}^*, [\mu]_2).$$

Sample $\mathbf{T} \leftarrow \mathbb{Z}_p^{(k+1) \times t}$, $\hat{\mathbf{u}} \leftarrow \mathbb{Z}_p^{nm}$ and $\mathbf{R} \leftarrow \mathbb{Z}_p^{k \times m}$ and output

$$\mathsf{sk}_f^* = \big(\, \mathbf{C}^\perp \cdot \mathsf{sk}_f^*[1] + \mathbf{a}^\perp \cdot \mathsf{sk}_f^*[2], [\mathbf{R}]_2 \,\big) \quad \text{and} \quad f \tag{12}$$

where

$$\mathsf{sk}_f^*[1] = \big(\, [\mathbf{A}^\top \underline{\mathbf{T}} + \mathbf{A}^\top \mathbf{W} \mathbf{M}]_2, [\mathbf{A}^\top \mathbf{T} \mathbf{L}_1 + \mathbf{A}^\top \mathbf{U}(\mathbf{I}_n \otimes \mathbf{R})]_2, [\mathbf{A}^\top \mathbf{T} \mathbf{L}_0 + \mathbf{A}^\top \mathbf{V} \mathbf{R}]_2 \,\big)$$
$$\mathsf{sk}_f^*[2] = \big(\, [-(\mathbf{p}_1^*)^\top + \widetilde{\mathbf{w}} \mathbf{M}]_2, [\hat{\mathbf{u}}^\top]_2, [(\mathbf{p}_2^*)^\top - \hat{\mathbf{u}}^\top (\mathbf{x}^* \otimes \mathbf{I}_m) + \widetilde{\mathbf{v}} \mathbf{R}]_2 \,\big)$$

Here $\underline{\mathbf{T}}$ refers to the matrix composed of the right most n' columns of $\mathbf{T}$. That is,

$$\mathsf{sk}_f^* = \left(\begin{array}{ll} [\mathbf{C}^\perp(\mathbf{A}^\top \underline{\mathbf{T}} + \mathbf{A}^\top \mathbf{W} \mathbf{M}) & +\mathbf{a}^\perp(-(\mathbf{p}_1^*)^\top + \widetilde{\mathbf{w}} \mathbf{M})]_2, \\ [\mathbf{C}^\perp(\mathbf{A}^\top \mathbf{T} \mathbf{L}_1 + \mathbf{A}^\top \mathbf{U}(\mathbf{I}_n \otimes \mathbf{R})) & +\mathbf{a}^\perp(\hat{\mathbf{u}}^\top)]_2 \\ [\mathbf{C}^\perp(\mathbf{A}^\top \mathbf{T} \mathbf{L}_0 + \mathbf{A}^\top \mathbf{V} \mathbf{R}) & +\mathbf{a}^\perp((\mathbf{p}_2^*)^\top - \hat{\mathbf{u}}^\top(\mathbf{x}^* \otimes \mathbf{I}_m) + \widetilde{\mathbf{v}} \mathbf{R})]_2 \end{array}, [\mathbf{R}]_2 \right)$$

A   Concrete Scheme for Quadratic Functions

We present a self-contained description of our functional encryption scheme for quadratic functions specified by $\mathbf{f} \in \mathbb{Z}_p^{n_1 \times n_2}$ where

$$\mathbf{z}_1, \mathbf{z}_2 \mapsto (\mathbf{z}_1 \otimes \mathbf{z}_2) \mathbf{f}^\top$$

The scheme is SA-SIM-secure under the bilateral k-Lin assumption and the k'-Lin assumption in $\mathbb{G}_1, \mathbb{G}_2$. For the most efficient concrete instantiation (cf. Fig. 1), we set $k = 2, k' = 1$.

- Setup$(p, 1^{n_1}, 1^{n_2})$: Run $\mathbb{G} = (\mathbb{G}_1, \mathbb{G}_2, \mathbb{G}_T, e) \leftarrow \mathcal{G}(p)$. Sample

$$\mathbf{A}_1 \leftarrow \mathbb{Z}_p^{k \times n_1}, \mathbf{A}_2 \leftarrow \mathbb{Z}_p^{k' \times n_2}, \mathbf{A}_0 \leftarrow \mathbb{Z}_p^{k' \times (k'+1)}, \mathbf{W} \leftarrow \mathbb{Z}_p^{(k'+1) \times (k'n_1 + kn_2)},$$

and output

$$\mathsf{mpk} = \big(\mathbb{G}, [\mathbf{A}_0]_1, [\mathbf{A}_0\mathbf{W}]_1, [\mathbf{A}_1]_1, [\mathbf{A}_1]_2, [\mathbf{A}_2]_2 \big) \quad \text{and} \quad \mathsf{msk} = \mathbf{W}$$

- Enc$(\mathsf{mpk}, (\mathbf{z}_1, \mathbf{z}_2))$: Sample $\mathbf{s}_1 \leftarrow \mathbb{Z}_p^k, \mathbf{s}_0, \mathbf{s}_2 \leftarrow \mathbb{Z}_p^{k'}$ and output

$$\mathsf{ct} = \big(\underbrace{[\mathbf{s}_1\mathbf{A}_1 + \mathbf{z}_1]_1}_{\mathbf{y}_1}, \underbrace{[\mathbf{s}_2\mathbf{A}_2 + \mathbf{z}_2]_2}_{\mathbf{y}_2}, \underbrace{[\mathbf{s}_0\mathbf{A}_0]_1}_{\mathbf{c}_0}, \underbrace{[\mathbf{s}_0\mathbf{A}_0\mathbf{W} + (\mathbf{s}_1 \otimes \mathbf{z}_2 \mid \mathbf{y}_1 \otimes \mathbf{s}_2)]_1}_{\mathbf{y}_0} \big)$$

$$\in \mathbb{G}_1^{n_1} \times \mathbb{G}_2^{n_2} \times \mathbb{G}_1^{k'+1} \times \mathbb{G}_1^{k'n_1 + kn_2}$$

- KeyGen$(\mathsf{msk}, \mathbf{f})$: Output

$$\mathsf{sk}_{\mathbf{f}} = \left[\mathbf{W} \cdot \begin{pmatrix} (\mathbf{A}_1 \otimes \mathbf{I}_{n_2})\mathbf{f}^\top \\ (\mathbf{I}_{n_1} \otimes \mathbf{A}_2)\mathbf{f}^\top \end{pmatrix} \right]_2 \in \mathbb{G}_2^{(k'+1) \times 1}$$

- Dec$(\mathsf{sk}_{\mathbf{f}}, \mathbf{f}, \mathsf{ct})$: Parse $\mathsf{sk}_{\mathbf{f}} = [\mathbf{k}^\top]_2$ and output the discrete log of

$$[(\mathbf{y}_1 \otimes \mathbf{y}_2) \cdot \mathbf{f}^\top]_T \cdot e([\mathbf{c}_0]_1, [\mathbf{k}^\top]_2) \cdot e\left([\mathbf{y}_0]_1, \left[\begin{pmatrix} (\mathbf{A}_1 \otimes \mathbf{I}_{n_2})\mathbf{f}^\top \\ (\mathbf{I}_{n_1} \otimes \mathbf{A}_2)\mathbf{f}^\top \end{pmatrix} \right]_2 \right)^{-1}$$

B   Security Proof for Sect. 4

We complete the security proof for the scheme Π in Sect. 4.2.

Theorem 1. *For all $\mathcal{A}$, there exist $\mathcal{B}_1$ and $\mathcal{B}_2$ with* $\mathsf{Time}(\mathcal{B}_1), \mathsf{Time}(\mathcal{B}_2) \approx \mathsf{Time}(\mathcal{A})$ *such that*

$$\mathsf{Adv}_{\mathcal{A}}^{\Pi}(\lambda) \leq \mathsf{Adv}_{\mathcal{B}_1}^{\mathrm{MDDH}_{k,k+1}^1}(\lambda) + \mathsf{Adv}_{\mathcal{B}_2}^{\mathrm{MDDH}_{k,mQ}^n}(\lambda) + 1/p$$

where n is length of public input $\mathbf{x}^*$ in the challenge, m is the parameter depending on size of function f and Q is the number of key queries.

Note that this yields a tight security reduction to the k-Lin assumption.

Game Sequence. We use $(\mathbf{x}^*, \mathbf{z}^*)$ to denote the semi-adaptive challenge and for notational simplicity, assume that all key queries f_j share the same parameters t and m. We prove Theorem 1 via a series of games.

<u>Game$_0$</u>: Real game.

Game$_1$: Identical to Game$_0$ except that ct* for $(\mathbf{x}^*, \mathbf{z}^*)$ is given by

$$\mathrm{ct}^* = \left(\boxed{\mathbf{c}^\top}_1, [(\mathbf{z}^*)^\top + \boxed{\mathbf{c}^\top}\mathbf{W}]_1, [\boxed{\mathbf{c}^\top}\mathbf{U}((\mathbf{x}^*)^\top \otimes \mathbf{I}_k) + \boxed{\mathbf{c}^\top}\mathbf{V}]_1 \right)$$

where $\mathbf{c} \leftarrow \mathbb{Z}_p^{k+1}$. We claim that Game$_0$ $\approx_c$ Game$_1$. This follows from $\mathrm{MDDH}_{k,k+1}^1$ assumption:

$$[\mathbf{A}^\top]_1, [\mathbf{s}^\top \mathbf{A}^\top]_1 \approx_c [\mathbf{A}^\top]_1, \boxed{[\mathbf{c}^\top]_1}.$$

In the reduction, we sample $\mathbf{W}, \mathbf{U}, \mathbf{V}$ honestly and use them to simulate mpk and KeyGen(msk, ·) along with $[\mathbf{A}^\top]_1$; the challenge ciphertext ct* is generated using the challenge term given above.

Game$_2$: Identical to Game$_1$ except that the j-th query f_j to KeyGen(msk, ·) is answered with

$$\mathrm{sk}_{f_j} = \left(\mathbf{C}^\perp \cdot \mathrm{sk}_{f_j}[1] + \mathbf{a}^\perp \cdot \mathrm{sk}_{f_j}[2], [\mathbf{R}_j]_2 \right)$$

with

$$\mathrm{sk}_{f_j}[1] = \left([\mathbf{A}^\top \underline{\mathbf{T}}_j + \mathbf{A}^\top \mathbf{W} \mathbf{M}_j]_2, [\mathbf{A}^\top \mathbf{T}_j \mathbf{L}_{1,j} + \mathbf{A}^\top \mathbf{U}(\mathbf{I}_n \otimes \mathbf{R}_j)]_2, [\mathbf{A}^\top \mathbf{T}_j \mathbf{L}_{0,j} + \mathbf{A}^\top \widetilde{\mathbf{V}} \mathbf{R}_j]_2 \right)$$

$$\mathrm{sk}_{f_j}[2] = \left([\mathbf{c}^\top \underline{\mathbf{T}}_j + \mathbf{c}^\top \mathbf{W} \mathbf{M}_j]_2, [\mathbf{c}^\top \mathbf{T}_j \mathbf{L}_{1,j} + \mathbf{c}^\top \mathbf{U}(\mathbf{I}_n \otimes \mathbf{R}_j)]_2, [\mathbf{c}^\top \mathbf{T}_j \mathbf{L}_{0,j} + \mathbf{c}^\top \mathbf{V} \mathbf{R}_j]_2 \right)$$

where $(\mathbf{L}_{1,j}, \mathbf{L}_{0,j}) \leftarrow \mathsf{lgen}(f_j)$, $\mathbf{T}_j \leftarrow \mathbb{Z}_p^{(k+1)\times t}$, $\mathbf{R}_j \leftarrow \mathbb{Z}_p^{k\times m}$, $\mathbf{c}$ is the randomness in ct* and $\mathbf{C}^\perp$ is defined such that $(\mathbf{A}|\mathbf{c})^\top (\mathbf{C}^\perp|\mathbf{a}^\perp) = \mathbf{I}_{k+1}$ (cf. Setup* in Sect. 4.2). By basic linear algebra, we have Game$_1$ = Game$_2$.

Game$_3$: Identical to Game$_2$ except that we replace Setup, Enc with Setup*, Enc* where ct* is given by

$$\mathrm{ct}^* = \left([\mathbf{c}^\top]_1, \boxed{[\widetilde{\mathbf{w}}^\top]_1, [\widetilde{\mathbf{v}}^\top]_1} \right)$$

and replace KeyGen(msk, ·) with KeyGen$_3^*$(msk*, ·), which works as KeyGen (msk, ·) in Game$_2$ except that, for the j-th query f_j, we compute

$$\mathrm{sk}_{f_j}[2] = \left(\begin{array}{l} [\underline{\widetilde{\mathbf{t}}}_j^\top - (\mathbf{z}^*)^\top \mathbf{M}_j + \widetilde{\mathbf{w}}^\top \mathbf{M}_j]_2, \; [\boxed{\widetilde{\mathbf{t}}_j^\top} \mathbf{L}_{1,j} + \boxed{\widetilde{\mathbf{u}}^\top}(\mathbf{I}_n \otimes \mathbf{R}_j)]_2, \\ [\boxed{\widetilde{\mathbf{t}}_j^\top} \mathbf{L}_{0,j} \boxed{-\widetilde{\mathbf{u}}^\top(\mathbf{I}_n \otimes \mathbf{R}_j)((\mathbf{x}^*)^\top \otimes \mathbf{I}_m)} + \widetilde{\mathbf{v}}^\top \mathbf{R}_j]_2 \end{array} \right)$$

where $\widetilde{\mathbf{w}}, \widetilde{\mathbf{v}}$ are given in msk* (output by Setup*) and $\widetilde{\mathbf{u}} \leftarrow \mathbb{Z}_p^{kn}, \mathbf{t}_j \leftarrow \mathbb{Z}_p^t, \mathbf{R}_j \leftarrow \mathbb{Z}_p^{k\times m}$. We claim that Game$_2$ $\approx_s$ Game$_3$. This follows from the following statement: for any full-rank $(\mathbf{A}|\mathbf{c})$, we have

$$(\mathbf{A}^\top \mathbf{U}, \mathbf{c}^\top \mathbf{U}, \mathbf{A}^\top \mathbf{W}, \mathbf{c}^\top \mathbf{W}, \quad \mathbf{A}^\top \mathbf{V}, \mathbf{c}^\top \mathbf{V}, \quad\quad \mathbf{A}^\top \mathbf{T}_j, \mathbf{c}^\top \mathbf{T}_j)$$
$$\equiv (\mathbf{A}^\top \mathbf{U}, \boxed{\widetilde{\mathbf{u}}^\top}, \mathbf{A}^\top \mathbf{W}, \boxed{\widetilde{\mathbf{w}}^\top - (\mathbf{z}^*)^\top}, \mathbf{A}^\top \mathbf{V}, \boxed{\widetilde{\mathbf{v}}^\top - \widetilde{\mathbf{u}}^\top(\mathbf{x}^* \otimes \mathbf{I}_k)}, \mathbf{A}^\top \mathbf{T}_j, \boxed{\widetilde{\mathbf{t}}_j^\top})$$

Game$_4$: Identical to Game$_3$ except that we replace KeyGen$_3^*$ with KeyGen$_4^*$ which works as KeyGen$_3^*$ except that, for the j-th query f_j, we compute

$$\mathrm{sk}_{f_j}[2] = \left([\underline{\widetilde{\mathbf{t}}}_j^\top - (\mathbf{z}^*)^\top \mathbf{M}_j + \widetilde{\mathbf{w}}^\top \mathbf{M}_j]_2, [\widetilde{\mathbf{t}}_j^\top \mathbf{L}_{1,j} + \boxed{\widehat{\mathbf{u}}_j^\top}]_2, [\widetilde{\mathbf{t}}_j^\top \mathbf{L}_{0,j} - \boxed{\widehat{\mathbf{u}}_j^\top}((\mathbf{x}^*)^\top \otimes \mathbf{I}_m) + \widetilde{\mathbf{v}}^\top \mathbf{R}_j]_2 \right)$$

where $\hat{\mathbf{u}}_j \leftarrow \mathbb{Z}_p^{nm}$ and $\mathbf{R}_j \leftarrow \mathbb{Z}_p^{k \times m}$. We claim that $\mathsf{Game}_3 \approx_c \mathsf{Game}_4$. This follows from $\mathrm{MDDH}_{k,mQ}^n$ assumption which tells us that

$$\left\{ [\tilde{\mathbf{u}}^\top (\mathbf{I}_n \otimes \mathbf{R}_j)]_2, [\mathbf{R}_j]_2 \right\}_{j \in [Q]} \approx_c \left\{ \boxed{[\hat{\mathbf{u}}_j^\top]_2}, [\mathbf{R}_j]_2 \right\}_{j \in [Q]}$$

where Q is the number of key queries.

$\underline{\mathsf{Game}_5}$: Identical to Game_4 except that we replace KeyGen_4^* with KeyGen^*; this is the ideal game. We claim that $\mathsf{Game}_4 \approx_s \mathsf{Game}_5$. This follows from the privacy of partial garbling scheme in Sect. 4.1.

We use $\mathsf{Adv}_{\mathcal{A}}^{\mathsf{xx}}(\lambda)$ to denote the advantage of adversary $\mathcal{A}$ in $\mathsf{Game}_{\mathsf{xx}}$. We prove the following lemmas showing the indistinguishability of adjacent games listed above.

Lemma 2 ($\mathsf{Game}_0 \approx_c \mathsf{Game}_1$). *For all $\mathcal{A}$, there exists $\mathcal{B}_1$ with $\mathsf{Time}(\mathcal{B}_1) \approx \mathsf{Time}(\mathcal{A})$ such that*

$$|\mathsf{Adv}_{\mathcal{A}}^1(\lambda) - \mathsf{Adv}_{\mathcal{A}}^0(\lambda)| \leq \mathsf{Adv}_{\mathcal{B}_1}^{\mathrm{MDDH}_{k,k+1}^1}(\lambda).$$

Lemma 3 ($\mathsf{Game}_2 \approx_c \mathsf{Game}_3$). *For all $\mathcal{A}$, we have $\mathsf{Adv}_{\mathcal{A}}^3(\lambda) \approx \mathsf{Adv}_{\mathcal{A}}^2(\lambda)$.*

The proof is the same as before, except we replace $\boxed{\mathbf{cW}}$, $\boxed{\mathbf{z}^* - \tilde{\mathbf{w}}}$ in $\mathsf{sk}_{f_j}[2]$ with $\boxed{\mathbf{cWM}_j}$, $\boxed{\mathbf{z}^* \mathbf{M}_j - \tilde{\mathbf{w}} \mathbf{M}_j}$

Proof (of Lemma 3). Recall that the difference between the two games lies in ct^* and $\mathsf{sk}_{f_j}[2]$: instead of computing

$$\mathsf{ct}^* = \left([\mathbf{c}^\top]_1, \boxed{[(\mathbf{z}^*)^\top + \mathbf{c}^\top \mathbf{W}]_1}, \boxed{[\mathbf{c}^\top \mathbf{U}((\mathbf{x}^*)^\top \otimes \mathbf{I}_k) + \mathbf{c}^\top \mathbf{V}]_1} \right)$$

$$\mathsf{sk}_{f_j}[2] = \left(\boxed{[\mathbf{c}^\top \mathbf{T}_j + \mathbf{c}^\top \mathbf{WM}_j]_2}, [\boxed{\mathbf{c}^\top \mathbf{T}_j} \mathbf{L}_{1,j} + \boxed{\mathbf{c}^\top \mathbf{U}}(\mathbf{I}_n \otimes \mathbf{R}_j)]_2, [\boxed{\mathbf{c}^\top \mathbf{T}_j} \mathbf{L}_{0,j} + \boxed{\mathbf{c}^\top \mathbf{VR}_j}]_2 \right)$$

in Game_2, we compute

$$\mathsf{ct}^* = \left([\mathbf{c}^\top]_1, \boxed{[\tilde{\mathbf{w}}^\top]_1}, \boxed{[\tilde{\mathbf{v}}^\top]_1} \right)$$

$$\mathsf{sk}_{f_j}[2] = \left([\boxed{\tilde{\mathbf{t}}_j^\top} - (\mathbf{z}^*)^\top \mathbf{M}_j + \boxed{\tilde{\mathbf{w}}^\top} \mathbf{M}_j]_2, [\boxed{\tilde{\mathbf{t}}_j^\top} \mathbf{L}_{1,j} + \boxed{\tilde{\mathbf{u}}^\top}(\mathbf{I}_n \otimes \mathbf{R}_j)]_2, \right.$$
$$\left. [\boxed{\tilde{\mathbf{t}}_j^\top} \mathbf{L}_{0,j} - \boxed{\tilde{\mathbf{u}}^\top}(\mathbf{I}_n \otimes \mathbf{R}_j)((\mathbf{x}^*)^\top \otimes \mathbf{I}_m) + \boxed{\tilde{\mathbf{v}}^\top} \mathbf{R}_j]_2 \right)$$

in Game_3.

This follows readily from the following statement: for all $\mathbf{x}^*, \mathbf{z}^*$,

$$(\mathbf{A}^\top \mathbf{U}, \boxed{\mathbf{c}^\top \mathbf{U}}, \quad \mathbf{A}^\top \mathbf{W}, \boxed{\mathbf{c}^\top \mathbf{W}}, \quad \mathbf{A}^\top \mathbf{V}, \boxed{\mathbf{c}^\top \mathbf{V}}, \quad \mathbf{A}^\top \mathbf{T}_j, \boxed{\mathbf{c}^\top \mathbf{T}_j})$$
$$\equiv (\mathbf{A}^\top \mathbf{U}, \boxed{\tilde{\mathbf{u}}^\top}, \quad \mathbf{A}^\top \mathbf{W}, \boxed{\tilde{\mathbf{w}}^\top - (\mathbf{z}^*)^\top}, \quad \mathbf{A}^\top \mathbf{V}, \boxed{\tilde{\mathbf{v}}^\top - \tilde{\mathbf{u}}^\top(\mathbf{x}^* \otimes \mathbf{I}_k)}, \quad \mathbf{A}^\top \mathbf{T}_j, \boxed{\tilde{\mathbf{t}}_j^\top})$$

where $\mathbf{U}, \mathbf{W}, \mathbf{V}, \tilde{\mathbf{w}}, \tilde{\mathbf{v}}$ are sampled as in Setup^* and $\tilde{\mathbf{u}} \leftarrow \mathbb{Z}_p^{kn}, \mathbf{T}_j \leftarrow \mathbb{Z}_p^{(k+1) \times t}, \mathbf{t}_j \leftarrow \mathbb{Z}_p^t$. We clarify that in the semi-adaptive security game, $(\mathbf{x}^*, \mathbf{z}^*)$ are chosen *after* seeing

$\mathbf{A}^\top\mathbf{U}, \mathbf{A}^\top\mathbf{W}, \mathbf{A}^\top\mathbf{V}$. Since the two distributions are identically distributed, the distinguishing advantage remains 0 even for adaptive choices of $\mathbf{x}^*, \mathbf{z}^*$ via a random guessing argument.

Finally, note that $\mathbf{A}^\top\mathbf{U}, \mathbf{A}^\top\mathbf{W}, \mathbf{A}^\top\mathbf{V}, \mathbf{A}^\top\mathbf{T}_j$ are used to simulate mpk, $\mathsf{sk}_{f_j}[1]$, whereas the boxed/gray terms are used to simulate $\mathsf{sk}_{f_j}[2]$. This readily proves the lemma. $\quad\square$

Lemma 4 (Game$_3 \approx_c$ Game$_4$). *For all $\mathcal{A}$, there exists $\mathcal{B}_2$ with* $\mathsf{Time}(\mathcal{B}_2) \approx \mathsf{Time}(\mathcal{A})$ *such that*

$$|\mathsf{Adv}_\mathcal{A}^4(\lambda) - \mathsf{Adv}_\mathcal{A}^3(\lambda)| \le \mathsf{Adv}_{\mathcal{B}_2}^{\mathrm{MDDH}_{k,mQ}^n}(\lambda)$$

where n is length of public input $\mathbf{x}$ in the challenge, m is the maximum size of function f and Q is the number of key queries.

Lemma 5 (Game$_4 \approx_s$ Game$_5$). *For all $\mathcal{A}$, we have* $\mathsf{Adv}_\mathcal{A}^5(\lambda) \approx \mathsf{Adv}_\mathcal{A}^4(\lambda)$.

The proof is the same as before except we replace $\mathbf{z}^*$ in $\mathsf{sk}_{f_j}[2]$, pgb, pgb* with $\mathbf{z}^*\mathbf{M}_j$ and $\tilde{\mathbf{w}}$ in $\mathsf{sk}_{f_j}[2]$ with $\tilde{\mathbf{w}}\mathbf{M}_j$.

Proof. Recall that the difference between the two games lies in $\mathsf{sk}_{f_j}[2]$: instead of computing

$$\mathsf{sk}_{f_j}[2] = \big(\,[\,\boxed{\tilde{\mathbf{t}}_j^\top - (\mathbf{z}^*)^\top\mathbf{M}_j} + \tilde{\mathbf{w}}\mathbf{M}_j]_2,\ [\,\boxed{\tilde{\mathbf{t}}_j^\top\mathbf{L}_{1,j} + \hat{\mathbf{u}}_j^\top}\,]_2,\ [\,\boxed{\tilde{\mathbf{t}}_j^\top\mathbf{L}_{0,j} - \hat{\mathbf{u}}^\top(\mathbf{x}^*\otimes\mathbf{I}_m)} + \tilde{\mathbf{v}}^\top\mathbf{R}]_2\,\big)$$

in KeyGen$_4^*$ (i.e., Game$_4$), we compute

$$\mathsf{sk}_{f_j}[2] = \big(\,[\,\boxed{\tilde{\mathbf{t}}_j^\top} + \tilde{\mathbf{w}}\mathbf{M}_j]_2,\ [\,\boxed{\hat{\mathbf{u}}_j^\top}\,]_2,\ [\,\boxed{\tilde{\mathbf{t}}_j^\top(\mathbf{L}_{1,j}(\mathbf{x}^*\otimes\mathbf{I}_m)+\mathbf{L}_{0,j})+\mathbf{e}_1\cdot\mathbf{z}^*\mathbf{M}_j f_j(\mathbf{x}^*)^\top - \hat{\mathbf{u}}_j^\top(\mathbf{x}^*\otimes\mathbf{I}_m)} + \tilde{\mathbf{v}}^\top\mathbf{R}]_2\,\big)$$

in KeyGen* (i.e., Game$_5$). By change of variable $\hat{\mathbf{u}}_j^\top \mapsto \hat{\mathbf{u}}_j^\top - \tilde{\mathbf{t}}_j^\top\mathbf{L}_{1,j}$ for all $j \in [Q]$ in Game$_4$, we can rewrite in the form:

$$\mathsf{sk}_{f_j}[2] = \big(\,[-\mathbf{p}_{j,1}^\top + \tilde{\mathbf{w}}\mathbf{M}_j]_2,\ [\hat{\mathbf{u}}_j^\top]_2,\ [\mathbf{p}_{j,2}^\top - \hat{\mathbf{u}}_j^\top(\mathbf{x}^*\otimes\mathbf{I}_m) + \tilde{\mathbf{v}}^\top\mathbf{R}]_2\,\big)$$

where

$$(\mathbf{p}_{j,1}\|\mathbf{p}_{j,2}) \leftarrow \begin{cases} \boxed{\mathsf{pgb}(f_j, \mathbf{x}^*, \mathbf{z}^*\mathbf{M}_j; \tilde{\mathbf{t}}_j)} & \text{in Game}_4 \\ \boxed{\mathsf{pgb}^*(f_j, \mathbf{x}^*, \mathbf{z}^*\mathbf{M}_j f_j(\mathbf{x}^*)^\top; \tilde{\mathbf{t}}_j)} & \text{in Game}_5 \end{cases}$$

Then the lemma immediately follows from the privacy of underlying partial garbling scheme which means $\mathsf{pgb}(f_j, \mathbf{x}^*, \mathbf{z}^*\mathbf{M}_j) \approx_s \mathsf{pgb}^*(f_j, \mathbf{x}^*, \mathbf{z}^*\mathbf{M}_j f_j(\mathbf{x}^*)^\top)$. $\quad\square$

References

1. Abdalla, M., Bourse, F., De Caro, A., Pointcheval, D.: Simple functional encryption schemes for inner products. In: Katz, J. (ed.) PKC 2015. LNCS, vol. 9020, pp. 733–751. Springer, Heidelberg (2015). https://doi.org/10.1007/978-3-662-46447-2_33
2. Abdalla, M., Gong, J., Wee, H.: Functional encryption for attribute-weighted sums from k-Lin. In: Micciancio, D., Ristenpart, T. (eds.) CRYPTO 2020. LNCS, vol. 12170, pp. 685–716. Springer, Cham (2020). https://doi.org/10.1007/978-3-030-56784-2_23

3. Agrawal, S., Libert, B., Stehlé, D.: Fully secure functional encryption for inner products, from standard assumptions. In: Robshaw, M., Katz, J. (eds.) CRYPTO 2016. LNCS, vol. 9816, pp. 333–362. Springer, Heidelberg (2016). https://doi.org/10.1007/978-3-662-53015-3_12

4. Ananth, P., Jain, A., Lin, H., Matt, C., Sahai, A.: Indistinguishability obfuscation without multilinear maps: new paradigms via low degree weak pseudorandomness and security amplification. In: Boldyreva, A., Micciancio, D. (eds.) CRYPTO 2019. LNCS, vol. 11694, pp. 284–332. Springer, Cham (2019). https://doi.org/10.1007/978-3-030-26954-8_10

5. Baltico, C.E.Z., Catalano, D., Fiore, D., Gay, R.: Practical functional encryption for quadratic functions with applications to predicate encryption. In: Katz, J., Shacham, H. (eds.) CRYPTO 2017. LNCS, vol. 10401, pp. 67–98. Springer, Cham (2017). https://doi.org/10.1007/978-3-319-63688-7_3

6. Boneh, D., Sahai, A., Waters, B.: Fully collusion resistant traitor tracing with short ciphertexts and private keys. In: Vaudenay, S. (ed.) EUROCRYPT 2006. LNCS, vol. 4004, pp. 573–592. Springer, Heidelberg (2006). https://doi.org/10.1007/11761679_34

7. Boneh, D., Sahai, A., Waters, B.: Functional encryption: definitions and challenges. In: Ishai, Y. (ed.) TCC 2011. LNCS, vol. 6597, pp. 253–273. Springer, Heidelberg (2011). https://doi.org/10.1007/978-3-642-19571-6_16

8. Boneh, D., Waters, B.: A fully collusion resistant broadcast, trace, and revoke system. In: Juels, A., Wright, R.N., De Capitani di Vimercati, S. (eds.), ACM CCS 2006, pp. 211–220. ACM Press, October/November 2006

9. Chen, J., Wee, H.: Semi-adaptive attribute-based encryption and improved delegation for boolean formula. In: Abdalla, M., De Prisco, R. (eds.) SCN 2014. LNCS, vol. 8642, pp. 277–297. Springer, Cham (2014). https://doi.org/10.1007/978-3-319-10879-7_16

10. Escala, A., Herold, G., Kiltz, E., Ràfols, C., Villar, J.: An algebraic framework for Diffie-Hellman assumptions. In: Canetti, R., Garay, J.A. (eds.) CRYPTO 2013. LNCS, vol. 8043, pp. 129–147. Springer, Heidelberg (2013). https://doi.org/10.1007/978-3-642-40084-1_8

11. Garg, S., Kumarasubramanian, A., Sahai, A., Waters, B.: Building efficient fully collusion-resilient traitor tracing and revocation schemes. In: Al-Shaer, E., Keromytis, A.D., Shmatikov, V. (eds.) ACM CCS 2010, pp. 121–130. ACM Press, October 2010

12. Gay, R.: A new paradigm for public-key functional encryption for degree-2 polynomials. In: Kiayias, A., Kohlweiss, M., Wallden, P., Zikas, V. (eds.) PKC 2020. LNCS, vol. 12110, pp. 95–120. Springer, Cham (2020). https://doi.org/10.1007/978-3-030-45374-9_4

13. Gay, R., Jain, A., Lin, H., Sahai, A.: Indistinguishability obfuscation from simple-to-state hard problems: new assumptions, new techniques, and simplification. Cryptology ePrint Archive, Report 2020/764 (2020)

14. Gong, J., Qian, H.: Simple and efficient FE for quadratic functions. Cryptology ePrint Archive, Report 2020/1026 (2020)

15. Gorbunov, S., Vaikuntanathan, V., Wee, H.: Predicate encryption for circuits from LWE. In: Gennaro, R., Robshaw, M. (eds.) CRYPTO 2015. LNCS, vol. 9216, pp. 503–523. Springer, Heidelberg (2015). https://doi.org/10.1007/978-3-662-48000-7_25

16. Goyal, R., Koppula, V., Waters, B.: New approaches to traitor tracing with embedded identities. In: Hofheinz, D., Rosen, A. (eds.) TCC 2019. LNCS, vol. 11892, pp. 149–179. Springer, Cham (2019). https://doi.org/10.1007/978-3-030-36033-7_6

17. Ishai, Y., Wee, H.: Partial garbling schemes and their applications. In: Esparza, J., Fraigniaud, P., Husfeldt, T., Koutsoupias, E. (eds.) ICALP 2014. LNCS, vol. 8572, pp. 650–662. Springer, Heidelberg (2014). https://doi.org/10.1007/978-3-662-43948-7_54

18. Jain, A., Lin, H., Matt, C., Sahai, A.: How to leverage hardness of constant-degree expanding polynomials over a $\mathbb{R}$ to build $i\mathcal{O}$. In: Ishai, Y., Rijmen, V. (eds.) Part I. LNCS, vol. 11476, pp. 251–281. Springer, Heidelberg (2019)

19. Jain, A., Lin, H., Sahai, A.: Simplifying constructions and assumptions for IO. IACR Cryptology ePrint Archive 2019:1252 (2019)
20. Lin, H.: Indistinguishability obfuscation from SXDH on 5-linear maps and locality-5 PRGs. In: Katz, J., Shacham, H. (eds.) CRYPTO 2017. LNCS, vol. 10401, pp. 599–629. Springer, Cham (2017). https://doi.org/10.1007/978-3-319-63688-7_20
21. Ryffel, T., Pointcheval, D., Bach, F., Dufour-Sans, E., Gay, R.: Partially encrypted deep learning using functional encryption. In: Advances in Neural Information Processing Systems, NeurIPS 2019, Vancouver, BC, Canada, 8–14 December 2019, pp. 4519–4530 (2019)
22. Wee, H.: Attribute-hiding predicate encryption in bilinear groups, revisited. In: Kalai, Y., Reyzin, L. (eds.) TCC 2017. LNCS, vol. 10677, pp. 206–233. Springer, Cham (2017). https://doi.org/10.1007/978-3-319-70500-2_8

On Perfect Correctness in (Lockable) Obfuscation

Rishab Goyal[1], Venkata Koppula[2], Satyanarayana Vusirikala[3(✉)],
and Brent Waters[4]

[1] MIT, Cambridge, USA
goyal@utexas.edu
[2] Weizmann Institute of Science, Rehovot, Israel
venkata.koppula@weizmann.ac.il
[3] University of Texas at Austin, Austin, USA
satya@cs.utexas.edu
[4] University of Texas at Austin and NTT Research, Austin, USA
bwaters@cs.utexas.edu

Abstract. In a lockable obfuscation scheme [28,39] a party takes as input a program P, a lock value α, a message msg and produces an obfuscated program $\tilde{P}$. The obfuscated program can be evaluated on an input x to learn the message msg if $P(x) = \alpha$. The security of such schemes states that if α is randomly chosen (independent of P and msg), then one cannot distinguish an obfuscation of P from a "dummy" obfuscation. Existing constructions of lockable obfuscation achieve provable security under the Learning with Errors assumption. One limitation of these constructions is that they achieve only statistical correctness and allow for a possible one sided error where the obfuscated program could output the msg on some value x where $P(x) \neq \alpha$.

In this work we motivate the problem of studying perfect correctness in lockable obfuscation for the case where the party performing the obfuscation might wish to inject a backdoor or hole in correctness. We begin by studying the existing constructions and identify two components that are susceptible to imperfect correctness. The first is in the LWE-based pseudo random generators (PRGs) that are non-injective, while the second is in the last level testing procedure of the core constructions.

We address each in turn. First, we build upon previous work to design *injective* PRGs that are provably secure from the LWE assumption. Next, we design an alternative last level testing procedure that has additional structure to prevent correctness errors. We then provide a surgical proof of security (to avoid redundancy) that connects our construction to the construction by Goyal, Koppula, and Waters (GKW) [28]. Specifically, we show how for a random value α an obfuscation under our new construction is indistinguishable from an obfuscation under the existing GKW construction.

© International Association for Cryptologic Research 2020
R. Pass and K. Pietrzak (Eds.): TCC 2020, LNCS 12550, pp. 229–259, 2020.
https://doi.org/10.1007/978-3-030-64375-1_9

1   Introduction

In cryptographic program obfuscation a user wants to take a program P and publish an obfuscated program $\widetilde{P}$. The obfuscated program should maintain the same functionality of the original while intuitively hiding anything about the structure of P beyond what can be determined by querying its input/output functionality.

One issue in defining semantics is whether we demand that $\widetilde{P}$ always match the functionality exactly on all inputs or we relax correctness to allow for some deviation with negligible probability. At first blush such differences in semantics might appear to be very minor. With a negligible correctness error it is straightforward for the obfsucator to parameterize an obfuscation such that the probability of a correctness error is some minuscule value such as 2^{-300} which would be much less than say the probability of dying from an asteroid strike (1 in 74 million).

The idea that statistical correctness is always good enough, however, rests on the presumption that the obfuscator itself wants to avoid errors. Consider for example, a party that is tasked with building a program that screens images from a video feed and raises an alert if any suspicious activity is detected. The party could first create a program P to perform this function and then release an obfuscated version $\widetilde{P}$ that could hide features of the proprietary vision recognition algorithm about how the program was built. But what if the party wants to abuse their role? For instance, they might want to publish a program $\widetilde{P}$ that unfairly flags a certain group or individual. Or perhaps is programmed with a backdoor to let a certain image pass.

In an obfuscation scheme with perfect correctness, it might be possible to audit such behavior. For example, an auditor could require that the obfuscating party produce their original program P along with the random coins used in obfuscating it. Then the auditor could check that the original program P meets certain requirements as well as seeing that $\widetilde{P}$ is indeed an obfuscation of P.[1] (We emphasize that if one does not want to reveal P to an auditor that such a proof can be done in zero knowledge or by attaching a non-interactive zero knowledge proof to the program. This proof will certify that the program meets some specification or has some properties; e.g. "there are at most three inputs that result in the output '010'.") However, for such a process to work it is imperative that the obfuscation algorithm be perfectly correct. Otherwise, a malicious obfuscator could potentially start with a perfectly legitimate program P, but purposefully choose coins that would flip the output of a program at a particular input point.

Another important context where perfect correctness matters is when a primitive serves as a component or building block in a larger cryptosystem. We present a few examples where a difference in perfect versus imperfect

---

[1] The above argument relies on the ability of one being able to test the original program meets a certain template or is otherwise well-formed. Our work does not address under which circumstances this is possible.

correctness in a primitive can manifest into fundamentally impacting security when complied into a larger system.

1. Dwork, Naor and Reingold [25] showed that the classical transformations of IND-CPA to IND-CCA transformations via NIZKs [22,33] may not work when the IND-CPA scheme is not perfectly correct. They addressed this by amplifying standard imperfect correctness to what they called almost-all-keys correctness.
2. Bitansky, Khurana, and Paneth [10] constructed zero knowledge arguments with low round complexity. For their work, they required lockable obfuscation with one-sided perfect correctness.[2]
3. Recently, [4,11] constructed constant-round post-quantum secure constant-round ZK arguments. These protocols use lockable obfuscation as a means to commit a message with pefect-binding property. Without both-sided perfect correctness, the commitment scheme and thereby the ZK argument scheme fails to be secure.

In this paper we study perfect correctness in lockable obfuscation, which is arguably the most powerful form of obfuscation which is provably secure under a standard assumption. Recall that a lockable obfuscation [28,39] scheme takes as input a program P, a message msg, a lock value α and produces an obfuscated program $\tilde{P}$. The semantics of evaluation are such that on input x the evaluation of the program outputs msg if and only if $P(x) = \alpha$. Lockable obfuscation security requires that the obfuscation of any program P with a randomly (and independently of P and msg) chosen value α will be indistinguishable from a "dummy" obfuscated program that is created without any knowledge of P and msg other than their sizes. While the power of lockable obfuscation does not reach that of indistinguishability obfuscation [8,26,37], it has been shown to be sufficient for many applications such as obfuscating conjunction and affine testers, upgrading public key encryption, identity-based encryption [14,20,38] and attribute-based encryption [36] to their anonymous versions and giving random oracle uninstantiability and circular security separation results, and most recently, building efficient traitor tracing systems [15,18].

The works of Goyal, Koppula, and Waters [28] and Wichs and Zirdelis [39] introduced and gave constructions of lockable obfuscation provably secure under the Learning with Errors [35] assumption. A limitation of both constructions (inherited from the bit-encryption cycle testers of [30]) is that they provide only statistical correctness. In particular, there exists a one-sided error in which it is possible that there exists an input x such that $P(x) \neq \alpha$ yet the obfuscated program outputs msg on input x.

Our Results. With this motivation in mind we seek to create a lockable obfuscation scheme that is perfectly correct and retains the provable security under

---

[2] In this particular example perfect correctness [28,39] was already present for the side they needed.

the LWE assumption. We begin by examining the GKW lockable obfuscation for branching programs and identify two points in the construction that are susceptible to correctness errors. The first is in the use of an LWE-based pseudo random generator that could be non-injective. The second is in the "last level testing procedure" comprised in the core construction. We address each one in turn. First, we build over the previous work to design and prove a new PRG construction that is both injective and probably secure from the LWE assumption. (We also create an injective PRG from the learning parity with noise (LPN) assumption as an added bonus.) Then we look to surgically modify the GKW construction to change the last level testing procedure to avoid the correctness pitfall. We accomplish this by adding more structure to a final level of matrices to avoid false matches, but doing so makes the new construction incompatible with the existing security proof. Instead of re-deriving the entire proof of security, we carefully show how an obfuscation under our new construction with a random lock value is indistinguishable from an obfuscation under the previous construction. Security then follows.

While the focus of this work has been on constructing lockable obfuscation schemes with perfect correctness building upon the schemes of [28, 39], we believe our techniques can also be applied to the recent obfuscation scheme by Chen, Vaikuntanathan, and Wee [19].

1.1 Technical Overview

We first present a short overview of the statistically correct lockable obfuscation scheme by Goyal, Koppula and Waters [29, Appendix D], (henceforth referred to as the GKW scheme), and discuss the barriers to achieving perfect correctness. Next, we discuss how to overcome each of these barriers in order to achieve perfect correctness.

Overview of the GKW Scheme. The GKW scheme can be broken down into three parts: (i) constructing a lockable obfuscation scheme for NC^1 circuits and 1-bit messages, (ii) bootstrapping to lockable obfuscation for poly-depth circuits, and (iii) extending to multi-bit message space. It turns out that steps (ii) and (iii) preserve the correctness properties of the underlying lockable obfuscation scheme, thus in order to build a *perfectly correct* lockable obfuscation scheme for poly-depth circuits and multi-bit messages, we only need to build a *perfectly correct* lockable obfuscation scheme for NC^1 and 1-bit messages.[3] We start by giving a brief overview of the lockable obfuscation scheme for NC^1, and then move to highlight the barriers to achieving perfect correctness.

One of the key ingredients in the GKW construction is a family of log-depth (statistically injective) PRGs with polynomial stretch (mapping ℓ bits to ℓ_{PRG} bits for an appropriately chosen polynomial ℓ_{PRG}). Consider a log-depth circuit C that takes as input ℓ_{in}-bits and outputs ℓ-bits. To obfuscate circuit C

---

[3] Strictly speaking, [29, Appendix C] shows how to extend the message space for semi-statistically correct lockable obfuscation schemes. However, the same transformation also works for perfectly correct schemes.

with lock value $\alpha \in \{0,1\}^\ell$ and message msg, the GKW scheme first chooses PRG from the family and computes an "expanded" lock value $\beta = \text{PRG}(\alpha)$. It then takes the circuit $\widehat{C} = \text{PRG}(C(\cdot))$ that takes as input ℓ_{in}-bits and outputs ℓ_{PRG}-bits, and generates the permutation branching program representation of $\widehat{C}$. Let $\text{BP}^{(i)}$ denote the branching program that computes i^{th} output bit of $\widehat{C}$. Since C and PRG are both log-depth circuits, we know (due to Barrington's theorem [9]) that $\text{BP}^{(i)}$ is of some polynomial length L and width 5.[4] The obfuscator continues by sampling $5\ell_{\text{PRG}}$ matrices, for each level except the last one, using lattice trapdoor samplers such that all the matrices at any particular level share a common trapdoor. Let $\mathbf{B}_{j,k}^{(i)}$ denote the matrix corresponding to level j, state k of the ith branching program $\text{BP}^{(i)}$. Next, it chooses the top level matrices $\left\{\mathbf{B}_{L,1}^{(i)}, \dots, \mathbf{B}_{L,5}^{(i)}\right\}$ for each $i \in [\ell_{\text{PRG}}]$ uniformly at random subject to the following "sum-constraint":

$$\sum_{i: \, \beta_i = 0} \mathbf{B}_{L,\text{rej}^{(i)}}^{(i)} + \sum_{i: \, \beta_i = 1} \mathbf{B}_{L,\text{acc}^{(i)}}^{(i)} = \begin{cases} \mathbf{0}^{n \times m} & \text{if msg} = 0, \\ \sqrt{q} \cdot \left[\mathbf{I}_n \, \| \, \mathbf{0}^{n \times (m-n)}\right] & \text{if msg} = 1. \end{cases}$$

Looking ahead, sampling the top level matrices in such a way helps to encode the expanded lock value β such that an evaluator can test for this relation if it has an input x such that $C(x) = \alpha$.

Next step in the obfuscation procedure is to encode the branching programs using the matrices and trapdoors sampled above. The idea is to choose a set of $\ell_{\text{PRG}} \cdot L$ "transition matrices" $\{\mathbf{C}_j^{(i,0)}, \mathbf{C}_j^{(i,1)}\}_{i,j}$ such that each matrix $\mathbf{C}_j^{(i,b)}$ is short and can be used to evaluate its corresponding state transition permutation $\sigma_{j,b}^{(i)}$. The obfuscation of C is set to be the ℓ_{PRG} base-level matrices $\{\mathbf{B}_{0,1}^{(i)}\}_i$ and $\ell_{\text{PRG}} \cdot L$ transition matrices $\{\mathbf{C}_j^{(i,0)}, \mathbf{C}_j^{(i,1)}\}_{i,j}$.

Evaluating the obfuscated program on input $x \in \{0,1\}^{\ell_{\text{in}}}$ is analogous to evaluating the ℓ_{PRG} branching programs on x. For each $i \in [\ell_{\text{PRG}}]$, the evaluation algorithm first computes $\mathbf{M}_i = \mathbf{B}_{0,1}^{(i)} \cdot \prod_{j=1}^L \mathbf{C}_j^{(i,x_{\text{inp}(j)})}$ and then sums them together as $\mathbf{M} = \sum_i \mathbf{M}_i$. To compute the final output, it looks at the entries of matrix $\mathbf{M}$, if all the entries are small (say less than $q^{1/4}$) it outputs 0, else if they are close to $\sqrt{q}$ it outputs 1, otherwise it outputs $\perp$.

To argue correctness, they first show that the matrix $\mathbf{M}$ computed by the evaluator is close to $\mathbf{\Gamma} \cdot \sum_i \mathbf{B}_{L,\text{st}^{(i)}}^{(i)}$ where $\mathbf{\Gamma}$ is some low-norm matrix and $\text{st}^{(i)}$ denotes the final state of $\text{BP}^{(i)}$.[5] It is easy to verify that if $C(x) = \alpha$, then $\widehat{C}(x) = \beta$, and therefore

---

[4] Recall, a permutation branching program of length L and width w can be represented using w states, $2L$ permutations $\sigma_{j,b}$ over states for each level $j \leq L$, an input-selector function $\text{inp}(\cdot)$ which determines the input read at each level, and an accepting and rejecting state. The program execution starts at state $\text{st} = 1$ of level 0, and iteratively carried out as $\text{st} = \sigma_{i,b}(\text{st})$ (where b is the input bit read at level i). Depending upon the final state (i.e., at level L), the program either accepts or rejects.

[5] That is, $\text{st}^{(i)} = \text{acc}^{(i)}$ if $\widehat{C}(x)_i = 0$ and $\text{rej}^{(i)}$ otherwise.

$$\mathbf{M} \approx \mathbf{\Gamma} \cdot \sum_i \mathbf{B}^{(i)}_{L,\mathsf{st}^{(i)}} = \begin{cases} \mathbf{0}^{n \times m} & \text{if msg} = 0, \\ \sqrt{q} \cdot \left[\mathbf{\Gamma} \,\|\, \mathbf{0}^{n \times (m-n)} \right] & \text{if msg} = 1. \end{cases}$$

As a result, if $C(x) = \alpha$, then the evaluation is correct. However, it turns out that even when $C(x) \neq \alpha$ the evaluation algorithm could still output $0/1$ (recall that if $C(x) \neq \alpha$, then the evaluation algorithm must output $\perp$). There are two sources of errors here.

Non-Injective PRGs. First, it is possible that the PRG chosen is not injective. In this event (which happens with negligible probability if PRG is chosen honestly), there exist two inputs $y \neq y'$ such that $\mathrm{PRG}(y) = \mathrm{PRG}(y')$. As a result, if there exist two inputs $x, x' \in \{0,1\}^{\ell_{\mathrm{in}}}$ such that $C(x) = y, C(x') = y'$, then the obfuscation of C with lock y and message msg, when evaluated on x', outputs msg instead of $\perp$. Note that this source of error can be eliminated if we use a perfectly injective PRG family instead of a statistically injective PRG family.

Sum-Constraints. The second source of error is due to the way we encode the lock value in the top-level matrices. Let $x \neq x'$ be two distinct inputs, and let $\alpha = C(x)$, $\alpha' = C(x')$, $\beta = \mathrm{PRG}(\alpha)$ and $\beta' = \mathrm{PRG}(\alpha')$. Suppose we obfuscate C with lock value α. Recall that the obfuscator samples the top-level matrices uniformly at random with the only constraint that the top-level matrices corresponding to the expanded lock value β either sum to 0 (if msg = 0), else they sum to certain medium-ranged matrix (i.e., entries $\approx \sqrt{q}$). Now this corresponds to sampling all but one top-level matrix uniformly at random (and without any constraint), and that one special matrix such that the constraint is satisfied. Therefore, it is possible (although with small probability) that summing together the top-level matrices for string β' is close to the top-level matrix sum for string β. That is,

$$\sum_{i:\ \beta_i = 0} \mathbf{B}^{(i)}_{L,\mathsf{rej}^{(i)}} + \sum_{i:\ \beta_i = 1} \mathbf{B}^{(i)}_{L,\mathsf{acc}^{(i)}} \approx \sum_{i:\ \beta'_i = 0} \mathbf{B}^{(i)}_{L,\mathsf{rej}^{(i)}} + \sum_{i:\ \beta'_i = 1} \mathbf{B}^{(i)}_{L,\mathsf{acc}^{(i)}}.$$

As a result, if we obfuscate C with lock α and message msg, and evaluate this on input x', then it could also output msg instead of $\perp$. This type of error is trickier to remove as it is crucial for security in the GKW construction that these matrices look completely random if one doesn't know the lock value α. To get around this issue, we provide an alternate top-level matrix sampling procedure that guarantees perfect correctness.

We next present our solutions to remove the above sources of imperfectness. First, we construct a perfectly injective PRG family that is secure under the LWE assumption. This resolves the first problem. Thereafter, we discuss our modifications to the GKW construction for resolving the *sum-constraint* error. Later we also briefly talk about our perfectly injective PRG family that is secure under the LPN assumption.

Perfectly Injective PRG Family. We will first show a perfectly injective PRG family based on the LWE assumption. The construction is a low-depth PRG family with unbounded (polynomial) stretch. The security of this construction relies on the Learning with Rounding (LWR) assumption, introduced by Banerjee, Peikert and Rosen. [7], which in turn can be reduced to LWE (with subexponential modulus/error ratio). First, let us recall the LWR assumption. This assumption is associated with two moduli p, q where $p < q$. The modulus q is the modulus of computation, and p is the rounding modulus. Let $\lfloor \cdot \rceil_p$ denote a mapping from $\mathbb{Z}_q$ to $\mathbb{Z}_p$ which maps integers based on their higher order bits. The LWR assumption states that for a uniformly random secret vector $\mathbf{s} \in \mathbb{Z}_q^n$ and uniformly random matrix $\mathbf{A} \in \mathbb{Z}_q^{n \times m}$, $\lfloor \mathbf{s}^T \cdot \mathbf{A} \rceil_p$ looks like a uniformly random vector in $\mathbb{Z}_p^m$, even when given $\mathbf{A}$. We will work with a 'binary secrets' version where the secret vector $\mathbf{s}$ is a binary vector.

Let us start by reviewing the PRG construction provided by Banerjee et al. [7]. In their scheme, the setup algorithm first chooses two moduli $p < q$ and outputs a uniformly random $n \times m$ matrix $\mathbf{A}$ with elements from $\mathbb{Z}_q$. The PRG evaluation takes as input an n bit string $\mathbf{s}$ and outputs $\lfloor \mathbf{s}^T \cdot \mathbf{A} \rceil_p$, where $\lfloor x \rceil_p$ essentially outputs the higher order bits of x. Assuming m is sufficiently larger than n and moduli p, q are appropriately chosen, for a uniformly random matrix $\mathbf{A} \leftarrow \mathbb{Z}_q^{n \times m}$, the function $\lfloor \mathbf{s}^T \cdot \mathbf{A} \rceil_p$ is injective with high probability (over the choice of $\mathbf{A}$). In order to achieve perfect injectivity, we sample the public matrix $\mathbf{A}$ in a special way.

In our scheme, the setup algorithm chooses a uniformly random matrix $\mathbf{B}$ and a low norm matrix $\mathbf{C}$. It sets $\mathbf{D}$ to be a diagonal matrix with medium-value entries ($\mathbf{D}$ is a fixed deterministic matrix). It sets $\mathbf{A} = [\mathbf{B} \mid \mathbf{B} \cdot \mathbf{C} + \mathbf{D}]$ and outputs it as part of the public parameters, together with the LWR moduli p, q. To evaluate the PRG on input $\mathbf{s} \in \{0, 1\}^n$, one outputs $\mathbf{y} = \lfloor \mathbf{s}^T \cdot \mathbf{A} \rceil_p$. Intuitively, the $\mathbf{D}$ matrix acts as a error correcting code, and if $\mathbf{s}_1 \neq \mathbf{s}_2$, then there is at least one coordinate such that $\lfloor \mathbf{s}_1^T \cdot \mathbf{D} \rceil_p$ and $\lfloor \mathbf{s}_2^T \cdot \mathbf{D} \rceil_p$ are far apart.

Suppose $\mathbf{s}_1$ and $\mathbf{s}_2$ are two bitstrings such that $\lfloor \mathbf{s}_1^T \cdot \mathbf{A} \rceil_p = \lfloor \mathbf{s}_2^T \cdot \mathbf{A} \rceil_p$. Then $\lfloor \mathbf{s}_1^T \cdot \mathbf{B} \rceil_p = \lfloor \mathbf{s}_2^T \cdot \mathbf{B} \rceil_p$, and as a result, $\lfloor \mathbf{s}_1^T \cdot \mathbf{B} \cdot \mathbf{C} \rceil_p$ and $\lfloor \mathbf{s}_2^T \cdot \mathbf{B} \cdot \mathbf{C} \rceil_p$ have close enough entries as $\mathbf{C}$ has small entries. However, this implies that $\lfloor \mathbf{s}_1^T \cdot \mathbf{D} \rceil_p$ and $\lfloor \mathbf{s}_2^T \cdot \mathbf{D} \rceil_p$ also have close enough entries, which implies that $\mathbf{s}_1 = \mathbf{s}_2$.

Pseudorandomness follows from the observation that $\mathbf{A}$ looks like a uniformly random matrix. Once we replace $[\mathbf{B} \mid \mathbf{B} \cdot \mathbf{C} + \mathbf{D}]$ with a uniformly random matrix $\mathbf{A}$, we can use the binary secrets version of LWR to argue that $\mathbf{s}^T \cdot \mathbf{A}$ is indistinguishable from a uniformly random vector. This is discussed in detail in Sect. 3.

Relation to the Perfectly Binding Commitment Scheme of [27]: The perfectly injective PRG family outlined above builds upon some core ideas from the perfectly binding commitments schemes in [27]. Below, we will describe the constructions from [27], and discuss the main differences in our PRG schemes.

In the LWE based commitment scheme, the sender first chooses a modulus q, matrices $\mathbf{B}, \mathbf{C}, \mathbf{D}$ and $\mathbf{E}$ of dimensions $n \times n$, where $\mathbf{B}$ is a uniformly random matrix, entries in $\mathbf{C}, \mathbf{E}$ are drawn from the low norm noise distribution, and $\mathbf{D}$

is some fixed diagonal matrix with medium-value entries. It sets $\mathbf{A} = [\mathbf{B} \,||\, \mathbf{B} \cdot \mathbf{C} + \mathbf{D} + \mathbf{E}]$. Next, it chooses a vector $\mathbf{s}$ from the noise distribution, vector $\mathbf{w}$ uniformly at random, vector $\mathbf{e}$ from the noise distribution and f from the noise distribution. To commit to a bit b, it sets $\mathbf{y} = \mathbf{A}^T \cdot \mathbf{s} + \mathbf{e}$, $z = \mathbf{w}^T \cdot \mathbf{s} + f + b(q/2)$, and the commitment is $(\mathbf{A}, \mathbf{w}, \mathbf{y}, z)$. The opening simply consists of the randomness used for constructing the commitment.

The main differences between our PRG construction and their commitment scheme are as follows: (i) we need to separate out their initial commitment step into PRG setup and evaluation phase, (ii) since the PRG evaluation is deterministic, we cannot add noise (unlike in the case of commitments). Therefore, we need to use Learning with Rounding. Finally, we need to carefully choose the rounding modulus p as we want to ensure that the rounding operation does not round off the contribution from the special matrix $\mathbf{D}$ while still allowing us to reduce to the LWR assumption.

Sum-Constraint on the Top-Level Matrices. We will now discuss how the top-level matrices can be sampled to ensure perfect correctness. In order to do so, let us first consider the following simplified problem which captures the essence of the issue. Given a string $\beta \in \{0,1\}^\ell$, we wish to sample 2ℓ matrices $\{\mathbf{M}_{i,b}\}_{i \in [\ell], b \in \{0,1\}}$ such that they satisfy the following three constraints:

1. $\sum_i \mathbf{M}_{i,\beta_i}$ has 'small' entries (say $< q^{1/4}$).
2. For all $\beta' \neq \beta$, $\sum_i \mathbf{M}_{i,\beta'_i}$ has 'large' entries (say greater than $q^{1/2}$).
3. For a uniformly random choice of string β, the set of 2ℓ matrices $\{\mathbf{M}_{i,b}\}_{i,b}$ 'look' like random matrices.

In the GKW construction, the authors use a simple sampler that the sampled matrices satisfy the first constraint, and by applying the Leftover Hash Lemma (LHL) they also show that the corresponding matrices satisfy the third constraint. However, to achieve perfect correctness, we need to build a matrix sampler such that its output always satisfy all the three constraints. To this end, we show that by carefully embedding LWE samples inside the output matrices we can achieve the second constraint as well. We discuss our approach in detail below.

We now define a sampler Samp that takes an ℓ-bit string β as input, and outputs 2ℓ matrices satisfying all the above constraints, assuming the Learning with Errors assumption (in addition to relying on LHL). The sampler first chooses 2ℓ uniformly random *square* matrices $\{\mathbf{A}_{i,b}\}_{i \in [\ell], b \in \{0,1\}}$ subject to the constraint that $\sum_i \mathbf{A}_{i,\beta_i} = \mathbf{0}^{n \times n}$. This can be achieved by simply sampling $2\ell - 1$ uniformly random $n \times n$ matrices, and setting $\mathbf{A}_{\ell,\beta_\ell} = -\sum_{i < \ell} \mathbf{A}_{i,\beta_i}$. Let $\mathbf{D} = q^{3/4} \left[\mathbf{I}_n \,||\, \mathbf{0}^{n \times (m-2n)}\right]$ be a $n \times (m-n)$ matrix with a few 'large' entries. The sampler then chooses a low norm $n \times (m-n)$ matrix $\mathbf{S}$ and low-norm $n \times (m-n)$ error matrices $\{\mathbf{E}_{i,b}\}_{i \in [\ell], b \in \{0,1\}}$. It sets the 2ℓ output matrices as

$$\mathbf{M}_{i,b} = \begin{cases} [\mathbf{A}_{i,b} \,||\, \mathbf{A}_{i,b} \cdot \mathbf{S} + \mathbf{E}_{i,b}] & \text{if } b = \beta_i \\ [\mathbf{A}_{i,b} \,||\, \mathbf{A}_{i,b} \cdot \mathbf{S} + \mathbf{E}_{i,b} + \mathbf{D}] & \text{if } b = 1 - \beta_i \end{cases}$$

In short, our sampler samples the first n columns of the output matrix in a similar way to GKW scheme, whereas the remaining $(m - n)$ columns are sampled in a special way such that if we sum up the matrices corresponding to string β then the last $(m - n)$ columns of the summed matrix have small entries, whereas summing up matrices corresponding to any other string $\beta' \neq \beta$, the last $(m - n)$ columns of the summed matrix have distinguishably large entries. Below we briefly argue why our sampler satisfies the three properties specified initially.

1. (First property): Note that $\sum_i \mathbf{A}_{i,\beta_i} = \mathbf{0}^{n \times n}$, therefore we have that

$$\mathbf{M}_\beta = \sum_i \mathbf{M}_{i,\beta_i} = \left[\mathbf{0}^{n \times n} \,\|\, \mathbf{0}^{n \times n} \cdot \mathbf{S} + \sum_i \mathbf{E}_{i,\beta_i} \right] = \left[\mathbf{0}^{n \times n} \,\|\, \sum_i \mathbf{E}_{i,\beta_i} \right].$$

   Since the error matrices are drawn from a low-norm distribution, the entries of $\mathbf{M}_\beta$ are 'small'.

2. (Second property): We need to check that $\mathbf{M}_{\beta'} = \sum_i \mathbf{M}_{i,\beta'_i}$ has 'large' entries for $\beta' \neq \beta$. Suppose β and β' differ at t positions ($t > 0$). Then

$$\sum_i \mathbf{M}_{i,\beta'_i} = \left[\sum_i \mathbf{A}_{\beta'} \,\|\, \mathbf{A}_{\beta'} \cdot \mathbf{S} + \mathbf{E}_{\beta'} + t \cdot \mathbf{D} \right],$$

   where $\mathbf{A}_{\beta'} = \sum_i \mathbf{A}_{i,\beta'_i}$ and $\mathbf{E}_{\beta'} = \sum_i \mathbf{E}_{i,\beta'_i}$. If $\mathbf{A}_{\beta'}$ has large entries (greater than $q^{1/2}$), then we are done. On the other hand, if $\mathbf{A}_{\beta'}$ has small entries (less than $q^{1/2}$), then we can argue that $\mathbf{A}_{\beta'} \cdot \mathbf{S} + \mathbf{E}_{\beta'}$ also has entries less than $q^{3/4}$, and therefore $\mathbf{A}_{\beta'} \cdot \mathbf{S} + \mathbf{E}_{\beta'} + t \cdot \mathbf{D}$ has large entries. This implies that $\mathbf{M}_{\beta'}$ has large entries, and hence the second constraint is also satisfied.

3. (Third property): To argue about the third property, we use the LWE assumption in conjunction with LHL. First, we can argue that the $\{\mathbf{A}_{i,b}\}$ matrices look like uniformly random matrices (using the leftover hash lemma). Next, using the LWE assumption, we can show that $\{[\mathbf{A}_{i,b} \,\|\, \mathbf{A}_{i,b} \cdot \mathbf{S} + \mathbf{E}_{i,b}]\}_{i,b}$ are indistinguishable from 2ℓ uniformly random matrices, and hence the third property is also satisfied.

We can also modify the above sampler slightly such that $\sum_i \mathbf{M}_{i,\beta_i}$ has 'medium' entries (that is, entries within the range $[q^{1/4}, q^{1/2})$). The sampler chooses random matrices $\{\mathbf{A}_{i,b}\}_{i,b}$ subject to the constraint that $\sum_i \mathbf{A}_{i,\beta_i} = q^{1/4} \mathbf{I}_n$, and the remaining steps are same as above. Let $\mathsf{Samp}_{\mathrm{med}}$ be the sampler for this 'medium-entries' variant.

We observe that if we plug in these samplers into the GKW scheme for sampling their top-level matrices, then that leads to a perfectly correct lockable obfuscation scheme. Specifically, let α be the lock used, PRG chosen from a perfectly injective PRG family, and $\beta = \mathrm{PRG}(\alpha)$ be the expanded lock value. The obfuscation scheme chooses matrices $\{\mathbf{M}_{i,b}\}_{i,b}$ using either Samp or $\mathsf{Samp}_{\mathrm{med}}$ depending on the message msg. That is, if $\mathsf{msg} = 0$, it chooses $\{\mathbf{M}_{i,b}\}_{i,b} \leftarrow \mathsf{Samp}(\beta)$, else it chooses $\{\mathbf{M}_{i,b}\}_{i,b} \leftarrow \mathsf{Samp}_{\mathrm{med}}(\beta)$. It then sets $\mathbf{B}^{(i)}_{L,\mathrm{acc}^{(i)}} = \mathbf{M}_{i,1}$

and $\mathbf{B}^{(i)}_{L,\text{rej}^{(i)}} = \mathbf{M}_{i,0}$ for each $i \in [\ell_{\text{PRG}}]$. From the properties of $\mathsf{Samp}/\mathsf{Samp}_{\text{med}}$, it follows that

$$\mathbf{M}_\beta = \sum_i \mathbf{M}_{i,\beta_i} = \sum_{i:\ \beta_i=0} \mathbf{B}^{(i)}_{L,\text{rej}^{(i)}} + \sum_{i:\ \beta_i=1} \mathbf{B}^{(i)}_{L,\text{acc}^{(i)}},$$

which has 'low' or 'medium' norm depending on msg bit. The remaining top level matrices are chosen uniformly at random. Everything else stays the same as in the GKW scheme.

For completeness, we now check that this scheme indeed satisfies perfect correctness. Consider an obfuscation of circuit C with lock α and message msg. If this obfuscation is evaluated on input x such that $C(x) = \alpha$, then the evaluation outputs msg as expected. If $C(x) = \alpha' \neq \alpha$, then $\text{PRG}(C(x)) = \beta' \neq \beta$ (since the PRG is injective). This means the top level sum is

$$\sum_{i:\ \beta'_i=0} \mathbf{B}^{(i)}_{L,\text{rej}^{(i)}} + \sum_{i:\ \beta'_i=1} \mathbf{B}^{(i)}_{L,\text{acc}^{(i)}} = \sum_i \mathbf{M}_{i,\beta'_i},$$

Using the second property of $\mathsf{Samp}/\mathsf{Samp}_{\text{med}}$, we know that this sum has 'large' entries, and therefore the evaluation outputs $\bot$. This completes our perfect correctness argument. Now for proving that our modification still give a secure lockable obfuscation, we do not re-derive a completely new security proof but instead we show that no PPT attacker can distinguish an obfuscated program generated using our scheme from the one generated by using the GKW scheme. Now combining this claim with the fact that the GKW scheme is secure under LWE assumption, we get that our scheme is also secure. Very briefly, the idea behind indistinguishability of these two schemes is that since the lock α is chosen uniformly at random, then $\text{PRG}(\alpha)$ is computationally indistinguishable from a uniformly random string β, and thus these top level matrices also look like uniformly random matrices for uniformly random β (using the third property of $\mathsf{Samp}/\mathsf{Samp}_{\text{med}}$). Now to complete argument we show the same hold for GKW scheme as well, thereby completing the proof. More details on this are provided in the main body.

Perfectly Injective PRGs from the LPN Assumption. Finally, we also build a family of perfectly injective PRGs based on the Learning Parity with Noise assumption. While the focus of this work has been getting an end-to-end LWE solution for perfectly correct lockable obfuscation, we also build perfectly injective PRGs based on the LPN assumption, which could be of independent interest. Recently, there has been a surge of interest towards new constructions of cryptographic primitives based on LPN [16,17,23,40–42], and we feel that our perfectly injective PRGs fit this theme. Our LPN solution uses a low-noise variant ($\beta \approx \frac{1}{\sqrt{n}}$) of the LPN assumption that has been used in previous public key encryption schemes [1]. Below we briefly sketch the main ideas behind our PRG construction.

To build perfectly injective PRGs from LPN, we take a similar approach to one taken in the LWE case. The starting idea is to use the PRG seed (as before) as the secret vector $\mathbf{s}$ and compute the PRG evaluation as $\mathbf{B}^T\mathbf{s}$) but now, unlike the LWE case, we do not have any rounding equivalent for LPN, that is we do not know how to avoid generating the error vector $\mathbf{e}$ during PRG evaluation. Therefore, to execute the idea we provide an (efficient) *injective* sampler for error vectors which takes as input a bit string and outputs an error vector $\mathbf{e}$ of appropriate dimension. (The injectivity property here states that the mapping between bit strings and the error vectors is injective.) So now in our PRG evaluation the input string is first divided in two disjoint components where the first component is directly interpreted as the secret vector $\mathbf{s}$ and second component is used to sample the error vector $\mathbf{e}$ using our injective sampler.

Although at first it might seem that building an injective sampler might not be hard, however it turns out there are a couple of subtle issues that we have taken care of while proving security as well as perfect injectivity. Concretely, for self-composability of our PRG (i.e., building PRGs which take as input bit strings of fixed length instead having a special domain sampling algorithm), we require that the size of support of distribution of error vectors $\mathbf{e}$ used is a 'perfect power of two'. As otherwise we can not hope to build a perfectly injective (error vector) sampler which takes as input a fixed length bit string and outputs the corresponding error vector. Now we know that the size of support of noise distribution in the LPN assumption might not be a perfect power of two, thus we might not be able to injectively sample error vectors from the fixed length bit strings. To resolve this issue, we define an alternate assumption which we call the 'restricted-exact-LPN' assumption and show that (a) it is as hard as standard LPN, (b) sufficient for our proof to go through, and (c) has an efficiently enumerable noise distribution whose support size is a perfect power of two (i.e., we can define an efficient injective error sampler for its noise distribution). More details are provided later in Sect. 5.

1.2 Related Works on Perfect Correctness

In this section, we discuss some related work and approaches for achieving perfect correctness for lockable obfuscation and its applications. First, a recent concurrent and independent work by Asharov et al. [6] also addresses the question of perfect correctness for obfuscation. They show how to generically achieve perfect correctness for any indistinguishability obfuscation scheme, assuming hardness of LWE. Below, we discuss other related prior works.

Perfect Correctness via Derandomization. Bitansky and Vaikuntanathan [13] showed how to transform any obfuscation scheme (and a large class of cryptosystems) to remove correctness errors using Nisan-Wigderson (NW) PRGs [34]. In their scheme, the obfuscator runs the erroneous obfuscation algorithm sufficiently many times, and for each execution of the obfuscator, the randomness used is derived pseudorandomly (by adding the randomness derived from the NW PRGs and the randomness from a standard cryptographic PRG). As the authors show, such a transformation leads to a perfectly correct scheme as long as certain circuit lower bound assumptions hold (in particular, they require that the NW-PRGs can fool certain bounded-size circuits). Our solution, on the other hand, does not rely on additional assumptions as well as it is as efficient as existing (imperfect) lockable obfuscation constructions [28,39].

Using a Random Oracle for Generating Randomness. A heuristic approach to prevent the obfuscator from using malicious randomness is to generate the random coins using a hash function H applied on the circuit. Such a heuristic might suffice for some applications such as the public auditing example discussed previously, but it does not seem to provide provable security in others. Note that our construction with perfect correctness is proven secure in the standard model, and does not need rely on ROs or a CRS.

Lastly, we want to point out that in earlier works by Bitansky and Vaikuntanathan [12], and Ananth, Jain and Sahai [3], it was shown how to transform any obfuscation scheme that has statistical correctness on $(1/2 + \epsilon)$ fraction of inputs (for some non-negligible ϵ) into a scheme that has statistical correctness for all inputs. However, this does not achieve perfect correctness. It is an interesting question whether their approach could be extended to achieve perfect correctness. Similar correctness amplification issues were also addressed by Ananth et al. [2].

2 Preliminaries

In this section, we review the notions of injective pseudorandom generators with setup and Lockable Obfuscation [28,39]. Due to space constraints, we review fundamentals of lattices and homomorphic encryption in the full version of the paper.

2.1 Injective Pseudorandom Generators with Setup

We will be considering PRGs with an additional setup algorithm that outputs public parameters. The setup algorithm will be important for achieving injectivity in our constructions. While this is weaker than the usual notion of PRGs (without setup), it turns out that for many of the applications that require injectivity of PRG, the setup phase is not an issue.

Setup(1^λ): The setup algorithm takes as input the security parameter λ and outputs public parameters pp, domain $\mathcal{D}$ and co-domain $\mathcal{R}$ of the PRG. Let params denote $(\mathsf{pp}, \mathcal{D}, \mathcal{R})$.

PRG(params, $s \in \mathcal{D}$) : The PRG evaluation algorithm takes as input the public parameters and the PRG seed $s \in \mathcal{D}$, and outputs $y \in \mathcal{R}$.

Perfect Injectivity. A pseudorandom generator with setup (Setup, PRG) is said to have perfect injectivity if for all $(\mathsf{pp}, \mathcal{D}, \mathcal{R}) \leftarrow \mathsf{Setup}(1^\lambda)$, for all $s_1 \neq s_2 \in \mathcal{D}$, $\mathrm{PRG}(\mathsf{params}, s_1) \neq \mathrm{PRG}(\mathsf{params}, s_2)$.

Pseudorandomness. A pseudorandom generator with setup (Setup, PRG) is said to be secure if for any PPT adversary $\mathcal{A}$, there exists a negligible function $\text{negl}(\cdot)$ such that for all $\lambda \in \mathbb{N}$,

$$\Pr\left[\mathcal{A}(\text{params}, t_b) = b \; : \; \begin{array}{c} \text{params} \leftarrow \text{Setup}(1^\lambda) \\ s \leftarrow \mathcal{D}, t_0 \leftarrow \mathcal{R}, b \leftarrow \{0,1\} \\ t_1 = \text{PRG}(\text{params}, s) \end{array}\right] \leq \frac{1}{2} + \text{negl}(\lambda).$$

2.2 Lockable Obfuscation

In this section, we recall the notion of lockable obfuscation defined by Goyal et al. [28]. Let n, m, d be polynomials, and $\mathcal{C}_{n,m,d}(\lambda)$ be the class of depth $d(\lambda)$ circuits with $n(\lambda)$ bit input and $m(\lambda)$ bit output. Let $\mathcal{M}$ be the message space. A lockable obfuscator for $\mathcal{C}_{n,m,d}$ consists of algorithms Obf and Eval with the following syntax.

- $\text{Obf}(1^\lambda, P, \text{msg}, \alpha) \to \widetilde{P}$. The obfuscation algorithm is a randomized algorithm that takes as input the security parameter λ, a program $P \in \mathcal{C}_{n,m,d}$, message $\text{msg} \in \mathcal{M}$ and 'lock string' $\alpha \in \{0,1\}^{m(\lambda)}$. It outputs a program $\widetilde{P}$.
- $\text{Eval}(\widetilde{P}, x) \to y \in \mathcal{M} \cup \{\bot\}$. The evaluator is a deterministic algorithm that takes as input a program $\widetilde{P}$ and a string $x \in \{0,1\}^{n(\lambda)}$. It outputs $y \in \mathcal{M} \cup \{\bot\}$.

Correctness. For correctness, we require that if $P(x) = \alpha$, then the obfuscated program $\widetilde{P} \leftarrow \text{Obf}(1^\lambda, P, \text{msg}, \alpha)$, evaluated on input x, outputs msg, and if $P(x) \neq \alpha$, then $\widetilde{P}$ outputs $\bot$ on input x. Formally,

Definition 1 (Perfect Correctness). *Let n, m, d be polynomials. A lockable obfuscation scheme for $\mathcal{C}_{n,m,d}$ and message space $\mathcal{M}$ is said to be perfectly correct if it satisfies the following properties:*

1. *For all security parameters λ, inputs $x \in \{0,1\}^{n(\lambda)}$, programs $P \in \mathcal{C}_{n,m,d}$ and messages $\text{msg} \in \mathcal{M}$, if $P(x) = \alpha$, then*

$$\text{Eval}(\text{Obf}(1^\lambda, P, \text{msg}, \alpha), x) = \text{msg}.$$

2. *For all security parameters λ, inputs $x \in \{0,1\}^{n(\lambda)}$, programs $P \in \mathcal{C}_{n,m,d}$ and messages $\text{msg} \in \mathcal{M}$, if $P(x) \neq \alpha$, then*

$$\text{Eval}(\text{Obf}(1^\lambda, P, \text{msg}, \alpha), x) = \bot.$$

Remark 1 (Weaker notions of correctness). We would like to point out that GKW additionally defined two weaker notions of correctness - statistical and semi-statistical correctness. They say that lockable obfuscation satisfies statistical correctness if for any triple (P, msg, α), the probability that there exists an x s.t. $P(x) \neq \alpha$ and the obfuscated program outputs msg on input x is negligible in security parameter. The notion of semi-statistical correctness is even weaker where each obfuscated program could potentially always output message msg for some input x s.t. $P(x) \neq \alpha$, but if one fixes the input x before obfuscation, then the probability of the obfuscated program outputting msg on input x is negligible.

Security. We now present the simulation based security definition for Lockable Obfuscation.

Definition 2. *Let n, m, d be polynomials. A lockable obfuscation scheme* (Obf, Eval) *for $\mathcal{C}_{n,m,d}$ and message space $\mathcal{M}$ is said to be secure if there exists a PPT simulator* Sim *such that for all PPT adversaries $\mathcal{A} = (\mathcal{A}_0, \mathcal{A}_1)$, there exists a negligible function $\mathsf{negl}(\cdot)$ such that the following function is bounded by $\mathsf{negl}(\cdot)$:*

$$\left| \Pr \left[\mathcal{A}_1(\tilde{P}_b, \mathsf{st}) = b : \begin{array}{c} (P \in \mathcal{C}_{n,m,d}, \mathsf{msg} \in \mathcal{M}, \mathsf{st}) \leftarrow \mathcal{A}_0(1^\lambda) \\ b \leftarrow \{0,1\}, \alpha \leftarrow \{0,1\}^{m(\lambda)} \\ \tilde{P}_0 \leftarrow \mathsf{Obf}(1^\lambda, P, \mathsf{msg}, \alpha) \\ \tilde{P}_1 \leftarrow \mathsf{Sim}(1^\lambda, 1^{|P|}, 1^{|\mathsf{msg}|}) \end{array} \right] - \frac{1}{2} \right|$$

3   Perfectly Injective PRGs from LWR

In this construction, we will present a construction based on the Learning With Rounding (LWR) assumption. At a high level, the construction works as follows: the setup algorithm chooses a uniformly random matrix $\mathbf{A} \in \mathbb{Z}_q^{n \times 2m}$, where m is much greater than n. The PRG evaluation outputs $\lfloor \mathbf{x}^T \cdot \mathbf{A} \rfloor_p$, where $p = 2^{\ell_{\mathsf{out}}}$. Note that this already gives us a PRG with statistical injectivity. However, to achieve perfect injectivity, we need to ensure that the matrix $\mathbf{A}$ is full rank, and that injectivity is preserved even after rounding. In order to achieve this, we need to make some modifications to the setup algorithm.

The new setup algorithm chooses a uniformly random matrix $\mathbf{B}$, a random matrix $\mathbf{R}$ with ± 1 entries. Let $\mathbf{D}$ be a fixed full rank matrix with 'medium sized' entries. It then outputs $\mathbf{A} = [\mathbf{B} \mid \mathbf{BR} + \mathbf{D}]$. The PRG evaluation is same as described above.

We will now describe the algorithms formally.

Setup(1^λ) The setup algorithm first sets the parameters $n, m, q, \ell_{\mathsf{out}}, \rho$ in terms of the security parameter. These parameters must satisfy the following constraints.

- $n = \mathsf{poly}(\lambda)$
- $q \leq 2^{n^\epsilon}$
- $m > 2n \log q$
- $p = 2^{\ell_{\mathsf{out}}}$
- $n < m \cdot \ell_{\mathsf{out}}$
- $(q/p)m < \rho < q$

One particular setting of parameters which satisfies the constraints above is as follows: set $n = \mathsf{poly}(\lambda)$, $q = 2^{n^\epsilon}$, $p = \sqrt{q}$, $m = n^2$ and $\rho = q/4$.

Next, it chooses a matrix $\mathbf{B} \leftarrow \mathbb{Z}_q^{n \times m}$, matrix $\mathbf{R} \leftarrow \{+1, -1\}^{m \times m}$. Let $\mathbf{D} = \rho \cdot [\mathbf{I}_n \mid \mathbf{0}^{n \times (m-n)}]$ and $\mathbf{A} = [\mathbf{B} \mid \mathbf{B} \cdot \mathbf{R} + \mathbf{D}]$. The setup algorithm outputs $\mathbf{A}$ as the public parameters. It sets the domain $\mathcal{D} = \{0,1\}^n$ and co-domain $\mathcal{R} = \{0,1\}^{m \cdot \ell_{\mathsf{out}}}$.

PRG($\mathbf{A}, \mathbf{s}$): The PRG evaluation algorithm takes as input the matrix $\mathbf{A}$ and the seed $\mathbf{s} \in \{0,1\}^n$. It computes $\mathbf{y} = \mathbf{s}^T \cdot \mathbf{A}$. Finally, it outputs $\lfloor \mathbf{y} \rfloor_p \in \mathbb{Z}_p^m$ as a bit string of length $2m \cdot \ell_{\mathsf{out}}$.

Depth of PRG *Evaluation Circuit and* PRG *Stretch.* First, note that the the PRG evaluation circuit only needs to perform a single matrix-vector multiplication followed by discarding the $\lceil \log_2 q/p \rceil$ least significant bits of each element. Clearly such a circuit can be implemented in $\mathbf{TC^0}$, the class of constant-depth, poly-sized circuits with unbounded fan-in and threshold gates (which is a subset of $\mathbf{NC^1}$). Additionally, the stretch provided by the above PRG could be arbitrarily set during setup. Thus, the above construction gives a PRG that provides a polynomial stretch with a $\mathbf{TC^0}$ evaluation circuit.

We now prove the following theorem where we show that our PRG construction satisfies perfect injectivity property. Due to space constraints, we argue the pseudorandomness property of the construction in the full version of the paper.

Theorem 1. *If the LWR assumption with parameters n, m, p and q holds, then the above construction is a perfectly injective PRG.*

Due to space constraints, we prove the Theorem in the full version of the paper.

4 Lockable Obfuscation with Perfect Correctness

4.1 Construction

In this section, we present our perfectly correct lockable obfuscation scheme. We note that the construction is similar to the statistically correct lockable obfuscation scheme described in Goyal et al. [28]. A part of the description has been taken verbatim from [28]. For any polynomials $\ell_{\mathsf{in}}, \ell_{\mathsf{out}}, d$ such that $\ell_{\mathsf{out}} = \omega(\log \lambda)$, we construct a lockable obfuscation scheme $\mathcal{O} = (\mathsf{Obf}, \mathsf{Eval})$ for the circuit class $\mathcal{C}_{\ell_{\mathsf{in}}, \ell_{\mathsf{out}}, d}$. The message space for our construction will be $\{0, 1\}$, although one can trivially extend it to $\{0, 1\}^{\ell(\lambda)}$ for any polynomial ℓ [28].

The tools required for our construction are as follows:

- A compact leveled homomorphic bit encryption scheme (LHE.Setup, LHE.Enc, LHE.Eval, LHE.Dec) with decryption circuit of depth $d_{\mathsf{Dec}}(\lambda)$ and ciphertexts of length $\ell_{\mathsf{ct}}(\lambda)$.
- A *perfectly injective* pseudorandom generator scheme (PRG.Setup, PRG. Eval), where PRG.Eval has depth $d_{\mathsf{PRG}}(\lambda)$, input length $\ell_{\mathsf{out}}(\lambda)$ and output length $\ell_{\mathsf{PRG}}(\lambda)$.

For notational convenience, let $\ell_{\mathsf{in}} = \ell_{\mathsf{in}}(\lambda)$, $\ell_{\mathsf{out}} = \ell_{\mathsf{out}}(\lambda)$, $\ell_{\mathsf{PRG}} = \ell_{\mathsf{PRG}}(\lambda)$, $d_{\mathsf{Dec}} = d_{\mathsf{Dec}}(\lambda)$, $d_{\mathsf{PRG}} = d_{\mathsf{PRG}}(\lambda)$ and $d = d(\lambda)$.

Fix any $\epsilon < 1/2$. Let χ be a B-bounded discrete Gaussian distribution with parameter σ such that $B = \sqrt{m} \cdot \sigma$. Let $n, m, \ell, \sigma, q, \mathsf{Bd}$ be parameters with the following constraints:

- $n = \mathsf{poly}(\lambda)$ and $q \le 2^{n^{\epsilon}}$ (for LWE security)
- $m \ge \widetilde{c} \cdot n \cdot \log q$ for some universal constant $\widetilde{c}$ (for SamplePre)
- $\sigma = \omega(\sqrt{n \cdot \log q \cdot \log m})$ (for Preimage Well Distributedness)
- $\ell_{\mathsf{PRG}} = n \cdot m \cdot \log q + \omega(\log n)$ (for applying Leftover Hash Lemma)

- $\ell_{\text{PRG}} \cdot (L + 1) \cdot (m^2 \cdot \sigma)^{L+1} < q^{1/8}$ (where $L = \ell_{\text{out}} \cdot \ell_{\text{ct}} \cdot 4^{d_{\text{Dec}} + d_{\text{PRG}}}$) (for correctness of scheme)

It is important that $L = \lambda^c$ for some constant c and $\ell_{\text{PRG}} \cdot (L + 1) \cdot (m^2 \cdot \sigma)^{L+1} < q^{1/8}$. This crucially relies on the fact that the LHE scheme is compact (so that ℓ_{ct} and ℓ_{PRG} are bounded by a polynomial independent of the size of the circuits supported by the scheme, and that the LHE decryption and PRG computation can be performed by a log depth circuit (i.e, have poly length branching programs). The constant c depends on the LHE scheme and PRG.

One possible setting of parameters is as follows: $n = \lambda^{4c/\epsilon}$, $m = n^{1+2\epsilon}$, $q = 2^{n^\epsilon}$, $\sigma = n$ and $\ell_{\text{PRG}} = n^{3\epsilon+3}$.

We will now describe the obfuscation and evaluation algorithms.

- $\text{Obf}(1^\lambda, P, \text{msg}, \alpha)$: The obfuscation algorithm takes as input a program $P \in \mathcal{C}_{\ell_{\text{in}}, \ell_{\text{out}}, d}$, message $\text{msg} \in \{0,1\}$ and $\alpha \in \{0,1\}^{\ell_{\text{out}}}$. The obfuscator proceeds as follows:
  1. It chooses the LHE key pair as $(\text{lhe.sk}, \text{lhe.ek}) \leftarrow \text{LHE.Setup}(1^\lambda, 1^{d \log d})$.[6]
  2. Next, it encrypts the program P. It sets $\mathbf{ct} \leftarrow \text{LHE.Enc}(\text{lhe.sk}, P)$.[7]
  3. It runs $\text{pp} \leftarrow \text{PRG.Setup}(1^\lambda)$, and assigns $\beta = \text{PRG.Eval}(\text{pp}, \alpha)$.
  4. Next, consider the following circuit Q which takes as input $\ell_{\text{out}} \cdot \ell_{\text{ct}}$ bits of input and outputs ℓ_{PRG} bits. Q takes as input ℓ_{out} LHE ciphertexts $\{\text{ct}_i\}_{i \leq \ell_{\text{out}}}$, has LHE secret key lhe.sk hardwired and computes the following — (1) it decrypts each input ciphertext ct_i (in parallel) to get string x of length ℓ_{out} bits, (2) it applies the PRG on x and outputs $\text{PRG.Eval}(\text{pp}, x)$. Concretely, $Q(\text{ct}_1, \ldots, \text{ct}_{\ell_{\text{out}}}) = \text{PRG.Eval}\big(\text{pp}, \text{LHE.Dec}(\text{lhe.sk}, \text{ct}_1) \| \cdots \| \text{LHE.Dec}(\text{lhe.sk}, \text{ct}_{\ell_{\text{out}}})\big)$.

     For $i \leq \ell_{\text{PRG}}$, we use $\text{BP}^{(i)}$ to denote the fixed-input selector permutation branching program that outputs the ith bit of output of circuit Q. Note that Q has depth $d_{\text{tot}} = d_{\text{Dec}} + d_{\text{PRG}}$. In the full version of the paper, we show that each branching program $\text{BP}^{(i)}$ has length $L = \ell_{\text{out}} \cdot \ell_{\text{ct}} \cdot 4^{d_{\text{tot}}}$ and width 5.
  5. The obfuscator creates matrix components which enable the evaluator to compute msg if it has an input strings (ciphertexts) $\text{ct}_1, \ldots, \text{ct}_{\ell_{\text{out}}}$ such that $Q(\text{ct}_1, \ldots, \text{ct}_{\ell_{\text{out}}}) = \beta$. Concretely, it runs the (randomized) routine Comp-Gen (defined in Figs. 1, 2). This routine takes as input the circuit Q in the form of ℓ_{PRG} branching programs $\{\text{BP}^{(i)}\}_i$, string β and message msg. Let $\left(\left\{ \mathbf{B}_{0,1}^{(i)} \right\}_i, \left\{ \mathbf{C}_j^{(i,0)}, \mathbf{C}_j^{(i,1)} \right\}_{i,j} \right) \leftarrow \text{Comp-Gen}(\{\text{BP}^{(i)}\}_i, \beta, \text{msg})$.

---

[6] We set the LHE depth bound to be $d \log d$, where the extra log factor is to account for the constant blowup involved in using a universal circuit. In particular, we can set the LHE depth bound to be $c \cdot d$ where c is some fixed constant depending on the universal circuit.

[7] Note that LHE scheme supports bit encryption. Therefore, to encrypt P, a multi-bit message, the FHE.Enc algorithm will be run independently on each bit of P. However, for notational convenience throughout this section we overload the notation and use FHE.Enc and FHE.Dec algorithms to encrypt and decrypt multi-bit messages respectively.

Comp-Gen

Input: $\{\mathsf{BP}^{(i)}\}_i$, $\beta \in \{0,1\}^{\ell_{\mathrm{PRG}}}$, $\mathsf{msg} \in \{0,1\}$

Output: Components $\left(\left\{\mathbf{B}_{0,1}^{(i)}\right\}_i, \{(\mathbf{C}_{\mathsf{level}}^{(i,0)}, \mathbf{C}_{\mathsf{level}}^{(i,1)})\}_{i \le \ell_{\mathrm{PRG}}, \mathsf{level} \le L}\right)$.

(a) Let $\mathsf{BP}^{(i)} = \left(\left\{\sigma_{j,b}^{(i)} : [5] \to [5]\right\}_{j \in [L], b \in \{0,1\}}, \mathsf{acc}^{(i)} \in [5], \mathsf{rej}^{(i)} \in [5]\right)$
for all $i \le \ell_{\mathrm{PRG}}$.

(b) First, it chooses a matrix for each state of each branching program. Recall, there are ℓ_{PRG} branching programs, and each branching program has L levels, and each level has 5 states. For each $i \le \ell_{\mathrm{PRG}}$, $j \in [0, L-1]$, it chooses a matrix of dimensions $5n \times m$ along with its trapdoors (independently) as $(\mathbf{B}_j^{(i)}, T_j^{(i)}) \leftarrow \mathsf{TrapGen}(1^{5n}, 1^m, q)$. The matrix $\mathbf{B}_j^{(i)}$ can be parsed as follows

$$\mathbf{B}_j^{(i)} = \begin{bmatrix} \mathbf{B}_{j,1}^{(i)} \\ \vdots \\ \mathbf{B}_{j,5}^{(i)} \end{bmatrix}$$

where matrices $\mathbf{B}_{j,k}^{(i)} \in \mathbb{Z}_q^{n \times m}$ for $k \le 5$. The matrix $\mathbf{B}_{j,k}^{(i)}$ corresponds to state k at level j of branching program $\mathsf{BP}^{(i)}$.

(c) Let $\mathbf{D} = q^{3/4} \cdot [\mathbf{I}_n \,\|\, \mathbf{0}^{n \times (m-2 \cdot n)}]$. For the top level, it first chooses the matrices $\mathbf{A}_{L,k}^{(i)}$ (of dimension $n \times n$) for each $i \le \ell_{\mathrm{PRG}}, k \le 5$, uniformly at random, subject to the following constraint:

$$\sum_{i:\beta_i=0} \mathbf{A}_{L,\mathsf{rej}^{(i)}}^{(i)} + \sum_{i:\beta_i=1} \mathbf{A}_{L,\mathsf{acc}^{(i)}}^{(i)} = \mathbf{0}^{n \times n} \text{ if } \mathsf{msg} = 0.$$

$$\sum_{i:\beta_i=0} \mathbf{A}_{L,\mathsf{rej}^{(i)}}^{(i)} + \sum_{i:\beta_i=1} \mathbf{A}_{L,\mathsf{acc}^{(i)}}^{(i)} = q^{1/4} \cdot \mathbf{I}_n \text{ if } \mathsf{msg} = 1.$$

It then samples a matrix $\mathbf{S} \leftarrow \chi^{n \times (m-n)}$, and matrices $\mathbf{E}_{L,\mathsf{rej}^{(i)}}^{(i)} \leftarrow \chi^{n \times (m-n)}, \mathbf{E}_{L,\mathsf{acc}^{(i)}}^{(i)} \leftarrow \chi^{n \times (m-n)}$ for each $i \le \ell_{\mathrm{PRG}}$. It then chooses matrices $\mathbf{F}_{L,k}^{(i)}$ as follows

$$\mathbf{F}_{L,\mathsf{acc}^{(i)}}^{(i)} = \mathbf{A}_{L,\mathsf{acc}^{(i)}}^{(i)} \cdot \mathbf{S} + \mathbf{E}_{L,\mathsf{acc}^{(i)}}^{(i)} + (1 - \beta_i) \cdot \mathbf{D}$$

$$\mathbf{F}_{L,\mathsf{rej}^{(i)}}^{(i)} = \mathbf{A}_{L,\mathsf{rej}^{(i)}}^{(i)} \cdot \mathbf{S} + \mathbf{E}_{L,\mathsf{rej}^{(i)}}^{(i)} + \beta_i \cdot \mathbf{D}$$

$$\mathbf{F}_{L,k}^{(i)} \leftarrow \mathbb{Z}_q^{n \times (m-n)} \text{ if } k \notin \{\mathsf{acc}^{(i)}, \mathsf{rej}^{(i)}\}$$

The top level matrices $\mathbf{B}_{L,k}^{(i)}$ for each $i \le \ell_{\mathrm{PRG}}, k \le 5$ are given by
$\mathbf{B}_{L,k}^{(i)} = \left[\mathbf{A}_{L,k}^{(i)} \,\|\, \mathbf{F}_{L,k}^{(i)}\right].$

The algorithm continues in Figure 2.

Fig. 1. Routine Comp-Gen

Comp-Gen

(d) Next, it generates the components for each level. For each level level $\in$ $[1, L]$, do the following:

   i. Choose matrices $\mathbf{S}_{\text{level}}^{(0)}, \mathbf{S}_{\text{level}}^{(1)} \leftarrow \chi^{n \times n}$ and $\mathbf{E}_{\text{level}}^{(i,0)}, \mathbf{E}_{\text{level}}^{(i,1)} \leftarrow \chi^{5n \times m}$ for $i \leq \ell_{\text{PRG}}$. If either $\mathbf{S}_{\text{level}}^{(0)}$ or $\mathbf{S}_{\text{level}}^{(1)}$ has determinant zero, then set it to be $\mathbf{I}_n$.

   ii. For $b \in \{0, 1\}$, set matrix $\mathbf{D}_{\text{level}}^{(i,b)}$ as a permutation of the matrix blocks of $\mathbf{B}_{\text{level}}^{(i)}$ according to the permutation $\sigma_{\text{level},b}^{(i)}(\cdot)$. More formally, for $i \leq \ell_{\text{PRG}}$, set

$$\mathbf{D}_{\text{level}}^{(i,b)} = \begin{bmatrix} \mathbf{B}_{\text{level},\sigma_{\text{level},b}^{(i)}(1)}^{(i)} \\ \vdots \\ \mathbf{B}_{\text{level},\sigma_{\text{level},b}^{(i)}(5)}^{(i)} \end{bmatrix}.$$

   iii. Set $\mathbf{M}_{\text{level}}^{(i,b)} = \left(\mathbf{I}_5 \otimes \mathbf{S}_{\text{level}}^{(b)}\right) \cdot \mathbf{D}_{\text{level}}^{(i,b)} + \mathbf{E}_{\text{level}}^{(i,b)}$ for $i \leq \ell_{\text{PRG}}$.

   iv. Compute $\mathbf{C}_{\text{level}}^{(i,b)} \leftarrow \mathsf{SamplePre}(\mathbf{B}_{\text{level}-1}^{(i)}, T_{\text{level}-1}^{(i)}, \sigma, \mathbf{M}_{\text{level}}^{(i,b)})$

(e) Output $\left(\left\{\mathbf{B}_{0,1}^{(i)}\right\}_i, \{(\mathbf{C}_{\text{level}}^{(i,0)}, \mathbf{C}_{\text{level}}^{(i,1)})\}_{i \leq \ell_{\text{PRG}}, \text{level} \leq L}\right).$

Fig. 2. Routine Comp-Gen Continued

6. The final obfuscated program consists of the LHE evaluation key $\mathsf{ek} = \mathsf{lhe.ek}$, LHE ciphertexts $\mathbf{ct}$, together with the components $\left(\left\{\mathbf{B}_{0,1}^{(i)}\right\}_i,\right.$ $\left.\left\{(\mathbf{C}_j^{(i,0)}, \mathbf{C}_j^{(i,1)})\right\}_{i,j}\right).$

– $\mathsf{Eval}(\tilde{P}, x)$: The evaluation algorithm takes as input $\tilde{P} = \left(\mathsf{ek}, \mathbf{ct}, \left\{\mathbf{B}_{0,1}^{(i)}\right\}_i,\right.$ $\left.\left\{(\mathbf{C}_j^{(i,0)}, \mathbf{C}_j^{(i,1)})\right\}_{i,j}\right)$ and input $x \in \{0, 1\}^{\ell_{\text{in}}}$. It performs the following steps.

1. The evaluator first constructs a universal circuit $U_x(\cdot)$ with x hardwired as input. This universal circuit takes a circuit C as input and outputs $U_x(C) = C(x)$. Using the universal circuit of Cook and Hoover [21], it follows that $U_x(\cdot)$ has depth $O(d)$.

2. Next, it performs homomorphic evaluation on $\mathbf{ct}$ using circuit $U_x(\cdot)$. It computes $\widetilde{\mathbf{ct}} = \mathsf{LHE.Eval}(\mathsf{ek}, U_x(\cdot), \mathbf{ct})$. Note that $\ell_{\text{ct}} \cdot \ell_{\text{out}}$ denotes the length of $\widetilde{\mathbf{ct}}$ (as a bitstring), and let $\widetilde{\mathbf{ct}}_i$ denote the ith bit of $\widetilde{\mathbf{ct}}$.

3. The evaluator then obliviously evaluates the ℓ_{PRG} branching programs on input $\widetilde{\mathbf{ct}}$ using the matrix components. It calls the component evaluation algorithm Comp-Eval (defined in Fig. 3). Let $y = \mathsf{Comp\text{-}Eval}\Big(\widetilde{\mathbf{ct}},$ $\left(\left\{\mathbf{B}_{0,1}^{(i)}\right\}_i, \left\{(\mathbf{C}_j^{(i,0)}, \mathbf{C}_j^{(i,1)})\right\}_{i,j}\right)\Big).$ The evaluator outputs y.

Comp-Eval

Input: Input   string z,   Components
$\left(\left\{ \mathbf{B}_{0,1}^{(i)} \right\}_i, \{ (\mathbf{C}_{\mathsf{level}}^{(i,0)}, \mathbf{C}_{\mathsf{level}}^{(i,1)}) \}_{i \leq \ell_{\mathrm{PRG}}, \mathsf{level} \leq L} \right).$
Output: $y \in \{0, 1, \bot\}.$

(a) For each $i \in [1, \ell_{\mathrm{PRG}}]$, do the following
    i. Set $\mathbf{M}^{(i)} = \mathbf{B}_{0,1}^{(i)}$.
    ii. For $j = 1$ to L, do the following
      - If $z_{\mathsf{inp}(j)} = 0$, set $\mathbf{M}^{(i)} = \mathbf{M}^{(i)} \cdot \mathbf{C}_j^{(i,0)}$. Else, set $\mathbf{M}^{(i)} = \mathbf{M}^{(i)} \cdot \mathbf{C}_j^{(i,1)}$.
(b) Compute $\mathbf{M} = \sum_i \mathbf{M}^{(i)}$ and do the following
    - If $\|\mathbf{M}\|_\infty \leq q^{1/8}$, output 0.
    - Otherwise, if $\|\mathbf{M}\|_\infty \leq q^{1/2}$, output 1.
    - Else output $\bot$.

Fig. 3. Routine Comp-Eval

4.2 Correctness

We will prove that the lockable obfuscation scheme described above satisfies the perfect correctness property (see Definition 1). To prove this, we need to prove that if $P(x) = \alpha$, then the evaluation algorithm always outputs the message, and if $P(x) \neq \alpha$, then it always outputs $\bot$.

First, we will prove the following lemma about the Comp-Gen and Comp-Eval routines. For any $z \in \{0,1\}^{\ell_{\mathrm{in}}(\lambda)}$, let $\mathrm{BP}(z) = \mathrm{BP}^{(1)}(z) \| \ldots \| \mathrm{BP}^{(\ell_{\mathrm{PRG}})}(z)$. Intuitively, this lemma states that for all fixed input branching programs $\{\mathrm{BP}^{(i)}\}_i$, strings β, input z, and messages msg, if $\mathrm{BP}(z) = \beta$, then the component evaluator outputs msg.

Lemma 1. *For any set of branching programs $\{\mathrm{BP}^{(i)}\}_{i \leq \ell_{\mathrm{PRG}}}$, string $\beta \in \{0,1\}^{\ell_{\mathrm{PRG}}}$, message $\mathsf{msg} \in \{0,1\}$ and input z,*

1. *if $\mathrm{BP}(z) = \beta$, then $\mathsf{Comp\text{-}Eval}(z, \mathsf{Comp\text{-}Gen}(\{\mathrm{BP}^{(i)}\}_i, \beta, \mathsf{msg})) = \mathsf{msg}$.*
2. *if $\mathrm{BP}(z) \neq \beta$, then $\mathsf{Comp\text{-}Eval}(z, \mathsf{Comp\text{-}Gen}(\{\mathrm{BP}^{(i)}\}_i, \beta, \mathsf{msg})) = \bot$.*

Proof. Recall that the component generation algorithm chooses matrices $\mathbf{B}_j^{(i)}$ for each $i \leq \ell_{\mathrm{PRG}}, j \leq L$, $\mathbf{S}_j^{(0)}, \mathbf{S}_j^{(1)}$ for each $j \leq L$ and $\mathbf{E}_j^{(i,0)}, \mathbf{E}_j^{(i,1)}$ for each $i \leq \ell_{\mathrm{PRG}}, j \leq L$. Note that the $\mathbf{S}_j^{(b)}$ and $\mathbf{E}_j^{(i,b)}$ matrices have l_∞ norm bounded by $\sigma \cdot m^{3/2}$ since they are chosen from truncated Gaussian distribution with parameter σ.

We start by introducing some notations for this proof.

- $\mathsf{st}_j^{(i)}$: the state of $\mathrm{BP}^{(i)}$ after j steps when evaluated on z
- $\mathbf{S}_j = \mathbf{S}_j^{(z_{\mathsf{inp}(j)})}$, $\quad \mathbf{E}_j^{(i)} = \mathbf{E}_j^{(i, z_{\mathsf{inp}(j)})}$, $\quad \mathbf{C}_j^{(i)} = \mathbf{C}_j^{(i, z_{\mathsf{inp}(j)})}$ for all $j \leq L$

- $\boldsymbol{\Gamma}_{j^*} = \prod_{j=1}^{j^*} \mathbf{S}_j$ for all $j^* \leq L$
- $\boldsymbol{\Delta}_{j^*}^{(i)} = \mathbf{B}_{0,1}^{(i)} \cdot \left(\prod_{j=1}^{j^*} \mathbf{C}_j^{(i)} \right), \quad \widetilde{\boldsymbol{\Delta}}_{j^*}^{(i)} = \boldsymbol{\Gamma}_{j^*} \cdot \mathbf{B}_{j^*, \mathsf{st}_{j^*}^{(i)}}^{(i)}, \quad \mathbf{Err}_{j^*}^{(i)} = \boldsymbol{\Delta}_{j^*}^{(i)} - \widetilde{\boldsymbol{\Delta}}_{j^*}^{(i)}$
  for all $j^* \leq L$
- For any string $x \in \{0,1\}^{\ell_{\mathrm{PRG}}}$, $\mathbf{A}_x = \sum_{i:x_i=0} \mathbf{A}_{L,\mathsf{rej}^{(i)}}^{(i)} + \sum_{i:x_i=1} \mathbf{A}_{L,\mathsf{acc}^{(i)}}^{(i)}$
- Similarly, $\mathbf{B}_x = \sum_{i:x_i=0} \mathbf{B}_{L,\mathsf{rej}^{(i)}}^{(i)} + \sum_{i:x_i=1} \mathbf{B}_{L,\mathsf{acc}^{(i)}}^{(i)}$ & $\mathbf{F}_x = \sum_{i:x_i=0} \mathbf{F}_{L,\mathsf{rej}^{(i)}}^{(i)}$
  $+ \sum_{i:x_i=1} \mathbf{F}_{L,\mathsf{acc}^{(i)}}^{(i)}$ & $\mathbf{E}_x = \sum_{i:x_i=0} \mathbf{E}_{L,\mathsf{rej}^{(i)}}^{(i)} + \sum_{i:x_i=1} \mathbf{E}_{L,\mathsf{acc}^{(i)}}^{(i)}$.

Observe that the Comp-Eval algorithm computes matrix $\mathbf{M} = \sum_{i=1}^{\ell_{\mathrm{PRG}}} \boldsymbol{\Delta}_L^{(i)}$. First, we show that for all $i \leq \ell_{\mathrm{PRG}}$, $j^* \leq L$, $\mathbf{Err}_{j^*}^{(i)}$ is small and bounded. This would help us in arguing that matrices $\mathbf{M} = \sum_{i=1}^{\ell_{\mathrm{PRG}}} \boldsymbol{\Delta}_L^{(i)}$ and $\widetilde{\mathbf{M}} = \sum_{i=1}^{\ell_{\mathrm{PRG}}} \widetilde{\boldsymbol{\Delta}}_L^{(i)}$ are very close to each other. We then prove the below bounds on $\mathbf{M}$ by proving the corresponding bounds on $\widetilde{\mathbf{M}}$ in each of the cases.

$$\|\mathbf{M}\|_\infty \begin{cases} < q^{1/8} & \text{when } \mathsf{BP}(z) = \beta \text{ and } \mathsf{msg} = 0 \\ \in (q^{1/8}, q^{1/2}) & \text{when } \mathsf{BP}(z) = \beta \text{ and } \mathsf{msg} = 1 \\ > q^{1/2} & \text{when } \mathsf{BP}(z) \neq \beta \end{cases}$$

First, we show that $\mathbf{Err}_{j^*}^{(i)}$ is bounded with the help of the following claim.

Claim 1. ([28, Claim 4.1]) $\forall\, i \in \{1, \ldots, \ell_{\mathrm{PRG}}\}, j^* \in \{1, \ldots, L\}$, $\left\|\mathbf{Err}_{j^*}^{(i)}\right\|_\infty \leq j^* \cdot \left(m^2 \cdot \sigma\right)^{j^*}$.

The remaining proof of the lemma will have two parts, (1) when $\mathsf{BP}(z) = \beta$ and (2) when $\mathsf{BP}(z) \neq \beta$. Recall that the Comp-Eval algorithm computes matrix $\mathbf{M} = \sum_{i=1}^{\ell_{\mathrm{PRG}}} \boldsymbol{\Delta}_L^{(i)}$. Let $\widetilde{\mathbf{M}} = \sum_{i=1}^{\ell_{\mathrm{PRG}}} \widetilde{\boldsymbol{\Delta}}_L^{(i)}$ and $\mathsf{Err} = \sum_{i=1}^{\ell_{\mathrm{PRG}}} \mathbf{Err}_L^{(i)}$. Also, we parse these matrices as $\mathbf{M} = \left[\mathbf{M}^{(1)} \,\|\, \mathbf{M}^{(2)}\right]$, $\widetilde{\mathbf{M}} = \left[\widetilde{\mathbf{M}}^{(1)} \,\|\, \widetilde{\mathbf{M}}^{(2)}\right]$ and $\mathsf{Err} = \left[\mathsf{Err}^{(1)} \,\|\, \mathsf{Err}^{(2)}\right]$, where $\mathbf{M}^{(1)}, \widetilde{\mathbf{M}}^{(1)}$ and $\mathsf{Err}^{(1)}$ are $n \times n$ (square) matrices.

First, note that $\mathbf{M} = \widetilde{\mathbf{M}} + \mathsf{Err}$. Using Claim 1, we can write that

$$\|\mathsf{Err}\|_\infty = \left\| \sum_{i=1}^{\ell_{\mathrm{PRG}}} \left(\boldsymbol{\Delta}_L^{(i)} - \widetilde{\boldsymbol{\Delta}}_L^{(i)} \right) \right\|_\infty \leq \sum_{i=1}^{\ell_{\mathrm{PRG}}} \left\| \boldsymbol{\Delta}_L^{(i)} - \widetilde{\boldsymbol{\Delta}}_L^{(i)} \right\|_\infty \leq \ell_{\mathrm{PRG}} \cdot L \cdot \left(m^2 \cdot \sigma\right)^L = \mathsf{Bd}. \tag{1}$$

Next, consider the following scenarios.

Part 1: $\mathsf{BP}(z) = \beta$. First, recall that the top level matrices always satisfy the following constraints during honest obfuscation:

$$\sum_{i=1}^{\ell_{\mathrm{PRG}}} \mathbf{B}_{L,\mathsf{st}_L^{(i)}}^{(i)} = \mathbf{B}_\beta = [\mathbf{A}_\beta \,\|\, \mathbf{A}_\beta \cdot \mathbf{S} + \mathbf{E}_\beta] = \begin{cases} \left[\mathbf{0}^{n \times n} \,\|\, \mathbf{E}_\beta\right] & \text{if } \mathsf{msg} = 0 \\ \left[q^{1/4} \cdot \mathbf{I}_n \,\|\, q^{1/4} \cdot \mathbf{S} + \mathbf{E}_\beta\right] & \text{if } \mathsf{msg} = 1 \end{cases}$$

Note that

$$\widetilde{\mathbf{M}} = \sum_{i=1}^{\ell_{\mathrm{PRG}}} \widetilde{\boldsymbol{\Delta}}_L^{(i)} = \sum_{i=1}^{\ell_{\mathrm{PRG}}} \boldsymbol{\Gamma}_L \cdot \mathbf{B}_{L,\mathrm{st}_L^{(i)}}^{(i)} = \boldsymbol{\Gamma}_L \cdot \sum_{i=1}^{\ell_{\mathrm{PRG}}} \mathbf{B}_{L,\mathrm{st}_L^{(i)}}^{(i)}$$

$$= \begin{cases} \left[\mathbf{0}^{n\times n} \,\|\, \boldsymbol{\Gamma}_L \cdot \mathbf{E}_\beta\right] & \text{if } \mathsf{msg} = 0 \\ \boldsymbol{\Gamma}_L \cdot \left[q^{1/4} \cdot \mathbf{I}_n \,\|\, q^{1/4} \cdot \mathbf{S} + \mathbf{E}_\beta\right] & \text{if } \mathsf{msg} = 1. \end{cases}$$

Next, we consider the following two cases dependending upon the message being obfuscated — (1) $\mathsf{msg} = 0$, (2) $\mathsf{msg} = 1$.

Case 1 ($\mathsf{msg} = 0$). In this case, we bound the l_∞ norm of the output matrix $\mathbf{M}$ (computed during evaluation) by $q^{1/8}$. We do this by bounding the norm of $\widetilde{\mathbf{M}}$ and using the error bound in Eq. 1. Recall that when $\mathsf{msg} = 0$, $\widetilde{\mathbf{M}} = \left[\mathbf{0}^{n\times n} \,\|\, \boldsymbol{\Gamma}_L \cdot \mathbf{E}_\beta\right]$. First, we bound the norms of $\boldsymbol{\Gamma}_L$ and $\mathbf{E}_\beta$ as follows.

$$\begin{aligned} \|\mathbf{E}_\beta\|_\infty &= \left\| \sum_{i:\beta_i=0} \mathbf{E}_{L,\mathrm{rej}^{(i)}}^{(i)} + \sum_{i:\beta_i=1} \mathbf{E}_{L,\mathrm{acc}^{(i)}}^{(i)} \right\|_\infty \\ &\leq \sum_{i:\beta_i=0} \left\| \mathbf{E}_{L,\mathrm{rej}^{(i)}}^{(i)} \right\|_\infty + \sum_{i:\beta_i=1} \left\| \mathbf{E}_{L,\mathrm{acc}^{(i)}}^{(i)} \right\|_\infty \leq \ell_{\mathrm{PRG}} \cdot \sigma \cdot m^{3/2} \\ &< \ell_{\mathrm{PRG}} \cdot \sigma \cdot m^2. \end{aligned} \qquad (2)$$

The last inequality follows from the fact that the matrices $\mathbf{E}_{L,\mathrm{acc}^{(i)}}^{(i)}, \mathbf{E}_{L,\mathrm{rej}^{(i)}}^{(i)}$ are sampled from truncated gaussian distribution. We can also write that,

$$\|\boldsymbol{\Gamma}_L\|_\infty = \left\| \prod_{j=1}^L \mathbf{S}_j \right\|_\infty \leq \prod_{j=1}^L \|\mathbf{S}_j\|_\infty \leq (\sigma \cdot n \cdot \sqrt{m})^L < (\sigma \cdot m^2)^L. \qquad (3)$$

This implies,

$$\left\| \widetilde{\mathbf{M}} \right\|_\infty = \|\boldsymbol{\Gamma}_L \cdot \mathbf{E}_\beta\|_\infty \leq \|\boldsymbol{\Gamma}_L\|_\infty \cdot \|\mathbf{E}_\beta\|_\infty < (\sigma\cdot m^2)^L \cdot \ell_{\mathrm{PRG}} \cdot \sigma \cdot m^2 = \ell_{\mathrm{PRG}} \cdot (\sigma\cdot m^2)^{L+1}.$$

Now we bound the l_∞ norm of $\mathbf{M}$. Recall that, $\|\mathsf{Err}\|_\infty \leq \ell_{\mathrm{PRG}} \cdot L \cdot (\sigma \cdot m^2)^L$. Therefore,

$$\begin{aligned} \|\mathbf{M}\|_\infty = \left\| \widetilde{\mathbf{M}} + \mathsf{Err} \right\|_\infty &\leq \left\| \widetilde{\mathbf{M}} \right\|_\infty + \|\mathsf{Err}\|_\infty < \ell_{\mathrm{PRG}} \cdot L \cdot (\sigma \cdot m^2)^{L+1} + \ell_{\mathrm{PRG}} \cdot L \cdot (\sigma \cdot m^2)^L \\ &< \ell_{\mathrm{PRG}} \cdot (L+1) \cdot (\sigma \cdot m^2)^{L+1} < q^{1/8}. \end{aligned}$$

The last inequality follows from the constraints described in the construction. Thus, matrix $\mathbf{M}$ (computed during evaluation) always satisfies the condition that $\|\mathbf{M}\|_\infty < q^{1/8}$ if $\mathsf{msg} = 0$.

Case 2 ($\mathsf{msg} = 1$). In this case, we prove that the l_∞ norm of the output matrix $\mathbf{M}$ (computed during evaluation) lies in $(q^{1/8}, q^{1/2})$. We do this by first computing upper and lower bounds on $\left\|\widetilde{\mathbf{M}}\right\|_\infty$ and using the bound on Err from Eq. 1. Recall that when $\mathsf{msg} = 1$, $\widetilde{\mathbf{M}} = \left[q^{1/4} \cdot \mathbf{\Gamma}_L \,\|\, q^{1/4} \cdot \mathbf{\Gamma}_L \cdot \mathbf{S} + \mathbf{\Gamma}_L \cdot \mathbf{E}_\beta\right]$. To prove a bound on $\left\|\widetilde{\mathbf{M}}\right\|_\infty$, we first prove bounds on individual components of $\widetilde{\mathbf{M}}$: $\mathbf{\Gamma}_L, \mathbf{S}, \mathbf{E}_\beta$.

By Eq. 3, we have $\|\mathbf{\Gamma}_L\|_\infty < (\sigma \cdot m^2)^L$. Note that during obfuscation we sample secret matrices $\mathbf{S}_{\mathsf{level}}^{(b)}$ (for each level and bit b) such that they are short and *always* invertible. Therefore, matrix $\mathbf{\Gamma}_L$ (which is product of L secret matrices) is also invertible. Thus, we can write that $\|\mathbf{\Gamma}_L\|_\infty \geq 1$. The lower bound of 1 follows from the fact that $\mathbf{\Gamma}_L$ is non-singular (and integral) matrix. By Eq. 2, we know that $\|\mathbf{E}_\beta\|_\infty < \ell_{\mathsf{PRG}} \cdot \sigma \cdot m^2$. Also, $\|\mathbf{S}\|_\infty \leq \sigma \cdot n \cdot \sqrt{m} < \sigma \cdot m^2$ as $\mathbf{S}$ is sampled from truncated gaussian distribution.

We finally prove bounds on $\left\|\widetilde{\mathbf{M}}\right\|_\infty$. We know that $\widetilde{\mathbf{M}}^{(1)} = q^{1/4} \cdot \mathbf{\Gamma}_L$ and $\widetilde{\mathbf{M}}^{(2)} = q^{1/4} \cdot \mathbf{\Gamma}_L \cdot \mathbf{S} + \mathbf{\Gamma}_L \cdot \mathbf{E}_\beta$.

$$\left\|\widetilde{\mathbf{M}}\right\|_\infty \geq \left\|\widetilde{\mathbf{M}}^{(1)}\right\|_\infty = q^{1/4} \cdot \|\mathbf{\Gamma}_L\|_\infty \geq q^{1/4}$$

$$\left\|\widetilde{\mathbf{M}}^{(1)}\right\|_\infty \leq q^{1/4} \cdot \|\mathbf{\Gamma}_L\|_\infty < q^{1/4} \cdot (\sigma \cdot m^2)^L$$

$$\left\|\widetilde{\mathbf{M}}^{(2)}\right\|_\infty \leq q^{1/4} \cdot \|\mathbf{\Gamma}_L\|_\infty \cdot \|\mathbf{S}\|_\infty + \|\mathbf{\Gamma}_L\|_\infty \cdot \|\mathbf{E}_\beta\|_\infty$$
$$< q^{1/4} \cdot (\sigma \cdot m^2)^{L+1} + \ell_{\mathsf{PRG}} \cdot (\sigma \cdot m^2)^{L+1}$$
$$< q^{1/4} \cdot (\ell_{\mathsf{PRG}} + 1) \cdot (\sigma \cdot m^2)^{L+1}$$

This implies,

$$\left\|\widetilde{\mathbf{M}}\right\|_\infty \leq \left\|\widetilde{\mathbf{M}}^{(1)}\right\|_\infty + \left\|\widetilde{\mathbf{M}}^{(2)}\right\|_\infty < q^{1/4} \cdot (\sigma \cdot m^2)^L + q^{1/4} \cdot (\ell_{\mathsf{PRG}} + 1) \cdot (\sigma \cdot m^2)^{L+1}$$
$$< q^{1/4} \cdot (\ell_{\mathsf{PRG}} + 2) \cdot (\sigma \cdot m^2)^{L+1} < q^{1/4} \cdot q^{1/8} < q^{3/8}$$

The last inequality follows from the constraints described in the construction. Next, we show that matrix $\mathbf{M}^{(1)}$ has large entries. In other words, matrix $\mathbf{M}$ has high l_∞ norm. Concretely,

$$\|\mathbf{M}\|_\infty = \left\|\widetilde{\mathbf{M}} + \mathsf{Err}\right\|_\infty \leq \left\|\widetilde{\mathbf{M}}\right\|_\infty + \|\mathsf{Err}\|_\infty = q^{3/8} + \mathsf{Bd} < q^{3/8} + q^{1/8} < q^{1/2}.$$

$$\|\mathbf{M}\|_\infty = \left\|\widetilde{\mathbf{M}} + \mathsf{Err}\right\|_\infty \geq \left\|\widetilde{\mathbf{M}}\right\|_\infty - \|\mathsf{Err}\|_\infty \geq \left\|\widetilde{\mathbf{M}}^{(1)}\right\|_\infty - \|\mathsf{Err}\|_\infty$$
$$\geq q^{1/4} - \mathsf{Bd} > q^{1/4} - q^{1/8} > q^{1/8}.$$

Hence if $\mathsf{msg} = 1$, $\|\mathbf{M}\|_\infty \in (q^{1/8}, q^{1/2})$ and the evaluation always outputs 1.

Part 2: $\mathsf{BP}(z) \neq \beta$. In this case, we prove that the l_∞ norm of output matrix $\mathbf{M}$ is at least $q^{1/2}$. Let $x = \mathsf{BP}(z)$ and δ_x be the edit distance between x and β, which is clearly greater than 0 if $x \neq \beta$. By construction, $\widetilde{\mathbf{M}} = \boldsymbol{\Gamma}_L \cdot [\mathbf{A}_x \,\|\, \mathbf{A}_x \cdot \mathbf{S} + \mathbf{E}_x + \delta_x \cdot \mathbf{D}]$ and $\mathbf{M} = \widetilde{\mathbf{M}} + \mathsf{Err}$. We now split this case into two subcases: 1) $\left\|\mathbf{M}^{(1)}\right\|_\infty > q^{1/2}$ and 2) $\left\|\mathbf{M}^{(1)}\right\|_\infty \leq q^{1/2}$.

Case 1. $\left\|\mathbf{M}^{(1)}\right\|_\infty > q^{1/2}$. In this case, $\|\mathbf{M}\|_\infty > q^{1/2}$ and the evaluator always outputs $\bot$.

Case 2. $\left\|\mathbf{M}^{(1)}\right\|_\infty \leq q^{1/2}$. In this case, we prove that $\mathbf{M}^{(2)}$ has high l_∞ norm. Recall that $\|\mathbf{S}\|_\infty \leq \sigma \cdot n \cdot \sqrt{m} < \sigma \cdot m^2$ as $\mathbf{S}$ is sampled from truncated gaussian distribution and $\|\mathbf{E}_x\|_\infty \leq \ell_{\mathsf{PRG}} \cdot \sigma \cdot m^2$ by an analysis similar to Eq. 2. Also, $\|\boldsymbol{\Gamma}_L\|_\infty < (\sigma \cdot m^2)^L$ by Eq. 3. We now prove an upper bound on norm of $\boldsymbol{\Gamma}_L \cdot [\mathbf{A}_x \cdot \mathbf{S} + \mathbf{E}_x]$.

$$\|\boldsymbol{\Gamma}_L \cdot \mathbf{A}_x\|_\infty \leq \left\|\mathbf{M}^{(1)}\right\|_\infty + \left\|\mathsf{Err}^{(1)}\right\|_\infty \leq q^{1/2} + \mathsf{Bd}$$

$$\begin{aligned}
\|\boldsymbol{\Gamma}_L \cdot \mathbf{A}_x \cdot \mathbf{S} + \boldsymbol{\Gamma}_L \cdot \mathbf{E}_x\|_\infty &\leq \|\boldsymbol{\Gamma}_L \cdot \mathbf{A}_x\|_\infty \cdot \|\mathbf{S}\|_\infty + \|\boldsymbol{\Gamma}_L\|_\infty \cdot \|\mathbf{E}_x\|_\infty \\
&\leq (q^{1/2} + \mathsf{Bd}) \cdot \sigma \cdot m^2 + \ell_{\mathsf{PRG}} \cdot (\sigma \cdot m^2)^{L+1} \\
&\leq q^{1/2} \cdot \sigma \cdot m^2 + \ell_{\mathsf{PRG}} \cdot L \cdot (\sigma \cdot m^2)^{L+1} + \ell_{\mathsf{PRG}} \cdot (\sigma \cdot m^2)^{L+1} \\
&< q^{1/2} \cdot \sigma \cdot m^2 + \ell_{\mathsf{PRG}} \cdot (L+1) \cdot (\sigma \cdot m^2)^{L+1} \\
&< q^{1/2} \cdot q^{1/8} + q^{1/8} < 1/2 \cdot q^{3/4}
\end{aligned}$$

$$(4)$$

The last 2 inequalities follow from the constraints described in the construction. As $\boldsymbol{\Gamma}_L \cdot \mathbf{D} = \left[q^{3/4} \cdot \boldsymbol{\Gamma}_L \,\|\, \mathbf{0}^{n \times (m - 2 \cdot n)}\right]$, we know that $\|\boldsymbol{\Gamma}_L \cdot \mathbf{D}\|_\infty = q^{3/4} \cdot \|\boldsymbol{\Gamma}_L\|_\infty$, which lies in $[q^{3/4}, q^{3/4} \cdot (\sigma \cdot m^2)^L]$ as discussed earlier. This along with Eq. 4 implies the following upper bound on $\left\|\widetilde{\mathbf{M}}^{(2)}\right\|_\infty$.

$$\begin{aligned}
\left\|\widetilde{\mathbf{M}}^{(2)}\right\|_\infty &= \|\boldsymbol{\Gamma}_L \cdot [\mathbf{A}_x \cdot \mathbf{S} + \mathbf{E}_x + \delta_x \cdot \mathbf{D}]\|_\infty \\
&\leq \|\boldsymbol{\Gamma}_L \cdot \mathbf{A}_x \cdot \mathbf{S} + \boldsymbol{\Gamma}_L \cdot \mathbf{E}_x\|_\infty + \delta_x \cdot \|\boldsymbol{\Gamma}_L \cdot \mathbf{D}\|_\infty \\
&< 1/2 \cdot q^{3/4} + \ell_{\mathsf{PRG}} \cdot \|\boldsymbol{\Gamma}_L \cdot \mathbf{D}\|_\infty \leq 1/2 \cdot q^{3/4} + q^{3/4} \cdot \ell_{\mathsf{PRG}} \cdot (\sigma \cdot m^2)^L \\
&< q^{3/4} \cdot q^{1/8} = q^{7/8}
\end{aligned}$$

The last inequality follows from the constraints described in the construction. We can also prove the following lower bound on $\left\|\widetilde{\mathbf{M}}^{(2)}\right\|_\infty$.

$$\begin{aligned}
\left\|\widetilde{\mathbf{M}}^{(2)}\right\|_\infty &= \|\boldsymbol{\Gamma}_L \cdot [\mathbf{A}_x \cdot \mathbf{S} + \mathbf{E}_x + \delta_x \cdot \mathbf{D}]\|_\infty \\
&\geq -\|\boldsymbol{\Gamma}_L \cdot \mathbf{A}_x \cdot \mathbf{S} + \boldsymbol{\Gamma}_L \cdot \mathbf{E}_x\|_\infty + \|\boldsymbol{\Gamma}_L \cdot \mathbf{D}\|_\infty > -1/2 \cdot q^{3/4} + q^{3/4} = 1/2 \cdot q^{3/4}
\end{aligned}$$

Now, we prove upper and lower bounds on $\mathbf{M}^{(2)} = \widetilde{\mathbf{M}}^{(2)} + \mathsf{Err}^{(2)}$.

$$q^{1/2} < 1/2 \cdot q^{3/4} - q^{1/8} < 1/2 \cdot q^{3/4} - \mathsf{Bd} \leq \left\|\mathbf{M}^{(2)}\right\|_\infty \leq q^{7/8} + \mathsf{Bd} < q^{7/8} + q^{1/8} < q/2$$

This implies, $\left\|\mathbf{M}^{(2)}\right\|_\infty > q^{1/2}$ in this case. Therefore, $\|\mathbf{M}\|_\infty > q^{1/2}$ and the evaluator always outputs $\bot$.

Using the above lemma, we can now argue the correctness of our scheme. First, we need to show correctness for the case when $P(x) = \alpha$.

Claim 2. *For any security parameter* $\lambda \in \mathbb{N}$, *any input* $x \in \{0,1\}^{\ell_{\mathrm{in}}}$, *any program* $P \in \mathcal{C}_{\ell_{\mathrm{in}},\ell_{\mathrm{out}},d}$ *and any message* $\mathsf{msg} \in \{0,1\}$, *if* $P(x) = \alpha$, *then*

$$\mathsf{Eval}(\mathsf{Obf}(1^\lambda, P, \mathsf{msg}, \alpha), x) = \mathsf{msg}.$$

Proof. First, the obfuscator encrypts the program P using an LHE secret key $\mathsf{lhe.sk}$, and sets $\mathsf{ct} \leftarrow \mathsf{LHE.Enc}(\mathsf{lhe.sk}, P)$. The evaluator evaluates the LHE ciphertext on universal circuit $U_x(\cdot)$, which results in an evaluated ciphertext $\widetilde{\mathsf{ct}}$. Now, by the correctness of the LHE scheme, decryption of $\widetilde{\mathsf{ct}}$ using $\mathsf{lhe.sk}$ outputs α. Therefore, $\mathsf{PRG.Eval}(\mathsf{pp}, \mathsf{LHE.Dec}(\mathsf{lhe.sk}, \widetilde{\mathsf{ct}})) = \beta$, where $\mathsf{pp} \leftarrow \mathsf{PRG.Setup}(1^\lambda)$.[8] Then, using Lemma 1, we can argue that Comp-Eval outputs msg, and thus Eval outputs msg.

Claim 3. *For all security parameters* λ, *inputs* $x \in \{0,1\}^{\ell_{\mathrm{in}}}$, *programs* $P \in \mathcal{C}_{\ell_{\mathrm{in}},\ell_{\mathrm{out}},d}$, $\alpha \in \{0,1\}^{\ell_{\mathrm{out}}}$ *such that* $P(x) \neq \alpha$ *and* $\mathsf{msg} \in \{0,1\}$,

$$\mathsf{Eval}(\mathsf{Obf}(1^\lambda, P, \mathsf{msg}, \alpha), x) = \bot$$

Proof. Fix any security parameter λ, program P, α, x such that $P(x) \neq \alpha$ and message msg. The evaluator evaluates the LHE ciphertext on universal circuit $U_x(\cdot)$, which results in an evaluated ciphertext $\widetilde{\mathsf{ct}}$. Now, by the correctness of the LHE scheme, decryption of $\widetilde{\mathsf{ct}}$ using $\mathsf{lhe.sk}$ does not output α. Therefore, by the perfect injectivity of PRG scheme, for all $\mathsf{pp} \leftarrow \mathsf{PRG.Setup}(1^\lambda)$, we have $\mathsf{PRG.Eval}(\mathsf{pp}, \mathsf{LHE.Dec}(\mathsf{lhe.sk}, \widetilde{\mathsf{ct}})) \neq \beta$. Then, using Lemma 1, we can argue that Comp-Eval outputs $\bot$, and thus Eval outputs $\bot$.

4.3 Security

In this subsection, we prove the security of the above construction. Concretely, we prove the following theorem.

Theorem 2. *Assuming that* LHE *is a secure leveled homomorphic encryption scheme, and* PRG *is a secure perfectly injective pseudorandom generator, lattice trapdoors are secure and* $(n, 2n \cdot \ell_{\mathrm{PRG}}, m - n, q, \chi)$-LWE-ss, $(n, 5m \cdot \ell_{\mathrm{PRG}}, n, q, \chi)$-LWE-ss *assumptions hold, the lockable obfuscation construction described in Sect. 4.1 is secure as per Definition 2.*

Proof. We prove the above theorem by proving that our construction is computationally indistinguishable from the construction provided in [28, Appendix D] that uses perfectly injective PRGs. Note that Goyal et al. [28] construct a

---

[8] As before, we are overloading the notation and using LHE.Dec to decrypt multiple ciphertexts.

simulator $\mathsf{Sim}(1^\lambda, 1^{|P|}, 1^{|\alpha|})$ and prove that their construction is computationally indstinguishable from the simulator. By a standard hybrid argument, this implies that our construction is computationally indstinguishable from the simulator. Formally, we prove the following theorem.

Theorem 3. *Assuming that* PRG *is a secure perfectly injective pseudorandom generator and* $(n, 2n \cdot \ell_{\mathrm{PRG}}, m - n, q, \chi)$*-LWE-ss assumption holds, the lockable obfuscation construction described in Sect. 4.1 is computationally indistinguishable[9] from [28, Appendix D] construction that uses perfectly injective PRGs.*

We prove the theorem using the following sequence of hybrids. The first hybrid corresponds to the security game in which the challenger uses our lockable obfuscation scheme (Sect. 4.1) for obfuscating the challenge program. The last hybrid corresponds to the security game in which the challenger uses lockable obfuscation scheme provided in [28]. We note that some portions of the proof are similar to those used in [28].

Game 0. This game correponds to the challenger using our lockable obfuscation scheme for obfuscating the challenge program.

1. The adversary sends a program P and message msg to the challenger.
2. The challenger first chooses the LWE parameters n, m, q, σ, χ and ℓ_{PRG}. Recall L denotes the length of the branching programs.
3. The challenger then chooses $(\mathsf{sk}, \mathsf{ek}) \leftarrow \mathsf{LHE.Setup}(1^\lambda, 1^{d \log d})$ and sets $\mathsf{ct} \leftarrow \mathsf{LHE.Enc}(\mathsf{sk}, P)$.
4. Next, it chooses a uniformly random string $\alpha \leftarrow \{0,1\}^{\ell_{\mathrm{out}}}$, runs $\mathsf{pp} \leftarrow \mathsf{PRG.Setup}(1^\lambda)$ and sets $\beta = \mathsf{PRG.Eval}(\mathsf{pp}, \alpha)$.
5. Next, consider the following program Q. It takes as input an LHE ciphertext ct, has sk hardwired and does the following: it decrypts the input ciphertext ct to get string x and outputs $\mathsf{PRG.Eval}(\mathsf{pp}, x)$. For $i \leq \ell_{\mathrm{PRG}}(\lambda)$, let $\mathsf{BP}^{(i)}$ denote the branching program that outputs the ith bit of $\mathsf{PRG.Eval}(\mathsf{pp}, x)$.
6. For $i = 1$ to ℓ_{PRG} and $j = 0$ to $L - 1$, it chooses $(\mathbf{B}_j^{(i)}, T_j^{(i)}) \leftarrow \mathsf{TrapGen}(1^{5n}, 1^m, q)$.
7. Let $\mathbf{D} = q^{3/4} \cdot \left[\mathbf{I}_n \,\|\, \mathbf{0}^{n \times (m - 2 \cdot n)} \right]$.

    (a) For the top level, it first chooses the matrices $\mathbf{A}_{L,k}^{(i)}$ (of dimension $n \times n$) for each $i \leq \ell_{\mathrm{PRG}}, k \leq 5$, uniformly at random, subject to the following constraints:

$$\sum_{i:\beta_i=0} \mathbf{A}_{L,\mathsf{rej}(i)}^{(i)} + \sum_{i:\beta_i=1} \mathbf{A}_{L,\mathsf{acc}(i)}^{(i)} = \mathbf{0}^{n \times n} \text{ if msg} = 0.$$

$$\sum_{i:\beta_i=0} \mathbf{A}_{L,\mathsf{rej}(i)}^{(i)} + \sum_{i:\beta_i=1} \mathbf{A}_{L,\mathsf{acc}(i)}^{(i)} = q^{1/4} \cdot \mathbf{I}_n \text{ if msg} = 1.$$

---

[9] Consider a game in which the adversary sends a program P and message msg to the challenger, which either obfuscates (P, msg) using [28] construction or our construction and sends back the obfuscated program. No PPT adversary can distinguish the two scenarios with non-negligible advantage.

(b) It then samples a matrix $\mathbf{S} \leftarrow \chi^{n \times (m-n)}$, and matrices $\mathbf{E}^{(i)}_{L,\mathsf{rej}^{(i)}} \leftarrow \chi^{n \times (m-n)}$, $\mathbf{E}^{(i)}_{L,\mathsf{acc}^{(i)}} \leftarrow \chi^{n \times (m-n)}$ for each $i \leq \ell_{\mathrm{PRG}}$. Next, it chooses matrices $\mathbf{F}^{(i)}_{L,k}$ as follows

$$\mathbf{F}^{(i)}_{L,\mathsf{acc}^{(i)}} = \mathbf{A}^{(i)}_{L,\mathsf{acc}^{(i)}} \cdot \mathbf{S} + \mathbf{E}^{(i)}_{L,\mathsf{acc}^{(i)}} + (1 - \beta_i) \cdot \mathbf{D}$$
$$\mathbf{F}^{(i)}_{L,\mathsf{rej}^{(i)}} = \mathbf{A}^{(i)}_{L,\mathsf{rej}^{(i)}} \cdot \mathbf{S} + \mathbf{E}^{(i)}_{L,\mathsf{rej}^{(i)}} + \beta_i \cdot \mathbf{D}$$
$$\mathbf{F}^{(i)}_{L,k} \leftarrow \mathbb{Z}^{n \times (m-n)}_q \text{ if } k \notin \{\mathsf{acc}^{(i)}, \mathsf{rej}^{(i)}\}$$

(c) The top level matrices $\mathbf{B}^{(i)}_{L,k}$ for each $i \leq \ell_{\mathrm{PRG}}, k \leq 5$ are set to $\mathbf{B}^{(i)}_{L,k} = \left[\mathbf{A}^{(i)}_{L,k} \,\|\, \mathbf{F}^{(i)}_{L,k} \right]$.

8. Next, it generates the components for each level. For each $i \in [1, \ell_{\mathrm{PRG}}]$ and each level $\mathsf{level} \in [1, L]$, do the following:

(a) Choose matrices $\mathbf{S}^{(0)}_{\mathsf{level}}, \mathbf{S}^{(1)}_{\mathsf{level}} \leftarrow \chi^{n \times n}$ and $\mathbf{E}^{(i,0)}_{\mathsf{level}}, \mathbf{E}^{(i,1)}_{\mathsf{level}} \leftarrow \chi^{5n \times m}$ for $i \leq \ell_{\mathrm{PRG}}$. If either $\mathbf{S}^{(0)}_{\mathsf{level}}$ or $\mathbf{S}^{(1)}_{\mathsf{level}}$ has determinant zero, then set it to be $\mathbf{I}_n$.

(b) For $b \in \{0, 1\}$, set matrix $\mathbf{D}^{(i,b)}_{\mathsf{level}}$ as a permutation of the matrix blocks of $\mathbf{B}^{(i)}_{\mathsf{level}}$ according to the permutation $\sigma^{(i)}_{\mathsf{level},b}(\cdot)$.

(c) Set $\mathbf{M}^{(i,b)}_{\mathsf{level}} = \left(\mathbf{I}_5 \otimes \mathbf{S}^{(b)}_{\mathsf{level}} \right) \cdot \mathbf{D}^{(i,b)}_{\mathsf{level}} + \mathbf{E}^{(i,b)}_{\mathsf{level}}$ for $i \leq \ell_{\mathrm{PRG}}$.

(d) Compute $\mathbf{C}^{(i,b)}_{\mathsf{level}} \leftarrow \mathsf{SamplePre}(\mathbf{B}^{(i)}_{\mathsf{level}-1}, T^{(i)}_{\mathsf{level}-1}, \sigma, \mathbf{M}^{(i,b)}_{\mathsf{level}})$

9. The challenger sends the final obfuscated program which consists of the LHE evaluation key ek, LHE encryption ct, together with the components $\left(\left\{ \mathbf{B}^{(i)}_{0,1} \right\}_i, \left\{ (\mathbf{C}^{(i,0)}_j, \mathbf{C}^{(i,1)}_j) \right\}_{i,j} \right)$ to the adversary.

10. The adversary outputs a bit b'.

Game 1: In this hybrid, the string β is chosen uniformly at random.

4. Next, it chooses a uniformly random string $\beta \leftarrow \{0,1\}^{\ell_{\mathrm{PRG}}}$.

Game 2: In this hybrid, the matrices $\mathbf{A}^{(i)}_{L,k}$ are chosen uniformly at random without any constraints.

7. (a) For the top level, it first chooses the matrices $\mathbf{A}^{(i)}_{L,k}$ (of dimension $n \times n$) for each $i \leq \ell_{\mathrm{PRG}}, k \leq 5$, uniformly at random without any constraints.

Game 3: In this hybrid, all the matrices $\mathbf{F}^{(i)}_{L,k}$ are chosen uniformly at random.

7. (b) It then samples matrices $\mathbf{R}^{(i)}_{L,\mathsf{rej}^{(i)}} \leftarrow \mathbb{Z}^{n \times (m-n)}_q, \mathbf{R}^{(i)}_{L,\mathsf{acc}^{(i)}} \leftarrow \mathbb{Z}^{n \times (m-n)}_q$ for each $i \leq \ell_{\mathrm{PRG}}$. Next, it chooses matrices $\mathbf{F}^{(i)}_{L,k}$ as follows.

$$\mathbf{F}^{(i)}_{L,\mathsf{acc}^{(i)}} = \mathbf{R}^{(i)}_{L,\mathsf{acc}^{(i)}} + (1 - \beta_i) \cdot \mathbf{D}, \qquad \mathbf{F}^{(i)}_{L,\mathsf{rej}^{(i)}} = \mathbf{R}^{(i)}_{L,\mathsf{rej}^{(i)}} + \beta_i \cdot \mathbf{D}$$
$$\mathbf{F}^{(i)}_{L,k} \leftarrow \mathbb{Z}^{n \times (m-n)}_q \text{ if } k \notin \{\mathsf{acc}^{(i)}, \mathsf{rej}^{(i)}\}$$

Game 4: In this hybrid, all the top level matrices $\mathbf{B}_{L,k}^{(i)}$ are chosen uniformly at random.

7. For the top level, for each $i \le \ell_{\mathrm{PRG}}$ and $k \le 5$, it chooses the matrices $\mathbf{B}_{L,k}^{(i)}$ uniformly at random from $\mathbb{Z}_q^{n \times m}$.

Game 5: In this hybrid, the top level matrices $\mathbf{B}_{L,k}^{(i)}$ are chosen according to GKW17 construction.

7. For the top level, for each $i \le \ell_{\mathrm{PRG}}$ and $k \le 5$, it chooses the matrices $\mathbf{B}_{L,k}^{(i)}$ uniformly at random from $\mathbb{Z}_q^{n \times m}$ subject to the following constraints.

$$\sum_{i \,:\, \beta_i = 0} \mathbf{B}_{L,\mathrm{rej}^{(i)}}^{(i)} + \sum_{i \,:\, \beta_i = 1} \mathbf{B}_{L,\mathrm{acc}^{(i)}}^{(i)} = \begin{cases} \mathbf{0} & \text{if msg} = 0. \\ \sqrt{q} \cdot \left[\mathbf{I}_n \,\|\, \mathbf{0}^{n \times (m-n)} \right] & \text{if msg} = 1. \end{cases}$$

Game 6: This hybrid corresponds to challenger using GKW17 lockable obfuscation scheme for obfuscating the challenge program.

7. Next, it chooses a uniformly random string $\alpha \leftarrow \{0,1\}^{\ell_{\mathrm{out}}}$, runs $\mathsf{pp} \leftarrow \mathrm{PRG.Setup}(1^\lambda)$ and sets $\beta = \mathrm{PRG.Eval}(\mathsf{pp}, \alpha)$.

Due to space constraints, we prove that Game 0 is indistinguishable from Game 6 in the full version of the paper.

5   Perfectly Injective PRGs from LPN

In this section, we give our construction of (perfectly) injective PRGs (with Setup) from the Learning Parity with Noise assumption.[10]

Overview. Let the input length of PRG be $n + \ell$. We parse input $x \in \{0,1\}^{n+\ell}$ as $x = y \,\|\, z$, where $|y| = n$ and $|z| = \ell$. Now, string y is parsed as $\mathbf{s}$, and z will be used to sample the error vector $\mathbf{e}$. Note that for injectivity argument to go through, it is important that the mapping between input y, z and vectors $\mathbf{s}, \mathbf{e}$ is also injective. Now both y and $\mathbf{s}$ are already of length n, thus we only need to make sure that our error vector sampling procedure is injective. Before describing our sampling procedure, we would like to point out that, in the PRG security game, the PRG seed is sampled uniformly at random, thus the distribution over error vectors will be a uniform distribution as well. This suggests that for basing pseudorandomness security we can't rely on the standard LPN assumption as the noise distribution is not Bernoulli, but uniform. However, we could instead

---

[10] Our PRG construction bears some resemblance to the IND-CCA secure encryption schemes provided by Döttling et al. [24] and Kiltz et al. [31], but requires new ideas. We point that if we try to build PRGs using the techniques from [24,31], then that only gives 'statistically injective' PRGs, whereas in this paper our goal is to get *perfectly injective* PRGs.

rely on the exact-LPN assumption (or xLPN) which is polynomially related to standard LPN assumption, and in which the noise distribution is uniform as the error vectors are sampled such that they have fixed hamming weight.

Next, we observe that the size of support of noise distribution in the xLPN assumption need not be a perfect *power of two*, thus we might not be able to injectively sample error vectors from the fixed length binary string z. To resolve this issue, we simply truncate the noise distribution to contain only lexically smallest error vectors such that the size of truncated set is equal to the nearest power of two. However, with this modification we need to rely on an alternate assumption which we call the restricted-exact-LPN assumption (or rxLPN). It turns out that the sample-preserving reduction of [5] also holds for rxLPN. This suggests that rxLPN and LPN assumptions are (polynomially) equivalent, therefore we could still reduce the security to the LPN assumption. Now to injectively map vectors with a fixed hamming weight to bitstrings, we employ a simple combinatorial trick to give a total ordering over vectors with efficient recursive sampling procedure. First, note that a total ordering over vectors can be trivially defined by denoting each vector with its corresponding integer representation. Now, our sampling procedure works as follows—let $x \in \{0,1\}^\ell$ and we want to sample vector $\mathbf{v} \in \mathbb{Z}_2^m$ such that $\mathsf{HW}(\mathbf{v}) = k$. The sampling algorithm first checks whether $\mathsf{int}(x) > {}^{m-1}C_k$ (where $\mathsf{int}(x)$ is the integer corresponding to string x). If the check succeeds, then it sets the first position in $\mathbf{v}$ to be 1, else it sets it 0, and continues. Also, if the check succeeds, then it updates $x = x - {}^{m-1}C_k$. In other words, each vector $\mathbf{v} \in \mathbb{Z}_2^m$ with $\mathsf{HW}(\mathbf{v}) = k$ is uniquely ranked from 0 to ${}^mC_k - 1$, and the sample algorithm outputs vector $\mathbf{v}$ with rank $\mathsf{int}(x)$. For example, $0^{m-k}1^k$ has rank 0 and 1^k0^{m-k} has rank ${}^mC_k - 1$. The sampling procedure has been formally described later in the full version of the paper.

Finally, to sample matrix $\mathbf{B}$ as a generator matrix of some good but random code, we employ ideas similar to that used in our LWE solution. To sample $\mathbf{B}$ in this special way, we simply choose a uniformly random matrix $\mathbf{A}$, a matrix $\mathbf{C}$ *with low hamming weight rows* and set $\mathbf{B} = [\mathbf{A} \mid \mathbf{AC} + \mathbf{G}]$, where $\mathbf{G}$ is the generator matrix of an error correcting code. Here the role of $\mathbf{G}$ is similar to the role of $\mathbf{D}$ in the previous solution, that is to map any non-zero vector to a high hamming weight vector. A crucial point here is that the rows of $\mathbf{C}$ must have low hamming weight. This is because if $\mathbf{A}^T\mathbf{s}$ has low hamming weight, then so does $\mathbf{C}^T\mathbf{A}^T\mathbf{s}$, and later this will be crucial in arguing that $\mathbf{B}$ is a generator matrix of a good code. Finally, for pseudorandomness of our construction, we want that $\mathbf{B}$ should look like a random matrix to any computationally bounded adversary. To this end, we use the Knapsack LPN assumption which was also shown to be (polynomially) equivalent to LPN assumption [32].[11] Due to space constraints, we defer the formal description of the construction to the full version of the paper.

---

[11] The Knapsack LPN assumption states that for a uniformly random matrix $\mathbf{A}$ and a matrix $\mathbf{E}$ such that each entry is 1 with probability p and $\mathbf{A}$ has fewer rows than columns, then $(\mathbf{A}, \mathbf{AE})$ look like uniformly random matrices.

Acknowledgements. We thank anonymous reviewers for useful feedback. The work is done in part while the first and second authors were at UT Austin. The first author is supported by IBM PhD Fellowship, and the Simons Institute for the Theory of Computing (supported by Simons-Berkeley research fellowship). The second author is supported by the Simons Institute for the Theory of Computing (supported by the Simons-Berkeley research fellowship), Binational Science Foundation (Grant No. 2016726), and by the European Union Horizon 2020 Research and Innovation Program via ERC Project REACT (Grant 756482) and via Project PROMETHEUS (Grant 780701). The third author is supported by Provost Fellowship. The fourth author is supported by NSF CNS-1908611, CNS-1414082, DARPA SafeWare and Packard Foundation Fellowship.

References

1. Alekhnovich, M.: More on average case vs approximation complexity. In: FOCS 2003 (2003)
2. Ananth, P., Jain, A., Naor, M., Sahai, A., Yogev, E.: Universal constructions and robust combiners for indistinguishability obfuscation and witness encryption. In: Robshaw, M., Katz, J. (eds.) CRYPTO 2016. LNCS, vol. 9815, pp. 491–520. Springer, Heidelberg (2016). https://doi.org/10.1007/978-3-662-53008-5_17
3. Ananth, P., Jain, A., Sahai, A.: Robust transforming combiners from indistinguishability obfuscation to functional encryption. In: Coron, J.-S., Nielsen, J.B. (eds.) EUROCRYPT 2017. LNCS, vol. 10210, pp. 91–121. Springer, Cham (2017). https://doi.org/10.1007/978-3-319-56620-7_4
4. Ananth, P., Placa, R.L.L.: Secure quantum extraction protocols. IACR Cryptol. ePrint Arch. (2019). https://eprint.iacr.org/2019/1323
5. Applebaum, B., Ishai, Y., Kushilevitz, E.: Cryptography with constant input locality. J. Cryptol. **22**(4), 429–469 (2009). https://doi.org/10.1007/s00145-009-9039-0
6. Asharov, G., Ephraim, N., Komargodski, I., Pass, R.: On perfect correctness without derandomization. IACR Cryptol. ePrint Arch. 2019, 1025 (2019)
7. Banerjee, A., Peikert, C., Rosen, A.: Pseudorandom functions and lattices. In: Pointcheval, D., Johansson, T. (eds.) EUROCRYPT 2012. LNCS, vol. 7237, pp. 719–737. Springer, Heidelberg (2012). https://doi.org/10.1007/978-3-642-29011-4_42
8. Barak, B., et al.: On the (Im)possibility of obfuscating programs. In: Kilian, J. (ed.) CRYPTO 2001. LNCS, vol. 2139, pp. 1–18. Springer, Heidelberg (2001). https://doi.org/10.1007/3-540-44647-8_1
9. Barrington, D.A.: Bounded-width polynomial-size branching programs recognize exactly those languages in NC1. In: STOC 1986 (1986)
10. Bitansky, N., Khurana, D., Paneth, O.: Weak zero-knowledge beyond the black-box barrier. In: STOC 2019 (2019)
11. Bitansky, N., Shmueli, O.: Post-quantum zero knowledge in constant rounds. In: STOC (2020)
12. Bitansky, N., Vaikuntanathan, V.: Indistinguishability obfuscation: from approximate to exact. In: Kushilevitz, E., Malkin, T. (eds.) TCC 2016-A. LNCS, vol. 9562, pp. 67–95. Springer, Heidelberg (2016). https://doi.org/10.1007/978-3-662-49096-9_4

13. Bitansky, N., Vaikuntanathan, V.: A note on perfect correctness by derandomization. In: Coron, J.-S., Nielsen, J.B. (eds.) EUROCRYPT 2017. LNCS, vol. 10211, pp. 592–606. Springer, Cham (2017). https://doi.org/10.1007/978-3-319-56614-6_20

14. Boneh, D., Franklin, M.: Identity-based encryption from the Weil pairing. In: Kilian, J. (ed.) CRYPTO 2001. LNCS, vol. 2139, pp. 213–229. Springer, Heidelberg (2001). https://doi.org/10.1007/3-540-44647-8_13

15. Boneh, D., Sahai, A., Waters, B.: Fully collusion resistant traitor tracing with short ciphertexts and private keys. In: Vaudenay, S. (ed.) EUROCRYPT 2006. LNCS, vol. 4004, pp. 573–592. Springer, Heidelberg (2006). https://doi.org/10.1007/11761679_34

16. Brakerski, Z., Lombardi, A., Segev, G., Vaikuntanathan, V.: Anonymous IBE, leakage resilience and circular security from new assumptions. In: Nielsen, J.B., Rijmen, V. (eds.) EUROCRYPT 2018. LNCS, vol. 10820, pp. 535–564. Springer, Cham (2018). https://doi.org/10.1007/978-3-319-78381-9_20

17. Brakerski, Z., Lyubashevsky, V., Vaikuntanathan, V., Wichs, D.: Worst-case hardness for LPN and cryptographic hashing via code smoothing. IACR Cryptology ePrint Archive 2018, 279 (2018)

18. Chen, Y., Vaikuntanathan, V., Waters, B., Wee, H., Wichs, D.: Traitor-tracing from LWE made simple and attribute-based. In: Beimel, A., Dziembowski, S. (eds.) TCC 2018. LNCS, vol. 11240, pp. 341–369. Springer, Cham (2018). https://doi.org/10.1007/978-3-030-03810-6_13

19. Chen, Y., Vaikuntanathan, V., Wee, H.: GGH15 beyond permutation branching programs: proofs, attacks, and candidates. In: Shacham, H., Boldyreva, A. (eds.) CRYPTO 2018. LNCS, vol. 10992, pp. 577–607. Springer, Cham (2018). https://doi.org/10.1007/978-3-319-96881-0_20

20. Cocks, C.: An identity based encryption scheme based on quadratic residues. In: Honary, B. (ed.) Cryptography and Coding 2001. LNCS, vol. 2260, pp. 360–363. Springer, Heidelberg (2001). https://doi.org/10.1007/3-540-45325-3_32

21. Cook, S.A., Hoover, H.J.: A depth-universal circuit. SIAM J. Comput. 14(4), 833–839 (1985)

22. Dolev, D., Dwork, C., Naor, M.: Nonmalleable cryptography. SIAM J. Comput. 45, 727–784 (2000)

23. Döttling, N., Garg, S., Hajiabadi, M., Masny, D.: New constructions of identity-based and key-dependent message secure encryption schemes. In: Abdalla, M., Dahab, R. (eds.) PKC 2018. LNCS, vol. 10769, pp. 3–31. Springer, Cham (2018). https://doi.org/10.1007/978-3-319-76578-5_1

24. Döttling, N., Müller-Quade, J., Nascimento, A.C.A.: IND-CCA secure cryptography based on a variant of the LPN problem. In: Wang, X., Sako, K. (eds.) ASIACRYPT 2012. LNCS, vol. 7658, pp. 485–503. Springer, Heidelberg (2012). https://doi.org/10.1007/978-3-642-34961-4_30

25. Dwork, C., Naor, M., Reingold, O.: Immunizing encryption schemes from decryption errors. In: Cachin, C., Camenisch, J.L. (eds.) EUROCRYPT 2004. LNCS, vol. 3027, pp. 342–360. Springer, Heidelberg (2004). https://doi.org/10.1007/978-3-540-24676-3_21

26. Garg, S., Gentry, C., Halevi, S., Raykova, M., Sahai, A., Waters, B.: Candidate indstinguishability obfuscation and functional encryption for all circuits. In: FOCS (2013)

27. Goyal, R., Hohenberger, S., Koppula, V., Waters, B.: A generic approach to constructing and proving verifiable random functions. In: Kalai, Y., Reyzin, L. (eds.) TCC 2017. LNCS, vol. 10678, pp. 537–566. Springer, Cham (2017). https://doi.org/10.1007/978-3-319-70503-3_18

28. Goyal, R., Koppula, V., Waters, B.: Lockable obfuscation. In: FOCS 2017 (2017)

29. Goyal, R., Koppula, V., Waters, B.: Lockable obfuscation. Cryptology ePrint Archive, Report 2017/274 (2017). https://eprint.iacr.org/2017/274

30. Goyal, R., Koppula, V., Waters, B.: Separating semantic and circular security for symmetric-key bit encryption from the learning with errors assumption. In: Coron, J.-S., Nielsen, J.B. (eds.) EUROCRYPT 2017. LNCS, vol. 10211, pp. 528–557. Springer, Cham (2017). https://doi.org/10.1007/978-3-319-56614-6_18

31. Kiltz, E., Masny, D., Pietrzak, K.: Simple chosen-ciphertext security from low-noise LPN. In: Krawczyk, H. (ed.) PKC 2014. LNCS, vol. 8383, pp. 1–18. Springer, Heidelberg (2014). https://doi.org/10.1007/978-3-642-54631-0_1

32. Micciancio, D., Mol, P.: Pseudorandom knapsacks and the sample complexity of LWE search-to-decision reductions. In: Rogaway, P. (ed.) CRYPTO 2011. LNCS, vol. 6841, pp. 465–484. Springer, Heidelberg (2011). https://doi.org/10.1007/978-3-642-22792-9_26

33. Naor, M., Yung, M.: Public-key cryptosystems provably secure against chosen ciphertext attacks. In: STOC 1990 (1990)

34. Nisan, N., Wigderson, A.: Hardness vs randomness. J. Comput. Syst. Sci. **49**(2), 149–167 (1994). https://doi.org/10.1016/S0022-0000(05)80043-1

35. Regev, O.: On lattices, learning with errors, random linear codes, and cryptography. In: STOC 2005 (2005)

36. Sahai, A., Waters, B.: Fuzzy identity-based encryption. In: Cramer, R. (ed.) EUROCRYPT 2005. LNCS, vol. 3494, pp. 457–473. Springer, Heidelberg (2005). https://doi.org/10.1007/11426639_27

37. Sahai, A., Waters, B.: How to use indistinguishability obfuscation: deniable encryption, and more. In: STOC 2014 (2014)

38. Shamir, A.: Identity-based cryptosystems and signature schemes. In: Blakley, G.R., Chaum, D. (eds.) CRYPTO 1984. LNCS, vol. 196, pp. 47–53. Springer, Heidelberg (1985). https://doi.org/10.1007/3-540-39568-7_5

39. Wichs, D., Zirdelis, G.: Obfuscating compute-and-compare programs under LWE. In: FOCS 2017 (2017)

40. Yu, Y., Steinberger, J.: Pseudorandom functions in almost constant depth from low-noise LPN. In: Fischlin, M., Coron, J.-S. (eds.) EUROCRYPT 2016. LNCS, vol. 9666, pp. 154–183. Springer, Heidelberg (2016). https://doi.org/10.1007/978-3-662-49896-5_6

41. Yu, Yu., Zhang, J.: Cryptography with auxiliary input and trapdoor from constant-noise LPN. In: Robshaw, M., Katz, J. (eds.) CRYPTO 2016. LNCS, vol. 9814, pp. 214–243. Springer, Heidelberg (2016). https://doi.org/10.1007/978-3-662-53018-4_9

42. Yu, Y., Zhang, J., Weng, J., Guo, C., Li, X.: Collision resistant hashing from learning parity with noise. IACR Cryptology ePrint Archive 2017, 1260 (2017)

Can a Public Blockchain Keep a Secret?

Fabrice Benhamouda[1], Craig Gentry[1], Sergey Gorbunov[2], Shai Halevi[1(✉)],
Hugo Krawczyk[1], Chengyu Lin[3], Tal Rabin[1,4], and Leonid Reyzin[5,6]

[1] Algorand Foundation, New York, USA
shaih@alum.mit.edu
[2] University of Waterloo, Waterloo, Canada
[3] Columbia University, New York, USA
[4] University of Pennsylvania, Philadelphia, USA
[5] Algorand Inc., Boston, USA
[6] Boston University, Boston, USA

Abstract. Blockchains are gaining traction and acceptance, not just for cryptocurrencies, but increasingly as an architecture for distributed computing. In this work we seek solutions that allow a *public* blockchain to act as a trusted long-term repository of secret information: Our goal is to deposit a secret with the blockchain, specify how it is to be used (e.g., the conditions under which it is released), and have the blockchain keep the secret and use it only in the specified manner (e.g., release only it once the conditions are met). This simple functionality enables many powerful applications, including signing statements on behalf of the blockchain, using it as the control plane for a storage system, performing decentralized program-obfuscation-as-a-service, and many more.

Using proactive secret sharing techniques, we present a scalable solution for implementing this functionality on a public blockchain, in the presence of a mobile adversary controlling a small minority of the participants. The main challenge is that, on the one hand, scalability requires that we use small committees to represent the entire system, but, on the other hand, a mobile adversary may be able to corrupt the entire committee if it is small. For this reason, existing proactive secret sharing solutions are either non-scalable or insecure in our setting.

We approach this challenge via "player replaceability", which ensures the committee is anonymous until after it performs its actions. Our main technical contribution is a system that allows sharing and re-sharing of secrets among the members of small dynamic committees, without knowing who they are until after they perform their actions and erase their secrets. Our solution handles a fully mobile adversary corrupting roughly 1/4 of the participants at any time, and is scalable in terms of both the number of parties and the number of time intervals.

Keywords: Blockchain · Evolving-committee proactive secret sharing · Mobile adversary · Player replaceability

© International Association for Cryptologic Research 2020
R. Pass and K. Pietrzak (Eds.): TCC 2020, LNCS 12550, pp. 260–290, 2020.
https://doi.org/10.1007/978-3-030-64375-1_10

1 Introduction

Imagine publishing a puzzle and handing over the solution to a public blockchain, to keep secret for a while and reveal it if no one solves the puzzle within a week. More generally, consider using the blockchain as a secure storage solution, allowing applications and clients to deposit secret data and specify the permissible use of that data. A blockchain providing such secret storage can enable a host of novel applications (Sect. 1.3). For example, the secret can be a signature key, enabling the blockchain to sign on behalf of some client or on behalf of the blockchain itself. Alternatively, the secret can provide a root of trust for key-management and certification solutions, allowing users and programs to enforce policies specifying how their private data can be used. Or the secret can be a decryption key for a fully homomorphic encryption scheme, enabling, in a sense, program-obfuscation-as-a-service via encrypted computation and consensus-enforced conditional decryption.

In this work we investigate the functionality of keeping a secret on a public blockchain. We seek a *scalable* solution, whose complexity is bounded by a fixed polynomial in the security parameter, regardless of how long the secret must be kept for or how many nodes participate in the blockchain. To achieve scalability, the work of maintaining the secret must be handled by a small committee. At the same time, the solution must remain secure even against a mobile adversary that can corrupt different participants at different times, as long as it corrupts no more than a small fraction of the participants at any given time.[1] Thus, the small size of the committee presents a challenge for security. An adversary would have enough "corruption budget" to corrupt all of the members of the committee; even if the committee is dynamic, the mobile adversary could corrupt it as soon as its known.

A beautiful approach for addressing the vulnerability of working with small committees is *player replaceability*, introduced by Chen and Micali [14] in the setting of reaching consensus in the Algorand blockchain. In such systems, committees are selected to do some work (such as agreeing on a block), but each committee member is charged with sending *a single message*. Most importantly, the member remains completely anonymous until it sends that message. The attacker, not knowing the identities of the selected members, cannot target them for corruption until after they complete their job. For example, the committee can be chosen by having parties self-select by locally solving moderately hard puzzles, or using "cryptographic sortition" [14] based on verifiable random functions (VRFs) [42].

Using this approach for our purpose is far from simple. How can one share a secret among the members of an unknown committee? In some contexts, one can devise solutions using the cryptographic sledgehammer of witness encryption [23], as sketched in [26]: In systems such as proof-of-stake blockchains, the statement "the committee votes to open the secret" can be expressed as an NP-

---

[1] This could mean a small fraction of the stake in a proof-of-stake blockchain, or of the computing power in a proof-of-work blockchain.

statement, and so one can use witness-encryption relative to that statement. While this approach shows polynomial-time feasibility, we are interested in solutions that can plausibly be used in practice, and therefore explore approaches that do not require obfuscation-like tools. Moreover, it is not clear how to extend this solution to systems such as proof-or-work blockchains, where it is unknown how to encode committee membership as an NP statement (because committee membership depends on statements such as "longest chain" or "first player to present a solution to the puzzle").

1.1   Using Proactive Secret Sharing

Our solution relies on proactive secret sharing (PSS) techniques [13,34,44], using well-coordinated messages and erasures to deal with mobile adversaries. Early work on proactive secret sharing assumed a fixed committee (say of size N), where parties are occasionally corrupted by the adversary and later recover and re-join the honest set. A drawback of these protocols in our context is that they require all the members to participate in every handover protocol, and are therefore not sufficiently scalable. Proactive secret sharing with dynamic committees (DPSS) was addressed in a number of previous works (e.g., [2,41, 45]).

Crucial to our solution is a new variant of proactive secret-sharing, that we call *evolving-committee PSS* (ECPSS). This variant is similar to DPSS, but with one important difference: DPSS schemes treat the committee membership as external input to the protocol, and rely on the promise that all these committees have honest majority. In contrast, in ECPSS the committee-selection is part of the construction itself, and it is up to protocol to ensure that the committees that are chosen maintain honest majority.

We show how to implement ECPSS using the approach of player replaceability. Our solution ensures that the committee members remain anonymous, until after they hand over fresh shares to a new committee and erase their own. This requires a method of selecting the members of the next committee and sending messages to them, without the senders knowing who the recipients are. Moreover, communication in our model must be strictly one way, since the adversary learns a node's identity once it sends a message. Committee members are not even allowed to know the identities of their peers (since some of them may be adversarial), so interactive protocols among the current members are also not allowed. Designing a solution in this challenging context is the main contribution of this work.

1.2   Overview of Our Solution

As common in PSS, the timeline of the system is partitioned into epochs, with a handover protocol at the beginning of each one. In each epoch i, the secret is shared among members of an epoch-i committee, and the committee changes from one epoch to the next, erasing its secret state once it passed the secret to the next committee. The committee in every epoch is small, consisting of

$c_i = O(\lambda)$ members out of the entire universe of N users. This lets us reduce the complexity of the handover protocol from $\Omega(N)$ to $O(c_i)$ broadcast messages. Our proactive solution is based on Shamir's secret sharing scheme [47], and uses the following components:

- We use the blockchain itself to provide synchrony, authenticated broadcast, and PKI. See Sect. 2.1.
- We use cryptographic sortition for choosing random but verifiable committees. See Sect. 2.3.[2]
- We use two public-key encryption (PKE) schemes, one for long-term keys and the other for ephemeral committee-specific keys. The long-term PKE needs to be anonymous [3]: namely, ciphertexts must not disclose the public keys that were used to generate them. Both anonymity and secrecy for these schemes must hold even under receiver-selected-opening attacks, see Sect. 2.4. (We note that these tools also require erasures.)
- We use non-interactive zero-knowledge (NIZK) proofs for statements about encrypted values lying on a low-degree polynomial (under the ephemeral scheme). The number of encrypted values in each one of these statements is small, essentially the size c_i of the committees from above.

Our solution uses anonymous public-key encryption to establish a communication mechanism that allow anyone to post a message to an unknown receiver. We refer to this communication mechanism as "target-anonymous channels." Once target-anonymous channels to the next-epoch committee are established, the current-epoch committee can use them to re-share the secret to the next-epoch committee.

Establishing target-anonymous channels to the next-epoch committee without revealing the committee to the adversary is a difficult problem. We solve it by using special-purpose committees, separate from the ones holding the secret. Namely, we have two types of committees:

- A *holding committee* that holds shares of the secret.
- A *nominating committee* whose role is to establish the target-anonymous channels, thereby "nominating" the members of the next holding committee.

Crucially, the nominating committee does not hold shares, and hence its members can self-select (because no channels to them need to be established). The self-selection can be accomplished, for example, by using cryptographic sortition. Once self-selected, each nominator chooses one member of the next holding committee, and publishes on the blockchain information that lets the current holding committee send messages to that member, without revealing its identity.

In more detail, after randomly choosing its nominee for the future holding committee, the nominator chooses and posts to the blockchain a new ephemeral public key, along with an encryption of the corresponding ephemeral secret key under the nominee's long-term public key. We use anonymous encryption to

---

[2] An alternative realization in the context of proof-of-work blockchains could use solving moderately-hard puzzles for that purpose.

ensure that the ephemeral keys and ciphertexts do not betray the identities (or long-term keys) of the nominees. Note that the ephemeral keys themselves may use a different encryption scheme, that need not be anonymous.

Once the ephemeral keys of the next committee are posted, everyone knows the size of that committee (call it c_{i+1}). Each member of the current holding committee re-shares its share using a t-of-c_{i+1} Shamir secret sharing (with $t \approx c_{i+1}/2$), uses the j-th ephemeral key to encrypt the j-th share, and broadcasts all these encrypted shares along with a proof that the sharing was done properly.

Members of the next holding committee recover their ephemeral secret keys by decrypting the posted ciphertexts with their long-term keys. Each member then collects all the shares that were encrypted under its ephemeral key and uses them to compute its share of the global secret in the new committee. Note that all these ciphertexts are publicly known, so they can serve also as a commitment to the share, enabling the holding committee members to prove correct re-sharing in the next iteration of the protocol.[3]

An important feature of this solution is that *it does not require the nominating committee members to prove anything* about how they chose their nominees or how the ephemeral keys were generated. Note that proving the selection would be of limited value, since even if we force corrupted members of the nominating committee to abide by the protocol, they can corrupt their nominees as soon as those are chosen. Moreover, asking the nominating committee to prove anything about their choice while maintaining anonymity would require that they prove size-N statements (i.e. proving that the receiver is one of the N parties in the system).[4]

In contrast, holding-committee members must prove that they re-share their shares properly. But the statements being proven (and their witnesses) are all short: Their size depends only on the committee size, and does not grow with the total number of parties or the history of the blockchain. Hence the NIZK complexity in our solution is just polynomial in the security parameter, even if we were to use the most naive NIZKs.

The lack of proofs by the nominating committee comes at a price, as it allows the adversary to double dip: An adversary controlling an f fraction of the parties will have roughly an f fraction of the nominating committee members (all of which can choose to nominate corrupted parties to the holding committee), and another f fraction of the holding committee members nominated by honest parties. Hence, our solution can only tolerate adversaries that control less than 29% of the total population. (In the appendix of the long version [6] we mention a variant of the protocol that does require proofs and is resilient to a higher percentage of adversarial parties, but in a weaker adversary model.)

We also comment that members of the holding committee must replace the secret key for their long-term keys and erase the old secret key before they

---

[3] If the ephemeral PKE scheme is also linearly-homomorphic, it may be possible to compress this commitment to a single ciphertext encrypting the share of that party.

[4] The communication can still be kept small using SNARKs, but the computation would have to be at least linear in N.

post their message in the protocol. Otherwise the adversary can corrupt them (because they will reveal themselves when posting messages) and use the old secret key to decrypt everything that was sent to them (in particular the shares that they received). This means that the term of "long-term keys" is also limited: these keys are used once and then discarded.

Aside: Anonymous PKE and Selective-Opening. In our setting, the anonymous PKE needs to provide security against selective-opening attacks (see discussion in Sect. 2.4). While it is well understood that semantic-security *does not* imply secrecy against selective-opening, the same is not true of anonymity. In Sect. 5 we show strong evidence that anonymity *is preserved* under selective-opening attacks. However, we do not fully resolve this question, and it remains an interesting problem for future work.

Aside: Parties vs. Stake or Computing Power. The description so far glossed over the question of what exactly is a party in the context of blockchains. Throughout this manuscript we mostly ignore this issue and think of parties as discrete entities, even though reality may be more complex. In a proof-of-stake (PoS) blockchain, parties are weighted by the amount of stake that they hold, with rich parties having more power than poor ones. Hence the sortition-based solution above must also be weighted accordingly, giving the rich more seats on the various committees. Similarly, in proof-of-work (PoW) blockchains, the parties with more computing power should get more seats on the committees. See Sect. 4 for more discussion about using stake to represent parties, and about the effect of parties sending tokens to each other (and hence changing their stake).

1.3 Applications

The solutions in this work can form the basis of many applications, both in blockchain-specific contexts and for traditional uses of threshold cryptography. Perhaps the most natural application is for signing global blockchain state, making it easy to verify without having to inspect the entire blockchain history. This is useful both for fast catch-up (when a new party joins the blockchain) and for a cross-blockchain token bridge (when one blockchain needs to verify statements about the state of another).

The secrets held by committee can more generally be used for "threshold cryptography as a service": for example, a threshold signature scheme deployed to support certification authorities, or authentication of credentials, or notarization services, etc. Another application is a verifiable randomness beacon, e.g., as used in [1,30]. Yet another versatile primitive is threshold Oblivious PRF, which can be used to implement a variety of secure storage systems, such as password-authenticated secrets (e.g., custodial services) [36], cloud key management [37], private information retrieval and search on encrypted data [20], oblivious pseudonyms [39], password managers [48], and more.

Even more generally, we can implement generic secure computation, letting the current committee pass to the next one the sum/product of two secrets rather than just passing the individual secrets themselves. (As it happens, our handover protocol is similar in many ways to the information-theoretic multiplication protocol from [24], making it rather easy to extend to secure computation.) A particularly powerful form of MPC-as-a-service is using threshold decryption of homomorphic encryption [10], which would enable applications akin to program obfuscation: Clients can encrypt their programs, anyone could apply these encrypted programs to arbitrary inputs, and the blockchain could decrypt the result (when accompanied by appropriate proofs). More limited in scope but with more practical implementations, threshold decryption of linearly-homomorphic encryption enables varied applications such as private set intersection [21], asset management and fraud prevention [29], and many more.

1.4   Related Work

Secret sharing was introduced in the works of Shamir [47] and Blakley [7]. The proactive setting stems from the mobile adversary model of Ostrovsky and Yung [44] followed by works of Canetti-Herzberg and Herzberg et al. in the static-committee setting [13,33,34]. The dynamic setting where the set of shareholders changes over time was contemplated in several works, such as [2,17,18,46]. We refer the reader to Maram et al. [41] for a detailed comparison of these works (in particular, see their Sect. 8 and Table 4).

Several works also deal with dynamic shareholder sets in the context of blockchain. The Ekiden design [15] provides privacy in smart contracts using a trusted execution environment (TEE). They also use threshold PRFs to derive periodic contract-specific symmetric keys for encrypting smart-contracts. Their scheme is described using a static committee but they suggest the use of proactive secret sharing and rotating committees for increased security. Calypso [38] uses blockchain and threshold encryption to build an auditable access control system for the management of keys and confidential data, and contemplates the possibility of shareholder committees changing periodically. Helix [1] selects per-block committees who agree on the next block in the chain using a PBFT protocol, and use threshold decryption *with a fixed static committee* to recover the transactions only after the block is finalized (and also to implement a verifiable source of randomness). Dfinity [30] also uses threshold cryptography (signatures in their case) and dynamic shareholder committees for implementing a randomness beacon, but the shared secret changes with each new committee.

Closest to our work are the works of Maram et al. (CHURP) [41] and Goyal et al. [27] that build proactive secret sharing over dynamic groups in a blockchain environment. The crucial difference between these works and ours is that they *assume a bound of t corrupted committee members*, without regard to how to ensure that such a bound holds. In fact their techniques are inapplicable in our setting, as they crucially build on active participation of the receiving committee in the handover protocol. As a result, in the mobile adversary model that we consider, their protocol is either non-scalable (requiring participation of all the stakeholders) or insecure (if using small committees). In contrast, our main goal is to maintain absolute secrecy of the new committee members during handover, to enable the use of small committees.

A concurrent independent work of Choudhuri et al. [16] deals with MPC in a "fluid" model where parties come and go and cannot be counted on to maintain state from one step to the next. This model share some commonalities with ours, but the solutions are very different. In particular their solution only provides security with abort, which is not enough for our purposes (as we need assurance of reconstruction). Their solution uses DPSS, where the composition of the committees is treated as input (under the promise that they are mostly honest), whereas a crucial part of our solution is choosing the committees.

Finally, our techniques are somewhat reminiscent of the protocol of Garay et al. [22] for MPC with sublinear communication (and indeed the resilience constant $1 - \sqrt{0.5}$ from Sect. 3.2 appears in their work as well).

2 Background and Definitions

2.1 Synchrony, Broadcast, PKI, and Adversary

We use the blockchain as a synchronization mechanism, an authenticated broadcast channel, and a PKI. For synchrony, we assume that all parties know what is the current block number on the blockchain. For communication, any party can broadcast a message to the blockchain at round i, and be assured that everyone will receive it no later than round $i + \delta$ (where δ is a known bound). Moreover, a party that received a message on the blockchain in round i is assured of its sender, and can also trust that all other parties received the same message at the same round.

This (authenticated) broadcast channel is the only communication mechanism in our model, and it is fully public. This means that anyone (including the adversary) can see who posts messages on it. We stress that we do not assume or use sender-anonymous channels, such channels may make the problem of keeping a secret on the blockchain much easier, but establishing them is notoriously hard, (if not impossible).

The same broadcast channel is also used for PKI, each party in our system periodically broadcasts a public key on the authenticated broadcast channel, hence letting everyone else know about that key.

Finally, we consider a mobile adversary that sees the messages on the broadcast channel and can corrupt any sender of any message at will. The power of the adversary is measured by its "corruption budget," which is defined as follows: The lifetime of the system is partitioned into epochs, and we assume that the PKI system have each party broadcasts a new key at least once per epoch. After corrupting a party, the adversary may decide to leave that party alone. If that happens then this party will broadcast a new key in the next epoch, and then it will no longer be under the adversary's control. In other words, the adversary controls a party from the time that it decides to corrupt it, until that party— after being left alone—broadcasts a new key (and have that key appears on the broadcast channel). The adversary's "corruption budget" is the largest percentage of parties that it controls at any point during the lifetime of the system. Our solutions in this work ensure security only against attackers whose corruption budget stays below some fraction f^* of the overall population. Specifically our main solution in Sect. 3 has $f^* = 1 - \sqrt{0.5} \approx 0.29$. (We sketch in the appendix of the long version [6] a variant with resilience $\frac{3-\sqrt{5}}{2} \approx 0.38$, but under a weaker adversary model.)

Importantly, our model assumes that parties can security erase their state, this requirement is inherent in all proactive protocols.

2.2   Evolving-Committee Proactive Secret Sharing

A t-of-n secret-sharing scheme [7,47] consists of sharing and reconstruction procedures, where a secret σ is shared among n parties, in a way that lets any t (or more) of them reconstruct the secret from their shares. In its simplest form, we only require the following secrecy and reconstruction properties against efficient adversaries that corrupt up to $t-1$ parties:

Definition 1 (Secret Sharing). *A t-of-n secret-sharing scheme must provide the following two properties.*

Semantic security: *An efficient adversary chooses two secrets σ_0, σ_1, then the sharing procedure is run and the adversary can see the shares held by all that parties that it corrupts. The adversary must have at most a negligible advantage in guessing if the value shared was σ_0 or σ_1.*

Reconstruction: *After receiving their shares from an honest dealer, the reconstruction protocol run by $\geq t$ honest parties will output the correct secret σ (except for negligible probability).*

In this work we use Shamir secret sharing [47], where the secret σ is shared among the n parties by choosing a random degree-$(t-1)$ polynomial F whose free term is σ (over some field $\mathcal{F}$ of size at least $n+1$), associating publicly with each party i a distinct point $\alpha_i \in \mathcal{F}$, then giving that party the value $\sigma_i = F(\alpha_i)$. Thereafter, collection of t parties or more can interpolate and recover the free term of F.

Robust secret sharing. In addition to the basic secrecy and reconstruction properties above, many applications of secret-sharing requires also *robust reconstruction*, namely that reconstruction succeeds in outputting the right secret whenever there are t or more correct shares, even if it is given some additional corrupted shares.

Definition 2. *A t-of-n secret-sharing scheme has robust reconstruction if polynomial-time adversaries can only win the following game with negligible probability (in n):*

- *The adversary specifies a secret σ, which is shared among the share holders;*
- *Later the adversary specifies a reconstruction set R of parties, consisting of at least t honest parties (and as many corrupted parties as it wants). The reconstruction procedure is run on the shares of the honest parties in R, as well as shares chosen by the adversary for the corrupted parties in R.*

The adversary wins if the reconstruction procedure fails to output the original secret σ.

Proactive secret sharing (PSS). A PSS scheme [13,34,44] is a method of maintaining a shared secret in the presence of a mobile adversary. The adversary model is that of Ostrovsky and Yung [44], with parties that are occasionally corrupted by the adversary and can later recover and re-join the honest set. PSS includes share-refresh protocol, which is run periodically in such a way that shares from different periods cannot be combined to recover the secret.

A PSS scheme provides the same secrecy and (robust) reconstruction properties from Definitions 1 and 2, and the power of the adversary is measured by the number of parties that it can corrupt between two runs of the share-refresh protocol. Typically, the requirement is that over an epoch from the beginning of one refresh operation until the end of the next one, the adversary controls at most $t-1$ of the n parties.

Dynamic PSS (DPSS). DPSS is a proactive scheme where the set of n secret holders may change from one epoch to the next. The share-refresh protocol is replaced by a share-handover protocol run between two (possibly overlapping) sets of n parties each, allowing the old set of holders to transfer the secret to the new set. DPSS still provides the same secrecy and (robust) reconstruction properties from Definitions 1 and 2 against a mobile adversary, this time under the assumption that the adversary controls at most $t-1$ of the n parties in each set.

Evolving-Committee PSS (ECPSS). Prior work on DPSS ignored the question of how these committee are formed. In all prior work the composition of the committee was treated as external input, and the restriction of $\leq t-1$ corrupted parties in each committee was a promise. In this work we take the next step, incorporating the committee-selection into the protocol itself, and *proving* that at most $t-1$ parties are corrupted whp (in our adversary model). We call this augmented notion *Evolving-Committee PSS* (ECPSS),

Definition 3. *An evolving-committee proactive secret sharing scheme (with parameters $t \leq n < N$) consists of the following procedures:*

Trusted Setup (optional). *Provide initial state for a universe of N parties;*
Sharing. *Shares a secret 2σ among an initial holding committee of size n;*
Committee-selection. *Select the next n-party holding committee, this protocol runs among all N parties;*
Handover. *An n-party protocol, takes the output of committee-selection and the current shares, and re-shares them among the next holding committee;*

Reconstruction. *Takes t or more shares from the current holding committee and reconstructs the secret σ (or outputs $\perp$ on failure.)*

An ECPSS protocol is scalable *if the messages sent during committee-selection and handover are bounded in total size by some fixed* $\mathsf{poly}(n, \lambda)$, *regardless of N.*

A run of the ECPSS scheme consists of initial (setup and) sharing, followed by periodic runs of committee-selection and handover, and concludes with reconstruction. Note that some variations are possible, for example n, t may vary from one committee to the next and even N could change over time.

In terms of security, we require that ECPSS provides the same secrecy and (robust) reconstruction properties from Definitions 1 and 2, within whatever adversary model that is considered. The main difference with DPSS is that ECPSS no longer enjoys the DPSS "promise" of mostly-honest committees, instead we have to *prove* that committees can keep a secret (i.e. that they are mostly honest) within the given adversary model. In our case, this is a traditional mobile-adversary model that only assumes some limit on the adversary's corruption power in the overall universe (as in Sect. 2.1 above).

An important feature of scalable ECPSS is that most parties neither send messages during committee-selection nor take part in the handover protocol. In our mobile-adversary model, this begs the question of how can such "passive" parties recover from compromise. Our EPSS must therefore rely on some external mechanism to let passive parties recover, a mechanism which is not part of the ECPSS protocol itself. In our setting we rely on the PKI component from Sect. 2.1 above, where each party broadcasts a new public key at least once per epoch, letting it recover from an exposure of its old secret key. When proving ECPSS security, however, we need not worry about this mechanism, we simply assume that such mechanism exists, and consider a party "magically recovered" if it is left alone by the adversary for a full epoch.

Finally, while it is convenient to consider the same epochs for both the ECPSS protocol and the underlying adversary model (and indeed we assume so in Sect. 3), it is not really required. The refresh protocol can run more often than the PKI-induced epochs. In our context such frequent secret-refresh may be required, indeed the secret must be refreshed every time that it is used by a higher-level application, since any use lets the adversary learn who was holding the secret. Such frequent refresh operations make it even more important to use efficient protocols, and in particular motivate our insistence on scalability.

2.3 Verifiable Random Functions and Cryptographic Sortition

A verifiable random function (VRF) [42] is a pseudorandom function that enables the key holder to prove (input, output) pairs. We refer the reader to [42] for the formal definition.[5] Constructions of VRFs are known under various number

---

[5] A convenient way of thinking about VRFs is as a hash of the signature in a unique-signature scheme.

theoretic assumptions (such as RSA, DDH, or hardness in paring groups), with or without the random-oracle heuristic.

VRFs can be used to implement *cryptographic sortition*, which is essentially a verifiable lottery [14] that the parties can use to self-select themselves to committees. Each party has a VRF key pair, the parties all know each other's public keys, and there is a publicly known input value that they all agree on. Each party computes the VRF on the public input using its secret key, thereby obtaining a random value that it can use to determine whether or not it was selected to the committee. Moreover the party can prove its self-selection to everyone by exhibiting the random value with the VRF proof.

In many settings (including ours) the adversary has some influence over the public input. In such settings, the VRF implementation sketched above falls short of implementing a "perfect" lottery, since the adversary can try many inputs until it finds one that it likes. We therefore consider a sortition functionality with initial phase where the adversary can reset the lottery, each time getting the lottery choices corresponding to the parties that it controls. Eventually the adversary decides that it is happy with its choices, and then the lottery functionality is activated for everyone. This functionality is described in Fig. 1.

Cryptographic Sortition

Parameters are probability $p \in (0, 1)$ and a set of N parties $P_1, \ldots, P_N$.

1. **Initialization.** For each $i = 1, \ldots, N$ choose a random independent bit b_i with $\Pr[b_i = 1] = p$. The adversary can repeatedly request to see all the bits for the corrupted parties, and can ask that all the bits will be chosen afresh. Once it is happy with its bits, the adversary can end this phase and move to Phase 2.
2a. **Lottery.** Once initialization ends, every party P_i can ask for its state, getting the bit b_i.
2b. **Verification.** All parties begin in *private mode*, and any party can ask at any time for its mode to be changed to *public mode*. A party P_i can ask for the state of any other party P_j, getting $\perp$ if P_j is still in private mode or the bit b_j if P_j is in public mode.

Fig. 1. The cryptographic sortition functionality.

2.4 Selective-Opening Security of Public-Key Encryption

Our solution relies crucially on implementing "target-anonymous" secure channels by broadcasting encrypted messages. In the mobile-adversary model, this means that the adversary gets to see public keys and encrypted messages, then decide on the nodes that it wants to corrupt, exposing their secret keys. This attack is known as the *receiver selective-opening attack* (cf. [4,5,11,19,32]), and it poses many challenges. In particular, it is known that secrecy under receiver selective-opening attack does not follow from semantic security [4,5,25,35], and implementing schemes that provably maintain secrecy in this setting is challenging. In our setting, we need schemes that provide both secrecy and anonymity in this model, and these two aspects seem to behave very differently. We begin with the secrecy aspect, which was researched more in the literature and is better understood.

Secrecy Under Selective Opening Attacks. We follow Hazay et al.'s definitions of indistinguishability-based receiver-selective-opening security (RIND-SO) [32], which build on [4,19]. In the RIND-SO security game, the adversary sees a vector of ciphertexts, encrypting messages that are drawn from some distribution $\mathcal{D}$. It obtains the opening of a selected subset of them (by obtaining secret keys), then receives from the challenger either the actual remaining plaintexts, or fake remaining plaintexts that are drawn afresh from $\mathcal{D}$ *conditioned on the opened plaintexts*. (This game requires that $\mathcal{D}$ be efficiently resamplable [9], namely it should be feasible to draw from $\mathcal{D}$ conditioned on the opened plaintexts.) RIND-SO security require that the adversary only has negligible advantage in telling these cases apart, see [32] for a formal definition.

While not following from standard semantic security (even for semi-adaptive adversaries), selective-opening security can be obtained from exponentially CPA-secure encryption via complexity leveraging. Encryption schemes with selective-opening security can also be built from receiver-non-committing encryption (RNCE) [11], but Nielsen [43] showed that an RNCE scheme must have secret-key at least as long as the total size of plaintexts that are encrypted to it. However, Hazay et al. [32] showed that RIND-SO security can be obtained from a weaker "tweaked" notion of RNCE, and that a construction due to Canetti et al. [12] achieves the desired notion under the Decision-Composite-residuosity (DCR) assumption.

Anonymity Under Selective Opening Attacks. Bellare et al. defined in [3] anonymity for static adversaries via indistinguishability between two keys, but in our setting we need anonymity also against selective opening. We are not aware of previous work that examined anonymity in this setting, and even defining what it means takes some care. In our setting it makes sense to require that the adversary's decision to open a key (i.e. corrupt its holder) is not significantly impacted by whether or not that key was used to encrypt a ciphertext. We consider adversary that can see public keys and ciphertexts and can open some fraction f of the public keys and learn the corresponding secret keys. We require that the adversary cannot learn the secret keys of much more than an f fraction of the keys that are actually used to encrypt the ciphertexts. This is defined via the following game between the adversary and a challenger, with parameters ϵ, m, t, n such that $\epsilon > 0$ is a constant and $\lambda \leq m, t \leq n(1 - \epsilon)$:

1. The challenger runs the key generation n times to get $(\mathsf{pk}_i, \mathsf{sk}_i) \leftarrow \mathsf{Gen}(1^\lambda, \$)$ for $i = 1, \ldots, n$, and sends $\mathsf{pk}_1, \ldots, \mathsf{pk}_n$ to the adversary;

2. The adversary chooses m plaintext messages $x_1, \ldots, x_m$;
3. The challenger chooses m distinct random indexes $A = \{i_1, \ldots, i_m\} \subset [n]$, uses pk_{i_j} to encrypt x_j, and sends to the adversary the ciphertexts $\mathsf{ct}_j \leftarrow \mathsf{Enc}_{\mathsf{pk}_{i_j}}(x_j)$ $(j = 1, \ldots, m)$.
4. The adversary adaptively chooses indexes $k_1, k_2, \ldots, k_t$ one at a times, and for each k_j it receives from the challenger the secret key sk_{k_j}.

The adversary wins this game if it opens more than $t/n + \epsilon$ fraction of the ciphertext-encrypting keys indexed by A.

Definition 4 (Adaptive Anonymous PKE). *A PKE scheme* $\mathcal{E} = (\mathsf{Gen}, \mathsf{Enc}, \mathsf{Dec})$ *is anonymous against selective-opening, if for every constant* $\epsilon > 0$ *and* $\lambda \leq m, t \leq n(1 - \epsilon)$, *no feasible adversary can win the above game with non-negligible probability (in* λ*).*

In the long version [6] we recall the static-adversary definition of Bellare et al. [3] and discuss its relations to our selective-opening notion. We show some evidence that our notion is implied by the definition from [3], hence we make the following conjecture:

Conjecture 1. An anonymous PKE against static adversaries is also selective-opening anonymous as per Definition 4.

2.5   Non-interactive Zero-Knowledge Proofs

We use the standard definition of NIZK [8] using a common reference string.

2.6   Instantiating the Building Blocks for Our Solution

As we sketched in the introduction, our solution uses two PKE schemes, external one for the long-term keys and internal one for the ephemeral keys. Denote these schemes by $\mathcal{E}_1$ (external) and $\mathcal{E}_2$ (internal), and denote their combination by $\mathcal{E}_3 = \mathcal{E}_1 \circ \mathcal{E}_2$. Namely, $\mathcal{E}_3$ uses long-term keys from $\mathcal{E}_1$, and encrypts a message by choosing an ephemeral key pair for $\mathcal{E}_2$, encrypting the ephemeral secret key by the long-term public key, and encrypting the message by the ephemeral public key. The properties of these schemes that we need are:

- $\mathcal{E}_1$ is anonymous under selective-opening, as per Definition 4.
- The combination $\mathcal{E}_3 = \mathcal{E}_1 \circ \mathcal{E}_2$ is RIND-SO secure as in [32].

In addition we would like the internal scheme $\mathcal{E}_2$ to be "secret-sharing friendly", in the sense that it allow efficient NIZK proofs that multiple values encrypted under multiple keys lie on a low-degree polynomial.[6] Below we sketch some plausible instantiations.

---

[6] The witness for such proof consists of the secret key for one of the keys and the encryption randomness for all the others.

Achieving Anonymity for $\mathcal{E}_1$. Since our solution does not require proving anything about the external scheme, we can use random-oracle-based instantiations, which makes it easier to deal with selective opening attacks. Moreover, under our Conjecture 1 it is enough to ensure static anonymity against static adversaries to get also anonymity under selective-opening. It is well known that most DL-based schemes and most LWE-based schemes are statically anonymous, and there are many variations of factoring-based schemes that are also anonymous.

Achieving Secrecy for $\mathcal{E}_3$. To get RIND-SO security for $\mathcal{E}_3$ we need both $\mathcal{E}_1$ and $\mathcal{E}_2$ to provide secrecy under selective opening. For $\mathcal{E}_1$ we may use random-oracle-based hybrid constructions, but for $\mathcal{E}_2$ we need efficient NIZK proofs and hence prefer not to use random oracles.

DCR-based instantiation. To get RIND-SO security for $\mathcal{E}_2$, we can use the "tweaked" receiver-noncommitting encryption from [32]. This method can be instantiated based on the decision-composite-residuosity (DCR) assumption. We begin with the DCR-based RNCE scheme of Canetti et al. [12], and apply the usual anonymization methods for factoring-based scheme to make it also anonymous (e.g., add a random multiple of n, see [31]).

This instantiation is also reasonably sharing-friendly, we can have a secret holder provide a Pedersen commitment to its secret, and prove that the encrypted shares are consistent with the commitment. A detailed description of such a scheme including the necessary zero-knowledge proofs can be found in [40, Sec. 6.2.4], and can be made non-interactive using the Fiat-Shamir heuristic.

DDH-based instantiation. A variation of the above can also be instantiated under DDH. In this variant, we roughly replace Shamir secret sharing with a Shamir-in-the-exponent sharing (hence the secret is a random group element g^s). This means that the share holders can recover g^s, but not s itself. This supports applications that recover an individual secret but may not suffice for more complex threshold functions. We can then use the DDH-based RCNE scheme from [12], and since we do not expect to recover s itself then we do not have the limitation from [12] of only encrypting short messages. This DDH-based scheme can be easily made anonymous, and also allow simple NIZK proofs via the Fiat-Shamir heuristic.

(We note that this approach does not work for the external $\mathcal{E}_1$, since there we need to recover the actual plaintext.)

It is likely that one could also exhibit plausible instantiations based on LWE, but we have not worked out the details of such instantiations.

3   Our Evolving-Committee PSS Scheme

Below let N denote the total number of parties in the system, and let C, t be two parameters denoting the expected size of the holding committee and the threshold, to be determined later (roughly $t \approx C/2 = O(\lambda)$). In the description below we assume that these parameters are fixed, but it is easy to adjust the protocol to a more dynamic setting.

We assume the model from Sect. 2.1, including the availability of a broadcast channel (with all parties having access to the entire broadcast history). We also assume access to one instance of the sortition functionality per epoch, a CRS known to all (fir the NIZK), and the PKI. For PKI we assume that every party has a "long-term"[7] public key for an anonymous PKE.

3.1 The Construction

Initial Setup and Sharing. For setup, we assume that all parties are given access to a common reference string for the NIZK, as well as the broadcast channel and the PKI. We also assume that the dealer is honest, and for simplicity we assume that sharing is run during initial setup.

1. On secret σ, the dealer chooses a random degree-$(t-1)$ polynomial F_0 with $F_0(0) = \sigma$.
2. The dealer also choose a random size-C committee $\mathcal{C}_0 \subset [N]$, associates with each party j in the first committee $\mathcal{C}_0$ an evaluation point α_j, and give that party α_j and the share $F_0(\alpha_j)$. (To save a bit on notations, we identify each index j with a point α_j in the secret-sharing field and write $F_i(j)$ rather than $F_i(\alpha_j)$.)
3. Finally, the dealer also broadcast the α's and commitments to all the shares, and give each party in $\mathcal{C}_0$ the decommitment string for its share.

We remark that an alternative sharing procedure can instead just use the same mechanism as the handover protocol below (with the honest dealer playing all the roles in the protocol).

Thereafter, we assume that at the end of every epoch i we have an c_i-member holding committee $\mathcal{C}_i$ holding a Shamir sharing of the global secret σ, and it needs to pass that secret to the next holding committee $\mathcal{C}_{i+1}$. We also assume that the broadcast channel includes commitments to all the shares, and that each party in $\mathcal{C}_i$ can open the commitment of its share.

Committee-Selection. Run by every party in the system $p \in [N]$:

1. Use the sortition functionality with HEAD probability C/N to draw a verifiable bit b_p. If $b_p = 0$ go to step 5. (We say that a party with $b_p = 1$ has a seat on the nominating committee, and note that the expected number of seats is C.)
2. Choose at random a nominee $q \in [N]$ and get from the PKI its "long-term" public key pk_q for the anonymous PKE $\mathcal{E}_1$.
3. Generates a new ephemeral key pair $(\mathsf{esk}, \mathsf{epk}) \leftarrow \mathcal{E}_2.\mathsf{Keygen}(\$)$, and use pk_q to encrypt the ephemeral secret key, $\mathsf{ct} \leftarrow \mathcal{E}_1.\mathsf{Enc}_{\mathsf{pk}_q}(\mathsf{esk})$.
4. Erase esk, set your sortition state to *public*, and broadcast $(\mathsf{epk}, \mathsf{ct})$.

---

[7] "Long-term" in quote since it is replaced at least once per epoch, we use the name to distinguish these keys from the "ephemeral" keys of $\mathcal{E}_2$ that are only used once in the protocol.

5. Watch the broadcast channel, let $(\mathsf{epk}_1, \mathsf{ct}_1), \ldots, (\mathsf{epk}_{c_{i+1}}, \mathsf{ct}_{c_{i+1}})$ be those broadcast pairs that were sent by parties with public sortition bits $b_{p'} = 1$, ordered lexicographically by the public key values $\mathsf{epk}_{\star}$. (Note that all honest parties have a consistent view of this list and in particular agree on the value c_{i+1}.)
6. For each such pair $(\mathsf{epk}_j, \mathsf{ct}_j)$, try to decrypt ct with your long-term secret key sk_p and see if the result is the secret key esk_j corresponding to epk_j. If so then store esk_j locally, it represents the j'th seat on the holding committee $\mathcal{C}_{i+1}$.

We note that each $(\mathsf{epk}, \mathsf{ct})$ establishes a "target-anonymous communication channel" to some party q. We also note that as part of the implementation of sortition, setting the sortition state to public would involve broadcasting the sortition proof together with $(\mathsf{epk}, \mathsf{ct})$.

The Handover Protocol. We use a technique similar to [24] to re-share the secret among the seats on the holding committee $\mathcal{C}_{i+1}$.

Previous-epoch holding committee members. By induction, the shares held by $\mathcal{C}_i$ define a degree-$(t-1)$ polynomial F_i with $F_i(0) = \sigma$, where each seat j holds a share $\sigma_j = F_i(j)$. Let $I = \{1, 2, \ldots, c_{i+1}\}$ be the non-zero evaluation points used for a t-of-c_{i+1} Shamir secret-sharing scheme. A party q holding seat j does the following:

1. Choose a random degree-$(t-1)$ polynomial G_j with $G_j(0) = \sigma_j$.
2. For each $k \in I$ Set $\sigma_{j,k} = G_j(k)$ and use the k'th ephemeral public key to encrypt it, setting $\mathsf{ct}_{j,k} = \mathsf{Enc}_{\mathsf{epk}_k}(\sigma_{j,k})$.
3. Let com_j be the commitment from the previous round to the share σ_j. Generates a NIZK proof for the statement that $(\mathsf{com}_j, \mathsf{ct}_{j,1}, \ldots, \mathsf{ct}_{j,c_{i+1}})$ are commitment/encryptions of values on a degree-$(t-1)$ polynomial w.r.t evaluation points $(0, 1, \ldots, c_{i+1})$ (and public keys $\mathsf{epk}_1, \ldots, \mathsf{epk}_{c_{i+1}}$) respectively.[8] Denote this proof by π_j.
4. Choose a new long-term key-pair, $(\mathsf{sk}'_q, \mathsf{pk}'_q) \leftarrow \mathcal{E}_1.\mathsf{Keygen}(\$)$, and erase the previous sk_q as well as all the protocol secrets (including all shares and ephemeral secret keys).
5. Broadcast a message that includes pk'_q (for the PKI) and $(\mathsf{ct}_{j,1}, \ldots, \mathsf{ct}_{j,c_{i+1}}, \pi_j)$.

Next-epoch holding committee members. Let $(\mathbf{ct}_1, \pi_1), \ldots, (\mathbf{ct}_{c_i}, \pi_{c_i})$ be the messages boradcast by prior-epoch committee members that include valid NIZK proofs, ordered lexicographically. Note again that all honest parties will agree on these messages and their respective prior-epoch evaluation points $j_1, \ldots, j_{c_i}$. Let $\lambda_{j_1}, \ldots, \lambda_{j_t}$ be the Lagrange coefficients for the first t points $j_1, \ldots, j_t$. Namely $F(0) = \sum_{k=1}^{t} \lambda_{j_k} \cdot F(j_k)$ holds for every polynomial F of degree $(t-1)$.

---

[8] The witness for this NIZK proof consists of the ephemeral secret key esk_j that was used to decrypt com_j, and the randomness that was used to encrypt the $\mathsf{ct}_{j,k}$'s.

Each party p with seat k on the holding committee $\mathcal{C}_{i+1}$ does the following:

1. Choose the first t ciphertext vectors $\mathbf{ct}_1, \ldots, \mathbf{ct}_t$, and extract the k'th ciphertext from each $\mathbf{ct}_{1,k}, \ldots, \mathbf{ct}_{t,k}$.
2. Use the ephemeral secret key esk_k to decrypt them to get the values $\sigma_{j_1,k} = G_{j_1}(k)$ through $\sigma_{j_t,k} = G_{j_t}(k)$.
3. Compute the share of the global secret corresponding to seat k as

$$\sum_{j \in \{j_1, \ldots, j_t\}} \lambda_j \cdot \sigma_{j,k}.$$

Moreover, the ciphertexts $\mathbf{ct}_{j_1,k}, \ldots, \mathbf{ct}_{j_t,k}$ are kept and used as the commitment value to this share (with the decommitment information being the ephemeral secret key esk_k).

Handover Correctness. To see that the values computed by the holding committee members in the handover protocols are indeed shares of the global secret, let us define the polynomial

$$F_{i+1} = \sum_{j \in \{j_1, \ldots, j_t\}} \lambda_j \cdot G_j,$$

where G_j is the polynomial chosen by the (holder of) the j'th seat on the holding-committee of period i. Since the G_j's all have degree-$(t-1)$, then so is F_{i+1}, and moreover we have

$$F_{i+1}(0) = \sum_{j \in \{j_1, \ldots, j_t\}} \lambda_j \cdot G_j(0) = \sum_{j \in \{j_1, \ldots, j_t\}} \lambda_j \cdot F_i(j) = F_i(0) = \sigma.$$

On the other hand, for each seat k on the holding committee of period $(i+1)$, we have

$$\sum_{j \in \{j_1, \ldots, j_t\}} \lambda_j \cdot \sigma_{j,k} = \sum_{j \in \{j_1, \ldots, j_t\}} \lambda_j \cdot G_j(k) = F_{i+1}(k).$$

Reconstruction. We use Shamir reconstruction, after checking validity relative to the commitments in the broadcast channel. Specifically, each party in the reconstruction set R provides its evaluation point and share of the global secret, as well as an NP-witness showing that this share is consistent with the relevant ciphertexts from the broadcast channel.[9] The procedure takes the first t evaluation points that have valid proofs, and uses interpolation to recover the secret from the corresponding shares.

---

[9] These NP witness is just the secret key of the ephemeral key that was used to send the shares to it.which need not be hidden anymore now that the secret is revealed.

3.2   The Parameters C And t

Below we analyze the parameters of our scheme vs. the fraction of corrupted parties that it can withstand. Jumping ahead, our scheme can withstand a fraction f of corrupted parties strictly below $f^* = 1 - \sqrt{0.5} \approx 0.29$, the committee-size parameter needs to be $C = \Omega\left(\frac{\lambda}{f(1-f)(f^*-f)^2}\right)$, and the threshold can be set as $t \approx C/2$. The process that we analyze is not very different from the one in [22, Thm 3] (and indeed we can tolerate the same fraction $f^* = 1 - \sqrt{0.5}$ as there). The main difference is that in our case the adversary can reset the sortition choice many times, which gives it some additional power but does not change the asymptotic behavior.

Our analysis uses tail bounds for the binomial distribution, so we begin by stating some properties of these bounds in the regime of interest. Let $p \in (0,1)$ and let k, n be integers with $pn < k \le n$, Our analysis is concerned with a setting where $p = o(1)$ (in the scheme we have $p = C/N$), and we use following Chernoff bounds:

$$\Pr\left[\mathrm{Bin}(n,p) > pn(1+\epsilon)\right] < \exp(-np\epsilon^2/(2+\epsilon)), \text{ and}$$
$$\Pr\left[\mathrm{Bin}(n,p) < pn(1-\epsilon)\right] < \exp(-np\epsilon^2/2). \tag{1}$$

In this analysis we ignore computational issues and assume that the adversary selects the keys to open without any information about membership in the nominating- and holding-committees. Our computational assumptions in Sect. 3.3 ensure that poly-time adversaries cannot do much better even if they do see the various keys and ciphertexts. In this information-theoretic analysis we can make the following simplifying assumptions:

- The adversary is computationally unbounded, but still can only reset the sortition functionality from Fig. 1 a bounded number of times, and it is subject to a budget of corrupting at most fN parties.
- Corrupted members of the nominating committee choose only corrupted members for the holding committee, and
- The adversary corrupts all the fN parties at the beginning of the handover protocol and these remain unchanged throughout.

To see why we can make the last assumption (in this information-theoretic setting), observe that any change in the number of corrupted seats that happens because the adversary make later choice of whom to corrupt implies in particular that the adversary gained information about the not-yet-corrupted members of the holding committee.

If we let c denote the number of seats on the holding committee, ϕ denote the number of corrupted seats, and t denote the threshold, then we need $\phi < t$ (for secrecy) and $c - \phi \ge t$ (for liveness). We show below how to set the parameter C (that determines the expected committee size) and the threshold t so as to get secrecy and liveness with high probability.

Recalling that our model of sortition from Sect. 2.3 allows the adversary to reset its choice many times, the process that we want to analyze is as follows:

1. The adversary corrupts $f \cdot N$ parties;
2. The adversary resets the sortition functionality a polynomial number of times, until it is happy that enough of its corrupted parties are selected to the nominating committee;
3. With the sortition so chosen, the honest (and corrupt) parties are selected to the nominating committee;
4. Each member of the nominating committee selects a holding-committee member, with the honest ones selecting at random (and corrupted members always selecting other corrupted members).

Let k_1, k_2, k_3 be three security parameters for the analysis, as follows. We will assume the adversary can reset the sortition functionality in the process above at most 2^{k_1} times.[10] We want to ensure secrecy except with probability 2^{-k_2} and liveness except with probability 2^{-k_3}. We will use parameters $\epsilon_1, \epsilon_2, \epsilon_3$, whose values we will fix later.

Let $B_1 = fC(1 + \epsilon_1)$; B_1 represents the maximum tolerable number of corrupted members in the nominating committee (note that the expected number is fC). Let $B_2 = f(1 - f)C(1 + \epsilon_2)$; B_2 represents the number of additional corrupted members in the holding committee (note that the expected number is $f(1 - f)C$). We will set the threshold at $t = B_1 + B_2 + 1$. Thus, ϵ_1 and ϵ_2 control the probability that secrecy fails. The parameter ϵ_3, discussed below, will control the probability that liveness fails. We will now discuss how to set $C, \epsilon_1, \epsilon_2, \epsilon_3$ to satisfy the following two conditions:

- Secrecy: $\Pr[\phi \geq t] \leq 2^{-k_2}$;
- Liveness: $\Pr[c - \phi < t] \leq 2^{-k_3}$.

The Parameter ϵ_1. As described above, the adversary corrupts fN parties, and then resets the sortition functionality at most 2^{k_1} times to try to get as many of these parties selected to the nominating committee as it can. The number of corrupted parties in the nominating committee *for each of these* 2^{k_1} *tries* is a binomial random variable $\text{Bin}(n = fN, p = \frac{C}{N})$. We can set the parameters C and ϵ_1 so as to ensure that

$$\Pr\left[\text{Bin}(fN, \tfrac{C}{N}) > B_1\right] < 2^{-k_1 - k_2 - 1},$$

in which case the union bound implies that

$$\Pr\left[\exists \text{ try with more than } B_1 \text{ corrupted parties selected}\right] < 2^{-k_2 - 1}.$$

Using Eq. 1, a sufficient condition for ensuring the bound above is to set ϵ_1 and C large enough so as to get $\exp\left(-fN \cdot \frac{C}{N} \cdot \frac{\epsilon_1^2}{2 + \epsilon_1}\right) < 2^{-k_1 - k_2 - 1}$, or equivalently

$$C > \frac{(k_1 + k_2 + 1)(2 + \epsilon_1) \ln 2}{f \epsilon_1^2}. \tag{2}$$

---

[10] Since in practice the adversary has very limited time in which to reset the sortition (e.g. less than 5 s in the Algorand network), it may be sufficient to use $k_1 = 64$.

The Parameter ϵ_2. We next bound the number of additional corrupted parties in the holding committee due to Step 4 above. Here we have a total of $(1-f)N$ honest parties, each one is selected to the nominating committee with probability C/N and then each selected honest party chooses a corrupted party to the holding committee with probability f. Hence the number of additional corrupted party is a binomial random variable with $n = (1-f)N$ and $p = fC/N$ (and, unlike in the analysis of ϵ_1, this time the adversary gets only one attempt—there is no resetting, because the adversary cannot predict how sortition will select honest parties). The expected number of additional corrupted parties is therefore $f(1-f)C$, and we get a high-probability bound on it by setting C and ϵ_2 so as to get

$$\Pr\left[\text{Bin}((1-f)N, \frac{fC}{N}) > B_2\right] < 2^{-k_2-1}.$$

Here too, we get a sufficient condition by applying Eq. 1. For this we need to set ϵ_2 and C large enough to get $\exp\left(-(1-f)N \cdot \frac{fC}{N}\right) \cdot \frac{\epsilon_2^2}{2+\epsilon_2}\right) < 2^{-k_2-1}$, or equivalently

$$C > \frac{(k_2+1)(2+\epsilon_2)\ln 2}{f(1-f)\epsilon_2^2}. \tag{3}$$

The Parameter ϵ_3 and the liveness condition. The conditions from Eqs. (2) and (3) ensure the secrecy condition except with probability 2^{-k_2}. It remains to set ϵ_3 and C to ensure liveness. Recall that the liveness condition holds as long as the number of honest members $(c-\phi)$ on the holding committee is at least t. Honest members come to the holding committee as follows: an honest party (out of $(1-f)N$ total) gets chosen to the nominating committee (with probability C/N), and then chooses an honest party (with probability $1-f$) to the holding committee. Thus, the number of honest members is a binomial random variable with $n = (1-f)N$ and $p = (1-f)C/N$. (Again, the adversary gets only one attempt, because the adversary cannot predict how sortition will select honest parties, so resetting doesn't help.) Since the expected value of this random variable is $(1-f)^2C$, it is sufficient to ensure that $t \le (1-f)^2C(1-\epsilon_3)$ for some $\epsilon_3 > 0$ such that

$$\Pr[\text{Bin}((1-f)N, (1-f)C/N) < (1-f)^2C(1-\epsilon_3)] < 2^{-k_3}.$$

By Eq. 1, this holds when $\exp\left(-(1-f)N \cdot (1-f)C/N \cdot \epsilon_3^2/2\right) < 2^{-k_3}$, i.e.,

$$C > \frac{2k_3\ln 2}{(\epsilon_3(1-f))^2}. \tag{4}$$

Recalling that our threshold was set to

$$t = B_1 + B_2 + 1 = fC(1+\epsilon_1) + f(1-f)C(1+\epsilon_2) + 1 \tag{5}$$
$$= C \cdot \left((2+\epsilon_1+\epsilon_2)f - (1+\epsilon_2)f^2\right) + 1,$$

the condition $t \le (1-f)^2C(1-\epsilon_3)$ is equivalent to:

$$\epsilon_3 \le \frac{1-(4+\epsilon_1+\epsilon_2)f+(2+\epsilon_2)f^2-\frac{1}{C}}{(1-f)^2}. \tag{6}$$

Putting it all together. Given the fraction f of corrupted parties and the security parameters k_1, k_2, k_3, we need to find some positive values for the other parameters $C, \epsilon_1, \epsilon_2, \epsilon_3, t$ that satisfy the bounds in Eqs. (2) to (6).

Clearly such positive values that satisfy Eq. (6) only exist when $1 - 4f + 2f^2$ is bounded away from zero, which means that f must be strictly smaller than $f^* = 1 - \sqrt{0.5} \approx 0.29$. When f is bounded below f^*, we can satisfy Eq. (6) by setting the ϵ's to $(f^* - f)/c$ for some moderate constant c, and then by Eqs. (2) to (4) we get $C = \Theta((k_1 + k_2 + k_3)/f(1 - f)(f^* - f)^2)$.

For example, the following table lists values of C and t that work for security parameters $k_1 = 64$ and $k_2 = k_3 = 128$ and different values of f (along with the ϵ's that were used to obtain these C and t values).

f	5%	10%	15%	20%	25%	30%
C	889	1556	3068	7759	38557	Impossible
t	425	788	1590	4028	19727	
ϵ_1	4.3835	1.8099	0.9216	0.46059	0.173688	
ϵ_2	3.3734	1.4936	0.8001	0.41728	0.163585	
ϵ_3	0.4703	0.3752	0.2829	0.18904	0.090453	

3.3 Analysis

Complexity. It is easy to see that the communication complexity of all the protocols in our construction (sharing, committee-selection, handover, and reconstruction) is some fixed polynomial in the security parameter, regardless of the number of epochs or the total number or parties N. Indeed there are only some $c = O(\lambda)$ parties in every committee, and each of them sends a single message including at most encryption nd proofs about size-$O(c)$ vectors.

Regarding computation, the only parts of the protocol that involve $O(N)$ objects are random selection of keys from a size-N public table (provided by the PKI). Every other operation involves at most size-$O(c)$ objects. Hence in a RAM model also the computation performed by each party depends only logarithmically on N.

Security. Below we denote by $\mathcal{E}_3 = \mathcal{E}_1 \circ \mathcal{E}_2$ the combination of the PKE schemes $\mathcal{E}_1, \mathcal{E}_2$ as in our scheme: $\mathcal{E}_3$ uses the keys from $\mathcal{E}_1$ and encrypts a message by choosing a fresh key pair for $\mathcal{E}_2$, encrypting the $\mathcal{E}_2$ secret key by the $\mathcal{E}_1$ public key, and encrypting the message by the $\mathcal{E}_2$ public key.

Theorem 1. *Let $f < 1 - \sqrt{0.5}$ be a constant, and consider the parameters $C = C(\lambda), t = t(\lambda)$ satisfying Eqs. 2 through 6.*

Let $\mathcal{E}_1, \mathcal{E}_2$ be two public-key encryption schemes, $\mathcal{E}_1$ is anonymous as per Definition 4 and the combination $\mathcal{E}_3 = \mathcal{E}_1 \circ \mathcal{E}_2$ is RIND-SO secure. Also let Π be a NIZK argument system and assume the sortition functionality from Fig. 1.

Then the construction in Sect. 3.1 with parameters C, t is a scalable ECPSS scheme satisfying secrecy and robust reconstruction (Definitions 1 and 2), in a model with erasures and the broadcast channel and PKI from Sect. 2.1, against polynomial-time mobile adversaries with corruption budget bounded by $f \cdot N$.

Proof Sketch. Below we only sketch the secrecy argument, which includes in particular a proof that the committees are mostly-honest. The robust-reconstruction argument is similar (but simpler).

Consider an adversary that specifies two secrets σ_0, σ_1 and then interacts with our ECPSS scheme, and we need to argue that it only has a negligible advantage in guessing which of σ_0, σ_1 was shared. As usual, the proof involves a game between the adversary and a challenger, and a sequence of hybrids that are proven indistinguishable via reductions to the secrecy of the various components. Below we tag each of these hybrids with the security property that is used to prove their indistinguishability from the previous hybrid in the sequence.

H_0 **(The real protocol).** This is a game where the challenger plays the role of all the honest parties, and in particular knows the global secret and all the shares.

H_1 **(NIZK Soundness).** In the next hybrid, the challenger aborts if at any point the honest parties accept a proof from the adversary even though the encrypted quantities in question do not lie on a degree-t polynomial. The challenger can detect this because it knows all the shares and it sees everything that the honest parties see. It follows from the NIZK soundness that the challenger only aborts with negligible probability.

H_2 **(Zero-knowledge).** Next the challenger uses the NIZK simulator to generate the honest-party proofs. Since it is zero-knowledge, the adversary cannot detect the difference.

H_3 **(Anonymous PKE).** In this hybrid the challenger aborts if the holding committee contains t or more corrupted seats, or fewer than t honest seats. We use the anonymity property of the long-term PKE to argue that this happens only with a negligible probability.

For this argument, first note that the set of corrupter nominators depends only on the sortition "ideal functionality," hence the bound B_1 from Sect. 3.2 holds for it. Next let S be the set of holding-committee members that were nominated by honest nominators. (More specifically, nominators that were honest at the time they broadcast their nomination message.) In Sect. 3.2 we bounded whp the number of corrupted members from S by the bound B_2 in an information-theoretic model, but now the adversary's view contains information about the set S (since the ephemeral keys are encrypted under their long-term public keys). Nonetheless, due to the anonymity of the PKE scheme $\mathcal{E}_1$, with overwhelming probability the adversary only corrupts $B_2(1 + o(1))$ members of this set.

H_4 **(PKE secrecy).** In this hybrid honest parties switch to encrypting a randomly chosen secret $\sigma_\$$ rather than the right one σ_b. We argue that the adversary cannot distinguish these hybrids by reduction to the hiding property of the combined PKE scheme $\mathcal{E}_1 \circ \mathcal{E}_2$. Note that in this hybrid we already know that the adversary corrupts less than t members of each holding committees, so we can re-sample the shares of the honest parties conditioned on those of the corrupted ones.

Finally we can undo the changes in these hybrids, arriving at a game where the adversary gets σ_{1-b} rather than σ_b.

4 Parties vs. Stake

In this paper we described the protocol in terms of individual parties, and the adversary's power in terms of corruption a fixed fraction of these parties. Our main application domain, however, is public proof-of-stake blockchains where the adversary's corruption budget is measured in stake. In this world every actual party holds some number of tokens, and the corruption budget of the adversary is expressed in tokens rather than in parties.

The easiest way of defining the adversary model and protocol actions in this world is to have a party with x tokens play the role of x parties in the protocol, and leave everything else as-is. If the party-to-stake mapping was static, then the stake-based adversary model would have been a weakening of the standard adversary, and hence every protocol that was secure in the party model against some f-fraction of corrupted parties would remains secure also in the stake model against f-fraction of corrupted stake. To see that, note that if a party owns x tokens and the adversary corrupts it, then the adversary is forced to corrupt all the x tokens at once, reducing its ability to corrupt different parties.

The thing that makes the stake model harder is that the stake assignment is not static, parties can move the stake among them dynamically. (This can be formulated using a UC-like environment that provides parties with tokens and move those tokens between them.) In this environment, it is not a priory clear that the proactive model makes sense at all: This model stipulates that corrupted parties can recover and join the ranks of honest parties. But when the adversary corrupts a party holding some stake, can't it just "take the money and run"? That is, can't the adversary simply transfer all the stake of a corrupted party into the adversary's own coffers, thereafter forever controlling it?

Making sense of party's recovery in the stake model hinges on the distinction between keys that control tokens (called *spending/withdrawal* keys) and keys that are used in the consensus (called *participation/validation* keys): PoS blockchain usually assume that stake-controlling keys are kept highly secure (e.g., offline, in a hardware device, or using some secret-sharing mechanism), and are only accessed infrequently. The cryptographic keys used for the protocol, on the other hand, must be accessed frequently and kept online. This model therefore assumes that the token-controlling keys are (almost) never compromised, but the consensus keys are easier to corrupt. In that model a corrupted party is one whose protocol key was compromised, but it can later recover by (cleaning up the node and) using the token-controlling key to choose and broadcast a new protocol key. It is instructive to consider the type of corruptions we are likely to confront in a PoS blockchain and their characteristics.

- *Mostly static adversarial base.* There may be a set of token keys that are held by the adversary, and hence their consensus keys remain adversarial throughout. While that set (and the stake that it holds) is not completely static, it changes rather slowly.
- *Somewhat dynamic node corruptions.* A second type of adversarial parties represent nodes where the stake key is held by honest participants but the consensus keys are subject to compromise due to security breaches. These tend to be more dynamic from the first set, but corruptions still require significant effort on the part of the attacker. It may be reasonable to assume that corruption of new nodes usually takes significant time.
- *Fully dynamic fail-stop.* A third set of "adversarial" nodes are fail-stop nodes, that are just knocked off due to denial-of-service (DoS) attacks. It seems reasonable to assume that the adversary can mount a DoS attack almost instantaneously and keep it going for a while.

Hence realistic protocols in PoS blockchains must be resilient to very dynamic DoS attacks, but can perhaps assume a mobile-but-slow-moving adversary when it comes to malicious corruptions. The next section sketches a protocol that can tolerate higher corrupted fraction in the face of such slow-moving adversary.

5   Static vs. Adaptive Anonymous PKE

Recall the definition of Bellare et al. for anonymous PKE against static adversaries:

Definition 5 (Anonymity [3]). *A PKE scheme $\mathcal{E} = (\mathsf{Gen}, \mathsf{Enc}, \mathsf{Dec})$ is anonymous if polynomial-time adversaries have at most a negligible advantage in the following game with a challenger:*

1. *The challenger runs the key generation twice to get $(\mathsf{pk}_i, \mathsf{sk}_i) \leftarrow \mathsf{Gen}(1^\lambda, \$)$ for $i = 0, 1$, and sends $\mathsf{pk}_0, \mathsf{pk}_1$ to the adversary.*
2. *The adversary responds with a plaintext message m.[11]*
3. *The challenger chooses a secret bit b, encrypts m relative to pk_b to get $\mathsf{ct} \leftarrow \mathsf{Enc}_{\mathsf{pk}_b}(m)$, and sends ct to the adversary.*
4. *The adversary outputs a guess b' for the bit b.*

The advantage of the adversary is $2 \cdot | \Pr[b = b'] - \frac{1}{2}|$.

We would like to prove Conjecture 1, that every PKE that satisfies Definition 5 also satisfies Definition 4. While we were not able to prove this conjecture, below we prove a special case of it for restricted class of adversaries that

---

[11] This message need not be in the plaintext space relative to these keys. Note that in that case the anonymity property implies that the scheme could also "encrypt" things outside of its plaintext space (although the result may not be decryptable).

"open" all the keys at once. That is, given the n public keys and m ciphertexts ($\lambda \leq m < n$), the adversary outputs a set D of $\ell = f \cdot n$ keys that it wants to open, and it gets all the secret keys for it at once. Note that this "semi-adaptive" adversary already exhibits all the problems with selective opening in the context of secrecy. In particular the examples showing that semantic security does not imply security under selective opening, apply also to these restricted adversaries.

Lemma 1. *Fix a constant $\epsilon > 0$. If there is an efficient semi-adaptive adversary that opens at most $\ell = fn$ keys but is able to open $t^* = (1 + \epsilon)fm$ keys in A with a noticeable probability $\alpha = \alpha(\lambda)$, then the PKE in use does not satisfy Definition 5.*

Proof. Fix an adversary $\mathcal{A}$, denote by A the set of public keys under which messages were encrypted and by D the set of keys that $\mathcal{A}$ opens, and let p_i be the probability of $|D \cap A| = i$ for that adversary (for all $i = 0, 1, \ldots, m$). The premise of the lemma is that $\sum_{i \geq t^*} p_i = \alpha = 1/\text{poly}(m)$.

We describe a reduction that uses this adversary in the anonymous-PKE game from Definition 5. The reduction has a parameter $\tau \leq m - 1$, and it gets two keys pk_0, pk_1 and a ciphertext ct encrypted under one of them. It chooses $n - 2$ more keys, selects a random subset $A' \subset [n]$ of size $m - 1$, and encrypts messages under the keys in A'. The reduction then gives the adversary the n keys and m ciphertexts (in random order), and gets from the adversary the set D of ℓ keys to open. If $|A' \cap D| \geq \tau$ and in addition pk_1 is opened but pk_0 is not, then the reduction outputs 1. Otherwise the reduction outputs 0.

Let x denote the key under which the message is encrypted and y denote the other key. The crux of the proof is showing that when the probability distribution $(p_0, p_1, \ldots, p_m)$ is far from an (n, m, ℓ)-hypergeometric distribution, there must exist some τ for which

$$\delta_\tau \stackrel{\text{def}}{=} \Pr[\text{reduction}_\tau \text{ outputs } 1 | x = \text{pk}_1] - \Pr[\text{reduction}_\tau \text{ outputs } 1 | x = \text{pk}_0]$$

is non-negligible (in m). Recall that the (n, m, ℓ)-hypergeometric distribution is $(p_0^*, p_1^*, \ldots, p_m^*)$ such that $p_i^* \stackrel{\text{def}}{=} \binom{i}{m}\binom{\ell-i}{n-m}/\binom{n}{\ell}$.

Observe that when $x = \text{pk}_1$, the reduction with τ outputs 1 if $|D \cap A| \geq \tau + 1$ (i.e., $\geq \tau$ for A' and one more for pk_1), and in addition $x = \text{pk}_1 \in D$ and $y = \text{pk}_0 \notin D$. Hence

$$\Pr[\text{reduction}_\tau \text{ outputs } 1 | x = \text{pk}_1] = \sum_{i=\tau+1}^{m} p_i \cdot \frac{i}{m} \cdot \left(1 - \frac{\ell - i}{n - m}\right). \tag{7}$$

On the other hand when $x = \text{pk}_0$, the reduction with τ outputs 1 if $|D \cap A| \geq \tau$, and in addition $y = \text{pk}_1 \in D$ and $x = \text{pk}_0 \notin D$. Hence

$$\Pr[\text{reduction}_\tau \text{ outputs } 1 | x = \text{pk}_0] = \sum_{i=\tau}^{m} p_i \cdot \left(1 - \frac{i}{m}\right) \cdot \frac{\ell - i}{n - m}. \tag{8}$$

Let us denote $u_i = \frac{i}{m} \cdot (1 - \frac{\ell-i}{n-m})$ and $v_i = (1 - \frac{i}{m}) \cdot \frac{\ell-i}{n-m}$. From Eqs. 7 and 8 we have

$$\delta_\tau = -p_\tau v_\tau + \sum_{i=\tau+1}^{m} p_i(u_i - v_i) = \left(-p_\tau \left(1 - \frac{\tau}{m}\right) + \sum_{i=\tau+1}^{m} p_i\left(\frac{i}{m} - \frac{\ell}{n}\right) \right) \cdot \frac{m}{n-m},$$
$$(9)$$

where the last equality follows because

$$u_i - v_i = \frac{i}{m} \cdot \frac{n-m-\ell+i}{n-m} - \frac{m-i}{m} \cdot \frac{\ell-i}{n-m} = \left(\frac{i}{m} - \frac{\ell}{n}\right) \cdot \frac{m}{n-m}.$$

Equation 9 yields a set of linear equations for expressing $\boldsymbol{\delta} = (\delta_0, \delta_1, \ldots, \delta_{m-1})$ in terms of $\boldsymbol{p} = (p_0, p_1, \ldots p_m)$. Let B be the $m \times (m+1)$ matrix representing these equations, namely $\boldsymbol{\delta} = \boldsymbol{p} \cdot B$. While it is not hard to show that the (n, m, ℓ)-hypergeometric distribution is the only one yielding $\boldsymbol{p}^* B = \boldsymbol{0}$, we still need to show that whenever $\boldsymbol{p}$ is noticeably far from $\boldsymbol{p}^*$ then δ is noticeably away from zero. To that end, we look again at Eq. 9 and give a name to the sum at the right-hand side. For every τ we denote:

$$\gamma_\tau \stackrel{\text{def}}{=} \sum_{i=\tau}^{m} p_i\left(\frac{i}{m} - \frac{\ell}{n}\right) = \sum_{i=\tau}^{m} p_i\left(\frac{i}{m} - f\right) \text{ and similarly } \gamma_\tau^* \stackrel{\text{def}}{=} \sum_{i=\tau}^{m} p_i^*\left(\frac{i}{m} - f\right).$$

Equation 9 can now be written as $\delta_\tau = \frac{m}{n-m}(\gamma_{\tau+1} - p_\tau(1 - \frac{\tau}{m}))$, and of course by definition we have $\gamma_\tau = p_\tau(\frac{\tau}{m} - f) + \gamma_{\tau+1}$. We similarly have $\gamma_\tau^* = p_\tau^*(\frac{\tau}{m} - f) + \gamma_{\tau+1}^*$, but here $\gamma_{\tau+1}^* - p_\tau^*(1 - \frac{\tau}{m}) = 0$. Note also that for $\tau \geq fm$ the term $\frac{\tau}{m} - f$ is non-negative. We next use the following two facts:

- By Chernoff bound, $\gamma_{t^*}^* < \sum_{i \geq t^*} p_i^*$ is exponentially small in $\epsilon f \cdot m = \Theta(m)$.
- By our assumption on the adversary γ_{t^*} is non-negligible since

$$\gamma_{t^*} = \sum_{i \geq t^*} p_i\left(\frac{i}{m} - f\right) \geq \sum_{i \geq t^*} p_i\left(\frac{t^*}{m} - f\right) = \epsilon f \sum_{i \geq t^*} p_i = \epsilon f \alpha.$$

This means that γ_{t^*} is exponentially (in m) larger than $\gamma_{t^*}^*$, i.e. there exists some constant $\eta > 0$ such that $\gamma_{t^*} \geq (1+\eta)^m \gamma_{t^*}^*$.

By the Claim 5 below, we either have $p_{t^*-1} \geq (1+\eta)^m(1-\frac{\eta}{2})p_{t^*-1}^*$, or else $\delta_{t^*-1} > \frac{\eta m}{2(n-m)}\gamma_{t^*}$, which is non-negligible (in m). In the former case (of large p_{t^*-1}) we get

$$\gamma_{t^*-1} = p_{t^*-1}\left(\frac{t^*-1}{m} - f\right) + \gamma_{t^*} \geq (1+\eta)^m(1-\frac{\eta}{2})p_{t^*-1}^*\underbrace{\left(\frac{t^*-1}{m} - f\right)}_{>0} + (1+\eta)^m\gamma_{t^*}^*$$
$$> (1+\eta)^m(1-\frac{\eta}{2})(p_{t^*-1}^*\left(\frac{t^*-1}{m} - f\right) + \gamma_{t^*}^*) = (1+\eta)^m(1-\frac{\eta}{2})\gamma_{t^*-1}^*.$$

In that case we can apply Claim 5 again to conclude that either $p_{t^*-2} > (1+\eta)^m(1-\frac{\eta}{2})^2 p_{t^*-2}^*$ or else δ_{t^*-2} is non-negligible. Repeating this process, we show by induction that either at least one of $\delta_{t^*-1}, \delta_{t^*-2}, \ldots, \delta_{fm}$ is non-negligible (in m), or else we have

$$\forall i \in [fm, t^* - 1], \ p_i > (1 + \eta)^m (1 - \frac{\eta}{2})^{t^*-i}.$$

But the last case cannot happen, since it means that the p_i's sum up to more than one. That is so because the hypergeometric distribution has probability at least $1/4$ of exceeding the expected value [28],[12] i.e., $\sum_{i \geq fm} p_i^* \geq 1/4$, and so

$$\sum_{i=0}^{m} p_i \geq \sum_{i=fm}^{t^*-1} p_i + \sum_{i=t^*}^{m} p_i \geq \sum_{i=fm}^{t^*} (1+\eta)^m (1-\eta/2)^{t^*-i} p_i^* + (1+\eta)^m \sum_{i=t^*}^{m} p_i^*$$

$$> (1+\eta)^m (1-\eta/2)^m \sum_{i \geq fm} p_i^* > \left(1+\eta/4\right)^m \cdot \frac{1}{4} > 1.$$

$\square$

Claim. For any $\tau \geq fm$, denote the ratio $R_{\tau+1} \overset{\text{def}}{=} \gamma_{\tau+1}/\gamma_{\tau+1}^*$ and let $\eta > 0$ be an arbitrary constant. Then either $p_\tau > R_{\tau+1}(1-\frac{\eta}{2})p_\tau^*$, or else $\delta_\tau \geq \frac{\eta m}{2(n-m)}\gamma_{\tau+1}$.

Proof. Recall that for the hypergeometric distribution we have $\gamma_{\tau+1}^* = p_\tau^*(1 - \frac{\tau}{m})$, and by definition of $R_{\tau+1}$'s we have $\gamma_{\tau+1} = R_{\tau+1}\gamma_{\tau+1}^*$. Assume that $p_\tau \leq R_{\tau+1}(1 - \frac{\eta}{2})p_\tau^*$, and we need to show that $\delta_\tau \geq \frac{\eta m}{2(n-m)}\gamma_{\tau+1}$. By Eq. 9 we have

$$\delta_\tau \cdot \frac{n-m}{m} = \gamma_{\tau+1} - p_\tau(1 - \frac{\tau}{m}) \geq R_{\tau+1}\gamma_{\tau+1}^* - R_{\tau+1}(1 - \frac{\eta}{2})p_\tau^*(1 - \frac{\tau}{m})$$

$$= R_{\tau+1}\underbrace{\left(\gamma_{\tau+1}^* - p_\tau^*(1 - \frac{\tau}{m})\right)}_{=0} + \frac{\eta}{2} \cdot R_{\tau+1} \cdot p_\tau^*(1 - \frac{\tau}{m}) = \frac{\eta}{2} \cdot R_{\tau+1}\gamma_{\tau+1}^* = \frac{\eta}{2} \cdot \gamma_{\tau+1}.$$

Hence $\delta_\tau \geq \frac{\eta m}{2(n-m)}\gamma_{\tau+1}$, as needed.

Acknowledgments. We thank Ran Cohen and the anonymous TCC reviewers for their comments, which greatly improved this paper.

References

1. Asayag, A., et al.: Helix: a scalable and fair consensus algorithm resistant to ordering manipulation. IACR Cryptology ePrint Archive (2018)
2. Baron, J., Defrawy, K.E., Lampkins, J., Ostrovsky, R.: Communication-optimal proactive secret sharing for dynamic groups. In: Malkin, T., Kolesnikov, V., Lewko, A.B., Polychronakis, M. (eds.) ACNS 2015. LNCS, vol. 9092, pp. 23–41. Springer, Cham (2015). https://doi.org/10.1007/978-3-319-28166-7_2
3. Bellare, M., Boldyreva, A., Desai, A., Pointcheval, D.: Key-privacy in public-key encryption. In: Boyd, C. (ed.) ASIACRYPT 2001. LNCS, vol. 2248, pp. 566–582. Springer, Heidelberg (2001). https://doi.org/10.1007/3-540-45682-1_33

---

[12] The proof in [28] is for the binomial distribution, but for our case of $m \ll n$ we get the same result upto a factor of $1 \pm o(1)$.

4. Bellare, M., Dowsley, R., Waters, B., Yilek, S.: Standard security does not imply security against selective-opening. In: Pointcheval, D., Johansson, T. (eds.) EURO-CRYPT 2012. LNCS, vol. 7237, pp. 645–662. Springer, Heidelberg (2012). https://doi.org/10.1007/978-3-642-29011-4_38

5. Bellare, M., Hofheinz, D., Yilek, S.: Possibility and impossibility results for encryption and commitment secure under selective opening. In: Joux, A. (ed.) EURO-CRYPT 2009. LNCS, vol. 5479, pp. 1–35. Springer, Heidelberg (2009). https://doi.org/10.1007/978-3-642-01001-9_1

6. Benhamouda, F., et al.: Can a blockchain keep a secret? Cryptology ePrint Archive, Report 2020/464 (2020). https://eprint.iacr.org/2020/464

7. Blakley, G.: Safeguarding cryptographic keys. In: Proceedings of the AFIPS Conference, pp. 313–318 (1979). https://doi.org/10.1109/AFIPS.1979.98

8. Blum, M., Feldman, P., Micali, S.: Non-interactive zero-knowledge and its applications (extended abstract). In: Simon, J. (ed.) Proceedings of the 20th Annual ACM Symposium on Theory of Computing, 2–4 May 1988, Chicago, Illinois, USA, pp. 103–112. ACM (1988). https://doi.org/10.1145/62212.62222

9. Böhl, F., Hofheinz, D., Kraschewski, D.: On definitions of selective opening security. In: Fischlin, M., Buchmann, J., Manulis, M. (eds.) PKC 2012. LNCS, vol. 7293, pp. 522–539. Springer, Heidelberg (2012). https://doi.org/10.1007/978-3-642-30057-8_31

10. Boneh, D., et al.: Threshold cryptosystems from threshold fully homomorphic encryption. In: Shacham, H., Boldyreva, A. (eds.) CRYPTO 2018. LNCS, vol. 10991, pp. 565–596. Springer, Cham (2018). https://doi.org/10.1007/978-3-319-96884-1_19

11. Canetti, R., Feige, U., Goldreich, O., Naor, M.: Adaptively secure multi-party computation. In: Proceedings of the twenty-eighth annual ACM symposium on Theory of computing, pp. 639–648 (1996). https://doi.org/10.1145/237814.238015

12. Canetti, R., Halevi, S., Katz, J.: Adaptively-secure, non-interactive public-key encryption. In: Kilian, J. (ed.) TCC 2005. LNCS, vol. 3378, pp. 150–168. Springer, Heidelberg (2005). https://doi.org/10.1007/978-3-540-30576-7_9

13. Canetti, R., Herzberg, A.: Maintaining security in the presence of transient faults. In: Desmedt, Y.G. (ed.) CRYPTO 1994. LNCS, vol. 839, pp. 425–438. Springer, Heidelberg (1994). https://doi.org/10.1007/3-540-48658-5_38

14. Chen, J., Micali, S.: Algorand: A secure and efficient distributed ledger. Theor. Comput. Sci. **777**, 155–183 (2019). https://doi.org/10.1016/j.tcs.2019.02.001

15. Cheng, R., et al.: Ekiden: a platform for confidentiality-preserving, trustworthy, and performant smart contracts. In: IEEE European Symposium on Security and Privacy, EuroS&P, pp. 185–200 (2019). https://doi.org/10.1109/EuroSP.2019.00023

16. Choudhuri, A.R., Goel, A., Green, M., Jain, A., Kaptchuk, G.: Fluid MPC: Secure multiparty computation with dynamic participants. Cryptology ePrint Archive, Report 2020/754 (2020). https://eprint.iacr.org/2020/754

17. Desmedt, Y., Jajodia, S.: Redistributing secret shares to new access structures and its applications. Technical report (1997)

18. Dolev, S., Garay, J.A., Gilboa, N., Kolesnikov, V.: Brief announcement: swarming secrets. In: Proceedings of the 29th ACM SIGACT-SIGOPS symposium on Principles of distributed computing, pp. 231–232 (2010). https://doi.org/10.1145/1835698.1835750

19. Dwork, C., Naor, M., Reingold, O., Stockmeyer, L.: Magic functions: In memoriam: Bernard M. Dwork 1923–1998. J. ACM (JACM) **50**(6), 852–921 (2003). https://doi.org/10.1145/950620.950623

20. Freedman, M.J., Ishai, Y., Pinkas, B., Reingold, O.: Keyword search and oblivious pseudorandom functions. In: Kilian, J. (ed.) TCC 2005. LNCS, vol. 3378, pp. 303–324. Springer, Heidelberg (2005). https://doi.org/10.1007/978-3-540-30576-7_17

21. Freedman, M.J., Nissim, K., Pinkas, B.: Efficient private matching and set intersection. In: Cachin, C., Camenisch, J.L. (eds.) EUROCRYPT 2004. LNCS, vol. 3027, pp. 1–19. Springer, Heidelberg (2004). https://doi.org/10.1007/978-3-540-24676-3_1

22. Garay, J., Ishai, Y., Ostrovsky, R., Zikas, V.: The price of low communication in secure multi-party computation. In: Katz, J., Shacham, H. (eds.) CRYPTO 2017. LNCS, vol. 10401, pp. 420–446. Springer, Cham (2017). https://doi.org/10.1007/978-3-319-63688-7_14

23. Garg, S., Gentry, C., Sahai, A., Waters, B.: Witness encryption and its applications. In: Proceedings of the forty-fifth annual ACM symposium on Theory of computing, pp. 467–476 (2013). https://doi.org/10.1145/2488608.2488667

24. Gennaro, R., Rabin, M.O., Rabin, T.: Simplified VSS and fast-track multiparty computations with applications to threshold cryptography. In: Coan, B.A., Afek, Y. (eds.) Proceedings of the Seventeenth Annual ACM Symposium on Principles of Distributed Computing, PODC 1998, Puerto Vallarta, Mexico, 28 June-2 July 1998, pp. 101–111. ACM (1998). https://doi.org/10.1145/277697.277716

25. Goldwasser, S., Micali, S.: Probabilistic encryption. J. Comput. Syst. Sci. **28**(2), pp. 270–299 (1984). https://doi.org/10.1016/0022-0000(84)90070-9

26. Goyal, R., Goyal, V.: Overcoming cryptographic impossibility results using blockchains. In: Kalai, Y., Reyzin, L. (eds.) TCC 2017. LNCS, vol. 10677, pp. 529–561. Springer, Cham (2017). https://doi.org/10.1007/978-3-319-70500-2_18

27. Goyal, V., Kothapalli, A., Masserova, E., Parno, B., Song, Y.: Storing and retrieving secrets on a blockchain. Cryptology ePrint Archive, Report 2020/504 (2020). https://eprint.iacr.org/2020/504

28. Greenberg, S., Mohri, M.: Tight lower bound on the probability of a binomial exceeding its expectation. Stat. Probab. Lett. **86**, 91–98 (2014). https://doi.org/10.1016/j.spl.2013.12.009

29. Gunasinghe, H., et al.: PrivIdEx: privacy preserving and secure exchange of digital identity assets. In: WWW, pp. 594–604 (2019). https://doi.org/10.1145/3308558.3313574

30. Hanke, T., Movahedi, M., Williams, D.: DFINITY technology overview series, consensus system. CoRR (2018). arXiv:1805.04548

31. Hayashi, R., Tanaka, K.: Anonymity on Paillier's trap-door permutation. In: Pieprzyk, J., Ghodosi, H., Dawson, E. (eds.) ACISP 2007. LNCS, vol. 4586, pp. 200–214. Springer, Heidelberg (2007). https://doi.org/10.1007/978-3-540-73458-1_16

32. Hazay, C., Patra, A., Warinschi, B.: Selective opening security for receivers. In: Iwata, T., Cheon, J.H. (eds.) ASIACRYPT 2015. LNCS, vol. 9452, pp. 443–469. Springer, Heidelberg (2015). https://doi.org/10.1007/978-3-662-48797-6_19

33. Herzberg, A., Jakobsson, M., Jarecki, S., Krawczyk, H., Yung, M.: Proactive public key and signature systems. In: Proceedings of the 4th ACM conference on Computer and communications security, pp. 100–110 (1997). https://doi.org/10.1145/266420.266442

34. Herzberg, A., Jarecki, S., Krawczyk, H., Yung, M.: Proactive secret sharing or: how to cope with perpetual leakage. In: Coppersmith, D. (ed.) CRYPTO 1995. LNCS, vol. 963, pp. 339–352. Springer, Heidelberg (1995). https://doi.org/10.1007/3-540-44750-4_27

35. Hofheinz, D., Rao, V., Wichs, D.: Standard security does not imply indistinguishability under selective opening. In: Hirt, M., Smith, A. (eds.) TCC 2016. LNCS, vol. 9986, pp. 121–145. Springer, Heidelberg (2016). https://doi.org/10.1007/978-3-662-53644-5_5

36. Jarecki, S., Kiayias, A., Krawczyk, H., Xu, J.: TOPPSS: cost-minimal password-protected secret sharing based on threshold OPRF. In: Gollmann, D., Miyaji, A., Kikuchi, H. (eds.) ACNS 2017. LNCS, vol. 10355, pp. 39–58. Springer, Cham (2017). https://doi.org/10.1007/978-3-319-61204-1_3

37. Jarecki, S., Krawczyk, H., Resch, J.K.: Updatable oblivious key management for storage systems. In: Proceedings of the 2019 ACM SIGSAC Conference on Computer and Communications Security (CCS 2019), pp. 379–393 (2019). https://doi.org/10.1145/3319535.3363196

38. Kokoris-Kogias, E., et al.: Verifiable management of private data under byzantine failures. IACR Cryptology ePrint Archive (2018). https://eprint.iacr.org/2018/209

39. Lehmann, A.: Scrambledb: Oblivious (chameleon) pseudonymization-as-a-service. In: Proceedings on Privacy Enhancing Technologies, 3, pp. 289–309. (2019). https://doi.org/10.2478/popets-2019-0048

40. Lindell, Y., Nof, A., Ranellucci, S.: Fast secure multiparty ECDSA with practical distributed key generation and applications to cryptocurrency custody. In: Proceedings of the 2018 ACM SIGSAC Conference on Computer and Communications Security, CCS 2018, pp. 1837–1854 (2018). https://doi.org/10.1145/3243734.3243788

41. Maram, S.K.D., et al.: CHURP: dynamic-committee proactive secret sharing. In: Proceedings of the 2019 ACM SIGSAC Conference on Computer and Communications Security, CCS 2019, London, UK, 11–15 November 2019 (2019). https://eprint.iacr.org/2019/017, https://doi.org/10.1145/3319535.3363203

42. Micali, S., Rabin, M.O., Vadhan, S.P.: Verifiable random functions. In: 40th Annual Symposium on Foundations of Computer Science (Cat. No.99CB37039), New York City, NY, USA, pp. 120–130 (1999). https://doi.org/10.1109/SFFCS.1999.814584

43. Nielsen, J.B.: Separating random oracle proofs from complexity theoretic proofs: the non-committing encryption case. In: Yung, M. (ed.) CRYPTO 2002. LNCS, vol. 2442, pp. 111–126. Springer, Heidelberg (2002). https://doi.org/10.1007/3-540-45708-9_8

44. Ostrovsky, R., Yung, M.: How to withstand mobile virus attacks (extended abstract). In: PODC (1991). https://doi.org/10.1145/112600.112605

45. Schultz, D.A., Liskov, B., Liskov, M.D.: Mobile proactive secret sharing. In: Proceedings of the twenty-seventh ACM symposium on Principles of distributed computing, pp. 458 (2008). https://doi.org/10.1145/1400751.1400856

46. Schultz, D.A., Liskov, B., Liskov, M.D.: MPSS: mobile proactive secret sharing. ACM Trans. Inf. Syst. Secur. **13**(4), 1–32 (2010). https://doi.org/10.1145/1880022.1880028

47. Shamir, A.: How to share a secret. ACM Commun. **22** 612–613 (1979). https://doi.org/10.1145/359168.359176

48. Shirvanian, M., Jarecki, S., Krawczyk, H., Saxena, N.: SPHINX: a password store that perfectly hides passwords from itself. In: ICDCS, pp. 1094–1104 (2017). https://doi.org/10.1109/ICDCS.2017.64

Blockchains from Non-idealized Hash Functions

Juan A. Garay[1], Aggelos Kiayias[2,3(✉)], and Giorgos Panagiotakos[1,4]

[1] Department of Computer Science and Engineering, Texas A&M University,
College Station, USA
garay@cse.tamu.edu
[2] School of Informatics, University of Edinburgh, Edinburgh, UK
akiayias@inf.ed.ac.uk
[3] IOHK, Hong Kong, China
[4] Department of Informatics and Telecommunications, University of Athens,
Athens, Greece
geo.panagiotakos@gmail.com

Abstract. The formalization of concrete, non-idealized hash function properties sufficient to prove the security of Bitcoin and related protocols has been elusive, as all previous security analyses of blockchain protocols have been performed in the random oracle model. In this paper we identify three such properties, and then construct a blockchain protocol whose security can be reduced to them in the standard model assuming a common reference string (CRS).

The three properties are: *collision resistance, computational randomness extraction* and *iterated hardness*. While the first two properties have been extensively studied, iterated hardness has been empirically stress-tested since the rise of Bitcoin; in fact, as we demonstrate in this paper, any attack against it (assuming the other two properties hold) results in an attack against Bitcoin.

In addition, iterated hardness puts forth a new class of search problems which we term *iterated search problems* (ISP). ISPs enable the concise and modular specification of blockchain protocols, and may be of independent interest.

1 Introduction

Blockchain protocols, introduced by Nakamoto [46], are seen as a prominent application of the "proof of work" (PoW) concept to the area of consensus protocol design. PoWs were initially introduced in the work of Dwork and Naor [27] as a spam protection mechanism, and subsequently found applications in other domains such as Sybil attack resilience [26] and denial of service protection [4,41], prior to their application to the domain of distributed consensus hinted at early on by Aspnes *et al.* [3].

A. Kiayias—Research partly supported by H2020 project PRIVILEDGE #780477.
G. Panagiotakos—Work partly done while at the University of Edinburgh.

R. Pass and K. Pietrzak (Eds.): TCC 2020, LNCS 12550, pp. 291–321, 2020.
https://doi.org/10.1007/978-3-030-64375-1_11

A PoW scheme is typified by a *proving* algorithm, that produces a solution given an input instance, as well as a *verification* algorithm that verifies the correctness of the witness with respect to the input. The fundamental property of a PoW scheme is that the proving algorithm allows for no significant shortcuts, i.e., it is hard to significantly make it more expedient, and hence any verified solution implies an investment of computational effort on behalf of the prover. Nevertheless, this "moderate hardness" property alone has been found to be insufficient for the utilization of PoWs in the context of various applications and other properties have been put forth to complement it. These include: (i) *amortization resistance*, which guarantees that the adversary cannot speed up the computation when solving multiple PoW instances together, and (ii) *fast verification*, which suggests a significant gap between the complexities of the proving and verification algorithms.

Despite the evolution of our understanding of the PoW primitive, as exemplified in recent works (e.g., [1,6,13,36]), there has been no definitive analysis of the primitive in the context of blockchain protocol security in the standard model. Intuitively, PoWs are useful in the consensus setting because they make message passing (moderately) hard and hence generate stochastic opportunities for the parties running the protocol to unify their view of the current state of the system. This fundamentally relies on an assumption about the aggregate computational power of the honest parties, but not on their actual number, in relation to the computational power of the parties that may deviate from the protocol (the "Byzantine" parties)—a hallmark of the peer-to-peer setting Bitcoin is designed for. Despite the fact that the Bitcoin blockchain has been analyzed formally [5,31,33,49], the required PoW properties have not been fully identified and most of the existing analysis has been carried out in the random oracle (RO) model [10]. The same is true for a wide variety of other protocols in the space, including [2,34,42].

We stress that despite the fact that the RO model has been widely used in the security analysis of practical protocols and primitives, it has also received significant criticism. For example, Canetti *et al.* [20] showed that there exist implementations of signatures and encryption schemes that are secure in the RO model but insecure for any implementation of the RO in the standard model; Nielsen [47] proved that efficient non-committing encryption has no instantiation in the standard model but a straightforward implementation in the RO model, while Goldwasser and Kalai [40] showed that the Fiat-Shamir heuristic [29] does not necessarily imply a secure digital signature, which is in contrast with the result by Pointcheval and Stern [50] in the RO model.

It follows that it is critical to discover security arguments for blockchain protocols that do not rely on the RO model. Note that we are looking for arguments as opposed to proofs since it is easy to observe that some computational assumption would still be needed for deriving the security of a blockchain protocol (recall that blockchain security cannot be inferred information theoretically as it fundamentally requires at minimum the collision resistance of the underlying hash function). In fact, the formalization of non-idealized, concrete hash function assumptions sufficient to prove security of Bitcoin and related protocols has been identified as a "fascinating open question" [18].

Following the above, the main question that motivates the present work is the following:

Is it possible to prove the security of blockchain protocols in the standard model under non-idealized assumptions about the underlying hash function?

Our Results. In this paper we answer the above question in the positive, by identifying three properties of a hash function family $\{H_k(\cdot)\}_k$ and then constructing a blockchain protocol whose security can be reduced to these properties (together with NIZKs; see below) in the standard model.

The first property is *collision resistance*. Specifically, it should be hard for an adversary given a random key k, to find two distinct messages m, m' for which it holds $H_k(m) = H_k(m')$. This property is useful in the blockchain context, since intuitively collision resistance ensures that the hash-chain maintained by the parties ensures the chronologically correct encoding of information.

The second property of the underlying hash function family is that it should be *computational randomness extracting* (CRE). Specifically, there is a way to isolate a finite subset of the domain of the hash function family so that for any given key k, the function H_k is a (weak) computational randomness extractor. This property is useful in a few different ways in blockchain security. Firstly, it will help for symmetry breaking, making sure that parties work concurrently on independent instances of the underlying problem. Secondly, it will ensure that the problem instances generated by honest parties (in the form of new blocks), will be sufficiently unpredictable in the eyes of the adversary. Regarding the plausibility of a CRE hash function, note that pseudorandom functions (PRFs) are known to imply weak computational randomness extractors [22], and assuming that a hash function implies a PRF is a fairly standard assumption [7, 25, 43].

The third property asks for the *iterative hardness* of the underlying hash function as multiple pre-images with near-zero hashes are stringed together in the form of a chain. This assumption is implicit in the context of the Bitcoin protocol. In fact, as we show, an attack against iterative hardness would result in an attack against the protocol (assuming a CRE hash function). This implies that there is (monetary) incentive to break this assumption, which coupled with the fact that no significant attacks have been demonstrated in the context of the Bitcoin protocol, establishes iterated hardness of the underlying hash (in this case SHA-256) as a plausible assumption.[1]

Armed with the above, we show a novel blockchain protocol whose security can be reduced to the collision resistance, computational randomness extraction and iterative hardness of the underlying hash function. Our design adopts Bitcoin's hash-based blockchain structure, as well as the longest-chain selection rule. However, contrary to previous analyses of this type of protocols [5, 31, 49]

---

[1] Refer to Sect. 3 for further discussion on this assumption.

in the RO model, iterative hardness provides no guarantee that blocks are "non-malleable," in the sense that it may be easy to mine multiple blocks on the same height of the chain once you have mined the first one. Our solution is to instead construct a PoW that *is* malleable, and leverage it to show a reduction that breaks the underlying iterated hardness assumption given a common-prefix attack to the blockchain protocol. In order to achieve this, we also have to hide the block witnesses by taking advantage of NIZK proofs with efficient simulation, thus managing to efficiently extract a sequence of iterated witnesses despite the fact that the attacker may not produce consecutive blocks.

In order to describe and analyze the protocol modularly, we put forth a new class of search problems, which we call *iterated search problems* (ISP). Taking advantage of ISPs one can produce concise and modular specifications of blockchain protocols, as evidenced by the description of our protocol (Sect. 4.3); as such, ISPs can be of independent interest.

In a nutshell, an ISP instance is defined by a problem statement set X, a witness set W and a relation R that determines when a witness satisfies the problem statement. The ISP is also equipped with a *successor* algorithm S that given a statement x and a witness w, can produce a successor problem statement x'; a *solving* algorithm M which given an initial problem statement x can find a sequence of witnesses; and a *verification* algorithm V that takes a problem statement x and witness w and outputs 1 if $(x, w) \in R$, and 0 otherwise. Each witness corresponds to the next statement defined by algorithm S on input the previous statement and witness, starting from x. The *iterated hardness* property of the ISP asks that if the solving algorithm takes t steps to solve k instances iteratively, no alternative algorithm can substantially speed this process up and produce k iterative solutions with non-negligible probability.

We perform our analysis in the static-adversary setting with synchronous rounds as in [31], and prove that our protocol can thwart adversaries and environments that roughly take less than half the computational steps the honest parties collectively are allowed per round. To our knowledge this is the first work that achieves such a result in the permissionless setting without idealized assumptions and no PKI[2]. In principle we can extend our results to the Δ-synchronous setting of [49], following the techniques found in Section 7 of [32]; we leave the details to the full version of the paper. Further, we leave as an open question the extension of our results to the dynamic setting of [33], as well as matching the (less than) 50% threshold on adversarial computational power of the Bitcoin blockchain which can be shown in the RO model.

Related Work. A related but distinct notion of hardness is *sequential* (i.e., non-parallelizable) iterated hardness. This notion has been considered as early as [51], mainly in the domains of timed-release cryptography [15] and protocol fairness [37], and recently formalized in [14] under the term *iterated sequential functions* (ISF) in the context of Verifiable Delay Functions (VDFs). In addition, a number of candidate hard problems have been proposed, including squaring

---

[2] See [30] for an extensive discussion on known results in the peer-to-peer/diffusion setting.

a group element of composite-modulus groups [51], hashing, and computing the modular square root of an element on a prime order group [44]. Nevertheless, we observe that if we base the Bitcoin protocol on an ISF (or VDF for that matter) it will be *insecure*. The fundamental issue is that it does not allow for parallelization, which is crucial for proving the security of any (Bitcoin-like) blockchain protocol. Indeed, an attacker with a single processor whose sequential speed is slightly faster than that of honest parties, can outperform potentially hundreds of them and mine longer chains first.

Another notion related to iterative hardness is the notion of "correlation intractability" (CI) [18]. The difference is that while CI only bounds the success probability in solving a single challenge, ISP fundamentally requires multiple instances. Further, while CI talks about any sparse relation, the iterative hardness definition is concerned with a specific non-sparse relation.

Finally, another related work focusing on sufficient conditions for the consensus problem in the permissionless setting (and no PKI, while matching the less than 50% threshold on adversarial computational power) is [36], which introduced the concept of *signatures of work* (SoW) as the basic underlying assumption. The only known implementation of SoWs however is in the RO model, hence it is unknown (and an interesting open question) whether SoWs can be realized under non-idealized hash function assumptions like the ones we consider here.

Due to space limitations, most of the proofs are presented in the full version [35] of the paper.

2 Preliminaries

In this section we present basic notation and definitions that we will use in the rest of the paper.

For $k \in \mathbb{N}^+$, $[k]$ denotes the set $\{1, \ldots, k\}$. For strings x, z, $x||z$ is the concatenation of x and z, and $|x|$ denotes the length of x. We denote sequences by $(a_i)_{i \in I}$, where I is the index set which will always be countable. For a set X, $x \leftarrow X$ denotes sampling a uniform element from X. For a distribution $\mathcal{U}$ over a set X, $x \leftarrow \mathcal{U}$ denotes sampling an element of X according to $\mathcal{U}$. By $\mathcal{U}_m$ we denote the uniform distribution over $\{0,1\}^m$. For random variable X, we denote by $H_\infty(X)$ the min-entropy of X. We denote the statistical distance between two random variables X, Z with range U by $\Delta[X, Z]$, i.e., $\Delta[X, Z] = \frac{1}{2} \sum_{v \in U} |\Pr[X = v] - \Pr[Z = v]|$. A *random variable ensemble* $(X_i)_{i \in I}$, is a sequence of random variables indexed by I. By $(X_i)_i \approx (Z_i)_i$ (resp. $\overset{c}{\approx}$) we denote that two ensembles are statistical (resp. computational) indistinguishable. We let λ denote the security parameter.

Protocol Execution and Security Model. In this paper we will follow a more concrete approach [8,11,12,37] to security evaluation. We will use functions t, ϵ, whose range is $\mathbb{N}, \mathbb{R}$, respectively, and have possibly many different arguments, to denote concrete bounds on the running time (number of steps) and probability of adversarial success of an algorithm in some given computational model, respectively. When we speak about running time this will include the execution time plus the length of the code (cf. [12]; note also that we will be considering uniform machines). We will always assume that t is a polynomial in the security parameter λ, although we will sometimes omit this dependency for brevity.

Instead of using interactive Turing machines (ITMs) as the underlying model of distributed computation, we will use (interactive) RAMs. The reason is that we need a model where subroutine access and simulation do not incur a significant overhead. ITMs are not suitable for this purpose, since one needs to account for the additional steps to go back-and-forth all the way to the place where the subroutine is stored. A similar choice was made by Garay *et al.* [37]; refer to [37] for details on using interactive RAMs in a UC-like framework. Given a RAM M, we will denote by $\mathsf{Steps}_M(1^\lambda, x)$ the random variable that corresponds to the number of steps taken by M given input 1^λ and x. We will say that M is t-bounded if it holds that $\Pr[\mathsf{Steps}_M(1^\lambda, x) \leq t(\lambda)] = 1$.

Finally, we remark that in our analyses there will be asymptotic terms of the form $\mathsf{negl}(\lambda)$ and concrete terms; throughout the paper, we will assume that λ is large enough to render the asymptotic terms insignificant compared to the concrete terms.

The Bitcoin Backbone Model. In this section, we give an overview of the security model that we are going to use throughout this work, introduced in [36]. This model is a variant of the synchronous model presented in [31] for the analysis of the Bitcoin backbone protocol, extended to accommodate a standard-model analysis of PoW-based blockchain protocols. In turn the model of [31] is based on Canetti's formulation of "real world" execution for multi-party cryptographic protocols [16,17].

An execution of some protocol Π is defined with respect to an "environment" program $\mathcal{Z}$, a "control" program C, and an "adversary" program $\mathcal{A}$. At a high level, $\mathcal{Z}$ is responsible for providing inputs to and obtaining outputs from different instances of Π, C is responsible for supervising the spawning and communication of all these programs, and $\mathcal{A}$ aims to disrupt the goals set by the protocol. The programs in question can be thought of as "interactive RAMs" communicating through registers in a well-defined manner.

We consider executions where the set of of parties $\{P_1, ..., P_n\}$ running Π is fixed and hardcoded to C. Moreover, we consider a "hybrid" model of computation [19], where the adversary $\mathcal{A}$ as well as all parties in the execution can access a number of "ideal" functionalities as subroutines; the functionalities are also modeled as RAMs and are presented later in detail. Initially $\mathcal{Z}$ is activated. $\mathcal{Z}$ can make special requests that result in the spawning of different parties and $\mathcal{A}$. In turn, $\mathcal{A}$ can corrupt different parties by sending messages of the form (Corrupt, P_i) to C, with the limitation that the total number of parties corrupted should be at most t; t is a parameter of the execution. We assume an active static adversary.

We are working in the *synchronous* model of computation, where the current round is known to all parties, and messages sent at one round are received at the beginning of the next one. The influence of the adversary in the network is going to be actively malicious following standard cryptographic practice. While we assume the adversary to be rushing and communication not to be authenticated, messages sent by honest parties are guaranteed to reach their destination.

All the above concerns are captured by the diffusion functionality $\mathcal{F}_{\text{diff}}$. The functionality maintains a Receive string defined for each party P_i. A party is allowed at any moment to fetch the messages sent to it at the previous round that are contained in its personal Receive string. Moreover, when the functionality receives an instruction to diffuse a message m from party P_i, it marks the party as complete for the current round, and forwards the message to the adversary; note that m is allowed to be empty. At any moment, the adversary $\mathcal{A}$ is allowed to specify the contents of the Receive string for each party P_i. The adversary has to specify when it is complete for the current round. When all parties are complete for the current round, the functionality inspects the contents of all Receive tapes and includes any messages that were diffused by the parties in the current round but not contributed by the adversary to the Receive tapes. The variable round is then incremented. In the protocol description, we will use DIFFUSE as the message transmission command.

In addition, we assume the existence of a *common reference string* (CRS) functionality that samples the CRS in a trusted manner from a known efficiently samplable distribution, and is available for all parties to fetch at the start of the execution. Note, that from our modeling it is implicit that the adversary and the honest parties get access to the CRS at the same round.

Based on the above, we denote by $\{\text{VIEW}_{\Pi,\mathcal{A},\mathcal{Z}}^{P,t,n}(z)\}_{z\in\{0,1\}^*}$ the random variable ensemble that corresponds to the view of party P at the end of an execution where $\mathcal{Z}$ takes z as input. We will consider stand-alone executions, hence z will always be of the form 1^λ, for $\lambda \in \mathbb{N}$. For simplicity, to denote this random variable ensemble we will use $\text{VIEW}_{\Pi,\mathcal{A},\mathcal{Z}}^{P,t,n}$. By $\text{VIEW}_{\Pi,\mathcal{A},\mathcal{Z}}^{t,n}$ we denote the concatenation of the views of all parties. The probability space where these variables are defined depends on the coins of all honest parties, $\mathcal{A}$, $\mathcal{Z}$ and the CRS generation procedure.

Furthermore, we are going to define a predicate on executions and prove our properties in disjunction with this predicate, i.e., either the property holds or the execution is not good.

Definition 1. Let $(t_\mathcal{A},\theta)$-good be a predicate defined on executions in the hybrid setting described above. Then E is $(t_\mathcal{A},\theta)$-good, where E is one such execution, if

- the total number of steps taken by $\mathcal{A}$ and $\mathcal{Z}$ per round is no more than $t_\mathcal{A}$;[3]
- the adversary sends at most θ messages per round.

Definition 2. Given a predicate Q and bounds $t_\mathcal{A},\theta,t,n \in \mathbb{N}$, with $t < n$, we say that protocol Π satisfies property Q for n parties assuming the number of corruptions is bounded by t, provided that for all PPT $\mathcal{Z},\mathcal{A}$, the probability that $Q(\text{VIEW}_{\Pi,\mathcal{A},\mathcal{Z}}^{t,n})$ is false and the execution is $(t_\mathcal{A},\theta)$-good is negligible in λ.

---

[3] The adversary cannot use the running time of honest parties that it has corrupted; it is activated instead of them during their turn.

Cryptographic Primitives and Building Blocks. We will make use of the following cryptographic primitives: Cryptographic hash functions, (computational) randomness extractors [22,48] and robust non-interactive zero-knowledge (NIZK) [52]. Refer to Appendix A for the corresponding security definitions.

Robust Public Transaction Ledgers. Our work is concerned with necessary and sufficient conditions to implement a public transaction ledger. Next, we give the transaction ledger definition introduced in [31], with the liveness property slightly strengthened, as in [49].

A *public transaction ledger* is defined with respect to a set of valid ledgers $\mathcal{L}$ and a set of valid transactions $\mathcal{T}$, each one possessing an efficient membership test. A ledger $\mathbf{x} \in \mathcal{L}$ is a vector of sequences of transactions $\text{tx} \in \mathcal{T}$. Ledgers correspond to chains of blocks in the Bitcoin protocol. It is possible for the adversary to create two transactions that are conflicting; valid ledgers must not contain conflicting transactions. Moreover, it is assumed that in the protocol execution there also exists an oracle Txgen that generates valid transactions, and is unambiguous, i.e., the adversary cannot create transactions that come in 'conflict' with the transactions generated by the oracle. A transaction is called *neutral* if there does not exist any transactions that come in conflict with it. Any ledger that contains neutral or non-conflicting transactions is considered to be valid.

Definition 3. *A protocol Π implements a robust public transaction ledger if it organizes the ledger as a chain of blocks of transactions and it satisfies the following two properties:*

- **Consistency** (parameterized by the "depth" parameter $k \in \mathbb{N}$): *If in a certain round an honest player reports a ledger that contains a transaction* tx *in a block more than k blocks away from the end of the ledger, where $k \in \mathbb{N}$ is the "depth" parameter (such transactions are called* stable*), then* tx *will be reported as stable and in the same position in the ledger by any honest player from this round on.*
- **Liveness** (parameterized by $k, u \in \mathbb{N}$—the "depth" and "wait time" parameters, resp.): *For every u consecutive rounds, there exists a round and an honest party, such that the transactions given as input to that party at this round that are either (i) issued by* Txgen *or (ii) neutral, will be reported by all honest parties as stable at the end of this round interval.*

3   Hash Functions Properties for Blockchain Security

In this section we describe the three falsifiable assumptions about hash functions which the security of our protocol is going to be based on. Two of these properties, namely, collision resistance [23] and weak computational randomness extraction [22], have been extensively studied in the hash function literature. The third one is new, and has to do with the moderate hardness of computing *sequences* of small hashes. We proceed to discuss each of the properties in detail.

We start with collision resistance. Most known blockchain protocols make use of a collision-resistant hash function in order to establish basic structural properties, e.g., that the adversary cannot create a blockchain that contains a cycle. That is exactly the way we are going to use this property here. We will use the following security definition [39].[4]

Definition 4. *Let* $\mathcal{H} = \{\{H_k : \{0,1\}^* \to \{0,1\}^\lambda\}_{k \in K(\lambda)}\}_{\lambda \in \mathbb{N}}$ *be a hash-function family, and* $\mathcal{A}$ *be a PPT adversary. Then* $\mathcal{H}$ *is* **collision resistant** *if and only if for any* $\lambda \in \mathbb{N}$ *and corresponding* $\{H_k\}_{k \in K}$ *in* $\mathcal{H}$,

$$\Pr_{k \leftarrow K}[(m, m') \leftarrow \mathcal{A}(1^\lambda, k) : (m \neq m') \wedge (H_k(m) = H_k(m'))] \leq \mathsf{negl}(\lambda).$$

Our second security assumption has to do with the existence of a fixed-length-input hash function family that is a *weak* computational randomness extractor. As explained in [22], this assumption is weaker than assuming a fixed-length-input pseudorandom function family (FI-PRF), a common assumption in the hash function literature [7,25,43]. We adapt the definition of a weak computational randomness extractor to the context of a hash function family.

Definition 5. *Let* $\mathcal{H} = \{\{H_k : \{0,1\}^{d\lambda} \to \{0,1\}^\lambda\}_{k \in K(\lambda)}\}_{\lambda \in \mathbb{N}}$, *for some* $d \in \mathbb{N}$, $d > 1$, *be a fixed-length input hash-function family.* $\mathcal{H}$ *is a* **computational randomness extracting** *(CRE) hash function family if for some* $c \in \mathbb{N}^+$, $c < d$, *the function family* $E = \{E_\lambda : \{0,1\}^{(c+1)\lambda} \times \{0,1\}^{(d-c-1)\lambda} \to \{0,1\}^\lambda\}_\lambda$, *where* $E_\lambda(x, i) \overset{\text{def}}{=} H_k(x\|i)$, *is a weak* $(c\lambda)$-*computational extractor, for any* $k \in K(\lambda)$.

This property will be useful in our protocol for two reasons. First, to ensure that the distributions of blocks generated by honest parties are identical and independent. Second, to establish that the blocks generated by honest parties, and which the adversary has the choice to mine on, look sufficiently random and hence the moderate hardness of the underlying problem is preserved.

Our third assumption about hash functions has to do with the hardness of finding sequences of small hashes in the hash-based (SHA-256) PoW construction proposed for Bitcoin. In more detail, given the hash x of some block, computing a valid PoW for this construction consists of finding witnesses w_1, w_2 such that $H_k(H_k(x\|w_1)\|w_2) < T$. In turn, our hardness property requires that any adversary should take a number of steps proportional to the number of PoWs computed, when these PoWs form a sequence starting from a uniformly random string x. The property is parameterized by t, the number of steps the adversary takes to generate each PoW on average.

Definition 6. *Let* $\mathcal{H} = \{\{H_k : \{0,1\}^{d\lambda} \to \{0,1\}^\lambda\}_{k \in K(\lambda)}\}_{\lambda \in \mathbb{N}}$, *for some* $d \in \mathbb{N}$, $d > 1$, *be a fixed-length input hash-function family, and let* T *be some hardness parameter.* $\mathcal{H}$ *is* t-**iteratively hard** *iff there exists a polynomial* $k_0(\cdot)$, *such that for any PPT RAM* $(\mathcal{A}_1, \mathcal{A}_2)$, $\lambda \in \mathbb{N}$, *and* $k \geq k_0(\lambda)$, *it holds that:*

---

[4] Throughout our exposition for simplicity we will assume that $\mathcal{H}$ takes one step to be evaluated. We note that our results can be generalized to the case where $\mathcal{H}$ takes more time.

$$\Pr_{\substack{\sigma \leftarrow K(\lambda); \\ x_0 \leftarrow [0,T]}} \left[\begin{array}{l} st \leftarrow \mathcal{A}_1(1^\lambda, \sigma); (w_i, w_i')_{i \in [k]} \leftarrow \mathcal{A}_2(1^\lambda, st, x_0) : \\ \forall i \in [k] : x_i := H_\sigma(H_\sigma(x_{i-1}||w_i)||w_i') < T \\ \wedge \ \mathsf{Steps}_{\mathcal{A}_2}(st, x_0) < k \cdot t \end{array} \right] \leq \mathsf{negl}(\lambda)$$

Our choice to base the security of our protocol on the iterated hardness of Bitcoin's PoW construction is not accidental. The fact that any attack on iterated hardness implies an attack on Bitcoin, as we show in Appendix B, as well as the fact that no attacks have been publicly disclosed in the last ten years that this construction has been actively used in Bitcoin, constitute empirical evidence in its favor. Note that this would not necessarily be the case if we based security on a stronger hardness property that was not necessary to prove Bitcoin secure, as it would then be possible that an attack against the property is known and the adversary does not have any incentive to reveal/deploy it, as it does not affect the security of the protocol in any way.[5]

We note that to prove the security of our protocol both properties in Definitions 5 and 6 should hold for the same hash function and for suitable parameters [6], which we discuss in the next section; collision resistance may hold for a different hash function. As argued above, SHA-256 is a natural candidate for these assumptions. Finally, in our protocol analysis we will also make use of a number of other standard assumptions, such as the existence of a NIZK-PoK scheme and that the honest parties control the majority of the computational power. The theorem we prove is as follows:

Theorem 3 (Informal). *Assume the existence of collision-resistant hash functions, a hash function family that is CRE and iteratively hard for appropriate parameters, a one-way trapdoor permutation and a dense cryptosystem (for the NIZK), and that $t_\mathcal{A}$ is (roughly) less than half the total running time of honest parties per round. Then there exists a protocol that implements a robust public transaction ledger.*

Finally, Gentry and Wichs [38] define as falsifiable the cryptographic assumptions that can be expressed as a game between an efficient challenger and an adversary. All cryptographic assumptions of Theorem 3 are falsifiable in this sense, with two caveats: First, due to the concrete security approach our work takes, the challenger should take as input the number of steps of the adversary. Second, in the computational randomness extraction property we quantify over all keys of the hash and all efficiently samplable distributions with sufficient min-entropy, which is not immediate to express in the framework of [38]. Instead, we could choose the key randomly, and expresses the extraction property w.r.t. a single family of source distributions that the adversary can influence. To simplify

---

[5] The profitability of an attack may also work as a counterincentive to revealing it. Nevertheless, there is merit in our argument if we take into consideration "white hat" actors who have tried breaking Bitcoin.

[6] Intuitively, the adversary should not be able to compute small hashes much faster than the rate at which honest parties generate blocks that is guaranteed by the computational extractor property.

our presentation we adopt the former version of the definition. However, we note that the proof techniques we use can be adapted to handle the latter.

4   Blockchains from Non-idealized Hash Functions

In this section we present and prove secure a protocol that implements a transaction ledger and is based on a hash function that satisfies the properties described in Sect. 3. We modularize our presentation and analysis by first introducing the concept of *iterated search problems* (ISP) in Sect. 4.1, and then presenting a technical overview in Sect. 4.2, followed by an ISP-based blockchain protocol in Sect. 4.3. Then, in Sect. 4.4, we introduce a "blockchain friendly" ISP security definition, that we show in Sect. 4.5 to be sufficient to prove our protocol secure. Finally, in Sect. 4.6 we construct a secure ISP based on the hash properties defined in Sect. 3, which in combination with our protocol can be shown to satisfy Theorem 3.

The choice of modularizing the protocol analysis has multiple benefits. In particular, it first allows us to formally capture all required properties that the moderately hard problem our protocol is built on should satisfy for the analysis to go through. We hope that this will motivate building other constructions in the future. Secondly, it makes it easier to take advantage of previous efforts to analyze relevant protocols [31,36,49]. While we adapt some of the proof techniques presented there, an important contribution of our work is that the ISP notion which we built on is considerably weaker and can be instantiated in the standard model from fairly simple assumptions.

4.1   Iterated Search Problems

In this section we introduce a class of problems inspired by Bitcoin's underlying computational problem. The straightforward properties that this class should have, are the ability to find a witness for a problem statement and to verify that the witness is correct, matching Bitcoin's block mining and block verification procedures, respectively. In addition, the notion models the ability to generate a new problem statement from a valid statement/witness pair. This captures the fact that in Bitcoin the problem that a miner solves depends on a previous block (i.e., a statement/witness pair). This concept has appeared before in the study of iterated *sequential* functions [14], whose name we draw from. Syntactically, the key difference here is that in each iteration we are not evaluating a function, but instead we are solving a search problem with possibly many witnesses. Moreover, as we already commented in Sect. 1 iterated sequential functions are *not* the correct abstractions for Bitcoin's underlying computational problem, as they allow for an attack against the protocol. We proceed to give a formal definition of ISPs.

Definition 7 (Iterated Search Problem). *An* iterated search problem *(ISP) $\mathcal{I}$ specifies a collection $(I_\lambda)_{\lambda \in \mathbb{N}}$ of distributions.[7] For every value of the*

---

[7] Here we follow the notation used in [21] to define *subset membership problems*. We remark that no other connection exists between the two papers.

security parameter $\lambda \geq 0$, I_λ *is a probability distribution of* instance descriptions. *An instance description* Λ *specifies*

1. *finite, non-empty sets* X, W, *and*
2. *a binary relation* $R \subset X \times W$.
We write $\Lambda[X, W, R]$ to indicate that the instance Λ specifies X, W and R as above.

An ISP also provides several algorithms. For this purpose, we require that the instance descriptions, as well as the elements of the sets X and W, can be uniquely encoded as bit strings of length polynomial in λ, and that both X and $(I_\lambda)_{\lambda \in \mathbb{N}}$ have polynomial-time samplers. The ISP algorithms are as follows, all parameterized by $\Lambda[X, W, R]$:

- *Verification* algorithm $V_\Lambda(x, w)$: A deterministic algorithm that takes as input a problem statement x and a witness w and outputs 1 if $(x, w) \in R$ and 0 otherwise.
- *Successor* algorithm $S_\Lambda(x, w)$: A deterministic algorithm that takes as input a problem statement[8] x and a valid witness w and outputs a new instance $x' \in X$.
- *Solving* algorithm $M_\Lambda(x, k)$: A probabilistic algorithm that takes as input a problem statement x and a number $k \in \mathbb{N}^+$ and outputs a sequence of k witnesses $(w_i)_{i \in [k]}$.

In the sequel, we will omit writing Λ as a parameter of V, S, M when it is clear from the context. In order to ease the presentation, we recursively extend the definitions of S and R to sequences of witnesses as follows: Let $S(x, \emptyset) := x$ and for any $k > 1$, $S(x, (w_i)_{i \in [k]}) := S(S(x, (w_i)_{i \in [k-1]}), w_k)$ and $(x, (w_i)_{i \in [k]}) \in R$ iff $\bigwedge_{i=1}^{k}(S(x, (w_j)_{j \in [i-1]}), w_i) \in R$. Further, we assume that M is *correct*, i.e., for $(w_i)_{i \in [k]} \leftarrow M(x, k)$, it holds that $(x, (w_i)_{i \in [k]}) \in R$.

Example. Next, we present as an example Bitcoin's underlying computational problem captured as an ISP.

Construction 1. *Let T be a protocol parameter representing how hard it is to solve a problem instance.[9] Then:*

- I_λ *is the uniform distribution over functions* $H : \{0, 1\}^* \to \{0, 1\}^\lambda$ *in some family of hash functions* $\mathcal{H}$, *i.e.,* $\Lambda = \{H\}$;
- $X = \{x | x < T \wedge x \in \{0, 1\}^\lambda\}$ *and* $W = \{0, 1\}^* \times \{0, 1\}^\lambda$;
- $R = \{(x, w) | H(H(x || m) || ctr) < T$, *for* $w = m || ctr\}$;
- $V(x, w)$ *checks whether* $H(H(x || m) || ctr) < T$, *for* $w = m || ctr$;

---

[8] We could formalize S more generally, to take as input a sequence of problem statements. However, for our exposition the current formulation suffices. Note, that a more general definition would be needed for the variable difficulty case [33], which we do not study here, where the next block's difficulty depends on the whole chain.

[9] For simplicity, in our exposition the hardness parameter for each ISP is fixed, and we do not capture it explicitly.

- $S(x, w) = H(H(x||m)||ctr)$, and
- $M(x, 1)$ tests whether $V(x, (m, ctr))$ is true, for different (m, ctr) pairs, until it finds a solution. $M(x, k)$ is defined inductively, by running successively $M(x, k - 1)$ and $M(x', 1)$, for $x' := S(x, M(x, k - 1))$. The output consists of the witnesses output by the two programs.

4.2 Technical Overview

Next, we give a complete overview of the technical results of this section regarding the implementation of a transaction ledger based on non-idealized hash functions.

First, we describe our ISP-based protocol in Sect. 4.3. The main challenge to overcome is that while the protocol's security is going to be based on iterated hardness (Definition 6), it operates in a setting where the adversary can also take advantage of the work of honest parties. This includes the adversary being able to see the information leaked by the honestly produced blocks, as well as honest parties directly working on the chain it is extending. In contrast, the iterated hardness experiment does not provide any guarantees about these cases, as the adversary does not receive any externally computed witnesses.

Towards this end, blocks in our protocol, instead of exposing the relevant computed witness, contain a proof of knowledge (PoK) of such a valid witness through a non-interactive zero-knowledge (NIZK) proof. At first, the fact that we use NIZK proofs for a language that is moderately hard may seem counterintuitive, due to the fact that a trivial simulator and extractor would exist for the zero-knowledge and soundness properties, since computing a new witness for a given statement takes polynomial time. Instead, following our general approach, we make concrete assumptions regarding the efficiency of both the simulator and the extractor. Informally, we require that the time it takes to simulate a proof or extract a witness is a lot smaller than the time it takes for honest parties to compute a witness (see Assumption 2). Note that in practice this can be achieved by making the underlying problem hard enough, which on the flip side will affect the performance of the resulting ledger being implemented.

Regarding chain selection, we adopt the longest-chain rule of the Bitcoin protocol. As we will see later, this will allow our protocol to operate even if the witnesses of the ISP are malleable. To make our analysis cleaner, the hash-chain structure of blocks is decoupled from the underlying computational problem.

As an intermediate step, in Sect. 4.4, we present a set of ISP properties sufficient to prove our protocol secure. First, an ISP is *iteratively hard* iff the ISP solving algorithm takes t steps to solve k instances iteratively, and no alternative algorithm can substantially speed up this process and produce k iterative solutions with non-negligible probability. Next, an ISP is (t, α)-*successful* when the number of steps of the solving algorithm is below t with probability at least α. The ISP is *next-problem simulatable* if the output of the successor algorithm applied on a witness w corresponding to an instance x can be simulated independently of x and the same is the case for the running time of the solver. Finally, an ISP is *witness-malleable* if, given a witness w for a problem instance x, it is possible to sample an alternative witness whose resulting distribution via the successor algorithm is computationally indistinguishable with the output of the successor over a random witness produced by the solving algorithm.

Armed with the above definitions we prove in Sect. 4.5 that our novel blockchain protocol implements a transaction ledger. We note that the main technical difficulty of our blockchain security proof is to construct a reduction that breaks the underlying iterated hardness assumption given a common-prefix attack to the blockchain protocol. The reduction takes advantage of the fact that the ISP is witness malleable and next-problem simulatable to cheaply simulate honest parties' work, as well as amenable to zero-knowledge proof simulation and extraction to extract a sequence of iterated witnesses despite the fact that the attacker may not produce consecutive blocks. After some more work, we are able to prove the following theorem:

Theorem 3 (Informal). *Assume the existence of collision-resistant hash functions, a one-way trapdoor permutation and a dense cryptosystem (for the NIZK) and a secure ISP problem with appropriate parameters, and that t_A is (roughly) less than half the total running time of honest parties per round. Then there exists a protocol that implements a robust public transaction ledger.*

Finally, in Sect. 4.6, we present a secure ISP problem assuming the existence of a hash function that satisfies both the computational extraction and iterated hardness properties presented in Sect. 3. The main characteristic of this new ISP (Construction 2) is that, similarly to the Bitcoin ISP (Construction 1), it uses a double hash, but, in contrast, it requires the inner hash value to be below the target threshold, as opposed to the outer value. In more detail, given a problem statement x and witnesses w_1, w_2, while the next problem is defined exactly as in Bitcoin, i.e., $H(H(x||w_1)||w_2)$, the witnesses are valid if $H(x||w_1) < T$ holds, compared to $H(H(x||w_1)||w_2) < T$. This swap allows the randomness of the outer hash witness to be freely selected by a uniform distribution. In turn, this gives us the ability to argue that (i) due to the randomness extraction property of the hash, the inner hash value is computationally indistinguishable from uniform and hence the solving run-time of the ISP can be simulated independently of the problem statement; (ii) again due to the randomness extraction property, the outer hash value is computationally indistinguishable from uniform, and (iii) witness malleability can be shown in a straightforward manner by choosing another witness for the outer hash at random. Moreover, regarding the hard-ISP property, we can take advantage of the iterative hardness of Bitcoin's ISP construction and the fact that Construction 2 is closely related to it. The main idea is that if there exists an attacker against our construction, then we can use it to break the iterative hardness property (Definition 6) by using the inner hash witnesses in Construction 2 as an outer hash witnesses in Construction 1. Putting everything together results in the following:

Lemmas 5 and 6 (Informal). *Assume the existence of a hash function family that is CRE and iteratively hard for appropriate parameters. Then, there exists a secure ISP problem.*

Finally, using the above results we are able to obtain Theorem 3.

4.3   Blockchain Protocol Description

Next, we are going to describe our new protocol. Our protocol, $\Pi_{\mathsf{PL}}^{\mathsf{new}}$, uses as building blocks three cryptographic primitives: An ISP $\mathcal{I} = (M, V, S)$, a collision-resistant hash function family $\mathcal{H}$, and a robust NIZK protocol $\Pi_{\mathsf{NIZK}} = (q, \mathsf{P}, \mathsf{V}, \mathsf{S} = (\mathsf{S}_1, \mathsf{S}_2), \mathsf{E})$ for the language[10]

$$L = \{(\Lambda[X, W, R], x, x') | \exists w \in W : (x, w) \in R \wedge S(x, w) == x'\}$$

where $\Lambda[X, W, R]$ is an ISP instance of $\mathcal{I}$. Π_{NIZK} also supports labels, which we denote as a superscript on P and V. The initialization of these primitives happens through the CRS all parties share at the start of the execution, which contains: An instance description $\Lambda[X, W, R]$, a statement x_{Gen}, the description of a hash function $H : \{0,1\}^* \rightarrow \{0,1\}^\lambda$ and the NIZK reference string Ω, each randomly sampled from $I_\lambda, X, \mathcal{H}, \{0,1\}^{q(\lambda)}$, respectively. Moreover, as in [31], our protocol is parameterized by the chain validation predicate $V(\cdot)$, the chain reading function $R(\cdot)$, and the input contribution function $I(\cdot)$ to capture higher-level applications, e.g., Bitcoin.

Next, we introduce some notation used in the description of our protocol. We use the terms block and chain to refer to tuples of the form $\langle s, m, x, \pi \rangle \in \{0,1\}^\lambda \times \{0,1\}^* \times X \times \{0,1\}^{\mathsf{poly}(\lambda)}$, and sequences of such tuples, respectively. The rightmost (resp., leftmost) block of chain $\mathcal{C}$ is denoted by $\mathsf{head}(\mathcal{C})$ (resp., $\mathsf{tail}(\mathcal{C})$). Each block contains the hash of the previous block s, a message m, the next problem x to be solved, and a NIZK proof π. We denote by $B_{\mathsf{Gen}} = \langle 0^\lambda, 0^\lambda, x_{\mathsf{Gen}}, 0^\lambda \rangle$ a special block called the genesis block; note that x_{Gen} is part of the CRS. A chain $\mathcal{C} = (\langle s_i, m_i, x_i, \pi_i \rangle)_{i \in [k]}$ is valid if: (i) The first block of $\mathcal{C}$ is equal to B_{Gen}; (ii) the contents of the chain $\mathbf{m}_{\mathcal{C}} = (m_1, \ldots, m_k)$ are valid according to the chain validation predicate V, i.e., $V(\mathbf{m}_{\mathcal{C}})$ is true; (iii) $s_{i+1} = H(s_i || m_i || x_i || i)$[11] for all $i \in [k]$, and (iv) $\mathsf{V}^{s_{i+1}}((\Lambda, x_{i-1}, x_i), \pi_i)$ is true for all $i \in [k] \setminus \{1\}$; see Algorithm 1. We call $H(s_i || m_i || x_i || i)$ the hash of block B_i and denote it by $H(B_i)$, and define $H(\mathcal{C}) \stackrel{\Delta}{=} H(\mathsf{head}(\mathcal{C}))$. We will consider two valid blocks or chains as equal, if all their parts match, except possibly for the NIZK proofs.

We proceed to describe the main function of the protocol, presented in Algorithm 4. At each round, each party chooses the longest valid chain among the ones it has received (Algorithm 2) and tries to extend it by computing a new witness. If it succeeds, it diffuses the new block to the network. In more detail, each party will run the solver M on the problem x defined in the last block $\langle s, m, x, \pi \rangle$ of the chosen chain $\mathcal{C}$. If it succeeds on finding a witness w, it will then compute a NIZK proof that it knows a witness w such that $(x, w) \in R$ and $S(x, w) = x'$, for some $x' \in X$. The proof should also have a label $H(H(\mathsf{head}(\mathcal{C})) || m' || x' || (|\mathcal{C}| + 1))$, where m' is the output of the input contribution function $I(\cdot)$, i.e., the message encoded in the block; see Algorithm 3. Then, the party diffuses the extended

---

[10] We assume that both V and S are efficiently computable. Hence, $L \in \mathcal{NP}$.

[11] We include a fixed length (λ-bit) encoding of the height of the block in the hash on purpose. This way, the contents of the hash chain form a suffix-free code [9], which in turn implies collision resistance. See Lemma 1.

Algorithm 1. The validate procedure, parameterized by B_{Gen}, the hash function $H(\cdot)$, the *chain validation predicate* $V(\cdot)$, and the verification algorithm V of Π_{NIZK}. The input is $\mathcal{C}$.

```
1:  function validate(C)
2:      b ← V(m_C) ∧ (tail(C) = B_Gen)          ▷ m_C describes the contents of chain C.
3:      if b = True then                         ▷ The chain is non-empty and meaningful w.r.t. V(·)
4:          s' ← H(B_Gen)                        ▷ Compute the hash of the genesis block.
5:          x' ← x_Gen
6:          C ← C^⌈1⌉                            ▷ Remove the genesis from C
7:          while (C ≠ ϵ ∧ b = True) do
8:              ⟨s, m, x, π⟩ ← tail(C)
9:              s'' ← H(tail(C))
10:             if (s = s' ∧ V^{s''}(Ω, (Λ, x', x), π)) then
11:                 s' ← s''                     ▷ Retain hash value
12:                 x' ← x
13:                 C ← C^⌈1⌉                    ▷ Remove the tail from C
14:             else
15:                 b ← False
16:     return (b)
```

chain to the network. Finally, if the party is queried by the environment, it outputs $R(\mathcal{C})$, where $\mathcal{C}$ is the chain selected by the party; the chain reading function $R(\cdot)$ interprets $\mathcal{C}$ differently depending on the higher-level application running on top of the Bitcoin backbone protocol. We assume that all honest parties take the same number of steps t_H per round.

Algorithm 2. The function that finds the "best" chain, parameterized by function $\max(\cdot)$. The input is $\{\mathcal{C}_1, \ldots, \mathcal{C}_k\}$.

```
1:  function maxvalid(C_1, ..., C_k)
2:      temp ← ε
3:      for i = 1 to k do
4:          if validate(C_i) then
5:              temp ← max(C, temp)
6:      return temp
```

In order to turn the above protocol into a protocol realizing a public transaction ledger, we define functions $V(\cdot), R(\cdot), I(\cdot)$ exactly as in [31]. For completeness we give these definitions in Table 1. We denote the new public ledger protocol by $\Pi_{\mathsf{PL}}^{\mathsf{new}}$.

4.4   ISP Security Properties

Next, we present a set of ISP properties sufficient to prove our protocol secure. Later in Sect. 4.6 we show how to instantiate them.

Algorithm 3. The *proof of work* function is parameterized by the hash function $H(\cdot)$, and the proving algorithm P of Π_{NIZK}. The input is $(m', \mathcal{C})$.

```
1: function pow(m′,C)
2:     ⟨s, m, x, π⟩ ← head(C)
3:     w ← M(x)                          ▷ Run the honest solving algorithm of the ISP.
4:     if w ≠ ⊥ then
5:         x′ ← S(x, w)                  ▷ Compute the next problem to be solved.
6:         s′ ← H(s||m||x|||C|)          ▷ Compute the hash of the last block.
7:         s″ ← H(s′||m′||x′|||C| + 1)   ▷ Compute the hash of the new block.
8:         π′ ← Pˢ″(Ω, (Λ, x, x′), w)    ▷ Compute the NIZK proof.
9:         B ← ⟨s′, m′, x′, π′⟩
10:    C ← CB                            ▷ Extend chain
11:    return C
```

Algorithm 4. The Bitcoin backbone protocol, parameterized by the *input contribution function* $I(\cdot)$ and the *chain reading function* $R(\cdot)$.

```
1:  C ← B_Gen                                         ▷ Initialize C to the genesis block.
2:  st ← ε
3:  round ← 0
4:  while TRUE do
5:      C̃ ← maxvalid(C, any chain C′ found in RECEIVE())
6:      ⟨st, m⟩ ← I(st, C̃, round, INPUT(), RECEIVE())   ▷ Determine the m-value.
7:      C_new ← pow(m, C̃)
8:      if C ≠ C_new then
9:          C ← C_new
10:         DIFFUSE(C)
11:     round ← round + 1
12:     if INPUT() contains READ then
13:         write R(m_C) to OUTPUT()
```

In the same spirit as in Boneh *et al.* [14]'s definition of an iterated sequential function, we can define the notion of a *hard* iterated search problem. Our definition is parameterized by t, δ and k_0, all functions of λ which we omit for brevity. Unlike the former definition, we take in account the *total* number of steps instead of only the sequential ones, and we require the error probability to be negligible after at least k_0 witnesses have been found instead of one. In that sense, our notion relaxes the strict convergence criterion of [14]. Finally, note that the adversary is allowed some precomputation time.

Definition 8. *An ISP* $\mathcal{I} = (V, M, S)$ *is* (t, δ, k_0)-*hard iff it holds that*

- *For* $\lambda \in \mathbb{N}$ *and for all polynomially large* $k \geq k_0$:

$$\Pr_{\substack{\Lambda[X,W,R] \leftarrow \mathcal{I}_\lambda; \\ x \leftarrow X}} \left[\begin{array}{l} (w_i)_{i \in [k]} \leftarrow M(x, k) : (x, (w_i)_i) \in R \\ \wedge\ \mathsf{Steps}_M(x, k) \leq k \cdot t \end{array} \right] \geq 1 - \mathsf{negl}(\lambda),\ and$$

Table 1. *The instantiation of functions* $V(\cdot), R(\cdot), I(\cdot)$ *for protocol* $\Pi_{\mathsf{PL}}^{\mathsf{new}}(\mathcal{I})$.

Content validation pre-dicate $V(\cdot)$	$V(\cdot)$ is true if its input $\langle m_1, \ldots, m_\ell \rangle$ is a valid ledger, i.e., it is in $\mathcal{L}$
Chain reading function $R(\cdot)$	$R(\cdot)$ returns the contents of the chain if they constitute a valid ledger, otherwise it is undefined
Input contribution function $I(\cdot)$	$I(\cdot)$ returns the largest subsequence of transactions in the input and receive registers that constitute a valid ledger, with respect to the contents of the chain $\mathcal{C}$ the party already has, preceded by a neutral random transaction

- *for any PPT RAM* $\mathcal{A} = (\mathcal{A}_1, \mathcal{A}_2)$, $\lambda \in \mathbb{N}$, *and all polynomially large* $k \geq k_0$, *it holds that*

$$\Pr_{\substack{\Lambda[X,W,R] \leftarrow I_\lambda; \\ x \leftarrow X}} \left[\begin{array}{l} st \leftarrow \mathcal{A}_1(1^\lambda, \Lambda); (w_i)_{i \in [k]} \leftarrow \mathcal{A}_2(1^\lambda, st, x) : \\ (x, (w_i)_i) \in R \wedge Steps_{\mathcal{A}_2}(st, x) < (1-\delta)k \cdot t \end{array} \right] \leq \mathsf{negl}(\lambda).$$

The next property, has to do with establishing an upper bound t on the the the running time of the verification algorithm V. Intuitively, the product $\theta \cdot t$ should be a lot smaller than the number of steps $t_\mathcal{H}$ per round available to honest parties, to avoid resource depletion attacks.

Definition 9. *An ISP* $\mathcal{I} = (V, M, S)$ *is* t-verifiable *iff algorithm* V *takes time at most* t *(on all inputs).*

In general, attacking an honest solver amounts to finding a certain set of inputs over which the honest solving algorithm fails to produce witnesses sufficiently fast. In order to combat this attack, we introduce the following property: We say that an ISP $\mathcal{I}$ is (t, α)-*successful* when the probability that M^{12} computes a witness in t steps is at least α.

Definition 10. *An ISP* $\mathcal{I} = (V, M, S)$ *is* (t, α)-successful *iff for* $\lambda \in \mathbb{N}$, $\Lambda[X, W, R] \in I_\lambda$, *and for all* $x \in X$ *it holds that:* $\Pr[\mathsf{Steps}_M(x) < t] \geq \alpha$.

The iterated hardness property (Definition 8) does not give any guarantees regarding composition. For blockchain protocols, however, this is necessary as many parties concurrently try to solve the same ISP. To address this issue, we introduce the next property that ensures that learning how long it took for a witness to be computed or what the next problem defined by such witness is, does not leak any information that could help the adversary find a witness himself. More formally, there exists an efficient simulator whose output is computationally indistinguishable from the distribution of the time it takes to compute a witness w for some statement x and the next statement $S(x, w)$. Note that, crucially, the simulator does not depend on the instance description Λ or the problem statement x, and that we consider a non-uniform distinguisher.

---

[12] For brevity, we use $M(x)$ instead of $M(x, 1)$ in this section.

Definition 11. *An ISP* $\mathcal{I} = (V, M, S)$ *is* t-next-problem simulatable *iff there exists a* t-bounded RAM Ψ *such that for any PPT RAM D, any $\lambda \in \mathbb{N}$, any $z \in \{0,1\}^{poly(\lambda)}$, any $\Lambda[X, W, R] \in I_\lambda$, and any $x \in X$, it holds that*

$$| \Pr[D(1^\lambda, z, \Lambda, x, (S(x, M(x)), \mathsf{Steps}_M(x))) = 1] - \Pr[D(1^\lambda, z, \Lambda, x, \Psi(1^\lambda)) = 1]| \leq \mathsf{negl}(\lambda).$$

The next property has to do with a party's ability to "cheaply" compute witnesses for a statement, if it already knows one. This will be important to ensure that even if the adversary has external help to produce some of the witnesses needed by the hard ISP experiment, as is the case for blockchain protocols, still the overall process remains hard with respect to the number of consecutive blocks the adversary actually produced. We call this ISP property *witness malleability*.

Definition 12. *An ISP* $\mathcal{I} = (V, M, S)$ *is* t-witness malleable *iff there exists a* t-bounded RAM Φ *such that for any PPT RAM D, any $\lambda \in \mathbb{N}$, any $z \in \{0,1\}^{poly(\lambda)}$, any $\Lambda[X, W, R] \in I_\lambda$, and any $(x, w) \in R$, it holds that $(x, \Phi(x, w)) \in R$, and*

$$| \Pr[D(1^\lambda, z, \Lambda, x, w, S(x, \Phi(x, w))) = 1] - \Pr[D(1^\lambda, z, \Lambda, x, w, S(x, M(x))) = 1]| \leq \mathsf{negl}(\lambda).$$

Finally, we call an ISP that satisfies all the above properties *secure*.

Definition 13. *An ISP* $\mathcal{I} = (V, M, S)$ *is* $(t_{\mathsf{ver}}, t_{\mathsf{succ}}, \alpha, t_{\mathsf{nps}}, t_{\mathsf{mal}}, t_{\mathsf{hard}}, \delta_{\mathsf{hard}}, k_{\mathsf{hard}})$-secure *iff it is* t_{ver}-verifiable, $(t_{\mathsf{succ}}, \alpha)$-successful, t_{nps}-next-problem simulatable, t_{mal}-witness malleable, and $(t_{\mathsf{hard}}, \delta_{\mathsf{hard}}, k_{\mathsf{hard}})$-hard.

An ISP scheme with trivial parameters is of limited use in a distributed environment; for example, if $\delta_{\mathsf{hard}} \ll 1$ or $t_{\mathsf{hard}} \ll t_{\mathsf{ver}}$. Hence, next we describe the parameters' ranges that make for a non-trivial secure ISP. First off, and ignoring negligible terms, one can show that $\alpha \leq \frac{t_{\mathsf{succ}}}{(1-\delta_{\mathsf{hard}})t_{\mathsf{hard}}}$ (see Lemma 4). On the other hand, the successful property always holds for $\alpha = 0$. Therefore, for a non-trivial ISP scheme it should hold that α is close to $\frac{t_{\mathsf{succ}}}{(1-\delta_{\mathsf{hard}})t_{\mathsf{hard}}}$. To avoid denial of service attacks, $\theta \cdot t_{\mathsf{ver}}$ must be sufficiently small compared to t_{hard}, the running time of the solving algorithm M. Furthermore, t_{mal} should be a lot smaller than t_{hard}, otherwise M can be used as a trivial simulator. We note, that the security of the protocol that we presented earlier relies on the fact that a secure ISP scheme with favorable parameters exists, mainly reflected in Assumption 2 (Sect. 4.5).

4.5 Security of the ISP-based Blockchain Protocol

In this subsection we prove that $\Pi_{\mathsf{PL}}^{\mathsf{new}}$ implements a robust public transaction ledger (cf. Definition 3), assuming the underlying ISP $\mathcal{I}$ is secure.

Security Proof of the ISP-based Protocol. We proceed to the main part of the protocol analysis. The first assumption we are going to make is that the underlying ISP $\mathcal{I}$ is secure, and that the runtimes of the procedures of the NIZK system are upper bounded.

Table 2. *The parameters in our analysis:* $\lambda, n, t, t_{\mathcal{H}}, t_{\mathcal{A}}, t'_{\mathcal{H}}, t'_{\mathcal{A}}, \theta, k_{hard}$ *are in* $\mathbb{N}$, $\alpha, f, \gamma, \beta, \delta, \delta_{\mathsf{Steps}}, \delta_{\mathsf{ISP}}$ *are in* $\mathbb{R}$.

λ :	security parameter
n :	number of parties
t :	number of parties corrupted
$t_{\mathcal{H}}$:	number of steps per round per honest party
$t_{\mathcal{A}}$:	total number of adversarial steps per round
$t'_{\mathcal{H}}$:	lower bound on number of steps running M per round per honest party
$t'_{\mathcal{A}}$:	round simulation cost, excluding honest calls to M
θ :	upper bound on the number of messages sent by the adversary per round
β :	upper bound on the rate at which the adversary computes witnesses per step
α :	probability that M outputs a witness after $t'_{\mathcal{H}}$ steps
f :	probability that at least one party computes a block in a round
γ :	probability that exactly one party computes a block in a round
δ :	upper bound on the total block generation rate
δ_{Steps} :	honest parties' advantage on number of steps
δ_{ISP} :	adversary's advantage on ISP witnesses computation rate
k_{hard} :	convergence parameter of ISP hardness

Assumption 1 (ISP Assumption). *For parameters* $t_{\mathsf{ver}}, t'_{\mathcal{H}}, \alpha, t_{\mathsf{nps}}, t_{\mathsf{mal}}, t_{\mathsf{hard}}$, $\delta_{\mathsf{hard}}, k_{\mathsf{hard}}, t_{\mathsf{P}}, t_{\mathsf{V}}, t_{\mathsf{S}}$, *and* t_{E} *we assume that:*

- *ISP* $\mathcal{I}$ *is* $(t_{\mathsf{ver}}, t'_{\mathcal{H}}, \alpha, t_{\mathsf{nps}}, t_{\mathsf{mal}}, t_{\mathsf{hard}}, \delta_{\mathsf{hard}}, k_{\mathsf{hard}})$-*secure;*[13]
- *running the prover (resp., verifier, simulator, extractor) of* Π_{NIZK} *takes* t_{P} *(resp.* $t_{\mathsf{V}}, t_{\mathsf{S}}, t_{\mathsf{E}})$ *steps.*

Next, we introduce some additional notation necessary to formalize our second assumption that has to do with the computational power of the honest parties and the adversary. For brevity, and to better connect our analysis to previous work [31,36,49], we denote by $\beta = ((1 - \delta_{\mathsf{hard}}) \cdot t_{\mathsf{hard}})^{-1}$, the upper bound on the rate at which the adversary can compute witnesses in the iterated hardness game. We introduce two variables, $t'_{\mathcal{H}}$ and $t'_{\mathcal{A}}$, that have to do with the effectiveness of honest parties and the adversary in producing witnesses for $\mathcal{I}$. $t'_{\mathcal{H}}$ is a lower bound on the number of steps each honest party takes per round running M. It holds that in any round at least $n - t$ parties will run M for at least $t'_{\mathcal{H}}$ steps. $t'_{\mathcal{A}}$ denotes the maximum time needed by a RAM machine to simulate the adversary, the environment and the honest parties in one round of the protocol execution, without taking into account calls made to M by the latter, and with the addition of one invocation of the NIZK extractor. They amount to:

$$t'_{\mathcal{A}} = t_{\mathcal{A}} + \theta \cdot t_{\mathsf{V}} + t_{\mathsf{E}} + n(t_{\mathsf{bb}} + t_{\mathsf{nps}} + t_{\mathsf{mal}} + t_{\mathsf{S}}) \quad \text{and} \quad t'_{\mathcal{H}} = t_{\mathcal{H}} - t_{\mathsf{bb}} - \theta t_{\mathsf{V}} - t_{\mathsf{P}},$$

where t_{bb} (bb for backbone) is an upper bound on the number of steps needed to run the code of an honest party in one round besides the calls to $M, \mathsf{P}, \mathsf{V}$ (Table 2).

---

[13] $t'_{\mathcal{H}}$ is related to our model and we formally define it in the next paragraph.

We are now ready to state our main computational assumption regarding the honest parties and the adversary. Besides assuming that the total number of steps the honest parties take per round exceed those of the adversary, and that the total block generation rate is bounded, we have to additionally assume that the efficiency of the solving algorithm M used by honest parties is comparable to that of the adversary; i.e, as explained earlier, α should be comparable to $\beta t'_{\mathcal{H}}$, otherwise the adversary will be able to compute long chains of blocks fast and break the security of the protocol. The observation we just made, corresponds to the first condition in our formalization, which we present next. To avoid confusion, we cast most of our analysis based on the δ parameter. Furthermore, note that under optimal conditions – i.e., δ_{ISP} close to 0 and $t_{\mathsf{P}}, t_{\mathsf{V}}, t_{\mathsf{E}}, t_{\mathsf{S}}, t_{\mathsf{nps}}, t_{\mathsf{mal}}$ a lot smaller than $t_{\mathcal{H}}$ – our assumption allows for an adversary that controls up to $1/3$ of the total computational power available (vs. $1/2$ in the RO model).

Assumption 2. *There exist $\delta_{\mathsf{ISP}}, \delta_{\mathsf{Steps}}$ and $\delta \in (0,1)$, such that for sufficiently large $\lambda \in \mathbb{N}$:*

- $\alpha \geq (1 - \delta_{\mathsf{ISP}})\beta t'_{\mathcal{H}} > \mathsf{negl}(\lambda)$ *(ISP generation gap)*
- $(n - t)t'_{\mathcal{H}}(1 - \delta_{\mathsf{Steps}}) \geq 2 \cdot t'_{\mathcal{A}}$ *(steps gap)*
- $\frac{\delta_{\mathsf{Steps}} - \delta_{\mathsf{ISP}}}{2} \geq \delta > \beta(t'_{\mathcal{A}} + nt_{\mathcal{H}})$ *(bounded block generation rate)*

Next, we focus on structural properties of blockchains in our protocol. We follow a similar approach to [36] based on a collisions resistant hash function. Observe that the hash structure of any blockchain in our protocol is similar to the Merkle-Damgard transform [24], defined as:

$$\mathsf{MD}(IV, (x_i)_{i \in [m]}) : z = IV; \text{ for } i = 1 \text{ to } m \text{ do } z = H(z\|x_i); \text{ return } z,$$

where H is the hash function described in the CRS, and IV is set to B_{Gen}. Based on this observation, as in [36], we can show that no efficient adversary can find distinct chains with the same hash value, as this would result to finding a collision on the underlying hash function. Due to space limitations we point to the full version of the paper for the proof.

Lemma 1. *Let $\mathcal{H}$ be a collision-resistant hash function family. The probability that any PPT RAM $\mathcal{A}$, given B_{Gen}, can find two distinct valid chains $\mathcal{C}_1, \mathcal{C}_2$ such that $H(\mathcal{C}_1) = H(\mathcal{C}_2)$, is negligible in λ.*

Lemma 1 implies that insertion and copy properties[14] of [31], that have to do with the way blocks are connected, do not occur with overwhelming probability in λ.

Definition 14. *An* insertion *occurs when, given a chain $\mathcal{C}$ with two consecutive blocks B and B_0, a block B^* created after B_0 is such that B, B^*, B_0 form three consecutive blocks of a valid chain. A* copy *occurs if the same block exists in two different positions.*

---

[14] A third property, called "prediction," also introduced in [31], is not needed in our proof as it is captured by the fact that the ISP is hard even in the presence of adversarial precomputation.

Corollary 1. *Let $\mathcal{H}$ be a collision-resistant hash function family. Then, for any PPT $\mathcal{A}, \mathcal{Z}$ no insertions or copies occur in $\text{VIEW}^{t,n}_{\Pi^{\text{new}}_{\text{PL}}, \mathcal{A}, \mathcal{Z}}$ with probability $1 - \text{negl}(\lambda)$.*

We proceed to the main part of the analysis. First, we introduce some useful notation. For each round j, we define the Boolean random variables X_j and Y_j as follows. Let $X_j = 1$ if and only if j was a *successful round*, i.e., at least one honest party computed a witness at round j, and let $Y_j = 1$ if and only if j was a *uniquely successful round*, i.e., *exactly one honest party* computed a witness at round j. With respect to a set of rounds R, let $X(R) = \sum_{j \in R} X_j$ and define $Y(R)$ similarly.

Moreover, with respect to some block B computed by an honest party P at some round r, let $Z^P_r(R)$ denote the maximum number of distinct blocks diffused by the adversary during R that have B as their ancestor and lie on the same chain; note that honest parties compute at most one block per round. If P is corrupted or did not compute any block at r, let $Z^P_r(R) = 0$. We extend the definition of random variable $X(R)$ to $X^P_r(R)$ similarly.

An important part of our analysis will be to establish lower and upper bounds for these random variables. First, in Lemma 3 we will show that the rate at which the adversary produces witnesses is upper bounded by $\beta \cdot t'_{\mathcal{A}}$. Then, in Lemma 4 we prove that the expected rate of successful and uniquely successful rounds is lower bounded by f and γ, respectively, both defined below:

$$f = 1 - (1 - \alpha)^{n-t} \text{ and } \gamma = (n - t) \cdot \alpha \cdot (1 - \beta t_{\mathcal{H}})^{n-1}$$

Finally, for our analysis to go through, γ should be twice as big as $\beta \cdot t'_{\mathcal{A}}$. As we demonstrate next, this follows from the fact that in Assumption 2 the honest parties take at least double the steps the adversary takes per round.

Lemma 2. *Assume an ISP that complies with Assumptions 1 and 2. It holds that $\gamma \geq 2(1 + \delta)\beta t'_{\mathcal{A}}$.*

Proof. For γ it holds that:

$$\gamma = (n - t) \cdot \alpha \cdot (1 - \beta t_{\mathcal{H}})^{n-1} \geq (n - t) \cdot \alpha \cdot (1 - \beta t_{\mathcal{H}} n)$$
$$\geq (n - t) \cdot (1 - \delta_{\text{ISP}}) \cdot \beta t'_{\mathcal{H}} \cdot (1 - \delta) \geq \frac{(1 - \delta_{\text{ISP}})(1 - \delta)}{(1 - \delta_{\text{Steps}})} \cdot 2 \cdot \beta t'_{\mathcal{A}} \geq 2(1 + \delta)\beta t'_{\mathcal{A}}$$

where we have first used Bernouli's inequality, and then the three conditions from Assumption 2. The last inequality follows from the fact that $\frac{\delta_{\text{Steps}} - \delta_{\text{ISP}}}{2} \geq \delta$. $\square$

As promised, we prove next that the adversary cannot mine blocks extending a single chain, with rate and probability better than that of breaking the iterative hardness property. Due to space limitations we only give a proof sketch, and point to the full version of the paper for the proof.

Lemma 3. *For any set of consecutive rounds R, where $|R| \geq k_{\text{hard}}/\beta t'_{\mathcal{A}}$, for any party P, and any round $i \in R$, the probability that $Z^P_i(R) \geq \beta t'_{\mathcal{A}}|R|$ is $\text{negl}(\lambda)$.*

(Proof Sketch.). W.l.o.g., let i be the first round of $R = \{i'|i \leq i' < i+s\}$, and let E be the event where in $\text{VIEW}^{t,n}_{\Pi^{\text{new}}_{\text{PL}},\mathcal{A},\mathcal{Z}}$ party P at round i mined a block B, and the adversary mined at least $\beta t'_{\mathcal{A}} s$ blocks until round $i+s$ that extend B and are part of a single chain. For the sake of contradiction, assume that the lemma does not hold, and thus $\Pr[E]$ is non-negligible. Using $\mathcal{A}$, we will construct an adversary $\mathcal{A}' = (\mathcal{A}'_1, \mathcal{A}'_2)$ that breaks the iterative hardness (Definition 8) of $\mathcal{I}$ with non-negligible probability.

$\mathcal{A}'$ is going to run internally $\mathcal{A}$ and $\mathcal{Z}$, while at the same time simulating the work honest parties do using the NIZK proof simulator. Moreover, $\mathcal{A}'$ is also going to use the witness malleability property, to trick $\mathcal{A}$ to produce blocks in a sequence, instead of interleaved adversarial and (simulated) honest blocks. Finally, using the NIZK extractor, $\mathcal{A}'$ is going to extract the witnesses from the adversarial blocks, and win the iterative hardness game. By a hybrid argument, we can show that the view of $\mathcal{A}, \mathcal{Z}$ is indistinguishable both in the real and the simulated run, and thus the probability that E happens will be the same in both cases, i.e., non-negligible.

We can do exactly the same reduction without simulating honest parties' work. Then, the total running time of the second stage of $\mathcal{A}'$ is $s \cdot (t'_{\mathcal{A}} + nt'_{\mathcal{H}})$-bounded. Hence, we can derive the following bound on the longest chain that can be produced by both honest and malicious parties during a certain number of rounds.

Corollary 2. *For any set of consecutive rounds R, where $|R| \geq k_{\text{hard}}/\beta(t'_{\mathcal{A}} + nt'_{\mathcal{H}})$, for any party P, and any round $i \in R$, the probability that $Z^P_i(R) + X^P_i(R) \geq \beta(t'_{\mathcal{A}} + nt'_{\mathcal{H}}) \cdot |R|$ is $\mathsf{negl}(\lambda)$.*

Next, we prove lower bounds on the rate of successful and uniquely successful rounds. In our proof we are going to take advantage of the next-problem simulatable property of $\mathcal{I}$ and the zero-knowledge property of the robust NIZK we are using. The main idea is to first use these two properties and similar arguments as in Lemma 3 to construct an "ideal" execution where: (i) honest parties' behavior is efficiently simulated using Ψ, and (ii) is computationally indistinguishable from the "real" execution. Then, since the outputs of different invocations of the runtime simulator $\Psi(1^\lambda)$ are independent, it will be much easier to establish lower bounds for $X(\cdot)$ and $Y(\cdot)$ in the ideal execution. Finally, due to the fact that the two executions are computationally indistinguishable, and the execution properties we examine can be efficiently checked, it will follow that the same bounds should also hold for the real execution with negligible difference in probability. Due to space limitations we point to the full version of the paper for the proof.

Lemma 4. *For any set of consecutive rounds R, with $|R| \geq \lambda/\gamma\delta^2$, the following two events occur with negligible probability in λ:*

- *the number of uniquely successful rounds in R is less or equal to $(1 - \frac{\delta}{4})\gamma \cdot |R|$;*
- *the number of successful rounds in R is less or equal to $(1 - \frac{\delta}{4})f \cdot |R|$.*

Following the strategy of [31], we are now ready to define the set of *typical executions* for this setting.

Definition 15 (Typical execution). *An execution is* typical *if and only if $\lambda \geq 9/\delta$ and for any set R of consecutive rounds with $|R| \geq \max\{4k_{\mathsf{hard}}, \lambda\}/\gamma\delta^2$, the following hold:*

1. *$Y(R) > (1 - \frac{\delta}{4})\gamma|R|$ and $X(R) > (1 - \frac{\delta}{4})f|R|$;*
2. *for any party P, any round $i \in R$: $Z_i^P(R) < \frac{\gamma}{2(1+\delta)} \cdot |R|$ and $Z_i^P(R) + X_i^P(R) < \beta(t'_{\mathcal{A}} + nt'_{\mathcal{H}}) \cdot |R|$; and*
3. *no insertions and no copies occurred.*

Theorem 1. *An execution is typical with probability $1 - \mathsf{negl}(\lambda)$.*

Having established that typical rounds happen with overwhelming probability, the rest of the proof follows closely that of [31]. The only difference is that to prove the corresponding common-prefix lemma, although we can match blocks mined in uniquely successful rounds to adversarial blocks in one of the two chains that constitute the fork, the typicality of the execution only provides a bound on the maximum number of blocks in a single chain. Hence, only half of the blocks matched must outnumber the uniquely successful rounds in this interval, which is also the reason why our proof only works with an adversary controlling up to $1/3$ of the parties. Due to space limitations we point to the full version of the paper for the details.

Next, we state our theorem. Note that both Consistency and Liveness depend on the convergence parameter k_{hard} of $\mathcal{I}$.

Theorem 2. *Assuming the existence of a collision-resistant hash function family, a one-way trapdoor permutation and a dense cryptosystem (for the NIZK), and a secure ISP problem $\mathcal{I}$ that comply with Assumptions 1 and 2, protocol $\Pi_{\mathsf{PL}}^{\mathsf{new}}$ implements a robust public transaction ledger with parameters $k = \max\{4k_{\mathsf{hard}}, \lambda\}/\gamma\delta$ and $u = 2k/(1 - \frac{\delta}{4})f$, except with negligible probability in λ.*

4.6   Realizing ISPs from Non-idealized Hash Functions

Next, we present a secure ISP problem assuming the existence of a hash function that satisfies both the computational extraction and iterated hardness properties presented in Sect. 3.

Construction 2. *Let $\mathcal{H}$ be a hash function family as in Definitions 5 and 6. Let $T \in \{0,1\}^\lambda$ be a hardness parameter. An instance of a secure ISP is as follows:*

- *I_λ is the uniform distribution over $K(\lambda)$, i.e., $\Lambda = \{k\}$;*
- *$X = \{0,1\}^\lambda, W = \{0,1\}^{2(d-1)\lambda}$;*
- *$R = \{(x,w)|H_k(x||w_1) < T \text{ for } w = w_1||w_2\}$;*
- *$M(x,1)$ iteratively samples w_1 from $\mathcal{U}_{(d-1)\lambda}$, and tests whether $H_k(x||w_1) < T$, until it finds a solution. It then samples a uniformly random w_2 from $\mathcal{U}_{(d-1)\lambda}$, and outputs $w_1||w_2$.*
- *$S(x,w) = H_k(H_k(x||w_1)||w_2)$, for $w = w_1||w_2$.*

Construction 2 is similar to Bitcoin's ISP construction (see Sect. 4.1, Construction 1), with the following differences:

1. In our construction $H_k(x||w_1)$ is required to be smaller than the hardness parameter T, while in Bitcoin $H_k(H_k(x||w_1)||w_2)$ is expected to be small, where w_1 is the hash of some message. This change allows a party who already knows a witness (w_1, w_2) for some statement, to produce a new one by changing w_2 arbitrarily.
2. Each time M tests a new possible witness, w_1 is sampled randomly, instead of just being increased by one, as in Bitcoin. This will help us later on to argue that each test succeeds with probability proportional to T.

Obviously, if used in "native" Bitcoin this construction is totally insecure, as by the time an honest party publishes a block, anyone can compute another valid block with minimal effort. However, it is good enough for our new protocol, where the witnesses are not exposed, and thus only a party who knows a witness can generate new witnesses for free. Next, we argue the security of the construction.

Assuming $\mathcal{H}$ is a computational randomness extractor is sufficient for the security properties that make up a secure ISP, besides hardness, to be satisfied. First, the fact that $H_k(x||w_1)$ is computationally indistinguishable from uniform, for any $x \in X$, implies that the runtime and the output of M are computationally indistinguishable from a process that sampled repeatedly a uniform value from $\{0,1\}^\lambda$ until it finds one that is smaller than T. This in turn implies that the runtime distribution of M is indistinguishable from the geometric distribution with parameter $T/2^\lambda$, and thus the successful ISP property is satisfied. Further, since w_2 is also chosen uniformly at random, we can show that a simulator that samples a random value from $\mathcal{U}_\lambda$ and the geometric distribution, satisfies the next-problem simulatability property. Finally, by resampling a new w_2 uniformly at random, an admissible witness is produced, and the witness malleability property follows. Thus, we are able to state the following lemma. Due to space limitations we point to the full version of the paper for the proof.

Lemma 5. *If $\mathcal{H}$ is a CRE hash family (Definition 5), then Construction 2 is $O(\lambda)$-next-problem simulatable, $O(\lambda)$-witness malleable, and $(t, \mathcal{C}_{T/2^\lambda}(O(t)))$-successful for any $t \in poly(\lambda)$, where $\mathcal{C}_{T/2^\lambda}$ is the cumulative geometric distribution with parameter $T/2^\lambda$.*

Regarding the hard-ISP property, we are going to take advantage of the iterative hardness of Bitcoin's ISP construction and the fact that Construction 2 is closely related to it. The main idea is that if there exists an attacker against our construction, then we can use it to break the iterative hardness property (Definition 6). In more detail, given as input a statement x, the iterated hardness attacker runs the attacker of our construction with input $H(x||w)$, where w is sampled at random. It is easy to see that if $((w_1, w_1'), \ldots, (w_m, w_m'))$ are the witnesses it is going to produce, then $((w, w_1), (w_1', w_2), \ldots, (w_{m-1}', w_m))$ are valid witnesses for Construction 1, and also against the iterative hardness property. The following lemma highlights this relation. Due to space limitations we point to the full version of the paper for the proof.

Lemma 6. *Assume Construction 2 is based on a hash family $\mathcal{H}$ that is CRE and t-iteratively hard. Then, for some polynomial $k_0(\cdot)$, any $\sigma \in (0,1)$ and $t' = \frac{2^\lambda}{(1-\sigma)T}$, Construction 2 is $(t', 1 - t'/t, k_0)$-hard.*

Due to Theorem 2 and the previous two lemmas, we can implement a ledger assuming the existence of a robust NIZK, a hash family that is collision-resistant, another hash function family that is both CRE and iteratively hard for appropriate parameters, and that the adversary controls less than a third of the total computational power. The following theorem holds.[15] Due to space limitations we point to the full version of the paper for the proof.

Theorem 3. *Assuming the existence of collision-resistant hash functions, a hash function family that is CRE and t_{hard}-iteratively hard, a one-way trapdoor permutation and a dense cryptosystem (for the NIZK), and that for some $\delta_{\mathsf{Steps}} \in (0,1)$, sufficiently large $\lambda \in \mathbb{N}$, and T equal to $\lfloor 2^\lambda \cdot \min\{\frac{\ln((1-\delta_{\mathsf{Steps}}^2/4)^{-1})}{t'_{\mathcal{H}}}, \frac{\delta_{\mathsf{Steps}}/4}{(t'_{\mathcal{A}}+nt'_{\mathcal{H}})(1+\delta_{\mathsf{Steps}}/2)}\}\rfloor$ it holds that :*

- $t_{\mathsf{hard}} \geq (1 + \delta_{\mathsf{Steps}}/2)^{-1} \cdot \frac{2^\lambda}{T}$; and
- $2 \cdot t'_{\mathcal{A}} \leq (1 - \delta_{\mathsf{Steps}}) \cdot (n - t)t'_{\mathcal{H}}$

protocol $\Pi_{\mathsf{PL}}^{\mathsf{new}}$ based on Construction 2 implements a robust public transaction ledger, except with negligible probability in λ.

A   Cryptographic Primitives and Building Blocks

In this section we provide formal definitions for additional cryptographic primitives used throughout the paper.

Randomness Extractors. We make use of the notion of *weak* computational randomness extractors, as formalized in [22].

Definition 16. *An extractor is a family of functions $\mathsf{Ext} = \{\mathsf{Ext}_\lambda : \{0,1\}^{n(\lambda)} \times \{0,1\}^{d(\lambda)} \to \{0,1\}^{m(\lambda)}\}_{\lambda \in \mathbb{N}}$, where $n(\cdot), d(\cdot)$ and $m(\cdot)$ are polynomials. The extractor is called weak $k(\cdot)$-computational if Ext_λ is PPT, and for all efficiently samplable probability ensembles $\{X_\lambda\}_\lambda$ with min-entropy $k(\lambda)$:*

$$(\mathsf{Ext}_\lambda(X_\lambda, U_{d(\lambda)}))_{\lambda \in \mathbb{N}} \stackrel{c}{\approx} (U_{m(\lambda)})_{\lambda \in \mathbb{N}}$$

where computational indistinguishability is defined w.r.t. a non-uniform distinguisher.

Robust Non-interactive Zero-Knowledge. We make use of the following composable notion of non-interactive zero-knowledge, introduced in [52].

---

[15] For simplicity, we assume that the cost in computational steps of evaluating H, and the hidden constant in the successful property of Lemma 5 are both 1. The theorem can be easily generalized for arbitrary costs.

Definition 17. *Given an NP relation* R, *let* $L = \{x : \exists w \ s.t. \ R(x, w) = 1\}$. $\Pi = (q, \mathsf{P}, \mathsf{V}, \mathsf{S} = (\mathsf{S}_1, \mathsf{S}_2), \mathsf{E})$ *is a robust NIZK argument for* L, *if* $\mathsf{P}, \mathsf{V}, \mathsf{S}, \mathsf{E} \in$ *PPT and* $q(\cdot)$ *is a polynomial such that the following conditions hold:*

1. *Completeness. For all* $x \in L$ *of length* λ, *all* w *such that* $R(x, w) = 1$, *and all* $\Omega \in \{0, 1\}^{q(\lambda)}$, $\mathsf{V}(\Omega, x, \mathsf{P}(\Omega, w, x))] = 1$.
2. *Multi-theorem zero-knowledge. For all PPT adversaries* $\mathcal{A}$, *we have that* $\mathrm{REAL}(\lambda) \approx \mathrm{SIM}(\lambda)$, *where*

$$\mathrm{REAL}(\lambda) = \{\Omega \leftarrow \{0, 1\}^{q(\lambda)}; out \leftarrow \mathcal{A}^{\mathsf{P}(\Omega, \cdot, \cdot)}(\Omega); Output \ out\},$$

$$\mathrm{SIM}(\lambda) = \{(\Omega, tk) \leftarrow \mathsf{S}_1(1^\lambda); out \leftarrow \mathcal{A}^{\mathsf{S}_2'(\Omega, \cdot, \cdot, tk)}(\Omega); Output \ out\},$$

and $\mathsf{S}_2'(\Omega, x, w, tk) \overset{def}{=} \mathsf{S}_2(\Omega, x, tk)$ *if* $(x, w) \in R$, *and outputs* failure *if* $(x, w) \notin R$.
3. *Extractability. There exists a PPT algorithm* E *such that, for all PPT* $\mathcal{A}$,

$$\Pr\left[\begin{array}{l}(\Omega, tk) \leftarrow \mathsf{S}_1(1^\lambda); (x, \pi) \leftarrow \mathcal{A}^{\mathsf{S}_2(\Omega, \cdot, tk)}(\Omega); w \leftarrow \mathsf{E}(\Omega, (x, \pi), tk) : \\ R(x, w) \neq 1 \wedge (x, \pi) \notin \mathcal{Q} \wedge \mathsf{V}(\Omega, x, \pi) = 1\end{array}\right] \leq \mathsf{negl}(\lambda)$$

where $\mathcal{Q}$ *contains the successful pairs* (x_i, π_i) *that* $\mathcal{A}$ *has queried to* S_2.

As in [28], we also require that the proof system supports labels. That is, algorithms $\mathsf{P}, \mathsf{V}, \mathsf{S}, \mathsf{E}$ take as input a label ϕ, and the completeness, zero-knowledge and extractability properties are updated accordingly. This can be achieved by adding the label ϕ to the statement x. In particular, we write $\mathsf{P}^\phi(\Omega, x, w)$ and $\mathsf{V}^\phi(\Omega, x, \pi)$ for the prover and the verifier, and $\mathsf{S}_2^\phi(\Omega, x, tk)$ and $\mathsf{E}^\phi(\Omega, (x, \pi), tk)$ for the simulator and the extractor.

Theorem 4. ([52]). *Assuming trapdoor permutations and a dense cryptosystem exist, robust NIZK arguments exist for all languages in* $\mathcal{NP}$.

B Iterated Hardness is Necessary

In this section, we demonstrate that an attack against iterated hardness implies an attack against the Bitcoin protocol, assuming the underlying hash function is collision-resistant and CRE (Definition 5). We phrase our attack against an abstraction of the Bitcoin protocol which appeared in [31], from which it is straightforward to extract a version of the protocol for our model. The main idea of the attack, is that if the hash function is CRE and not iteratively hard for appropriate parameters, then while honest parties' chains will grow at a fixed rate due to the CRE property, Bitcoin protocol's adversary can use the iterated hardness adversary to quickly produce a longer chain and break consistency. Due to space limitations we point to the full version of the paper for the proof.

Theorem 5. *Let* $n, t, t_\mathcal{H}, t_\mathcal{A}$ *such that* $t_\mathcal{A} = c \cdot (n - t)t_\mathcal{H}$, *for some* $c \in (0, 1)$. *If* $\mathcal{H}$ *is collision-resistant and CRE, and the Bitcoin protocol from [31] satisfies Consistency with parameter* k, *then* $\mathcal{H}$ *is* $\frac{c}{2} \cdot \frac{(n-t)t_\mathcal{H}}{(1-T/2^\lambda)^{(n-t)t_\mathcal{H}}}$-*iteratively hard, for any polynomial* k.

As expected, as the computational power of the adversary decreases, the iteratively hard hash function needs to be less secure.

References

1. Alwen, J., Tackmann, B.: Moderately hard functions: definition, instantiations, and applications. In: Kalai, Y., Reyzin, L. (eds.) TCC 2017. LNCS, vol. 10677, pp. 493–526. Springer, Cham (2017). https://doi.org/10.1007/978-3-319-70500-2_17
2. Andrychowicz, M., Dziembowski, S.: PoW-based distributed cryptography with no trusted setup. In: Gennaro, R., Robshaw, M. (eds.) CRYPTO 2015. LNCS, vol. 9216, pp. 379–399. Springer, Heidelberg (2015). https://doi.org/10.1007/978-3-662-48000-7_19
3. Aspnes, J., Jackson, C., Krishnamurthy, A.: Exposing computationally-challenged Byzantine impostors. Technical Report YALEU/DCS/TR-1332, Yale University Department of Computer Science, July 2005
4. Back, A.: Hashcash-a denial of service counter-measure (2002)
5. Badertscher, C., Maurer, U., Tschudi, D., Zikas, V.: Bitcoin as a transaction ledger: a composable treatment. In: Katz, J., Shacham, H. (eds.) CRYPTO 2017. LNCS, vol. 10401, pp. 324–356. Springer, Cham (2017). https://doi.org/10.1007/978-3-319-63688-7_11
6. Ball, M., Rosen, A., Sabin, M., Vasudevan, P.N.: Proofs of work from worst-case assumptions. In: Shacham, H., Boldyreva, A. (eds.) CRYPTO 2018. LNCS, vol. 10991, pp. 789–819. Springer, Cham (2018). https://doi.org/10.1007/978-3-319-96884-1_26
7. Bellare, M., Canetti, R., Krawczyk, H.: Pseudorandom functions revisited: the cascade construction and its concrete security. In: 37th Annual Symposium on Foundations of Computer Science, FOCS 1996, Burlington, Vermont, USA, 14–16 October 1996, pp. 514–523 (1996)
8. Bellare, M., Desai, A., Jokipii, E., Rogaway, P.: A concrete security treatment of symmetric encryption. In: FOCS 1997, pp. 394–403 (1997)
9. Bellare, M., Jaeger, J., Len, J.: Better than advertised: improved collision-resistance guarantees for md-based hash functions. In: CCS 2017, pp. 891–906. ACM, New York (2017)
10. Bellare, M., Rogaway, P.: Random oracles are practical: a paradigm for designing efficient protocols. In: CCS 1993 (1993)
11. Bellare, M., Rogaway, P.: The exact security of digital signatures-how to sign with RSA and Rabin. In: Maurer, U. (ed.) EUROCRYPT 1996. LNCS, vol. 1070, pp. 399–416. Springer, Heidelberg (1996). https://doi.org/10.1007/3-540-68339-9_34
12. Bernstein, D.J., Lange, T.: Non-uniform cracks in the concrete: the power of free precomputation. In: Sako, K., Sarkar, P. (eds.) ASIACRYPT 2013. LNCS, vol. 8270, pp. 321–340. Springer, Heidelberg (2013). https://doi.org/10.1007/978-3-642-42045-0_17
13. Bitansky, N., Goldwasser, S., Jain, A., Paneth, O., Vaikuntanathan, V., Waters, B.: Time-lock puzzles from randomized encodings. In: Sudan, M. (ed.) Proceedings of the 2016 ACM Conference on Innovations in Theoretical Computer Science, Cambridge, MA, USA, 14–16 January 2016, pp. 345–356. ACM (2016)
14. Boneh, D., Bonneau, J., Bünz, B., Fisch, B.: Verifiable delay functions. In: Shacham, H., Boldyreva, A. (eds.) CRYPTO 2018. LNCS, vol. 10991, pp. 757–788. Springer, Cham (2018). https://doi.org/10.1007/978-3-319-96884-1_25

15. Boneh, D., Naor, M.: Timed commitments. In: Bellare, M. (ed.) CRYPTO 2000. LNCS, vol. 1880, pp. 236–254. Springer, Heidelberg (2000). https://doi.org/10. 1007/3-540-44598-6_15

16. Canetti, R.: Security and composition of multiparty cryptographic protocols. J. Cryptol. **13**(1), 143–202 (2000)

17. Canetti, R.: Universally composable security: a new paradigm for cryptographic protocols. In: 42nd Annual Symposium on Foundations of Computer Science, FOCS 2001, 14–17 October 2001, Las Vegas, Nevada, USA, pp. 136–145. IEEE Computer Society (2001)

18. Canetti, R., Chen, Y., Reyzin, L., Rothblum, R.D.: Fiat-Shamir and correlation intractability from strong KDM-secure encryption. In: Nielsen, J.B., Rijmen, V. (eds.) EUROCRYPT 2018. LNCS, vol. 10820, pp. 91–122. Springer, Cham (2018). https://doi.org/10.1007/978-3-319-78381-9_4

19. Canetti, R., Fischlin, M.: Universally composable commitments. In: Kilian, J. (ed.) CRYPTO 2001. LNCS, vol. 2139, pp. 19–40. Springer, Heidelberg (2001). https:// doi.org/10.1007/3-540-44647-8_2

20. Canetti, R., Goldreich, O., Halevi, S.: The random oracle methodology, revisited. J. ACM **51**(4), 557–594 (2004)

21. Cramer, R., Shoup, V.: Universal hash proofs and a paradigm for adaptive chosen ciphertext secure public-key encryption. In: Knudsen, L.R. (ed.) EUROCRYPT 2002. LNCS, vol. 2332, pp. 45–64. Springer, Heidelberg (2002). https://doi.org/10. 1007/3-540-46035-7_4

22. Dachman-Soled, D., Gennaro, R., Krawczyk, H., Malkin, T.: Computational extractors and pseudorandomness. In: Cramer, R. (ed.) TCC 2012. LNCS, vol. 7194, pp. 383–403. Springer, Heidelberg (2012). https://doi.org/10.1007/978-3-642-28914-9_22

23. Damgård, I.B.: Collision free hash functions and public key signature schemes. In: Chaum, D., Price, W.L. (eds.) EUROCRYPT 1987. LNCS, vol. 304, pp. 203–216. Springer, Heidelberg (1988). https://doi.org/10.1007/3-540-39118-5_19

24. Damgård, I.B.: A design principle for hash functions. In: Brassard, G. (ed.) CRYPTO 1989. LNCS, vol. 435, pp. 416–427. Springer, New York (1990). https:// doi.org/10.1007/0-387-34805-0_39

25. Dodis, Y., Gennaro, R., Håstad, J., Krawczyk, H., Rabin, T.: Randomness extraction and key derivation using the CBC, Cascade and HMAC modes. In: Franklin, M. (ed.) CRYPTO 2004. LNCS, vol. 3152, pp. 494–510. Springer, Heidelberg (2004). https://doi.org/10.1007/978-3-540-28628-8_30

26. Douceur, J.R.: The sybil attack. In: Druschel, P., Kaashoek, F., Rowstron, A. (eds.) IPTPS 2002. LNCS, vol. 2429, pp. 251–260. Springer, Heidelberg (2002). https:// doi.org/10.1007/3-540-45748-8_24

27. Dwork, C., Naor, M.: Pricing via processing or combatting Junk Mail. In: Brickell, E.F. (ed.) CRYPTO 1992. LNCS, vol. 740, pp. 139–147. Springer, Heidelberg (1993). https://doi.org/10.1007/3-540-48071-4_10

28. Faust, S., Mukherjee, P., Nielsen, J.B., Venturi, D.: Continuous non-malleable codes. In: Lindell, Y. (ed.) TCC 2014. LNCS, vol. 8349, pp. 465–488. Springer, Heidelberg (2014). https://doi.org/10.1007/978-3-642-54242-8_20

29. Fiat, A., Shamir, A.: How to prove yourself: practical solutions to identification and signature problems. In: Odlyzko, A.M. (ed.) CRYPTO 1986. LNCS, vol. 263, pp. 186–194. Springer, Heidelberg (1987). https://doi.org/10.1007/3-540-47721-7_12

30. Garay, J., Kiayias, A.: SoK: a consensus taxonomy in the blockchain era. In: Jarecki, S. (ed.) CT-RSA 2020. LNCS, vol. 12006, pp. 284–318. Springer, Cham (2020). https://doi.org/10.1007/978-3-030-40186-3_13

31. Garay, J., Kiayias, A., Leonardos, N.: The bitcoin backbone protocol: analysis and applications. In: Oswald, E., Fischlin, M. (eds.) EUROCRYPT 2015. LNCS, vol. 9057, pp. 281–310. Springer, Heidelberg (2015). https://doi.org/10.1007/978-3-662-46803-6_10

32. Garay, J.A., Kiayias, A., Leonardos, N.: The bitcoin backbone protocol: analysis and applications. IACR Cryptol. ePrint Arch. **2014**, 765 (2014)

33. Garay, J., Kiayias, A., Leonardos, N.: The bitcoin backbone protocol with chains of variable difficulty. In: Katz, J., Shacham, H. (eds.) CRYPTO 2017. LNCS, vol. 10401, pp. 291–323. Springer, Cham (2017). https://doi.org/10.1007/978-3-319-63688-7_10

34. Garay, J.A., Kiayias, A., Leonardos, N., Panagiotakos, G.: Bootstrapping the blockchain, with applications to consensus and fast PKI setup. In: Abdalla, M., Dahab, R. (eds.) PKC 2018. LNCS, vol. 10770, pp. 465–495. Springer, Cham (2018). https://doi.org/10.1007/978-3-319-76581-5_16

35. Garay, J.A., Kiayias, A., Panagiotakos, G.: Blockchains from non-idealized hash functions. Cryptology ePrint Archive, Report 2019/315 (2019). https://eprint.iacr.org/2019/315

36. Garay, J.A., Kiayias, A., Panagiotakos, G.: Consensus from signatures of work. In: Jarecki, S. (ed.) CT-RSA 2020. LNCS, vol. 12006, pp. 319–344. Springer, Cham (2020). https://doi.org/10.1007/978-3-030-40186-3_14

37. Garay, J.A., MacKenzie, P., Prabhakaran, M., Yang, K.: Resource fairness and composability of cryptographic protocols. J. Cryptol. **24** (2011)

38. Gentry, C., Wichs, D.: Separating succinct non-interactive arguments from all falsifiable assumptions. In: Fortnow, L., Vadhan, S.P. (eds.) STOC 2011. ACM (2011)

39. Goldreich, O.: Foundations of Cryptography, vol. 1. Cambridge University Press, New York (2006)

40. Goldwasser, S., Kalai, Y.T.: On the (in)security of the Fiat-Shamir paradigm. In: Foundations of Computer Science (FOCS 2003). IEEE Computer Society (2003)

41. Juels, A., Brainard, J.G.: Client puzzles: a cryptographic countermeasure against connection depletion attacks. In: NDSS 1999. The Internet Society (1999)

42. Katz, J., Miller, A., Shi, E.: Pseudonymous secure computation from time-lock puzzles. IACR Cryptology ePrint Archive 2014:857 (2014)

43. Krawczyk, H.: Cryptographic extraction and key derivation: the HKDF scheme. In: Rabin, T. (ed.) CRYPTO 2010. LNCS, vol. 6223, pp. 631–648. Springer, Heidelberg (2010). https://doi.org/10.1007/978-3-642-14623-7_34

44. Lenstra, A.K., Wesolowski, B.: A random zoo: sloth, unicorn, and trx. Cryptology ePrint Archive, Report 2015/366 (2015). https://eprint.iacr.org/2015/366

45. Maurer, U. (ed.): EUROCRYPT 1996. LNCS, vol. 1070. Springer, Heidelberg (1996). https://doi.org/10.1007/3-540-68339-9

46. Nakamoto, S.: Bitcoin: a peer-to-peer electronic cash system (2008). http://bitcoin.org/bitcoin.pdf

47. Nielsen, J.B.: Separating random oracle proofs from complexity theoretic proofs: the non-committing encryption case. In: Yung, M. (ed.) CRYPTO 2002. LNCS, vol. 2442, pp. 111–126. Springer, Heidelberg (2002). https://doi.org/10.1007/3-540-45708-9_8

48. Nisan, N., Zuckerman, D.: Randomness is linear in space. J. Comput. Syst. Sci. **52**(1), 43–52 (1996)

49. Pass, R., Seeman, L., Shelat, A.: Analysis of the blockchain protocol in asynchronous networks. In: Coron, J.-S., Nielsen, J.B. (eds.) EUROCRYPT 2017. LNCS, vol. 10211, pp. 643–673. Springer, Cham (2017). https://doi.org/10.1007/978-3-319-56614-6_22

50. Pointcheval, D., Stern, J.: Security proofs for signature schemes. In: Maurer, U. (ed.) EUROCRYPT 1996. LNCS, vol. 1070, pp. 387–398. Springer, Heidelberg (1996). https://doi.org/10.1007/3-540-68339-9_33
51. Rivest, R.L., Shamir, A., Wagner, D.A.: Time-lock puzzles and timed-release crypto. Technical report, Cambridge, MA, USA (1996)
52. De Santis, A., Di Crescenzo, G., Ostrovsky, R., Persiano, G., Sahai, A.: Robust non-interactive zero knowledge. In: Kilian, J. (ed.) CRYPTO 2001. LNCS, vol. 2139, pp. 566–598. Springer, Heidelberg (2001). https://doi.org/10.1007/3-540-44647-8_33

Ledger Combiners for Fast Settlement

Matthias Fitzi[1(✉)], Peter Gaži[1], Aggelos Kiayias[1,2], and Alexander Russell[1,3]

[1] IOHK, Hong Kong, China
{Matthias.Fitzi,Peter.Gazi,Aggelos.Kiayias,Alexander.Russell}@iohk.io
[2] University of Edinburgh, Edinburgh, UK
[3] University of Connecticut, Storrs, USA

Abstract. Blockchain protocols based on variations of the longest-chain rule—whether following the proof-of-work paradigm or one of its alternatives—suffer from a fundamental latency barrier. This arises from the need to collect a sufficient number of blocks on top of a transaction-bearing block to guarantee the transaction's stability while limiting the rate at which blocks can be created in order to prevent security-threatening forks. Our main result is a black-box security-amplifying combiner based on parallel composition of m blockchains that achieves $\Theta(m)$-fold security amplification for conflict-free transactions or, equivalently, $\Theta(m)$-fold reduction in latency. Our construction breaks the latency barrier to achieve, for the first time, a ledger based purely on Nakamoto longest-chain consensus guaranteeing worst-case constant-time settlement for conflict-free transactions: settlement can be accelerated to a constant multiple of block propagation time with negligible error.

Operationally, our construction shows how to view any family of blockchains as a unified, virtual ledger without requiring any coordination among the chains or any new protocol metadata. Users of the system have the option to inject a transaction into a single constituent blockchain or—if they desire accelerated settlement—all of the constituent blockchains. Our presentation and proofs introduce a new formalism for reasoning about blockchains, the *dynamic ledger*, and articulate our constructions as transformations of dynamic ledgers that amplify security. We also illustrate the versatility of this formalism by presenting robust-combiner constructions for blockchains that can protect against complete adversarial control of a minority of a family of blockchains.

1 Introduction

Since the appearance of Bitcoin [33] in 2009, dozens of projects from both academia and industry have proposed protocols for maintaining decentralized, robust transaction ledgers in a permissionless setting. The prominent design paradigm in this space comes from the Bitcoin protocol itself, often referred to as "Nakamoto-style" ledger consensus. This approach adopts the *blockchain*—a linearly ordered sequence of blocks, each of which commits to the previous history and may contain new transactions—as the fundamental data structure for maintaining the ledger. The core consensus algorithm then calls for eligible protocol

© International Association for Cryptologic Research 2020
R. Pass and K. Pietrzak (Eds.): TCC 2020, LNCS 12550, pp. 322–352, 2020.
https://doi.org/10.1007/978-3-030-64375-1_12

participants to create transaction-bearing blocks, append them to the longest chain they observe, and broadcast the result; this implicitly declares a "vote" for a unique ordered sequence of past transactions—the ledger. As a result, the immutability of a particular portion of the ledger is not immediate, but rather grows gradually with the number of blocks (representing votes) amassed on top of it in the blockchain. This paradigm has been featured in both theoretical proposals as well as deployed systems and can be instantiated with a wide variety of Sybil-resistant mechanisms such as proof of work (Bitcoin, Ethereum [7] and a vast majority of deployed blockchains), proof of stake [2,3,11,12,24], proof of space [10,34], and others.

In terms of performance, one of the key measures of interest for any distributed ledger protocol is *latency*, also called *settlement time*. Roughly speaking, this is the time elapsed between the moment a signed transaction is injected into the protocol and the time it becomes universally recognized as immutable. While Nakamoto-style consensus protocols have attracted attention both for their simplicity and for various desirable security features,[1] they appear to face a fundamental barrier when it comes to latency. Informally, for a transaction to become accepted as stable, a sufficient number of blocks (representing an agreement over a representative fraction of the parties, weighted according to the Sybil-resistant mechanism in place) must be collected on top of the block containing this transaction. However, blocks can only be created at a limited rate dictated by the delays introduced by the underlying communication network: if blocks are routinely created by participants that have not yet received recent previous blocks, forks in the blockchain appear even without adversarial interference. These forks then result in a division of the honest majority and represent a threat to the protocol's security. This relationship is now quite well understood [35].

One way to address this disadvantage without giving up on the Nakamoto paradigm (and its advantages) is to carefully design overlay structures on top of the plain Nakamoto-style blockchain. Several such proposals exist, and can be roughly split into two categories. The first group of proposals (e.g., [27,36, 38]) still produces a full ledger of all settled transactions, but relies on stronger assumptions for their latency improvement, such as a higher threshold of honest participants. The second category are so-called layer-2 designs implementing payment [14,41] or state [15] channels that only need limited interaction with the slow blockchain; however, they divert from the original goal of maintaining a distributed ledger of all executed transactions. Hence, the following fundamental question remains:

What is the fastest achievable settlement time for Nakamoto-style consensus?

This question has also been recently addressed by elegant concurrent work on the Prism protocol [5], albeit with somewhat different goals; we give a detailed comparison between our work and [5] in Sect. 1.2.

---

[1] For example, they can provide security in the Byzantine setting with simple honest majority [9,36,38], and resilience against fluctuating participation [2,37].

1.1 Our Contributions

We approach the challenge of designing low-latency ledgers by introducing a black-box technique for "combining" a family of existing ledgers into a new, virtual ledger that provides amplified security properties. Our technique results in a system with striking simplicity: The construction gives *a deterministic rule for interpreting an arbitrary family of m constituent ledgers as a single virtual ledger*. Participants of the system maintain their current view of each constituent ledger and, via this interpretation, a view of the master combined ledger. Users simply inject their transactions into the constituent ledgers as usual. We show that when users inject transactions into a single constituent ledger they are provided with settlement guarantees (in the virtual ledger) roughly consistent with those offered by the constituent ledgers. On the other hand, when a conflict-free transaction is injected into all of the constituent ledgers, it enjoys a $1/\Theta(m)$ *multiplicative improvement in settlement time*. Of course, settlement time cannot be reduced beyond the time required for a block to be transmitted across the network; however, our results adapt smoothly to this limit; in particular, by taking m to scale with the security parameter of the system, we obtain $O(1)$ settlement time for conflict-free transactions (except with negligible probability). We remark that in cryptocurrency ledgers, such as Bitcoin, transaction issuers always have the option to submit conflict-free transactions so that the assumption is not a limitation. While the results do not require any specific coordination among the ledgers, they naturally require a measure of stochastic independence; we discuss this in detail below.

We present our results by formulating an abstract notion which we call a *dynamic ledger*. Our constructions transform a family of such dynamic ledgers into an associated dynamic ledger (as indicated above) in a way that amplifies the security properties. Typical blockchain algorithms are direct instantiations of this abstraction: our techniques can thus be applied in wide generality to existing blockchains such Bitcoin, Ethereum, Ouroboros, etc.

Such a transformation is a "combiner" in the classical cryptographic sense of the word: an operator for cryptographic primitives that acts in a black-box manner on a number of underlying implementations of a primitive with the objective of realizing a strengthened implementation of the same primitive. This folklore idea in cryptography first received an explicit treatment by Herzberg [23]. One of the objectives for developing combiners—especially prominent in the context of hash functions—was the concept of *robustness*. In particular, a robust combiner maintains the security of the combined implementation despite the security failure of any number (up to a threshold) of the underlying input implementations. Another objective for developing combiners is *amplification*: In an amplification combiner, the goal is to improve a certain security property of the combined implementation to a level that goes significantly beyond the security offered by the underlying input implementations. The combiner discussed above is of the amplification variety; later in the paper, we also show how to achieve robustness in our setting.

With this summary behind us, we describe our contributions in more detail.

A Model for Abstract Ledgers. We provide a new mathematical abstraction of a distributed ledger that can be used to reflect an arbitrary ledger protocol, but is particularly well-suited for describing Nakamoto-style blockchains with eventual-consensus behavior (regardless of their underlying Sybil-resistant election mechanism). Its main design goals are generality and simplicity, so as to allow for a clean study of generic constructions with such ledgers that is unencumbered by the execution details of the underlying protocols.

Roughly speaking, our abstraction—called a *dynamic ledger*—determines at every point in time (i) a set of transactions that are contained in the ledger; and (ii) a mapping that assigns to each transaction a real value called its *rank*. The rank plays several roles: it is used to order the transactions in the ledger, describe their stability, and maintain a loose connection to actual time; the most natural example of a rank is the timestamp of the transaction's block in Bitcoin. (In fact, a simple monotonicity transform is necessary; see Sect. 4.2.)

A dynamic ledger satisfies three fundamental properties: *liveness, absolute persistence*, and *relative persistence*. The former two properties are direct analogues of the well-established notions of persistence and liveness introduced by previous formalizations of blockchain protocols; the notion of relative persistence is novel. In a nutshell, it is a weakening of absolute persistence that guarantees that the rank of a transaction cannot significantly change in the future; in particular the relative order of the transaction with respect to sufficiently distant transactions is determined. This is particularly useful for reasoning about transaction settlement in the typical setting of interest: when transaction validity depends only on its ordering with respect to *conflicting* transactions. Looking ahead, relative persistence is exactly the notion that allows us to achieve the full benefits of our amplification combiner; it appears to be of independent interest as well, as it also arises naturally in our robust combiner.

A Combiner for Consistency Amplification and Latency Reduction; the Combined Rank Function. Our main technical contribution, discussed briefly above, is an amplification combiner for latency reduction of abstract ledgers. This combiner builds a "combined ledger" (or virtual ledger) as a deterministic function of m underlying dynamic ledgers. Participants insert their transaction into any number of the underlying ledgers, depending on the desired settlement-time guarantees.

The major challenge is the definition and analysis of the combiner rank function. Rank is an abstract notion of position in the ledger that is tethered to absolute time by the security guarantees: for example, in a ledger at time T the probability that a transaction appearing at rank r is later disrupted is a function of $T - r$; the standard case, where the underlying ledgers provide "linear consistency," guarantees consistency error $\exp(-\Omega(T - r))$. Note that, in general, there is no guarantee that transactions will appear in all underlying ledgers so the combined rank function must somehow assign rank in a fashion that appropriately reflects both deep transactions appearing in a single ledger and shallower transactions appearing in many ledgers. This state of affairs introduces two conflicting goals: in order to achieve linear amplification we insist that when a transaction appears in all m ledgers, our constructed ledger yields settlement error $\exp(-\Omega(m(T - r)))$—note the factor of m in the exponent; on the other hand, a transaction appearing in a single ledger will be assigned some finite rank and thus for large values of T we cannot hope to beat $\exp(-\Omega(T - r))$, the consistency guarantee of a single ledger. To realize this, our construction (and combined rank function) is determined by a parameter L which, intuitively, determines the transition between these two regimes. One should think of L proportional to the security parameter of the system, so that $2^{-\Theta(L)}$ is an acceptable bound for undesirable events; thus, injecting a transaction into all the ledgers achieves this $2^{-\Theta(L)}$ security bound $\Theta(m)$ times faster than transactions submitted to a single ledger.

It is a rather remarkable fact that the behavior we demand is provided by the exponential weighting functions that arise naturally in the theory of regret minimization (e.g., the multiplicative weights algorithm [1]). The actual form of our combined rank function is

$$\exp(-\mathsf{combinedRank}(\mathsf{tx})/L) = \frac{1}{m} \sum_{i=1}^{m} \exp(-\mathsf{rank}_i(\mathsf{tx})/L).$$

The (log scale) consistency error achieved by this rank function, when coupled with underlying ledgers that offer linear consistency, is informally illustrated by the blue line in the figure below. The solid black line is the consistency error offered by the underlying ledgers; one can clearly see the region of rapid growth (prior to L) followed by the region where the slope stabilizes to that of the single ledger bounds, as it must. The dotted line has slope exactly m times that of the "single ledger" line, corresponding intuitively to "perfect amplification."

We analyze two extreme scenarios and show that while insertion of a transaction into a single ledger leads to a settlement time comparable to the one provided by the underlying ledgers, inserting the transaction into all m ledgers results in a speed-up by a linear factor $\Theta(m)$. In the natural setting where there is a cost associated with including a transaction in each ledger, we emphasize that the construction yields a trade-off between transaction fee and settlement time: transactions appearing in

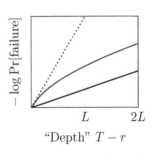

more chains settle faster. The choice can be made on a per-transaction basis by its sender. Moreover, by considering a sufficient number of parallel chains m, this allows us to achieve relative settlement in constant time except with negligible error.

Clearly, amplification-type results can only be obtained under some sort of independence assumption on the underlying ledgers. We characterize a generic (black-box) assumption, called *subindependence*, which is weaker than full independence of the ledgers and sufficient for our results. We also show how subindependence can be naturally achieved by existing techniques in both proof-of-work and proof-of-stake settings; details appear in Sect. 4.1.

Our construction does not require any coordination between the underlying ledgers, it can be deployed on top of existing blockchains without direct cooperation from parties maintaining the ledgers, so long as these ledgers maintain their persistence and liveness guarantees, are sufficiently independent, and allow for inclusion of a sufficiently general class of transaction data.

Finally, we show how our construction can be applied to the most familiar setting of proof-of-work (PoW) blockchains. Specifically, applying our combiner to $m = \lambda$ PoW blockchains yields a construction C providing constant-time relative settlement except with probability negligible in λ, articulated in Theorem 1 below. For concreteness, we work in the synchronous (p, q)-flat PoW model that assumes the existence of n parties, each of which is allowed to issue q PoW queries per round that independently succeed with probability p (see, e.g., [20] for details).

Theorem 1 (Informal). *Let $\epsilon > 0$ and let λ denote the security parameter. There exists a construction C that, if executed in the synchronous (p, q)-flat PoW model with n parties out of which at least a $(1/2 + \varepsilon)$-fraction is honest, achieves relative settlement in time $O(1)$ except with an error probability negligible in λ.*

Hidden in the asymptotic description above is the dependence of p, q, and n on the security parameter λ which must in fact satisfy some natural conditions. We give a formal statement corresponding to Theorem 1, together with a precise description of the construction C, as Corollary 7 in Sect. 4.3.

A simplified illustration of the settlement speed-up provided by our construction is given in the Appendix of the full paper [17].

A Robust Ledger Combiner. As our final contribution, we describe a class of constructions of robust ledger combiners: a black-box construction on top of m ledgers that maintains relative persistence and liveness guarantees even if the contents of a δ-fraction of these ledgers (chosen adaptively) are arbitrarily corrupted, for δ up to $1/2$. The individual constructions in this class are parametrized by the choice of an estimator function that is a part of the combiner's rank function; we show that the concrete choice of this estimator represents a trade-off between δ and the *stability* of the combiner, a metric of how much the ranks of individual transactions in the combiner change as a result of a corruption respecting the δ-threshold. This construction serves as an additional illustration of the generality of our ledger abstraction. We refer the reader to the full paper [17] for the details.

1.2   Related Work

The formal modeling of robust transaction ledgers and blockchain protocols goes back to the property-based analysis of Bitcoin due to Garay et al. [20] and Pass et al. [35]. These works identified the central properties of common prefix, chain growth, and chain quality and demonstrated how they imply the desired persistence and liveness of the resulting ledger. A composable analysis of a blockchain protocol (namely Bitcoin) in the UC framework [8] along with the realized ledger functionality first appeared in [4] and, later, essentially the same functionality was shown to be realized by proof-of-stake protocols in [2,3].

The notion of combiners was formally proposed in [23]. Robust combiners for hash functions were further studied in [6,40] and also applied to other primitives such as oblivious transfer [22]. Amplification combiners were introduced by [16] who also observed that classical results in security amplification can be seen as such combiners. Indistinguishability amplification for random functions and permutations achieved by certain combiners from a class of so-called *neutralizing* constructions was studied both in the information-theoretic [21,28–30,43] and computational [13,26,31,32,39] settings.

Various approaches are known to reduce settlement times of Nakamoto-style blockchains. One approach is to deviate from the single-chain structure, arranging blocks in a directed acyclic graph (DAG) as first suggested by Lerner [25]. Sompolinsky et al. [42] gave a DAG-based construction that substantially reduces settlement times at the expense of giving up on a total order on all transactions in the ledger. Another approach explores "hybrid" protocols where committee-based consensus reduces latency in the optimistic case [36,38]. In context of proof-of-stake, Algorand [9] reduces settlement times over eventual-consensus proof-of-stake protocols by finalizing each block via a Byzantine Agreement subprotocol before moving to the next one. However, Algorand cannot tolerate fluctuating participation or adversarial stake ratio up to $1/2$. Moreover, its constant-time settlement guarantees are only provided *in expectation*, in contrast to our worst-case guarantees.

Concurrent work on the Prism protocol [5] also addressed the efficiency of Nakamoto consensus. (We remark that a preliminary version of this paper [18] was published as an IACR eprint in 2018.) Prism is a concrete, PoW-based ledger protocol optimizing both throughput and latency compared to Bitcoin. Prism similarly approaches the problem by introducing "parallel blockchains," though in a different form. Our approach has some notable advantages in comparison with Prism: (i) our construction is generic and can be deployed on top of existing ledgers with arbitrary Sybil-resistant mechanisms; (ii) we provide worst-case constant-time settlement except with a negligible error probability while Prism (similarly to Algorand) only provides *expected* constant-time settlement; (iii) we base our results on the generic subindependence assumption that is weaker than full independence, which is assumed in Prism (though not achieved by their PoW mechanism). On the other hand, Prism has an important feature which clearly sets it apart from our work: it explicitly models and optimizes throughput. A more detailed comparison between our work and Prism is given in our full paper.

2 The Ledger Abstraction

In this section we define *abstract ledgers* which describe the functionality provided by distributed ledger protocols such as Bitcoin. Our goal here is to capture this behavior in an abstract, high-level manner, which allows us to express our composition results unencumbered by the details of the individual protocols.

2.1 Ledgers and Dynamic Ledgers

We start by defining an abstraction of an individual snapshot of the state of a ledger protocol, which we call a *ledger*. A ledger reflects a collection of *transactions* which are given a linear order by way of a general function called *rank*. As a basis for intuition about our definitions and proofs, we mention that, roughly speaking, Bitcoin realizes such a ledger where the rank function is given by the timestamp corresponding to the block containing the transaction; we give a more detailed discussion in Sect. 4.2.

Our ledger will operate over a *transaction space* which we define first.

Definition 1 (Transaction space). *A transaction space is a pair* $(\mathcal{T}, \prec_{\mathcal{T}})$, *where* $\mathcal{T}$ *is a set of "transactions" and* $\prec_{\mathcal{T}}$ *is a linear order on* $\mathcal{T}$. *A conflict relation* C *on a transaction space* $\mathcal{T}$ *is a symmetric binary relation on* $\mathcal{T}$; *if* $(\mathrm{tx}_1, \mathrm{tx}_2) \in C$ *for two transactions* $\mathrm{tx}_1, \mathrm{tx}_2 \in \mathcal{T}$, *we say that* tx_1 *conflicts with* tx_2, *we write* $\mathrm{conflict}(\mathrm{tx}) \subseteq \mathcal{T}$ *for the set of transactions conflicting with* tx.

The linear order $\prec_{\mathcal{T}}$ on the ambient transaction space $\mathcal{T}$ is largely incidental; it is only used in our setting to break ties among transactions with a common rank. Thus, in practice this linear order can be instantiated with a simple "syntactic" property—such as a lexicographic ordering—rather than an ordering that reflects any semantics about the transactions.

In contrast, if a transaction space is equipped with a conflict relation, this is intended to carry semantic value; in a conventional UTXO transaction model (such as that of many deployed blockchains) two transactions conflict if they share UTXO inputs. As we discuss below, a conflict structure permits a more flexible notion of settlement that is only required to provide strong guarantees for non-conflicting transactions.

Definition 2 (Ledger). *A ledger* $\mathbf{L}$ *for a transaction space* $(\mathcal{T}, \prec_{\mathcal{T}})$ *is a pair* (T, rank) *where:* $T \subseteq \mathcal{T}$ *is a subset of* transactions *and* $\mathrm{rank}: \mathcal{T} \to \mathbb{R}^+ \cup \{\infty\}$ *is a function taking finite values precisely on the set* T; *that is,* $T = \{\mathrm{tx} \in \mathcal{T} \mid \mathrm{rank}(\mathrm{tx}) \neq \infty\}$. *The value* $\mathrm{rank}(\mathrm{tx})$ *is referred to as the* rank *of the transaction* tx. *Notationally, if* $\mathbf{L}$ *is a ledger we routinely overload the symbol* $\mathbf{L}$ *to stand for its set of transactions (the above set* T).

The linear order $\prec_{\mathcal{T}}$ *and the rank function* $\mathrm{rank}(\cdot)$ *induce a linear order* $\prec_{\mathbf{L}}$ *on the ledger by the rule*

$$x \prec_{\mathbf{L}} y :\Leftrightarrow (\mathrm{rank}(x) < \mathrm{rank}(y) \vee (\mathrm{rank}(x) = \mathrm{rank}(y) \wedge x \prec_{\mathcal{T}} y)) \,.$$

(Thus the underlying total order $\prec_T$ is only used to "break ties.")

For a ledger $\mathbf{L} = (T, \mathsf{rank})$ and a threshold r, we let $\mathbf{L} \lceil r \rceil \overset{\text{def}}{=} (T', \mathsf{rank}')$ denote the ledger consisting of transactions $T' \overset{\text{def}}{=} \{\mathsf{tx} \in T \mid \mathsf{rank}(\mathsf{tx}) \leq r\}$ with the inherited rank function: $\mathsf{rank}'(\mathsf{tx}) = \mathsf{rank}(\mathsf{tx})$ for all $\mathsf{tx} \in T'$ and equal to ∞ otherwise. Similarly, for a transaction $\mathsf{tx} \in \mathbf{L}$, let $\mathbf{L} \lceil \mathsf{tx} \rceil$ denote the ledger $\{\mathsf{tx}' \mid \mathsf{tx}' \preceq_{\mathbf{L}} \mathsf{tx}\}$ with the inherited rank function.

The above notion of a ledger captures a static state; we extend it to describe evolution in time as follows.

Definition 3 (Dynamic ledger). *Consider the sequence of time slots $t \in \mathbb{N}$ and any sequence of sets of transactions $A^{(0)}, A^{(1)}, \ldots$ (each a subset of a common transaction space T) denoting the transactions that arrive at each time slot. A dynamic ledger is a sequence of random variables $\mathbf{D} \overset{\text{def}}{=} \mathbf{L}^{(0)}, \mathbf{L}^{(1)}, \ldots,$ that satisfy the following properties parametrized by security functions $\mathrm{p}_R^+ : (\mathbb{R}^+)^2 \to [0,1]$ and $\mathrm{p}_R^-, \mathrm{p}_A, \mathrm{l} : \mathbb{R}^+ \to [0,1]:$*

Liveness. *For every $r \geq 0$, $t_0 \geq 0$, and $t \geq t_0 + r$,*

$$\Pr\left[L_{r,t_0,t}\right] \overset{\text{def}}{=} \Pr\left[A^{(t_0)} \not\subseteq \mathbf{L}^{(t)} \lceil t_0 + r \rceil\right] \leq \mathrm{l}(r).$$

Absolute Persistence. *For each rank $r \geq 0$, time $t_0 \geq 0$, and $t \geq t_0$, we have $\mathbf{L}^{(t_0)} \lceil t_0 - r \rceil = \mathbf{L}^{(t)} \lceil t_0 - r \rceil$ except with small failure probability. Specifically, for all $r, t_0 \geq 0$,*

$$\Pr\left[P_{r,t_0}\right] \overset{\text{def}}{=} \Pr\left[\exists t \geq t_0, \mathbf{L}^{(t_0)} \lceil t_0 - r \rceil \neq \mathbf{L}^{(t)} \lceil t_0 - r \rceil\right] \leq \mathrm{p}_A(r).$$

Relative Persistence. *For each $r^+, r^- \geq 0$, time $t_0 \geq 0$, and $t \geq t_0$, we have $\mathbf{L}^{(t_0)} \lceil t_0 - r^- - r^+ \rceil \subseteq \mathbf{L}^{(t)} \lceil t_0 - r^- \rceil \subseteq \mathbf{L}^{(t_0)}$ except with small failure probability. Specifically, for each $r^-, r^+, t_0 \geq 0$:*

$$\Pr\left[\exists t \geq t_0, \mathbf{L}^{(t_0)} \lceil t_0 - r^- - r^+ \rceil \not\subseteq \mathbf{L}^{(t)} \lceil t_0 - r^- \rceil\right] \leq \mathrm{p}_R^+(r^-, r^+),$$

$$\Pr\left[\exists t \geq t_0, \mathbf{L}^{(t)} \lceil t_0 - r^- \rceil \not\subseteq \mathbf{L}^{(t_0)}\right] \leq \mathrm{p}_R^-(r^-).$$

As indicated, we let P_{r,t_0} and $L_{r,t_0,t}$ denote the absolute-persistence failure event with parameters (r, t_0) and the liveness failure event with parameters (r, t_0, t), respectively.

The above definition deserves a detailed discussion. A dynamic ledger is a sequence of ledgers—one for each time slot t—which reflects the current state of the ledger structure $\mathbf{L}^{(t)}$ at that time. Throughout the paper, we will use the superscript notation $\cdot^{(t)}$ to denote the time coordinate.

Absolute persistence and *liveness* capture the standard design features of distributed ledger protocols: absolute persistence mandates that at time t_0, the state of the ledger up to rank $t_0 - r$ is fixed for all future times, except with error

$p_A(r)$. Liveness, on the other hand, guarantees that any transaction appearing in $A^{(t_0)}$ will be a part of a (later) ledger at time $t \geq t_0 + r$ with a rank at most $t_0 + r$, except with error at most $l(r)$. Note that the liveness guarantee only pertains to transactions tx appearing in the sets $A^{(t_0)}$, which may not necessarily "explain" all of the transactions in the ledger; in particular, we do not always insist that $\mathbf{L}^{(t)} \subseteq \bigcup_{s \leq t} A^{(s)}$. This extra flexibility permits us to simultaneously study differing liveness guarantees for various subclasses of transactions processed by a particular ledger (see Sect. 3.2).

The remaining property, *relative persistence*, is more complex: It is a weakening of absolute persistence by *not* requiring future stability for the prefix of the currently seen ledger $\mathbf{L}^{(t_0)}$ up to rank $t_0 - r^- - r^+$; it merely asks that no transaction tx *currently contained* in it will rise to a rank exceeding $t_0 - r^-$; likewise, it insists that no transaction tx′ currently absent in the ledger will ever achieve a rank below $t_0 - r^-$, potentially overtaking tx. This property bears a direct connection to the notion of transaction settlement as we discuss in Sect. 2.3. Looking ahead, we note that relative persistence provides sufficient guarantees for settling transactions that are only invalidated by "conflicting" transactions, and our combiner will achieve stronger relative-persistence than absolute-persistence guarantees, allowing for our latency-reduction results in Sect. 3.

Note that absolute persistence for some r clearly implies relative persistence with $r^+ = 0$ and $r^- = r$. A natural parametrization that makes our notions meaningful is where each $f \in \{p_A, p_R^-, l\}$ is monotonically decreasing and satisfies $f(0) \geq 1$ (similarly, p_R^+ should be monotonically decreasing in each coordinate and $p_R^+(r^-, r^+) \geq 1$ whenever $0 \in \{r^-, r^+\}$). Of course each of these functions represents a probability upper-bound, though we entertain values above 1 purely to simplify notation. A persistence or liveness function is *exponential* if it has the form $f(x) = \exp(-\alpha x + \beta)$ for some $\alpha > 0$ and $\beta \geq 0$; ledgers with exponential security will be our main focus.

Finally, our intention is to use dynamic ledgers to model blockchain consensus protocols. In this case, the chain held by each (honest) party $\mathsf{P} \in \mathcal{P}$ is modeled as a dynamic ledger $\mathbf{D}_\mathsf{P} = \mathbf{L}_\mathsf{P}^{(0)}, \mathbf{L}_\mathsf{P}^{(1)}, \ldots$, satisfying the properties of persistence and liveness from Definition 3. Of course, this by itself does not capture all the desired goals of blockchain protocols, as it does not reflect consensus properties across parties; how to reflect this in our model is discussed in the full paper [17].

2.2 Composition of Dynamic Ledgers

In the sequel, we will be interested in combining several dynamic ledgers to form a new "virtual" ledger. This notion of combining makes no assumptions on the ledgers to be combined other than a common transaction space. Moreover, it requires no explicit coordination among the ledgers or maintenance of special metadata: in fact, the "subledgers" involved in the construction do not even need to "know" that they are being viewed as a part of a combined ledger. Concretely, a *virtual ledger construction* is a deterministic, stateless rule for interpreting a family of m individual ledgers as a single ledger. This is formally captured in the following definition.

Definition 4 (Virtual Ledger Constructions). *A virtual ledger construction* $C[\cdot]$ *is a mapping that takes a tuple of dynamic ledgers* $(\mathbf{D}_1, \ldots, \mathbf{D}_m)$ *over the same transaction space* $\mathcal{T}$ *and returns a dynamic ledger* $C[\mathbf{D}_1, \ldots, \mathbf{D}_m] = \mathbf{L}^{(0)}, \mathbf{L}^{(1)}, \ldots$ *over* $\mathcal{T}$ *determined by three functions* $(\mathsf{a}_C, \mathsf{t}_C, \mathsf{r}_C)$ *as described below. We write* $\mathbf{D}_i = \mathbf{L}_i^{(0)}, \mathbf{L}_i^{(1)}, \ldots$ *with arriving transaction sets denoted* $A_i^{(0)}, A_i^{(1)}, \ldots$ *and the rank function of each* $\mathbf{L}_i^{(t)}$ *being* $\mathsf{rank}_i^{(t)}$. *Then*

(i) the arriving transaction sets are given by $A^{(t)} = \mathsf{a}_C(A_1^{(t)}, \ldots, A_m^{(t)})$;
(ii) the ledger contents are given by $\mathbf{L}^{(t)} = \mathsf{t}_C(\mathbf{L}_1^{(t)}, \ldots, \mathbf{L}_m^{(t)})$; *and*
(iii) the rank is given by $\mathsf{rank}^{(t)}(\mathsf{tx}) = \mathsf{r}_C(\mathsf{rank}_1^{(t)}(\mathsf{tx}), \ldots, \mathsf{rank}_m^{(t)}(\mathsf{tx}))$.

Since the above requirements are formulated independently for each t, it is well-defined to treat $C[\cdot]$ *as operating on ledgers rather than dynamic ledgers; we sometimes overload the notation in this sense.*

Looking ahead, our amplification combiner will consider $\mathsf{t}_C(\mathbf{L}_1^{(t)}, \ldots, \mathbf{L}_m^{(t)}) = \bigcup_i \mathbf{L}_i^{(t)}$ along with two related definitions of a_C given by $\bigcup_i A_i^{(t)}$ and $\bigcap_i A_i^{(t)}$; see Sect. 3. The robust combiner will adopt a more sophisticated notion of t_C.

In each of these cases, the important structural properties of the construction are captured by the rank function r_C.

2.3   Transaction Validity and Settlement

In the discussion below, we assume a general notion of *transaction validity* that can be decided inductively: given a ledger $\mathbf{L}$, the validity of a transaction $\mathsf{tx} \in \mathbf{L}$ is determined by the transactions in the state $\mathbf{L}\lceil\mathsf{tx}\rceil$ of $\mathbf{L}$ up to tx and their ordering. Intuitively, only valid transactions are then accounted for when interpreting the state of the ledger on the application level. The canonical example of such a validity predicate in the case of so-called UTXO transactions is formalized in the full version of this paper [17]. Note that protocols such as Bitcoin allow only valid transactions to enter the ledger; as the Bitcoin ledger is represented by a simple chain it is possible to evaluate the validity predicate upon block creation for each included transaction. This may not be the case for more general ledgers, such as the result of applying one of our combiners or various DAG-based constructions.

While we focus our analysis on persistence and liveness as given in Definition 3, our broader goal is to study *settlement*. Intuitively, settlement is the delay necessary to ensure that a transaction included in some $A^{(t)}$ enters the dynamic ledger and, furthermore, that its validity stabilizes for all future times.

Definition 5 (Absolute settlement). *For a dynamic ledger* $\mathbf{D} \overset{\text{def}}{=} \mathbf{L}^{(0)}, \mathbf{L}^{(1)}, \ldots$ *we say that a transaction* $\mathsf{tx} \in A^{(\tau)} \cap \mathbf{L}^{(t)}$ *(for* $\tau \leq t$*) is (absolutely) settled at time t if for all* $\ell \geq t$ *we have: (i)* $\mathbf{L}^{(t)}\lceil\mathsf{tx}\rceil \subseteq \mathbf{L}^{(\ell)}$, *(ii) the linear orders* $\prec_{\mathbf{L}^{(t)}}$ *and* $\prec_{\mathbf{L}^{(\ell)}}$ *agree on* $\mathbf{L}^{(t)}\lceil\mathsf{tx}\rceil$, *and (iii) for any* $\mathsf{tx}' \in \mathbf{L}^{(\ell)}$ *such that* $\mathsf{tx}' \prec_{\mathbf{L}^{(\ell)}} \mathsf{tx}$ *we have* $\mathsf{tx}' \in \mathbf{L}^{(t)}\lceil\mathsf{tx}\rceil$.

Note that for any absolutely settled transaction, its validity is determined and it is guaranteed to remain unchanged in the future.

It will be useful to also consider a weaker notion of *relative settlement* of a transaction: Intuitively, tx is *relatively settled* at time t if we have the guarantee that no (conflicting) transaction tx' that is not part of the ledger at time t can possibly eventually precede tx in the ledger ordering.

Definition 6 (Relative settlement). *Let $\mathcal{T}$ be a transaction space with a conflict relation. For a dynamic ledger $\mathbf{D} \overset{\mathrm{def}}{=} \mathbf{L}^{(0)}, \mathbf{L}^{(1)}, \ldots,$ over $\mathcal{T}$ we say that a transaction tx $\in A^{(\tau)}$ is relatively settled at time $t \geq \tau$ if for any $\ell \geq t$ we have: (i) tx $\in \mathbf{L}^{(\ell)}$; (ii) for any transaction tx' such that tx' $\prec_{\mathbf{L}^{(\ell)}}$ tx and tx' $\in$ conflict(tx) we have tx' $\in \mathbf{L}^{(t)}$.*

We define an analogous notion when $\mathcal{T}$ is not equipped with a conflict relation, by replacing (ii) with the stronger condition that applies to all transactions: for any transaction tx' such that tx' $\prec_{\mathbf{L}^{(\ell)}}$ tx we have tx' $\in \mathbf{L}^{(t)}$.

We illustrate the usefulness of relative settlement on the example of the well-known UTXO transactions. If a UTXO-transaction tx satisfies that: (i) all its inputs appear as outputs of a preceding valid, absolutely settled transaction, (ii) tx itself is relatively settled, and finally, (iii) no conflicting transaction (using the same inputs) is currently part of the ledger; then the validity of tx can be reliably decided and is guaranteed not to change in the future.

In a dynamic ledger with liveness, absolute and relative persistence described by l, p_A and (p_R^+, p_R^-) respectively, there is a clear direct relationship of both types of settlement to these properties. Namely, a transaction tx $\in A^{(\tau)}$ is absolutely (resp. relatively) settled in time $\tau + r_l + r_p$ (resp. $\tau + r_l + r^+ + r^-$) except with error $p_A(r_p) + l(r_l)$ (resp. $l(r_l) + p_R^+(r^-, r^+) + p_R^-(r^-)$).

While the time τ when the transaction tx entered the system is not necessarily observable by inspecting the ledger, settlement itself is an observable event: tx is absolutely (resp. relatively) settled at time T if it is seen as part of the ledger $\mathbf{L}^{(T)}\lceil T - r_p \rceil$ (resp. $\mathbf{L}^{(T)}\lceil T - r^+ - r^- \rceil$), except with error $p_A(r_p)$ (resp. $p_R^+(r^-, r^+) + p_R^-(r^-)$).

For ledgers that provide better guarantees for relative persistence than for absolute persistence, relative settlement can occur faster than absolute settlement.

3 The Security-Amplifying Combiner for Latency Reduction

We describe a general combiner which transforms m underlying ledgers to a virtual ledger in which transactions settle more quickly. As discussed previously, by logging a transaction in *all* of the underlying ledgers, users can be promised a $\Theta(m)$ (multiplicative) reduction in settlement time; on the other hand, by logging a transaction in a single one of the underlying ledgers, the promised settlement time is roughly consistent with the underlying ledger settlement time.

3.1 The Subindependence Assumption

Given m dynamic ledgers $\mathcal{D} = (\mathbf{D}_1, \ldots, \mathbf{D}_m)$, informally, we say that the dynamic ledgers satisfy ε-*subindependence* if, for any collection of events $F_1, \ldots, F_m$ capturing either persistence or liveness failures—with the understanding that F_i refers solely to properties of $\mathbf{L}_i$—we have $\Pr\left[\bigwedge_i F_i\right] \leq \prod_i \Pr[F_i]$ conditioned on some event occurring with probability at least $1 - \varepsilon$.

Definition 7 (Subindependence). *Let $\mathcal{D} = (\mathbf{D}_1, \ldots, \mathbf{D}_m)$ be a collection of m dynamic ledgers. Ledgers $\mathcal{D}$ satisfy ε-persistence subindependence if for any subset $I \subseteq \{1, \ldots, m\}$ and any collection of persistence failure events $\{P^{(i)}_{r_i, t_i} \mid i \in I\}$, where the event $P^{(i)}_\star$ refers to $\mathbf{D}_i$, there is an event E with $\Pr[E] \geq 1 - \varepsilon$ such that we have $\Pr\left[\bigwedge_i P^{(i)}_{r_i, t_i} \mid E\right] \leq \prod_i \mathrm{p}^{(i)}_A(r_i)$. We similarly define ε-liveness subindependence.*

Throughout our proofs, we treat ε as negligible quantity and, for purposes of a clean exposition, do not include the additive error terms related to ε in our concluding error bounds. (See Sect. 4.1 for further discussion, including how to interpret the notion of "negligible" in this context.) Consistent with this treatment, we leave ε implicit in our notation, and simply say that the dynamic ledgers $\mathcal{D}$ possess subindependence if they possess both persistence and liveness subindependence.

As we discuss in Sect. 4.1, in situations such as those that arise in blockchains one cannot hope for *exact independence* among persistence failure events for the simple reason that an adaptive adversary may decide—as a result of the success of her attacks on some subset of the ledgers—to cease attacking the others; this creates a (harmless) negative correlation between failure events. Intuitively, the subindependence conditions express the inability of an attacker to outperform the simple setting where she aggressively attacks each of the ledgers in isolation of the others. We discuss how subindependence can be naturally achieved in both PoW and PoS settings in Sect. 4.1.

3.2 The Parallel Ledger Construction

We consider m dynamic ledgers $\mathcal{D} \stackrel{\text{def}}{=} (\mathbf{D}_1, \ldots, \mathbf{D}_m)$ over the same transaction space $\mathcal{T}$ and sequence of time slots $t \in \{0, 1, \ldots\}$, where each dynamic ledger $\mathbf{D}_i = \mathbf{L}_i^{(0)}, \mathbf{L}_i^{(1)}, \ldots$ and its sequence of arriving transactions is denoted as $A_i^{(0)}, A_i^{(1)}, \ldots$.

Definition 8 (Construction P[$\mathcal{D}$]). *Our main construction $\mathsf{P}[\mathbf{D}_1, \ldots, \mathbf{D}_m]$ (which we also write $\mathsf{P}[\mathcal{D}]$ when convenient) is defined by*

$$\mathsf{ac}(A_1^{(t)}, \ldots, A_m^{(t)}) = \bigcup_i A_i^{(t)}, \qquad \mathsf{tc}(\mathbf{L}_1^{(t)}, \ldots, \mathbf{L}_m^{(t)}) = \bigcup_i \mathbf{L}_i^{(t)},$$

and the rank function $\overline{\text{rank}}_L^{(t)}$ defined as follows: For a tuple $\mathbf{r} = (r_1, \ldots, r_m) \in (\mathbb{R} \cup \{\infty\})^m$ and a constant L, define

$$\overline{\text{rank}}_L(\mathbf{r}) \overset{\text{def}}{=} -L \ln \left(\frac{1}{m} \sum_{r_i \leq \theta(\mathbf{r})} \exp(-r_i/L) \right), \tag{1}$$

where $\theta(\mathbf{r}) = \min_i r_i + L \ln m$, and $\exp(-\infty/L)$ is defined to be 0. We overload the notation to apply to transactions, so that the resulting rank function can serve the purposes of a virtual ledger construction: Let tx be a transaction appearing with rank r_i in ledger $\mathbf{L}_i^{(t)}$ for some fixed t; then define $\overline{\text{rank}}_L^{(t)}(\text{tx}) = \overline{\text{rank}}_L(\mathbf{r})$.

The definition (1) can be rephrased into an alternate, and somewhat more intuitive, equation: if $I_\theta \overset{\text{def}}{=} \{i \mid r_i \leq \theta(\mathbf{r})\}$ then

$$\frac{1}{m} \sum_{i \in I_\theta} \exp(-r_i/L) = \exp(-\overline{\text{rank}}_L(\mathbf{r})/L). \tag{2}$$

In particular the notion is a simple average if rank is interpreted under an exponential functional: $\exp(-\text{rank}(\cdot)/L)$. Note, additionally, that for any $\mathbf{r} = (r_1, \ldots, r_m)$, we have $\min_{i \in [m]} r_i \leq \overline{\text{rank}}_L(\mathbf{r}) \leq (\min_{i \in [m]} r_i) + L \ln m$ and, furthermore, the inequality can be naturally interpreted if some or all of the r_i are ∞. The first inequality is tight when all r_i are equal.

A final remark about truncation by the threshold $\theta(\mathbf{r})$: While the "large-scale" features of the parallel ledger—including relative persistence and liveness—do not depend on truncation, absolute persistence depends on eventual stability of the rank function. The truncation operation guarantees this, ensuring that only a bounded portion of the ledger is relevant for determining the final rank of a transaction.

Preemptive Rank Function. When the dynamic ledgers $\mathcal{D}$ are defined over a transaction space with a conflict relation, we consistently work with a slightly different notion of *preemptive rank* for the amplification construction above. Specifically, we say that a transaction tx is *dominant* in a ledger $\mathbf{L}$ if it appears in the ledger and no earlier transaction conflicts with tx (that is tx $\in \mathbf{L}$ and tx$' \prec_{\mathbf{L}}$ tx $\Rightarrow$ tx$' \notin \text{conflict(tx)}$). Let ρ_i be the rank of tx in ledger $\mathbf{L}_i$ and define $r_i = \rho_i$ if tx is dominant in $\mathbf{L}_i$, and $r_i = \infty$ otherwise. Then the *preemptive rank* $\overline{\text{rank}}_L^*(\text{tx})$ of tx is defined to be $\overline{\text{rank}}_L(r_1, \ldots, r_m)$.

Fast and Slow Submission. We consider two ways of submitting tx to $\mathsf{P}[\mathcal{D}]$:

The "fast" mechanism: A transaction tx is simultaneously submitted to all of the underlying dynamic ledgers $\{\mathbf{D}_i\}_{i=1}^m$, appearing in $\bigcap_{i \in [m]} A_i^{(t)}$.

The "slow" mechanism: A transaction tx is submitted to (at least) one of the dynamic ledgers $\mathbf{D}_i$, appearing in $\bigcup_{i \in [m]} A_i^{(t)}$.

An important feature of our protocol is that a single deployment supports both of these mechanisms and their use can be decided by transaction producers on a per-transaction basis. As we will see, these two mechanisms exhibit markedly different liveness guarantees: Participants desiring fast liveness and settlement[2] can adopt the fast mechanism by submitting their transactions to all m of the ledgers; participants with less urgency can adopt the slow mechanism, simply submitting their transactions to a single ledger.

To formally capture this in a clean way, we will introduce a slight variant, $\mathsf{P}_F[\mathcal{D}]$, which allows us to specifically study the improved liveness properties of transactions when they happen to be submitted for insertion into all of the constituent ledgers $\mathbf{D}_i$ at the same time. Specifically, $\mathsf{P}_F[\mathcal{D}]$ has precisely the same definition as $\mathsf{P}[\mathcal{D}]$ with the exception that $\mathsf{a}_\mathsf{C}(A_1^{(t)}, \ldots, A_m^{(t)}) = \bigcap_i A_i^{(t)}$. Thus, note that the two virtual ledgers $\mathsf{P}[\mathcal{D}]$ and $\mathsf{P}_F[\mathcal{D}]$ contain exactly the same elements with exactly the same ranks. They differ only in the sets of transactions (determined by a_C) for which they provide liveness guarantees: "slow" liveness guarantees for $\bigcup_i A_i^{(t)}$ correspond to bounds on $\mathsf{P}[\mathcal{D}]$ while "fast" liveness guarantees for transactions in $\bigcap_i A_i^{(t)}$ correspond to liveness guarantees for $\mathsf{P}_F[\mathcal{D}]$. This bookkeeping slight of hand is merely a way to use a single abstraction to express both a general liveness guarantee and an accelerated guarantee for transaction submitted to all ledgers $\mathbf{D}_i$.

We remark that fast settlement guarantees are provided anytime a transaction has been submitted to all of the underlying ledgers: the proof does not require that they be submitted at exactly the same time. In terms of the definitions above, the proof would apply even if we defined $\overline{A}_i^{(t)} \overset{\text{def}}{=} \bigcup_{s \leq t} A_i^{(s)}$, $F^{(t)} \overset{\text{def}}{=} \bigcap_i \overline{A}_i^{(t)}$, and $A^{(t)}$ (the set for which fast settlement is guaranteed) to be $F^{(t)} \setminus F^{(t-1)}$. Thus a transaction would be guaranteed fast settlement as soon as it has been submitted to all relevant ledgers. We work with the simple formulation $(\bigcap_i A_i^{(t)})$ merely as a matter of convenience.

3.3 Main Result and Proof Outline

Our main result follows, formulated for exponentially secure ledgers as defined in Sect. 2.1.

Theorem 2. *Let $\mathcal{D} = (\mathbf{D}_1, \ldots, \mathbf{D}_m)$ be a family of m subindependent dynamic ledgers defined over a common transaction space $\mathcal{T}$ with a conflict relation, each possessing exponential liveness $\mathsf{l}(r) = \exp(-\alpha_l r + \beta_l)$ and absolute persistence $\mathsf{p}(r) = \exp(-\alpha_\mathsf{p} r + \beta_\mathsf{p})$. Consider the combined dynamic ledgers $\mathsf{P}_F[\mathcal{D}]$ and $\mathsf{P}[\mathcal{D}]$ with the (preemptive) rank function $\overline{\mathrm{rank}}_L^*$ for a parameter $L \geq m$. Then for $\mathsf{P}_F[\mathcal{D}]$, there is a constant $C > 1$ so that if $L \geq Cm \ln m$, we have*

$$\Pr\left[\exists \mathrm{tx} \in A^{(t_0)} \text{ not relatively settled at time } t_0 + 2r\right] \tag{3}$$
$$\leq \exp(-r\Omega(m) + O(m)) + \exp\left(-\Omega(r) - \Omega(L \ln(m))\right).$$

---

[2] Recall the difference between *liveness* and *settlement* in our terminology (cf. Sect. 2.3).

At the same time, for P[$\mathcal{D}$] *we have*

$$\Pr\left[\exists \text{tx} \in A^{(t_0)} \text{ not absolutely settled at } t_0 + 2r\right] \le m\exp(-\Omega(r) + O(L\ln m)).$$

The constants hidden in the $\Omega()$ and $O()$ notation depend on $\alpha_{\mathrm{p}}, \alpha_{\mathrm{l}}, \beta_{\mathrm{p}}, \beta_{\mathrm{l}}$, but they are independent of m, L, and r.

Note that in (3), the first term vanishes with the desired m-fold speedup, and dominates the total error as long as roughly $rm < L$. Beyond that, the second term is dominant and the error vanishes at the pace of a single constituent ledger. This is essential for enabling both slow and fast settlement, as discussed in Sect. 1.1. Note that as L can be chosen to scale with the security parameter so that $\exp(-\Theta(L))$ is an acceptable error probability, the region $rm < L$ is thus exactly where the settlement speedup is desired.

On a high level, the proof for $\mathsf{P}_F[\mathcal{D}]$ goes as follows. For a transaction tx $\in$ $A^{(t_0)}$, we can expect that: (1) At time $t_0 + 2r$, tx appears in at least $4m/5$ of the m ledgers with rank at most $t_0 + r$. (2) At most $m/5$ of these $4m/5$ ledgers will exhibit an absolute persistence failure allowing a change of their state up to rank $t_0 + r$ after time $t_0 + 2r$, affecting the rank of tx. Based on the above two events, at any time after $t_0 + 2r$ there can be at most $2m/5$ ledgers that do not contain tx with rank at most $t_0 + r$. Then: (3) For any competing transaction tx$'$ $\in$ conflict(tx) not present at time $t_0 + 2r$, these $2m/5$ ledgers will never contribute enough to the rank of tx$'$ to overtake tx in $\mathsf{P}_F[\mathcal{D}]$. More precisely, each of the three above events is shown to fail with at most the error probability in the theorem statement.

The result for P[$\mathcal{D}$] is proven along the following lines. Assume a transaction tx inserted to (at least) one of the ledgers $\mathbf{L}_i$ at time t_0. For any $t \ge t_0 + r - L\ln m$, we have tx $\in \mathbf{L}_i^{(t)}\lceil t_0 + r - L\ln m\rceil$ except for probability $\mathrm{l}(r - L\ln m)$, and, by the properties of the rank function, also tx $\in \mathbf{L}^{(t)}\lceil t_0 + r\rceil$. Let $T \ge t = t_0 + 2r$ and assume tx $\in \mathbf{L}^{(t)}\lceil t_0 + r\rceil$ as by the above liveness guarantee. As $\mathbf{L}^{(T)}\lceil t_0 + r\rceil$ is fully determined by the ledgers $\mathbf{L}_j^{(T)}\lceil t_0 + r + L\ln m\rceil$, a persistence failure $\mathbf{L}^{(T)}\lceil t_0 + r\rceil \ne \mathbf{L}^{(t)}\lceil t_0 + r\rceil$ implies a persistence failure of some $\mathbf{L}_j^{(t)}\lceil t_0 + r + L\ln m\rceil$, which has a probability at most $m\,\mathsf{p}_A(-r + L\ln m)$.

The bound for $\mathsf{P}_F[\mathcal{D}]$ in particular gives us the following corollary.

Corollary 1. *In the setting of Theorem 2, if the number of chains m scales with the security parameter then $\mathsf{P}_F[\mathcal{D}]$ achieves constant-time settlement except with an error probability negligible in the security parameter.*

In the rest of this section, we establish the above results in full detail. In Sect. 3.4 we study the central part of our combiner—its rank function; and based on it, Sect. 3.5 obtains our persistence and liveness bounds in their most general form. Section 3.6 specializes them to the setting of interest with exponentially-secure underlying ledgers; and finally Sect. 3.7 concludes the derivation of Theorem 2 and Corollary 1.

3.4   Properties of $\overline{\text{rank}}$

Before discussing the persistence and liveness guarantees of our construction, we derive some general properties of its rank function.

Lemma 1. *Let* $\mathbf{r} = (r_1, \ldots, r_m) \in (\mathbb{R} \cup \{\infty\})^m$ *and* $T \geq \min_i r_i$. *Let* $I_T = \{i \mid r_i \leq T\}$ *and, for each* $i \in I_T$, *define* $d_i = T - r_i$. *Writing* $D = T - \overline{\text{rank}}_L(\mathbf{r})$,

$$\sum_{i \in I_T} d_i \geq D + L \ln\left(m - \frac{m-1}{\exp(D/L)}\right).$$

We note the following weaker, but convenient, bound: when $D \geq 0$, *the sum* $\sum_{i \in I_T} d_i$ *is no more than* $D + L \ln\left((mD + L)/(D + L)\right)$.

Proof. Let $I_\theta = \{i \mid r_i \leq \theta(\mathbf{r})\}$. Writing $R = -\overline{\text{rank}}_L(\mathbf{r})/L$, from Eq. (2) we have

$$m \exp(T/L) \exp(R) = \exp(T/L) \sum_{i \in I_\theta} \exp(-r_i/L) \leq \sum_{i \in I_\theta \setminus I_T} 1 + \sum_{i \in I_T \cap I_\theta} \exp(d_i/L)$$

$$\overset{(*)}{\leq} (|I_\theta| - 1) + \exp\left(\sum_{i \in I_T} d_i/L\right) \leq (m - 1) + \exp\left(\sum_{i \in I_T} d_i/L\right)$$

$$(4)$$

where the inequality $\overset{(*)}{\leq}$ above follows from the fact that for any $a_i \geq 0$ we have $\sum_{i=1}^{\ell} \exp(a_i) \leq (\ell - 1) + \exp(\sum_{i=1}^{\ell} a_i)$, and $d_i \geq 0$ for all $i \in I_T$. (This follows by expanding the power series of e^x and noting that $\sum a_i^k \leq (\sum a_i)^k$ for positive a_i.) Inequality (4) then yields

$$\sum_{i \in I_T} \frac{d_i}{L} \geq \ln\left[m \exp\left[\frac{T}{L} + R\right] - (m-1)\right] = \left[\frac{T}{L} + R\right] + \ln\left[m - \frac{m-1}{\exp(T/L + R)}\right]$$

and hence

$$\sum_{i \in I_T} d_i \geq (T - \overline{\text{rank}}_L(\mathbf{r})) + L \ln\left(m - \frac{m-1}{\exp([T - \overline{\text{rank}}_L(\mathbf{r})]/L)}\right),$$

completing the proof. The second lower bound indicated in the theorem follows from the fact that $\exp(1 + x) \geq 1 + x$ for $x \geq 0$.   □

We note a corollary of this, which also reflects the number of contributing terms in the sum defining $\overline{\text{rank}}$.

Corollary 2. *Let* $\mathbf{r} = (r_1, \ldots, r_m) \in (\mathbb{R} \cup \{\infty\})^m$ *and* $T \geq \min_i r_i$. *Let*

$$I_T = \{i \mid r_i \leq T\}, \qquad I_\theta = \{i \mid r_i \leq \theta(\mathbf{r})\}, \qquad m' = |I_\theta|,$$

and, for each $i \in I_T$, *define* $d_i = T - r_i$. *Then*

$$\sum_{i \in I_T} d_i \geq [T - \overline{\text{rank}}_L(\mathbf{r})] + L \ln\left(m - \frac{m'-1}{\exp([T - \overline{\text{rank}}_L(\mathbf{r})]/L)}\right).$$

Proof. This follows from the proof of Lemma 1 by working with the version of Eq. (4) that retains dependence on $|I_\theta|$.   □

For two rank tuples $\mathbf{r} = (r_1, \ldots, r_m)$ and $\mathbf{s} = (s_1, \ldots, s_m)$ in $(\mathbb{R} \cup \{\infty\})^m$, we define $\mathbf{r} \vee \mathbf{s}$ to be the tuple $(\min(r_1, s_1), \ldots, \min(r_m, s_m))$.

Lemma 2. (Rank addition). *Consider two rank tuples* $\mathbf{r} = (r_1, \ldots, r_m)$ *and* $\mathbf{s} = (s_1, \ldots, s_m)$ *in* $(\mathbb{R} \cup \{\infty\})^m$. *Then*

$$\exp(-\overline{\mathrm{rank}}(\mathbf{r} \vee \mathbf{s})/L) \leq \exp(-\overline{\mathrm{rank}}(\mathbf{r})/L) + \exp(-\overline{\mathrm{rank}}(\mathbf{s})/L); \qquad (5)$$

and moreover, for any $\alpha \in (0, 1)$,

$$\overline{\mathrm{rank}}(\mathbf{r}) \geq \overline{\mathrm{rank}}(\mathbf{r} \vee \mathbf{s}) + \ln(1/\alpha)L \implies \overline{\mathrm{rank}}(\mathbf{s}) \leq \overline{\mathrm{rank}}(\mathbf{r} \vee \mathbf{s}) + \ln(1/(1-\alpha))L. \quad (6)$$

Proof. The validity of Eq. (5) can be observed by simply expanding the $\overline{\mathrm{rank}}$ function according to its definition. For the implication (6), note that if $\overline{\mathrm{rank}}(\mathbf{r}) \geq \overline{\mathrm{rank}}(\mathbf{r} \vee \mathbf{s}) + \ln(1/\alpha)L$ then (5) gives us

$$\exp\left(-\overline{\mathrm{rank}}(\mathbf{r} \vee \mathbf{s})/L\right) \leq \alpha \cdot \exp\left(-\overline{\mathrm{rank}}(\mathbf{r} \vee \mathbf{s})/L\right) + \exp\left(-\overline{\mathrm{rank}}(\mathbf{s})/L\right)$$

and hence $\exp\left(-\overline{\mathrm{rank}}(\mathbf{s})/L\right) \geq (1-\alpha) \cdot \exp\left(-\overline{\mathrm{rank}}(\mathbf{r} \vee \mathbf{s})/L\right)$, implying $\overline{\mathrm{rank}}(\mathbf{s}) \leq \overline{\mathrm{rank}}(\mathbf{r} \vee \mathbf{s}) + \ln(1/(1-\alpha))L$ as desired.   □

3.5   Persistence and Liveness of the Parallel Ledgers

We begin with a lemma that establishes relative persistence guarantees under general circumstances: it requires only a super-additive persistence function and does not require that the transaction space have a conflict relation.

Definition 9 (Super-additive functions). *Recall that a function* $f : \mathbb{R} \to \mathbb{R}$ *is convex if, for any* $x_1, \ldots, x_n$ *and* $\lambda_1, \ldots, \lambda_n$ *for which* $\lambda_i \geq 0$ *and* $\sum_i \lambda_i = 1$, *we have* $f(\sum_i \lambda_i x_i) \leq \sum_i \lambda_i f(x_i)$. *A persistence function* p *is super-additive if* $\log \mathrm{p}$ *is convex. It follows that* p *satisfies the inequality*

$$\prod_{i=1}^{m} \mathrm{p}(r_i) \leq \mathrm{p}\left(\frac{1}{m} \sum_i r_i\right)^m. \qquad (7)$$

Note that any exponential persistence function (as defined in Sect. 2.1) is super-additive.

Lemma 3 (Relative persistence of P[$\mathcal{D}$]). *Consider* P[$\mathcal{D}$], *the parallel composition of* m *subindependent ledgers, each with super-additive absolute persistence* $\mathrm{p}_A(\cdot)$. *For any* $\delta > 0$ *and time* T, *the probability that an adversary can inject a transaction* tx *that does not appear in any of the ledgers so as to achieve* $\overline{\mathrm{rank}}_L(\mathrm{tx}) \leq T - D$ *is at most*

$$i(D; \delta, L) \overset{\text{def}}{=} \left(\frac{D + L\ln m}{\delta}\right)^m \cdot \mathrm{p}_A\left(\frac{1}{m}\left(D + L\ln\left(\frac{mD + L}{D + L}\right)\right) - \delta\right)^m.$$

Moreover, the ledger $\mathsf{P}[\mathcal{D}]$ *satisfies the following relative persistence guarantees: for any* $t_0, r \geq 0$,

$$\Pr\left[\exists t \geq t_0, \mathbf{L}^{(t)}\lceil t_0 - r\rceil \not\subseteq \mathbf{L}^{(t_0)}\right] \leq \overline{\mathsf{p}_R}(r; L) \stackrel{\text{def}}{=} i(r; \delta, L)$$

and, for the constant $r^* = \ln(2)L$,

$$\Pr\left[\exists t \geq t_0, \mathbf{L}^{(t_0)}\lceil t_0 - (r + r^*)\rceil \not\subseteq \mathbf{L}^{(t)}\lceil t_0 - r\rceil\right] \leq \overline{\mathsf{p}_R^+}(r, r^*; L) \stackrel{\text{def}}{=} i(r; \delta, L).$$

Proof. In light of Lemma 1, in order for a transaction tx to be injected into the m ledgers so as to achieve $\overline{\mathrm{rank}}_L(\mathrm{tx}) \leq T - D$, it must appear with a rank tuple $(T - d_1, \ldots, T - d_m)$ for which

$$\sum_i d_i \geq D + L \ln\left(\frac{mD + L}{D + L}\right).$$

In preparation for applying a union bound, we identify a finite family of tuples $\mathcal{R}$ so that for any tuple of positive reals $\mathbf{x} = (x_1, \ldots, x_m)$ with $\sum x_i \geq \Lambda$ there is a "bounding" tuple $\mathbf{r} \in \mathcal{R}$ so that $\mathbf{r} \leq \mathbf{x}$ and $\sum_i r_i \approx \Lambda$. (Here the $\leq$ indicates that $r_i \leq x_i$ for all i.) For two real numbers x and $\delta > 0$, define $\lfloor x \rfloor_\delta$ to be the largest integer multiple of δ that is less than or equal to x; that is, $\lfloor x \rfloor_\delta \stackrel{\text{def}}{=} \max\{k \in \delta\mathbb{Z} \mid k \leq x\}$. Observe that for any tuple $\mathbf{x} = (x_1, \ldots, x_m)$ for which $\sum_i x_i \geq \Lambda$, the tuple $\lfloor \mathbf{x} \rfloor_\delta \stackrel{\text{def}}{=} (\lfloor x_1 \rfloor_\delta, \ldots, \lfloor x_m \rfloor_\delta)$ contains only integer multiples of δ, is coordinate-wise no larger than $\mathbf{x}$, and satisfies $\Lambda - \delta m \leq \sum_i \lfloor x_i \rfloor_\delta \leq \Lambda$. For $\Lambda \geq 0$, let $\mathcal{R}(\Lambda, \delta) = \{\mathbf{r} = (r_1, \ldots, r_m) \mid r_i \in \delta\mathbb{Z}, r_i \geq 0, \Lambda - \delta m \leq \sum_i r_i \leq \Lambda\}$. With this in place, it follows that if tx appears with ranks $(T - d_1, \ldots, T - d_m)$ and $T - \overline{\mathrm{rank}}_L(\mathrm{tx}) \geq D$ then there is a tuple

$$\mathbf{r} \in \mathcal{R} \stackrel{\text{def}}{=} \mathcal{R}\left(D + L\ln\left\lceil\frac{mD + L}{D + L}\right\rceil, \delta\right)$$

for which $\mathbf{r} \leq \mathbf{d}$ and hence $(T - d_1, \ldots, T - d_m) \leq (T - r_1, \ldots, T - r_m)$.

For a tuple $\mathbf{r} = (r_1, \ldots, r_m)$ consider the event, denoted $E_\mathbf{r}$, that the adversary can inject a transaction so that it appears with rank no more than $T - r_i$ in ledger i. By subindependence and the convexity of $\log \mathsf{p}_A(\cdot)$,

$$\Pr[E_\mathbf{r}] \leq \prod_{i=1}^m \mathsf{p}_A(r_i) \leq \mathsf{p}_A\left(\frac{1}{m}\sum_{i=1}^m r_i\right)^m,$$

from inequality (7) above. Then we have

$$\Pr\left[\mathrm{tx\ injected\ so\ that\ }\overline{\mathrm{rank}}_L(\mathrm{tx}) \leq T - D\right] \leq |\mathcal{R}| \cdot \max_{\mathbf{r} \in \mathcal{R}} \Pr[E_\mathbf{r}].$$

To conclude the argument, invoking the upper bound $|\mathcal{R}| \leq ((D + L\ln m)/\delta)^m$ we see that the probability $\Pr[\mathrm{tx\ injected\ so\ that\ }\overline{\mathrm{rank}}_L(\mathrm{tx}) \leq T - D]$ is bounded above by

$$\left(\frac{D + L\ln m}{\delta}\right)^m \cdot \mathsf{p}_A\left(\frac{1}{m}\left(D + L\ln\left\lceil\frac{mD + L}{D + L}\right\rceil\right) - \delta\right)^m.$$

The bound on $\mathsf{p}_R^-(r)$ follows immediately.

As for $p_R^+(r, \ln(2)L; L)$, consider a transaction tx with rank $T - (r + \ln(2)L)$. In order for such a transaction to rise to rank $T - r$, some subset S of appearances of the transaction must be removed with sufficient rank to permit the resulting rank to rise to $T - r$. In light of Lemma 2, this removal must involve rewriting the underlying blockchains at ranks corresponding to $\overline{\text{rank}}$ at least $T - (r + \ln(2)L) + \ln(2)L = T - r$, as desired. (This corresponds to the setting $\alpha = 1/2$ in Lemma 2.) $\square$

We state a corollary of the above result which pertains to the problem of injecting a transaction into a *particular* subset of the ledgers. This relies directly on Corollary 2, and will be a critical component of the $\Theta(m)$-amplification results below.

Corollary 3 (Relative persistence of $\mathsf{P}[\mathcal{D}]$ (with targeted insertion).
Consider $\mathsf{P}[\mathcal{D}]$, the parallel composition of m subindependent ledgers, each with super-additive absolute persistence $p_A(\cdot)$. Let $\mathcal{I}$ denote a subset of m' of the ledgers and let D satisfy $\exp(D/L) > (m'-1)/(m-1)$. Then for any $\delta > 0$ and time T, the probability that an adversary can inject a transaction tx that does not appear in any of the ledgers so as to appear only in ledgers $\mathcal{I}$ and achieve $\overline{\text{rank}}_L(\text{tx}) \leq T - D$ is no more than

$$i(D, m'; \delta, L) \stackrel{\text{def}}{=} \left(\frac{D + L \ln m}{\delta} \right)^{m'} \cdot p_A \left(\frac{1}{m'} \left(D + L \ln \left(m - \frac{m'-1}{\exp(D/L)} \right) \right) - \delta \right)^{m'}.$$

Proof. This follows from the proof of Lemma 3 by suitably adjusting the bound on $|\mathcal{R}|$ to the restricted set of chains and applying the bound from Corollary 2. $\square$

We return to the general setting to formulate a bound on absolute persistence.

Lemma 4 (Absolute persistence of $\mathsf{P}[\mathcal{D}]$). *Consider $\mathsf{P}[\mathcal{D}]$, the parallel composition of m subindependent ledgers, each with absolute persistence $p_A(\cdot)$. Then the parallel ledger $\mathsf{P}[\mathcal{D}]$ has absolute persistence $\overline{p}_A(r) \leq m \, p_A(r - L \ln m)$.*

Proof. As above, we let $\mathsf{P}[\mathbf{D}_1, \ldots, \mathbf{D}_m] = \mathbf{L}^{(0)}, \mathbf{L}^{(1)}, \ldots$. Consider a time t_0 and $r \geq L \ln m$. We observe that for any time $t \geq t_0$, $\mathbf{L}^{(t)} \lceil t_0 - r \rceil$ is completely determined by the ledgers $\mathbf{L}_i^{(t)} \lceil t_0 - r + L \ln m \rceil$. To see this, consider a transaction tx in the general ledger $\mathbf{L}^{(t)}$ of rank $s \leq t_0 - r$. Letting s_i denote the rank of tx in the constituent ledgers $\mathbf{L}_i^{(t)}$, recall that $\min_i s_i \leq s \leq t_0 - r$ and, furthermore, that $s = \overline{\text{rank}}(\text{tx})$ depends only on those s_i for which

$$s_i \leq \theta(\mathbf{s}) = \min_i s_i + L \ln m \leq s + L \ln m \leq t_0 - r + L \ln m;$$

in particular $\overline{\text{rank}}(\text{tx})$ is determined only by the ledgers $\mathbf{L}_i^{(t)} \lceil t_0 - r + L \ln m \rceil$.

To conclude, a persistence failure in $\mathbf{L}^{(t)} \lceil t_0 - r \rceil$ implies a persistence failure in some $\mathbf{L}_i^{(t)} \lceil t_0 - r + L \ln m \rceil$ and thus $\overline{p}_A(r) \leq m \, p_A(r - L \ln m)$, as desired. $\square$

As the ledger $\mathsf{P}_F[\mathcal{D}]$ is identical to $\mathsf{P}[\mathcal{D}]$ aside from the definition of a_C, it possesses the persistence guarantees described in Lemma 3, Corollary 3, and Lemma 4.

Liveness. We now direct our attention to liveness. We separately consider two distinct ways of submitting a transaction to the parallel ledger, the "fast" and the "slow" mechanisms as defined in Sect. 3.2. Recall that formally, the "fast" case corresponds to the liveness function of the virtual ledger $\mathsf{P}_F[\mathcal{D}]$, while the "slow" case corresponds to the liveness of the virtual ledger $\mathsf{P}[\mathcal{D}]$. We study these liveness functions next.

Definition 10 (Census). *Consider* $\mathsf{P}[\mathbf{D}]$, *and let* $\mathrm{tx} \in \mathcal{T}$ *be a transaction. The* (r, T)-*census of* tx, *denoted by* $C_r^{(T)}(\mathrm{tx})$, *is the number of ledgers for which* $\mathrm{tx} \in \mathbf{L}_i^{(T)}[r]$. *When* T *can be inferred from context, we shorten this to the* r-*census* $C_r(\mathrm{tx})$.

Lemma 5 (Liveness of $\mathsf{P}_F[\mathcal{D}]$). *Consider* $\mathsf{P}_F[\mathcal{D}]$, *the parallel composition of* m *subindependent ledgers, each with liveness* $\mathsf{l}(\cdot)$. *Then, for any* t_0 *and* t *for which* $t \geq t_0 + r$ *and any* $\gamma \in [0, 1]$,

$$\Pr[\exists \mathrm{tx} \in \bigcap_i A_i^{(t_0)} \text{ with } (t_0 + r, t)\text{-census} \leq (1 - \gamma)m] \leq \binom{m}{\gamma m} \mathsf{l}(r)^{\gamma m}.$$

It follows that for any $\gamma \in (0, 1)$ *the ledger* $\mathsf{P}_F[\mathcal{D}]$ *has liveness*

$$\bar{\mathsf{l}}^{\mathsf{P}_F}(r) = \binom{m}{\gamma m} \mathsf{l}\left(r - L \ln\left(\frac{1}{1 - \gamma}\right)\right)^{m\gamma}.$$

Proof. Consider times $t \geq t_0$ and a delay $r \geq 0$. For a parameter $\gamma \in (0, 1)$ we consider the (census) event that the transactions in $\bigcap_i A_i^{(t_0)}$ appear in at least $(1 - \gamma)m$ of the ledgers $\mathbf{L}_i^{(t)}\lceil t_0 + r \rceil$. In this case, any transaction $\mathrm{tx} \in A^{t_0}$ has rank $\overline{\mathrm{rank}}(\mathrm{tx}) \leq t_0 + r + L \ln(1/(1 - \gamma))$ in the ledger $\mathbf{L}^{(t)}$. It follows that the probability that there exists a transaction in $A^{(t_0)}$ that does not appear in $\mathbf{L}^{(t)}\lceil t_0 + r + L \ln(1/(1 - \gamma)) \rceil$ is no more than $\binom{m}{\gamma m} \mathsf{l}(r)^{\gamma m}$. Reparametrizing this (by setting $r' = r + L \ln(1/\gamma)$) yields the statement of the lemma. □

Lemma 6 (Liveness of $\mathsf{P}[\mathcal{D}]$). *Consider* $\mathsf{P}[\mathcal{D}]$, *the parallel composition of* m *ledgers, each with liveness* $\mathsf{l}(\cdot)$. *Then the parallel ledger* $\mathsf{P}[\mathcal{D}]$ *has liveness* $\bar{\mathsf{l}}^{\mathsf{P}}(r) = \mathsf{l}(r - L \ln m)$.

Proof. Consider times $t \geq t_0$ and a delay $r \geq 0$. Observe that if a transaction tx appears in any $\mathbf{L}_i^{(t)}\lceil t_0 + r \rceil$ then it appears in $\mathbf{L}^{(t)}\lceil t_0 + r + L \ln m \rceil$. This yields the statement of the lemma. □

3.6   Ledgers with Exponential Security

To achieve guarantees with more immediate interpretability and prepare for our main amplification results, we consider the most interesting case for persistence and liveness functions: $r \mapsto \exp(-\alpha r + \beta)$ for $\alpha, \beta \geq 0$. Note that such a function is superadditive according to Definition 9. The following statements follow directly from Corollary 3 with $\delta = 1$, and from Lemmas 4–6.

Corollary 4 (Relative persistence with targeted insertion). *Consider* $P[\mathcal{D}]$ *or* $P_F[\mathcal{D}]$, *the parallel composition of* m *ledgers, each with absolute persistence* $p_A(r) = \exp(-\alpha_p r + \beta_p)$. *Let* $\mathcal{I}$ *denote a subset of* m' *of the ledgers and let* D *satisfy* $\exp(D/L) > (m'-1)/(m-1)$. *Then for any* $\delta > 0$ *and time* T, *the probability that an adversary can inject a transaction* tx *that does not appear in any of the ledgers so as to appear only in ledgers* $\mathcal{I}$ *and achieve* $\overline{\mathrm{rank}}_L(\mathrm{tx}) \leq T - D$ *is no more than*

$$(D + L\ln m)^{m'} \cdot \exp\left(-\alpha_p\left[D + L\ln\left(m - \frac{m'-1}{\exp(D/L)}\right)\right] + (\alpha_p + \beta_p)m'\right).$$

Corollary 5 (Absolute persistence). *Consider* $P[\mathcal{D}]$ *or* $P_F[\mathcal{D}]$, *the parallel composition of* m *ledgers with absolute persistence* $p_A(r) = \exp(-\alpha_p r + \beta_p)$. *Then the ledgers* $P[\mathcal{D}]$ *and* $P_F[\mathcal{D}]$ *both have absolute persistence* $\overline{p}_A(r) \leq m^{\alpha_p L+1} \exp(-\alpha_p r + \beta_p)$.

Corollary 6 (Liveness). *Consider* $P[\mathcal{D}]$ *and* $P_F[\mathcal{D}]$, *constructed with* m *ledgers* $\mathcal{D}$ *that each possess liveness* $l(r) = \exp(-\alpha_l r + \beta_l)$. *Then, for any* $\gamma \in (0,1)$ *and times* t_0 *and* t *for which* $t_0 + r \leq t$,

$$\Pr[\exists \mathrm{tx} \in A^{(t_0)} \text{ with } (t_0 + r, t)\text{-census} \leq (1-\gamma)m] \leq \binom{m}{\gamma m}\exp(-\gamma m(\alpha_l r - \beta_l))$$

and the liveness function $\overline{l}^{\,P_F}(\cdot)$ *of* $P_F[\mathcal{D}]$ *satisfies*

$$\overline{l}^{\,P_F}(r) = \binom{m}{\gamma m}\exp\left(-\alpha_l \gamma m\left(r - L\ln\left(\frac{1}{1-\gamma}\right)\right) + \beta_l \gamma m\right).$$

The liveness function $\overline{l}^{\,P}(\cdot)$ *of* $P[\mathcal{D}]$ *satisfies* $\overline{l}^{\,P}(r) = m^{\alpha L}\exp(-\alpha_l r + \beta_l)$.

Theorem 3 (Restatement of Theorem 2 for $P[\mathcal{D}]$**).** *Consider* $P[\mathcal{D}]$ *for a family of* m *subindependent ledgers* $\mathcal{D} = (\mathbf{D}_1, \ldots, \mathbf{D}_m)$, *each possessing exponential liveness* $l(r) = \exp(-\alpha_l r + \beta_l)$ *and (absolute) persistence* $p(r) = \exp(-\alpha_p r + \beta_p)$. *We assume all ledgers are defined over a common transaction space* $\mathcal{T}$ *with a conflict relation and the general ledger is defined over the (preemptive) rank function* $\overline{\mathrm{rank}}_L^*$ *for a parameter* $L \geq m$. *Then*

$$\Pr\begin{bmatrix}\exists \mathrm{tx} \in A^{(t_0)} \text{ not absolutely} \\ \text{settled at time } t_0 + 2r\end{bmatrix} \leq m\exp(-\Omega(r) + O(L\ln m)).$$

The constants hidden in the $\Omega()$ *and* $O()$ *notation depend on* $\alpha_p, \alpha_l, \beta_p, \beta_l$, *but they are independent of* m, L, *and* r.

Proof. Assume a transaction tx inserted to (at least) one of the ledgers $\mathbf{L}_i$ at time t_0. By Corollary 6, at any point in time $t \geq t_0 + r$, we have that $\mathrm{tx} \in \mathbf{L}^{(t)}\lceil t_0 + r \rceil$ except for probability $\overline{l}(r) \leq \exp(-\Omega(r) + O(L\ln m))$. Let $T \geq t = t_0 + 2r$. By Corollary 5, $\mathbf{L}^{(T)}\lceil t_0 + r \rceil = \mathbf{L}^{(t)}\lceil t_0 + r \rceil$ remains persistent except for error $\overline{p_A}(r) \leq m\exp(-\Omega(r) + O(L\ln m))$. The stated bound now follows by union bound over the errors $\overline{l}(r)$ and $\overline{p_A}(r)$. $\square$

3.7 Fast Settlement with Preemption: Achieving Linear Amplification and Constant Settlement Time

We show how to achieve $\Theta(m)$ amplification for liveness and settlement time. This construction applies to transaction spaces with a conflict relation, and focuses on the setting of ledgers with exponential security, as discussed in the section above.

The Settlement Function. To contrast the constructions against the underlying ledgers, it is convenient to introduce a settlement function $s(r)$, which provides an error bound for the event that a transaction submitted at a time t_0 has not (relatively) settled by time $t_0 + r$. Assuming that the underlying ledgers provide exponential liveness and persistence yields settlement

$$s(r) \leq p_A(r/2) + l(r/2) = \exp(-\Theta(r)) \quad \text{(settlement of underlying ledgers } \mathbf{D}_i\text{).}$$

Our goal is to demonstrate that the fast ledger $\mathsf{P}_F[\mathcal{D}]$ provides linear amplification, yielding settlement function $\tilde{s}$ of the form

$$\tilde{s}_{\mathsf{P}_F}(r) \leq \exp(-\Theta(mr)) + \exp(-\tilde{\Theta}(r+L)) \quad \text{(settlement of fast ledger } \mathsf{P}_F[\mathcal{D}]\text{).}$$

(Here the $\tilde{\Theta}()$ notation neglects an additive term linear in m but logarithmic in L and r.) Note that this scales as $\exp(-\Theta(rm))$ so long as $rm \leq L$.

As discussed earlier, participants are free to use the "slow" logging mechanism (that is, simply logging their transaction in a single of the underlying ledgers), in which case they will achieve

$$\tilde{s}_{\mathsf{P}}(r) \leq \exp(-\Theta(r) + O(L \ln m)) \quad \text{(settlement of slow ledger } \mathsf{P}[\mathcal{D}]\text{).}$$

Thus parameter L determines the transition between fast and slow settlement. For $r \approx L/m$, one achieves fast settlement; for $r \approx L \log m$, the system provides settlement guarantees asymptotically consistent with those of the underlying ledgers themselves.

Theorem 4 (Restatement of Theorem 2 for $\mathsf{P}_F[\mathcal{D}]$). *Let $\mathcal{D} = (\mathbf{D}_1, \ldots, \mathbf{D}_m)$ be a family of m subindependent dynamic ledgers defined over a common transaction space $\mathcal{T}$ with a conflict relation, each possessing exponential liveness $l(r) = \exp(-\alpha_l r + \beta_l)$ and absolute persistence $p(r) = \exp(-\alpha_p r + \beta_p)$. Consider the combined dynamic ledger $\mathsf{P}_F[\mathcal{D}]$ with the (preemptive) rank function $\overline{\mathrm{rank}}_L^*$ for a parameter $L \geq m$. We have*

$$\Pr \begin{bmatrix} \exists \mathrm{tx} \in A^{(t_0)} \text{ not rela-} \\ \text{tively settled at time } t_0 + \\ 2r \end{bmatrix} \leq \begin{array}{l} \exp(-r\Omega(m) + O(m)) + \\ \exp\left(-\Omega(r) - \Omega(L \ln(m)) + O(m \ln(L+r))\right), \end{array}$$

thus there is a constant $C > 1$ so that if $L \geq Cm \ln m$ this probability is

$$\exp(-r\Omega(m) + O(m)) + \exp\left(-\Omega(r) - \Omega(L \ln(m))\right).$$

The constants hidden in the $\Omega()$ and $O()$ notation depend on $\alpha_p, \alpha_l, \beta_p, \beta_l$ (and constants selected during the proof), but they are independent of m, L, and r.

Proof. Consider the set of transactions $A^{(t_0)}$. In light of Corollary 6, at time $T = t_0 + 2r$ these transactions will appear in at least $(1 - \gamma)m$ of the ledgers with rank $t_0 + r$ except with probability

$$\binom{m}{\gamma m} \exp(-\alpha_1 r + \beta_1)^{m\gamma} \leq \exp(-\gamma m[\alpha_1 r - \beta_1 - \ln(e/\gamma)]).$$

Specifically the $(t_0 + r, r_0 + 2r)$-census of these transactions is at least $(1 - \gamma)m$. Observe that so long as r exceeds a constant determined by α, β, and γ, this has the desired scaling.

We now consider the possibility that a transaction from $A^{(t_0+2r)}$ (or later) that conflicts with some transaction in $A^{(t_0)}$ can achieve rank less than those in $A^{(t_0)}$. We observe that almost all of the $(1 - \gamma)m$ ledgers guaranteed above (that contain the transactions of $A^{(t_0)}$ at rank at most $t_0 + r$) are fixed for all future times up to this rank. Specifically, the probability that more than γm of these ledgers are not persistent through rank $t_0 + r$ (in the view of future times $T \geq t_0 + 2r$) is at most

$$\binom{m}{\gamma m} \exp(-\alpha_p r + \beta_p)^{\gamma m} \leq \exp(-\gamma m[\alpha_p r - \beta_p - \ln(e/\gamma)]).$$

As above, for a constant r that depends only on α_p, β_p, and γ, we achieve the desired scaling.

Observe that—except with this small error probability $\exp(-\Omega(mr))$—all transactions in $A^{(t_0)}$ have $\overline{\mathrm{rank}}_L^*$ no more than $t_0 + r + \ln(1/(1 - 2\gamma))L$ at all future times.

In order for a transaction appearing after $t_0 + 2r$ to compete with a transaction in $A^{(t_0)}$, then, it must achieve a $\overline{\mathrm{rank}}_L^*$ of $t_0 + r + \ln(1/(1 - 2\gamma))L$ using only $2\gamma m$ of the ledgers. At time $T = t_0 + 2r$, we apply Corollary 4 with the setting of $D = r - \ln(1/(1 - 2\gamma))L$; further assuming that $\gamma < 1/4$, this event can occur with probability no more than

$$(r + L \ln m)^{2\gamma m}.$$

$$\exp\left(-\alpha_p \left[r - L \ln\left(\frac{1}{1 - 2\gamma}\right) + L \ln\left(m - \frac{2\gamma m}{1 - 2\gamma}\right)\right] + (\alpha_p + \beta_p)2\gamma m\right).$$

As we assume $m \leq L$, this is no more than

$$(r + L^2)^{2\gamma m} \exp\left(-\alpha_p r - \alpha_p L \left[\ln\left(m\frac{1 - 4\gamma}{1 - 2\gamma}\right) - 1\right] + (\alpha_p + \beta_p)2\gamma m\right)$$

$$= \exp\left(-\alpha_p r - \alpha_p L [\ln(m) + O(1)] + O(m \ln(L + r))\right).$$

By choosing $L = Cm \log m$ for large enough C, we obtain the form recorded in the statement of the theorem.   □

Remark 1. By setting $\gamma = 1/5$ in the proof above, we obtain a version that reflects the leading constants in the exponent. The three contributing terms are:

$\exp(-(m/5)[\alpha_l r - (\beta_l + 3)])$	Failure of $A^{(t_0)}$ to achieve $(t_0 + r, t_0 + 2r)$-census $\geq 4m/5$;
$\exp(-(m/5)[\alpha_p r - (\beta_p + 3)])$	Persistence failure exceeding $m/5$ of these transactions at rank $t_0 + r$;
$\exp(-\alpha_p r - \alpha_p L[\ln(\frac{m}{3e})] + \frac{m}{5}(2\beta_p + 4\ln(r + L))$	Persistence failure of remaining rank by insertion into $2m/5$ chains.

3.7.1 Worst-Case Constant-Time Settlement

In the setting where we have the luxury to select m so that it scales with the security parameter of the system, the construction above provides *constant time* settlement. Specifically, examining the statement (and following remarks with explicit bounds) of Theorem 2 above, by merely taking r large enough to ensure that $\alpha_l r \geq \beta_l + 4$ and $\alpha_p r \geq \beta_p + 4$ the first two failure terms above both decay exponentially in m. Likewise, by suitably adjusting L so that

$$L \geq \frac{m + (m/5)(2\beta_p + 4\ln(r + L))}{\alpha_p \ln(m/3e)}$$

the third term also falls off exponentially in m. (This is always possible with $L = O(m \log m)$.) Thus this achieves settlement in constant time except with probability negligible in the security parameter, establishing the following corollary stated earlier.

Corollary 1 (restated). *In the setting of Theorem 2, if the number of chains m scales with the security parameter then $\mathsf{P}_F[\mathcal{D}]$ achieves constant-time settlement except with an error probability negligible in the security parameter.*

In the full paper [17] we additionally explore the amplification problem in a stronger setting, called the *coordinated model*, assuming that any transaction attempted to be included into any of the ledgers is also immediately attempted to be included into all of the remaining ledgers. This allows to adopt a simpler rank function and achieve simpler results.

4   Implementation Considerations

4.1   Achieving Subindependence

Proof of Stake. Subindependence is easier to achieve in the proof-of-stake setting. In PoS, block creation rights are attributed to protocol participants via a stake-based lottery governed by randomness that is derived as a part of the protocol. Hence, a straightforward solution for obtaining (sub)independence in a setup with m PoS blockchains is to derive independent lottery randomness for selecting block creators for each of the chains (even in situations where these are sampled from the same stake distribution). This approach has been proposed before, e.g., in [19], and hence we omit the details.

Proof of Work. Blockchain subindependence in the proof-of-work setting can be achieved by generalizing the 2-for-1-PoW idea from [20] where two independent PoW-oracle queries are obtained from a single invocation of the random oracle. Similarly to [5], we propose a construction for an m-for-1-PoW to achieve m PoW-queries (one for each chain) by invocation of one single random oracle query—however, introducing some dependence between the m resulting queries. Still, the construction is sufficient to serve as a common PoW to maintain m *subindependent* ledgers.

The Construction. Given a hash function $H : \{0,1\}^* \to \{0,1\}^\kappa$ modeled as a random oracle, we partition a hash output $Y = H(X)$ into two bit-segments $Y = (Y_1, Y_2)$ of size $\kappa/2$ each. The first segment decides whether the query is *successful* (by the test $Y_1 < T$ for some threshold T with $p \stackrel{\text{def}}{=} T/2^{\kappa/2}$), the second segment *assigns* the invocation to a particular PoW instance $i \in [m]$ (by computing $i = 1 + (Y_2 \bmod m)$). The single invocation $H(X)$ is then defined to be *successful for instance* i if it is both successful and is assigned to instance i (i.e., $Y_1 < T$ and $i = 1 + (Y_2 \bmod m)$). Formally, we write $\mathsf{PoW}_p^m(X) \stackrel{\text{def}}{=} (S_1, \ldots, S_m)$ where $S_i \stackrel{\text{def}}{=} (Y_1 < T \wedge i = 1 + (Y_2 \bmod m)) \in \{0,1\}$ for the bit vector of successes of the query X with respect to all instances. Note that the random variables S_i are fully determined by X and the internal randomness of the random oracle.

Analysis. We compare $\mathsf{PoW}_p^m(X)$ to an "ideal" oracle $\mathsf{IPoW}_{p'}^m(X)$ that for each new query X samples a fresh response $\mathsf{IPoW}_{p'}^m(X) \stackrel{\text{def}}{=} (\tilde{S}_1, \ldots, \tilde{S}_m)$ such that each binary random variable $\tilde{S}_i$ takes value 1 with probability p' and all $\tilde{S}_i$ are independent; repeated queries are answered consistently. Responses to new queries $\mathsf{IPoW}_{p'}^m(X)$ hence also depend only on the input and the internal randomness of $\mathsf{IPoW}_{p'}^m$. Let $\delta(\cdot, \cdot)$ denote the standard notion of statistical distance (sometimes called the total variation distance) of random variables. Then we have the following simple observation.

Lemma 7. *For any $x \in \{0,1\}^*$ and $p \in (0,1)$, we have*

$$\delta\left(\mathsf{PoW}_p^m(x), \mathsf{IPoW}_{p/m}^m(x)\right) \leq p^2 .$$

The above lemma already justifies the use of PoW_p^m for achieving subindependence in practical scenarios. To observe this, note that the use of $\mathsf{IPoW}_{p/m}^m$ would lead to full independence of the individual PoW lotteries, and by Lemma 7 the real execution with PoW_p^m will only differ from this ideal behavior with probability at most $Q \cdot p^2$, where Q is the total number of PoW-queries. With current values of $p \approx 10^{-22}$ in, e.g., Bitcoin,[3] and the block creation time adjusting to 10 minutes, this difference would manifest on expectation in about 10^{18} years. Note that any future increase of the total mining difficulty while maintaining the block creation time would only increase this period. Nonetheless, in the full paper [17], we prove the following, fully-parameterized result.

---

[3] https://btc.com/stats/diff.

Lemma 8. *Consider the collection of m dynamic ledgers $\mathcal{D} = (\mathbf{D}_1, \ldots, \mathbf{D}_m)$ produced by a parallel m-fold execution of Bitcoin using PoW_p^m as the joint PoW oracle as described above, with n parties, each making q queries to PoW_p^m per round. Let λ denote a security parameter and assume throughout that $q \geq \lambda^5$, $m \leq \lambda$, $pq \leq \lambda$, and the honest parties dominate the adversarial parties sufficiently to invoke existing analysis yielding exponential persistence and liveness bounds for an individual chain. Then the ledgers $\mathcal{D}$ satisfy ε-subindependence with $\varepsilon = \mathsf{poly}(\lambda) \cdot \exp(-\Omega(\lambda))$.*

4.2   Realizing Rank via Timestamped Blockchains

An important consideration when deploying our virtual ledger construction over existing blockchains is how to realize the notion of rank. We note that typical Nakamoto-style PoS blockchains (e.g., the Ouroboros family, Snow White) assume a common notion of time among the participants and explicitly label blocks with slot numbers with a direct correspondence to absolute time. These slot numbers (or, preferably, a notion of common time associated with each slot number) directly afford a notion of rank that provides the desired persistence and liveness guarantees. To formalize this property, we introduce the notion of a timestamped blockchain.

Definition 11. *A* timestamped blockchain *is one satisfying the following conventions:*

- Block timestamps. *Every block contains a declared timestamp.*
- Monotonicity. *In order for a block to be considered valid, its timestamp can be no less than the timestamps of all prior blocks in the blockchain. (Thus valid blockchains consist of blocks in monotonically increasing order.)*

Informally, we say that an algorithm is a timestamped blockchain algorithm *if it calls for participants to broadcast timestamped blockchains and to "respect timestamps." More specifically, the algorithm satisfies the following:*

- Faithful honest timestamping. *Honest participants always post blocks with timestamps determined by their local clocks.*
- Ignore future blocks. *Honest participants ignore blocks that contain a timestamp which is greater than their local time by more than a fixed constant. (These blocks might be considered later when the local clock of the participant "catches up" with the timestamp.)*

As mentioned above, typical Nakamoto-style PoS blockchains are timestamped by design. For PoW blockchains the situation varies case by case. For instance, Bitcoin provides block timestamps, but these follow a more complex convention which guarantees that the timestamp associated with each block exceeds the *median* timestamp of the previous 11 blocks. Note, then, that one can assign a "logical timestamp" to block B_t equal to the maximum timestamp on the blocks $\{B_i : i \leq t\}$; these logical timestamps are then monotonically non-decreasing. Ignoring future blocks is also a part of the Bitcoin protocol.

For blockchains that do not provide timestamps satisfying the above notion natively, the full paper [17] describes a straightforward transformation that modifies any longest-chain rule blockchain algorithm into a timestamped blockchain, and demonstrates security of the transformation.

Timestamped Blockchains as Dynamic Ledgers. Timestamped blockchains can be interpreted as dynamic ledgers in the natural way: for a fixed party P and time t, the ledger $\mathbf{L}^{(t)}$—corresponding to the index t in the dynamic ledger—consists of all the transactions present in the blocks constituting the blockchain $B_{\mathsf{P},t}$ held by P at time t that have a timestamp not greater than t. The rank of each transaction $\mathsf{tx} \in \mathbf{L}^{(t)}$ is then defined to be the timestamp of the earliest block in $B_{\mathsf{P},t}$ containing it. Observe that standard exponentially vanishing error bounds on the persistence and liveness of such blockchains then translate to exponential failure bounds for the respective properties of the dynamic ledger.

4.3   A Proof-of-Work Instantiation

In this section we summarize the implications of our results for the proof-of-work setting by proving Corollary 7, which is a more detailed version of Theorem 1. Recall the definition of the (p, q)-flat PoW model from Theorem 1.

Corollary 7. *Let $\epsilon > 0$ and let λ denote the security parameter. Let $\mathcal{D} = (\mathbf{D}_1, \ldots, \mathbf{D}_m)$ be a family of $m = \lambda$ dynamic ledgers induced from m PoW-based blockchains using PoW_p^m as their joint PoW oracle, having a common transaction space with a conflict relation, and run by a combined population of $n = \mathsf{poly}(\lambda)$ parties in the synchronous (p, q)-flat PoW model, out of which at least a $(1/2 + \epsilon)$-fraction is honest. Let the assumptions of Lemma 8 be satisfied, i.e., $q \geq \lambda^5$, $pq \leq \lambda$.*

Consider the combined dynamic ledger $\mathsf{P}_F[\mathcal{D}]$ with the (preemptive) rank function $\overline{\mathsf{rank}}_L^*$. Then for $\mathsf{P}_F[\mathcal{D}]$, there is a constant $C > 1$ so that if $L = Cm \ln m$, $\mathsf{P}_F[\mathcal{D}]$ achieves constant-time relative settlement except with an error probability negligible in the security parameter λ. (Observe that with such choice of L the system still provides meaningful single-chain settlement guarantees.)

Proof (sketch). The statement is an instantiation of Corollary 1 (which is itself based on Theorem 2) to the case of $m = \lambda$ PoW-based ledgers using a joint PoW_p^m oracle. The required subindependence of this mining mechanism follows from Lemma 8.   □

References

1. Arora, S., Hazan, E., Kale, S.: The multiplicative weights update method: a meta-algorithm and applications. Theory Comput. **8**(6), 121–164 (2012)
2. Badertscher, C., Gaži, P., Kiayias, A., Russell, A., Zikas, V.: Ouroboros genesis: composable proof-of-stake blockchains with dynamic availability. In: Lie, D., Mannan, M., Backes, M., Wang, X. (eds.) ACM CCS 2018, pp. 913–930. ACM Press, October 2018

3. Badertscher, C., Gaži, P., Kiayias, A., Russell, A., Zikas, V.: Ouroboros chronos: Permissionless clock synchronization via proof-of-stake. Cryptology ePrint Archive, Report 2019/838 (2019). https://eprint.iacr.org/2019/838

4. Badertscher, C., Maurer, U., Tschudi, D., Zikas, V.: Bitcoin as a transaction ledger: a composable treatment. In: Katz, J., Shacham, H. (eds.) CRYPTO 2017. LNCS, vol. 10401, pp. 324–356. Springer, Cham (2017). https://doi.org/10.1007/978-3-319-63688-7_11

5. Bagaria, V.K., Kannan, S., Tse, D., Fanti, G.C., Viswanath, P.: Prism: Deconstructing the blockchain to approach physical limits. In: Cavallaro, L., Kinder, J., Wang, X., Katz, J. (eds.) ACM CCS 2019, pp. 585–602. ACM Press, November 2019

6. Boneh, D., Boyen, X.: On the impossibility of efficiently combining collision resistant hash functions. In: Dwork, C. (ed.) CRYPTO 2006. LNCS, vol. 4117, pp. 570–583. Springer, Heidelberg (2006). https://doi.org/10.1007/11818175_34

7. Buterin, V.: A next-generation smart contract and decentralized application platform (2009). Online manuscript

8. Canetti, R.: Universally composable security: a new paradigm for cryptographic protocols. In: 42nd FOCS, pp. 136–145. IEEE Computer Society Press, October 2001

9. Chen, J., Micali, S.: Algorand (2016). arXiv preprint arXiv:1607.01341

10. Cohen, B., Pietrzak, K.: The chia network blockchain (2019). Online manuscript

11. Daian, P., Pass, R., Shi, E.: Snow White: robustly reconfigurable consensus and applications to provably secure proof of stake. In: Goldberg, I., Moore, T. (eds.) FC 2019. LNCS, vol. 11598, pp. 23–41. Springer, Cham (2019). https://doi.org/10.1007/978-3-030-32101-7_2

12. David, B., Gaži, P., Kiayias, A., Russell, A.: Ouroboros praos: an adaptively-secure, semi-synchronous proof-of-stake blockchain. In: Nielsen, J.B., Rijmen, V. (eds.) EUROCRYPT 2018, vol. 10821. LNCS, pp. 66–98. Springer, Heidelberg (2018). https://doi.org/10.1007/978-3-319-78375-8_3

13. Dodis, Y., Impagliazzo, R., Jaiswal, R., Kabanets, V.: Security amplification for *interactive* cryptographic primitives. In: Reingold, O. (ed.) TCC 2009. LNCS, vol. 5444, pp. 128–145. Springer, Heidelberg (2009). https://doi.org/10.1007/978-3-642-00457-5_9

14. Dziembowski, S., Eckey, L., Faust, S., Malinowski, D.: Perun: virtual payment hubs over cryptocurrencies. In: 2019 IEEE Symposium on Security and Privacy (SP), pp. 327–344 (2019)

15. Dziembowski, S., Faust, S., Hostáková, K.: General state channel networks. In: Lie, D., Mannan, M., Backes, M., Wang, X. (eds.) ACM CCS 2018, pp. 949–966. ACM Press, October 2018

16. Fischlin, M., Lehmann, A.: Security-amplifying combiners for collision-resistant hash functions. In: Menezes, A. (ed.) CRYPTO 2007. LNCS, vol. 4622, pp. 224–243. Springer, Heidelberg (2007). https://doi.org/10.1007/978-3-540-74143-5_13

17. Fitzi, M., Gaži, P., Kiayias, A., Russell, A.: Ledger combiners for fast settlement. Cryptology ePrint Archive, Report 2020/675 (2020)

18. Fitzi, M., Gaži, P., Kiayias, A., Russell, A.: Parallel chains: Improving throughput and latency of blockchain protocols via parallel composition. Cryptology ePrint Archive, Report 2018/1119 (2018)

19. Fitzi, M., Gaži, P., Kiayias, A., Russell, A.: Proof-of-stake blockchain protocols with near-optimal throughput. Cryptology ePrint Archive, Report 2020/037 (2020)

20. Garay, J., Kiayias, A., Leonardos, N.: The bitcoin backbone protocol: analysis and applications. In: Oswald, E., Fischlin, M. (eds.) EUROCRYPT 2015. LNCS, vol. 9057, pp. 281–310. Springer, Heidelberg (2015). https://doi.org/10.1007/978-3-662-46803-6_10

21. Gaži, P., Maurer, U.: Free-start distinguishing: combining two types of indistinguishability amplification. In: Kurosawa, K. (ed.) ICITS 2009. LNCS, vol. 5973, pp. 28–44. Springer, Heidelberg (2010). https://doi.org/10.1007/978-3-642-14496-7_4

22. Harnik, D., Kilian, J., Naor, M., Reingold, O., Rosen, A.: On robust combiners for oblivious transfer and other primitives. In: Cramer, R. (ed.) EUROCRYPT 2005. LNCS, vol. 3494, pp. 96–113. Springer, Heidelberg (2005). https://doi.org/10.1007/11426639_6

23. Herzberg, A.: On tolerant cryptographic constructions. In: Menezes, A. (ed.) CT-RSA 2005. LNCS, vol. 3376, pp. 172–190. Springer, Heidelberg (2005). https://doi.org/10.1007/978-3-540-30574-3_13

24. Kiayias, A., Russell, A., David, B., Oliynykov, R.: Ouroboros: a provably secure proof-of-stake blockchain protocol. In: Katz, J., Shacham, H. (eds.) CRYPTO 2017. LNCS, vol. 10401, pp. 357–388. Springer, Cham (2017). https://doi.org/10.1007/978-3-319-63688-7_12

25. Lerner, S.: Dagcoin draft (2015). Online manuscript

26. Luby, M., Rackoff, C.: Pseudo-random permutation generators and cryptographic composition. In: 18th ACM STOC, pp. 356–363. ACM Press, May 1986

27. Magri, B., Matt, C., Nielsen, J.B., Tschudi, D.: Afgjort: a partially synchronous finality layer for blockchains. Cryptology ePrint Archive, Report 2019/504 (2019)

28. Maurer, U., Oswald, Y.A., Pietrzak, K., Sjödin, J.: Luby-Rackoff ciphers from weak round functions? In: Vaudenay, S. (ed.) EUROCRYPT 2006. LNCS, vol. 4004, pp. 391–408. Springer, Heidelberg (2006). https://doi.org/10.1007/11761679_24

29. Maurer, U., Pietrzak, K.: Composition of random systems: when two weak make one strong. In: Naor, M. (ed.) TCC 2004. LNCS, vol. 2951, pp. 410–427. Springer, Heidelberg (2004). https://doi.org/10.1007/978-3-540-24638-1_23

30. Maurer, U., Pietrzak, K., Renner, R.: Indistinguishability amplification. In: Menezes, A. (ed.) CRYPTO 2007. LNCS, vol. 4622, pp. 130–149. Springer, Heidelberg (2007). https://doi.org/10.1007/978-3-540-74143-5_8

31. Maurer, U., Tessaro, S.: Computational indistinguishability amplification: tight product theorems for system composition. In: Halevi, S. (ed.) CRYPTO 2009. LNCS, vol. 5677, pp. 355–373. Springer, Heidelberg (2009). https://doi.org/10.1007/978-3-642-03356-8_21

32. Myers, S.: Efficient amplification of the security of weak pseudo-random function generators. J. Cryptol. 16(1), 1–24 (2003)

33. Nakamoto, S.: Bitcoin: a peer-to-peer electronic cash system (2008). Online manuscript

34. Park, S., Kwon, A., Fuchsbauer, G., Gaži, P., Alwen, J., Pietrzak, K.: SpaceMint: a cryptocurrency based on proofs of space. In: Meiklejohn, S., Sako, K. (eds.) FC 2018. LNCS, vol. 10957, pp. 480–499. Springer, Heidelberg (2018). https://doi.org/10.1007/978-3-662-58387-6_26

35. Pass, R., Seeman, L., Shelat, A.: Analysis of the blockchain protocol in asynchronous networks. In: Coron, J.-S., Nielsen, J.B. (eds.) EUROCRYPT 2017. LNCS, vol. 10211, pp. 643–673. Springer, Cham (2017). https://doi.org/10.1007/978-3-319-56614-6_22

36. Pass, R., Shi, E.: Hybrid consensus: efficient consensus in the permissionless model. Cryptology ePrint Archive, Report 2016/917 (2016)

37. Pass, R., Shi, E.: The sleepy model of consensus. In: Takagi, T., Peyrin, T. (eds.) ASIACRYPT 2017. LNCS, vol. 10625, pp. 380–409. Springer, Cham (2017). https://doi.org/10.1007/978-3-319-70697-9_14

38. Pass, R., Shi, E.: Thunderella: blockchains with optimistic instant confirmation. In: Nielsen, J.B., Rijmen, V. (eds.) EUROCRYPT 2018. LNCS, vol. 10821, pp. 3–33. Springer, Cham (2018). https://doi.org/10.1007/978-3-319-78375-8_1

39. Pietrzak, K.: Composition does not imply adaptive security. In: Shoup, V. (ed.) CRYPTO 2005. LNCS, vol. 3621, pp. 55–65. Springer, Heidelberg (2005). https://doi.org/10.1007/11535218_4

40. Pietrzak, K.: Non-trivial black-box combiners for collision-resistant hash-functions don't exist. In: Naor, M. (ed.) EUROCRYPT 2007. LNCS, vol. 4515, pp. 23–33. Springer, Heidelberg (2007). https://doi.org/10.1007/978-3-540-72540-4_2

41. Poon, J., Dryja, T.: The bitcoin lightning network: Scalable off-chain instant payments (2016). Online manuscript

42. Sompolinsky, Y., Lewenberg, Y., Zohar, A.: SPECTRE: A fast and scalable cryptocurrency protocol. Cryptology ePrint Archive, Report 2016/1159 (2016)

43. Vaudenay, S.: Decorrelation: a theory for block cipher security. J. Cryptol. **16**(4), 249–286 (2003)

Asynchronous Byzantine Agreement with Subquadratic Communication

Erica Blum[1][(✉)], Jonathan Katz[1][(✉)], Chen-Da Liu-Zhang[2][(✉)], and Julian Loss[1][(✉)]

[1] University of Maryland, College Park, USA
erblum@cs.umd.edu, jkatz2@gmail.com, lossjulian@gmail.com
[2] ETH Zurich, Zurich, Switzerland
lichen@inf.ethz.ch

Abstract. Understanding the communication complexity of Byzantine agreement (BA) is a fundamental problem in distributed computing. In particular, for protocols involving a large number of parties (as in, e.g., the context of blockchain protocols), it is important to understand the dependence of the communication on the number of parties n. Although adaptively secure BA protocols with $o(n^2)$ communication are known in the synchronous and partially synchronous settings, no such protocols are known in the fully asynchronous case.

We show asynchronous BA protocols with (expected) subquadratic communication complexity tolerating an adaptive adversary who can corrupt $f < (1 - \epsilon)n/3$ of the parties (for any $\epsilon > 0$). One protocol assumes initial setup done by a trusted dealer, after which an unbounded number of BA executions can be run; alternately, we can achieve subquadratic *amortized* communication with no prior setup. We also show that some form of setup is needed for (non-amortized) subquadratic BA tolerating $\Theta(n)$ corrupted parties.

As a contribution of independent interest, we show a secure-computation protocol in the same threat model that has $o(n^2)$ communication when computing no-input functionalities with short output (e.g., coin tossing).

1   Introduction

Byzantine agreement (BA) [31] is a fundamental problem in distributed computing. In this context, n parties wish to agree on a common output even when f of those parties might be adaptively corrupted. Although BA is a well-studied problem, it has recently received increased attention due to its application to blockchain (aka state machine replication) protocols. Such applications typically involve a large number of parties, and it is therefore critical to understand how the communication complexity of BA scales with n. While protocols with adaptive security and $o(n^2)$ communication complexity have been obtained in both

---

J. Katz—Portions of this work were done while at George Mason University.

R. Pass and K. Pietrzak (Eds.): TCC 2020, LNCS 12550, pp. 353–380, 2020.
https://doi.org/10.1007/978-3-030-64375-1_13

the synchronous [29] and partially synchronous [1] settings, there are currently no such solutions for the *asynchronous* model.[1] This leads us to ask:

> *Is it possible to design an asynchronous BA protocol with subquadratic communication complexity that tolerates $\Theta(n)$ adaptive corruptions?*

We give both positive and negative answers to this question.

Positive Results. We show asynchronous BA protocols with (expected) subquadratic communication complexity that can tolerate adaptive corruption of any $f < (1 - \epsilon)n/3$ of the parties, for arbitrary $\epsilon > 0$. (This corruption threshold is almost optimal, as it is known [7] that asynchronous BA is impossible altogether for $f \geq n/3$, even assuming prior setup and static corruptions.) Our solutions rely on two building blocks, each of independent interest:

1. We show a BA protocol Π_{BA} tolerating f adaptive corruptions and having subquadratic communication complexity. This protocol assumes prior setup by a trusted dealer for each BA execution, but the size of the setup is independent of n.
2. We construct a secure-computation protocol Π_{MPC} tolerating f adaptive corruptions, and relying on a subquadratic BA protocol as a subroutine. For the special case of no-input functionalities, the number of BA executions depends only on the security parameter, and the communication complexity is subquadratic when the output length is independent of n.

We can combine these results to give an affirmative answer to the original question. Specifically, using a trusted dealer, we can achieve an *unbounded* number of BA executions with $o(n^2)$ communication per execution. The idea is as follows. Let L be the number of BA executions required by Π_{MPC} for computing a no-input functionality. The dealer provides the parties with the setup needed for $L + 1$ executions of Π_{BA}; the total size of this setup is linear in L but independent of n. Then, each time the parties wish to carry out Byzantine agreement, they will use one instance of their setup to run Π_{BA}, and use the remaining L instances to refresh their initial setup by running Π_{MPC} to simulate the dealer. Since the size of the setup for Π_{BA} is independent of n, the total communication complexity is subquadratic in n.

Alternately, we can avoid a trusted dealer (though we do still need to assume a PKI) by having the parties run an arbitrary adaptively secure protocol to generate the initial setup. This protocol may not have subquadratic communication complexity; however, once it is finished the parties can revert to the solution above which has subquadratic communication per BA execution. Overall, this gives BA with *amortized* subquadratic communication.

Impossibility Result. We justify our reliance on a trusted dealer by showing that some form of setup is necessary for (non-amortized) subquadratic BA tolerating $\Theta(n)$ corrupted parties. Moreover, this holds even when secret channels and erasures are available.

---

[1] Tolerating $f < n/3$ *static* corruptions is easy; see Sect. 1.1.

1.1   Related Work

The problem of BA was introduced by Lamport, Shostak and Pease [31]. Without some form of setup, BA is impossible (even in a synchronous network) when $f \geq n/3$. Fischer, Lynch, and Patterson [23] ruled out deterministic protocols for asynchronous BA even when $f = 1$. Starting with the work of Rabin [38], randomized protocols for asynchronous BA have been studied in both the setup-free setting [14,34] as well as the setting with a PKI and a trusted dealer [11].

Dolev and Reischuk [21] show that any BA protocol achieving subquadratic communication complexity (even in the synchronous setting) must be randomized. BA with subquadratic communication complexity was first studied in the synchronous model by King et al., who gave setup-free *almost-everywhere* BA protocols with polylogarithmic communication complexity for the case of $f < (1-\epsilon)n/3$ static corruptions [30] and BA with $O(n^{1.5})$ communication complexity for the same number of adaptive corruptions [29]. Subsequently, several works [1,26,32,33,35] gave improved protocols with subquadratic communication complexity (in the synchronous model with an adaptive adversary) using the "player replaceability paradigm," which requires setup in the form of verifiable random functions.

Abraham et al. [1] show a BA protocol with adaptive security and subquadratic communication complexity in the *partially synchronous* model. They also give a version of the Dolev-Reischuk bound that rules out subquadratic BA (even with setup, and even in the synchronous communication model) against a strong adversary who is allowed to remove messages sent by honest parties from the network after those parties have been adaptively corrupted. Our lower bound adapts their ideas to the standard asynchronous model where honest parties' messages can be arbitrarily delayed, but cannot be deleted once they are sent. (We refer to the work of Garay et al. [24] for further discussion of these two models.) In concurrent work, Rambaud [39] proves an impossibility result similar to our own; we refer to Sect. 7 for further discussion.

Cohen et al. [19] show an adaptively secure asynchronous BA protocol with $o(n^2)$ communication. However, they consider a non-standard asynchronous model in which the adversary cannot arbitrarily schedule delivery of messages. In particular, the adversary in their model cannot reorder messages sent by honest parties in the same protocol step. We work in the standard asynchronous model. On the other hand, our work requires stronger computational assumptions and a trusted dealer (unless we settle for amortized subquadratic communication complexity).

We remark for completeness that asynchronous BA with subquadratic communication complexity for a *static* adversary corrupting $f < n/3$ of the parties is trivial using a committee-based approach, assuming a trusted dealer. Roughly, the dealer chooses a random committee of $\Theta(\kappa)$ parties (where κ is a security parameter) who then run BA on behalf of everyone. Achieving subquadratic BA *without* any setup in the static-corruption model is an interesting open question.

Asynchronous secure multi-party computation (MPC) was first studied by Ben-Or, Canetti and Goldreich [4]. Since then, improved protocols have been proposed with both unconditional [36,37,40] and computational [16,17,27,28] security. These protocols achieve optimal output quality, and incur a total communication complexity of at least $\Theta(n^3\kappa)$ assuming the output has length κ. Our MPC protocol gives a trade-off between the communication complexity and the output quality. In particular, we achieve subquadratic communication complexity when the desired output quality is sublinear (as in the case of no-input, randomized functions).

1.2 Overview of the Paper

In Sect. 2 we discuss our model and recall some standard definitions. We show how to achieve asynchronous reliable consensus and reliable broadcast with subquadratic communication in Sect. 3. In Sect. 4 we present an asynchronous BA protocol with subquadratic communication complexity, assuming prior setup by a trusted dealer for each execution. In Sect. 5 we show a communication-efficient asynchronous protocol for secure multi-party computation (MPC). We describe how these components can be combined to give our main results in Sect. 6. We conclude with our lower bound in Sect. 7.

2 Preliminaries and Definitions

We denote the security parameter by κ, and assume $\kappa < n = \mathsf{poly}(\kappa)$. In all our protocols, we implicitly assume parties take 1^κ as input; in our definitions, we implicitly allow properties to fail with probability negligible in κ. We let PPT stand for probabilistic polynomial time. We use standard digital signatures, where a signature on a message m using secret key sk is computed as $\sigma \leftarrow \mathsf{Sign}_{\mathsf{sk}}(m)$; a signature is verified relative to public key pk by calling $\mathsf{Vrfy}_{\mathsf{pk}}(m, \sigma)$. For simplicity, we assume in our proofs that the adversary cannot forge valid signatures on behalf of honest parties. When replacing the signatures with real-world instantiations, our theorems follow except with an additive negligible failure probability.

Model. We consider a setting where n parties $P_1, \ldots, P_n$ run a distributed protocol over a network in which all parties are connected via pairwise authenticated channels. We work in the *asynchronous* model, meaning the adversary can arbitrarily schedule the delivery of all messages, so long as all messages are eventually delivered. We consider an *adaptive* adversary that can corrupt some bounded number f of the parties at any point during the execution of some protocol, and cause them to deviate arbitrarily from the protocol specification. However, we assume the "atomic send" model, which means that (1) if at some point in the protocol an honest party is instructed to send several messages (possibly to different parties) simultaneously, then the adversary can corrupt that party either before or after it sends all those messages, but not in the midst of sending those messages; and (2) once an honest party sends a message, that message is guaranteed to be delivered eventually even if that party is later corrupted. In addition, we assume secure erasure.

In many cases we assume an incorruptible dealer who can initialize the parties with setup information in advance of any protocol execution. Such setup may include both public information given to all parties, as well as private information given to specific parties; when we refer to the size of a setup, we include the total private information given to all parties but count the public information only once. A public key infrastructure (PKI) is one particular setup, in which all parties hold the same vector of public keys $(\mathsf{pk}_1, \ldots, \mathsf{pk}_n)$ and each honest party P_i holds the honestly generated secret key sk_i corresponding to pk_i.

Byzantine Agreement. We include here the standard definition of Byzantine agreement. Definitions of other primitives are given in the relevant sections.

Definition 1 (Byzantine agreement). *Let Π be a protocol executed by parties $P_1, \ldots, P_n$, where each party P_i holds an input v_i and parties terminate upon generating output. Π is an f-secure* Byzantine agreement *protocol if the following hold when at most f parties are corrupted:*

- **Validity:** *if every honest party has the same input value v, then every honest party outputs v.*
- **Consistency:** *all honest parties output the same value.*

3 Building Blocks

In this section we show asynchronous protocols with subquadratic communication for reliable consensus, reliable broadcast, graded consensus, and coin flipping.

3.1 Reliable Consensus

Reliable consensus is a weaker version of Byzantine agreement where termination is not required. The definition follows.

Definition 2 (Reliable consensus). *Let Π be a protocol executed by parties $P_1, \ldots, P_n$, where each party P_i holds an input v_i and parties terminate upon generating output. Π is an f-secure* reliable consensus *protocol if the following hold when at most f parties are corrupted:*

- **Validity:** *if every honest party has the same input value v, then every honest party outputs v.*
- **Consistency:** *either no honest party terminates, or all honest parties output the same value.*

We show a reliable consensus protocol Π_{RC} with subquadratic communication. The protocol can be viewed as a variant of Bracha's reliable broadcast protocol [7,8] for the case where every party has input. The protocol assumes prior setup initialized by a trusted dealer. The trusted setup has expected size $O(\kappa^2)$ and takes the following form. First, the dealer selects two secret committees C_1, C_2 by independently placing each party in C_1 (resp., C_2) with probability κ/n. Then, for each party P_i in C_1 (resp., C_2), the dealer generates a public/private key pair $(\mathsf{pk}_{1,i}, \mathsf{sk}_{1,i})$ (resp., $(\mathsf{pk}_{2,i}, \mathsf{sk}_{2,i})$) for a digital signature scheme and gives the associated private key to P_i; the public keys (but not the identities of the members of the committees) are given to all parties.

The protocol itself is described in Fig. 1. It begins by having each party in C_1 send its signed input to all the parties. The parties in C_2 then send a signed **ready** message on a value v the first time they either (1) receive v from $\kappa - t$ parties in C_1 or (2) receive **ready** messages on v from $t + 1$ parties in C_2. All parties terminate upon receiving **ready** messages on the same value from $\kappa - t$ parties in C_2. Each committee has expected size $O(\kappa)$, and each member of a committee sends a single message to all parties; thus, $O(\kappa n)$ messages are sent (in expectation) during the protocol.

Security relies on the fact that an adversary cannot corrupt too many members of C_1 (resp., C_2) "until it is too late," except with negligible probability. For a static adversary this is immediate. For an adaptive adversary this follows from the fact that each member of a committee sends only a single message and erases its signing key after sending that message; thus, once the attacker learns that some party is in a committee, adaptively corrupting that party is useless.

Protocol Π_{RC}

We describe the protocol from the point of view of a party P_i with input v_i, assuming the setup described in the text. Set $t = (1 - \epsilon) \cdot \kappa/3$.

1. If $P_i \in C_1$: Compute $\sigma_i \leftarrow \mathsf{Sign}_{\mathsf{sk}_{1,i}}(v_i)$, erase $\mathsf{sk}_{1,i}$, and send $(\mathbf{echo}, (i, v_i, \sigma_i))$ to all parties.
2. If $P_i \in C_2$: As long as no **ready** message has yet been sent, do: upon receiving $(\mathbf{echo}, (j, v, \sigma_j))$ with $\mathsf{Vrfy}_{\mathsf{pk}_{1,j}}(v, \sigma_j) = 1$ on the same value v from at least $\kappa - t$ distinct parties, or receiving $(\mathbf{ready}, (j, v, \sigma_j))$ with $\mathsf{Vrfy}_{\mathsf{pk}_{2,j}}(v, \sigma_j) = 1$ on the same value v from strictly more than t distinct parties, compute $\sigma_i \leftarrow \mathsf{Sign}_{\mathsf{sk}_{2,i}}(v)$, erase $\mathsf{sk}_{2,i}$, and send $(\mathbf{ready}, (i, v, \sigma_i))$ to all parties.
3. Upon receiving $(\mathbf{ready}, (j, v, \sigma_j))$ with $\mathsf{Vrfy}_{\mathsf{pk}_{2,j}}(v, \sigma_j) = 1$ on the same value v from at least $\kappa - t$ distinct parties and, output v and terminate.

Fig. 1. A reliable consensus protocol, parameterized by ϵ.

Theorem 1. *Let $0 < \epsilon < 1/3$ and $f \le (1 - 2\epsilon) \cdot n/3$. Then Π_{RC} is an f-secure reliable consensus protocol with expected setup size $O(\kappa^2)$ and expected communication complexity $O((\kappa + \mathcal{I}) \cdot \kappa n)$, where $\mathcal{I}$ is the size of each party's input.*

Proof. Recall that $t = (1 - \epsilon) \cdot \kappa/3$. Say a party is *1-honest* if it is in C_1 and is not corrupted when executing step 1 of the protocol, and *1-corrupted* if it is in C_1 but corrupted when executing step 1 of the protocol. Define 2-honest and 2-corrupted analogously. Lemma 11 shows that with overwhelming probability C_1 (resp., C_2) contains fewer than $(1 + \epsilon) \cdot \kappa$ parties; there are more than $\kappa - t$ parties who are 1-honest (resp., 2-honest); and there are fewer than $t < \kappa - t$ parties who are 1-corrupted (resp., 2-corrupted). For the rest of the proof we assume these hold. We also use the fact that once a 1-honest (resp., 2-honest) party P sends a message, that message is the only such message that will be accepted by honest parties on behalf of P (even if P is adaptively corrupted after sending that message).

We first prove that Π_{RC} is f-valid. Assume all honest parties start with the same input v. Each of the parties that is 1-honest sends an echo message on v to all other parties, and so every honest party eventually receives valid echo messages on v from more than $\kappa - t$ distinct parties. Since there are fewer than $\kappa - t$ parties that are 1-corrupted, no honest party receives valid echo messages on $v' \neq v$ from $\kappa - t$ or more distinct parties. It follows that every 2-honest party sends a ready message on v to all other parties. A similar argument then shows that all honest parties output v and terminate.

Toward showing consistency, we first argue that if honest P_i, P_j send ready messages on v_i, v_j, respectively, then $v_i = v_j$. Assume this is not the case, and let P_i, P_j be the first honest parties to send ready messages on distinct values v_i, v_j. Then P_i (resp., P_j) must have received at least $\kappa - t$ valid ready messages on v_i (resp., v_j). But then at least

$$(\kappa - t) + (\kappa - t) = (1 + \epsilon) \cdot \kappa + t$$

valid ready messages were received by P_i, P_j overall. But this is impossible, since the maximum number of such messages is at most $|C_2|$ plus the number of 2-corrupted parties (because 2-honest parties send at most one ready message), which is strictly less than $(1 + \epsilon) \cdot \kappa + t$.

Now, assume an honest party P_i outputs v. Then P_i must have received valid ready messages on v from at least $\kappa - t$ distinct parties in C_2, more than $\kappa - 2t > t$ of whom are 2-honest. As a consequence, all 2-honest parties eventually receive valid ready messages on v from more than t parties, and so all 2-honest parties eventually send a ready message on v. Thus, all honest parties eventually receive valid ready messages on v from at least $\kappa - t$ parties, and so output v also.

3.2   Reliable Broadcast

Reliable broadcast allows a sender to consistently distribute a message to a set of parties. In contrast to full-fledged broadcast (and by analogy to reliable consensus), reliable broadcast does not require termination.

Definition 3 (Reliable broadcast). *Let Π be a protocol executed by parties $P_1, \ldots, P_n$, where a designated sender P^* initially holds input v^*, and parties terminate upon generating output. Π is an f-secure reliable broadcast protocol if the following hold when at most f parties are corrupted:*

– **Validity:** *if P^* is honest at the start of the protocol, then every honest party outputs v^*.*
– **Consistency:** *either no honest party terminates, or all honest parties output the same value.*

It is easy to obtain a reliable broadcast protocol Π_{RBC} (cf. Fig. 2) from reliable consensus: the sender P^* simply signs its message and sends it to all parties, who then run reliable consensus on what they received. In addition to the setup for the underlying reliable consensus protocol, Π_{RBC} assumes P^* has a public/private key pair $(\mathsf{pk}^*, \mathsf{sk}^*)$ with pk^* known to all other parties.

Protocol Π_{RBC}

1. P^* does: compute $\sigma^* \leftarrow \mathsf{Sign}_{\mathsf{sk}^*}(v^*)$, erase sk^*, and send (v^*, σ^*) to all parties.
2. Upon receiving (v^*, σ^*) with $\mathsf{Vrfy}_{\mathsf{pk}^*}(v, \sigma) = 1$, input v to Π_{RC} (with parameter ϵ).
3. Upon receiving output v from Π_{RC}, output v and terminate.

Fig. 2. A reliable broadcast protocol, implicitly parameterized by ϵ.

Theorem 2. *Let $0 < \epsilon < 1/3$ and $f \leq (1 - 2\epsilon) \cdot n/3$. Then Π_{RBC} is an f-secure reliable broadcast protocol with expected setup size $O(\kappa^2)$ and expected communication complexity $O((\kappa + \mathcal{I}) \cdot \kappa n)$, where $\mathcal{I}$ is the size of the sender's input.*

Proof. Consistency follows from consistency of Π_{RC}. As for validity, if P^* is honest at the outset of the protocol then P^* sends (v^*, σ^*) to all parties in step 1; even if P^* is subsequently corrupted, that is the only valid message from P^* that other parties will receive. As a result, every honest party runs Π_{RC} using input v, and validity of Π_{RC} implies validity of Π_{RBC}.

3.3 Graded Consensus

Graded consensus [22] can be viewed as a weaker form of consensus where parties output a grade along with a value, and agreement is required to hold only if some honest party outputs a grade of 1. Our definition does not require termination upon generating output.

Definition 4 (Graded consensus). *Let Π be a protocol executed by parties $P_1, \ldots, P_n$, where each party P_i holds an input v_i and is supposed to output a value w_i along with a grade $g_i \in \{0, 1\}$. Π is an f-secure graded-consensus protocol if the following hold when at most f parties are corrupted:*

– **Graded validity:** *if every honest party has the same input value v, then every honest party outputs $(v, 1)$.*

– **Graded consistency:** *if some honest party outputs* $(w, 1)$, *then every honest party* P_i *outputs* (w, g_i).

We formally describe a graded-consensus protocol Π_{GC} inspired by the graded consensus protocol of Canetti and Rabin [14], and prove the following theorem in the full version of the paper.

Theorem 3. *Let* $0 < \epsilon < 1/3$ *and* $f \leq (1 - 2\epsilon) \cdot n/3$. *Then* Π_{GC} *is an* f-*secure graded-consensus protocol with expected setup size* $O(\kappa^3)$ *and expected communication complexity* $O((\kappa + \mathcal{I}) \cdot \kappa^2 n)$, *where* $\mathcal{I}$ *is the size of each party's input.*

3.4 A Coin-Flip Protocol

We describe here a protocol that allows parties to generate a sequence of random bits (coins) $\mathsf{Coin}_1, \ldots, \mathsf{Coin}_T$ for a pre-determined parameter T. We denote the sub-protocol to generate the ith coin by $\mathsf{CoinFlip}(i)$. Roughly speaking, the protocol guarantees that (1) when all honest parties invoke $\mathsf{CoinFlip}(i)$, all honest parties output the same value Coin_i and (2) until the first honest party invokes $\mathsf{CoinFlip}(i)$, the value of Coin_i is uniform.

Our coin-flip protocol assumes setup provided by a trusted dealer that takes the following form: For each iteration $1, \ldots, T$, the dealer chooses uniform $\mathsf{Coin}_i \in \{0, 1\}$; chooses a random subset E_i of the parties by including each party in E_i with probability κ/n; and then gives authenticated secret shares of Coin_i (using a perfectly secret $\lceil \kappa/3 \rceil$-out-of-$|E_i|$ secret-sharing scheme) to the members of E_i. (Authentication is done by having the dealer sign the shares.) Since each share (including the signature) has size $O(\kappa)$, the size of the setup is $O(\kappa^2 T)$.

The coin-flip protocol itself simply involves having the parties in the relevant subset send their shares to everyone else. The communication complexity is thus $O(\kappa^2 n)$ per iteration.

Lemma 1. *Let* $0 < \epsilon < 1/3$ *and* $f \leq (1 - 2\epsilon) \cdot n/3$. *Then as long as at most* f *parties are corrupted,* $\mathsf{CoinFlip}(i)$ *satisfies the following:*

1. *all honest parties obtain the same value* Coin_i,
2. *until the first honest party invokes* $\mathsf{CoinFlip}(i)$, *the value of* Coin_i *is uniform from the adversary's perspective.*

Proof. Lemma 11 implies that, except with negligible probability, E_i contains more than $\lceil \kappa/3 \rceil$ honest parties and fewer than $(1 - \epsilon) \cdot \kappa/3$ corrupted parties. The stated properties follow.

4 (Single-Shot) BA with Subquadratic Communication

In this section we describe a BA protocol Π_{BA} with subquadratic communication complexity. (See Fig. 3.) Π_{BA} assumes setup that is then used for a single execution of the protocol. The setup for Π_{BA} corresponds to the setup required

---

Protocol Π_{BA}

We describe the protocol from the point of view of a party with input $v \in \{0,1\}$.

Set $b := v$ and ready := false. Then for $k = 1$ to $\kappa + 1$ do:

1. Run Π_{GC} on input b, and let (b,g) denote the output.
2. Invoke $\mathsf{CoinFlip}(k)$ to obtain Coin_k.
3. If $g = 0$ then set $b := \mathsf{Coin}_k$.
4. Run Π_{GC} on input b, and let (b,g) denote the output.
5. If $g = 1$ and ready = false, then set ready := true and run Π_{RC} on input b.
6. Set $k := k + 1$ and goto step 1.

Termination: If Π_{RC} ever terminates with output b', output b' and terminate.

Fig. 3. A Byzantine agreement protocol, implicitly parameterized by ϵ.

for $O(\kappa)$ executions of graded consensus, $O(\kappa)$ iterations of the coin-flip sub-protocol, and a single execution of reliable consensus. Using the protocols from the previous section, Π_{BA} thus requires setup of size $O(\kappa^4)$ overall.

Following ideas by Mostéfaoui et al. [34], our protocol consists of a sequence of $\Theta(\kappa)$ iterations, where each iteration invokes a graded-consensus subprotocol and a coin-flip subprotocol. In each iteration there is a constant probability that honest parties reach agreement; once agreement is reached, it cannot be undone in later iterations. The coin-flip protocol allows parties to adopt the value of a common coin if agreement has not yet been reached (or, at least, if parties are unaware that agreement has been reached). Reliable consensus is used so parties know when to terminate.

We prove security via a sequence of lemmas. Throughout the following, we fix some value $0 < \epsilon < 1/3$ and let $f \leq (1 - 2\epsilon)n/3$ be a bound on the number of corrupted parties.

Lemma 2. *If at most f parties are corrupted during an execution of Π_{BA}, then with all but negligible probability some honest party sets* ready = true *within the first κ iterations.*

Proof. Consider an iteration k of Π_{BA} such that no honest party set ready = true in any previous iteration. (This is trivially true in the first iteration). We begin by showing that some honest party sets ready = true in that iteration with probability at least $1/2$. Consider two cases:

- If some honest party outputs $(b,1)$ in the first execution of Π_{GC} during iteration k, then graded consistency of Π_{GC} guarantees that every other honest party outputs $(b,1)$ or $(b,0)$ in that execution. The value b is independent of Coin_k, because b is determined prior to the point when the first honest party invokes $\mathsf{CoinFlip}(i)$; thus, $\mathsf{Coin}_k = b$ with probability $1/2$. If that occurs, then all honest parties input b to the second execution of Π_{GC} and, by graded validity, every honest party outputs $(g,1)$ in the second execution of Π_{GC} and sets $\mathsf{ready} = \mathsf{true}$.

- Say no honest party outputs grade 1 in the first execution of Π_{GC} during iteration k. Then all honest parties input Coin_k to the second execution of Π_{GC} and, by graded validity, every honest party outputs $(g,1)$ in the second execution of Π_{GC} and sets $\mathsf{ready} = \mathsf{true}$.

Thus, in each iteration where no honest party has yet set $\mathsf{ready} = \mathsf{true}$, some honest party sets $\mathsf{ready} = \mathsf{true}$ in that iteration with probability at least $1/2$. We conclude that the probability that no honest party has set $\mathsf{ready} = \mathsf{true}$ after κ iterations is negligible.

Lemma 3. *Assume at most f parties are corrupted during execution of Π_{BA}. If some honest party executes Π_{RC} using input b in iteration k, then (1) honest parties who execute Π_{GC} in any iteration $k' > k$ use input b, and (2) honest parties who execute Π_{RC} in any iteration $k' \geq k$ use input b.*

Proof. Consider the first iteration k in which some honest party P sets $\mathsf{ready} = \mathsf{true}$, and let b denote P's input to Π_{RC}. P must have received $(b,1)$ from the second execution of Π_{GC} in iteration k. By graded consistency, all other honest parties must receive $(b,0)$ or $(b,1)$ from that execution of Π_{GC} as well. Thus, any honest parties who execute Π_{RC} in iteration k use input b, and any honest parties who run[2] the first execution of Π_{GC} in iteration $k+1$ will use input b as well. Graded validity ensures that any honest party who receives output from that execution of Π_{GC} will receive $(b,1)$, causing them to use input b to the next execution of Π_{GC} as well as Π_{RC} (if they execute those protocols), and so on.

Lemma 4. *Assume at most f parties are corrupted during an execution of Π_{BA}. If some honest party sets $\mathsf{ready} = \mathsf{true}$ within the first κ iterations and executes Π_{RC} using input b, then all honest parties terminate with output b.*

Proof. Let $k \leq \kappa$ be the first iteration in which some honest party sets $\mathsf{ready} = \mathsf{true}$ and executes Π_{RC} using input b. By Lemma 3, any other honest party who executes Π_{RC} must also use input b, and furthermore all honest parties who execute Π_{GC} in any subsequent iteration use input b there as well. We now consider two cases:

- If no honest party terminates before all honest parties receive output from the second execution of Π_{GC} in iteration $k+1$, then graded validity of Π_{GC} ensures that all honest parties receive $(b,1)$ as output from that execution, and thus all parties execute Π_{RC} using input b at this point if they have not done so already. Validity of Π_{RC} then ensures that all honest parties output b and terminate.

---

[2] Note that some honest parties may terminate before others, and in particular it may be the case that not all honest parties run some execution of Π_{GC}.

– If some honest party P has terminated before all honest parties receive output from the second execution of Π_{GC} in iteration $k + 1$, validity of Π_{RC} implies that P must have output b. In that case, consistency of Π_{RC} guarantees that all parties will eventually output b and terminate.

This completes the proof.

Theorem 4. *Let $0 < \epsilon < 1/3$ and $f \leq (1 - 2\epsilon) \cdot n/3$. Then Π_{BA} is an f-secure BA protocol with expected setup size $O(\kappa^4)$ and expected communication complexity $O(\kappa^4 n)$.*

Proof. By Lemma 2, with overwhelming probability some honest party sets ready = true within the first κ iterations and thus executes Π_{RC} using some input b. It follows from Lemma 4 that all honest parties eventually output b and terminate. This proves consistency.

Assume all honest parties have the same input v. Unless some honest party terminates before all honest parties have concluded the first iteration, one can verify (using graded validity of Π_{GC}) that in the first iteration all honest parties output $(v, 1)$ from the first execution of Π_{GC}; use input v to the second execution of Π_{GC}; output $(v, 1)$ from the second execution of Π_{GC}; and execute Π_{RC} using input v. But the only way some honest party could terminate before all honest parties have concluded the first iteration is if that party executes Π_{RC} using input v. Either way, Lemma 4 shows that all honest parties will terminate with output v, proving validity.

5   MPC with Subquadratic Communication

In this section we give a protocol for asynchronous secure multiparty computation (MPC). Our protocol uses a Byzantine agreement protocol as a subroutine; importantly, the number of executions of Byzantine agreement is independent of the number of parties as well as the output length, as long as the desired input quality is low enough. Our MPC protocol also relies on a sub-protocol for (a variant of the) *asynchronous common subset* problem; we give a definition, and a protocol with subquadratic communication complexity, in the next section.

5.1   Validated ACS with Subquadratic Communication

A protocol for the asynchronous common subset (ACS) problem [5,12] allows n parties to agree on a subset of their initial inputs of some minimum size. We consider a *validated* version of ACS (VACS), where it is additionally ensured that all values in the output multiset satisfy a given predicate Q [10,15].

Definition 5. *Let Q be a predicate, and let Π be a protocol executed by parties $P_1, \ldots, P_n$, where each party outputs a multiset of size at most n, and terminates upon generating output. Π is an f-secure Q-validated ACS protocol with ℓ-output quality if the following hold when at most f parties are corrupted and every honest party's input satisfies Q:*

– **Q-Validity:** *if an honest party outputs S, then each $v \in S$ satisfies $Q(v) = 1$.*
– **Consistency:** *every honest party outputs the same multiset.*
– **ℓ-Output quality:** *all honest parties output a multiset of size at least ℓ that contains inputs from at least $\ell - f$ parties who were honest at the start of the protocol.*

Our VACS protocol $\Pi_{\mathsf{VACS}}^{\ell,Q}$ (see Fig. 4) is inspired by the protocol of Ben-Or et al. [5]. During the setup phase, a secret committee C is chosen by independently placing each party in C with probability s/n, where $s = \frac{3}{2+\epsilon}\ell$ and ℓ is the desired output quality. Each party in the committee acts as a sender in a reliable-broadcast protocol, and then the parties run $|C|$ instances of Byzantine agreement to agree on the set of reliable-broadcast executions that terminated. The expected communication complexity and setup size for $\Pi_{\mathsf{VACS}}^{\ell,Q}$ are thus (in expectation) a factor of $O(\ell)$ larger than those for reliable broadcast and Byzantine agreement.

Protocol $\Pi_{\mathsf{VACS}}^{\ell,Q}$

We describe the protocol from the point of view of a party P with input v. We assume prior setup in which a committee C is chosen (see text).

1. Execute $|C|$ instances of reliable broadcast, denoted $\mathsf{RBC}_1, \ldots, \mathsf{RBC}_{|C|}$. If P is the ith member of C, then P executes the ith instance of Π_{RBC} as the sender using input v.
2. On output v_i from RBC_i with $Q(v_i) = 1$, if P has not yet begun executing the ith instance BA_i of Byzantine agreement, then begin that execution using input 1.
3. When P has output 1 in ℓ instances of Byzantine agreement, then begin executing any other instances of Byzantine agreement that have not yet begun using input 0.
4. Once P has terminated in all instances of Byzantine agreement, let $\mathsf{CoreSet}$ be the indices of those instances that resulted in output 1. After receiving output v_i from RBC_i for all $i \in \mathsf{CoreSet}$, output the multiset $\{v_i\}_{i \in \mathsf{CoreSet}}$.

Fig. 4. A VACS protocol (implicitly parameterized by ϵ) with ℓ-output quality and predicate Q.

Using the protocols from the previous sections, we thus obtain:

Theorem 5. *Let $0 < \epsilon < 1/3$, $f \le (1 - 2\epsilon) \cdot n/3$, and $\ell \le (1 + \epsilon/2) \cdot 2n/3$. Then $\Pi_{\mathsf{VACS}}^{\ell,Q}$ is an f-secure Q-validated ACS protocol with ℓ-output quality. It has expected setup size $O(\ell\kappa^4)$ and expected communication complexity $O(\ell \cdot (\mathcal{I} + \kappa^3) \cdot \kappa n)$, where $\mathcal{I}$ is the size of each party's input, and uses $O(\ell)$ invocations of Byzantine agreement in expectation.*

Proof. Say v is in the multiset output by some honest party, where v was output by RBC_i. BA_i must have resulted in output 1, which (by validity of BA) can only occur if some honest party used input 1 when executing BA_i. But then $Q(v) = 1$. This proves Q-validity of $\Pi_{\mathsf{VACS}}^{\ell,Q}$.

By consistency of BA, all honest parties agree on $\mathsf{CoreSet}$. If $i \in \mathsf{CoreSet}$, then BA_i must have resulted in output 1 which means that some honest party P must have used input 1 to BA_i. (Validity or BA_i ensures that if all honest parties used input 0, the output of BA must be 0). But then P must have terminated in RBC_i; consistency of RBC_i then implies that all honest parties eventually terminate RBC_i with the same output v_i. Consistency of $\Pi_{\mathsf{VACS}}^{\ell,Q}$ follows.

Lemma 11 shows that with overwhelming probability there are more than $\frac{2+\epsilon}{3} \cdot \frac{3}{2+\epsilon} \ell = \ell$ honest parties in C at step 1 of the protocol. Validity of RBC implies that in the corresponding instances of RBC, all honest parties terminate with an output satisfying Q. If every honest party begins executing all the corresponding instances of BA, those ℓ instances will all yield output 1. The only way all honest parties might not begin executing all those instances of BA is if some honest party outputs 1 in some (other) ℓ instances of BA, but then consistency of BA implies that all honest parties output 1 in those same ℓ instances. We conclude that every honest party outputs 1 in at least ℓ instances of BA, and so outputs a multiset S of size at least ℓ. Since each instance of RBC (and so each corrupted party) contributes at most one value to S, this proves ℓ-output quality.

5.2   Secure Multiparty Computation

We begin by reviewing the definition of asynchronous MPC by Canetti [13]. Let g be an n-input function, possibly randomized, where if the inputs of the parties are $\mathbf{x} = (x_1, \ldots, x_n)$ then all parties should learn $y \leftarrow g(x_1, \ldots, x_n)$. In the real-world execution of a protocol Π computing g, each party P_i initially holds 1^κ and an input x_i, and an adversary $\mathcal{A}$ has input 1^κ and auxiliary input z. The parties execute Π, and may be adaptively corrupted by $\mathcal{A}$ during execution of the protocol. At the end of the execution, each honest party outputs its local output (as dictated by the protocol), and $\mathcal{A}$ outputs its view. We let $\mathrm{REAL}_{\Pi,\mathcal{A}}(\kappa, \mathbf{x}, z)$ denote the distribution over the resulting vector of outputs as well as the set of corrupted parties.

Security of Π is defined relative to an ideal-world evaluation of g by a trusted party. The parties hold inputs as above, and we now denote the adversary by $\mathcal{S}$. The ideal execution proceeds as follows:

- **Initial corruption.** $\mathcal{S}$ may adaptively corrupt parties and learn their inputs.
- **Computation with ℓ-output quality.** $\mathcal{S}$ sends a set $\mathsf{CoreSet} \subseteq \{P_1, \ldots, P_n\}$ of size at least ℓ to the trusted party. In addition, $\mathcal{S}$ sends to the trusted party an input x_i' for each corrupted $P_i \in \mathsf{CoreSet}$.
  For $P_i \notin \mathsf{CoreSet}$, let $x_i' = \bot$; if $P_i \in \mathsf{CoreSet}$ is honest, then let $x_i' = x_i$. The trusted party computes $y \leftarrow g(x_1', \ldots, x_n')$ and sends $(y, \mathsf{CoreSet})$ to each party.
- **Additional corruption.** $\mathcal{S}$ may corrupt additional parties.[3]

---

[3] $\mathcal{S}$ learns nothing additional, because we assume secure erasure (in both the ideal- and real-world executions).

- **Output stage.** Each honest party outputs $(y, \mathsf{CoreSet})$.
- **Post-execution corruption.** $\mathcal{S}$ may corrupt additional parties, and then outputs an arbitrary function of its view.

We let $\mathrm{IDEAL}^{\ell}_{g,\mathcal{S}}(\kappa, \mathbf{x}, z)$ be the distribution over the vector of outputs and the set of corrupted parties following an ideal-world execution as above.

Definition 6. Π f-securely computes g with ℓ-output quality *if for any* PPT *adversary* $\mathcal{A}$ *corrupting up to* f *parties, there is a* PPT *adversary* $\mathcal{S}$ *such that:*

$$\{\mathrm{IDEAL}^{\ell}_{g,\mathcal{S}}(\kappa, \mathbf{x}, z)\}_{\kappa \in \mathbb{N}; \mathbf{x}, z \in \{0,1\}^*} \approx_c \{\mathrm{REAL}_{\Pi, \mathcal{A}}(\kappa, \mathbf{x}, z)\}_{\kappa \in \mathbb{N}; \mathbf{x}, z \in \{0,1\}^*}.$$

We construct an MPC protocol $\Pi^{\ell}_{\mathsf{MPC}}$ that offers a tradeoff between communication complexity and output quality; in particular, it has subquadratic communication complexity when the output quality and the output length of the functionality being computed are sublinear in the number of parties. We provide a high-level overview of our protocol next, with a full description in Fig. 5.

Let $t = (1 - \epsilon) \cdot \kappa/3$. Our protocol assumes trusted setup as follows:

1. A random committee C is selected by including each party in C independently with probability κ/n. This is done in the usual way by giving each member of the committee a secret key for a signature scheme, and giving the corresponding public keys to all parties. In addition:
   (a) We assume a threshold fully homomorphic encryption (TFHE) scheme [2, 6] $\mathsf{TFHE} = (\mathsf{KGen}, \mathsf{Enc}, \mathsf{Dec}, \mathsf{Eval})$ with non-interactive decryption whose secret key is shared in a t-out-of-$|C|$ manner among the parties in C. (We refer to Appendix B.1 for appropriate definitions of TFHE.)
   Specifically, we assume a TFHE public key ek is given to all parties, while a share dk_i of the corresponding secret key is given to the ith party in C.
   (b) The setup for $\Pi^{\ell}_{\mathsf{MPC}}$ includes setup for $|C|$ instances of Π_{RBC} (with the ith party in C the sender for the ith instance of Π_{RBC}), as well as one instance of Π_{RC}.
2. All parties are given a list of $|C|$ commitments to each of the TFHE shares dk_i; the randomness ω_i for the ith commitment is given to the ith member of C.
3. All parties are given the TFHE encryption of a random κ-bit value r. We denote the resulting ciphertext by $c_{\mathsf{rand}} \leftarrow \mathsf{Enc}_{ek}(r)$.
4. Parties are given the setup for one instance of VACS protocol $\Pi^{\ell,Q}_{\mathsf{VACS}}$. We further assume that each party in the committee that is chosen as part of the setup for that protocol is given a secret key for a signature scheme, and all parties are given the corresponding public keys.
5. All parties are given a common reference string (CRS) for a universally composable non-interactive zero-knowledge (UC-NIZK) proof [20] (see below).

The overall expected size of the setup is $O((\ell + \kappa) \cdot \mathsf{poly}(\kappa))$.

Fix a (possibly randomized) functionality g the parties wish to compute. We assume without loss of generality that g uses exactly κ random bits (one can always use a PRG to ensure this). To compute g, each party P_i begins by encrypting its input x_i using the TFHE scheme, and signing the result; it also computes an NIZK proof of correctness for the resulting ciphertext. The parties then use VACS (with ℓ-output quality) to agree on a set S containing at least ℓ of those ciphertexts. Following this, parties carry out a local computation in which they evaluate g homomorphically using the set of ciphertexts in S as the inputs and the ciphertext c_{rand} (included in the setup) as the randomness. This results in a ciphertext c^* containing the encrypted result, held by all parties. Parties in C enable decryption of c^* by using reliable broadcast to distribute shares of the decrypted value (along with a proof of correctness). Finally, the parties use reliable consensus to agree on when to terminate.

In the description above, we have omitted some details. In particular, the protocol ensures adaptive security by having parties erase certain information once it is no longer needed. This means, in particular, that we do not need to rely on equivocal TFHE [18].

In our protocol, parties generate UC-NIZK proofs for different statements. (Note that UC-NIZK proofs are proofs of knowledge; they are also non-malleable.) In particular, we define the following languages, parameterized by values (given to all parties) contained in the setup:

1. $(i, c_i) \in L_1$ if there exist x_i, r_i such that $c_i = \text{Enc}_{ek}(x_i; r_i)$.
2. $(i, c^*, d_i) \in L_2$ if $d_i = \text{Dec}_{dk_i}(c^*)$ and $\text{com}_i = \text{Com}(dk_i; \omega_i)$. (Here, com_i is the commitment to dk_i included in the setup.)

We prove the following theorem in the full version of the paper.

Protocol Π_{MPC}^{ℓ}

Let $t = (1 - \epsilon) \cdot \kappa/3$. We describe the protocol from the point of view of a party P_i with input x_i, assuming the setup described in the text.

1. Compute $c_i \leftarrow \text{Enc}_{ek}(x_i)$ along with a UC-NIZK proof π_i that $(i, c_i) \in L_1$. Erase x_i and the randomness used to generate c_1 and π_i.
   Execute $\Pi_{\text{VACS}}^{\ell, Q}$ using input $(i, \text{Sign}_{sk_i}(c_i), c_i, \pi_i)$, where $Q(i, \sigma, c, \pi) = 1$ iff $\text{Vrfy}_{pk_i}(c, \sigma) = 1$ and π is a correct proof for (i, c). Let S' denote the multiset output by $\Pi_{\text{VACS}}^{\ell, Q}$. Let $S \subseteq S'$ be the set obtained by including, for all i, only the lexicographically first tuple $(i, \star, \star, \star)$ in S'. Let $I = \{i \mid \exists (i, \star, \star, \star) \in S\}$.
2. Define the circuit $\mathcal{C}_g$ taking $|I| + 1$ inputs, where $\mathcal{C}_g(\{x_i\}_{i \in I}, r) = g(\{x_i\}_{i \in I}, \{\perp\}_{i \notin I}; r)$. Compute $c^* := \text{Eval}_{ek}(\mathcal{C}_g, \{c_i\}_{i \in I}, c_{\text{rand}})$.
   If $P_i \in C$, compute $d_i := \text{Dec}_{dk_i}(c^*)$ and a UC-NIZK proof π_i' that $(i, c^*, d_i) \in L_2$. Erase dk_i, ω_i, and the randomness used to generate π_i'.
   Execute $|C|$ instances of Π_{RBC}. If P_i is the ith member of C, it executes the ith instance of Π_{RBC} as the sender using input (i, d_i, π_i').
3. Upon receiving t outputs $\{(j, d_j, \pi_j')\}$ from the Π_{RBC} instances, with valid proofs and distinct j, compute $y_i := \text{Rec}(\{d_j\})$ and execute Π_{RC} with input y_i. When Π_{RC} terminates with output y, output (y, I) and terminate.

Fig. 5. An MPC protocol with ℓ-output quality, parameterized by ϵ.

Theorem 6. *Let $0 < \epsilon < 1/3$, $f \leq (1 - 2\epsilon) \cdot n/3$, and $\ell \leq (1 + \epsilon/2) \cdot 2n/3$. Assuming appropriate security of the NIZK proofs and TFHE, protocol $\Pi_{\mathsf{MPC}}^{\ell}$ f-securely computes g with ℓ-output quality. $\Pi_{\mathsf{MPC}}^{\ell}$ requires setup of expected size $O((\ell + \kappa) \cdot \mathsf{poly}(\kappa))$, has expected communication complexity $O((\ell + \kappa) \cdot (\mathcal{I} + \mathcal{O}) \cdot \mathsf{poly}(\kappa) \cdot n)$, where $\mathcal{I}$ is the size of each party's input and $\mathcal{O}$ is the size of the output, and invokes Byzantine agreement $O(\ell)$ times in expectation.*

6 Putting it All Together

The BA protocol Π_{BA} from Sect. 4 requires prior setup by a trusted dealer that can be used only for a *single* BA execution. Using multiple, independent instances of the setup it is, of course, possible to support any *bounded* number of BA executions. But a new idea is needed to support an *unbounded* number of executions.

In this section we discuss how to use the MPC protocol from Sect. 5 to achieve this goal. The key idea is to use that protocol to *refresh the setup* each time a BA execution is done. We first describe how to modify our MPC protocol to make it suitable for our setting, and then discuss how to put everything together to obtain the desired result.

6.1 Securely Simulating a Trusted Dealer

As just noted, the key idea is for the parties to use the MPC protocol from Sect. 5 to simulate a trusted dealer. In that case the parties are evaluating a no-input (randomized) functionality, and so do not need any output quality; let $\Pi_{\mathsf{MPC}} = \Pi_{\mathsf{MPC}}^{0}$. Importantly, Π_{MPC} has communication complexity subquadratic in n.

Using Π_{MPC} to simulate a dealer, however, requires us to address several technicalities. As described, Π_{MPC} evaluates a functionality for which all parties receive the *same* output. But simulating a dealer requires the parties to compute a functionality where parties receive *different* outputs. The standard approach for adapting MPC protocols to provide parties with different outputs does not work in our context: specifically, using symmetric-key encryption to encrypt the output of each party P_i using a key that P_i provides as part of its input does not work since Π_{MPC} has no output quality (and even $\Pi_{\mathsf{MPC}}^{\ell}$ only guarantees ℓ-output quality for $\ell < n$). Assuming a PKI, we can fix this by using public-key encryption instead (in the same way); this works since the public keys of the parties can be incorporated into the functionality being computed—since they are common knowledge—rather than being provided as inputs to the computation.

Even when using public-key encryption as just described, however, additional issues remain. Π_{MPC} has (expected) subquadratic communication complexity only when the output length $\mathcal{O}$ of the functionality being computed is sublinear in the number of parties. Even if the dealer algorithm generates output whose length is independent of n, naively encrypting output for every party (encrypting a "null" value of the appropriate length for parties whose output is empty) would result in output of total length linear in n. Encrypting the output only for parties with non-empty output does not work either since, in general, this might reveal which parties get output, which in our case would defeat the purpose of the setup!

We can address this difficulty by using *anonymous public-key encryption* [3]. Roughly, an anonymous public-key encryption (APKE) scheme has the property that a ciphertext leaks no information about the public key pk used for encryption, except to the party holding the corresponding secret key sk (who is able to decrypt the ciphertext using that key). Using APKE to encrypt the output for each party who obtains non-empty output, and then randomly permuting the resulting ciphertexts, allows us to compute a functionality with sublinear output length while hiding which parties receive output. This incurs—at worst—an additional multiplicative factor of κ in the output length.

Summarizing, we can simulate an arbitrary dealer algorithm in the following way. View the output of the dealer algorithm as $\mathsf{pub}, \{(i, s_i)\}$, where pub represents the public output that all parties should learn, and each s_i is a private output that only P_i should learn. Assume the existence of a PKI, and let pk_i denote a public key for an APKE scheme, where the corresponding secret key is held by P_i. Then use $\varPi_{\mathsf{MPC}}$ to compute $\mathsf{pub}, \{\mathsf{Enc}_{\mathsf{pk}_i}(s_i)\}$, where the ciphertexts are randomly permuted. As long as the length of the dealer's output is independent of n, the output of this functionality is also independent of n.

6.2   Unbounded Byzantine Agreement with Subquadratic Communication

We now show how to use the ideas from the previous section to achieve an *unbounded* number of BA executions with subquadratic communication. We describe two solutions: one involving a trusted dealer who initializes the parties with a one-time setup, and another that does not require a dealer (but does assume a PKI) and achieves expected subquadratic communication in an amortized sense.

For the first solution, we assume a trusted dealer who initializes the parties with the setup for one instance of $\varPi_{\mathsf{BA}}$ and one instance of $\varPi_{\mathsf{MPC}}$. (We also assume a PKI, which could be provided by the dealer as well; however, when we refer to the setup for $\varPi_{\mathsf{MPC}}$ we do not include the PKI since it does not need to be refreshed.) Importantly, the setup for $\varPi_{\mathsf{MPC}}$ allows the parties to compute any no-input functionality; the size of the setup is fixed, independent of the size of the circuit for the functionality being computed or its output length. For an execution of Byzantine agreement, the parties run $\varPi_{\mathsf{BA}}$ using their inputs and then use $\varPi_{\mathsf{MPC}}$ to refresh their setup by simulating the dealer algorithm. (We stress that the parties refresh the setup for both $\varPi_{\mathsf{BA}}$ and $\varPi_{\mathsf{MPC}}$.) The expected communication complexity per execution of Byzantine agreement is the sum of the communication complexities of $\varPi_{\mathsf{BA}}$ and $\varPi_{\mathsf{MPC}}$. The former is subquadratic; the latter is subquadratic if we follow the approach described in the previous section. Thus, the parties can run an unbounded number of subquadratic BA executions while only involving a trusted dealer once.

Alternately, we can avoid a trusted dealer by having the parties simulate the dealer using an arbitrary adaptively secure MPC protocol. (We still assume a PKI.) The communication complexity of the initial MPC protocol may be arbitrarily high, but all subsequent BA executions will have subquadratic (expected) communication complexity as above. In this way we achieve an unbounded number of BA executions with amortized (expected) subquadratic communication complexity.

7   A Lower Bound for Asynchronous Byzantine Agreement

We show that some form of setup is necessary for adaptively secure asynchronous BA with (non-amortized) subquadratic communication complexity. Our bound holds even if we allow secure erasure, and even if we allow secret channels between all the parties. (However, we assume an attacker can tell when a message is sent from one party to another.)

A related impossibility result was shown by Abraham et al. [1, Theorem 4]; their result holds even with prior setup and in the synchronous model of communication. However, their result relies strongly on an adversary who can delete messages sent by honest parties after those parties have been adaptively corrupted. In contrast, our bound applies to the standard communication model where honest parties' messages cannot be deleted once they are sent.

In concurrent work [39], Rambaud shows a bound that is slightly stronger than ours: His result holds even in the partially synchronous model, and rules out subquadratic communication complexity even with a PKI. We note, however, that his analysis treats signatures in an idealized manner, and thus it does not apply, e.g., to protocols using unique signatures for coin flipping.

We provide an outline of our proof that omits several technical details, but conveys the main ideas. Let Π be a setup-free protocol for asynchronous BA with subquadratic communication complexity. We show an efficient attacker $\mathcal{A}$ who succeeds in violating the security of Π. The attacker exploits the fact that with high probability, a uniform (honest) party P will communicate with only $o(n)$ other parties during an execution of Π. The adversary $\mathcal{A}$ can use this to "isolate" P from the remaining honest parties in the network and cause an inconsistency. In more detail, consider an execution in which P holds input 1, and the remaining honest parties S' all hold input 0. $\mathcal{A}$ tricks P into thinking that it is running in an alternate (simulated) execution of Π in which all parties are honest and hold input 1, while fooling the parties in S' into believing they are running an execution in which all honest parties hold 0 and at most f (corrupted) parties abort. By validity, P will output 1 and the honest parties in S' will output 0, but this contradicts consistency.

To "isolate" P as described, $\mathcal{A}$ runs two simulated executions of Π alongside the real execution of the protocol. (Here, it is crucial that Π is setup-free, so $\mathcal{A}$ can run the simulated executions on behalf of all parties.) $\mathcal{A}$ delays messages sent by honest parties to P in the real execution indefinitely; this is easy to do in the asynchronous setting. When a party $Q \in S'$ sends a message to P in the simulated execution, $\mathcal{A}$ corrupts Q in the real execution and then sends that message on Q's behalf. Analogously, when P sends a message to some honest party $Q \in S'$ in the real execution, $\mathcal{A}$ "intercepts" that message and forwards it to the corresponding party in the simulation. (A subtlety here is that messages sent between two honest parties cannot be observed via eavesdropping, because we allow secret channels, and can not necessarily be observed by adaptively corrupting the recipient Q after it receives the message, since we allow erasure. Instead, $\mathcal{A}$ must corrupt Q *before* it receives the message sent by P.) It only remains to argue that, in carrying out this strategy, $\mathcal{A}$ does not exceed the corruption bound.

A BA protocol is (f, δ)-secure if the properties of Definition 1 simultaneously hold with probability at least δ when f parties are corrupted.

Theorem 7. *Let $\frac{2}{3} < \delta < 1$ and $f \geq 2$. Let Π be a setup-free BA protocol that is (f, δ)-secure in an asynchronous network. Then the expected number of messages that honest parties send in Π is at least $(\frac{3\delta - 2}{8\delta})^2 \cdot (f - 1)^2$.*

Proof. If $f \geq n/3$ the theorem is trivially true (as asynchronous BA is impossible); thus, we assume $f < n/3$ in what follows. We present the proof assuming f is even and show that in this case, the expected number of messages is at least $c^2 f^2$. The case of odd f can be reduced to the case of even f since any (f, δ)-secure protocol is also an $(f - 1, \delta)$-secure protocol.

Let $c = \frac{3\delta - 2}{8\delta}$. Fix an (f, δ)-secure protocol Π whose expected number of messages is less than $c^2 f^2$. Fix a subset $S \subset [n]$ with $|S| = \frac{f}{2}$. Let S' denote the remaining parties. Consider an execution (Ex1) of Π that proceeds as follows: At the start of the execution, an adversary corrupts all parties in S and they immediately abort. The parties in S' remain honest and run Π using input 0. By δ-security of Π we have:

Lemma 5. *In Ex1 all parties in S' output 0 with probability at least δ.*

Now consider an execution (Ex2) of Π involving an adversary $\mathcal{A}$. (As explained in the proof intuition, $\mathcal{A}$'s goal is to make P believe it is running in an execution in which all parties are honest and have input 1, and to make the honest parties in S' believe they are running in Ex1.) At the start of the execution, $\mathcal{A}$ chooses a uniform $P \in S$ and corrupts all parties in S except for P. All parties in S' are initially honest and hold input 0, while P holds input 1. $\mathcal{A}$ maintains two simulated executions that we label *red* and *blue*. (See Fig. 6.) In the blue execution, $\mathcal{A}$ plays the role of all parties other than P; all these virtual parties run Π honestly with input 1. In the red execution, $\mathcal{A}$ simulates an execution in which all parties in S immediately abort, and all parties in S' run Π honestly with input 0. $\mathcal{A}$ uses these two simulations to determine how to interact with the honest parties in the real execution. Specifically, it schedules delivery of messages as follows:

- **S' to P, real execution.** Messages sent by honest parties in S' to P in the real execution are delayed, and delivered only after all honest parties have generated output.

- P **to** S'**, real execution.** When P sends a message to an honest party $Q \in S'$ in the real execution, $\mathcal{A}$ delays the message and then corrupts Q. Once Q is corrupted, $\mathcal{A}$ delivers the message to Q in the real execution (and can then read the message). $\mathcal{A}$ also delivers that same message to Q in the blue simulation.
- S' **to** P**, blue execution.** When a party $Q \in S'$ sends a message m to P in the blue execution, $\mathcal{A}$ corrupts Q in the real execution (if Q was not already corrupted), and then sends m to P (on behalf of Q) in the real execution. (Messages that Q may have sent previously to P in the real execution continue to be delayed.)
- S **to** P**, blue execution.** When a party $Q \in S$ sends a message m to P in the blue execution, Q sends m to P in the real execution (recall that parties in $S \setminus \{P\}$ are corrupted in Ex2).
- S' **to** S'**, real execution.** Messages sent by honest parties in S' to other parties in S' in the real execution are delivered normally. If the receiver is corrupted, the message is relayed to $\mathcal{A}$, who simulates this same message in the red execution.
- S' **to** $S \setminus \{P\}$**, real execution.** Messages sent by honest parties in S' to the (corrupted) parties in $S \setminus \{P\}$ in the real execution are ignored.
- S' **to** S'**, red execution.** If a party $Q \in S'$ is corrupted in the real execution, then whenever a message m is sent by a party Q to another party in S' in the red execution, Q sends m in the real execution.

If $\mathcal{A}$ would ever need to corrupt more than f parties in total, then it simply aborts. (However, the real execution continues without any further interference from $\mathcal{A}$.)

Lemma 6. *In Ex2, the distribution of the joint view of all parties in S' who remain uncorrupted is identical to the distribution of their joint view in Ex1. In particular, with probability at least δ in Ex2 all parties in S' who remain uncorrupted output 0.*

Proof. The only messages received by the parties in S' in either Ex1 or Ex2 are those that arise from an honest execution of Π among the parties in S', all of whom hold input 0. Moreover, in Ex2 the decision as to whether or not a party in S' is corrupted is independent of the joint view of all uncorrupted parties in S'. The final statement follows from Lemma 5.

We also show that with positive probability, $\mathcal{A}$ does not abort.

Lemma 7. *In Ex2, $\mathcal{A}$ does not abort with probability at least $1 - 4c$.*

Proof. $\mathcal{A}$ aborts if it would exceed the corruption bound. Initially, only the $f/2$ parties in S are corrupted. Let M denote the total number of messages sent either by the parties in S' to the parties in S or by parties in S to parties in S' in the blue execution. By assumption, $\mathbf{Exp}[M] < c^2 f^2$. Let X be the event that $M \leq \frac{c}{2} f^2$. Lemma 9 implies that

$$\Pr[X] \geq \Pr\left[M \leq \frac{\mathbf{Exp}[M]}{2c}\right] \geq 1 - 2c.$$

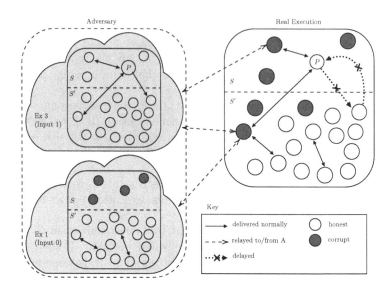

Fig. 6. Adversarial strategy in Ex2. In the real execution (shown at right) corrupted parties in S interact with P as if they are honest with input 1, and ignore honest parties in S'. Corrupted parties in S' interact with P as if they are honest with input 1, and interact with S' as if they are honest with input 0. All messages between P and honest parties in S' are delayed indefinitely. The adversary maintains two simulated executions (shown at left) to determine which messages corrupted parties will send in the real execution. (Color figure online)

Let Y be the event that, among the first $cf^2/2$ messages sent by parties in S' to parties in S or vice versa, a uniformly chosen $P \in S$ sends and/or receives at most $f/2$ of those messages. By the pigeonhole principle, at most cf parties in S can receive and/or send $f/2$ or more of those messages, and so $\Pr[Y] \geq 1 - cf/|S| = 1 - 2c$.[4] Thus, $\Pr[X \wedge Y] = \Pr[X] + \Pr[Y] - \Pr[X \cup Y] \geq (1 - 2c) + (1 - 2c) - 1 = 1 - 4c$. The lemma follows by observing that when X and Y occur, at most $f/2$ parties in S' are corrupted.

Finally, consider an execution (Ex3) in which a uniform $P \in S$ is chosen and then Π is run honestly with all parties holding input 1.

Lemma 8. *In Ex2, conditioned on the event that $\mathcal{A}$ does not abort, the view of P is distributed identically to the view of P in Ex3. In particular, with probability at least δ in Ex2, P outputs 1.*

---

[4] It is convenient to view the communication between S and S' as an undirected, bipartite multi-graph in which each node represents a party and an edge (U, V) represents a message sent between parties $U \in S$ and $V \in S'$. As the number of edges in this graph is at most $cf^2/2$, there can not be more than cf nodes in S whose total degree is at least $f/2$.

Proof. In Ex2, the view of P is determined by the virtual execution in which all parties run Π honestly using input 1. The final statement follows because in Ex3, (f, δ)-security of Π implies that P outputs 1 with probability at least δ.

We now complete the proof of the theorem. In execution Ex2, let Z_1 be the event that $\mathcal{A}$ does not abort; by Lemma 7, $\Pr[Z_1] \geq 1 - 4c$. Let Z_2 be the event that P does not output 0 in Ex2; using Lemma 8 we have

$$\Pr[Z_2] \geq \Pr[Z_2 \mid Z_1] \cdot \Pr[Z_1] \geq \delta \cdot (1 - 4c).$$

Let Z_3 be the event that all uncorrupted parties in S' output 0 in Ex2. By Lemma 6, $\Pr[Z_3] \geq \delta$. Recalling that $2/3 < \delta < 1$, we see that

$$\Pr[Z_2 \wedge Z_3] = \Pr[Z_2] + \Pr[Z_3] - \Pr[Z_2 \cup Z_3] \geq 2\delta - 4c\delta - 1 = \frac{\delta}{2} > \frac{1}{3} > 1 - \delta,$$

contradicting (f, δ)-security of Π.

A   Concentration Inequalities

We briefly recall the following standard concentration bounds.

Lemma 9 (Markov bound). *Let X be a non-negative random variable. Then for $a > 0$,*

$$\Pr[X \geq a] \leq \frac{E[X]}{a}.$$

Lemma 10 (Chernoff bound). *Let $X_1, ..., X_n$ be independent Bernoulli random variables with parameter p. Let $X := \sum_i X_i$, so $\mu := E[X] = p \cdot n$. Then, for $\delta \in [0, 1]$*

- $\Pr[X \leq (1 - \delta) \cdot \mu] \leq e^{-\delta^2 \mu/2}$.
- $\Pr[X \geq (1 + \delta) \cdot \mu] \leq e^{-\delta^2 \mu/(2+\delta)}$.

Let $\chi_{s,n}$ denote the distribution that samples a subset of the n parties, where each party is included independently with probability s/n. The following lemma will be useful in our analysis.

Lemma 11. *Fix $s \leq n$ and $0 < \epsilon < 1/3$, and let $f \leq (1 - 2\epsilon) \cdot n/3$ be a bound on the number of corrupted parties. If $C \leftarrow \chi_{s,n}$, then:*

1. *C contains fewer than $(1 + \epsilon) \cdot s$ parties except with probability $e^{-\frac{\epsilon^2 s}{2+\epsilon}}$.*
2. *C contains more than $(1 + \epsilon/2) \cdot 2s/3$ honest parties except with probability at most $e^{-\epsilon^2 s/12 \cdot (1+\epsilon)}$.*
3. *C contains fewer than $(1 - \epsilon) \cdot s/3$ corrupted parties except with probability at most $e^{-\epsilon^2 s/(6-9\epsilon)}$.*

Proof. Let $H \subseteq [n]$ be the indices of the honest parties. Let X_j be the Bernoulli random variable indicating if $P_j \in C$, so $\Pr[X_j = 1] = s/n$. Define $Z_1 = \sum_j P_j$, $Z_2 := \sum_{j \in H} X_j$, and $Z_3 := \sum_{j \notin H} X_j$. Then:

1. Since $E[Z_1] = s$, setting $\delta = \epsilon$ in Lemma 10 yields

$$\Pr\left[Z_1 \geq (1 + \epsilon) \cdot s\right] \leq e^{-\epsilon^2 s/(2+\epsilon)}.$$

2. Since $E[Z_2] \geq (n - f) \cdot s/n \geq (1 + \epsilon) \cdot 2s/3$, setting $\delta = \frac{\epsilon}{2+2\epsilon}$ in Lemma 10 yields

$$\Pr\left[Z_2 \leq \frac{(1 + \epsilon/2) \cdot 2s}{3}\right] \leq e^{-\epsilon^2 s/12 \cdot (1+\epsilon)}.$$

3. Since $E[Z_3] \leq f \cdot s/n \leq (1 - 2\epsilon) \cdot s/3$, setting $\delta = \frac{\epsilon}{1-2\epsilon}$ in Lemma 10 yields

$$\Pr\left[Z_3 \geq \frac{(1 - \epsilon) \cdot s}{3}\right] \leq e^{-\epsilon^2 s/(6-9\epsilon)}.$$

B   Additional Definitions

B.1   Threshold Fully Homomorphic Encryption

For our protocol we require a threshold (compact) fully homomorphic encryption (TFHE) scheme. Our definitions follow prior work [2,6,9,25,41].

Definition 7. *A threshold fully homomorphic encryption (TFHE) scheme consists of the following algorithms:*

- *The key-generation algorithm* KGen *takes as input the security parameter along with integers t, N. It outputs an encryption key ek and decryption keys $dk_1, \ldots, dk_N$.*
- *The encryption algorithm* Enc *takes as input the encryption key ek and a message m. It outputs a ciphertext c.*
- *The (deterministic) homomorphic evaluation algorithm* Eval *takes as input the encryption key ek, an n-input circuit C, and n ciphertexts $c_1, \ldots, c_n$; it outputs a ciphertext c.*
- *The (deterministic) partial decryption algorithm* Dec *takes as input a decryption key dk_i and a ciphertext c. It outputs a decryption share d_i.*
- *The reconstruction algorithm* Rec *takes as input decryption shares $\{d_i\}$ and outputs a message m.*

We require:

Correctness: *For any integers n, t, N, messages $\{m_i\}_{i \in [n]}$, n-input circuit C, and set $I \subseteq [N]$ with $|I| = t$, if we run $(ek, \{dk_i\}_{i \in [N]}) \leftarrow \mathsf{KGen}(1^\kappa, 1^t, 1^N)$ followed by*

$$c := \mathsf{Eval}_{ek}(C, \mathsf{Enc}_{ek}(m_1), \ldots, \mathsf{Enc}_{ek}(m_n)),$$

then $\mathsf{Rec}(\{\mathsf{Dec}_{dk_i}(c)\}_{i \in I}) = C(m_1, \ldots, m_n)$.

Compactness: *There is a polynomial p such that for all (ek, dk) output by* $\mathsf{KGen}(1^\kappa, 1^t, 1^N)$ *and all $\{m_i\}$, the length of*

$$\mathsf{Eval}_{ek}(C, \mathsf{Enc}_{ek}(m_1), \ldots, \mathsf{Enc}_{ek}(m_n))$$

is at most $p(|C(m_1, \ldots, m_n)|, \kappa)$.

For our application, it is easiest to define security in terms of simulation.

Definition 8. *We say a TFHE scheme is simulation secure if there is a probabilistic polynomial-time simulator* Sim *such that for any probabilistic polynomial-time adversary $\mathcal{A}$, the following experiments are computationally indistinguishable:*

$\mathrm{REAL}_{\mathcal{A}, C}(1^\kappa, 1^t, 1^N)$:

1. *Compute $(ek, \{dk_i\}_{i=1}^N) \leftarrow \mathsf{KGen}(1^\kappa, 1^t, 1^N)$ and give ek to $\mathcal{A}$.*
2. *$\mathcal{A}$ adaptively chooses a subset $S \subset [N]$ with $|S| < t$ as well as messages $m_1, \ldots, m_n$ and a circuit C. In return, $\mathcal{A}$ is given $\{dk_i\}_{i \in S}$ and $\{c_i \leftarrow \mathsf{Enc}_{ek}(m_i)\}_{i=1}^n$.*
3. *$\mathcal{A}$ outputs $\{(m_i', r_i')\}_{i \in S}$. Define $c_i' := \mathsf{Enc}_{ek}(m_i'; r_i')$ for $i \in S$.*
4. *Let $c^* := \mathsf{Eval}_{ek}(\{c_i\}_{i=1}^n, \{c_i'\}_{i \in S})$ and give $\{\mathsf{Dec}_{dk_i}(c^*)\}_{i \notin S}$ to $\mathcal{A}$.*

$\mathrm{IDEAL}_{\mathcal{A}, C}(1^\kappa, 1^t, 1^N)$:

1. *Compute $ek \leftarrow \mathsf{Sim}(1^\kappa, 1^t, 1^N)$ and give ek to $\mathcal{A}$.*
2. *$\mathcal{A}$ adaptively chooses a subset S of parties with $|S| < t$ as well as messages $m_1, \ldots, m_n$ and a circuit C. In return, $\mathsf{Sim}(1^n)$ is run to compute $\{dk_i\}_{i \in S}$ and $\{c_i\}_{i=1}^n$ that are given to $\mathcal{A}$.*
3. *$\mathcal{A}$ outputs $\{(m_i', r_i')\}_{i \in S}$.*
4. *Let $y = C(\{m_i\}_{i=1}^n, \{m_i'\}_{i \in S})$. Compute $\{d_i\}_{i \notin S} \leftarrow \mathsf{Sim}(y)$ and give the result to $\mathcal{A}$.*

B.2   Anonymous Public-Key Encryption

We recall the definition of anonymous public-key encryption from [3].

Definition 9. *A CPA-secure public-key encryption scheme $\mathcal{PE} = (\mathsf{KGen}, \mathsf{Enc}, \mathsf{Dec})$ is anonymous if the following is negligible for any PPT adversary $\mathcal{A}$:*

$$\left| \Pr\left[\begin{array}{c} (\mathsf{pk}_0, \mathsf{sk}_0) \leftarrow \mathsf{KGen}(1^\kappa); (\mathsf{pk}_1, \mathsf{sk}_1) \leftarrow \mathsf{KGen}(1^\kappa); \\ m \leftarrow \mathcal{A}(\mathsf{pk}_0, \mathsf{pk}_1); b \leftarrow \{0,1\}; c \leftarrow \mathsf{Enc}_{\mathsf{pk}_b}(m) \end{array} : A(c) = b \right] - \frac{1}{2} \right|.$$

References

1. Abraham, I., et al.: Communication complexity of Byzantine agreement, revisited. In: Robinson, P., Ellen, F. (eds.) 38th ACM PODC, pp. 317–326. ACM, July/August 2019

2. Asharov, G., Jain, A., López-Alt, A., Tromer, E., Vaikuntanathan, V., Wichs, D.: Multiparty computation with low communication, computation and interaction via threshold FHE. In: Pointcheval, D., Johansson, T. (eds.) EUROCRYPT 2012. LNCS, vol. 7237, pp. 483–501. Springer, Heidelberg (2012). https://doi.org/10.1007/978-3-642-29011-4_29

3. Bellare, M., Boldyreva, A., Desai, A., Pointcheval, D.: Key-privacy in public-key encryption. In: Boyd, C. (ed.) ASIACRYPT 2001. LNCS, vol. 2248, pp. 566–582. Springer, Heidelberg (2001). https://doi.org/10.1007/3-540-45682-1_33

4. Ben-Or, M., Canetti, R., Goldreich, O.: Asynchronous secure computation. In: 25th ACM STOC, pp. 52–61. ACM Press, May 1993

5. Ben-Or, M., Kelmer, B., Rabin, T.: Asynchronous secure computations with optimal resilience (extended abstract). In: Anderson, J., Toueg, S. (eds.) 13th ACM PODC, pp. 183–192. ACM, August 1994

6. Boneh, D., et al.: Threshold cryptosystems from threshold fully homomorphic encryption. In: Shacham, H., Boldyreva, A. (eds.) CRYPTO 2018, Part I. LNCS, vol. 10991, pp. 565–596. Springer, Cham (2018). https://doi.org/10.1007/978-3-319-96884-1_19

7. Bracha, G.: Asynchronous Byzantine agreement protocols. Inf. Comput. **75**, 130–143 (1987)

8. Bracha, G., Toueg, S.: Asynchronous consensus and broadcast protocols. J. ACM **32**(4), 824–840 (1985)

9. Brakerski, Z., Vaikuntanathan, V.: Efficient fully homomorphic encryption from (standard) LWE. In: Ostrovsky, R. (ed.) 52nd FOCS, pp. 97–106. IEEE Computer Society Press, October 2011

10. Cachin, C., Kursawe, K., Petzold, F., Shoup, V.: Secure and efficient asynchronous broadcast protocols. In: Kilian, J. (ed.) CRYPTO 2001. LNCS, vol. 2139, pp. 524–541. Springer, Heidelberg (2001). https://doi.org/10.1007/3-540-44647-8_31

11. Cachin, C., Kursawe, K., Shoup, V.: Random oracles in constantipole: practical asynchronous Byzantine agreement using cryptography (extended abstract). In: Neiger, G. (ed.) 19th ACM PODC, pp. 123–132. ACM, July 2000

12. Canetti, R.: Studies in secure multiparty computation and applications. Ph.D. thesis, Weizmann Institute of Science (1996)

13. Canetti, R.: Security and composition of multiparty cryptographic protocols. J. Cryptol. **13**(1), 143–202 (2000)

14. Canetti, R., Rabin, T.: Fast asynchronous Byzantine agreement with optimal resilience. In: 25th ACM STOC, pp. 42–51. ACM Press, May 1993

15. Choudhury, A., Hirt, M., Patra, A.: Unconditionally secure asynchronous multiparty computation with linear communication complexity. Cryptology ePrint Archive, Report 2012/517 (2012). http://eprint.iacr.org/2012/517

16. Choudhury, A., Patra, A.: Optimally resilient asynchronous MPC with linear communication complexity. In: Proceedings of the International Conference on Distributed Computing and Networking (ICDCN), pp. 1–10 (2015)

17. Cohen, R.: Asynchronous secure multiparty computation in constant time. In: Cheng, C.-M., Chung, K.-M., Persiano, G., Yang, B.-Y. (eds.) PKC 2016, Part II. LNCS, vol. 9615, pp. 183–207. Springer, Heidelberg (2016). https://doi.org/10.1007/978-3-662-49387-8_8

18. Cohen, R., Shelat, A., Wichs, D.: Adaptively secure MPC with sublinear communication complexity. In: Boldyreva, A., Micciancio, D. (eds.) CRYPTO 2019, Part II. LNCS, vol. 11693, pp. 30–60. Springer, Cham (2019). https://doi.org/10.1007/978-3-030-26951-7_2

19. Cohen, S., Keidar, I., Spiegelman, A.: Sub-quadratic asynchronous Byzantine agreement WHP, Not a COINcidence (2020). https://arxiv.org/abs/2002.06545
20. De Santis, A., Di Crescenzo, G., Ostrovsky, R., Persiano, G., Sahai, A.: Robust non-interactive zero knowledge. In: Kilian, J. (ed.) CRYPTO 2001. LNCS, vol. 2139, pp. 566–598. Springer, Heidelberg (2001). https://doi.org/10.1007/3-540-44647-8_33
21. Dolev, D., Reischuk, R.: Bounds on information exchange for Byzantine agreement. J. ACM **32**(1), 191–204 (1985)
22. Feldman, P., Micali, S.: Optimal algorithms for byzantine agreement. In: 20th ACM STOC, pp. 148–161. ACM Press, May 1988
23. Fischer, M.J., Lynch, N.A., Paterson, M.: Impossibility of distributed consensus with one faulty process. J. ACM **32**(2), 374–382 (1985)
24. Garay, J.A., Katz, J., Kumaresan, R., Zhou, H.-S.: Adaptively secure broadcast, revisited. In: Gavoille, C., Fraigniaud, P (eds.) 30th ACM PODC, pp. 179–186. ACM, June 2011
25. Gentry, C.: A fully homomorphic encryption scheme. Ph.D. thesis, Stanford University (2009)
26. Guo, Y., Pass, R., Shi, E.: Synchronous, with a chance of partition tolerance. In: Boldyreva, A., Micciancio, D. (eds.) CRYPTO 2019, Part I. LNCS, vol. 11692, pp. 499–529. Springer, Cham (2019). https://doi.org/10.1007/978-3-030-26948-7_18
27. Hirt, M., Nielsen, J.B., Przydatek, B.: Cryptographic asynchronous multi-party computation with optimal resilience. In: Cramer, R. (ed.) EUROCRYPT 2005. LNCS, vol. 3494, pp. 322–340. Springer, Heidelberg (2005). https://doi.org/10.1007/11426639_19
28. Hirt, M., Nielsen, J.B., Przydatek, B.: Asynchronous multi-party computation with quadratic communication. In: Aceto, L., Damgård, I., Goldberg, L.A., Halldórsson, M.M., Ingólfsdóttir, A., Walukiewicz, I. (eds.) ICALP 2008, Part II. LNCS, vol. 5126, pp. 473–485. Springer, Heidelberg (2008). https://doi.org/10.1007/978-3-540-70583-3_39
29. King, V., Saia, J.: Breaking the $O(n^2)$ bit barrier: scalable byzantine agreement with an adaptive adversary. In: Richa, A.W., Guerraoui, R. (eds.) 29th ACM PODC, pp. 420–429. ACM, July 2010
30. King, V., Saia, J., Sanwalani, V., Vee, E.: Scalable leader election. In: 17th SODA, pp. 990–999. ACM-SIAM, January 2006
31. Lamport, L., Shostak, R., Pease, M.: The Byzantine generals problem. ACM Trans. Program. Lang. Syst. **4**(3), 382–401 (1982)
32. Micali, S.: Very simple and efficient Byzantine agreement. In: Papadimitriou, C.H. (ed.) ITCS 2017. LIPIcs, vol. 4266, pp. 6:1–6:1, 67, January 2017
33. Micali, S., Vaikuntanathan, V.: Optimal and player-replaceable consensus with an honest majority. Technical report, MIT (2017)
34. Mostéfaoui, A., Hamouma, M., Raynal, M.: Signature-free asynchronous Byzantine consensus with $t < n/3$ and $O(n^2)$ messages. In: Halldórsson, M.M., Dolev, S. (eds.) 33rd ACM PODC, pp. 2–9. ACM, July 2014
35. Pass, R., Shi, E.: The sleepy model of consensus. In: Takagi, T., Peyrin, T. (eds.) ASIACRYPT 2017, Part II. LNCS, vol. 10625, pp. 380–409. Springer, Cham (2017). https://doi.org/10.1007/978-3-319-70697-9_14
36. Patra, A., Choudhury, A., Pandu Rangan, C.: Efficient asynchronous multiparty computation with optimal resilience. Cryptology ePrint Archive, Report 2008/425 (2008). http://eprint.iacr.org/2008/425

37. Prabhu, B., Srinathan, K., Rangan, C.P.: Asynchronous unconditionally secure computation: an efficiency improvement. In: Menezes, A., Sarkar, P. (eds.) INDOCRYPT 2002. LNCS, vol. 2551, pp. 93–107. Springer, Heidelberg (2002). https://doi.org/10.1007/3-540-36231-2_9
38. Rabin, M.O.: Randomized Byzantine generals. In: 24th FOCS, pp. 403–409. IEEE Computer Society Press, November 1983
39. Rambaud, M.: Lower bounds for authenticated randomized Byzantine consensus under (partial) synchrony: the limits of standalone digital signatures. https://perso.telecom-paristech.fr/rambaud/articles/lower.pdf
40. Srinathan, K., Pandu Rangan, C.: Efficient asynchronous secure multiparty distributed computation. In: Roy, B., Okamoto, E. (eds.) INDOCRYPT 2000. LNCS, vol. 1977, pp. 117–129. Springer, Heidelberg (2000). https://doi.org/10.1007/3-540-44495-5_11
41. van Dijk, M., Gentry, C., Halevi, S., Vaikuntanathan, V.: Fully homomorphic encryption over the integers. In: Gilbert, H. (ed.) EUROCRYPT 2010. LNCS, vol. 6110, pp. 24–43. Springer, Heidelberg (2010). https://doi.org/10.1007/978-3-642-13190-5_2

Expected Constant Round Byzantine Broadcast Under Dishonest Majority

Jun Wan[1]([⊠]), Hanshen Xiao[1], Elaine Shi[2,3], and Srinivas Devadas[1]

[1] Massachusetts Institute of Technology, Cambridge, MA 02139, USA
{junwan,hsxiao,devadas}@mit.edu
[2] Cornell University, Ithaca, NY 14850, USA
runting@gmail.com
[3] Carnegie Mellon University, Pittsburgh, PA 15213, USA
https://eprint.iacr.org/2020/590.pdf

Abstract. Byzantine Broadcast (BB) is a central question in distributed systems, and an important challenge is to understand its round complexity. Under the honest majority setting, it is long known that there exist randomized protocols that can achieve BB in expected constant rounds, regardless of the number of nodes n. However, whether we can match the expected constant round complexity in the corrupt majority setting—or more precisely, when $f \geq n/2 + \omega(1)$—remains unknown, where f denotes the number of corrupt nodes. In this paper, we are the first to resolve this long-standing question. We show how to achieve BB in expected $O((n/(n-f))^2)$ rounds. Our results hold under a weakly adaptive adversary who cannot perform "after-the-fact removal" of messages already sent by a node before it becomes corrupt. We also assume trusted setup and the Decision Linear (DLIN) assumption in bilinear groups.

1 Introduction

Byzantine Agreement (BA) is one of the most fundamental problems in fault tolerant distributed computing [4,8,27] and of increasing interest given recent advances in cryptocurrencies [3,14,23]. In this paper, we consider the "broadcast" formulation of Byzantine Agreement, henceforth also called Byzantine Broadcast (BB): imagine that there are n nodes among which there is a designated sender. The sender is given an input bit $b \in \{0, 1\}$ and wants to send this bit to every other node. Although up to $f < n - 1$ nodes can be corrupted and deviate arbitrarily from the prescribed protocol, we would like to nonetheless ensure two key properties: 1) *consistency* requires that all honest nodes must output the same bit (even when the sender is corrupt); and 2) *validity* requires that all honest nodes output the sender's input bit if the sender is honest[1].

---

[1] An alternative formulation is the "agreement" version where every node receives an input bit b, and validity requires that if all honest nodes receive the same input bit b, then honest nodes must output b. However, this agreement notion is known to be impossible under corrupt majority.

© International Association for Cryptologic Research 2020
R. Pass and K. Pietrzak (Eds.): TCC 2020, LNCS 12550, pp. 381–411, 2020.
https://doi.org/10.1007/978-3-030-64375-1_14

An important question to understand is the *round complexity* of Byzantine Broadcast. Dolev and Strong [12] showed that assuming (idealized) digital signatures, there is a deterministic protocol achieving $f + 1$ rounds; and moreover, $f + 1$ rounds is the best one can hope for in any *deterministic* protocol. It is also widely understood that *randomization* can help overcome the $(f + 1)$-round barrier in the honest majority setting. Specifically, many elegant works have shown expected constant-round protocols assuming honest majority [2,15,16,26].

For a long while, the community was perplexed about the following natural question: *can we achieve sublinear-round Byzantine Broadcast under dishonest majority?* The ingenious work by Garay et al. [19] was the first to demonstrate a positive result although their construction achieves sublinear round complexity only under a narrow parameter regime: specifically, they constructed an expected $\Theta((f - n/2)^2)$-round protocol, and the subsequent work of Fitzi and Nielsen [18] improved it to $\Theta(f - n/2)$ rounds. In other words, these constructions achieve sublinear number of rounds only if $f \leq n/2 + o(n)$. This is somewhat unsatisfying since even for $f = 0.51n$, their results would be inapplicable.

Very recently, the frontier of our understanding was again pushed forward due to Chan, Pass, and Shi [9]. Assuming trusted setup and standard cryptographic assumptions, their protocol achieves Byzantine Broadcast with probability $1 - \delta$ for any $f \leq (1 - \epsilon) \cdot n$ in $\mathsf{poly} \log(1/\epsilon, 1/\delta)$ rounds (both in expectation and worst-case), where $\epsilon, \delta \in (0, 1)$ are two parameters that the protocol takes as input. Although their work represents exciting progress on a long stagnant front, it fails to match the asymptotic (expected) round complexity of known honest majority protocols—for honest majority, it is long known how to achieve *expected constant* round complexity [2,26]. We thus ask the following question: can we achieve Byzantine Broadcast in *expected constant* rounds in the corrupt majority setting?

1.1   Our Contributions

We present a Byzantine Broadcast protocol that achieves expected $O((\frac{n}{n-f})^2)$ rounds. This means that for $f = (1 - \epsilon)n$ where $\epsilon \in (0, 1)$ may be an arbitrarily small constant, our protocol achieves expected constant rounds. Our protocol works even under an adaptive adversary, assuming a trusted setup and standard cryptographic assumptions in an algebraic structure called bilinear groups. In this paper, we assume that when the adaptive adversary corrupts a node v in some round r, it cannot erase the message v has already sent in round r but it can make the now-corrupt v inject additional messages into round r—such a model is also referred to as *weakly adaptive* in earlier works.

To the best of our knowledge, our work is the first to achieve an expected constant-round BB protocol for any $f \geq n/2 + \omega(1)$. Previously, no result was known even for the *static* corruption setting, and even under any setup assumptions. We compare our results with the state-of-art results in Table 1 and summarize our results in Theorem 1.

Table 1. A comparison between our results and previous work under dishonest majority.

	Garay et al. [19]	Fitzi et al. [18]	Chan et al. [9]	This paper
Expected round complexity	$\Theta((2f-n)^2)$	$\Theta(2f-n)$	Same as worst-case	$\Theta((\frac{n}{n-f})^2)$
Worst-case round complexity with $1-\delta$ failure probability	$\Theta(\log(\frac{1}{\delta})+(2f-n)^2)$	$\Theta(\log(\frac{1}{\delta})+(2f-n))$	$\Theta(\log(\frac{1}{\delta})\cdot\frac{n}{n-f})$	$\Theta(\frac{\log(1/\delta)}{\log(n/f)}\cdot\frac{n}{n-f})$

Theorem 1 (Expected constant round BB under adaptive corruption).
Assume trusted setup and that the decisional linear assumption holds in suitable bilinear groups[2] Then, there exists a BB protocol with expected $O((\frac{n}{n-f})^2)$ round complexity for any non-uniform p.p.t. adversary that can adaptively corrupt $f < n-1$ nodes.

Throughout the paper, we assume a *synchronous* network, i.e., honest nodes can deliver messages to each other within a single round. This assumption is necessary since without it, Byzantine Broadcast is long known to be impossible under more than $n/3$ corruptions [13].

1.2 Interpreting Our Result

Below we situate our result in context to help the reader understand how tight the bound is as well as the assumptions we make.

On the Tightness of the Bound and the Resilience Parameter. Theorem 1 says that if the number of honest nodes is an arbitrarily small constant fraction (e.g., 0.01%), we can achieve expected constant rounds. The restriction on the number of honest nodes is necessary in light of an elegant lower bound proven by Garay et al. [19]: they showed that even randomized protocols cannot achieve BB in less than $\Theta(n/(n-f))$ number of rounds, *even assuming static corruption* and allowing reasonable setup assumptions. Note that their lower bound says that when almost all nodes can be corrupt except $O(1)$ nodes who remain honest, then even randomized protocols must incur linear number of rounds. Comparing their lower bound and our upper bound side by side, one can see that for the (narrow) regime $n-f = o(n)$, there is still an asymptotical gap between our upper bound and their lower bound. Whether we can construct an upper bound that matches their lower bound in this regime remains open, even under static corruptions and allowing any reasonable setup assumptions.

On the Weakly Adaptive Model. Our result holds in the weakly adaptive model [1,21,31]. In this model, the adversary can adaptively corrupt a node; and if some node u becomes newly corrupt in round r, the adversary can inject new messages on behalf of u in the same round r; however, the adversary cannot erase

---

[2] We formally define the decisional linear assumption in the online full version. The reader can also refer to Groth et al. [24] for the definition.

the messages u already sent in round r prior to becoming corrupt. The weakly adaptive model is akin to the atomic message model first introduced by Garay et al. [20] as a way to overcome a lower bound pertaining to a particular adaptive, simulation-based notion of security proven by Hirt and Zikas [25]. The only slight difference is that in the atomic message model, not only is the adversary unable to perform "after-the-fact" message removal, it also must wait for one network delay after a node i becomes corrupt, before it is able to inject messages on behalf of i. In this sense, the weakly adaptive model is a slightly weaker model than the atomic model by Garay et al. (and this makes our upper bound slightly stronger).

In comparison, the classical consensus literature often considered a *strongly adaptive* model [12,16,19]—this was also the widely accepted model in the early distributed systems and multi-party protocols literature (see also Definition 1 in Feldman's thesis [17] and Fig. 4, page 176 of Canetti's excellent work [7]). In the strongly adaptive model, the adversary is allowed to perform "after-the-fact" message removal, i.e., if the adversary adaptively corrupts a node u in round r, it can erase all messages u had sent in round r prior to becoming corrupt. Thus, a strongly adaptive adversary has strictly more power than a weakly adaptive one. The weakly adaptive model was inspired by the line of work on blockchains and sublinear-communication, large-scale consensus protocols. Many famous protocols including Nakamoto's consensus [30,34], and other subsequent blockchain protocols [1,10,11,32,33,35] were proven secure in the weakly adaptive model, and it is widely known that their security fails to hold in the strongly adaptive model. The recent work by Abraham et al. [1] showed that this is not a coincidence—in the strongly adaptive model, no consensus protocol can achieve sublinear communication overhead!

We adopt the weakly adaptive model inspired by the blockchain line of work. The techniques in this paper do not easily extend to the strongly adaptive model; there is an attack that breaks our protocol under the strongly adaptive model.

It remains an open question whether in the strongly adaptive model, expected constant round BB is possible under even 51% corruption. In fact, in the strongly adaptive model under 51% corruption, even sublinear-round protocols were not known. In a companion work [36], we show that assuming trusted setup, the existence of time-lock puzzles and other reasonable cryptographic assumptions, one can construct BB with polylogarithmic round complexity in the strongly adaptive model. It is interesting to note that the techniques used in that work [36] depart completely from the ones in this paper. In light of our companion paper [36], it remains open 1) whether any sublinear-round BB is possible under 51% strongly adaptive corruption, without time lock puzzles; and 2) whether expected constant round BB is possible under 51% strongly adaptive corruption and any reasonable assumptions. New upper- or lower-bounds in these directions would be exciting.

On the Necessity of Trusted Setup. We assume a trusted setup to get our weakly adaptive BB. Due to the famous lower bound by Lamport et al. [28], some setup assumption is necessary to get consensus under at least $n/3$ (even static) corruptions. We do not understand if our trusted setup can be weakened, and we leave it as another exciting open question. We stress, however, that *expected constant-round BB under 51% corruption is an open question whose answer has eluded the community for more than three decades, under any assumption, allowing any (reasonable) setup, and even under static corruption*. We therefore believe that despite our trusted setup and weakly adaptive restrictions, our result is an important step forward in this line of work.

2 Technical Overview

2.1 Preliminaries

Problem Definition. The problem of Byzantine Broadcast has been widely explored. Suppose there are n *nodes* (sometimes also called *parties*) in a distributed system, indexed from 1 to n, respectively. The communication within the system is modeled by a synchronous network, where a message sent by an honest node in some round r is guaranteed to be delivered to an honest recipient at the beginning of the next round $r + 1$. Among the n nodes in the system, there is a designated sender whose identity is common knowledge. Before the protocol begins, the sender receives an input bit b. All nodes then engage in interactions where the sender aims to send the bit b to everyone. At the end of the protocol, each node u outputs a bit b_u. Henceforth, we assume that the protocol is parameterized with a security parameter λ. We say that a protocol achieves Byzantine Broadcast if it satisfies the following guarantees except with negligibly small in λ probability.

- *Consistency*: for any two honest nodes u and v, $b_u = b_v$.
- *Validity*: if the designated sender is honest, for any honest node u, $b_u = b$.

Although our main definition is for agreeing on a single bit, our approach easily extends to multi-valued BB too.

Adversary Model. At any point of time during the protocol's execution a node can either be *honest* or *corrupt*. Honest nodes correctly follow the protocol, while corrupt nodes are controlled by an adversary and can deviate from the prescribed protocol arbitrarily. We allow the adversary to be *rushing*, i.e., it can observe the messages honest nodes want to send in round r before deciding what messages corrupt nodes send in the same round r.

We consider an adaptive adversary in our paper. In any round r, it can adaptively corrupt honest nodes after observing the messages they want to send in round r, as long as the total number of corrupted nodes does not exceed an upper bound f. If a node $v \in [n]$ becomes newly corrupt in round r, the adversary can make it inject new messages of its choice in the present round r; however, the adversary cannot perform "after-the-fact removal", i.e., erase the messages v sent in round r before it became corrupt.

Modeling Setup. We will allow setup assumptions as well as standard cryptography. Our protocol makes use of a public-key infrastructure and digital signatures, and for simplicity in this paper we assume that the signature scheme is *ideal*. We adopt a standard idealized signature model, i.e., imagine that there is a trusted functionality that keeps track of all messages nodes have signed and answers verification queries by looking up this trusted table. Under such an idealized signature model, no signature forgery is possible. When we replace the ideal signature with a real-world instantiation that satisfies the standard notion of "unforgeability under chosen-message attack", all of our theorems and lemmas will follow accounting for an additive, negligibly small failure probability due to the failure of the signature scheme—this approach has been commonly adopted in prior works too and is well-known to be cryptographically sound (even against adaptive adversaries).

For other cryptographic primitives we adopt, e.g., verifiable random functions, we do not assume idealized primitives since the computationally sound reasoning for these primitives is known to have subtleties.

2.2   Technical Roadmap

Byzantine Broadcast under dishonest majority is challenging even under static corruption because the standard random committee election technique fails to work. More concretely, in the honest majority setting and assuming static corruption, a well-known random committee election technique can allow us to compile any polynomial-round BB to a poly-logarithmic round BB protocol. However, as already pointed out by Chan et al. [9], this technique is inapplicable to the corrupt majority setting even under a static adversary.[3] Similarly, we also know of no way to extend the recent techniques of Chan et al. [9] to obtain our result. Instead, we devise novel techniques that redesign the consensus protocol from the ground up.

Trust Graph Maintenance (Section 3). First, we devise a new method for nodes to maintain a *trust graph* over time. While previous work [5,22] also used consistency graph in multiparty protocols and secret sharing, our trust graph is of a different nature from prior work. We are the first to tie the round complexity of distributed consensus with the diameter of a trust graph, and upper bound the diameter.

The vertices in the trust graph represent nodes in the BB protocol; and an edge between u and v indicates that u and v mutually trust each other. Initially, every node's trust graph is the complete graph; however, during the protocol, if some nodes misbehave, they may get removed completely or get disconnected from other nodes in honest nodes' trust graphs. On the other hand, honest nodes will forever remain direct neighbors to each other in their respective trust graphs.

---

[3] As Chan et al. [9] point out, the random committee election approach fails to work for corrupt majority (even for static corruption), because members outside the committee cannot rely on a majority voting mechanism to learn the outcome.

There are a few challenges we need to cope with in designing the trust graph mechanism. First, if a node v misbehaves in a way that leaves a cryptographic evidence implicating itself (e.g., double-signing equivocating votes), then honest nodes can distribute this evidence and remove v from their trust graphs. Sometimes, however, v may misbehave in a way that does not leave cryptographic evidence: for example, v can fail to send a message it is supposed to send to u, and in this case u cannot produce an evidence to implicate v. In our trust graph mechanism, we allow u to complain about v without providing an evidence, and a receiver of this complaint can be convinced that at least one node among u and v is corrupt (but it may not be able to tell which one is corrupt). In any case, the receiver of this complaint may remove the edge (u, v) from its trust graph. We do not allow a node u to express distrust about an edge (v, w) that does not involve itself—in this way a corrupt node cannot cause honest nodes to get disconnected in their trust graphs.

A second challenge we are faced with is that honest nodes may not have agreement for their respective trust graphs at any point of time—in fact, reaching agreement on their trust graphs may be as hard as the BB problem we are trying to solve in the first place. However, if honest nodes always share their knowledge to others, we can devise a mechanism that satisfies the following *monotonicity* condition: any honest node's trust graph in round $t > r$ is a subgraph of any honest node's trust graph in round r. In our protocol we will have to work with this slightly imperfect condition rather than complete agreement.

Finally, although an honest node is convinced that besides their direct neighbors in its own trust graph, no one else can be honest, it still must wait to hear what nodes multiple hops away say during the protocol. This is because their direct neighbors may still trust their own neighbors, and the neighbors' neighbors may care about their own neighbors, etc. For information to flow from a node v that is r hops away from u in u's trust graph may take up to r rounds, and this explains why the diameter of the trust graph is critical to the round complexity of our protocol. We will devise algorithms for ensuring that honest nodes' trust graphs have *small diameter*. To maintain small diameter, we devise a mechanism for nodes to post-process their trust graphs: for example, although a node u may not have direct evidence against v, if many nodes complain about v, u can be indirectly convinced that v is indeed corrupt and remove v.

The TrustCast Building Block (Section 4). A common technique in the consensus literature is to bootstrap full consensus from weaker primitives, often called "reliable broadcast" or "gradecast" depending on the concrete definitions [6,16,26]. Typically, these weaker primitives aim to achieve consistency whether the sender is honest or not; but they may not achieve liveness if the sender is corrupt [6,16,26]. Based on a weaker primitive such as "reliable broadcast" or "gradecast", existing works would additionally rely on random leader election to bootstrap full consensus. Roughly speaking, every epoch a random leader is chosen, and if the leader is honest, liveness will ensue. Additionally, relying on the consistency property of this weaker primitive, with enough care we can devise mechanisms for ensuring consistency within the same epoch and across epochs—in other words, honest nodes must make the same decision no matter whether they make decisions in the same epoch or different epochs.

In our work we devise a TrustCast building block which is also a weakening of full consensus and we would like to bootstrap consensus from this weaker primitive. Our definition of TrustCast, however, is tied to the trust graph and departs significantly from prior works. Specifically, TrustCast allows a sender $s \in [n]$ to send a message to everyone: *if s wants to continue to remain in an honest node u's trust graph, u must receive some valid message from s at the end of the protocol*, although different honest nodes may receive inconsistent messages from s if s is corrupt. At a high level, the sender s has three choices:

1. it can either send the same valid message to all honest nodes;
2. (*technical challenge*) or it can fail to send a valid message to some honest node, say u,—in this case u will remove s from its trust graph immediately and in the next round all honest nodes will remove s from their trust graphs;
3. or u can send equivocating messages to different honest nodes, but in the next round honest nodes will have compared notes and discovered the equivocation, and thus they remove s from their trust graphs.

The first case will directly lead to progress in our protocol. In the second and third cases, s will be removed from honest nodes' trust graphs; we also make progress in the sense that s can no longer hamper liveness in the future.

An important technical challenge for designing the TrustCast protocol lies in the second case above: in this case, u may not have a cryptographic evidence to implicate s and thus u cannot directly convince others to remove s. However, in this case, it turns out that u can be convinced that some of its direct neighbors must be corrupt, and it will instead convince others to remove the edge (u, v) for every direct neighbor v that it believes to be corrupt. Once these edges are removed, s will land in a "remote" part of the graph such that honest nodes can be convinced that it is corrupt and remove it altogether.

3   Trust Graph Maintenance

3.1   Overview of Trust Graph Maintenance and Invariants

At a very high level, the novelty of our approach lies in the way parties maintain and make use of an undirected *trust graph* over time. In a trust graph, the vertices correspond to all or a subset of the parties participating in the consensus protocol. An edge (u, v) in the trust graph intuitively means that the nodes $u \in [n]$ and $v \in [n]$ mutually trust each other. Since a node in the graph corresponds to a party in the system, to avoid switching between the words "node" and "party", we will just use the word "node".

Initially, every honest node's trust graph is the complete graph over the set $[n]$, i.e., everyone mutually trusts everyone else. However, over the course of the protocol, a node may discover misbehavior of other nodes and remove nodes or edges from its own trust graph accordingly. We will assume that at any point of time, *an honest node u's trust graph must be a single connected component containing u*—effectively u would always discard any node disconnected from itself from its own trust graph.

Notations. Throughout the paper, we will use G_u^r to denote the node u's updated trust graph in round r (after processing the graph-messages received in round r and updating the trust graph). More precisely, G_u^r is the trust graph exported by u's trust graph module to u's consensus module. Sometimes, if the round we refer to is clear, we may also write G_u omitting the round r. We also use $N(v, G)$ to denote the set of neighbors of v in the graph G. In cases where the graph G we refer to is clear, we just abbreviate it to $N(v)$. For convenience, we always assume that a node is a neighbor of itself. Therefore, $v \in N(v)$ holds.

Finally, we follow the notations in Sect. 2.1 where n is the number of nodes in the system, f is the upper bound for the number of corrupt nodes and $h = n - f$ is the lower bound for the number of honest nodes.

Important Invariants of the Trust Graph. A very natural requirement is that corrupt nodes can never cause honest nodes to suspect each other; in fact, we want the following invariant:

> **Honest clique invariant:** at any time, in any honest node's trust graph, all honest nodes form a clique. This implies that all honest nodes must forever remain direct neighbors to each other in their trust graphs.

The round complexity of our protocol is directly related to the diameter of honest nodes' trust graphs and thus we want to make sure that honest nodes' trust graphs have small diameter. To understand this more intuitively, we can consider an example in which three nodes, u, v, and s execute Byzantine Broadcast with s being the sender. All three nodes behave honestly except that s drops all messages to u. In this case, although u is convinced that s is corrupt and thus removes the edge (u, s) from its trust graph, it cannot prove s's misbehavior to v. Since v still has reasons to believe that s might be honest, v will seek to reach agreement with s. Now, if u tries to reach agreement with v, it has to care about what s says. But since s drops all messages to u, any information propagation from s to u must incur 2 rounds with v acting as the relay.

This example can generalize over multiple hops: although an honest node $u \in [n]$ knows that except for its direct neighbors in its trust graph, everyone else must be corrupt; it must nonetheless wait for information to propagate from nodes multiple hops away in its trust graph. For a node w that is r hops away from u in u's trust graph, information from w may take r rounds to reach u. Summarizing, for our protocol to be round efficient, we would like to maintain the following invariant:

> **Small diameter invariant:** at any point of time, every honest node u's trust graph must have small diameter.

Finally, we stress that a difficult challenge we are faced with, is the fact that honest nodes may never be in full agreement w.r.t. their trust graphs at any snapshot of time—in fact, attempting to make honest nodes agree on their trust graphs could be as difficult as solving the Byzantine Broadcast problem itself. However, from a technical perspective, what will turn out to be very helpful to us, is the following monotonicity invariant:

Monotonicity invariant: an honest node u's trust graph in round $t > r$ must be a subset of an honest node v's trust graph in round r. Here, we say that an undirected graph $G = (V, E)$ is a subset of another undirected graph $G' = (V', E')$ iff $V \subseteq V'$ and $E \subseteq E'$.

The above trust graph monotonicity invariant can be maintained because of the following intuition: whatever messages an honest node $v \in [n]$ sees in round r, v can relay them such that all other honest nodes must have seen them by round $r + 1$—in this way the honest node u would perform the same edge/node removal in round $r + 1$ as what v performed in round r.

3.2   Conventions and Common Assumptions

Throughout our paper, we assume that message echoing among honest nodes is implicit (and our protocol will not repeatedly state the echoing):

Implicit echoing assumption: All honest nodes echo every fresh message they have heard from the network, i.e., as soon as an honest node u receives a message m at the beginning of some round r, if this message is well-formed and has not been received before, u relays it to everyone.

Each node has a *consensus module* (see Sects. 4 and 5) and a *trust graph module* which will be described in this section. Messages generated by the trust graph module and the consensus module will have different formats. Henceforth, we may call messages generated by the trust graph module *graph messages*; and we may call all other messages *consensus messages*. Below, we state some assumptions about the modules and their interfaces. We assume that all messages generated by the consensus module are of the following format:

Message format of the consensus module: All protocol messages generated by the consensus module are of the form $(\mathsf{T}, e, \mathsf{payload})$ along with a signature from the sender, where T is a string that denotes the type of the message, $e \in \mathbb{N}$ denotes the epoch number (the meaning of this will be clear later in Sect. 5), and $\mathsf{payload}$ is a string denoting an arbitrary payload. Each type of message may additionally require its payload to satisfy some wellformedness requirements.

For example, (vote, e, b) and $(\mathsf{comm}, e, \mathcal{E})$ represent vote messages and commit messages, respectively, in our Byzantine Broadcast protocol (see Sect. 5), where vote and comm denote the type of the message, e denotes the epoch number, and the remainder of the message is some payload.

In our consensus module, nodes can misbehave in different ways, and some types of misbehaviors can generate cryptographic evidence to implicate the offending node. We define equivocation evidence below.

Equivocation evidence. In our consensus module, honest nodes are not supposed to double-sign two different messages with the same type and epoch number—if any node does so, it is said to have equivocated. Any node that has equivocated must be malicious. The collection of two messages signed by the same node $u \in [n]$, with the same type and epoch but different payloads, is called an *equivocation evidence* for u.

3.3 Trust Graph Maintenance Mechanism

Note that if the trust graph always remains the complete graph, obviously it would satisfy the aforementioned three invariants. However, keep in mind that the goal for trust graph maintenance is to make sure that corrupt nodes do not hamper liveness. In our protocol, once a node starts to misbehave in certain ways, each honest node would remove them from its trust graph such that they would no longer care about reaching agreement with them. In our scheme, every node maintains its trust graph in the following manner:

Trust graph maintenance mechanism

- *Node removal upon equivocation evidence.* First, upon receiving an equivocation evidence implicating some node $v \in [n]$, a node removes v from its trust graph as well as all v's incident edges. After the removal, call the post-processing mechanism described below to update the trust graph.
- *Pairwise distrust messages and edge removal.* Sometimes, the consensus module of node u can observe that a direct neighbor v in its trust graph has not followed the honest protocol (e.g., u is expecting some message from v but v did not send it); however, u may not have a cryptographic evidence to prove v's misbehavior to others. In this case, u's consensus module calls the Distrust(v) operation.
  - When u's trust graph module receives a Distrust(v) call, it signs and echoes a distrust message (`distrust`, (u, v)).
  - When a node $w \in [n]$ receives a message of the form (`distrust`, (u, v)) signed by u (w and u might be the same user), w removes the edge (u, v) from its own trust graph[a] and calls the post-processing procedure.
- *Post-processing for maintaining $O(n/h)$ diameter.* The diameter of the trust graph can grow as nodes and edges are being removed. To maintain the property that honest nodes' trust graphs have small diameter, each node performs the following post-processing every time it removes a node or an edge from its trust graph (recall that h denotes the number of honest nodes and $N(v)$ represents the set of v's neighbors in a graph):

- **Repeat:** find an edge (v, w) in the trust graph such that $|N(v) \cap N(w)| < h$, and remove the edge; until no such edge can be found. Afterwards, remove all nodes disconnected from u in u's trust graph.
- **Until** no such node or edge exists.
- u then removes any node that is disconnected from u in u's trust graph.

---

[a] Since each node will receive its own messages at the beginning of the next round, when a node u calls $\mathsf{Distrust}(v)$, the edge (u, v) will be removed from its own trust graph at the beginning of the next round.

Remark 1. Note that a $(\mathtt{distrust}, (u, v))$ message is only valid if it is signed by u, i.e., the first node in the pair of nodes—this makes sure that corrupt nodes cannot misuse distrust messages to cause an edge between two honest nodes to be removed (in any honest node's trust graph).

Suppose that an honest node never declares $\mathsf{Distrust}$ on another honest node—note that this is a condition that our protocol must respect and it will be proved in Theorem 4 of Sect. 4. We first show that the honest clique invariant is satisfied. An edge is removed from the trust graph iff (1) a $\mathsf{Distrust}$ is declared on the edge or (2) the edge is removed during post processing. Since an honest node never declares $\mathsf{Distrust}$ on another honest node, we only need to show that we never remove edges between honest nodes during post processing.

Lemma 1. *The post processing does not remove any edge between honest nodes.*

Proof. We will prove by contradiction. Let us consider post-processing on a node u's trust graph G_u. Suppose the edge (v, w) is removed during post-processing where v and w are both honest nodes. W.l.o.g., we can assume that this is the first time any edge between honest nodes is removed during post processing. This means that before post processing, all honest nodes are fully connected in G_u, i.e., all honest nodes are the neighbors of both v and w. Thus, we have $|N(v, G_u) \cap N(w, G_u)| \geq h$. This violates our assumption that (v, w) is removed during post processing, because (v, w) is removed iff $|N(v, G_u) \cap N(w, G_u)| < h$.

The monotonicity invariant is not as apparent. We need to show that if an honest node u removes an edge during post-processing, another honest node v would remove this edge as well in the next round. The observation is that the post-processing algorithm does not change the subgraph relationship—if G is a subgraph of H and we apply post-processing on both G and H to get G' and H', then G' would still be a subgraph of H'. Since an edge can only be removed by calling $\mathsf{Distrust}$ and post processing, we can prove the monotonicity invariant using induction. Due to the page limit, we skip the proof for the monotonicity lemma. The detailed proof for Lemma 2 can be found in the online version [37].

Lemma 2. *The trust graph maintenance mechanism satisfies the monotonicity invariant, i.e., for any honest node u, v and any round number r, G_v^{r+1} is a subgraph of G_u^r.*

Finally, the most challenging part is to prove that the post-processing mechanism will output a graph with diameter at most $O(n/h)$. To prove this, we will show that if the graph's diameter is larger than $2n/h$, there must exist an edge (v, w) such that $|N(v) \cap N(w)| < h$—henceforth, we call such an edge a fictitious edge. At a very high level, observe that if the graph's diameter is greater than $2n/h$, there must exist a path from some u to some u' whose length is greater than $2n/h$. Now, we can divide nodes into layers based on their distance from u, where S_i denotes all nodes at distance i from u. Since there must be more than $2n/h$ layers, we can show that there must exist two adjacent layers S_i and S_{i+1} such that the union of the two contains fewer than h nodes. Therefore, any edge between the two layers is a fictitious edge. This is the high level intuition and might be inaccurate in the boundary condition. Through a more involved argument (see our online version [37] for detail), we can provide a tight upper bound and show that after the post-processing, the graph's diameter is at most $d = \lceil n/h \rceil + \lfloor n/h \rfloor - 1$.

Lemma 3. *The post-processing guarantees that the diameter of the trust graph is upper bounded by $d = \lceil n/h \rceil + \lfloor n/h \rfloor - 1$.*

The following theorem follows directly from Lemma 1, 2 and 3.

Theorem 2 (Efficient trust graph mechanism). *Suppose that an honest node never declares Distrust on another honest node (which is proven to be true in Sect. 4). Then, the efficient trust graph maintenance mechanism satisfies the honest clique invariant, the monotonicity invariant, and moreover, at any point of time, any honest node's trust graph has diameter at most $d = \lceil n/h \rceil + \lfloor n/h \rfloor - 1$.*

Finally, observe that the trust graph module's communication (including implicit echoing of graph messages) is upper bounded by $\widetilde{O}(n^4)$ (the $\widetilde{O}$ hides the $\log n$ terms needed to encode a node's identifier). This is because there are at most $O(n^2)$ number of effective distrust messages and everyone will echo each such message seen to all nodes.

4 New Building Block: The TrustCast Protocol

Starting from this section, we will be describing the consensus module. In this section, we first describe an important building block called TrustCast which will play a critical role in our BB protocol. Before describing the consensus module, we first clarify the order in which the trust module and consensus module are invoked within a single round:

1. At the beginning of the round, a node u receives all incoming messages.
2. Next, u's trust graph module processes all the graph-messages and updates its local trust graph:
   - Process all the freshly seen Distrust messages and remove the corresponding edges from its trust graph.
   - Check for new equivocation evidence: if any equivocation evidence is seen implicating any $v \in [n]$, remove v and all edges incident to v from the node's own trust graph.

   Recall also that every time an edge or node is removed from a node's trust graph, a post-processing procedure is called to make sure that the trust graph still has $O(n/h)$ diameter (see Sect. 3.3).
3. Now, u's consensus module processes the incoming consensus messages, and computes a set of messages denoted M to send in this round. The rules for computing the next messages M are specified by our Byzantine Broadcast protocol (Sect. 5) which calls the TrustCast protocol (this section) as a building block. The protocol is allowed to query the node's current trust graph (i.e., the state after the update in the previous step).
4. Finally, u sends M to everyone; additionally, for every fresh message first received in this round, u relays it to everyone.

Henceforth, in our consensus module description, whenever we say "at the beginning of round r", we actually mean in round r after Step (2), i.e., after the trust graph module makes updates and yields control to the consensus module.

4.1   The TrustCast Protocol

Motivation and Intuition. We introduce a TrustCast protocol that will be used as a building block in our Byzantine Broadcast protocol. In the TrustCast protocol, a sender $s \in [n]$ has a message m and wants to share m with other parties. At the end of the TrustCast protocol, any honest node either *receives a message from s or removes s from its trust graph*. The TrustCast protocol does not guarantee consistency: if the sender is corrupt, different honest parties may output different messages from the sender. However, if the sender is indeed honest, then all honest parties will output the message that the sender sends. Very remotely, the TrustCast protocol resembles the notion of a "reliable broadcast" [6] or a "gradecast" [16,26] which is a weakening of Byzantine Broadcast—many existing works in the consensus literature bootstrap full consensus (or broadcast) from either reliable broadcast or gradecast. Similarly, we will bootstrap Byzantine Broadcast from TrustCast; however, we stress that our definition of the TrustCast abstraction is novel, especially in the way the abstraction is tied to the trust graph.

Abstraction and Notations. A TrustCast protocol instance must specify a sender denoted $s \in [n]$; furthermore, it must also specify a verification function Vf for receiving nodes to check the validity of the received message. Therefore, we will use the notation $\mathsf{TrustCast}^{\mathsf{Vf},s}$ to specify the verification function and the sender of a TrustCast instance. Given a node $u \in [n]$ and a message m, we also use the following convention

$$u.\mathsf{Vf}(m) = \mathsf{true} \text{ in round } r$$

to mean that message m passes the verification of Vf w.r.t. node u in round r.

In our Byzantine Broadcast protocol, whenever a sender s calls $\mathsf{TrustCast}^{\mathsf{Vf},s}$ to propagate a message m, the verification function Vf and the message m must respect the following two conditions—only if these conditions are satisfied can we guarantee that honest nodes never distrust each other (see Theorem 4).

- *Validity at origin.* Assuming that the leader s is honest, it must be that $s.\mathsf{Vf}(m) = \mathsf{true}$ in round 0, i.e., at the beginning of the $\mathsf{TrustCast}^{\mathsf{Vf},s}$ protocol.
- *Monotonicity condition.* We say that Vf satisfies the monotonicity condition if and only if the following holds. Let $r < t$ and suppose that $u, v \in [n]$ are honest. Then, if $u.\mathsf{Vf}(m) = \mathsf{true}$ in round r, it must hold that $v.\mathsf{Vf}(m) = \mathsf{true}$ in round t as well. Note that in the above, u and v could be the same or different parties.

The first condition guarantees that an honest sender always verifies the message it sends. The second condition, i.e., the Monotonicity condition, guarantees that if an honest node successfully verifies a message, then that message would pass verification of all other honest nodes in future rounds. Together, the two conditions imply that the honest sender's message would pass verification of all honest nodes.

TrustCast Protocol. We describe the $\mathsf{TrustCast}^{\mathsf{Vf},s}(m)$ protocol below where a sender $s \in [n]$ wants to propagate a message of the form $m = (\mathsf{T}, e, \mathsf{payload})$ whose validity can be ascertained by the verification function Vf. Recall that by our common assumptions (see Sect. 3.2), honest nodes echo every fresh message seen. Moreover, if an honest node $u \in [n]$ sees the sender's signatures on two messages with the same (T, e) but different payloads, then u removes the sender s from its trust graph. For brevity, these implicit assumptions will not be repeated in the protocol description below.

Protocol $\mathsf{TrustCast}^{\mathsf{Vf},s}(m)$

Input: The sender s receives an input message m and wants to propagate the message m to everyone.

Protocol: In round 0, the sender s sends the message m along with a signature on m to everyone.

Let $d = \lceil n/h \rceil + \lfloor n/h \rfloor - 1$, for each round $1 \leq r \leq d$, every node $u \in [n]$ does the following:

$(\star)$ If no message m signed by s has been received such that $u.\mathsf{Vf}(m) = \mathsf{true}$ in round r, then for any v that is a direct neighbor of u in u's trust graph: if v is at distance less than r from the sender s, call $\mathsf{Distrust}(v)$.

Outputs: At the beginning of round $d + 1$, if (1) the sender s is still in u's trust graph and (2) u has received a message m such that $u.\mathsf{Vf}(m) = \mathsf{true}$, then u outputs m.

To better understand the protocol, consider the example where the sender s is a direct neighbor of an honest node u in u's trust graph. This means that u "trusts" s, i.e., u thinks that s is an honest node. Therefore, u expects to receive s's message in the first round of the TrustCast protocol. If u has not received from s in the first round, it knows that s must be corrupted. It would thus remove the edge (u, s) from u's trust graph.

Similarly, if s is at distance r from u in u's trust graph, then u should expect to receive a valid message signed by s in at most r rounds. In case it does not, then u can be convinced that all of its direct neighbors that are at distance $r-1$ or smaller from s in its trust graph must be malicious—therefore u calls Distrust to declare distrust in all such neighbors. Note that the distrust messages generated in round r will be processed at the beginning of round $r + 1$. We now utilize the above intuition to prove that the TrustCast protocol satisfies the following properties:

- At the end of the TrustCast protocol, any honest node either receives a message from s or removes s from its trust graph (Theorem 3).
- In the TrustCast protocol, we never remove edges between two honest nodes in any honest node's trust graph (Theorem 4).

In the rest of the paper, we always use the variable d to represent $\lceil n/h \rceil + \lfloor n/h \rfloor - 1$.

Theorem 3. *Let $u \in [n]$ be an honest node. At the beginning of round $d + 1$, either the sender s is removed from u's trust graph or u must have received a message m signed by s such that $u.\mathsf{Vf}(m) = \mathsf{true}$ in some round r.*

Proof. By the definition of the $\mathsf{TrustCast}^{\mathsf{Vf},s}$ protocol, if in round r, the node u has not received a message m signed by s such that $u.\mathsf{Vf}(m) = \mathsf{true}$ in round r, then u will call $\mathsf{Distrust}(v)$ for each of its neighbors v that is within distance $r - 1$ from s. The $\mathsf{Distrust}(v)$ operation generates a distrust message that will be processed at the beginning of round $r + 1$, causing u to remove the edge (u, v) from its trust graph. After removing the edge (u, v), the trust graph module will also perform some post-processing which may further remove additional edges and nodes. After this procedure, s must be at distance at least $r + 1$ from u or removed from u's trust graph.

By setting the round number r to d, we can conclude that at the beginning of round $d + 1$, if u has not received a message m such that $u.\mathsf{Vf}(m) = \mathsf{true}$, then s must be either at distance at least $d + 1$ from u or removed from u's trust graph. Yet, u's trust graph must contain a single connected component containing u, with diameter at most d. So s must be removed from u's trust graph.

Theorem 4. *If the validity at origin and the monotonicity conditions are respected, then an honest node u will never call $\mathsf{Distrust}(v)$ where v is also honest.*

Proof. We can prove by contradiction: suppose that in round $r \in [1, d]$, an honest node u calls Distrust(v) where $v \in [n]$ is also honest. This means that in round r, u has not received a message m signed by s such that $u.\mathsf{Vf}(m) = \mathsf{true}$ in round r. Due to the implicit echoing and the monotonicity condition of Vf, it means that in round $r - 1$, v has not received a message m signed by s such that $v.\mathsf{Vf}(m) = \mathsf{true}$ in round $r - 1$. We may now consider two cases:

- **Case 1: suppose** $r - 1 = 0$. If the validity at origin condition holds, then v cannot be the sender s. In this case u cannot call Distrust(v) in round 0 because v is at distance at least 1 from the sender s.
- **Case 2: suppose** $r - 1 > 0$. By definition of the $\mathsf{TrustCast}^{\mathsf{Vf}, s}$ protocol, in round $r - 1$, v would send Distrust(w) for any w within distance $r - 2$ from s in G_v^{r-1}. Suppose v sends distrust messages on $w_1, \cdots, w_l$ and we denote the graph $G' \leftarrow G_v^{r-1} / \{(v, w_1), \cdots, (v, w_l)\}$. Then, in G', the distance between v and s should be at least r. Let us now consider node u and u's trust graph. By trust graph monotonicity and Lemma 2, u's trust graph at the beginning of round r, i.e., G_u^r, should be a subset of G_v^{r-1}. Further, u would receive v's distrust messages on $w_1, \cdots, w_l$ in round r. Thus,

$$G_u^r \subseteq G_v^{r-1} / \{(v, w_1), \cdots, (v, w_l)\}.$$

This implies that the distance between v and s in G_u^r should be at least r, contradicting our assumption that the distance between v and s is $r - 1$.

In either case, we have reached a contradiction.

In this section, we provided a TrustCast protocol with nice properties (Theorem 3 and 4) related to the trust graph. In the next section, we will show how to bootstrap full consensus from the TrustCast protocol.

Remark 2. Later, when TrustCast is invoked by a parent protocol, it could be invoked in an arbitrary round r_{init} of the parent protocol; moreover, at invocation, honest nodes' trust graphs need not be complete graphs. In this section, our presentation assumed that the initial round is renamed to round 0 (and all the subsequent rounds are renamed correspondingly). We say that a sender s *trustcasts* message m with verification function Vf if s calls $\mathsf{TrustCast}^{\mathsf{Vf}, s}$ on message m. If the verification function Vf is clear in the context, we just say s *trustcasts* a message m.

5 Byzantine Broadcast Under an Adaptive Adversary

In this section, we present a Byzantine Broadcast (BB) protocol that achieves security under a weakly adaptive adversary.

Leader Election. One common trick used in existing Byzantine Broadcast protocols is to select a leader in each epoch and let the leader broadcast its proposal. However, ideal leader election is hard to implement under an adaptive adversary. This is because the adaptive adversary will learn the leader's identity upon receiving the leader's proposal. It can then corrupt the leader and generate an equivocating proposal. At the high level, we want an honest leader to fulfill its duty before its identity is known to the adversary. To achieve this, we need to use verifiable random functions (VRFs) and a new building block called AckCast, which is a simple extension of TrustCast.

Commit Evidence. In our Byzantine Broadcast protocol, each node uses the TrustCast protocol to send messages until it becomes confident as to which bit to commit on. Afterwards, it needs to convince other nodes to also commit on this bit using what we call a *commit evidence*. In other words, once a node generates a valid commit evidence, all other nodes that receive it will commit on the corresponding bit. We want the commit evidence to satisfy that.

- It is impossible for two nodes to generate valid commit evidences on different bits.
- If the leader in this epoch is honest, at least one honest node should be able to generate a commit evidence on the leader's proposed bit.

The first property guarantees consistency while the second property guarantees liveness. We first show what we define to be a commit evidence in our protocol. After we describe our protocol in Sect. 5.3, we will prove that this definition satisfies the two properties above.

Fix an epoch e and a bit $b \in \{0, 1\}$. We say that a collection $\mathcal{E}$ containing signed messages of the form $(\texttt{vote}, e, b)$ is an epoch-e commit evidence for b w.r.t. G_u^r iff for every $v \in G_u^r$, $\mathcal{E}$ contains a signed message $(\texttt{vote}, e, b)$ from v. Recall that G_u^r is u's trust graph at the beginning of round r (after processing graph-messages).

Fix $u \in [n]$ and the round r. We say that a commit evidence for (e, b) w.r.t. G_u^r is *fresher* than a commit evidence for (e', b') w.r.t. G_u^r iff $e' > e$. Henceforth, we will assume that $\perp$ is a valid epoch-0 commit evidence for either bit.

Remark 3. In our protocol description, if we say that "node $u \in [n]$ sees a commit evidence for (e, b) in round r", this means that at the beginning of the round r, after having processed graph-messages, node u has in its view a commit evidence for (e, b) w.r.t. G_u^r.

Lemma 4 (Commit evidence monotonicity lemma). *Let $u, v \in [n]$ be honest nodes. A commit evidence for (e, b) w.r.t. G_u^r must be a commit evidence for (e, b) w.r.t. G_v^t for any $t > r$. Note that in the above, u and v can be the same or different node(s).*

Proof. Due to the trust graph monotonicity lemma, we have $G_u^t \subseteq G_v^r$ since $t > r$. The lemma then follows directly.

Protocol Intuition. Our protocol proceeds in incrementing epochs where each epoch consists of three phases, called **Propose**, **Vote**, and **Commit**, respectively. Each phase has $O(d)$ ($d = \lceil n/h \rceil + \lfloor n/h \rfloor - 1$) rounds. Intuitively, each phase aims to achieve the following objectives:

- **Propose:** the leader uses the TrustCast protocol to share the freshest commit evidence it has seen.
- **Vote:** each node uses the TrustCast protocol to relay the leader's proposal it receives in the propose phase. At the end of the vote phase, each node checks whether it can construct a commit evidence.
- **Commit:** nodes use the TrustCast protocol to share their commit evidence.

Besides the three phases, there is also a termination procedure (with the entry point **Terminate**) that runs in the background and constantly checks whether the node should terminate. Also, to apply the TrustCast protocol, we need to define the corresponding verification functions such that the *monotonicity condition* and the *validity at origin condition* (defined in Sect. 4.1) are satisfied.

In this section, we first review VRFs [29] in Sect. 5.1. We will apply VRF as a cryptographic primitive in the leader election step. In Sect. 5.2, we introduce our AckCast protocol. Finally, in Sect. 5.3, we introduce our Byzantine Broadcast protocol under an adaptive adversary, followed by its proof of correctness.

5.1 Preliminary: Verifiable Random Functions

In this section, we review the definition and notations of VRFs in [29]. A VRF includes the following (possibly randomized) algorithms:

- $(pp, \{\mathsf{pk}_u, \mathsf{sk}_u\}_{u \in [n]}) \leftarrow \mathsf{Gen}(1^\lambda)$: takes in a security parameter λ and generates public parameters pp, and a public and secret key pair $(\mathsf{pk}_u, \mathsf{sk}_u)$ for each node $u \in [n]$; each sk_u is of the form $\mathsf{sk}_u := (s_u, \rho_u)$ where s_u is said to be the *evaluation key* and ρ_u is said to be the *proof key* for u.
- $(y, \pi) \leftarrow \mathsf{Eval}(pp, \mathsf{sk}_u, x)$: we shall assume that $\mathsf{Eval} := (E, P)$ has two sub-routines E and P where $\mathsf{Eval}.E$ is *deterministic* and $\mathsf{Eval}.P$ is possibly randomized. Given the public parameters pp, the secret key $\mathsf{sk}_u = (s_u, \rho_u)$, and input $x \in \{0, 1\}^{|x|}$, compute $y := \mathsf{Eval}.E(pp, s_u, x)$ and $\pi := \mathsf{Eval}.P(pp, s_u, \rho_u, x)$, and output (y, π).
- $\{0, 1\} \leftarrow \mathsf{Ver}(pp, \mathsf{pk}_u, x, y, \pi)$: receives the public parameters pp, a public key pk_u, an input x, a purported outcome y, and a proof π, outputs either 0 indicating rejection or 1 indicating acceptance.

For a VRF scheme to satisfy correctness, we require that for any $v \in [n]$ and any input x, the following holds with probability 1: let $(pp, \{\mathsf{pk}_u, \mathsf{sk}_u\}_{u \in [n]}) \leftarrow \mathsf{Gen}(1^\lambda)$, and let $(y, \pi) \leftarrow \mathsf{Eval}(pp, \mathsf{sk}_v, x)$, then $\mathsf{Ver}(pp, \mathsf{pk}_v, x, y, \pi) = 1$.

Suppose the adversary can request to create new VRF instances, query existing instances with specified inputs, selectively corrupt instances and obtain the secret keys of these instances.

- We say that a VRF scheme satisfies **pseudorandomness under selective opening** iff the adversary is unable to distinguish the VRF's evaluation outcomes on any future message from randomly generated values.
- We say that a VRF scheme satisfies **unforgeability**, if the adversary cannot forge the VRF outcome and proof on behalf of any honest node on a point that has not been queried.

Due to the page limit, we are unable to review the full definition of VRF. The detailed definition and the cryptographic games are included in the online version [37]. Abraham et al. [1] proved the following theorem where the bilinear group assumptions needed are the same as those adopted by Groth et al. [24].

Theorem 5 (Existence of adaptively secure VRFs [1]). *Assuming standard bilinear group assumptions and a trusted setup, we can construct a VRF scheme satisfying pseudorandomness under selective opening and unforgeability.*

VRF Technical Lemma. Abraham et al. [1] showed the following theorem regarding VRFs that satisfy pseudorandomness under selective opening attacks. To describe the theorem, we need to first describe the following experiments:

- *Ideal experiment.* In the ideal experiment, an adversary $\mathcal{A}$ interacts with an idealized oracle $\mathcal{F}$. The execution continues in epochs. At the beginning of each epoch e, $\mathcal{F}$ picks a random answer for every query of the form (u, e) for $u \in [n]$, and returns all n answers to $\mathcal{A}$. When $\mathcal{A}$ calls $\mathcal{F}$.Corrupt(u), $\mathcal{F}$ records that u has been corrupted.
- *Real experiment.* In the real experiment, an adversary $\mathcal{A}$ interacts with an oracle $\mathcal{F}'$. First, $\mathcal{F}'$ calls VRF.Gen(1^λ) and gives the resulting $pp, \mathsf{pk}_1, \ldots, \mathsf{pk}_n$ to $\mathcal{A}$, but keeps $\mathsf{sk}_1, \ldots, \mathsf{sk}_n$ to itself.
  At the beginning of every epoch e, $\mathcal{F}'$ computes for every $u \in [n]$ a tuple $(y_u, \pi_u) := \mathsf{VRF.Eval}(pp, \mathsf{sk}_u, e)$ and returns (y_u, π_u) to $\mathcal{A}$. Whenever $\mathcal{A}$ calls $\mathcal{F}'$.Corrupt(u), $\mathcal{F}'$ records that u has been corrupted but also discloses sk_u to $\mathcal{A}$ as well as all the randomness used by Eval earlier pertaining to u.

Now, let bad be any polynomial-time computable function defined over the following variables:

1. the sequence of answers (not including the proof part for the real experiment) to all (u, e) queries sorted by lexicographical ordering of the queries, and
2. the nodes corrupted by $\mathcal{A}$ and the epoch in which they become corrupt.

Lemma 5 (Technical lemma regarding VRF [1]). *Suppose that the VRF satisfies pseudorandomness under selective opening. Then, if there exists a non-uniform p.p.t. adversary $\mathcal{A}$ that can cause the bad event* bad *to take place in the real experiment with probability p, there must exist a non-uniform p.p.t. adversary $\mathcal{A}'$ that can cause* bad *to happen in the ideal experiment with probability at least $p - \mathsf{negl}(\lambda)$.*

5.2   New Building Block: AckCast Protocol

We describe an additional helpful building block called AckCast that is a simple extension of the previous TrustCast. In AckCast, a sender $s \in [n]$ trustcasts a message and then every node acknowledges (ACK) the message (also using TrustCast). If a node receives ACKs on different messages, which must contain equivocating signatures from the sender, then the sender must be corrupted and can be removed from the trust graph. At the end of the AckCast protocol, we guarantee that for any honest node u, either

- s is no longer in u's trust graph, or
- u has received a unique and valid message from s; moreover, u has heard an ACK for the same message from every node in u's trust graph.

AckCast$^{\mathsf{Vf},s}$:
1. The sender $s \in [n]$ trustcasts the message m with TrustCast$^{\mathsf{Vf},s}$;
2. For every honest node $u \in [n]$,
   - if the previous TrustCast$^{\mathsf{Vf},s}$ outputs a message m signed by s such that $u.\mathsf{Vf}(m) = \mathsf{true}$, then set $m' \leftarrow (\mathsf{ack}, s, m)$.
   - else, set $m' \leftarrow (\mathsf{ack}, s, \perp)$.

   u trustcasts the message m' with TrustCast$^{\mathsf{Vf}',u}$, where $v.\mathsf{Vf}'(\mathsf{ack}, s, m) = \mathsf{true}$ in round r iff
   (a) either s is no longer in G_v^r or m must agree with what s has trustcast (in v's view); and
   (b) either $m = \perp$ or $v.\mathsf{Vf}(m) = \mathsf{true}$ in round r.

It can be observed that if Vf satisfies the monotonicity condition, then Vf' also satisfies the monotonicity condition. Further, Vf' also satisfies the validity at origin condition by the property of the first TrustCast$^{\mathsf{Vf},s}$. We list these observations in Lemmas 6 and fct:validitymulticastack. Due to the page limit, the detailed proof is omitted and can be found in our online version [37].

Lemma 6. *If Vf satisfies the monotonicity condition, then Vf' also satisfies the monotonicity condition.*

Lemma 7. *Vf' satisfies the validity at origin property, i.e., when an honest node u trustcasts (ack, s, m) with TrustCast$^{\mathsf{Vf}',u}$ in some round r during AckCast$^{\mathsf{Vf},s}$, it must be that $u.\mathsf{Vf}'(\mathsf{ack}, s, m) = \mathsf{true}$ in round r.*

Given Lemmas 6 and 7, we can show that AckCast satisfies what we want.

Lemma 8. *Assume that Vf satisfies the monotonicity condition and that the message m input to s satisfies the validity at origin condition. Then, at the end of the AckCast protocol, for any honest node u, either*

1. *s is no longer in u's trust graph or*
2. *u has heard s trustcast a unique message m such that $u.\mathsf{Vf}(m) = \mathsf{true}$ at the end of the protocol; moreover, u must have received an ACK of the form (ack, s, m) from every node in its trust graph.*

Proof. Since Vf satisfies the monotonicity condition and the validity at origin condition, by Lemmas 6 and 7, Vf' also satisfies the monotonicity condition and the validity at origin condition. Thus, by Theorem 3, for any two honest nodes u and v, u must have received a valid ACK from v that passes Vf' in TrustCast$^{\mathsf{Vf}',v}$. In other words, by the end of the AckCast protocol, any honest node u must have received valid ACKs that passes Vf' from all nodes in its trust graph.

Now, we want to show that the ACKs u receives match what s trustcasts. If s is still in u's trust graph by the end of AckCast, by Theorem 3, u must have received a valid message from s. By the definition of Vf', each ACK message received by u must agree with what s has trustcast. This completes our proof.

5.3   Protocol

Strawman Attempt. We first discuss a strawman attempt using a VRF that achieves security against an adaptive adversary. In every epoch, every node u computes $(y_u, \pi_u) := \mathsf{VRF}(pp, \mathsf{sk}_u, e)$. y_u is said to be u's charisma and we define the leader to be the node with the maximum charisma. The issue with this approach is that the adversary, upon observing that u has the maximum charisma and is the leader, can immediately corrupt u, and make u send an equivocating proposal. Such an attack will not affect consistency, however, it will hamper liveness due to the following: every honest node, upon seeing u's equivocating proposal, removes u from its trust graph; and now they would vote for $\perp$ in the Vote phase. An adversary with a corruption budget of f can continue this attack for f epochs in which an honest node becomes the leader, and thus liveness can take as long as $\Omega(f)$ epochs to ensue.

To defeat the aforementioned attack, we are inspired by techniques from the standard Byzantine Broadcast literature [2,26] but it is not trivial to adapt these techniques to our setting. At a high level, during the Propose phase of each epoch, everyone multicasts a proposal using AckCast pretending that they might be the elected leader. Because AckCast rather than TrustCast is used, effectively everyone would also trustcast an ACK for everyone's proposal. Note that at this time, the VRF outcomes have not been revealed and the adversary cannot effectively single out and target the leader.

Our key idea is to require that a valid proposal must contain everyone's ACK message. In this way, when nodes reveal their VRF outcomes (i.e., their charisma), the adversary may immediately corrupt the leader, but it is already too late for the now-corrupt leader to insert a new equivocating proposal, because there is no time for this new equivocating proposal to acquire ACKs from everyone. To integrate this idea into our protocol invovles further technicalities, but with this intuition in mind, we can now present our protocol formally.

Protocol. Our protocol is described below.

Setup. Run $(pp, \{\mathsf{pk}_u, \mathsf{sk}_u\}_{u \in [n]}) \leftarrow \mathsf{VRF.Gen}(1^\lambda)$. Publish $(pp, \mathsf{pk}_1, \ldots, \mathsf{pk}_n)$ and give sk_u to each $u \in [n]$.

Assumption. For the initial sender $s \in [n]$ in epoch 1, we redefine the outcome of $\mathsf{VRF.Eval}(pp, \mathsf{sk}_s, 1)$ to be $(\infty, \perp)$, and we assume that $\mathsf{VRF.Ver}(pp, \mathsf{pk}_s, 1, \infty, \perp) = 1$. This makes sure that the initial sender s has the maximum charisma in epoch $e = 1$. We shall also assume that by construction, the function VRF will append to the outcome y the unique identifier of the node u. In this way, the evaluation outcomes for two different nodes must be *distinct*.

Main Protocol. For each epoch $e = 1, 2, \ldots$:

1. **Propose:** ($O(d)$ rounds) Every node $u \in [n]$ performs the following:
   - Choose a bit to propose and an evidence as follows:
     - If $e = 1$ and u is the initial sender, u chooses $P := (b, \perp)$ where b is its input bit.
     - Else if a non-$\perp$ commit evidence (for some bit) has been seen, let $\mathcal{E}(e, b)$ denote the freshest such commit evidence and let $P := (b, \mathcal{E}(e, b))$.
     - Else, u chooses a random bit b and let $P := (b, \perp)$.
   - u ackcasts the proposal $(\texttt{prop}, e, P)$ by calling $\mathsf{AckCast}^{\mathsf{Vf}_{\mathrm{prop}}, u}$ where

$$v.\mathsf{Vf}_{\mathrm{prop}}(\texttt{prop}, e, (b, \mathcal{E})) = \mathsf{true} \text{ in round } r \text{ iff}$$

   (a) $\mathcal{E}$ is a valid commit evidence vouching for the bit b proposed; and
   (b) for every $w \in G_v^r$, $\mathcal{E}$ is at least as fresh as any commit evidence trustcast by w in the **Commit** phase of *all* previous epochs $e' < e$—recall that $\perp$ is a commit evidence for epoch 0.

2. **Elect:** (1 round) Every node u computes $(y, \pi) := \mathsf{VRF.Eval}(pp, \mathsf{sk}_u, e)$, and sends the signed tuple $(\texttt{elect}, e, y, \pi)$ to everyone.

3. **Prepare:** ($O(d)$ rounds) Every node $u \in [n]$ does the following:
   - Let $S \subseteq [n]$ be the set of nodes v satisfying the following:[a]
     (a) u has received from v a signed tuple of the form $(\texttt{elect}, e, y_v, \pi_v)$ where $\mathsf{VRF.Ver}(pp, \mathsf{pk}_v, e, y_v, \pi_v) = 1$—henceforth, y_v is said to be v's charisma;
     (b) u has received from v a signed proposal of the form $(\texttt{prop}, e, (b, \_))$. Moreover, everyone that remains in u's trust graph has ACKed this proposal in $\mathsf{AckCast}^{\mathsf{Vf}_{\mathrm{prop}}, v}$ earlier.
   - Find the node $L \in S$ whose charisma y_L is maximized based on lexicographical ordering.
   - Trustcast the tuple $(\texttt{prep}, e, b, L, y_L, \pi_L)$ by calling $\mathsf{TrustCast}^{\mathsf{Vf}_{\mathrm{prep}}, u}$ where

$$v.\mathsf{Vf}_{\mathrm{prep}}(\texttt{prep}, e, b, L, y, \pi) = \mathsf{true} \text{ in round } r \text{ iff}$$

   (a) Everyone in G_v^r has ACKed a proposal of the form $(\texttt{prop}, e, (b, \_))$ by the end of the $\mathsf{AckCast}^{\mathsf{Vf}_{\mathrm{prop}}, L}$ instance; and
   (b) $\mathsf{VRF.Ver}(pp, \mathsf{pk}_L, e, y, \pi) = 1$.

   Henceforth, given a prepare message of the form $(\texttt{prep}, e, b, L, y, \pi)$, y is said to be the charisma of the prepare message.

4. **Vote:** ($O(d)$ rounds) Every node $u \in [n]$ performs the following:
   - Compare the $(\texttt{prep}, e, \_, \_, \_, \_)$ messages that have been trustcast by all nodes v that still remain in u's trust graph, and pick the one $(\texttt{prep}, e, b^*, L^*, y^*, \pi^*)$ whose charisma value y^* is the maximum.

- Trustcast a vote of the form $(\texttt{vote}, e, (b^*, L^*, y^*, \pi^*))$ by calling $\mathsf{TrustCast}^{\mathsf{Vf}_{\mathrm{vote}}, u}$ where

$$v.\mathsf{Vf}_{\mathrm{vote}}(\texttt{vote}, e, (b, L, y, \pi)) = \mathsf{true} \text{ in round } r \text{ iff}$$

   (a) Everyone in G_v^r has ACKed a proposal for b signed by L by the end of the $\mathsf{AckCast}^{\mathsf{Vf}_{\mathrm{prop}}, L}$;
   (b) $\mathsf{VRF.Ver}(pp, \mathsf{pk}_L, e, y, \pi) = 1$;
   (c) For everyone $w \in G_v^r$, y must be at least as large as the charisma of the prepare message trustcast to v by w.

5. **Commit:** $(O(d)$ rounds) Every node $u \in [n]$ performs the following:
   - If everyone still in u's trust graph voted for the same bit $b \in \{0, 1\}$ (as defined by the outputs of the $\mathsf{TrustCast}^{\mathsf{Vf}_{\mathrm{vote}}, u}$ protocols during the **Vote** phase), then **output** the bit b, and trustcast a commit message $(\texttt{comm}, e, \mathcal{E})$ by calling $\mathsf{TrustCast}^{\mathsf{Vf}_{\mathrm{comm}}, u}$, where $\mathcal{E}$ contains a signed vote message of the form $(\texttt{vote}, e, (b, \_))$ from everyone in u's trust graph.
   - Else, use $\mathsf{TrustCast}^{\mathsf{Vf}_{\mathrm{comm}}, u}$ to trustcast the message $(\texttt{comm}, e, \bot)$.
   We define the verification function $\mathsf{Vf}_{\mathrm{comm}}$ below. $v.\mathsf{Vf}_{\mathrm{comm}}(\texttt{comm}, e, \mathcal{E}) = \mathsf{true}$ in round r iff:
   (a) either v has seen a tuple $(\texttt{elect}, e, y, \pi)$ signed by some $w \notin G_v^r$ such that (1) $\mathsf{VRF.Ver}(pp, \mathsf{pk}_w, e, y, \pi) = 1$, and (2) for everyone $w' \in G_v^r \cup S$, y is greater than the charisma of the prepare message trustcast by w'.
   (b) or $\mathcal{E}$ must be a valid epoch-e commit evidence.
Terminate: In every round r, every node u checks the following: if there is some (e, b) such that u has seen, from everyone in G_u^r, a signed message of the form $(\texttt{comm}, e, \mathcal{E})$ where $\mathcal{E}$ is a valid commit evidence for (e, b), then terminate (recall that by our implicit assumptions, the node u will echo these messages to everyone before terminating).

---

[a] We want to make sure that as long as a node remains honest in the propose phase, it will be in the set S of any honest node u.

5.4   Consistency, Liveness and Validity Proof

To apply the properties of the $\mathsf{TrustCast}$ protocol, we must show that our verification functions respect the *monotonicity condition* and *validity at origin*. The *monotonicity condition* follows from the trust graph's *monotonicity invariant* and our *implicit echoing* assumption. The *validity at origin* property can be verified mechanically. We defer the detailed proofs to the online version [37].

Given that the verification functions respect the *monotonicity condition* and *validity at origin*, we first prove that our Byzantine Broadcast protocol achieves consistency, i.e., honest nodes always output the same bit. We divide the proof into two parts. First, we show that within the same epoch, two honest nodes cannot commit on different bits. Secondly, we show that even across different epochs, consistency is still guaranteed.

Lemma 9 (Consistency within the same epoch). *If an honest node $u \in [n]$ sees an epoch-e commit evidence for the bit $b \in \{0,1\}$ in some round r, and an honest node $v \in [n]$ sees an epoch-e commit evidence for the bit $b' \in \{0,1\}$ in some round t, it must be that $b = b'$.*

Proof. Let $\mathcal{E}$ be the epoch-e commit evidence seen by u in round r and let $\mathcal{E}'$ be the epoch-e commit evidence seen by v in round t. Due to the honest clique invariant of the trust graph, $\mathcal{E}$ must contain signatures on $(\texttt{vote}, e, b)$ from every honest node, and $\mathcal{E}'$ must contain signatures on $(\texttt{vote}, e, \widetilde{b})$ from every honest node. However, each honest node will only vote for a single bit in any given epoch e. It holds that $b = b'$.

Lemma 10 (Consistency across epochs). *If an honest node $u \in [n]$ outputs the bit b in some epoch e, then in every epoch $e' > e$, no honest node $v \in [n]$ can ever see a commit evidence for $(e', 1 - b)$.*

Proof. We will use induction to show that honest nodes will never receive commit evidence for the bit $1 - b$ in any epoch after e. By the protocol definition, for u to output b in epoch e, it must have seen a commit evidence for (e, b) at the beginning of the **Commit** phase in epoch e. We have already shown in Lemma 9 that any two nodes cannot commit on different bits within the same epoch. Therefore, there cannot exist any commit evidence for $1 - b$ in epoch e. Thus, we have shown the base case of our induction.

Suppose no honest node has seen any commit evidence for $1 - b$ between epoch e and e' ($e' \geq e$), we will show that no commit evidence will be seen for $1 - b$ in epoch $e' + 1$ as well. Note that in epoch e, u will use $\textsf{TrustCast}^{\textsf{Vf}_{\textsf{comm}}, u}$ to trustcast its commit evidence for (e, b), and all honest nodes will receive it by the end of epoch e. Since no commit evidence for $1 - b$ has been seen afterwards, for any honest node, the freshest commit evidence it has seen is on b. Now, during epoch $e' + 1$, every honest node will reject $L_{e'+1}$'s proposal (where reject means not passing the $\textsf{Vf}_{\textsf{prop}}$ function) unless it is for the same bit b; and if they do reject $L_{e'+1}$'s proposal, they will vote on $\bot$. Therefore, in epoch $e' + 1$, no honest node will vote for $1 - b$, and no honest node will ever see a commit evidence for $(e' + 1, 1 - b)$. This completes our induction proof.

Theorem 6 (Consistency). *If honest nodes u and v output b and b', respectively, it must be that $b = b'$.*

Proof. For an honest node to output b in epoch e, it must observe a commit evidence for (e, b) in epoch e. Consider the earliest epoch e in which an honest node, say, u', outputs a bit b. By definition, every other honest node will output in epoch e or greater. By Lemma 9, no honest node will output $1 - b$ in epoch e. By Lemma 10, no honest node will output $1 - b$ in epoch $e' > e$.

Next, we show that our protocol achieves liveness and terminates in expected constant rounds. Observe that if an honest node terminates, then all other honest nodes would terminate in the next round.

Lemma 11. *If some honest node terminates in round r, then all honest nodes will have terminated by the end of round $r + 1$.*

Proof. If an honest node terminates in round r, it must have received consistent commit evidence from every node in its trust graph. By the implicit echoing assumption, it would forward those commit evidences to all other honest nodes before round $r + 1$. By the trust graph monotonicity invariant and the commit evidence monotonicity lemma (Lemma 4), all other honest nodes would gather enough commit evidence in round $r + 1$ and terminate as well.

During the execution, even before nodes reveal their charisma for some epoch e, we can already define a node u's epoch-e charisma as the honestly computed VRF outcome $\mathsf{VRF.Eval}(pp, \mathsf{sk}_u, e)$. This definition is well-formed no matter whether the node is honest or corrupt.

Definition 1 (Lucky epoch). *Henceforth, we say that epoch e is lucky iff the node with the maximum epoch-e charisma has not been corrupted until it has sent a signed $(\mathtt{elect}, e, \_, \_)$ message.*

Lemma 12. *Suppose that the VRF satisfies unforgeability. Except with negligible probability, the following holds: if e is a lucky epoch, then one round after the end of epoch e, all honest nodes will terminate.*

Proof. By Lemma 11, if any honest node terminates during epoch e, all honest nodes will terminate in the next round. Therefore, it suffices to prove the lemma assuming that no honest node has terminated by the end of epoch e, i.e., we may assume that all honest nodes will participate in all the TrustCast protocols till the end of epoch e. Thus, we can safely use the properties of TrustCast.

Suppose epoch e is a lucky epoch. This means that the node L with the maximum epoch-e charisma has not been corrupted until it has sent the signed elect message $(\mathtt{elect}, e, y, \pi)$. Since the adaptive adversary cannot remove messages already sent, all honest nodes will receive the elect message. Every honest node will then trustcast $(\mathtt{prep}, e, b, L, y, \pi)$ where b is L's proposed bit in the **Propose** phase of epoch e. Since L remains honest throughout the propose phase, all nodes have consistent views on L's proposed bit and they can only Ack b. After the propose phase, honest nodes no longer Ack any new proposal. Thus, even if L becomes corrupt immediately after sending the elect message, it cannot gather Ack messages from honest nodes on the bit $1 - b$.

By Theorem 3, after the **Vote** phase, for any two honest nodes u and v, u must have received a vote from v that passes $\mathsf{Vf}_{\mathrm{vote}}$. Due to condition (c) of the $\mathsf{Vf}_{\mathrm{vote}}$ check, the vote from v must vote for the same bit b that L proposes. Thus, at the end of the **Vote** phase, any honest node would receive votes on b from every node in its trust graph, which forms a commit evidence for b.

Again, by Theorem 3, after the **Commit** phase, for any two honest nodes u and v, u must have received a commit message from v that passes $\mathsf{Vf}_{\mathrm{comm}}$. Recall that a $\perp$ commit message passes $\mathsf{Vf}_{\mathrm{comm}}$ w.r.t. node u iff there exists a node not in u's trust graph, whose charisma is greater than all the prepare messages u has received. However, since epoch e is a lucky epoch, all honest nodes generate their prepare message from L, who has the largest charisma in epoch e. Therefore, all the commit messages received must be non-$\perp$ commit messages. And since all honest nodes vote on b in the **Vote** phase, the commit message must be on b. In conclusion, unless the adversary can successfully forge a VRF result which happens with negligible probability, any honest node will receive commit messages from every node in its trust graph on b. This satisfies the termination condition and all honest nodes will terminate.

Lemma 13. *Suppose that the VRF satisfies pseudorandomness under selective opening. Then, let $\mathbf{R}_{\mathrm{lucky}}$ be a random variable denoting the first lucky epoch. It must be that there is a negligible function $\mathsf{negl}(\cdot)$ such that for every R,*

$$\Pr[\mathbf{R}_{\mathrm{lucky}} \geq R] \leq \Pr[\mathsf{Geom}(h/n) \geq R] + \mathsf{negl}(\lambda)$$

where $\mathsf{Geom}(h/n)$ denotes a geometric random variable with probability h/n.

Proof. We can consider an ideal-world protocol defined just like the real-world protocol except for the following: whenever a node needs to compute $\mathsf{VRF.Eval}(pp, \mathsf{pk}_u, e)$, it will instead call an ideal functionality $\mathcal{F}.\mathsf{Eval}(u, e)$. Upon receiving this call, $\mathcal{F}$ picks y, at random if this is the first time $\mathsf{Eval}(u, e)$ is queried, and records the tuple (u, e, y). Now $\mathcal{F}$ returns the answer y that has been recorded for the query (u, e), and the tuple $(y, \perp)$ will be used in place of the outcome of the VRF evaluation. Similarly, whenever a node needs to call $\mathsf{VRF.Ver}(pp, \mathsf{pk}_u, e, y, \pi)$, the call is replaced with a call to $\mathcal{F}.\mathsf{Ver}(u, e, y)$, which simply checks if the tuple (u, e, y) has been recorded—if so, return 1; else return 0.

In this ideal world protocol, since leaders are elected completely randomly, it is not hard to see that $\Pr[\mathbf{R}_{\mathrm{lucky}} \geq R] = \Pr[\mathsf{Geom}(h/n) \geq R]$.

By the VRF technical lemma (Lemma 5), it is impossible to distinguish between the results of VRFs (the real-world protocol) and a uniformly random distribution (the ideal world protocol) for any polynomially bounded adversary. It thus follows that in the real-world protocol,

$$\Pr[\mathbf{R}_{\mathrm{lucky}} \geq R] \leq \Pr[\mathsf{Geom}(h/n) \geq R] + \mathsf{negl}(\lambda)$$

as long as the adversary is polynomially bounded.

Theorem 7 (Liveness). *Assume that the VRF adopted satisfies pseudorandomness under selective opening and unforgeability. Then, the protocol described in Sect. 5.3 achieves liveness in $O((n/h)^2)$ number of rounds.*

Proof. Follows directly from Lemma 12 and Lemma 13.

Finally, we show that the protocol also achieves validity. Note that the definition of validity needs to be slightly adjusted under the adaptive adversary model. Since an adaptive adversary can corrupt arbitrary nodes at any time, the validity requirement only makes sense when the initial sender remains honest throughout the entire protocol.

Theorem 8 (Validity). *Assume that the VRF adopted satisfies unforgeability. For the protocol described in Sect. 5.3, the following holds except with negligible probability: if the designated sender s is (forever) honest, then everyone will output the sender's input bit.*

Proof. Recall that by our construction, s is guaranteed to have the maximum charisma in epoch 1. The proof of Lemma 12 implies that if s is (forever) honest, at most one round after epoch $e = 1$, all honest nodes will have terminated with an output that agrees with s's proposal.

5.5   Round Complexity Analysis

Finally, we analyze the round complexity and communication complexity of the protocol, showing that the protocol terminates in expected $O((n/h)^2)$ rounds and has $\widetilde{O}(n^4)$ communication complexity.

In Theorem 7, we proved that as soon as some epoch has an honest leader, all honest nodes will terminate at most 1 round after the epoch's end. Each epoch has $O(d) = O(n/h)$ number of rounds, and with random leader election, in expectation we need $O(n/h)$ number of rounds till we encounter an honest leader. Thus, the expected round complexity is $O((n/h)^2)$. We can also show that with probability $1-\delta$, the round complexity is bounded by $\log(\frac{1}{\delta}) \cdot \frac{n}{h} / \log(\frac{1}{1-h/n})$.

The total number of consensus messages generated by honest nodes in each epoch (not counting implicit echoing) is at most $O(n)$. Each message is at most $\widetilde{O}(n)$ in size (the $\widetilde{O}$ hides the $\log n$ terms needed to encode a node's identifier). Each such consensus message will be delivered to $O(n)$ nodes and each node will echo every fresh message to everyone. Therefore, the total amount of communication pertaining to the consensus module (including implicit echoing of consensus messages) is $\widetilde{O}(n^4)$.

On top of this, honest nodes also need to echo messages sent by corrupt nodes and there can be (unbounded) polynomially many such messages. However, we can easily make the following optimization: for consensus messages with the same type and same epoch, every honest node echoes at most two messages originating from the same node (note that this is sufficient to form an equivocation evidence to implicate the sender). With this optimization, the per-epoch total communication for sending consensus messages is upper bounded by $\widetilde{O}(n^4)$. As mentioned earlier in Sect. 3, the total amount of communication for the trust graph module is also upper bounded by $\widetilde{O}(n^4)$. Thus, the total communication is upper bounded by $\widetilde{O}(n^4 \cdot E)$ where E denotes the number of epochs till termination. Note that in expectation $E = n/h$; moreover, with probability $1 - \delta$, E is upper bounded by $\log(\frac{1}{\delta})/\log(\frac{1}{1-h/n})$.

6   Conclusion and Future Work

Our paper presents a Byzantine Broadcast protocol with amortized $O(1)$ round complexity that works even under dishonest majority. The round complexity is constant and the communication complexity is $\widetilde{O}(n^4)$ (for the entire system). We believe this is the first protocol that gives constant round complexity for Byzantine Broadcast under dishonest majority.

It has been shown by Garay et al. [19] that no randomized protocols can achieve BB in less than $O(n/(n - f))$ number of rounds, even assuming static corruption and allowing standard setup assumptions. Therefore, for the (narrow) regime $n - f = o(n)$, there is still an asymptotical gap between our upper bound and their lower bound. Bridging this gap is an exciting direction for future work.

Acknowledgement. We are extremely grateful to Zachary Newman, Ling Ren and the anonymous TCC reviewers for their detailed and insightful comments and suggestions that helped greatly in improving the paper. We are especially grateful to our shepherd Ran Cohen who spent a significant amount of time trying to help us improve the paper. This work is in part supported by an NSF grant under the award number CNS-1561209, and a Packard Fellowship.

References

1. Abraham, I., et al.: Communication complexity of Byzantine agreement, revisited. In: PODC (2019)
2. Abraham, I., Devadas, S., Dolev, D., Nayak, K., Ren, L.: Synchronous Byzantine agreement with optimal resilience, expected $O(n^2)$ communication, and expected $O(1)$ rounds. In: Financial Cryptography and Data Security (FC) (2019)
3. Abraham, I., Malkhi, D., Nayak, K., Ren, L., Spiegelman, A.: Solida: a blockchain protocol based on reconfigurable Byzantine consensus. In: OPODIS (2017)
4. Adya, A., et al.: FARSITE: federated, available, and reliable storage for an incompletely trusted environment. ACM SIGOPS Oper. Syst. Rev. **36**(SI), 1–14 (2002)
5. Bishop, A., Pastro, V., Rajaraman, R., Wichs, D.: Essentially optimal robust secret sharing with maximal corruptions. In: Fischlin, M., Coron, J.-S. (eds.) EUROCRYPT 2016. LNCS, vol. 9665, pp. 58–86. Springer, Heidelberg (2016). https://doi.org/10.1007/978-3-662-49890-3_3
6. Bracha, G.: Asynchronous Byzantine agreement protocols. Inf. Comput. **75**, 2 (1987)
7. Canetti, R.: Security and composition of multiparty cryptographic protocols. J. Cryptol. **13**(1), 143–202 (2000)
8. Castro, M., Liskov, B.: Practical Byzantine fault tolerance. In: OSDI (1999)
9. Chan, T.-H.H., Pass, R., Shi, E.: Sublinear-round Byzantine agreement under corrupt majority. In: Kiayias, A., Kohlweiss, M., Wallden, P., Zikas, V. (eds.) PKC 2020. LNCS, vol. 12111, pp. 246–265. Springer, Cham (2020). https://doi.org/10.1007/978-3-030-45388-6_9
10. Daian, P., Pass, R., Shi, E.: Snow White: robustly reconfigurable consensus and applications to provably secure proof of stake. In: Goldberg, I., Moore, T. (eds.) FC 2019. LNCS, vol. 11598, pp. 23–41. Springer, Cham (2019). https://doi.org/10.1007/978-3-030-32101-7_2

11. David, B., Gaži, P., Kiayias, A., Russell, A.: Ouroboros praos: an adaptively-secure, semi-synchronous proof-of-stake blockchain. In: Nielsen, J.B., Rijmen, V. (eds.) EUROCRYPT 2018. LNCS, vol. 10821, pp. 66–98. Springer, Cham (2018). https://doi.org/10.1007/978-3-319-78375-8_3
12. Dolev, D., Strong, H.R.: Authenticated algorithms for byzantine agreement. SIAM J. Comput. **12**(4), 656–666 (1983)
13. Dwork, C., Lynch, N., Stockmeyer, L.: Consensus in the presence of partial synchrony. J. ACM **35**, 288–323 (1988)
14. Farell, R.: An analysis of the cryptocurrency industry (2015)
15. Feldman, P., Micali, S.: Byzantine agreement in constant expected time. In: FOCS (1985)
16. Feldman, P., Micali, S.: An optimal probabilistic protocol for synchronous byzantine agreement. SIAM J. Comput. **26**, 873–933 (1997)
17. Felman, P.N.: Optimal algorithms for Byzantine agreement. Ph.D. dissertation, MIT (1988)
18. Fitzi, M., Nielsen, J.B.: On the number of synchronous rounds sufficient for authenticated Byzantine agreement. In: Keidar, I. (ed.) DISC 2009. LNCS, vol. 5805, pp. 449–463. Springer, Heidelberg (2009). https://doi.org/10.1007/978-3-642-04355-0_46
19. Garay, J., Katz, J., Koo, C.-Y., Ostrovsky, R.: Round complexity of authenticated broadcast with a dishonest majority. In: FOCS (2007)
20. Garay, J., Katz, J., Kumaresan, R., Zhou, H.-S.: Adaptively secure broadcast, revisited, pp. 179–186 (2011)
21. Garay, J., Kiayias, A., Leonardos, N.: The bitcoin backbone protocol: analysis and applications. In: Oswald, E., Fischlin, M. (eds.) EUROCRYPT 2015, Part II. LNCS, vol. 9057, pp. 281–310. Springer, Heidelberg (2015). https://doi.org/10.1007/978-3-662-46803-6_10
22. Gennaro, R., Ishai, Y., Kushilevitz, E., Rabin, T.: On 2-round secure multiparty computation. In: Yung, M. (ed.) CRYPTO 2002. LNCS, vol. 2442, pp. 178–193. Springer, Heidelberg (2002). https://doi.org/10.1007/3-540-45708-9_12
23. Gilad, Y., Hemo, R., Micali, S., Vlachos, G., Zeldovich, N.: Algorand: scaling Byzantine agreements for cryptocurrencies. In: SOSP (2017)
24. Groth, J., Ostrovsky, R., Sahai, A.: New techniques for noninteractive zero-knowledge. J. ACM **59**(3), 11:1–11:35 (2012)
25. Hirt, M., Zikas, V.: Adaptively secure broadcast. In: Gilbert, H. (ed.) EUROCRYPT 2010. LNCS, vol. 6110, pp. 466–485. Springer, Heidelberg (2010). https://doi.org/10.1007/978-3-642-13190-5_24
26. Katz, J., Koo, C.-Y.: On expected constant-round protocols for Byzantine agreement. In: Dwork, C. (ed.) CRYPTO 2006. LNCS, vol. 4117, pp. 445–462. Springer, Heidelberg (2006). https://doi.org/10.1007/11818175_27
27. Lamport, L.: The part-time parliament. TOCS **16**(2), 133–169 (1998)
28. Lamport, L., Shostak, R., Pease, M.: The Byzantine generals problem. TOPLAS **4**(3), 382–401 (1982)
29. Micali, S., Vadhan, S., Rabin, M.: Verifiable random functions. In: FOCS (1999)
30. Nakamoto, S.: Bitcoin: a peer-to-peer electronic cash system (2008)
31. Pass, R., Seeman, L., Shelat, A.: Analysis of the blockchain protocol in asynchronous networks. In: Coron, J.-S., Nielsen, J.B. (eds.) EUROCRYPT 2017. LNCS, vol. 10211, pp. 643–673. Springer, Cham (2017). https://doi.org/10.1007/978-3-319-56614-6_22
32. Pass, R., Shi, E.: Fruitchains: a fair blockchain. In: PODC (2017)

33. Pass, R., Shi, E.: Hybrid consensus: efficient consensus in the permissionless model. In: DISC (2017)
34. Pass, R., Shi, E.: Rethinking large-scale consensus (invited paper). In: CSF (2017)
35. Pass, R., Shi, E.: The sleepy model of consensus. In: Takagi, T., Peyrin, T. (eds.) ASIACRYPT 2017. LNCS, vol. 10625, pp. 380–409. Springer, Cham (2017). https://doi.org/10.1007/978-3-319-70697-9_14
36. Wan, J., Xiao, H., Devadas, S., Shi, E.: Round-efficient Byzantine broadcast under strongly adaptive and majority corruptions (2020)
37. Wan, J., Xiao, H., Shi, E., Devadas, S.: Expected constant round byzantine broadcast under dishonest majority. Cryptology ePrint Archive, Report 2020/590

Round-Efficient Byzantine Broadcast Under Strongly Adaptive and Majority Corruptions

Jun Wan[1(✉)], Hanshen Xiao[1], Srinivas Devadas[1], and Elaine Shi[2,3]

[1] Massachusetts Institute of Technology, Cambridge, USA
{junwan,hsxiao,devadas}@mit.edu
[2] CMU, Pittsburgh, USA
runting@gmail.com
[3] Cornell, Ithaca, USA

Abstract. The round complexity of Byzantine Broadcast (BB) has been a central question in distributed systems and cryptography. In the honest majority setting, expected constant round protocols have been known for decades even in the presence of a strongly adaptive adversary. In the corrupt majority setting, however, no protocol with sublinear round complexity is known, even when the adversary is allowed to *strongly adaptively* corrupt only 51% of the players, and even under reasonable setup or cryptographic assumptions. Recall that a strongly adaptive adversary can examine what original message an honest player would have wanted to send in some round, adaptively corrupt the player in the same round and make it send a completely different message instead.

In this paper, we are the first to construct a BB protocol with sublinear round complexity in the corrupt majority setting. Specifically, assuming the existence of time-lock puzzles with suitable hardness parameters and that the decisional linear assumption holds in suitable bilinear groups, we show how to achieve BB in $\left(\frac{n}{n-f}\right)^2 \cdot \mathsf{poly} \log \lambda$ rounds with $1 - \mathsf{negl}(\lambda)$ probability, where n denotes the total number of players, f denotes the maximum number of corrupt players, and λ is the security parameter. Our protocol completes in polylogarithmically many rounds even when 99% of the players can be corrupt.

1 Introduction

Byzantine Broadcast (BB), first defined by Lamport et al. [LSP82], is a foundational abstraction in distributed systems and cryptography, and has been studied for more than three decades. In Byzantine Broadcast, a designated sender wants to send a bit $b \in \{0, 1\}$ to n nodes, and we would like to guarantee *consistency*, i.e., all honest nodes output the same bit; and *validity*, i.e., if the designated sender is honest, all honest nodes must output the sender's input. In BB, an important performance metric is the protocol's round complexity. Due to the elegant work of Dolev and Strong [DS83], it is long known that any *deterministic* BB protocol must incur at least $\Omega(n)$ number of rounds, and indeed Dolev

© International Association for Cryptologic Research 2020
R. Pass and K. Pietrzak (Eds.): TCC 2020, LNCS 12550, pp. 412–456, 2020.
https://doi.org/10.1007/978-3-030-64375-1_15

and Strong [DS83] also demonstrate a round-optimal deterministic protocol with $\Theta(n)$ rounds. It is also well-known that with randomization, expected constant-round BB protocols exist in the honest-majority setting [FM97, KK09, ADD+19]. On the other hand, for quite a long time, no sublinear (randomized) protocol was known for the corrupt majority setting. In 2007, after progress had been stagnant for a long while, Garay et al. [GKKO07] first showed a glimpse of hope for the corrupt majority setting, by constructing a protocol that achieved $O((2f - n)^2)$ round complexity where f denotes the number of corrupt nodes. Subsequently, Fitzi et al. [FN09] improved their result to $O(2f - n)$ rounds. Both Garay et al. [GKKO07] and Fitzi et al. [FN09], however, were somewhat unsatisfying, since the regime under which they give sublinear round complexity is rather narrow: even the latter work [FN09] requires $f/n - \frac{1}{2}$ to be $o(1)$ fraction to achieve sublinear round complexity. Even when $f = 51\% \cdot n$, both these works would incur at least linear number of rounds. Progress became somewhat stagnant again until very recently, Chan et al. [CPS20] made some long-awaited progress, demonstrating a new BB protocol that achieved $O(\frac{n}{n-f}) \cdot \text{poly} \log \lambda$ number of rounds even in the corrupt majority setting, where the protocol's failure probability is guaranteed to be negligibly small in the security parameter λ. Interestingly, their result is also optimal up to a poly-logarithmic factor due to an $\Omega(\frac{n}{n-f})$ lower bound by Garay et al. [GKKO07] even for randomized protocols and even assuming static corruptions. Subsequently, a companion work by Wan et al. [WXSD20] showed how to construct expected $O((\frac{n}{n-f})^2)$-round BB under corrupt majority; and this result can be viewed as a further improvement of Chan et al. [CPS20] for a broad range of parameters, e.g., when 1% (or any arbitrarily small constant fraction) of the nodes are honest.

Nonetheless, the constructions by Chan et al. [CPS20] and Wan et al. [WXSD20] remain somewhat unsatisfying, since to achieve their result, the two works [CPS20, WXSD20] had to significantly weaken the adversary's capabilities relative to the prior results in this space. All aforementioned works [DS83, GKKO07, FN09] prior to Chan et al. [CPS20] secured against a *strongly adaptive* adversary, i.e., the adversary can observe the messages in flight from honest nodes in a round, adaptively corrupt a subset of nodes and erase an arbitrary subset of their messages in flight, and moreover, make the newly corrupt nodes send additional messages in the same round. In fact, the strongly adaptive model is the well-accepted model in the early days of distributed consensus and multi-party protocols (see also Definition 1 in Feldman's thesis [Fel88] and Figure 4, page 176 of Canetti's excellent work [Can00]). By contrast, the approaches of Chan et al. [CPS20] and Wan et al. [WXSD20] defend only against a *weakly adaptive* adversary—such an adversary can observe the messages honest nodes want to send in a round, adaptively corrupt a subset of the nodes, and make the newly corrupt nodes send additional messages in the same round; however, the adversary cannot perform "after-the-fact-removal", i.e., it cannot retroactively erase the messages any node had sent before it became corrupt in the same round. The weakly adaptive model is akin to the atomic message model first introduced by Garay et al. [GKKZ11] as a way to overcome a lower bound pertaining to a particular adaptive, simulation-based notion of security proven by Hirt and Zikas [HZ10]. The only slight difference is that in the atomic message model, not only is the adversary unable to perform "after-the-fact" message removal, it also must wait for one network delay after a node i becomes corrupt, before it is able to inject messages on behalf of i. More recently, a line of works inspired by blockchains [GKL15, PSS17, PS17c, PS17d, DPS16, ACD+19, CPS19a] also adopted the weakly adaptive model to get bandwidth-efficient protocols—it turns out that the weakly adaptive relaxation is necessary for constructing Byzantine Agreement with sublinear communication complexity [ACD+19].

In some settings, however, the weakly adaptive model may be unsatisfactory, e.g., if the adversary can control intermediate routers in the network, it indeed can examine the honest messages in flight, then corrupt a subset of the nodes and fail to deliver any subset of their messages already in flight. Thus, the state of the art begs the following natural question,

> Are there (randomized) BB protocols with sublinear round complexity, and secure in the presence of a strongly adaptive adversary that is allowed to corrupt a majority of the nodes?

1.1 Our Results and Contributions

Main Result. We give the first affirmative answer to the above question, and to achieve this we rely on the existence of a trusted setup, the decisional linear assumption in suitable bilinear groups, as well as the existence of time-lock puzzles with suitable hardness parameters. Our main result is stated in the following theorem.

Theorem 1.1 (Main result). *Assuming the existence of a trusted setup, the decisional linear assumption in suitable bilinear groups (see Appendix A.1), as well as the existence of time-lock puzzles [RSW96] with hardness parameter ξ, there exists a protocol that achieves BB in $\left(\frac{n}{n-f}\right)^2 \cdot \frac{\mathsf{poly}\log\lambda}{\xi}$ number of rounds with probability $1 - \mathsf{negl}(\lambda)$ where $\mathsf{negl}(\cdot)$ is a suitable negligible function (of the security parameter λ).*

More concretely, a time-lock puzzle with hardness parameter ξ ensures that the puzzle solution remains hidden from any machine running in time that is at most ξ fraction of the honest evaluation time, even when the machine has access to unbounded polynomial parallelism. As a typical example, consider the case when $\xi \in (0,1)$ is a constant just like what prior works have assumed [RSW96, BBBF18], and moreover, suppose that $\frac{n}{n-f}$ is also a constant (e.g., 99% may be corrupt)—in this case, our protocol's round complexity is simply $\mathsf{poly}\log\lambda$.

To the best of our knowledge, no prior work can achieve sublinear-round BB in the strongly adaptive setting under any reasonable setup assumption, and even for only 51% corruption. In this sense our result significantly improves our understanding of the round complexity of BB.

Interpreting the Result. Our result currently requires a trusted setup. We do not know if the trusted setup is necessary, but some form of setup is necessary: without any setup, Byzantine Broadcast is impossible under $1/3$ or more corruptions due to an elegant lower bound by Lamport et al. [LSP82]. Besides trusted setup, we also assume the existence of time-lock puzzles; therefore, another open question is to understand whether time-lock puzzles are necessary. In fact, without time-lock puzzles, *even sublinear-round BB* under 51% strongly adaptive corruption remains open. New upper- or lower-bounds along this direction would be very exciting and seem very challenging.

Another natural question is whether we can improve the round complexity to expected constant. Due to the companion result of Wan et al. [WXSD20], we know that expected constant round is possible with a weakly adaptive adversary, and assuming trusted setup and the decisional linear assumption in suitable bilinear groups. Naturally, it seems tempting to ask for the same in the strongly adaptive setting. Unfortunately, with our techniques, we do not know how to go beyond polylogarithmic number of rounds. In fact, even our underlying message distribution primitive itself already takes polylogarithmically many rounds as we explain in Sect. 2 and the subsequent technical sections. Therefore, whether expected constant round BB is possible for 51% *strongly* adaptive corruption remains an open question—constructing an upper bound seems challenging even assuming static corruption, and allowing any reasonable setup assumptions; similarly, whether there is possibly a lower bound also seems challenging.

1.2 Technical Highlights

We give a high-level overview of our main techniques.

Delayed-Exposure Message Distribution. One major new technique we introduce is a delayed-exposure message distribution mechanism. Specifically, we devise a novel poly-logarithmic round, randomized protocol that allows all n honest nodes to each distribute a time-lock puzzle that embeds a message they want to send; moreover, by the end of poly-logarithmically many rounds, all honest nodes can obtain the solutions of all other honest nodes' puzzles. On the other hand, even if the adversary has unbounded parallelism, it cannot learn any information about honest nodes' messages encoded in the puzzles within one round of time; and thus the adversary cannot make informed adaptive corruptions based on the message contents.

To solve this problem, we need to overcome several technical challenges. First, although we allow the adversary to have access to unbounded parallelism, it is unrealistic to expect that honest machines are also equipped with up to n amount of parallelism. Like in the standard distributed protocol literature, we assume that the honest nodes are *sequential* RAM machines and thus they cannot solve puzzles in parallel. However, if they solved all the puzzles sequentially it would take linear number of rounds which is what we want to avoid in the first place.

Second, the honest nodes do not even have a consistent view of the puzzles being distributed which makes it difficult to coordinate who solves which puzzles. To overcome these challenges, we devise a novel *age-based sampling* technique where nodes sample puzzles to solve and the probability of sampling grows exponentially w.r.t. how long ago the puzzle was first seen. We defer the detailed construction and its analysis to later sections.

We stress that the delayed-exposure primitive can be of independent interest in other protocol design contexts—in this sense, besides our new construction, we also make a conceptual contribution in defining this new primitive and formulating its security properties (see Sect. 4).

Applying the Delayed-Exposure Distribution Mechanism. Once we have the delayed-exposure distribution mechanism, we can combine it with techniques proposed in the recent work by Chan et al. [CPS20], and upgrade their weakly adaptive protocol to a strongly adaptive one while still preserving a polylogarithmic round complexity. For this upgrade, the most challenging aspect is how to prove security. The most natural approach towards proving security is to first prove that the real-world protocol securely emulates a natural ideal-world counterpart, and then argue the security of the ideal-world protocol (which does not use cryptography) using an information-theoretic argument. Unfortunately, this approach fails partly because the time-lock puzzles only provide transient secrecy of the messages they encode. Instead, we work around this issue by devising a sequence of hybrids from the real-world execution to an ideal-world execution without cryptography, and we show that for every adjacent pair of hybrids, the probability of certain relevant bad events can only increase. Eventually, we upper bound the probability of bad events in the ideal world using an information theoretic argument.

Soundness of Cryptography w.r.t. an Adaptive Adversary. Last but not the least, in our construction and when arguing about the sequence of hybrids, one technicality that arises is that the adversary is strongly adaptive, and therefore some of the cryptographic building blocks we use must be commensurate and secure against selective opening attacks. This technicality will show up throughout the paper in our definitions, constructions, and proofs.

1.3 Additional Related Work

Several other works [KY, CMS89] proved lower bounds on the *worst-case* round complexity of randomized BA; and an online full version [CPS19b] of the recent work by Chan et al. [CPS20] presented a complete version of these proofs. Note that these lower bounds are incomparable to Garay et al.'s lower bound [GKKO07]. Cohen et al. [CHM+19] prove lower bounds on the round complexity of randomized Byzantine agreement (BA) protocols, bounding the halting probability of such protocols after one and two rounds.

A line of works in the literature [HZ10, GKKZ11, CCGZ16] have focused on a simulation-based notion of adaptive security for Byzantine Broadcast, where the concern is that the adversary should not be able to observe what the sender wants to broadcast, and then adaptively corrupt the sender to flip the bit. This simulation-based notion is stronger than the property-based security definitions in this paper. To achieve this strong notion of security, Garay et al. [GKKZ11] adopted the "atomic message model". As mentioned earlier, the atomic message model is almost the same as our weakly adaptive model, except that in the atomic message model, when a node i becomes newly corrupt, the adversary must wait for a network delay before it can inject corrupt messages on behalf of i.

In this paper, we consider the "broadcast" version of consensus commonly called Byzantine Broadcast. There is also another "agreement" version of the formulation, commonly called Byzantine Agreement. In the agreement version, each node has an input bit b and they all want to agree on a bit. The consistency requirement is unchanged, and the validity requirement instead stipulates that if all honest nodes have the same input bit b, then all honest nodes must output b. It turns out that the agreement version of the formulation is only possible assuming honest majority, and that is why our paper does not discuss this formulation.

A line of work has focused on a repeated consensus abstraction either called State Machine Replication [Sch90, PS17b, PS17a, CL99, Lam98, GKL15] or blockchains. Imprecisely speaking, a blockchain protocol must reach consensus repeatedly over time whereas Byzantine Broadcast achieves single-shot consensus. There are typically two approaches for constructing a blockchain protocol: 1) through sequential/parallel composition of a single-shot abstraction (e.g., Byzantine Broadcast); and 2) direct blockchain construction [CL99, Lam98, YMR+19, CS20].

Finally, our paper is not the first that uses time-lock puzzles in the context of distributed consensus. Prior works have used time-lock puzzles to construct "proof-of-work" type of consensus protocols [KMS14, EFL17].

2 Technical Roadmap

For simplicity, in our informal technical roadmap, we may assume that the adversary may adaptively corrupt an arbitrarily large constant fraction of the nodes. In other words, we assume that $f = (1 - \epsilon)n$ in the remainder of this section for an arbitrarily small constant $\epsilon \in (0, 1)$. Our full protocol in the subsequent sections will be stated formally for more general parameters.

The most natural starting point appears to be the very recent work by Chan et al. [CPS20] which achieves BB with polylogarithmic round complexity in a weakly adaptive corruption model even in the presence of majority corruptions. Unfortunately, their protocol needed the weakly adaptive restriction not just in the proofs; in fact, their protocol is prone to an explicit attack that breaks consistency assuming a strongly adaptive adversary.

2.1 Chan et al. Breaks Under a Strongly Adaptive Adversary

To aid understanding, we first describe Chan et al.'s approach [CPS20] at a very high level. Their main idea is a new method of committee election relying on an adaptively secure Verifiable Random Function (VRF) [MVR99, ACD+19] which they call "bit-specific" committee election. More concretely, during setup, a VRF public- and secret-key pair denoted (pk_u, sk_u) is selected for every node $u \in [n]$ and the corresponding public keys $pk_1, \ldots, pk_n$ are published in the sky. Recall that a designated sender wants to broadcast a bit to all other nodes. Using the VRF, we can define two committees called the 0-committee and the 1-committee, each responsible for voting for the 0-bit and the 1-bit, respectively. Specifically, the b-committee consists of all nodes whose VRF evaluation outcome on the input b is smaller than an appropriate difficulty parameter. The difficulty parameter is chosen such that each committee's size is polylogarithmic in expectation. Now, committee members for each bit b will engage in poly-logarithmically many rounds of voting based on certain voting rules; moreover, all nodes, including committee members and non-committee members, keep relaying the votes they have seen. We will not go into the details of the voting rules, but what is important here is that the security of their scheme critically relies on the fact that the committee members remain secret until they actually cast a vote for the corresponding bit b. More specifically, after the setup phase, each node knows whether it is a member of the 0-committee (or the 1-committee resp.) but this knowledge is kept secret until the node has cast a vote for the bit 0 (or the bit 1 resp.). Further, when a vote for b is cast, the vote is attached with a VRF proof that vouches for the fact that the voter is a member of the b-committee.

In Chan et al.'s scheme [CPS20], if somehow the adversary could predict who is in which committee, then security could be broken, since the adversary would have enough budget to corrupt all members of the 0-committee (or the 1-committee resp.) before their vote gets propagated to everyone. However, since the VRF scheme satisfies pseudorandomness under adaptive corruptions, essentially the adversary cannot effectively guess which nodes are in either committee until the nodes actually cast a vote for the corresponding bit b, divulging the fact that they are in the b-committee. Even though upon observing a node u's vote for a bit b, the adversary can act instantly and corrupt the voter u (who must be a member of the b-committee), it is already too late—u's vote is guaranteed to propagate to all other nodes since a weakly adaptively adversary cannot retroactively erase the vote u had already sent prior to corruption.

Now, if the adversary is actually strongly adaptive, then an explicit attack is to wait till a node u casts a vote for b, act immediately and corrupt u in the same round, and cause u's vote to be delivered to a subset of the honest recipients but not all of them—without going into details, such an attack would break the consistency of Chan et al.'s protocol.

It might be tempting to try to fix the above problem with naïve solutions along the following vein: have all honest nodes first commit to their messages (which is either a valid vote or a dummy message), wait for a while, and then open their messages to reveal whether it is a vote. However, such naïve attempts do not fundamentally fix the problem, because a strongly adaptive adversary can always immediately erase a vote as soon as it is opened.

2.2 A Strawman Scheme

A first strawman idea is to use time-lock puzzles to transiently hide message contents and thereby defeat the agility of the strongly adaptive adversary. Imagine that in some round, some members of the b-committee want to cast a vote for b (henceforth called voters), and other nodes do not want to cast votes (henceforth called non-voters). Recall that the adversary cannot predict a-priori which nodes are members of the b-committee, but if the votes are cast in the clear, then the voter immediately reveals itself to be a b-committee member.

Our idea is 1) for voters to lock the votes temporarily in a time-lock puzzle and send the resulting puzzle rather than the clear-text vote; and 2) for non-voters to send chaff of the same length, also temporarily locked in puzzles. Even if the adversary may have unbounded parallelism, it cannot distinguish within one round of time which nodes are voters and which ones are non-voters. Although the adversary can adaptively corrupt a subset of nodes and prevent their puzzles from being delivered, such adaptive corruption is basically performed in a blindfolded manner. Finally, if a node is not corrupt in the round in which the puzzle is sent, essentially the puzzle is let through and honest nodes can solve it later given enough time and obtain the message locked inside it.

In the strawman scheme, each voting round is prolonged to the time needed for a single node to solve *all* puzzles (plus one more round for sending the puzzles). If every honest node had n parallel processors, then it could solve all puzzles in parallel consuming only a constant number of rounds. However, it is quite unreasonable to assume that all honest nodes have so much parallelism—in particular, note that the amount of parallelism must scale linearly with the number of nodes. Therefore, we would like a better solution where the honest nodes may run on sequential machines, and yet the adversary is allowed unbounded polynomial parallelism.

2.3 Our Approach

In our approach, all nodes propagate their own puzzle to everyone else in the first round. If a node remains honest till the end of the first round, then its puzzle is guaranteed to be received by all honest nodes—henceforth we call such puzzles *honest puzzles*. Puzzles sent by nodes that are corrupt before the end of the first round are said to be *corrupt puzzles*.

We now repeat logarithmically many iterations: in each iteration, all nodes share the workload of solving the puzzles, and send solutions to each other. After logarithmically many iterations, we will show that except with negligible probability, all honest puzzles will have been solved and their solutions received by all honest nodes (but we do not guarantee that corrupt puzzles are also solved).

To make this idea work, however, is non-trivial, and we are faced with several challenges. One difficulty arises from the fact that the honest nodes do not have common knowledge of the set of puzzles at the start of the protocol, since corrupt nodes can reveal their puzzles only to a subset of the honest nodes. Similarly, at the end of each iteration, honest nodes also do not have common knowledge of which set of puzzles have been solved. Therefore, nodes must coordinate and share the work-load of solving puzzles, regardless of their different views of what the remaining puzzles are. Our idea is for nodes to randomly select a somewhat small subset of puzzles to solve in every iteration but how to choose a random subset is somewhat tricky.

Idealized Randomized Process Assuming Perfect Knowledge of Leftover Honest Puzzles. Although we use randomness to overcome the inconsistency in nodes' views of the remaining puzzle set, it still helps to first think of how a random strategy might work in a perfect, imaginary world where everyone always knows which are the set of *leftover* honest puzzles at the beginning of each iteration—here, a puzzle is said to be *leftover* if no so-far honest node has solved it and propagated its solution. In such a perfect world, we could use the following randomized strategy: in the first iteration, there are at most n honest puzzles to start with. Now, everyone chooses each of the n puzzles with some probability p_1 such that the expected number of puzzles each node solves is $p_1 \cdot n$. Note that the adversary can examine which puzzles' solutions each node is propagating at the end of the first iteration, and then adaptively decide on a set of nodes to corrupt, and make these nodes fail to propagate their puzzle solutions. If all honest nodes that tried to solve a specific puzzle Z are corrupt, then Z will be leftover. A smart adversary can try to pick a set of nodes to corrupt such that the set of leftover honest puzzles is maximized. One can prove that as long as $p_1 \cdot n$ is a sufficiently large constant, even if the adversary chooses the worst-case set of size $(1 - \epsilon)n$ to corrupt, there cannot be more than $n/2$ leftover honest puzzles except with negligible probability. In other words, the adversary cannot simultaneously deny too many honest puzzles from being solved. Now, in the second iteration, there at most $n/2$ honest puzzles left, and we can repeat the same but setting $p_2 = 2p_1$, i.e., the probability of sampling each honest puzzle doubles. Again, one can show that after two iterations, there cannot be more than $n/4$ leftover honest puzzles except with negligible probability, and this goes on for logarithmically many rounds at which point all honest puzzles are solved except with negligible probability.

Working with Imperfect Knowledge and Corrupt Puzzles. Our actual protocol needs to somehow "embed" the above idealized random process in a world where there can be corrupt puzzles, and moreover, honest nodes do not have a consistent view of which puzzles are solved. This turns out to be tricky— for example, the simplest idea is for nodes to always pick puzzles from the set of puzzles they have seen by the end of the first round (recall that during the first round nodes propagate their own puzzles to each other). However, if in the first round, the adversary discloses $\Theta(n)$ corrupt puzzles (henceforth denoted Q) only to one honest node u, then no one else will be helping to solve these corrupt puzzles Q; and if the probability p keeps doubling in each iteration, u will need to solve $\Theta(n)$ puzzles in the last iteration. So we want u to be able to propagate Q to others, so that when others receive them, they can start solving them too. But this introduces a new issue: the adversary can suddenly disclose a new set of $\Theta(n)$ puzzles late in the protocol, i.e., when the probability p has doubled logarithmically many times and is close to 1. In this case, the same node would have to solve too many puzzles.

To overcome the above issues, our approach adjusts the sampling probability based on the puzzle's *age*. Roughly speaking, we define a puzzle's age as how many iterations ago the puzzle was first seen. Given a puzzle of age α, we will sample it with probability $p_1 \cdot 2^\alpha$. In other words, the older the puzzle is, the more likely it will get sampled, and the probability of being sampled doubles with every iteration. Finally, if a node v is detected to have double-signed more than one puzzle, all of v's puzzles will henceforth be ignored.

We will prove later in the technical sections that except with negligible probability, in every iteration, the number of leftover puzzles of age α in the union of the honest nodes' views is upper bounded by $n/2^{\alpha-1}$, as long as each iteration is long enough such that honest nodes can indeed solve all puzzles they have sampled. Note that since puzzles of age α are each sampled with probability $p_1 \cdot 2^\alpha$, the expected number of puzzles of age α that are chosen is $\Theta(np_1) = \Theta(1)$. By the Chernoff bound, we can show that except with $\mathsf{negl}(\lambda)$ probability, no more than $\mathsf{poly}\log \lambda$ puzzles of each age α are chosen. Since the protocol runs for logarithmically many iterations, there can be at most logarithmically many different ages. Therefore, in each iteration, every node must solve only polylogarithmically many puzzles (except with negligible probability).

Other Subtleties. So far, we have implicitly assumed that there is a way to convince another node that some purported puzzle solution is indeed the correct solution, since otherwise the adversary can convince honest nodes to accept wrong solutions. To make sure this is indeed the case, honest nodes sign the message they want to distribute and then lock both the message and the signature inside a puzzle. In this way, a valid solution for a correctly constructed puzzle would be verifiable. However, this is not enough since the adversary can still construct bad puzzles, and when honest nodes solve them, they cannot convince others that the solution is valid. This issue can be fixed if we simply attach a zero-knowledge proof to the puzzle vouching for the fact that it correctly encodes a message and a signature from the purported sender.

Putting it All Together. In summary, to obtain Byzantine Broadcast, we first construct a *delayed-exposure message distribution* mechanism called Distribute. In a Distribute protocol, at the beginning every node u receives an input message m_u, and each node would like to distribute its input messages to others. If a node u remains honest at the end of the first round of the protocol, we say its input m_u is an *honest* message.

The Distribute protocol guarantees the following: 1) *liveness*, i.e., all honest messages must be delivered to every honest node at the end of the protocol; and 2) *momentary secrecy*, i.e., by the end of the first round, no probabilistic polynomial-time adversary, even when allowed unbounded parallelism, could have learned any information about the honest messages (although eventually, given sufficiently long polynomial time, the adversary could solve the puzzles and learn the input messages). The protocol works as follows (described below for the special case when $f = (1 - \epsilon)n$ where $\epsilon \in (0, 1)$ is a constant):

- **Round 1:** Every node $u \in [n]$ computes a signature σ_u on its input message m_u, and computes a puzzle Z_u that encodes (m_u, σ_u). Further, u computes a non-interactive zero-knowledge proof denoted π_u that the puzzle Z_u indeed encodes a pair where the second term is a valid signature on the first one (w.r.t. u's public key).

  Node u now propagates (Z_u, π_u) to everyone along with a signature on the pair.

- **Repeat $\Theta(\log n)$ iterations:** Each iteration has duration $\mathcal{T}_{\text{solve}} \cdot \text{poly} \log \lambda + 1$ where $\mathcal{T}_{\text{solve}}$ is the time it takes for a sequential machine to solve a single puzzle. During each iteration, a node samples each puzzle of age α to solve with independent probability $\min(p_1 \cdot 2^\alpha, 1)$, and once solved it propagates the solution (m, σ) to others if σ is a valid signature for m from the purported sender of m.

  At any time, if a node v is detected to have double-signed two different puzzles, all puzzles signed by v will henceforth be ignored.

- **Output.** Finally, for each node $v \in [n]$, if a valid pair (m, σ) has been observed where σ is a valid signature on m under v's public key, then (m, σ) is output as the message received from v; if no such valid pair has been seen, output $\perp$ as the received message from v.

Intuitively, the security properties of Distribute ensure that honest messages will indeed be delivered, and moreover, the adversary cannot base its corruption decisions based on the contents of the messages, and must make corruptions blindly. To get Byzantine Broadcast, we can now plug in the Distribute protocol to distribute batches of votes in the protocol by Chan et al. [CPS20]. Just like in the strawman scheme in Sect. 2.2, here, nodes who do not want to transmit batches of votes must transmit chaff using the Distribute protocol. Through this transformation, we effectively constrain a strongly adaptive adversary such that its capability is roughly the same as a weakly adaptive adversary. We defer the details of the Byzantine Broadcast (BB) protocol to the subsequent technical sections.

Challenges in Proving Security. Although the intuition is clear, formally reasoning the security of our BB protocol is actually rather subtle due to the use of cryptography. Ideally, we would like to abstract the cryptography away and reason about the core randomized process captured by the protocol in an ideal-world execution. Unfortunately, the real-world protocol does *not* securely emulate the most natural ideal-world protocol that captures the core randomized process. For example, one concrete challenge is the following: we would like to argue that the first-round messages of a Distribute protocol can be simulated by a simulator without knowing the actual input messages of the honest nodes. Unfortunately, the simulated messages can only fool the adversary for a small amount of time, and the adversary could eventually discover that they were being simulated.

To tackle this challenge, our actual proof defines a sequence of hybrids from the real-world experiment with cryptography, to an ideal-world experiment without cryptography. Instead of arguing that the adversary's view is computationally indistinguishable in adjacent hybrids, we argue that the probability of certain bad events happening in the next hybrid is an upper bound of the probability in the previous hybrid (ignoring negligible differences). This means that bad events cannot happen with higher probability in the real-world than in the ideal-world. Finally, since the ideal-world execution does not involve cryptography, we can argue through a probabilistic argument that the probability of relevant bad events is negligibly small.

Finally, another subtlety in both our construction and proofs is the fact that the adversary is adaptive; and therefore we need to rely on cryptographic primitives with suitable adaptive notions of security.

Remark 1 (On how general our Distributeprimitive is). One natural question is whether our Distribute primitive can be used to upgrade any weakly adaptive protocol to a strongly adaptive one preserving its security properties. Our result does not imply such a general weakly to strongly adaptive compiler, partly due to the technical challenges mentioned earlier, specifically, the fact that we cannot prove that the real-world protocol emulates some natural ideal-world protocol. As an exciting future direction, it would be great to understand how general our Distribute primitive is, i.e., for which class of protocols it is applicable. Further, another exciting question is whether we can get a general weakly to strongly adaptive compiler (see also Sect. 7).

3 Preliminaries

3.1 Definitions

Protocol Execution Model. We assume a standard protocol execution model with n nodes numbered $1, 2, \ldots, n$, respectively. An adversary denoted $\mathcal{A}$ can adaptively corrupt nodes during the middle of the execution. The nodes that have not been corrupted are called honest nodes. All corrupt nodes are under the control of $\mathcal{A}$, i.e., the messages they receive are forwarded to $\mathcal{A}$, and $\mathcal{A}$ controls what messages they will send once they become corrupt.

We assume a *synchronous* network model, i.e., honest nodes can send messages to each other within one *round*. More precisely, if an honest node u sends a message to v during round r, as long as u and v are still honest at the beginning of round $r+1$, then v would have received the message by the beginning of round $r+1$. We assume that in each round, a node first reads incoming messages from the network, then it performs some local computation and sends messages.

The adversary $\mathcal{A}$ is allowed to examine the messages honest nodes send during a round r, and then decide who to corrupt in round r, and what messages corrupt nodes send in round r. If a node u becomes newly corrupt in round r, any message it wanted to send in round r can be erased by $\mathcal{A}$; further, $\mathcal{A}$ can make the newly corrupt u send additional messages of its choice in the same round r. Recall that such an adversary is said to be *strongly adaptive*.

We assume that the protocol's execution may be parameterized by a security parameter denoted $\lambda \in \mathbb{N}$. We would like the protocol to ensure the desired security properties with $1 - \mathsf{negl}(\lambda)$ probability for some negligible function $\mathsf{negl}(\cdot)$.

Modeling Honest and Adversarial Machines. We model honest nodes as probablistic, sequential Random Access Machines (RAMs), and model the adversary as a non-uniform probabilistic, parallel machine with unbounded polynomial parallelism running in unbounded polynomial parallel time.

In constructing our protocol, we will leverage certain cryptographic primitives whose security is only guaranteed against an adversary that is restricted to run in a small, bounded number of parallel steps. Therefore, we define a T-bounded adversary as follows:

Definition 3.1. We say that $\mathcal{A}$ is a T-bounded, non-uniform *p.p.t.* parallel machine iff $\mathcal{A}$ is a non-uniform probabilistic parallel machine with unbounded polynomial parallelism, but restricted to run in at most T parallel steps. Note that here the usage of the term *p.p.t.* actually means polynomially bounded in total work—since in the parallel algorithms literature, the terms "work" and "sequential time" are used interchangeably to describe a PRAM algorithm's work, we preserve the familiar short-hand *p.p.t.*.

Note that although some of our underlying cryptographic primitives are secure only against T-bounded adversaries, we need to prove our protocol secure against an adversary running in unbounded parallel time. This is partly why our proofs are non-trivial (see Sect. 6.2 for more details).

Duration of a Round. Finally, we discuss the duration of a *round* in our execution model. The standard distributed systems and cryptography literature implicitly assumes that a round is of polynomial duration and it is long enough such that an honest node can perform the prescribed cryptographic operations, e.g., verify signatures on all messages received, verify the zero-knowledge proofs attached to the messages received, sign the messages it wants to send, and so on. We make the same assumption in this paper, with the exception of the Solve algorithm of our time-lock puzzle scheme. Specifically, we will later on parametrize our time-lock puzzle such that a sequential machine (e.g., an honest node's machine) would take multiple rounds to solve a single puzzle.

Byzantine Broadcast. Recall that there are n nodes, and without loss of generality, we call node 1 the designated sender. Prior to protocol start, the designated sender receives an input $b \in \{0, 1\}$ from $\mathcal{A}$. At the end of the protocol, every node $u \in [n]$ outputs a bit b_u. We would like to guarantee the following security properties with $1 - \mathsf{negl}(\lambda)$ probability over the randomized execution:

- *Consistency:* if a forever-honest node u outputs a bit b_u and a forever-honest node v outputs a bit b_v, it must be that $b_u = b_v$;
- *Validity:* if the designated sender is forever-honest, it must be that every forever-honest node outputs the sender's input bit b.

In the above, forever-honest means that the corresponding node remains honest till the end of the protocol.

Notations. Throughout the paper, we use n to denote the total number of nodes, f to denote the maximum number of corrupt nodes, and $h = n - f$ to denote the number of honest nodes. Since we care about the asymptotical behavior of the round complexity w.r.t. n, without loss of generality, we may assume $n \geq \log^2 \lambda$ where λ is the security parameter as mentioned.

3.2 Time-Lock Puzzles

We review the notion of time-lock puzzles [BGJ+16, RSW96, LPS17].

Definition 3.2 (Time-lock puzzles). Let S be a finite domain of size at most $2^{\mathsf{poly}(\lambda)}$. A time-lock puzzle (TLP) with solution space S is a tuple of algorithms (Gen, Solve) as defined below:

- $Z \leftarrow \mathsf{Gen}(1^\lambda, T, s)$: a probabilistic algorithm that takes a security parameter λ, a time parameter T, and a solution $s \in S$, and outputs a puzzle Z.
- $s \leftarrow \mathsf{Solve}(Z)$: a deterministic algorithm that takes in a puzzle Z, and outputs a solution s.

Correctness. We require that for every λ, every $s \in S$, every T, $\mathsf{Solve}(\mathsf{Gen}(1^\lambda, T, s))$ outputs the correct solution s with probability 1.

Efficiency. We require that on a sequential Random-Access Machine, $\mathsf{Gen}(1^\lambda, T, s)$ runs in at most $\mathsf{poly}(\lambda, \log T)$ steps for any $s \in S$; and moreover $\mathsf{Solve}(Z)$ runs in at most T number of steps for any Z in the support of $\mathsf{Gen}(1^\lambda, T, \cdot)$.

ξ-hardness. An TLP scheme (Gen, Solve) is said to be ξ-hard iff there exists a polynomial $\widetilde{T}$ such that for all polynomials $T(\cdot) \geq \widetilde{T}(\cdot)$ and every ξT-bounded, non-uniform $p.p.t.$ parallel machine $\mathcal{A}$, there exists a negligible function $\mathsf{negl}(\cdot)$, such that for all $\lambda \in \mathbb{N}$ and for all $s_0, s_1 \in S$ it holds that

$$\left| \Pr\left[\mathcal{A}(\mathsf{Gen}(1^\lambda, T, s_0)) = 1 \right] - \Pr\left[\mathcal{A}(\mathsf{Gen}(1^\lambda, T, s_1)) = 1 \right] \right| \leq \mathsf{negl}(\lambda).$$

3.3 Verifiable Random Functions

A verifiable random function (VRF) [MVR99] includes the following (possibly randomized) algorithms:

- $(\mathsf{crs}, \{\mathsf{pk}_u, \mathsf{sk}_u\}_{u \in [n]}) \leftarrow \mathsf{Gen}(1^\lambda)$: takes in a security parameter λ and generates public parameters crs, and a public and secret key pair $(\mathsf{pk}_u, \mathsf{sk}_u)$ for each node $u \in [n]$; each sk_u is of the form $\mathsf{sk}_u := (s_u, \rho_u)$ where s_u is said to be the *evaluation key* and ρ_u is said to be the *proof key* for u.

- $(y, \sigma) \leftarrow \mathsf{Eval}(\mathsf{crs}, \mathsf{sk}_u, x)$: we shall assume that $\mathsf{Eval} := (E, P)$ has two sub-routines E and P where $\mathsf{Eval}.E$ is *deterministic* and $\mathsf{Eval}.P$ is possibly randomized. Given the public parameters crs, the secret key $\mathsf{sk}_u = (s_u, \rho_u)$, and input $x \in \{0,1\}^{|x|}$, compute $y := \mathsf{Eval}.E(\mathsf{crs}, s_u, x)$ and $\sigma := \mathsf{Eval}.P(\mathsf{crs}, s_u, \rho_u, x)$, and output (y, σ).
- $\{0,1\} \leftarrow \mathsf{Vf}(\mathsf{crs}, \mathsf{pk}_u, x, y, \sigma)$: receives the public parameters crs, a public key pk_u, an input x, a purported outcome y, and a proof σ, outputs either 0 indicating rejection or 1 indicating acceptance.

For the VRF scheme to satisfy correctness, we require that for any $v \in [n]$, for any input x, the following holds with probability 1: let $(\mathsf{crs}, \{\mathsf{pk}_u, \mathsf{sk}_u\}_{u \in [n]}) \leftarrow \mathsf{Gen}(1^\lambda)$, and let $(y, \sigma) \leftarrow \mathsf{Eval}(\mathsf{crs}, \mathsf{sk}_v, x)$, then it must be that $\mathsf{Vf}(\mathsf{crs}, \mathsf{pk}_v, x, y, \sigma) = 1$.

3.3.1 Pseudorandomness Under Selective Opening

To define pseudorandomness under selective opening, we shall consider two games. The first game is intended to capture that the evaluation outcome, i.e., the y term output by Eval, is pseudorandom even when $\mathcal{A}$ can selectively corrupt nodes and open the first component of the corrupted nodes' secret keys. The second game captures the notion that the proof σ does not reveal anything additional even under an adaptive adversary.

First Game: Pseudorandomness of the Evaluation Outcome. We consider a selective opening adversary $\mathcal{A}$ that interacts with a challenger denoted $\mathcal{C}$ in the following experiment $\mathsf{Expt}_b^{\mathcal{A}}(1^\lambda)$ indexed by the bit $b \in \{0,1\}$.

$\mathsf{Expt}_b^{\mathcal{A}}(1^\lambda)$:

- First, the challenger $\mathcal{C}$ runs the $\mathsf{Gen}(1^\lambda)$ algorithm and remembers the secret key components $(s_1, \ldots, s_n)$ for later use. Note that $\mathcal{C}$ need not give public parameters to $\mathcal{A}$.
- Next, the adversary $\mathcal{A}$ can adaptively make queries of the following forms:
  - **Evaluate**: $\mathcal{A}$ submits a query (u, x), now $\mathcal{C}$ computes $y \leftarrow \mathsf{Eval}.E(\mathsf{crs}, s_u, x)$ and gives y to $\mathcal{A}$.
  - **Corrupt**: $\mathcal{A}$ specifies an index $u \in [n]$ to corrupt, and $\mathcal{C}$ parses $\mathsf{sk}_u := (s_u, \rho_u)$ and reveals s_u to $\mathcal{A}$.
  - **Challenge**: $\mathcal{A}$ specifies an index $u^* \in [n]$ and an input x. If $b = 0$, the challenger returns a completely random string of appropriate length. If $b = 1$, the challenger computes $y \leftarrow \mathsf{Eval}.E(\mathsf{crs}, s_{u^*}, x)$ and returns y to the adversary.

We say that $\mathcal{A}$ is compliant iff with probability 1, every challenge tuple (u^*, x) it submits satisfies the following: 1) $\mathcal{A}$ does not make a corruption query on u^* throughout the game; and 2) $\mathcal{A}$ does not make any evaluation query on the tuple (u^*, x).

If no efficient and compliant adversary can effectively distinguish $\mathsf{Expt}_0^{\mathcal{A}}(1^\lambda)$ and $\mathsf{Expt}_1^{\mathcal{A}}(1^\lambda)$, then we can be sure that the evaluation outcome of the VRF is pseudorandom even with an adaptive adversary.

Second Game: Zero-Knowledge of the Proofs. We also need to make sure that the proof part is zero-knowledge even w.r.t. an adaptive adversary. Therefore, we define another game below where the adversary $\mathcal{A}$ tries to distinguish whether it is playing in the real-world experiment or in the ideal-world experiment:

- *Real-world experiment* Real*:* In the real-world experiment, the challenger runs the $\mathsf{Gen}(1^\lambda)$ algorithm and gives the public parameters crs and all public keys $\mathsf{pk}_1, \ldots, \mathsf{pk}_n$ to $\mathcal{A}$, but keeps $\mathsf{sk}_1, \ldots, \mathsf{sk}_n$ to itself. Next, $\mathcal{A}$ can adaptively make the following queries:
    - **Evaluate:** $\mathcal{A}$ submits a query (u, x), now $\mathcal{C}$ computes $(y, \sigma) \leftarrow \mathsf{Eval}(\mathsf{crs}, \mathsf{sk}_u, x)$ and gives (y, σ) to $\mathcal{A}$.
    - **Corrupt:** $\mathcal{A}$ specifies an index $u \in [n]$ to corrupt. $\mathcal{C}$ reveals not only sk_u to $\mathcal{A}$, but also all the randomness used in the Eval algorithm for any earlier **Evaluate** query pertaining to u.

- *Ideal-world experiment* $\mathsf{Ideal}^{\mathcal{S}_0, \mathcal{S}_1, \mathcal{S}_2, \mathcal{S}_3}$*:* First, the challenger $\mathcal{C}$ runs a simulated setup algorithm

$$(s_1, \ldots, s_n) \leftarrow \mathcal{S}_0(1^\lambda);$$
$$(\mathsf{crs}, \mathsf{pk}_1, \ldots, \mathsf{pk}_n, \tau) \leftarrow \mathcal{S}_1(1^\lambda);$$

it gives the public parameters crs and all public keys $\mathsf{pk}_1, \ldots, \mathsf{pk}_n$ to $\mathcal{A}$, but keeps the trapdoor τ to itself.

Next, $\mathcal{A}$ can adaptively make the following queries:

    - **Evaluate:** $\mathcal{A}$ submits a query (u, x), and now the simulator computes $y := \mathsf{Eval}.E(\mathsf{crs}, s_u, x)$, and $\sigma \leftarrow \mathcal{S}_2(\tau, \mathsf{pk}_u, x, y)$ and gives y, σ to $\mathcal{A}$.
    - **Corrupt:** $\mathcal{A}$ specifies an index $u \in [n]$ to corrupt. Let $\mathcal{I}$ denote the indices of the earlier **Evaluate** queries that correspond to the node $u \in [n]$; and moreover, for $i \in \mathcal{I}$, let the i-th query be of the form (u, x_i) and the result be of the form (y_i, σ_i).
    The challenger $\mathcal{C}$ calls $(\rho_u, \{\psi_i\}_{i \in \mathcal{I}}) \leftarrow \mathcal{S}_3(\tau, \mathsf{pk}_u, s_u, \{x_i, \sigma_i\}_{i \in \mathcal{I}})$, and returns the secret key $\mathsf{sk}_u := (s_u, \rho_u)$ as well as $\{\psi_i\}_{i \in \mathcal{I}}$ to $\mathcal{A}$.

Definition 3.3 (Pseudorandomness under selective opening). We say that a VRF scheme satisfies pseudorandomness under selective opening iff:

1. for any compliant non-uniform p.p.t. adversary $\mathcal{A}$, its views in $\mathsf{Expt}_0^{\mathcal{A}}(1^\lambda)$ and $\mathsf{Expt}_1^{\mathcal{A}}(1^\lambda)$ are computationally indistinguishable.
2. there exist p.p.t. simulators $(\mathcal{S}_0, \mathcal{S}_1, \mathcal{S}_2, \mathcal{S}_3)$ such that the outcome of $\mathcal{S}_0(1^\lambda)$ is identically distributed as the $(s_0, \ldots, s_n)$ components generated by the real-world $\mathsf{Gen}(1^\lambda)$ algorithm, and moreover, $\mathcal{A}$'s views in the above Real and $\mathsf{Ideal}^{\mathcal{S}_0, \mathcal{S}_1, \mathcal{S}_2, \mathcal{S}_3}$ are computationally indistinguishable.

3.3.2   Unforgeability

We say that a VRF scheme satisfies unforgeability, if there exists a negligible function $\mathsf{negl}(\cdot)$ such that no non-uniform $p.p.t.$ adversary $\mathcal{A}$ can win the following game with more than $\mathsf{negl}(\lambda)$ probability:

- First, the challenger $\mathcal{C}$ runs the $\mathsf{Gen}(1^\lambda)$ algorithm and gives the public parameters crs and all public keys $\mathsf{pk}_1, \ldots, \mathsf{pk}_n$ to $\mathcal{A}$, but keeps $\mathsf{sk}_1, \ldots, \mathsf{sk}_n$ to itself.
- The adversary $\mathcal{A}$ can adaptively make the following queries:
    - **Evaluate:** $\mathcal{A}$ submits a query (u, x), now $\mathcal{C}$ computes $(y, \sigma) \leftarrow \mathsf{Eval}(\mathsf{crs}, \mathsf{sk}_u, x)$ and gives (y, σ) to $\mathcal{A}$.
    - **Corrupt:** $\mathcal{A}$ specifies an index $u \in [n]$ and $\mathcal{C}$ reveals sk_u to $\mathcal{A}$ as well as random coins used in earlier **Evaluate** queries pertaining to u.
- Finally, $\mathcal{A}$ outputs a tuple (u, x, y, σ). It is said to win the game if either $\mathsf{Vf}(\mathsf{crs}, \mathsf{pk}_u, x, y, \sigma) = 1$, but $y \neq y'$ where $(y', \_) := \mathsf{Eval}(\mathsf{crs}, \mathsf{sk}_u, x)$; or if u has not been corrupted before and $\mathcal{A}$ has not made any **Evaluate** query of the form (u, x).

In other words, we want that except with negligible probability, $\mathcal{A}$ cannot forge the VRF outcome and proof on behalf of any honest node on a point that has not been queried; furthermore, even for corrupted nodes, $\mathcal{A}$ cannot forge an VRF outcome and proof such that the evaluation outcome is different from the honest evaluation outcome.

Abraham et al. [ACD+19] proved the following theorem where the bilinear group assumptions needed are the same as those adopted by Groth et al. [GOS12].

Theorem 3.4 (Existence of adaptively secure VRFs [ACD+19]). *Assuming standard bilinear group assumptions and a trusted setup, we can construct a VRF scheme satisfying pseudorandomness under selective opening and unforgeability.*

4   Delayed-Exposure Message Distribution

4.1   Definitions

4.1.1   Syntax

We first introduce the syntax of the $\mathsf{Distribute}(1^\lambda, m_1, \ldots, m_n)$ protocol. At the beginning of the protocol, every node $u \in [n]$ is given a message $m_u \in \{0, 1\}^\ell$ of length $\ell(\lambda, n)$ which is upper bounded by a fixed polynomial in λ and n. In the $\mathsf{Distribute}$ protocol, every node makes an attempt to multicast its message m_u to everyone else. At the end of R_{distr} number of rounds, everyone outputs $(m'_1, \ldots, m'_n)$ where $m'_u \in \{0, 1\}^\ell \cup \{\bot\}$ denotes the message received from node $u \in [n]$, and $\bot$ indicates that nothing has been received from u.

In the following we will allow setup assumptions for constructing our $\mathsf{Distribute}$ protocol, specifically, we assume that the setup algorithm $\mathsf{Gen}(1^\lambda)$ outputs a common reference string denoted crs. Moreover, there is a public-key infrastructure (PKI) later used for digital signatures. We assume that during the setup phase, we run the key generation algorithm of a digital signature scheme which outputs a public- and secret-key pair for every node $u \in [n]$, henceforth denoted vk_u and ssk_u, respectively. We assume that the crs and the PKI consisting of $\{\mathsf{vk}_u, \mathsf{ssk}_u\}_{u \in [n]}$ can be reused across multiple instances of the Distribute protocol.

4.1.2 Security

At the beginning of the Distribute protocol, either everyone is honest, or a subset of nodes have already been corrupted by the adversary $\mathcal{A}$. During the Distribute protocol, the adversary $\mathcal{A}$ can adaptively corrupt more nodes, and upon newly corrupting a node $u \in [n]$, the adversary $\mathcal{A}$ receives u's internal state.

Liveness. Liveness requires the following: let $\widetilde{H}$ denote the set of nodes that remain honest till the beginning of the second round of the Distribute protocol; except with negligible in λ probability, it holds that for every node $u \in \widetilde{H}$, all forever-honest nodes[1] output m_u as the message received from u.

Momentary Secrecy. Roughly speaking, we want that even when the adversary $\mathcal{A}$ may have unbounded polynomial parallelism, the honest nodes' messages remain secret to $\mathcal{A}$ till the beginning of the second round of Distribute. Formally, we define the following $\mathsf{Expt}(1^\lambda, \{m_u^*\}_{u \in [n]})$ experiment.

Experiment $\mathsf{Expt}(1^\lambda, \{m_u^*\}_{u \in [n]})$: The experiment $\mathsf{Expt}(1^\lambda, \{m_u^*\}_{u \in [n]})$ is defined as follows:

- **Setup.** Run the honest setup algorithm which outputs a common reference string denoted crs and a key pair $(\mathsf{vk}_u, \mathsf{ssk}_u)$ for every $u \in [n]$. The crs and the public verification keys $\{\mathsf{vk}_u\}_{u \in [n]}$ are given to $\mathcal{A}$;
- **Query.** The query phase runs for an arbitrary polynomial amount of time. During this time, $\mathcal{A}$ may adaptively make the following queries where multiple sessions of the Distribute protocol are allowed to be initiated concurrently:
  - *Session.* $\mathcal{A}$ specifies a session identifier sid, as well as a set of input messages $\{m_u\}_{u \in H}$ where H denotes the so-far honest nodes. Now, the so-far honest nodes execute the honest Distribute protocol using the inputs $\{m_u\}_{u \in H}$ and session identifier sid, and interact with $\mathcal{A}$.
  - *Corrupt.* At any time, $\mathcal{A}$ specifies a new node $u \in [n]$ to corrupt, and at this moment ssk_u and all random coins used by node u so far in the protocol are given to $\mathcal{A}$;
- **Challenge.** Finally, $\mathcal{A}$ outputs challenge with a challenge session identifier sid^*: it is required that sid^* be a fresh one that has never been queried before. Let H^* denote the honest nodes at the moment. Now, compute the first-round messages denoted M^* that H^* would send in the real-world Distribute protocol

---

[1] Forever honest w.r.t. the Distribute protocol means that the node remains honest till the end of the protocol.

with the session identifier sid^*, and using the inputs $\{m_u^*\}_{u \in H^*}$. Output $\mathcal{A}$'s view[2] in the experiment as well as M^*.

We say that the Distribute protocol satisfies momentary secrecy iff for any non-uniform $p.p.t.$ parallel machine $\mathcal{A}$ and any non-uniform $p.p.t.$ $2\mathcal{T}_\emptyset$-bounded parallel distinguisher $\mathcal{D}$, there is a negligible function $\mathsf{negl}(\cdot)$ for the following to be true for any choice of λ, and any $\{m_u^*\}_{u \in [n]}$ and $\{\widetilde{m}_u^*\}_{u \in [n]}$,

$$\left| \Pr\left[\mathcal{D}(1^\lambda, \mathsf{Expt}(1^\lambda, \{m_u^*\}_{u \in [n]})) = 1\right] - \Pr\left[\mathcal{D}(1^\lambda, \mathsf{Expt}(1^\lambda, \{\widetilde{m}_u^*\}_{u \in [n]}))) = 1\right]\right|$$
$$\leq \mathsf{negl}(\lambda).$$

4.2 Construction

Assumptions. In the construction below, we assume that there is a public-key infrastructure (PKI) available, and *nodes sign all messages* that they want to send. Only messages attached with valid signatures from the purported senders are considered valid, and all invalid messages are discarded. We also make an *implicit echoing* assumption: we assume that every honest node will echo every fresh message received to everyone, such that if a forever-honest node $u \in [n]$ observes some message at the beginning of round r, then every so-far honest node will have received it by the beginning of round $r + 1$.

NP Language. We will make use of a non-interactive zero-knowledge proof (NIZK) system that is secure against adaptive corruptions. The formal definition of such a NIZK system is given in Sect. A.2. We now describe the NP language used in our NIZK proofs. A statement is of the form $\mathsf{stmt} := (u, Z)$, and a witness is of the form $w := (m, \sigma, \rho)$. We assume that $(\lambda, \mathcal{T}_{\mathrm{solve}}, \mathsf{vk}_1, \ldots, \mathsf{vk}_n)$ are global parameters and do not repeat it in the statement. A statement $\mathsf{stmt} := (u, Z)$ is in the language vouched for by a valid witness $w := (m, \sigma, \rho)$ iff there exists (m, σ, ρ) such that $Z = \mathsf{TLP.Gen}(1^\lambda, \mathcal{T}_{\mathrm{solve}}, (m, \sigma); \rho)$ and moreover $\Sigma.\mathsf{Vf}(\mathsf{vk}_u, m, \sigma) = 1$.

Protocol. Let $\mathsf{TLP} := (\mathsf{Gen}, \mathsf{Solve})$ denote a time-lock puzzle with hardness parameter ξ as defined in Sect. 3.2, and let $\mathcal{T}_\emptyset$ denote the duration of one synchronous round. Let $\mathsf{NIZK} := (\mathsf{Gen}, \mathsf{P}, \mathsf{V})$ denote a non-interactive zero-knowledge proof system as defined in Sect. A.2. Let $\Sigma := (\mathsf{Gen}, \mathsf{Sign}, \mathsf{Vf})$ denote a digital signature scheme. The Distribute protocol is described below.

Input: Each node $u \in [n]$ receives the input $m_u \in \{0,1\}^\ell$. Without loss of generality, henceforth we shall assume that the message m_u itself is tagged with the sender's identifier $u \in [n]$. Below, we may assume that we always prefix the message m_u with the string inp.

Setup: Run $\mathsf{crs}_{\mathrm{nizk}} \leftarrow \mathsf{NIZK.Gen}(1^\lambda)$ and publish $\mathsf{crs}_{\mathrm{nizk}}$. Recall that there is a PKI and nodes sign all messages they send, henceforth we use vk_u and ssk_u to denote the public- and secret-key of node u, respectively.

---

[2] Here, $\mathcal{A}$'s view may contain any output $\mathcal{A}$ has produced so far which might have taken an arbitrary polynomial time to compute prior to the start of the challenge phase.

Protocol:

1. **Initial round**: every node $u \in [n]$ does the following:

   - let $\sigma := \Sigma.\mathsf{Sign}(\mathsf{ssk}_u, m_u)$; call $Z_u \leftarrow \mathsf{TLP.Gen}(1^\lambda, \mathcal{T}_{\mathrm{solve}}, (m_u, \sigma); \rho)$ where $\mathcal{T}_{\mathrm{solve}} := 2\mathcal{T}_\emptyset/\xi$ and ρ explicitly denotes the randomness consumed by the $\mathsf{TLP.Gen}$ algorithm;
   - call $\pi_u \leftarrow \mathsf{NIZK.P}(\mathsf{crs}_{\mathrm{nizk}}, (u, Z_u), (m_u, \sigma, \rho))$;
   - sign and multicast the tuple $(\mathsf{puz}, Z_u, \pi_u)$ to everyone.

   Henceforth, we assume that whenever an honest node receives a message of the form $(\mathsf{puz}, Z_u, \pi_u)$ signed by u, it calls $\mathsf{NIZK.V}(\mathsf{crs}_{\mathrm{nizk}}, (u, Z_u), \pi_u)$ and if the verification fails, the message is discarded immediately without being processed. If the verification succeeds, the puzzle Z_u is considered as received and we say that it belongs to u.

2. **Solve phase**: Henceforth, every $\mathcal{T}_{\mathrm{epoch}} := \mathcal{T}_{\mathrm{solve}} \cdot \lceil \frac{2n}{h} \cdot \ln(\frac{16n}{h}) \cdot \log^2 \lambda \cdot (\log n + 3) \rceil + 1$ rounds is called an *epoch*: round 1 is the beginning of the first epoch; round $\mathcal{T}_{\mathrm{epoch}} + 1$ is the beginning of the second epoch, and so on.

   Repeat the following for a total of $E = \lceil \log_2 n \rceil + 1$ epochs.

   - At the beginning of each epoch, let S denote the set of all puzzles received so far and belonging to *active* nodes. For $Z \in S$, define the puzzle's *age* $\alpha(Z)$ as follows: $\alpha(Z) := \lceil \frac{r - r'}{\mathcal{T}_{\mathrm{epoch}}} \rceil$ where r denotes the beginning round of the epoch and $r' \leq r$ denotes the first round in which Z was observed.
   - For each $Z \in S$ sequentially, perform the following: flip a random coin that comes up heads with probability $p := \min\left(\frac{2^{\alpha(Z)} \cdot \ln(16n/h)}{h}, 1 \right)$; if the coin comes up heads, then solve the puzzle Z by calling $(m, \sigma) \leftarrow \mathsf{TLP.Solve}(Z)$. Once solved, multicast the solution (m, σ) to everyone[a].

   Output: at any time, upon observing a tuple (m, σ) where σ is a valid signature on m from the purported sender (henceforth denoted $v \in [n]$), if no message from v has been output yet, output m as the message received from v and mark v as *inactive*. At the end of the protocol, if no message from some $v \in [n]$ has been output, then we output a canonical message $\perp$ as the message from v.

   Detect equivocation: at any time, if multiple puzzles have been received from the same node $v \in [n]$, mark v as *inactive*[b].

---

[a] We may assume that if more than $\frac{2n}{h} \cdot \ln(\frac{16n}{h}) \cdot \log^2 \lambda \cdot (\log n + 3)$ number of puzzles are chosen to be solved in some epoch, the node simply aborts outputting failure — we will show in the proof of Lemma 4.3 later that this does not happen except with negligible probability.

[b] Both the **Output** and **Equivocation** entry points are processed at the beginning of every round before all other actions of the round.

Clearly, the total round complexity of the Distribute protocol is

$$\left((\lceil \log_2 n \rceil + 1) \cdot \frac{\mathcal{T}_{\text{solve}}}{\mathcal{T}_0} \cdot \left(\lceil \frac{2n}{h} \cdot \ln(\frac{16n}{h}) \cdot \log^2 \lambda \cdot (\log n + 3) \rceil + 1 \right) + 1 \right)$$

Assume that n is polynomially bounded in λ, then the round complexity is upper bounded by $O(\frac{n}{\xi \cdot h}) \cdot$ poly log λ.

4.3   Proofs: Liveness

Henceforth, we use the term "m is *in honest view*" to mean that some forever-honest node has seen m.

Fact 4.1. *If some forever-honest node observes a puzzle Z at the beginning of epoch e, then all so-far honest nodes will have observed Z by the beginning of epoch $e + 1$.*

Proof. Follows directly from the implicit echoing assumption, i.e., honest nodes echo every fresh message they see. □

Fact 4.2. *Assume that the NIZK scheme satisfies perfect knowledge extraction, the TLP scheme satisfies correctness. Then, except with negligible probability, the following must hold: if any forever-honest node solves a puzzle Z belonging to $v \in [n]$ by the beginning of the last round of epoch e, then no puzzle from v will still be active in any so-far honest node's view at the beginning of epoch $e + 1$.*

Proof. If the NIZK satisfies perfect knowledge extraction, then it must be that the solved solution is a (m, σ) pair such that σ is a valid signature from v on m. Since an honest node has solved the puzzle and found the solution by the beginning of the last round of epoch e, it will multicast (m, σ) to everyone in the last round of epoch e, and by the beginning of epoch $e + 1$, every so-far honest node will have observed (m, σ) and will have marked v as inactive. □

Given Fact 4.1, we know that honest nodes' perception of a puzzle's age can differ by at most 1. We say that a puzzle Z's *minimum age* is $\alpha \geq 0$ in epoch e, iff all forever-honest nodes have observed it by the beginning of epoch $e - \alpha$, but at least one forever-honest node has not observed it by the beginning of epoch $e - \alpha - 1$.

Henceforth, if at the beginning of some epoch e, a so-far honest has seen a puzzle belonging to an active node, then the puzzle is said to be *active*. Due to the equivocation detection rule, it must be that from each active node, at most one active puzzle has been seen.

Lemma 4.3. *Let $\alpha \geq 0$ and $n \geq \log^2 \lambda$. Except with negligible in λ probability, the following holds: at the beginning of every epoch, there can be at most $n/2^{\alpha - 1}$ active puzzles belonging to distinct nodes, and with minimum age α, in honest view.*

Proof. We first state some simplifying assumptions that can be made without loss of generality. We may assume that honest nodes use a puzzle's minimum age to determine the probability p with which a puzzle is selected to be solved. Note that in the real-world protocol, a node does not necessarily know the minimum age of the puzzle, but we may assume it for proving this lemma since making p smaller will only increase the probability of the bad event stated in the lemma that we care about bounding. Furthermore, let us first assume that any forever-honest node has enough time to solve all puzzles it chooses to solve during any epoch e, and not only so, they can be solved by the beginning of the last round of the epoch e—later we will show that indeed this is the case except with negligible probability.

For $\alpha = 0$, the lemma trivially holds. Henceforth, we may assume that $\alpha \geq 1$. Fix any epoch e, and let $S_{\alpha-1}$ denote all active puzzles whose minimum age is $\alpha-1 \geq 0$ at the beginning of epoch e. This means that all so-far honest nodes will choose to solve any puzzle in $S_{\alpha-1}$ with probability $p = \min(\frac{2^{\alpha-1} \cdot \ln(16n/h)}{h}, 1)$ in epoch e. We would like to upper bound the probability that at least $n/2^{\alpha}$ puzzles in $S_{\alpha-1}$ are not selected by any forever-honest node in epoch e. Due to Fact 4.2, if $\frac{2^{\alpha-1} \cdot \ln(16n/h)}{h} \geq 1$, then there cannot be any active puzzles of minimum age α left in any honest node's view at the beginning of the next epoch. Henceforth, we may also assume that $p = \frac{2^{\alpha-1} \cdot \ln(16n/h)}{h} < 1$.

Consider a fixed honest node u and an active puzzle from a fixed node v: the probability that u does not select an active puzzle from v is at most $1 - p$. The probability that any fixed set of h forever-honest nodes (denoted W) all do not select an active puzzle from v is $(1 - p)^h$. For any fixed set of $n/2^{\alpha-1}$ nodes denoted Γ that has a puzzle of minimum age $\alpha - 1$ in honest view in epoch e, the probability that a fixed set of h forever-honest nodes' puzzle choices do not intersect with Γ is at most $(1 - p)^{h \cdot n/2^{\alpha-1}}$.

The probability that there exists a choice for the set W (consisting of h forever-honest nodes), and a set $\Gamma \subset [n]$ of size $n/2^{\alpha-1}$ (who have a puzzle of age $\alpha-1$ in honest view in epoch e), such that W's puzzle choices do not intersect with Γ is upper bounded by the following expression:

$$(1-p)^{h \cdot n/2^{\alpha-1}} \cdot \binom{n}{h} \cdot \binom{n}{n/2^{\alpha-1}}$$

$$\leq \left(1 - \frac{2^{\alpha-1} \cdot \ln(16n/h)}{h}\right)^{hn/2^{\alpha-1}} \cdot \binom{n}{h} \cdot \binom{n}{n/2^{\alpha-1}}$$

$$= \left(1 - \frac{2^{\alpha-1} \cdot \ln(16n/h)}{h}\right)^{\frac{h}{2^{\alpha-1} \cdot \ln(16n/h)} \cdot \ln(\frac{16n}{h}) \cdot n} \cdot \binom{n}{h} \cdot \binom{n}{n/2^{\alpha-1}}$$

$$\leq \exp\left(-\ln\left(\frac{16n}{h}\right) \cdot n\right) \cdot \binom{n}{h} \cdot \binom{n}{n/2^{\alpha-1}}$$

$$= \left(\frac{h}{16n}\right)^n \cdot \binom{n}{h} \cdot \binom{n}{n/2^{\alpha-1}} \tag{$*$}$$

$$= \left(\frac{h}{16n}\right)^n \cdot \binom{n}{h} \cdot \binom{n}{n - n/2^{\alpha-1}}$$

$$\leq \left(\frac{h}{16n}\right)^n \cdot \left(\frac{en}{h}\right)^h \cdot \left(\frac{en}{n(1 - 1/2^{\alpha-1})}\right)^{n(1 - 1/2^{\alpha-1})}$$

$$\leq \left(\frac{h}{16n}\right)^n \cdot \left(\frac{en}{h}\right)^n \cdot \left(\frac{en}{n(1 - 1/2^{\alpha-1})}\right)^n$$

$$= \left(\frac{h}{16n} \cdot \frac{en}{h} \cdot \frac{en}{n(1 - 1/2^{\alpha-1})}\right)^n \leq \exp(-\Theta(n))$$

In the above derivation, if $\alpha = 1$, then the last term $\binom{n}{n/2^{\alpha-1}}$ in the expression (∗) is equal to 1. Therefore, in the derivation steps after the expression (∗), we can simply assume that $\alpha > 1$ which only makes the expression $\binom{n}{n/2^{\alpha-1}}$ larger.
[To reviewer: We expanded the derivation to make it more detailed.]
So far, we have assumed that if a forever-honest node selects some puzzle to solve in some epoch e, it will actually have enough time to solve the puzzle by the beginning of the last round of epoch e. We now show that the allotted epoch duration $T_{\text{epoch}} := T_{\text{solve}} \cdot \lceil \frac{2n}{h} \cdot \ln(\frac{16n}{h}) \cdot \log^2 \lambda \cdot (\log n + 3) \rceil + 1$ is indeed long enough to meet this requirement except with negligible probability. Basically, if in epoch e, the number of puzzles of minimum age α left in honest view is at most $n/2^{\alpha-1}$, and an honest node selects each puzzle with probability $p = \min(\frac{2^{\alpha-1} \cdot \ln(16n/h)}{h}, 1)$, we can bound the total number of puzzles of minimum age α an honest node selects to solve with the following two cases:

- Case 1: if $\frac{2^{\alpha-1} \cdot \ln(16n/h)}{h} \geq 1$, then $2^{\alpha-1} \geq h/\ln(16n/h)$. The total number of puzzles of minimum age α selected to solve is upper bounded by $n/2^{\alpha-1} \leq \frac{n}{h} \cdot \ln(16n/h)$.
- Case 2: if $\frac{2^{\alpha-1} \cdot \ln(16n/h)}{h} < 1$, then the expected number of puzzles of minimum age α selected to solve is upper bounded by

$$\frac{n}{2^{\alpha-1}} \cdot \frac{2^{\alpha-1} \cdot \ln(16n/h)}{h} = \frac{n}{h} \cdot \ln(16n/h).$$

By the Chernoff bound, the probability that the number of puzzles of minimum age α selected to solve is more than

$$\frac{n}{h} \cdot \ln(16n/h) + \sqrt{\frac{n}{h} \cdot \ln(16n/h)} \cdot \log^2 \lambda \leq \frac{n}{h} \cdot \ln(16n/h) \cdot \log^2 \lambda \qquad (**)$$

is upper bounded by $\exp(-\Omega(\log^4 \lambda))$.

Recall that the number of ages is upper bounded by the number of epochs, that is $\lceil \log_2 n \rceil + 1$. Now, taking a union bound over all possible ages, except with $\exp(-\Omega(\log^4 \lambda))$ probability, the total number of puzzles an honest node chooses to solve in an epoch is upper bounded by

$$\frac{2n}{h} \cdot \ln(\frac{16n}{h}) \cdot \log^2 \lambda \cdot \lceil \log_2 n \rceil \leq \frac{2n}{h} \cdot \ln(\frac{16n}{h}) \cdot \log^2 \lambda \cdot (\log n + 3)$$

Finally, taking a union bound over the number of epochs which is polynomially bounded in λ, we have that except with $\exp(-\Omega(\log^4 \lambda))$ probability, the above bad event will never happen throughout all epochs.

[To reviewer: We added more steps of derivation in the above calculations.]

Thus, the allotted epoch duration $\mathcal{T}_{\text{epoch}} := \mathcal{T}_{\text{solve}} \cdot \lceil \frac{2n}{h} \cdot \ln(\frac{16n}{h}) \cdot \log^2 \lambda \cdot (\log n + 3) \rceil + 1$ is sufficiently long such that except with negligible in λ probability, an honest node has time to solve all puzzles it chooses in every epoch. □

Remark 2. The expression $(\ast\ast)$ is by no means the tightest possible bound; but it is outside the scope of this paper to understand what the best possible constant c is in the $O(\log^c(\lambda, n))$ round complexity bound. With our current techniques, we only know how to achieve poly-logarithmic round complexity in the strongly adaptive setting under corrupt majority. It is an exciting open question whether we can improve the result to, say, expected constant rounds, or prove impossibility.

[To reviewer: We added an explanation why we did not focus on calculating the tightest expression.]

Theorem 4.4 (Liveness). *Assume that $n \geq \log^2 \lambda$, that the* NIZK *scheme satisfies soundness, the* TLP *scheme satisfies correctness, and the signature scheme Σ satisfies existential unforgeability under chosen-message attack. Then, the above* Distribute *protocol satisfies liveness.*

Proof. Let $\widetilde{H}$ denote the set of nodes that remain honest till the beginning of the second round of the Distribute protocol. For every $u \in \widetilde{H}$, every so-far honest node will have received an honestly generated puzzle Z_u from u at the beginning of the second round, i.e., the beginning of the first epoch of the Solve phase. At the beginning of the next round after the final epoch E, Z_u, if still active, would have age E in every honest node's view, i.e., its minimum age is E. Due to Lemma 4.3, except with negligible probability, the number of active puzzles from nodes in $\widetilde{H}$ is then upper bounded by $n/2^{E-1} < 1$. Now, since honest nodes do not double sign puzzles, except with negligible probability, it must be that every forever-honest node has output a message for everyone in $\widetilde{H}$. □

4.4 Proofs: Momentary Secrecy

Experiment $\mathsf{Hyb}(1^\lambda, \{m_u^*\}_{u \in [n]})$. The hybrid experiment $\mathsf{Hyb}(1^\lambda, \{m_u^*\}_{u \in [n]})$ is defined almost identically as $\mathsf{Expt}^\mathcal{A}(1^\lambda, \{m_u^*\}_{u \in [n]})$, except with the following modifications:

- Run the simulated NIZK setup algorithm $\mathsf{Gen}_0(1^\lambda)$ which outputs a crs and a trapdoor τ;
- Whenever an honest node u is supposed to compute a NIZK proof by calling

$$\pi_u \leftarrow \mathsf{NIZK}.\mathsf{P}(\mathsf{crs}_{\mathsf{nizk}}, \mathsf{stmt} = (u, Z_u), w = (m_u, \sigma, \rho); \mathsf{coins}),$$

now we instead call the simulated prover

$$\pi_u \leftarrow \mathsf{NIZK.P_0(crs_{nizk}}, \tau, \mathsf{stmt} = (u, Z_u); \mathsf{coins}).$$

Note that $\mathsf{P_0}$ uses the trapdoor τ but does not use the witness to output a simulated proof;

- Whenever a node u newly becomes corrupt and the experiment needs to explain the random coins used earlier by u, it calls the NIZK's Explain algorithm, that is,

$$\mathsf{NIZKcoins} \leftarrow \mathsf{NIZK.Explain}\,(\mathsf{crs_{nizk}}, \tau, \mathsf{stmt} = (u, Z_u), w = (m_u, \sigma, \rho); \mathsf{coins})$$

to output an explanation of the coins used in generating the earlier NIZK proofs. These coins are returned to $\mathcal{A}$ along with all other random coins consumed by the newly corrupted node u earlier.

[To reviewer: Indeed, there is no VRF here, the VRF was an editorial typo due to historical reasons, since we changed our protocol completely at some point. Thank you for spotting this. We also polished the entire paragraph to make it more clear.]

For details of the NIZK syntax and security definitions (including the NIZK.Explain algorithm which is part of the NIZK's security definition), please refer to Appendix A.2.

Claim 4.5. *Assume that the* NIZK *scheme satisfies non-erasure computational zero-knowledge. Then, the outputs of the experiments* $\mathsf{Expt}(1^\lambda, \{m_u^*\}_{u\in[n]})$ *and* $\mathsf{Hyb}(1^\lambda, \{m_u^*\}_{u\in[n]})$ *are computationally indistinguishable.*

Proof. Follows directly from the computational zero-knowledge of the NIZK system.   □

Experiment $\mathsf{Ideal}(1^\lambda)$. The ideal experiment $\mathsf{Ideal}(1^\lambda)$ is almost identical to $\mathsf{Hyb}(1^\lambda, \_)$, except with the following modification:

- At the beginning of the challenge phase, let H^* denote the so-far honest nodes. We compute the first-round message $(\mathsf{puz}, Z_u, \pi_u)$ for every $u \in H^*$ as below: call $Z_u \leftarrow \mathsf{TLP.Gen}(1^\lambda, \mathcal{T}_{\mathsf{solve}}, (0, \sigma))$ where $\sigma \leftarrow \Sigma.\mathsf{Sign}(\mathsf{ssk}_u, 0)$. Further, call the NIZK's simulated prover $\widetilde{\mathsf{P}}$ which uses τ but not the witness to generate a simulated proof π_u.

Claim 4.6. *Assume that the* TLP *scheme satisfies* ξ*-hardness. Then, for any* $\{m_u^*\}_{u\in[n]}$*, no non-uniform parallel* $2\mathcal{T}_0$*-bounded distinguisher* $\mathcal{D}$ *can distinguish the outputs of the experiments* $\mathsf{Ideal}(1^\lambda)$ *and* $\mathsf{Hyb}(1^\lambda, \{m_u^*\}_{u\in[n]})$ *except with negligible probability.*

Proof. We can consider a sequence of hybrids for $i \in [0, h]$, such that in the i-th hybrid, during the challenge session, the first $\min(i, |H^*|)$ nodes in H^* (by lexicographical ordering) will use the input $(0, \sigma)$ where $\sigma \leftarrow \Sigma.\mathsf{Sign}(\mathsf{ssk}_u, 0)$

to compute a puzzle. If there exists a non-uniform parallel $2T_\emptyset$-bounded distinguisher $\mathcal{D}$ that can distinguish the outputs of the experiments $\mathsf{Ideal}(1^\lambda)$ and $\mathsf{Hyb}(1^\lambda, \{m_u^*\}_{u \in [n]})$ with more than negligible probability, by the hybrid argument, there must exist a pair of adjacent hybrids indexed j and $j+1$ that $\mathcal{D}$ can distinguish with non-negligible probability.

We can construct a non-uniform p.p.t. parallel machine $\mathcal{B}$ which breaks the ξ-hardness of the TLP scheme. $\mathcal{B}$ simulates the experiment for $\mathcal{A}$ and let u be the $(j+1)$-th node in H^* at the beginning of the challenge session. At the beginning of the challenge session, for every v that is among the first j nodes in H^*, $\mathcal{B}$ computes their puzzles using the input $(0, \sigma)$ where $\sigma \leftarrow \Sigma.\mathsf{Sign}(\mathsf{ssk}_v, 0)$; and for everyone else in H^* that is not among the first $j+1$ nodes, $\mathcal{B}$ will compute their puzzles using the input (m_v^*, σ') where $\sigma' \leftarrow \Sigma.\mathsf{Sign}(\mathsf{ssk}_v, m_v^*)$.

After this computation is done, $\mathcal{B}$ now computes the first-round message for the $(j+1)$-th node in H^*. To do so, $\mathcal{B}$ interacts with a TLP challenger which either returns a puzzle either for the string $(0, \sigma)$ where $\sigma \leftarrow \Sigma.\mathsf{Sign}(\mathsf{ssk}_u, 0)$, or for the string (m_u^*, σ') where $\sigma' \leftarrow \Sigma.\mathsf{Sign}(\mathsf{ssk}_u, m_u^*)$. This answer will be used as the puzzle for the $(j+1)$-th node in H^*.

At this moment, $\mathcal{B}$ gives the view of $\mathcal{A}$, including all random coins consumed by $\mathcal{A}$ and all outputs of $\mathcal{A}$ so far, as well as the first-round messages of H^* in the challenge session to the distinguisher $\mathcal{D}$, and in at most $2T_\emptyset$ time, it outputs the same answer as $\mathcal{D}$. □

At this moment, by the hybrid argument, we have that no non-uniform p.p.t. $2T_\emptyset$-bounded parallel machine $\mathcal{D}$ can distinguish the outputs of $\mathsf{Expt}^{\mathcal{A}}(1^\lambda, \{m_u^*\}_{u \in [n]})$ and $\mathsf{Ideal}(1^\lambda)$ with more than negligible probability. By a symmetric argument, the same holds for $\mathsf{Expt}^{\mathcal{A}}(1^\lambda, \{\widetilde{m}_u^*\}_{u \in [n]})$ and $\mathsf{Ideal}(1^\lambda)$. Thus, we can conclude that no non-uniform p.p.t. $2T_\emptyset$-bounded parallel machine $\mathcal{D}$ can distinguish the outputs of $\mathsf{Expt}^{\mathcal{A}}(1^\lambda, \{m_u^*\}_{u \in [n]})$ and $\mathsf{Expt}^{\mathcal{A}}(1^\lambda, \{\widetilde{m}_u^*\}_{u \in [n]})$ with more than negligible probability.

5   Byzantine Broadcast Protocol

5.1   Protocol

Without loss of generality, we may assume that $u = 1$ is the designated sender for the Byzantine Broadcast. Our protocol will make use of a VRF scheme which is defined in Sect. 3.3, and will rely on the Distribute protocol that is defined and constructed in Sect. 4.

Vote. A vote from a node $u \in [n]$ for the bit $b \in \{0, 1\}$ is a tuple of the form $(\mathsf{vote}, b, u, D, \sigma)$ such that $\mathsf{VRF.Vf}(\mathsf{crs}_{\mathrm{vrf}}, \mathsf{pk}_u, b, D, \sigma) = 1$, and moreover, it must be that either $D < D_p$ or $u = 1$. Here D_p denotes a *difficulty parameter* whose choice will be specified shortly.

Batch of Votes. An r-batch of votes for a bit $b \in \{0, 1\}$ is a collection of valid votes from r distinct nodes, and moreover, it must be that one of these votes comes from the designated sender.

Protocol. Our Byzantine Broadcast protocol is described below. Recall that $h = n - f$ denotes the number of honest nodes.

Initially, every node u's Extracted$_u$ set is set to $\emptyset$. The designated sender $u = 1$ computes and records a vote for its input bit b by computing $(D, \sigma) \leftarrow$ VRF.Eval(crs$_{\text{vrf}}$, sk$_1$, b).

Parameters. Let ℓ be the length of the first term of the VRF's evaluation outcome. The difficulty parameter D_p is set such that the probability that a random string of length ℓ is less than D_p with probability $p \in (\frac{\log^2 \lambda}{h}, \frac{3\log^2 \lambda}{h}) \cap (0, 1)$. The number of phases $R := 6\log^2 \lambda \cdot \frac{n}{h}$.

Setup. We use two instances of the Distribute protocol, denoted Distribute^0 and Distribute^1 respectively, and each instance is used by nodes to distribute batches of votes for the bit 0 and 1, respectively. For $b \in \{0, 1\}$, call the setup of Distribute which outputs (crs$_{\text{distr}}^b$, $\{$vk$_u^b$, ssk$_u^b\}_{u \in [n]}$). Call (crs$_{\text{vrf}}$, $\{$pk$_u$, sk$_u\}_{u \in [n]}$) $\leftarrow$ VRF.Gen(1^λ). Now, publish the public parameters (crs$_{\text{distr}}^0$, crs$_{\text{distr}}^1$, crs$_{\text{vrf}}$) and give each node u the secret keys ssk$_u^0$, ssk$_u^1$, and sk$_u$.

Phase $r \in [1 \ldots R]$. Each phase consists of $R_{\text{distr}} + 1$ rounds where R_{distr} denotes the round complexity of the Distribute protocol.

1. In the first round, every node u performs the following: for each bit $b \in \{0, 1\}$, if node u has seen a valid r-batch of votes for b and $b \notin$ Extracted$_u$, then it multicasts any such r-batch for b to everyone, and sets Extracted$_u \leftarrow$ Extracted$_u \cup \{b\}$.
2. The next step lasts for R_{distr} rounds. Each node $u \neq 1$ does the following: for each bit $b \in \{0, 1\}$, it invokes a new session of the Distribute^b protocol with a new session identifier r to distribute either an $(r + 1)$-batch of votes or a dummy message:

   - If it has recorded a valid r-batch of votes for b and node u has never computed a vote for b before, then it attempts to vote for b by computing $(D, \sigma) \leftarrow$ VRF.Eval(crs$_{\text{vrf}}$, sk$_u$, b). If $D < D_p$, then execute the following:
     - let Extracted$_u \leftarrow$ Extracted$_u \cup \{b\}$;
     - invoke Distribute^b to distribute a valid $(r + 1)$-batch of votes for b, possibly by adding its own vote (vote, b, u, D, σ).
   - Else if the node did not decide to distribute an $(r+1)$-batch of votes for b in the above, then invoke Distribute^b to distribute a dummy message $\bot$ which is encoded as a string of the same length as an $(r + 1)$-batch of votes for b.

At any time, if any valid vote is received over the network or output by the Distribute^0 or Distribute^1 protocols, the vote is then recorded by the node.

Output. At the end of the R phases, if $|$Extracted$_u| = 1$ node u outputs the unique bit in Extracted$_u$; else output the default bit 0.

Round Complexity. The total round complexity of the above protocol is upper bounded by $R \cdot R_{\text{distr}} = \left(\frac{n}{h}\right)^2 \cdot \frac{1}{\xi} \cdot \mathsf{poly} \log \lambda$. As a special case, in the case 99% or any arbitrarily large constant fraction of nodes are corrupt, and assuming that the hardness parameter ξ is a constant, the round complexity of the protocol is $\mathsf{poly} \log \lambda$.

6 Proofs for Our Byzantine Broadcast Protocol

6.1 Additional Terminology

For convenience, we will use the following terminology.

- We say that an execution satisfies consistency for the bit $b \in \{0,1\}$, iff the following holds: if some forever-honest node u has b in its Extracted$_u$ set at the end, then every forever-honest node v have b in its Extracted$_v$ set at the end, too. To show consistency, we just have to prove that except with negligible probability over the choice of the randomized execution, consistency holds for $b = 0$ as well as $b = 1$.
- For convenience, we say that a node u *mines* a vote for $b \in \{0,1\}$ if it calls $(D, \sigma) \leftarrow \mathsf{VRF.Eval}(\mathsf{crs}_{\mathrm{vrf}}, \mathsf{sk}_u, b)$ to attempt to compute a vote for b, and recall that whether a mining attempt is successful depends on whether the outcome D is less than the difficulty parameter D_p. All honest mining attempts are made in the second round of some phase, i.e., the first round of the Distribute protocol of that phase.
- We say that a node $u \in [n]$ is in the 0-committee iff the first term in the output of $\mathsf{VRF.Eval}(\mathsf{crs}_{\mathrm{vrf}}, \mathsf{sk}_u, 0)$ is smaller than D_p. Members of the 1-committee is similarly defined.

We will consider two types of bad events. We will later prove that if, except with negligible probability, neither type of bad event happens for both bits, then consistency is respected except with negligible probability.

- *Type A bad event for the bit b:* In the second round of some phase r, all so-far honest nodes have made attempts to mine a vote for b (in the second round of some phase $r' \leq r$); and yet, the adversary $\mathcal{A}$ manages to corrupt every member of the b-committee either before it even made a mining attempt for b, or by the beginning of the third round of the phase in which it makes a mining attempt for b.
- *Type B bad event for the bit b:* Either at least R nodes are members of the b-committee, or no node is a member of the b-committee.

6.2 Proof Overview: Challenges and Intuition

We would like to use probablistic reasoning to argue that the above two types of bad events do not happen except with negligible probability. The probabilistic reasoning could be accomplished using standard measure concentration bounds if all the cryptography we employ were "ideal". Unfortunately the cryptography we employ is far from ideal. One problem we encounter is that our delayed-exposure distribution primitive Distribute guarantees secrecy against only an adversary who is restricted to run in a small number of parallel steps. An adversary who can take more parallel steps can completely break the secrecy of Distribute by solving the time-lock puzzles. For our final protocol, of course, we want to prove security against any *parallel p.p.t. adversary* who is allowed to take an *unbounded* number of parallel steps.

Partly due to this reason, the most natural proof strategy completely fails: we are not able describe an ideal protocol (without cryptography), and show that the real-world protocol *securely emulates* the ideal protocol by a standard, *simulation-based* notion. What comes to the rescue is that we only need to prove that certain security properties hold in the real-world protocol; and proving these properties eventually boils down to showing that certain bad events (as defined above) happen with negligible probability. Therefore, instead of proving that the real-world protocol *securely emulates* some ideal protocol, our strategy is to prove that the probability of bad events is not higher in the real-world protocol than in the ideal protocol (barring negligible differences). To do this, we will define a polynomially long sequence of hybrids, starting from the real-world protocol, all the way to the ideal protocol which does not have any cryptography: we will prove that for every pair of adjacent hybrids, the probability of bad events in the former is not higher than the probability of bad events in the latter (barring negligible differences).

We now elaborate on our blueprint—below in our proof overview, we mainly focus on how we bound the probability of Type-A bad events since this is the most technical part of the proof. First, we make several modifications to the real-world protocol and obtain a hybrid called $\mathsf{Hyb}'_\star$. $\mathsf{Hyb}'_\star$ *is no longer a consensus protocol, it should simply be viewed as a game in which the adversary $\mathcal{A}$ is trying to cause Type-A bad events to happen.* The modifications we made ensure that the probability of Type-A bad events can only increase in $\mathsf{Hyb}'_\star$ in comparison with the real-world protocol. Importantly, in $\mathsf{Hyb}'_\star$, we introduce a *final guessing phase*: if at the end of the protocol, $\mathcal{A}$ has corrupted $f' < f$ number of nodes, i.e., it has more corruption budget left, we give $\mathcal{A}$ an extra opportunity to guess who, among the remaining honest nodes that have not made a mining attempt for b, are members of the b-committee. If $\mathcal{A}$ can correctly guess all remaining honest b-committee members in at most $f - f'$ tries, we also declare that $\mathcal{A}$ wins, i.e., a Type-A bad event has happened.

At this moment, it is not clear why we introduce the final guessing phase yet. This will become clear in the next hybrid $\mathsf{Hyb}_\star$. In $\mathsf{Hyb}_\star$, we modify the final guessing phase, such that the remaining honest nodes who have not made a mining attempt for b yet would use true random coins rather than VRFs to determine if they are a member of the b-committee. In this way, the game becomes ideal (i.e., without cryptography) after the final guessing phase starts. Partly relying on the security of VRF, one can show that any parallel *p.p.t.* $\mathcal{A}$

cannot cause Type-A bad events to happen more often in Hyb'_* than in Hyb_* (barring negligible differences).

Now, in the remainder of the proof, our idea is to start from the end of the experiment, and make each phase "ideal" one by one. In other words, in each hybrid, we will make the final guessing phase start one phase earlier, until at the very end, the final guessing phase starts upfront and therefore the whole game becomes ideal (i.e., no cryptography). In the process, we make sure that $\mathcal{A}$'s probability of causing bad events does not decrease (barring negligible differences).

At this moment, it is a good time to revisit how we can overcome the aforementioned problem where the overall adversary is a parallel machine running in unbounded parallel steps but our Distribute primitive only gives secrecy against an adversary who is restricted to run in a small number of parallel steps. With the above proof strategy, informally speaking, at some point, we need to compare the probability of Type-A bad event in the following two adjacent hybrids—henceforth let r^* be the phase immediately preceding the final guessing phase:

1. in the first hybrid, in phase r^*, honest nodes run the real Distribute protocol using real inputs;
2. in the second hybrid, in phase r^*, honest nodes run the Distribute protocol using input $\mathbf{0}$.

In both of these hybrids, the adversary $\mathcal{A}$ can win the game if it either wins in the final guessing phase, or if $\mathcal{A}$ can guess, by the beginning of the third round of phase r^*, which honest nodes successfully made mining attempts for b in phase r^*. To succeed in the latter, $\mathcal{A}$ might try to gain some leverage by attacking the Distribute protocol of phase r^*, but because of the short-fuse deadline $\mathcal{A}$ must make the guess by, the Distribute protocol in phase r^* is unhelpful to $\mathcal{A}$ due to the momentary secrecy property. Even though after phase r^*, $\mathcal{A}$ may completely break the secrecy of the Distribute protocol of phase r^*, recall that the games becomes ideal immediately after phase r^*. Therefore, breaking the secrecy of the phase-r^* Distribute protocol no longer helps $\mathcal{A}$ after phase r^*.

Last but not the least, besides the aforementioned technicalities, yet another is that $\mathcal{A}$ is adaptive, and we need to handle the adaptivity with particular care in our proofs. Now, without further ado, we present our formal proofs.

6.3   Bounding the Probability of Type-A Bad Events

Let Real denote an execution of the real-world protocol in which the adversary $\mathcal{A}$'s goal is to cause a Type-A bad event to happen. In the remainder of this section, we will consider a sequence of hybrid experiments starting with Real such that for each pair of adjacent experiments, the probability of a Type-A bad event in the latter is an upper bound of the probability of a Type-A bad event in the former (ignoring negligible differences). In the end, we will upper bound the probability of a Type-A bad event in the final experiment called Hyb_1. Hyb_1 essentially gets rid of the cryptography and therefore we can upper bound the probability of a Type-A bad event in Hyb_1 with a simple information-theoretic, probabilistic argument.

In the following we fix an arbitrary $b \in \{0, 1\}$, and we care about bounding Type-A bad events for the bit b. Henceforth whenever we say Type-A bad event, it means a Type-A bad event for the bit b. Also, recall that we use the notation $f = n - h$ to denote the maximum number of corruptions allowed.

6.3.1 Experiment $\mathsf{Hyb}'_\star$

Since we only care about bounding Type-A bad events for the bit b, we make some simplifications to the protocol without decreasing the probability of a Type-A bad event. We therefore define a hybrid experiment $\mathsf{Hyb}'_\star$:

1. At the beginning of the protocol, for each $u \in [n]$, we compute $(D_u, \sigma_u) \leftarrow \mathsf{VRF.Eval}(\mathsf{crs}_{\mathrm{vrf}}, \mathsf{sk}_u, 1 - b)$ and disclose to $\mathcal{A}$ the pair (D_u, σ_u) which is the evaluation outcome and proof for the bit $1 - b$. Of course, upon the new corruption of some node v, we now need to explain to $\mathcal{A}$ the coins in the above evaluation for v too.
2. During the protocol, in each phase, we only run the $\mathsf{Distribute}^b$ protocol but not the $\mathsf{Distribute}^{1-b}$ protocol; similarly, we need not run the setup for $\mathsf{Distribute}^{1-b}$ either.
3. If some honest node u tried to call $\mathsf{Distribute}^b$ to send a valid $(r + 1)$-batch of votes for b in the second round of phase r and u remains honest till the beginning of the third round of phase r, the experiment declares that $\mathcal{A}$ has failed to cause a Type-A bad event, and simply aborts outputting $\mathsf{adv\text{-}fail}$.
4. Immediately after the second round of phase R, for every honest node u who has already made a mining attempt for b, we disclose its VRF secret key sk_b to $\mathcal{A}$ even if u has not been corrupted by $\mathcal{A}$ (and note that these nodes do not count towards the corruption budget).

   Now, we allow $\mathcal{A}$ an extra **final guessing phase**, in which $\mathcal{A}$ can adaptively specify nodes to corrupt one by one; all nodes specified must not have made a mining attempt for b yet. Every time $\mathcal{A}$ specifies a new node u to corrupt, it learns its VRF secret key sk_u. The experiment stops when $\mathcal{A}$ has made f corruption queries in total. At this moment, if A has corrupted all members of the b-committee who have not made a mining attempt for b at the beginning of the final guessing phase, then declare that a Type-A bad event has happened.

Claim 6.1. *If for some non-uniform p.p.t. parallel machine $\mathcal{A}$, a Type-A bad event happens with probability μ in the real-world experiment Real, then there exists a non-uniform p.p.t. parallel machine $\mathcal{A}'$ such that a Type-A bad event happens with probability at least μ in $\mathsf{Hyb}'_\star$.*

Proof. We can add these modifications one by one and in each step argue that if there is a non-uniform *p.p.t.* parallel machine $\mathcal{A}$ in the previous experiment that can cause a Type-A bad event to occur with probability μ, then there is a non-uniform *p.p.t.* parallel machine $\mathcal{A}'$ in the modified experiment that can cause a Type-A bad event to occur with probability at least $\mu - \mathsf{negl}(\lambda)$.

First, we can add the modification 4. It is not hard to see that this phase only gives the adversary more opportunities in causing a Type-A bad event. In some sense, the final guessing phase is saying, at the end of the protocol, if not so-far honest nodes have made mining attempts for b (in this case a Type-A bad event cannot happen), we will pretend as if all of them made mining attempts for b and give $\mathcal{A}$ another opportunity to guess who the b-committee members are.

With modification 4, we can essentially imagine that all so-far honest nodes will have made mining attempts for b by the end of the protocol. Therefore, modification 3 is cosmetic, it basically checks for Type-A bad events constantly in the background and does not change the probability of Type-A bad event.

Next, we can add modifications 1 and 2. It is not hard to see that if there is a non-uniform $p.p.t.$ parallel machine $\mathcal{A}$ in the previous experiment that can cause a Type-A bad event to occur with probability μ, then we can construct a non-uniform $p.p.t.$ parallel machine $\mathcal{A}'$ in the modified experiment that can cause a Type-A bad event to occur with probability at least μ. Basically $\mathcal{A}'$ simply simulates the $\mathsf{Distribute}^{1-b}$ instances for $\mathcal{A}$ using its knowledge of all the VRF evaluations and proofs for $1 - b$. Whenever $\mathcal{A}$ corrupts some v, $\mathcal{A}'$ learns the explanation of the coins that contributed towards v's VRF proofs for $1 - b$, in this way, $\mathcal{A}'$ can provide the necessary explanation to $\mathcal{A}$ too.   □

6.3.2 Experiment $\mathsf{Hyb}_\star$

Experiment $\mathsf{Hyb}_\star$ is almost the same as $\mathsf{Hyb}'_\star$, except that when the final guessing phase starts, every so-far honest node who has not made a mining attempt for b yet chooses a random D from an appropriate domain instead of using the honest VRF outcome to determine whether it is a member of the b-committee. Furthermore, during the final guessing phase, when $\mathcal{A}$ corrupts any node, we no longer disclose the node's VRF key to $\mathcal{A}$.

Lemma 6.2. *Assume that the VRF scheme satisfies pseudorandomness under selective opening (see Definition 3.3). Then, suppose that there is a non-uniform $p.p.t.$ parallel machine $\mathcal{A}$ that can cause a Type-A bad event to happen in $\mathsf{Hyb}'_\star$ with probability μ, then there is a non-uniform $p.p.t.$ parallel machine $\mathcal{A}'$ that can cause a Type-A bad event to happen in $\mathsf{Hyb}_\star$ with probability at least $\mu - \mathsf{negl}(\lambda)$ for some appropriate negligible function $\mathsf{negl}(\cdot)$.*

Proof. We prove this lemma through a sequence of intermediate hybrids described below.

Hybrid $\widetilde{\mathsf{H}}_\star$. The experiment $\widetilde{\mathsf{H}}_\star$ is defined in almost the same way as $\mathsf{Hyb}'_\star$ except with the following modifications:

- During the setup, we will replace the VRF's setup with the simulated setup algorithms $\mathcal{S}_0$ which generates the $(s_1, \ldots, s_n)$ part of the secret keys, and $\mathcal{S}_1$ which generates $(\mathsf{crs}, \mathsf{pk}_1, \ldots, \mathsf{pk}_n, \tau)$. The adversary $\mathcal{A}$ is given the public components $\mathsf{crs}, \mathsf{pk}_1, \ldots, \mathsf{pk}_n$.

- Whenever an honest node u needs to evaluate the VRF on input b', we compute the VRF outcome y honestly using sk_u, but call $\mathcal{S}_2(\tau, \mathsf{pk}_u, b', y)$ instead to compute a simulated proof using the trapdoor τ.
- Whenever an honest node u gets corrupted, we call the $\mathcal{S}_3$ algorithm which returns ρ_u and all the randomness u used in earlier VRF evaluations. Now return $\mathsf{sk}_u := (s_u, \rho_u)$ to $\mathcal{A}$. If this is before the final guessing round, also return the random coins output by $\mathcal{S}_3$ to $\mathcal{A}$, as well as randomness the newly corrupted node used in the Distribute protocol instances so far. Immediately after the second round of phase R, call $\mathcal{S}_3$ for every honest node v who has already made a mining attempt for b, and return s_u and the term ρ_v output by $\mathcal{S}_3$ to $\mathcal{A}$.

Claim 6.3. *Assume that the VRF scheme satisfies pseudorandomness under selective opening (see Definition 3.3). Then, $\mathcal{A}$'s views in $\widetilde{\mathsf{H}}_\star$ and $\mathsf{Hyb}'_\star$ are computationally indistinguishable.*

Proof. Follows directly from the second part of the definition of pseudorandomness under selective opening. □

Hybrid $\widetilde{\mathsf{H}}_f$. The experiment $\widetilde{\mathsf{H}}_f$ is almost the same as $\widetilde{\mathsf{H}}_\star$ except with the following modification: when the last node u becomes corrupt during the final guessing phase, for u and all remaining honest nodes who have not made a mining attempt for b, we choose a random number of appropriate length to determine whether the node is in the b-committee. Moreover, for the last corruption u in the final guessing stage, we do not disclose u's secret key or coins to $\mathcal{A}$.

Claim 6.4. *Assume that the VRF scheme satisfies pseudorandomness under selective opening. Then, if there exists a non-uniform p.p.t. parallel machine $\mathcal{A}$ that can cause a Type-A bad event to happen in $\widetilde{\mathsf{H}}_\star$ with probability μ, then there is a non-uniform p.p.t. parallel machine $\mathcal{A}'$ that can cause a Type-A bad event to happen in $\widetilde{\mathsf{H}}_f$ with probability at least $\mu - \mathsf{negl}(\lambda)$ for some negligible function $\mathsf{negl}(\cdot)$.*

Proof. Whenever $\mathcal{A}$ makes the last corruption query during the final guessing phase, whether a Type-A bad event has occurred is already determined no matter whether we disclose the secret key of the newly corrupt node to $\mathcal{A}$. Therefore, henceforth we simply assume that nothing is disclosed to $\mathcal{A}$ upon the last corruption during the final guessing phase.

Basically we define $\mathcal{A}'$ to be the same as $\mathcal{A}$ and it runs $\mathcal{A}$ till it makes the last corruption query during the final guessing phase. We show that if $\mathcal{A}$ can cause a Type-A bad event to happen in $\widetilde{\mathsf{H}}_\star$ with more than negligibly higher probability than $\mathcal{A}'$ in experiment $\widetilde{\mathsf{H}}_f$, we can construct a reduction $\mathcal{B}$ to break the first game in the definition of pseudorandomness under selective opening.

Essentially $\mathcal{B}$ interacts with its challenger $\mathcal{C}$ as defined in the first game in the definition of pseudorandomness under selective opening. Moreover, $\mathcal{B}$ simulates the experiment $\widetilde{\mathsf{H}}_\star$ to $\mathcal{A}$ right till the moment $\mathcal{A}$ makes the last corruption query in the final guessing phase.

- During setup, $\mathcal{B}$ asks its challenger $\mathcal{C}$ to run the setup who generates $(s_1, \ldots, s_n)$. $\mathcal{B}$ now runs $\mathcal{S}_1$ to generate $\mathsf{crs}, \mathsf{pk}_1, \ldots, \mathsf{pk}_n, \tau$ and it gives the terms $\mathsf{crs}, \mathsf{pk}_1, \ldots, \mathsf{pk}_n$ to $\mathcal{A}$.
- Whenever the experiment needs to evaluate the first term of the VRF outcome, $\mathcal{B}$ instead forwards the query to its challenger $\mathcal{C}$, and then it simulates the proof part by calling $\mathcal{S}_2$ just like in $\widetilde{\mathsf{H}}_*$.
- Whenever $\mathcal{A}$ corrupts an honest node u (except for the last corruption query in the final guessing phase), $\mathcal{B}$ issues a corruption query to $\mathcal{C}$, learns s_u, and then calls the $\mathcal{S}_3$ algorithm which returns ρ_u and all the randomness u used in earlier VRF evaluations. Now return $\mathsf{sk}_u := (s_u, \rho_u)$ to $\mathcal{A}$, and if this is before the final guessing round, also return the random coins output by $\mathcal{S}_3$ to $\mathcal{A}$, as well as the coins u used in Distribute protocol instances so far.
- Immediately after the second round of phase R, for every honest node v who has already made a mining attempt for b, $\mathcal{B}$ issues a corruption query to $\mathcal{C}$ for v, learns the s_v, and then calls $\mathcal{S}_3$ to obtain ρ_v. It returns the pair (s_v, ρ_v) to $\mathcal{A}$.
- When $\mathcal{A}$ makes the last corruption query during the final guessing stage, $\mathcal{B}$ sends multiple challenge queries on the input b to $\mathcal{C}$ to obtain the evaluation outcomes for the last corrupted node, as well as all remaining honest nodes who have not made a mining attempt for b.

Besides the above, $\mathcal{B}$ simulates the rest of the $\widetilde{\mathsf{H}}_*$ faithfully.

These evaluation outcomes are used to determine whether a Type-A event has happened at this moment. Note that if $\mathcal{C}$ returned random answers, the experiment is the same as $\mathcal{A}'$ interacting with $\widetilde{\mathsf{H}}_f$; otherwise it is the same as $\mathcal{A}$ interacting with $\widetilde{\mathsf{H}}_*$.

We stress that in the above, we are using a multi-challenge version of the first-game of the pseudorandomness under selective opening notion, where in the challenge phase, the adversary can specify multiple challenge queries rather than a single one. As argued in Chan et al. [ACD+19], the multi-challenge version is equivalent to the single challenge version by a standard hybrid argument. □

Hybrid $\widetilde{\mathsf{H}}_{f-1}$. The experiment $\widetilde{\mathsf{H}}_{f-1}$ is almost the same as $\widetilde{\mathsf{H}}_f$ except with the following modification: when the second to last corruption query u is made in the final guessing phase (or if fewer than 2 corruption queries are made in the final guessing phase, then for all of them):

- we do not return anything to $\mathcal{A}$ upon the corruption query; and
- we use a random number for the node u as well as all remaining honest nodes who have not made a mining attempt for b, to determine if the corresponding node is a member of the b-committee.

Claim 6.5. *Assume that the VRF scheme satisfies pseudorandomness under selective opening. Then, if there exists a non-uniform p.p.t. parallel machine $\mathcal{A}$ that can cause a Type-A bad event to happen in H_f with probability μ, then there is a non-uniform p.p.t. parallel machine $\mathcal{A}'$ that can cause a Type-A bad event to happen in H_{f-1} with probability at least $\mu - \mathsf{negl}(\lambda)$ for some negligible function $\mathsf{negl}(\cdot)$.*

Proof. Basically, $\mathcal{A}'$ runs $\mathcal{A}$ till it makes the second to last corruption query u in the final guessing phase. $\mathcal{A}'$ also makes the same corruption query u as the second to last query, but for the last corruption query, it just chooses to corrupt an arbitrary honest node that has not made a mining attempt for b.

We can construct a reduction $\mathcal{B}$ in a similar way as in the proof of Claim 6.4, except that now $\mathcal{B}$ stops at the second to last corruption query (for the node u) in the final guessing stage, and then $\mathcal{B}$ asks $\mathcal{C}$ for the evaluation outcome on the input b for u as well as any remaining honest node who has not made a mining attempt for b. The returned evaluation outcomes are used to decide whether the corresponding node is a member of the b-committee. It is not hard to see that if $\mathcal{C}$ returns random answers, the experiment above would have the same probability of causing a Type-A bad event as in $\widetilde{\mathsf{H}}_{f-1}$; else it has the same probability of causing a Type-A bad event as in $\widetilde{\mathsf{H}}_f$.   □

Hybrid $\widetilde{\mathsf{H}}_1$. We can define a sequence of hybrids $\widetilde{\mathsf{H}}_f, \widetilde{\mathsf{H}}_{f-1}, \ldots, \widetilde{\mathsf{H}}_1$, until eventually we arrive at $\widetilde{\mathsf{H}}_1$, which is almost the same as $\mathsf{Hyb}_\star$ except that we are using the simulated setup and simulated VRF proofs in $\widetilde{\mathsf{H}}_1$. Specifically, in experiment $\widetilde{\mathsf{H}}_i$, when $\mathcal{A}$ is making the last but $(f-i+1)$-th corruption query in the final guessing phase, we switch to using random outcomes for all remaining honest nodes who have not made a mining attempt for b (including the one being corrupted right now), to determine if the corresponding node is in the b-th committee; and moreover at this moment we do not disclose anything more to $\mathcal{A}$.

Claim 6.6. *Assume that the VRF scheme satisfies pseudorandomness under selective opening. Then, if there exists a non-uniform p.p.t. parallel machine $\mathcal{A}$ that can cause a Type-A bad event to happen in H_i with probability μ, then there is a non-uniform p.p.t. parallel machine $\mathcal{A}'$ that can cause a Type-A bad event to happen in H_{i-1} with probability at least $\mu - \mathsf{negl}(\lambda)$ for some negligible function $\mathsf{negl}(\cdot)$.*

Proof. The proof is essentially identical to that of Claim 6.5.   □

Claim 6.7. *Assume that the VRF scheme satisfies pseudorandomness under selective opening. Then, $\mathcal{A}$'s views in $\widetilde{\mathsf{H}}_1$ and $\mathsf{Hyb}_\star$ are computationally indistinguishable.*

Proof. Directly follows from the second part of the pseudorandomness under selective opening notion.   □

With the above sequence of hybrid experiments, we have concluded the proof of Lemma 6.2.   □

6.3.3   Experiments Hyb'_r and Hyb_r

We define a sequence of hybrids below $\{\mathsf{Hyb}'_r, \mathsf{Hyb}_r\}_{r \in [1,R]}$.

Experiment Hyb'_r. Experiment Hyb'_r is almost identical as $\mathsf{Hyb}_\star$ except the following modifications:

- In phase r of the protocol, we pretend instead that so-far honest nodes use the inputs $\mathbf{0}$ for the phase-r Distribute^b protocol, and compute their first-round messages (denoted M) of the Distribute^b protocol. We give M to $\mathcal{A}$, and let it run till the beginning of the third round of phase r (i.e., the second round of the phase-r Distribute protocol). $\mathcal{A}$ outputs, among other terms, a set of new nodes to corrupt by the beginning of the third round of phase R.
- At this moment, every remaining honest node who has not yet made a mining attempt for b will use a random string of appropriate length to determine if it is a member of the b-committee. We now let $\mathcal{A}$ engage in a final guessing phase as defined before.

The definition of a Type-A bad event in Hyb_r is the same as in $\mathsf{Hyb}_\star$.

Experiment Hyb_r. Experiment Hyb_r is almost the same as $\mathsf{Hyb}_\star$ except that at the beginning of the second round of phase r, the experiment discloses all honest nodes' secret keys for the Distribute^b instance to $\mathcal{A}$. $\mathcal{A}$ now enters the final guessing phase, in which all remaining honest nodes who have not yet made mining attempts for b switch to using random coins to determine if they are a member of the b-committee.

Claim 6.8. *Assume that the* Distribute *protocol satisfies momentary secrecy. Then, there exists a negligible function* $\mathsf{negl}(\cdot)$ *such that the following holds: if for some non-uniform p.p.t.* $\mathcal{A}$, *Type-A bad events happen with probability* μ *in* $\mathsf{Hyb}_\star$, *then there must exist a non-uniform p.p.t.* $\mathcal{A}'$ *such that Type-A bad events happen with probability at least* $\mu - \mathsf{negl}(\lambda)$ *in* Hyb'_R.

Proof. Consider the following experiment Expt^β in which a reduction $\mathcal{B}$ interacts with a challenger $\mathcal{C}$ as well as the adversary $\mathcal{A}$.

- For the Distribute^b instance, it will embed the public parameters passed to it by $\mathcal{C}$.
- Whenever $\mathcal{B}$ needs to play on behalf of honest nodes in Distribute^b protocols (not including in phase R), it forwards the query to $\mathcal{C}$ instead providing the inputs of the so-far honest nodes, and acts as a relay between $\mathcal{C}$ and $\mathcal{A}$ for messages of the Distribute^b protocol.
- Whenever some honest node is corrupted by $\mathcal{A}$, it forwards the corruption query to $\mathcal{C}$, and forwards the internal states returned by $\mathcal{C}$ to $\mathcal{A}$; besides this, $\mathcal{B}$ also gives $\mathcal{A}$ the secret keys and random coins pertaining to the VRF of the newly corrupt node.
- Finally, during phase R, $\mathcal{B}$ invokes a challenge session with $\mathcal{C}$. Depending on the bit β, $\mathcal{C}$ will either use the honest nodes' real inputs in the challenge Distribute^b protocol if $\beta = 0$; else if $\beta = 1$, it will use the vector $\mathbf{0}$ as honest inputs to the challenge Distribute^b protocol. Let M^β be the first-round messages of the challenge Distribute^b protocol computed by $\mathcal{C}$. Let view^β be the joint view of $\mathcal{A}$ and $\mathcal{B}$ at this point.
- ($\diamond$): Now, give M^β to $\mathcal{A}$, run it till the beginning of the next round, and $\mathcal{A}$ outputs, among other terms, a set K^β of nodes to corrupt.

- At this moment, any remaining honest node who has not made a mining attempt for b uses random coins to decide if it is a member of the b-committee, and we let $\mathcal{A}$ engage in the final guessing phase.

Besides the above, $\mathcal{B}$ simply runs the experiment $\mathsf{Hyb}_\star$ faithfully. Observe that if $\beta = 0$, the experiment is the same as $\mathsf{Hyb}_\star$ till the beginning of the third round of phase R (i.e., second round of the phase-R Distribute protocol); else if $\beta = 1$, the experiment is the same Hyb'_R till the beginning of the third round of phase R.

Let X denote the total number of honest nodes who have not made a mining attempt for b by the beginning of the third round of phase R, let Y denote the total number of nodes corrupted by the beginning of the third round of phase R, and let Z be a bit indicating whether at the beginning of the third round of phase R, adv-fail has occurred—recall that if the set K does not contain all honest b-committee members who made a mining attempt for b in phase R, then adv-fail would occur.

Recall that after the beginning of the third round of phase R, the experiment enters a final guessing phase in which all honest nodes who have not made a mining attempt for b yet uses random coins to decide if they are members of the b committee. To prove that the probability of Type-A bad events in Hyb'_R can must be at least as high as in $\mathsf{Hyb}_\star$ barring negligible differences, it suffices to show that for any $x \in [n]$, $0 \leq y \leq x$, and $z \in \{0, 1\}$,

$$\left| \Pr_{\mathsf{Expt}^0} [X = x, Y = y, Z = z] - \Pr_{\mathsf{Expt}^1} [X = x, Y = y, Z = z] \right| \leq \mathsf{negl}(\lambda)$$

Suppose not. Then, there must exist $x \in [n]$, $0 \leq y \leq x$, and $z \in \{0, 1\}$, such that $\Pr_{\mathsf{Expt}^0} [X = x, Y = y, Z = z]$ and $\Pr_{\mathsf{Expt}^1} [X = x, Y = y, Z = z]$ differ by a non-negligible amount. Now, we can construct a non-uniform p.p.t. parallel $2T_\emptyset$-bounded distinguisher $\mathcal{D}$ that can distinguish (M^0, view^0) and (M^1, view^1) with more than negligible probability. Basically $\mathcal{D}$ takes M^β and view^β, and runs whatever $\mathcal{A}$ runs in the $(\diamond)$ step for exactly one round which is $T_\emptyset$ amount of time. At this moment, among $\mathcal{A}$'s output, there is an additional set K of nodes to corrupt. Finally, $\mathcal{D}$ tallies the counts X, Y, and the bit Z; here the tallying includes the set K. $\mathcal{D}$ outputs 1 if $(X, Y, Z) = (x, y, z)$; else it outputs 0. The tallying can be computed in logarithmic in n parallel time. Due to our assumption on the duration of an round, that is, an honest node must be able to process all n received messages within a round (see Sect. 3.1), the tallying can be computed in a single round, that is, at most $T_\emptyset$ time. Therefore, $\mathcal{D}$ runs in at most $2T_\emptyset$ time in total.

Remark 3. We stress that $\mathcal{A}$'s views are NOT computationally indistinguishable in the two hybrids since $\mathcal{A}$ can run in unbounded parallel time. We are merely arguing that the probability of Type-A bad events are not decreased by switching the phase-R Distribute messages. It is NOT true that $(M^0, \mathsf{view}^0, K^0)$ and $(M^1, \mathsf{view}^1, K^1)$ are computationally indistinguishable, because (M^0, K^0)

and (M^1, K^1) can potentially be distinguished by an adversary running in sufficiently long time. However, *any property on* $(M^0, \text{view}^0, K^0)$ *or* $(M^1, \text{view}^1, K^1)$ *that can be checked in small parallel runtime should happen with almost the same probability* regardless of the choice of β.   □

Claim 6.9. *Assume that the VRF scheme satisfies pseudorandomness under selective opening. Then, there exists a negligible function* $\mathsf{negl}(\cdot)$ *such that the following holds: if for some non-uniform p.p.t.* $\mathcal{A}$, *Type-A bad events happen with probability* μ *in* Hyb'_R, *then there must exist a non-uniform p.p.t.* $\mathcal{A}'$ *such that Type-A bad events happen with probability at least* $\mu - \mathsf{negl}(\lambda)$ *in* Hyb_R.

Proof. First, disclosing all honest secret keys for the $\mathsf{Distribute}^b$ protocol at the beginning of the second round of phase R discloses strictly more information to $\mathcal{A}$ than in the earlier Hyb'_R. Next, we can repeat the same argument as in the proof of Lemma 6.2, that we can switch to using random coins to decide whether the following nodes are members of the b-committee: the nodes that remain honest at the beginning of the second round of phase R and have not yet made any mining attempts for b.   □

Claim 6.10. *Assume that the* $\mathsf{Distribute}$ *protocol satisfies momentary secrecy, and that the VRF scheme satisfies pseudorandomness under selective opening. Then, there exists a negligible function* $\mathsf{negl}(\cdot)$ *such that the following holds: if for some non-uniform p.p.t.* $\mathcal{A}$, *Type-A bad events happen with probability* μ *in* $\mathsf{Hyb}_\star$, *then there must exist a non-uniform p.p.t.* $\mathcal{A}'$ *such that Type-A bad events happen with probability at least* $\mu - \mathsf{negl}(\lambda)$ *in* Hyb_1.

Proof. The proof works through a sequence of hybrids from Hyb_R to Hyb'_{R-1}, to Hyb_{R-1}, to Hyb'_{R-2} and so on, where to argue each adjacent pair of hybrids we use either the same proof as Claim 6.8 or the same proof as Claim 6.9.   □

Lemma 6.11. *Let* b *be an arbitrary bit. For any non-uniform p.p.t. parallel machine* $\mathcal{A}$, *the probability of a Type-A bad event for* b *in* Real *is negligibly small.*

Proof. Notice that in Hyb_1, even for an unbounded adversary making $f = n - h$ corruptions, the expected number of forever-honest nodes that belong to the b-committee is $\Theta(\log^2 \lambda)$. By the Chernoff bound, the probability that $\mathcal{A}$ succeeds in guessing and corrupting all members of the b-committee is upper bounded by $\mathsf{negl}(\lambda)$.

Now, the earlier sequence of hybrids established that the probability of a Type-A bad event for b in Real must be upper bounded by the probability of a Type-A bad event in Hyb_1 against an unbounded adversary plus $\mathsf{negl}(\lambda)$.   □

6.4 Consistency Proofs

The following lemma bounds the probability of a Type-B bad event for either $b = 0$ or $b = 1$.

Lemma 6.12. *Fix an arbitrary $b \in \{0, 1\}$. Assume that the VRF scheme satisfies pseudorandomness under selective opening. Then, Type-B bad events do not happen except with negligible probability.*

Proof. If we used random coins to decide if each node is a member of the b-committee, then the probability that at least $R = 6 \log^2 \lambda \cdot \frac{n}{h}$ nodes are members of the b-committee is upper bounded by a negligible function in λ by the Chernoff bound. Similarly, the probability that no node is a member of the b-committee is also negligibly small in λ. Now, rather than true randomness, we are using the VRF which gives pseudorandomness, and because the function that determines how many nodes are in the b-committee is a polynomial function on the outcomes of the VRF, it holds that the same holds when the true random coins are replaced with pseudorandom ones. □

So far, we have concluded that neither Type-A nor Type-B bad events happen except with negligible probability, for either bit $b \in \{0, 1\}$. To prove consistency, it suffices to show that if neither types of bad events happen for both bits except with negligible probability, then consistency follows. This is stated and proven in the following theorem.

Theorem 6.13 (Consistency). *Assume that $n \geq \log^2 \lambda$, that the VRF scheme satisfies pseudorandomness under selective opening as well as unforgeability, and that the Distribute protocol satisfies liveness and momentary secrecy. Then, the Byzantine Broadcast protocol defined earlier in this section satisfies consistency.*

Proof. Due to Lemmas 6.11 and 6.12, the liveness of the Distribute protocol, as well as the unforgeability of the VRF, it suffices to prove that the following hold in some execution, then the execution satisfies consistency.

1. for either $b = 0$ or $b = 1$, neither Type-A nor Type-B bad events happen for b;
2. the liveness property of Distribute is never broken;
3. for either $b = 0$ or $b = 1$, if any so-far honest node u has not made a mining attempt for b, then there is no valid vote from u for b in any honest node's view.

Observe that an inconsistency can only take place if some forever-honest node u includes a bit b in its Extracted$_u$ set but some other honest node v does not include b in its Extracted$_v$ set. We now consider the following cases:

- *Case 1:* u first added the bit b to its Extracted$_u$ set in some phase r but *not* in the first round of phase r. According to our protocol, in phase r, u must have observed an r-batch of votes for b, made a successful mining attempt for the bit b, and moreover, it must have tried to distribute an $(r + 1)$-batch of votes for b. Since Type-B bad events do not happen and votes are not forged, it must be that $r < R$.

  Since u is forever honest, by the liveness property of Distribute, it must be that by the end of the phase-r Distribute protocol, all forever-honest nodes will have observed the $(r + 1)$-batch of votes from u. Therefore, every forever-honest node v will have added b to its Extracted$_v$ set in the first round of phase $r + 1 \leq R$.

- *Case 2*: u first added the bit b to its Extracted$_u$ set in some phase r but in the first round of phase r. This means that u has observed an r-batch of votes for b in the first round of phase r. Since Type-B bad events do not happen and votes are not forged, it must be that $r < R$.

  Because u is forever honest, it must be that at the beginning of the second round of phase r, all so-far nodes have observed the same r-batch of votes for b that u saw. Now, all so-far honest nodes will make a mining attempt for b if they have not done so already. Now, since Type-A and Type-B bad events do not happen, there must exist a so-far honest node v that made a successful mining attempt for the bit b in the second round of some phase $r' \leq r$, and moreover, the adversary did not yet corrupt v at the beginning of the third round of phase r'. Now, by liveness of the Distribute protocol, by the beginning of phase $r' + 1 \leq R$, all forever-honest nodes will have observed the $(r' + 1)$ batch of votes for b that v tried to distribute in phase r', and therefore, by the end of the first round of phase $r' + 1$, every forever-honest node w will have added the bit b to its Extracted$_w$ set.   □

6.5   Validity Proofs

Theorem 6.14 (Validity). *Suppose that $n \geq \log^2 \lambda$, that the VRF scheme satisfies pseudorandomness under selective opening as well as unforgeability, and that the* Distribute *protocol satisfies liveness and momentary secrecy. Suppose also that the designated sender is forever-honest and its input is $b' \in \{0,1\}$. Then, except with negligible probability, if any forever-honest node outputs b at the end of the protocol, it must be that $b = b'$.*

Proof. If the designated sender $u = 1$ is forever-honest, let b be its input bit, then node $u = 1$ must distribute a valid 1-batch of votes for b in the first round of the first phase. Thus, by the beginning of the second round of the first phase, all so-far honest nodes will have made a mining attempt for b. Because Type-A and Type-B bad events do not happen except with negligible probability, it must be that except with negligible probability, at least one node u successfully mines a vote for b in phase 1 and the node u remains honest till at least the beginning of the third round of the first phase. By the liveness property of Distribute, it must be that except with negligible probability, by the beginning of the second phase, every so-far honest node v will have observed a valid 2-batch of votes for b, and will have added the bit b to its Extracted$_v$ set. Finally, validity follows by observing that due to the unforgeability of the VRF, no valid batch of votes for $1 - b$ can appear in any honest node's view except with negligible probability. □

7   Conclusion and Open Questions

Our work is the first to show a sublinear-round Byzantine Broadcast protocol secure in the presence of *corrupt majority* and *strongly adaptive* corruptions.

Our work leaves open several exciting directions for future work:

- Recall that Garay et al. [GKKO07] show an $\Omega(\frac{n}{n-f})$ lower bound even for randomized protocols and static corruptions. Our round complexity is $\left(\frac{n}{n-f}\right)^2$ poly log λ assuming that the puzzle's hardness parameter ξ is a constant. Although our round complexity is only polylogarithmic even with, say, 99% corruption, it is an intriguing question whether we can match the elegant lower bound of Garay et al. [GKKO07].
- Another interesting and natural direction is whether we can get rid of cryptographic assumptions such as time-lock puzzles.
- In the honest majority setting, it is long known how to construct expected constant-round protocols even for strongly adaptive adversaries [FM97, KK09, ADD+19]. Therefore, an interesting question is whether we can attain expected constant-round protocols in the corrupt majority setting under strongly adaptive corruptions.
- Finally, as mentioned earlier, it would be interesting to understand how general our current Distribute primitive is, and whether one can devise a general compiler that upgrades any weakly adaptive protocol to a strongly adaptive one while preserving its security.

Acknowledgment. We are extremely grateful to the TCC reviewers for their detailed and insightful comments and suggestions that helped greatly in improving the paper. We are especially grateful to our shepherd Ran Cohen who spent a significant amount of time to help us improve the paper. We acknowledge helpful technical discussions with Kai-Min Chung, Ilan Komargodski, Hoeteck Wee, and Rafael Pass about time-lock puzzles. This work is in part supported by an NSF grant under the award number CNS-1561209, and a Packard Fellowship.

A   Additional Preliminaries

A.1   The Decisional Linear Assumption

Suppose that $\mathcal{G}(1^\lambda)$ is a group generator that samples a bilinear group $(\mathbb{G}, \mathbb{G}_T)$ of prime order p, along with a pairing operation $e : \mathbb{G} \times \mathbb{G} \to \mathbb{G}_T$, and a random generator $g \in \mathbb{G}$. The decisional linear assumption posits that the following two probability ensembles are computationally indistinguishable:

1. Run $\mathcal{G}(1^\lambda)$ to generate a bilinear group $(\mathbb{G}, \mathbb{G}_T)$ of prime order p, along with a pairing operation $e : \mathbb{G} \times \mathbb{G} \to \mathbb{G}_T$, and a random generator $g \in \mathbb{G}$. Sample random x, y, r, s at random from $\mathbb{Z}_p$. Output the tuple $(g, g^x, g^y, g^{xr}, g^{ys}, g^{r+s})$ as well as the group description.
2. Run $\mathcal{G}(1^\lambda)$ to generate a bilinear group $(\mathbb{G}, \mathbb{G}_T)$ of prime order p, along with a pairing operation $e : \mathbb{G} \times \mathbb{G} \to \mathbb{G}_T$, and a random generator $g \in \mathbb{G}$. Sample random x, y, r, s, d at random from $\mathbb{Z}_p$. Output the tuple $(g, g^x, g^y, g^{xr}, g^{ys}, g^d)$ as well as the group description.

A.2 Adaptively Secure Non-interactive Zero-Knowledge Proofs

We use $f(\lambda) \approx g(\lambda)$ to mean that there exists a negligible function $\nu(\lambda)$ such that $|f(\lambda) - g(\lambda)| < \nu(\lambda)$.

A non-interactive proof system henceforth denoted NIZK for an NP language $\mathcal{L}$ consists of the following algorithms.

- crs $\leftarrow$ Gen($1^\lambda, \mathcal{L}$): Takes in a security parameter λ, a description of the language $\mathcal{L}$, and generates a common reference string crs.
- $\pi \leftarrow$ P(crs, stmt, w): Takes in crs, a statement stmt, a witness w such that (stmt, w) $\in \mathcal{L}$, and produces a proof π.
- $b \leftarrow$ V(crs, stmt, π): Takes in a crs, a statement stmt, and a proof π, and outputs 0 (reject) or 1 (accept).

Perfect Completeness. A non-interactive proof system is said to be perfectly complete, if an honest prover with a valid witness can always convince an honest verifier. More formally, for any (stmt, w) $\in \mathcal{L}$, we have that

$$\Pr\left[\text{crs} \leftarrow \text{Gen}(1^\lambda, \mathcal{L}), \ \pi \leftarrow \text{P(crs, stmt, } w) : \text{V(crs, stmt, } \pi) = 1\right] = 1.$$

Non-erasure Computational Zero-Knowledge. Non-erasure zero-knowledge requires that under a simulated CRS, there is a simulated prover that can produce proofs without needing the witness. Further, upon obtaining a valid witness to a statement a-posteriori, the simulated prover can explain the simulated NIZK with the correct witness.

We say that a proof system (Gen, P, V) satisfies non-erasure computational zero-knowledge iff there exist a probabilistic polynomial-time algorithms (Gen$_0$, P$_0$, Explain) such that

$$\Pr\left[\text{crs} \leftarrow \text{Gen}(1^\lambda), \mathcal{A}^{\text{Real(crs,} \cdot, \cdot)}(\text{crs}) = 1\right] \approx \Pr\left[(\text{crs}_0, \tau_0) \leftarrow \text{Gen}_0(1^\lambda), \mathcal{A}^{\text{Ideal(crs}_0, \tau_0, \cdot, \cdot)}(\text{crs}_0) = 1\right],$$

where Real(crs, stmt, w) runs the honest prover P(crs, stmt, w) with randomness r and obtains the proof π, and then outputs (π, r); Ideal(crs$_0$, τ_0, stmt, w) runs the simulated prover $\pi \leftarrow$ P$_0$(crs$_0$, τ_0, stmt, ρ) with randomness ρ and without a witness, and then runs $r \leftarrow$ Explain(crs$_0$, τ_0, stmt, w, ρ) and outputs (π, r).

Perfect Knowledge Extraction. We say that a proof system (Gen, P, V) satisfies perfect knowledge extraction, if there exists probabilistic polynomial-time algorithms (Gen$_1$, Extr), such that for all (even unbounded) adversary $\mathcal{A}$,

$$\Pr\left[\text{crs} \leftarrow \text{Gen}(1^\lambda) : \mathcal{A}(\text{crs}) = 1\right] = \Pr\left[(\text{crs}_1, \tau_1) \leftarrow \text{Gen}_1(1^\lambda) : \mathcal{A}(\text{crs}_1) = 1\right],$$

and moreover,

$$\Pr\left[(\text{crs}_1, \tau_1) \leftarrow \text{Gen}_1(1^\lambda); (\text{stmt}, \pi) \leftarrow \mathcal{A}(\text{crs}_1); w \leftarrow \text{Extr(crs}_1, \tau_1, \text{stmt}, \pi) : \begin{array}{l} \text{V(crs}_1, \text{stmt}, \pi) = 1 \\ \text{but (stmt, } w) \notin \mathcal{L} \end{array}\right] = 0.$$

Theorem A.1 (Instantiation of NIZK [GOS12]). *Assume that the decisional linear assumption holds in suitable bilinear groups. Then, there exists a proof system that satisfies perfect completeness, non-erasure computational zero-knowledge, and perfect knowledge extraction.*

References

[ACD+19] Abraham, I., et al.: Communication complexity of Byzantine agreement, revisited. In: PODC (2019)

[ADD+19] Abraham, I., Devadas, S., Dolev, D., Nayak, K., Ren, L.: Synchronous Byzantine agreement with optimal resilience, expected $o(n^2)$ communication, and expected o(1) rounds. In: Financial Cryptography and Data Security (FC) (2019)

[BBBF18] Boneh, D., Bonneau, J., Bünz, B., Fisch, B.: Verifiable delay functions. In: Shacham, H., Boldyreva, A. (eds.) CRYPTO 2018, Part I. LNCS, vol. 10991, pp. 757–788. Springer, Cham (2018). https://doi.org/10.1007/978-3-319-96884-1_25

[BGJ+16] Bitansky, N., Goldwasser, S., Jain, A., Paneth, O., Vaikuntanathan, V., Waters, B.: Time-lock puzzles from randomized encodings. In: Proceedings of the 2016 ACM Conference on Innovations in Theoretical Computer Science (ITCS), pp. 345–356 (2016)

[Can00] Canetti, R.: Security and composition of multiparty cryptographic protocols. J. Cryptol. **13**(1), 143–202 (2000)

[CCGZ16] Cohen, R., Coretti, S., Garay, J., Zikas, V.: Probabilistic termination and composability of cryptographic protocols. In: Robshaw, M., Katz, J. (eds.) CRYPTO 2016, Part III. LNCS, vol. 9816, pp. 240–269. Springer, Heidelberg (2016). https://doi.org/10.1007/978-3-662-53015-3_9

[CHM+19] Cohen, R., Haitner, I., Makriyannis, N., Orland, M., Samorodnitsky, A.: On the round complexity of randomized Byzantine agreement. In: 33rd International Symposium on Distributed Computing, DISC 2019, Budapest, Hungary, 14–18 October 2019, pp. 12:1–12:17 (2019)

[CL99] Castro, M., Liskov, B.: Practical Byzantine fault tolerance. In: OSDI (1999)

[CMS89] Chor, B., Merritt, M., Shmoys, D.B.: Simple constant-time consensus protocols in realistic failure models. J. ACM **36**(3), 591–614 (1989)

[CPS19a] Hubert Chan, T.-H., Pass, R., Shi, E.: Consensus through herding. In: Ishai, Y., Rijmen, V. (eds.) EUROCRYPT 2019. LNCS, vol. 11476, pp. 720–749. Springer, Cham (2019). https://doi.org/10.1007/978-3-030-17653-2_24

[CPS19b] Hubert Chan, T.-H., Pass, R., Shi, E.: Sublinear-round byzantine agreement under corrupt majority (2019). Online full version of this paper. https://eprint.iacr.org/2019/886

[CPS20] Chan, T.-H.H., Pass, R., Shi, E.: Sublinear-round byzantine agreement under corrupt majority. In: Kiayias, A., Kohlweiss, M., Wallden, P., Zikas, V. (eds.) PKC 2020, Part II. LNCS, vol. 12111, pp. 246–265. Springer, Cham (2020). https://doi.org/10.1007/978-3-030-45388-6_9

[CS20] Chan, B.Y., Shi, E.: Streamlet: textbook streamlined blockchains. Cryptology ePrint Archive, Report 2020/088 (2020). https://eprint.iacr.org/2020/088

[DPS16] Daian, P., Pass, R., Shi, E.: Snow white: robustly reconfigurable consensus and applications to provably secure proofs of stake. Cryptology ePrint Archive, Report 2016/919 (2016)

[DS83] Dolev, D., Raymond Strong, H.: Authenticated algorithms for Byzantine agreement. SIAM J. Comput. - SIAMCOMP **12**(4), 656–666 (1983)

[EFL17] Eckey, L., Faust, S., Loss, J.: Efficient algorithms for broadcast and consensus based on proofs of work. Cryptology ePrint Archive, Report 2017/915 (2017). https://eprint.iacr.org/2017/915

[Fel88] Felman, P.N.: Optimal algorithms for Byzantine agreement. Ph.D. dissertation, MIT (1988)

[FM97] Feldman, P., Micali, S.: An optimal probabilistic protocol for synchronous Byzantine agreement. SIAM J. Comput. **26**, 873–933 (1997)

[FN09] Fitzi, M., Nielsen, J.B.: On the number of synchronous rounds sufficient for authenticated Byzantine agreement. In: Keidar, I. (ed.) DISC 2009. LNCS, vol. 5805, pp. 449–463. Springer, Heidelberg (2009). https://doi.org/10.1007/978-3-642-04355-0_46

[GKKO07] Garay, J., Katz, J., Koo, C.-Y., Ostrovsky, R.: Round complexity of authenticated broadcast with a dishonest majority. In: 48th Annual IEEE Symposium on Foundations of Computer Science (FOCS), November 2007

[GKKZ11] Garay, J.A., Katz, J., Kumaresan, R., Zhou, H.-S.: Adaptively secure broadcast, revisited. In: Proceedings of the 30th Annual ACM SIGACT-SIGOPS Symposium on Principles of Distributed Computing, PODC 2011, pp. 179–186. ACM, New York (2011)

[GKL15] Garay, J., Kiayias, A., Leonardos, N.: The bitcoin backbone protocol: analysis and applications. In: Oswald, E., Fischlin, M. (eds.) EUROCRYPT 2015. LNCS, vol. 9057, pp. 281–310. Springer, Heidelberg (2015). https://doi.org/10.1007/978-3-662-46803-6_10

[GOS12] Groth, J., Ostrovsky, R., Sahai, A.: New techniques for noninteractive zero-knowledge. J. ACM **59**(3), 11:1–11:35 (2012)

[HZ10] Hirt, M., Zikas, V.: Adaptively secure broadcast. In: Gilbert, H. (ed.) EUROCRYPT 2010. LNCS, vol. 6110, pp. 466–485. Springer, Heidelberg (2010). https://doi.org/10.1007/978-3-642-13190-5_24

[KK09] Katz, J., Koo, C.-Y.: On expected constant-round protocols for Byzantine agreement. J. Comput. Syst. Sci. **75**(2), 91–112 (2009)

[KMS14] Katz, J., Miller, A., Shi, E.: Pseudonymous secure computation from time-lock puzzles. IACR Cryptology ePrint Archive 2014:857 (2014)

[KY] Karlin, A., Yao, A.C.-C.: Probabilistic lower bounds for byzantine agreement. Manuscript

[Lam98] Lamport, L.: The part-time parliament. ACM Trans. Comput. Syst. **16**(2), 133–169 (1998)

[LPS17] Lin, H., Pass, R., Soni, P.: Two-round and non-interactive concurrent non-malleable commitments from time-lock puzzles. In: 58th IEEE Annual Symposium on Foundations of Computer Science, FOCS 2017, Berkeley, CA, USA, 15–17 October 2017, pp. 576–587 (2017)

[LSP82] Lamport, L., Shostak, R., Pease, M.: The Byzantine generals problem. ACM Trans. Program. Lang. Syst. **4**(3), 382–401 (1982)

[MVR99] Micali, S., Vadhan, S., Rabin, M.: Verifiable random functions. In: FOCS (1999)

[PS17a] Pass, R., Shi, E.: Hybrid consensus: efficient consensus in the permissionless model. In: DISC (2017)

[PS17b] Pass, R., Shi, E.: Rethinking large-scale consensus. In: 30th IEEE Computer Security Foundations Symposium, CSF 2017, Santa Barbara, CA, USA, 21–25 August 2017, pp. 115–129 (2017)

[PS17c] Pass, R., Shi, E.: Rethinking large-scale consensus (invited paper). In: CSF (2017)

[PS17d] Pass, R., Shi, E.: The sleepy model of consensus. In: Takagi, T., Peyrin, T. (eds.) ASIACRYPT 2017. LNCS, vol. 10625, pp. 380–409. Springer, Cham (2017). https://doi.org/10.1007/978-3-319-70697-9_14

[PSS17]   Pass, R., Seeman, L., Shelat, A.: Analysis of the blockchain protocol in asynchronous networks. In: Coron, J.-S., Nielsen, J.B. (eds.) EUROCRYPT 2017. LNCS, vol. 10211, pp. 643–673. Springer, Cham (2017). https://doi.org/10.1007/978-3-319-56614-6_22

[RSW96]   Rivest, R.L., Shamir, A., Wagner, D.A.: Time-lock puzzles and timed-release crypto. Technical report, USA (1996)

[Sch90]   Schneider, F.B.: Implementing fault-tolerant services using the state machine approach: a tutorial. ACM Comput. Surv. **22**(4), 299–319 (1990)

[WXSD20]   Wan, J., Xiao, H., Shi, E., Devadas, S.: Expected constant round byzantine broadcast under dishonest majority. Cryptology ePrint Archive, Report 2020/590 (2020). https://eprint.iacr.org/2020/590

[YMR+19]   Yin, M., Malkhi, D., Reiter, M.K., Gueta, G.G., Abraham, I.: HotStuff: BFT consensus with linearity and responsiveness. In: Proceedings of the 2019 ACM Symposium on Principles of Distributed Computing (PODC), pp. 347–356. Association for Computing Machinery, New York (2019)

A Lower Bound for One-Round Oblivious RAM

David Cash, Andrew Drucker, and Alexander Hoover[(✉)]

University of Chicago, Chicago, USA
{davidcash,alexhoover}@uchicago.edu, andy.drucker@gmail.com

Abstract. We initiate a fine-grained study of the round complexity of Oblivious RAM (ORAM). We prove that any one-round balls-in-bins ORAM that does not duplicate balls must have either $\Omega(\sqrt{N})$ bandwidth or $\Omega(\sqrt{N})$ client memory, where N is the number of memory slots being simulated. This shows that such schemes are strictly weaker than general (multi-round) ORAMs or those with server computation, and in particular implies that a one-round version of the original square-root ORAM of Goldreich and Ostrovksy (J. ACM 1996) is optimal. We prove this bound via new techniques that differ from those of Goldreich and Ostrovksy, and of Larsen and Nielsen (CRYPTO 2018), which achieved an $\Omega(\log N)$ bound for balls-in-bins and general multi-round ORAMs respectively. Finally we give a weaker extension of our bound that allows for limited duplication of balls, and also show that our bound extends to multiple-round ORAMs of a restricted form that include the best known constructions.

1   Introduction

Oblivious RAM (ORAM), introduced by Goldreich and Ostrovsky [11], is a primitive for hiding access patterns to an array held by an untrusted party. It is of interest in complexity theory, where one is concerned with the power of oblivious RAM programs which access memory in a manner independent of their inputs, and also for applications like outsourcing encrypted data and protecting secure processors against untrusted memory. ORAM has been studied extensively, with many variants which all in some form define an ORAM to be a stateful, secret-keyed algorithm that provides a client-side interface for reading and writing to an array. The algorithm does not have enough state to store the array itself, so it is allowed to interact with a more powerful but untrusted party that can (e.g. a larger physical memory, or a cloud server). For clarity, we refer to this party as a *server*. Security requires that the addresses being read and written to are hidden from the server.

This work concerns *balls-in-bins* ORAMs, which are a restricted form of ORAM that is powerful enough to capture the best-known (optimal) constructions. At a high level such ORAMs obey two constraints: (1) they interact with a server that acts only as a passive array, accepting read and write requests to cells of the array (below we call such servers *array-only*), and (2) the ORAM treats

© International Association for Cryptologic Research 2020
R. Pass and K. Pietrzak (Eds.): TCC 2020, LNCS 12550, pp. 457–485, 2020.
https://doi.org/10.1007/978-3-030-64375-1_16

array values as abstract symbols, only moving them from one cell to another[1]. In particular, we do not consider schemes where the server processes data, such as by applying homomorphic encryption.

Intuitively, ORAMs with an array-only server simulate access to a "virtual" array with N_1 cells for the client by reading and writing to a "physical" array with N_2 cells held at the server, for N_2 usually larger than N_1 ($N_2 = \Theta(N_1 \mathrm{polylog} N_1)$ is typical). They typically work by translating one virtual operation into several physical operations, inserting dummies and shuffling real data to hide the intended addresses of the physical operations. The state can be used to hold some values from the array.

ORAM constructions aim to minimize the (bandwidth) *overhead*, which is defined to be the number of physical operations per virtual operation. A very simple (stateless even) ORAM can work by simply storing the N_1 cells in place at the server, and simulating accesses by scanning the entire array at the server, incurring overhead N_1 (here $N_1 = N_2$). While it is not usually explicitly mentioned, another extreme ORAM can use a large state of N_1 array cells to trivially store the virtual array without any server interaction, achieving zero overhead.

Much research on ORAM has targeted more efficient overhead. In their original work, Goldreich and Ostrovsky gave a more advanced construction with $O(\log^3 N_1)$ overhead, and recent work gave a construction with overhead $O(\log N_1)$ [1,22], which is known to be optimal [18] for ORAMs with array-only servers.

ROUND-COMPLEXITY OF ORAMs. We initiate the detailed study of the *round complexity* of balls-in-bins ORAMs. It has been observed several times that many of the physical operations (i.e., those processed by the array-only server) of ORAMs can be batched together in parallel rather than issued one-at-a-time, as the ORAM is defined to issue those operations independent of their outcomes. (To be more precise, one generalizes the notion of an array-only server to accept batches of array operations; We fix the details later.) Reducing rounds is desirable for efficiency and simplicity of implementation. But in all efficient constructions there appears to be an inherent limit to this type of batching optimization, as ORAMs adapt some of their physical operations based on the outcome of prior physical operations.

The issue of rounds of general, non-balls-in-bins ORAM, has been considered by Williams and Sion [26] and Garg, Mohassel, and Papamanthou [9], who constructed single-round ORAMs that used server computation (i.e. their server is not array-only). The latter work also noted that both of the families of ORAM schemes with poly-logarithmic bandwidth (hierarchical [1,12,14,17,19,22] and tree-based [5,21,24,25]) had $O(\log N_1)$ round complexity, where N_1 is again the number of cells in the virtual array to be simulated.

---

[1] Most of our results require that the balls be moved to exactly one location rather than copied, i.e. do not allow for *duplication* of balls.

OUR CONTRIBUTIONS. This work proves an overhead lower bound for balls-in-bins ORAMs that operate in a single round[2]. It then gives extensions of this result to somewhat more general ORAMs that can store multiple copies of each ball. Finally this work applies the one-round bound to obtain a bound on multi-round balls-in-bins ORAMs of a restricted form that we call "partition-restricted" that captures the best-known bounded-round constructions, showing that they are optimal for ORAMs of this form.

Towards sketching our one-round bound, we observe first that the one-round setting is particularly sensitive to the amount of ORAM state compared to multi-round ORAM. If one is studying $O(1)$-rounds schemes, the state can always be stashed at the server, at the cost of one round, as long as the state size is less than the bandwidth overhead. But in the one-round case (or k-round, for fixed k) we will see that the size of the state is crucially relevant.

Our first main result is an unconditional proof that any one-round balls-in-bins ORAM which does not duplicate balls must either have $\Omega(\sqrt{N_1})$ state or $\Omega(\sqrt{N_1})$ bandwidth overhead. This bound is tight up to logarithmic factors for state, as an optimal construction is a one-round version of the square-root ORAM [11] with $O(\sqrt{N_1} \log N_1)$ state.

Our techniques differ from those of prior ORAM lower bounds, which fall into two categories. The first date back to the original Goldreich and Ostrovsky work, and give bounds on balls-in-bins ORAMs via counting arguments, showing that any particular physical access sequence can only satisfy a bounded number of virtual request sequences. The second comes from a recent line of work initiated by Larsen and Nielsen [18], who proved bounds against general ORAMs via a novel usage of information transfer arguments to show that many consecutive operations must frequently overlap in order to be correct and oblivious.

Our bounds follow intuition similar to the techniques of Larsen and Nielsen, but are for balls-in-bins schemes. At a high level, we show that a one-round requirement and correctness force an ORAM to request overlapping sets of array cells, unless it has $\Omega(\sqrt{N_1})$ client memory or bandwidth. This actually follows from a simple attack but a subtle analysis. Below we first present a simplified version of the bound for ORAM schemes that have almost no client memory (and in particular are only allowed to maintain a program counter). This was the simplest type of ORAM we could find that was non-trivial to bound, and already encapsulates the main difficulties. We then extend our proof to schemes with more client memory. Our version of balls-in-bins schemes does not allow for multiple of copies of balls to be made, but we can give a weaker bound for a bounded number of copies. This latter bound is tight for a constant number of copies, but is loose for larger numbers of copies, becoming trivial if a ball is copied $N_1^{1/4}$ time.

Finally, we sketch how prior ORAMs can be viewed in our formalism for rounds, and show that the square-root ORAM matches our bound. We then

---

[2] In this work, a "round" is interpreted to be a read request for several cells, followed by a write request to several cells; We discuss the motivation for this below. Being permissive on the notion of a round only makes our lower bounds stronger.

observe that for any constant k, a natural "k-th root" version of that ORAM gives a $(k-1)$-round of a special form with $O(kN_1^{1/k})$ overhead and $O(N_1^{1/k})$ state[3]. While we cannot prove anything non-trivial even for two-round ORAM, we can show that these ORAMs fall into a class of "partition-restricted" ORAMs, and are optimal for that class. The observation is simple: Since these ORAMs predictably access only a relatively small region of memory in their first $(k-2)$ rounds, we can view that region as state and collapse them to one-round schemes to which our one-round bound applies.

In the full version, we additionally consider another restricted class of balls-in-bins ORAM that we call *static*. These ORAMs can not move balls between physical cells on the server after writing them, which seems to not have been considered explicitly previously. Intuitively, such ORAMs can be thought of as "balls-in-bins" PIR schemes, and it is possible that one could hope for a weak type of protection (say, for a bounded number of operations, or with some non-negligible security bound). We observe the counting argument of Goldreich and Ostrovsky easily gives a strong bound for unbounded operation sequences, but that our techniques give a sharper bound for concrete parameters and provide a lower bound for bounded operation sequences. For instance, we show that even if a static ORAM is only required to remain oblivious for $N_1 + Q + 1$ operations, it must have overhead or state $\Omega(Q)$, for $Q \leq \sqrt{N_1}$, which follows from proofs similar to our main results. Additionally, we prove that to support an arbitrary number of operations, the ORAM must have overhead or state $\Omega(N_1)$.

RELATED WORK. Goldreich and Ostrovsky were the first to define ORAM and proved the first $\Omega(\log n)$ lower bound for the bandwidth of balls-in-bins ORAMs [11], without any restriction on the number of rounds. Boyle and Naor [2] pointed out some key assumptions in the original proof and asked if they could be overcome. Soon after, Larsen and Nielsen removed the assumptions and obtained the same $\Omega(\log n)$ bound using novel information transfer techniques [18]. After their result, the same bound has been extended with fewer assumptions [15] and to other oblivious data structures [16].

Most of the lower bound work has been on amortized bandwidth and does not consider any restrictions or bounds on round complexity. However, recent work by Chan, Chung, and Shi [3] showed a round lower bound for Oblivious *Parallel* RAM (OPRAM). Showing that any OPRAM must have $\Omega(\log m)$ rounds, where m is the number of processors. OPRAM bounds are distinct from non-parallel ORAM bounds, as they concern the different issue of coordination amongst processors.

Many ORAM constructions have been given in the literature that pay attention to rounds. In their work introducing ORAM, Goldreich and Ostrovsky define a 2-round ORAM as a warm-up for their hierarchical construction [11]. More recently, Goodrich et al. [13] presented a family of constant round ORAM constructions. Several works gave one-round ORAM constructions with server computation [4–10,20,26]. This line of work allows the server holding the data to

---

[3] One can also obtain a similar construction by modifying tree-based ORAMs [23,24] to use $(k-1)$ levels of recursion.

perform some computation as part of the protocol, rather than the server being an array which can only read and write to requested cells. The previous lower bounds for ORAM do not apply to this model, and neither do ours.

ORGANIZATION. Section 2 gives definitions. Sections 3, 4, and 5 give our lower bounds for counter-only, general one-round, and multiple-copy schemes respectively. In Sect. 6 we recall the square root construction and its bounded-round variants in our notation, and finally we conclude with a discussion of open problems in Sect. 7.

2 Preliminaries

ORAM SYNTAX. We give a definition of the ORAM primitive that tailored to the single-round case, and then later extend it to some fixed number of rounds. Our definition most closely follows that of Wang, Chan, and Shi [25], with changes that we discuss below.

We start with an intuitive sketch of Definition 1 below, which is itself quite short. It models a one-round ORAM simulating a virtual array with N_1 cells, with each cell storing a *block* from a set $\mathcal{B}_1$ (e.g. $\mathcal{B}_1 = \{0,1\}^{w_1}$). An ORAM scheme should accept *read operations* (which consist of an address $a \in [N_1]$) and *write operations* (which consist of an address/block pair $(a, d) \in [N_1] \times \mathcal{B}_1$). Correctness requires that in the course of processing a sequence of operations, the last written block written at that address should be returned for read operations (we will formalize this statement later), and obliviousness will require that the addresses a in the sequence are hidden.

The scheme will interact with an array-only server holding a physical array consisting of N_2 cells, each storing a block from the set $\mathcal{B}_2$, which may or may not equal $\mathcal{B}_1$ (parameters with subscripts 1 and 2 will correspond to the virtual array and physical array respectively). The ORAM scheme interacts with the server by sending read and write operations, this time with addresses in $[N_2]$ and blocks in $\mathcal{B}_2$. The server is assumed to always respond correctly. We assume an ORAM comes with associated sets StSp and RSp for the *state space* and *randomness space* respectively. The state space is the set of all possible settings for the data that the ORAM can hold between processing read/operations (so, for example, if StSp $= \mathcal{B}_1^{N_1}$ then the ORAM can hold the entire virtual array and ignore the server entirely). The randomness space will not be restricted or particularly relevant for quantitative bounds but making it explicit (rather than declaring the ORAM has access to a random tape) fixes a sample space on which every random variable is defined. We remark that secret keys can be sampled (and persistently stored) in the randomness space in addition to any coins that may be used.

Our results require a precise definition of rounds for an ORAM. Intuitively, a round should consist of sending a tuple of read/write operations from the ORAM to the server, which applies the writes and then responds with the results of the read operations. Afterwards, the client updates its local state and continues, either with more rounds or by replying for the virtual operation (i.e. outputting a block in $\mathcal{B}_1$ in the case of a read, or simply stopping in the case of a write).

We opt for a definition that is somewhat more permissive by defining a round to consist of a tuple of read operations (below specified by Access) followed by a tuple of write operations and a returned block (both below specified by Out; these may depend on what is returned by the read operations). This version of the definition simplifies the accounting for rounds without weakening our lower bounds.

Definition 1. *Let* $\mathcal{B}_1, \mathcal{B}_2, \mathsf{StSp}, \mathsf{RSp}$ *be sets with* $\perp \in \mathsf{StSp}, \perp \notin \mathcal{B}_1$, *and let* N_1, N_2 *be positive integers. For* $j = 1, 2$ *define the sets*

$$\mathsf{RdOps}_j = [N_j], \quad \mathsf{WrOps}_j = [N_j] \times \mathcal{B}_j, \quad and \quad \mathsf{Ops}_j = \mathsf{RdOps}_j \cup \mathsf{WrOps}_j.$$

A one-round ORAM scheme (with respect to $\mathcal{B}_1, \mathcal{B}_2, N_1, N_2, \mathsf{StSp}, \mathsf{RSp})$ *is a pair of functions* $\mathsf{O} = (\mathsf{Access}, \mathsf{Out})$,

$$\mathsf{Access} : \mathsf{Ops}_1 \times \mathsf{StSp} \times \mathsf{RSp} \to \mathsf{RdOps}_2^*$$
$$\mathsf{Out} : \mathcal{B}_2^* \times \mathsf{Ops}_1 \times \mathsf{StSp} \times \mathsf{RSp} \to (\mathcal{B}_1 \cup \{\perp\}) \times \mathsf{WrOps}_2^* \times \mathsf{StSp}.$$

This models the following usage: A sample from RSp (e.g. keys and a random tape) is chosen and then kept private at the client, and the state is initialized to a canonical value $\perp \in \mathsf{StSp}$. The function Access takes as input a requested virtual operation along with the current state and the randomness, and outputs a list of physical read operations on the server memory. The function Out takes the results of these operations (i.e. the blocks from read operations), the virtual operation being requested, and the state and randomness. Its first output is the result of the operation (either the block resulting from a read, or $\perp$ for a write). Its second output is a set of write operations that should be applied at the server. When we use Out in the games defined in Fig. 1, we write elements in WrOps_2^* as $(\mathsf{wrts}, \mathbf{d}_w)$, which denote the ordered sets of locations and data to write respectively. Finally, Out also outputs an updated state, in preparation for the next operation.

As mentioned before the definition, this syntax is actually somewhat stronger than one-round, since the client is allowed defer its writes until after it sees the results of the reads. The definition of Wang et al. makes a similar choice, where the ORAM is allowed to "piggyback" its interaction with the server between operations, receiving the next operation before being required to output the result of the previous one [25]. Our bounds apply to either model but we found ours simpler. Finally we remark that allowing Access to update the state is unnecessary, as Out gets all of the information available to it.

ORAM CORRECTNESS AND OBLIVIOUSNESS. We next define correctness and obliviousness of an ORAM scheme. In both cases, every definition we are aware of only explicitly considered non-adaptive definitions, where an adversary chooses operations all at once. We give adaptive definitions, and note that standard arguments can separate the adaptive and non-adaptive versions. Our bounds

```
Game G_O^cor(A)

    ω $← RSp
    M₁ ← (⊥)^N₁;  M₂ ← (⊥)^N₂
    st ← ⊥;  WIN ← false
    Run A^RD,WR
    Return WIN

Oracle RD(a)
    rds ← Access(a, st, ω)
    d_r ← M₂[rds]
    (d_out, (wrts, d_w), st) ← Out(d_r, a, st, ω)
    M₂[wrts] ← d_w
    d_ideal ← M₁[a]
    If d_ideal ≠ d_out then WIN ← true
    Return (rds, wrts)

Oracle WR(a, d)
    rds ← Access((a, d), st, ω)
    d_r ← M₂[rds]
    (d_out, (wrts, d_w), st) ← Out(d_r, (a, d), st, ω)
    M₂[wrts] ← d_w
    M₁[a] ← d
    Return (rds, wrts)
```

Fig. 1. Game G_O^{cor} for an ORAM scheme $O = (Access, Out)$.

will ultimately only need a non-adaptive adversary and thus be stronger, but practical constructions should likely aim for the stronger definition.

The correctness definition uses game $G_O^{cor}(A)$ from Fig. 1, which we sketch now. At a high level, it allows the adversary to adaptively request that virtual operations be run, and gets to see the physical addresses touched. The adversary wins if it ever catches the ORAM returning an incorrect block on a read operation.

This game starts by choosing an element of randomness space, and initializes two arrays: M_1 with N_1 cells, and M_2 with N_2 cells. The first array will model the "ideal" virtual array that should be maintained in the course of operation, and the second will hold the physical array that the server would maintain. An initial state is fixed, and the adversary is given access to two oracles, and attempts to trigger a "win" flag.

The first oracle accepts a virtual read operation $a \in RdOps_1$, and the game processes the query by running Access and Out on the appropriate inputs, updating M_2 as a real server would. It also performs the "ideal" virtual read operation on M_1, and sets the win flag if the ideal output differs from what the ORAM output. Finally it returns the addresses from the read and write operations, simulating what a server would see.

The second oracle is similar but processes write operations. It applies the correct write to the ideal array $\mathbf{M}_1$, and also simulates the ORAM running with physical array $\mathbf{M}_2$. It also returns the addresses of the physical operations.

Definition 2. *Let* $\mathsf{O} = (\mathsf{Access}, \mathsf{Out})$ *be a one-round ORAM scheme with respect to* $\mathcal{B}_1, \mathcal{B}_2, N_1, N_2, \mathsf{StSp}, \mathsf{RSp}$, *and let* A *be an adversary. The* correctness *advantage of* A *against* O *is defined to be*

$$\mathbf{Adv}_{\mathsf{O}}^{\mathrm{cor}}(A) = \Pr[\mathbf{G}_{\mathsf{O}}^{\mathrm{cor}}(A) = 1],$$

where $\mathbf{G}_{\mathsf{O}}^{\mathrm{cor}}$ *is defined in Fig. 1. We say that* O *is* perfectly correct *if this advantage is zero for any adversary* A.

Game $\mathbf{G}_{\mathsf{O}}^{\mathrm{obl}\text{-}b}(A)$

   $\omega \xleftarrow{\$} \mathsf{RSp}$
   $\mathbf{M}_2 \leftarrow (\perp)^{N_2}$
   $\mathsf{st} \leftarrow \perp$
   $b' \leftarrow A^{\mathrm{RD}, \mathrm{WR}}$
   Return b'

Oracle $\mathrm{RD}(a_0, a_1)$
   $\mathsf{rds} \leftarrow \mathsf{Access}(a_b, \mathsf{st}, \omega)$
   $\mathbf{d}_r \leftarrow \mathbf{M}_2[\mathsf{rds}]$
   $(d_{\mathrm{out}}, (\mathsf{wrts}, \mathbf{d}_w), \mathsf{st}) \leftarrow \mathsf{Out}(\mathbf{d}_r, a_b, \mathsf{st}, \omega)$
   $\mathbf{M}_2[\mathsf{wrts}] \leftarrow \mathbf{d}_w$
   Return $(\mathsf{rds}, \mathsf{wrts})$

Oracle $\mathrm{WR}((a_0, d_0), (a_1, d_1))$
   $\mathsf{rds} \leftarrow \mathsf{Access}((a_b, d_b), \mathsf{st}, \omega)$
   $\mathbf{d}_r \leftarrow \mathbf{M}_2[\mathsf{rds}]$
   $(d_{\mathrm{out}}, (\mathsf{wrts}, \mathbf{d}_w), \mathsf{st}) \leftarrow \mathsf{Out}(\mathbf{d}_r, (a_b, d_b), \mathsf{st}, \omega)$
   $\mathbf{M}_2[\mathsf{wrts}] \leftarrow \mathbf{d}_w$
   Return $(\mathsf{rds}, \mathsf{wrts})$

Fig. 2. Games $\mathbf{G}_{\mathsf{O}}^{\mathrm{obl}\text{-}b}$, $b = 0, 1$, for an ORAM scheme $\mathsf{O} = (\mathsf{Access}, \mathsf{Out})$.

The obliviousness definition uses games $\mathbf{G}_{\mathsf{O}}^{\mathrm{obl}\text{-}b}(A)$, $b = 0, 1$, from Fig. 2. These are left-right indistinguishability games, where the adversary can now query its oracles with two operations (either both read or both writes). The oracle processes one of the operations, updating a physical array $\mathbf{M}_2$, and returns the physical addresses touched, modeling what a curious server would see.

Definition 3. *Let* $\mathsf{O} = (\mathsf{Access}, \mathsf{Out})$ *be a one-round ORAM scheme with respect to* $\mathcal{B}_1, \mathcal{B}_2, N_1, N_2, \mathsf{StSp}, \mathsf{RSp}$, *and let* A *be an adversary. The* obliviousness *advantage of* A *against* O *is defined to be*

$$\mathbf{Adv}_{\mathsf{O}}^{\mathrm{obl}}(A) = \Pr[\mathbf{G}_{\mathsf{O}}^{\mathrm{obl}\text{-}1}(A) = 1] - \Pr[\mathbf{G}_{\mathsf{O}}^{\mathrm{obl}\text{-}0}(A) = 1].$$

We say that O *is* perfectly oblivious *if this advantage is zero for any adversary* A.

In the obliviousness definition the data written to the physical array is not revealed to the distinguishing adversary. Standard encryption can be applied to upgrade a scheme to a model where data is also hidden. This definition also reveals to the adversary if operations are reads or writes, and implicitly when one operation ends and the next begins (see Hubáček et al. [15], which considered models where this distinction is not revealed).

ORAM RESOURCE MEASURES. We will be interested in the *overhead* and *state size* of an ORAM. We will consider worst-case and amortized overhead.

Definition 4. *Let* $O = (\mathsf{Access}, \mathsf{Out})$ *be a one-round ORAM with respect to* $\mathcal{B}_1, \mathcal{B}_2, N_1, N_2, \mathsf{StSp}, \mathsf{RSp}$. *We say that* O *has* worst-case overhead p *if* Access *and* Out *always output at most p operations. We say that* O *has amortized overhead* p *if for every $Q \geq 0$ and every adversary A issuing Q queries in* $\mathbf{G}_O^{\mathrm{cor}}$, *the total the number of operations returned in oracle queries is at most pQ with probability* 1.

We define the state size *of* O *to be* $\log |\mathsf{StSp}|$.

BALLS-IN-BINS ORAM. Our results will only apply to a restricted class of schemes that handle memory in a symbolic "balls-in-bins" manner. This was originally informally defined by Goldreich and Ostrovsky, and we follow most closely the definition of Boyle and Naor [2].

Definition 5. *Let* $O = (\mathsf{Access}, \mathsf{Out})$ *be a one-round ORAM with respect to* $\mathcal{B}_1, \mathcal{B}_2, N_1, N_2, \mathsf{StSp}, \mathsf{RSp}$. *We say that* O *is* balls-in-bins *if it is of the following special form:*

- $\mathcal{B}_2$ *is the disjoint union of* $\mathcal{B}_1$ *and a set of bitstrings* $\{0,1\}^{w_2}$. *We call the members of* $\mathcal{B}_1$ *balls.*
- StSp *has the form* $\{0,1\}^m \times (\mathcal{B}_1 \cup \{\bot\})^r$. *That is, a state of* O *consists of* m *bits along with an array of r balls/$\bot$ entries. For a state* $\mathsf{st} = (\sigma, \mathbf{reg})$, *the entries in* $\mathbf{reg}$ *are called* registers.
- *The function* Out *satisfies the following:*
  If $\mathsf{Out}(\mathbf{d}_r, (a,d), \mathsf{st}, \omega) = (d_{\mathrm{out}}, \mathsf{wrts}, \mathbf{d}_w, \mathsf{st}')$, *where* $\mathsf{st} = (\sigma, \mathbf{reg})$ *and* $\mathsf{st}' = (\sigma', \mathbf{reg}')$, *then*
    - $\mathbf{reg}'$ *and* $\mathbf{d}_w$ *are formed by moving d and the balls from* $\mathbf{reg}$ *and* $\mathbf{d}_r$, *and then populating their remaining entries with arbitrary non-ball values. (Any ball may be moved to at most one place.)*
    - d_{out} *appears in* $\mathbf{d}_r$ *or* $\mathbf{reg}$.

Intuitively, this definition requires that whenever the ORAM returns a block for a read, the history of that block can be traced back to when it is written, as at each step the ORAM can only move the balls between physical cells and/or registers.

We note that this definition does not allow for copying a ball multiple times, and our main bound does not hold if such copies are allowed. In Sect. 5 we give a relaxed definition and prove a weaker bound in the presence of duplicate balls.

Our warm-up bound will consider even more restricted balls-in-bins ORAMs that maintains almost no state. Restricting the scheme to no state at all is not interesting, as then it cannot even vary its requests as they are repeated. Thus we define a *counter only* scheme to maintain only a program counter of the number of operations performed.

Definition 6. *We say that a one-round ORAM* O *is* counter-only *if it satisfies all of the conditions for a balls-in-bins scheme, except that it has* StSp = $\{0,1\}^*$ *(i.e. no registers), and its state at all times is a simple counter of the number operations run (initialized to zero, and then incremented on each run of* Out*).*

We remark that a counter-only scheme can still have a secret key (say a PRF key, or even a random function), which is modeled in the randomness space. Giving the ORAM a counter allows it to change its operations as time progresses, and non-trivial constructions are possible. For us it has the advantage of forcing the ORAM to behave in a simple combinatorial manner, as at each step the possible physical cells accessed for each operation are fixed once the randomness is fixed.

3 Warm-Up: Lower Bound for Counter-Only Schemes

We first give a bound for the restricted case of counter-only schemes with perfect correctness and perfect obliviousness, and in the next section remove all of these restrictions.

Theorem 1. *Let* O = (Access, Out) *be a counter-only one-round balls-in-bins ORAM scheme with respect to* $\mathcal{B}_1, \mathcal{B}_2, N_1, N_2,$ StSp, RSp. *Assume* $|\mathcal{B}_1| \geq N_1$. *Suppose* O *is perfectly correct, perfectly oblivious, and has worst-case overhead* p. *Then*

$$p \geq C\sqrt{N_1},$$

where C *is an absolute constant.*

Proof. For concreteness we prove the theorem with $C = 0.1$. Let O have the syntax from the theorem, and assume it is perfectly correct and $p < C\sqrt{N_1}$. We construct a non-adaptive randomized adversary A and show that O cannot be perfectly oblivious, i.e. that $\mathbf{Adv}_O^{\mathrm{obl}}(A) > 0$. The adversary works as follows:

1. For $i = 1, \ldots, N_1$, query $\mathrm{WR}((i, b_i), (i, b_i))$, where $b_1, \ldots, b_{N_1}$ are arbitrary distinct balls from $\mathcal{B}_1$. Ignore the responses.
2. Let $T = \sqrt{N_1}$. Choose $J \overset{\$}{\leftarrow} [N_1]^T$, a sequence of T i.i.d. uniform virtual addresses, and query

$$\mathrm{RD}(J[1], J[1]), \ldots, \mathrm{RD}(J[T], J[T]).$$

   Let $\mathsf{rds}_1, \ldots, \mathsf{rds}_T \subseteq [N_2]$ be the physical addresses read for each query.
3. Choose $t \overset{\$}{\leftarrow} [T]$, set $j_0^* \leftarrow J[t]$, and $j_1^* \overset{\$}{\leftarrow} [N_1]$. Query $\mathrm{RD}(j_0^*, j_1^*)$ and let rds^* be the physical addresses read.
4. Output 0 if there exists an address $a \in \mathsf{rds}^*$ that also appears in rds_t but not in any of $\mathsf{rds}_1, \ldots, \mathsf{rds}_{t-1}$. Otherwise output 1.

We claim that

$$\Pr[\mathbf{G}_O^{\text{obl-0}}(A) = 1] \leq 0.2 \tag{1}$$

and

$$\Pr[\mathbf{G}_O^{\text{obl-1}}(A) = 1] \geq 0.9 \tag{2}$$

which together will prove the theorem.

We start with the latter inequality (2), which is intuitively simple; it follows because the read operation for j_1^* can only overlap in the required way (meaning at a "fresh" physical address that was not previously touched) with p of the previous reads, and the random variable t is chosen independently of these overlaps. Formally, condition on ω, J and j_1^*; then t (which is still used in the final step) remains uniform. The set rds^* can overlap at a point a in the required way with at most p of the sets $\text{rds}_1, \ldots, \text{rds}_T$. Thus the probability the adversary will output 0 is bounded by $p/T \leq 0.1$.

Proving (1) is more subtle. We sketch our approach before giving the formal proof. Our plan is to focus on the starting physical position of the "test" ball $b^* = b_{J[t]}$ after step 1 of the adversary, and argue that with good probability this position will work as the address a in step 4, that is, it is accessed for the first time at query t in step 2, and then again in step 3.

To argue that this position is touched for the first time at query t in step 2, we use a counting argument. Since $p < C\sqrt{N_1}$, at most $p(t-1) < CN_1$ balls in total could have been touched in the $t-1$ prior operations. Thus most balls are untouched, remaining where they started. We are picking one at random and thus have a good probability of accessing the starting position of b^* for the first time in the t-th query.

More difficult is arguing that the starting position of b^* is touched again in 3. A counting argument no longer works for b^*, because now b^* *was* previously touched with probability 1 (it is no longer independent), and the ORAM has a chance to move it. At this point perfect correctness and the assumption that O is counter-only combine to come to the rescue. Note that since O is counter-only, once ω and b^* have been chosen, the locations read in step 3 are fixed, independent of the "history" in step 2. The crucial observation is that the starting location of b^* must be read in step 3 if there is *any* history that would leave b^* in its starting place. This is due to perfect correctness, since the ORAM must be correct for that history, even if it is not the one that actually happened! All that remains is to apply another counting argument showing that most balls have a history in which they do not move, and the combine (via a union bound) with the argument about step 2.

Now for the formal proof of (1). We will prove this holds conditioned on any fixed ω, t, and $J[1], \ldots, J[t-1]$; The only remaining choices are $J[t], \ldots, J[T]$, which are still uniform. By our assumption that O is balls-in-bins and has no registers, after the first stage of the adversary we have that every ball $b_1, \ldots, b_{N_1}$ lies in exactly one entry of $\mathbf{M}_2$; Let $q_1, \ldots, q_{N_1} \in [N_2]$ be their respective indices. We will show that with probability at least 0.8 in the conditional space, $a = q_{J[t]}$

satisfies the conditions for outputting 0 in the final step of the adversary. This establishes that 1 is output with probability at most 0.2 in this game.

We do this in two steps, following the sketch. We write $q^* = q_{J[t]}$ for the index of b^* index. We first show that

$$\Pr[q^* \in \mathsf{rds}_t \setminus \bigcup_{k=1}^{t-1} \mathsf{rds}_k] \geq 0.9 \tag{3}$$

and then that

$$\Pr[q^* \in \mathsf{rds}^*] \geq 0.9. \tag{4}$$

(In both cases, the probability is over $J[t] \in [N_1]$ only, the latter because the construction is counter-only.) A union bound gives the claimed 0.8 probability.

We proceed with the first step. Since $J[1], \ldots, J[t-1]$ and ω are fixed, the sets $\mathsf{rds}_1, \ldots, \mathsf{rds}_{t-1}$ are also fixed. We have

$$\Pr[q^* \notin \bigcup_{k=1}^{t-1} \mathsf{rds}_k] \geq 1 - \frac{(t-1)p}{N_1} \geq 0.9,$$

because $J[t]$ is uniform in the conditional space and q^* is thus uniform on a set of size N_1, while the union of the rds_k is of size at most $(t-1)p$. By the perfect correctness and balls-in-bin assumptions on O, we must have that $q^* \in \mathsf{rds}_t$ whenever q^* is not in any of $\mathsf{rds}_1, \ldots, \mathsf{rds}_{t-1}$, because ball b^* will still reside at index q^* of $\mathbf{M}_2$. Thus the event in the probability is actually equivalent to $q^* \in \mathsf{rds}_t \setminus \bigcup_{k=1}^{t-1} \mathsf{rds}_k$, and we have completed (3), the first step in proving (1).

We now prove the second step (4). The argument from the first step does not apply, because the test ball is being read twice (once in the second stage, and then again at the third stage of the adversary). Instead, here we will apply the assumption that O is counter-only and one round (so far everything we have proved would hold with small modifications even if O were an arbitrary multi-round scheme).

The set rds^* is computed by $\mathsf{Access}(J[t], \mathsf{st}, \omega)$ where $\mathsf{st} = N_1 + T + 1$ is the counter. The key observation is that this set must contain q^* if there exists *any* value $\hat{J} \in [N_1]^T$ such that $q^* \notin \bigcup_{k=1}^{T} \mathsf{Access}(\hat{J}[k], N_1 + k, \omega)$. This is true because after these accesses ball b^* would not be touched and hence still reside at index q^*. Thus q^* must be touched by $\mathsf{Access}(J[t], \mathsf{st}, \omega)$ (as O is perfectly correct) in case it has not moved. (Note we have used that O is counter-only here; If it had more state, then the set $\mathsf{Access}(J[t], \mathsf{st}, \omega)$ could change based on the "history", but it can not change when O is counter-only.)

Thus we only need to lower-bound the number of values of $J[t]$ for which there exists $\hat{J} \in [N_1]^T$ such that $q^* \notin \bigcup_{k=1}^{T} \mathsf{Access}(\hat{J}[k], k + N_1, \omega)$. This is easy: Just take some arbitrary choice of $\hat{J}$. The union of their access sets will have size at most $pT \leq 0.1 N_1$, so we get that there are $0.9 N_1$ values for $J[t]$ will work. This establishes (4) and (1).   □

4   Lower Bound for General Balls-in-Bins Schemes

We extend the previous theorem to general balls-in-bins schemes. The step form the previous proof that falls apart is (4), which relied on the final "test" access issued by the scheme to be independently of the request history. This no longer holds when the scheme has state beyond a counter, and indeed state can enable an ORAM to sometimes avoid the repeated test index.

The previous strategy can be made to work even with state. Intuitively, the scheme will not be able to remember "too much" of the history, and so its bounded state can only help avoid the test with a relatively small advantage. We formalize this intuition by bounding, for any state, the number of histories for which a particular state can be used to evade the attack, and ultimately union bound over all possible states.

Theorem 2. Let $O = (\mathsf{Access}, \mathsf{Out})$ be a one-round balls-in-bins ORAM scheme with respect to $\mathcal{B}_1, \mathcal{B}_2, N_1, N_2, \mathsf{StSp}, \mathsf{RSp}$. Assume $|\mathcal{B}_1| \geq N_1 \geq 10^6$. Suppose O has worst-case overhead $1 \leq p < C\sqrt{N_1}$ and state size s and for every adversary A, $\mathbf{Adv}_O^{cor}(A) < 0.001$ and $\mathbf{Adv}_O^{obl}(A) < 0.4$. Then

$$ps \geq CN_1,$$

where C is an absolute constant.

Before giving the proof, we note that this bound is tight up to logarithmic factors for constructions with $p = O(\sqrt{N_1})$, with the matching construction being a modification of the "square-root ORAM" that we recall in Sect. 6. We leave open to determine the optimal state size for constructions with larger p. We also note that $\mathsf{StSp} = \{0,1\}^m \times (\mathcal{B}_1 \cup \{\bot\})^r$ for balls-in-bins ORAM, and for the following proof, we need only assume $m + r \log N_1 < 0.001 N_1 / p$ for a contradiction, which is slightly stronger than the stated result.

Proof. The proof proceeds as before, with the same adversary A, except we have it issue $T = 0.001 N_1 / p$ queries in the second stage. We will show that, if $p < 0.001 \sqrt{N_1}$ and $s < 0.0001 N_1 / p$, then

$$\Pr[\mathbf{G}_O^{obl\text{-}0}(A) = 1] \leq 0.55 \tag{5}$$

and

$$\Pr[\mathbf{G}_O^{obl\text{-}1}(A) = 1] \geq 0.999. \tag{6}$$

The bound (6) is proved exactly as before, so we only need to establish (5). We do so via the same strategy, proving analogues of (3) and (4). Throughout the proof, we assume $\mathsf{StSp} = \{0,1\}^m \times (\mathcal{B}_1 \cup \{\bot\})^r$ because the ORAM is balls-in-bins.

Let $\mathsf{rds}_1, \ldots, \mathsf{rds}_T$ and q^* be defined as before. Then an analogue of (3) holds via a very similar proof; In fact we have

$$\Pr[q^* \in \mathsf{rds}_t \setminus \bigcup_{k=1}^{t-1} \mathsf{rds}_k] \geq 0.997 \tag{7}$$

with our parameters now. The only modification to the argument is we must subtract the correctness error 0.001 and also the probability that the test ball is in one of the registers in StSp. By assumption, $r \leq 0.001N_1$, which gives the bound above.

Thus, proving the theorem is reduced to proving an analogue of (4). Specifically, we prove that

$$\Pr[q^* \in \mathsf{rds}^*] \geq 0.5. \tag{8}$$

Combining (7) and (8) via a union bound establishes (5), showing that O will output 0 with at least probability 0.45.

We now prove (8). This requires analyzing how many balls the ORAM can move from their starting positions while maintaining correctness, so we begin with some definitions to quantify this. We define a function $B(\hat{J}, \hat{\omega})$ which takes as input a tuple $\hat{J} \in [N_1]^T$ and $\hat{\omega} \in \mathsf{RSp}$, and counts the number of balls in $\hat{J}$ that will move during the second stage of the adversary (these are the "bad" balls for our attack). Formally, $B(\hat{J}, \hat{\omega})$ works as follows:

1. Run the game $\mathbf{G}_{\mathsf{O}}^{\mathrm{obl}\text{-}0}(A)$ with $\omega = \hat{\omega}$, until the end of the first stage. At this point, every ball is either in a unique position in $\mathbf{M}_2$, or in a register. Let $q_1, \ldots, q_{N_1}$ be the indexes of the balls in $\mathbf{M}_2$ or $\perp$ if the corresponding ball is in a register.
2. Continue the game, now also using $J = \hat{J}$ until the end of the second stage of the adversary. Let st be the state of O.
3. Output the number of $j \in \hat{J}$ such that $q_j \notin \mathsf{Access}(j, \mathsf{st}, \hat{\omega})$. (This includes j for which $q_j = \perp$.)

We also define related functions:

- $B(\hat{J}, \hat{\omega}, \hat{\mathsf{st}})$ that is exactly the same as B, except it uses the input state $\hat{\mathsf{st}}$ in step 3 instead of the state computed in step 2.
- $B_{\mathrm{all}}(\hat{J}, \hat{\omega})$ that is exactly the same as B, except for the last step, in which case it outputs the count of $j \in [N_1]$ that satisfy the condition (and not just the $j \in \hat{J}$).
- $B_{\mathrm{all}}(\hat{J}, \hat{\omega}, \hat{\mathsf{st}})$ that is B_{all}, except modified to use $\hat{\mathsf{st}}$ as the state in step 3. This function does not depend on $\hat{J}$, as it can be computed by running step 1, and then skipping to step 3.

The latter three functions will be useful for counting the total number of balls that move, not just those in $\hat{J}$ (in the case of B_{all}). The versions with a hard-coded state $\hat{\mathsf{st}}$ will be useful for steps in the proof where we want to argue about the existence of a good state.

It suffices to show that

$$\Pr_{J,\omega}[B(J,\omega) > 0.25T] \leq 1/5. \tag{9}$$

Assuming this, we have

$$
\Pr_{J,\omega,t}[q^* \notin \mathsf{rds}^*] \leq \Pr_{J,\omega,t}[q^* \notin \mathsf{rds}^* | B(J,w) \leq 0.25T]
$$
$$
+ \Pr_{J,\omega,t}[q^* \notin \mathsf{rds}^* \wedge B(J,w) > 0.25T]
$$
$$
\leq 1/4 + \Pr_{J,\omega}[B(J,w) > 0.25T] \leq 1/4 + 1/5 < 1/2.
$$

We now prove (9). Our strategy is to condition on whether or not $B_{\mathrm{all}}(J,\omega)$ is large and handle the cases separately. We have that $\Pr_{J,\omega}[B(J,\omega) > 0.25T]$ is at most

$$
\Pr_{J,\omega}[B_{\mathrm{all}}(J,\omega) > 0.03N_1] + \Pr_{J,\omega}[B(J,\omega) > 0.25T \wedge B_{\mathrm{all}}(J,\omega) \leq 0.03N_1]. \tag{10}
$$

The first term is bounded using Markov's inequality. We assert that for any fixed $\hat{J} \in [N_1]^T$,

$$
\mathbb{E}_{\omega}[B_{\mathrm{all}}(\hat{J},\omega)] \leq r + pT + \varepsilon N_1 \leq 0.003N_1,
$$

where $\varepsilon = \mathbf{Adv}_{\mathsf{O}}^{\mathrm{cor}}(A)$. This expectation is over ω only. This follows because B will count at most r balls from registers, pT balls moved during the second stage, and (in expectation) at most εN_1 balls on which O errs with our adversary. Each of these contribute at most $0.001N_1$ to the expectation. By Markov's inequality, we get that first term of (10) is at most 0.1.

We complete the proof by bounding the second term of (10). For this, we are aiming to show that, that O is unlikely to enter a state where not too many balls have been moved in total and yet many balls from J have been moved. The challenge is that the state depends on J. We will show that any particular state cannot be useful for too many J, and then take a union bound over all states; It is (only) here that use the fact that O does not have a large state space. Intuitively, without such a bound on the state space, the state st, which depends on J, could be chosen so that $B_{\mathrm{all}}(J,\omega) \leq 0.03N_1$ and yet still $B(J,\omega) > 0.25T$, because $0.25T \ll 0.03N_1$.

Formally, we bound the second term for every fixed $\hat{\omega}$. We observe that it is at most

$$
\Pr_{J}[\exists \hat{\mathsf{st}} \in \mathsf{StSp} : B(J,\hat{\omega},\hat{\mathsf{st}}) > 0.25T \wedge B_{\mathrm{all}}(J,\hat{\omega},\hat{\mathsf{st}}) \leq 0.03N_1],
$$

where we have used the versions of B and B_{all} with a hard-coded state as input. We then union bound over $\hat{\mathsf{st}} \in \mathsf{StSp}$, so this probability is at most

$$
\sum_{\hat{\mathsf{st}} \in \mathsf{StSp}} \Pr_{J}[B(J,\hat{\omega},\hat{\mathsf{st}}) > 0.25T \wedge B_{\mathrm{all}}(J,\hat{\omega},\hat{\mathsf{st}}) \leq 0.03N_1].
$$

For a fixed $\hat{\mathsf{st}}$, the probability is at most the chance that at least $0.25T$ of the i.i.d. uniform entries of J land in a pre-determined set of size at most $0.03N_1$

(since ω and st are fixed, $B_{\text{all}}(J, \omega, \text{st})$ is fixed, counting this set, as it does not depend on J). If we denote by X the number of such entries, we have

$$\Pr[X > 0.25T] \leq \Pr[X > 0.03(1 + 7.33)T].$$

By a Chernoff bound this probability is at most

$$\left(\frac{e^{7.33}}{(8.33)^{8.33}}\right)^{0.03T} \leq 0.75^T.$$

Summing over $\hat{\text{st}} \in \text{StSp}$ gives

$$|\text{StSp}| \cdot 0.75^T \leq 2^{0.0001N_1/p} 0.75^{0.001N_1/p} < 0.1$$

for $N_1 \geq 10^6$, because $p < 0.001\sqrt{N_1}$. This completes the bound of the second term of (10). Combining with the bound on the first term completes the proof, giving (9), as desired. $\qquad\square$

4.1   Bound for ORAMs with Amortized Overhead

Theorem 2 only applies to ORAMs with worse-cast overhead, but the ideas extend easily to ORAMs with only amortized overhead. As-is, the attack from the previous theorem cannot handle an amortized adversary; For example, the final test read could have exceptionally high overhead, which would allow for the test set to overlap with many of the previous sets. To work around this, our high-level approach is to have the adversary repeat the reading stage of the attack many times and then choose one at random to test for overlaps. An averaging argument shows that with high probability over this random choice, the chosen stage will not have too much overhead and thus the previous reasoning will apply.

Theorem 3. *Let* $\mathsf{O} = (\mathsf{Access}, \mathsf{Out})$ *be a one-round balls-in-bins ORAM scheme with respect to* $\mathcal{B}_1, \mathcal{B}_2, N_1, N_2, \mathsf{StSp}, \mathsf{RSp}$. *Assume* $|\mathcal{B}_1| \geq N_1 \geq 30 \cdot 10^6$. *Suppose* O *has amortized overhead* $1 \leq p < C\sqrt{N_1}$, *state size* s, *and for every adversary* A, $\mathbf{Adv}_{\mathsf{O}}^{\text{cor}}(A) < 0.001$ *and* $\mathbf{Adv}_{\mathsf{O}}^{\text{obl}}(A) < 0.15$. *Then*

$$ps \geq CN_1,$$

where C *is an absolute constant.*

Proof. We will take $C = 0.001/30$ so that most calculations remain similar to the previous proof. Define an adversary A as follows:

1. For $i = 1, \ldots, N_1$, query $\text{WR}((i, b_i), (i, b_i))$, where $b_1, \ldots, b_{N_1}$ are arbitrary distinct balls from $\mathcal{B}_1$. Ignore the responses.
2. Let $T = CN/p$. For $k = 1, \ldots, N_1$, repeat the following:
   (a) Let $J_k \xleftarrow{\$} [N_1]^T$ and query

$$\text{RD}(J_k[1], J_k[1]), \ldots, \text{RD}(J_k[T], J_k[T]).$$

   Call the sets of physical cells accessed $\mathsf{rds}_1^k, \ldots, \mathsf{rds}_T^k$.

(b) Choose $t_k, t'_k \xleftarrow{\$} [T]$ and $J'_k \xleftarrow{\$} [N_1]^T$. Query

$$\mathrm{RD}(J'_k[1], J'_k[1]), \ldots, \mathrm{RD}(J_k[t_k], J'_k[t'_k]), \ldots, \mathrm{RD}(J'_k[T], J'_k[T]).$$

This is a sequence reading J'_k (on both the left and right), except on one random query, namely the t'_k-th query. There, the attack is using a random entry from J_k on the left as a test. We call the set of physical addresses returned by this operation rds^*_k.

3. Choose $i \xleftarrow{\$} [N_1]$. Output 0 if there exists an address $a \in \mathsf{rds}^*_i$ that also appears in rds^i_t but not in any of $\mathsf{rds}^i_1, \ldots, \mathsf{rds}^i_{t-1}$. Otherwise output 1.

This adversary is based on the same idea as in the two previous proofs. The only differences are that it copies the attack N_1 times and only tests one at random. Notice that this adversary always queries $N_1 + 2TN_1 < 3TN_1$ queries. By the definition of amortized overhead, this means less than $3pTN_1$ operations can be returned across the entire sequence.

Throughout the proof, we use notation $J, J', t, t', \mathsf{rds}_1, \ldots, \mathsf{rds}_T, \mathsf{rds}^*$ for the respective variables at the chosen "test window" i to avoid cluttered indices. The rest of the proof will not need to refer to those values with other indices $k \neq i$.

From here we proceed as the previous proof. Assume $p < C\sqrt{N}$ and $s < 0.1CN_1/p$. We will prove

$$\Pr[\mathbf{G}^{\mathsf{obl}\text{-}0}_{\mathsf{O}}(A) = 1] \le 0.7 \tag{11}$$

and

$$\Pr[\mathbf{G}^{\mathsf{obl}\text{-}1}_{\mathsf{O}}(A) = 1] \ge 0.85. \tag{12}$$

We begin showing (12). Assume everything is fixed but i, t, t'. Then,

$$\Pr_{i,t,t'}[\mathbf{G}^{\mathsf{obl}\text{-}1}_{\mathsf{O}}(A) = 0] \le \Pr_{i,t,t'}[|\mathsf{rds}^*| \ge 30p] + \Pr_{i,t,t'}[\mathbf{G}^{\mathsf{obl}\text{-}1}_{\mathsf{O}}(A) = 0 \,\|\,|\mathsf{rds}^*| < 30p]$$

$$\le 0.1 + 30p/T \le 0.15.$$

The final inequality comes because if $\Pr_{i,t'}[|\mathsf{rds}^*| \ge 30p] > 0.1$, then there are $0.1TN_1$ sets with size at least $30p$, which means the total overhead is at least $3pTN_1 > (2T+1)pN_1$.

Now, we move on to prove (11). We will use the same technique to extend the original proof. First, we will use the same notation defining q^* as as the location of the tested ball in the chosen internal i. Then, we will show

$$\Pr[q^* \in \mathsf{rds}_t \setminus \bigcup_{k=1}^{t-1} \mathsf{rds}_k] \ge 0.8. \tag{13}$$

This follows from a similar argument as before. Define $\varepsilon = \mathbf{Adv}_O^{\mathsf{cor}}(A) < 0.001$.

$$\Pr[q^* \notin \mathsf{rds}_t \setminus \bigcup_{k=1}^{t-1} \mathsf{rds}_k] \leq \Pr[q^* \in \bigcup_{k=1}^{t-1} \mathsf{rds}_k | \left|\bigcup_{k=1}^{t-1} \mathsf{rds}_k\right| < 30Tp]$$

$$+ \Pr[\left|\bigcup_{k=1}^{t-1} \mathsf{rds}_k\right| \geq 30Tp] + \frac{r}{N_1} + \varepsilon N_1$$

$$\leq \frac{30pT}{N_1} + 0.1 + 0.001 + 0.001 \leq 0.15.$$

Otherwise, at least $0.1N_1$ of the repeated attacks would access a total of $3N_1Tp$, which gives a contradiction.

The final part of the previous proof which must be extended is

$$\Pr[q^* \in \mathsf{rds}^*] \geq 0.45.$$

We extend this claim by considering the expectation and probabilities over i in the same way. We have to redefine and extend all the functions based on $B(J, \omega)$ to follow the query pattern of our new adversary. The new functions also must take new inputs i, t', which specify where to stop running and count the balls, exactly analogous to how the adversary chooses where to plant the repeated read. The positions of the balls will now be marked at the beginning of each attack and the functions will count using those positions given i.

The claims will still be true with these analogous definitions except, we must show, for all fixed $\hat{J} \in [N_1]^{2N_1T}$, then with probability 0.9 over the uniformly random choice of i,

$$\mathbb{E}_{\omega,t'}[B_{\mathsf{all}}(\hat{J}, \omega, i, t')] \leq r + 30pT + \varepsilon N_1 \leq 0.003N_1.$$

As has been establish, with probability 0.9 at most $30pT$ balls accessed in any attack interval. Assuming this, the expectation must be at most $0.003N_1$ or else the ORAM will be incorrect with probability more than 0.001 against an adversary in this interval.

Once this is established, we take all other probabilities assuming this expectation use a union bound. This achieves the bound

$$\Pr[B(J, \omega, i, t') > 0.25T] \leq 0.3,$$

which implies,

$$\Pr[q^* \notin \mathsf{rds}^*] \leq 0.55.$$

This concludes the proof of (11), because we output 0 with probability at least $1 - 0.55 - 0.15 = 0.3$.   □

5   Lower Bound for Balls-in-Bins Schemes with Duplicates

The techniques used for the previous proof can be extended to allow the ORAM scheme to have up to D copies of any ball. We start by defining precisely how such an ORAM is allowed to copy balls, and then we extend our previous proof idea to such ORAM schemes.

Current constructions do not make use of duplication. However, it could be an avenue to achieve low overhead for constant round schemes in principle. We prove a lower bound using our same techniques from the previous sections and show for constant duplication, we achieve a similar bound for one-round ORAM.

Unfortunately, our techniques do not give tight bounds against high duplication. For example, our bound is trivial for ORAM copying a single ball $N_1^{0.25}$ times. In our proof technique, we attempt to force the ORAM to overlap two reads on a specific physical address in a special way. When a ball can be located in many locations, the ORAM can often avoid this behavior by accessing the locations of other copies.

Definition 7. *Let* $O = (\mathsf{Access}, \mathsf{Out})$ *be a one-round balls-in-bins ORAM with respect to* $\mathcal{B}_1, \mathcal{B}_2, N_1, N_2, \mathsf{StSp} = \{0,1\}^m \times (\mathcal{B}_1 \cup \{\bot\})^r, \mathsf{RSp}$, *except that we relax the balls-in-bins restriction to allow* Out *to copy balls to multiple locations.*

For a deterministic adversary A *in* $\mathbf{G}_O^{\mathrm{obl\text{-}0}}$, $\mathbf{G}_O^{\mathrm{obl\text{-}1}}$, *or* $\mathbf{G}_O^{\mathrm{cor}}$ *and for every* $b \in \mathcal{B}_1$, *after* A *is finished querying its oracles, define*

$$Q_b(A) = \{i \mid \mathbf{M}_2[i] = b\}$$

and

$$R_b(A) = \{i \mid \mathbf{reg}[i] = b\},$$

where $\mathbf{M}_2$ *is the final server memory state in the game, and* $\mathbf{reg}$ *is the final register state of* O.

We say O *is* D-*duplicate if for all adversaries* A *which query* WR N_1 *times with* N_1 *unique balls in* $\mathbf{G}_O^{\mathrm{obl\text{-}0}}$, $\mathbf{G}_O^{\mathrm{obl\text{-}1}}$, *or* $\mathbf{G}_O^{\mathrm{cor}}$, *and for all* $b \in \mathcal{B}_1$

$$|Q_b(A)| + |R_b(A)| \leq D.$$

Theorem 4. *Let* $O = (\mathsf{Access}, \mathsf{Out})$ *be a one-round* D-*duplicate balls-in-bins ORAM scheme with respect to* $\mathcal{B}_1, \mathcal{B}_2, N_1, N_2, \mathsf{StSp}, \mathsf{RSp}$. *Assume* $|\mathcal{B}_1| \geq N_1 \geq 10^6$ *and* $1 \leq D < 0.5\sqrt{N_1}$. *Suppose* O *has worst-case overhead* $0 < p < C\sqrt{N}/D^2$, *state size* s, *and for every adversary* A, $\mathbf{Adv}_O^{\mathrm{cor}}(A) < 0.001/D$ *and* $\mathbf{Adv}_O^{\mathrm{obl}}(A) < 0.4$. *Then*

$$ps \geq CN_1/D^3,$$

where C *is an absolute constant.*

Proof. This proof proceeds in the same structure as before. Assume for a contradiction that $p < 0.001\sqrt{N_1}/D^2$ and $s < 0.0001N_1/(D^3p)$. We construct an adversary A that works as follows:

1. For $i = 1, \ldots, N_1$, query $\mathrm{WR}((i, b_i), (i, b_i))$, where $b_1, \ldots, b_{N_1}$ are arbitrary distinct balls from $\mathcal{B}_1$. Ignore the responses.
2. Let $T = 0.001N_1/(D^2p) \geq \sqrt{N_1}$. Choose $J \xleftarrow{\$} [N_1]^{DT}$, a sequence of DT i.i.d. uniform virtual addresses. For $i = 1, \ldots, D$, choose $t_i \xleftarrow{\$} [(i-1)T+1, \ldots, iT]$. Define $j_0^* = J[t_1]$.

3. For $k = 1, \ldots, DT$, if $k = t_i$ for some i then query

$$\text{RD}(j_0^*, J[k]),$$

and otherwise query

$$\text{RD}(J[k], J[k]).$$

Let $\text{rds}_1, \ldots, \text{rds}_{DT} \subseteq [N_2]$ be the physical addresses read for each query.

4. Let $j_1^* \xleftarrow{\$} [N_1]$ and $t_{D+1} = TD + 1$. Query $\text{RD}(j_0^*, j_1^*)$ and let $\text{rds}_{t_{D+1}}$ be the addresses read.

5. Output 0 if there exists a pair of indices $i, j \in [D+1]$ with $i < j$ and an address $a \in \text{rds}_{t_j}$ that also appears in rds_{t_i} but not in any of $\text{rds}_1, \ldots, \text{rds}_{t_i-1}$. Otherwise output 1.

This attack follows a similar structure as those outlined in previous sections. However, it accesses the targeted ball $D + 1$ times total. Intuitively, we are showing that each of these accesses must touch one of the D initial locations of the balls. If that is true, then there is some pair which accesses the same location by the pigeonhole principle. This pair is identified be the adversary with high probability and that gives our advantage.

We claim that

$$\Pr[\mathbf{G}_O^{\text{obl-0}}(A) = 1] \leq 0.55 \tag{14}$$

and

$$\Pr[\mathbf{G}_O^{\text{obl-1}}(A) = 1] \geq 0.999 \tag{15}$$

which prove the theorem.

We prove similar claims to the previous proofs, but will need to make a pigeonhole argument as well. For a fixed random string ω, by definition O is has at most D duplicates of any ball and has no registers, after the first stage of the adversary we have that every ball $b_1, \ldots, b_{N_1}$ lies in at most D entry of $\mathbf{M}_2$; Let $Q_1, Q_2, \ldots, Q_{N_1} \subseteq [N_2]$ be the sets of their respective indices, each with size at most D.

We begin by proving (14). First, we show

$$\Pr[|Q_{j_0^*} \cap \text{rds}_{t_1}| \geq 1] \geq 0.997, \tag{16}$$

which follows from arguments used in previous proofs. There are at most pT accesses before t_1, only r registers, and O can error on only ε fraction of the inputs. Therefore, over the random choice of t_1, which is independent from previous accesses. None of the at most D balls were touched prior to this access with probability at most $D(pT + r + \varepsilon N_1)/N_1 \leq 0.003$.

We will prove that for every $2 \leq i \leq D + 1$,

$$\Pr[|Q_{j_0^*} \cap \text{rds}_{t_i}| \geq 1] \geq 1 - \frac{0.5}{D} \tag{17}$$

which together with (16) proves that there is some index q^* that lies in two different reads t_i and t_j with probability 0.497 using a union bound.

Then, given this q^*, i and j exists, we will prove, for the smallest pair $i < j$ with the desired overlap,

$$\Pr[q^* \in \mathsf{rds}_{t_i} \setminus \bigcup_{k=1}^{t_i-1} \mathsf{rds}_k] \geq 0.997, \tag{18}$$

which finishes the proof for Eq. (14).

Now we shift our focus to prove Eq. (17) which requires the proof techniques used in the previous extension. We redefine the function $B(\hat{J}, \hat{\omega})$ for this new setting, so it can take in a sequence of variable length $\hat{J} \in [N_1]^{\leq DT}$ and $\hat{\omega} \in \mathsf{RSp}$. Let $\hat{J}$ be length k, then B works as follows:

1. Run the game $\mathbf{G}_\mathsf{O}^{\mathsf{obl\text{-}0}}(A)$ with $\omega = \hat{\omega}$, $J = \hat{J} \times \perp^{DT-k}$, until the end of the first stage. At this point, every ball is in some set of indices in $\mathbf{M}_2$, or in a register. Let $Q_1, \ldots, Q_{N_1}$ be the sets of indices of the balls $b_1, \ldots, b_{N_1}$ respectively in $\mathbf{M}_2$.
2. Continue the game for another k queries (i.e. $\hat{J}$ is finished). Let st be the state of O.
3. Output the number of $j \in \hat{J}$ such that $|Q_j \cap \mathsf{Access}(j, \mathsf{st}, \omega')| = 0$.

Similarly, we redefine $B(\hat{J}, \hat{\omega}, \hat{\mathsf{st}})$, $B_{\mathsf{all}}(\hat{J}, \hat{\omega})$, and $B_{\mathsf{all}}(\hat{J}, \hat{\omega}, \hat{\mathsf{st}})$ with the updated check condition at the end. Even with this redefinition, it suffices to show, for every $i \geq 2$,

$$\Pr_{J,\omega}[B(J, \omega) > 0.25t_i] \leq 0.2/D. \tag{19}$$

Assuming this, we have for any fixed $i \geq 2$,

$$\begin{aligned}
\Pr_{J,\omega,t}[|Q_{j_0^*} \cap \mathsf{rds}_i| = 0] &\leq \Pr_{J,\omega,t}[|Q_{j_0^*} \cap \mathsf{rds}_i| = 0 \wedge B(J, w) \leq 0.25t_i] \\
&\quad + \Pr_{J,\omega,t}[|Q_{j_0^*} \cap \mathsf{rds}_i| = 0 \wedge B(J, w) > 0.25t_i] \\
&\leq 0.25/D + \Pr_{J,\omega}[B(J, w) > 0.25t_i] \\
&\leq 0.25/D + 0.2/D < 0.5/D.
\end{aligned}$$

In this probability, we note that J is taken according to the distribution that A submits to to the left part of its oracles up to rds_{t_i} which is independently random outside of the locations $t_1, \ldots, t_{i-1}$.

First, we bound (19), by conditioning on the size of $B_{\mathsf{all}}(J, \omega)$. We have that $\Pr_{J,\omega}[B(J, \omega) > 0.25t_i]$ is at most

$$\Pr_{J,\omega}[B_{\mathsf{all}}(J, \omega) > 0.03N_1] + \Pr_{J,\omega}[B(J, \omega) > 0.25t_i \wedge B_{\mathsf{all}}(J, \omega) \leq 0.03N_1]. \tag{20}$$

The first term is bounded using Markov's inequality. We assert that for any fixed $\hat{J} \in [N_1]^{\leq DT}$,

$$\mathbb{E}_\omega[B_{\mathsf{all}}(\hat{J}, \omega)] \leq r + pDT + \varepsilon N_1 \leq 0.003N_1/D,$$

where $\varepsilon = \mathbf{Adv}_O^{\mathrm{cor}}(A)$. Just as before, this follows because B will count at most r balls from registers, pDT balls moved during the second stage, and (in expectation) at most εN_1 balls on which O errs with our adversary. Each of these contribute at most $0.001N_1/D$ to expectation. By Markov's inequality, we get that first term of (20) is at most $0.1/D$.

We complete the proof by bounding the second term of (20), in a similar way to before. Intuitively, since the entries of J are distributed according to A, for a set $\hat{\mathrm{st}}$ this is the probability that at least $0.25t_i$ of its entries land in a pre-determined set of size at most $0.03N_1$, or equivalently a tail bound on flipping a biased coin $t_i - i$ times. We subtract i, because $i - 1$ values are the same. So, long as 0.25 of the remaining values are covered by $B(J,\omega)$, then 0.25 of all the values will be covered, giving us an upper bound. Formally, upper bound with an existential quantifier over the state and union bound as in the previous section, but we omit the details here.

Take the probability of heads to be 0.03, and let X be the total number of heads seen after t_i independent coin flips. Then, we have, for a fixed $\hat{\omega}$ and fixed $\hat{\mathrm{st}}$,

$$\Pr_J[B(J,\hat{\omega},\hat{\mathrm{st}}) > 0.25(t_i - i)] \leq \Pr[X > 0.25(t_i - D)]$$

$$\leq \Pr[X > (1 + 7.33)0.03(t_i - D)].$$

Using a Chernoff bound, this probability is at most

$$\left(\frac{e^{7.33}}{(8.33)^{8.33}}\right)^{0.03(t_i - D)} \leq 0.75^{(t_i - D)} \leq 0.75^{T-D}.$$

Then, a union bound of all states gives us our final requirement,

$$|\mathsf{StSp}| \cdot 0.75^{(T-D)} \leq 2^{0.0001N_1/(D^3 p)}0.75^{0.001N_1/(D^2 p)-D} < 0.1$$

when $D < 0.5\sqrt{N_1}$ and $N_1 \geq 10^6$. This concludes the proof of (17).

We show (18) next. Fix q^*, i and j as before. Then,

$$\Pr[q^* \in \mathsf{rds}_{t_i} \setminus \bigcup_{k=1}^{t_i-1} \mathsf{rds}_k] \geq 1 - \varepsilon - \frac{(p+r) \cdot (t_i - 1)}{N_1} \geq 0.997$$

because O can error on a most ε faction of the inputs, and there are at most $(p+r) \cdot (t_i - 1)$ balls touched before t_i is read. Also, t_i and thus q^* is uniform and independent from all other reads except for t_k when $k < i$. However, if $q^* \in t_k$ from some k, then we would have taken t_k and t_i as the pair to fix instead. Together with (17) this proves (14).

To prove (15), we condition on ω, J and j_1^*, then the each of the sets rds_{t_j} can overlap with at most p of the $(j - 1)T$ previous sets in the desired way. Summing over all possible endpoints shows the probability of outputting 0 is bounded by $Dp/T < 0.001$, which proves 1 is output with probability at least 0.999, completing the proof of the theorem. $\square$

6 Constant-Round ORAM

We define k-round ORAM in our notation and then review (within our formalism) the "square-root construction" given in the original paper on Oblivious RAM by Goldreich and Ostrovsky [11]. We will also present an $O(kN_1^{1/k})$-overhead construction using k-rounds which can be seen as a middle ground between the square-root and hierarchical constructions. A similar construction was given by Goodreich et al. [13], which explores constant round ORAM as an extension of the square root construction for all constants. However, the number of rounds is less explicit than the construction we present.

We then prove a simple corollary of Theorem 2, which shows the constant-round $O(kN_1^{1-1/k})$-overhead constructions are optimal up to logarithmic factors for a restricted class of ORAM we call "partition-restricted" ORAM. This restriction requires that the reads of all rounds except the last fall into a relatively small, pre-determined zone of physical memory. We then note that the given constant-round constructions have this property, but that it does not extend to logarithmic round constructions which do not respect this restriction. This corollary suggests that to achieve better overhead performance for constant rounds, would require new techniques in ORAM constructions.

CONSTANT ROUND ORAM DEFINITIONS. The k-round definition we give is a natural extension of the one-round definition. We aim for a simple and permissive definition, so we allow the ORAM to issue a sequence of k reads. After each read, the results are accumulated before the final round, which produces the writes and the operation output. We note that allowing writes in the intervening rounds would not strengthen the ORAM, as they can always be deferred without increasing bandwidth in our model.

We remark that other definitions are not typically so permissive. In practice, one would need to store the read results in the ORAM memory which often needs to be small.

Definition 8. *Let* $\mathcal{B}_1, \mathcal{B}_2, \mathsf{RSp}, \mathsf{StSp}$ *be sets, and* N_1, N_2 *be positive integers. For* $j = 1, 2$ *define the sets*

$$\mathsf{RdOps}_j = [N_j], \quad \mathsf{WrOps}_j = [N_j] \times \mathcal{B}_j, \quad and \quad \mathsf{Ops}_j = \mathsf{RdOps}_j \cup \mathsf{WrOps}_j.$$

A k-round ORAM scheme *(with respect to* $\mathcal{B}_1, \mathcal{B}_2, N_1, N_2, \mathsf{StSp}, \mathsf{RSp}$*) is a tuple of functions* $\mathsf{O} = (\mathsf{Access}_1, \ldots, \mathsf{Access}_k, \mathsf{Out})$,

$$\mathsf{Access}_i : \mathcal{B}_2^* \times \mathsf{Ops}_1 \times \mathsf{StSp} \times \mathsf{RSp} \to \mathsf{RdOps}_2^* \quad (i = 1, \ldots, k)$$
$$\mathsf{Out} : \mathcal{B}_2^* \times \mathsf{Ops}_1 \times \mathsf{StSp} \times \mathsf{RSp} \to (\mathcal{B}_1 \cup \{\bot\}) \times \mathsf{WrOps}_2^* \times \mathsf{StSp}.$$

We next adapt the correctness and obliviousness definitions to constant-round ORAM. We use the definitions and their associated games as-is, except that in the games we redefine the notation Access to mean the following algorithm, for $\mathsf{op} \in \mathsf{Ops}_1, \mathsf{st} \in \mathsf{StSp}, \omega \in \mathsf{RSp}$:

$$\frac{\mathsf{Access}(\mathsf{op}, \mathsf{st}, \omega)}{\mathbf{d}_r \leftarrow \perp}$$

For $i = 1, \ldots, k$:

    rds $\leftarrow$ rds $\cup$ $\mathsf{Access}_i(\mathbf{d}_r, \mathsf{op}, \mathsf{st}, \omega)$

    $\mathbf{d}_r \leftarrow \mathbf{M}_2[\mathsf{rds}]$

Return rds.

This models the accumulated reads mentioned above, where each Access_i gets to see the output of reads for $\mathsf{Access}_1, \ldots, \mathsf{Access}_{i-1}$. The games then provide Out with *all* of the accumulated read results, exactly as specified in their code. The rest of the games are exactly the same.

The state size of a k-round ORAM is measured exactly as before. For worst-case and amortized overhead, we use the same definitions, but with the version of Access defined above.

A VERSION OF THE SQUARE-ROOT ORAM. The square-root construction of Goldreich and Ostrovsky is usually described as a multi-round ORAM with no state. Here we show that it can be viewed as an amortized one-round scheme with larger state that matches our lower bounds. Below we extend this to a family of constant-round schemes. As the ideas are very standard in the ORAM literature, we omit the full details.

The ORAM works with an arbitrary set of balls $\mathcal{B}_1$ and virtual memory size N_1, and with physical memory of $N_2 = N_1 + \sqrt{N_1}$ cells with $\mathcal{B}_2 = \mathcal{B}_1$. The randomness space is defined so that an unbounded sequence of random permutations π on $[N_2]$ can be generated[4]. The state of the ORAM consists of a counter st.c (initially 0, and always between 0 and $\sqrt{N_1}$) and a tuple st.Cache of at most $\sqrt{N_1}$ virtual-address/ball pairs.

The ORAM maintains the physical array to hold the N_1 balls at physical addresses $\pi(1), \ldots, \pi(N_1)$, with virtual address a stored at physical address $\pi(a)$, where π is the current random permutation. The physical addresses $\pi(N_1 + 1), \ldots, \pi(N_1 + \sqrt{N_1})$ will be "dummies", which are accessed to cover for when the same virtual address been accesses multiple times. The ORAM stores in st.Cache the virtual-address/ball pairs involved in the most recent $\sqrt{N_1}$ operations. To process a read operation, if the requested virtual address a is not in the cache, then ORAM accesses the ball at physical address $\pi(a)$. If on the other hand a is stored in the cache, then the ORAM accesses the next dummy, namely $\pi(N_1 + \mathsf{st}.c)$. After retrieval, balls are held in the cache. After $\sqrt{N_1}$ operations, the cache may be full, so the ORAM downloads the entire physical memory, samples a fresh π, and places the balls in the physical memory according to π.

This ORAM is perfectly oblivious: Independent of the addresses, the ORAM will access random distinct physical addresses for at most $\sqrt{N_1}$ reads (or no addresses for writes), followed by a reads and writes to all N_2 physical cells. It

---

[4] To be totally rigorous in our formalism, one needs to give the ORAM the ability to remember which permutation π in the sequence is being used, e.g. by providing an unbounded counter that does not count as state.

has amortized overhead $p = (\sqrt{N_1} + (N_1 + \sqrt{N_1}))/N_1 = O(\sqrt{N_1})$ and a state with $m = \log N_1$ bits and $r = \sqrt{N_1}$ registers, making it tight for Theorem 2 up to logarithmic factors.

k^{th}-ROOT ORAM CONSTRUCTION. The ideas in the square-root ORAM generalize to give a $k - 1$-round construction with amortized overhead $O(kN_1^{1/k})$ and state size $O(N_1^{1/k})$. This construction is simply a re-parameterization of the well-known hierarchical ORAM of Goldreich and Ostrovsky [11], adjusted to a constant number of levels, so we only sketch the construction, assuming their construction is familiar.

The ORAM holds in its state a cache containing at most $N^{1/k}$ virtual-address/ball pairs. At the physical memory, it maintains $k-1$ "levels", which are regions of physical memory. Level i consists of $O(\log(\frac{1}{\varepsilon})N_1^{(i+1)/k})$ cells storing a hash table capable of holding $N_1^{(i+1)/k}$ balls, except with probability ε, which we consider an independent error parameter. Thus the final $(k - 1)$-th layer can hold N_1 balls.

An access happens over $k-1$ rounds. Initially it the ORAM checks the cache, and remembers if the requested virtual address is found or not. Then in the i-th round, the hash table on level i is to be accessed. If the ball has not yet been found, then the table is accessed at the points determined by the hash function for that level. If the ball has been found then a dummy is accessed. Eventually the ball is found and added to the cache (and in the case of writes the ORAM just add them directly).

Eventually the cache will overflow, so the ORAM periodically rebuilds the hash tables according to a schedule that also ensures none of the levels overflow. Namely, after $N_1^{i/k}$ operations, levels $1, \ldots, i$ are downloaded and all of the balls they contain are stored in a rebuilt table on level i. (In our setting we again avoid the complexity of using oblivious sorts; We allow ORAMs to simply to rebuild locally and upload the tables.)

This completes the sketch of the kth-root ORAM. It has state size $O(N_1^{1/k})$ and overhead $O(kN_1^{1/k})$. We can calculate the overhead by observing that after $N_1^{i/k}$ operations, the ORAM performs a rebuild requiring $O(N_1^{(i+1)/k})$ operations. Thus after N_1 operations, this type of rebuild will accumulate a total cost of $O(N_1^{1-i/k} \cdot N_1^{(i+1)/k}) = O(N_1^{1+1/k})$ physical operations. This amortizes to $O(N_1^{1/k})$ overhead, and summing over k gives $O(kN_1^{1/k})$.

BOUND FOR RESTRICTED k-ROUND ORAM. We now partially address the question of whether the kth-root ORAMs are optimal. Our one-round bounds of course do not apply, and adapting them appears to be non-trivial. Instead, we observe that these ORAMs obey a simple restricted property, and then prove that the kth-root ORAM is optimal amongst multi-round ORAMs with this property.

We call this property *partition-restricted*. Intuitively, a multi-round ORAM is ℓ-*partition-restricted* if all of its rounds always access some predetermined regions of ℓ physical cells. For example, the kth-root ORAM is ℓ-partition-restricted for

$\ell = O(N_1^{1-1/k})$, as the first $k - 2$ rounds will access tables of that size or less (recall the kth-root ORAM has $k - 1$ rounds total).

For such ORAMs we make a simple observation: One can move the physical memory of the first $(k - 2)$ rounds into the state of the ORAM, and transform it into a one-round ORAM to which our bound applies.

Definition 9. *Let* $\mathsf{O} = (\mathsf{Access}, \mathsf{Out})$ *be a* k-*round ORAM scheme with respect to* $\mathcal{B}_1, \mathcal{B}_2, N_1, N_2, \mathsf{StSp} = \{0, 1\}^m \times (\mathcal{B}_1 \cup \{\bot\})^r, \mathsf{RSp}$ *We say that* O *is* ℓ-*partition-restricted if there exists a set* $P \subseteq [N_2]$ *of size at most* ℓ *such that for every input* $(\mathbf{d}_r, \mathsf{op}, \mathsf{st}, \omega)$ *and* $i = 1, \ldots, k - 1$ *we have* $\mathsf{Access}_i(\mathbf{d}_r, \mathsf{op}, \mathsf{st}, \omega) \subseteq P$.

We now show that ℓ-partition-restricted multi-round ORAMs reduce to one-round ORAMs.

Corollary 1. *Let* $\mathsf{O} = (\mathsf{Access}, \mathsf{Out})$ *be a* k-*round balls-in-bins ORAM scheme with respect to* $\mathcal{B}_1, \mathcal{B}_2, N_1, N_2, \mathsf{StSp}, \mathsf{RSp}$. *Assume* $|\mathcal{B}_1| \geq N_1 \geq 30 \cdot 10^6$ *and* $\mathcal{B}_2 = \mathcal{B}_1 \cup \{\bot\}$. *Suppose* O *has amortized overhead* $1 \leq p < C\sqrt{N_1}$, *state size* s, O *is partition-restricted to* ℓ *server cells, and for every adversary* A, $\mathbf{Adv}_{\mathsf{O}}^{\mathrm{cor}}(A) < 0.001$ *and* $\mathbf{Adv}_{\mathsf{O}}^{\mathrm{obl}}(A) < 0.15$. *Then*

$$p(s + \ell \log N_1) \geq CN_1,$$

where C *is an absolute constant.*

This corollary proves that the kth-root is optimal up to logarithmic factors for this restricted class of ORAM. It is notable that this bound is actually independent of the number of rounds the ORAM uses. It only requires that all but the final access are restricted. This means the registers of the client can be outsourced on the server and read as an additional round. So, we assume there are no registers in StSp and achieve the same bound.

Proof. Assume for a contradiction that $(s + \ell \log N_1) < CN_1/p$. Then, we can construct a one-round ORAM O' with state space $\mathsf{StSp}' = \mathsf{StSp} \times (\mathcal{B}_1 \cup \{\bot\})^\ell$. Since O is partition-restricted to ℓ server cells there is a set P which can capture the first $k - 1$ access. The new ORAM O' simulates O but whenever O reads or writes to the set P, O' simulates this by reading or writing to the ℓ extra registers in StSp'. Because the first $k - 1$ accesses will always read from P, O' only requires accessing the server to simulate the final access, making it one-round.

Notice that $\max_A \mathbf{Adv}_{\mathsf{O}'}^{\mathrm{cor}}(A) \leq \max_A \mathbf{Adv}_{\mathsf{O}}^{\mathrm{cor}}(A)$ and $\max_A \mathbf{Adv}_{\mathsf{O}'}^{\mathrm{obl}}(A) \leq \max_A \mathbf{Adv}_{\mathsf{O}}^{\mathrm{obl}}(A)$. This follows because any adversary against O' can ignore all accesses before the final access and have the same advantage against O.

Since O' is one-round, $p(s + \ell \log N_1) < C \cdot N_1$, and $1 \leq p < C\sqrt{N_1}$ this contradicts Theorem 3.   ☐

7   Conclusion and Open Problems

Lower bounds for ORAM schemes have been largely focused on bandwidth cost for ORAM with an unrestricted number of rounds and constant client memory.

However, there are still open questions when schemes are restricted to have a fixed number of rounds.

We prove near-optimal results for one-round ORAM with large client memory in this paper. However, it is possible that do not we have a tight bound for one-round ORAM with constant client memory. It seems likely that one-round ORAM with constant memory should require $\Omega(N_1)$ overhead.

There is the problem of extending our work out of the balls-in-bins model. Our techniques do not immediately give lower bounds in an information theoretic model for ORAM, but possibly could be extended with techniques similar to those used by Larsen and Nielsen [18]. Many of the proof steps extend to equivalent statements with compression arguments, however it is unclear how to extend Eq. (8) to the information theoretic setting.

This issue is related to an issue which arose with bounded duplicate ORAM. If we bound the duplication, the proof extends but gets weakens significantly. We are unaware of any duplicate balls-in-bins ORAM constructions that match our bound, and it seems likely the loss to duplicates is an artifact of the proof.

Extension beyond partition-restricted to two-round or even an arbitrary k-round is still open. One might hope that the k-round construction from Sect. 6 is tight up to poly-log factors and that the true lower bound for k-round is $\Omega(kN_1^{1/k})$ with constant client memory.

Acknowledgements. We thank the anonymous referees for many suggestions on improving the presentation of this paper. The first and third authors were supported in part by NSF CNS-1928767.

References

1. Asharov, G., Komargodski, I., Lin, W.-K., Nayak, K., Peserico, E., Shi, E.: OptORAMa: optimal oblivious RAM. In: Canteaut, A., Ishai, Y. (eds.) EURO-CRYPT 2020. LNCS, vol. 12106, pp. 403–432. Springer, Cham (2020). https://doi.org/10.1007/978-3-030-45724-2_14

2. Boyle, E., Naor, M.: Is there an oblivious RAM lower bound? In: Sudan, M., (ed.) ITCS 2016: 7th Conference on Innovations in Theoretical Computer Science, pp. 357–368, Association for Computing Machinery, Cambridge, 14–16 January 2016

3. Chan, T.-H.H., Chung, K.-M., Shi, E.: On the depth of oblivious parallel RAM. In: Takagi, T., Peyrin, T. (eds.) ASIACRYPT 2017. LNCS, vol. 10624, pp. 567–597. Springer, Cham (2017). https://doi.org/10.1007/978-3-319-70694-8_20

4. Dautrich Jr., J.L., Stefanov, E., Shi, E.: Burst ORAM: minimizing ORAM response times for bursty access patterns. In: Fu, K., Jung, J. (eds.) USENIX Security 2014: 23rd USENIX Security Symposium, pp. 749–764, USENIX Association, San Diego, 20–22 August 2014

5. Devadas, S., van Dijk, M., Fletcher, C.W., Ren, L., Shi, E., Wichs, D.: Onion ORAM: a constant bandwidth blowup oblivious RAM. In: Kushilevitz, E., Malkin, T. (eds.) TCC 2016. LNCS, vol. 9563, pp. 145–174. Springer, Heidelberg (2016). https://doi.org/10.1007/978-3-662-49099-0_6

6. Fletcher, C., Naveed, M., Ren, L., Shi, E., Stefanov, E.: Bucket ORAM: single online roundtrip, constant bandwidth oblivious RAM. Cryptology ePrint Archive, Report 2015/1065 (2015). http://eprint.iacr.org/2015/1065

7. Garg, S., Lu, S., Ostrovsky, R.: Black-box garbled RAM. Cryptology ePrint Archive, Report 2015/307 (2015). http://eprint.iacr.org/2015/307

8. Garg, S., Lu, S., Ostrovsky, R., Scafuro, A.: Garbled RAM from one-way functions. In: Servedio, R.A., Rubinfeld, R. (eds.) 47th Annual ACM Symposium on Theory of Computing, pp. 449–458. ACM Press. Portland, 14–17 June 2015

9. Garg, S., Mohassel, P., Papamanthou, C.: TWORAM: Efficient oblivious RAM in two rounds with applications to searchable encryption. In: Robshaw, M., Katz, J. (eds.) Advances in Cryptology, CRYPTO 2016, Part III, LNCS, vol. 9816, pp. 563–592, Santa Barbara, 14–18 August 2016. Springer, Heidelberg (2016). https://doi.org/10.1007/978-3-662-53015-3_20

10. Gentry, C., Halevi, S., Lu, S., Ostrovsky, R., Raykova, M., Wichs, D.: Garbled RAM revisited. In: Nguyen, P.Q., Oswald, E. (eds.) EUROCRYPT 2014. LNCS, vol. 8441, pp. 405–422. Springer, Heidelberg (2014). https://doi.org/10.1007/978-3-642-55220-5_23

11. Goldreich, O., Ostrovsky, R.: Software protection and simulation on oblivious RAMs. J. ACM **43**(3), 431–473 (1996)

12. Goodrich, M.T., Mitzenmacher, M.: Privacy-preserving access of outsourced data via oblivious RAM simulation. In: Aceto, L., Henzinger, M., Sgall, J. (eds.) ICALP 2011. LNCS, vol. 6756, pp. 576–587. Springer, Heidelberg (2011). https://doi.org/10.1007/978-3-642-22012-8_46

13. Goodrich, M.T., Mitzenmacher, M., Ohrimenko, O., Tamassia, R.: Practical oblivious storage. In: Proceedings of the Second ACM Conference on Data and Application Security and Privacy, CODASPY 2012, pp. 13–24, Association for Computing Machinery, New York (2012)

14. Goodrich, M.T., Mitzenmacher, M., Ohrimenko, O., Tamassia, R.: Privacy-preserving group data access via stateless oblivious RAM simulation. In: Rabani, Y. (ed.) 23rd Annual ACM-SIAM Symposium on Discrete Algorithms, ACM-SIAM, pp. 157–167, Kyoto, 17–19 January 2012

15. Hubáček, P., Koucký, M., Král, K., Slívová, V.: Stronger lower bounds for online ORAM. In: Hofheinz, D., Rosen, A. (eds.) TCC 2019. LNCS, vol. 11892, pp. 264–284. Springer, Cham (2019). https://doi.org/10.1007/978-3-030-36033-7_10

16. Jacob, R., Larsen, K.G., Nielsen, J.B.: Lower bounds for oblivious data structures. In: Chan, T.M. (ed.) 30th Annual ACM-SIAM Symposium on Discrete Algorithms, ACM-SIAM, pp. 2439–2447, San Diego, 6–9 January 2019

17. Kushilevitz, E., Lu, S., Ostrovsky, R.: On the (in)security of hash-based oblivious RAM and a new balancing scheme. In: Rabani, Y. (ed.) 23rd Annual ACM-SIAM Symposium on Discrete Algorithms, ACM-SIAM, pp. 143–156, Kyoto, 17–19 January 2012

18. Larsen, K.G., Nielsen, J.B.: Yes, there is an oblivious RAM lower bound!. In: Shacham, H., Boldyreva, A. (eds.) CRYPTO 2018. LNCS, vol. 10992, pp. 523–542. Springer, Cham (2018). https://doi.org/10.1007/978-3-319-96881-0_18

19. Lu, S., Ostrovsky, R.: Distributed oblivious RAM for secure two-party computation. In: Sahai, A. (ed.) TCC 2013. LNCS, vol. 7785, pp. 377–396. Springer, Heidelberg (2013). https://doi.org/10.1007/978-3-642-36594-2_22

20. Lu, S., Ostrovsky, R.: How to garble RAM programs? In: Johansson, T., Nguyen, P.Q. (eds.) EUROCRYPT 2013. LNCS, vol. 7881, pp. 719–734. Springer, Heidelberg (2013). https://doi.org/10.1007/978-3-642-38348-9_42

21. Moataz, T., Mayberry, T., Blass, E.-O.: Constant communication ORAM with small blocksize. In: Ray, I., Li, N., Kruegel, C. (eds.) ACM CCS 2015: 22nd Conference on Computer and Communications Security, pp. 862–873. ACM Press, Denver, 12–16 October 2015

22. Patel, S., Persiano, G., Raykova, M., Yeo, K.: PanORAMa: oblivious RAM with logarithmic overhead. In: Thorup, M. (ed.) 59th Annual Symposium on Foundations of Computer Science, pp. 871–882, IEEE Computer Society Press, Paris, 7–9 October 2018

23. Shi, E., Chan, T.-H.H., Stefanov, E., Li, M.: Oblivious RAM with $O((\log N)^3)$ worst-case cost. In: Lee, D.H., Wang, X., (eds.) Advances in Cryptology - ASIACRYPT 2011. LNCS, vol. 7073, pp. 197–214, Seoul, South, Springer, Heidelberg, 4–8 December 2011. https://doi.org/10.1007/978-3-642-25385-0_11

24. Stefanov, E., et al.: Path ORAM: an extremely simple oblivious RAM protocol. In: Sadeghi, A.-R., Gligor, V.D., Yung, M., (eds.) ACM CCS 2013: 20th Conference on Computer and Communications Security, pp. 299–310. ACM Press, Berlin, 4–8 November 2013

25. Wang, X., Chan, T.-H.H., Shi, E.: Circuit ORAM: on tightness of the Goldreich-Ostrovsky lower bound. In: Ray, I., Li, N., Kruegel, C. (eds.) ACM CCS 2015: 22nd Conference on Computer and Communications Security, pp. 850–861. ACM Press, Denver 12–16 October 2015

26. Williams, P., Sion, R., Single round access privacy on outsourced storage. In: Yu, T., Danezis, G., Gligor, V.D. (eds.) ACM CCS 2012: 19th Conference on Computer and Communications Security, pp. 293–304. ACM Press, Raleigh, 16–18 October 2012

Lower Bounds for Multi-server Oblivious RAMs

Kasper Green Larsen[1], Mark Simkin[1], and Kevin Yeo[2(✉)]

[1] Computer Science Department, Aarhus University, Aarhus, Denmark
{larsen,simkin}@cs.au.dk
[2] Google LLC, Mountain View, USA
kwlyeo@google.com

Abstract. In this work, we consider the construction of oblivious RAMs (ORAM) in a setting with *multiple servers* and the adversary may corrupt a subset of the servers. We present an $\Omega(\log n)$ overhead lower bound for any k-server ORAM that limits any PPT adversary to distinguishing advantage at most $1/4k$ when only one server is corrupted. In other words, if one insists on negligible distinguishing advantage, then multi-server ORAMs cannot be faster than single-server ORAMs even with polynomially many servers of which only one unknown server is corrupted. Our results apply to ORAMs that may err with probability at most $1/128$ as well as scenarios where the adversary corrupts larger subsets of servers. We also extend our lower bounds to other important data structures including oblivious stacks, queues, deques, priority queues and search trees.

1 Introduction

With the ever increasing amount of data, it is becoming infeasible for users to store their data on consumer machines such as phones or laptops. Therefore, there has been significant movement to outsourcing data to larger cloud storage providers. In this work, we focus on *privacy-preserving storage protocols* that considers the setting where a client outsource the storages of data to a server such as a cloud storage provider in a privacy-preserving manner. For privacy, the client wishes to maintain privacy for the outsourced data from the adversarial server as the outsourced data might be sensitive. In addition, the client wishes to maintain the ability to perform operations over the outsourced data in an efficient manner. As a first step, the client might consider encrypting the data locally and only sending ciphertexts of the data to the server while storing the private key exclusively in client memory. As a result, the server never sees the data in the plaintext. However, the adversarial server will still observe the patterns of access

K. G. Larsen—Supported by a Villum Young Investigator Grant and an AUFF Starting Grant.
M. Simkin—Supported by the European Unions's Horizon 2020 research and innovation program under grant agreement No 669255 (MPCPRO) and No 731583 (SODA).

R. Pass and K. Pietrzak (Eds.): TCC 2020, LNCS 12550, pp. 486–503, 2020.
https://doi.org/10.1007/978-3-030-64375-1_17

performed by the client to the encrypted data. Several works in the past decade (see [21,23,26,31] as some examples) have shown that access pattern leakage can be used to compromise the privacy of the encrypted data. Therefore, it is an important problem to also efficiently hide the patterns of access to encrypted data to maintain privacy.

To solve the problem of hiding patterns of access to data, Goldreich and Ostrovsky [17] introduced the oblivious RAM (ORAM) primitive. Oblivious RAMs consider the problem of enabling a client to outsource an array with n entries, each consisting of exactly r bits, to the server, while enabling the client to both retrieve and perform update operations on any of the n array entries. The server itself consists of a memory of cells, each storing w bits. The client performs array update and retrieval operations by reading and writing to the server memory cells in a manner that hides the underlying operation being performed.

In terms of access pattern privacy, oblivious RAMs provide the guarantee that the adversarial server will learn no information about the sequence of array operations performed by the client except the total number of array operations performed. In more detail, any adversary that is given two plaintext sequences of array operations of equal length and observes the pattern of server cell accesses incurred by an ORAM, cannot determine which of the two plaintext sequences induced the observed ORAM access pattern.

The ORAM primitive is extremely powerful because it can be used in a blackbox manner to convert any non-oblivious algorithm/data structure into an oblivious version. In particular, every plaintext retrieval or update of memory performed by the non-oblivious algorithm/data structure will be replaced with an ORAM operation. Therefore, an important problem is constructing efficient ORAMs that may be used to also construct efficient algorithms/data structures for more complex tasks. For this reason, ORAM has been a well-studied topic over the past decade.

Efficiency of ORAMs is typically measured in terms of the bandwidth overhead. The bandwidth overhead is defined as the multiplicative factor of the extra number of server cells that must be accessed to process a single ORAM operation, i.e. if the ORAM accesses t server cells on an ORAM operation, then the bandwidth overhead is tr/w. Goldreich and Ostrovsky [17] presented the first ORAM with poly-logarithmic amortized bandwidth overhead per operation. A series of works [18,19,28,44,47,48] continued improving the efficiency until recent works by Patel et al. [40] introduced an ORAM with $O(\log n \log \log n)$ bandwidth overhead and Asharov et al. [1] presented an ORAM with $O(\log n)$ bandwidth. Other variants of ORAM such as statistically-secure ORAMs [9,10], parallel ORAMs [2,5,7] and garbled RAMs [14,15,38] have also been studied. Additionally, there has been work for efficiently constructing other oblivious data structures [49] including priority queues [25,46]. To summarize, there are optimal $\Theta(\log n)$ constructions for oblivious arrays (RAMs), stacks, queues, deques and priority queues in the single-server setting.

There has also been a lot of work proving lower bounds on the efficiency of ORAMs. Goldreich and Ostrovsky [17] presented an $\Omega(\log n)$ lower bound with certain restrictions of statistical adversaries and a no-coding assumption using a "balls-and-bins" model. Larsen and Nielsen [35] improve these lower bounds by considering computational adversaries where ORAMs can encode memory in any possible manner. Further works investigate the question of whether relaxations of the original ORAM setting allow for more efficient constructions and prove that the essentially same lower bound holds for other oblivious data structures [24, 34], weaker differentially private guarantees [43] and weaker adversaries [22]. A natural open question that remains is whether one can find a meaningful relaxation that allows us to break the logarithmic barrier. In this work, we investigate whether having access to multiple non-colluding servers can help us achieve this goal.

The ability to construct asymptotically faster schemes using multiple non-colluding servers has been exhibited previously in another privacy-preserving data structure known as *private information retrieval* (PIR). PIR was introduced by Chor *et al.* [8] for the information-theoretic setting with multiple non-colluding servers and Kushilevitz and Ostrovsky [30] for the computationally-secure setting with a single server. PIR and ORAM mainly differ in the capability of the client and server to hold state. PIR requires that both the client and server are stateless (beyond the server being able to hold a static database). In particular, clients are not even able to hold a private key that may be used between multiple queries. In contrast, ORAM enables both the client and server to be stateful and use information between multiple queries. For more information comparing ORAM and PIR, we refer readers to Sect. 1.2 of [41]. In the single-server variant of information-theoretic PIR, there are several proofs showing at least linear $\Omega(n)$ bandwidth is required for each query [16,27]. These are matched by the simplest construction of information-theoretic PIR where the client downloads the entire database on each query. On the other hand, PIR in the two non-colluding servers scenario may be constructed using sublinear bandwidth. The original works by Chor *et al.* [8] showed that there existed two-server statistically-secure PIR constructions with $O(\sqrt{n})$ and $O(n^{1/3})$ bandwidth. In more recent works, it has been shown that there exist PIR schemes in the two non-colluding servers setting with sub-polynomial bandwidth [11].

As the multi-server setting considers weaker adversaries, the lower bounds for the single-server setting [35,43] do not directly apply. Therefore, it seems plausible that oblivious data structures can be constructed in this model with faster efficiency than their single-server counterparts. While there have been several works [4,6,12,20,29,37] that consider oblivious RAMs in the two (or more) non-colluding servers model, all of them have an overhead of at least $\Omega(\log n)$, meaning that they are not asymptotically faster than single-server oblivious RAMs and data structures. This leads to the natural question of whether it is possible to construct $o(\log n)$ overhead oblivious RAMs and data structures in the multiple non-colluding servers setting.

Before presenting our results, we find it insightful to discuss two simple strategies for implementing multi-server ORAMs. In a setup with k servers, one naive approach is to pick a uniform random server and simply store the array there, without any obfuscation. This gives a great overhead of $O(1)$ (for $r = \Theta(w)$), but unfortunately security is very weak: A single adversarial server can distinguish two sequences of operations with probability $1/k$. Another simple strategy is to just ignore the first $k-1$ servers and run an optimal single-server ORAM on the last server. This gives an overhead of $O(\log n)$ but fails to exploit the multi-server setting. Is there anything in between these two extremes?

Our main result is a surprising negative resolution to this question, that is, if one insists on $o(\log n)$ overhead, then the *only* solution is to pick a random server and store the array there without any obfuscation, resulting in $1/k$ distinguishing probability for an adversarial server!

1.1   Our Results

Before we formally present our main contributions of this paper, we start by briefly describing the setting for which our lower bounds will apply. Our scenario consists of $k \geq 2$ servers that a client may use to host storage of parts of an oblivious RAM construction. We strictly consider weak, probabilistically polynomial time adversaries that can corrupt exactly one server and see all the probes performed by the ORAM on the corrupted server. As we are proving lower bounds, our results also apply to stronger adversaries that may be able to corrupt a large number of servers such as a constant fraction of all k servers. By the same argument, our lower bound also applies to computationally unbounded adversaries.

We note our ORAM lower bounds apply to the natural setting where operations arrive in an online manner. That is, the ORAM must complete one operation before receiving the next operation. Furthermore, the adversary is aware of when the processing of one operation ends and the processing of another operation begins.

Finally, we prove our lower bounds in the *cell probe model* of Yao [51]. In this model, the memory of the k servers is viewed as cells of w bits. The only measured cost is the number of probes performed to server cells. Computation, accessing memory stored on the client, generating randomness and querying the random oracle (if one exists) is completely free. Once again, since we are proving lower bounds, our results also apply to more natural cost models where these operations are charged appropriately.

We now present our main result:

Theorem 1 (Informal). *Any online k-server ORAM with n blocks of memory, consisting of $r \geq 1$ bits each, must have expected amortized overhead of $\Omega(\log(nr/m))$ on sequences of $\Theta(n)$ operations where the client has m bits of memory. This holds for probabilistically polynomial time adversaries that corrupt exactly one server and have a distinguishing advantage of at most $1/4k$ for any pair of length n sequences.*

For the natural setting where $r \leq m \leq n^{1-\epsilon}$ for any constant $\epsilon > 0$, the above lower bound simplifies to $\Omega(\log n)$. The above lower bound holds in the random oracle model, for any number of servers k and for any cell size w.

Using the above result, we show that multi-server ORAMs cannot be asymptotically faster than single-server ORAMs for any reasonable number of servers.

Corollary 1 (Informal). *For any $k = \mathbf{poly}(n)$, any k-server ORAM where probabilistically polynomial time adversaries that corrupt one of the k servers have negligible distinguishing advantage, must have $\Omega(\log n)$ overhead, which is asymptotically equivalent to the optimal single-server ORAM.*

Finally, we note that our lower bounds may be extended to other important data structures including stacks, queues, deques, priority queues and search trees.

Theorem 2 (Informal). *Any online k-server oblivious stacks, queues, deques, priority queues or search trees storing at most n elements, consisting of $r \geq 1$ bits each, must have expected amortized overhead of $\Omega(\log(nr/m))$ on sequences of n operations where the client has m bits of memory. This holds for probabilistically polynomial time adversaries that corrupt exactly one server and have a distinguishing advantage of at most $1/4k$ for any pair of length n sequences of operations.*

1.2 Our Techniques

In this section, we present an overview of the new techniques needed to prove our lower bound. To do this, we briefly overview the previous lower bound for ORAMs in the single-server setting by Larsen and Nielsen [35]. In addition, we show why the original proof fails for the setting when there exists multiple servers where the adversary may corrupt a single server. Larsen and Nielsen [35] used the information transfer technique introduced by Patrascu and Demaine [45]. For a sequence of n ORAM operations, each either a READ or a WRITE into one of n array entries, the information transfer tree is a complete binary tree with exactly n leaf nodes where the first operation is assigned to the leftmost node, the second operation is assigned to the second leftmost node and so forth. As we consider the cell probe model, each operation consists of a series of cell probes. Here a cell probe is simply an access to a server memory cell. For each probe p to a cell c, we identify both the operation that incurred p as well as the most recent, past operation that overwrote the contents of cell c. The cell probe p is *assigned* to the lowest common ancestor of the two leaf nodes associated with the operation performing p and the most recent, past operation that overwrote the probed cell. If the probed cell was never overwritten previously, the probe is not assigned to any node in the tree. Note that all cell probes are assigned to at most one node in the tree. Therefore, a lower bound on the number of total assigned probes results in a cell probe lower bound.

Consider any internal node v in the information transfer tree and the n_d left and right leaf nodes of the subtree rooted at v. Consider the sequence z of

n_d WRITE operations associated with the left leaf nodes each consist of writing uniformly at random chosen r-bit strings into n_d unique indices. Furthermore, suppose the operations in the right subtree of z perform n_d READ operations that retrieve the n_d different random bit strings written in the left subtree. If most of the n_d READ operations in the right subtree return the right answer, then a large portion of the $r \cdot n_d$ bits of entropy generated in WRITE operations in the left subtree must be transferred to the answers of READ operations in the right subtree. Information may only be transferred between the left and right subtree through client storage and the probes assigned to the root of the subtree v. As client storage is typically small, this implies a large number of probes must be assigned to v with high probability. Otherwise, one can construct an impossible compression scheme of the $r \cdot n_d$ random bits generated in the left subtree. Suppose there exists another sequence y of n ORAM operations that assigns significantly less probes to v. We can construct a simple and efficient adversary that distinguishes the two sequences by simply counting the number of probes assigned to v in polynomial time, which contradicts the obliviousness assumption. The application of this argument to many nodes of the information transfer tree suffices to prove the single-server ORAM lower bound.

Moving to the multi-server setting with $k \geq 2$ servers, the adversary is able to only see the probes performed to one server. For any multi-server ORAM construction that performs most of its probes to a single server, we can extend the adversary from the single-server setting by corrupting a server uniformly at random. As a result, the adversary is able to distinguish with probability $\Omega(1/k)$ unless y also assigns similarly large number of probes with high probability to the corrupted server. However, there might exist intelligent schemes that evenly distribute all probes across all k servers such that the adversary will only be able to see a small number of probes. Even worse, the probes might be distributed such that the probability any server sees even one probe is small when the number of servers is large such as $k = \Omega(n^2)$. Therefore, the challenge is proving that sequence y must also assign a large number of probes to v even when the adversary corrupts only a single server.

We now give intuition as to why these simpler counting adversaries do not suffice to prove lower bounds for k-server ORAMs with the current techniques. Going back to the proof framework of [35], we can consider an impossible sequence y that assigns a small number of probes to v in expectation. We need to show that the adversary can distinguish sequences y and z where z is the worst-case sequence for node v that maximizes the number of probes assigned to node v described in the previous paragraph. In the proof of [35], it was critically shown that the number of probes assigned by z to v is large with very high probability. This is a strong statement about the distribution of probes (as opposed to just bounding the expected number of probes assigned to v) that showed the counting adversary to distinguish with an impossible advantage. We note that this argument heavily utilizes the fact that the contents of cells of probes assigned to node v encode almost all the information generated in the left subtree of v. Unfortunately, these techniques do not work for multi-server ORAM schemes that can arbitrarily distribute probes to different servers. There is no requirement or guarantee that by restricting to probes that are both assigned to node v and all occur on a single server, the contents of these probed cells still encode the r-bit random strings generated in the left subtree of v. For example, a multi-server scheme might distribute the r-bit random strings across several servers using an information-theoretic secret sharing scheme. Therefore, the necessary guarantees needed for the simple counting adversary to successfully distinguish sequences y and z might not be true in the multiple server setting.

The main idea of our proof technique is to consider a more sophisticated adversary that groups the number of observable probe counts to the corrupted server that are assigned to node v into geometrically increasing sets, $[2^0, 2^1)$, $[2^1, 2^2)$, ..., $[2^j, \infty)$ for sufficiently large j. The new adversary will attempt to distinguish sequences y and z by finding a grouping of probe counts that are more likely for sequence y instead of sequence z. If sequence z results in a probe count in group $[2^i, 2^{i+1})$ with probability p, then sequence y must also result in a probe count in that group with probability at least $p - \varepsilon$ if the adversary should not be able to distinguish the sequences y and z with probability greater than ε. As a result, we can show that the expectation of the probe counts assigned to v to each server by y must be similarly large as under z, completing the proof.

1.3   Related Works

There has been two previous works showing that proving lower bounds for certain oblivious data structures in weaker settings will be difficult. Boyle and Naor [3] show that proving lower bounds for offline ORAMs that receive all operations ahead of time is as hard as proving sorting circuit lower bounds. Weiss and Wichs [50] prove that lower bounds for read-only ORAMs would imply unknown lower bounds in either sorting circuits and/or locally decodable codes.

There are also many works that have proved lower bounds in the cell probe model for data structures without privacy guarantees. Yao [51] introduced the cell probe model as a model for proving lower bounds. Fredman and Saks [13] presented the chronogram technique to prove almost logarithmic lower bounds. Patrascu and Demanie [45] introduced the information transfer technique to prove logarithmic lower bounds. Panigrahy et al. [39] present the cell-sampling technique to prove almost logarithmic lower bounds for static data structures. Larsen [32,33] presented the first super-logarithmic lower bounds for data structures with $\Theta(\log n)$-bit outputs. The first super-logarithmic lower bounds for decision data structures was proved in [36]. The above list only several examples of the many works in cell probe lower bounds.

2   Formal Model

We prove our lower bounds in a variant of the oblivious cell probe model of Larsen and Nielsen [35], adapted to a setting with k servers. In this model, an ORAM consists of k servers $S_1, \ldots, S_k$, each with a server memory of w-bit cells, where each cell has an integer address in $[K]$ for some $K \leq 2^w$. We also assume $k \leq 2^w$ such that a cell has enough bits to store the index of a server. An ORAM is furthermore equipped with a client memory of m bits, which is free to access. A multi-server ORAM processes READ and WRITE operations by reading and writing to memory cells at the servers. For READ operations, the ORAM terminates by announcing the answer to the READ based on what it has probed.

We refer to the reading and writing of a memory cell simply as probing it - also to distinguish reading and writing cells from READ and WRITE operations. The running time is defined as the number of cells it probes when processing READ and WRITE operations. Randomized ORAMs furthermore have access to an arbitrarily long uniform random bit string R, which is referred to as the random oracle bit string. The bit string R is drawn before any operations are performed on the ORAM and is chosen independently of the future operations. We say that a randomized ORAM has failure probability δ if for every sequence of operations $\mathrm{op}_1, \ldots, \mathrm{op}_M$, and for every query op_i in that sequence, the probability that op_i is answered correctly is at least $1 - \delta$.

When processing READ and WRITE operations, the cells probed and the contents written to cells in each step may be an arbitrary deterministic function of the client memory, random oracle bit string and contents of all other cells probed so far while processing the current operation. The ORAM is also allowed to update the client memory in each step, again setting the contents to an arbitrary deterministic function of the current memory, random oracle bit string and contents of cells probed so far. Allowing an arbitrary deterministic function abstracts away the instruction set of a normal RAM and allows arbitrary computations free of charge.

To define the security requirements of a multi-server ORAM, let

$$y := (\mathrm{op}_1, \ldots, \mathrm{op}_M)$$

denote a sequence of M READ and WRITE operations. Let

$$A(y) := (A(\mathrm{op}_1), \ldots, A(\mathrm{op}_M))$$

denote the corresponding *probe sequence*, where each $A(\mathrm{op}_i)$ is the list of probes made while processing op_i. Note that $A(y)$ is a deterministic function of the random oracle bit string and the sequence y. Each probe in a list $A(\mathrm{op}_i)$ is described by a tuple (s, a), where s is the index of the server where the probe is made and a is the address of the memory cell accessed at the server. For a server S_i, we let $A_{|S_i}(\mathrm{op}_j)$ denote the sub list of $A(\mathrm{op}_j)$ containing only the probes (s, a) with $s = i$. We similarly define $A_{|S_i}(y) = (A_{|S_i}(\mathrm{op}_1), \ldots, A_{|S_i}(\mathrm{op}_M))$ as the probes seen by server S_i. A multi-server ORAM is secure if it satisfies the following security guarantee:

Definition 1 (Security). *A multi-server ORAM is (ε, δ)-secure if the following two properties hold:*

Indistinguishability: *For any two sequences of operations y and z of the same length n and for any server S_i, their probe sequences $A_{|S_i}(y)$ and $A_{|S_i}(z)$ cannot be distinguished with probability better than ε by an algorithm which is polynomial time in n. Formally, if $\mathcal{A}_{|S_i,n}$ denotes the image of $A_{|S_i}$ on sequences of length n and $f : \mathcal{A}_{|S_i,n} \to \{0,1\}$ denotes a polynomial time computable function, then it must be the case that $|\Pr[f(A_{|S_i}(y)) = 1] - \Pr[f(A_{|S_i}(z)) = 1]| \leq \varepsilon$ for any two sequences y and z of length n. Here the probability is taken over the randomness R of the ORAM.*

Correctness: *The ORAM has failure probability at most δ.*

3 Lower Bound

We use the information transfer technique by Patrascu and Demaine [45], modified to multiple servers. We consider various sequences of n READ and WRITE operations to an ORAM $\mathcal{O}$ with memory size n. The READ and WRITE operations store and retrieve r-bit strings and the servers have cell size w bits. We prove the following theorem

Theorem 3. *Any ORAM with k servers that is $(1/4k, 1/128)$-secure, has server cell size w bits, has client memory size m bits and that supports storing r-bit values in n entries, must make an expected amortized $\Omega(r \log(nr/m)/w)$ probes per operation over sequences of n operations.*

First we define the information transfer tree $\mathcal{T}$. For any sequence of n operations $x = \mathrm{op}_1, \ldots, \mathrm{op}_n$, we construct a binary tree $\mathcal{T}$ with the operations as leaves. When processing the operations op_i, we assign the probes in $A(\mathrm{op}_i)$ to the nodes of $\mathcal{T}$. For each probe $p = (s, a) \in A(\mathrm{op}_i)$, consider the last time the cell (s, a) was probed during $\mathrm{op}_1, \ldots, \mathrm{op}_n$. If op_j with $j \leq i$ denotes the last operation in which the cell was probed, we assign p to the lowest common ancestor of op_i and op_j in $\mathcal{T}$. If p is the first probe to access (s, a) we do not assign it to any node of $\mathcal{T}$. For each node v of $\mathcal{T}$, we let $P(x, v)$ denote the set of probes assigned to v while processing x (note the $P(x, v)$ is a random variable due to the randomness R of the ORAM).

Observe that any probe is assigned to at most one node of $\mathcal{T}$.

We now consider a fixed "dummy" sequence of operations:

$$y := \mathrm{READ}(0), \mathrm{READ}(0), \mathrm{READ}(0), \cdots, \mathrm{READ}(0)$$

which always just reads the first ORAM memory cell. We say that the root of $\mathcal{T}$ has depth 0 and the leaves have depth $\log n$. For simplicity, we also assume n is a power of two. For a node $v \in \mathcal{T}$, we use $d(v)$ to denote its depth. We will prove the following:

Lemma 1. *If $\mathcal{O}$ is $(1/4k, 1/128)$-secure and has client memory size m, then for any node $v \in \mathcal{T}$ of depth $d = d(v) \leq \log(nr/m) - 6$, it holds that $\mathbb{E}_R[|P(y, v)|] = \Omega(nr/(w2^d))$.*

Lemma 1 immediately gives our result, since by linearity of expectation we get that the total number of probes T made by $\mathcal{O}$ satisfies:

$$
\begin{aligned}
\mathbb{E}[T] &\geq \sum_{v \in \mathcal{T}} \mathbb{E}[|P(y,v)|] \\
&\geq \sum_{d=0}^{\log(nr/m)-6} \sum_{v \in \mathcal{T}:d(v)=d} \mathbb{E}[|P(y,v)|] \\
&\geq \sum_{d=0}^{\log(nr/m)-6} 2^d \cdot \Omega(nr/(w2^d)) \\
&= \Omega(nr\log(nr/m)/w).
\end{aligned}
$$

Thus what remains is to prove Lemma 1. To do so, consider a node $v \in \mathcal{T}$ of depth $d(v) \leq \log(nr/m) - 6$. We consider a distribution $\mathcal{D}_v$ over sequences of n operations $\mathrm{op}_1, \ldots, \mathrm{op}_n$. The distribution is as follows: For every op_i that is outside the subtree rooted at v, we let $\mathrm{op}_i = \mathrm{READ}(0)$. We let the $n_d = n/2^{d+1}$ operations in v's left subtree be $\mathrm{WRITE}(1, r_1), \ldots, \mathrm{WRITE}(n_d, r_{n_d})$ where each r_i is a uniform random r-bit string. We let the n_d operations in v's right subtree be $\mathrm{READ}(1), \ldots, \mathrm{READ}(n_d)$. As in previous ORAM lower bounds, we first argue that under distribution $\mathcal{D}_v$, there must be many probes assigned to v in expectation:

Lemma 2. *Let $z \sim \mathcal{D}_v$ be a sequence of n operations. If $\mathcal{O}$ is $(1/4k, 1/128)$-secure and has client memory size m, then $\Pr_{z,R}[|P(z,v)| \geq (1/12)nr/(w2^d)] \geq 3/4$.*

We defer the proof of Lemma 2 to Sect. 3.1 as it follows previous proofs uneventfully.

We will now use the security guarantees of $\mathcal{O}$ and Lemma 2 to prove Lemma 1. To do so, start by partitioning the set $P(x,v)$ into k sets $P_{|S_1}(x,v), \ldots, P_{|S_k}(x,v)$ where $P_{|S_i}(x,v)$ contains all probes to a cell at server S_i while processing a sequence of operations x. Let $z \sim \mathcal{D}_v$. For each $j \in \{0, \ldots, \log(nr/(48w2^d))\}$ define $q_{i,j}$ as

$$
q_{i,j} := \Pr_{z,R}[|P_{|S_i}(z,v)| \in [2^j, 2^{j+1})].
$$

when $j < \log(nr/(48w2^d))$, and define

$$
q_{i,\log(nr/(48w2^d))} := \Pr_{z,R}[|P_{|S_i}(z,v)| \geq nr/(48w2^d)].
$$

Similarly, define

$$
\hat{q}_{i,j} := \Pr_{R}[|P_{|S_i}(y,v)| \in [2^j, 2^{j+1})].
$$

and

$$
\hat{q}_{i,\log(nr/(48w2^d))} := \Pr_{R}[|P_{|S_i}(y,v)| \geq nr/(48w2^d)].
$$

We first observe that for all i, j, we must have $\hat{q}_{i,j} \geq q_{i,j} - 1/4k$. To see this, observe that if $\hat{q}_{i,j} < q_{i,j} - 1/4k$ then for an $x \in \{y, z\}$, the server S_i can

distinguish whether $x = y$ or $x = z$ with probability greater than $1/4k$ as follows:
When seeing $A_{|S_i}(x)$, output 1 if $|P_{|S_i}(x, v)| \in [2^j, 2^{j+1})$ and 0 otherwise. Notice
that this information can be computed from $A_{|S_i(x)}$. As a technical caveat, note
that z is random and not a fixed sequence as in the definition of the security
guarantee. But if the adversary can distinguish the random z from y, then by
averaging, there must exist a fixed sequence in the support of z which can also
be distinguished from y with the same advantage. Hence $\hat{q}_{i,j} \geq q_{i,j} - 1/4k$ for
all i, j.

We now split the proof in two cases. Assume first that $\sum_i q_{i,\log(nr/(48w2^d))} \geq 1/2$. In this case, we have $\sum_i \hat{q}_{i,\log(nr/(48w2^d))} \geq 1/2 - k/4k = 1/4$. By linearity
of expectation, this implies $\mathbb{E}_R[|P(y, v)|] \geq (1/4)(nr/48w2^d) = \Omega(nr/(w2^d))$ as
claimed. Next, assume that $\sum_i q_{i,\log(nr/(48w2^d))} < 1/2$. By Lemma 2, we have

$$\Pr_{z,R}[|P(z, v)| \geq (1/12)nr/(w2^d)] \geq 3/4.$$

Now let E denote the event that for all i, we have:

$$|P_{|S_i}(z, v)| < nr/(48w2^d).$$

Note that

$$\Pr_{z,R}[\neg E] = \sum_i \Pr[|P_{|S_i}(z, v)| \geq nr/(48w2^d)] = \sum_i q_{i,\log(nr/(48w2^d))} < 1/2$$

where the last inequality is by the assumption made previously. Therefore,
$\Pr_{z,R}[E] > 1/2$. We then have:

$$\Pr_{z,R}[|P(z, v)| \geq (1/12)nr/(w2^d) \wedge E] \geq 1 - 1/4 - (1 - \Pr_{z,R}[E]) = \Pr_{z,R}[E] - 1/4$$

Therefore

$$\begin{aligned}
\Pr_{z,R}[|P(z, v)| \geq (1/12)nr/(w2^d) \mid E] &= \Pr_{z,R}[|P(z, v)| \geq (1/12)nr/(w2^d) \wedge E] / \Pr_{z,R}[E] \\
&\geq (\Pr_{z,R}[E] - 1/4) / \Pr_{z,R}[E] \\
&= 1 - 1/(4 \Pr_{z,R}[E]) \\
&\geq 1/2.
\end{aligned}$$

This implies that

$$\mathbb{E}_{z,R}[|P(z, v)| \mid E] \geq (1/24)nr/(w2^d).$$

We will show that this means that

$$\mathbb{E}_R[|P(y, v)|] = \Omega(nr/(w2^d)).$$

To see this, consider what happens if we modify the definition of $P(z, v)$ such
that we set $P(z, v) = \emptyset$ if there is at least one server S_i such that $|P_{|S_i}(z, v)| \geq$

$nr/(48w2^d)$. Let $P^*(z,v)$ denote this modified version of $P(z,v)$ and let $q^*_{i,j}$ denote the corresponding versions of the $q_{i,j}$'s. We clearly have $q^*_{i,j} \le q_{i,j}$ for all i,j. Moreover, conditioned on E, we have $P(z,v) = P^*(z,v)$. It follows that

$$\mathbb{E}_{z,R}[|P^*(z,v)|] = \Pr_{z,R}[E]\mathbb{E}_{z,R}[|P(z,v)| \mid E] \ge (1/48)nr/(w2^d).$$

At the same time, we also have

$$\mathbb{E}_{z,R}[|P^*(z,v)|] \le \sum_{i=1}^{k} \sum_{j=0}^{\log(nr/(48w2^d))-1} q^*_{i,j}2^{j+1}$$

Using that $q^*_{i,j} \le q_{i,j}$, this means that

$$\sum_{i=1}^{k} \sum_{j=0}^{\log(nr/(48w2^d))-1} q_{i,j}2^{j+1} \ge (1/48)nr/(w2^d).$$

Now $\hat{q}_{i,j} \ge q_{i,j} - 1/4k$ thus

$$\sum_{i=1}^{k} \sum_{j=0}^{\log(nr/(48w2^d))-1} \hat{q}_{i,j}2^{j+1} \ge (1/48)nr/(w2^d) - \sum_{i=1}^{k} \sum_{j=0}^{\log(nr/(48w2^d))-1} 2^{j+1}/4k$$

$$= (1/48)nr/(w2^d) - \sum_{i=1}^{k} 2^{\log(nr/(48w2^d))+1}/4k$$

$$= (1/48)nr/(w2^d) - (1/96)nr/(w2^d)$$

$$= (1/96)nr/(w2^d).$$

But

$$\mathbb{E}_R[|P(y,v)|] \ge \sum_{i=1}^{k} \sum_{j=0}^{\log(nr/(48w2^d))} \hat{q}_{i,j}2^j$$

$$\ge (1/2) \sum_{i=1}^{k} \sum_{j=0}^{\log(nr/(48w2^d))-1} \hat{q}_{i,j}2^{j+1}$$

$$= \Omega(nr/(w2^d)).$$

This completes the proof of Lemma 1.

3.1 Proof of Lemma 2

We prove this via an encoding argument. An encoder Alice and a decoder Bob share access to the random oracle bit string R used by $\mathcal{O}$. Alice receives as input the $n_d = n/2^{d+1}$ random bit strings $r_1, \ldots, r_{n_d}$ given as arguments to the WRITE operations in v's left subtree and wants to transmit them to Bob. By Shannon's source coding theorem, if Alice sends a prefix free code, then the expected length of the message must be at least $n_d r = nr/2^{d+1}$ bits. They proceed as follows:

Encoding. Alice constructs the sequence of operations $z = \text{op}_1, \ldots, \text{op}_n$ where the WRITE operations in v's left subtree write the values $r_1, \ldots, r_{n_d}$ to entries $1, \ldots, n_d$, and the READ operations in v's right subtree read the entries $1, \ldots, n_d$. All op_i outside v's subtree are simply READ(0) operations. Thus z is distributed according to $\mathcal{D}_v$. Alice runs the sequence of operations on $\mathcal{O}$ and constructs the set $P(z, v)$ and also counts how many of the READ operations in v's right subtree that fail to return the correct answer. Let f denote the number of READ operations that err. Her message to Bob is as follows:

1. If $f \geq n_d/16$ or $|P(z, v)| \geq (1/12)nr/(w2^d)$, then Alice sends a 0-bit, followed by $n_d r = nr/2^{d+1}$ bits giving a naive encoding of $r_1, \ldots, r_{n_d}$. This costs $1 + nr/2^{d+1}$ bits.
2. Otherwise, Alice starts by sending a 1-bit. Alice encodes all $f \leq n_d/16$ erring queries by encoding f using $\log(n)$ bits and the identity of the f queries using $\log \binom{n_d}{f}$ bits. The answer of the f erring queries are trivially encoded using fr bits. For each probe $p = (s, a)$, Alice sends s, a and the contents of the cell with address a at server S_s as it was immediately after processing the operations in v's subtree. She also sends the contents of the client memory as it was immediately after processing v's left subtree. This costs $1 + |P(z, v)|(\log k + 2w) + \log(n) + \log \binom{n_d}{f} + fr + m$. Using Stirling's approximation, we get that the cost is at most $1 + |P(z, v)|(\log k + 2w) + \log(n) + f \log(n_d e/f)$. This is maximized when $f = n_d/16$ meaning the encoding size is at most $1 + |P(z, v)|(\log k + 2w) + (1/16)nr/2^{d+1} + (1/16)\log(16e)n/2^{d+1}$. As $\log(16e) < 6$, we get the above is at most $1 + |P(z, v)|(\log k + 2w) + (7/16)nr/2^{d+1}$. Using the assumption on the size of $|P(z, v)|$ and that k fits in a single word, we get the encoding is at most $1 + 3w(1/12)nr/2^d + (7/16)nr/2^{d+1} + m = 1 + (15/16)nr/2^{d+1} + m$. We required $d \leq \log(nr/m) - 6$, hence $m \leq nr/2^{d+6}$ and it follows that the cost is no more than $1 + (31/32)nr/2^{d+1}$.

Decoding. Bob starts by checking the first bit of Alice's message. If this is a 0-bit, Bob immediately recovers $r_1, \ldots, r_{n_d}$ from the remaining part of Alice's message. Otherwise, Bob identifies the f erring queries and naively decodes their answers. Next, Bob reconstructs the set $P(z, v)$ and the contents of those cells as they were right after processing v's left subtree. Bob now runs $\mathcal{O}$ using the randomness R on the sequence z until just before v's left subtree (this is solely READ(0) operations, so Bob knows these). He then skips over all operations in the left subtree and continues running the READ(1), ..., READ(n_d) in v's right subtree. While processing these operations, Bob checks each cell that is probed. If the cell is in $P(z, v)$, Bob knows the contents from Alice's message. If it is not in $P(z, v)$, then Bob already knows the contents as they were not updates during v's left subtree by definition of $P(z, v)$. Thus Bob can process all the READ operations and recovers $r_1, \ldots, r_{n_d}$.

Analysis. Let $\alpha = \Pr[|P(z, v)| < (1/12)nr/(w2^d)]$. Then the probability that Alice sends a non-trivial encoding (step 2.) is at least $1 - (1 - \alpha) - 1/8 = \alpha - 1/8$. This follows by a union bound and Markov's inequality since $\mathbb{E}[f] = n_d/128$ due to $\mathcal{O}$ having error probability at most $1/128$ implying that $\Pr[f > n_d/16] \leq 1/8$. The expected length of the encoding is hence at most

$$1 + (1 - \alpha + 1/8)nr/2^{d+1} + (\alpha - 1/8)(31/32)nr/2^{d+1}.$$

This is less than $n_d r$ for any constant $\alpha > 1/8$. We thus conclude that $\Pr[|P(z,v)| \geq (1/12)nr/(w2^d)] \geq 3/4$.

4   Extension to Oblivious Data Structures

In this section, we show that the above lower bound may be extended to other oblivious data structures including stacks, queues, deques, priority queues and search trees using techniques by Jacob $et\ al.$ [24]. We describe how to modify the lower bound to handle stacks and queues. Since one can use deques, priority queues and search trees to simulate a stack and/or queue, we only need to prove a lower bound for oblivious stacks and queues.

For the "dummy" sequence of operations in the lower bound, we will use the following sequence for both stacks and queues:

$$\text{PUSH}(\bar{0}), \text{POP}(), \text{PUSH}(\bar{0}), \text{POP}(), \ldots, \text{PUSH}(\bar{0}), \text{POP}()$$

where $\bar{0}$ is the all-zeroes bit string of length r. The lower bound also requires designing a worst case sequence for each node v in the information transfer tree. If we let n_d be the number of operations in the left and right subtree of v, then we make the operations of the leaf nodes of the subtree rooted at v be

$$\text{PUSH}(r_1), \ldots, \text{PUSH}(r_{n_d}), \text{POP}(), \ldots, \text{POP}()$$

where each r_i is also a uniformly random r-bit string. Outside v's subtree, we make alternating $\text{PUSH}(\bar{0}), \text{POP}()$ operations. This sequence has the desired property (for both stacks and queues) that the queries to the right subtree of v have to retrieve the random strings generated from the left subtree of v. The rest of the lower bound proof proceeds identically using these new hard operational sequences for stacks and queues.

Theorem 4. *Any oblivious stack, queue, deque, priority queue or search tree with k servers that is $(1/4k, 1/128)$-secure, has server cell size w bits, has client memory size m bits and that supports storing up to n r-bit elements, must make an expected amortized $\Omega(r \log(nr/m)/w)$ probes per operation over sequences of n operations.*

5   Conclusions

In this work, we study oblivious data structures that enable performing operations without revealing information about these operations. There has been a long line of work for oblivious data structures that has led to tight $\Theta(\log n)$

constructions for many oblivious data structures. However, this means there is a significant gap between plaintext and oblivious operations for many data structures such as arrays (RAMs). A natural next question is: are there any settings where we can achieve meaningful privacy with smaller $o(\log n)$ overhead? This question was investigated in [42,43] that considered weaker differentially private access hiding only operational sequences that differ in very few operations. Additionally, [22] considered weaker adversaries that may not view the beginning and ending of operations. In both cases, the weakening of the adversaries was not sufficient to achieve $o(\log n)$ overhead. We continue along this line of research by showing weaker adversaries that only corrupt one server in the multi-server model does not suffice to achieve $o(\log n)$ overhead.

References

1. Asharov, G., Komargodski, I., Lin, W.-K., Nayak, K., Peserico, E., Shi, E.: OptORAMa: Optimal oblivious RAM. Cryptology ePrint Archive, Report 2018/892
2. Boyle, E., Chung, K.-M., Pass, R.: Oblivious parallel RAM and applications. In: Kushilevitz, E., Malkin, T. (eds.) TCC 2016. LNCS, vol. 9563, pp. 175–204. Springer, Heidelberg (2016). https://doi.org/10.1007/978-3-662-49099-0_7
3. Boyle, E., Naor, M.: Is there an oblivious RAM lower bound? In: Proceedings of the 2016 ACM Conference on Innovations in Theoretical Computer Science, pp. 357–368. ACM (2016)
4. Bunn, P., Katz, J., Kushilevitz, E., Ostrovsky, R.: Efficient 3-party distributed ORAM. IACR Cryptology ePrint Archive 2018:706 (2018)
5. Chan, T.-H.H., Guo, Y., Lin, W.-K., Shi, E.: Oblivious hashing revisited, and applications to asymptotically efficient ORAM and OPRAM. In: Takagi, T., Peyrin, T. (eds.) ASIACRYPT 2017. LNCS, vol. 10624, pp. 660–690. Springer, Cham (2017). https://doi.org/10.1007/978-3-319-70694-8_23
6. Chan, T.-H.H., Katz, J., Nayak, K., Polychroniadou, A., Shi, E.: More is less: perfectly secure oblivious algorithms in the multi-server setting. In: Peyrin, T., Galbraith, S. (eds.) ASIACRYPT 2018. LNCS, vol. 11274, pp. 158–188. Springer, Cham (2018). https://doi.org/10.1007/978-3-030-03332-3_7
7. Chen, B., Lin, H., Tessaro, S.: Oblivious parallel RAM: improved efficiency and generic constructions. In: Kushilevitz, E., Malkin, T. (eds.) TCC 2016. LNCS, vol. 9563, pp. 205–234. Springer, Heidelberg (2016). https://doi.org/10.1007/978-3-662-49099-0_8
8. Chor, B., Goldreich, O., Kushilevitz, E., Sudan, M.: Private information retrieval. In: Proceedings of the 36th Annual Symposium on Foundations of Computer Science, 1995, pp. 41–50. IEEE (1995)
9. Chung, K.-M., Liu, Z., Pass, R.: Statistically-secure ORAM with $\tilde{O}(\log^2 n)$ overhead. In: Sarkar, P., Iwata, T. (eds.) ASIACRYPT 2014. LNCS, vol. 8874, pp. 62–81. Springer, Heidelberg (2014). https://doi.org/10.1007/978-3-662-45608-8_4
10. Damgård, I., Meldgaard, S., Nielsen, J.B.: Perfectly secure oblivious ram without random oracles. In: Ishai, Y. (ed.) TCC 2011. LNCS, vol. 6597, pp. 144–163. Springer, Heidelberg (2011). https://doi.org/10.1007/978-3-642-19571-6_10
11. Dvir, Z., Gopi, S.: 2-Server PIR with subpolynomial communication. J. ACM (JACM) 63(4), 39 (2016)

12. Faber, S., Jarecki, S., Kentros, S., Wei, B.: Three-party ORAM for secure computation. In: Iwata, T., Cheon, J.H. (eds.) ASIACRYPT 2015. LNCS, vol. 9452, pp. 360–385. Springer, Heidelberg (2015). https://doi.org/10.1007/978-3-662-48797-6_16

13. Fredman, M., Saks, M.: The cell probe complexity of dynamic data structures. In: Proceedings of the Twenty-first Annual ACM Symposium on Theory of Computing, pp. 345–354. ACM (1989)

14. Garg, S., Lu, S., Ostrovsky, R., Scafuro, A.: Garbled RAM from one-way functions. In: Proceedings of the Forty-seventh Annual ACM Symposium on Theory of Computing, pp. 449–458. ACM (2015)

15. Gentry, C., Halevi, S., Lu, S., Ostrovsky, R., Raykova, M., Wichs, D.: Garbled RAM revisited. In: Nguyen, P.Q., Oswald, E. (eds.) EUROCRYPT 2014. LNCS, vol. 8441, pp. 405–422. Springer, Heidelberg (2014). https://doi.org/10.1007/978-3-642-55220-5_23

16. Goldreich, O., Karloff, H., Schulman, L.J., Trevisan, L.: Lower bounds for linear locally decodable codes and private information retrieval. In: Proceedings 17th IEEE Annual Conference on Computational Complexity, pp. 175–183. IEEE (2002)

17. Goldreich, O., Ostrovsky, R.: Software protection and simulation on oblivious RAMs. J. ACM (JACM) 43(3), 431–473 (1996)

18. Goodrich, M.T., Mitzenmacher, M.: Privacy-preserving access of outsourced data via oblivious RAM simulation. In: Aceto, L., Henzinger, M., Sgall, J. (eds.) ICALP 2011. LNCS, vol. 6756, pp. 576–587. Springer, Heidelberg (2011). https://doi.org/10.1007/978-3-642-22012-8_46

19. Goodrich, M.T., Mitzenmacher, M., Ohrimenko, O., Tamassia, R.: Privacy-preserving group data access via stateless oblivious RAM simulation. In: Proceedings of the Twenty-third Annual ACM-SIAM Symposium on Discrete Algorithms, pp. 157–167. Society for Industrial and Applied Mathematics (2012)

20. Gordon, S.D., Katz, J., Wang, X.: Simple and efficient two-server ORAM. In: Peyrin, T., Galbraith, S. (eds.) ASIACRYPT 2018. LNCS, vol. 11274, pp. 141–157. Springer, Cham (2018). https://doi.org/10.1007/978-3-030-03332-3_6

21. Grubbs, P., Lacharité, M.-S., Minaud, B., Paterson, K.G.: Learning to reconstruct: statistical learning theory and encrypted database attacks. Cryptology ePrint Archive, Report 2019/011

22. Hub'avcek, P., Koucký, M., Král, K., Slívová, V.: Stronger lower bounds for online ORAM. CoRR, abs/1903.03385 (2019)

23. Islam, M.S., Kuzu, M., Kantarcioglu, M.: Access pattern disclosure on searchable encryption: ramification, attack and mitigation. In: NDSS (2012)

24. Jacob, R., Larsen, K.G., Nielsen, J.B.: Lower bounds for oblivious data structures. In: SODA 2019 (2019)

25. Jafargholi, Z., Larsen, K.G., Simkin, M.: Optimal oblivious priority queues and offline oblivious RAM. Cryptology ePrint Archive, Report 2019/237 (2019). https://eprint.iacr.org/2019/237

26. Kellaris, G., Kollios, G., Nissim, K., O'Neill, A.: Generic attacks on secure outsourced databases. In: CCS 2016 (2016)

27. Kerenidis, I., De Wolf, R.: Exponential lower bound for 2-query locally decodable codes via a quantum argument. J. Comput. Syst. Sci. 69(3), 395–420 (2004)

28. Kushilevitz, E., Lu, S., Ostrovsky, R.: On the (in) security of hash-based oblivious RAM and a new balancing scheme. In: Proceedings of the Twenty-third Annual ACM-SIAM Symposium on Discrete Algorithms, pp. 143–156. Society for Industrial and Applied Mathematics (2012)

29. Kushilevitz, E., Mour, T.: Sub-logarithmic distributed oblivious ram with small block size. arXiv preprint arXiv:1802.05145 (2018)
30. Kushilevitz, E., Ostrovsky, R.: Replication is not needed: single database, computationally-private information retrieval. In: Proceedings of the 38th Annual Symposium on Foundations of Computer Science, 1997, pp. 364–373. IEEE (1997)
31. Lacharité, M.-S., Minaud, B., Paterson, K.G.: Improved reconstruction attacks on encrypted data using range query leakage. In: IEEE S&P 2018 (2018)
32. Larsen, K.G.: The cell probe complexity of dynamic range counting. In: Proceedings of the Forty-fourth Annual ACM Symposium on Theory of Computing, pp. 85–94. ACM (2012)
33. Larsen, K.G.: Higher cell probe lower bounds for evaluating polynomials. In: 2012 IEEE 53rd Annual Symposium on Foundations of Computer Science, pp. 293–301. IEEE (2012)
34. Larsen, K.G., Malkin, T., Weinstein, O., Yeo, K.: Lower bounds for oblivious near-neighbor search. arXiv preprint arXiv:1904.04828 (2019)
35. Larsen, K.G., Nielsen, J.B.: Yes, there is an oblivious RAM lower bound!. In: Shacham, H., Boldyreva, A. (eds.) CRYPTO 2018. LNCS, vol. 10992, pp. 523–542. Springer, Cham (2018). https://doi.org/10.1007/978-3-319-96881-0_18
36. Larsen, K.G., Weinstein, O., Yu, H.: Crossing the logarithmic barrier for dynamic boolean data structure lower bounds. In: Proceedings of the 50th Annual ACM SIGACT Symposium on Theory of Computing, pp. 978–989. ACM (2018)
37. Lu, S., Ostrovsky, R.: Distributed oblivious RAM for secure two-party computation. In: Sahai, A. (ed.) TCC 2013. LNCS, vol. 7785, pp. 377–396. Springer, Heidelberg (2013). https://doi.org/10.1007/978-3-642-36594-2_22
38. Lu, S., Ostrovsky, R.: Black-box parallel garbled RAM. In: Katz, J., Shacham, H. (eds.) CRYPTO 2017. LNCS, vol. 10402, pp. 66–92. Springer, Cham (2017). https://doi.org/10.1007/978-3-319-63715-0_3
39. Panigrahy, R., Talwar, K., Wieder, U.: Lower bounds on near neighbor search via metric expansion. In: 2010 IEEE 51st Annual Symposium on Foundations of Computer Science, pp. 805–814. IEEE (2010)
40. Patel, S., Persiano, G., Raykova, M., Yeo, K.: PanORAMa: oblivious RAM with logarithmic overhead. In: FOCS 2018 (2018)
41. Patel, S., Persiano, G., Yeo, K.: Private stateful information retrieval. In: Proceedings of the 2018 ACM SIGSAC Conference on Computer and Communications Security, pp. 1002–1019. ACM (2018)
42. Patel, S., Persiano, G., Yeo, K.: What storage access privacy is achievable with small overhead? In: Proceedings of the 38th ACM SIGMOD-SIGACT-SIGAI Symposium on Principles of Database Systems, pp. 182–199. ACM (2019)
43. Persiano, G., Yeo, K.: Lower bounds for differentially private RAMs. In: Ishai, Y., Rijmen, V. (eds.) EUROCRYPT 2019. LNCS, vol. 11476, pp. 404–434. Springer, Cham (2019). https://doi.org/10.1007/978-3-030-17653-2_14
44. Pinkas, B., Reinman, T.: Oblivious RAM revisited. In: Rabin, T. (ed.) CRYPTO 2010. LNCS, vol. 6223, pp. 502–519. Springer, Heidelberg (2010). https://doi.org/10.1007/978-3-642-14623-7_27
45. Pătraşcu, M., Demaine, E.D.: Logarithmic lower bounds in the cell-probe model. SIAM J. Comput. 35(4), 932–963 (2006)
46. Shi, E.: Path oblivious heap. Cryptology ePrint Archive, Report 2019/274 (2019). https://eprint.iacr.org/2019/274
47. Stefanov, E., Shi, E., Song, D.: Towards practical oblivious RAM. arXiv preprint arXiv:1106.3652 (2011)

48. Stefanov, E., et al.: Path ORAM: an extremely simple oblivious RAM protocol. In: Proceedings of the 2013 ACM SIGSAC Conference on Computer and Communications Security, pp. 299–310. ACM (2013)
49. Wang, X.S., et al.: Oblivious data structures. In: Proceedings of the 2014 ACM SIGSAC Conference on Computer and Communications Security, pp. 215–226. ACM (2014)
50. Weiss, M., Wichs, D.: Is there an oblivious RAM lower bound for online reads? In: Beimel, A., Dziembowski, S. (eds.) TCC 2018. LNCS, vol. 11240, pp. 603–635. Springer, Cham (2018). https://doi.org/10.1007/978-3-030-03810-6_22
51. Yao, A.C.-C.: Should tables be sorted? J. ACM (JACM) 28(3), 615–628 (1981)

On Computational Shortcuts
for Information-Theoretic PIR

Matthew M. Hong[1], Yuval Ishai[2], Victor I. Kolobov[2(✉)],
and Russell W. F. Lai[3]

[1] IIIS, Tsinghua University, Beijing, China
hoou8547@hotmail.com
[2] Technion, Haifa, Israel
{yuvali,tkolobov}@cs.technion.ac.il
[3] Friedrich-Alexander University Erlangen-Nuremberg, Nuremberg, Germany
russell.lai@cs.fau.de

Abstract. Information-theoretic *private information retrieval* (PIR)
schemes have attractive concrete efficiency features. However, in the standard PIR model, the computational complexity of the servers must scale
linearly with the database size.

We study the possibility of bypassing this limitation in the case where
the database is a truth table of a "simple" function, such as a union of
(multi-dimensional) intervals or convex shapes, a decision tree, or a DNF
formula. This question is motivated by the goal of obtaining lightweight
homomorphic secret sharing (HSS) schemes and secure multiparty computation (MPC) protocols for the corresponding families.

We obtain both positive and negative results. For "first-generation"
PIR schemes based on Reed-Muller codes, we obtain computational
shortcuts for the above function families, with the exception of DNF
formulas for which we show a (conditional) hardness result. For "third-
generation" PIR schemes based on matching vectors, we obtain stronger
hardness results that apply to all of the above families. Our positive
results yield new information-theoretic HSS schemes and MPC protocols with attractive efficiency features for simple but useful function families. Our negative results establish new connections between information-
theoretic cryptography and fine-grained complexity.

1 Introduction

Secure multiparty computation (MPC) [15,27,49,61] allows two or more parties
to compute a function of their secret inputs while only revealing the output.

M.M. Hong—Work done in part while visiting Technion.
Y. Ishai—Supported by ERC Project NTSC (742754), NSF-BSF grant 2015782, BSF
grant 2018393, and a grant from the Ministry of Science and Technology, Israel and
Department of Science and Technology, Government of India.
R.W.F. Lai—Work done in part while visiting Technion. Supported by the State of
Bavaria at the Nuremberg Campus of Technology (NCT). NCT is a research cooper-
ation between the Friedrich-Alexander-Universität Erlangen-Nürnberg (FAU) and the
Technische Hochschule Nürnberg Georg Simon Ohm (THN).

R. Pass and K. Pietrzak (Eds.): TCC 2020, LNCS 12550, pp. 504–534, 2020.
https://doi.org/10.1007/978-3-030-64375-1_18

Much of the large body of research on MPC is focused on minimizing *communication complexity*, which often forms an efficiency bottleneck. In the setting of computational security, fully homomorphic encryption (FHE) essentially settles the main questions about *asymptotic* communication complexity of MPC [23,24,46,47]. However, the information-theoretic (IT) analog of the question, *i.e.*, how communication-efficient IT MPC protocols can be, remains wide open, with very limited negative results [2,5,35,37,38,45,53]. These imply superlinear lower bounds only when the number of parties grows with the total input length. Here we will mostly restrict our attention to the simple case of a constant number of parties with security against a single, *passively* corrupted, party.

On the upper bounds front, the communication complexity of classical IT MPC protocols from [15,27] scales linearly with the *circuit size* of the function f being computed. With few exceptions, the circuit size remains a barrier even today. One kind of exceptions includes functions f whose (probabilistic) degree is smaller than the number of parties [6,9]. Another exception includes protocols that have access to a trusted source of correlated randomness [20,32,36,53]. Finally, a very broad class of exceptions that applies in the standard model includes "complex" functions, whose circuit size is super-polynomial in the input length. For instance, the minimal circuit size of most Boolean functions $f : \{0,1\}^n \to \{0,1\}$ is $2^{\tilde{\Omega}(n)}$. However, *all* such functions admit a 3-party IT MPC protocol with only $2^{\tilde{O}(\sqrt{n})}$ bits of communication [10,43]. This means that for most functions, communication is super-polynomially smaller than the circuit size. Curiously, the *computational complexity* of such protocols is bigger than 2^n even if f has circuits of size $2^{o(n)}$. These kind of gaps between communication and computation will be in the center of the present work.

Beyond the theoretical interest in the asymptotic complexity of IT MPC protocols, they also have appealing *concrete efficiency* features. Indeed, typical implementations of IT MPC protocols in the honest-majority setting are faster by orders of magnitude than those of similar computationally secure protocols for the setting of dishonest majority.[1] Even when considering *communication* complexity alone, where powerful tools such as FHE asymptotically dominate existing IT MPC techniques, the latter can still have better *concrete* communication costs when the inputs are relatively short. These potential advantages of IT MPC techniques serve to further motivate this work.

1.1 Homomorphic Secret Sharing and Private Information Retrieval

We focus on low-communication MPC in a simple client-server setting, which is captured by the notion of *homomorphic secret sharing* (HSS) [16,18,21]. HSS can be viewed as a relaxation of FHE which, unlike FHE, exists in the IT setting. In an HSS scheme, a client shares a secret input $x \in \{0,1\}^n$ between k servers. The

---

[1] It is often useful to combine an IT protocol with a lightweight use of symmetric cryptography in order to reduce communication costs (see, e.g., [3,33,48]); we will use such a hybrid approach in the context of optimizing concrete efficiency.

servers, given a function f from some family $\mathcal{F}$, can *locally* apply an evaluation function on their input shares, and send the resulting output shares to the client. Given the k output shares, the client should recover $f(x)$. In the process, the servers should learn nothing about x, as long as at most t of them collude.

As in the case of MPC, we assume by default that $t = 1$ and consider a constant number of servers $k \geq 2$. A crucial feature of HSS schemes is *compactness* of output shares, typically requiring their size to scale linearly with the output size of f and independently of the complexity of f. This makes HSS a good building block for low-communication MPC. Indeed, HSS schemes can be converted into MPC protocols with comparable efficiency by distributing the input generation and output reconstruction [18].

An important special case of HSS is (multi-server) *private information retrieval* (PIR) [29]. A PIR scheme allows a client to retrieve a single bit from an N-bit database, which is replicated among $k \geq 2$ servers, such that no server (more generally, no t servers) learns the identity of the retrieved bit. A PIR scheme with database size $N = 2^n$ can be seen as an HSS scheme for the family $\mathcal{F}$ of *all* functions $f : \{0,1\}^n \rightarrow \{0,1\}$.

PIR in the IT setting has been the subject of a large body of work; see [63] for a partial survey. Known IT PIR schemes can be roughly classified into three generations. The first-generation schemes, originating from the work of Chor et al. [29], are based on Reed-Muller codes. In these schemes the communication complexity is $N^{1/\Theta(k)}$. In the second-generation schemes [13], the exponent vanishes super-linearly with k, but is still constant for any fixed k. Finally, the third-generation schemes, originating the works of Yekhanin [62] and Efremenko [43], have sub-polynomial communication complexity of $N^{o(1)}$ with only $k = 3$ servers or even $k = 2$ servers [41]. (An advantage of the 3-server schemes is that the server answer size is constant.) These schemes are based on a nontrivial combinatorial object called a *matching vectors* (MV) family.

As noted above, a PIR scheme with database size $N = 2^n$ can be viewed as an HSS scheme for the family $\mathcal{F}$ of all functions f (in truth-table representation). Our work is motivated by the goal of extending this to more expressive (and succinct) function representations. While a lot of recent progress has been made on the computational variant of the problem for functions represented by circuits or branching programs [17,18,22,39,44,54], almost no progress has been made for IT HSS. Known constructions are limited to the following restricted types: (1) HSS for general truth tables, corresponding to PIR, and (2) HSS for low-degree polynomials, which follow from the multiplicative property of Shamir's secret-sharing scheme [15,27,34,57]. Almost nothing is known about the existence of non-trivial IT HSS schemes for other useful function families, which we aim to explore in this work.

1.2   HSS via Computational Shortcuts for PIR

Viewing PIR as HSS for truth tables, HSS schemes for more succinct function representations can be equivalently viewed as a computationally efficient PIR schemes for *structured* databases, which encode the truth tables of succinctly described functions. While PIR schemes for general databases require linear computation in N [14], there are no apparent barriers that prevent *computational shortcuts* for *structured databases*. In this work we study the possibility of designing useful HSS schemes by applying such shortcuts to existing IT PIR schemes. Namely, by exploiting the structure of truth tables that encode simple functions, the hope is that the servers can answer PIR queries with $o(N)$ computation.

We focus on the two main families of IT PIR constructions: (1) first-generation "Reed-Muller based" schemes, or RM PIR for short; and (2) third-generation "matching-vector based" schemes, or MV PIR for short. RM PIR schemes are motivated by their simplicity and their good concrete communication complexity on small to medium size databases, whereas MV PIR schemes are motivated by their superior asymptotic efficiency. Another advantage of RM PIR schemes is that they naturally scale to bigger security thresholds $t > 1$, increasing the number of servers by roughly a factor of t but maintaining the per-server communication complexity. For MV PIR schemes, the comparable t-private variants require at least 2^t servers [7].

1.3 Our Contribution

We obtain the following main results. See Sect. 2 for a more detailed and more technical overview.

Positive Results for RM PIR. We show that for some natural function families, such as unions of multi-dimensional intervals or other convex shapes (capturing, e.g., geographical databases), decision trees, and DNF formulas with disjoint terms, RM PIR schemes do admit computational shortcuts. In some of these cases the shortcut is essentially optimal, in the sense that the computational complexity of the servers is equal to the size of the PIR queries plus the size of the function representation (up to polylogarithmic factors). In terms of concrete efficiency, the resulting HSS schemes can in some cases be competitive with alternative techniques from the literature, including lightweight computational HSS schemes based on symmetric cryptography [19], even for large domain sizes such as $N = 2^{40}$. This may come at the cost of either using more servers ($k \geq 3$ or even $k \geq 4$, compared to $k = 2$ in [19]) or alternatively applying communication balancing techniques from [11,29,60] that are only efficient for short outputs.

Negative Results for RM PIR. The above positive result may suggest that "simple" functions admit shortcuts. We show that this can only be true to a limited extent. Assuming the Strong Exponential Time Hypothesis (SETH) assumption [26], a conjecture commonly used in fine-grained complexity [59], we show that there is no computational shortcuts for general DNF formulas. More broadly, there are no shortcuts for function families that contain hard counting problems.

Negative Results for MV PIR. Somewhat unexpectedly, for MV PIR schemes, the situation appears to be significantly worse. Here we can show conditional hardness results even for the *all-1 database*. Of course, one can trivially realize an HSS scheme for the constant function $f(x) = 1$. However, our results effectively rule out obtaining efficient HSS for richer function families via the MV PIR route, even for the simple but useful families to which our positive results for RM PIR apply. This shows a qualitative separation between RM PIR and MV PIR.

Our negative results are obtained by exploiting a connection between shortcuts in MV PIR and counting problems in graphs that we prove to be ETH-hard. While this only rules out a specific type of HSS constructions, it can still be viewed as a necessary step towards broader impossibility results. For instance, proving that (computationally efficient) HSS for simple function families cannot have $N^{o(1)}$ share size *inevitably requires* proving computational hardness of the counting problems we study, simply because if these problems were easy then such HSS schemes would exist. We stress that good computational shortcuts for MV PIR schemes, matching our shortcuts for RM PIR schemes, is a desirable goal. From a theoretical perspective, they would give rise to better information-theoretic HSS schemes for natural function classes. From an applied perspective, they could give concretely efficient HSS schemes and secure computation protocols (for the same natural classes) that outperform all competing protocols on moderate-sized input domains. (See the full version for communication break-even points.) Unfortunately, our negative results give strong evidence that, contrary to prior expectations, such shortcuts for MV PIR do not exist.

Positive Results for Tensored and Parallel MV PIR. Finally, we show how to bypass our negative result for MV PIR via a "tensoring" operator and parallel composition. The former allows us to obtain the same shortcuts we get for RM PIR while maintaining the low communication cost of MV PIR, but at the cost of increasing the number of servers. This is done by introducing an exploitable structure similar to that in RM PIR through an operation that we called tensoring. In fact, tensoring can be applied to any PIR schemes with certain natural structural properties to obtain new PIR with shortcuts. The parallel composition approach is restricted to specific function classes and has a significant concrete overhead. Applying either transformation to an MV PIR scheme yields schemes that no longer conform to the baseline template of MV PIR, and thus the previous negative result does not apply.

2   Overview of Results and Techniques

Recall that the main objective of this work is to study the possibility of obtaining non-trivial IT HSS schemes via computational shortcuts for IT PIR schemes. In this section we give a more detailed overview of our positive and negative results and the underlying techniques.

From here on, we let $N = 2^n$ be the size of the (possibly structured) database, which in our case will be a truth table encoding a function $f : \{0,1\}^n \to \{0,1\}$ represented by a bit-string $\hat{f}$ of length $\ell = |\hat{f}| \leq N$. We are mostly interested in the case where $\ell \ll N$. We will sometimes use ℓ to denote a natural size parameter which is upper bounded by $|\hat{f}|$. For instance, $\hat{f}$ can be a DNF formula with ℓ terms over n input variables. We denote by $\mathcal{F}$ the *function family* associating each $\hat{f}$ with a function f and a size parameter ℓ, where $\ell = |\hat{f}|$ by default.

For both HSS and PIR, we consider the following efficiency measures:

- Input share size $\alpha(N)$: Number of bits that the client sends to each server.
- Output share size $\beta(N)$: Number of bits that each server sends to the client.
- Evaluation time $\tau(N, \ell)$: Running time of server algorithm, mapping an input share in $\{0,1\}^{\alpha(N)}$ and function representation $\hat{f} \in \{0,1\}^{\ell}$ to output share in $\{0,1\}^{\beta(N)}$.

When considering PIR (rather than HSS) schemes, we may also refer to $\alpha(N)$ and $\beta(N)$ as *query size* and *answer size* respectively. The computational model we use for measuring the running time $\tau(N, \ell)$ is the standard RAM model by default; however, both our positive and negative results apply (up to polylogarithmic factors) also to other standard complexity measures, such as circuit size.

Any PIR scheme PIR can be viewed as an HSS scheme for a truth-table representation, where the PIR database is the truth-table $\hat{f}$ of f. For this representation, the corresponding evaluation time τ must grow linearly with N. If a more expressive function family $\mathcal{F}$ supports faster evaluation time, we say that PIR admits a computational shortcut for $\mathcal{F}$. It will be useful to classify computational shortcuts as *strong* or *weak*. A strong shortcut is one in which the evaluation time is optimal up to polylogarithmic factors, namely $\tau = \tilde{O}(\alpha+\beta+\ell)$. (Note that $\alpha + \beta + \ell$ is the total length of input and output.) Weak shortcuts have evaluation time of the form $\tau = O(\ell \cdot N^{\delta})$, for some constant $0 < \delta < 1$. A weak shortcut gives a meaningful speedup whenever $\ell = N^{o(1)}$.

2.1   Shortcuts in Reed-Muller PIR

The first generation of PIR schemes, originating from the work of Chor et al. [29], represent the database as a low-degree multivariate polynomial, which the servers evaluate on each of the client's queries. We refer to PIR schemes of this type as *Reed-Muller* PIR (or RM PIR for short) since the answers to all possible queries form a Reed-Muller encoding of the database. While there are several variations of RM PIR in the literature, the results we describe next are insensitive to the differences. In the following focus on a slight variation of the original k-server RM PIR scheme from [29] (see [11]) that has answer size $\beta = 1$, which we denote by $\mathsf{PIR}_{\mathsf{RM}}^k$. For the purpose of this section we will mainly focus on the computation performed by the servers, for the simplest case of $k = 3$ ($\mathsf{PIR}_{\mathsf{RM}}^3$), as this is the aspect we aim to optimize. For a full description of the more general case we refer the reader to Sect. 4.

Let $\mathbb{F} = \mathbb{F}_4$ be the Galois field of size 4. In the $\mathsf{PIR}_{\mathsf{RM}}^3$ scheme, the client views its input $i \in [N]$ as a pair of indices $i = (i_1, i_2) \in [\sqrt{N}] \times [\sqrt{N}]$ and computes two vectors $q_1^j, q_2^j \in \mathbb{F}^{\sqrt{N}}$ for each server $j \in \{1, 2, 3\}$, such that $\{q_1^j\}$ depend on i_1 and $\{q_2^j\}$ depend on i_2. Note that this implies that $\alpha(N) = O(\sqrt{N})$. Next, each server j, which holds a description of a function $f: [\sqrt{N}] \times [\sqrt{N}] \to \{0, 1\}$, computes an answer $a_j = \sum_{i'_1, i'_2 \in [\sqrt{N}]} f(i'_1, i'_2) q_1^j[i'_1] q_2^j[i'_2]$ with arithmetic over $\mathbb{F}$ and sends the client a single bit which depends on a_j (so $\beta(N) = 1$). The client reconstructs $f(i_1, i_2)$ by taking the exclusive-or of the 3 answer bits.

Positive Results for RM PIR. The computation of each server j, $a_j = \sum_{i'_1, i'_2 \in [\sqrt{N}]} f(i'_1, i'_2) q_1^j[i'_1] q_2^j[i'_2]$, can be viewed as an evaluation of a multivariate degree-2 polynomial, where $\{f(i'_1, i'_1)\}$ are the coefficients, and the entries of q_1^j, q_2^j are the variables. Therefore, to obtain a computational shortcut, one should look for *structured* polynomials that can be evaluated in time $o(N)$. A simple but useful observation is that computational shortcuts exist for functions f which are *combinatorial rectangles*, that is, $f(i_1, i_2) = 1$ if and only if $i_1 \in I_1$ and $i_2 \in I_2$, where $I_1, I_2 \subseteq [\sqrt{N}]$. Indeed, we may write

$$a_j = \sum_{i'_1, i'_2 \in [\sqrt{N}]} f(i'_1, i'_2) q_1^j[i'_1] q_2^j[i'_2] = \sum_{(i'_1, i'_2) \in (I_1, I_2)} q_1^j[i'_1] q_2^j[i'_2] \qquad (1)$$

$$= \left(\sum_{i'_1 \in I_1} q_1^j[i'_1] \right) \left(\sum_{i'_2 \in I_2} q_2^j[i'_2] \right). \qquad (2)$$

Note that if a server evaluates the expression using Eq. (1) the time is $O(N)$, but if it instead uses Eq. (2) the time is just $O(\sqrt{N}) = O(\alpha(N))$. Following this direction, we obtain non-trivial IT HSS schemes for some natural function classes such as disjoint unions of intervals and decision trees.

Theorem 1 (Decision trees, formal version Theorem 9). $\mathsf{PIR}_{\mathsf{RM}}^k$ *admits a weak shortcut for decision trees (more generally, disjoint DNF formulas). Concretely, for n variables and ℓ leaves (or terms), we have $\tau(N, \ell) = O(\ell \cdot N^{1/(k-1)})$, where $N = 2^n$.*

Theorem 2 (Union of disjoint intervals, formal version Theorems 10 and 11). *For every positive integers $d \geq 1$ and $k \geq 3$ such that $d|k-1$, $\mathsf{PIR}_{\mathsf{RM}}^k$ admits a strong shortcut for unions of ℓ disjoint d-dimensional intervals in $([N^{1/d}])^d$. Concretely, $\tau(N, \ell) = O(N^{1/(k-1)} + \ell)$.*

Better shortcuts running in $\tilde{O}(N^{1/(k-1)} + \ell \cdot N^{1/3(k-1)})$ are also possible. Moreover, by expressing (discretized) convex bodies as unions of intervals, we generalize the result for interval functions to convex body membership functions.

Negative Results for RM PIR. All of the previous positive results apply to function families $\mathcal{F}$ for which there is an efficient *counting algorithm* that given $\hat{f} \in \mathcal{F}$ returns the number of satisfying assignments of f. We show that this is not a coincidence: efficient counting can be reduced to finding a shortcut for $\hat{f}$ in $\mathsf{PIR}_{\mathsf{RM}}^k$. This implies that computational shortcuts are impossible for function representations for which the counting problem is hard. Concretely, following a similar idea from [52], we show that a careful choice of PIR query can be used to obtain the *parity* of all evaluations of f as the PIR answer. The latter is hard to compute even for DNF formulas, let alone stronger representation models, assuming standard conjectures from fine-grained complexity: either the *Strong Exponential Time Hypothesis* (SETH) or, with weaker parameters, even the standard *Exponential Time Hypothesis* (ETH) [25,26].

Theorem 3 (No shortcuts for DNF under ETH, formal version Corollaries 2 and 3). *Assuming (standard) ETH, $\mathsf{PIR}_{\mathsf{RM}}^k$ does not admit a strong shortcut for DNF formulas for sufficiently large k. Moreover, assuming SETH, for any $k \geq 3$, $\mathsf{PIR}_{\mathsf{RM}}^k$ does not admit a weak shortcut for DNF formulas.*

2.2   Hardness of Shortcuts for Matching-Vector PIR

Recall that MV PIR schemes are the only known PIR schemes achieving subpolynomial communication (that is, $N^{o(1)}$) with a constant number of servers. We give strong evidence for hardness of computational shortcuts for MV PIR. We start with a brief technical overview of MV PIR.

We consider here a representative instance of MV PIR from [12,43], which we denote by $\mathsf{PIR}_{\mathsf{MV,SC}}^3$. This MV PIR scheme is based on two crucial combinatorial ingredients: a family of *matching vectors* and a *share conversion* scheme, respectively. We describe each of these ingredients separately.

A family of matching vectors MV consists of N pairs of vectors $\{u_x, v_x\}$ such that each matching inner product $\langle u_x, v_x \rangle$ is 0, and each non-matching inner product $\langle u_x, v_{x'} \rangle$ is nonzero. More precisely, such a family is parameterized by integers m, h, N and a subset $S \subset \mathbb{Z}_m$ such that $0 \notin S$. A matching vector family is defined by two sequences of N vectors $\{u_x\}_{x \in [N]}$ and $\{v_x\}_{x \in [N]}$, where $u_x, v_x \in \mathbb{Z}_m^h$, such that for all $x \in [N]$ we have $\langle u_x, v_x \rangle = 0$, and for all $x, x' \in [N]$ such that $x \neq x'$ we have $\langle u_x, v_{x'} \rangle \in S$. We refer to this as the *S-matching* requirement. Typical choices of parameters are $m = 6$ or $m = 511$ (products of two primes), $|S| = 3$ (taking the values $(0,1), (1,0), (1,1)$ in Chinese remainder notation), and $h = N^{o(1)}$ (corresponding to the PIR query length).

A share conversion scheme SC is a local mapping (without interaction) of shares of a secret y to shares of a related secret y', where $y \in \mathbb{Z}_m$ and y' is in some other Abelian group $\mathbb{G}$. Useful choices of $\mathbb{G}$ include $\mathbb{F}_2^2$ and $\mathbb{F}_2^9$ corresponding to $m = 6$ and $m = 511$ respectively. The shares of y and y' are distributed using linear secret-sharing schemes $\mathcal{L}$ and $\mathcal{L}'$ respectively, where $\mathcal{L}'$ is typically additive secret sharing over $\mathbb{G}$. The relation between y and y' that SC should comply with is defined by S as follows: if $y \in S$ then $y' = 0$ and if $y = 0$ then $y' \neq 0$. More concretely, if $(y_1, \ldots, y_k)$ are $\mathcal{L}$-shares of y, then each server j can run the share conversion scheme on (j, y_j) and obtain $y_j' = \mathsf{SC}(j, y_j)$ such that $(y_1', \ldots, y_k')$ are $\mathcal{L}'$-shares of some y' satisfying the above relation. What makes share conversion nontrivial is the requirement that the relation between y and y' hold regardless of the randomness used by $\mathcal{L}$ for sharing y.

Suppose MV and SC are compatible in the sense that they share the same set S. Moreover, suppose that SC applies to a 3-party linear secret-sharing scheme

$\mathcal{L}$ over $\mathbb{Z}_m$. Then we can define a 3-server PIR scheme $\mathsf{PIR}^3_{\mathsf{MV},\mathsf{SC}}$ in the following natural way. Let $f : [N] \to \{0,1\}$ be the servers' database and $x \in [N]$ be the client's input. The queries are obtained by applying $\mathcal{L}$ to independently share each entry of u_x. Since $\mathcal{L}$ is linear, the servers can locally compute, for each $x' \in [N]$, $\mathcal{L}$-shares of $y_{x,x'} = \langle u_x, v_{x'} \rangle$. Note that $y_{x,x} = 0 \in \mathbb{Z}_m$ and $y_{x,x'} \in S$ (hence $y_{x,x'} \neq 0$) for $x \neq x'$. Letting $y_{j,x,x'}$ denote the share of $y_{x,x'}$ known to server j, each server can now apply share conversion to obtain a $\mathcal{L}'$-share $y'_{j,x,x'} = \mathsf{SC}(j, y_{j,x,x'})$ of $y'_{x,x'}$, where $y'_{x,x'} = 0$ if $x \neq x'$ and $y'_{x,x'} \neq 0$ if $x = x'$. Finally, using the linearity of $\mathcal{L}'$, the servers can locally compute $\mathcal{L}'$-shares $\tilde{y}_j$ of $\tilde{y} = \sum_{x' \in [N]} f(x') \cdot y'_{x,x'}$, which they send as their answers to the client. Note that $\tilde{y} = 0$ if and only if $f(x) = 0$. Hence, the client can recover $f(x)$ by applying the reconstruction of $\mathcal{L}'$ to the answers and comparing $\tilde{y}$ to 0. When $\mathcal{L}'$ is additive over $\mathbb{G}$, each answer consists of a single element of $\mathbb{G}$.

Shortcuts for MV PIR Imply Subgraph Counting. The question we ask in this work is whether the server computation in the above scheme can be sped up when f is a "simple" function, say one for which our positive results for RM PIR apply. Somewhat unexpectedly, we obtain strong evidence against this by establishing a connection between computational shortcuts for $\mathsf{PIR}^3_{\mathsf{MV},\mathsf{SC}}$ for useful choices of $(\mathsf{MV},\mathsf{SC})$ and the problem of counting induced subgraphs. Concretely, computing a server's answer on the all-1 database and query x^j requires computing the parity of the number of subgraphs with certain properties in a graph defined by x^j. By applying results and techniques from parameterized complexity [28,42], we prove ETH-hardness of computational shortcuts for variants of the MV PIR schemes from [12,43]. In contrast to the case of RM PIR, these hardness results apply even for functions as simple as the constant function $f(x) = 1$.

The variants of MV PIR schemes to which our ETH-hardness results apply differ from the original PIR schemes from [12,43] only in the parameters of the matching vectors, which are worse asymptotically, but still achieve $N^{o(1)}$ communication complexity. The obstacle which prevents us from proving a similar hardness result for the original schemes from [12,43] seems to be an artifact of the proof, instead of an inherent limitation (more on this later). We therefore formulate a clean hardness-of-counting conjecture that would imply a similar hardness result for the original constructions from [12,43].

We now outline the ideas behind the negative results, deferring the technical details to Sect. 5. Recall that the computation of each server j in $\mathsf{PIR}^3_{\mathsf{MV},\mathsf{SC}}$ takes the form

$$\sum_{x' \in [N]} f(x') \cdot \mathsf{SC}(j, y_{j,x,x'}),$$

where $y_{j,x,x'}$ is the j-th share of $\langle u_x, v_{x'} \rangle$. Therefore, for the all-1 database ($f = 1$), for every S-matching vector family MV and share conversion scheme SC from $\mathcal{L}$ to $\mathcal{L}'$ we can define the $(\mathsf{MV},\mathsf{SC})$-counting problem $\#(\mathsf{MV},\mathsf{SC})$.

Definition 1 (Server computation problem). *For a Matching Vector family* MV *and share conversion* SC, *the problem* $\#(\mathsf{MV},\mathsf{SC})$ *is defined as follows.*

- INPUT: *a valid $\mathcal{L}$-share y_j of some $u_x \in \mathbb{Z}_m^h$ (element-wise)*,
- OUTPUT: $\sum_{x' \in [N]} SC(j, y_{j,x,x'})$, *where $y_{j,x,x'}$ is the share of $\langle u_x, v_{x'} \rangle$.*

Essentially, the server computes N inner products of the input and the matching vectors using the homomorphic property of the linear sharing, maps the results using the share conversion and adds the result to obtain the final output.

Let $\mathsf{MV}_{\mathrm{Grol}}^w$ be a matching vectors family due to Grolmusz [40,50], which is used in all third-generation PIR schemes (see Sect. 5, Fact 1). For presentation, we focus on the special case $\#(\mathsf{MV}_{\mathrm{Grol}}^w, \mathsf{SC}_{\mathrm{Efr}})$, where $\mathsf{SC}_{\mathrm{Efr}}$ is a share conversion due to Efremenko [43], which we present in Sect. 3.3. Note that all the results that follow also hold for the share conversion of [12], denoted by $\mathsf{SC}_{\mathrm{BIKO}}$. The family we consider, $\mathsf{MV}_{\mathrm{Grol}}^w$, is associated with the parameters $r \in \mathbb{N}$ and $w \colon \mathbb{N} \to \mathbb{N}$, such that the size of the matching vector family is $\binom{r}{w(r)}$, and the length of each vector is $h = \binom{r}{\leq \Theta(\sqrt{w(r)})}$. By choosing $w(r) = \Theta(\sqrt{r})$ and r such that $N \leq \binom{r}{w(r)}$, the communication complexity of $\mathsf{PIR}_{\mathsf{MV}_{\mathrm{Grol}}^w, \mathsf{SC}_{\mathrm{Efr}}}^k$ is $h = 2^{O(\sqrt{n \log n})}$, where $N = 2^n$, which is the best asymptotically among known PIR schemes.

Next, we relate $\#(\mathsf{MV}_{\mathrm{Grol}}^w, \mathsf{SC}_{\mathrm{Efr}})$ to $\oplus\mathrm{INDSUB}(\Phi, w)$, the problem of deciding the parity of the number of w-node subgraphs of a graph G that satisfy graph property Φ. Here we consider the parameter w to be a function of the number of nodes of G. We will specifically interested in graph properties $\Phi = \Phi_{m,\Delta}$ that include graphs whose number of edges modulo m is equal to Δ. Formally:

Definition 2 (Subgraph counting problem). *For a graph property Φ and parameter $w \colon \mathbb{N} \to \mathbb{N}$ (function of the number of nodes), the problem $\oplus\mathrm{INDSUB}(\Phi, w)$ is defined as follows.*

- INPUT: *Graph G with r nodes.*
- OUTPUT: *The parity of the number of induced subgraphs H of G such that: (1) H has $w(r)$ nodes; (2) $H \in \Phi$.*

We let $\Phi_{m,\Delta}$ denote the set of graphs H such that $|E(H)| \equiv \Delta \mod m$.

The following main technical lemma for this section relates obtaining computational shortcuts for $\mathsf{PIR}_{\mathsf{MV},\mathsf{SC}}^k$ to counting induced subgraphs.

Lemma 1 (From MV PIR to subgraph counting). *If $\#(\mathsf{MV}_{\mathrm{Grol}}^w, \mathsf{SC}_{\mathrm{Efr}})$ can be computed in $N^{o(1)} \left(= r^{o(w)}\right)$ time, then $\oplus\mathrm{INDSUB}(\Phi_{511,0}, w)$ can be decided in $r^{o(w)}$ time, for any nondecreasing function $w \colon \mathbb{N} \to \mathbb{N}$.*

The Hardness of Subgraph Counting. The problem $\oplus\mathrm{INDSUB}(\Phi_{511,0}, w)$ is studied in parameterized complexity theory [42] and falls into the framework of *motif counting problems* described as follows in [56]: *Given a large structure and a small pattern called the motif, compute the number of occurrences of the motif in the structure.* In particular, the following result can be derived from Döfer *et al.* [42].

Theorem 4. *[42, Corollary of Theorem 22]* $\oplus\text{INDSUB}(\Phi_{511,0}, w)$ *cannot be solved in time* $r^{o(w)}$ *unless* ETH *fails.*

Theorem 4 is insufficient for our purposes since it essentially states that no machine running in time $r^{o(w)}$ can successfully decide $\oplus\text{INDSUB}(\Phi_{511,0}, w)$ for any pair (r, w). It other words, it implies hardness of counting for *some* weight parameter w, while for our case, we have specific function $w(r)$.

Fortunately, in [28] it was shown the counting of cliques, a very central motif, is hard for cliques of any size as long as it is bounded from above by $O(r^c)$ for an arbitrary constant $c < 1$ ($\sqrt{r}$, $\log r$, $\log^* r$, etc.), assuming ETH. Indeed, after borrowing results from [28] and via a more careful analysis of the proof of [42, Theorem 22], we can prove the following stronger statement about its hardness.

Theorem 5. *For some efficiently computable function* $w = \Theta(\log r/\log\log r)$, $\oplus\text{INDSUB}(\Phi_{511,0}, w)$ *cannot be solved in time* $r^{o(w)}$, *unless* ETH *fails.*

Denote by MV^* the family $\text{MV}_{\text{Grol}}^w$ with $w(r) = \Theta(\log r/\log\log r)$ as in Theorem 5. Lemma 1 and Theorem 5 imply the impossibility result for strong shortcuts for PIR schemes instantiated with MV^*. Note that such an instantiation of $\text{MV}_{\text{Grol}}^w$ yields PIR schemes with subpolynomial communication $2^{O(n^{3/4}\text{polylog }n)}$.

Theorem 6. *[No shortcuts in Efremenko MV PIR, formal version Theorem 15]* $\#(\text{MV}^*, \text{SC}_{\text{Efr}})$ *cannot be computed in* $N^{o(1)}$ $\left(= r^{o(w)}\right)$ *time, unless* ETH *fails. Consequently, there are no strong shortcuts for the all-1 database for* $\text{PIR}_{\text{MV}^*, \text{SC}_{\text{Efr}}}^3$.

It is natural to ask whether hardness for other ranges of parameters such as $w = \Theta(\sqrt{r})$ holds for $\oplus\text{INDSUB}(\Phi_{511,0}, w)$ in the spirit of Theorem 5. This is also of practical concern because the best known $\text{MV}_{\text{Grol}}^w$ constructions fall within such ranges. In particular, if we can show $\oplus\text{INDSUB}(\Phi_{511,0}, \Theta(\sqrt{r}))$ cannot be decided in $r^{o(\sqrt{r})}$ time, it will imply that $\text{PIR}_{\mathcal{P},\mathcal{C}}^k$ for $\mathcal{P} = \text{MV}_{\text{Grol}}^{\Theta(\sqrt{r})}$ and $\mathcal{C} = \text{SC}_{\text{Efr}}$ does not admit strong shortcuts for the all-1 database, since $\alpha(n) = N^{o(1)}$ but $\tau(n) = N^{\Omega(1)}$.

In fact, the problem $\oplus\text{INDSUB}(\Phi_{511,0}, w)$ is plausibly hard, and can be viewed as a variant of the fine-grained-hard Exact-k-clique problem [59]. Consequently, we make the following conjecture.

Conjecture 1 (Hardness of counting induced subgraphs). $\oplus\text{INDSUB}(\Phi_{m,\Delta}, w)$ cannot be decided in $r^{o(w)}$ time, for any integers $m \geq 2$, $0 \leq \Delta < m$, and for every function $w(r) = O(r^c)$, $0 \leq c < 1$.

For the impossibility results in this paper, we are only concerned with $w(r) = \Theta(\sqrt{r})$, and $(m, \Delta) = (511, 0)$ or $(m, \Delta) = (6, 4)$.

2.3   HSS from Generic Compositions of PIRs

Our central technique for obtaining shortcuts in PIR schemes is by exploiting the structure of the database. For certain PIR schemes where the structure is not exploitable, such as those based on matching vectors, we propose to introduce exploitable structures artificially by composing several PIR schemes. Concretely, we present two generic ways, tensoring and parallel PIR composition, to obtain a PIR which admits shortcuts for some function families by composing PIRs which satisfy certain natural properties. For details, we refer to the full version.

Tensoring. First we define a *tensoring operation* on PIR schemes, which generically yields PIRs with shortcuts, at the price of increasing the number of servers.

Theorem 7 (Tensoring, informal). *Let* PIR *be a k-server PIR scheme satisfying some natural properties. Then there exists a k^d-server PIR scheme* PIR$^{\otimes d}$ *with the same (per server) communication complexity that admits the same computational shortcuts as* PIR$_{\mathsf{RM}}^{d+1}$ *does.*

When PIR is indeed instantiated with a matching-vector PIR, Theorem 7 gives HSS schemes for disjoint DNF formulas or decision trees with the best asymptotic efficiency out of the ones we considered.

Corollary 1 (Decision trees from tensoring, informal). *There is a 3^d-server HSS for decision trees, or generally disjoint DNF formulas, with $\alpha(N) = \tilde{O}\left(2^{6\sqrt{n \log n}}\right)$, $\beta(N) = O(1)$ and $\tau(N, \ell) = \tilde{O}\left(N^{1/d+o(1)} + \ell \cdot N^{1/3d}\right)$, where n is the number of variables and ℓ is the number of leaves in the decision tree.*

Parallel PIR Composition. For the special case of interval functions, we can do even better with the second technique. We show that by making *parallel invocations* to HSS for point functions, it is possible to obtain HSS for the class of *sparsely-supported DNF functions*. In particular, this yields an HSS for union of intervals with the best asymptotic complexity among our constructions. This approach however does not generalize to better asymptotic results for decision trees or DNF formulas due to known lower bounds for covering codes [30].

Theorem 8 (Intervals from parallel composition, informal). *There is a 3-server HSS for unions of ℓ d-dimensional intervals with $\alpha(N) = \tilde{O}\left(2^{6\sqrt{n \log n}}\right)$, $\beta(N) = O(\log(\frac{1}{\epsilon}))$ and $\tau(N, \ell) = \tilde{O}\left(\log(\frac{1}{\epsilon})\ell \cdot 2^{6\sqrt{n \log n}}\right)$.*

2.4 Concrete Efficiency

Motivated by a variety of real-world applications, the concrete efficiency of PIR has been extensively studied in the applied cryptography and computer security communities; see, e.g., [1,31,51,55,58] and references therein. Many of the application scenarios of PIR can potentially benefit from the more general HSS functionality we study in this work. To give a sense of the concrete efficiency benefits we can get, consider following MPC task: The client holds a secret input x and wishes to know if x falls in a union of a set of 2-dimensional intervals held by k servers, where at most t servers may collude ($t = 1$ by default). This can be generalized to return a payload associated with the interval to which x belongs. HSS for this "union of rectangles" function family can be useful for securely querying a geographical database.

We focus here on HSS obtained from the $\mathsf{PIR}_{\mathsf{RM}}^k$ scheme, which admits strong shortcuts for multi-dimensional intervals and at the same time offers attractive concrete communication complexity. For the database sizes we consider, the concrete communication and computation costs are much better than those of (computational) single-server schemes based on fully homomorphic encryption. Classical secure computation techniques are not suitable at all for our purposes, since their communication cost would scale linearly with the number of intervals. The closest competing solutions are obtained via symmetric-key-based *function secret sharing* (FSS) schemes for intervals [17,19] (see full version for details).

We instantiate the FSS-based constructions with $k = 2$ servers, since the communication complexity in this case is only $O(\lambda n^2)$ for a security parameter λ [19]. For $k \geq 3$ (and $t = k - 1$), the best known FSS schemes require $O(\lambda \sqrt{N})$ communication [17]. Our comparison focuses on communication complexity which is easier to measure analytically. Our shortcuts make the computational cost scale linearly with the server input size, with small concrete constants. Below we give a few data points to compare the IT-PIR and the FSS-based approaches.

For a 2-dimensional database of size $2^{30} = 2^{15} \times 2^{15}$ (which is sufficient to encode a $300 \times 300 \, \mathrm{km}^2$ area with $10 \times 10 \, \mathrm{m}^2$ precision), the HSS based on $\mathsf{PIR}_{\mathsf{RM}}^k$ with shortcuts requires 16.1, 1.3, and 0.6 KB of communication for $k = 3, 4$ and 5 respectively, whereas FSS with $k = 2$ requires roughly 28 KB. For these parameters, we expect the concrete computational cost of the PIR-based HSS to be smaller as well.

We note that in $\mathsf{PIR}_{\mathsf{RM}}^k$ the payload size contributes additively to the communication complexity. If the payload size is small (a few bits), it might be beneficial to base the HSS on a "balanced" variant of $\mathsf{PIR}_{\mathsf{RM}}^k$ proposed by Woodruff and Yekhanin [60]. Using the Baur-Strassen algorithm [8], we can get the same shortcuts as for $\mathsf{PIR}_{\mathsf{RM}}^k$ with roughly half as many servers, at the cost of longer output shares that have comparable size to the input shares. Such balanced schemes are more attractive for short payloads than for long ones. For a 2-dimensional database of size $2^{30} = 2^{15} \times 2^{15}$, the HSS based on balanced $\mathsf{PIR}_{\mathsf{RM}}^k$ with 1-bit payload requires 1.5 and 0.2 KB communication for $k = 2$ and 3 respectively.

Our approach is even more competitive in the case of a higher corruption threshold $t \geq 2$, since (as discussed above) known FSS schemes perform more poorly in this setting, whereas the cost of $\mathsf{PIR}_{\mathsf{RM}}^k$ scales linearly with t. Finally, $\mathsf{PIR}_{\mathsf{RM}}^k$ is more "MPC-friendly" than the FSS-based alternative in the sense that its share generation is non-cryptographic and thus is easier to distribute via an MPC protocol.

3   Preliminaries

Let $m, n \in \mathbb{N}$ with $m \leq n$. We use $\{0, 1\}^n$ to denote the set of bit strings of length n, $[n]$ to denote the set $\{1, \ldots, n\}$, and $[m, n]$ to denote the set $\{m, m+1, \ldots, n\}$.

The set of all finite-length bit strings is denoted by $\{0,1\}^*$. Let $v = (v_1, \ldots, v_n)$ be a vector. We denote by $v[i]$ or v_i the i-th entry v. Let S, X be sets with $S \subseteq X$. The set membership indicator $\chi_{S,X} : X \to \{0,1\}$ is a function which outputs 1 on input $x \in S$, and outputs 0 otherwise. When X is clear from the context, we omit X from the subscript and simply write χ_S.

3.1 Function Families

To rigorously talk about a function and its description as separate objects, we define function families in a fashion similar to that in [17].

Definition 3 (Function Families). *A function family is a collection of tuples* $\mathcal{F} = \{\mathcal{F}_n = (\mathcal{X}_n, \mathcal{Y}_n, P_n, E_n)\}_{n \in \mathbb{N}}$ *where* $\mathcal{X}_n \subseteq \{0,1\}^*$ *is a domain set,* $\mathcal{Y}_n \subseteq \{0,1\}^*$ *is a range set,* $P_n \subseteq \{0,1\}^*$ *is a collection of function descriptions, and* $E_n : P_n \times \mathcal{X}_n \to \mathcal{Y}_n$ *is an algorithm, running in time* $O(|\mathcal{X}_n|)$, *defining the function described by each* $\hat{f} \in P_n$.
  Concretely, each $\hat{f} \in P_n$ *describes a corresponding function* $f : \mathcal{X}_n \to \mathcal{Y}_n$ *defined by* $f(x) = E_n(\hat{f}, x)$. *Unless specified, from now on we assume that* $\mathcal{X}_n = \{0,1\}^n$ *and* $\mathcal{Y}_n = \mathbb{F}_2$. *When there is no risk of confusion, we will describe a function family by* $\mathcal{F}_n$ *instead of* $\mathcal{F} = \{\mathcal{F}_n\}_{n \in \mathbb{N}}$, *write* f *instead of* $\hat{f}$, *and write* $f \in \mathcal{F}_n$ *or* $f \in \mathcal{F}$ *instead of* $\hat{f} \in P_n$.

Definition 4 (All Boolean Functions). *The family of all Boolean functions is a tuple* $\mathrm{ALL}_n = (\mathcal{X}_n, \mathcal{Y}_n, P_n, E_n)$ *where* P_n *is a set containing the truth table* $\hat{f}$ *of* f *for each* $f : \mathcal{X}_n \to \mathcal{Y}_n$, *and* E_n *is the selection algorithm such that* $E_n(\hat{f}, x) = \hat{f}[x]$.

We next define combinatorial rectangle functions, each of which is parameterized with a combinatorial rectangle, and it outputs 1 whenever the input lies in the rectangle. This family is central to the shortcuts that we obtain for the Reed-Muller PIR and the PIRs obtained by tensoring.

Definition 5 (Combinatorial Rectangles). *Let* $d \in \mathbb{N}$, $\mathcal{X}^1, \ldots, \mathcal{X}^d$ *be sets and* $cr : \mathcal{X}^1 \times \cdots \times \mathcal{X}^d \to \mathbb{F}_2$ *be a function. We say that* cr *is a* $(d\text{-dimensional})$ combinatorial rectangle function *if the truth table of* cr *forms a* $(d\text{-dimensional})$ combinatorial rectangle. *In other words, for each* $i \in [d]$, *there exist subsets* $\mathcal{S}^i \subseteq \mathcal{X}^i$ *such that* $cr(x_1, \ldots, x_d) = 1$ *if and only if* $x_i \in \mathcal{S}^i$ *for all* $i \in [d]$. *A combinatorial rectangle function* cr *can be described by* $\hat{cr} = (\mathcal{S}^1, \ldots, \mathcal{S}^d)$ *of length* $|\hat{cr}| = O(n)$, *and an evaluation algorithm* E_{CR} *such that* $E_{\mathrm{CR}}(\hat{cr}, x) = cr(x)$.

Definition 6 (Sum of Combinatorial Rectangles). *Let* $\ell, d \in \mathbb{N}$. *The family of* ℓ-sum d-dimensional combinatorial rectangle functions *is a tuple* $\mathrm{SUMCR}_n^{\ell,d} = (\mathcal{X}_n, \mathcal{Y}_n, P_n, E_n)$ *where* $\mathcal{X}_n = \mathcal{X}_n^1 \times \cdots \times \mathcal{X}_n^d$ *for some sets* $\mathcal{X}_n^1, \ldots, \mathcal{X}_n^d$, $P_n = \{\hat{cr}\}_{\hat{cr}=(\hat{cr}_1, \ldots, \hat{cr}_\ell)}$ *is the set of all* ℓ-tuples of descriptions of combinatorial rectangle functions with domain $\mathcal{X}_n$, and $E(\hat{cr}, x) = \sum_{i=1}^{\ell} E_{\mathrm{CR}}(\hat{cr}_i, x) = \sum_{i=1}^{\ell} cr_i(x)$. *That is,* $\mathrm{SUMCR}_n^{\ell,d}$ *defines all functions of the form* $f = cr_1 + \ldots + cr_\ell$.

We next define natural special cases of combinatorial rectangle functions. The first are interval functions which output 1 when the input falls into specified intervals. The second are DNF formulas.

Definition 7 (Interval Functions). *Let $\ell, d \in \mathbb{N}$ with $d|n$. The family of ℓ-sum d-dimensional interval functions is a tuple $\mathrm{SUMINT}_n^{\ell,d} = (\mathcal{X}_n, \mathcal{Y}_n, P_n, E_n)$ where*

- *$\mathcal{X}_n = \left(\{0,1\}^{n/d}\right)^d$,*
- *$\mathcal{Y}_n = \mathbb{F}_2$,*
- *$P_n = \left\{ (a_i^j, b_i^j)_{i \in [\ell], j \in [d]} : a_i^j, b_i^j \in \{0,1\}^{n/d} \right\}$, and*
- *$E\left((a_i^j, b_i^j)_{i \in [\ell], j \in [d]}, x\right) = \sum_{i=1}^{\ell} \chi_{\prod_{j=1}^d [a_i^j, b_i^j]}(x)$.*

In a similar fashion we define $\mathrm{INT}_n^{\ell,d} = (\mathcal{X}_n, \mathcal{Y}_n, P_n, E_n')$ to be the family of ℓ-union d-dimensional interval functions, where

$$E_n'\left((a_i^j, b_i^j)_{i \in [\ell], j \in [d]}, x\right) = \bigvee_{i=1}^{\ell} \chi_{\prod_{j=1}^d [a_i^j, b_i^j]}(x).$$

Moreover, let $\mathrm{INT}_n^{\ell,d} = (\mathcal{X}_n, \mathcal{Y}_n, P_n', E_n')$ be the family of disjoint ℓ-union d-dimensional interval functions, where $P_n' \subseteq P_n$ is restricted to only include cases such that at most a single indicator $\chi_{\prod_{j=1}^d [a_i^j, b_i^j]}$ outputs 1 for a given x.

The function family $\mathrm{SEG}_n^{\ell} := \mathrm{DINT}_n^{\ell,1}$ corresponds to a disjoint union of one-dimensional intervals.

Next, we say that $\mathcal{F}_n^{\ell}$ is a *subfamily* of $\mathcal{G}_n^{\ell}$ if their domain and range sets, $\mathcal{X}_n$ and $\mathcal{Y}_n$, match, and any function $f \in \mathcal{F}_n^{\ell}$ can be expressed as a sum (over $\mathcal{Y}_n$) of $O(1)$ functions from $\mathcal{G}_n^{\ell}$.

Proposition 1 (Intervals are Rectangles). $\mathrm{SUMINT}_n^{\ell,d}$ *is a subfamily of $\mathrm{SUMCR}_n^{\ell,d}$. In particular, any single interval function with description $\{(a_i, b_i)\}_{i \in [d]}$ corresponds to the combinatorial rectangle with description $\{S_i = \{a_i, a_i + 1, \ldots, b_i\}\}_{i \in [d]}$.*

Definition 8 (DNF Formulas). *Let $\ell \in \mathbb{N}$. The family of functions computed by ℓ-sum disjunctive terms is a tuple $\mathrm{SUMDNF}_n^{\ell} = (\mathcal{X}_n, \mathcal{Y}_n, P_n, E_n)$ where $P_n = \{(c_1, \ldots, c_{\ell})\}_{c_1, \ldots, c_{\ell}}$ consists of all ℓ-tuples of disjunctive terms over n Boolean variables, and E_n is such that $E_n((c_1, \ldots, c_{\ell}), (x_1, \ldots, x_n)) = \sum_{i=1}^{\ell} c_i(x_1, \ldots, x_n)$. $c_1, \ldots, c_{\ell}$ are called the* terms *of the DNF formula.*

In a similar fashion, the family of functions computed by ℓ-term DNFs is a tuple $\mathrm{DNF}_n^{\ell} = (\mathcal{X}_n, \mathcal{Y}_n, P_n, E_n')$ where E_n' is such that $E_n((c_1, \ldots, c_{\ell}), (x_1, \ldots, x_n)) = \bigcup_{i=1}^{\ell} c_i(x_1, \ldots, x_n)$.

Finally, the family of functions computed by ℓ-term disjoint DNFs is a tuple $\mathrm{DDNF}_n^{\ell} = (\mathcal{X}_n, \mathcal{Y}_n, P_n', E_n')$ where $P_n' \subseteq P_n$ is restricted to only include cases such that at most a single term c_i outputs 1 for any given x.

Functions computed by decision trees of ℓ leaves can also be computed by ℓ-term disjoint DNF formulas. Therefore the shortcuts we obtain for (disjoint) DNFs apply to decision trees as well.

While the dimension d is not part of the description of DNF formulas over n boolean variables $x_1, \ldots, x_n$, by introducing a intermediate "dimension" parameter d and partitioning the n variables into d parts, we can represent the DNF formula as a d-dimensional truth table. More concretely, every dimension corresponds to the evaluations of $\frac{n}{d}$ variables. Through this way, we can embed the function into combinatorial rectangles.

Proposition 2 (DNFs are Rectangles). *For any dimension $d \in [n]$, the family* SUMDNF_n^ℓ *is a subfamily of* $\mathrm{SUMCR}_n^{\ell,d}$.

Remark 1 (Disjoint union and general union). The ability to evaluate the sum variants of DNF and INT implies the ability to evaluate the disjoint union because disjoint union can be carried out as a summation. However, the general operation of union is more tricky if the addition is over $\mathbb{F}_2$. It is possible to perform union by (1) having summations over $\mathbb{Z}_m$ for a large enough m such as $m > \ell$, which blows up the input and output share size by a factor of $O(\log \ell)$; or by (2) sacrificing perfect correctness for ϵ-correctness, using random linear combinations, thus multiplying the output share size by $O(\log(1/\epsilon))$. Note that this only works for disjunctions and not for more complex predicates. For instance, for depth-3 circuits we don't have a similar technique.

3.2 Secret Sharing

A secret sharing scheme $\mathcal{L} = (\mathsf{Share}, \mathsf{Dec})$ is a tuple of algorithms. Share allows a secret message $s \in K$ to be shared into n parts, $s^1, \ldots, s^n \in K'$ such that they can be distributed among servers $S_1, \ldots, S_n$ in a secure way. Typically, any single share s^j reveals no information about s in the information-theoretic sense. Dec allows authorized server sets to recover s from their respective shares $\{s^j\}$.

We only consider *linear* secret sharing schemes $\mathcal{L} : K \rightarrow K'$ in which K and K' are additive groups and the shares satisfy that $\{s_{\mathcal{L}}^j + s_{\mathcal{L}}^{\prime j}\}$ is a valid sharing of $s + s'$ under $\mathcal{L}$. We will use linear secret sharing schemes over finite fields and over rings of the form $\mathbb{Z}_m$. Another feature of these schemes that we will require, is that the client's reconstruction algorithm for s is a linear function of (some of) the shares $s^1, \ldots, s^n$. Linear secret sharing schemes can be viewed as *homomorphic secret sharing* schemes, endowed with a linear homomorphism Eval, which we will define more formally in Definition 9.

An *additive* secret-sharing scheme $\mathcal{L}_{\mathsf{add}}$ over an Abelian group splits a secret into random group elements that add up to the secret. For other types of linear secret-sharing, our results will mostly treat them abstractly and will not be sensitive to the details of their implementation; see [12] for formal definitions of the flavors of "Shamir's scheme" and "CNF scheme" we will refer to.

3.3   HSS and PIR

Definition 9 (Information-Theoretic HSS). *An information-theoretic k-server homomorphic secret sharing scheme for a function family $\mathcal{F}_n$, or k-HSS for short, is a tuple of algorithms* (Share, Eval, Dec) *with the following syntax:*

- Share(x): *On input $x \in \mathcal{X}_n$, the sharing algorithm* Share *outputs k input shares, $(x^1, \ldots, x^k)$, where $x^i \in \{0,1\}^{\alpha(N)}$, and some decoding information η.*
- Eval$(\rho, j, \hat{f}, x^j)$: *On input $\rho \in \{0,1\}^{\gamma(\text{n})}$, $j \in [k]$, $\hat{f} \in P_n$, and the share x^j, the evaluation algorithm* Eval *outputs $y^j \in \{0,1\}^{\beta(N)}$, corresponding to server j's share of $f(x)$. Here ρ are public random coins common to the servers and j is the label of the server.*
- Dec$(\eta, y^1, \ldots, y^k)$: *On input the decoding information η and $(y^1, \ldots, y^k)$, the decoding algorithm* Dec *computes a final output $y \in \mathcal{Y}_n$.*

We require the tuple (Share, Eval, Dec) to satisfy correctness and security.

Correctness. Let $0 \le \epsilon < 1$. We say that the HSS scheme is ϵ-correct if for any $f \in \mathcal{F}_n$ and $x \in \mathcal{X}_n$

$$
\Pr\left[\mathsf{Dec}\left(\eta, y^1, \ldots, y^k\right) = f(x) : \begin{array}{c} \rho \in_R \{0,1\}^{\gamma(n)} \\ (x^1, \ldots, x^k, \eta) \leftarrow \mathsf{Share}(x) \\ \forall j \in [k]\; y^j \leftarrow \mathsf{Eval}(\rho, j, \hat{f}, x^j) \end{array} \right] \ge 1 - \epsilon.
$$

If the HSS scheme is 0-correct, then we say the scheme is perfectly correct.

Security. Let $x, x' \in \mathcal{X}_n$ be such that $x \neq x'$. We require that for any $j \in [k]$ the following distributions are identical

$$
\{x^j : (x^1, \ldots, x^k, \eta) \leftarrow \mathsf{Share}(x)\} \equiv \{x'^j : (x'^1, \ldots, x'^k, \eta') \leftarrow \mathsf{Share}(x')\}.
$$

For perfectly correct HSS we may assume without loss of generality that Eval uses no randomness and so $\gamma(n) = 0$. In general, we will omit the randomness parameter ρ from Eval for perfectly correct HSS and PIR. Similarly, whenever Dec does not depend on η we omit this parameter from Share and Dec as well.

An HSS is said to be *additive* [21] if Dec simply computes the sum of the output shares over some additive group. This property is useful for composing HSS for simple functions into one for more complex functions. We will also be interested in the following weaker notion which we term *quasiadditive HSS*.

Definition 10 (Quasiadditive HSS). *Let HSS =* (Share, Eval, Dec) *be an HSS for a function family $\mathcal{F}$ such that $\mathcal{Y}_n = \mathbb{F}_2$. We say that HSS is* quasiadditive *if there exists an Abelian group $\mathbb{G}$ such that* Eval *outputs elements of $\mathbb{G}$, and* Dec$(y^1, \ldots, y^k)$ *computes an addition $\tilde{y} = y^1 + \ldots + y^k \in \mathbb{G}$ and outputs 1 if and only if $\tilde{y} \neq 0$.*

Share$_\mathrm{RM}(x)$:

1. Let $d = k - 1$. Divide $x \in \{0,1\}^n$ into d pieces $x = (x_1, \ldots, x_d) \in \left(\{0,1\}^{n/d}\right)^d$.

2. For every $i \in [d]$ compute a unit vector $e_i \in \mathbb{F}_2^{N^{1/d}}$ as $e_i[z] = \begin{cases} 1, & z = x_i \\ 0, & z \neq x_i \end{cases}$.

3. Let $\mathbb{F} = \mathbb{F}_{2^\kappa}$ be a field with $2^\kappa > k$ elements. Let $\alpha_1, \ldots, \alpha_k \in \mathbb{F}$ be distinct nonzero field elements. Draw random vectors $r_1, \ldots, r_d \in_R \mathbb{F}^{N^{1/d}}$ and compute $q_i^j := e_i + r_i \alpha_j$ for $i \in [d]$ and $j \in [k]$.

4. The share of each server $j \in [k]$ is $x^j := (q_1^j, \ldots, q_d^j)$. Output $(x^1, \ldots, x^k)$.

Eval$_\mathrm{RM}(j, \hat{f}, x^j = (q_1^j, \ldots, q_d^j))$:

1. Let $\lambda_j := \prod_{\ell \neq j} \alpha_\ell / (\alpha_\ell - \alpha_j)$ be the j'th Lagrange coefficient. Compute

$$\tilde{y}^j = \lambda_j \sum_{(x_1', \ldots, x_d') \in \{0,1\}^n} f(x_1', \ldots, x_d') \prod_{i=1}^d (q_i^j)[x_i']$$

2. Output $y^j = \sigma(\tilde{y}^j)$, where $\sigma : \mathbb{F} \to \mathbb{F}_2$ is a homomorphism with respect to addition such that $\sigma(z) = z$ for $z \in \mathbb{F}_2$.

Dec$_\mathrm{RM}(y^1, \ldots, y^k)$: Output $y = y^1 + \ldots + y^k$.

HSS Parameters: Input share size $\alpha(N) = O(N^{1/d})$, output share size $\beta(N) = 1$.

Fig. 1. The scheme PIR$_\mathrm{RM}^k$.

Definition 11 (PIR). *If the tuple* HSS $=$ (Share, Eval, Dec) *is a perfectly correct k-HSS for the function family* ALL$_n$, *we say that* HSS *is a k-server private information retrieval scheme, or k-PIR for short.*

Finally, the local computation Eval is modelled by a RAM program.

Definition 12 (Computational shortcut in PIR). *Let* PIR $=$ (Share, Eval, Dec) *be a PIR with share length $\alpha(N)$, and $\mathcal{F}$ be a function family. We say that* PIR *admits a* strong *shortcut for $\mathcal{F}$ if there is an algorithm for* Eval *which runs in quasilinear time $\tau(N, \ell) = \tilde{O}(\alpha(N) + \beta(N) + \ell)$ for every function $f \in \mathcal{F}$, where $\ell = |\hat{f}|$ is the description length of f. In similar fashion, we say that* PIR *admits a* (weak) *shortcut for $\mathcal{F}$ if there is an algorithm for* Eval *which runs in time $\tau(N, \ell) = O(\ell \cdot N^\delta)$, for some constant $0 < \delta < 1$.*

4 Shortcuts for Reed-Muller PIR

Let $3 \leq k \in \mathbb{N}$ and $d = k - 1$ be constants. The k-server Reed-Muller based PIR scheme PIR$_\mathrm{RM}^k = $ (Share$_\mathrm{RM}$, Eval$_\mathrm{RM}$, Dec$_\mathrm{RM}$) is presented in Fig. 1.

We observe that, in k-server Reed-Muller PIR $\mathsf{PIR}_{\mathsf{RM}}^{k}$, the sum of products

$$\sum_{(x'_1,\ldots,x'_d)\in\{0,1\}^n} f(x'_1,\ldots,x'_d) \prod_{i=1}^{d} (q_i^j)[x'_i]$$

can be written as a product of sums if f is a combinatorial rectangle function. Consequently $\mathsf{PIR}_{\mathsf{RM}}^{k}$ admits a computational shortcut for d-dimensional combinatorial rectangles, which gives rise to shortcuts for intervals and DNFs as they are special cases of combinatorial rectangles (Propositions 1 and 2).

Lemma 2. $\mathsf{PIR}_{\mathsf{RM}}^{k}$ *admits a strong shortcut for the function family of single d-dimensional combinatorial rectangle, i.e.,* $\mathrm{SUMCR}_n^{1,d}$. *More concretely,* $\tau(N,\ell) = O(\alpha(N)) = O(N^{1/d})$.

Proof. Naturally, the client and server associate $x = (x_1,\ldots,x_d)$ as the input to the functions f from $\mathrm{SUMCR}_n^{1,d}$. Let $\hat{f} = \hat{\mathrm{cr}} = \{S_1,\ldots,S_d\}$ be the combinatorial rectangle representing f. Given $\hat{f}$, the computation carried out by server j is

$$\mathsf{Eval}_{\mathsf{RM}}(j,\hat{f},x^j = (q_1^j,\ldots,q_d^j)) = \sigma\left(\lambda_j \sum_{(x'_1,\ldots,x'_d)\in S_1\times\ldots\times S_d} \prod_{i=1}^{d} q_i^j[x'_i]\right) \quad (3)$$

$$= \sigma\left(\lambda_j \prod_{i=1}^{d} \sum_{x'_i\in S_i} q_i^j[x'_i]\right) \quad (4)$$

If the server evaluates the expression using Eq. (3) the time is $O(N)$, but if it instead uses Eq. (4) the time is $O(d \max_i\{|S_i|\}) = O(2^{\frac{n}{d}}) = O(\alpha(N))$.

Theorem 9. $\mathsf{PIR}_{\mathsf{RM}}^{k}$ *admits a weak shortcut for the function family* $\mathrm{SUMCR}_N^{\ell,d}$. *More concretely,* $\tau(N,\ell) = O(\ell\alpha(N)) = O(\ell N^{1/d})$. *The same shortcut exists for decision trees with ℓ leaves, or, more generally,* SUMDNF_n^{ℓ} *and* DDNF_n^{ℓ}.

Proof. This is implied by Lemma 2, by noting that $f = \mathrm{cr}_1 + \ldots \mathrm{cr}_\ell$ over the common input x. In particular, the final Eval algorithm makes ℓ calls to the additive HSS given by Lemma 2, so the running time is $O(\ell\alpha(N)) = O(\ell 2^{\frac{n}{d}})$.

An algorithm, presented in the full version, improves the efficiency of Theorem 9 for decision trees to $\tilde{O}(\alpha(n) + \ell \cdot \alpha(n)^{1/3})$.

4.1 Intervals and Convex Shapes

By Proposition 1, one obtains weak shortcuts for d-dimensional intervals. In fact, one can obtain *strong shortcuts* by the standard technique of precomputing the prefix sums in the summation Eq. (4).

Theorem 10. $\mathsf{PIR}_{\mathsf{RM}}^{k}$ *admits a strong shortcut for the function family* $\mathrm{SUMINT}_n^{\ell,d}$. *More concretely,* $\tau(N,\ell) = O(\alpha(N) + \ell) = O(N^{1/d} + \ell)$. *The same shortcut applies to* $\mathrm{DINT}_n^{\ell,d}$.

Segments and Low-Dimensional Intervals. Every segment can be split into at most $(2d - 1)$ d-dimensional intervals. The splitting (deferred to the full version) works by comparing the input $x \in \{0,1\}^n$ with the endpoints $a, b \in (\{0,1\}^{n/d})^d$ in a block-wise manner.

Theorem 11. $\mathsf{PIR}_{\mathsf{RM}}^k$ *admits a strong shortcut for the function families* SEG_n^ℓ. *Generally, for every integer* $d'|d$, $\mathsf{PIR}_{\mathsf{RM}}^k$ *admits a strong shortcut for the function families* $\mathrm{DINT}_n^{d',\ell}$ *(or* $\mathrm{SUMINT}_n^{d',\ell}$*). More concretely,* $\tau(N, \ell) = O(N^{1/d} + \ell)$.

Shortcut for Convex Shapes. At a high level, convex body functions are functions whose preimage of 1 forms a convex body in the d-dimensional cube $\mathcal{X}_n := (\{0,1\}^{n/d})^d$. The following theorem follows from the fact that we can efficiently split a d-dimensional convex body into $O(N^{(d-1)/d})$ d-dimensional intervals in a "Riemann-sum" style.

Theorem 12 (Convex bodies, Informal). *There is a perfectly correct k-server HSS for the function class of ℓ-unions of convex shapes with* $\alpha(n) = O(N^{1/(k-1)})$, $\beta(n) = 1$ *and* $\tau(n) = O(\ell N^{(k-2)/(k-1)})$.

We show that the bound is essentially the best achievable by splitting the shape into union of intervals. Finally, we show that on the other hand, for more regular shapes like circles, strong shortcuts are possible if one settles for an approximated answer. Detailed discussion of such results are deferred to the full version.

Theorem 13 (Circle approximation, Informal). *There is a perfectly correct k-server HSS for the function class of ℓ-unions of ϵ-approximations of circles with* $\alpha(n) = O(N^{1/(k-1)})$, $\beta(n) = 1$ *and* $\tau(n) = O(\alpha(n) + \frac{1}{\epsilon}\ell)$.

4.2 Compressing Input Shares

The scheme $\mathsf{PIR}_{\mathsf{RM}}^3$ described above can be strictly improved by using a more dense encoding of the input. This results in a modified scheme $\mathsf{PIR}_{\mathsf{RM'}}^3$ with $\alpha'(N) = \sqrt{2} \cdot N^{1/2}$, a factor $\sqrt{2}$ improvement over $\mathsf{PIR}_{\mathsf{RM}}^3$. This is the best known 3-server PIR scheme with $\beta = 1$ (up to lower-order additive terms [11]). In the full version, we show that with some extra effort, similar shortcuts apply also to the optimized $\mathsf{PIR}_{\mathsf{RM'}}^3$.

4.3 Negative Results for RM PIR

Although we have shortcuts for disjoint DNF formulas, similar shortcut for more expressive families with *counting hardness* is unlikely. The idea is similar in spirit to [52, Claim 5.4]. The lower bounds for $\mathsf{PIR}_{\mathsf{RM}}^3$ also hold for $\mathsf{PIR}_{\mathsf{RM'}}^3$.

Theorem 14. *Let $\mathcal{F}$ be a function family for which $\mathsf{PIR}_{\mathsf{RM}}^k$ admits a weak shortcut with* $\tau(N, \ell) = T$. *Then, there exists an algorithm* $\mathsf{Count}_2 : P_n \to \mathbb{F}_2$ *running in time* $O(T + |\hat{f}|)$, *that when given $\hat{f} \in P_n$, computes the parity of* $|\{x \in \mathcal{X}_n : f(x) = 1\}|$.

Proof. Recall that the server computes the following expression in $\mathsf{PIR}_{\mathsf{RM}}^k$:

$$\sigma\left(\lambda_j \sum_{(x_1',\ldots,x_{k-1}')\in\mathcal{X}^n} f(x_1',\ldots,x_{k-1}')\prod_{i=1}^{k-1}(q_i^j)[x_i']\right).$$

To compute the required parity, instead of using $e_1,\ldots,e_n$ in the original $\mathsf{Share}_{\mathsf{RM}}$ in step 3 (see Fig. 1), we use the vectors $1^{N^{1/d}},\ldots,1^{N^{1/d}}$, *i.e.*, the all-one vectors. After calling Eval on all the respective shares and decoding the output, one obtains

$$\sum_{(x_1',\ldots,x_{k-1}')\in\{0,1\}^n} f(x_1',\ldots,x_{k-1}') = |\{x\in\mathcal{X}_n : f(x)=1\}| \pmod 2.$$

The total time of the algorithm is $O(T + |\hat{f}|)$.

We recall the following conjecture commonly used in complexity theory.

Conjecture 2 (Strong Exponential Time Hypothesis (SETH)). SAT cannot be decided with high probability in time $O(2^{(1-\epsilon)n})$ for any $\epsilon > 0$.

By the isolation lemma from [25], SETH is known to imply that $\oplus\mathsf{SAT}$, which is similar to SAT except that one need to compute the parity of the number of satisfying assignments, cannot by solved in time $O(2^{(1-\epsilon)n})$. The number of satisfying assignments to a CNF formula equals $2^n - r$, where r is the number of satisfying assignments to its negation. Since the negation of a CNF formula is in DNF, $\oplus\mathsf{DNF}$ cannot be decided in $O(2^{(1-\epsilon)n})$ as well. Therefore we have the following corollary.

Corollary 2. *For any k, there exists a polynomially bounded ℓ such that $\mathsf{PIR}_{\mathsf{RM}}^k$ does not admit a weak shortcut for the function family DNF_n^ℓ, unless SETH fails.*

Proof. By Theorem 14, if there is a weak shortcut for any polynomially bounded ℓ, *i.e.*, an algorithm computing Eval for any function in DNF_n^ℓ in time $O(N^{1-\epsilon})$, then one can decide $\oplus\mathsf{DNF}$ in time $O(N^{1-\epsilon})$.

Note that the hardness for DNF_n^ℓ is not contradictory to the fact that larger field size or random linear combinations help evaluating general DNFs (see Remark 1) because our proof heavily relies on the fact that we work over a small field (which has several efficiency benefits) and that the shortcut is deterministic.

Conjecture 3 (Exponential Time Hypothesis (ETH)). SAT requires time $O(2^{\delta n})$, for some $\delta > 0$, to be decided with high probability.

In a similar fashion, assuming the ETH, we can obtain the weaker result that strong shortcuts are impossible given k is large, namely when $k > \frac{1}{\delta}$.

Corollary 3. *Assume ETH. For some large enough k and some polynomially bounded ℓ, $\mathsf{PIR}_{\mathsf{RM}}^k$ does not admit a strong shortcut for the function family DNF_n^ℓ.*

5   On Shortcuts for Matching Vector PIR

Matching vectors (MV) based PIR schemes in the literature can be cast into a template due to [12]. As described in the introduction, this template has two ingredients: (1) a *matching vector family*; (2) a *share conversion*. A complete specification is given in the full version.

We describe the server computation in more detail, in particular, we present the structure of the matching vector family on which MV PIR is based. In $\mathsf{PIR}^k_{\mathsf{MV},\mathsf{SC}}$ each server j is given as input $x^j \in \mathbb{Z}_m^h$ which is a secret share of u_x. Then, for every $x' \in [N]$, the server j homomorphically obtains $y_{j,x,x'}$ which is the j-th share of $\langle u_x, v_{x'} \rangle$. Next, each server j computes a response

$$\sum_{x' \in [N]} f(x') \mathsf{SC}(j, y_{j,x,x'}).$$

Therefore, for the all-1 database ($f(x) = 1$), for every S-matching vector family MV and share conversion scheme SC from $\mathcal{L}$ to $\mathcal{L}'$ we can define the $(\mathsf{MV}, \mathsf{SC})$-counting problem, $\#(\mathsf{MV}, \mathsf{SC})$, see Definition 1.

We consider $\#(\mathsf{MV}^w_{\mathrm{Grol}}, \mathsf{SC})$, where $\mathsf{MV}^w_{\mathrm{Grol}}$ is a matching vectors family due to Grolmusz [40], which is used in all third-generation PIR schemes, which we present in Fact 1, and $\mathsf{SC} \in \{\mathsf{SC}_{\mathrm{Efr}}, \mathsf{SC}_{\mathrm{BIKO}}\}$.

$\#(\mathsf{MV}, \mathsf{SC})$ displays a summation of converted shares of inner products. The actual computation carried out is determined by the structure of $v_{x'}$ and hence the instance of the MV used. Here we describe the *graph-based* matching vector family, first given in [40].

Instantiation of Grolmusz's Family. There is an explicitly constructable S-Matching Vector family for $m = p_1 p_2$ with $\alpha(N) = N^{o(1)}$ based on the intersecting set family in [50] for the *canonical set* $S = S_m = \{(0,1), (1,0), (1,1)\} \subseteq \mathbb{Z}_{p_1} \times \mathbb{Z}_{p_2}$ (in Chinese remainder notation). Here we give a more detailed description of their structure in the language of hypergraphs.

Fact 1 (The parameterized $\mathsf{MV}^w_{\mathrm{Grol}}$, modified from [40]). *Let $m = p_1 p_2$ where $p_1 < p_2$ are distinct primes. For any integer r and parameter function $w(r)$, one can construct an S-matching vector family $\{u_x, v_x \in \mathbb{Z}_m^h\}_{x \in [N]}$ where $N = \binom{r}{w(r)}$ and $h = \binom{r}{\leq d}$ for $d \leq p_2 \sqrt{w(r)}$. Moreover, the construction is hypergraph-based in the following sense:*

Let $[r]$ be the set of vertices. Every index $x \in [N]$ corresponds to a set $T_x \subset [r]$ of $w(r)$ nodes. The vector v_x has entries in $\{0, 1\}$ and its coordinates are labelled with $\zeta \subset [r]$ which are hyperedges of size at most d nodes. Moreover, $v_x[\zeta] = 1$ iff the vertices of the hyperedge ζ are all inside T_x. Therefore the inner product can be evaluated as

$$\langle u_x, v_{x'} \rangle = \sum_{\zeta \subseteq T_{x'}, |\zeta| \leq d} u_x[\zeta] = \sum_{\zeta \subseteq T_x, |\zeta| \leq d} u_{x'}[\zeta] = \sum_{\zeta \subseteq T_x \cap T_{x'}, |\zeta| \leq d} 1.$$

In other words, the inner product is carried out by a summation over all the hyperedges lying within a given vertex subset $T_{x'}$. Under this view, we will call $|T_{x'}| = w(r)$ the clique size parameter.

By setting MV_{Grol}^w with $w = \Theta(\sqrt{r})$, we obtain from Fact 1 and the definition of $PIR_{MV_{Grol}^w, SC}^k$, a PIR scheme with $\alpha(N) = 2^{O(2p_2\sqrt{n\log n})}$, which is state of the art in terms of asymptotic communication complexity. We prove Fact 1 in the full version.

5.1   A Reduction from a Subgraph Counting Problem for SC_{Efr}

In this section we relate the server computation to a subgraph counting problem. For this we rely on the hypergraph-based structure of the matching vector family, in combination with the share conversion SC_{Efr}. More concretely, we relate $\#(MV_{Grol}^w, SC_{Efr})$ to the problem $\oplus INDSUB(\Phi_{511,0}, w)$, see Definition 2 and the preceding discussion.

We prove the following which relates obtaining computational shortcuts for $PIR_{MV,SC}^k$ to counting induced subgraphs.

Lemma 3 (Hardness of (MV_{Grol}^w, SC_{Efr})-counting). *If $\#(MV_{Grol}^w, SC_{Efr})$ can be computed in $N^{o(1)} \left(= r^{o(w)}\right)$ time, then $\oplus INDSUB(\Phi_{511,0}, w)$ can be decided in $r^{o(w)}$ time, for any nondecreasing function $w: \mathbb{N} \to \mathbb{N}$.*

In particular, if we can show $\oplus INDSUB(\Phi_{511,0}, \Theta(\sqrt{r}))$ cannot be decided in $r^{o(\sqrt{r})}$ time under some complexity assumption, it will imply that $PIR_{MV_{Grol}^{\Theta(\sqrt{r})}, SC_{Efr}}^k$ does not admit strong shortcuts for the all-1 database under the same assumption, as $\alpha(N) = N^{o(1)}$ holds and $\tau(N, \ell) = N^{o(1)}$ is impossible.

Proof (Proof of Lemma 3). Let $m = 511$. Recall that $N = \binom{r}{w}$ and $h = \binom{r}{\le d}$ where $d \le p_2\sqrt{w}$. Suppose A is an algorithm solving $\#(MV_{Grol}^w, SC_{Efr})$ with these parameters that runs in time $N^{o(1)} = r^{o(w)}$. By definition of $Share_{Efr}$, the input to A is a vector $x^j \in \mathbb{Z}_m^h$. To homomorphically obtain a share of $\langle u_x, v_{x'} \rangle$, where x is the client's input, the server first computes $\langle x^j, v_{x'} \rangle$. For any instance G in $\oplus INDSUB(\Phi_{m,0}, w)$ with $|V(G)| = r$, we define the following vector $q \in \mathbb{Z}_m^h$: for every hyperedge ζ where $|\zeta| \le d$,

$$q[\zeta] = \begin{cases} 0 & \text{if } \zeta \notin E(G) \\ 1 & \text{if } \zeta \in E(G). \end{cases} \tag{5}$$

Note that for any $|\zeta| \ne 2$ we have $q[\zeta] = 0$. By Fact 1 and how q is constructed, for every $x' \in [N]$,

$$\langle q, v_{x'} \rangle = \sum_{\zeta \subset T_{x'}, |\zeta| \le d} q[\zeta] = \sum_{\zeta \subset T_{x'}, \zeta \in E(G)} 1.$$

Therefore the value of the inner product is the number of edges in the subgraph induced by the nodes in $T_{x'}$. For $\ell = 1, \ldots, (m-1)$, we feed $\ell \cdot q$ into the algorithm A. The output will be

$$\sum_{x' \in [N]} \mathsf{SC}_{\mathrm{Efr}}(j, \langle \ell \cdot q, v_{x'} \rangle) = \sum_{x' \in [N]} a_j \gamma^{\langle \ell \cdot q, v_{x'} \rangle} = a_j \sum_{x' \in [N]} \gamma^{\ell \langle q, v_{x'} \rangle}$$

$$= a_j \sum_{b \in \{0, \ldots, m-1\}} \sum_{x' : \langle q, v_{x'} \rangle = b} \gamma^{b\ell}$$

$$= a_j \sum_{b \in \{0, \ldots, m-1\}} c_b (\gamma^\ell)^b,$$

where $c_b \in \{0, 1\}$ (recall that the field $\mathbb{F}_{2^9}$ has characteristic 2) is the parity of the number of induced w-subgraphs, whose number of edges is congruent to b modulo m. This is because c_b counts the number of elements in the set $\{x' \in [N] : \langle q, x' \rangle = b\} = \{x' \in [N] : \sum_{\zeta \subset T_{x'}, \zeta \in E(G)} 1 = b\}$. Consequently, the bit c_0 is the answer bit to the problem $\oplus\mathrm{INDSUB}(\Phi_{m,0}, w)$. Note that after each call to A, we obtain evaluation of the degree-$(m-1)$ polynomial $Q(\Gamma) = a_j \sum_{b \in \{0, \ldots, m-1\}} c_b \Gamma^b$ at $\Gamma = \gamma^\ell$. Since the points $\{\gamma^\ell\}_{\ell=0}^{m-1}$ are distinct, we can perform interpolation to recover c_b for any $b \in \{0, \ldots, m-1\}$. In particular, we can compute the desired bit c_0. The overall running time is $O(m^2) + mr^{o(w)} = r^{o(w)}$.

In the full version, we show that a similar reduction holds for $\mathsf{SC}_{\mathrm{BIKO}}$ as well, except that we consider the problem $\oplus\mathrm{INDSUB}(\Phi_{6,4}, w)$.

5.2 Hardness of Subgraph Counting

As described in Sect. 2.2, we have the following plausible conjecture, and it turns out that its hardness can be based on ETH for a suitable choice of parameter.

Conjecture 4 (Hardness of counting induced subgraphs). $\oplus\mathrm{INDSUB}(\Phi_{m,\Delta}, w)$ cannot be decided in $r^{o(w)}$ time, for any integers $m \geq 2$, $0 \leq \Delta < m$, and for every function $w(r) = O(r^c)$, $0 \leq c < 1$.

Note that Conjecture 4 does not rule out *weak* shortcuts. However, it seems that even weak shortcuts would be difficult to find when instantiated with matching vectors from Fact 1. Indeed, for the related problem of hyperclique counting, algorithms which are faster than the naïve one are known only for the special case when hyperedges are *edges* (e.g. [4]).

Basing on ETH. Proving Conjecture 4 is difficult as it is a fine-grained lower bound. However, by assuming ETH, we can prove Conjecture 4 partially, in the sense that for a specific choice of $w(r)$, the lower bound does hold.

Lemma 4. *There is an efficiently computable function $w(r) = \Theta(\log r / \log \log r)$, such that if $\oplus\mathrm{INDSUB}(\Phi_{511,0}, w)$ or $\oplus\mathrm{INDSUB}(\Phi_{6,4}, w)$ can be decided in $r^{o(w(r))}$ time, then ETH fails.*

Proof. This follows from $\mathsf{ETH} \overset{Lemma\,5}{\leq} \mathrm{CLIQUE}(k(r)) \overset{Lemma\,6}{\leq} \oplus\mathrm{INDSUB}(\varPhi, w)$ for $\varPhi \in \{\varPhi_{511,0}, \varPhi_{6,4}\}$.

Next, we sketch how to perform the steps of the reduction in the proof of Lemma 4.

Reducing Clique Decision to ETH. Let $\mathrm{CLIQUE}(k(r))$ be the problem that, given a graph G with r nodes, decide whether a clique of size $k(r)$ exists in G. As a direct corollary of [28, Theorem 5.7], we have the following lemma.

Lemma 5. *There is an efficiently computable function* $k(r) = \Theta(\log r/\log \log r)$, *such that if* $\mathrm{CLIQUE}(k(r))$ *can be solved in* $r^{o(k(r))}$ *time, then* ETH *fails.*

Reducing Induced Subgraph Counting to Clique Decision. By reproducing the reduction in [42], we have the following (proofs deferred to the full version).

Lemma 6. *Let* $k(r) = \Theta(\log r/\log \log r)$ *as in Lemma 5. Then, there is an efficiently computable size parameter* $w(r) = \Theta(\log r/\log \log r)$ *such that if* $\oplus\mathrm{INDSUB}(\varPhi_{511,0}, w)$ *or* $\oplus\mathrm{INDSUB}(\varPhi_{6,4}, w)$ *can be decided in* $r^{o(w(r))}$ *time, then one can decide* $\mathrm{CLIQUE}(k(r))$ *in* $r^{o(k(r))}$ *time.*

While Lemma 5 could be proven to hold for $k(r) = \Theta(\sqrt{r})$ as well, as discussed in Sect. 2.2, by reproducing the reduction in [42], Lemma 6 only holds for $k(r) = o(\log r)$.

Hardness of Subgraph Counting. Finally, our main theorem follows from Conjecture 4 and Lemmas 3 and 4. To this end, denote by MV^* the family $\mathsf{MV}^w_{\mathrm{Grol}}$ obtained by instantiating $w(r)$ with this specific parameter.

Theorem 15. $\#(\mathsf{MV}^*, \mathsf{SC})$ *cannot be computed in* $N^{o(1)} \left(= r^{o(w)}\right)$ *time, unless* ETH *fails. Moreover, assuming Conjecture 4, the same holds for* $\mathsf{MV}^w_{\mathrm{Grol}}$ *with* $w = \Theta(\sqrt{r})$. *Here* SC *is either* $\mathsf{SC}_{\mathrm{Efr}}$ *or* $\mathsf{SC}_{\mathrm{BIKO}}$.

6   Concrete Efficiency

While this paper deals with *computational* shortcuts, in this section we will make comparisons exclusively with respect to *communication*. The main reason we compare communication is that for our main positive results, computation scales at most quasi-linearly with the size of the inputs, and thus is essentially the best one can hope for. Moreover, it is hard to make exact "apples to apples" comparisons for computation (what are the units?) Perhaps most importantly, for the problems to which our positive results apply (e.g., unions of convex shapes), the (asymptotic and concrete) computational efficiency of our schemes dominate those of competing approaches (FHE, brute-force PIR, garbled circuits, GMW-style protocols). Due to the concrete inefficiency of HSS from generic composition of PIRs, we will focus exclusively on HSS from shortcuts for $\mathsf{PIR}^k_{\mathsf{RM}}$.

Cryptographic Share Compression. In the full version we describe a simple method [33] to compress the queries of $\mathsf{PIR}^k_{\mathsf{RM}} = (\mathsf{Share}, \mathsf{Eval}, \mathsf{Dec})$, at the cost of making the scheme only computationally secure, utilizing share conversion from Shamir secret sharing to CNF secret sharing (c.f. [12] for relevant definitions).

Communication Complexity. In Table 1 we compare the communication complexity for unions of disjoint two dimensional intervals. For two dimensional intervals, FSS requires queries of length $O(\lambda(\log N)^2)$ [19].

Table 1. Total communication complexity for the task where the client holds a secret index x in a grid $[\sqrt{N}] \times [\sqrt{N}]$ and it wishes to privately learn (with security threshold $t = 1$) if it is contained in a collection of ℓ two dimensional intervals held by k servers. The computational cost for FSS and Reed-Muller is $\tilde{O}(\mathsf{comm} + \ell)$, where comm is the communication complexity. The latter is obtained via our shortcuts. Note that for $k = 4$ the aforementioned computational cost is obtainable only when considering grids with dimensions $[N^{1/3}] \times [N^{2/3}]$. For grids with dimensions $[\sqrt{N}] \times [\sqrt{N}]$ the computational cost becomes $\tilde{O}(\mathsf{comm} + \ell\sqrt{\mathsf{comm}})$. See [19, Corollary 3.20] for how the numbers in last column were computed. Share compression was applied to Reed-Muller.

Domain size	Reed-Muller [29] (k = 3)	Reed-Muller [29] (k = 4)	Reed-Muller [29] (k = 5)	FSS [19] (k = 2)
2^{10}	0.05 KB	0.05 KB	0.06 KB	3.1 KB
2^{15}	0.1 KB	0.1 KB	0.1 KB	7.0 KB
2^{20}	0.6 KB	0.2 KB	0.3 KB	12.5 KB
2^{25}	2.9 KB	0.5 KB	0.4 KB	19.5 KB
2^{30}	16.1 KB	1.3 KB	0.6 KB	28.1 KB
2^{35}	90.6 KB	3.7 KB	1.1 KB	38.3 KB
2^{40}	512.1 KB	11.5 KB	2.2 KB	50.0 KB
2^{70}	16.0 GB	11.3 MB	362.3 KB	153.1 KB

It is worth mentioning that private geographical queries were already considered in [58]. However, there the two dimensional plane is tessellated with overlapping shapes of the same size, which reduces the problem to the task of evaluating multipoint functions. Therefore, this approach can be seen as a simply reducing the size of the problem. In contrast, here we allow for a better tradeoff between precision and computation. Our solution is more expressive, as it allows for shapes of high and low precision simultaneously.

Larger Security Threshold. In this section we consider the applicability of our PIR-based HSS to security models with larger security threshold. Specifically, we will consider the case where we allow at most *two* colluding servers. However, lending to its PIR backbone, our HSS constructions scale well for higher security thresholds.

Indeed, there is an analogue of $\mathsf{PIR}_{\mathsf{RM}}^k$ with 2 security threshold, such that for $O(\sqrt{N})$ and $O(N^{1/3})$ total communication, the number of required servers is 5 and 7, respectively. Moreover, this PIR scheme retains all the computational shortcuts of $\mathsf{PIR}_{\mathsf{RM}}^k$ and its shares can be compressed as well. Alternatively, employing multiparty FSS [17] (for multipoint functions) requires only 3 servers. However, in stark contrast to two party FSS, multiparty FSS requires $O(\lambda\sqrt{N})$ total communication. Moreover, it is not clear how to obtain an FSS for one dimensional intervals in this setting, let alone two dimensional intervals. We conclude our HSS wins by two orders of magnitude.

Another approach to increase the security threshold of FSS is via the generic tensoring technique of [7], which preserves the communication complexity. Nevertheless, this scales worse with larger security threshold t, requiring 2^t servers, compared to $2t+1$ servers via Reed-Muller PIR. Furthermore, this approach is not computationally efficient, requiring $O(N)$ computation. We provide a description of the tensoring of [7] in the full version.

In Table 2 we compare the communication complexity of FSS with our HSS for the simple task of PIR, as more expressive function families are unavailable for higher security thresholds for FSS.

Table 2. Total communication complexity for the task where the client holds a secret index x in $[N]$ and it wishes to privately learn (with security threshold $t = 2$) if its contained in a collection of ℓ points in $[N]$ held by k servers. The computational cost for FSS and Reed-Muller is $\tilde{O}(\mathsf{comm} + \ell)$, where comm is the communication complexity. Data for FSS was obtained from [17, Theorem 7]. Share compression was applied to Reed-Muller.

Domain size	Reed-Muller [29] (t = 2, k = 5)	FSS [19] (t = 2, k = 3)
2^{10}	0.2 KB	3.0 KB
2^{15}	0.6 KB	17.0 KB
2^{20}	1.2 KB	96.0 KB
2^{25}	4.7 KB	543.1 KB
2^{30}	24.4 KB	3.0 MB
2^{35}	136.2 KB	17.0 MB
2^{40}	768.4 KB	96.0 MB
2^{70}	24.0 GB	3.0 TB

Other Settings. In the full version, we show how to make our schemes more efficient whenever the payload size is small (a few bits), by basing our shortcuts on a "balanced" variant of $\mathsf{PIR}_{\mathsf{RM}}^k$, proposed by Woodruff and Yekhanin [60]. In addition, we discuss our schemes in the context of distributed share generation and argue that our schemes are more "MPC-friendly" than the FSS-based alternative.

References

1. Angel, S., Chen, H., Laine, K., Setty, S.T.V.: PIR with compressed queries and amortized query processing. In: IEEE Symposium on Security and Privacy (2018)
2. Applebaum, B., Holenstein, T., Mishra, M., Shayevitz, O.: The communication complexity of private simultaneous messages, revisited. In: Nielsen, J.B., Rijmen, V. (eds.) EUROCRYPT 2018. LNCS, vol. 10821, pp. 261–286. Springer, Cham (2018). https://doi.org/10.1007/978-3-319-78375-8_9
3. Araki, T., Furukawa, J., Lindell, Y., Nof, A., Ohara, K.: High-throughput semi-honest secure three-party computation with an honest majority. In: CCS 2016 (2016)
4. Austrin, P., Kaski, P., Kubjas, K.: Tensor network complexity of multilinear maps. In: ITCS 2019 (2019)
5. Ball, M., Holmgren, J., Ishai, Y., Liu, T., Malkin, T.: On the complexity of decomposable randomized encodings, or: how friendly can a garbling-friendly PRF be? In: ITCS 2020, pp. 86:1–86:22 (2020)
6. Barkol, O., Ishai, Y.: Secure computation of constant-depth circuits with applications to database search problems. In: Shoup, V. (ed.) CRYPTO 2005. LNCS, vol. 3621, pp. 395–411. Springer, Heidelberg (2005). https://doi.org/10.1007/11535218_24
7. Barkol, O., Ishai, Y., Weinreb, E.: On locally decodable codes, self-correctable codes, and t-private PIR. Algorithmica 58, 831–859 (2010)
8. Baur, W., Strassen, V.: The complexity of partial derivatives. Theor. Comput. Sci. 22, 317–330 (1983)
9. Beaver, D., Feigenbaum, J., Kilian, J., Rogaway, P.: Security with low communication overhead. In: Menezes, A.J., Vanstone, S.A. (eds.) CRYPTO 1990. LNCS, vol. 537, pp. 62–76. Springer, Heidelberg (1991). https://doi.org/10.1007/3-540-38424-3_5
10. Beimel, A., Ishai, Y., Kumaresan, R., Kushilevitz, E.: On the cryptographic complexity of the worst functions. In: Lindell, Y. (ed.) TCC 2014. LNCS, vol. 8349, pp. 317–342. Springer, Heidelberg (2014). https://doi.org/10.1007/978-3-642-54242-8_14
11. Beimel, A., Ishai, Y., Kushilevitz, E.: General constructions for information-theoretic private information retrieval. J. Comput. Syst. Sci. 71, 213–247 (2005)
12. Beimel, A., Ishai, Y., Kushilevitz, E., Orlov, I.N.: Share conversion and private information retrieval. In: IEEE 27th Conference on Computational Complexity (2012)
13. Beimel, A., Ishai, Y., Kushilevitz, E., Raymond, J.-F.: Breaking the $O(n^{1/(2k-1)})$ barrier for information-theoretic private information retrieval. In: FOCS 2002 (2002)
14. Beimel, A., Ishai, Y., Malkin, T.: Reducing the servers computation in private information retrieval: PIR with preprocessing. In: Bellare, M. (ed.) CRYPTO 2000. LNCS, vol. 1880, pp. 55–73. Springer, Heidelberg (2000). https://doi.org/10.1007/3-540-44598-6_4
15. Ben-Or, M., Goldwasser, S., Wigderson, A.: Completeness theorems for non-cryptographic fault-tolerant distributed computation (extended abstract). In: STOC 1988 (1988)
16. Benaloh, J.C.: Secret sharing homomorphisms: keeping shares of a secret secret (extended abstract). In: Odlyzko, A.M. (ed.) CRYPTO 1986. LNCS, vol. 263, pp. 251–260. Springer, Heidelberg (1987). https://doi.org/10.1007/3-540-47721-7_19

17. Boyle, E., Gilboa, N., Ishai, Y.: Function secret sharing. In: Oswald, E., Fischlin, M. (eds.) EUROCRYPT 2015. LNCS, vol. 9057, pp. 337–367. Springer, Heidelberg (2015). https://doi.org/10.1007/978-3-662-46803-6_12

18. Boyle, E., Gilboa, N., Ishai, Y.: Breaking the circuit size barrier for secure computation under DDH. In: Robshaw, M., Katz, J. (eds.) CRYPTO 2016. LNCS, vol. 9814, pp. 509–539. Springer, Heidelberg (2016). https://doi.org/10.1007/978-3-662-53018-4_19

19. Boyle, E., Gilboa, N., Ishai, Y.: Function secret sharing: improvements and extensions. In: CCS 2016 (2016)

20. Boyle, E., Gilboa, N., Ishai, Y.: Secure computation with preprocessing via function secret sharing. In: Hofheinz, D., Rosen, A. (eds.) TCC 2019. LNCS, vol. 11891, pp. 341–371. Springer, Cham (2019). https://doi.org/10.1007/978-3-030-36030-6_14

21. Boyle, E., Gilboa, N., Ishai, Y., Lin, H., Tessaro, S.: Foundations of homomorphic secret sharing. In: ITCS 2018 (2018)

22. Boyle, E., Kohl, L., Scholl, P.: Homomorphic secret sharing from lattices without FHE. In: Ishai, Y., Rijmen, V. (eds.) EUROCRYPT 2019. LNCS, vol. 11477, pp. 3–33. Springer, Cham (2019). https://doi.org/10.1007/978-3-030-17656-3_1

23. Brakerski, Z., Döttling, N., Garg, S., Malavolta, G.: Leveraging linear decryption: rate-1 fully-homomorphic encryption and time-lock puzzles. In: Hofheinz, D., Rosen, A. (eds.) TCC 2019. LNCS, vol. 11892, pp. 407–437. Springer, Cham (2019). https://doi.org/10.1007/978-3-030-36033-7_16

24. Brakerski, Z., Vaikuntanathan, V.: Efficient fully homomorphic encryption from (standard) LWE. In: FOCS 2011 (2011)

25. Calabro, C., Impagliazzo, R., Kabanets, V., Paturi, R.: The complexity of unique k-SAT: an isolation lemma for k-CNFs. J. Comput. Syst. Sci. **74**, 386–393 (2008)

26. Calabro, C., Impagliazzo, R., Paturi, R.: The complexity of satisfiability of small depth circuits. In: Chen, J., Fomin, F.V. (eds.) IWPEC 2009. LNCS, vol. 5917, pp. 75–85. Springer, Heidelberg (2009). https://doi.org/10.1007/978-3-642-11269-0_6

27. Chaum, D., Crépeau, C., Damgård, I.: Multiparty unconditionally secure protocols (extended abstract). In: STOC 1988 (1988)

28. Chen, J., Huang, X., Kanj, I.A., Xia, G.: Strong computational lower bounds via parameterized complexity. J. Comput. Syst. Sci. **72**, 1346–1367 (2006)

29. Chor, B., Goldreich, O., Kushilevitz, E., Sudan, M.: Private information retrieval. J. ACM **45**, 965–981 (1998)

30. Cooper, J.N., Ellis, R.B., Kahng, A.B.: Asymmetric binary covering codes. J. Comb. Theor. Ser. A **100**, 232–249 (2002)

31. Corrigan-Gibbs, H., Boneh, D., Mazières, D.: Riposte: an anonymous messaging system handling millions of users. In: IEEE Symposium on Security and Privacy (2015)

32. Couteau, G.: A note on the communication complexity of multiparty computation in the correlated randomness model. In: Ishai, Y., Rijmen, V. (eds.) EUROCRYPT 2019. LNCS, vol. 11477, pp. 473–503. Springer, Cham (2019). https://doi.org/10.1007/978-3-030-17656-3_17

33. Cramer, R., Damgård, I., Ishai, Y.: Share conversion, pseudorandom secret-sharing and applications to secure computation. In: Kilian, J. (ed.) TCC 2005. LNCS, vol. 3378, pp. 342–362. Springer, Heidelberg (2005). https://doi.org/10.1007/978-3-540-30576-7_19

34. Cramer, R., Damgård, I., Maurer, U.: General secure multi-party computation from any linear secret-sharing scheme. In: Preneel, B. (ed.) EUROCRYPT 2000. LNCS, vol. 1807, pp. 316–334. Springer, Heidelberg (2000). https://doi.org/10.1007/3-540-45539-6_22

35. Damgård, I., Larsen, K.G., Nielsen, J.B.: Communication lower bounds for statistically secure MPC, with or without preprocessing. In: Boldyreva, A., Micciancio, D. (eds.) CRYPTO 2019. LNCS, vol. 11693, pp. 61–84. Springer, Cham (2019). https://doi.org/10.1007/978-3-030-26951-7_3

36. Damgård, I., Nielsen, J.B., Nielsen, M., Ranellucci, S.: The tinytable protocol for 2-party secure computation, or: gate-scrambling revisited. In: Katz, J., Shacham, H. (eds.) CRYPTO 2017. LNCS, vol. 10401, pp. 167–187. Springer, Cham (2017). https://doi.org/10.1007/978-3-319-63688-7_6

37. Damgård, I., Nielsen, J.B., Polychroniadou, A., Raskin, M.: On the communication required for unconditionally secure multiplication. In: Robshaw, M., Katz, J. (eds.) CRYPTO 2016. LNCS, vol. 9815, pp. 459–488. Springer, Heidelberg (2016). https://doi.org/10.1007/978-3-662-53008-5_16

38. Data, D., Prabhakaran, M.M., Prabhakaran, V.M.: On the communication complexity of secure computation. In: Garay, J.A., Gennaro, R. (eds.) CRYPTO 2014. LNCS, vol. 8617, pp. 199–216. Springer, Heidelberg (2014). https://doi.org/10.1007/978-3-662-44381-1_12

39. Dodis, Y., Halevi, S., Rothblum, R.D., Wichs, D.: Spooky encryption and its applications. In: Robshaw, M., Katz, J. (eds.) CRYPTO 2016. LNCS, vol. 9816, pp. 93–122. Springer, Heidelberg (2016). https://doi.org/10.1007/978-3-662-53015-3_4

40. Dvir, Z., Gopalan, P., Yekhanin, S.: Matching vector codes. In: FOCS 2010 (2010)

41. Dvir, Z., Gopi, S.: 2-server PIR with sub-polynomial communication. In: FOCS 2015 (2015)

42. Dörfler, J., Roth, M., Schmitt, J., Wellnitz, P.: Counting induced subgraphs: an algebraic approach to #W[1]-hardness. In: MFCS 2019 (2019)

43. Efremenko, K.: 3-query locally decodable codes of subexponential length. In: STOC 2009 (2009)

44. Fazio, N., Gennaro, R., Jafarikhah, T., Skeith, W.E.: Homomorphic secret sharing from Paillier encryption. In: Okamoto, T., Yu, Y., Au, M.H., Li, Y. (eds.) ProvSec 2017. LNCS, vol. 10592, pp. 381–399. Springer, Cham (2017). https://doi.org/10.1007/978-3-319-68637-0_23

45. Feige, U., Kilian, J., Naor, M.: A minimal model for secure computation (extended abstract). In: Leighton, F.T., Goodrich, M.T. (eds.) STOC 1994, pp. 554–563 (1994)

46. Gentry, C.: Fully homomorphic encryption using ideal lattices. In: STOC 2009 (2009)

47. Gentry, C., Halevi, S.: Compressible FHE with applications to PIR. In: Hofheinz, D., Rosen, A. (eds.) TCC 2019. LNCS, vol. 11892, pp. 438–464. Springer, Cham (2019). https://doi.org/10.1007/978-3-030-36033-7_17

48. Gilboa, N., Ishai, Y.: Compressing cryptographic resources. In: Wiener, M. (ed.) CRYPTO 1999. LNCS, vol. 1666, pp. 591–608. Springer, Heidelberg (1999). https://doi.org/10.1007/3-540-48405-1_37

49. Goldreich, O., Micali, S., Wigderson, A.: How to play any mental game or a completeness theorem for protocols with honest majority. In: STOC 1987 (1987)

50. Grolmusz, V.: Superpolynomial size set-systems with restricted intersections mod 6 and explicit Ramsey graphs. Combinatorica 20, 71–86 (2000)

51. Gupta, T., Crooks, N., Mulhern, W., Setty, S.T.V., Alvisi, L., Walfish, M.: Scalable and private media consumption with popcorn. In: USENIX 2016 (2016)

52. Harsha, P., Ishai, Y., Kilian, J., Nissim, K., Venkatesh, S.: Communication versus computation. In: Díaz, J., Karhumäki, J., Lepistö, A., Sannella, D. (eds.) ICALP 2004. LNCS, vol. 3142, pp. 745–756. Springer, Heidelberg (2004). https://doi.org/10.1007/978-3-540-27836-8_63

53. Ishai, Y., Kushilevitz, E., Meldgaard, S., Orlandi, C., Paskin-Cherniavsky, A.: On the power of correlated randomness in secure computation. In: Sahai, A. (ed.) TCC 2013. LNCS, vol. 7785, pp. 600–620. Springer, Heidelberg (2013). https://doi.org/10.1007/978-3-642-36594-2_34

54. Lai, R.W.F., Malavolta, G., Schröder, D.: Homomorphic secret sharing for low degree polynomials. In: Peyrin, T., Galbraith, S. (eds.) ASIACRYPT 2018. LNCS, vol. 11274, pp. 279–309. Springer, Cham (2018). https://doi.org/10.1007/978-3-030-03332-3_11

55. Melchor, C.A., Barrier, J., Fousse, L., Killijian, M.-O.: XPIR: private information retrieval for everyone. In: PoPET 2016 (2016)

56. Roth, M.: Counting Problems on Quantum Graphs. Ph.D. thesis (2019)

57. Shamir, A.: How to share a secret. Commun. ACM **22**, 612–613 (1979)

58. Wang, F., Yun, C., Goldwasser, S., Vaikuntanathan, V., Zaharia, M.: Splinter: practical private queries on public data. In: USENIX 2017 (2017)

59. Williams, V.V.: On some fine-grained questions in algorithms and complexity. In: Proceedings of the ICM (2018)

60. Woodruff, D.P., Yekhanin, S.: A geometric approach to information-theoretic private information retrieval. In: CCC 2005 (2005)

61. Yao, A.C.: How to generate and exchange secrets (extended abstract). In: FOCS 1986 (1986)

62. Yekhanin, S.: Towards 3-query locally decodable codes of subexponential length. In: STOC 2007 (2007)

63. Yekhanin, S.: Private information retrieval. Commun. ACM **53**, 68–73 (2010)

Characterizing Deterministic-Prover Zero Knowledge

Nir Bitansky[1] and Arka Rai Choudhuri[2](✉)

[1] Tel Aviv University, Tel Aviv, Israel
nirbitan@tau.ac.il
[2] Johns Hopkins University, Baltimore, USA
achoud@cs.jhu.edu

Abstract. Randomness is typically thought to be essential for zero knowledge protocols. Following this intuition, Goldreich and Oren (Journal of Cryptology 94) proved that auxiliary-input zero knowledge cannot be achieved with a deterministic prover. On the other hand, positive results are only known in the honest-verifier setting, or when the prover is given at least a restricted source of entropy. We prove that removing (or just bounding) the verifier's auxiliary input, deterministic-prover zero knowledge becomes feasible:

- Assuming non-interactive witness-indistinguishable proofs and subexponential indistinguishability obfuscation and one-way functions, we construct deterministic-prover zero-knowledge arguments for NP ∩ coNP against verifiers with bounded non-uniform auxiliary input.
- Assuming also keyless hash functions that are collision-resistant against bounded-auxiliary-input quasipolynomial-time attackers, we construct similar arguments for all of NP.

Together with the result of Goldreich and Oren, this characterizes when deterministic-prover zero knowledge is feasible. We also demonstrate the necessity of strong assumptions, by showing that deterministic prover zero knowledge arguments for a given language imply witness encryption for that language. We further prove that such arguments can always be collapsed to two messages and be made laconic. These implications rely on a more general connection with the notion of predictable arguments by Faonio, Nielsen, and Venturi (PKC 17).

1 Introduction

Goldwasser, Micali, and Rackoff [18] founded the concept of *zero-knowledge proofs* on two main elements: *interaction and randomness*. While both interaction and verifier randomness are known to be essential for zero knowledge, the answer as to whether the prover must also be randomized is not as definite. Goldreich and Oren [16] showed that prover randomness is essential in order to achieve *auxiliary-input zero-knowledge* for non-trivial languages. According to this notion, motivated by composition [15], anything that a verifier can learn

© International Association for Cryptologic Research 2020
R. Pass and K. Pietrzak (Eds.): TCC 2020, LNCS 12550, pp. 535–566, 2020.
https://doi.org/10.1007/978-3-030-64375-1_19

from the proof, on top of the auxiliary information z it already possesses, can be efficiently simulated given the same auxiliary information z.

So when is deterministic-prover zero knowledge possible? So far, deterministic prover zero knowledge have only been shown to exist in the *honest-verifier setting*. Here Faonio, Nielsen, and Venturi [12] proved that any NP language $\mathcal{L}$ that has a *witness encryption scheme* [13], also has a deterministic-prover honest-verifier (perfect) zero-knowledge argument, or proof, if the language $\mathcal{L}$ has a *hash proof system* [10]. A similar result was recently shown by Dahari and Lindell [11]. In the same work, Dahari and Lindell also show a statistically sound honest-verifier zero knowledge protocol with an unbounded honest prover for all of NP assuming doubly-enhanced injective one-way functions. In the malicious verifier setting, they give a protocol satisfying a non-standard distributional notion of zero knowledge. In their definition, the prover has access to a pair of witnesses sampled from a distribution, which satisfy a certain entropy guarantee.

Whether zero knowledge with a truly deterministic prover is possible considering any meaningful form of malicious verifiers remains unknown.

1.1   This Work

We prove that deterministic-prover zero knowledge for non-trivial languages is feasible for the class of malicious verifiers with bounded auxiliary input.

Theorem 1 (Informal). *Assuming non-interactive witness-indistinguishable proofs and subexponentially-secure indistinguishability obfuscation and one-way functions, there exist two-message deterministic-prover arguments for NP $\cap$ coNP that are zero-knowledge against bounded-auxiliary-input verifiers.*[1]

Theorem 2 (Informal). *Assuming also keyless hash functions that are collision-resistant against bounded-auxiliary-input quasipolynomial-time attackers, there exist similar arguments for all of NP.*

By zero knowledge against bounded-auxiliary-input verifiers we formally mean that for any polynomial bound b, there exists a corresponding deterministic-prover argument that is zero knowledge against (malicious) verifiers with non-uniform auxiliary input of size at most b. This, in particular, includes the class of *uniform verifiers*, considered in the original zero-knowledge definition of [18]. We stress that the running time of the verifier may be an arbitrary polynomial, potentially larger than b. Also, indistinguishability of simulated and real proofs holds against non-uniform distinguishers of arbitrary polynomial size. Same goes for soundness, which holds against non-uniform provers of arbitrary polynomial size.

---

[1] Indistinguishability obfuscation implies non-interactive witness indistinguishable proofs, but with a randomized verifier [8], which is insufficient for our purpose. The verifier can be derandomized under a worst-case Nisan-Wigderson [21] type derandomization assumption [9]. Non-interactive witness indistinguishable proofs with a deterministic verifier are also known from standard assumptions on bilinear maps [19].

Together with the impossibility result of Goldreich and Oren for unbounded auxiliary input, the above results give a complete picture of when exactly deterministic-prover zero knowledge is feasible. We note that two-message zero knowledge against unbounded auxiliary input is by itself known to be impossible. Our result indeed circumvents this impossibility (for bounded auxiliary input), but this was already known (with a randomized prover) [6].

On the Necessity of Strong Assumptions and Predictable Arguments. To demonstrate the feasibility of deterministic-prover zero knowledge, we rely on hardness assumptions that are arguably strong. We show that this is inherent. Specifically, we show that deterministic prover zero-knowledge arguments for NP imply witness encryption for NP, which at this point is only known based on strong assumptions, such as indistinguishability obfuscation.

The implication to witness encryption, in fact, follows from a more general implication to *predictable arguments*. Predictable arguments, introduced by Faonio, Nielsen, and Venturi [12], are arguments where the honest verifier's (private) random coins efficiently determine a unique accepting transcript—in order to convince the verifier, the prover must be consistent with this transcript throughout the entire protocol. We prove that any deterministic-prover zero-knowledge argument against bounded-auxiliary-input verifiers can be turned into a predictable argument. The transformation, in fact, preserves the honest prover algorithm, and in particular also zero knowledge.

Theorem 3 (Informal). *Any deterministic-prover zero-knowledge argument against bounded-auxiliary-input verifiers can be made predictable.*

We also give a transformation that only requires honest-verifier zero knowledge and works provided that the argument is expressive enough (e.g., for all NP or even just NP ∩ coNP). The fact that deterministic-prover zero knowledge arguments imply witness encryption, then follows from [12] where predictable arguments are shown to imply witness encryption.

Corollary 1 (of Predictability). *Any deterministic-prover zero-knowledge argument against bounded-auxiliary-input verifiers for a language $\mathcal{L}$ implies a witness encryption scheme for $\mathcal{L}$.*

We use additional known results regarding predictable arguments [12] to deduce similar results for deterministic-prover zero knowledge:

Corollary 2 (of Predictability). *Any deterministic-prover zero-knowledge argument against bounded-auxiliary-input verifiers can be reduced to two messages and made laconic.*

Here by *laconic* [12,17] we mean that the prover sends a *single* bit and the soundness error is negligibly close to $1/2$; or more generally, the prover sends ℓ bit in order to obtain a soundness error negligibly close to $2^{-\ell}$.

Non-Black-Box Zero-Knowledge Simulation. The zero-knowledge simulator in our constructed arguments makes non-black-box use of the verifier's code. This is known to be inherent—black-box simulation is impossible in the setting of two (or even three) message zero knowledge against bounded-auxiliary-input verifiers [6,15].

1.2   Technical Overview

We now give an overview of the main ideas and techniques behind our results.

The Deterministic-Prover Zero-Knowledge Protocol. Our starting point is the protocol against honest verifiers based on witness encryption [12]. In their protocol, the verifier simply sends a witness encryption of a random message u with respect to the statement $x \in \mathcal{L}$ to be proven, and expects to get u back from the prover. Witness encryption guarantees that a prover that has a corresponding witness w, can obtain u and convince the verifier. However, if the statement is false, namely $x \notin \mathcal{L}$, u is hidden, and soundness is guaranteed.

While honest verifiers are easy to simulate in this scheme, it is not clear how to simulate malicious verifiers. For this purpose, we aim to add to the protocol *a trapdoor way of obtaining u*. A simulator that has the code of the verifier should be able to extract the message u. In contrast, a malicious prover who doesn't have the code (specifically, the verifier's randomness) should still fail to find u when $x \notin \mathcal{L}$.

Explainable Verifiers. To explain the idea behind the protocol in its simplest form, let us start by assuming that the first message v sent by verifier to the prover is always *explainable* [7]. That is, there exist honest verifier coins r that explain this message as an honest verifier message $v = V(x; r)$. The difference between this setting and the honest verifier setting is that the explaining coins r may be distributed arbitrarily and also computationally hard to find.

Our basic idea is for the verifier to send the prover yet another witness encryption of u where *the witness is basically the malicious verifier code* V^*. Our realization of this idea is inspired by Barak's uniform simulation technique [1]. Let b be the given bound on the description size of the verifier including its (bounded) auxiliary input hardwired. Then, the honest verifier samples a long random string $R \leftarrow \{0,1\}^{b+2\lambda}$. Then in addition to the witness encryption of u under the statement $x \in \mathcal{L}$, it sends a witness encryption of u under the statement:

"There exists a program Π of size $b + \lambda$ (namely short) that outputs R."

To argue that the protocol remains sound, we note that except with negligible probability $2^{-\lambda}$ over the choice of r, such a short program does not exist. In this case, witness encryption will guarantee that u remains hidden and soundness is preserved. Furthermore, a simulator in possession of the b-size code V^* of the malicious verifier can now use it to simulate. Specifically, let ℓ be the amount of coins r^* used by V^*, then the simulator will sample r^* using a pseudorandom generator that stretches a seed s^* of length $\approx \lambda$ to a pseudorandom r^* of length ℓ. Looking at the string R that $V^*(x; r^*)$ outputs, the simulator now possesses a size-$(b + \lambda)$ program Π that computes R—the code of V^* with the seed s^* hardwired. This in turn leads to valid simulation.

Witness Encryption for Unbounded NP Relations and IO. One thing to notice about the latter protocol is that in fact the existence of program Π that outputs R is not an NP statement, unless we restrict the running time of Π to some specific polynomial. However, while the non-uniform description size (equivalently, auxiliary input size) of the malicious verifier V^* is a-priori bounded, its running time is not bounded by any specific polynomial.

Accordingly, we need a strong notion of witness encryption for unbounded non-deterministic relations. Specifically, encryption under a statement x should take time polynomial in $|x|$ (and the security parameter), and not depend on the time required to verify a witness for x. In contrast, decrypting with a witness w should take time proportional to the time required to verify w. Such witness encryption schemes directly follow from known indistinguishability obfuscation (IO) schemes for Turing Machines, which are in turn constructed from subexponentially-secure IO for circuits [5, 14, 20].

Malicious Verifiers. Having constructed a protocol against explainable verifiers, we use compilers from the literature to turn it into a protocol against arbitrary verifiers. These compilers use non-interactive witness-indistinguishable proofs (NIWIs) in order to enforce explainable behavior on the verifier's side. Being non-interactive verifying, these proofs require no randomness from the honest zero-knowledge prover.

The first such compiler [7] works for NP ∩ coNP and requires no additional hardness assumptions. The second compiler is taken from [3] (where it was used in a different context) and relies in addition on keyless hash functions that are collision resistant against attackers with bounded auxiliary input and quasipolynomial running time, as well as subexponentially secure commitments (which in turn follow from subexponentially secure IO and one-way functions). In the body, we reanalyze these compilers to show that they can be used to enforce *robust explainability*, which roughly means that the verifier's messages are almost always explainable on any efficiently samplable distribution on its coins, a property required for our simulation strategy. See more details in Sect. 3.

From Deterministic-Prover Zero Knowledge to Predictable Arguments. We now explain how deterministic-prover zero knowledge implies predictable arguments, which in turn imply witness encryption (as well as the additional properties stated in Corollary 2). We start with an oversimplified transformation that captures the main idea, but does not fully work, and then explain how to augment it. This oversimplified transformation, in fact, starts from deterministic-prover *honest-verifier* zero knowledge.

Let (P, V) be our argument, and let Sim be the honest-verifier simulator. We consider a new verifier V' that works as follows. It applies the simulator $\mathsf{Sim}(x)$ to obtain simulated randomness $\tilde{r}$ for the honest verifier along with simulated prover messages $\tilde{\mathsf{p}}_1, \ldots, \tilde{\mathsf{p}}_k$. The verifier V' then certifies that the prover messages lead to an accepting transcript with respect to the verifier coins r. If they do not lead to an accepting transcript, V' automatically rejects; otherwise, it interacts with the prover, and rejects the moment it receives a message $\mathsf{p}_i \neq \tilde{\mathsf{p}}_i$. The described protocol is predictable by construction. Also, since we do not change the honest prover, it is zero knowledge against the same class of verifiers as the original protocol. We now turn to argue that the protocol is complete and sound.

To see that the protocol has almost perfect completeness, consider a distinguisher that has the witness w hardwired. Given a transcript $\mathsf{p}_1, \ldots, \mathsf{p}_k$ and verifier coins r, it can perfectly emulate a conversation between the deterministic prover $\mathsf{P}(x, w)$ and honest verifier $\mathsf{V}(x; r)$ and check whether the produced prover messages are consistent with the input transcript $\mathsf{p}_1, \ldots, \mathsf{p}_k$, and that the transcript is accepting. We deduce that with overwhelming probability the simulator produces simulated messages $\tilde{\mathsf{p}}_1, \ldots, \tilde{\mathsf{p}}_k$, and randomness r, such that the honest prover would produce the same messages, and the transcript will be accepting. To see soundness, notice that if the simulated coins r are pseudorandom and the simulated prover messages $\tilde{\mathsf{p}}_1, \ldots, \tilde{\mathsf{p}}_k$ are accepting, then by the soundness of the original protocol (P, V), it should be hard for an efficient prover to produce messages consistent with $\tilde{\mathsf{p}}_1, \ldots, \tilde{\mathsf{p}}_k$ (or with any accepting transcript).

Above, when proving soundness we actually made the implicit assumption that the honest verifier simulator $\mathsf{Sim}(x)$ produces pseudorandom verifier coins, even when given a no instance $x \notin \mathcal{L}$. Indeed, with respect to random, or pseudorandom, coins, we can argue that it is hard to find accepting transcripts. While this is a natural property, it does not follow directly from honest verifier zero knowledge. To circumvent this difficulty, we slightly augment the above transformation, while relying on zero-knowledge against (not necessarily honest) bounded-auxiliary-input verifiers.

Specifically, the verifier V' uses a pseudorandom generator to sample coins r for the honest verifier V, using a short seed s. It then applies the same procedure as above, except that it runs the simulator $\mathsf{Sim}(\mathsf{V}_s, x)$ for the deterministic verifier V_s that first derives the coins r from the seed s, and then applies V. By choosing an appropriate pseudorandom generator, we can guarantee that the non-uniform description of V_s is short enough. This transformation guarantees that the simulated coins are pseudorandom, even for a no instance, and allows the above proof to go through. The necessity of zero-knowledge to hold even for verifiers that are not necessarily honest comes from the fact that our description of V_s deviates from the honest verifier strategy. We give another construction of predictable arguments from deterministic-prover arguments that are only honest-verifier zero knowledge, provided that the arguments supports expressive enough languages. See Sect. A for details.

A Word on Two-Message Laconic Arguments. As stated in Corollary 2, we use the implication to predictable arguments to also derive that any deterministic-prover zero knowledge argument for bounded-auxiliary-input verifiers can be made two message and laconic. This corollary is obtained by applying as is general transformations on predictable arguments [12]. The only thing we need to prove is that these transformations preserve zero knowledge. The only hurdle here is that the mentioned transformations involve parallel repetition for the sake of soundness amplification. We observe that (unlike many-round zero knowledge) two-message zero knowledge against bounded-auxiliary-input verifiers is closed under parallel repetition.

On Deterministic Prover Zero-Knowledge Proofs. While our results (in conjunction with prior works) provide a complete picture of deterministic zero-knowledge arguments, our results do not have any bearing on deterministic zero-knowledge *proofs*, where soundness is required to hold against unbounded provers. Completing the picture for *proofs* remains an interesting open problem.

2 Definitions

In this work, we will consider PPT machines with both, bounded and unbounded non-uniform auxiliary input. For simplicity of notation, rather than considering explicit auxiliary input in our definitions, we consider two basic notions of non-uniformity. The corresponding zero knowledge definition will in particular capture the auxiliary input setting. See Remark 1.

1. *non-uniform* PPT: this is the standard notion of non-uniform PPT machines. Formally, a non-uniform PPT $M = \{M_\lambda\}_\lambda$ is a family of probabilistic Turing machines (one for each λ), where there exists a polynomial poly, such that the description size $|M_\lambda|$ and the running time of M_λ are bounded by $\mathsf{poly}(\lambda)$.
2. *b-non-uniform* PPT: These are PPT machines with non-uniform description of size $b(\lambda)$ and arbitrary polynomial running time (possibly larger than $b(\lambda)$). Formally, a b-non-uniform PPT $M = \{M_\lambda\}_\lambda$ is a family of probabilistic Turing machines (one for each λ), where $|M_\lambda| \leq b(\lambda)$ and there exists a polynomial poly, such that the running time of M_λ is bounded by $\mathsf{poly}(\lambda)$.

In both of the above, we often omit from M_λ the subscript λ when it is clear from the context. If we simply say a PPT machine, we mean a uniform one.

Throughout this work, we will talk about computational indistinguishability with respect to non-uniform distinguishers.

Definition 1 (Computational Indistinguishability). *Two ensembles $X = \{X_\alpha\}_{\alpha \in S}$ and $Y = \{Y_\alpha\}_{\alpha \in S}$ are said to be computationally indistinguishable, denoted by $X \approx_c Y$, if for every non-uniform PPT distinguisher $\mathcal{D}$, every polynomial p, all sufficiently large λ and every $\alpha \in \{0,1\}^{\mathsf{poly}(\lambda)} \cap S$*

$$\left| \Pr\left[\mathcal{D}(1^\lambda, X_\alpha) = 1\right] - \Pr\left[\mathcal{D}(1^\lambda, Y_\alpha) = 1\right] \right| < \frac{1}{\mathsf{p}(\lambda)},$$

where the probability are taken over the samples of X_α, Y_α and coin tosses of $\mathcal{D}$.

We shall sometimes find it convenient to talk about the stronger notion of statistical indistinguishability, defined below.

Definition 2 (Statistical Indistinguishability). *Two ensembles* $X = \{X_\alpha\}_{\alpha \in S}$ *and* $Y = \{Y_\alpha\}_{\alpha \in S}$ *are said to be statistically indistinguishable, denoted by* $X \approx_s Y$, *if for every polynomial* p, *all sufficiently large* λ *and every* $\alpha \in \{0,1\}^{\mathsf{poly}(\lambda)} \cap S$

$$\Delta(X_\alpha, Y_\alpha) < \frac{1}{\mathsf{p}(\lambda)},$$

where $\Delta(X_\alpha, Y_\alpha)$ *corresponds to the statistical distance between* X_α *and* Y_α.

2.1 Deterministic-Prover Zero Knowledge Against Bounded-Auxiliary-Input Verifiers

We define the notion of deterministic-prover zero-knowledge arguments against verifiers with bounded auxiliary-input (DPZK). We shall denote by $\mathsf{Out}_A \langle A(a), B(b) \rangle$ the output of party A on execution of the protocol between A with input a, and B with input b. By $\mathsf{View}_A \langle A(a), B(b) \rangle$, we denote the view of party A consisting of the protocol transcript along with its random tape.

Definition 3. *An interactive protocol* (P, V) *between a **deterministic** polynomial time prover* P *and* PPT *verifier* V, *for a language* $\mathcal{L}$ *is a deterministic prover b-bounded-auxiliary-input zero knowledge argument if the following holds.*

Completeness: *For every* $x \in \mathcal{L}$,

$$\Pr[\mathsf{Out}_\mathsf{V} \langle \mathsf{P}(x, w), \mathsf{V}(x) \rangle = 1] = 1.$$

Soundness: *For any non-uniform* PPT P^*, *there exists a negligible function* $\mathsf{negl}(\cdot)$ *such that for all* $\lambda \in \mathbb{N}$ *and* $x \in \{0,1\}^\lambda \setminus \mathcal{L}$,

$$\Pr[\mathsf{Out}_\mathsf{V} \langle \mathsf{P}^*, \mathsf{V}(x) \rangle = 1] \leq \mathsf{negl}(\lambda).$$

Zero Knowledge: *There exists a* PPT *simulator* Sim, *such that for every b-non-uniform* PPT *verifier* V^* *of running time at most* $t(\lambda)$,

$$\left\{ \mathsf{View}_{\mathsf{V}^*} \langle \mathsf{P}(x, w), \mathsf{V}^* \rangle \right\}_{\substack{\lambda \in \mathbb{N}, \\ x \in \mathcal{L} \cap \{0,1\}^\lambda, \\ w \in R_\mathcal{L}(x)}} \approx_c \left\{ \mathsf{Sim}(\mathsf{V}^*, 1^t, x) \right\}_{\substack{\lambda \in \mathbb{N}, \\ x \in \mathcal{L} \cap \{0,1\}^\lambda, \\ w \in R_\mathcal{L}(x)}}.$$

Remark 1 (Universal Simulation). In the above definition, there exists one universal simulator Sim that gets the code of the verifier as input. We note that this definition is known [16] to imply the alternative definition of (bounded) auxiliary-input zero knowledge that requires that any for any t-time V^* there is a PPT simulator $\mathsf{Sim}_{\mathsf{V}^*}$ such that given (bounded) auxiliary input z, $\mathsf{Sim}_{\mathsf{V}^*}(x, z, 1^t)$ simulates $\mathsf{V}^*(z)$.

2.2   Indistinguishability Obfuscation (IO)

We now give a definition of indistinguishability obfuscator for Turing Machines, which can be constructed from indistinguishability obfuscators for circuits [5,14,20].

Definition 4 (Indistinguishability Obfuscator for Turing Machines). *A succinct indistinguishability obfuscator for Turing machines consists of a PPT machine* iOM *that works as follows:*

- iOM *takes as input the security parameter* 1^λ, *the Turing machine* M *to obfuscate, an input length* n, *and time bound* t.
- iOM *outputs a Turing machine* $\widetilde{M}$ *which is an obfuscation of* M *corresponding to input length* n *and time bound* t. $\widetilde{M}$ *takes as input* $x \in \{0,1\}^n$.

The scheme should satisfy the following requirements:

Correctness. *For all* $\lambda \in \mathbb{N}$, *for all* $M \in \mathcal{M}_\lambda$, *for all inputs* $x \in \{0,1\}^n$, *time bounds* t' *such that* $t' \leq t$, *let* y *be the output of* $M(x)$ *after at most* t *steps, then*

$$\Pr\left[\widetilde{M} \leftarrow \mathrm{iOM}(1^\lambda, 1^n, 1^{\log t}, M) \;:\; \widetilde{M}(x) = y\right] = 1.$$

Security. *It holds that*

$$\left\{\mathrm{iOM}(1^\lambda, 1^n, 1^{\log t}, M_0)\right\}_{\substack{\lambda,t,n,\\ M_0,M_1}} \approx_c \left\{\mathrm{iOM}(1^\lambda, 1^n, 1^{\log t}, M_1)\right\}_{\substack{\lambda,t,n,\\ M_0,M_1}},$$

where $\lambda \in \mathbb{N}$, $n \leq t \leq 2^\lambda$, *and* M_0, M_1 *are any pair of machines of the same size such that for any input* $x \in \{0,1\}^n$ *both halt after the same number of steps with the same output.*

Efficiency and Succinctness. *We require that the running time of* iOM *and the length of its output, namely the obfuscated machine* $\widetilde{M}$, *is* $\mathsf{poly}(|M|, \log t, n, \lambda)$. *We also require that the running time* $\tilde{t}_x$ *of* $\widetilde{M}(x)$ *is* $\mathsf{poly}(t_x, |M|, n, \lambda)$, *where* t_x *is the running time of* $M(x)$.

2.3   Witness Encryption

The following definition of witness encryption is taken from [13].

Definition 5. *A witness encryption scheme for an* NP *language* $\mathcal{L}$, *with corresponding witness relation* $R_\mathcal{L}$, *consists of the following two polynomial-time algorithms:*

Encryption. *The probabilistic algorithm* $\mathsf{WE.Enc}(1^\lambda, x, m)$ *takes as input a security parameter* 1^λ, *a string* $x \in \{0,1\}^*$, *and a message* $m \in \{0,1\}$. *It outputs a ciphertext* ct.

Decryption. *The algorithm* $\mathsf{WE.Dec}(\mathsf{ct}, w)$ *takes as input a ciphertext* ct, *a string* $w \in \{0,1\}^*$. *It outputs either a message* $m \in \{0,1\}$.

544 N. Bitansky and A. R. Choudhuri

The above algorithms satisfy the following conditions:

- **Correctness.** *For any security parameter λ, for any $m \in \{0,1\}$, and for any $(x,w) \in R_{\mathcal{L}}$, we have that*

$$\Pr\left[\mathsf{ct} \leftarrow \mathsf{WE.Enc}(1^\lambda, x, m) \ : \ \mathsf{WE.Dec}(\mathsf{ct}, w) = m\right] = 1.$$

- **Security.** *For any non-uniform PPT adversary $\mathcal{A}$, there exists a negligible function $\mathsf{negl}(\cdot)$ such that for any $\lambda \in \mathbb{N}$, and any $x \notin \mathcal{L}$, we have that*

$$\left\{\mathsf{WE.Enc}(1^\lambda, x, 0)\right\}_{\lambda \in \mathbb{N}, x \notin \mathcal{L}} \approx_c \left\{\mathsf{WE.Enc}(1^\lambda, x, 1)\right\}_{\lambda \in \mathbb{N}, x \notin \mathcal{L}}.$$

We note that the above scheme can be extended to encrypt strings, rather than just bits, by encrypting each bit independently. Witness encryption for all of NP can be constructed from IO for circuits [13].

2.4 Non-interactive Witness Indistinguishability (NIWI)

Definition 6 ([2]). *A non-interactive witness-indistinguishable proof system $\mathsf{NIWI} = (\mathsf{NIWI.Prov}, \mathsf{NIWI.Ver})$ for an NP relation $R_{\mathcal{L}}$ consists of two polynomial-time algorithms:*

- *a probabilistic prover $\mathsf{NIWI.Prov}(x, w, 1^\lambda)$ that given an instance x, witness w, and security parameter 1^λ, produces a proof π.*
- *a deterministic verifier $\mathsf{NIWI.Ver}(x, \pi)$ that verifies the proof.*

We make the following requirements:

Completeness *for every $\lambda \in \mathbb{N}, (x,w) \in R_{\mathcal{L}}$,*

$$\Pr\left[\pi \leftarrow \mathsf{NIWI.Prov}(x, w, 1^\lambda) \ : \ \mathsf{NIWI.Ver}(x, \pi) = 1\right] = 1$$

Soundness *for every $x \notin \mathcal{L}$ and $\pi \in \{0,1\}^*$,*

$$\mathsf{NIWI.Ver}(x, \pi) = 0.$$

Witness Indistinguishability. *It holds that*

$$\left\{\mathsf{NIWI.Prov}(x, w_0, 1^\lambda)\right\}_{\substack{\lambda, x, \\ w_0, w_1}} \approx_c \left\{\mathsf{NIWI.Prov}(x, w_1, 1^\lambda)\right\}_{\substack{\lambda, x, \\ w_0, w_1}},$$

where $\lambda \in \mathbb{N}, x \in \{0,1\}^\lambda, w_0, w_1 \in R_{\mathcal{L}}(x)$.

2.5 Collision Resistance Against Bounded Non-uniform Adversaries

We describe here the notion of keyless collision resistance against quasi-polynomial b-non-uniform adversaries, extending the definition in [3].

Syntax. A keyless collision resistance hash function is associated with an input function $\ell(\lambda) > \lambda$ and a polynomial time algorithm H such that $\mathsf{H}(1^\lambda, X)$ is a deterministic algorithm that takes as input an $X \in \{0,1\}^{\ell(\lambda)}$ and outputs a hash $Y \in \{0,1\}^\lambda$.

Definition 7. *We say that* H *is collision-resistant against quasi-polynomial adversaries if for any b-non-uniform probabilistic $2^{\mathsf{poly}(\log \lambda)}$-time $\mathcal{A}$, there exists a negligible function* negl, *such that for any* $\lambda \in \mathbb{N}$,

$$\Pr\left[(x_1, x_2) \leftarrow \mathcal{A}(1^\lambda) \ : \ x_1 \neq x_2, \mathsf{H}(1^\lambda, x_1) = \mathsf{H}(1^\lambda, x_2)\right] \leq \mathsf{negl}(\lambda).$$

2.6 Non-interactive Commitment Schemes

We define below bit commitment schemes.

Definition 8 (Non-interactive Bit Commitment Schemes). *A polynomial time computable function:* $\mathsf{Com} : \{0,1\} \times \{0,1\}^\lambda \mapsto \{0,1\}^{\ell(\lambda)}$ *is a bit commitment if it satisfies the properties below:*

Binding: *For any $r, r' \in \{0,1\}^\lambda, b, b' \in \{0,1\}$, if $\mathsf{Com}(b; r) = \mathsf{Com}(b'; r')$ then $b = b'$.*

Computational Hiding: *The following holds:*

$$\left\{\mathsf{Com}(0) : r \leftarrow_\$ \{0,1\}^\lambda\right\} \approx_c \left\{\mathsf{Com}(1; r) : r \leftarrow_\$ \{0,1\}^\lambda\right\}.$$

where computational indistinguishability is with respect to arbitrary non-uniform PPT *distinguisher.*

We note that the above scheme can be extended to commit to strings, rather than just bits, by committing to each bit independently. Looking ahead, we require that the underlying string that is committed can be extracted in quasi-polynomial time. Such commitments can be constructed from subexponentiall-secure injective one-way functions (which in turn can be constructed from subexponential IO and one-way functions).

2.7 Explainable Verifiers

We define here the a variant of the notion of explainable verifiers [7] called robustly-explainable verifiers. Roughly speaking, explainable verifiers are ones whose messages almost always lie in the support of the honest verifier messages (or are abort). Robustly-explainable verifiers are such where this occurs when they use random coins sampled from an arbitrary efficient sampler (and not necessarily the uniform distribution).

Definition 9 (Explainable Message). *Let $\langle \mathsf{P}, \mathsf{V} \rangle$ be a two-message protocol. We say that a given message m is explainable with respect to x, if there exist honest verifier coins r such that $m \in \{V(x; r), \bot\}$.*

Definition 10 (Robustly-Explainable Verifier). *Let* $\langle \mathsf{P}, \mathsf{V} \rangle$ *be a protocol. A* b-*non-uniform* PPT *verifier* V^* *using* $\ell(\lambda)$ *random coins is robustly-explainable if for any* PPT *sampler* R *on* $\ell(\lambda)$ *bits, there exists a negligible* $\mathsf{negl}(\lambda)$ *such that for any* $\lambda \in \mathbb{N}$ *and* $x \in \lambda$,

$$\Pr\left[r \leftarrow R(1^\lambda), m = \mathsf{V}^*(x; r) : m \text{ is explainable} \right] \geq 1 - \mathsf{negl}(\lambda).$$

2.8 Pseudorandom Generators

Definition 11 (Psedudorandom Generators). *A deterministic function* $\mathsf{PRG} : \{0,1\}^\lambda \rightarrow \{0,1\}^{p(\lambda)}$ *is called a pseudorandom generator (PRG) if:*

1. *(efficiency):* PRG *can be computed in polynomial time,*
2. *(expansion):* $p(\lambda) > \lambda$,
3. $\left\{ x \leftarrow \{0,1\}^\lambda : \mathsf{PRG}(x) \right\} \approx_c \left\{ U_{p(\lambda)} \right\}$, *where* $U_{p(\lambda)}$ *is the uniform distribution over* $p(\lambda)$ *bits.*

3   A Deterministic-Prover Zero-Knowledge Protocol

In this section we present our deterministic prover zero knowledge (DPZK) protocol. As explained in the introduction, we start by describing the protocol for robustly-explainable verifiers. We then show how to compile this protocol to one that is secure against malicious verifiers.

3.1   DPZK for Robustly-Explainable Verifiers

We use the following components for the deterministic prover zero knowledge (DPZK) protocol for an NP language $\mathcal{L}$ against b-non-uniform explainable verifiers.

- A witness encryption scheme (WE.Enc, WE.Dec) for language $\mathcal{L}$.
- An indistinguishability obfuscation (IO) scheme iOM for Turing Machines (TM).

Additionally, we will use the machine described below that outputs the hardcoded secret u given as input the description of a "short" Turing machine that outputs a hardcoded public value R.

Machine: Prog

Hardcoded: R, u
Input: $\mathsf{M} \in \{0,1\}^{\rho(\lambda)}$

if M outputs R

output u

else

output $\bot$

In what follows, let $\rho(\lambda) = b(\lambda) + \lambda + \omega(1)$, $\ell(\lambda) = \rho(\lambda) + \lambda$. The protocol is described in Fig. 1. We prove the properties of the protocol below.

Protocol: DPZK for robustly-explainable verifiers

Common input: Input $x \in \mathcal{L}$, security parameter 1^λ

P's auxiliary input: witness w such that $(x, w) \in R_\mathcal{L}$

1. Verifier V computes the first message as

    (a) $R \leftarrow_\$ \{0,1\}^{\ell(\lambda)}$
    (b) $t := \lambda^{\log \lambda}$
    (c) $u \leftarrow_\$ \{0,1\}^\lambda$
    (d) $\widetilde{\mathsf{Prog}} \leftarrow \mathsf{iOM}\left(1^\lambda, 1^\rho, 1^{\log t}, \mathsf{Prog}\,[R, u]\right)$
    (e) $\mathsf{ct} \leftarrow \mathsf{WE.Enc}(u, x)$
    send $(R, \mathsf{ct}, \widetilde{\mathsf{Prog}})$ to the prover P.

2. Prover P computes the second message as

    (a) $\widetilde{u} := \mathsf{WE.Dec}(\mathsf{ct}, x, w)$
    send $\widetilde{u}$ to the verifier V.

3. Verifier V performs the check

    (a) if $\widetilde{u} = u$, accept. Else, reject.

Fig. 1. Deterministic prover zero-knowledge for robustly-explainable verifiers.

Completeness. Completeness follows from the correctness of witness encryption.

Soundness. We now prove that the above protocol is sound against computationally bounded provers.

Proposition 1. *Assuming security of the indistinguishability obfuscation scheme and the witness encryption scheme, the protocol is sound.*

Proof. We consider a sequence of hybrids transitioning from the real protocol to an ideal protocol where the probability that the prover convinces the verifier of accepting is clearly negligible.

Hyb_0: This is the real protocol.
Hyb_1: In this hybrid, we modify the program Prog to Prog' that always output $\bot$.

By our choice of parameters and a union bound, the probability that there exists a machine $M \in \{0,1\}^\rho$ that outputs R is at most $2^{\rho-\ell} = 2^{-\lambda}$. Therefore, except with negligible probability Prog and Prog' are functionally equivalent. The indistinguishability of Hyb_1 and Hyb_0 then follows from the indistinguishability of the IO scheme.

Hyb_2: In this hybrid, we additionally change the ciphertext ct of the witness encryption scheme to be the encryption of 0.

Since $x \notin \mathcal{L}$, the indistinguishability between Hyb_2 and Hyb_1 follows from the security of the witness encryption scheme.

It is left to observe that in Hyb_2 the prover obtains no information about u, and thus convinces the verifier with probability at most $2^{-\lambda}$.   □

Zero Knowledge. We prove

Proposition 2. *Assuming the existence of pseudorandom generators, the protocol is zero knowledge against b-non-uniform verifiers.*

Proof. We describe the simulation strategy below. In what follows V^* is a b-non-uniform malicious verifier of polynomial running time at most $t(\lambda)$. Additionally, let k be the amount of random coins r^* used by V^*. The simulator Sim will use a PRG $\mathsf{PRG} : \{0,1\}^\lambda \mapsto \{0,1\}^k$.

$\underline{\mathsf{Sim}(V^*, 1^t, x)}$:

1. Construct verifier V_s^* that has the seed s hardwired. V_s^* computes $\mathsf{PRG}(s)$ and uses it as random coins for V^*. Additionally, V_s^* truncates V^*'s output to R.
2. Initialize V^* with random coins $\mathsf{PRG}(s)$.
3. Given $\widetilde{\mathsf{Prog}}$ from V^*, use the description of V_s^* as input to $\widetilde{\mathsf{Prog}}$ and obtain u.
4. u is then used as the simulated prover message, along with verifier randomness $\mathsf{PRG}(s)$.

First, consider an execution between the prover and augmented verifier $\langle P(x,w), V_s^* \rangle$, and let v and p denote the verifier and prover messages in such an execution. Then by pseudorandomness of PRG,

$$\mathsf{View}_{V^*}\langle P(x,w), V^* \rangle \approx_c \mathsf{p}, \mathsf{PRG}(s).$$

Next, by the fact that V^* is robustly explainable, we know that except with negligible probability, $\mathsf{v} = (R, \mathsf{ct}, \widetilde{\mathsf{Prog}})$ is explainable; namely, has the structure prescribed by the honest verifier algorithm. Noting that V_s^* is a program of length $b + \lambda + O(1) < \rho(\lambda)$ and running time at most $t(\lambda)$ that outputs R. By the fact that v is explainable, $\widetilde{\mathsf{Prog}}(V_s^*) = \mathsf{WE.Dec}(\mathsf{ct}, x, w)$. It follows that

$$\mathsf{p}, \mathsf{PRG}(s) \approx_s \mathsf{Sim}(V^*, 1^t, x),$$

and overall

$$\mathsf{View}_{V^*}\langle P(x,w), V^* \rangle \approx_c \mathsf{Sim}(V^*, 1^t, x),$$

as required.   □

3.2   From Explainable to Malicious Verifiers

In this section we give generic compilers going from robust-explainable to malicious verifiers. These compilers were constructed in [7] where they were used to enforce explainability and in [3] where they were used in a different context. We prove that these compilers, in fact, enforce robust explainability. The statements, and correspondingly the underlying assumptions, change based on whether we want a DPZK for NP ∩ coNP, or for all of NP. We discuss the two cases separately.

3.2.1   DPZK for NP ∩ coNP

We consider languages $\mathcal{L} \in$ NP ∩ coNP, which in turn means that in addition to relation $R_{\mathcal{L}}$, there is also a NP-relation $R_{\overline{\mathcal{L}}}$ to certify that a statement $x \notin \mathcal{L}$. We use the following primitives in our construction:

- A two-message deterministic-prover zero-knowledge (DPZK) protocol $(e\mathsf{P}, e\mathsf{V})$ secure against robustly-explainable verifiers. Let the verifier and prover messages be denoted by v and p, respectively.
- A non-interactive witness indistinguishable proof (NIWI) (NIWI.Prov, NIWI.Ver) for the language

$$\mathcal{L}_{\mathsf{NIWI}} = \Big\{ (\mathsf{v}, x) \ \Big| \ \exists (r, \bar{w}) \text{ s.t. } \mathsf{v} = e\mathsf{V}(x; r) \text{ OR } R_{\overline{\mathcal{L}}}(x, \bar{w}) = 1 \Big\},$$

namely, either the verifier's message is explainable, or the statement is not in the language. Henceforth, we shall refer to the second half of the 'OR' statement, that the statement is not in the language, to be the *trapdoor statement*.

The protocol is presented in Fig. 2.

Completeness. Completeness follows directly from the completeness of the underlying protocol and the NIWI proof.

Zero Knowledge. We show how any b-non-uniform malicious verifier V^* for the above protocol can be converted to a robustly-explainable $b + O(1)$-non-uniform verifier against the original protocol.

Claim 1. There exist an efficient simulator S and a verifier $e\mathsf{V}^*$ such that

1. $e\mathsf{V}^*$ is a robustly explainable verifier against $\langle e\mathsf{P}, e\mathsf{V} \rangle$.
2. $e\mathsf{V}^*$ is $(b + O(1))$-non-uniform and efficiently constructable from $e\mathsf{V}^*$.
3. For every $x \in \mathcal{L}$,

$$\mathsf{View}_{\mathsf{V}^*} \langle \mathsf{P}(x, w), \mathsf{V}^* \rangle \equiv \mathsf{S}(\mathsf{View}_{e\mathsf{V}^*} \langle e\mathsf{P}(x, w), e\mathsf{V}^* \rangle).$$

Protocol: (P,V) for $\mathcal{L} \in$ NP $\cap$ coNP

Common input: Input $x \in \mathcal{L}$, security parameter 1^λ

P's auxiliary input: witness w such that $(x, w) \in R_{\mathcal{L}}$

1. Verifier V computes the first message as

   (a) $r \leftarrow_{\$} \{0,1\}^{p(n)}$
   (b) $\mathsf{v} := e\mathsf{V}(x; r)$
   (c) $x_{\mathsf{NIWI}} := (\mathsf{v}, x)$
   (d) $w_{\mathsf{NIWI}} := (r, \bot)$
   (e) $\mathsf{wi} \leftarrow \mathsf{NIWI.Prov}(x_{\mathsf{NIWI}}, w_{\mathsf{NIWI}})$
   send $(\mathsf{v}, \mathsf{wi})$ to the prover P.

2. Prover P computes the second message as

   (a) $\widetilde{x}_{\mathsf{NIWI}} := (\mathsf{v}, x)$
   (b) if $\mathsf{NIWI.Ver}(\widetilde{x}_{\mathsf{NIWI}}, \mathsf{wi}) \neq 1$, output $\bot$.
   (c) $\mathsf{p} := e\mathsf{P}(x, w, \mathsf{v})$.
   send p to the verifier V.

3. Verifier V performs the check

   (a) if $e\mathsf{V}(x, \mathsf{p}; r) = 1$, accept. Else, reject.

Fig. 2. Deterministic-prover zero knowledge for $\mathcal{L} \in$ NP $\cap$ coNP.

Proof. We construct $\mathsf{S}, e\mathsf{V}^*$.

$e\mathsf{V}^*$:

1. Emulates V^* and obtains $(\mathsf{v}, \mathsf{wi})$.
2. If wi is not a valid proof for the statement (v, x), send $e\mathsf{P}$ the message $\bot$.
3. Else, send $e\mathsf{P}$ v, and get p.
4. Complete emulation of V^* with message p.

$\underline{\mathsf{S}}$:

1. Outputs the randomness of the emulated V^* (can be derived from the randomness of $e\mathsf{V}^*$,
2. as well as the received prover message p (possibly $\bot$).

The third property asserted in the claim follows by construction of $\mathsf{S}, e\mathsf{V}^*$ and the fact that the prover P checks on its own whether the verifier's proof is accepting. It is left to see that $e\mathsf{V}^*$ is robustly explainable, $(b + O(1))$-non-uniform, and efficiently constructable from V^*. Robust explainability follows directly by the (unconditional) soundness of the NIWI—eV^* either outputs an explainable message or $\perp$. $(b + O(1))$-non-uniformity and efficient construction follow from the fact that V^* is b-non-uniform and eV^* uses it as a black box and described by the four code lines above. □

Claim 1 directly gives rise to a zero knowledge Sim for the protocol (P, V). In what follows, let $e\text{Sim}$ be the simulator of the underlying DPZK protocol against robustly-explainable verifiers.

$\underline{\text{Sim}(V^*, 1^t, x)}$:

1. Construct the explainable verifier eV^*.
2. Output $S(e\text{Sim}(eV^*, 1^t, x))$.

The validity of the simulator Sim follows directly from that of $e\text{Sim}$ and Claim 1.

Soundness. For soundness, we show that any cheating prover P^* breaking the soundness of the above protocol, can be converted into a prover eP^* that breaks the soundness of the underlying protocol. eP^* will have the witness $\bar{w}$ for $x \notin \mathcal{L}$ hardwired.

$\underline{eP^*}$:

1. Obtain message v from eV.
2. Use $\bar{w}$ as the witness to compute the NIWI proof wi.
3. Emulate P^* with (v, wi) and obtain p.
4. Send p to the verifier eV.

First note that since $\mathcal{L} \in \text{NP} \cap \text{coNP}$, the statement $x \notin \mathcal{L}$ has a witness $\bar{w}$ as required. The only difference in the views of P^* and its emulated version in eP^* is in the NIWI proof. From the witness indistinguishability of the NIWI, P^*'s success probability does not change by more than a negligible amount.

3.2.2 DPZK for All of NP

As mentioned to in the introduction, for the case of NP, we require stronger primitives. Specifically, we use the following primitives for our construction:

- A two round deterministic prover zero knowledge (DPZK) protocol (eP, eV) secure against robustly-explainable verifiers. Let the verifier and prover messages be denoted by v and p, respectively.
- A non-interactive commitment scheme Com with perfect binding and computational hiding. Additionally, as mentioned earlier, we require that the plaintext underlying a commitment can be extracted in quasi-polynomial time. Such commitments can be constructed from subexponentiall-secure injective one-way functions (which in turn can be constructed from subexponential IO and one-way functions).
- A keyless collision-resistant hash function H secure against $(b + O(1))$-non-uniform quasi-polynomial time adversaries.

– A non-interactive witness-indistinguishable proof (NIWI) (NIWI.Prov, NIWI.Ver) for the language

$$\mathcal{L}_{\mathsf{NIWI}} = \Big\{(\mathsf{v}, x, c) \ \Big| \ \exists (r, r_{\mathsf{Com}}, x_1, x_2) \ \text{s.t.} \ \mathsf{v} = e\mathsf{V}(x; r) \ \text{OR}$$

$$\big(c = \mathsf{Com}((x_1, x_2); r_{\mathsf{Com}}) \wedge x_1 \neq x_2 \wedge \mathsf{H}(1^\lambda, x_1) = \mathsf{H}(1^\lambda, x_2)\big)\Big\},$$

namely, either the verifier's message is explainable, or the commitment sent by the verifier contains a collision in H. As before, we shall refer to the second half of the 'OR' statement as the *trapdoor statement*.

The protocol is presented in Fig. 3.

Protocol: (P,V) for $\mathcal{L} \in \mathsf{NP}$

Common input: Input $x \in \mathcal{L}$, security parameter 1^λ

P's auxiliary input: witness w such that $(x, w) \in R_{\mathcal{L}}$

1. Verifier V compute the first message as

   (a) $r \leftarrow_\$ \{0, 1\}^{p(n)}$
   (b) $c := \mathsf{Com}(0; r_{\mathsf{Com}})$
   (c) $\mathsf{v} := e\mathsf{V}(x; r)$
   (d) $x_{\mathsf{NIWI}} := (x, \mathsf{v}, c, \mathsf{H})$
   (e) $w_{\mathsf{NIWI}} := (r, \perp, \perp)$
   (f) $\mathsf{wi} \leftarrow \mathsf{NIWI.Prov}(x_{\mathsf{NIWI}}, w_{\mathsf{NIWI}})$.
   send $(\mathsf{v}, \mathsf{wi}, c)$ to the prover P.

2. Prover P computes the second message as

   (a) $\widetilde{x}_{\mathsf{NIWI}} := (x, \mathsf{v}, c, \mathsf{H})$
   (b) if $\mathsf{NIWI.Ver}(\widetilde{x}_{\mathsf{NIWI}}, \mathsf{wi}) \neq 1$, output $\perp$.
   (c) $\mathsf{p} := e\mathsf{P}(x, w, \mathsf{v})$.
   send p to the verifier V.

3. Verifier V performs the check

   (a) if $e\mathsf{V}(x, \mathsf{p}; r) = 1$, accept. Else, reject.

Fig. 3. Deterministic prover zero-knowledge for $\mathcal{L} \in \mathsf{NP}$.

Completeness. Follows directly from the completeness of the underlying protocol and the NIWI.

Zero Knowledge. For zero knowledge, we follow the same strategy as in the previous subsection and show how any b-non-uniform verifier V^* for the above protocol can be converted into a robustly-explainable $(b + O(1))$-non-uniform verifier against the original protocol.

We argue that Claim 1 also holds for this protocol with the exact same S and eV^*. The only difference is in the proof of robust explainability of the verifier eV^*, which is based on complexity leveraging.

Robust Explainability of eV^*. Fix some PPT sampler R for coins for eV^* and assume toward contradiction that with noticeable probability it outputs a message v that is not explainable when initialized with random coins sampled using R. We show that there exists a $(b + O(1))$-non-uniform quasi-polynomial time attacker that finds a collision in H. Recall the eV^* only outputs a non-$\perp$ message provided that the emulated V^* produces a valid NIWI. By the unconditional soundness of the NIWI, it follows that whenever eV^* outputs a non-explainable message, it must be that c is a valid commitment to a collision in H. This collision is then be extracted from the commitment in quasi-polynomial time. Note that the corresponding collision finder can be described by eV^* and R, which have non-uniform description of size $b + O(1)$. $\qquad\square$

Zero knowledge of (P, V) now follows from that of (eP, eV) and the existence of S and eV^*, exactly as in the previous subsection.

Soundness. We show that any cheating prover P^* breaking the soundness of the above protocol, can be converted into a prover eP^* that breaks the soundness of the underlying robustly-explainable protocol. The reduction is similar to that in the previous subsection with some required changed. eP^* will have a collision (x_1, x_2) as (part of the) witness for the *trapdoor statement* hardwired in its code.

eP^*:

1. Obtain message v from eV.
2. Compute $c = \text{Com}(x_1, x_2; r_{\text{Com}})$.
3. Use $(x_1, x_2, r_{\text{Com}})$ as the witness to compute the NIWI proof wi.
4. Emulate P^* with (v, wi) and obtain p.
5. Send p to the verifier eV.

The difference in the views of P^* and its emulated version in eP^* is the commitment to (x_1, x_2) rather than zero, and in the witness used for the NIWI proof. Using the hiding of the commitment (against non-uniform PPT attackers) and the witness indistinguishability of the NIWI, P^*'s success probability does not change by more than a negligible amount.

Remark 2. We emphasize that for soundness, we require that all the underlying primitives to are secure against non-uniform adversaries since our soundness reduction is non-uniform.

4   Predictable Arguments and DPZK

In this section, we show that any deterministic-prover zero-knowledge (DPZK) argument against bounded-non-uniform verifier can be made *predictable*. The notion of predictable arguments was introduced in [12], where it is in particular shown to imply witness encryption. In the next section, we address additional properties of DPZK that follow from this connection.

We start by recalling the definition of predictable arguments (PA) [12]. While they also address predictable argument of knowledge, we restrict attention to predictable arguments that are only sound.

Definition 12 (Predictable Argument). *A ρ-round predictable argument is an argument specified by a tuple of algorithms* (Chal, Resp) *as described below:*

1. *The verifier* PA.V *samples* $(c, b) \leftarrow$ Chal$(1^\lambda, x)$, *where* $c := (c_1, \cdots, c_\rho)$ *and* $b := (b_1, \cdots, b_\rho)$.
2. *For all $i \in [\rho]$ in increasing sequence:*
   (a) PA.V *sends c_i to the* PA.P*;*
   (b) *The prover* PA.P *computes $a_i :=$ Resp$(1^\lambda, x, w, c_1, \cdots, c_i)$ and sends a_i to* PA.V.
   (c) PA.V *checks if $a_i = b_i$, and returns 0 otherwise.*
3. *If all challenges are answered correctly,* PA.V *returns 1.*

The protocol is required to satisfy:

Correctness. *There exists a negligible function* negl$(\cdot)$ *such that for all $x \in \mathcal{L}$ such that $R_L(x, w) = 1$, we have*

$$\Pr[\mathsf{Out}_{\mathsf{PA.V}}\langle \mathsf{PA.P}(x, w), \mathsf{PA.V}(x)\rangle = 1] \geq 1 - \mathsf{negl}(\lambda).$$

Soundness. *For any non-uniform* PPT *prover* P*, there exists a negligible function* negl$(\cdot)$ *such that for all $x \notin \mathcal{L}$,*

$$\Pr[\langle \mathsf{PA.P}^*, \mathsf{PA.V}(x)\rangle = 1] \leq \mathsf{negl}(\lambda).$$

A **deterministic-prover zero-knowledge predictable argument (PA-DPZK)** is a deterministic-prover zero-knowledge argument that is also a predictable argument.

We prove the following:

Theorem 4. *Let* (P, V) *be a deterministic-prover zero-knowledge argument for $\mathcal{L}$ against bounded-non-uniform verifiers. There exists a verifier* V' *such that* (P, V') *is a predictable argument.*

Note that since we do not change the honest prover P it follows that (P, V') is also deterministic-prover zero knowledge against the same class of verifiers.

Relying on the following result by Faonio, Nielsen, and Venturi,

Theorem 5 ([12]). *If there exists a Predictable Argument (PA) for a language $\mathcal{L}$, then there exists a witness encryption scheme for $\mathcal{L}$.*

our theorem holds for all $\lambda^{\Omega(1)}$-non-uniform verifiers, and we deduce

Corollary 3. *If there exists a deterministic-prover zero-knowledge argument for $\mathcal{L}$ against $\lambda^{\Omega(1)}$-non-uniform verifiers, then there exists a witness encryption scheme for $\mathcal{L}$.*

We now proceed with the proof.

Proof of Theorem 4. Let (P, V) be a ρ-round DPZK argument for $\mathcal{L}$ against b-non-uniform verifiers, for $b(\lambda) \geq 2\lambda + \omega(1)$. Let $\mathsf{PRG} : \{0,1\}^\lambda \to \{0,1\}^\ell$ be a pseudorandom generator, where $\ell(\lambda)$ is the amount of coins used by V. For a given seed $s \in \{0,1\}^\lambda$, we define the deterministic verifier $\mathsf{V}_s(x)$ that derives coins $r = \mathsf{PRG}(s)$ for V then emulates $\mathsf{V}(x;r)$.

The transformed verifier V' is presented in Fig. 4.

The New Verifier V'

Input: x, security parameter 1^λ

1. Sample $s \leftarrow_{\!\!s} \{0,1\}^\lambda$ and construct V_s.
2. Sample $\{\widetilde{\mathsf{p}}_i\}_{i=1}^\rho \leftarrow \mathsf{Sim}(\mathsf{V}_s, 1^t, x)$, where t is the running time of V_s.
3. Emulate an execution of $\mathsf{V}_s(x)$ with prover messages $\{\widetilde{\mathsf{p}}_i\}_{i=1}^\rho$; let $\{\widetilde{\mathsf{v}}_i\}_{i=1}^\rho$ be the resulting verifier messages.
4. If the verifier V_s rejects in the above execution, reject.
5. Proceed interacting with the prover P: at each round $i \in [\rho]$:
   - send $\mathsf{v}_i (= \widetilde{\mathsf{v}}_i)$ to P,
   - if the prover answers with $\mathsf{p}_i = \widetilde{\mathsf{p}}_i$, proceed to the next round,
   - else, reject.
6. Accept.

Fig. 4. The Verifier in the Predictable Protocol

First, note that the protocol satisfies the structural requirement of a predictable argument. We now move to prove completeness and soundness with respect to the new verifier V'.

Completeness. We show that $(\mathsf{P}, \mathsf{V}')$ is complete based on (a) the completeness of $(\mathsf{P}, \mathsf{V}')$; (b) zero knowledge of $(\mathsf{P}, \mathsf{V}')$; and (c) pseudorandomness of PRG.

Fix any statement $x \in \mathcal{L}$ and corresponding prover witness w. We need to show that in an interaction $\langle \mathsf{P}(x, w), \mathsf{V}'(x) \rangle$, V' rejects with negligible probability. First, by the completeness of (P, V) and the pseudorandomness of PRG, an interaction $\langle \mathsf{P}(x, w), \mathsf{V}_s(x) \rangle$ is accepting except with negligible probability over the choice of s. Noting that $V_s(x)$ is b-non-uniform, we can invoke zero knowledge, to deduce that the simulated prover messages $\{\widetilde{p}_i\}_{i=1}^{\rho}$ make V_s accept with overwhelming probability over the choice of s.

We next argue that the deterministic prover $P(x, w)$ produces messages $\{p_i = \widetilde{p}_i\}_{i=1}^{\rho}$ with overwhelming probability (over the coins of Sim that sampled them). This again follows from zero knowledge. Indeed, we can consider a zero-knowledge distinguisher that has (x, w, s) hardwired, and given messages p_i emulates a conversation of the deterministic $P(x, w)$ with $V_s(x)$, and outputs "real" if the corresponding prover messages coincide with p_i, or "simulated" otherwise. If the simulated messages $\widetilde{p}_i$ are inconsistent with the real prover messages p_i, the distinguisher will tell them apart.

Soundness. We show that (P, V') is sound based on (a) the pseudorandomness of PRG; and (b) the soundness of (P, V).

First, note that by pseudorandomness the protocol (P, V_s) where s is chosen at random is also sound, since otherwise a cheating prover can be directly used to distinguish real verifier coins form pseudorandom ones. Next, note that any cheating prover against V' directly implies a cheating prover against V_s (for a random s) by construction. Indeed, V' emulates V_s and accepts only when the prover is consistent with a simulated strategy $\widetilde{p}_i$ that convinces V_s.[2] Soundness follows.

$\square$

5   Round Reduction and Laconicity

Faonio, Nielsen, and Venturi [12] proved that the round complexity of any predictable argument can be collapsed to one (two messages overall) and that any predictable argument can be made laconic—namely, the prover message is a single bit (or more generally ℓ bits to achieve soundness $\approx 2^{-\ell}$). In this section, we review their transformations and show that they preserve zero knowledge against bounded-non-uniform verifiers. As a corollary of this and the previous section, we deduce that any deterministic-prover zero knowledge argument against bounded-non-uniform verifiers can be collapsed to one round and made laconic.

5.1   Round Reduction

We start by recalling the round-collapsing transformation from [12]. In what follows, let (P', V') be a ρ-round predictable argument, the following transformation provides a one round predictable argument (P, V) with a large soundness error (to be dealt with later on). Roughly, the verifier randomly chooses a "cut-off"

---

[2] Here we implicitly rely on the fact that the simulator produces an accepting transcript for the deterministic verifier V_s. The deterministic nature of the verifier ensures that the simulator cannot manipulate the verifier's randomness and therefore must produce an accepting transcript is consistent with $V(\cdot; PRG(s))$.

point i^* for the underlying protocol, and sends all the verifier messages up to, and including, the i^*-th round verifier message to the prover. Being a predictable argument, the verifier is able to do so without requiring the corresponding intermediate prover messages. The prover then iteratively computes the response for each round of the underlying protocol and send over all the prover messages with the verifier accepting if and only if each prover messages corresponds to the predicted prover message.

In [12], it is proven that this protocol has soundness error at most $1 - \rho^{-1} +$ $\mathsf{negl}(\lambda)$. The protocol is then repeated $\omega(\rho \log \lambda)$ times to achieve negligible soundness, using a parallel repetition theorem for one round arguments [4].

Protocol: One Round (P, V)

Common input: Input $x \in \mathcal{L}$, security parameter 1^λ

P's auxiliary input: witness w such that $(x, w) \in R_{\mathcal{L}}$

1. Verifier V
   (a) Samples $i^* \leftarrow_\$ [\rho]$,
   (b) Samples $(\mathsf{v}_i, \mathsf{b}_i)_{i \in [\rho]} \leftarrow_\$ \mathsf{V}(x)$.
   (c) Sends $\mathsf{v}_1, \cdots, \mathsf{v}_{i^*}$ to the prover P.
2. Prover P
   (a) For each $i \in [i^*]$, compute $\mathsf{p}_i := \mathsf{P}(x, w, \{\mathsf{v}_j\}_{j \in [i]})$.
   (b) Send $\mathsf{p}_1, \cdots, \mathsf{p}_{i^*}$ to the verifier V.
3. Verifier V accepts if and only if for all $j \in [i^*]$, $\mathsf{p}_j = \mathsf{b}_j$.

Fig. 5. Round collapsing transformation.

Proposition 3. *The round collapsing transformation preserves zero knowledge against b-non-uniform verifiers.*

Proof. We prove the proposition in two steps. First, we show that the transformation in Fig. 5 preserves zero-knowledge. Then we show that two-message zero-knowledge against bounded-non-uniform adversaries is closed under parallel repetition.

To prove the first part, let V^* be a b-non-uniform verifier. We show the following claim.

Claim 2. There exist an efficient simulator S and a verifier V'^* against $\langle P', V' \rangle$ such that

1. V'^* is $(b + O(1))$-non-uniform and efficiently constructable from V^*.
2. For every $x \in \mathcal{L}$,

$$\mathsf{View}_{V^*} \langle P(x, w), V^* \rangle \equiv \mathsf{S}(\mathsf{View}_{V'^*} \langle P'(x, w), V'^* \rangle).$$

This claim gives rise to a simulator Sim for (P, V), which simply invokes Sim' of (P, V) on V'^* and then invokes S.

Proof of Claim. We construct S, V'^*.

$\underline{V'^*}$:

1. Emulates V^* and obtains $(v_1, \ldots, v_{i^*})$.
2. At each round $i \in [i^*]$, forward v_i to P'.
3. Abort after round i^*.

$\underline{\mathsf{S}}$:

1. Outputs the randomness of the emulated V^* (can be derived from the randomness of V'^*),
2. as well as the received prover messages $p_1, \ldots, p_{i^*}$.

The second property asserted in the claim follows by construction of S, V'^* and the construction of P from P' in Fig. 5. It is left to see that V'^* is $(b + O(1))$-non-uniform and efficiently constructable from V^*. $(b + O(1))$-non-uniformity and efficient construction follow from the fact that V^* is b-non-uniform and V'^* uses it as a black box and described by the three code lines above. □

We now prove that closure under parallel repetition.

Claim 3. For any two-message zero knowledge system (P, V) against b-non-uniform verifiers and a any polynomial ℓ, the ℓ-fold parallel repetition $(P_{\otimes \ell}, V_{\otimes \ell})$ is zero knowledge against $(b - O(\log \lambda))$-non-uniform verifiers.

Proof. In what follows, let Sim be the simulator for the original argument (P, V), and let $V^*_{\otimes \ell}$ be any $(b - \lambda - O(\log \lambda))$-non-uniform verifier of polynomial running time $t(\lambda)$. We now describe the simulator $\mathsf{Sim}_{\otimes \ell}$ for $(P_{\otimes \ell}, V_{\otimes \ell})$. The simulator will use a pseudorandom generator $\mathsf{PRG} : \{0,1\}^\lambda \rightarrow \{0,1\}^k$, where k is the amount of coins used by $V^*_{\otimes \ell}$.

$\underline{\mathsf{Sim}_{\otimes\ell}(\mathsf{V}^*_{\otimes\ell}, 1^t, x)}$:

1. Sample a $s \leftarrow_\$ \{0,1\}^\lambda$.
2. For each $i \in [\ell]$:
   (a) Construct the deterministic verifier $\mathsf{V}^*_{s,i}$ that first derives coins $\mathsf{PRG}(s)$, uses them to emulate $\mathsf{V}^*_{\otimes\ell}$, obtains $\mathsf{v}_1, \ldots, \mathsf{v}_\ell$, and outputs v_i. Let $t' = t + \mathsf{poly}(\lambda)$ be a bound on its running time.
   (b) Sample $\tilde{\mathsf{p}}_i \leftarrow_\$ \mathsf{Sim}(\mathsf{V}^*_{s,i}, 1^{t'}, x)$.
3. Output $\tilde{\mathsf{p}}_1, \ldots, \tilde{\mathsf{p}}_\ell, \mathsf{PRG}(s)$.

We now prove the validity of $\mathsf{Sim}_{\otimes\ell}$. First, consider an execution between the prover $\mathsf{P}(x,w)$ and verifier $\mathsf{V}^*_s = (\mathsf{V}^*_{s,1}, \ldots, \mathsf{V}^*_{s,\ell})$, and let $\mathsf{p}_1, \ldots, \mathsf{p}_\ell$ denote the prover messages in such an execution. Then by pseudorandomness of PRG,

$$\mathsf{View}_{\mathsf{V}^*_{\otimes\ell}}\langle \mathsf{P}(x,w), \mathsf{V}^*_{\otimes\ell}\rangle \approx_c \mathsf{p}_1, \ldots, \mathsf{p}_\ell, \mathsf{PRG}(s).$$

Noting that $\mathsf{V}^*_{s,i}$ is a program of length at most b and running time at most $t'(\lambda)$, we can invoke the simulation guarantee (P, V). Specifically, we can deduce that

$$\mathsf{p}_1, \ldots, \mathsf{p}_\ell, \mathsf{PRG}(s) \approx_c \tilde{\mathsf{p}}_1, \ldots, \tilde{\mathsf{p}}_\ell, \mathsf{PRG}(s).$$

This can be shown by a standard hybrid argument and follows from the fact that $\mathsf{p}_i \approx_c \tilde{\mathsf{p}}_i = \mathsf{Sim}(\mathsf{V}^*_{s,i}, 1^{t'}, x)$ and that the distinguisher can have (x, w, s) hardwired in order to simulate any other p_j or $\tilde{\mathsf{p}}_i$. Overall

$$\mathsf{View}_{\mathsf{V}^*_{\otimes\ell}}\langle \mathsf{P}(x,w), \mathsf{V}^*_{\otimes\ell}\rangle \approx_c \mathsf{Sim}_{\otimes\ell}(\mathsf{V}^*_{\otimes\ell}, 1^t, x).$$

$\square$

This complete the proof of Proposition 3. $\square$

5.2   Laconic Prover Messages

As in the previous section, we start by recalling the laconic prover transformation from [12]. In what follows, let $(\mathsf{P}', \mathsf{V}')$ be a one round predictable argument, the following transformation provides a laconic prover predictable argument (P, V) with a soundness error negligibly close to $1/2$, where the prover sends only a single bit (Fig. 6). Roughly, the verifier samples a sufficiently large random string γ and sends it to the prover along with the verifier message. The prover responds with a single bit corresponding to the inner product of γ and its own response to the verifier message, with the verifier accepting if only if the bit matches its own computed inner product of γ with the predicted prover message.

Protocol: Laconic Prover (P, V)

Common input: Input $x \in \mathcal{L}$, security parameter 1^λ

P's auxiliary input: witness w such that $(x, w) \in R_{\mathcal{L}}$

1. Verifier V

   (a) Sample $(\mathsf{v}, \mathsf{b}) \leftarrow_\$ \mathsf{V}'(x)$.
   (b) Sample $\gamma \leftarrow_\$ \{0, 1\}^{|\mathsf{b}|}$.
   (c) Send v, γ to the prover P.

2. Prover P

   (a) Compute $\mathsf{p} := \mathsf{P}'(x, w, \mathsf{v})$.
   (b) Send $\mathsf{q} := \langle \mathsf{p}, \gamma \rangle$ to the verifier V.

3. Verifier V accepts if and only if $\mathsf{q} = \langle \mathsf{b}, \gamma \rangle$.

Fig. 6. Laconic prover transformation.

In [12], it is proven that this protocol has soundness error at most $\frac{1}{2} + \mathsf{negl}(\lambda)$. As we have seen in the previous subsection (Claim 3), the soundness can be amplified in a manner that preserves zero knowledge. Specifically, ℓ repetitions yields a protocol with soundness error at most $2^{-\ell} + \mathsf{negl}(\lambda)$. Therefore, we focus on proving that a single instance of the above transformation preserves zero knowledge.

Proposition 4. *The round collapsing transformation preserves zero knowledge against b-non-uniform verifiers.*

Proof. Let V^* be a b-non-uniform verifier. We show the following claim.

Claim 4. *There exist an efficient simulator S and a verifier V'^* against $\langle \mathsf{P}', \mathsf{V}' \rangle$ such that*

1. V'^* *is* $(b + O(1))$-*non-uniform and efficiently constructable from* V^*.
2. *For every* $x \in \mathcal{L}$,

$$\mathsf{View}_{\mathsf{V}^*} \langle \mathsf{P}(x, w), \mathsf{V}^* \rangle \equiv \mathsf{S}(\mathsf{View}_{\mathsf{V}'^*} \langle \mathsf{P}'(x, w), \mathsf{V}'^* \rangle).$$

This claim gives rise to a simulator Sim for (P, V), which simply invokes Sim' of $(\mathsf{P}', \mathsf{V}')$ on V'^* and then invokes S.

Proof of Claim. We construct $\mathsf{S}, \mathsf{V}'^*$.

$\underline{\mathsf{V}'^*:}$

1. Emulate V^* and obtains (v, γ).
2. Forward v to P'.

$\underline{\mathsf{S}:}$

1. Outputs the randomness of the emulated V^* (can be derived from the randomness of V'^*),
2. as well as $\langle \mathsf{p}, \gamma \rangle$, where p is the received prover message and γ is derived from the randomness of V^*.

The proof is similar to that of Claim 2 in the previous subsection. The second property asserted in the claim follows by construction of $\mathsf{S}, \mathsf{V}'^*$ and the construction of P from P'. It is left to see that V'^* is $(b+O(1))$-non-uniform and efficiently constructable from V^*. $(b + O(1))$-non-uniformity and efficient construction follow from the fact that V^* is b-non-uniform and V'^* uses it as a black box and described by the two code lines above. □

This completes the proof of Proposition 4. □

Acknowledgments. Nir Bitansky is a member of the Check Point Institute of Information Security. Supported by the Alon Young Faculty Fellowship, by Len Blavatnik and the Blavatnik Family foundation, and an ISF grant 18/484.

This work was done in part when Arka Rai Choudhuri was visiting Tel Aviv University and supported by the Check Point Institute of Information Security. He is also supported in part by DARPA/ARL Safeware Grant W911NF-15-C-0213, NSF Grants CNS-1908181, CNS-1414023, CNS-1814919, NSF CAREER 1942789, Samsung Global Research Outreach award, Johns Hopkins University Catalyst award and the Office of Naval Research Grant N00014-19-1-2294.

A   Predictable Arguments from Honest-Verifier ZK

In Sect. 4, we showed how to transform any deterministic-prover zero-knowledge (DPZK) protocol into one that is also a predictable argument (PA). In this section, we show that if we start with a weaker notion of deterministic-prover honest verifier zero-knowledge (DP-HVZK)[3] and the existence of an appropriate hard language, we can transform the DP-HVZK protocol into a predictable argument. One caveat of this transformation is that the languages of the DP-HVZK and PA in our transformation will be related, but not identical. As long as the DP-HVZK we start from is for an expressive enough class of languages (e.g. for $\mathsf{NP} \cap \mathsf{coNP}$), we will get a PA for the same class.

---

[3] Only zero-knowledge against honestly behaving verifiers.

Definition 13. (Hard-on-Average Language). *A language $\mathcal{L}$ is hard-on-average if there exist two PPT samplers $Y_{\mathcal{L}}, N_{\mathcal{L}}$ where the support of the first is $\mathcal{L}$ and of the second is $\{0,1\}^* \setminus \mathcal{L}$ such that*

$$\left\{ x : x \leftarrow Y_{\mathcal{L}}(1^\lambda) \right\}_{\lambda \in \mathbb{N}} \approx_c \left\{ x : x \leftarrow N_{\mathcal{L}}(1^\lambda) \right\}_{\lambda \in \mathbb{N}}.$$

We establish the following theorem.

Theorem 6. *If there exists a deterministic-prover honest-verifier zero-knowledge argument (DP-HVZK) for $\mathcal{L} \vee \mathcal{L}_{\mathsf{hard}}$, where $\mathcal{L}_{\mathsf{hard}}$ is a hard-on-average language, then there exists a predictable argument (PA) for $\mathcal{L}$.*

By the fact that both NP and NP $\cap$ coNP are closed under OR, we deduce the following corollaries.

Corollary 4. *Assuming DP-HVZK for all of NP and hard-on-average languages in NP, there is a witness encryption scheme for all of NP.*

Corollary 5. *Assuming DP-HVZK for all of NP $\cap$ coNP and hard-on-average languages in NP $\cap$ coNP, there is a witness encryption scheme for all of NP $\cap$ coNP.*

We note that hard-on-average languages in NP are known to follow from one-way functions, and hard-on-average languages in NP $\cap$ coNP are known to follow from one-way permutations.

We now proceed with the proof.

Proof of Theorem 6. To build a predictable argument for $\mathcal{L}$, we use the following primitives:

- A hard language $\mathcal{L}_{\mathsf{hard}}$ given by samplers $(Y_{\mathcal{L}_{\mathsf{hard}}}, N_{\mathcal{L}_{\mathsf{hard}}})$.
- A ρ-round DP-HVZK protocol $\langle \mathsf{P}', \mathsf{V}' \rangle$ for the language $\mathcal{L}_{OR}$ defined below, where the verifier V' sends messages v_i in round i, and the prover P' sends message p_i in round i. We denote by Sim' the corresponding honest-verifier simulator. The language $\mathcal{L}_{OR}$ is defined below,

$$\mathcal{L}_{OR} = \left\{ (x, \tilde{x}) \mid \exists (w, \tilde{w}) \text{ s.t. } R_{\mathcal{L}}(x, w) = 1 \text{ OR } R_{\mathcal{L}_{\mathsf{hard}}}(\tilde{x}, \tilde{w}) = 1 \right\},$$

namely, either the statement x is in $\mathcal{L}$, or $\tilde{x}$ is in $\mathcal{L}_{\mathsf{hard}}$.

The transformation is presented in Fig. 7.
Before we proceed with the completeness and soundness, we note that the protocol structure follows that of a predictable argument.

Completeness. We show that (P, V) is complete based on the honest verifier zero-knowledge property of $(\mathsf{P}', \mathsf{V}')$.

Fix any $x \in \mathcal{L}$ and the corresponding witness w, a yes-instance $\tilde{x} \in \mathcal{L}_{\mathsf{hard}}$, and let $x' = (x, \tilde{x})$. Let $\tilde{\mathsf{p}}_1, \ldots, \tilde{\mathsf{p}}_\rho$ denote the messages and $\tilde{r}$ denote the verifier randomness simulated by $\mathsf{Sim}'(x')$. We argue that the deterministic prover

$\mathsf{P}(x, w)$ produces messages $\{\mathsf{p}_i = \widetilde{\mathsf{p}}_i\}_{i=1}^{\rho}$ with overwhelming probability (over the coins of Sim'). This follows from zero knowledge. Consider a distinguisher that has (x, w) hardwired, and given messages p_i and verifier randomness $\widetilde{r}$ emulates a conversation of the deterministic $\mathsf{P}'(x, w)$ with $\mathsf{V}'(x; \widetilde{r})$, and outputs "real" if the corresponding prover messages coincide with p_i, or "simulated" otherwise. If the simulated messages $\widetilde{\mathsf{p}}_i$ are inconsistent with the real prover messages p_i, the distinguisher will tell them apart.

Soundness. We show that (P, V) is sound based on the completeness, soundness and zero knowledge of $(\mathsf{P}', \mathsf{V}')$, as well as the hardness of $\mathcal{L}_{\mathsf{hard}}$.

Fix any $x \notin \mathcal{L}$ and cheating prover P^*. We prove that P^* fails to convince $\mathsf{V}(x)$ of accepting, except with negligible probability. We consider several hybrid experiments transitioning from a real interaction to an ideal interaction. We will show that when moving from one hybrid to the next the prover's chance of convincing the verifier does not decrease by more than a negligible amount. Then we will show that the chance that $\mathsf{V}(x)$ is convinced the final (ideal interaction) hybrid is negligible.

Protocol: PA (P, V)

Common input: Input $x \in \mathcal{L}$, security parameter 1^{λ}

P's auxiliary input: witness w such that $(x, w) \in R_{\mathcal{L}}$

Verifier V computes

1. $\widetilde{x} \leftarrow Y_{\mathcal{L}_{\mathsf{hard}}}(1^{\lambda})$
2. $x' := (x, \widetilde{x})$.
3. $\left(\{(\mathsf{v}_i, \widetilde{\mathsf{p}}_i)\}_{i=1}^{\rho}, \widetilde{r}\right) \leftarrow \mathsf{Sim}'(x')$.

sends $\widetilde{x}$ to the prover P in the first message.

In each round $i \in [\rho]$,

1. Verifier V sends v_i to the prover P.
2. Prover P computes
   (a) $x' := (x, \widetilde{x})$
   (b) $w' := (w, \bot)$
   (c) $\mathsf{p}_i := \mathsf{P}'(x', w', \{\mathsf{v}_j\}_{j=1}^i)$
   sends p_i to the verifier V.
3. If for any $i \in [\rho]$, $\mathsf{p}_i \neq \widetilde{\mathsf{p}}_i$, V rejects.

If verifier V has not rejected in all rounds, accept.

Fig. 7. Transforming DP-HVZK to PA

Hyb_0: This is a real interaction between P^* and $\mathsf{V}(x)$.

Hyb_1: In this hybrid, once V samples a simulated transcript $\widetilde{\mathsf{p}}_1, \ldots, \widetilde{\mathsf{p}}_\rho, \widetilde{r}$ $\leftarrow_\$ \mathsf{Sim}(x')$, it emulates an execution of $\mathsf{V}'(x'; \widetilde{r})$ with the simulated prover messages and checks whether it is accepting. If it is not, V rejects immediately.

We argue that the probability that P^* convinces $\mathsf{V}(x)$ to accept in this hybrid is negligibly close to that in Hyb_0. For this purpose, we argue that with overwhelming probability $\mathsf{Sim}(x')$ samples an accepting transcript. This is shown based on completeness and zero knowledge of $(\mathsf{P}', \mathsf{V}')$. Specifically, recall that $\mathsf{V}(x)$ samples $\widetilde{x} \in \mathcal{L}_{\mathsf{hard}}$ and thus $x' = (x, \widetilde{x}) \in \mathcal{L}_{OR}$. By the completeness of $(\mathsf{P}', \mathsf{V}')$, in an interaction between $\mathsf{V}'(x')$ and $\mathsf{P}'(x', w')$ where $w' = (\bot, \widetilde{w})$ and $\widetilde{w}$ is a witness for $\widetilde{x}$, the prover convince V' with overwhelming probability. It then follows from zero knowledge of $(\mathsf{P}', \mathsf{V}')$ that $\mathsf{Sim}(x')$ also generates an accepting transcript with overwhelming probability; otherwise, we can non-uniformly fix $\widetilde{x}, \widetilde{w}$ and construct a distinguisher that violates zero knowledge.

Hyb_2: In this hybrid, the verifier V does not insist that the prover P^* is consistent with the simulated messages $\widetilde{\mathsf{p}}_1, \ldots, \widetilde{\mathsf{p}}_\rho$. Instead, it emulates $\mathsf{V}'(x'; \widetilde{r})$, and accepts if the messages sent by P^* convince V'.

The probability that V accepts in this hybrid is at least as large as the probability it accepts in Hyb_1. Indeed, any execution that would have been accepted in the previous hybrid Hyb_1 is in particular an execution in which $\mathsf{V}'(x'; \widetilde{r})$ is convinced and thus is also accepted in the current Hyb_2.

Hyb_3: In this hybrid, the verifier V does not check that the simulated $\widetilde{\mathsf{p}}_1, \ldots, \widetilde{\mathsf{p}}_\rho, \widetilde{r}$ make $\mathsf{V}'(x'; \widetilde{r})$ accept. (In particular, the simulated prover messages $\widetilde{\mathsf{p}}_1, \ldots, \widetilde{\mathsf{p}}_\rho$ are ignored altogether, and only the simulated coins $\widetilde{r}$ are used).

The probability that $\mathsf{V}(x)$ accepts in this hybrid is at least as large as the probability it accepts in the previous hybrid, as we have only removed a verifier test.

Hyb_4: In this hybrid, instead of sampling simulated coins $\widetilde{r}$ using $\mathsf{Sim}'(x')$, V samples truly random coins r.

The probability that $\mathsf{V}(x)$ accepts in this hybrids is negligibly close to that in the previous hybrid. This follows from zero knowledge of $(\mathsf{P}', \mathsf{V}')$. Indeed, since $x' \in \mathcal{L}_{OR}$, the simulated honest verifier coins $\widetilde{r}$ are pseudorandom.

Hyb_5: In this hybrid, $\mathsf{V}(x)$ samples a no-instance $\widetilde{x} \leftarrow N_{\mathcal{L}_{\mathsf{hard}}}$ instead of a yes-instance. By the indistinguishability of $Y_{\mathcal{L}_{\mathsf{hard}}}$ and $N_{\mathcal{L}_{\mathsf{hard}}}$, the probability that P^* convinces $\mathsf{V}(x)$ to accept in this hybrid is negligibly close to that in Hyb_4.

We now argue that the probability that P^* convinces $\mathsf{V}(x)$ to accept in Hyb_5 is negligible. Note that in Hyb_5 it holds that both $x \notin \mathcal{L}$ and $\widetilde{x} \notin \mathcal{L}_{\mathsf{hard}}$ and thus $x' = (x, \widetilde{x}) \notin \mathcal{L}_{OR}$. For P^* to convince $\mathsf{V}(x)$ of accepting in Hyb_5, it must convince $\mathsf{V}'(x'; r)$ of accepting, when V' uses truly random coins. By the soundness of $(\mathsf{P}', \mathsf{V}')$ this occurs with negligible probability. Soundness follows.   □

References

1. Barak, B.: How to go beyond the black-box simulation barrier. In: 42nd FOCS, pp. 106–115. IEEE Computer Society Press (October 2001)
2. Barak, B., Ong, S.J., Vadhan, S.: Derandomization in cryptography. In: Boneh, D. (ed.) CRYPTO 2003. LNCS, vol. 2729, pp. 299–315. Springer, Heidelberg (2003). https://doi.org/10.1007/978-3-540-45146-4_18
3. Barak, B., Pass, R.: On the possibility of one-message weak zero-knowledge. In: Naor, M. (ed.) TCC 2004. LNCS, vol. 2951, pp. 121–132. Springer, Heidelberg (2004). https://doi.org/10.1007/978-3-540-24638-1_7
4. Bellare, M., Impagliazzo, R., Naor, M.: Does parallel repetition lower the error in computationally sound protocols? In: 38th FOCS, pp. 374–383. IEEE Computer Society Press (October 1997)
5. Bitansky, N., et al.: Indistinguishability obfuscation for RAM programs and succinct randomized encodings. SIAM J. Comput. **47**(3), 1123–1210 (2018)
6. Bitansky, N., Canetti, R., Paneth, O., Rosen, A.: On the existence of extractable one-way functions. In: Shmoys, D.B. (ed.) 46th ACM STOC, pp. 505–514. ACM Press (May/June 2014)
7. Bitansky, N., Khurana, D., Paneth, O.: Weak zero-knowledge beyond the black-box barrier. In: Charikar, M., Cohen, E. (eds.) 51st ACM STOC, pp. 1091–1102. ACM Press (June 2019)
8. Bitansky, N., Paneth, O.: ZAPs and non-interactive witness indistinguishability from indistinguishability obfuscation. In: Dodis, Y., Nielsen, J.B. (eds.) TCC 2015. LNCS, vol. 9015, pp. 401–427. Springer, Heidelberg (2015). https://doi.org/10.1007/978-3-662-46497-7_16
9. Bitansky, N., Vaikuntanathan, V.: A note on perfect correctness by derandomization. In: Coron, J.-S., Nielsen, J.B. (eds.) EUROCRYPT 2017. LNCS, vol. 10211, pp. 592–606. Springer, Cham (2017). https://doi.org/10.1007/978-3-319-56614-6_20
10. Cramer, R., Shoup, V.: Universal hash proofs and a paradigm for adaptive chosen ciphertext secure public-key encryption. In: Knudsen, L.R. (ed.) EUROCRYPT 2002. LNCS, vol. 2332, pp. 45–64. Springer, Heidelberg (2002). https://doi.org/10.1007/3-540-46035-7_4
11. Dahari, H., Lindell, Y.: Deterministic-prover zero-knowledge proofs. Cryptology ePrint Archive, Report 2020/141 (2020). https://eprint.iacr.org/2020/141
12. Faonio, A., Nielsen, J.B., Venturi, D.: Predictable arguments of knowledge. In: Fehr, S. (ed.) PKC 2017. LNCS, vol. 10174, pp. 121–150. Springer, Heidelberg (2017). https://doi.org/10.1007/978-3-662-54365-8_6
13. Garg, S., Gentry, C., Sahai, A., Waters, B.: Witness encryption and its applications. In: Boneh, D., Roughgarden, T., Feigenbaum, J. (eds.) 45th ACM STOC, pp. 467–476. ACM Press (June 2013)
14. Garg, S., Srinivasan, A.: A simple construction of iO for turing machines. In: Beimel, A., Dziembowski, S. (eds.) TCC 2018. LNCS, vol. 11240, pp. 425–454. Springer, Cham (2018). https://doi.org/10.1007/978-3-030-03810-6_16
15. Goldreich, O., Krawczyk, H.: On the composition of zero-knowledge proof systems. SIAM J. Comput. **25**(1), 169–192 (1996)
16. Goldreich, O., Oren, Y.: Definitions and properties of zero-knowledge proof systems. J. Cryptol. **7**(1), 1–32 (1994)

17. Goldreich, O., Vadhan, S., Wigderson, A.: On interactive proofs with a laconic prover. In: Orejas, F., Spirakis, P.G., van Leeuwen, J. (eds.) ICALP 2001. LNCS, vol. 2076, pp. 334–345. Springer, Heidelberg (2001). https://doi.org/10.1007/3-540-48224-5_28

18. Goldwasser, S., Micali, S., Rackoff, C.: The knowledge complexity of interactive proof systems. SIAM J. Comput. **18**(1), 186–208 (1989)

19. Groth, J., Ostrovsky, R., Sahai, A.: Non-interactive zaps and new techniques for NIZK. In: Dwork, C. (ed.) CRYPTO 2006. LNCS, vol. 4117, pp. 97–111. Springer, Heidelberg (2006). https://doi.org/10.1007/11818175_6

20. Koppula, V., Lewko, A.B., Waters, B.: Indistinguishability obfuscation for turing machines with unbounded memory. In: Servedio, R.A., Rubinfeld, R. (eds.) 47th ACM STOC, pp. 419–428. ACM Press (June 2015)

21. Nisan, N., Wigderson, A.: Hardness vs randomness. J. Comput. Syst. Sci. **49**(2), 149–167 (1994)

NIZK from SNARG

Fuyuki Kitagawa[1], Takahiro Matsuda[2], and Takashi Yamakawa[1(✉)]

[1] NTT Secure Platform Laboratories, Tokyo, Japan
{fuyuki.kitagawa.yh,takashi.yamakawa.ga}@hco.ntt.co.jp
[2] National Institute of Advanced Industrial Science and Technology (AIST),
Tokyo, Japan
t-matsuda@aist.go.jp

Abstract. We give a construction of a non-interactive zero-knowledge (NIZK) argument for all NP languages based on a succinct non-interactive argument (SNARG) for all NP languages and a one-way function. The succinctness requirement for the SNARG is rather mild: We only require that the proof size be $|\pi| = \mathsf{poly}(\lambda)(|x| + |w|)^c$ for some constant $c < 1/2$, where $|x|$ is the statement length, $|w|$ is the witness length, and λ is the security parameter. Especially, we do not require anything about the efficiency of the verification.

Based on this result, we also give a generic conversion from a SNARG to a zero-knowledge SNARG assuming the existence of CPA secure public-key encryption. For this conversion, we require a SNARG to have efficient verification, i.e., the computational complexity of the verification algorithm is $\mathsf{poly}(\lambda)(|x| + |w|)^{o(1)}$. Before this work, such a conversion was only known if we additionally assume the existence of a NIZK.

Along the way of obtaining our result, we give a generic compiler to upgrade a NIZK for all NP languages with non-adaptive zero-knowledge to one with adaptive zero-knowledge. Though this can be shown by carefully combining known results, to the best of our knowledge, no explicit proof of this generic conversion has been presented.

1 Introduction

A *non-interactive zero-knowledge (NIZK)* argument [7] is a non-interactive argument system that enables a prover to convince a verifier of the truth of an NP statement without revealing any information about its witness. Since it is known that a NIZK in the plain model where no setup is needed exists only for trivial languages [32], NIZKs are typically constructed in the common reference string (CRS) model where a trusted party generates a CRS and provides it to both the prover and verifier. In the following, we refer to NIZKs in the CRS model simply as NIZKs. Thus far, NIZKs for all NP languages have been constructed based on various standard assumptions including factoring [26], pairings [14,36], and lattices [45]. Besides the theoretical importance on its own, NIZKs have found numerous applications in cryptography including chosen-ciphertext security [23,43], leakage- and tamper-resilient cryptography [21,22,40], advanced types of digital signatures [2,16,47], multi-party computation [31], to name a few.

© International Association for Cryptologic Research 2020
R. Pass and K. Pietrzak (Eds.): TCC 2020, LNCS 12550, pp. 567–595, 2020.
https://doi.org/10.1007/978-3-030-64375-1_20

A *succinct non-interactive argument (SNARG)* is another notion of a non-interactive argument, which satisfies *succinctness*, i.e., the proof size is (asymptotically) smaller than the statement size and the witness size. Micali [42] gave a construction of SNARGs for all NP languages in the random oracle model. On the other hand, Gentry and Wichs [29] ruled out a black-box reduction proving the adaptive soundness of a SNARG from any falsifiable assumption in the standard model. Since then, there have been proposed constructions of SNARGs for all NP languages based on non-falsifiable assumptions on pairings [28,34,35], lattices [9,10][1], or hash functions [4]. On the application side, SNARGs have natural applications in the context of verifiable computation. They also have been gaining a renewed attention in the context of blockchains (e.g., [3,8]).[2]

As mentioned above, there are constructions of NIZKs based on various standard assumptions while there is no known construction of SNARGs based on a standard assumption and there is even a strong impossibility for that. Given this situation, we may think that a SNARG is a stronger primitive than a NIZK. However, it is not known if a SNARG implies a NIZK, and they have been treated as incomparable primitives. For example, Bitansky et al. [4] gave a generic conversion from a SNARG to a zero-knowledge SNARG by additionally assuming the existence of NIZKs. If a SNARG implies a NIZK, we could drop the additional assumption of the NIZK. Besides, since both NIZKs and SNARGs are important and fundamental primitives that have been well-studied, we believe that it is interesting on its own if we find a new relationship between them.

1.1 Our Results

We give a construction of a NIZK for all NP languages based on a SNARG for all NP languages and a one-way function (OWF). The succinctness requirement for the SNARG is rather mild: We only require that its proof size be $|\pi| = \mathsf{poly}(\lambda)(|x| + |w|)^c$ for some constant $c < 1/2$, where $|x|$ is the statement length, $|w|$ is the witness length, and λ is the security parameter. Especially, we do not require anything about the efficiency of the verification.

Based on this result, we also give a generic conversion from a SNARG to a zero-knowledge SNARG assuming the existence of CPA secure public-key encryption. For this conversion, we require a SNARG to have efficient verification, i.e., the computational complexity of the verification algorithm is $\mathsf{poly}(\lambda)(|x| + |w|)^{o(1)}$ (and thus the proof size is also $|\pi| = \mathsf{poly}(\lambda)(|x| + |w|)^{o(1)}$). Before this work, such a conversion was only known if we additionally assume the existence of a NIZK [4].

Along the way of obtaining our result, we give a generic compiler to upgrade a NIZK for all NP languages with non-adaptive zero-knowledge to one with adaptive zero-knowledge. Though this can be shown by carefully combining known

---

[1] The lattice based constructions are in the designated verifier model where a designated party that holds a verification key can verify proofs.

[2] Actually, what is often used in blockchains is a SNARK [4], which is a stronger variant of a SNARG that satisfies extractability. We often refer to a SNARK as a SNARG since we do not discuss extractability in this paper.

results, to the best of our knowledge, no explicit proof of this generic conversion has been presented.[3,4]

We note that we use the adaptive computational soundness as a default notion of soundness for non-interactive arguments in this paper, and our results are proven in this setting. We leave it as an interesting open problem to study if similar implications hold for NIZKs and SNARGs with non-adaptive computational soundness.

To the best of our knowledge, all known constructions of a SNARG in the CRS model satisfies the zero-knowledge property from the beginning. Therefore, we do not obtain a concrete construction of a NIZK from an assumption that was not known to imply NIZKs by using our result. Nonetheless, it is in general important to study generic relationships between different primitives from a theoretical point of view, and we believe that our results contribute to deepening our understanding on the two important and fundamental primitives of NIZKs and SNARGs.

1.2   Technical Overview

In this section, we give an overview of the construction of a NIZK from a SNARG. Once this is done, it is straightforward to obtain a generic conversion from a SNARG to a zero-knowledge SNARG by combining it with the result of [4].

First, we observe that the succinctness of a SNARG implies that a SNARG proof at least "loses" some information about the witness though it may leak some partial information. Based on this observation, our basic idea is to combine a SNARG with a leakage-resilient primitive [1] whose security holds even if a certain fraction of a secret key is leaked. If the SNARG proof size is small enough, then we may be able to use the security of the leakage-resilient primitive to fully hide the witness considering a SNARG proof as a leakage. For example, suppose that we have a leakage-resilient secret-key encryption (LR-SKE) scheme whose semantic security holds as long as the amount of leakage from the secret key is at most a half of the secret key size. Then, a naive (failed) idea to construct a NIZK is to let a NIZK proof consist of an encryption ct of the witness by the LR-SKE scheme and a SNARG proof proving that there exists a secret key of the LR-SKE scheme that decrypts ct to a valid witness. Soundness of this construction is easy to reduce to the soundness of the SNARG. In addition, if the SNARG is fully succinct, then we can show that the SNARG proof size is at most a half of the secret key size if we set the secret key size of LR-SKE to be sufficiently large. Then, it seems possible to argue that the information of the witness is completely hidden by the security of LR-SKE. However, there is a flaw

---

[3] Dwork and Naor [24] showed a similar compiler for a NIZK *proof* in the common *random* string model. But their compiler does not work for a NIZK *argument* in the common *reference* string model.

[4] A recent work by Couteau, Katsumata, and Ursu [20] implicitly relies on a similar observation. However, they do not state it in a general form, and they only analyze their specific instantiations.

in the above idea: The security of a LR-SKE scheme holds only if the leakage does not depend on the challenge ciphertext. On the other hand, in the above construction, the SNARG proof clearly depends on the challenge ciphertext ct, and thus we cannot use the security of a LR-SKE scheme. Though the above naive idea fails, this highlights a potential idea of combining a SNARG with a leakage-resilient primitive to obtain a NIZK. Indeed, we implement this idea by modifying the NIZK construction based on the hidden-bits paradigm [26].

NIZK via the Hidden-Bits Paradigm. First, we recall the construction of a NIZK based on the hidden-bits paradigm [26] following the formalization by Quach, Rothblum, and Wichs [46]. Readers familiar with their formalization can safely skip this paragraph. The construction uses two building blocks: a NIZK in the hidden-bit model (HBM-NIZK) and a hidden-bits generator (HBG).

In an HBM-NIZK, a trusted party picks a random string $\rho \in \{0,1\}^k$ and gives it to the prover. Then a prover, who holds a statement x and a witness w, generates a proof π along with a subset $I \subseteq [k]$, which specifies which bits of ρ to be revealed to the verifier. Then, the verifier is given a statement x, a proof π, a subset I, and a string ρ_I that is the substring of ρ on the positions corresponding to I, and accepts or rejects. We require an HBM-NIZK to satisfy two security requirements: soundness and zero-knowledge. Intuitively, soundness requires that no cheating prover can convince the verifier of a false statement x with non-negligible probability, and the zero-knowledge property requires that the verifier learns nothing beyond that x is a true statement. Feige, Lapidot, and Shamir [26] constructed an HBM-NIZK for all NP languages that satisfies these security requirements (without relying on any assumption).

An HBG is a primitive introduced in [46], which consists of the following algorithms:

- HBG.Setup($1^\lambda, 1^k$) generates a CRS crs where k denotes the length of hidden-bits to be generated.
- HBG.GenBits(crs) generates a succinct commitment com whose length is much shorter than k, "hidden-bits" $r \in \{0,1\}^k$, and a tuple of proofs $\{\pi_i\}_{i \in [k]}$. Intuitively, each π_i can be thought of as a certificate of the i-th bit of r.
- HBG.Verify(crs, com, i, r_i, π_i) verifies the proof π_i to ensure that the i-th hidden-bit is r_i.

We require an HBG to satisfy two security requirements: binding and hiding. The binding property requires that for any fixed commitment com, there exist "committed bits" $r^* \in \{0,1\}^k$ and no PPT adversary can generate a proof π_i such that HBG.Verify(crs, com, $i, \bar{r_i^*}, \pi_i$) accepts, where $\bar{r_i^*}$ denotes the negation of r_i^*.[5] Combined with the succinctness of com, this implies that there should be a "sparse" set $\mathcal{V}^{crs} \in \{0,1\}^k$ (dependent on crs) of size much smaller than 2^k such that no PPT adversary can generate a set of proofs $\{\pi_i\}_{i \in I}$ for bits that are not consistent with any element of $\mathcal{V}^{crs}$ even if it can control the value of com. The

---

[5] The original definition in [46] required a stronger requirement of *statistical* binding where the property should hold against all computationally unbounded adversaries.

hiding property requires that for any subset $I \subseteq [k]$, no PPT adversary given $\{(r_i, \pi_i)\}_{i \in I}$ can distinguish $r_{\bar{I}}$ from a fresh random string $r'_{\bar{I}} \xleftarrow{\$} \{0,1\}^{|\bar{I}|}$, where $r_{\bar{I}}$ denotes the substring of r on the positions corresponding to $\bar{I} = [k] \setminus I$.

Combining the above two primitives, Quach et al. [46] constructed a NIZK as follows: The setup algorithm generates a CRS crs $\xleftarrow{\$}$ HBG.Setup($1^\lambda, 1^k$) of the HBG and a random string $s \xleftarrow{\$} \{0,1\}^k$ and outputs them as a CRS of the NIZK where $k = \mathsf{poly}(\lambda)$ is a parameter that is set appropriately as explained later. Then the prover generates $(\mathsf{com}, r, \{\pi_i\}_{i \in [k]}) \xleftarrow{\$}$ HBG.GenBits(crs), sets $\rho := r \oplus s$, runs the prover of the underlying HBM-NIZK w.r.t. the hidden-bits ρ to generate (I, π_{hbm}), and outputs $(I, \pi_{\mathsf{hbm}}, \mathsf{com}, r_I, \{\pi_i\}_{i \in I})$ as a proof of the NIZK. Then the verifier runs the verification of the underlying HBG to check the validity of r_I and the verification algorithm of the underlying HBM-NIZK under the revealed hidden-bits $\rho_I := r_I \oplus s_I$.

The security of the above NIZK is argued as follows: For each fixed r, any cheating prover against the above NIZK can be easily converted into a cheating prover against the underlying HBM-NIZK. Moreover, by the binding property of the underlying HBG, the prover has to use r in the subset $\mathcal{V}^{\mathsf{crs}}$ to pass the verification. Then, by taking the union bound, the success probability of a cheating prover against the above NIZK is at most $|\mathcal{V}^{\mathsf{crs}}| \ll 2^k$ times larger than that of a cheating prover against the underlying HBM-NIZK. Thus, by setting k to be sufficiently large so that the success probability of a cheating prover against the underlying HBM-NIZK is at most $|\mathcal{V}^{\mathsf{crs}}|^{-1}\mathsf{negl}(\lambda)$, we can prove the soundness. Intuitively, the zero-knowledge property of the above NIZK is easy to reduce to that of the underlying HBM-NIZK by observing that the hiding property of the underlying HBG ensures that the verifier obtains no information about $r_{\bar{I}}$. We note that this simple reduction works only for *non-adaptive* zero-knowledge where an adversary declares a challenge statement before seeing a CRS. Roughly speaking, this is because in the definition of the hiding property of a HBG, the subset I is fixed before the CRS is chosen whereas an adversary against adaptive zero-knowledge may choose I depending on the CRS. Quach et al. [46] showed that adaptive zero-knowledge can be also proven assuming that the underlying HBM-NIZK satisfies a stronger notion of zero-knowledge called special zero-knowledge. We omit to explain the details since we will show a generic compiler from non-adaptive to adaptive zero-knowledge.

HBG from a SNARG? Our first attempt is to construct an HBG from a SNARG combined with a leakage-resilient weak pseudorandom function (LR-wPRF) [37]. A (one-bit-output) LR-wPRF is a function family $\mathcal{F} = \{F_K : \{0,1\}^m \to \{0,1\}\}_{K \in \{0,1\}^\kappa}$ such that $(x^*, F_K(x^*))$ for $x^* \xleftarrow{\$} \{0,1\}^m$ looks pseudorandom from an adversary that is given an arbitrary polynomial number of input-output pairs $(x, F_K(x))$ for $x \xleftarrow{\$} \{0,1\}^m$ and a leakage from K (that does not depend on x^*) of at most ℓ-bit for a certain leakage bound $\ell < \kappa$. Hazay et al. [37] constructed an LR-wPRF for any polynomial $\ell = \mathsf{poly}(\lambda)$ based solely on the existence of a OWF.

Then, our first (failed) attempt for constructing an HBG from a SNARG and an LR-wPRF is as follows:

- HBG.Setup($1^\lambda, 1^k$) samples $(x_1, \ldots, x_k) \in \{0,1\}^{m \times k}$ and outputs it as a CRS crs.
- HBG.GenBits(crs) randomly picks a key $K \xleftarrow{\$} \{0,1\}^\kappa$ of the LR-wPRF, and outputs a commitment com of K by a statistically binding commitment scheme, hidden-bits $r := (F_K(x_1), \ldots, F_K(x_k))$, and proofs $\{\pi_i\}_{i \in [k]}$ that are generated by the SNARG to certify r.
- HBG.Verify(crs, com, i, r_i, π_i) verifies the proof π_i by the verification algorithm of the SNARG.

The binding property easily follows from the statistical binding property of the underlying commitment scheme and the soundness of the underlying SNARG. For the hiding property, we would like to rely on the security of the underlying LR-wPRF by viewing the SNARG proofs as a leakage. However, there are the following two problems:

1. An adversary against the hiding property can obtain all proofs $\{\pi_i\}_{i \in I}$ corresponding to the subset I whose size may be linear in k. On the other hand, for ensuring the succinctness of the commitment, we have to set $k \gg \kappa$. Thus, the total size of $\{\pi_i\}_{i \in I}$ may be larger than κ, in which case it is impossible to rely on the security of the LR-wPRF.
2. Even if the above problem is resolved, we still cannot apply the security of the LR-wPRF since com also depends on K and its size must be larger than that of K.

To resolve these issues, our idea is to drop the commitment com from the output of HBG.GenBits(crs), and generate a single SNARG proof π that proves that "there exists $K \in \{0,1\}^\kappa$ such that $r_i = F_K(x_i)$ for all $i \in I$" in one-shot instead of generating π_i for each $i \in I$ separately. Then, the only leakage of K given to an adversary against the hiding property is the SNARG proof π, whose size is sublinear in $|I|$ by the succinctness of the SNARG. Thus, it seems possible to apply the security of the LR-wPRF if we set parameters appropriately. However, this idea is not compatible with the syntax of an HBG. This is why we modify the syntax of an HBG to introduce what we call an *HBG with subset-dependent proofs* (SDP-HBG).

HBG with Subset-Dependent Proofs. Roughly speaking, an SDP-HBG is a (weaker) variant of an HBG with the following modifications:

1. A proof is generated depending on a subset I, which specifies positions of bits to be revealed. This is in contrast to the original definition of an HBG where proofs are generated for each position $i \in [k]$. To formalize this, we introduce the proving algorithm separated from the bits generation algorithm.
2. The bits generation algorithm does not output a commitment, and we require a relaxed version of the binding property that we call the *somewhat binding* property as explained later.

More precisely, an SDP-HBG consists of the following algorithms:

- $\mathsf{HBG}^{\mathsf{sdp}}.\mathsf{Setup}(1^\lambda, 1^k)$ generates a CRS crs.
- $\mathsf{HBG}^{\mathsf{sdp}}.\mathsf{GenBits}(\mathsf{crs})$ generates "hidden-bits" $r \in \{0,1\}^k$ and a state st.
- $\mathsf{HBG}^{\mathsf{sdp}}.\mathsf{Prove}(\mathsf{st}, I)$ generates a proof π that certifies the sub-string r_I.
- $\mathsf{HBG}^{\mathsf{sdp}}.\mathsf{Verify}(\mathsf{crs}, I, r_I, \pi)$ verifies the proof π to ensure that the substring of r on the positions corresponding to the subset I is indeed r_I.

We require an SDP-HBG to satisfy the somewhat binding property and the hiding property. The somewhat binding property requires that there exists a "sparse" subset $\mathcal{V}^{\mathsf{crs}} \in \{0,1\}^k$ (dependent on crs) of size much smaller than 2^k such that no PPT malicious prover can generate a proof for bits that are not consistent with any element of $\mathcal{V}^{\mathsf{crs}}$. As mentioned earlier, a similar property easily follows by combining the succinctness of the commitment and the binding property in the original HBG, and this was the essential property to prove soundness in the construction of a NIZK from an HBG. The hiding property is similar to that for an HBG except that an adversary is given a single proof π corresponding to the subset I instead of $\{\pi_i\}_{i \in I}$. Namely, it requires that for any subset $I \in [k]$, no PPT adversary given $\{r_i\}_{i \in I}$ and π that certifies $\{r_i\}_{i \in I}$ can distinguish $r_{\overline{I}}$ from a fresh random string $r'_{\overline{I}} \xleftarrow{\$} \{0,1\}^{|\overline{I}|}$, where $r_{\overline{I}}$ denotes the sub-string of r on the positions corresponding to $\overline{I} = [k] \setminus I$.

To see that an SDP-HBG is a weaker primitive than an HBG, in Sect. 4.2, we formally show that an original HBG indeed implies an SDP-HBG.

SDP-HBG from a SNARG and an LR-wPRF. Next, we construct an SDP-HBG from a SNARG and an LR-wPRF. Since the idea is already explained, we directly give the construction below:

- $\mathsf{HBG}^{\mathsf{sdp}}.\mathsf{Setup}(1^\lambda, 1^k)$ samples $(x_1, \ldots, x_k) \in \{0,1\}^{m \times k}$ and outputs it as a CRS crs.
- $\mathsf{HBG}^{\mathsf{sdp}}.\mathsf{GenBits}(\mathsf{crs})$ randomly picks a key $K \xleftarrow{\$} \{0,1\}^\kappa$ of the LR-wPRF and outputs hidden-bits $r := (F_K(x_1), \ldots, F_K(x_k))$ and a state $\mathsf{st} := K$.
- $\mathsf{HBG}^{\mathsf{sdp}}.\mathsf{Prove}(\mathsf{st}, I)$ outputs a SNARG proof π that proves that there exists $K \in \{0,1\}^\kappa$ such that $r_i = F_K(x_i)$ for all $i \in I$.
- $\mathsf{HBG}^{\mathsf{sdp}}.\mathsf{Verify}(\mathsf{crs}, I, r_I, \pi)$ verifies the proof π by the verification algorithm of the SNARG.

The somewhat binding property is easy to reduce to the soundness of the underlying SNARG if $\kappa \ll k$. The hiding property is easy to reduce to the security of the underlying LR-PRF if $|\pi| \leq \ell$ where ℓ is the leakage bound by noting that the proof π corresponding to the subset I does not depend on $x_{\overline{I}}$, and thus we can think of $x_{\overline{I}}$ as challenge inputs and π as a leakage. Therefore, what remains is to show that we can appropriately set the parameters to satisfy these two inequalities. Here, for simplicity we assume that the SNARG is fully succinct, i.e., $|\pi| = \mathsf{poly}(\lambda)$ independently of the statement/witness size.[6] Especially, $|\pi|$

---

[6] Though the full succinctness just says $|\pi| = \mathsf{poly}(\lambda)(|x| + |w|)^{o(1)}$, this implies $|\pi| = \mathsf{poly}(\lambda)$ as long as we have $|x| = \mathsf{poly}(\lambda)$ and $|w| = \mathsf{poly}(\lambda)$.

can be upper bounded by a polynomial in λ that does not depend on k. Then, we first set $\ell = \mathsf{poly}(\lambda)$ so that $|\pi| \leq \ell$. According to this choice of ℓ, $\kappa = \mathsf{poly}(\lambda)$ is determined. Here, we emphasize that κ does not depend on k. Thus, for sufficiently large $k = \mathsf{poly}(\lambda)$, we have $\kappa \ll k$ as desired.[7] The crucial point is that no matter how large k is, this does not affect $|\pi|$ thanks to the full succinctness of the SNARG. We note that we assume nothing about the leakage-rate (i.e., ℓ/κ) of the LR-wPRF, and thus we can use the LR-wPRF based on a OWF in [37], which achieves a relatively poor leakage-rate of $O(\frac{\log \lambda}{\lambda})$. For the case of slightly-succinct SNARGs, a more careful analysis is needed, but we can extend the above proof as long as $|\pi| = \mathsf{poly}(\lambda)(|x| + |w|)^c$ holds for some constant $c < 1/2$.

As seen above, the underlying SNARG in fact needs to prove only a statement of an NP language with a specific form that is dependent on the LR-wPRF (which is in turn based on a OWF). Thus, if the latter is determined beforehand, the SNARG is required to support this particular language (and not all NP languages).[8]

NIZK from an SDP-HBG. Then, we show that an SDP-HBG suffices for constructing a NIZK. In fact, the construction and security proof are essentially the same as that from an HBG in [46]:

- The setup algorithm generates a CRS $\mathsf{crs} \xleftarrow{\$} \mathsf{HBG}^{\mathsf{sdp}}.\mathsf{Setup}(1^\lambda, 1^k)$ of the SDP-HBG and a random string $s \xleftarrow{\$} \{0,1\}^k$, and outputs them as a CRS of the NIZK;
- The prover generates $(r, \mathsf{st}) \xleftarrow{\$} \mathsf{HBG}^{\mathsf{sdp}}.\mathsf{GenBits}(\mathsf{crs})$, sets $\rho := r \oplus s$, runs the prover of the underlying HBM-NIZK w.r.t. the hidden-bits ρ to generate $(I \subseteq [k], \pi_{\mathsf{hbm}})$, generates $\pi_{\mathsf{bgen}} \xleftarrow{\$} \mathsf{HBG}^{\mathsf{sdp}}.\mathsf{Prove}(\mathsf{st}, I)$, and outputs $(I, \pi_{\mathsf{hbm}}, r_I, \pi_{\mathsf{bgen}})$ as a proof of the NIZK;
- The verifier runs the verification of the underlying SDP-HBG to check the validity of r_I and the verification of the underlying HBM-NIZK under the revealed hidden-bits $\rho_I := r_I \oplus s_I$.

It is easy to see that essentially the same proofs as the NIZK from an HBG work for soundness and non-adaptive zero-knowledge. However, it is not clear how to prove the adaptive zero-knowledge for this construction. As mentioned earlier, for the construction of a NIZK from an HBG, Quach et al. [46] proved its adaptive zero-knowledge assuming that the underlying HBM-NIZK satisfies a stronger notion of zero-knowledge called special zero-knowledge. However, their proof does not extend to the proof of adaptive zero-knowledge for the above NIZK from an SDP-HBG even if we rely on the special zero-knowledge for the underlying HBM-NIZK. Roughly speaking, the problem comes from the fact that the SDP-HBG enables us to generate a proof π_{bgen} corresponding to a subset I

---

[7] It suffices that we have this for sufficiently large k since we can take $k = \mathsf{poly}(\lambda)$ arbitrarily largely in the construction of a NIZK.

[8] A similar remark applies to the underlying NIZK with non-adaptive zero-knowledge used in the non-adaptive-to-adaptive conversion for a NIZK.

only after I is fixed. This is in contrast to an HBG where we can generate π_i that certifies the i-th hidden bit for each $i \in [k]$ before I is fixed. Specifically, the proof of adaptive zero-knowledge from an HBG in [46] crucially relies on the fact that if $I \subseteq I^*$, then a set of proofs $\{\pi_i\}_{i \in I}$ can be derived from $\{\pi_i\}_{i \in I^*}$ in a trivial manner. On the other hand, we do not have a similar property in SDP-HBG since it generates a proof for a subset I in one-shot instead of generating a proof in a bit-by-bit manner. Thus, we have to come up with an alternative way to achieve adaptive zero-knowledge.

Non-adaptive to Adaptive Zero-Knowledge. Based on existing works, we give a generic compiler from non-adaptive to adaptive zero-knowledge. First, we observe that we can construct an HBG by combining a commitment, a pseudorandom generator (PRG), and a NIZK in a straightforward manner. We note that essentially the same construction was already mentioned by Dwork and Naor [24] where they constructed a verifiable PRG, which is a similar but slightly different primitive from an HBG. Our crucial observation is that non-adaptive zero-knowledge is sufficient for this construction of an HBG. Then, we can apply the construction of [46] instantiated with the above HBG and an HBM-NIZK with special zero-knowledge to obtain a NIZK with adaptive zero-knowledge.

1.3 Related Work

Known Constructions of NIZKs. Here, we review known constructions of a NIZK for all NP languages. Below, we just write NIZK to mean NIZK for all NP languages for simplicity. In this paragraph, we omit a NIZK that is also a SNARG since such schemes are mentioned in the next paragraph. Blum, Feldman, and Micali [7] introduced the concept of NIZK and constructed a NIZK based on the quadratic residuosity assumption. Feige, Lapidot, and Shamir [26] established the hidden-bits paradigm and constructed a NIZK based on trapdoor permutations. The requirements on trapdoor permutations for realizing a NIZK have been revisited and refined in a series of works [15,30,33]. Canetti, Halevi, and Katz [14] constructed a NIZK based on pairing by instantiating the hidden-bits paradigm. Groth, Ostrovsky, and Sahai [36] constructed a pairing-based NIZK based on a completely different approach, which yields the first NIZK with perfect zero-knowledge. Sahai and Waters [48] constructed the first NIZK with a deterministic proving algorithm and perfect zero-knowledge based on indistinguishability obfuscation and a OWF. Recently, there has been a line of researches [12,13,38] aiming at realizing the Fiat-Shamir transform [27] in the standard model. Peikert and Shiehian [45] constructed a NIZK based on a standard lattice-based assumption following this approach. Very recently, Couteau, Katsumata, and Ursu [20] constructed a NIZK based on a certain exponential hardness assumption on pairing-free groups. We note that it still remains open to construct a NIZK from polynomial hardness assumption on pairing-free groups.

We omit NIZKs in a different model than the CRS model including preprocessing, designated prover, and designated verifier models since our focus in this paper is constructions in the CRS model. We refer to [39,41] for a survey on NIZKs in these models.

Known Constructions of SNARGs. Here, we review known constructions of a SNARG for all NP languages. Below, we just write SNARG to mean SNARG for all NP languages. We note that some of the following constructions are actually a *SNARK*, which satisfies a stronger notion of soundness called extractability, but we just call them a SNARG since we do not discuss extractability in this paper. Also, other than [18,42], here we only mention works that do not rely on random oracles. For the recent advances on practical SNARGs (SNARKs) including those in the random oracle model, see, e.g., the recent papers [11,17, 19,25] and references therein.

Micali [42] constructed a zero-knowledge SNARG in the random oracle model. Chiesa, Manohar, and Spooner [18] proved that the Micali's construction is also secure in the quantum random oracle model. Groth [34,35] and Gennaro, Gentry, Perno, and Raykova [28] proposed zero-knowledge SNARGs in the CRS model based on non-falsifiable assumptions on pairing groups. There are several constructions of (zero-knowledge) SNARGs in the designated-verifier model where verification can be done only by a designated verifier who possesses a secret verification key. These include constructions based on an extractable collision-resistant hash function [4], homomorphism-extractable encryption [5], linear-only encryption [6,9,10], etc.

NIZKs/SNARGs and OWFs. Pass and shelat [44] showed that a NIZK for a hard-on-average language implies the existence of (non-uniform) OWFs. On the other hand, Wee [49] gave an evidence that a SNARG for a hard-on-average language is unlikely to imply the existence of OWFs. Therefore, it is considered reasonable to additionally assume the existence of OWFs for constructing a NIZK from a SNARG.

2 Preliminaries

In this section, we review the basic notation and definitions of cryptographic primitives.

Basic Notation. For a natural number $n > 0$, we define $[n] := \{1, \ldots, n\}$. Furthermore, for $I \subseteq [n]$, we define $\overline{I} := [n] \setminus I$.

For a string x, $|x|$ denotes the bit-length of x. For bits $b, b' \in \{0, 1\}$, $(b' \stackrel{?}{=} b)$ is defined to be 1 if $b' = b$ holds and 0 otherwise.

For a set S, $|S|$ denotes its size, and $x \stackrel{\$}{\leftarrow} S$ denotes sampling x uniformly at random from S. Furthermore, for natural numbers i, k such that $i \in [k]$ and a sequence $z \in S^k$, z_i denotes the i-th entry in z. Also, for $I \subseteq [k]$, we define $z_I := (z_i)_{i \in I}$, namely the subsequence of z in the positions I.

For a probabilistic (resp. deterministic) algorithm A, $y \stackrel{\$}{\leftarrow} A(x)$ (resp. $y \leftarrow A(x)$) denotes $\mathcal{A}$ on input x outputs y. If we need to specify a randomness r used in A, we write $y \leftarrow A(x; r)$ (in which case the computation is deterministic). If $\mathcal{O}$ is a function or an algorithm, then $A^{\mathcal{O}}$ means that A has oracle access to $\mathcal{O}$.

Throughout the paper, we use λ to denote the security parameter, and a "PPT adversary" is a non-uniform PPT adversary (equivalently, a family of polynomial-sized circuits). A function $\epsilon(\lambda)$ with range $[0, 1]$ is said to be negligible if $\epsilon(\lambda) = \lambda^{-\omega(1)}$, and $\mathsf{negl}(\lambda)$ denotes an unspecified negligible function of λ. $\mathsf{poly}(\lambda)$ denotes an unspecified (constant-degree) polynomial of λ.

2.1 NIZK and SNARG

Here, we define several notions of a non-interactive argument for an NP language $\mathcal{L}$. Throughout this paper, for an NP language $\mathcal{L}$, we denote by $\mathcal{R} \subseteq \{0,1\}^* \times \{0,1\}^*$ the corresponding efficiently computable binary relation. For $(x, w) \in \mathcal{R}$, we call x a statement and w a witness.

Definition 2.1 (Non-interactive Arguments). *A non-interactive argument for an* NP *language $\mathcal{L}$ consists of the three PPT algorithms* (Setup, Prove, Verify):

$\mathsf{Setup}(1^\lambda) \overset{\$}{\to} \mathsf{crs}$: *The setup algorithm takes the security parameter 1^λ as input, and outputs a CRS* crs.

$\mathsf{Prove}(\mathsf{crs}, x, w) \overset{\$}{\to} \pi$: *The prover's algorithm takes a CRS* crs, *a statement x, and a witness w as input, and outputs a proof π.*

$\mathsf{Verify}(\mathsf{crs}, x, \pi) \to \top$ *or* $\bot$: *The verifier's algorithm takes a CRS* crs, *a statement x, and a proof π as input, and outputs $\top$ to indicate acceptance of the proof or $\bot$ otherwise.*

A non-interactive argument must satisfy the following requirements:

Completeness: *For all pairs $(x, w) \in \mathcal{R}$, we have*

$$\Pr\left[\mathsf{Verify}(\mathsf{crs}, x, \pi) = \top : \begin{array}{l} \mathsf{crs} \overset{\$}{\leftarrow} \mathsf{Setup}(1^\lambda); \\ \pi \overset{\$}{\leftarrow} \mathsf{Prove}(\mathsf{crs}, x, w) \end{array}\right] = 1.$$

Soundness: *We define the following four variants of soundness.*

 Adaptive Computational Soundness: *For all PPT adversaries $\mathcal{A}$, we have*

$$\Pr\left[x \notin \mathcal{L} \wedge \mathsf{Verify}(\mathsf{crs}, x, \pi) = \top : \begin{array}{l} \mathsf{crs} \overset{\$}{\leftarrow} \mathsf{Setup}(1^\lambda); \\ (x, \pi) \overset{\$}{\leftarrow} \mathcal{A}(\mathsf{crs}) \end{array}\right] = \mathsf{negl}(\lambda).$$

 Adaptive Statistical Soundness: *This is defined similarly to adaptive computational soundness, except that $\mathcal{A}$ can be any computationally unbounded adversary.*

 Non-adaptive Computational (resp. Statistical) Soundness: *This is defined similarly to adaptive computational (resp. statistical) soundness, except that $\mathcal{A}$ must declare $x \notin \mathcal{L}$ before it is given* crs.

If we only require completeness and soundness as defined above, a non-interactive argument trivially exists for all NP languages, since a witness itself can be used as a proof. Thus, we consider two other properties that make non-interactive arguments non-trivial. First, we define non-interactive zero-knowledge arguments (NIZKs).

Definition 2.2 (NIZK). *A non-interactive argument* (Setup, Prove, Verify) *for an* NP *language $\mathcal{L}$ is a* non-interactive zero-knowledge argument *(NIZK) if it satisfies the following property in addition to completeness and soundness.*

(**Computational**) **Zero-Knowledge:** *We define the following four variants of zero-knowledge property.*

Adaptive Multi-theorem Zero-Knowledge: *There exists a PPT simulator $\mathcal{S} = (\mathcal{S}_1, \mathcal{S}_2)$ that satisfies the following. For all PPT adversaries $\mathcal{A}$, we have*

$$\left| \Pr[\mathsf{Expt}_{\mathcal{A}}^{\mathsf{azk\text{-}real}}(\lambda) = 1] - \Pr[\mathsf{Expt}_{\mathcal{A},\mathcal{S}}^{\mathsf{azk\text{-}sim}}(\lambda) = 1] \right| = \mathsf{negl}(\lambda),$$

where the experiments $\mathsf{Expt}_{\mathcal{A}}^{\mathsf{azk\text{-}real}}(\lambda)$ and $\mathsf{Expt}_{\mathcal{A},\mathcal{S}}^{\mathsf{azk\text{-}sim}}(\lambda)$ are defined as follows, and in the experiments, $\mathcal{A}$'s queries (x,w) must satisfy $(x,w) \in \mathcal{R}$.

$\mathsf{Expt}_{\mathcal{A}}^{\mathsf{azk\text{-}real}}(\lambda)$:	$\mathsf{Expt}_{\mathcal{A},\mathcal{S}}^{\mathsf{azk\text{-}sim}}(\lambda)$:
$\mathsf{crs} \xleftarrow{\$} \mathsf{Setup}(1^\lambda)$	$(\mathsf{crs}, \mathsf{st}) \xleftarrow{\$} \mathcal{S}_1(1^\lambda)$
$b' \xleftarrow{\$} \mathcal{A}^{\mathcal{O}_0(\cdot,\cdot)}(\mathsf{crs})$	$b' \xleftarrow{\$} \mathcal{A}^{\mathcal{O}_1(\cdot,\cdot)}(\mathsf{crs})$
where $\mathcal{O}_0(x,w) := \mathsf{Prove}(\mathsf{crs}, x, w)$	*where* $\mathcal{O}_1(x,w) := \mathcal{S}_2(\mathsf{st}, x)$
Return b'.	Return b'.

Though we treat adaptive multi-theorem zero-knowledge as defined above as a default notion of zero-knowledge, we also define weaker notions of zero-knowledge.

Adaptive Single-Theorem Zero-Knowledge: *This is defined similarly to adaptive multi-theorem zero-knowledge, except that $\mathcal{A}$ is allowed to make only a single query.*

Non-adaptive Multi-theorem Zero-Knowledge: *There exists a PPT simulator $\mathcal{S}$ that satisfies the following. For all PPT adversaries $\mathcal{A} = (\mathcal{A}_1, \mathcal{A}_2)$ we have*

$$\left| \Pr[\mathsf{Expt}_{\mathcal{A}}^{\mathsf{nazk\text{-}real}}(\lambda) = 1] - \Pr[\mathsf{Expt}_{\mathcal{A},\mathcal{S}}^{\mathsf{nazk\text{-}sim}}(\lambda) = 1] \right| = \mathsf{negl}(\lambda),$$

where the experiments $\mathsf{Expt}_{\mathcal{A}}^{\mathsf{nazk\text{-}real}}(\lambda)$ and $\mathsf{Expt}_{\mathcal{A},\mathcal{S}}^{\mathsf{nazk\text{-}sim}}(\lambda)$ are defined below. In the experiments, ℓ (the number of statement/witness pairs) is arbitrarily chosen by $\mathcal{A}_1$, and $\mathcal{A}_1$'s output must satisfy $(x_i, w_i) \in \mathcal{R}$ for all $i \in [\ell]$.

$\mathsf{Expt}_{\mathcal{A}}^{\mathsf{nazk\text{-}real}}(\lambda)$:	$\mathsf{Expt}_{\mathcal{A},\mathcal{S}}^{\mathsf{nazk\text{-}sim}}(\lambda)$:
$(\{(x_i, w_i)\}_{i \in [\ell]}, \mathsf{st}) \xleftarrow{\$} \mathcal{A}_1(1^\lambda)$	$(\{(x_i, w_i)\}_{i \in [\ell]}, \mathsf{st}) \xleftarrow{\$} \mathcal{A}_1(1^\lambda)$
$\mathsf{crs} \xleftarrow{\$} \mathsf{Setup}(1^\lambda)$	$(\mathsf{crs}, \{\pi_i\}_{i \in [\ell]}) \xleftarrow{\$} \mathcal{S}(1^\lambda, \{x_i\}_{i \in [\ell]})$
$\pi_i \xleftarrow{\$} \mathsf{Prove}(\mathsf{crs}, x_i, w_i)$ *for* $i \in [\ell]$	
$b' \xleftarrow{\$} \mathcal{A}_2(\mathsf{crs}, \{\pi_i\}_{i \in [\ell]}, \mathsf{st})$	$b' \xleftarrow{\$} \mathcal{A}_2(\mathsf{crs}, \{\pi_i\}_{i \in [\ell]}, \mathsf{st})$
Return b'.	Return b'.

Non-adaptive Single-Theorem Zero-Knowledge: *This is defined similarly to non-adaptive multi-theorem zero-knowledge, except that ℓ must be 1.*

It is well-known that a NIZK with adaptive single-theorem zero-knowledge can be generically converted into a NIZK with adaptive multi-theorem zero-knowledge using a PRG [26]. It is easy to see that the same construction works in the non-adaptive setting. Thus, we have the following lemma.

Lemma 2.1. *If there exist a OWF and a NIZK for all NP languages with adaptive (resp. non-adaptive) single-theorem zero-knowledge, then there exists a NIZK for all NP languages with adaptive (resp. non-adaptive) multi-theorem zero-knowledge. The resulting NIZK satisfies the same notion of soundness (which is either of adaptive/non-adaptive statistical/computational soundness) as the building-block NIZK.*

Remark 2.1. Pass and shelat [44] showed that a NIZK for a hard-on-average language implies the existence of a (non-uniform) OWF. Therefore, we can weaken the assumption of the existence of a OWF to the existence of a hard-on-average NP language. We just assume the existence of a OWF for simplicity. A similar remark also applies to Theorem 3.1 and Lemmas 3.1 and 3.2.

Next, we define SNARGs. The following definition is taken from [29] with a minor modification in the definition of slight succinctness (see Remark 2.2).

Definition 2.3 ((Fully/Slightly Succinct) SNARG). *A non-interactive argument* (Setup, Prove, Verify) *for an* NP *language* $\mathcal{L}$ *is a fully (resp. δ-slightly) succinct non-interactive argument (SNARG) if it satisfies full (resp. δ-slight) succinctness defined as follows in addition to completeness and soundness.*

Succinctness: *We define the following two variants of succinctness.*
  Full Succinctness: *For all* $(x, w) \in \mathcal{R}$, crs $\xleftarrow{\$}$ Setup(1^λ), *and* $\pi \xleftarrow{\$}$ Prove(crs, x, w), *we have* $|\pi| = \mathsf{poly}(\lambda)(|x| + |w|)^{o(1)}$.
  δ-Slight Succinctness : *For all* $(x, w) \in \mathcal{R}$, crs $\xleftarrow{\$}$ Setup(1^λ), *and* $\pi \xleftarrow{\$}$ Prove(crs, x, w), *we have* $|\pi| = \mathsf{poly}(\lambda)(|x| + |w|)^{\delta}$.

Remark 2.2. The notion of δ-slight succinctness is meaningful only when $\delta < 1$ since otherwise we can use a witness itself as a proof. We note that our definition of δ-slight succinctness for any $\delta < 1$ is stronger than slight succinctness defined in [29] where they require $|\pi| = \mathsf{poly}(\lambda)(|x| + |w|)^{\delta} + o(|x| + |w|)$ for some $\delta < 1$. Namely, they allow the proof size to grow according to any function dominated by $|x| + |w|$ asymptotically as long as that is independent of the security parameter λ.

We define an additional property for SNARG.

Definition 2.4 (Efficient Verification of SNARG). *A SNARG* (Setup, Prove, Verify) *for an* NP *language* $\mathcal{L}$ *has efficient verification if the following is satisfied.*

Efficient Verification: *For all* $(x, w) \in \mathcal{R}$, $\mathsf{crs} \xleftarrow{\$} \mathsf{Setup}(1^\lambda)$, *and* $\pi \xleftarrow{\$}$ $\mathsf{Prove}(\mathsf{crs}, x, w)$, *the running time of* $\mathsf{Verify}(\mathsf{crs}, x, \pi)$ *is* $\mathsf{poly}(\lambda)(|x| + |w|)^{o(1)}$.

Remark 2.3. The efficient verification property immediately implies full succinctness.

Remark 2.4. The efficient verification property is usually a default requirement for SNARGs. On the other hand, we do not assume a SNARG to have efficient verification unless otherwise mentioned. This is because efficient verification is not needed for the construction of a NIZK in this paper.

2.2   NIZK in the Hidden-Bits Model

Here, we define a NIZK in the hidden-bits model introduced in [26]. The following definition is taken from [46].

Definition 2.5 (NIZK in the Hidden-Bits Model). *Let $\mathcal{L}$ be an* NP *language and $\mathcal{R}$ be its associated relation. A non-interactive zero-knowledge proof in the hidden-bits model (HBM-NIZK) for $\mathcal{L}$ consists of the pair of PPT algorithms* $(\mathsf{NIZK}^{\mathsf{hbm}}.\mathsf{Prove}, \mathsf{NIZK}^{\mathsf{hbm}}.\mathsf{Verify})$ *and a polynomial $k = k(\lambda, n)$, which specifies the hidden-bits length.*

$\mathsf{NIZK}^{\mathsf{hbm}}.\mathsf{Prove}(1^\lambda, \rho, x, w) \xrightarrow{\$} (I, \pi)$: *The prover's algorithm takes the security parameter 1^λ, a string $\rho \in \{0, 1\}^{k(\lambda, n)}$, a statement $x \in \{0, 1\}^n$, and a witness w as input, and outputs a subset of indices $I \subseteq [k]$ and a proof π.*
$\mathsf{NIZK}^{\mathsf{hbm}}.\mathsf{Verify}(1^\lambda, I, \rho_I, x, \pi) \rightarrow \top$ *or* $\bot$: *The verifier's algorithm takes the security parameter 1^λ, a subset $I \subseteq [k]$, a string ρ_I, a statement x, and a proof π as input, and outputs $\top$ to indicate acceptance of the proof or $\bot$ otherwise.*

An HBM-NIZK must satisfy the following requirements.

Completeness: *For all pairs* $(x, w) \in \mathcal{R}$, *we have*

$$\Pr\left[\begin{array}{c} \mathsf{NIZK}^{\mathsf{hbm}}.\mathsf{Verify}(1^\lambda, I, \rho_I, x, \pi) \\ = \top \end{array} : \begin{array}{c} \rho \xleftarrow{\$} \{0, 1\}^{k(\lambda, |x|)}; \\ (I, \pi) \xleftarrow{\$} \mathsf{NIZK}^{\mathsf{hbm}}.\mathsf{Prove}(1^\lambda, \rho, x, w) \end{array}\right]$$
$$= 1.$$

ϵ**-Soundness :** *For all polynomials $n = n(\lambda)$ and computationally unbounded adversaries $\mathcal{A}$, we have*

$$\Pr\left[\begin{array}{c} x \in \{0, 1\}^n \setminus \mathcal{L} \\ \wedge \, \mathsf{NIZK}^{\mathsf{hbm}}.\mathsf{Verify}(1^\lambda, I, \rho_I, x, \pi) = \top \end{array} : \begin{array}{c} \rho \xleftarrow{\$} \{0, 1\}^{k(\lambda, n)}; \\ (x, I, \pi) \xleftarrow{\$} \mathcal{A}(\rho) \end{array}\right] \leq \epsilon(\lambda).$$

Zero-Knowledge: *There exists a PPT simulator $\mathsf{NIZK}^{\mathsf{hbm}}.\mathsf{Sim}$ that satisfies the following. For all computationally unbounded adversaries $\mathcal{A} = (\mathcal{A}_1, \mathcal{A}_2)$, we have*

$$\left| \Pr[\mathsf{Expt}_{\mathcal{A}}^{\mathsf{hbmzk\text{-}real}}(\lambda) = 1] - \Pr[\mathsf{Expt}_{\mathcal{A}, \mathsf{NIZK}^{\mathsf{hbm}}.\mathsf{Sim}}^{\mathsf{hbmzk\text{-}sim}}(\lambda) = 1] \right| = \mathsf{negl}(\lambda),$$

where the experiments $\mathsf{Expt}_{\mathcal{A}}^{\mathsf{hbmzk\text{-}real}}(\lambda)$ *and* $\mathsf{Expt}_{\mathcal{A},\mathsf{NIZK}^{\mathsf{hbm}}.\mathsf{Sim}}^{\mathsf{hbmzk\text{-}sim}}(\lambda)$ *are defined as follows, and* $\mathcal{A}_1$'s *output must satisfy* $(x, w) \in \mathcal{R}$.

$\underline{\mathsf{Expt}_{\mathcal{A}}^{\mathsf{hbmzk\text{-}real}}(\lambda):}$

$(x, w, \mathsf{st}) \xleftarrow{\$} \mathcal{A}_1(1^\lambda)$

$\rho \xleftarrow{\$} \{0,1\}^{k(\lambda, |x|)}$

$(I, \pi) \xleftarrow{\$} \mathsf{NIZK}^{\mathsf{hbm}}.\mathsf{Prove}(1^\lambda, \rho, x, w)$

$b' \xleftarrow{\$} \mathcal{A}_2(I, \rho_I, \pi, \mathsf{st})$

Return b'.

$\underline{\mathsf{Expt}_{\mathcal{A},\mathsf{NIZK}^{\mathsf{hbm}}.\mathsf{Sim}}^{\mathsf{hbmzk\text{-}sim}}(\lambda):}$

$(x, w, \mathsf{st}) \xleftarrow{\$} \mathcal{A}_1(1^\lambda)$

$(I, \rho_I, \pi) \xleftarrow{\$} \mathsf{NIZK}^{\mathsf{hbm}}.\mathsf{Sim}(1^\lambda, x)$

$b' \xleftarrow{\$} \mathcal{A}_2(I, \rho_I, \pi, \mathsf{st})$

Return b'.

Lemma 2.2 ([26]). *For any* NP *language* $\mathcal{L}$, *there exists an HBM-NIZK satisfying completeness,* $2^{-\Omega(k)}$*-soundness, and zero-knowledge.*

Remark 2.5. Though Quach et al. [46] also defined a stronger definition of zero-knowledge called *special zero-knowledge*, we omit its definition since we do not use it in security proofs given in this version. We note that we use an HBM-NIZK with special zero-knowledge in a proof of Lemma 3.2, which is given in the full version.

2.3 Leakage-Resilient Weak Pseudorandom Function

Here, we review the definition of a leakage-resilient weak pseudorandom function (LR-wPRF) [37]. Though the definition is essentially the same as that in [37], we make it more explicit that we can arbitrarily set the leakage bound $\ell = \ell(\lambda)$ instead of treating ℓ as a fixed parameter hardwired in a scheme. [9] Specifically, we define parameters of an LR-wPRF including the key length, input length, and output length as polynomials of λ and ℓ. This implicitly means that an evaluation of an LR-wPRF also depends on ℓ since it is given a key and an input whose length depends on ℓ.

Definition 2.6 (Leakage-Resilient Weak Pseudorandom Function). *Let* $\kappa = \kappa(\lambda, \ell)$, $m = m(\lambda, \ell)$, *and* $n = n(\lambda, \ell)$ *be polynomials. A* leakage-resilient weak pseudorandom function (LR-wPRF) *with the key length* κ, *input length* m, *and output length* n, *is a family of efficiently computable functions* $\mathcal{F} = \{F_K : \{0,1\}^m \to \{0,1\}^n\}_{K \in \{0,1\}^\kappa}$ *such that for all polynomials* $\ell = \ell(\lambda)$ *and PPT adversaries* $\mathcal{A} = (\mathcal{A}_1, \mathcal{A}_2)$, *we have*

$$\left| \Pr[\mathsf{Expt}_{\mathcal{F},\mathcal{A}}^{\mathsf{LRwPRF\text{-}0}}(\lambda, \ell) = 1] - \Pr[\mathsf{Expt}_{\mathcal{F},\mathcal{A}}^{\mathsf{LRwPRF\text{-}1}}(\lambda, \ell) = 1] \right| = \mathsf{negl}(\lambda),$$

where the experiment $\mathsf{Expt}_{\mathcal{F},\mathcal{A}}^{\mathsf{LRwPRF\text{-}b}}(\lambda, \ell)$ *(with* $b \in \{0,1\}$*) is described in Fig. 1.*

Hazay et al. [37] showed how to construct an LR-wPRF from a OWF. Their result can be stated in the following form that is convenient for our purpose.

---

[9] Syntactically, this treatment of the leakage bound ℓ is similar to a cryptographic primitive in the bounded retrieval model (BRM). Unlike the BRM, however, we do not pose any efficiency requirement on the scheme regarding the dependency on the given leakage bound ℓ.

$$\begin{array}{llll}
\mathsf{Expt}_{\mathcal{F},\mathcal{A}}^{\mathsf{LRwPRF\text{-}b}}(\lambda,\ell): & F_K(\$): & \mathsf{Chal}(\$): \\
\quad L \leftarrow 0 & \quad x \xleftarrow{\$} \{0,1\}^{m(\lambda,\ell)} & \quad x^* \xleftarrow{\$} \{0,1\}^{m(\lambda,\ell)} \\
\quad K \xleftarrow{\$} \{0,1\}^{\kappa(\lambda,\ell)} & \quad \text{Return } (x, F_K(x)). & \quad \begin{cases} y^* := F_K(x^*) & \text{if } b=0 \\ y^* \xleftarrow{\$} \{0,1\}^{n(\lambda,\ell)} & \text{if } b=1 \end{cases} \\
\quad \mathsf{st} \xleftarrow{\$} \mathcal{A}_1^{F_K(\$),\mathsf{Leak}(\cdot)}(1^\lambda, 1^\ell) & \mathsf{Leak}(f): & \quad \text{Return } (x^*, y^*). \\
\quad b' \xleftarrow{\$} \mathcal{A}_2^{\mathsf{Chal}(\$)}(\mathsf{st}) & \quad L \leftarrow L + |f(K)| & \\
\quad \text{Return } b'. & \quad \text{If } L > \ell \text{ then return } \bot. & \\
& \quad \text{Return } f(K). &
\end{array}$$

Fig. 1. The experiment for defining the leakage-resilience for a wPRF.

Theorem 2.1 ([37]). *If there exists a OWF, then there exists an LR-wPRF with the key length $\kappa = \ell \cdot \mathsf{poly}(\lambda)$, input length $m = \ell \cdot \mathsf{poly}(\lambda)$, and output length $n = 1$.*

Remark 2.6. Actually, Hazay et al. showed that we can set $\kappa = O(\ell\lambda/\log\lambda)$, $m = O(\ell\lambda)$, and n to be any polynomial in λ. We state the theorem in the above form since this is sufficient for our purpose.

3   Non-adaptive to Adaptive Zero-Knowledge for NIZK

In this section, we show the following theorem.

Theorem 3.1. *If there exist a OWF and a NIZK for all NP languages that satisfies adaptive computational (resp. statistical) soundness and non-adaptive single-theorem zero-knowledge, then there exists a NIZK for all NP languages that satisfies adaptive computational (resp. statistical) soundness and adaptive multi-theorem zero-knowledge.*

Remark 3.1. The theorem remains true even if we start from a NIZK with non-adaptive statistical soundness since we can convert it into one with adaptive statistical soundness while preserving the zero-knowledge property by a simple parallel repetition. On the other hand, we do not know whether the theorem remains true if we start from a NIZK with *non-adaptive computational* soundness.

HBG from Non-adaptive NIZK. First, we show that we can construct an HBG by combining a non-interactive commitment scheme, a PRG, and a NIZK in a straightforward manner.[10] We note that Dwork and Naor [24] already mentioned a similar construction.[11] Our crucial observation is that non-adaptive multi-theorem zero-knowledge is sufficient for this purpose. Moreover, as stated in Lemma 2.1, we can generically upgrade non-adaptive single-theorem zero-knowledge to non-adaptive multi-theorem zero-knowledge. Therefore, we obtain the following lemma.

---

[10] A formal definition of HBG can be found in the full version.

[11] Dwork and Naor [24] constructed what they call a *verifiable pseudorandom generator* from a NIZK, which is a similar primitive to an HBG.

Lemma 3.1. *If there exist a OWF and a NIZK for all* NP *languages that satisfies adaptive computational (resp. statistical) soundness and non-adaptive single-theorem zero-knowledge, then there exists an HBG that satisfies succinct commitment, computational (resp. statistical) binding, and computational hiding.*

Since the construction and security proof are straightforward, we omit them here and give them in the full version.

Adaptive NIZK from HBG. Quach et al. [46] gave a construction of a NIZK with adaptive statistical soundness and adaptive multi-theorem zero-knowledge based on an HBG with statistical binding and computational hiding. It is easy to see that the same construction works for a computationally binding HBG to construct an adaptively computationally sound NIZK. Namely, we have the following lemma.

Lemma 3.2. *If there exist a OWF and an HBG that satisfies succinct commitment, computational (resp. statistical) binding, and computational hiding, then there exists a NIZK for all* NP *languages that satisfies adaptive computational (resp. statistical) soundness and adaptive multi-theorem zero-knowledge.*

Since the construction and proof are essentially the same as those in [46], we omit them here, and give them in the full version.

Theorem 3.1 can be obtained by combining Lemmata 3.1 and 3.2.

4 Hidden-Bits Generator with Subset-Dependent Proofs

In this section, we introduce a weaker variant of an HBG that we call an *HBG with subset-dependent proofs* (SDP-HBG). We also give a construction of an SDP-HBG from the combination of a SNARG and an LR-wPRF (and thus, from a SNARG and a OWF).

4.1 Definition

Here, we define an SDP-HBG.

Definition 4.1 (SDP-HBG). *A hidden-bits generator with subset dependent proofs (SDP-HBG) consists of the four PPT algorithms* $(\mathsf{HBG}^{\mathsf{sdp}}.\mathsf{Setup}, \mathsf{HBG}^{\mathsf{sdp}}.\mathsf{GenBits}, \mathsf{HBG}^{\mathsf{sdp}}.\mathsf{Prove}, \mathsf{HBG}^{\mathsf{sdp}}.\mathsf{Verify})$:

$\mathsf{HBG}^{\mathsf{sdp}}.\mathsf{Setup}(1^\lambda, 1^k) \xrightarrow{\$} \mathsf{crs}$: *The setup algorithm takes the security parameter* 1^λ *and the length parameter* 1^k *as input, and outputs a CRS* crs.

$\mathsf{HBG}^{\mathsf{sdp}}.\mathsf{GenBits}(\mathsf{crs}) \xrightarrow{\$} (r, \mathsf{st})$: *The bits generation algorithm takes a CRS* crs *as input, and outputs a string* $r \in \{0,1\}^k$ *and a state* st.

$\mathsf{HBG}^{\mathsf{sdp}}.\mathsf{Prove}(\mathsf{st}, I) \xrightarrow{\$} \pi$: *The proving algorithm takes a state* st *and a subset* $I \subseteq [k]$ *as input, and outputs a proof* π.

$\mathsf{HBG}^{\mathsf{sdp}}.\mathsf{Verify}(\mathsf{crs}, I, r_I, \pi) \rightarrow \top$ *or* $\bot$: *The verification algorithm takes a CRS* crs, *a subset* $I \subseteq [k]$, *a string* $r_I \in \{0,1\}^{|I|}$, *and a proof* π *as input, and outputs* $\top$ *indicating acceptance or* $\bot$ *otherwise.*

We require an SDP-HBG to satisfy the following properties:

Correctness: *For any natural number k and $I \subseteq [k]$, we have*

$$\Pr \left[\mathsf{HBG}^{\mathsf{sdp}}.\mathsf{Verify}(\mathsf{crs}, I, r_I, \pi) = \top : \begin{array}{l} \mathsf{crs} \xleftarrow{\$} \mathsf{HBG}^{\mathsf{sdp}}.\mathsf{Setup}(1^\lambda, 1^k); \\ (r, \mathsf{st}) \xleftarrow{\$} \mathsf{HBG}^{\mathsf{sdp}}.\mathsf{GenBits}(\mathsf{crs}); \\ \pi \xleftarrow{\$} \mathsf{HBG}^{\mathsf{sdp}}.\mathsf{Prove}(\mathsf{st}, I) \end{array} \right] = 1.$$

Somewhat Computational Binding: *There exists a constant $\gamma < 1$ such that (1) for any polynomial $k = k(\lambda)$ and crs generated by $\mathsf{HBG}^{\mathsf{sdp}}.\mathsf{Setup}(1^\lambda, 1^k)$, there exists a subset $\mathcal{V}^{\mathsf{crs}} \subseteq \{0,1\}^k$ such that $|\mathcal{V}^{\mathsf{crs}}| \leq 2^{k^\gamma \mathsf{poly}(\lambda)}$, and (2) for any PPT adversary $\mathcal{A}$, we have*

$$\Pr \left[\begin{array}{l} r_I \notin \mathcal{V}_I^{\mathsf{crs}} \\ \wedge\, \mathsf{HBG}^{\mathsf{sdp}}.\mathsf{Verify}(\mathsf{crs}, I, r_I, \pi) = \top \end{array} : \begin{array}{l} \mathsf{crs} \xleftarrow{\$} \mathsf{HBG}^{\mathsf{sdp}}.\mathsf{Setup}(1^\lambda, 1^k); \\ (I, r_I, \pi) \xleftarrow{\$} \mathcal{A}(\mathsf{crs}) \end{array} \right]$$
$$= \mathsf{negl}(\lambda),$$

where $\mathcal{V}_I^{\mathsf{crs}} := \{r_I : r \in \mathcal{V}^{\mathsf{crs}}\}$.

Computational Hiding: *For any polynomial $k = k(\lambda)$, $I \subseteq [k]$, and PPT adversary $\mathcal{A}$, we have*

$$\left| \Pr[\mathcal{A}(\mathsf{crs}, I, r_I, \pi, r_{\overline{I}}) = 1] - \Pr[\mathcal{A}(\mathsf{crs}, I, r_I, \pi, r'_{\overline{I}}) = 1] \right| = \mathsf{negl}(\lambda),$$

where we generate $\mathsf{crs} \xleftarrow{\$} \mathsf{HBG}^{\mathsf{sdp}}.\mathsf{Setup}(1^\lambda, 1^k)$, $(r, \mathsf{st}) \xleftarrow{\$} \mathsf{HBG}^{\mathsf{sdp}}.\mathsf{GenBits}(\mathsf{crs})$, $\pi \xleftarrow{\$} \mathsf{HBG}^{\mathsf{sdp}}.\mathsf{Prove}(\mathsf{st}, I)$, and $r' \xleftarrow{\$} \{0,1\}^k$.

An SDP-HBG can be seen as a weaker variant of an ordinary HBG, in the sense that the former can be naturally constructed from the latter. A proof can be found in the full version.

4.2   Construction

Here, we give a construction of an SDP-HBG from a SNARG and a OWF.

Theorem 4.1 *If there exist a OWF and a δ-slightly succinct SNARG for all NP languages for some $\delta < 1/2$ that satisfies adaptive computational soundness, then there exists an SDP-HBG that satisfies somewhat computational binding and computational hiding.*

Our construction of an SDP-HBG uses the following ingredients.

- An LR-wPRF $\mathcal{F} = \{F_K : \{0,1\}^m \to \{0,1\}\}_{K \in \{0,1\}^\kappa}$, built from a OWF via Theorem 2.1, with the key length $\kappa = \kappa(\lambda, \ell) = \ell \cdot \mathsf{poly}(\lambda)$, input length $m = m(\lambda, \ell) = \ell \cdot \mathsf{poly}(\lambda)$, and output length 1.
- A δ-slightly succinct SNARG $(\mathsf{SNARG.Setup}, \mathsf{SNARG.Prove}, \mathsf{SNARG.Verify})$ for some $\delta < 1/2$ for the language $\mathcal{L}$ associated with the relation $\mathcal{R}$ defined as follows:

$$\left((k', \{x_i\}_{i \in [k']}, \{r_i\}_{i \in [k']}), K \right) \in \mathcal{R} \iff r_i = F_K(x_i) \text{ for all } i \in [k'].$$

In our construction of an SDP-HBG, the leakage bound ℓ of the underlying LR-wPRF is chosen depending on the length parameter k input to the setup algorithm of the SDP-HBG, so that

(a) $\kappa \le k^\gamma \cdot \text{poly}(\lambda)$ holds for some constant $\gamma < 1$, and
(b) for any $k' \le k$, $x_i \in \{0,1\}^m$ for $i \in [k']$, $r_i \in \{0,1\}$ for $i \in [k']$, and $K \in \{0,1\}^\kappa$, if $\text{crs}_{\text{snarg}} \xleftarrow{\$} \text{SNARG.Setup}(1^\lambda)$ and $\pi \xleftarrow{\$} \text{SNARG.Prove}(\text{crs}_{\text{snarg}}, (k', \{x_i\}_{i \in [k']}, \{r_i\}_{i \in [k']}), K)$, then we have $|\pi| \le \ell$.

Below we explain how we choose such ℓ.

Recall that the δ-slight succinctness of the SNARG ensures that the size of a proof π generated from a statement/witness pair $(x, w) \in \mathcal{R}$ satisfies $|\pi| \le (|x| + |w|)^\delta \cdot \text{poly}(\lambda)$. In our case, the bit-length of a statement $x = (k', \{x_i\}_{i \in [k']}, \{r_i\}_{i \in [k']})$ is bounded by $\log k + k \cdot (m+1) \le k \cdot (m+2) = k\ell \cdot \text{poly}(\lambda)$, and the bit-length of a witness $w = K$ is just $\kappa = \ell \cdot \text{poly}(\lambda)$. Hence, the size of a proof π generated by SNARG.Prove for (x, w) is bounded by

$$|\pi| \le (k\ell \cdot \text{poly}(\lambda) + \ell \cdot \text{poly}(\lambda))^\delta \cdot \text{poly}(\lambda) \le (k\ell)^\delta \cdot p,$$

for some polynomial $p = \text{poly}(\lambda)$ that is independent of k and ℓ.

Then we set the leakage bound $\ell = \ell(\lambda, k)$ as

$$\ell := k^{\frac{\delta}{1-\delta}} \cdot p^{\frac{1}{1-\delta}}.$$

Since we assume $\delta < 1/2$, we have $\frac{\delta}{1-\delta} < 1$. Thus the property (a) is satisfied with $\gamma := \frac{\delta}{1-\delta}$. Furthermore, we have

$$|\pi| \le (k\ell)^\delta \cdot p = k^{\frac{\delta}{1-\delta}} p^{\frac{1}{1-\delta}} = \ell.$$

Hence, the property (b) is also satisfied, as desired.

Using the above ingredients, our construction of an SDP-HBG ($\text{HBG}^{\text{sdp}}.\text{Setup}$, $\text{HBG}^{\text{sdp}}.\text{GenBits}$, $\text{HBG}^{\text{sdp}}.\text{Prove}$, $\text{HBG}^{\text{sdp}}.\text{Verify}$) is described in Fig. 2. In the description, x_I is a short hand for $\{x_i\}_{i \in I}$.

It is easy to see that the construction satisfies correctness. The security properties of the SDP-HBG are guaranteed by the following theorem.

Theorem 4.2. *The above SDP-HBG satisfies somewhat computational binding and computational hiding.*

Proof. We start by showing somewhat computational binding, then computational hiding.

Somewhat Computational Binding. For a CRS $\text{crs} = (\text{crs}_{\text{snarg}}, \{x_i\}_{i \in [k]})$ output from $\text{HBG}^{\text{sdp}}.\text{Setup}(1^\lambda, 1^k)$, we define $\mathcal{V}^{\text{crs}} := \{(F_K(x_1), \ldots, F_K(x_k)) \mid K \in \{0,1\}^\kappa\}$. Then, since $|K| = \kappa \le k^\gamma \text{poly}(\lambda)$, we have $|\mathcal{V}^{\text{crs}}| \le 2^{k^\gamma \text{poly}(\lambda)}$. Furthermore, it is straightforward to see that by the soundness of the underlying SNARG, no PPT adversary can generate a valid proof for (I, r_I) that is inconsistent with any element of $\mathcal{V}$. More specifically, any PPT adversary that given $\text{crs} = (\text{crs}_{\text{snarg}}, \{x_i\}_{i \in [k]})$ outputs a tuple (I, r_I, π) satisfying $\text{SNARG.Verify}(\text{crs}_{\text{snarg}}, (|I|,$

HBG^{sdp}.Setup$(1^\lambda, 1^k)$:	HBG^{sdp}.GenBits(crs) :
crs$_{\mathsf{snarg}} \xleftarrow{\$} $ SNARG.Setup(1^λ)	$(\mathsf{crs}_{\mathsf{snarg}}, \{x_i\}_{i \in [k]}) \leftarrow \mathsf{crs}$
$\forall i \in [k] : x_i \xleftarrow{\$} \{0,1\}^m$	$K \xleftarrow{\$} \{0,1\}^\kappa$
Return crs $= (\mathsf{crs}_{\mathsf{snarg}}, \{x_i\}_{i \in [k]})$.	$\forall i \in [k] : r_i \leftarrow F_K(x_i)$
	Return $(r = \{r_i\}_{i \in [k]}, \mathsf{st} = (\mathsf{crs}, K, r))$.
HBG^{sdp}.Prove(st, I) :	HBG^{sdp}.Verify$(\mathsf{crs}, I, r_I, \pi)$:
$(\mathsf{crs}, K, r) \leftarrow \mathsf{st}$	$(\mathsf{crs}_{\mathsf{snarg}}, \{x_i\}_{i \in [k]}) \leftarrow \mathsf{crs}$
$(\mathsf{crs}_{\mathsf{snarg}}, \{x_i\}_{i \in [k]}) \leftarrow \mathsf{crs}$	$X := (|I|, x_I, r_I)$
$X := (|I|, x_I, r_I)$	Return SNARG.Verify$(\mathsf{crs}_{\mathsf{snarg}}, X, \pi)$.
$\pi \xleftarrow{\$} $ SNARG.Prove$(\mathsf{crs}_{\mathsf{snarg}}, X, K)$	
Return π.	

Fig. 2. The construction of an SDP-HBG based on an LR-wPRF and a SNARG.

$x_I, r_I), \pi) = \top$ and $r_I \notin \mathcal{V}_I^{\mathsf{crs}}$, can be straightforwardly turned into a PPT adversary that breaks the adaptive soundness of the underlying SNARG, since $r_I \notin \mathcal{V}_I^{\mathsf{crs}}$ implies $(|I|, x_I, r_I) \notin \mathcal{L}$.

Computational Hiding. It is easy to reduce the computational hiding of our SDP-HBG to the security of the underlying LR-wPRF in which the leakage bound is ℓ, by noting that the leakage from K is π whose size is at most ℓ. Formally, given any polynomial $k = k(\lambda)$, $I \subseteq [k]$, and PPT adversary $\mathcal{A}$, consider the following PPT adversary $\mathcal{B} = (\mathcal{B}_1, \mathcal{B}_2)$ that attacks the security of the underlying LR-wPRF with the leakage bound ℓ.

$\mathcal{B}_1^{F_K(\$), \mathsf{Leak}(\cdot)}(1^\lambda)$: (where $K \xleftarrow{\$} \{0,1\}^\kappa$) $\mathcal{B}_1$ makes $|I|$ queries to the oracle $F_K(\$)$, and regards the returned values from the oracle as $\{(x_i, r_i = F_K(x_i))\}_{i \in [I]}$. Next, $\mathcal{B}_1$ computes $\mathsf{crs}_{\mathsf{snarg}} \xleftarrow{\$} $ SNARG.Setup(1^λ), and defines the circuit $f :$ $\{0,1\}^\kappa \to \{0,1\}^\ell$ by $f(\cdot) := $ SNARG.Prove$(\mathsf{crs}_{\mathsf{crs}}, (|I|, x_I, r_I), \cdot)$. Then, $\mathcal{B}_1$ submits $f(\cdot)$ to the oracle $\mathsf{Leak}(\cdot)$, and receives π. Finally, $\mathcal{B}_1$ sets $\mathsf{st}_\mathcal{B}$ as all the information known to $\mathcal{B}_1$, and terminates with output $\mathsf{st}_\mathcal{B}$.

$\mathcal{B}_2^{\mathsf{Chal}(\$)}(\mathsf{st}_\mathcal{B})$: $\mathcal{B}_2$ submits $k - |I|$ queries to the challenge oracle $\mathsf{Chal}(\$)$, and regards the returned values from the oracle as $\{(x_i, r_i)\}_{i \in \overline{I}}$. Note that $r_i = F_K(x_i)$ if $b = 0$ and $r_i \xleftarrow{\$} \{0,1\}$ if $b = 1$, where b is $\mathcal{B}$'s challenge bit. Now, $\mathcal{B}_2$ sets $\mathsf{crs} := (\mathsf{crs}_{\mathsf{snarg}}, \{x_i\}_{i \in [k]})$, and runs $\mathcal{A}(\mathsf{crs}, I, r_I, \pi, r_{\overline{I}})$. When $\mathcal{A}$ terminates with output b', $\mathcal{B}_2$ outputs b' and terminates.

Since $|f(\cdot)| = \ell$, $\mathcal{B}$ complies with the rule of the LR-wPRF security experiment with the leakage bound ℓ. Furthermore, it is straightforward to see that if $b = 0$, then the pairs $\{(x_i, r_i)\}_{i \in \overline{I}}$ that $\mathcal{B}_2$ receives from the challenge oracle satisfy $F_K(x_i) = r_i$, and $\mathcal{B}$ simulates the computational hiding experiment in the case $r_{\overline{I}}$ is the real randomness generated by HBG^{sdp}.GenBits(crs), perfectly for $\mathcal{A}$. On the other hand, if $b = 1$, then $\{r_i\}_{i \in \overline{I}}$ are random bits, and $\mathcal{B}_2$ simulates the experiment of the opposite case (i.e. $r_{\overline{I}} = \{r_i\}_{i \in \overline{I}}$ is random) perfectly for $\mathcal{A}$. Hence, $\mathcal{B}$'s advantage in breaking the security of the underlying LR-wPRF is exactly the same as $\mathcal{A}$'s advantage in breaking the computational hiding property of our SDP-HBG. $\qquad\square$

5   NIZK from SDP-HBG

In this section, we show the following theorem.

Theorem 5.1. *If there exists an SDP-HBG, then there exists a NIZK for all* NP *languages that satisfies adaptive computational soundness and non-adaptive single-theorem zero-knowledge.*

Combining Theorems 3.1, 4.1 and 5.1, we obtain the following theorem.

Theorem 5.2. *If there exist a OWF and a δ-slightly succinct SNARG for all* NP *languages for some $\delta < 1/2$ that satisfies adaptive computational soundness, then there exists a NIZK for all* NP *languages that satisfies adaptive soundness and adaptive multi-theorem zero-knowledge.*

In the following, we prove Theorem 5.1. The construction of our NIZK is almost the same as the scheme by Quach, Rothblum, and Wichs [46], except that we use an SDP-HBG instead of an HBG.

Construction. Our NIZK uses the following ingredients:

- An SDP-HBG ($\mathsf{HBG}^{\mathsf{sdp}}.\mathsf{Setup}, \mathsf{HBG}^{\mathsf{sdp}}.\mathsf{GenBits}, \mathsf{HBG}^{\mathsf{sdp}}.\mathsf{Prove}, \mathsf{HBG}^{\mathsf{sdp}}.\mathsf{Verify}$).
- An HBM-NIZK ($\mathsf{NIZK}^{\mathsf{hbm}}.\mathsf{Prove}, \mathsf{NIZK}^{\mathsf{hbm}}.\mathsf{Verify}$) for an NP language $\mathcal{L}$ with ϵ-soundness.

Let $\gamma < 1$ be the constant regarding the somewhat computational binding of the SDP-HBG, which satisfies $|\mathcal{V}^{\mathsf{crs_{bgen}}}| \leq 2^{k^{\gamma}\mathsf{poly}(\lambda)}$ for all $\mathsf{crs_{bgen}}$ generated by $\mathsf{HBG}^{\mathsf{sdp}}.\mathsf{Setup}(1^{\lambda}, 1^{k})$. When we use an HBM-NIZK with the random-string length k, we can make $\epsilon = 2^{-\Omega(k)}$ as stated in Lemma 2.2. Therefore, we can take $k = k(\lambda) = \mathsf{poly}(\lambda)$ so that $|\mathcal{V}^{\mathsf{crs}}| \cdot \epsilon = \mathsf{negl}(\lambda)$ holds. We fix such k in the following.

Then, our construction of a NIZK for $\mathcal{L}$ is described in Fig. 3.

It is easy to see that the construction satisfies completeness. The security properties of the NIZK is guaranteed by the following theorem.

Theorem 5.3. *The above NIZK satisfies adaptive computational soundness and non-adaptive single-theorem zero-knowledge.*

Proof. We start by showing soundness, and then zero-knowledge.

Adaptive Computational Soundness. Let $\mathcal{A}$ be any PPT adversary that attacks the adaptive soundness of our NIZK. Let Win be the event that $\mathcal{A}$ succeeds in breaking the adaptive soundness (i.e. $\mathsf{NIZK}.\mathsf{Verify}(\mathsf{crs}, x, \pi) = \top$ and $x \notin \mathcal{L}$). Suppose $\mathcal{A}$ on input $\mathsf{crs} = (\mathsf{crs_{bgen}}, s)$ outputs a pair $(x, \pi = (I, \pi_{\mathsf{hbm}}, r_I, \pi_{\mathsf{bgen}}))$. Let $\mathcal{V}^{\mathsf{crs_{bgen}}} \subseteq \{0,1\}^{k}$ be the set with which the somewhat computational binding of the underlying SDP-HBG is considered. We have

$$\Pr[\mathsf{Win}] = \Pr[\mathsf{Win} \wedge r_I \notin \mathcal{V}_I^{\mathsf{crs_{bgen}}}] + \Pr[\mathsf{Win} \wedge r_I \in \mathcal{V}_I^{\mathsf{crs_{bgen}}}].$$

It is straightforward to see that $\Pr[\mathsf{Win} \wedge r_I \notin \mathcal{V}_I^{\mathsf{crs_{bgen}}}] = \mathsf{negl}(\lambda)$ holds by the somewhat computational binding of the underlying SDP-HBG.

NIZK.Setup(1^λ) :	NIZK.Prove(crs, x, w) :
$\mathsf{crs_{bgen}} \xleftarrow{\$} \mathsf{HBG^{sdp}.Setup}(1^\lambda, 1^k)$	$(\mathsf{crs_{bgen}}, s) \leftarrow \mathsf{crs}$
$s \xleftarrow{\$} \{0,1\}^k$	$(r, \mathsf{st}) \xleftarrow{\$} \mathsf{HBG^{sdp}.GenBits(crs_{bgen})}$
Return $\mathsf{crs} := (\mathsf{crs_{bgen}}, s)$.	$\rho \leftarrow s \oplus r$
	$(I, \pi_\mathsf{hbm}) \xleftarrow{\$} \mathsf{NIZK^{hbm}.Prove}(\rho, x, w)$
	$\pi_\mathsf{bgen} \xleftarrow{\$} \mathsf{HBG^{sdp}.Prove(st}, I)$
	Return $\pi := (I, \pi_\mathsf{hbm}, r_I, \pi_\mathsf{bgen})$.
NIZK.Verify(crs, x, π) :	
$(\mathsf{crs_{bgen}}, s) \leftarrow \mathsf{crs}$	
$(I, \pi_\mathsf{hbm}, r_I, \pi_\mathsf{bgen}) \leftarrow \pi$	
$\rho_I \leftarrow s_I \oplus r_I$	
If (a) $\wedge$ (b) then return $\top$ else return $\bot$:	
– (a) $\mathsf{NIZK^{hbm}.Verify}(I, \rho_I, x, \pi_\mathsf{hbm}) = \top$	
– (b) $\mathsf{HBG^{sdp}.Verify(crs_{bgen}}, I, r_I, \pi_\mathsf{bgen}) = \top$	

Fig. 3. The construction of a NIZK based on an SDP-HBG and an HBM-NIZK.

Hence, it remains to show $P := \Pr[\mathsf{Win} \wedge r_I \in \mathcal{V}_I^{\mathsf{crs_{bgen}}}] = \mathsf{negl}(\lambda)$. Fix $\mathsf{crs_{bgen}^*}$ in the image of $\mathsf{HBG^{sdp}.Setup}(1^\lambda, 1^k)$ and $\mathcal{A}$'s randomness $r_\mathcal{A}^*$ that maximize the above probability P. Let $\mathcal{V}^* := \mathcal{V}^{\mathsf{crs_{bgen}^*}}$. Let $F(\cdot)$ be the function that on input $s \in \{0,1\}^k$, computes $(x, \pi = (I, \pi_\mathsf{hbm}, r_I, \pi_\mathsf{bgen})) \leftarrow \mathcal{A}(\mathsf{crs} = (\mathsf{crs_{bgen}^*}, s); r_\mathcal{A}^*)$, and outputs $(x, I, \pi_\mathsf{hbm}, r_I)$. (Looking ahead, F is essentially an adversary against the ϵ-soundness of the underlying HBM-NIZK.) Let P' be the following probability:

$$P' := \Pr\left[\begin{array}{l}\mathsf{NIZK^{hbm}.Verify}(I, s_I \oplus r_I, x, \pi_\mathsf{hbm}) = \top \\ \wedge\, r_I \in \mathcal{V}_I^* \wedge x \notin \mathcal{L}\end{array} : \begin{array}{l}s \xleftarrow{\$} \{0,1\}^k; \\ (x, I, \pi_\mathsf{hbm}, r_I) \leftarrow F(s)\end{array}\right].$$

$\mathcal{S}(1^\lambda, x)$:
$(I, \rho_I, \pi_\mathsf{hbm}) \xleftarrow{\$} \mathsf{NIZK^{hbm}.Sim}(x)$
$\mathsf{crs_{bgen}} \xleftarrow{\$} \mathsf{HBG^{sdp}.Setup}(1^\lambda, 1^k)$
$(r, \mathsf{st}) \xleftarrow{\$} \mathsf{HBG^{sdp}.GenBits(crs_{bgen})}$
$\pi_\mathsf{bgen} \xleftarrow{\$} \mathsf{HBG^{sdp}.Prove(st}, I)$
$s_I := \rho_I \oplus r_I$
$s_{\overline{I}} \xleftarrow{\$} \{0,1\}^{k-|I|}$
$\mathsf{crs} := (\mathsf{crs_{bgen}}, s)$
$\pi := (I, \pi_\mathsf{hbm}, r_I, \pi_\mathsf{bgen})$
Return (crs, π).

Fig. 4. The simulator for showing non-adaptive single-theorem zero-knowledge in the proof of Theorem 5.3.

Clearly, we have $P \leq P'$. We also have

$$P' = \sum_{r' \in \mathcal{V}^*} \Pr \left[\begin{array}{l} \mathsf{NIZK^{hbm}.Verify}(I, s_I \oplus r_I, x, \pi_{\mathsf{hbm}}) = \top \\ \wedge \ r_I = r_I' \wedge x \notin \mathcal{L} \end{array} : \begin{array}{l} s \xleftarrow{\$} \{0,1\}^k; \\ (x, I, \pi_{\mathsf{hbm}}, r_I) \leftarrow F(s) \end{array} \right]$$

$$\leq |\mathcal{V}^*| \cdot \max_{r^* \in \mathcal{V}^*} \Pr \left[\begin{array}{l} \mathsf{NIZK^{hbm}.Verify}(I, s_I \oplus r_I, x, \pi_{\mathsf{hbm}}) = \top \\ \wedge \ r_I = r_I^* \wedge x \notin \mathcal{L} \end{array} : \begin{array}{l} s \xleftarrow{\$} \{0,1\}^k; \\ (x, I, \pi_{\mathsf{hbm}}, r_I) \leftarrow F(s) \end{array} \right]$$

$$= |\mathcal{V}^*| \cdot \max_{r^* \in \mathcal{V}^*} \Pr \left[\begin{array}{l} \mathsf{NIZK^{hbm}.Verify}(I, \rho_I, x, \pi_{\mathsf{hbm}}) = \top \\ \wedge \ r_I = r_I^* \wedge x \notin \mathcal{L} \end{array} : \begin{array}{l} \rho \xleftarrow{\$} \{0,1\}^k; \\ (x, I, \pi_{\mathsf{hbm}}, r_I) \leftarrow F(\rho \oplus r^*) \end{array} \right]$$

$$\leq |\mathcal{V}^*| \cdot \max_{r^* \in \mathcal{V}^*} \Pr \left[\begin{array}{l} \mathsf{NIZK^{hbm}.Verify}(I, \rho_I, x, \pi_{\mathsf{hbm}}) = \top \\ \wedge \ x \notin \mathcal{L} \end{array} : \begin{array}{l} \rho \xleftarrow{\$} \{0,1\}^k; \\ (x, I, \pi_{\mathsf{hbm}}, r_I) \leftarrow F(\rho \oplus r^*) \end{array} \right]$$

$$\leq |\mathcal{V}^*| \cdot \epsilon(k) = \mathsf{negl}(\lambda),$$

where the last inequality uses the ϵ-soundness of the underlying HBM-NIZK which we consider for the adversary $\mathcal{B}(\rho)$ that outputs $F(\rho \oplus r^*)$ other than r_I, and the last equality is due to our choice of k. Hence, we have $P = \Pr[\mathsf{Win} \wedge r_I \in \mathcal{V}_I^{\mathsf{crs_{bgen}}}] = \mathsf{negl}(\lambda)$ as well.

Combined together, we have seen that $\mathcal{A}$'s advantage in breaking the adaptive soundness of our NIZK is negligible. This implies that our NIZK satisfies adaptive soundness.

Non-adaptive Single-Theorem Zero-Knowledge. Let $\mathsf{NIZK^{hbm}.Sim}$ be the simulator that is guaranteed to exist by the zero-knowledge of the underlying HBM-NIZK. Using $\mathsf{NIZK^{hbm}.Sim}$, we first give the description of the simulator $\mathcal{S}$ in Fig. 4 for showing the non-adaptive single-theorem zero-knowledge of our NIZK.

We prove the non-adaptive single-theorem zero-knowledge of the above NIZK via a sequence of games argument using four games, among which the first game Game_1 (resp. the final game Game_4) is exactly the real (resp. simulated) experiment. Let $\mathcal{A} = (\mathcal{A}_1, \mathcal{A}_2)$ be any PPT adversary that attacks the non-adaptive single-theorem zero-knowledge of the above NIZK. For $j \in [4]$, let T_j be the event that $\mathcal{A}_2$ finally outputs 1 in Game_j. The description of the games is as follows.

Game_1: This is exactly the real experiment $\mathsf{Expt}_{\mathcal{A}}^{\mathsf{nazk\text{-}real}}$. We have $\Pr[\mathsf{T}_1] = \Pr[\mathsf{Expt}_{\mathcal{A}}^{\mathsf{nazk\text{-}real}}(\lambda) = 1]$.

Game_2: We change the ordering of the steps of Game_1, and furthermore "program" s by first choosing $\rho \xleftarrow{\$} \{0,1\}^k$ and then setting $s := \rho \oplus r$, without changing the distribution of $\mathcal{A}$'s view. Specifically, this game proceeds as follows.

    1. Run $(x, w, \mathsf{st}_{\mathcal{A}}) \xleftarrow{\$} \mathcal{A}_1(1^\lambda)$.

    2. Pick $\rho \xleftarrow{\$} \{0,1\}^k$.

    3. Compute $(\pi_{\mathsf{hbm}}, I) \xleftarrow{\$} \mathsf{NIZK^{hbm}.Prove}(\rho, x, w)$.

    4. Compute $\mathsf{crs_{bgen}} \xleftarrow{\$} \mathsf{HBG^{sdp}.Setup}(1^\lambda, 1^k)$.

    5. Compute $(r, \mathsf{st}) \xleftarrow{\$} \mathsf{HBG^{sdp}.GenBits}(\mathsf{crs_{bgen}})$.

6. Compute $\pi_{\mathsf{bgen}} \overset{\$}{\leftarrow} \mathsf{HBG}^{\mathsf{sdp}}.\mathsf{Prove}(\mathsf{st}, I)$.
7. Set $s_I := \rho_I \oplus r_I$.
8. Set $s_{\overline{I}} := \rho_{\overline{I}} \oplus r_{\overline{I}}$.[12]
9. Set $\mathsf{crs} := (\mathsf{crs}_{\mathsf{bgen}}, s)$ and $\pi := (I, \pi_{\mathsf{hbm}}, r_I, \pi_{\mathsf{bgen}})$.
10. Run $b' \overset{\$}{\leftarrow} \mathcal{A}_2(\mathsf{crs}, \pi, \mathsf{st}_{\mathcal{A}})$.

It is easy to see that the distribution of $\mathcal{A}$'s view has not been changed from Game_1. Hence, we have $\Pr[\mathsf{T}_1] = \Pr[\mathsf{T}_2]$.

Game_3: This game is identical to the previous game, except that the 8th step "$s_{\overline{I}} := \rho_{\overline{I}} \oplus r_{\overline{I}}$" is replaced with "$s_{\overline{I}} \overset{\$}{\leftarrow} \{0,1\}^{k-|I|}$".
It is straightforward to see that $|\Pr[\mathsf{T}_2] - \Pr[\mathsf{T}_3]| = \mathsf{negl}(\lambda)$ holds by the computational hiding of the underlying SDP-HBG.

Game_4: This game is identical to the previous game, except that $(\rho, \pi_{\mathsf{hbm}}, I)$ is generated as $(\rho_I, \pi_{\mathsf{hbm}}, I) \overset{\$}{\leftarrow} \mathsf{NIZK}^{\mathsf{hbm}}.\mathsf{Sim}(x)$, instead of picking $\rho \overset{\$}{\leftarrow} \{0,1\}^k$ and then executing $(\pi_{\mathsf{hbm}}, I) \overset{\$}{\leftarrow} \mathsf{NIZK}^{\mathsf{hbm}}.\mathsf{Prove}(\rho, x, w)$.
It is immediate to see that $|\Pr[\mathsf{T}_3] - \Pr[\mathsf{T}_4]| = \mathsf{negl}(\lambda)$ holds by the zero-knowledge of the underlying HBM-NIZK.
It is also straightforward to see that Game_4 is identical to the simulated experiment $\mathsf{Expt}_{\mathcal{A},\mathcal{S}}^{\mathsf{nazk\text{-}sim}}$. Hence, we have $\Pr[\mathsf{T}_4] = \Pr[\mathsf{Expt}_{\mathcal{A},\mathcal{S}}^{\mathsf{nazk\text{-}sim}}(\lambda) = 1]$.

Combined together, $\mathcal{A}$'s advantage against the non-adaptive single-theorem zero-knowledge can be estimated as follows:

$$\left| \Pr[\mathsf{Expt}_{\mathcal{A}}^{\mathsf{nazk\text{-}real}}(\lambda) = 1] - \Pr[\mathsf{Expt}_{\mathcal{A},\mathcal{S}}^{\mathsf{nazk\text{-}sim}}(\lambda) = 1] \right| = \left| \Pr[\mathsf{T}_1] - \Pr[\mathsf{T}_4] \right|$$

$$\leq \sum_{j\in[3]} \left| \Pr[\mathsf{T}_j] - \Pr[\mathsf{T}_{j+1}] \right| = \mathsf{negl}(\lambda).$$

This proves that our NIZK is non-adaptive single-theorem zero-knowledge. □

Remark 5.1. (On adaptive zero-knowledge.) One may think that we can prove that the above construction satisfies adaptive single-theorem zero-knowledge by relying on the special zero-knowledge property of the underlying HBM-NIZK, since a similar statement is proven for the construction of a NIZK based on an (ordinary) HBG in [46]. However, we believe that this is not possible. Roughly speaking, the problem comes from the fact that the SDP-HBG enables us to generate a proof π_{bgen} corresponding to a subset I only after I is fixed. This is in contrast to an HBG where we can generate π_i that certifies the i-th hidden bit for each $i \in [k]$ before I is fixed. Specifically, the proof of adaptive zero-knowledge from an HBG in [46] crucially relies on the fact that if $I \subseteq I^*$, then a set of proofs $\{\pi_i\}_{i\in I}$ can be derived from $\{\pi_i\}_{i\in I^*}$ in a trivial manner. On the other hand, we do not have a similar property in SDP-HBG since it generates a proof for a subset I in one-shot instead of generating a proof in a bit-by-bit manner. We note that if SDP-HBG satisfies an adaptive version of computational

---

[12] Splitting the step "$s := \rho \oplus r$" into Steps 7 and 8 is to make it easier to describe the change in the next game and also see the correspondence with the procedure of the simulator $\mathcal{S}$.

hiding where an adversary can choose a subset I depending on a CRS $\mathsf{crs}_{\mathsf{bgen}}$, then we can prove the adaptive zero-knowledge of the above scheme relying on special zero-knowledge of HBM-NIZK. However, such an adaptive version of computational hiding cannot be proven by a similar proof to the one in Sect. 4.2 due to the fact that a leakage function cannot depend on a challenge input in the security game of LR-wPRF. Therefore, instead of directly proving that the above scheme satisfies adaptive zero-knowledge, we rely on the generic conversion from non-adaptive to adaptive zero-knowledge as stated in Theorem 3.1.

6 Zero-Knowledge SNARG

In this section, we consider a zero-knowledge SNARG (zkSNARG) which is a SNARG that also satisfies the zero-knowledge property.

Bitansky et al. [4] gave a construction of a zkSNARG in the designated verifier model based on a SNARG (with efficient verification) in the designated verifier model, a NIZK argument of knowledge, and a circuit-private FHE scheme. As noted in [4], if we consider a publicly verifiable SNARG (which is the default notion of a SNARG in this paper), then we need not rely on FHE. Moreover, a NIZK argument of knowledge can be constructed by combining any NIZK and CPA secure PKE. Thus, we obtain the following theorem:

Lemma 6.1. *Assume that there exist a fully succinct SNARG for all* NP *languages with adaptive computational soundness and efficient verification, a NIZK for all* NP *languages with adaptive computational soundness and adaptive multi-theorem zero-knowledge, and a CPA secure PKE scheme. Then, there exists a fully succinct SNARG for all* NP *languages with adaptive computational soundness, adaptive multi-theorem zero-knowledge, and efficient verification.*

Since this lemma follows from a straightforward extension of existing works, we omit the proof here and give it in the full version.

Combining Lemma 6.1 and Theorem 5.2, we obtain the following theorem.

Theorem 6.1. *If there exist a CPA secure PKE scheme and a fully succinct SNARG for all* NP *languages with adaptive computational soundness and efficient verification, then there exists a fully succinct SNARG for all* NP *languages with adaptive computational soundness, adaptive multi-theorem zero-knowledge, and efficient verification.*

Remark 6.1. We cannot prove a similar statement for a SNARG without efficient verification since efficient verification is essential in the construction of a zkSNARG in Lemma 6.1.

Acknowledgement. The second author was partially supported by JST CREST Grant Number JPMJCR19F6 and JSPS KAKENHI Grant Number 19H01109.

References

1. Akavia, A., Goldwasser, S., Vaikuntanathan, V.: Simultaneous hardcore bits and cryptography against memory attacks. In: Reingold, O. (ed.) TCC 2009. LNCS, vol. 5444, pp. 474–495. Springer, Heidelberg (2009). https://doi.org/10.1007/978-3-642-00457-5_28

2. Bellare, M., Micciancio, D., Warinschi, B.: Foundations of group signatures: formal definitions, simplified requirements, and a construction based on general assumptions. In: Biham, E. (ed.) EUROCRYPT 2003. LNCS, vol. 2656, pp. 614–629. Springer, Heidelberg (2003). https://doi.org/10.1007/3-540-39200-9_38

3. Ben-Sasson, E., et al.: Zerocash: decentralized anonymous payments from Bitcoin. In: 2014 IEEE Symposium on Security and Privacy, pp. 459–474. IEEE Computer Society Press (May 2014)

4. Bitansky, N., et al.: The hunting of the SNARK. J. Cryptol. **30**(4), 989–1066 (2017)

5. Bitansky, N., Chiesa, A.: Succinct arguments from multi-prover interactive proofs and their efficiency benefits. In: Safavi-Naini, R., Canetti, R. (eds.) CRYPTO 2012. LNCS, vol. 7417, pp. 255–272. Springer, Heidelberg (2012). https://doi.org/10.1007/978-3-642-32009-5_16

6. Bitansky, N., Chiesa, A., Ishai, Y., Paneth, O., Ostrovsky, R.: Succinct non-interactive arguments via linear interactive proofs. In: Sahai, A. (ed.) TCC 2013. LNCS, vol. 7785, pp. 315–333. Springer, Heidelberg (2013). https://doi.org/10.1007/978-3-642-36594-2_18

7. Blum, M., Feldman, P., Micali, S.: Non-interactive zero-knowledge and its applications (extended abstract). In: 20th ACM STOC, pp. 103–112. ACM Press (May 1988)

8. Boneh, D., Bonneau, J., Bünz, B., Fisch, B.: Verifiable delay functions. In: Shacham, H., Boldyreva, A. (eds.) CRYPTO 2018. LNCS, vol. 10991, pp. 757–788. Springer, Cham (2018). https://doi.org/10.1007/978-3-319-96884-1_25

9. Boneh, D., Ishai, Y., Sahai, A., Wu, D.J.: Lattice-based SNARGs and their application to more efficient obfuscation. In: Coron, J.-S., Nielsen, J.B. (eds.) EUROCRYPT 2017. LNCS, vol. 10212, pp. 247–277. Springer, Cham (2017). https://doi.org/10.1007/978-3-319-56617-7_9

10. Boneh, D., Ishai, Y., Sahai, A., Wu, D.J.: Quasi-optimal SNARGs via linear multi-prover interactive proofs. In: Nielsen, J.B., Rijmen, V. (eds.) EUROCRYPT 2018. LNCS, vol. 10822, pp. 222–255. Springer, Cham (2018). https://doi.org/10.1007/978-3-319-78372-7_8

11. Bünz, B., Fisch, B., Szepieniec, A.: Transparent SNARKs from DARK compilers. In: Canteaut, A., Ishai, Y. (eds.) EUROCRYPT 2020. LNCS, vol. 12105, pp. 677–706. Springer, Cham (2020). https://doi.org/10.1007/978-3-030-45721-1_24

12. Canetti, R., et al.: Fiat-Shamir: from practice to theory. In: Charikar, M., Cohen, E. (eds.) 51st ACM STOC, pp. 1082–1090. ACM Press (June 2019)

13. Canetti, R., Chen, Y., Reyzin, L., Rothblum, R.D.: Fiat-Shamir and correlation intractability from strong KDM-secure encryption. In: Nielsen, J.B., Rijmen, V. (eds.) EUROCRYPT 2018. LNCS, vol. 10820, pp. 91–122. Springer, Cham (2018). https://doi.org/10.1007/978-3-319-78381-9_4

14. Canetti, R., Halevi, S., Katz, J.: A forward-secure public-key encryption scheme. J. Cryptol. **20**(3), 265–294 (2007)

15. Canetti, R., Lichtenberg, A.: Certifying trapdoor permutations, revisited. In: Beimel, A., Dziembowski, S. (eds.) TCC 2018. LNCS, vol. 11239, pp. 476–506. Springer, Cham (2018). https://doi.org/10.1007/978-3-030-03807-6_18

16. Chaum, D., van Heyst, E.: Group signatures. In: Davies, D.W. (ed.) EUROCRYPT 1991. LNCS, vol. 547, pp. 257–265. Springer, Heidelberg (1991). https://doi.org/10.1007/3-540-46416-6_22

17. Chiesa, A., Hu, Y., Maller, M., Mishra, P., Vesely, N., Ward, N.: Marlin: preprocessing zkSNARKs with universal and updatable SRS. In: Canteaut, A., Ishai, Y. (eds.) EUROCRYPT 2020. LNCS, vol. 12105, pp. 738–768. Springer, Cham (2020). https://doi.org/10.1007/978-3-030-45721-1_26

18. Chiesa, A., Manohar, P., Spooner, N.: Succinct arguments in the quantum random oracle model. In: Hofheinz, D., Rosen, A. (eds.) TCC 2019. LNCS, vol. 11892, pp. 1–29. Springer, Cham (2019). https://doi.org/10.1007/978-3-030-36033-7_1

19. Chiesa, A., Ojha, D., Spooner, N.: FRACTAL: post-quantum and transparent recursive proofs from holography. In: Canteaut, A., Ishai, Y. (eds.) EUROCRYPT 2020. LNCS, vol. 12105, pp. 769–793. Springer, Cham (2020). https://doi.org/10.1007/978-3-030-45721-1_27

20. Couteau, G., Katsumata, S., Ursu, B.: Non-interactive zero-knowledge in pairing-free groups from weaker assumptions. In: Canteaut, A., Ishai, Y. (eds.) EUROCRYPT 2020. LNCS, vol. 12107, pp. 442–471. Springer, Cham (2020). https://doi.org/10.1007/978-3-030-45727-3_15

21. Damgård, I., Faust, S., Mukherjee, P., Venturi, D.: Bounded tamper resilience: how to go beyond the algebraic barrier. In: Sako, K., Sarkar, P. (eds.) ASIACRYPT 2013. LNCS, vol. 8270, pp. 140–160. Springer, Heidelberg (2013). https://doi.org/10.1007/978-3-642-42045-0_8

22. Dodis, Y., Haralambiev, K., López-Alt, A., Wichs, D.: Efficient public-key cryptography in the presence of key leakage. In: Abe, M. (ed.) ASIACRYPT 2010. LNCS, vol. 6477, pp. 613–631. Springer, Heidelberg (2010). https://doi.org/10.1007/978-3-642-17373-8_35

23. Dolev, D., Dwork, C., Naor, M.: Nonmalleable cryptography. SIAM J. Comput. 30(2), 391–437 (2000)

24. Dwork, C., Naor, M.: Zaps and their applications. SIAM J. Comput. 36(6), 1513–1543 (2007)

25. Ephraim, N., Freitag, C., Komargodski, I., Pass, R.: SPARKs: succinct parallelizable arguments of knowledge. In: Canteaut, A., Ishai, Y. (eds.) EUROCRYPT 2020. LNCS, vol. 12105, pp. 707–737. Springer, Cham (2020). https://doi.org/10.1007/978-3-030-45721-1_25

26. Feige, U., Lapidot, D., Shamir, A.: Multiple noninteractive zero knowledge proofs under general assumptions. SIAM J. Comput. 29(1), 1–28 (1999)

27. Fiat, A., Shamir, A.: How To prove yourself: practical solutions to identification and signature problems. In: Odlyzko, A.M. (ed.) CRYPTO 1986. LNCS, vol. 263, pp. 186–194. Springer, Heidelberg (1987). https://doi.org/10.1007/3-540-47721-7_12

28. Gennaro, R., Gentry, C., Parno, B., Raykova, M.: Quadratic span programs and succinct NIZKs without PCPs. In: Johansson, T., Nguyen, P.Q. (eds.) EUROCRYPT 2013. LNCS, vol. 7881, pp. 626–645. Springer, Heidelberg (2013). https://doi.org/10.1007/978-3-642-38348-9_37

29. Gentry, C., Wichs, D.: Separating succinct non-interactive arguments from all falsifiable assumptions. In: Fortnow, L., Vadhan, S.P. (eds.) 43rd ACM STOC, pp. 99–108. ACM Press (June 2011)

30. Goldreich, O.: Basing non-interactive zero-knowledge on (enhanced) trapdoor permutations: the state of the art. In: Goldreich, O. (ed.) Studies in Complexity and Cryptography. Miscellanea on the Interplay between Randomness and Computation. LNCS, vol. 6650, pp. 406–421. Springer, Heidelberg (2011). https://doi.org/10.1007/978-3-642-22670-0_28

31. Goldreich, O., Micali, S., Wigderson, A.: How to play any mental game or a completeness theorem for protocols with honest majority. In: Aho, A. (eds.) 19th ACM STOC, pp. 218–229. ACM Press (May 1987)

32. Goldreich, O., Oren, Y.: Definitions and properties of zero-knowledge proof systems. J. Cryptol. 7(1), 1–32 (1994)

33. Goldreich, O., Rothblum, R.D.: Enhancements of trapdoor permutations. J. Cryptol. 26(3), 484–512 (2013)

34. Groth, J.: Short pairing-based non-interactive zero-knowledge arguments. In: Abe, M. (ed.) ASIACRYPT 2010. LNCS, vol. 6477, pp. 321–340. Springer, Heidelberg (2010). https://doi.org/10.1007/978-3-642-17373-8_19

35. Groth, J.: On the size of pairing-based non-interactive arguments. In: Fischlin, M., Coron, J.-S. (eds.) EUROCRYPT 2016. LNCS, vol. 9666, pp. 305–326. Springer, Heidelberg (2016). https://doi.org/10.1007/978-3-662-49896-5_11

36. Groth, J., Ostrovsky, R., Sahai, A.: New techniques for noninteractive zero-knowledge. J. ACM 59(3), 11:1–11:35 (2012)

37. Hazay, C., López-Alt, A., Wee, H., Wichs, D.: Leakage-resilient cryptography from minimal assumptions. J. Cryptol. 29(3), 514–551 (2016)

38. Kalai, Y.T., Rothblum, G.N., Rothblum, R.D.: From obfuscation to the security of Fiat-Shamir for proofs. In: Katz, J., Shacham, H. (eds.) CRYPTO 2017. LNCS, vol. 10402, pp. 224–251. Springer, Cham (2017). https://doi.org/10.1007/978-3-319-63715-0_8

39. Katsumata, S., Nishimaki, R., Yamada, S., Yamakawa, T.: Exploring constructions of compact NIZKs from various assumptions. In: Boldyreva, A., Micciancio, D. (eds.) CRYPTO 2019. LNCS, vol. 11694, pp. 639–669. Springer, Cham (2019). https://doi.org/10.1007/978-3-030-26954-8_21

40. Katz, J., Vaikuntanathan, V.: Signature schemes with bounded leakage resilience. In: Matsui, M. (ed.) ASIACRYPT 2009. LNCS, vol. 5912, pp. 703–720. Springer, Heidelberg (2009). https://doi.org/10.1007/978-3-642-10366-7_41

41. Kim, S., Wu, D.J.: Multi-theorem preprocessing NIZKs from lattices. In: Shacham, H., Boldyreva, A. (eds.) CRYPTO 2018. LNCS, vol. 10992, pp. 733–765. Springer, Cham (2018). https://doi.org/10.1007/978-3-319-96881-0_25

42. Micali, S.: Computationally sound proofs. SIAM J. Comput. 30(4), 1253–1298 (2000)

43. Naor, M., Yung, M.: Public-key cryptosystems provably secure against chosen ciphertext attacks. In: 22nd ACM STOC, pp. 427–437. ACM Press (May 1990)

44. Pass, R., Shelat, A.: Unconditional characterizations of non-interactive zero-knowledge. In: Shoup, V. (ed.) CRYPTO 2005. LNCS, vol. 3621, pp. 118–134. Springer, Heidelberg (2005). https://doi.org/10.1007/11535218_8

45. Peikert, C., Shiehian, S.: Noninteractive zero knowledge for NP from (plain) learning with errors. In: Boldyreva, A., Micciancio, D. (eds.) CRYPTO 2019. LNCS, vol. 11692, pp. 89–114. Springer, Cham (2019). https://doi.org/10.1007/978-3-030-26948-7_4

46. Quach, W., Rothblum, R.D., Wichs, D.: Reusable designated-verifier NIZKs for all NP from CDH. In: Ishai, Y., Rijmen, V. (eds.) EUROCRYPT 2019. LNCS, vol. 11477, pp. 593–621. Springer, Cham (2019). https://doi.org/10.1007/978-3-030-17656-3_21

47. Rivest, R.L., Shamir, A., Tauman, Y.: How to leak a secret. In: Boyd, C. (ed.) ASIACRYPT 2001. LNCS, vol. 2248, pp. 552–565. Springer, Heidelberg (2001). https://doi.org/10.1007/3-540-45682-1_32

48. Sahai, A., Waters, B.: How to use indistinguishability obfuscation: deniable encryption, and more. In: Shmoys, D.B. (eds.) 46th ACM STOC, pp. 475–484. ACM Press (May/June 2014)

49. Wee, H.: On round-efficient argument systems. In: Caires, L., Italiano, G.F., Monteiro, L., Palamidessi, C., Yung, M. (eds.) ICALP 2005. LNCS, vol. 3580, pp. 140–152. Springer, Heidelberg (2005). https://doi.org/10.1007/11523468_12

Weakly Extractable One-Way Functions

Nir Bitansky[✉], Noa Eizenstadt[✉], and Omer Paneth[✉]

Tel Aviv University, Tel Aviv, Israel
nirbitan@tau.ac.il, noae@mail.tau.ac.il, omerpa@tauex.tau.ac.il

Abstract. A family of one-way functions is extractable if given a random function in the family, an efficient adversary can only output an element in the image of the function if it knows a corresponding preimage. This knowledge extraction guarantee is particularly powerful since it does not require interaction. However, extractable one-way functions (EFs) are subject to a strong barrier: assuming indistinguishability obfuscation, no EF can have a knowledge extractor that works against all polynomial-size non-uniform adversaries. This holds even for non-black-box extractors that use the adversary's code.

Accordingly, the literature considers either EFs based on non-falsifiable knowledge assumptions, where the extractor is not explicitly given, but it is only *assumed* to exist, or EFs against a restricted class of adversaries with a bounded non-uniform advice. This falls short of cryptography's gold standard of security that requires an explicit reduction against non-uniform adversaries of arbitrary polynomial size.

Motivated by this gap, we put forward a new notion of *weakly extractable* one-way functions (WEFs) that circumvents the known barrier. We then prove that WEFs are inextricably connected to the long standing question of three-message zero knowledge protocols. We show that different flavors of WEFs are sufficient and necessary for three-message zero knowledge to exist. The exact flavor depends on whether the protocol is computational or statistical zero knowledge and whether it is publicly or privately verifiable.

Combined with recent progress on constructing three message zero-knowledge, we derive a new connection between keyless multi-collision resistance and the notion of *incompressibility* and the feasibility of non-interactive knowledge extraction. Another interesting corollary of our result is that in order to construct three-message zero knowledge arguments, it suffices to construct such arguments where the honest prover strategy is *unbounded*.

N. Bitansky—Member of the Check Point Institute of Information Security. Supported by the Alon Young Faculty Fellowship, by Len Blavatnik and the Blavatnik Family foundation, by the Blavatnik Interdisciplinary Cyber Research Center at Tel Aviv University, and an ISF grant 484/18.

N. Eizenstadt—Supported by ISF grant 484/18.

O. Paneth—Member of the Check Point Institute of Information Security. Supported by an Azrieli Faculty Fellowship, by Len Blavatnik and the Blavatnik Foundation, by the Blavatnik Interdisciplinary Cyber Research Center at Tel Aviv University, and ISF grant 1789/19.

R. Pass and K. Pietrzak (Eds.): TCC 2020, LNCS 12550, pp. 596–626, 2020.
https://doi.org/10.1007/978-3-030-64375-1_21

1   Introduction

An extractable one-way function is a family of functions $\{f_k\}$ that satisfies two properties: *One-wayness:* Given an image $y = f_k(x)$ for random key k and input x, it is hard to find a corresponding pre-image $x' \in f_k^{-1}(y)$; and *Extraction:* Given a random key k, it is hard to produce an image y *obliviously*, without *knowing* a corresponding preimage x'. This is formalized by requiring that for any efficient algorithm A that given k produces an image y, there is an efficient extractor $\mathcal{E}$ (that depends on A) that given the same key k, extracts a preimage x'.

While their extraction property is reminiscent of *proofs of knowledge* [FS89, BG92], EFs are essentially different—they draw their power from the fact that *extraction can be done without interaction.*

The Good. The non-interactive nature of EFs gives rise to killer applications such as encryption with strong CCA security [Dam91,BP04], three-message zero knowledge [HT98,CD08], and by extending one-wayness to collision-resistance, also succinct non-interactive arguments of knowledge (SNARKs) [BCC+14].

The Bad. Constructing EFs has proven to be an elusive task. A first barrier is that without interaction, traditional *black-box extraction* techniques, like rewinding, (provably) do not work. Accordingly, extraction must use *the code* of the adversary in a non-black-box way. Bitansky, Canetti, Paneth, and Rosen [BCPR16], following Goldreich's intuition [HT98], demonstrated an even stronger barrier that holds for non-black-box extractors. Assuming indistinguishability obfuscation, they show that no efficient extractor can work against all polynomial-size non-uniform adversaries; that is, even when the extractor is given the adversary's code.

The Ugly. One approach that avoids the above barriers is to simply *assume* the existence of an extractor for every adversary, without giving an explicit extraction strategy. An EF with such non-explicit extractors follows, for example, from the *knowledge of exponent assumption* [Dam91]. Such *knowledge assumptions* translate in applications to security reductions that are, at least in part, nonexplicit. Knowledge assumptions are arguably unsatisfying, and in particular are not *falsifiable* [Nao03].

Another way to circumvent known barriers is to restrict the class of adversaries. Bitansky et al. construct EFs *with an explicit extractor* against adversaries with bounded non-uniform advice, under standard assumptions.[1] The restriction on the adversaries carries over to applications—they obtain three-message zero-knowledge, but only against verifiers with bounded non-uniformity. This of course falls short of the gold standard in cryptography of security against non-uniform adversaries of arbitrary polynomial size.

Given this state of affairs, we ask:

> *Is there hope for explicit extraction from general non-uniform adversaries?*

---

[1] More accurately, they constructed *generalized* EFs under standard assumption and (plain) EFs assuming publicly verifiable delegation, which by now is also known based on standard assumptions [KPY19].

1.1   This Work

We put forward a new definition of *weakly extractable* one-way functions (WEFs) that circumvents the [BCPR16] extraction barrier. We then show that WEFs are deeply connected to three-message zero knowledge protocols, establishing a loose equivalence between the two notions.

The New Definition. Our notion of WEFs is inspired by simulation-based definitions of multi-party computation. We relax the extraction requirement as follows: instead of requiring that the extractor $\mathcal{E}$, given a random key k and the code of the adversary A, is able to find a preimage $x' \in f_k^{-1}(y)$ for the adversary's image $y = A(k)$, we allow the extractor to sample a *simulated key* $\tilde{k}$ on its own together with an extracted preimage $x' \in f_{\tilde{k}}^{-1}(y)$ for $y = A(\tilde{k})$. The simulated key $\tilde{k}$ must be indistinguishable from a randomly sampled key k.

For this relaxation to be meaningful we must also strengthen the one-wayness requirement. Instead of one-wayness for a random key, we require that f_k is hard to invert on *any* key k. More generally, we can require hardness for any key from some NP set of *valid* keys. In this case, we further require that the extractor's simulated keys be valid and thus extraction cannot simply sample "easy to invert" keys. Rather, just as in standard EFs, the WEF extractor must use the code of the adversary to extract a preimage or it could be used to break one-wayness.

Our main motivation for studying WEFs is that they are weak enough to circumvent the impossibility of [BCPR16] (see the technical overview for more details) yet, appear to capture a natural and meaningful notion of extraction. We confirm this intuition by showing that WEFs are sufficient for one of the central applications of EFs: three-message zero knowledge arguments.

Theorem 1 (Informal). *Assuming WEFs, two-message witness-indistinguishable arguments, and non-interactive commitments, there exist three-message ZK arguments for NP.*

The existence of three-message zero knowledge arguments (with negligible soundness error) is one of the central questions in the area. The main barrier to constructing such arguments is that they require non-black box simulation [GK96]. In addition to constructions based on EFs, the only known construction secure against arbitrary polynomial size non-uniform adversaries was given recently by Bitansky, Kalai and Paneth [BKP18] based on *keyless multi-collision resistant hash functions* (and other, more standard, assumptions). A feature of the WEF-based zero knowledge argument, which [BKP18] protocol lacks, is that it is *publicly verifiable*. This means that the verifier's decision can be inferred from the message transcript alone.

A Tighter Connection. We continue to show a tighter connection between the notions of WEF and three-message zero knowledge. We show that a slight generalization of WEF is sufficient as well as *necessary* for three-message zero knowledge. Our generalization follows Bitansky et al.'s [BCPR16] generalization of EFs, allowing for a more general forms of hardness than one-wayness. They consider a relation $\mathcal{R}_k(y, x')$ on images $y = f_k(x)$ and *solutions* x', and replace one-wayness with the hardness of finding solutions. Likewise, the extractor only has to find x' that satisfies the relation $\mathcal{R}_k$, rather than a preimage.[2] We generalize WEFs in an analogous way.

We establish the following equivalence between generalized WEFs (GWEFs) and three-message zero knowledge arguments:

Theorem 2 (Informal). *Assuming two-message witness- indistinguishable and non interactive commitments arguments, GWEFs exist if and only if publicly verifiable three-message zero knowledge arguments exist.*

Finally, we ask if there is some natural notion of WEF that corresponds to three-message ZK arguments that are privately verifiable, such as the argument of [BKP18]. Again following [BCPR16], we consider a notion of *privately verifiable* GWEFs where the hard relation $\mathcal{R}_k$ is not publicly verifiable—efficiently testing whether $(f_k(x), x') \in \mathcal{R}_k$ requires the preimage x (see the technical overview for a more details on privately verifiable GWEFs).

In the privately verifiable settings, we show the following loose equivalence:

Theorem 3 (Informal).

1. *Assuming privately verifiable GWEFs and secure function evaluation, there exist privately verifiable three-message computational zero-knowledge arguments for NP.*
2. *Assuming privately verifiable three-message <u>statistical</u> zero-knowledge arguments for NP and non-interactive commitments, there exist privately verifiable GWEFs.*

Recently, building on [BKP18] and relying on the same assumptions, three-message statistical zero-knowledge arguments were constructed in [BP19]. Thus, as a corollary from Theorem 3 we obtain privately verifiable GWEFs from keyless multi-collision resistant hashing (and other standard assumptions). This connects between the notion of *incompressibility*, which stands behind keyless multi-collision-resistance and the notion of knowledge extraction. We further note that keyless collision-resistance is a falsifiable assumption, which should be contrasted with the fact that standard EFs all crucially rely on non-falsifiable assumptions such as the knowledge of exponent assumption.

On WEFs Candidates. As mentioned above, the negative result of Bitansky et al. [BCPR16] does not extend to WEFs. Therefore, even assuming indistinguishability obfuscation, existing candidate constructions, such as the one based on the knowledge of exponent assumption, may be weakly extractable. In the current work, however, we do not provide any evidence in support of that.

---

[2] In this formulation, we think of the preimage x as the private randomness used to sample y. Looking ahead, we will also discuss GWEFs with private verification, where it will be useful to refer to the private randomness x explicitly.

Demonstrating, under standard assumptions, a WEF with an explicit extractor against non-uniform adversaries is left as an open question. We view the privately verifiable GWEFs from keyless multi-collision resistant hashing that follows from Theorem 3 as a first step in this direction.

On Zero Knowledge with an Unbounded Honest Prover. Our GWEF constructions from zero knowledge arguments, in fact, work even if the *honest prover* is unbounded. Combined with our results in the reverse direction, this has an interesting implication—to obtain three-message zero knowledge arguments *with an efficient honest prover*, it suffices to obtain such argument with *with an unbounded honest prover*.

1.2   Technical Overview

We now provide an overview of the main technical ideas behind our results. We start by explaining how the definition of WEFs circumvents the [BCPR16] barrier. We then discuss the equivalence between GWEFs and (publicly verifiable) three-message zero knowledge. Finally, we discuss the case of private verification.

Circumventing the Impossibility. The [BCPR16] impossibility constructs a distribution $\mathcal{A}$ over obfuscated adversaries, and shows that if the extractor works given a random key k and adversary A sampled from $\mathcal{A}$, then it must also work when the adversary A is sampled *after the key k* from an alternative distribution $\mathcal{A}_k$ over adversaries that have a random image $f_k(x)$ hardwired in their code. This argument crucially relies on the fact that *the extractor does not control the key k*.

GWEFs to Publicly Verifiable Zero Knowledge. The construction of publicly verifiable zero knowledge from GWEFs is mostly similar to previous constructions (e.g., [CD08, BCC+14]). We sketch it here briefly, highlighting the differences. To prove some NP statement $\varphi \in \mathcal{L}$, the protocol follows the Feige-Lapidot-Shamir *trapdoor paradigm* [FLS90]. The prover sends a random key k for a GWEF, and the verifier responds with a random image $y = f_k(x)$. The prover then provides a witness-indistinguishable proof of knowledge that either the statement φ is true, or that (a) the chosen key k is valid (and thus hard), and (b) it knows a solution x' for y; namely, $(y, x') \in \mathcal{R}_k$.

   The protocol is publicly verifiable, as it only requires verifying the witness indistinguishable proof, which is publicly verifiable. Soundness follows from the fact that for a valid key k and a random image $f_k(x)$, it is hard to find a solution x' satisfying $\mathcal{R}_k$. For zero knowledge, the simulator uses the extractor $\mathcal{E}(V^*)$ to extract from the verifier a solution x' together with a corresponding simulated key k and an NP certificate for the key's validity. It then uses x' and the certificate of validity as its witness in the witness-indistinguishable proof. The protocol, as described, implicitly assumes that the malicious verifier's message y can indeed be explained as an image $y = f_k(x)$. We bridge this gap using standard techniques, based on two-message witness-indistinguishability and commitments, for compiling protocols against explainable verifiers to ones against malicious verifiers [BKP19].

Publicly Verifiable Zero Knowledge to GWEFs. The main idea behind the construction of GWEFs from three-message zero knowledge is a natural one—a key k for a function f_k consists of the first zero knowledge message zk_1 as well a statement $\varphi \in \mathcal{L}$ for some language $\mathcal{L}$ (to be specified), an image under the function $f_k(x)$ is the honest verifier response $y = \mathsf{zk}_2$, when using x as its randomness. The corresponding hard relation $\mathcal{R}_k(y, x')$ accepts as a solution x' any message zk_3 that convinces the verifier. Indeed, given that the zero knowledge is publicly verifiable, this can be tested efficiently.

The set of valid keys (for which the relation is hard) consists of false statements $\varphi \notin \mathcal{L}$. Indeed, finding a solution $x' = \mathsf{zk}_3$ to a random image $y = \mathsf{zk}_2$ under a valid key $k = (\mathsf{zk}_1, \varphi)$, amounts to producing an accepting proof for the false statement φ, which is computationally hard due to the soundness of the argument.

The extractor $\mathcal{E}(A)$ samples a false φ on its own, and runs the zero knowledge simulator $S(\varphi, V_A)$ on the code of the verifier V_A induced by the adversary A to produce a simulated transcript $(\mathsf{zk}_1, \mathsf{zk}_2, \mathsf{zk}_3)$. It then sets the simulated key to be (zk_1, φ) and the extracted preimage to be zk_3. To argue that the extractor indeed works we have to argue that the simulator produces an accepting transcript. We note that had φ been a *true* statement, then this would have followed from the zero knowledge and completeness of the underlying argument. Indeed, the honest prover necessarily generates accepting transcripts due to completeness, and the simulated transcript must be indistinguishable.

To establish faithful extraction, we choose the language $\mathcal{L}$ so to guarantee indistinguishable distributions over true-statements and false-statements. Since the simulator is efficient, and cannot tell them apart, it will also generate accepting transcripts on false-statements like the one sampled by the extractor. We also require that false-statements are taken from an NP set. The existence of a language $\mathcal{L}$ satisfying these properties follow from non-interactive commitments.

Privately Verifiable GWEFs. We now move to discuss privately verifiable GWEFs and their connection to privately verifiable zero knowledge. Here the hard relation $\mathcal{R}_k$ is not publicly verifiable—efficiently testing whether $(f_k(x), x') \in \mathcal{R}_k$ requires the preimage x.

In the setting of privately verifiable GWEF, where testing a solution x' for y requires private information (a preimage), there are two knowledge-related questions: (1) the usual one: must the adversary know a solution for the produced image y? but also (2) can it even recognize such a solution? The definition we consider essentially says that if the adversary can generate an image y, for which it can verify solutions, then it must also know a solution. If it cannot even verify a solution, we only require that the extractor generates x' that the adversary cannot distinguish from a solution.

Following this intuition, we further relax the previous extraction definition as follows. The extractor $\mathcal{E}$ may sometime fail to extract. However, there is an additional extractor $\widetilde{\mathcal{E}}$ that is guaranteed to always succeed and produce a key k and candidate solution x' that are indistinguishable from those generated by $\mathcal{E}$. The extractor $\widetilde{\mathcal{E}}$ is given the extra freedom to solve invalid keys (indeed invalid keys may be indistinguishable from valid keys, if the NP certificate of validity is hidden). Note that in the publicly verifiable setting, or if the adversary generates images y whose solutions it can recognize, the original extractor $\mathcal{E}$ must indeed always succeed just like the alternative $\widetilde{\mathcal{E}}$ (otherwise, we can tell them apart).

Privately Verifiable GWEFs to Privately Verifiable Zero Knowledge. The construction of privately verifiable zero knowledge from privately verifiable GWEFs follows the construction of [BCPR16] from privately verifiable GEFs. In a nutshell, in the case of privately verifiable GWEFs, the prover cannot directly prove that it found a solution x', as testing a solution requires the private randomness x used to generate $y = f_k(x)$. Instead, the verifier and prover execute a secure function evaluation protocol, which allows to perform this verification in an "encrypted manner". This results in privately verifiable zero knowledge due to the private state of the verifier in the secure function evaluation protocol.

Soundness of the protocol is argued similarly to [BCPR16]. For zero knowledge, we rely on the relaxed extraction guarantee described above. The simulator uses $\mathcal{E}$ to generate a simulated key k along with an NP certificate of validity, and extracted a solution x'. Only in the analysis, we switch to indistinguishably generating the keys using the alternative extractor $\widetilde{\mathcal{E}}$, and use the fact that it successfully extracts.

Privately Verifiable Statistical Zero Knowledge to Privately Verifiable GWEFs. The construction of GWEFs from Privately Verifiable Zero Knowledge is essentially the same as that from publicly verifiable zero knowledge. We address the difference in the analysis, explaining why statistical zero knowledge is needed, and how the alternative extractor relaxation aids the construction.

Recall that in the GWEF construction from publicly verifiable zero knowledge, to prove hardness it is crucial that a valid key corresponds to a false statement φ. To show that the extractor faithfully extracts, we had to show that the simulator faithfully generates an accepting transcript. We argued that in two steps: (1) the simulator generates accepting transcripts on true statements, and (2) even though the extractor generates false statements, the simulator would still succeed as it cannot tell false statements from true ones.

In the private verification setting, (1) is not clear. Indeed, testing whether a transcript is accepting cannot be done efficiently, and thus computational zero knowledge is insufficient for arguing that the simulator would also generate accepting transcripts. This is where we resort to statistical zero knowledge—indeed, an unbounded distinguisher can generate verifier coins consistent with the transcript and test acceptance. However, the second argument (2) should also be treated with care. The fact that the simulator generates accepting transcripts on true statements does not necessarily mean that it generates such transcripts on false statements. Indeed these are inherently only computational indistinguishable. However, this argument is sufficient for establishing our relaxed extraction guarantee: the alternative extractor $\widetilde{\mathcal{E}}$ simply chooses true statements rather than false statements. Since these are computationally indistinguishable, and the extracted solution x' is efficiently generated from the statement, we are guaranteed that the two extractors are indeed indistinguishable.

1.3   Open Questions

The notions of WEFs and GWEFs suggest a new avenue for dealing with knowledge extraction in the non-interactive settings. We address a few of the open questions that arise.

- Can we use our new notions of extraction to go beyond zero knowledge and obtain results on the round complexity of secure computation? One concrete approach is to construct (G)WEFs with a unique hard property. That is, a GWEFs and a property π such that an image y uniquely determines the value $\pi(x')$ for any solution x' but given only y the value $\pi(x')$ is pseudo-random. Indeed, this can be seen as a generalization of WEF that are injective and will lead to *extractable commitments* in two messages.
- Can we construct any form of collision resistant (G)WEFs? Can these suffice for applications such as succinct non-interactive arguments of knowledge (SNARKs)?
- Is there an implication in the reverse direction from (G)WEF to keyless multi-collision-resistance, or, more generally to some non-trivial notion of incompressibility.

2   Preliminaries

We rely on the following standard computational concepts and notation:

- A PPT is a probabilistic polynomial-time algorithm.
- We follow the standard practice of modeling any efficient adversary strategy as a family of polynomial size circuits. For an adversary A corresponding to a family of polynomial-size circuits $\{A_n\}_{n\in\mathbb{N}}$.
- A distinguisher algorithm is one that has a single output bit.
- We say that a function $f : \mathbb{N} \to \mathbb{R}$ is negligible if for all constants $c > 0$, there exists $N \in \mathbb{N}$ such that for all $n > N$, $f(n) < n^{-c}$. We sometimes denote negligible functions by negl.
- We say that a function $f : \mathbb{N} \to \mathbb{R}$ is noticeable if there exist constants $c > 0$ and $N \in \mathbb{N}$ such that for all $n > N$, $f(n) \geq n^{-c}$.
- Two ensembles of random variables $\mathcal{X} = \{X_i\}_{n\in\mathbb{N},i\in I_n}$, $\mathcal{Y} = \{Y_i\}_{n\in\mathbb{N},i\in I_n}$ over the same set of indices $I = \bigcup_{n\in\mathbb{N}} I_n$ are said to be *computationally indistinguishable*, denoted by $\mathcal{X} \approx_c \mathcal{Y}$, if for every polynomial-size distinguisher $D = \{D_n\}_{n\in\mathbb{N}}$ there exists a negligible function $\mu(\cdot)$ such that for all $n \in \mathbb{N}, i \in I_n$,

$$\mathbb{E}D(X_i) - \mathbb{E}D(Y_i) \leq \mu(n).$$

The ensembles are statistically indistinguishable if the above holds also for unbounded (rather than polynomial-size distinguishers).
- For a finite set S, denote by $x \leftarrow S$ the process of uniformly sampling x from S.

– For a distribution X, we denote by $x \in X$ the fact that x is in the support of X.

Let $\mathcal{R} = \{(\varphi, \omega)\}$ be a relation. Denote by $\mathcal{L}(\mathcal{R})$ the corresponding language:

$$\mathcal{L}(\mathcal{R}) := \{\varphi \mid \exists \omega \text{ such that } (\varphi, \omega) \in \mathcal{R}\}.$$

For any φ, we denote by $\mathcal{R}(\varphi)$ the set of witnesses corresponding to φ:

$$\mathcal{R}(\varphi) := \{\omega \mid (\varphi, \omega) \in \mathcal{R}\}.$$

2.1   Hard on Average Relations

We define hard-on-average problems with solved instance and co-instance samplers. Such a hard problem is given by two efficient samplers Y, N and corresponding NP relations $\mathcal{R}_Y, \mathcal{R}_N$. Y outputs yes-instances along with a witness and N outputs no-instances along with a witness. The two types of instances are computationally indistinguishable.

Definition 1 (Hard on Average Problem). *A hard-on-average problem consists of PPT samplers Y, N supported on NP relations $\mathcal{R}_Y, \mathcal{R}_N$. We require*

1. **Disjointness:** $\mathcal{L}(\mathcal{R}_Y) \cap \mathcal{L}(\mathcal{R}_N) = \emptyset$.
2. **Indistinguishability:**

$$\{\varphi \mid (\varphi, \omega) \leftarrow Y(1^n)\}_n \approx_c \{\bar{\varphi} \mid (\bar{\varphi}, \bar{\omega}) \leftarrow N(1^n)\}_n.$$

The notion is, in fact, equivalent to non-interactive commitments, but will be useful for presenting our constructions of generalized weakly extractable one-way functions, in a conceptually clear manner. To see this equivalence, we can consider the two NP languages corresponding to commitments of 0 and 1, and consider their respective relations. Analogously, we can construct commitments, where committing to 1 is done by sampling from Y, and committing to 0 is done by sampling from N.

2.2   Non-interactive Commitments

Definition 2 (Non-interactive Commitment [Blu81]). *A non-interactive commitment scheme consists of a polynomial-time commitment algorithm $Com(x; r)$ that given a message $x \in \{0,1\}^*$ and randomness $r \in \{0,1\}^n$ outputs a commitment c. We make the following requirements:*

1. **Perfect Binding:** *For every security parameter $n \in \mathbb{N}$, and string $c \in \{0,1\}^*$ there exists at most a single $x \in \{0,1\}^*$ such that c is a commitment to x:*

$$\forall n \in \mathbb{N}, r_0, r_1 \in \{0,1\}^n \text{ if } Com(w_0; r_0) = Com(w_1; r_1) \text{ then } w_0 = w_1.$$

2. **Computational Hiding:** *for any sequence $\mathcal{I} = \{n \in \mathbb{N}, w_0, w_1 \in \{0,1\}^{\text{poly}(n)}\}$:*

$$\left\{ c_0 : \begin{array}{c} r \leftarrow \{0,1\}^n \\ c_0 \leftarrow Com(w_0; r) \end{array} \right\}_{(n,w_0,w_1) \in \mathcal{I}} \approx_c \left\{ c_1 : \begin{array}{c} r \leftarrow \{0,1\}^n \\ c_1 \leftarrow Com(w_1; r) \end{array} \right\}_{(n,w_0,w_1) \in \mathcal{I}}.$$

Non-interactive commitments can be constructed from any injective one-way function (or a certifiable collection thereof) [Blu81].

2.3   Zero-Knowledge and Witness Indistinguishable Protocols

Throughout, for an interactive protocol between a prover P and verifier V (one of which possibly malicious), we denote by $\langle P(\omega), V \rangle(\varphi)$ the transcript of an interaction with prover private input ω (possibly empty), and common input φ. We denote by $Acc/Rej \overset{\text{out}}{\leftarrow} \langle P(\omega), V \rangle(\varphi)$ the output of the (honest) verifier.

Definition 3 (Zero-Knowledge Arguments). *We say that a pair of interactive PPT machines $\langle P, V \rangle$ is a zero-knowledge argument system for a NP relation $\mathcal{R}$ if the following holds:*

1. **Completeness:** *For every element $\varphi \in \mathcal{L}(\mathcal{R})$, and a witness $\omega \in \mathcal{R}(\varphi)$:*

$$\Pr\left[Acc \overset{\text{out}}{\leftarrow} \langle P(\omega), V \rangle(\varphi) \right] = 1.$$

2. **Soundness:** *For any family of polynomial-size circuits $P^* = \{P_n^*\}_n$, and every $\varphi \in \{0,1\}^n \setminus \mathcal{L}$:*

$$\Pr\left[Acc \overset{\text{out}}{\leftarrow} \langle P_n^*, V \rangle(\varphi) \right] \leq \text{negl}(n).$$

3. **Zero Knowledge:** *There exists a PPT simulator S such that for any non-uniform family of polynomial-size circuits $V^* = \{V_n^*\}_n$,*

$$\{\langle P(\omega), V_n^* \rangle(\varphi)\}_{\varphi,\omega} \approx_c \{S(V_n^*, \varphi)\}_{\varphi,\omega},$$

where $(\varphi, \omega) \in \mathcal{R}$ and $|\varphi| = n$.

The argument is **statistical zero knowledge** *if the above indistinguishability is statistical (rather than computational).*

The protocol is **publicly verifiable** *is the verifier's decision can be determined solely from the protocol's transcript (without the private coins of the verifier).*

Definition 4 (Argument of Knowledge). *An argument system $\langle P, V \rangle$ is an argument of knowledge for a relation $\mathcal{R}$ if there exists a PPT extractor $\mathcal{E}$ such that for any non-uniform family of polynomial-size circuits $P^* = \{P_n^*\}_{n \in \mathbb{N}}$, any noticeable function $\varepsilon(n)$, any $n \in \mathbb{N}$, and any $\varphi \in \{0,1\}^n$:*

$$if \quad \Pr\left[Acc \overset{\text{out}}{\leftarrow} \langle P_n^*, V \rangle(\varphi) \right] = \varepsilon(n)$$

then

$$\Pr\left[\begin{matrix} \omega \leftarrow \mathcal{E}^{P_n^*}(1^{1/\varepsilon(n)}, \varphi) \\ \omega \in \mathcal{R}(\varphi) \end{matrix} \right] \geq \varepsilon(n) - \text{negl}(n).$$

2.4   Offline-Online Witness Indistinguishable Arguments

An offline-online interactive argument is a protocol $\langle P, V \rangle$ that can be divided into two phases: an offline phase independent of the proven statement, and an online phase where the statement (and witness) become available and the proof is completed. We define such witness-indistinguishable arguments (and arguments of knowledge). Our formal definition follows that of [BP19]. Below, we consider sub-protocols $\langle \mathsf{offP}, \mathsf{offV} \rangle (1^n)$ where both prover and verifier may have an output; we denote this by $(O_P, O_V) \overset{\mathsf{out}}{\leftarrow} \langle \mathsf{offP}, \mathsf{offV} \rangle (1^n)$.

Definition 5 (Offline-Online Witness-Indistinguishable Arguments).
An interactive protocol $\langle P, V \rangle$ is an offline-online witness-indistinguishable argument for an NP relation $\mathcal{R}$ if it consists of two sub-protocols $P = (\mathsf{offP}, \mathsf{onP}), V = (\mathsf{offV}, \mathsf{onV})$, that satisfy:

1. **Completeness:** *For any $(\varphi, \omega) \in \mathcal{R}$ where $|\varphi| = n$:*

$$\Pr\left[\langle Acc \overset{\mathsf{out}}{\leftarrow} \mathsf{onP}(st_P, \omega), \mathsf{onV}(st_V) \rangle (\varphi) \ \middle| \ (st_P, st_V) \overset{\mathsf{out}}{\leftarrow} \langle \mathsf{offP}, \mathsf{offV} \rangle (1^n) \right] = 1.$$

2. **Adaptive Soundness:** *For any non-uniform family of polynomial-size circuits $P^* = \{\mathsf{offP}_n^*, \mathsf{onP}_n^*\}_n$, and for all $n \in \mathbb{N}$:*

$$\Pr\left[Acc \overset{\mathsf{out}}{\leftarrow} \langle \mathsf{onP}_n^*(st_P), \mathsf{onV}(st_V) \rangle (\varphi) \ \middle| \ ((st_P, \varphi), st_V) \overset{\mathsf{out}}{\leftarrow} \langle \mathsf{offP}_n^*, \mathsf{offV} \rangle (1^n) \right]$$
$$\leq \mathrm{negl}(n),$$

where $\varphi \notin \mathcal{L}$ and $|\varphi| = n$.

3. **Adaptive Witness-Indistinguishability** *For any non-uniform family of polynomial size circuits $V^* = \{V_n^*\}_n$, all $n \in \mathbb{N}$:*

$$\Pr\left[b \overset{\mathsf{out}}{\leftarrow} \langle \mathsf{onP}(st_P, \omega_b), \mathsf{onV}_n^*(st_V) \rangle (\varphi) \ \middle| \ \begin{array}{l} (st_P, (st_V, \varphi, \omega_0, \omega_1)) \overset{\mathsf{out}}{\leftarrow} \langle \mathsf{offP}, \mathsf{offV}_n^* \rangle (1^n), \\ b \leftarrow \{0, 1\} \end{array} \right] \leq \frac{1}{2} + \mathrm{negl}(n),$$

where $(\varphi, \omega_0), (\varphi, \omega_1) \in \mathcal{R}$ and $|\varphi| = n$.

Definition 6 (Adaptive Argument of Knowledge). *We say that the system is an **Adaptive Argument of Knowledge** if there exists a PPT extractor $\mathcal{E}$ such that for any non-uniform family of polynomial-size circuits $P^* = \{\mathsf{offP}_n^*, \mathsf{onP}_n^*\}_{n \in \mathbb{N}}$, and for all $n \in \mathbb{N}$:*

$$\text{if} \quad \Pr\left[\begin{array}{l} Acc \overset{\mathsf{out}}{\leftarrow} \langle \mathsf{onP}_n^*(st_P), \mathsf{onV}(st_V) \rangle (\varphi) \ | \\ ((st_P, \varphi), st_V) \overset{\mathsf{out}}{\leftarrow} \langle \mathsf{offP}_n^*, \mathsf{offV} \rangle (1^n) \end{array} \right] = \varepsilon$$

then

$$\Pr\left[\begin{array}{l} Acc \overset{\mathsf{out}}{\leftarrow} \langle \mathsf{onP}_n^*(st_P), \mathsf{onV}(st_V) \rangle (\varphi) \ | \\ \omega \leftarrow \mathcal{E}^{(\mathsf{offP}_n^*, \mathsf{onP}_n^*)}(1^{1/\varepsilon}, \varphi, st_P, st_V) \\ \omega \in \mathcal{R}(\varphi) \end{array} \middle| \ ((st_P, \varphi), st_V) \overset{\mathsf{out}}{\leftarrow} \langle \mathsf{offP}_n^*, \mathsf{offV} \rangle (1^n) \right] \geq \varepsilon - \mathrm{negl}(n)$$

where $|\varphi| = n$. This further holds for randomized circuits offP*, onP*, provided that the first prover message of offP is deterministic.[3]

Assuming non-interactive commitments, there exist three-message systems as the one defined above that are adaptive arguments of knowledge, and have two offline (prover and verifier) messages and a single online (prover) message [FLS90].

Two-message systems (that are only sound) are known under a variety of assumptions like trapdoor permutations, or concrete number-theoretic or lattice assumptions (e.g. [DN00, GOS06, KKS18]).

2.5 Secure Function Evaluation

We define two-message secure function evaluation.

Definition 7 (Two-Message Secure Function Evaluation Scheme). *A secure function evaluation scheme consists of three algorithms (Enc, Dec, Eval), where Enc, Eval are probabilistic and Dec is deterministic, satisfying:*

1. **Correctness:** *For any $n \in \mathbb{N}$, $x \in \{0,1\}^n$ and circuit C:*

$$\Pr\left[Dec_{sk}(\widehat{ct}) = C(x) \mid (sk, ct) \leftarrow Enc(x), \widehat{ct} \leftarrow Eval(ct, C)\right] = 1.$$

2. **Semantic Security:**

$$\left\{ct \mid (sk, ct) \leftarrow Enc(w_0)\right\}_{n,w_0,w_1} \approx_c \left\{ct \mid (sk, ct) \leftarrow Enc(w_1)\right\}_{n,w_0,w_1},$$

where $n \in \mathbb{N}$, $w_0, w_1 \in \{0,1\}^n$.

3. **Circuit Privacy:**

$$\left\{Eval(ct, C_0)\right\}_{n,C_0,C_1,ct} \approx_c \left\{Eval(ct, C_1)\right\}_{n,C_0,C_1,ct},$$

where $n \in \mathbb{N}$, $C_0, C_1 \in \{0,1\}^{\text{poly}(n)}$ compute the same function, and $ct \in \{0,1\}^{\ell(n)}$, where $\ell(n)$ is the size of encryptions of messages of length n.

Such secure function evaluation schemes are known from a variety of assumptions such as DDH [NP01] and LWE [BD18].

3 Extractable-One Way Functions: A New Definition

In this section, we provide our new definition of extractable one-way functions against adversaries with arbitrary polynomial-size non-uniform advice. We start by recalling the concept of *generalized extractable one-way functions* (GEF) [BCPR16], which considers general (hard) relations, rather than the specific preimage relation. We then present our new definition of generalized weakly extractable one-way functions (GWEF).

---

[3] The requirement for randomized circuits is not essential, but simplifies the analysis.

Definition 8 (GEF [BCPR16]). *A polynomial-time computable family of functions*

$$\mathcal{F} = \left\{ f_k : \{0,1\}^{\ell(n)} \to \{0,1\}^{\ell'(n)} \mid n \in \mathbb{N}, k \in \{0,1\}^{m(n)} \right\},$$

associated with an efficient key sampler K, is a generalized extractable one-way function with respect to a polynomial-time relation $\mathcal{R}^{\mathcal{F}}$ if the following holds:

1. $\mathcal{R}^{\mathcal{F}}$-**Hardness:** *For any non-uniform family of polynomial-size circuits $A = \{A_n\}_n$ and every $n \in \mathbb{N}$,*

$$\Pr\left[(f_k(x), x') \in \mathcal{R}_k^{\mathcal{F}} \mid k \leftarrow K(1^n), x \leftarrow \{0,1\}^{\ell(n)}, x' \leftarrow A_n(k, f_k(x)) \right]$$
$$\leq \mathrm{negl}(n).$$

2. $\mathcal{R}^{\mathcal{F}}$-**Extractability:** *There exists a PPT extractor $\mathcal{E}$ such that for any non-uniform family of polynomial size circuits $A = \{A_n\}_n$ and every $n \in \mathbb{N}$,*

$$\Pr\left[\begin{array}{c} \exists x : y = f_k(x), \\ (y, x') \notin \mathcal{R}_k^{\mathcal{F}} \end{array} \middle| \begin{array}{c} k \leftarrow K(1^n) \\ y \leftarrow A_n(k), \\ x' \leftarrow \mathcal{E}(k, A_n) \end{array} \right] \leq \mathrm{negl}(n).$$

Definition 9 (Privately Verifiable GEF). *A GEF is (only) privately verifiable if the relation $\mathcal{R}_k^{\mathcal{F}}$ is not necessarily polynomial-time, but there exists a polynomial-time tester $\mathcal{M}$ such that for any (k, x, x'):*

$$\mathcal{M}(k, x, x') = 1 \quad \text{iff} \quad (f_k(x), x') \in \mathcal{R}_k^{\mathcal{F}}.$$

On the Amount of Non-uniformity. The definition of [BCPR16] also considers PPT adversaries with *bounded* non-uniform advice. In contrast, the above definition is formulated for non-uniform circuit adversaries of arbitrary polynomial size, which is equivalent to considering PPT adversaries with arbitrary polynomial-size non-uniform advice. As discussed in the introduction, while security against such adversaries is the gold standard in cryptography, such extractable functions are shown in [BCPR16] to be impossible assuming indistinguishability obfuscation.

The New Definition for Arbitrary Non-uniformity. The main relaxation we introduce in order to overcome the impossibility is to only require that extraction holds with respect to *simulated keys*, indistinguishable from real keys. That is, we allow the extractor to also simulate the key, for which it may use the code of the adversary.

Having relaxed extraction, we also strengthen the hardness requirement—we ask that one-wayness holds with respect to *any* key from a predefined set of valid keys $\mathcal{L}(\mathcal{K})$, certifiable by an NP relation $\mathcal{K}$, rather than only when the key is chosen at random by the (real) key sampler. (As noted in the introduction, without this strengthening, extraction relative to extractor-simulated keys becomes trivial, assuming trapdoor one-way functions. Indeed, this stronger form of one-wayness will be crucial for the application of three-message zero-knowledge.) We shall require that the simulated keys are also valid and are generated by the extractor along with an NP certificate for their validity.

Definition 10 (GWEF). *An efficiently computable family of functions*

$$\mathcal{F} = \left\{ f_k : \{0,1\}^{\ell(n)} \to \{0,1\}^{\ell'(n)} \mid n \in \mathbb{N}, f_k \in \{0,1\}^{m(n)} \right\},$$

associated with an efficient key sampler K and NP relation $\mathcal{K}$, is a generalized weakly extractable one-way function with respect to a polynomial-time relation $\mathcal{R}^{\mathcal{F}}$ if the following holds:

1. **Worst-case $\mathcal{R}^{\mathcal{F}}$-Hardness:** *For any non-uniform family of polynomial-size circuits $A = \{A_n\}_n$, every $n \in \mathbb{N}$, and every $k \in \mathcal{L}(\mathcal{K}) \cap \{0,1\}^{m(n)}$,*

$$\Pr\left[(f_k(x), x') \in \mathcal{R}^{\mathcal{F}} \mid x \leftarrow \{0,1\}^{\ell(n)}, x' \leftarrow A_n(k, f_k(x)) \right] \le \mathrm{negl}(n).$$

2. **Weak $\mathcal{R}^{\mathcal{F}}$-Extractability:** *There exists a PPT extractor $\mathcal{E}$ such that for any non-uniform family of polynomial-size circuits $A = \{A_n\}_n$, we have:*
   (a) **Extraction:** *For all $n \in \mathbb{N}$,*

$$\Pr\left[\begin{array}{c} \exists x : y = f_k(x), \\ (y, x') \notin \mathcal{R}_k^{\mathcal{F}} \end{array} \middle| \begin{array}{c} (k, v, x') \leftarrow \mathcal{E}(1^n, A_n) \\ y \leftarrow A_n(k) \end{array} \right] \le \mathrm{negl}(n) .$$

   (b) **Key Indistinguishability:**

$$\{k \mid k \leftarrow K(1^n)\}_n \approx_c \{k \mid (k, v, x') \leftarrow \mathcal{E}(1^n, A_n)\}_n .$$

   (c) **Validity:** *For all $n \in \mathbb{N}$,*

$$\Pr_{k,v,x' \leftarrow \mathcal{E}(1^n, A_n)} [(k, v) \in \mathcal{K}] \ge 1 - \mathrm{negl}(n).$$

Remark 1 (On Validity of Keys). We note that we do not insist that random keys sampled by K are valid. Indeed, requiring this is typically not useful in settings where keys are not necessarily generated by trusted parties. We note, however, that due to key-indistinguishability, it is possible to add this additional requirement generically, by having the $K(1^n)$ sample using $\mathcal{E}(1^n, C_n)$, for any fixed circuit C_n.

3.1 Privately Verifiable GWEF

We now turn to define private-verifiable GWEF. Here we relax the definition even further, allowing that simulated keys generated by the extractor are not necessarily valid. Rather, we require that there exists another extractor $\tilde{\mathcal{E}}$ that does output valid keys, and such that the key k and extracted w sampled by $\tilde{\mathcal{E}}$ are indistinguishable from those sampled by $\mathcal{E}$. However, $\tilde{\mathcal{E}}$, may not necessarily succeed in producing w that satisfies the relation $\mathcal{R}_k^{\mathcal{F}}$.

We present the definition, and then further discuss the intuition behind it.

Definition 11 (Privately Verifiable GWEF). *A GWEF is (only) privately verifiable if the relation $\mathcal{R}_k^{\mathcal{F}}$ is not necessarily polynomial-time, but there exists a polynomial-time tester $\mathcal{M}(k, x, w)$ for $(f_k(x), w) \in \mathcal{R}_k^{\mathcal{F}}$ as in Definition 9. In addition, Weak $\mathcal{R}^{\mathcal{F}}$-Extractability is augmented.*

Weak $\mathcal{R}^{\mathcal{F}}$-Extractability: *There exist PPT extractors $\mathcal{E}, \widetilde{\mathcal{E}}$ such that for any non-uniform family of polynomial size circuits $A = \{A_n\}_n$, we have:*

1. **Extraction:** *For all $n \in \mathbb{N}$,*

$$\Pr \left[\begin{array}{c} \exists x : y = f_k(x), \\ (y, w) \notin \mathcal{R}_k^{\mathcal{F}} \end{array} \middle| \begin{array}{c} (k, w) \leftarrow \mathcal{E}(1^n, A_n) \\ y \leftarrow A_n(k) \end{array} \right] \leq \mathrm{negl}(n) \ .$$

2. **Key Indistinguishability:**

$$\{k \mid k \leftarrow K(1^n)\}_n \approx_c \{k \mid (k, w) \leftarrow \mathcal{E}(1^n, A_n)\}_n \ .$$

3. **$\widetilde{\mathcal{E}}$-Validity:** *For all $n \in \mathbb{N}$,*

$$\Pr \left[(k, v) \in \mathcal{K} \mid (k, v, w) \leftarrow \widetilde{\mathcal{E}}(1^n, A_n) \right] \geq 1 - \mathrm{negl}(n).$$

4. **Extractor Indistinguishability:**

$$\{k, w \mid (k, w) \leftarrow \mathcal{E}(1^n, A_n)\}_n \approx_c \left\{k, w \mid (k, v, w) \leftarrow \widetilde{\mathcal{E}}(1^n, A_n)\right\}_n \ .$$

More on the Definition. In the setting of privately verifiable GWEF, where testing a solution w for y requires private information (a preimage), there are two knowledge-related questions: (1) the usual one: must the adversary know a solution for the produced image y? but also (2) can it even recognize such a solution? The definition we consider essentially says that if the adversary can generate an image y, for which it can verify solutions, then it must also know a solution. If it cannot even verify a solution, we only require that the extractor generates w that the adversary cannot distinguish from a solution.

4   From Three-Message ZK to GWEF

In this section, we present our constructions of generalized weakly extractable one-way functions from three-message zero-knowledge arguments.

4.1   Publicly Verifiable GWEF

In this section, we construct publicly verifiable three-message zero-knowledge protocols from GWEF.

Theorem 4. *Assuming publicly verifiable three-message zero-knowledge argument system for NP and non-interactive commitments, there exists a GWEF.*

Ingredients and Notation:

- $\mathcal{H} = (Y, N, \mathcal{R}_Y, \mathcal{R}_N)$, a hard-on-average problem with solved instances and co-instances. (Recall that such problems follow from non-interactive commitments.)
- $\langle P, V \rangle$, a ZK argument system for $\mathcal{R}_Y$. We denote the protocol's messages by $\mathsf{zk}_1, \mathsf{zk}_2, \mathsf{zk}_3$.

We now define our GWEF $\mathcal{F}$ with associated key sampler K, key-relation $\mathcal{K}$, and hard relation $\mathcal{R}^{\mathcal{F}}$. These are given in Fig. 1.

Security Analysis. We now show that the described function family $\mathcal{F}$ (and associated $K, \mathcal{K}, \mathcal{R}^{\mathcal{F}}$) satisfy the requirements of a GWEF.

Hardness. We show hardness based on the soundness of the argument system and disjointness property of $\mathcal{H}$.

Proposition 1. $\mathcal{F}$ *satisfies* $\mathcal{R}^{\mathcal{F}}$-*hardness.*

Proof. Assume toward contradiction there exists a family of polynomial-size circuits $A = \{A_n\}_n$ and a noticeable function $\varepsilon(n)$, such that for infinitely many n, there exists a valid key $k = (\bar{\varphi}, \mathsf{zk}_1) \in \mathcal{L}(\mathcal{K})$, such that

$$\Pr\left[(y, x') \in \mathcal{R}_k^{\mathcal{F}} \,\middle|\, \begin{array}{l} x \leftarrow \{0,1\}^n \\ y = f_k(x) \\ x' = A(k, y) \end{array}\right] \geq \varepsilon(n).$$

Sampler $K(1^n)$:

- Sample $(\varphi, \omega) \leftarrow Y(1^n)$
- Let S be the zero-knowledge simulator, and let V_0 be the honest verifier circuit with hardwired randomness 0^n. Sample $(\mathsf{zk}_1, \mathsf{zk}_2, \mathsf{zk}_3) \leftarrow S(V_0, \varphi)$.
- Return $k = (\varphi, \mathsf{zk}_1)$.

Key relation $\mathcal{K}$:

- $(k, v) \in \mathcal{K}$ iff $k = (\varphi, \mathsf{zk}_1)$ such that $(\varphi, v) \in \mathcal{R}_N$.

Function $f_k(r)$ in family $\mathcal{F} = \{f_k : \{0,1\}^n \to \{0,1\}^*\}_{n,k}$:

- Parse $k = (\varphi, \mathsf{zk}_1)$.
- Emulate the verifier V with statement φ, first prover message zk_1, and randomness r. Let zk_2 be the produced verifier message.
- Output zk_2.

$\mathcal{R}^{\mathcal{F}}$:

- $(y, x') \in \mathcal{R}_k^{\mathcal{F}}$ iff
  - Parsing $y = \mathsf{zk}_2$, $x' = \mathsf{zk}_3$, and $k = (\varphi, \mathsf{zk}_1)$.
  - The transcript $(\mathsf{zk}_1, \mathsf{zk}_2, \mathsf{zk}_3)$ with respect to statement φ is accepting.

Fig. 1. GWEF

That is, parsing $y = \mathsf{zk}_2, x' = \mathsf{zk}_3$, the transcript $(\mathsf{zk}_1, \mathsf{zk}_2, \mathsf{zk}_3)$ is accepting with respect to statement $\bar{\varphi}$.

We construct a corresponding prover $P^* = \{P_n^*\}_n$ (Fig. 2) that convinces the verifier of accepting the statement $\bar{\varphi}$ with probability $\varepsilon(n) - \mathrm{negl}(n)$. Since $k \in \mathcal{K}$, it holds that $\bar{\varphi} \in \mathcal{L}(\mathcal{R}_N)$. By the disjointness property of $\mathcal{H}$, this means that $\bar{\varphi} \notin \mathcal{L}(\mathcal{R}_Y)$ and thus, P^* will violate the soundness of the underlying argument system.

$P_n^*(\bar{\varphi})$

1. Sends zk_1 to the verifier.
2. Obtains a response zk_2 from the verifier.
3. Emulates $A_n(k, y)$, where $y = \mathsf{zk}_2$, and obtains zk_3. Sends zk_3 to the verifier.

Fig. 2. ZK malicious prover GWEF

Note that the view of A_n when emulated by P_n^* is identical to its view when breaking the hardness of $\mathcal{R}^{\mathcal{F}}$. Thus P_n^* convinces the verifier of accepting the false statement with probability $\varepsilon(n) - \mathrm{negl}(n)$.

Weak Extractability. We now prove weak extractability, based on the zero-knowledge and completeness properties of the argument system and indistinguishability of $\mathcal{H}$.

Proposition 2. $\mathcal{F}$ *satisfies weak extractability.*

Proof. We start by defining the extractors $\mathcal{E}$, which is described in Fig. 3.

$\mathcal{E}(1^n, A)$:

- Sample $(\bar{\varphi}, \bar{\omega}) \leftarrow N(1^n)$.
- Consider the verifier circuit V^*, that given a first prover message zk_1, computes $\mathsf{zk}_2 = A(\bar{\varphi}, \mathsf{zk}_1)$, and responds with zk_2.
- Sample a simulated transcript $(\mathsf{zk}_1, \mathsf{zk}_2, \mathsf{zk}_3) \leftarrow S(V^*, \bar{\varphi})$, where S is the zero-knowledge simulator.
- Output (k, v, x') where $k = (\bar{\varphi}, \mathsf{zk}_1)$, $v = \bar{\omega}$, and $x' = \mathsf{zk}_3$.

Fig. 3. GWEF extractor

We prove the three properties—extraction, key-indistinguishability and validity—required by weak extractability (Definition 10). From hereon, fix a family of polynomial size circuits $A = \{A_n\}_n$.

Claim (Extraction). For all $n \in \mathbb{N}$,

$$\Pr \left[\begin{array}{l} \exists x : y = f_k(x), \\ (y, x') \notin \mathcal{R}_k^{\mathcal{F}} \end{array} \middle| \begin{array}{l} (k, x') \leftarrow \mathcal{E}(1^n, A_n) \\ y \leftarrow A_n(k) \end{array} \right] \leq \mathrm{negl}(n) .$$

Proof. We start by recalling that whenever y is in the image of f_k, it is the case that $y = \mathsf{zk}_2$, such that zk_2 is the response of the honest verifier to zk_1, using some randomness r, where zk_1 is given by the key $k = (\varphi, \mathsf{zk}_1)$.

Our goal is to show that except with negligible probability, the extractor produces zk_3, such that the simulated transcript $(\mathsf{zk}_1, \mathsf{zk}_2, \mathsf{zk}_3)$ is accepting with respect to statement $\bar{\varphi}$. We show that this follows from the zero-knowledge and completeness of the underlying argument, and the hardness of the language $\mathcal{H}$.

To see this, consider an alternative experiment where (φ, ω) are sampled from the yes-instances sampler Y. From the ZK guarantee of the simulator, the generated transcript is computationally indistinguishable from the honest interaction. Note that by the (perfect) completeness of the zero-knowledge argument, whenever $A_n(k)$ outputs $y = \mathsf{zk}_2$ in the image of f_k, the interaction results in an accepting transcript. By the zero-knowledge property, it follows that except with negligible probability, the simulator also generates accepting transcripts whenever A_n outputs y in the image of f_k.

It is left to note that from the indistinguishability of the hard samplers Y, N, the simulated transcripts of the experiment are indistinguishable from the ones used by the extractor. Therefore they are accepting with the same probability, and thus $\mathcal{E}$ successfully extracts x' such that $(y, x') \in \mathcal{R}_k^{\mathcal{F}}$, as required.

Claim (Key Indistinguishability).

$$\{k \mid k \leftarrow K(1^n)\}_n \approx_c \{k \mid (k, v, x') \leftarrow \mathcal{E}(1^n, A_n)\}_n .$$

Proof. Recall that $k = (\varphi, \mathsf{zk}_1)$ where the statement φ is sampled from $Y(1^n)$ in the key sampler, and from $N(1^n)$ in the simulated case. Consider the hybrid experiment where φ is sampled from $Y(1^n)$ in the simulated case. The message zk_1 is then sampled from $S(V_0, \varphi)$, where V_0 is the honest verifier with hardwired randomness 0^n, by the key sampler, and from $S(V^*, \varphi)$, where V^* is the verifier constructed from A_n, by the hybrid extractor. Using zero-knowledge guarantee, and the fact that the honest prover's first message zk_1 is independent of the verifier, we have:

$$\{\mathsf{zk}_1 \mid (\mathsf{zk}_1, \mathsf{zk}_2, \mathsf{zk}_3) \leftarrow S(V_0, \varphi)\} \approx_c \{\mathsf{zk}_1 \mid (\mathsf{zk}_1, \mathsf{zk}_2, \mathsf{zk}_3) \leftarrow \langle P, V_0 \rangle(\varphi)\} \equiv$$
$$\{\mathsf{zk}_1 \mid (\mathsf{zk}_1, \mathsf{zk}_2, \mathsf{zk}_3) \leftarrow \langle P, V^* \rangle(\varphi)\} \approx_c \{\mathsf{zk}_1 \mid (\mathsf{zk}_1, \mathsf{zk}_2, \mathsf{zk}_3) \leftarrow S(V^*, \varphi)\} ,$$

where throughout $\varphi \leftarrow Y(1^n)$.

From the hardness of the samplers, Y-instances are indistinguishable from N- instances, and therefore the simulated transcripts are distinguishable. The extractor indistinguishability follows.

Claim (Validity). For all $n \in \mathbb{N}$:

$$\Pr\left[(k, v) \in \mathcal{K} \mid (k, v, x') \leftarrow \mathcal{E}(1^n, A_n)\right] \geq 1 - \mathrm{negl}(n).$$

Recall that $\mathcal{E}$ always samples $(\bar{\varphi}, \bar{\omega}) \leftarrow N(1^n)$ and sets $k = (\bar{\varphi}, \mathsf{zk}_1)$ and $v = \bar{\omega}$. Thus $(k, v) \in \mathcal{K}$ by definition.

4.2 Privately Verifiable GWEF

In this section, we construct privately verifiable GWEF from privately verifiable three-message zero knowledge protocols.

Theorem 5. *Assuming privately verifiable three-message statistical zero-knowledge argument system for NP and non-interactive commitments, there exists a privately verifiable GWEF.*

Adjustments from GWEF. In this construction we use privately verifiable ZK, rather than publicly verifiable one. Therefore, unlike the previous construction, the verifier's randomness is required in order to efficiently decide whether the transcript is accepting or not. To overcome it, SZK is needed. This will guarantee that the simulated transcripts are indeed accepting (and are not simply hard to distinguish). Note that the definition of the privately GWEF extractor is relaxed as well, allowing two different extractors. One of which will guarantee extraction, and will use the ZK simulator on true statements, and the other will guarantee validity, and will use false statements. From the hardness of the problem $\mathcal{H}$, both extractors will be indistinguishable, as required.

Ingredients and Notation:

- $\mathcal{H} = (Y, N, \mathcal{R}_Y, \mathcal{R}_N)$, a hard-on-average problem with solved instances and co-instances. (Recall that such problems follow from non-interactive commitments.)
- $\langle P, V \rangle$, an SZK argument system for $\mathcal{R}_Y$. We denote the protocol's messages by $\mathsf{zk}_1, \mathsf{zk}_2, \mathsf{zk}_3$.
- *Com*, a non-interactive string commitment scheme.

We now define our privately verifiable GWEF $\mathcal{F}$ with associated key sampler K, key-relation $\mathcal{K}$, hard relation $\mathcal{R}^{\mathcal{F}}$, and corresponding tester $\mathcal{M}$. These are given in Fig. 4.

<u>Sampler $K(1^n)$:</u>

- Sample $(\varphi, \omega) \leftarrow Y(1^n)$.
- Let S be the zero-knowledge simulator, and let V_0 be the honest verifier circuit with hardwired randomness 0^n. Sample $(\mathsf{zk}_1, \mathsf{zk}_2, \mathsf{zk}_3) \leftarrow S(V_0, \varphi)$.
- Return $k = (\varphi, \mathsf{zk}_1)$.

<u>Key relation $\mathcal{K}$:</u>

- $(k, v) \in \mathcal{K}$ iff $k = (\varphi, \mathsf{zk}_1)$ such that $(\varphi, v) \in \mathcal{R}_N$.

<u>Function $f_k(r, r')$ in family $\mathcal{F} = \left\{ f_k : \{0, 1\}^{n \times n} \to \{0, 1\}^* \right\}_{n,k}$:</u>

- Parse $k = (\varphi, \mathsf{zk}_1)$.
- Emulate the verifier V with statement φ, first prover message zk_1, and randomness r. Let zk_2 be the produced verifier message.
- Compute a commitment $c = Com(r; r')$ to the verifier's randomness r.
- Output (zk_2, c).

<u>$\mathcal{R}^{\mathcal{F}}$ and private tester $\mathcal{M}$:</u>

- $(y, x') \in \mathcal{R}_k^{\mathcal{F}}$ iff
  - Parsing $y = (\mathsf{zk}_2, c)$, $x' = \mathsf{zk}_3$, and $k = (\varphi, \mathsf{zk}_1)$.
  - c is a commitment to a string r, such that the verifier V accepts the transcript $(\mathsf{zk}_1, \mathsf{zk}_2, \mathsf{zk}_3)$ with respect to statement φ and verifier randomness r.
- The tester $\mathcal{M}(k, x, x')$, parses $x = (r, r')$, computes $y = f_k(x)$, and efficiently tests if $(y, x') \in \mathcal{R}_k^{\mathcal{F}}$ using r, r'.

Fig. 4. Privately verifiable GWEF

Security Analysis We now show that the described function family $\mathcal{F}$ (and associated $K, \mathcal{K}, \mathcal{R}^{\mathcal{F}}, \mathcal{M}$) satisfy the requirements of a GWEF.

Hardness. We show hardness based on the soundness of the argument system, disjointness property of $\mathcal{H}$, and hiding of the commitment scheme.

Proposition 3. $\mathcal{F}$ *satisfies* $\mathcal{R}^{\mathcal{F}}$*-hardness.*

Proof. Assume toward contradiction there exists a family of polynomial-size circuits $A = \{A_n\}_n$ and a noticeable function $\varepsilon(n)$, such that for infinitely many n, there exists a valid key $k = (\bar{\varphi}, \mathsf{zk}_1) \in \mathcal{L}(\mathcal{K})$, such that

$$\Pr \left[(y, x') \in \mathcal{R}_k^{\mathcal{F}} \; \middle| \; \begin{array}{l} x \leftarrow \{0, 1\}^{n \times n} \\ y = f_k(x) \\ x' = A(k, y) \end{array} \right] \geq \varepsilon(n).$$

That is, parsing $y = (\mathsf{zk}_2, c), x = (r, r'), x' = \mathsf{zk}_3$, the verifier V accepts $(\mathsf{zk}_1, \mathsf{zk}_2, \mathsf{zk}_3)$ with respect to statement $\bar{\varphi}$ and verifier randomness r.

We construct a corresponding prover $P^* = \{P_n^*\}_n$ (Fig. 5) that convinces the verifier of accepting the statement $\bar{\varphi}$ with probability $\varepsilon(n) - \mathrm{negl}(n)$. Since $k \in \mathcal{K}$, it holds that $\bar{\varphi} \in \mathcal{L}(\mathcal{R}_N)$. By the disjointness property of $\mathcal{H}$, this means that $\bar{\varphi} \notin \mathcal{L}(\mathcal{R}_Y)$ and thus, P^* will violate the soundness of the underlying argument system.

$$P_n^*(\bar{\varphi})$$

1. Sends zk_1 to the verifier.
2. Obtains a response zk_2 from the verifier.
3. Simulates the commitment c as a commitment to 0^n, emulates $A_n(k, y)$, where $y = (zk_2, c)$, and obtains zk_3. Sends zk_3 to the verifier.

Fig. 5. ZK malicious prover GWEF

We then consider a hybrid experiment in which the prover P_n^* obtains a commitment c to the verifier's randomness r, rather than simulating the commitment c as a commitment to 0^n on its own. By the hiding of the commitment, the prover in this hybrids experiment convinces the verifier of accepting with the same probability as in a real interaction up to a negligible difference $negl(n)$.

It is left to note that the view of A_n when emulated by P_n^* in this hybrid experiment is identical to its view, when breaking the hardness of $\mathcal{R}^{\mathcal{F}}$. Thus in the hybrids experiment, the verifier is convinces with probability $\varepsilon(n)$.

It follows that in a real interaction P_n^* convinces the verifier of accepting the false statement with probability $\varepsilon(n) - negl(n)$.

Weak Extractability. We now prove weak extractability, based on the statistical zero-knowledge and completeness properties of the argument system, indistinguishability of $\mathcal{H}$, and binding of the commitment Com.

Proposition 4. $\mathcal{F}$ satisfies weak extractability.

Proof. We start by defining the extractors $\mathcal{E}, \widetilde{\mathcal{E}}$. These are described in Fig. 6.

We now prove the four properties—extraction, key-indistinguishability, $\widetilde{\mathcal{E}}$-validity, and extractor-indistinguishability—required by weak extractability (Definition 11). From hereon, fix a family of polynomial size circuits $A = \{A_n\}_n$.

$\mathcal{E}(1^n, A)$:

- Sample $(\varphi, \omega) \leftarrow Y(1^n)$.
- Consider the verifier circuit V^*, that given a first prover message zk_1, computes $(\mathsf{zk}_2, c) = A(\varphi, \mathsf{zk}_1)$, and responds with zk_2.
- Sample a simulated transcript $(\mathsf{zk}_1, \mathsf{zk}_2, \mathsf{zk}_3) \leftarrow S(V^*, \varphi)$, where S is the (statistical) zero-knowledge simulator.
- Output (k, x') where $k = (\varphi, \mathsf{zk}_1)$, and $x' = \mathsf{zk}_3$.

$\widetilde{\mathcal{E}}(1^n, A)$:

- Sample $(\bar{\varphi}, \bar{\omega}) \leftarrow N(1^n)$.
- Consider the verifier circuit V^*, that given a first prover message zk_1, computes $(\mathsf{zk}_2, c) = A(\bar{\varphi}, \mathsf{zk}_1)$, and responds with zk_2.
- Sample a simulated transcript $(\mathsf{zk}_1, \mathsf{zk}_2, \mathsf{zk}_3) \leftarrow S(V^*, \bar{\varphi})$, where S is the (statistical) zero-knowledge simulator.
- Output (k, v, x') where $k = (\bar{\varphi}, \mathsf{zk}_1)$, $v = \bar{\omega}$, and $x' = \mathsf{zk}_3$.

Fig. 6. GWEF extractors

Claim (Extraction). For all $n \in \mathbb{N}$,

$$\Pr\left[\begin{array}{c} \exists x : y = f_k(x), \\ (y, x') \notin \mathcal{R}_k^{\mathcal{F}} \end{array} \middle| \begin{array}{c} (k, x') \leftarrow \mathcal{E}(1^n, A_n) \\ y \leftarrow A_n(k) \end{array}\right] \leq \mathrm{negl}(n) .$$

Proof. We start by recalling that whenever y is in the image of f_k, it is the case that $y = (\mathsf{zk}_2, c)$, such that:

- zk_2 is the response to zk_1 of the honest verifier, using some randomness r, where zk_1 is given by $k = (\varphi, \mathsf{zk}_1)$.
- c is a commitment to the verifier randomness r.

Our goal is to show that except with negligible probability, whenever this occurs, the extractor produces zk_3, such that the honest verifier accepts the simulated $(\mathsf{zk}_1, \mathsf{zk}_2, \mathsf{zk}_3)$ with respect to statement φ and randomness r. We show that this follows from the statistical zero-knowledge and completeness of the underlying argument.

To see this, consider an alternative experiment where $\mathsf{zk}_1, \mathsf{zk}_3$ are generated by the honest zero knowledge prover $P(\varphi)$. Note that by the (perfect) completeness of the zero-knowledge argument, in this experiment, whenever $A_n(k)$, where $k = (\varphi, \mathsf{zk}_1)$, outputs $y = (\mathsf{zk}_2, c)$ in the image of f_k, the prover outputs a message zk_3 such that the corresponding transcript $(\mathsf{zk}_1, \mathsf{zk}_2, \mathsf{zk}_3)$ is accepting with respect to the corresponding verifier randomness r, which by the binding of Com is uniquely defined by the commitment c.

By statistical zero knowledge, it follows that except with negligible probability $\mathrm{negl}(n)$, the simulator also generates accepting transcripts whenever A_n

outputs y in the image of f_k. In this case, $\mathcal{E}$ successfully extracts x' such that $(y, x') \in \mathcal{R}_k^{\mathcal{F}}$, as required.

Claim (Key Indistinguishability).

$$\{k \mid k \leftarrow K(1^n)\}_n \approx_c \{k \mid (k, x') \leftarrow \mathcal{E}(1^n, A_n)\}_n.$$

Proof. Recall that $k = (\varphi, \mathsf{zk}_1)$ where the statement φ is sampled from $Y(1^n)$ in both distributions. The message zk_1 is sampled from $S(V_0, \varphi)$, where V_0 is the honest verifier with hardwired randomness 0^n, by K, and from $S(V^*, \varphi)$, where V^* is the verifier constructed from A_n, by $\mathcal{E}$.

Using zero-knowledge guarantee, and the fact that the honest prover's first message zk_1 is independent of the verifier, we have:

$$\{\mathsf{zk}_1 \mid (\mathsf{zk}_1, \mathsf{zk}_2, \mathsf{zk}_3) \leftarrow S(V_0, \varphi)\} \approx_s \{\mathsf{zk}_1 \mid (\mathsf{zk}_1, \mathsf{zk}_2, \mathsf{zk}_3) \leftarrow \langle P, V_0 \rangle(\varphi)\} \equiv$$
$$\{\mathsf{zk}_1 \mid (\mathsf{zk}_1, \mathsf{zk}_2, \mathsf{zk}_3) \leftarrow \langle P, V^* \rangle(\varphi)\} \approx_s \{\mathsf{zk}_1 \mid (\mathsf{zk}_1, \mathsf{zk}_2, \mathsf{zk}_3) \leftarrow S(V^*, \varphi)\},$$

where throughout $\varphi \leftarrow Y(1^n)$.

Claim ($\widetilde{\mathcal{E}}$-Validity). For all $n \in \mathbb{N}$:

$$\Pr\left[(k, v) \in \mathcal{K} \mid k, v, x' \leftarrow \widetilde{\mathcal{E}}(1^n, A_n)\right] \geq 1 - \mathrm{negl}(n).$$

Proof Recall that $\widetilde{\mathcal{E}}$ always samples $(\bar{\varphi}, \bar{\omega}) \leftarrow N(1^n)$ and sets $k = (\bar{\varphi}, \mathsf{zk}_1)$ and $v = \bar{\omega}$. Thus $(k, v) \in \mathcal{K}$ by definition with all but negligible probability.

Claim (Extractor Indistinguishability)

$$\{k, x' \mid (k, x') \leftarrow \mathcal{E}(1^n, A_n)\}_n \approx_c \left\{k, x' \mid (k, v, x') \leftarrow \widetilde{\mathcal{E}}(1^n, A_n)\right\}_n.$$

Proof Observe that the extractors $\mathcal{E}$ and $\widetilde{\mathcal{E}}$ generate (k, x') efficiently from φ sampled using $Y(1^n)$ and $\bar{\varphi}$ sampled using $N(1^n)$, respectively. Thus, extractor indistinguishability follows from the indistinguishability of Y-instances from N-instances.

5   From GWEF to Three-Message ZK

In this section, we show that GWEF (with additional standard assumptions) are sufficient for constructing three-message zero-knowledge arguments.

5.1   Publicly Verifiable ZK

In this section, we construct publicly verifiable three-message zero-knowledge arguments from GWEFs. The construction itself is mostly similar to previous constructions (e.g., [CD08, BCC+14]), but requires a new analysis, following the weaker extractability guarantee.

Theorem 6. *Assume there exist GWEF, non-interactive commitments, and two-message witness indistinguishable arguments. Then there exists a publicly verifiable three-message ZK argument.*

Ingredients and Notation:

- $\mathcal{F}$, a GWEF with associated key sampler K, valid key relation $\mathcal{K}$, and a hard relation $\mathcal{R}^{\mathcal{F}}$.
- *Com*, a non-interactive string commitment scheme.
- $\langle(\mathsf{off}P, \mathsf{on}P), (\mathsf{off}V, \mathsf{on}V)\rangle$ an offline-online WIAOK system for NP with two offline messages and a single online message. (Recall that such systems follow from non-interactive commitments. We denote its corresponding messages by $\mathsf{wi}_1, \mathsf{wi}_2, \mathsf{wi}_3$)
- $\langle\mathsf{on}P', (\mathsf{off}V', \mathsf{on}V')\rangle$ an offline-online WI system for NP with a single offline (verifier) message and a single online (prover) message. We denote its corresponding messages by $\mathsf{wi}'_1, \mathsf{wi}'_2$

The protocol is described in Fig. 7.

Security Analysis. The security analysis is omitted from this extended abstract and can be found in the full version of the paper.

5.2 Privately Verifiable ZK

In this section, we construct privately verifiable three-message zero-knowledge arguments from privately verifiable GWEFs. The construction is similar to that of [BCPR16], but requires a new analysis, following the weaker extractability guarantee.

Theorem 7. *Assume there exist privately verifiable GWEF and secure function evaluation. Then there exists a privately verifiable three-message ZK argument.*

Adjustments from Public Verification. There are two main differences between this construction and the publicly verifiable one. First, as membership in $\mathcal{R}$ can no longer be tested efficiently given only (y, x'), it will be done homomorphically over the verifier's encrypted input. Second, as membership is already tested homomorphically, the validity of the image can be tested in the same circuit, thus sparing the two-message WI used in the public version.

Ingredients and Notation:

- $\mathcal{F}$, a privately verifiable GWEF with associated a key sampler K, valid key relation $\mathcal{K}$, hard relation $\mathcal{R}^{\mathcal{F}}$ and an efficient tester $\mathcal{M}$. We denote by $\mathcal{M}_{k,y,x'}$ the augmented $\mathcal{R}^{\mathcal{F}}$-tester that on input x returns 1 if either $y \neq f_k(x)$ or $\mathcal{M}(k, x, x') = 1$.
- *(Enc, Dec, Eval)*, a secure function evaluation scheme.
- $\langle(\mathsf{off}P, \mathsf{on}P), (\mathsf{off}V, \mathsf{on}V)\rangle$ an offline-online WIAOK system for NP with two offline messages and a single online message. (Recall that such systems follow from non-interactive commitments, which in turn follow from secure function evaluation [LS19]).

The protocol is described in Fig. 8.

$$\langle P(\omega), V \rangle(\varphi)$$

Common Input: statement $\varphi \in \mathcal{L}(\mathcal{R})$.
Prover Input: witness $\omega \in \mathcal{R}(\varphi)$.

1. P computes:
   - $k \leftarrow K(1^n)$, a GWEF key.
   - wi_1, the first prover message in the offline WI $\langle \mathsf{off}P, \mathsf{off}V \rangle(1^n)$.
   - wi'_1, the first offline message the verifier $\mathsf{off}V'$.
   - $c \leftarrow Com(\omega)$, a commitment to the witness ω.
   Sends $\mathsf{zk}_1 = (k, \mathsf{wi}_1, \mathsf{wi}'_1, c)$.
2. V computes:
   - $x \leftarrow \{0,1\}^{\ell(n)}$, a random string.
   - $y = f_k(x)$, the image of x under the GWEF.
   - wi_2, the second verifier message in the offline WI $\langle \mathsf{off}P, \mathsf{off}V \rangle(1^n)$.
   - wi'_2, the second prover message in the online WI $\langle \mathsf{on}P'(x), \mathsf{on}V' \rangle(\Gamma)$ for the statement $\Gamma = \Gamma_1(\varphi, c) \vee \Gamma_2(k, y)$:

$$\exists \bar{\omega} : \left(c \in Com(\bar{\omega}) \bigwedge \bar{\omega} \notin \mathcal{R}(\varphi) \right) \bigvee \exists x : y = f_k(x) \ ,$$

   where the witness x is used.
   Sends $\mathsf{zk}_2 = (y, \mathsf{wi}_2, \mathsf{wi}'_2)$.
3. P computes:
   - The decision of the online verifier in $\langle \mathsf{on}P'(x'), \mathsf{on}V' \rangle(\Gamma)$. If it rejects, then P aborts.
   - wi_3, the third prover message in the online WI $\langle \mathsf{on}P(\omega), \mathsf{on}V \rangle(\Psi)$ for the statement $\Psi = \Psi_1(\varphi) \vee \Psi_2(k, c, y)$:

$$\varphi \in \mathcal{L}(\mathcal{R}) \bigvee \left(k \in \mathcal{L}(\mathcal{K}) \bigwedge \exists \omega' : c \in Com(\omega') \bigwedge \exists x' : (y, x') \in \mathcal{R}_k^{\mathcal{F}} \right) \ ,$$

   where the prover uses the witness $\omega \in \mathcal{R}(\varphi)$.
   Sends $\mathsf{zk}_3 = \mathsf{wi}_3$
4. V accepts iff the online verifier in $\langle \mathsf{on}P(\omega), \mathsf{on}V \rangle(\Psi)$ accepts.

Fig. 7. Privately verifiable three-message ZK protocol for $\mathcal{R} \in \mathrm{NP}$

$$\langle P(\omega), V \rangle(\varphi)$$

Common Input: statement $\varphi \in \mathcal{L}(\mathcal{R})$.
Prover Input: witness $\omega \in \mathcal{R}(\varphi)$.

1. P computes:
   - $k \leftarrow K(1^n)$, a GWEF key.
   - wi_1, the first prover message in the offline WI $\langle \text{off}P, \text{off}V \rangle(1^n)$.
   Sends $\text{zk}_1 = (k, \text{wi}_1)$.
2. V computes:
   - $x \leftarrow \{0,1\}^{\ell(n)}$, a random string.
   - $(sk, ct) \leftarrow Enc(x)$, an SFE encryption of x.
   - $y = f_k(x)$, the image of x under the GWEF.
   - wi_2, the second verifier message in the offline WI $\langle \text{off}P, \text{off}V \rangle(1^n)$.
   Sends $\text{zk}_2 = (y, ct, \text{wi}_2)$.
3. P computes:
   - $\widehat{ct} \leftarrow Eval(ct, 1)$, an evaluation of the constant 1 circuit, padded to the size of the circuit $\mathcal{M}_{k,y,x'}$.
   - wi_3, the third prover message in the online WI $\langle \text{on}P(\omega), \text{on}V \rangle(\Psi)$ for the statement $\Psi = \Psi_1(\varphi) \vee \Psi_2(k, y, ct, \widehat{ct})$:

   $$\varphi \in \mathcal{L}(\mathcal{R}) \bigvee \left(k \in \mathcal{L}(\mathcal{K}) \bigwedge \exists x' : \widehat{ct} \in Eval(ct, \mathcal{M}_{k,y,x'}) \right) \ ,$$

   where the prover uses the witness $\omega \in \mathcal{R}(\varphi)$.
   Sends $\text{zk}_3 = (\widehat{ct}, \text{wi}_3)$
4. V computes:
   - $Dec_{sk}(\widehat{ct})$, the decryption of the test bit.
   - The decision of the online verifier in $\langle \text{off}P(\omega), \text{off}V \rangle(\Psi)$.
   It accepts if both accept.

Fig. 8. Privately verifiable three-message ZK protocol for $\mathcal{R} \in \text{NP}$

Security Analysis. The completeness of the protocol follows readily from the completeness and correctness of the underlying primitives. We focus on proving that the protocols is an argument of knowledge and that it is zero knowledge.

Proposition 5 (Argument of Knowledge). *The protocol is an argument of knowledge (and in particular, sound). Specifically, there exists a PPT extractor* $ZK.\mathcal{E}$ *such that for any non-uniform family of polynomial-size circuits* $P^* = \{P_n^*\}_{n \in \mathbb{N}}$, *any noticeable function* $\varepsilon(n)$, *any* $n \in \mathbb{N}$, *and any* $\varphi \in \{0,1\}^n$:

$$\text{if} \quad \Pr\left[Acc \overset{\text{out}}{\leftarrow} \langle P_n^*, V \rangle(\varphi) \right] = \varepsilon(n)$$

then

$$\Pr\left[\begin{matrix} \omega \leftarrow ZK.\mathcal{E}^{P_n^*}(1^{1/\varepsilon(n)}, \varphi) \\ \omega \in \mathcal{R}(\varphi) \end{matrix} \right] \geq \varepsilon(n) - \text{negl}(n) .$$

Proof. We define the extractor $ZK.\mathcal{E}$ in Fig. 9.

$$\text{ZK.}\mathcal{E}^{P^*}(1^{1/\varepsilon}, \varphi)$$

Oracle: a prover circuit P^*.
Input: parameter $1^{1/\varepsilon}$ and statement φ.

1. Emulates the prover P^* and obtain its first message (k, wi_1).
2. Constructs prover circuits for the offline-online WI protocol:
   (a) $\text{off}P^*(1^n)$:
       - Sends wi_1 to $\text{on}V$.
       - Samples $x \leftarrow \{0,1\}^{\ell(n)}$ and $(sk, ct) \leftarrow Enc(x)$, and computes $y = f_k(x)$.
       - Given wi_2 from verifier $\text{off}V$, feeds (y, wi_2, ct) to the emulated P^* as the response of verifier V, and obtains $(\widehat{ct}, \text{wi}_3)$.
       - Outputs statement $\Psi = \Psi_1(\varphi) \vee \Psi_2(k, y, ct, \widehat{ct})$ and internal state $st_P = \text{wi}_3$.
   (b) $\text{on}P^*(\Psi; \text{wi}_3)$:
       - Sends wi_3 to $\text{on}V$.
3. Emulates an execution $((st_P, \Psi), st_V) \overset{\text{out}}{\leftarrow} \langle \text{off}P^*, \text{off}V \rangle(1^n)$.
4. Applies the WI extractor $\omega \leftarrow WI.\mathcal{E}^{(\text{off}P^*, \text{on}P^*)}(1^{1/\varepsilon}, \Psi, st_P, st_V)$.
5. Outputs the extracted ω.

Fig. 9. Argument of knowledge extractor for the three-message ZK protocol

We now prove the validity of the extractor. Let $P^* = \{P_n^*\}_{n \in \mathbb{N}}$ be a non-uniform family of polynomial-size circuits, and assume the for every n, there exists φ such that P_n^* convinces the verifier V of accepting φ with probability $\varepsilon(n)$. We prove that $\text{ZK.}\mathcal{E}^{P_n^*}(1^\varepsilon, \varphi)$ outputs $\omega \in \mathcal{R}(\varphi)$ with probability at least $\varepsilon(n) - \text{negl}(n)$.

First note that each execution of $\text{ZK.}\mathcal{E}$ perfectly emulates an interaction $\langle P_n^*, V \rangle(\varphi)$.

Claim. Let $\widehat{ct}$ and Ψ be the evaluated cipher-text and statement induced by the execution of $\text{ZK.}\mathcal{E}$. Then, with probability at least $\varepsilon(n) - \text{negl}(n)$, the extracted witness ω satisfies Ψ and in addition $Dec_{sk}(\widehat{ct}) = 1$.

Proof. Since $\text{ZK.}\mathcal{E}$ perfectly emulates an interaction $\langle P_n^*, V \rangle(\varphi)$, the verifier V accepts in the induced interaction with probability $\varepsilon(n)$. Whenever this occurs:

- The WI verifier $(\text{off}V, \text{on}V)$ accepts.
- It holds that $Dec_{sk}(\widehat{ct}) = 1$.

Noting that the prover $(\text{off}P_n^*, \text{on}P_n^*)$ constructed by $\text{ZK.}\mathcal{E}$ has a deterministic first message, it follows by the adaptive argument of knowledge guarantee of the WI system that except with negligible probability $\text{negl}(n)$, whenever the WI verifier accepts, $\text{WI.}\mathcal{E}$ succeeds in extracting a witness for Ψ. The claim follows.

To complete the proof of Proposition 5, and conclude that the extracted ω is a witness for $\Psi_1(\varphi) = (\varphi \in \mathcal{L})$, we prove:

Claim. Except with negligible probability $\text{negl}(n)$, either the extracted witness ω does not satisfy $\Psi_2(k, y, ct, \widehat{ct})$ or $Dec_{sk}(\widehat{ct}) \neq 1$.

Proof. Assume toward contradiction that for infinitely many n, the extracted witness ω satisfies Ψ_2 and $Dec_{sk}(\widehat{ct}) = 1$ with probability $\delta(n)$. That is, $\omega = (v, x')$ such that:

- $(k, v) \in \mathcal{K}$, the key is valid.
- $\widehat{ct} \in Eval(ct, \mathcal{M}_{k,y,x'})$, the cipher-text $\widehat{ct}$ is a homomorphic evaluation of the augmented $\mathcal{R}^{\mathcal{F}}$-tester $\mathcal{M}_{k,y,x'}$.

The second condition implies that $\mathcal{M}(k, x, x') = 1$, and accordingly $(y, x') \in \mathcal{R}^{\mathcal{F}}_k$. Indeed, recalling that $(ct, sk) \in Enc(x)$ and that $Dec_{sk}(\widehat{ct}) = 1$, this follows from the correctness of the SFE scheme.

We now construct a polynomial-size adversary $A = \{A_n\}_n$ that breaks the $\mathcal{R}^{\mathcal{F}}$-hardness of $\mathcal{F}$ with probability $\delta(n) - \text{negl}(n)$, relative to the valid key k (deterministically defined by the first prover message) (Fig. 10).

$$A_n(y)$$

Input: $\tilde{y}$ (an image under f_k).

A_n emulates the extractor $\text{ZK}.\mathcal{E}^{P^*_n}(1^{1/\varepsilon(n)}, \varphi)$ with the following exceptions:

1. The extractor does not sample (x, y, ct) on its own.
2. A_n samples $\tilde{ct} \leftarrow Enc(0^{\ell(n)})$.
3. A_n then uses $(\tilde{ct}, \tilde{y})$ in the emulation in place of (ct, y).
4. When the emulated extractor $\text{ZK}.\mathcal{E}$ outputs ω, A_n outputs $x' = \omega$.

Fig. 10. Adversary for the $\mathcal{R}^{\mathcal{F}}$ hardness

Claim. For infinitely many n,

$$\Pr\left[\begin{matrix} x' \leftarrow A_n(f_k(x)) \\ (f_k(x), x') \in \mathcal{R}^{\mathcal{F}}_k \end{matrix} \ \middle| \ x \leftarrow \{0,1\}^{\ell(n)} \right] \geq \delta(n) - \text{negl}(n).$$

Proof. To see this we first consider an alternative experiment, where A_n also obtains an SFE encryption $ct \leftarrow Enc(x)$ of x and uses it in the emulation of $\text{ZK}.\mathcal{E}$, instead of using $\tilde{ct}$. We argue that in this alternative experiment, A_n outputs x' such that $(f_k(x), x') \in \mathcal{R}^{\mathcal{F}}_k$ with the same probability as in the original experiment up to a negligible difference $\text{negl}(n)$.

Indeed, this follows directly from the semantic security of SFE encryptions. Any noticeable difference between the experiments directly leads to a distinguisher between encryptions of $0^{\ell(n)}$ and x. (Note that given x, we can efficiently test the condition $(f_k(x), x') \in \mathcal{R}^{\mathcal{F}}_k$, using $\mathcal{M}(f_k(x), x, x')$).

It is left to observe that in this alternative experiment the extractor $\text{ZK}.\mathcal{E}$ is perfectly emulated, and thus by our assumption on $\text{ZK}.\mathcal{E}$, A_n it outputs the required x' with probability at least $\delta(n) - \text{negl}(n)$.

This complete the proof of Proposition 5.

Proposition 6 (Zero Knowledge). *The protocol $\langle P, V \rangle$ is zero knowledge.*

Proof. We start by describing the simulator S in Fig. 11. In what follows, let $\mathcal{E}, \widetilde{\mathcal{E}}$ be the GWEF extractors guaranteed by Definition 11.

$$S(V_n^*, \varphi)$$

1. Sample:
   - wi_1, the first prover message in the offline WI.
   - $(k, v, x') \leftarrow \widetilde{\mathcal{E}}(1^n, V_n^*(\cdot, \mathsf{wi}_1))$, a key k, a certificate v for the keys validity, and an extracted solution x'. Here $V_n^*(\cdot, \mathsf{wi}_1)$ is a circuit that given key k, runs $(y, ct, \mathsf{wi}_2) \leftarrow V_n^*(k, \mathsf{wi}_1)$ and outputs y.
   - Let $\mathsf{zk}_1 = (k, \mathsf{wi}_1)$.
2. Compute the response $\mathsf{zk}_2 = (y, ct, \mathsf{wi}_2)$ of the verifier V^* to prover message zk_1.
3. Compute:
   - $\widehat{ct} \leftarrow \mathit{Eval}(ct, \mathcal{M}_{k,y,x'})$.
   - wi_3, the third prover message in the online WI for statement $\Psi_1(\varphi) \vee \Psi_2(k, y, ct, \widehat{ct})$, using the witness (v, x') for Ψ_2.
   - Let $\mathsf{zk}_3 = (\widehat{ct}, \mathsf{wi}_3)$.
4. Output the transcript $(\mathsf{zk}_1, \mathsf{zk}_2, \mathsf{zk}_3)$.

Fig. 11. Simulator for the three-message ZK protocol

We now prove the validity of the simulator S, using a sequence of hybrids.

H_1: The transcript $(\mathsf{zk}_1, \mathsf{zk}_2, \mathsf{zk}_3)$ is generated by S.

H_2: Instead of generating wi_3, using the witness (v, x') for Ψ_2, it is generated using a witness ω for $\Psi_1 = (\varphi \in \mathcal{L})$. We note that by the $\widetilde{\mathcal{E}}$-validity property of the GWEF, $v \in \mathcal{K}(k)$ with overwhelming probability. Thus, like ω, (v, x') is also a valid witness for the statement Ψ. By the adaptive witness-indistinguishability of the WI system, this hybrid is computationally indistinguishable from H_1.

H_3: Instead of generating k, x' using $\widetilde{\mathcal{E}}$, we generate it using $\mathcal{E}$. By the extractor-indistinguishability, this hybrid is computationally indistinguishable from H_2.

H_4: Instead of generating $\widehat{ct} \leftarrow \mathit{Eval}(ct, \mathcal{M}_{k,y,x'})$, we generate $\widehat{ct} \leftarrow \mathit{Eval}(ct, \mathbf{1})$. By the extraction guarantee of $\mathcal{E}$ we have that the probability that y is in the image of f_k, but the extractor $\mathcal{E}$ fails to extract $x' \in \mathcal{R}_k^{\mathcal{F}}(y)$, is negligible. We observe that if it is the case that y is in the image and $x' \in \mathcal{R}_k^{\mathcal{F}}(y)$, then by definition $\mathcal{M}_{k,y,x'} \equiv \mathbf{1}$; indeed, for any preimage x of y, it returns 1, since $\mathcal{M}(k, x, x') = 1$, and for any x that is not a preimage $\mathcal{M}_{k,y,x'} \equiv \mathbf{1}$ returns 1. Furthermore, if y is not in the image then no x is a preimage and again $\mathcal{M}_{k,y,x'} \equiv \mathbf{1}$. Since the two circuits are of equal size and compute the same function, the indistinguishability of the two hybrids follows by circuit privacy.

H_5: Here the transcript is generated as in a real interaction between P and V^*. The only difference between this hybrids and the previous ones is that in this hybrid the GWEF key f_k is sampled from $K(1^n)$ instead of by $\mathcal{E}$. Indistinguishability of the hybrids follows by the key-indistinguishability property.

References

[BCC+14] Bitansky, N., et al.: The hunting of the SNARK. IACR Cryptology ePrint Archive, Report 2014/580 (2014)

[BCPR16] Bitansky, N., Canetti, R., Paneth, O., Rosen, A.: On the existence of extractable one-way functions. SIAM J. Comput. **45**(5), 1910–1952 (2016)

[BD18] Brakerski, Z., Döttling, N.: Two-message statistically sender-private OT from LWE. In: Beimel, A., Dziembowski, S. (eds.) TCC 2018. LNCS, vol. 11240, pp. 370–390. Springer, Cham (2018). https://doi.org/10.1007/978-3-030-03810-6_14

[BG92] Bellare, M., Goldreich, O.: On defining proofs of knowledge. In: Brickell, E.F. (ed.) CRYPTO 1992. LNCS, vol. 740, pp. 390–420. Springer, Heidelberg (1993). https://doi.org/10.1007/3-540-48071-4_28

[BKP18] Bitansky, N., Kalai, Y.T., Paneth, O.: Multi-collision resistance: a paradigm for keyless hash functions. In: Proceedings of the 50th Annual ACM SIGACT Symposium on Theory of Computing, STOC 2018, Los Angeles, CA, USA, 25–29 June 2018, pp. 671–684. ACM (2018)

[BKP19] Bitansky, N., Khurana, D., Paneth, O.: Weak zero-knowledge beyond the black-box barrier. In: Proceedings of the 51st Annual ACM SIGACT Symposium on Theory of Computing, STOC 2019, Phoenix, AZ, USA, 23–26 June 2019, pp. 1091–1102. ACM (2019)

[Blu81] Blum, M.: Coin flipping by telephone. In: Advances in Cryptology: A Report on CRYPTO 81, CRYPTO 81, IEEE Workshop on Communications Security, Santa Barbara, California, USA, 24–26 August 1981, pp. 11—15. U.C. Santa Barbara, Department of Electrical and Computer Engineering, ECE Report No 82–04 (1981)

[BP04] Bellare, M., Palacio, A.: Towards plaintext-aware public-key encryption without random oracles. In: Lee, P.J. (ed.) ASIACRYPT 2004. LNCS, vol. 3329, pp. 48–62. Springer, Heidelberg (2004). https://doi.org/10.1007/978-3-540-30539-2_4

[BP19] Bitansky, N., Paneth, O.: On round optimal statistical zero knowledge arguments. In: Boldyreva, A., Micciancio, D. (eds.) CRYPTO 2019. LNCS, vol. 11694, pp. 128–156. Springer, Cham (2019). https://doi.org/10.1007/978-3-030-26954-8_5

[CD08] Canetti, R., Dakdouk, R.R.: Extractable perfectly one-way functions. In: Aceto, L., Damgård, I., Goldberg, L.A., Halldórsson, M.M., Ingólfsdóttir, A., Walukiewicz, I. (eds.) ICALP 2008. LNCS, vol. 5126, pp. 449–460. Springer, Heidelberg (2008). https://doi.org/10.1007/978-3-540-70583-3_37

[Dam91] Damgård, I.: Towards practical public key systems secure against chosen ciphertext attacks. In: Feigenbaum, J. (ed.) CRYPTO 1991. LNCS, vol. 576, pp. 445–456. Springer, Heidelberg (1992). https://doi.org/10.1007/3-540-46766-1_36

[DN00] Dwork, C., Naor, M.: Zaps and their applications. In: 41st Annual Symposium on Foundations of Computer Science, FOCS 2000, Redondo Beach, California, USA, 12–14 November 2000, pp. 283–293. IEEE Computer Society (2000)

[FLS90] Feige, U., Lapidot, D., Shamir, A.: Multiple non-interactive zero knowledge proofs based on a single random string (extended abstract). In: 31st Annual Symposium on Foundations of Computer Science, St. Louis, Missouri, USA, 22–24 October 1990, vol. I, pp. 308–317. IEEE Computer Society (1990)

[FS89] Feige, U., Shamir, A.: Zero knowledge proofs of knowledge in two rounds. In: Brassard, G. (ed.) CRYPTO 1989. LNCS, vol. 435, pp. 526–544. Springer, New York (1990). https://doi.org/10.1007/0-387-34805-0_46

[GK96] Goldreich, O., Krawczyk, H.: On the composition of zero-knowledge proof systems. SIAM J. Comput. **25**(1), 169–192 (1996)

[GOS06] Groth, J., Ostrovsky, R., Sahai, A.: Non-interactive zaps and new techniques for NIZK. In: Dwork, C. (ed.) CRYPTO 2006. LNCS, vol. 4117, pp. 97–111. Springer, Heidelberg (2006). https://doi.org/10.1007/11818175_6

[HT98] Hada, S., Tanaka, T.: On the existence of 3-round zero-knowledge protocols. In: Krawczyk, H. (ed.) CRYPTO 1998. LNCS, vol. 1462, pp. 408–423. Springer, Heidelberg (1998). https://doi.org/10.1007/BFb0055744

[KKS18] Kalai, Y.T., Khurana, D., Sahai, A.: Statistical witness indistinguishability (and more) in two messages. In: Nielsen, J.B., Rijmen, V. (eds.) EUROCRYPT 2018. LNCS, vol. 10822, pp. 34–65. Springer, Cham (2018). https://doi.org/10.1007/978-3-319-78372-7_2

[KPY19] Kalai, Y.T., Paneth, O., Yang, L.: How to delegate computations publicly. In: Proceedings of the 51st Annual ACM SIGACT Symposium on Theory of Computing, STOC 2019, Phoenix, AZ, USA, 23–26 June 2019, pp. 1115–1124. ACM (2019)

[LS19] Lombardi, A., Schaeffer, L.: A note on key agreement and non-interactive commitments. IACR Cryptology ePrint Archive: Report 2019/279 (2019)

[Nao03] Naor, M.: On cryptographic assumptions and challenges. In: Boneh, D. (ed.) CRYPTO 2003. LNCS, vol. 2729, pp. 96–109. Springer, Heidelberg (2003). https://doi.org/10.1007/978-3-540-45146-4_6

[NP01] Naor, M., Pinkas, B.: Efficient oblivious transfer protocols. In: Proceedings of the 12th Annual Symposium on Discrete Algorithms, Washington, DC, USA, 7–9 January 2001, pp. 448–457. ACM/SIAM (2001)

Towards Non-interactive Witness Hiding

Benjamin Kuykendall[(✉)] and Mark Zhandry

Princeton University and NTT Research, Princeton, USA
{brk,mzhandry}@princeton.edu

Abstract. Witness hiding proofs require that the verifier cannot find a witness after seeing a proof. The exact round complexity needed for witness hiding proofs has so far remained an open question. In this work, we provide compelling evidence that witness hiding proofs are achievable *non-interactively* for wide classes of languages. We use non-interactive witness indistinguishable proofs as the basis for all of our protocols. We give four schemes in different settings under different assumptions:

- A *universal* non-interactive proof that is witness hiding as long as any proof system, possibly an inefficient and/or non-uniform scheme, is witness hiding, has a known bound on verifier runtime, and has short proofs of soundness.
- A *non-uniform* non-interactive protocol justified under a worst-case complexity assumption that is witness hiding and efficient, but may not have short proofs of soundness.
- A new security analysis of the *two-message argument* of Pass [Crypto 2003], showing witness hiding for any non-uniformly hard distribution. We propose a heuristic approach to removing the first message, yielding a non-interactive argument.
- A witness hiding non-interactive proof system for languages with *unique witnesses*, assuming the non-existence of a weak form of witness encryption for any language in NP ∩ coNP.

Keywords: Witness hiding · Non-interactive proofs

1 Introduction

Zero knowledge proofs [23] prove that an NP statement is true without revealing anything except the truthfulness of the statement. Such proofs, however, must depart from the usual mathematical notion of a proof by allowing multiple rounds of interaction between the prover and verifier. In fact, such proofs require at least three back-and-forth messages [5,21] between the prover and verifier—and likely more if restricted to black-box constructions [25,29]—without an additional resource such as a common reference string or a random oracle.

Weaker Security Properties. In order to achieve fewer rounds, and in particular to achieve the usual mathematical notion of a non-interactive proof, weaker security guarantees are necessary. Many such notions have been proposed [5–7,14,15,33].

© International Association for Cryptologic Research 2020
R. Pass and K. Pietrzak (Eds.): TCC 2020, LNCS 12550, pp. 627–656, 2020.
https://doi.org/10.1007/978-3-030-64375-1_22

Perhaps the most prominent example is witness indistinguishability, which guarantees that the proofs generated using any two witnesses are computationally indistinguishable. Non-interactive witness indistinguishable (NIWI) proofs are known from standard assumptions such as bilinear maps.

However, for general languages, it is unclear what guarantee is provided by witness indistinguishability. If the particular instance has a unique witness, then witness indistinguishability is completely meaningless, and a NIWI proof could simply be the witness itself. Even in settings with multiple witnesses, it is unclear in general what the proof recipient may learn from the proof. For example, perhaps *some* witness can be extracted from such a proof, even if the prover's own witness remains hidden.

For these reasons, NIWI proofs are typically applied to specially crafted languages where witness indistinguishability yields stronger security properties. As a result, NIWIs have been demonstrated to be useful as a building block for higher-level cryptosystems. Yet, they remain of limited use for any given language[1].

This work will focus on a different relaxation of zero knowledge called *witness hiding* [16]. Witness hiding guarantees that the verifier cannot learn any witness for the NP statement, though they may potentially reveal more than just the truthfulness of the statement. Unlike witness indistinguishability, witness hiding provides a clear, intuitive guarantee for arbitrary statements, including the case of unique witnesses.

Though the security guarantees of witness hiding proofs are apparently much weaker than zero knowledge, it has been surprisingly difficult to actually construct witness hiding proofs in fewer than three rounds. In fact, only recently have constructions for *two-message* witness hiding for all of NP been given [9,13,28]. This state of affairs may be at least partially explained by black-box barriers to witness hiding in few rounds [27]. On the other hand, certain restricted settings are known to have *non-interactive* witness hiding proofs, such as NIWI proofs in the special case when instances have two "independent" witnesses [6,16,26], or for particular protocols [8,12].

Given the difficulty of even achieving two-message witness hiding and the limited positive results for the non-interactive setting, the central question in this paper is:

Is non-interactive witness hiding possible,
and if so, what is needed to construct it?

---

[1] The situation is similar to that of obfuscation, which historically been used to protect intellectual property in software. Here, the ideal notion of Virtual Black Box obfuscation is impossible in general [4], so we consider an indistinguishability notion instead. This weaker notion sees use as a cryptographic building block, but has limited to no meaning for obfuscating general programs, and as such provides no guarantee for the original application to protecting intellectual property.

1.1 Results

In this work, we give a number of positive results for witness hiding in one or two messages. Our protocols work in different settings and rely on different assumptions. Taken together, however, we believe they strongly suggest that non-interactive witness hiding should be possible for all of NP.

In Sect. 3 we review the two-round proof system of [32] and provide a new proof of soundess. While it was already known that the protocol is witness hiding for quasipolynomially hard distributions, we analyze distributions with standard albeit non-uniform hardness. To achieve this, we weaken the model on interaction, considering the *delayed input* setting where the verifier only gets the instance x after sending its first message.

Theorem 1. *Assume quasipolynomially hard one-way-functions and perfectly sound NIWIs for NP. Then for any distribution of instances for which it is hard for efficient non-uniform adversaries to find witnesses, the argument system of [32] is witness hiding argument in the delayed input model.*

In Sect. 4 we build a non-uniform scheme, meaning that for each distribution and some choice of advice shared by the prover and verifier, the proof system is witness hiding. The result uses super-polynomially secure primitives and relies on a new complexity assumption that can be considered as a quantitative strengthening of MA $\not\subseteq$ coNP. The choice of parameters is given in the body of the paper.

Theorem 2. *Assume some language in coNP, for all but finitely many input lengths, lacks an MA-type proof system where the verifier is allowed some specified super-polynomial runtime and witness size. Assume NIWIs for NP with some specified super-polynomial security. Then for any distribution of instances for which it is super-polynomially hard for efficient adversaries to find witnesses, there exists a choice of advice such that our construction is witness hiding.*

In Sect. 5 we build an explicit universal NIWH proof system parameterized by a runtime. If any NIWH scheme exists with a verifier that runs within the time bound and satisfies a *provable soundness* condition we define in the body, then the universal scheme will be witness hiding. Even if the secure scheme has an inefficient prover, the universal scheme will still be efficient. Even if the secure scheme is non-uniform, the universal scheme will still be uniform; although provable soundness must be defined differently in this setting, requiring short proofs of soundness for each input length. We argue that this proof can be extended to arbitrary falsifiable security properties other than witness hiding. In this sense the construction is actually the "best possible" non-interactive proof.

Theorem 3. *Take any distribution D. Assume there exists a non-interactive proof system P, V with an unbounded prover but verifier runtime s. Assume soundness of V is provable in some fixed logical proof system. If P, V is witness hiding for D, then an explicit universal construction (independent of P, V and D but depending on s) is witness hiding as well.*

In Sect. 6 we present a non-interactive proof system for any language with unique witnesses. As part of the construction, a distribution E over instances of an NP ∩ coNP problem is used. Security is as follows: a successful adversary against witness hiding yields a weak form of witness encryption where the instances are drawn from E. This alone is slightly hard to interpret as a positive result. But by combining with the best-possible proof system above, we can avoid a concrete choice of E.

Theorem 4. *Assume some language* $T \in$ *NP* ∩ *coNP lacks a witness encryption scheme with average case correctness relative to some ensemble* E *for all input lengths large enough. Then the best possible proof system above, with a time parameter calculated in the proof, is witness hiding for any distribution over instances with unique witnesses which are hard for efficient adversaries to find.*

1.2   Technical Details

To begin, we recall how non-interactive witness hiding proofs are used to construct non-interactive zero knowledge (and hence witness hiding) proofs in the common reference string model. The common reference string will consist of a commitment to 0: $\mathsf{CRS} = \mathsf{Comm}(0; r)$, where r are the random coins. To prove an NP statement x using witness w, compute a NIWI proof π of the statement

$$x' = x \vee (\exists r : \mathsf{CRS} = \mathsf{Comm}(1; r)).$$

Assuming the commitment Comm is perfectly binding, x' is equivalent to x since the second clause is false. Therefore, a proof of x' also proves x. To show zero knowledge, one switches to an experiment where $\mathsf{CRS} = \mathsf{Comm}(1; r)$, which is undetectable by the hiding property of the commitment. At this point, x' can be proven with witness r, and witness indistinguishability guarantees this proof is indistinguishable from the honest one. But the new proof is independent of the witness for x.

Witness Hiding Arguments in One and Two Messages (Sect. 3). Building on this idea, we consider the following proof system which eschews the common reference string. Let y be any *false* instance of an NP language. To prove a statement x, compute a NIWI proof of the statement

$$x' = x \vee y$$

As before, this proof is sound because y is false. But what about witness hiding? In the example above using commitments, we switch to a setting where we can generate proofs without knowing a witness for x. In the case now, this would seem to require switching y to be true. But if y is chosen by a single party, this could compromise security. Indeed, a malicious prover could generate y to be true and therefore use the satisfying assignment to generate an invalid proof. Meanwhile, a malicious verifier could ensure that y is always false, preventing us from switching to a true y to prove witness hiding. Addressing these two concerns simultaneously is the goal of each of our constructions.

The work of Pass in [32] presents a solution in two rounds. First, the verifier chooses a true statement y, specifically in the form

$$y_b = \exists r \; : \; f(r) = b$$

where f is a one-way function. Then the prover sends a NIWI[2] of $x \vee y_b$ along with a perfectly binding commitment to a witness.

The proofs of soundness and witness hiding proceed through *complexity leveraging*: the reductions will inefficiently invert the one-way function and commitment. To prove witness hiding, we simulate the proof by brute forcing $r = f^{-1}(b)$ then run the witness hiding adversary on the simulated proof.[3] To prove soundness, we open the commitment by brute force, in turn breaking the one-way function. In order for these attacks to yield contradictions, we need *quasipolynomial* security guarantees: in particular, witness hiding is only guaranteed when finding a witness is hard for quasipolynomial time adversaries.

We present a novel security analysis of the Pass construction that avoids complexity leveraging by using non-uniformity instead. Unfortunately, this analysis only works in the *delayed input model* where the verifier does not learn the instance x until after their message is sent.

Previous works also achieve witness hiding proof in two messages. The work of [28] is also only secure in the delayed input model, so their result is comparable. The proof system of [9] is secure in the usual communication model; however, it require strong primitives such as fully homomorphic encryption and compute-and-compare obfuscation. The protocol presented here also allows the verifier's first message to be reused for an arbitrary number of proofs and for public verification of protocol transcripts, unlike protocols in other works.

We observe that under slightly stronger conditions, we can make the verifier use public coins. Suppose that f is in fact a one-way permutation; then the verifier can sample b directly from the image. This will yield the same distribution of first messages. Since r is not needed for verification, the protocol can still be executed. Witness hiding and soundness follow from the exact same analysis as before. Thus we get a public coin two-message witness hiding protocol under general and plausible assumptions.

We next modify the proof to obtain a heuristic non-interactive protocol. We simply have the public coin verifier's first message be deterministically generated from the security parameter, say setting $b = H(1^\lambda)$ for some hash function H. Witness hiding still follows immediately from the analysis above. By fixing the first message, we also eliminate the delayed-input limitation of the two-round protocol. Further, computational soundness can be easily justified in the random oracle model for H.

A random oracle model proof of soundness requires some discussion, as it is well known that non-interactive *zero knowledge* exists in the random oracle

---

[2] An appropriate two-message witness hiding proof or "zap" suffices for their work; we stick with the NIWI for simplicity of explication.

[3] This proof actually yields a stronger property called "quasipolynomial simulatability". But we are only interested in witness hiding here.

model. However, we note that such a zero knowledge system inherently requires the simulator to program random oracle outputs. In particular, zero knowledge cannot hold in the standard model without assuming additional resources like a common reference string. As the simulator is needed to prove witness hiding, this means that proving witness hiding of such a protocol requires the full power of programming the random oracle. In contrast, in our scheme witness hiding holds in the standard model without any reliance on the random oracle. Instead, only soundness requires the random oracle. Moreover, soundness requires only for r to be unpredictable. But this follows simply from the hardness of inverting f and the fact that the random oracle output is truly random. Thus, we obtain soundness in a very mild version of the random oracle model. We note that while Lindell [31] constructed NIZKs where zero knowledge similarly does not require the random oracle, the construction also (inherently) requires a common reference string to achieve zero knowledge hence witness hiding. Our non-interactive protocol does not require a common reference string.

Beyond idealized models, the computational soundness of this scheme poses a significant barrier to removing interaction. Any concrete choice of a hash function that outputs true instances yields a non-uniform adversary against soundness. By taking a witness to $y = H(1^\lambda)$ as advice, the adversary can generate a proof of $x \vee y$ for any x.[4] The same barrier applies to the derandomization techniques that remove interaction from ZAPs; for instance, following [6] and taking y as the output of a hitting set generator would require statistical soundness.

Lacking an explicit means to choose a value of y a priori, we turn to the non-uniform setting. We keep the basic scheme the same, but simply let $y \in$ UNSAT be an advice string for both prover and verifier, guaranteeing soundness. It remains to prove witness hiding.

On Non-uniform Witness Hiding (Sect. 4). We move to the non-uniform setting, where both parties have access to a non-uniform advice string. We will set y to be this advice string. We will also allow adversaries to be non-uniform. We now ask: is there some y such that the protocol above is witness hiding? Suppose to the contrary that the protocol is *not* witness hiding for *any* false y. Then we observe that an adversarial verifier V^* that takes a proof π and extracts a witness for x *itself* serves as a witness to the fact that y is false. Indeed, if y were true, then no such V^* could exist by analogous arguments to above.

So if the protocol fails to be witness hiding for every false y, then we have witnesses for a coNP-complete language. This *suggests* that failure to be witness hiding for any y implies coNP $\subseteq$ NP, a widely unexpected outcome. Unfortunately, the verifier sketched above fails to be an NP verifier in three ways:

- It is probabilistic, running the randomized adversary on random inputs.
- It may not succeed for all input sizes, as breaking security only requires successful adversaries for infinitely many input sizes.

---

[4] The same barrier does not apply to soundness against uniform adversaries. In fact, a closely related construction (described in [3], but analysed in a different setting) can be used to achieve witness hiding proofs sound against uniform adversaries assuming *keyless* collision-resistant hash functions.

- It requires super-polynomial time and witness size, as adversaries can have arbitrary polynomial size and run in arbitrary polynomial time.

Nonetheless, we can strengthen our assumptions to subsume these differences. Define the complexity class $\mathsf{ioMA}(t)$, the analog of MA where the verifier is now allowed to run in time $t(n)$ and is only correct for infinitely many n. We formally describe the verifier sketched above and conclude that either $\mathsf{coNP} \subseteq \mathsf{ioMA}(t)$ for any super-polynomial t—a surprising complexity result— or else for every n there exists *some* false y such that the protocol above is witness hiding.

Unfortunately, we cannot use this protocol in a uniform setting as the y needed to achieve witness hiding may be hard to compute. Furthermore, the choice of y is not universal; it depends on the underlying distribution D from which the statements are drawn. Thus the construction is not a single witness hiding proof system for NP, but rather a family of proof systems, one for each hard distribution. Non-uniform protocols should be viewed as *existential* results: unlike common reference string protocols, the non-uniform model does not require the joint input to be sampleable.

Nevertheless, this result at least suggests a fundamental difficulty of *ruling out* non-interactive witness hiding protocols. Indeed, ruling out such protocols in the non-uniform setting would yield a surprising complexity implication, coming close to showing that the polynomial hierarchy collapses. Given that non-interactive witness hiding cannot be ruled out, we believe our result is also strongly suggestive that it should be possible to actually find a non-interactive witness hiding proof system, under plausible computational assumptions. Finding an explicit procedure for generating appropriate y clearly would suffice to make this scheme uniform; however, it is unclear how to do so.

Best-Possible Proofs (Sect. 5). As discussed above, our non-uniform construction offers compelling evidence for the existence of non-interactive witness hiding proofs, but gives little indication of how to go about constructing them. Here, we partially close this gap, showing that an inexplicit construction satisfying the right properties is sufficient to build an *explicit* witness hiding protocol.

More concretely, we seek a universal non-interactive proof system, which guarantees witness hiding as long as *some* witness hiding protocol exists. Our inspiration will be the notion of best-possible obfuscation, by Goldwasser and Rothblum [24]. There, they showed that the indistinguishability notion of obfuscation is actually as good of an obfuscator as any other notion of obfuscation, subject to certain minutia regarding program size.

Consider the following first attempt. On input a statement x, a proof will be a NIWI proof of the statement

$$x' := \exists V, \pi' : V(x, \pi')$$

Here, V is a verifier for an arbitrary sound proof system and π' is a proof of x relative to V. The intuition behind witness hiding is that if a witness hiding non-interactive proof system (P, V) exists, then V together with $\pi' = P(x, w)$ is a witness for x'. Such a witness would of course be witness hiding by assumption and can be used to generate the NIWI proof of x'. However, we do not actually need to know (P, V) in order to generate the proof: we can use *any* sound proof system to generate the NIWI proof of x'. For example, take (I, V_L) to be the standard NP proof system: I simply outputs the witness, and V_L checks the NP relation. Of course, this proof system does not hide the witness, but once we use it to generate the NIWI proof of x', witness indistinguishability kicks in and implies that the resulting proof is "as good" as if it had been generated using (P, V). Thus, we obtain witness hiding regardless of the starting proof system.

While the above does indeed demonstrate witness hiding, the protocol is not sound. The problem is that the statement x' does not actually guarantee that V is the verifier of a sound proof system (recall that although soundness is often described as a property of a proof system, it is actually a property of the verifier alone). A cheating prover could simply pick V to accept all inputs; then the proof verifies for any choice of x'.

We need to augment the proof system to check that V is sound. For an arbitrary Turing machine V, there is no way to actually this: the problem is undecidable. Even restricting to circuits, making this determination efficiently would imply a collapse of the polynomial hierarchy. Instead, we require that V is accompanied by a proof attesting to its soundness. In more detail, consider a sound logical system S that is powerful enough to reason about programs and soundness. A witness (z, V, π) for x' then consists of a witness z for x under V, the code of the verifier V, and an S-proof π that V is sound. In order for this to be an NP relation, we need a polynomial bound on the length of the witness (z, V, π). In particular, we need a bound s on the runtime of V.

Our resulting proof system is sound, assuming the soundness of S. It will also be witness hiding, as long as *some* witness hiding proof system exists whose verifier runs in time at most s and whose soundness can be proving using S. The witness hiding proof system can even have inefficient provers, and our proof system will inherit the witness hiding security and still be efficient. Thus, to demonstrate witness hiding of our protocol, one only has to reason about the *existence* of witness hiding proofs.

The discussion above extends to the case where V is a circuit instead of a Turing machine; this allows us to base witness hiding off of the existence of a non-uniform scheme. But in the non-uniform case, the proof of soundness may be different for each input length. Thus the need for short proofs of soundness becomes a significant obstacle. However, the best-possible proof system remains uniform, even if a non-uniform scheme is used to prove security.

Given this extension to non-uniform schemes, one may hope to combine our best-possible proof system with our non-uniform proof system from the previous section, thereby obtaining a concrete witness hiding proof. Unfortunately, this appears challenging. In order to use our best-possible proof system, we require a proof of soundness in S. But such a proof would demonstrate that the advice string y in the non-uniform proof system is a false statement. Such a proof would be at odds with our justification for the soundness of the protocol. Recall that our soundness proof assumes that a carefully constructed MA-type proof system

P_{nu} rejects y. But a proof of soundness implies y has a short proof of satisfiability in $\mathcal{S}$, which in turn defines an NP proof system $P_{\mathcal{S}}$. Thus to find a choice of advice that suffices for the non-uniform protocol and demonstrates provable soundness, we would need to demonstrate a sequence of y that are rejected by P_{nu} but accepted by $P_{\mathcal{S}}$. It is unclear if such instances exist.

*Non-interactive Witness Hiding vs. Witness Encryption (*Sect. 6*).* To alleviate this difficulty, our next idea is to explicitly choose y with short proofs of unsatisfiability. Concretely, choose y from a distribution over non-instances of some language T in NP $\cap$ coNP. Making this change means we can no longer rely on the assumption coNP $\subsetneq$ MA to prove completeness; but an interesting connection to witness encryption will yield another route to proving security.

We will have the prover sample y from some distribution E over *false* instances and prove the statement $x' = x \vee y$ as before. Since a malicious prover could have chosen a true statement y, this protocol so far is not sound. However, we augment the proof π by also including the witness z for the falseness of y.

Now certainly the protocol is sound, since z means that x' is equivalent to x. But why might this protocol be witness hiding? After all, by including z in the proof, we seem to have again broken any arguments that work by switching y to be true. It appears we are back at square one.

First, we limit ourselves to distributions D over x with *unique* witnesses.[5] Now suppose we actually did *not* include z. Then we can easily prove witness hiding by switching y to be a true instance and using the witness for y to generate the proof. This implies that given π alone it is hard to find the witness for x.

Now suppose that the overall proof is not witness hiding. This means given π alone, the witness w for x is hidden, but given *both* π and z it is possible to recover w. If so, we can turn the protocol plus witness hiding adversary into a type of *witness encryption scheme* for statements $\neg y$. Recall that witness encryption [19] allows for encrypting messages to NP statements; any witness for the statement can recover the message, but messages encrypted to false statements are computationally hidden.

Consider the following first attempt at a witness "key encapsulation" scheme: to encrypt to an instance $\neg y$, sample a random (x, w) from D. Then construct the proof π that $x \vee y$ using the witness w for x. The ciphertext is π and the encapsulated key is w. If $\neg y$ is false (meaning y is true), then we know that π computationally hides w by the NIWI. Thus we get witness encryption security. On the other hand, if $\neg y$ is true and one knows a witness z for $\neg y$, one can run the witness hiding adversary to recover w. Uniqueness of w guarantees that the recovered w is the actual encapsulated key. Of course, w is not pseudorandom as one can verify that w is a valid witness. Instead, we will extract a Goldreich-Levin hardcore bit from w; this hardcore bit will then be used to mask the message bit.

---

[5] Recall that for languages with multiple *independent* witnesses, a NIWI proof is already witness hiding, so the unique witness setting covers the other end of the spectrum; we will leave it as an interesting open problem extending our results below to "in between" languages with multiple *dependent* witnesses.

Now, the above scheme fails to satisfy the definition of witness encryption for two reasons:

- The witness hiding adversary might work with only non-negligible probability. This yields a decryption algorithm that succeeds with only non-negligible probability.
- Correctness is only guaranteed with respect to witnesses sampled according to E, not truly arbitrary witnesses.

Nevertheless, such a witness encryption scheme has interesting consequences. If, for distribution D, there is no language T and distribution E that make our protocol witness hiding, then we get such a witness encryption scheme for every language and distribution over instances in NP ∩ coNP. This would be enough to build public key encryption, assuming any hard-on-average problem in NP ∩ coNP. By hard-on-average, we mean that there is a second distribution F over true instances (and valid witnesses) such that y sampled from E or F are computationally indistinguishable. This gives public key encryption from tools that are otherwise not known to imply public key encryption, namely NIWIs and any hard-on-average problem in NP ∩ coNP. It is also enough to build identity-based encryption from any unique signature scheme, following [19].

Another interesting consequence of our connection to witness encryption is the following: general witness encryption is currently known only from very strong and new mathematical tools [2,19]. While many in the community believe witness encryption exists, the case is far from settled. We do not take a position either way, but consider the plausible scenario that there is *some* language in NP ∩ coNP and some distribution for which no witness encryption scheme exists (in the sense obtained above).[6]

Under this assumed *non*-existence of witness encryption, for appropriate choice of length parameters we immediately see that our best-possible proof system is a non-interactive witness hiding proof system. In fact, it is possible to use any choice of polynomial-length length parameters by re-scaling the security parameters appropriately. Thus we obtain a fully concrete scheme with provable security under plausible assumptions.

1.3   Discussion

We observe that our protocols are superficially related to the "proofs of ignorance" approach of Kalai and Deshpande [13]. In their work, they prove x by

---

[6] It is worth noting that many problems in NP ∩ coNP do have witness encryption schemes based on their own hardness: for example, the quadratic residuosity problem gives rise to the Goldwasser-Micali pubic key encryption scheme [22], which can be adapted to a witness encryption scheme for the language of quadratic non-residues. However, hardness in NP ∩ coNP is not known to generically imply witness encryption or even public key encryption. For example, the presumed hard problems of deciding who wins in a stochastic game [11] or determining whether a given knot is the unknot [30] are both in NP ∩ coNP, but neither is known to yield public key encryption.

proving $x \vee y$ and supplying a "proof of ignorance" that the prover does not know a witness for y. For example, the witness w for $\neg y$ in our second construction certainly demonstrates that the prover does not know a witness for y. On the other hand, turning "proofs of ignorance," as defined by [13], into witness hiding, used a very strong KDM security assumption, which was demonstrated to be false [18]. Our justifications for witness hiding proceed by entirely different arguments.

Haitner, Rosen and Shaltiel provide a black-box barrier to witness hiding in few rounds [27]. However, their barrier does not apply to our schemes. Their barrier only applies to specific (but common) approaches to witness hiding by parallel repetition; our schemes do not use parallel repetition. Further, our schemes are certainly non-black-box, using the adversary's code itself to either violate a complexity assumption or build another protocol. Some of our proofs are also not by reduction to the original search problem, again avoiding the barrier.

2 Preliminaries

2.1 Basic Building Blocks

Let p.p.t. be the set of probabilistic polynomial time Turing machines. Let negl be the set of negligible functions. We use the standard definition of NP.

Definition 1 (Conventions for NP languages). *Note the verifier characterizes the language: given a two-input machine V that runs in time polynomial in the length of the first input, put $L_V = \{x \: : \: \exists y \; V \; accepts \; (x,w)\}$. Define the NP witness relation for L as $R_L = \{(x,w) \: : \: V \; accepts \; (x,w)\}$.*

Definition 2 (probability ensemble). *A probability ensemble D is a map from $\mathbb{N}$ to distributions over strings. All probability ensembles in this paper will be of polynomial length, meaning there exists a polynomial p such that for all λ and $x \in \mathrm{Sup}(D(\lambda))$ we have $|x| \leq p(\lambda)$. They will also be poly-time sampleable. Let $\Delta(S)$ be the set of probability ensembles with support contained in S.*

Definition 3 (search hardness). *Fix $L \in$ NP, $D \in \Delta(R_L)$. Say the search problem over D is hard when $\forall A \in$ p.p.t.*

$$\Pr_{(x,w) \sim D(\lambda)} [(x, A(x)) \in R_L] = \mathrm{negl}(\lambda).$$

Analogously, say the *search problem over D is hard against non-uniform adversaries* when the same condition holds $\forall A \in$ p.p.t. / poly.

Definition 4 (hard-on-average). *Fix $L \in$ NP, $D_0 \in \Delta(\overline{L})$, $D_1 \in \Delta(L)$. Say L is hard-on-average when D_0 and D_1 are computationally indistinguishable.*

2.2   Proof Systems

The proof systems used in this paper differ in three aspects. First, they use different number of messages. Second, they have different soundness guarantees. Third, they have different guarantees on what information is revealed to the verifier. We do not define a full taxonomy of proof systems but rather only what we will use in the later parts of the paper.

Definition 5 (non-interactive argument system). *Fix an NP relation R_L. We say a pair of p.p.t. algorithms P, V is a non-interactive argument system for L when the following two properties hold:*

   Completeness: $\forall (x, w) \in R_L$, $\Pr[V(x, P(x, w))] = 1$.
   Soundness: $\forall \widetilde{P} \in$ p.p.t., $\exists \mu \in$ negl, $\forall x \notin L$, $\Pr[V(x, \widetilde{P}(x))] \leq \mu(|x|)$.

Definition 6 (non-interactive proof system). *We say a non-interactive argument system P, V is a non-interactive proof system for L when the following stronger soundness property holds:*

   Soundness: $\exists \mu \in$ negl, $\forall x \notin L$, $\forall \pi$, $\Pr[V(x, \pi)] \leq \mu(|x|)$.

In particular, we say a proof system has *perfect soundness* when the soundness property holds with $\mu = 0$. Analogously, a *non-uniform non-interactive proof system* is a pair of p.p.t./ poly algorithms for which the same properties hold.

Next we define the delayed input model in the two-message case. We define the steps of the verifier V by two algorithms V_0, V_1. First, V_0 runs on input $|x|$ and outputs the first message m and some internal state q; second, the prover P runs on input x, m and outputs the second message π; third, V_1 runs on input x, q, π and either accepts or rejects. We define completeness and soundness in this model.

Definition 7 (delayed-input two-message argument system). *Fix $L \in$ NP. A triple of p.p.t. algorithms V_0, P, V_1 is a two-message argument system for L when the following two properties hold:*

   Completeness: $\forall (x, w) \in R_L$:

$$\Pr[V_1(x, q, P(x, w, m)) \mid (q, m) \leftarrow V_0(|x|)] = 1.$$

   Soundness: $\forall \widetilde{P} \in$ p.p.t., $\exists \mu \in$ negl, $\forall x \notin L$

$$\Pr[V_1(x, q, \widetilde{P}(x, m)) \mid (q, m) \leftarrow V_0(|x|)]] \leq \mu(|x|).$$

Definition 8 (witness indistinguishable [6,10]). *Say the prover P is witness indistinguishable for $L \in$ NP when for any sequence $I = \{(x, w_1, w_2)\}$ such that $(x, w_i) \in R_L$, the ensembles Π_1, Π_2 are computationally indistinguishable, where:*

$$\Pi_i = \{\pi \leftarrow P(x, w_i)\}_{(x, w_1, w_2) \in I}.$$

We assume NIWIs for arbitrary NP relations. Thus when R_L is clear from context, we say simply "a NIWI for x using witness w" to denote $P(x, w)$ and "verify that π is a valid proof of x" to denote $V(x, \pi)$. Implicit is an encoding scheme to write x as an instance of an NP-complete problem and w as the corresponding witness.

Definition 9 (witness hiding). *Fix $L \in$ NP, $D \in \Delta(R_L)$. Say the prover P is* witness hiding *for D when $\forall A \in$ p.p.t./ poly*

$$\Pr_{(x,w)\sim D(\lambda)}[(x, A(x, P(x, w))) \in R_L] = \mathrm{negl}(\lambda).$$

Though this definition is used in prior work [13,28], it is weaker than the original definition of witness hiding given by Feige and Shamir [17]. Their definition requires an explicit witness extractor M that, by making black-box calls to the adversary A and the sampler for D, achieves $\Pr[(x, A(x, P(x, w))) \in R_L] - \Pr[(x, M^{A,D}(x)) \in R_L] \leq \mathrm{negl}(\lambda)$. The extractor definition entails explicit black-box security reductions that are not achieved for all of our constructions.

2.3   Fine-Grained Notions

For Sect. 4 we define *fine-grained* notions of the above. To make these modifications, we change our notions of "efficient adversaries" and "negligible functions" to concrete measures. Let $\mathrm{SIZE}(S)$ be the class of circuit families of size $S(\lambda)$.

Definition 10 ((S, ε)-hardness of search problem). *Fix $L \in$ NP, $D \in \Delta(R_L)$. Say the* search problem over D is (S, ε)-hard *when $\forall \lambda \in \mathbb{N}$, $\forall A \in \mathrm{SIZE}(S)$*

$$\Pr_{(x,w)\sim D(\lambda)}[(x, A(x)) \in R_L] \leq \varepsilon(\lambda).$$

In the standard definitions of proof systems, using the length of the input to quantify the security suffices. But in the finer-grained model, we choose an explicit security parameter λ and provide 1^λ as input to the prover.

Definition 11 ((S, ε)-witness indistinguishable). *Fix $L \in$ NP. We say a proof system (P, V) is (S, ε)-witness indistinguishable for L when $\forall \lambda, x, w_1, w_2$ such that $(x, w_i) \in R_L$ and $\forall A \in \mathrm{SIZE}(S)$*

$$\left| \Pr_{\pi \leftarrow P(x, w_1, 1^\lambda)}[A(x, \pi)] - \Pr_{\pi \leftarrow P(x, w_2, 1^\lambda)}[A(x, \pi)] \right| \leq \varepsilon(\lambda).$$

Definition 12 ((S, ε)-witness hiding). *Fix $L \in$ NP, $D \in \Delta(R_L)$. Say a prover P is (S, ε)-witness hiding for D when $\forall \lambda \in \mathbb{N}$, $A \in \mathrm{SIZE}(S)$*

$$\Pr_{(x,w)\sim D(\lambda)}[(x, A(x, P(x, w, 1^\lambda))) \in R_L] = \varepsilon(\lambda).$$

We also say a proof system is (S, ε)-*witness hiding for all λ large enough* when there exists λ_0 such that for all $\lambda > \lambda_0$ the condition holds.

3   Witness Hiding Arguments in One and Two Messages

We review the two-message proof system of Pass from [32]. The referenced work proves a property called quasipolynomial time simulatability. We repeat this analysis, showing how it implies witness hiding for subexponentially hard distributions. The proof system takes the form of a NIWI of $x \lor y$ for a clause in the form $y = \exists r : f(r) = b$ where f is a one-way function. A perfectly binding commitment to the witness is included for the proof of soundness. The choice of b is made by the verifier. The analysis is completed using complexity leveraging.

We also present a new analysis in the delayed input model. This allows us to replace complexity leveraging with non-uniform choices. This result is incomparable to the original.

The introduction discusses several further properties of the protocol. The protocol allows the verifier's first message to be reused for an arbitrary number of proofs, and allows for public verification of transcripts. Further, if the distribution of b is uniformly random, for example if f is chosen to be a permutation, then the scheme is public coin. Finally, the scheme is amenable to a heuristic implementation by a hash function: simply choose $b = H(1^\lambda)$. In the (non-programmable) random oracle model this is secure.

3.1   Prerequisites

We require surjective one-way functions and commitment schemes with guarantees amenable to complexity leveraging: this entails security against one class of adversaries, but also requires that they can be inverted in some larger runtime.

Definition 13 (one-way function). *Say a one-way function f is* secure *against adversaries running in time T_0 if $\forall A \in \text{SIZE}(T)$, $\text{Pr}_{x \sim \mathcal{U}}[f(A(f(x))) = f(x)]$. We say f is* invertible *in time T_1 if there exists a Turing machine B running in time T_1 such that $\forall x, f(B(f(x))) = f(x)$.*

Definition 14 (perfectly binding commitment). *Say a commitment scheme* Comm *is* perfectly binding *if $\forall x_1 \neq x_2, \forall r_1, \forall r_2$, $\text{Comm}(x_1, r_1) \neq \text{Comm}(x_2, r_2)$. Say* Comm *is* hiding *if commitments to any pairs of sequences of messages, one of each length, are computationally indistinguishable by non-uniform adversaries. We say* Comm *is* extractable *in time T_1 if there exists a Turing machine B running in time T_1 such that $\forall x, \forall r, B(\text{Comm}(x, r)) = x$.*

3.2   Construction from Pass 2003

Fix $L \in \mathsf{NP}$ and $D \in \Delta(R_L)$. Consider the following scheme for a two-message witness hiding argument in the delayed input model. Let $f : \{0,1\}^k \to \{0,1\}^\ell$ a surjective one-way function and Comm a perfectly binding commitment scheme.

$\mathsf{TwoMessage.V_0}(|x|)$: sample $r \sim \{0,1\}^k$. Put $b = f(r)$. Save and output b.

TwoMessage.$P(x, w, b)$: put $c = \text{Comm}((0^\ell, w))$. Compute π a NIWI for

$$S_{b,c} := \exists r', w' \; : \; c = \text{Comm}((r', w')) \wedge (b = f(r') \vee (x, w') \in R_L)$$

using the witness $(0^\ell, w)$. Output $\tau = (c, \pi)$.

TwoMessage.$V_1(x, b, (c, \pi))$: check that π is a valid proof of $S_{b,c}$.

3.3   Security from Complexity Leveraging

We sketch the proof of [32] for completeness.

Theorem 5. *Assume the search problem over D is hard against adversaries running in time T_{search}. Assume f is one-way against adversaries running in time T_{owf} but invertible in time T_{invert}. Assume Comm is hiding against non-uniform polynomial time adversaries and extractable in time T_{extract}. Assume a perfectly sound NIWI. If the following inequalities hold for all polynomials p:*

$$T_{\text{search}} = O(T_{\text{invert}} + p(n)),$$
$$T_{\text{owf}} = O(T_{\text{extract}} + p(n))$$

then TwoMessage is a perfectly complete witness hiding argument system against adversaries running in time $o(T_{\text{search}})$.

In particular, if D, f, and the extraction algorithm for Comm are quasipolynomially hard in their input lengths and security parameters, then input lengths and security parameters can be set to satisfy the above inequalities as in the original paper.

Proof. Completeness follows from the completeness of the underlying NIWI. Witness hiding follows by considering π generated using an alternative witness. Soundness is by reduction to the one-way function game.

Completeness: if $(x, w) \in R_L$ then $(0^n, w)$ is a valid witness for $S_{b,c}$. Thus by the completeness of the NIWI system conclude that the verifier accepts.

Witness Hiding: let A be an attacker on witness hiding. We build B simulating the prover in order to break the search problem against D as follows. Sample $x \sim D$ and send it to A, which will reply with some value b. Invert the OWF to find r such that $f(r) = b$. Then compute π' a NIWI of $S_{b,c}$ using witness $(r, 0)$. Let $c = \text{Comm}((r, 0))$. Send (c, b) to A. Interpret the output of A as a possible witness for x.

Argue that $\text{Adv}_B = \text{Adv}_A \pm \text{negl}$ from the witness indistinguishability of the NIWI and the hiding property of the commitment. Standard witness indistinguishability and hiding against non-uniform adversaries suffice (though we omit the proof).

Soundness: fix $x \notin L$ and a possibly malicious prover A outputting (c, π) given honest b. We construct a one-way function adversary B as follows. First, extract the commitment c which yields (r', w') by binding. By the soundness of the NIWI system we know that (r', w') is a witness for $S_{b,c}$. But since $x \notin L$ conclude that $(x, w') \notin R_L$. Thus it must be the case that $f(r') = b$. Output r'.

3.4 Security from Non-uniform Hardness

The witness hiding proof above can be adjusted to avoid the use of complexity leveraging if we assume the D search problem is hard against non-uniform adversaries and move to the delayed input model.

Theorem 6. *Assume the search problem over D is hard against poly-size circuits. Assume f is one-way against adversaries running in time T_{owf}. Assume* Comm *is hiding against non-uniform polynomial time adversaries and extractable in time T_{extract}. Assume a perfectly sound NIWI. If the following inequality holds for all polynomials p:*

$$T_{\mathrm{owf}} = O(T_{\mathrm{extract}} + p(n))$$

then TwoMessage *is a perfectly complete witness hiding argument system against efficient poly-size circuits.*

Proof. Completeness and soundness follow identically. For witness hiding, we build a non-uniform adversary, hard-coding the OWF pre-image.

Witness Hiding: let A be an attacker on witness hiding; it plays the role of a malicious verifier and outputs w' a witness for $x \in L$ with probability Adv_A. Recall from the definition that A consists of two algorithms: first, A_0 which takes input $|x|$ and outputs b and some internal state q; second, the honest prover P runs on input x, b yielding c, π; third, A_1 which takes (b, q), (c, π) and x and outputs w.

Let r_0 be the explicit choice of randomness by A_0. Then we can break the experiment that defines Adv_A into two parts:

$$\underset{r_0}{\mathrm{E}}[\Pr[(x, A_1(x, q, \tau)) \in R_L \mid (b, q) = A_0(|x|, r_0)]] = \mathrm{Adv}_A,$$

where $\tau = $ TwoMessage.$\mathsf{P}(x, w, b)$ and the inner probability is over choice of $x \sim D$, $z' \sim \{0, 1\}^n$, internal randomness of the NIWI prover, and internal randomness of A_1. Now for each input size we can fix some (b, q) such that

$$\Pr[(x, A_1(x, q, \tau)) \in R_L] \geq \mathrm{Adv}_A.$$

We define a non-uniform adversary B against the search problem over D. For inputs size λ, the advice is a tuple (b, q, r) with b, q as chosen above and r such that $f(b) = r$. On input x, set $c = \mathrm{Comm}((r, 0))$ and compute a NIWI of $S_{b,c}$ using witness $(r, 0)$. Run A on the new proof. The conclusion that $\mathrm{Adv}_B = \mathrm{Adv}_A \pm \mathrm{negl}$ follows as above.

4   Non-uniform Witness Hiding

We present a non-interactive *non-uniform* witness hiding proof system. By writing a proof of x as a NIWI of $x \vee y$ for a false statement y fixed non-uniformly, we easily guarantee completeness and soundness. To achieve witness hiding, we give an MA-type verifier relative to which the code of an adversary is itself a witness to the falseness of y.

We begin by quantifying how this proof system differs from the standard complexity class MA. Then we state our construction formally and prove the desired security properties. The construction is unfortunately existential: it is unclear how to instantiate the scheme, even heuristically. However, it provides strong barriers to ruling out non-interactive witness hiding protocols.

4.1 Assumption

Throughout, UNSAT denotes the language of unsatisfiable boolean formulae. An arbitrary coNP-complete language can be used to yield the same result. Now recall the standard definition of MA. (e.g. adapted from Def. 8.10 of [1]).

Definition 15 (MA). *We say L has an MA proof system when some p.p.t. Turing machine V has the following properties for some polynomial q:*

Completeness: $\forall x \in L, |x| = \lambda, \exists a \in \{0,1\}^{q(\lambda)}, \Pr[V(x,a)] \geq 2/3$,
Soundness: $\forall x \notin L, \forall a, \Pr[V(x,a)] \leq 1/3$.

From this definition, we get the standard complexity assumption MA $\not\subseteq$ coNP. Unfortunately, this assumption does not appear sufficient for our NIWH system.

We need to make two changes. First, we allow the verifier to run in some super-polynomial time $T(\lambda)$ and use witnesses of size $R(\lambda)$. Second, while standard assumptions only require that the verifier fail for some input length, we want a proof system that works for all input lengths. Thus we require that any proof system fails for all inputs large enough. Both changes are captured by the following definition.

Definition 16 (ioMA(T,R)). *Take any T, R. Say L has an ioMA(T,R) proof system when some V running in time $T(\lambda)$ has both of the following properties for infinitely many values of λ:*

Completeness: $\forall x \in L, |x| = \lambda, \exists a \in \{0,1\}^{R(\lambda)}, \Pr[V(x,a)] \geq 2/3$,
Soundness: $\forall x \notin L, |x| = \lambda, \forall a \Pr[V(x,a)] \leq 1/3$.

The complexity assumption coNP $\not\subseteq$ ioMA(T,R) is simply a quantitative strengthening of coNP $\not\subseteq$ MA; we believe it to be justifiable under the same motivation.

4.2 Construction

Fix $L \in$ NP and $D \in \Delta(R_L)$. We propose the following scheme for a non-interactive witness-hiding proof. The scheme is parameterized by a sequence of circuits $(y_\lambda)_{\lambda \in \mathbb{N}}$ with each $y_\lambda \in$ UNSAT and $|y_\lambda| = \lambda$. The y_λ serve as advice for the prover and verifier.

NonUniform.Prove$(x, w, 1^\lambda; y_\lambda)$: output a NIWI for $x \in L \lor y_\lambda \in$ SAT using witness w and security parameter λ.
NonUniform.Verify$(x, \pi; y_\lambda)$: verify π is a valid proof of $x \in L \lor y_\lambda \in$ SAT.

4.3   Security

Completeness and soundness follow directly from the completeness and soundness of the underlying NIWI, for any choice of $y_\lambda \in$ UNSAT. To prove witness-hiding we use the complexity assumption. The proof and the security of the resulting NIWH proof system are parameterized by the strength of the complexity assumption and the security of the NIWI.

Theorem 7. *Fix a constant* $\alpha > 0$. *Assume the search problem over* D *is* (S, ε)-*hard. Assume a perfectly sound* $(S_{\text{NIWI}}, \varepsilon_{\text{NIWI}})$-*NIWI. Assume* coNP $\not\subseteq$ ioMA(T, R). *Assume the following inequalities between parameters hold, for some fixed* $q(\lambda) = \text{poly}(\lambda)$ *and constant* β *chosen in the proof:*

$$S(\lambda) \geq S_{\text{NIWI}}(\lambda) + q(\lambda),$$
$$T(\lambda) \geq \beta((\varepsilon + \varepsilon_{\text{NIWI}})^{-1}\alpha^{-2})(S_{\text{NIWI}}(\lambda) + \text{poly}(\lambda)),$$
$$R(\lambda) \geq S_{\text{NIWI}}(\lambda).$$

Then there exists a sequence of y_λ *(depending on* D*) such that* NonUniform *is a perfectly sound proof system with* $(S_{\text{NIWI}}, (1 + \alpha)(\varepsilon + \varepsilon_{\text{NIWI}}))$-*witness-hiding for all* λ *large enough.*

In particular: take S_{NIWI} slightly super-polynomial in λ and $\varepsilon_{\text{NIWI}} = \text{negl}(\lambda)$. The required T, R, S will be fixed super-polynomial functions as given by the inequalities in the theorem statement. Then under the appropriate assumptions the theorem yields a standard NIWH system; that is, with witness hiding $\text{negl}(\lambda)$ against all $\text{poly}(\lambda)$ adversaries.

Proof. We prove completeness, soundness, and witness hiding.

Completeness: if $(x, w) \in R_L$ then w is a witness for $x \in L \lor y_\lambda \in$ SAT. By completeness of the NIWI system conclude that NonUniform.Verify accepts (x, π).

Soundness: consider $x \notin L$. Since $y_\lambda \in$ UNSAT, we know the statement $x \in L \lor y_\lambda \in$ SAT is false. Thus by the soundness of the NIWI system we conclude NonUniform.Verify does not accept (x, π) for any value of π.

Witness-Hiding: we prove witness-hiding by constructing an ioMA(T, R)-type protocol for UNSAT. We show the protocol is unconditionally sound and efficient. We show the protocol is complete if and only if there is no choice of $(y_\lambda)_{\lambda \in \mathbb{N}}$ such that NonUniform is witness-hiding. The verifier is parameterized by a choice of α (in the theorem statement) and k (chosen below).

UnsatVerifier(t, A): Interpret A as a circuit. If $|A| \geq S_{\text{NIWI}}$ reject. Sample k tuples $(x_i, w_i) \sim D(|t|)$ and compute the sample probability

$$p = \frac{1}{k} \sum_{i \in [k]} \mathbb{1}[(x_i, A(x_i, \text{NonUniform.Prove}(x_i, w_i; t))) \in R_L].$$

Accept if and only $p > (1 + \alpha/2)(\varepsilon + \varepsilon_{\text{NIWI}})$.

Soundness of UnsatVerifier: fix $(t, z) \in R_{\text{SAT}}$. Let π be a NIWI proof of $x \in L \vee t \in \text{SAT}$ using witness z. If $|A| < S_{\text{NIWI}}$ then by witness indistinguishability we know

$$\Pr[(x_i, A(x_i, \text{NonUniform.Prove}(x_i, w_i; t))) \in R_L] \leq \Pr[(x_i, A(x_i, \pi)) \in R_L] + \varepsilon_{\text{NIWI}}.$$

Now note that $(x_i, A(x_i, \pi)) \in R_L$ is computed by a circuit of size at most $|A|$, plus the size of the circuit that computes the NIWI, plus the size of the verifier circuit for R_L. Setting q accordingly, then it is bounded in particular by $S \geq S_{\text{NIWI}} + q(\lambda)$. Thus by the hardness of the D-search problem

$$\Pr[(x_i, A(x_i, \pi)) \in R_L] < \varepsilon.$$

Together the two inequalities yield

$$\Pr[(x_i, A(x_i, \text{NonUniform.Prove}(x_i, w_i; t))) \in R_L] \leq \varepsilon + \varepsilon_{\text{NIWI}}.$$

This shows that $\mathbb{E}[p] \leq \varepsilon + \varepsilon_{\text{NIWI}}$. To bound the tail probability use a standard Chernoff bound (e.g. Cor. A.15 in [1]).

$$\Pr[|p - \varepsilon + \varepsilon_{\text{NIWI}}| \geq \frac{\alpha}{2}(\varepsilon + \varepsilon_{\text{NIWI}})] \leq 2 \exp(-\alpha^2 \Omega(k(\varepsilon + \varepsilon_{\text{NIWI}}))).$$

Thus choosing $k = \beta((\varepsilon + \varepsilon_{\text{NIWI}})^{-1}\alpha^{-2})$ for some constant β suffices for the verifier to reject with probability $2/3$.

Runtime of UnsatVerifier: from our choice of k and the size of A observe the verifier runs in time

$$k(|A| + \text{poly}(\lambda)) = \beta((\varepsilon + \varepsilon_{\text{NIWI}})^{-1}\alpha^{-2})(S_{\text{NIWI}} + q).$$

Completeness of UnsatVerifier: fix $r \in \text{UNSAT}$, $|r| = \lambda$. Assume NonUniform with advice r is not sufficiently witness hiding. Then there exists A with $|A| < S_{\text{NIWI}}$ such that

$$\Pr[(x_i, A(x_i, \text{NonUniform.Prove}(x_i, w_i; r))) \in R_L] \geq (1 + \alpha)(\varepsilon + \varepsilon_{\text{NIWI}}).$$

Applying the same Chernoff bound shows that the verifier will accept with overwhelming probability.

Conclude by using the assumption: since we know for all $\lambda > \lambda_0$ that UnsatVerifier cannot be complete, there must be some $y \in \text{UNSAT}$, $|y| = \lambda$ such that NonUniform with advice y_λ is witness hiding.

5 Best-Possible Proofs

We present a construction for a non-interactive witness hiding proof system that is secure as long as any such scheme is secure. In fact, assuming even the existence a proof system with an inefficient prover, the scheme given in this section will be efficient and uniform as long as the original scheme is *provably sound* in a sense made precise later. We discuss how a non-uniform notion of provable soundness can be used to base the same construction off of the existence of a non-uniform witness hiding proof system. We do not know if the scheme given in the previous section meets this requirement.

This construction enjoys security properties beyond witness hiding. In fact, assuming the existence of a provably sound non-interactive proof that achieves any falsifiable security notion, this construction will have the property as well as long as length parameters are picked appropriately. Thus the construction is in fact the "best possible" non-interactive proof that can be achieved, in the same sense as [24].

Unfortunately, this paper does not provide a NIWH for all NP that has provable soundness. Thus, we are left in an odd state of affairs where we know a universal construction but lack the existential proof needed to claim it is secure.

5.1   Prerequisites

Let S be a proof system for a language powerful enough to encode Turing machines. Assume that S-proofs can be checked in time polynomial in their length. Further assume that S is sound, meaning that any provable statement in S is true in the metatheory (or, for the purposes of this work, simply true). A concrete choice of S would be Peano arithmetic or any standard deductive system for axiomatic set theory.

Fix some verifier V corresponding to the language $L_V \in$ NP. Let D be another polynomial-time verifier. We want a proof that $L_V = L_D$ inside of S. This leads to the following definition.

Definition 17 (soundness for L_V). *We say D is L_V-sound if the following statement holds*

$$\forall x \in \{0,1\}^* \ (\exists y \ D(x,y) \Rightarrow \exists w \ V(x,w)).$$

We require that such a statement can be encoded in the language of S. We also require that the there be a proof that V is L_V-sound. This is a relatively mild assumption, achievable by both concrete choices of proof systems proposed.

5.2   Construction

We begin by constructing V', another verifier for L_V. Fix polynomials q, s, ℓ.

$V'(x, w')$: Interpret $(z, D, \pi) \leftarrow w'$ where
   z is a string of length $q(|x|)$,
   D is a Turing machine description of length $s(|x|)$,
   π is an S-proof of length $\ell(|x|)$.
Verify that π is a valid proof that D is L_V-sound. If not, reject. Otherwise, simulate D on input (x, z) for s steps and output the result.

Theorem 8. V' *is an NP verifier for* L_V *for sufficiently large choices of* q, s, ℓ.

Proof. Three things to show:

Polynomial time: the runtime is, as desired,

$$\mathrm{poly}(q(|x|), s(|x|), \ell(|x|)) = \mathrm{poly}(|x|).$$

Completeness: for any $x \in L_V$ let w_x be the shortest witness such that $V(x, w)$ accepts. Since V is an NP verifier, we know that $\max_{x \,:\, |x|=n} |w_x|$ is bounded by some polynomial; choose q larger. Further, the size of V as a Turing machine description is some constant; choose s larger. The runtime of V is bounded by some polynomial; choose s larger. The size of the proof π_V that V is L_V-sound is some constant as well; choose ℓ larger.
Then take any $x \in L$. By construction $V'(x, (w_x, V, \pi_V))$ will accept.
Soundness: assume $V'(x, (z, D, \pi))$ accepts. By the soundness of $\mathcal{S}$, we know that D must be L_V-sound. Since D accepts (x, z), we know by the definition of L_V-soundness that there exists w such that V accepts (x, w). By the soundness of V as an NP verifier, conclude that $x \in L$.

Our final proof will be a NIWI corresponding to V', constructed using the witness given in the completeness proof above.

BestPossible.Prove(x, w): output a NIWI that $\exists w'$ such that $V'(x, w')$ accepts using witness (w, V, π_V) with V and π_V as described above.
BestPossible.Verify(x, π): check π is a valid NIWI of the desired statement.

5.3 Security

Theorem 9. *Let* $D \in \Delta(R_{L_V})$. *Assume the search problem over* D *is hard for non-uniform adversaries. Assume there exists a non-interactive proof system* (NIWH.Prove, NIWH.Verify) *with non-uniform witness hiding for* D *such that for every* x *the following holds for some polynomials* q, s, ℓ *and for all* $|x|$ *large enough:*

the length of NIWH.Prove(x, w) *is at most* $q(|x|)$,
the size of NIWH.Verify *written as a Turing machine at most* $s(|x|)$,
the length of an S-*proof of soundness is at most* $\ell(|x|)$.

Assume the NIWI system used in the construction is perfectly sound. Then conclude BestPossible *with parameters* (q, s, ℓ) *is a perfectly complete and sound NIWH against non-uniform adversaries with an efficient prover.*

Proof. We prove completeness, soundness, and witness hiding.

Completeness: follows from completeness of the NIWI system and the analysis of the witness $(w, V_{|x|}, \pi_{V, |x|})$ from the previous theorem.
Soundness: since the NIWI system is perfectly sound, we know that if BestPossible.Verify accepts, then $\exists w'$ such that $V'(x, w')$. From the previous theorem, we know V' is an NP-verifier for L_V. Thus conclude $x \in L_V$.

Witness Hiding: let A be an attacker (resp. non-uniform attacker) against the witness hiding of BestPossible. We build B an adversary against the witness hiding of NIWH. First, for input size $|x|$, let D be the Turing machine computing NIWH.Verify and π the S-proof that D is L_V-sound. Then build B as follows: on input (x, π), construct π' a NIWI of $\exists w'$ such that $V'(x, w')$ accepts using witness $(x, (\pi', D, \pi))$. Run A on π' and output the result.

By witness indistinguishability, π' as constructed by B is indistinguishable from $\pi = \mathsf{BestPossible.Prove}(x, w)$. Thus we have

$$
\begin{aligned}
\mathrm{Adv}_B &= \Pr_{(x,w)\sim D(\lambda)}[(x, B(x, \pi))] \\
&= \Pr_{(x,w)\sim D(\lambda)}[(x, A(x, \pi'))] \\
&= \Pr_{(x,w)\sim D(\lambda)}[(x, A(x, \pi))] \pm \mathrm{negl}(\lambda) \\
&= \mathrm{Adv}_A \pm \mathrm{negl}(\lambda).
\end{aligned}
$$

5.4   Additional Properties

Note that non-uniformity is not required in the above proof as long as NIWH.Verify is uniform and there exists an S-proof that it is sound for all input sizes. In this setting, we get an analogue to the above theorem where the resulting adversary is uniform.

Further note that we never run NIWH.Prove. In fact, the whole proof goes through even if NIWH.Prove is inefficient. Regardless, BestPossible will be efficient.

Finally, note that our use of witness hiding was minimal. Observe that witness hiding can be replaced with any falsifiable notion of security. In the sense that this single construction (with appropriate parameters) achieves any desired notion shows that it is the "best possible" non-interactive proof.

5.5   Basing Security on Non-uniform Proofs

In the above construction, consider replacing Turing machines with circuits of size at most s. We replace the soundness condition with the following:

Definition 18 (soundness for inputs of length n). *Say a circuit D is L_V-sound for inputs of length n if the following statement holds*

$$
\forall x \in \{0,1\}^n \ (\exists y \ D(x, y) \Rightarrow \exists w \ V(x, w)).
$$

Assuming some non-uniform NIWH proof system exists and for each n the S-proof of L_V-soundness for inputs of length n is length at most $\ell(n)$, a slightly modified version of BestPossible is secure. However, this modification is unnecessary because a non-uniform scheme with this soundness condition actually implies NIWH scheme with an inefficient prover, and per the last section, this suffices for the theorem.

The construction is as follows: let P, V a non-uniform NIWH scheme with advice a_n. Let π_n an $\mathcal{S}$-proof of soundness for inputs of length n. Define V': on input $(x, (\pi', a, \pi))$, check that π is an $\mathcal{S}$-proof that $V(\cdot; a)$ is L_V-sound for inputs of length n. If not, reject. Otherwise run $V(x, \pi'; a)$ and output the result. The inefficient prover P' can simply use brute force to find an acceptable a and π and output $(P(x, w; a), a, \pi)$.

In the construction of Sect. 4 it is unclear if, for any choice of advice, that soundness for inputs of length n has short proofs. Recall the basic steps of Theorem 7: we showed the protocol was secure as long as the advice $y_\lambda \in$ UNSAT. We constructed an MA-type verifier UnsatVerifier for the language UNSAT. We concluded that the scheme is witness hiding as long as UnsatVerifier does not accept y_λ. Thus to achieve probable soundness, we need to prove the existence of y_λ that fulfills the following three conditions:

(a). $y_\lambda \in$ UNSAT,
(b). UnsatVerifier rejects y_λ,
(c). $\exists$ a poly-size $\mathcal{S}$-proof that $y_\lambda \in$ UNSAT.

By the soundness of $\mathcal{S}$, we know that (c) implies (a). But it is still unclear how to achieve (b) and (c) simultaneously. In general, NP $\neq$ coNP establishes that proofs of unsatisfiability are long in the worst case. But this does not rule out short proofs for some appropriate statement.

6 Witness Encryption vs. Non-interactive Witness Hiding

Again, we present a non-interactive witness hiding proof system comprised of a NIWI of $x \vee y$; but in this scheme the prover picks y. To maintain soundness, the prover also provides an NP proof that y is false. To prove witness hiding, we restrict to the case where x has a unique witness. Then, an adversary against witness hiding is an algorithm that, from the proof and a witness to $\neg y$, recovers w. By using w to encode a bit, the adversary serves as the decryptor for a weak *witness encryption* scheme.

We begin by defining witness encryption and a weakened notion of it. We proceed to give the construction and finally prove the desired properties. Recall that witness encryption is currently only known from extremely strong cryptographic tools, namely multilinear maps and obfuscation. Thus it is plausible that our weakened form of witness encryption does not exist for some language in $L \in$ NP $\cap$ coNP. But then this protocol would indeed be witness hiding. Further, we avoid choosing L concretely by using our best-possible protocol from the previous section.

6.1 Definitions

Consider the usual notion of witness encryption, as introduced by [19]. Fix a language $L \in$ NP with verifier V.

Definition 19 (witness encryption). *We say* (Encrypt, Decrypt) *is an* witness encryption scheme for L *when the following two properties hold.*

Correctness: $\forall \lambda \in \mathbb{N}$, $\forall m \in \{0, 1\}$, $\forall (x, w) \in R_L$

$$\Pr[\textit{Decrypt}(x, w, \textit{Encrypt}(x, m)) = m] = 1.$$

Soundness security: $\forall A \in$ p.p.t., $\exists \mu \in$ negl, $\forall x \notin L$,

$$\Pr_{m \sim \{0,1\}}[A(\textit{Encrypt}(x, m)) = m] = \frac{1}{2} + \text{negl}(\lambda).$$

Consider a relaxed notion of correctness relative to some distribution T over (x, w) such that $V(x, w)$ is true.

Definition 20 (average case correctness for witness encryption).

Average case correctness: $\exists f \notin$ negl, $\forall \lambda \in \mathbb{N}$, $\forall m \in \{0, 1\}$,

$$\Pr_{(x,w) \sim T}[\textit{Decrypt}(x, w, \textit{Encrypt}(x, m)) = m] = f(\lambda).$$

This definition is weaker in two ways. First, it only guarantees any notion of correctness for infinitely many values of λ (as opposed to for all λ in the original definition). Second, decryption can fail. Since the failure probability is over the choice of instance, it may be the case that some instances always fail. Regardless, even with these limitations, we feel this is a strong cryptographic primitive.

6.2   Construction

Fix $L \in$ NP and $D \in \Delta(R_L)$. Assume R_L restricted to D has unique witnesses: $\forall (x, w) \in \sup D$ if $(x, w') \in R_L$ accepts then $w' = w$. We propose the following scheme for a non-interactive witness hiding proof. Fix $T \in$ NP $\cap$ coNP, or equivalently R_T, $R_{\overline{T}}$ two NP relations and a probability ensemble E over $(y, z) \in R_T$.

VsWE.Prove(x, w): sample $(y, z) \sim E$. Compute π a NIWI for the statement $x \in L \vee y \notin T$ using the witness w. Output $\tau = (y, z, \pi)$.

VsWE.Verify(x, τ): parse $(y, z, \pi) \leftarrow \tau$. Accept iff $V_T(y, z)$ accepts and π is a valid proof of the statement $x \in L \vee y \notin T$.

6.3   Security

Completeness and soundness of the scheme follow easily from the properties of the underlying NIWI. Then we argue that if the scheme is not witness hiding, then an adversary yields a witness encryption scheme in the weak sense above.

Theorem 10. *Assume the search problem over D is hard against non-uniform adversaries. Assume a perfectly sound NIWI. Then VsWE is a perfectly sound proof system. Further, any adversary that breaks the witness hiding of VsWE with non-negligible probability yields a witness encryption scheme for the language T with average case correctness with respect to E and the usual sense of soundness security for infinitely many lengths.*

Proof. Completeness and soundness follow from the corresponding properties of the NIWI. Witness hiding is justified by constructing a witness encryption decryptor from a witness hiding adversary.

Completeness: if $(x, w) \in R_L$, then w is a witness for $x \in L \lor y \notin T$. Thus by completeness of the NIWI system conclude that π is valid. Further by construction $V_T(y, z)$ accepts for all $(y, z) \sim E$. Conclude the verifier accepts.

Soundness: fix $x \notin L$. Consider any (y, z, π). Two cases: (1) if $y \in T$ then $x \in L \lor y \notin T$ is false. By NIWI soundness, π fails to verify; (2) if $y \notin T$ then $V_T(y, z)$ cannot accept. In either case, the verifier rejects.

Witness Hiding: let A be an attacker that breaks witness hiding, meaning that $p = \Pr[V_L(x, A(x, y, z, \pi))]$ is non-negligible. Then we construct a one-bit witness encryption scheme WE_A for the language T as follows.

$\mathsf{WE}_A.\mathsf{Encrypt}(y, m)$: sample $(x, w) \sim D$. Let π a NIWI for the statement $x \in L \lor y \notin T$ using the witness w. Sample $r \sim \{0, 1\}^{|w|}$. Output $c = (x, \pi, r, \langle w, r \rangle \oplus m)$.
$\mathsf{WE}_A.\mathsf{Decrypt}(y, z, c)$: parse $(x, \pi, r, b) = c$. Let $w' = A(x, y, z, \pi)$. If $V_L(x, w)$ rejects then output $\bot$. Otherwise output $\langle w', r \rangle \oplus b$.

It remains to show that WE_A is correct and secure.

Average Case Correctness of WE_A: with probability p over choice of y and (x, w), we have w' a valid witness for $x \in L$. Then by the unique witness property we have $w' = w$. By construction this yields $\langle w', r \rangle \oplus b = m$.

Soundness Security of WE_A: Fix a p.p.t. adversary B and sequence of inputs $\{y_\lambda\}_{\lambda \in \mathbb{N}}$, $y_\lambda \notin T$. Consider the following quantity:

$$\mathrm{Adv}_{B,Y}(\lambda) := |\Pr[B(\mathsf{WE}_A.\mathsf{Encrypt}(y_\lambda, 0))] - \Pr[B(\mathsf{WE}_A.\mathsf{Encrypt}(y_\lambda, 1))]|.$$

Let z_λ be a witness for $y_\lambda \notin T$. Such witnesses exist since $T \in \mathsf{coNP}$. Proceed by a series of games, parameterized by λ, for which the challengers are as follows.

$\mathcal{G}_0$: Sample $(x, w) \sim D(1^\lambda)$. Let π a NIWI for the statement $x \in L \lor y_\lambda \notin T$ using the witness w. Sample $r \sim \{0, 1\}^{|w|}$. Output $c = (x, \pi, r, \langle w, r \rangle \oplus m)$ with $m = 0$.
$\mathcal{G}_1$: Same as $\mathcal{G}_0$ but derive π using witness z_λ.
$\mathcal{G}_2$: Same as $\mathcal{G}_1$ but output $b \sim \{0, 1\}$ instead of $\langle w, r \rangle \oplus m$.
$\mathcal{G}_3$: Same as $\mathcal{G}_1$ but with $m = 1$.
$\mathcal{G}_4$: Same as $\mathcal{G}_0$ but with $m = 1$.

To show $\mathcal{G}_0 \approx \mathcal{G}_1$. This follows from the witness indistinguishability of the underlying NIWI proof system. Let A_{01} be a p.p.t. adversary that distinguishes between games 0 and 1. Then we have

$$\mathrm{Adv}_{A_{01}}(\lambda) = |\Pr_{c \leftarrow \mathcal{G}_0}[A_{01}(y_\lambda, c)] - \Pr_{c \leftarrow \mathcal{G}_1}[A_{01}(y_\lambda, c)]|.$$

Now for each λ choose (x_λ, w_λ) that achieve

$$\mathrm{Adv}_{A_{01}}(\lambda) \leq \left| \Pr_{c \leftarrow \mathcal{G}_0}[A_{01}(y_\lambda, c)|(x, w) = (x_\lambda, w_\lambda)]\right.$$
$$\left. - \Pr_{c \leftarrow \mathcal{G}_1}[A_{01}(y_\lambda, c)|(x, w) = (x_\lambda, w_\lambda)]\right|.$$

This allows us to define a sequence of NIWI games as follows:

$$\mathcal{I} = \{(x_\lambda \in L \vee y_\lambda \notin T, w_\lambda, z_\lambda)\}_{\lambda \in \mathbb{N}}.$$

Then we give a non-uniform p.p.t. adversary A_{NIWI} against the NIWI game on sequence $\mathcal{I}$. A_{NIWI} takes $y_\lambda, x_\lambda, w_\lambda$ as an advice string. It receives a proof π as input. It samples $r \sim \{0, 1\}^{|w|}$ and outputs $A_{01}(y_\lambda, (x_\lambda, \pi, r, \langle w_\lambda, r \rangle \oplus m))$ with $m = 0$.

Note that A_{NIWI} simulates $\mathcal{G}_0|(x, w) = (x_\lambda, w_\lambda)$ when the challenger uses witness w_λ and $\mathcal{G}_0|(x, w) = (x_\lambda, w_\lambda)$ when it uses witness z_λ. Thus $\mathrm{Adv}_{A_{\mathrm{NIWI}}}(\lambda) \geq \mathrm{Adv}_{A_{01}}(\lambda)$. Conclude by NIWI security that $\mathrm{Adv}_{A_{01}}$ is negligible.

To show $\mathcal{G}_1 \approx \mathcal{G}_2$. This follows from the fact that $\langle w, r \rangle$ is determined by the Goldreich-Levin hardcore predicate associated with $(x, w) \mapsto x$. Let A_{12} be a p.p.t. adversary that distinguishes between games 1 and 2 with

$$\mathrm{Adv}_{A_{12}}(\lambda) = \left|\Pr_{c \leftarrow \mathcal{G}_1}[A_{12}(y_\lambda, c)] - \Pr_{c \leftarrow \mathcal{G}_2}[A_{12}(y_\lambda, c)]\right|.$$

We give a non-uniform p.p.t. adversary A_{HCP} that guesses the hardcore predicate. A_{HCP} takes non-uniform input y_λ, z_λ. The challenger picks $(x, w) \sim D$, $q \sim \{0, 1\}^{|x|}$, $r \sim \{0, 1\}^{|w|}$ and A_{HCP} gets input (x, q, r). It derives π from x, y_λ, z_λ. It picks $b \sim \{0, 1\}$ and computes $a = A_{12}(y_\lambda, (x, \pi, r, b))$. If $a = 1$ then it outputs $b \oplus \langle x, q \rangle \oplus m$ with $m = 0$. Otherwise it outputs a random bit.

Let $t = \langle w, r \rangle \oplus m$. Considering the designs of $\mathcal{G}_1$ and $\mathcal{G}_2$ we have

$$\Pr_{c \leftarrow \mathcal{G}_1}[A_{12}(y_\lambda, c)] = \Pr[a = 1 | b = t],$$

$$\Pr_{c \leftarrow \mathcal{G}_2}[A_{12}(y_\lambda, c)] = \frac{1}{2}(\Pr[a = 1 | b = t] + \Pr[a = 1 | b \neq t]).$$

Now using these values we have

$$\Pr[A_{\mathsf{HCP}}(x, q, r) = \langle(x, w), (r, q)\rangle] = \Pr[a = 1 | b = t] \Pr[b = t] + \frac{1}{2} \Pr[a = 0]$$

$$= \frac{1}{2}(1 + \Pr_{c \leftarrow \mathcal{G}_1}[A_{12}(y_\lambda, c)] - \Pr_{c \leftarrow \mathcal{G}_2}[A_{12}(y_\lambda, c)])$$

$$= \frac{1}{2} \pm \mathrm{Adv}_{A_{12}}.$$

However, since $\langle(x, w), (r, q)\rangle$ is the Goldreich-Levin hardcore predicate [20] of the one-way function $(x, w) \mapsto x$, we know that

$$\Pr[A_{\mathsf{HCP}}(x, q, r) = \langle(x, w), (r, q)\rangle] = \frac{1}{2} + \mathrm{negl}(\lambda).$$

Conclude that $\mathrm{Adv}_{A_{12}}$ is negligible.

Conclude. By repeating the above arguments with $m = 1$, observe that $\mathcal{G}_2 \approx \mathcal{G}_3$ and $\mathcal{G}_3 \approx \mathcal{G}_4$. Then note that $\mathcal{G}_0$ and $\mathcal{G}_4$ are the honest soundness security game with plaintexts $m = 0$ and $m = 1$ respectively. As $\mathcal{G}_0 \approx \mathcal{G}_4$ conclude that $\mathrm{Adv}_{B,Y}$ is negligible.

6.4 Applicability for Best-Possible Proofs

We do not have a candidate for a specific language $T \in \mathsf{NP} \cap \mathsf{coNP}$ for which witness encryption with average case correctness does not exist. However, even lacking such a candidate, we argue that the construction of Sect. 5 is secure for any choice of polynomial length parameters. In particular, it is witness hiding for D with unique witnesses assuming any T exists.

Theorem 11. *Let D as above. Assume some $T \in \mathsf{NP} \cap \mathsf{coNP}$ lacks a witness encryption scheme with average case correctness relative to some ensemble E for all input lengths large enough. Then the BestPossible with known length parameters, calculated below, is witness hiding for D.*

Proof. Let $t'(n, m)$ be the runtime of VsWE.Verify where n is the length of x and m is the length of y encoded as an instance of a fixed NP-complete language; note $t' = \mathrm{poly}(n, m)$. We will run the best-possible proof with witness-length parameter $q = n$, runtime parameter $s = t'(n, n)$, and proof-length parameter n and adjust the length of y appropriately.

Recall that T has an NP verifier V_T. Let $q'(\lambda)$ be the maximum over inputs of length λ of the length of the shortest witness; note $q' = \mathrm{poly}(\lambda)$. Let $s'(\lambda)$ be the size of V_T as a Turing machine; note $s' = O(1)$. Writing y as an instance of our NP-complete language we have $m = \mathrm{poly}(\lambda)$.

Now lift the proof of soundness from Theorem 10 into the deductive system $\mathcal{S}$. The size of this proof depends on the size of V_T, but should still be $\ell'(\lambda) = O(1)$.

So we have s' and ℓ' constant; thus $n > s', \ell'$ for all n large enough. Further we have that q' is polynomial in λ. Choose $\lambda(n)$ so that $q'(\lambda) < n$ and $m(\lambda) < n$.

Define the ensemble E' such that $E'(n) = E(\lambda(n))$. Then use E' to instantiate VsWE.

Note that an average case correct witness encryption scheme relative to E' for infinitely many n immediately gives an average case correct witness encryption scheme relative to E for infinitely many λ. Now apply Theorem 10. By construction, s, q, ℓ are large enough for inputs large enough to describe the appropriate witness, verifier, and soundness proof. Conclude BestPossible is witness hiding.

References

1. Arora, S., Barak, B.: Computational Complexity: A Modern Approach, 1st edn. Cambridge University Press, New York (2009)
2. Badrinarayanan, S., Miles, E., Sahai, A., Zhandry, M.: Post-zeroizing obfuscation: new mathematical tools, and the case of evasive circuits. In: Fischlin, M., Coron, J.-S. (eds.) EUROCRYPT 2016. LNCS, vol. 9666, pp. 764–791. Springer, Heidelberg (2016). https://doi.org/10.1007/978-3-662-49896-5_27
3. Ball, M., Dachman-Soled, D., Kulkarni, M.: New techniques for zero-knowledge: leveraging inefficient provers to reduce assumptions, interaction, and trust. In: Micciancio, D., Ristenpart, T. (eds.) CRYPTO 2020. LNCS, vol. 12172, pp. 674–703. Springer, Cham (2020). https://doi.org/10.1007/978-3-030-56877-1_24
4. Barak, B., et al.: On the (Im)possibility of obfuscating programs. In: Kilian, J. (ed.) CRYPTO 2001. LNCS, vol. 2139, pp. 1–18. Springer, Heidelberg (2001). https://doi.org/10.1007/3-540-44647-8_1
5. Barak, B., Lindell, Y., Vadhan, S.P.: Lower bounds for non-black-box zero knowledge. In: 44th FOCS, pp. 384–393. IEEE Computer Society Press, October 2003. https://doi.org/10.1109/SFCS.2003.1238212
6. Barak, B., Ong, S.J., Vadhan, S.: Derandomization in cryptography. In: Boneh, D. (ed.) CRYPTO 2003. LNCS, vol. 2729, pp. 299–315. Springer, Heidelberg (2003). https://doi.org/10.1007/978-3-540-45146-4_18
7. Barak, B., Pass, R.: On the possibility of one-message weak zero-knowledge. In: Naor, M. (ed.) TCC 2004. LNCS, vol. 2951, pp. 121–132. Springer, Heidelberg (2004). https://doi.org/10.1007/978-3-540-24638-1_7
8. Bellare, M., Palacio, A.: GQ and Schnorr identification schemes: proofs of security against impersonation under active and concurrent attacks. In: Yung, M. (ed.) CRYPTO 2002. LNCS, vol. 2442, pp. 162–177. Springer, Heidelberg (2002). https://doi.org/10.1007/3-540-45708-9_11
9. Bitansky, N., Khurana, D., Paneth, O.: Weak zero-knowledge beyond the black-box barrier. In: Charikar, M., Cohen, E. (eds.) 51st ACM STOC, pp. 1091–1102. ACM Press, June 2019. https://doi.org/10.1145/3313276.3316382
10. Bitansky, N., Paneth, O.: ZAPs and non-interactive witness indistinguishability from indistinguishability obfuscation. In: Dodis, Y., Nielsen, J.B. (eds.) TCC 2015. LNCS, vol. 9015, pp. 401–427. Springer, Heidelberg (2015). https://doi.org/10.1007/978-3-662-46497-7_16
11. Condon, A.: The complexity of stochastic games. Inf. Comput. **96**(2), 203–224 (1992). https://doi.org/10.1016/0890-5401(92)90048-K
12. Deng, Y., Song, X., Yu, J., Chen, Y.: On instance compression, schnorr/guillouquisquater, and the security of classic protocols for unique witness relations. Cryptology ePrint Archive, Report 2017/390 (2017). http://eprint.iacr.org/2017/390

13. Deshpande, A., Kalai, Y.: Proofs of ignorance and applications to 2-message witness hiding. Cryptology ePrint Archive, Report 2018/896 (2018). https://eprint.iacr.org/2018/896
14. Dwork, C., Naor, M.: Zaps and their applications. In: 41st FOCS, pp. 283–293. IEEE Computer Society Press, November 2000. https://doi.org/10.1109/SFCS.2000.892117
15. Dwork, C., Stockmeyer, L.J.: 2-round zero knowledge and proof auditors. In: 34th ACM STOC, pp. 322–331. ACM Press, May 2002. https://doi.org/10.1145/509907.509958
16. Feige, U., Shamir, A.: Witness indistinguishable and witness hiding protocols. In: 22nd ACM STOC, pp. 416–426. ACM Press, May 1990. https://doi.org/10.1145/100216.100272
17. Feige, U., Shamir, A.: Zero knowledge proofs of knowledge in two rounds. In: Brassard, G. (ed.) CRYPTO 1989. LNCS, vol. 435, pp. 526–544. Springer, New York (1990). https://doi.org/10.1007/0-387-34805-0_46
18. Freitag, C., Komargodski, I., Pass, R.: Impossibility of strong KDM security with auxiliary input. Cryptology ePrint Archive, Report 2019/293 (2019). https://eprint.iacr.org/2019/293
19. Garg, S., Gentry, C., Sahai, A., Waters, B.: Witness encryption and its applications. In: Boneh, D., Roughgarden, T., Feigenbaum, J. (eds.) 45th ACM STOC, pp. 467–476. ACM Press, June 2013. https://doi.org/10.1145/2488608.2488667
20. Goldreich, O., Levin, L.A.: A hard-core predicate for all one-way functions. In: 21st ACM STOC, pp. 25–32. ACM Press, May 1989. https://doi.org/10.1145/73007.73010
21. Goldreich, O., Oren, Y.: Definitions and properties of zero-knowledge proof systems. J. Crypt. 7(1), 1–32 (1994). https://doi.org/10.1007/BF00195207
22. Goldwasser, S., Micali, S.: Probabilistic encryption and how to play mental poker keeping secret all partial information. In: 14th ACM STOC, pp. 365–377. ACM Press, May 1982. https://doi.org/10.1145/800070.802212
23. Goldwasser, S., Micali, S., Rackoff, C.: The knowledge complexity of interactive proof systems. SIAM J. Comput. 18(1), 186–208 (1989)
24. Goldwasser, S., Rothblum, G.N.: On best-possible obfuscation. In: Vadhan, S.P. (ed.) TCC 2007. LNCS, vol. 4392, pp. 194–213. Springer, Heidelberg (2007). https://doi.org/10.1007/978-3-540-70936-7_11
25. Gordon, S.D., Wee, H., Xiao, D., Yerukhimovich, A.: On the round complexity of zero-knowledge proofs based on one-way permutations. In: Abdalla, M., Barreto, P.S.L.M. (eds.) LATINCRYPT 2010. LNCS, vol. 6212, pp. 189–204. Springer, Heidelberg (2010). https://doi.org/10.1007/978-3-642-14712-8_12
26. Groth, J., Ostrovsky, R., Sahai, A.: Non-interactive zaps and new techniques for NIZK. In: Dwork, C. (ed.) CRYPTO 2006. LNCS, vol. 4117, pp. 97–111. Springer, Heidelberg (2006). https://doi.org/10.1007/11818175_6
27. Haitner, I., Rosen, A., Shaltiel, R.: On the (Im)Possibility of Arthur-Merlin witness hiding protocols. In: Reingold, O. (ed.) TCC 2009. LNCS, vol. 5444, pp. 220–237. Springer, Heidelberg (2009). https://doi.org/10.1007/978-3-642-00457-5_14
28. Jain, A., Kalai, Y.T., Khurana, D., Rothblum, R.: Distinguisher-dependent simulation in two rounds and its applications. In: Katz, J., Shacham, H. (eds.) CRYPTO 2017. LNCS, vol. 10402, pp. 158–189. Springer, Cham (2017). https://doi.org/10.1007/978-3-319-63715-0_6
29. Katz, J.: Which languages have 4-round zero-knowledge proofs? In: Canetti, R. (ed.) TCC 2008. LNCS, vol. 4948, pp. 73–88. Springer, Heidelberg (2008). https://doi.org/10.1007/978-3-540-78524-8_5

30. Lackenby, M.: The efficient certification of knottedness and thurston norm (2016). https://arxiv.org/abs/1604.00290
31. Lindell, Y.: An efficient transform from sigma protocols to NIZK with a CRS and non-programmable random oracle. In: Dodis, Y., Nielsen, J.B. (eds.) TCC 2015. LNCS, vol. 9014, pp. 93–109. Springer, Heidelberg (2015). https://doi.org/10.1007/978-3-662-46494-6_5
32. Pass, R.: On deniability in the common reference string and random Oracle model. In: Boneh, D. (ed.) CRYPTO 2003. LNCS, vol. 2729, pp. 316–337. Springer, Heidelberg (2003). https://doi.org/10.1007/978-3-540-45146-4_19
33. Pass, R.: Simulation in Quasi-polynomial time, and its application to protocol composition. In: Biham, E. (ed.) EUROCRYPT 2003. LNCS, vol. 2656, pp. 160–176. Springer, Heidelberg (2003). https://doi.org/10.1007/3-540-39200-9_10

FHE-Based Bootstrapping
of Designated-Prover NIZK

Zvika Brakerski[1], Sanjam Garg[2], and Rotem Tsabary[1($\boxtimes$)]

[1] Weizmann Institute of Science, Rehovot, Israel
rotem.tsabary@weizmann.ac.il
[2] University of California, Berkeley, Berkeley, USA

Abstract. We present a novel tree-based technique that can convert any designated-prover NIZK proof system (DP-NIZK) which maintains zero-knowledge only for single statement, into one that allows to prove an unlimited number of statements in ZK, while maintaining all parameters succinct. Our transformation requires leveled fully-homomorphic encryption. We note that single-statement DP-NIZK can be constructed from any one-way function. We also observe a two-way derivation between DP-NIZK and attribute-based signatures (ABS), and as a result derive now constructions of ABS and homomorphic signatures (HS).

Our construction improves upon the prior construction of lattice-based DP-NIZK by Kim and Wu (Crypto 2018) since we only require leveled FHE as opposed to HS (which also translates to improved LWE parameters when instantiated). Alternatively, the recent construction of NIZK without preprocessing from either circular-secure FHE (Canetti et al. STOC 2019) or polynomial Learning with Errors (Peikert and Shiehian, Crypto 2019) could be used to obtain a similar final statement. Nevertheless, we note that our statement is formally incomparable to these works (since leveled FHE is not known to imply circular secure FHE or the hardness of LWE). We view this as evidence for the potential in our technique, which we hope can find additional applications in future works.

1 Introduction

In non-interactive zero-knowledge proof systems for NP (NIZK) [BFM88], a prover can provide a non-interactive proof of the validity of an NP statement

Z. Brakerski and R. Tsabary—Supported by the Binational Science Foundation (Grant No. 2016726), and by the European Union Horizon 2020 Research and Innovation Program via ERC Project REACT (Grant 756482) and via Project PROMETHEUS (Grant 780701).

S. Garg—Supported in part from AFOSR Award FA9550-19-1-0200, NSF CNS Award 1936826, DARPA SIEVE Award, and research grants by the Sloan Foundation, Visa Inc., and Center for Long-Term Cybersecurity (CLTC, UC Berkeley). Any opinions, findings and conclusions or recommendations expressed in this material are those of the author(s) and do not necessarily reflect the views of the funding agencies.

© International Association for Cryptologic Research 2020
R. Pass and K. Pietrzak (Eds.): TCC 2020, LNCS 12550, pp. 657–683, 2020.
https://doi.org/10.1007/978-3-030-64375-1_23

(efficiently, using a witness), that convinces a verifier, without revealing any information about the witness or anything other than the validity of the statement. This is not possible to achieve in the plain model, and therefore usually some common setup is considered, in particular it is often assumed that an honestly generated common reference string (CRS) is accessible to both the prover and the verifier [FLS90]. In this work we consider proof systems with statistical soundness and computational zero-knowledge.

NIZK with Preprocessing. In some cases it suffices to consider a relaxed notion, *NIZK with preprocessing* [SMP87], where the trusted party that generates the CRS also produces additional secret information either for the prover or for the verifier or for both. As pointed out by Kim and Wu [KW18], multi-theorem preprocessing NIZK could replace plain NIZK in a number of applications, e.g. for achieving MPC with low round complexity.

In the case of secret information for the prover, known as *designated-prover* NIZK or DP-NIZK, the prover's key should be kept secret in order to maintain zero-knowledge. In the mirror case of *designated-verifier* NIZK (DV-NIZK), the verifier's secret is for the purposes of securing the soundness. In both cases, the preprocessing might make the CRS *non-reusable*. That is, if the same secret key of the prover (resp. verifier) is used in the proofs of multiple statements then ZK (resp. soundness) might not hold for all of these statements. Therefore, we make the distinction between single-theorem and multi-theorem NIZK in the preprocessing model. We note that throughout this introduction, writing DP/DV-NIZK refers by default to the multi-theorem version.

The seminal work of [FLS90] shows, among other things, how to transform any single-statement NIZK proof system into a multi-statement NIZK. [KNYY19] recently showed that a similar bootstrapping strategy works also in the designated-verifier model. As pointed out by [KW18], the transformation fails to work in the designated-prover model since it critically relies on the fact that the prover algorithm is publicly computable. In this work we focus on multi-statement DP-NIZK.

1.1   Our Results

We present a new technique for bootstrapping DP-NIZK from single-theorem to multi-theorem, using leveled fully homomorphic encryption (FHE) as a building block. We recall that leveled FHE schemes are ones that allow to evaluate depth d circuits, for any (polynomially bounded) d specified at key generation time. We start by noticing that single-theorem DP-NIZK can be constructed straightforwardly from any one-way function using garbled circuits and commitment schemes (we did not find this simple construction in the literature). We then apply a succinctness transformation similar to that proposed by Gentry et al. [Gen09, GGI+15] to shrink the CRS size and make it independent of the complexity of the statement that needs to be proven. This transformation uses (leveled) FHE. Finally, as our main contribution, we present a tree based construction which transforms single-theorem succinct DP-NIZK into multi-theorem (succinct) DP-NIZK, essentially by committing to an implicit tree of CRS values, each of which is used to prove the validity of its children. We provide more information and a technical overview in Sect. 1.3 below.

In addition, in this work, we observe a two-way implication between DP-NIZK and the notion of attribute-based signatures (ABS) [MPR11,BF14,BZ14, BGI13], assuming one-way functions exist. Combining this new observation with the known connection between ABS and HS [Tsa17], we get a construction of homomorphic signatures from leveled FHE. We note the parameters of the obtained HS scheme are fairly unfavorable, in particular the length of the signature grows with the size of the evaluated function. However, this schemes has the so-called context-hiding property. Such HS schemes suffice for some applications (not surprisingly, the [KW18] construction of DP-NIZK is an example of such as application). See Sect. 1.4 below.

1.2 Our Parameters and Assumptions Compared to Prior Work

Comparison with DP-NIZK Constructions from LWE. [KW18] presented a construction of DP-NIZK using homomorphic signatures for $\mathbf{NC}^1$ as building block. Such HS schemes were constructed under the learning with errors (LWE) assumption [Reg05] by Gorbunov, Vaikuntanathan and Wee [GVW15]. Comparing our result with their work, we point out that our techniques are very different. Succinctness and bootstrapping that play a central role in our construction, do not appear to be a component of the [KW18] construction. In terms of assumptions, we require leveled FHE and they require homomorphic signatures. The two assumptions are formally incomparable, but when instantiating concretely with LWE, our construction is favorable in terms of the required assumption. Leveled FHE can be constructed based on the hardness of LWE, with a fixed polynomial modulus-to-noise ratio, and with parameters that grow moderately with d [BV14]. The modulus-to-noise ratio (when measured as a function of the dimension of the LWE problem) effectively determines the hardness of the LWE instance at hand. The smaller the ratio is, the harder the problem becomes, and the better approximation to worst-case lattice problems one will be able to achieve if the assumption is broken. In terms of parameter growth, the only parameter effected by d is the public key, which grows linearly with d. In contrast to FHE, it is not known how to *bootstrap* homomorphic signatures. Bootstrapping allows the modulus-to-noise ratio to be fixed, regardless of the evaluation depth. Therefore, since [KW18] requires the use of HS rather than FHE, they require modulus to noise ratio of $\text{poly}(s)$, where s is the size of the verification circuit for the $\mathbf{NP}$ relation for which proofs are provided. This is worse than the parameters presented in this work.

We should also compare our construction to the recent constructions of NIZK without preprocessing by Canetti et al. [CCH+19] and by Peikert and Shiehian [PS19]. The former constructs NIZK from any *circular secure* FHE scheme. That is, one that can securely encrypt its own secret key. This is not known to be implied by LWE, but it is an assumption that is fairly common in the FHE literature. The latter constructs NIZK from LWE with fixed polynomial modulus-to-noise ratio. Their construction uses LWE-based leveled FHE as building block, but then uses specific properties of the LWE-based scheme so their construction is not generic. Formally, none of these constructions are implied by generic leveled FHE, which suggests that our techniques have a novel aspect that hopefully can serve as stepping stone for future contributions.

Other DP-NIZK Constructions. Katsumata et al. [KNYY19] showed how to construct DP-NIZK (with computational soundness) based on a (new) assumption on groups with bilinear maps, however a later work by these authors [KNYY20] subsumed that result and showed how to remove the preprocessing and remain with essentially the same properties.

1.3   Technical Overview

As we outlined above, our construction has three components:

1. A single-theorem DP-NIZK construction from any one-way function via garbled circuits and commitments.
2. A succinctness transformation from single-theorem DP-NIZK to succinct single-theorem DP-NIZK. This is similar to the succinctness transformations in [Gen09, GGI+15].
3. Tree-based bootstrapping from succinct single-theorem NIZK to (succinct) multi-theorem DP-NIZK.

In what follows, we describe each of these components in more detail. We consider an **NP** language L and we let V be the verifier for an **NP** relation of L. That is, V is a polynomial time algorithm s.t. $V(x, w) = 1$ if and only if w is a valid witness for $x \in L$. We slightly overload the notation and also use V to denote the circuit that implements the algorithm V on instances x of length n, where n is clear from the context.

Single-Theorem DP-NIZK from OWF. We create a DP-NIZK scheme for instances of size n with respect to the language L. The DP-NIZK setup generates a common reference string crs and prover secret key k_P as follows. We start by generating a garbled circuit G of the circuit V. We then commit to each of the labels of the garbled circuit, let $c_{i,b}$ be a commitment to the label $\ell_{i,b}$. The garbled circuit G and the committed labels are placed in crs, and the openings of all commitments are provided as the secret k_P. In order to prove that $x \in L$ for some instance x, a prover P with witness w simply opens the commitments to the labels corresponding to (x, w). The verifier executes the garbled circuit and verifies that the output is indeed 1. One minor subtlety is that the verifier needs to be convinced that the prover indeed opened to the correct x, but needs to know nothing about w. This is achieved by providing the labels corresponding to x in the "correct" order, i.e. $c_{i,0}$ followed by $c_{i,1}$, but for the w labels $c_{i,0}$ and $c_{i,1}$ will be randomly permuted.

Remark 1. As was pointed out to us by TCC 2020 reviewers, there is an alternative way to obtain single-theorem DP-NIZK from OWF by instantiating the hidden-bit model [FLS90]. The hidden bit-model requires that the CRS constitutes a commitment to a sequence of bits drawn (by a trusted party) from a certain distribution, which can be opened by the prover. This can be instantiated for designated prover straightforwardly by having in the CRS commitments to the hidden bits, and giving the openings of the commitments to the prover.

This alternative has the advantage of not requiring use of garbled circuits, but it has the drawback of being designated for a specific **NP** complete language such as hamiltoniciy, or variants of SAT [KP95]. Although in a different context, [Dam92] also considers the goal of constructing proofs directly for arbitrary circuits. In contrast, the garbled circuit approach can apply directly to any witness relation and does not require an **NP** reduction to be used.

Succinctness Transformation. The idea here is to use (leveled) FHE as follows. In the setup process, generate $\mathsf{crs}^0, k_P{}^0$ for a non-compact scheme, and also generate a key pair for the FHE scheme ($\mathsf{hpk}, \mathsf{hsk}$). Place $\mathsf{hpk}, \mathsf{crs}^0$ and a commitment c for hsk in the new CRS and $\mathsf{hsk}, k_P{}^0$ and the opening for the commitment c in the new k_P. Now, to prove that $x \in L$ using w, encrypt w using the FHE, let ct_w be the encryption. Then consider the ciphertext ct which is the homomorphic evaluation of $V(x, \cdot)$ on the ciphertext ct_w. The prover will use $k_P{}^0$ to prove that when decrypting ct with the hsk committed to by the commitment c, the outcome is 1. The verifier will calculate ct locally using homomorphic evaluation, and then will verify the proof using crs^0. This guarantees that soundness holds, up to subtleties like ensuring that any ciphertext ct_w, even dishonestly generated, corresponds to some encrypted value. We note that soundness for DP-NIZK is easier to show than for NIZK without preprocessing as in [Gen09, GGI+15] since the homomorphic encryption keys, and commitments thereof, are guaranteed to be honestly generated.

In terms of succinctness, we only use the underlying scheme to prove statements about the decryption circuit of the FHE scheme, which is independent of the statement length n, and therefore we would hope that the complexity of V does not play a role in the parameters of the new scheme. This is not entirely correct since in leveled FHE, the length of hpk can depend on the depth of V. However, we note that hpk is reusable, and we can generate many instances of the proof system with the same hpk. Thus, the parameters contain a part which may not be succinct but is reusable, and another part that is succinct but possibly not reusable. This will suffice for our purposes as we see below.

Tree-Based Bootstrapping. The basic idea is to implicitly generate exponentially many (in the security parameter) single-theorem (crs, k_P) values, so that the prover can use a fresh value for each new theorem. Of course the verifier will need a way to retrieve the correct crs and verify that it is indeed one of those implicit crs values and not some value maliciously chosen by a dishonest prover. To resolve this issue, we generate additional instances of the single-theorem

DP-NIZK and use them to prove that the crs values were generated honestly according to some predetrmined (pseudo)randomness that is given via a PRF.

In more detail, we consider a depth-λ binary tree, where each node is associated with an independent instance of the single-theorem DP-NIZK, and all of those instances are implicitly determined by a PRF seed that generates the randomness for the DP-NIZK setup algorithm. Every intermediate node is used in order to prove the (single) statement that the CRS of its two children were generated honestly according to the PRF seed, and the CRS of the tree-root is given as part of the CRS of the multi-theorem DP-NIZK. To prove a statement, the prover randomly chooses one of the tree leaves and uses the corresponding CRS to generate the proof for the statement. It then provides, in addition, all of the proofs on the path from the tree root to this leaf, as an evidence that this leaf indeed appears in the predetermined tree.

Note that the setup algorithm of any node is encoded into the NP relation that is proved by its parent node, and a non-efficient setup might cause a blow-up that is exponential with the tree depth. This is where we crucially use the decomposability of the setup algorithm that was discussed when we described the succinctness transformation. In the tree construction, we will generate the reusable-but-not-succinct part of the single-statement CRS once for all of the nodes in a given level of the tree, and then each node will be associated with a new instance of the succinct-but-not-reusable part of the single-statement CRS.

The zero-knowledge comes from the zero-knowledge of the single-statement DP-NIZK (as long as the prover does not choose the same leaf more than once) and from the pseudorandomness of the PRF seed. In fact, we have to generate a fresh PRF seed for every level of the tree, and to use the pseudorandomness of the seed of the ith level to claim that the single-statement DP-NIZK instances of the ith level are zero-knowledge. We then can claim that the zero-knowledge of the ith level instances guarantees that the PRF seed of the $i + 1$th level remains secret since it is only used as a witness, and the proof proceed via 2λ similar hybrids.

If we only cared about zero-knowledge, we could let the prover sample the PRF seeds on its own (or even to use real randomness instead of PRF outputs). But such scheme would not be sound, since the prover can possibly sample a bad CRS of the single-statement DP-NIZK for which soundness does not hold. To resolve this issue, during setup we sample a random string r along with the PRF seeds for all of the tree levels, and publish r and commitments to the seeds. The prover is then forced to use as "randomness" for the single-statement DP-NIZK setup the PRF outputs XORed with the truly random string r, where we enforce this as part of the NP relation that is verified. That is, we require that the witnesses of all of the proofs along the tree will include the proper decommitments to the PRF seeds. With this approach the PRF seeds remain hidden from the verifier due to the hiding of the commitments, so we don't compromise zero-knowledge, and in addition the *truly* random string r restricts the prover to use as "randomness" for the single-statement DP-NIZK setup only strings which the marginal distribution of each of them independently is uniform. We therefore need the underlying single-statement DP-NIZK to be sound for any set of 2^λ CRS values that were sampled with "randomness" that is randomized via the same uniform string r. To obtain this, we use the fact that the underlying single-statement DP-NIZK is *statistically* sound and therefore its soundness can be amplified via parallel repetition λ times.

1.4 DP-NIZK, Attribute-Based Signatures and Homomorphic Signatures

An attribute-based signatures scheme (ABS, [MPR11,BGI13,BF14,BZ14]) is a digital signature scheme that supports multiple keys with varying permissions, where signatures do not reveal information about the permissions of the signing key that was used. A homomorphic signature (HS, [CJL09,BFKW09,GKKR10, BF11a,BF11b,GVW15]) is a digital signature that supports homomorphic evaluations over the signed message, where evaluated signatures should not reveal information about the message associated with the pre-evaluated signature other than the result of the function that was computed homomomorphically.

The relation between ABS, HS and NIZK was studied in various works. [MPR11,BF14,SAH16,SKAH18] show reductions of the form "OWF+NIZK $\rightarrow$ ABS", [KW18] show that "HS $\rightarrow$ DPNIZK" and [Tsa17] shows that "ABS $\leftrightarrow$ HS" for certain types of ABS and HS. Our new DPNIZK construction can be translated to new ABS and HS constructions as follows.

Attribute-Based Signatures from OWF and DP-NIZK. While we believe that some of the aforementioned constructions [MPR11,BF14,SAH16,SKAH18] of ABS from OWF+NIZK can possibly be initialized from OWF+DPNIZK (and in turn also imply HS from OWF+DPNIZK via [Tsa17]), to the best of our knowledge a statement of the flavor "OWF+DPNIZK $\rightarrow$ ABS" does not explicitly appear in previous literature, so we briefly describe such a reduction now.

The ABS public key and master secret key are an instance of a standard signature scheme. To generate an ABS key for a policy f, generate and instance of DPNIZK and a commitment scheme. Commit to f and use the master secret key to sign (with a standard signature) the DPNIZK CRS and the commitment to f. To sign a message x with a constrained key, provide a DPNIZK proof respective to the instance that appears in the key, proving that "there exists a valid decommitment for some f such that $f(x) = 1$". The commitments scheme and standard signature schemes can be instantiated from one-way functions.

Attribute-Based Signatures from FHE. Applying the transformation which is described above to our DPNIZK construction results in an ABS scheme with the following characteristics:

- *Efficiency.* The size of public parameters and the master key is some $\text{poly}(\lambda)$ and in particular independent of the message and policy space, while keys and signatures grow with the policy size.
- *Unforgeability.* The unforgeability is based on the statistical soundness of DPNIZK, the (possibly statistical) binding of the commitment scheme and

the unforgeability of the standard signature scheme. Since any ABS is in particular a standard signature scheme, this is the best possible unforgeability.
- *Policy Privacy.* The privacy is based on the hiding of the commitment and on the zero-knowledge of DPNIZK, which in turn relies on the security of the underlying FHE.

Homomorphic Signatures from FHE. We apply the "ABS → HS" transformation of [Tsa17] and derive a single-hop HS scheme with the following characteristics:

- *Efficiency.* The size of public parameters and the master key is some $\text{poly}(\lambda)$ and in particular independent of the message and policy space. However, both post-evaluation and pre-evaluation signatures grow with the function to be computed. That is, when one signs a message they also commit to the maximal size of functions to be homomorphically-computed over it.
- *Unforgeability.* Can be based on any OWF.
- *Context-Hiding.* Relies on the security of the FHE.

DP-NIZK from Attribute-Based Signatures. As mentioned above, the work of [Tsa17,KW18] implies a derivation of the form "ABS → DPNIZK". To simplify and complete the picture, we now briefly describe a direct and simple transformation. In the setup of the DP-NIZK scheme, sample a symmetric key sk and initialize the ABS scheme. If $V(\cdot, \cdot)$ is the verification circuit of the NP relation, then consider the circuit $V'(\cdot, \cdot) = V(\cdot, \mathsf{Dec}_{\mathsf{sk}}(\cdot))$ and generate an ABS key for the policy V'. The secret prover key consists of sk and the ABS key for V'. To prove a statement x with a witness w, consider w' the encryption of w under key sk and provide an ABS signature for the message (x, w').

2   Preliminaries

2.1   Notations

For $n \in \mathbb{N}$ we let $[n]$ denote the ordered set $\{1, \ldots, n\}$. For a bit-string $m \in \{0,1\}^n$ we let U_m^d denote the universal circuit that takes as input a description of a circuit $f : \{0,1\}^n \to \{0,1\}$ of depth at most d, and outputs $f(m)$. for a bit-string $m \in \{0,1\}^n$ we let m_i denote the ith bit of m.

2.2   Pseudorandom Function (PRF)

Definition 1. *A Pseudorandom Function (PRF) is a pair of polynomial-time algorithms* (Setup, Eval) *where* Setup *is randomized and* Eval *is deterministic, such that for any* PPT *adversary* $\mathcal{A}$ *it holds that*

$$\left| Pr\left[\mathcal{A}^{\mathsf{Eval}_k(\cdot)}(1^\lambda) = 1 \right] - Pr\left[\mathcal{A}^{\mathcal{O}(\cdot)}(1^\lambda) = 1 \right] \right| = \mathrm{negl}(\lambda)$$

where the probability is over $k \leftarrow \mathsf{Setup}(1^\lambda)$ *and the coins of* $\mathcal{A}$, *and* $\mathcal{O}(\cdot)$ *is a random function.*

2.3 Collision Resistant Hash Function (CRH)

Definition 2. *An efficient function family ensemble* $\mathcal{H} = \{\mathcal{H}_{n,\lambda} : \{0,1\}^n \rightarrow \{0,1\}^\lambda\}_{n,\lambda \in \mathbb{N}}$ *is a secure collision-resistant hash (CRH) function family if for any* PPT *algorithm* $\mathcal{A}$ *and any* n, *for large enough* λ *it holds that*

$$Pr\left[x \neq y,\ H(x) = H(y)\ :\ H \leftarrow \mathcal{H}_{n,\lambda},\ (x,y) \leftarrow \mathcal{A}(1^{\lambda+n}, H)\right] = \text{negl}(\lambda).$$

2.4 Statistically Binding Equivocable Commitments

Definition 3. *A commitment scheme* (Gen, Commit, Ver) *is a tuple of* PPT *algorithms as follows.*

- Gen$(1^\lambda, 1^n) \rightarrow$ crs *takes as input a security parameter* λ *and message length* n, *and outputs a common reference string* crs.
- Commit$($crs$, m) \rightarrow (c, d)$ *takes as input a common reference string* crs *and a message* $m \in \{0,1\}^n$, *and outputs a commitment* c *and decommitment* d.
- Ver$($crs$, c, m, d) \rightarrow \{accept, reject\}$ *takes as input a common reference string* crs, *a commitment* c, *a message* m *and a decommitment* d, *and either accepts or rejects.*

Correctness. A commitment scheme is correct if for every $m \in \{0,1\}^n$ *it holds that*

$$\mathsf{Ver}(crs, c, m, d) = accept$$

where crs $\leftarrow$ Gen$(1^\lambda, 1^n)$ *and* $(c, d) \leftarrow$ Commit$($crs$, m)$.

Statistical Binding. A commitment scheme is statistically binding if for any sufficiently large λ *and any* n *the following holds*

$$Pr_{crs \leftarrow \mathsf{Gen}(1^\lambda, 1^n)}\left[\exists(r, m_0, m_1, d)\ :\ \begin{array}{c} c := \mathsf{Commit}(crs, m_0\ ;\ r) \\ \mathsf{Ver}(crs, c, m_1, d) = accept \\ m_0 \neq m_1 \end{array} \right] = \text{negl}(\lambda).$$

Hiding. A commitment scheme is hiding if for any sufficiently large λ *and any* n, *for any* PPT *adversary* $\mathcal{A}$ *and any pair of messages* $m_0, m_1 \in \{0,1\}^n$ *it holds that*

$$|Pr\left[\mathcal{A}(crs, c_0) = 1\right] - Pr\left[\mathcal{A}(crs, c_1) = 1\right]| = \text{negl}(\lambda)$$

where crs $\leftarrow$ Gen$(1^\lambda, 1^n)$, $(c_b, d_b) \leftarrow$ Commit$($crs$, m_b)$ *for* $b \in \{0,1\}$ *and the probability is over the coins of* Gen, Commit *and* $\mathcal{A}$.

Equivocability. A commitment scheme is equivocable if there exists a PPT *simulator* $\mathcal{S} = (\mathcal{S}^A, \mathcal{S}^B)$ *such that for any sufficiently large* λ *and any* n, *for any* PPT *distinguisher* Ψ, *any pair of messages* $m_0, m_1 \in \{0,1\}^n$ *and any* $b \in \{0,1\}$ *it holds that*

$$|Pr\left[\Psi(crs, c_b, d_b) = 1\right] - Pr\left[\Psi(crs', c', d_b') = 1\right]| = \text{negl}(\lambda)$$

where crs $\leftarrow$ Gen$(1^\lambda, 1^n)$, $(c_b, d_b) \leftarrow$ Commit$($crs$, m_b)$ *for* $b \in \{0,1\}$, $(crs', c', \mathsf{td}_{c'}) \leftarrow \mathcal{S}^A(1^\lambda, 1^n)$ *and* $d_b' \leftarrow \mathcal{S}^B(crs', c', \mathsf{td}_{c'}, m_b)$ *for* $b \in \{0,1\}$, *and the probability is over the coins of* Gen, Commit, $\mathcal{S}$ *and* Ψ.

2.5 Garbled Circuits

Definition 4. *A garbling scheme for circuits is a tuple of* PPT *algorithms* (Garble, Eval) *with the following syntax.*

- Garble$(1^\lambda, C) \rightarrow (\widetilde{C}, \{\mathsf{lab}_{i,b}\}_{i\in[n],b\in\{0,1\}})$ *is a probabilistic algorithm that takes as input a security parameter* λ *and a boolean circuit* $C : \{0,1\}^n \rightarrow \{0,1\}$, *and outputs a garbled circuit* $\widetilde{C}$ *and* $2n$ *labels* $\{\mathsf{lab}_{i,b}\}_{i\in[n],b\in\{0,1\}}$, *where each of the labels is of size* $\lambda = \mathrm{poly}(\lambda)$ *for some fixed polynomial* poly.
- Eval$(\widetilde{C}, \{\mathsf{lab}_i\}_{i\in[n]}) \rightarrow b$ *is a deterministic algorithm that takes as input a garbled circuit* $\widetilde{C}$ *and* n *labels* $\{\mathsf{lab}_i\}_{i\in[n]}$, *and outputs a bit* $b \in \{0,1\}$.

Correctness. *The scheme is correct if for every circuit* $C : \{0,1\}^n \rightarrow \{0,1\}$, *every input* $x \in \{0,1\}^n$ *and every* $\left(\widetilde{C}, \{\mathsf{lab}_{i,b}\}_{i\in[n],b\in\{0,1\}}\right) \leftarrow$ Garble$(1^\lambda, C)$, *it holds that*

$$\mathsf{Eval}\left(\widetilde{C}, \{\mathsf{lab}_{i,x_i}\}_{i\in[n]}\right) = C(x).$$

Security. *The scheme is secure if there exists a* PPT *simulator* $\mathcal{S}$ *such that for every circuit* $C : \{0,1\}^n \rightarrow \{0,1\}$ *and every input* $x \in \{0,1\}^n$ *it holds that*

$$\left(\widetilde{C}, \{\mathsf{lab}_{i,x_i}\}_{i\in[n]}\right) \equiv_\lambda \mathcal{S}\left(1^\lambda, 1^{|C|}, C(x)\right),$$

where $\left(\widetilde{C}, \{\mathsf{lab}_{i,b}\}_{i\in[n],b\in\{0,1\}}\right) \leftarrow$ Garble$(1^\lambda, C)$ *and* $\equiv_\lambda$ *denotes computational indistinguishability with respect to the security parameter* λ.

2.6 Homomorphic Encryption

Definition 5. *A leveled fully homomorphicencryption scheme* FHE *is a tuple of* PPT *algorithms* (Keygen, Enc, Eval, Dec) *with the following syntax.*

- Keygen$(1^\lambda, 1^d) \rightarrow (\mathsf{pk}, \mathsf{sk})$ *is a probabilistic algorithm that takes as input a security parameter* λ *and depth* d, *and outputs a public key* pk *and secret key* sk.
- Enc$(\mathsf{pk}, m) \rightarrow \mathsf{ct}$ *is a probabilistic algorithm that takes as input a public key* pk *and a message* $m \in \{0,1\}^*$, *and outputs a ciphertext* ct.
- Eval$(\mathsf{ct}, C) \rightarrow \mathsf{ct}'$ *is a deterministic algorithm that takes as input a ciphertext* ct *and a boolean circuit* $C : \{0,1\}^* \rightarrow \{0,1\}$, *and outputs an evaluated ciphertext* ct'.
- Dec$(\mathsf{sk}, \mathsf{ct}')$ *is a deterministic algorithm that takes as input a secret key* sk *and an evaluated ciphertext* ct', *and outputs a bit* $b \in \{0,1\}$.

Correctness. The scheme is correct if for every $n, d \in \mathbb{N}$, every message $m \in \{0, 1\}^n$ and every circuit $C : \{0, 1\}^n \rightarrow \{0, 1\}$ of depth at most d, it hold that

$$Pr[\ (\mathsf{pk}, \mathsf{sk}) \leftarrow \mathsf{Keygen}(1^\lambda, 1^d),$$
$$\mathsf{ct} \leftarrow \mathsf{Enc}(\mathsf{pk}, m),$$
$$\mathsf{ct}' \leftarrow \mathsf{Eval}(\mathsf{ct}, C),$$
$$\mathsf{Dec}(\mathsf{sk}, \mathsf{ct}') \neq C(m)\ ] = \mathsf{negl}(\lambda),$$

where the probability is over the coins of Keygen *and* Enc.

Security. The scheme is secure if for any PPT adversary $\mathcal{A}$, any $n \in \mathbb{N}$ and any pair of messages $m_0, m_1 \in \{0, 1\}^n$, it holds that

$$|Pr\left[\mathcal{A}\left(\mathsf{Enc}(\mathsf{pk}, m_0)\right) = 1\right] - Pr\left[\mathcal{A}\left(\mathsf{Enc}(\mathsf{pk}, m_1)\right) = 1\right]| = \mathsf{negl}(\lambda)$$

where $\mathsf{pk} \leftarrow \mathsf{Keygen}(1^\lambda, 1^d)$ *and the probability is over the coins of* Keygen, Enc *and* $\mathcal{A}$.

Compactness. The scheme is compact if there exists a polynomial $p = p(\cdot)$ such that for all security parameters λ and all $n, d \in \mathbb{N}$, $m \in \{0, 1\}^n$ and $C : \{0, 1\}^n \rightarrow \{0, 1\}$ of depth at most d, for all $(\mathsf{pk}, \mathsf{sk}) \leftarrow \mathsf{Keygen}(1^\lambda, 1^d)$, the output length of $\mathsf{Eval}(\widetilde{m}, C)$ is at most p bits long where $\widetilde{m} \leftarrow \mathsf{Enc}(\mathsf{pk}, m)$, and the size of sk is at most p bits.

For our application we need an FHE scheme where the correctness also holds for maliciously chosen ciphertexts. Formally,

Definition 6 (FHE with correctness for all ciphertexts). *An FHE shceme has correctness for all ciphertexts if for all $n, d \in \mathbb{N}$, for every string $\mathsf{ct} \in \{0, 1\}^p$ and every circuit $C : \{0, 1\}^n \rightarrow \{0, 1\}$ of depth at most d, it holds that*

$$Pr[\ (\mathsf{pk}, \mathsf{sk}) \leftarrow \mathsf{Keygen}(1^\lambda, 1^d),$$
$$\mathsf{ct}'_C \leftarrow \mathsf{Eval}(\mathsf{ct}, C),$$
$$\mathsf{ct}'_I \leftarrow \mathsf{Eval}(\mathsf{ct}, I),$$
$$\mathsf{Dec}(\mathsf{sk}, \mathsf{ct}'_C) \neq C\left(\mathsf{Dec}(\mathsf{sk}, \mathsf{ct}'_I)\right)\ ] = \mathsf{negl}(\lambda),$$

where I is the identity circuit and the probability is over the coins of Keygen.

We now show that any FHE scheme with standard correctness implies a scheme with correctness for all ciphertexts (which preserves the compactness property).

Lemma 1. *Let* FHE $= (\mathsf{Keygen}, \mathsf{Enc}, \mathsf{Eval}, \mathsf{Dec})$ *be an FHE scheme with standard correctness and let* PKE $= (\mathsf{Keygen}, \mathsf{Enc}, \mathsf{Dec})$ *be a public-key encryption scheme. hen there exists an FHE scheme* FHE$' = (\mathsf{Keygen}', \mathsf{Enc}', \mathsf{Eval}', \mathsf{Dec}')$ *with correctness for all ciphertexts.*

Proof. Define $\mathsf{FHE}' = (\mathsf{Keygen}', \mathsf{Enc}', \mathsf{Eval}', \mathsf{Dec}')$ as follows:

- $\mathsf{Keygen}'(1^\lambda, 1^d)$: Sample $(\mathsf{hpk}, \mathsf{hsk}) \leftarrow \mathsf{FHE.Keygen}(1^\lambda, 1^{d'})$ and $(\mathsf{pk}, \mathsf{sk}) \leftarrow \mathsf{PKE.Keygen}(1^\lambda)$, then compute $\tilde{\mathsf{sk}} \leftarrow \mathsf{FHE.Enc}(\mathsf{hpk}, \mathsf{sk})$ and output $(\mathsf{pk}', \mathsf{sk}') := ((\mathsf{hpk}, \mathsf{pk}, \tilde{\mathsf{sk}}), \mathsf{hsk})$ where $d' = \mathrm{poly}(d, \lambda)$ is the maximal depth of C' as defined in Eval' below.
- $\mathsf{Enc}'(\mathsf{pk}', m)$: Compute and output $\mathsf{ct}' := m' \leftarrow \mathsf{PKE.Enc}(\mathsf{pk}, m)$.
- $\mathsf{Eval}'(\mathsf{ct}', C)$: Define the circuit $C_{\mathsf{ct}'}(\circ) := C(\mathrm{PKE.Dec}_\circ(\mathsf{ct}'))$. Compute and output $\mathsf{ct}'' := \mathsf{FHE.Eval}(\tilde{\mathsf{sk}}, C_{\mathsf{ct}'})$.
- $\mathsf{Dec}'(\mathsf{sk}', \mathsf{ct}')$: Output $\mathsf{FHE.Dec}(\mathsf{hsk}, \mathsf{ct}')$.

Fix $n, d \in \mathbb{N}$, a string $\mathsf{ct}' \in \{0,1\}^p$ and a circuit $C : \{0,1\}^n \to \{0,1\}$ of depth at most d. Consider $(\mathsf{pk}', \mathsf{sk}') \leftarrow \mathsf{Keygen}'(1^\lambda, 1^d)$, $\mathsf{ct}''_I \leftarrow \mathsf{Eval}'(\mathsf{ct}', I)$ and $\mathsf{ct}''_C \leftarrow \mathsf{Eval}'(\mathsf{ct}', C)$, then it holds that

$$\mathsf{ct}''_C = \mathsf{FHE.Eval}(\tilde{\mathsf{sk}}, C_{\mathsf{ct}'})$$

$$\mathsf{ct}''_I = \mathsf{FHE.Eval}(\tilde{\mathsf{sk}}, I_{\mathsf{ct}'})$$

and therefore

$$\begin{aligned}
\mathsf{Dec}'(\mathsf{sk}', \mathsf{ct}''_C) &= \mathsf{FHE.Dec}(\mathsf{hsk}, \mathsf{ct}''_C) \\
&= \mathsf{FHE.Dec}(\mathsf{hsk}, \mathsf{FHE.Eval}(\tilde{\mathsf{sk}}, C_{\mathsf{ct}'})) \\
&= C_{\mathsf{ct}'}(\mathsf{sk}) \\
&= C(\mathrm{PKE.Dec}_{\mathsf{sk}}(\mathsf{ct}'))
\end{aligned}$$

and

$$\begin{aligned}
C\left(\mathsf{Dec}'(\mathsf{sk}', \mathsf{ct}''_I)\right) &= C\left(\mathsf{FHE.Dec}(\mathsf{hsk}, \mathsf{ct}''_I)\right) \\
&= C\left(\mathsf{FHE.Dec}(\mathsf{hsk}, \mathsf{FHE.Eval}(\tilde{\mathsf{sk}}, I_{\mathsf{ct}'}))\right) \\
&= C\left(I_{\mathsf{ct}'}(\mathsf{sk})\right) \\
&= C\left(\mathrm{PKE.Dec}_{\mathsf{sk}}(\mathsf{ct}')\right).
\end{aligned}$$

3   Definitions of Designated-Prover NIZK

Definition 7 (DP-NIZK Proofs). *A designated-prover non-interactive zero-knowledge (DP-NIZK) proof Π_{DPNIZK} for an ensemble of **NP** languages $\mathcal{C} \subseteq \{C : \{0,1\}^* \times \{0,1\}^* \to \{0,1\}\}$ (where C is a verification circuit and $\mathcal{L}_C = \{x : \exists w \; C(x, w) = 1\}$ is the **NP** language determined by C) is defined by a tuple of* PPT *algorithms with the following syntax.*

- Setup$(1^\lambda, \mathsf{params}) \to (\mathsf{crs}, k_P)$ *takes as input the security parameter λ and possibly some parameters params of $\mathcal{C}$ (e.g. the maximal circuit depth), and outputs a common reference string crs and a proving key k_P.*
- Prove$_{\mathsf{crs}}(C, k_P, x, w) \to \pi$ *takes as input a common reference string crs, a circuit $C \in \mathcal{C}$, a proving key k_P, a statement x and a witness w. It outputs a proof π.*

- $\mathsf{Verify}_{crs}(C, x, \pi) \rightarrow \{0, 1\}$ *takes as input a common reference string* crs, *a circuit* $C \in \mathcal{C}$, *a statement* x *and a proof* π, *and either accepts (with output 1) or rejects (with output 0) the proof.*

Moreover, Π_{DPNIZK} *should satisfy the following properties:*

(Perfect) Completeness. For all sufficiently large λ, *for all circuits* $C \in \mathcal{C}$, *for all pairs* (x, w) *for which* $C(x, w) = 1$ *and for all* $(crs, k_P) \leftarrow \mathsf{Setup}(1^\lambda, \mathsf{params})$, *it holds that*

$$Pr\left[\mathsf{Verify}_{crs}\left(C, x, \mathsf{Prove}_{crs}(C, k_P, x, w)\right) = 1\right] = 1.$$

(Statistical) Soundness. For all sufficiently large λ *and for all* $C \in \mathcal{C}$ *it holds that*

$$Pr_{crs \leftarrow \mathsf{Setup}(1^\lambda, \mathsf{params})}\left[\exists (x, \pi) \ : \ x \notin \mathcal{L}_C \wedge \mathsf{Verify}_{crs}(C, x, \pi) = 1\right] = \mathrm{negl}(\lambda).$$

(Programmable CRS) Zero-Knowledge. For all PPT *adversaries* $\mathcal{A}$ *there exists a* PPT *simulator* $\mathcal{S} = (\mathcal{S}_1, \mathcal{S}_2)$ *such that*

$$\left| Pr\left[\mathcal{A}^{\mathsf{Prove}_{crs}(\cdot, k_P, \cdot, \cdot)}(crs) = 1\right] - Pr\left[\mathcal{A}^{\mathcal{O}(\cdot, crs', \tau, \cdot, \cdot)}(crs') = 1\right]\right| = \mathrm{negl}(\lambda),$$

where $(crs, k_P) \leftarrow \mathsf{Setup}(1^\lambda, \mathsf{params})$, $(crs', \tau) \leftarrow \mathcal{S}_1(1^\lambda, \mathsf{params})$ *and*

$$\mathcal{O}(C, crs', \tau, x, w) = \begin{cases} \mathcal{S}_2(C, crs', \tau, x) & C(x, w) = 1 \\ \bot & o.w. \end{cases},$$

and the probability is over the coins of $\mathcal{A}, \mathcal{S}, \mathsf{Setup}, \mathsf{Prove}$. *We also consider the a relaxed notion of* single-statement *zero knowledge, in which the (programmable CRS) zero-knowledge condition holds only for adversaries* $\mathcal{A}$ *that make at most a single query to the oracle.*

We sometimes require the following additional property.

Efficient Setup. A DP-NIZK proof system is efficient *if for all* λ *there exists a* $p = \mathrm{poly}(\lambda)$ *such that for all* params, *the complexity of* $\mathsf{Setup}(1^\lambda, \mathsf{params})$ *is* p *(and in particular does not depend on* params*).*

3.1 Single-Statement Global-Setup DP-NIZK Proofs

Definition 8 (Single-Statement Global-Setup DP-NIZK Proofs). *A single-statement global-setup DP-NIZK proof* Π_{1DPNIZK} *for an ensemble of* **NP** *languages* $\mathcal{C} \subseteq \{C : \{0,1\}^* \times \{0,1\}^* \rightarrow \{0,1\}\}$ *(where* C *is a verification circuit and* $\mathcal{L}_C = \{x \ : \ \exists w \ C(x, w) = 1\}$ *is the* **NP** *language determined by* C) *is defined by a tuple of* PPT *algorithms with the following syntax.*

- $\mathsf{GlobalSetup}(1^\lambda, \mathsf{params}) \rightarrow (crs, \mathsf{msk})$ *takes as input the security parameter* λ *and possibly some parameters* params *of* $\mathcal{C}$ *(e.g. the maximal circuit depth), and outputs a common reference string* crs *and a master secret key* msk.

- Setup$_{crs}$(msk) → (pk, k_P) *takes as input a common reference string* crs *and a master secret key* msk, *and outputs a public key* pk *and a proving key* k_P.
- Prove$_{crs}$(C, (pk, k_P), x, w) → π *takes as input a common reference string* crs, *a circuit* $C \in \mathcal{C}$, *a public key* pk, *a proving key* k_P, *a statement* x *and a witness* w. *It outputs a proof* π.
- Verify$_{crs}$(C, pk, x, π) → {0, 1} *takes as input a common reference string* crs, *a circuit* $C \in \mathcal{C}$, *a public key* pk, *a statement* x *and a proof* π, *and either accepts (with output 1) or rejects (with output 0) the proof.*

Moreover, Π_{1DPNIZK} *should satisfy the following properties:*

(Perfect) Completeness. For all sufficiently large λ, *for all* $C \in \mathcal{C}$ *and for all pairs* (x, w) *for which* $C(x, w) = 1$, *it holds that*

$$
\begin{aligned}
&(crs, \text{msk}) \leftarrow \text{GlobalSetup}(1^\lambda, \text{params}); \\
&(\text{pk}, k_P) \leftarrow \text{Setup}_{crs}(\text{msk}); \\
&\pi \leftarrow \text{Prove}_{crs}(C, (\text{pk}, k_P), x, w); \\
&\text{Verify}_{crs}(C, \text{pk}, x, \pi) = 1.
\end{aligned}
$$

(Statistical) Soundness. For all sufficiently large λ, *for all* $C \in \mathcal{C}$ *and for all* $(crs, \text{msk}) \leftarrow \text{GlobalSetup}(1^\lambda)$ *it holds that*

$$
Pr_{\text{pk} \leftarrow \text{Setup}_{crs}(\text{msk})} \left[\exists (x, \pi) \; : \; \begin{matrix} x \notin \mathcal{L}_C \\ \text{Verify}_{crs}(C, \text{pk}, x, \pi) = 1 \end{matrix} \right] = \text{negl}(\lambda).
$$

(Statistical) ϵ-Soundness. We also define a generalized notion of soundness as follows. For all sufficiently large λ, *for all* $C \in \mathcal{C}$ *for all* $(crs, \text{msk}) \leftarrow \text{GlobalSetup}(1^\lambda)$ *it holds that*

$$
Pr_{\text{pk} \leftarrow \text{Setup}_{crs}(\text{msk})} \left[\exists (x, \pi) \; : \; \begin{matrix} x \notin \mathcal{L}_C \\ \text{Verify}_{crs}(C, \text{pk}, x, \pi) = 1 \end{matrix} \right] = \epsilon(\lambda).
$$

(Programmable CRS) Single-Statement Zero-Knowledge. For all PPT *adversaries* $\mathcal{A}$ *there exists a* PPT *simulator* $\mathcal{S} = (\mathcal{S}_1, \mathcal{S}_2)$ *such that*

$$
\begin{aligned}
&\left| Pr \left[\mathcal{A}^{\{\text{pk}^i\} \leftarrow \text{Setup}_{crs}(\text{msk}), \; \text{Prove}_{crs}(\cdot, \text{pk}^i, k_P^i, \cdot, \cdot)}(crs) = 1 \right] \right. \\
&\left. - Pr \left[\mathcal{A}^{\{\text{pk}^i\} \leftarrow \mathcal{O}_1, \; \mathcal{O}_2(\cdot, \text{pk}^i, \cdot, \cdot)}(crs) = 1 \right] \right| = \text{negl}(\lambda),
\end{aligned}
$$

where

$$
\mathcal{O}_1 = (\text{pk}^i, \tau^i) \leftarrow \mathcal{S}_1(crs); \quad \text{Output pk}^i;
$$

and

$$
\mathcal{O}_2(C, \text{pk}^i, x, w) = \begin{cases} \mathcal{S}_2(crs, C, \text{pk}^i, \tau^i, x) & C \in \mathcal{C} \wedge C(x, w) = 1 \\ \bot & o.w. \end{cases},
$$

the probability is over the coins of $\mathcal{A}, \mathcal{S}, \text{Setup}, \text{Prove}$ *and* crs $\leftarrow$ GlobalSetup(1^λ, params), *and for every* i *the adversary* $\mathcal{A}$ *makes at most a single query of the form* Prove$_{crs}$($\cdot$, pk^i, k_P^i, $\cdot$, $\cdot$).

Efficiency. For all λ *there exists a* $p = \mathrm{poly}(\lambda)$ *such that for all* params *and all* $(crs, msk) \leftarrow$ GlobalSetup$(1^\lambda, params)$, *the complexity of* Setup$_{crs}$(msk) *is* p *(and in particular does not depend on* params*)*.

Remark 2. A global-setup DP-NIZK can be viewed as a generalization of standard DP-NIZK in the following manner. When the algorithm GlobalSetup is trivial (i.e. when it outputs crs $=$ msk $= 1^\lambda$), then the tuple of algorithms (Setup, Prove, Verify) qualify as a DP-NIZK proof system with efficient setup and single-statement zero-knowledge.

Remark 3. Every 1DPNIZK with standard statistical soundness can be amplified to 1DPNIZK with statistical ϵ-soundness for any $\epsilon = \frac{1}{2^{\mathrm{poly}(\lambda)}}$ via parallel composition of Setup, Prove, Verify for $log\left(\frac{1}{\epsilon}\right) = \mathrm{poly}(\lambda)$ times. The single-statement zero-knowledge simulator of the amplified proof system is derived via parallel composition of the simulator of the underlying 1DPNIZK proof system.

4 Our Construction

4.1 Single-Statement Global-Setup DP-NIZK from FHE

Theorem 1. *Assuming the existence of the following building blocks, for every* $d \in \mathbb{N}$ *there exists a single-statement global-setup DP-NIZK proof system as in Definition 8 for the ensemble* $\mathcal{C}_d$ *of* **NP** *relations that are verifiable by circuits* C *of depth at most* d.

1. *A leveled fully-homomorphic scheme* FHE $=$ (Keygen, Enc, Eval, Dec) *with correctness for all ciphertexts as in Definitions 5 and 6. For every* λ *let* $p = \mathrm{poly}(\lambda)$ *denote the size of* FHE *evaluated-ciphertexts and secret-keys as described in the "compactness" section of Definition 5.*
2. *A garbing scheme* GC $=$ (Garble, Eval) *as in Definition 4 where each label is of size* $\lambda = \mathrm{poly}(\lambda)$ *bits.*
3. *A statistically-binding equivocable commitment scheme* SBCS $=$ (Gen, Commit, Ver) *as in Definition 3.*

In the rest of this section we prove Theorem 1. We let params $= d$ be the depth bound of circuits in $\mathcal{C}_d$.

Construction 9 (Single-Statement Global-Setup DP-NIZK).

- GlobalSetup$(1^\lambda, 1^d)$:
  1. *Compute* (hpk, hsk) $\leftarrow$ FHE.Keygen$(1^\lambda, 1^d)$.
  2. *Output* crs $:=$ hpk *and* msk $:=$ hsk.
- Setup$_{crs}$(msk):
  1. *Parse* msk $=$ hsk *and let* $D_{\mathsf{hsk}} : \{0,1\}^p \to \{0,1\}$ *be the boolean circuit that has* hsk *hard-wired in it, takes as input an* FHE *evaluated-ciphertext* ct, *and decrypts* ct *with* hsk. *Compute*

$$\left(\widetilde{D_{\mathsf{hsk}}}, \{\mathsf{lab}_{i,b}\}_{i \in [p], b \in \{0,1\}}\right) \leftarrow \mathsf{GC.Garble}\left(1^\lambda, D_{\mathsf{hsk}}\right).$$

2. *For* $i \in [p]$ *and* $b \in \{0,1\}$ *compute* $crs_{i,b} \leftarrow$ SBCS.Setup$(1^\lambda, 1^\lambda)$ *and* $(c_{i,b}, d_{i,b}) \leftarrow$ SBCS.Commit$(crs_{i,b}, \mathsf{lab}_{i,b})$.
3. *Output*

$$\mathsf{pk} := \left(\widetilde{D_{hsk}}, \{crs_{i,b}, c_{i,b}\}_{i \in [p], b \in \{0,1\}} \right), \qquad k_P := \{\mathsf{lab}_{i,b}, \ d_{i,b}\}_{i \in [p], b \in \{0,1\}}.$$

- Prove$_{crs}(C, (\mathsf{pk}, k_P), x, w)$:
  1. *If* $C \notin \mathcal{C}_d$ *or* $C(x, w) \neq 1$ *then output* $\bot$.
  2. *Encrypt* $\mathsf{ct}_w \leftarrow$ FHE.Enc$_{hpk}(w)$.
  3. *Let* C'_x *be the circuit* $C_x(\circ) := C(x, \circ)$ *and compute homomorphically*

  $$\mathsf{ct}_b \leftarrow \text{FHE.Eval}_{hpk}(\mathsf{ct}_w, C_x).$$

  4. *Note that* $\mathsf{ct}_b \in \{0,1\}^p$. *For* $i \in [p]$ *let* $\widetilde{b}_i$ *denote the ith bit of* ct_b. *Output*

  $$\pi := \left(\mathsf{ct}_w, \{\mathsf{lab}_{i, \widetilde{b}_i}, \ d_{i, \widetilde{b}_i}\}_{i \in [p]} \right).$$

- Verify$_{crs}(C, \mathsf{pk}, x, \pi)$:
  1. *Parse* $crs = \mathsf{hpk}$, $\mathsf{pk} = \left(\widetilde{D_{hsk}}, \{crs_{i,b}, c_{i,b}\}_{i \in [p], b \in \{0,1\}} \right)$ *and* $\pi = (\mathsf{ct}_w, \{\mathsf{lab}_i, \ d_i\}_{i \in [p]})$.
  2. *Compute* $\mathsf{ct}_b \leftarrow$ FHE.Eval$_{hpk}(\mathsf{ct}_w, C_x)$ *(where* C_x *is as defined above).*
  3. *Note that* $\mathsf{ct}_b \in \{0,1\}^p$. *For* $i \in [p]$ *let* $\widetilde{b}_i$ *denote the ith bit of* ct_b. *Verify the label decommitments: for* $i \in [p]$ *compute*

  $$\text{SBCS.Ver} \left(crs_{i, \widetilde{b}_i}, c_{i, \widetilde{b}_i}, \mathsf{lab}_i, d_i \right),$$

  if any of those verifications fail then output 0 (reject).
  4. *Compute and output* GC.Eval $\left(\widetilde{D_{sk}}, \{\mathsf{lab}_i\}_{i \in [p]} \right)$.

Proof of Completeness. Fix λ, d, C, x, w where $C \in \mathcal{C}_d$ and $C(x, w) = 1$. Consider

$$(\mathsf{crs}, \mathsf{msk}) \leftarrow \text{GlobalSetup}(1^\lambda, 1^d),$$

$$(\mathsf{pk}, k_P) \leftarrow \text{Setup}_{crs}(\mathsf{msk}),$$

$$\pi \leftarrow \text{Prove}_{crs}(C, (\mathsf{pk}, k_P), x, w).$$

Parse $crs = \mathsf{hpk}$, $\mathsf{pk} = \left(\widetilde{D_{hsk}}, \{crs_{i,b}, c_{i,b}\}_{i \in [p], b \in \{0,1\}} \right)$ and $\pi = (\mathsf{ct}_w, \{\mathsf{lab}_i, \ d_i\}_{i \in [p]})$.

Consider the execution of Verify$_{crs}(C, \mathsf{pk}, x, \pi)$. Since FHE.Eval is deterministic, the value ct_b that is computed in Prove and in Verify is identical. Therefore the correctness of SBCS implies that all of the decommitment verifications in step (3) of Verify pass. Moreover, due to the correctness of FHE it holds that

$$\text{FHE.Dec}_{hsk}(\mathsf{ct}_b) = \text{FHE.Dec}_{hsk} \left(\text{FHE.Eval}_{hpk}(\mathsf{ct}_w, C_x) \right)$$
$$= \text{FHE.Dec}_{hsk} \left(\text{FHE.Eval}_{hpk}(\text{FHE.Enc}_{hpk}(w), C_x) \right)$$
$$= C_x(w) = C(x, w) = 1,$$

and the correctness of GC implies that the output in step (4) of Verify is FHE.Dec$_{hsk}(\mathsf{ct}_b) = 1$. $\qquad \square$

Proof of Soundness. Fix $\lambda, d \in \mathbb{N}$, $C \in \mathcal{C}_d$ and $(\mathsf{crs}, \mathsf{msk}) \leftarrow \mathsf{GlobalSetup}(1^\lambda, 1^d)$, and consider the random variable $\mathsf{pk} \leftarrow \mathsf{Setup}_{\mathsf{crs}}(\mathsf{msk})$. Assume that there exist (x, π) such that $x \notin \mathcal{L}_C$ and $\mathsf{Verify}_{\mathsf{crs}}(C, \mathsf{pk}, x, \pi) = 1$.

Parse $\mathsf{crs} = \mathsf{hpk}$, $\mathsf{pk} = \left(\widetilde{D}_{\mathsf{hsk}}, \{\mathsf{crs}_{i,b}, c_{i,b}\}_{i \in [p], b \in \{0,1\}} \right)$ and $\pi = (\mathsf{ct}_w, \{\mathsf{lab}'_i, d'_i\}_{i \in [p]})$, and recall that the values in the pk were computed as follows

$$\left(\widetilde{D}_{\mathsf{hsk}}, \{\mathsf{lab}_{i,b}\}_{i \in [p], b \in \{0,1\}} \right) \leftarrow \mathsf{GC.Garble}\left(1^\lambda, D_{\mathsf{hsk}}\right)$$

and

$$\forall i \in [p] : \quad (c_{i,b}, d_{i,b}) \leftarrow \mathsf{SBCS.Commit}(\mathsf{crs}_{i,b}, \mathsf{lab}_{i,b}).$$

Let $\mathsf{ct}_b \leftarrow \mathsf{FHE.Eval}_{\mathsf{hpk}}(\mathsf{ct}_w, C_x)$ be the value that is computed during Verify and for $i \in [p]$ let $\widetilde{b}_i$ denote the ith bit of ct_b.

Assume towards contradiction that for all $i \in [p]$ it holds that $\mathsf{lab}'_i = \mathsf{lab}_{i, \widetilde{b}_i}$, then by the correctness of GC and FHE, and since Verify outputs 1, it holds that

$$
\begin{aligned}
1 &= \mathsf{GC.Eval}\left(\widetilde{D}_{\mathsf{hsk}}, \{\mathsf{lab}'_i\}_{i \in [p]} \right) \\
&= \mathsf{GC.Eval}\left(\widetilde{D}_{\mathsf{hsk}}, \{\mathsf{lab}_{i, \widetilde{b}_i}\}_{i \in [p]} \right) \\
&= \mathsf{FHE.Dec}_{\mathsf{hsk}}(\mathsf{ct}_b) \\
&= \mathsf{FHE.Dec}_{\mathsf{hsk}}\left(\mathsf{FHE.Eval}_{\mathsf{hpk}}(\mathsf{ct}_w, C_x) \right) \\
&= C_x\left(\mathsf{FHE.Dec}_{\mathsf{hsk}}(\mathsf{FHE.Eval}_{\mathsf{hpk}}(\mathsf{ct}_w, I)) \right) \\
&= C\left(x, \mathsf{FHE.Dec}_{\mathsf{hsk}}(\mathsf{FHE.Eval}_{\mathsf{hpk}}(\mathsf{ct}_w, I)) \right),
\end{aligned}
$$

and therefore the string $w := \mathsf{FHE.Dec}_{\mathsf{hsk}}(\mathsf{FHE.Eval}_{\mathsf{hpk}}(\mathsf{ct}_w, I))$ satisfies $C(x, w) = 1$, with contradiction to the assumption that $x \notin \mathcal{L}_C$.

Therefore, it must be the case that there exists some $j \in [p]$ for which $\mathsf{lab}'_j \neq \mathsf{lab}_{j, \widetilde{b}_j}$. Since all of the verifications in step (3) of Verify pass successfully, it in particular holds that

$$\mathsf{SBCS.Ver}\left(\mathsf{crs}_{j, \widetilde{b}_j}, c_{j, \widetilde{b}_j}, \mathsf{lab}'_j, d'_j \right) = 1.$$

Therefore, denoting $\mathsf{crs}^* := \mathsf{crs}_{j, \widetilde{b}_j}$, $m_0^* := \mathsf{lab}_{j, \widetilde{b}_j}$, $m_1^* := \mathsf{lab}'_j$ and $d^* := d'_j$, and letting r^* be the randomness used during $\mathsf{pk} \leftarrow \mathsf{Setup}_{\mathsf{crs}}(\mathsf{msk})$ when computing $c_{j, \widetilde{b}_j} \leftarrow \mathsf{SBCS.Commit}(\mathsf{crs}_{j, \widetilde{b}_j}, \mathsf{lab}_{j, \widetilde{b}_j} \; ; \; r^*)$, it holds that

$$
Pr_{\mathsf{pk} \leftarrow \mathsf{Setup}_{\mathsf{crs}}(\mathsf{msk})} \left[\exists(x, \pi) : \begin{array}{c} x \notin \mathcal{L}_C \\ \mathsf{Verify}_{\mathsf{crs}}(C, \mathsf{pk}, x, \pi) = 1 \end{array} \right] \leq
$$

$$
Pr_{\mathsf{crs}^* \leftarrow \mathsf{SBCS.Setup}(1^\lambda, 1^\lambda)} \left[\exists(r^*, m_0^*, m_1^*, d^*) : \begin{array}{c} c^* \leftarrow \mathsf{SBCS.Commit}(\mathsf{crs}^*, m_0^* \; ; \; r^*) \\ m_0^* \neq m_1^* \\ \mathsf{SBCS.Verify}\left(\mathsf{crs}^*, c^*, m_1^*, d^*\right) = 1 \end{array} \right]
$$

$$= \mathsf{negl}(\lambda)$$

where the last equation is due to the binding of SBCS. $\square$

Proof of Single-Statement Zero-Knowledge. Let $\mathsf{SBCS}.\mathcal{S} = (\mathsf{SBCS}.\mathcal{S}^A, \mathsf{SBCS}.\mathcal{S}^B)$ be the equivocability simulator of SBCS and let $\mathsf{GC}.\mathcal{S}$ be the simulator of the garbling scheme. Define the single-statement zero-knowledge simulator $\mathcal{S} = (\mathcal{S}_1, \mathcal{S}_2)$ as follows:

- $\mathcal{S}_1(\mathsf{crs})$:
  1. Set $\mathsf{hsk} := 0^p$, where p is the upper-bound on the size of FHE secret-keys and evaluated ciphertexts, as in Definition 5.
  2. Let $D_{\mathsf{hsk}} : \{0,1\}^p \to \{0,1\}$ be the boolean circuit that has hsk hard-wired in it, takes as input an FHE evaluated-ciphertext ct, and decrypts ct with hsk. Compute

  $$\left(\widetilde{D_{\mathsf{hsk}}}, \{\mathsf{lab}_i\}_{i \in [p]} \right) \leftarrow \mathcal{S}_{\mathsf{GC}} \left(1^\lambda, 1^{|D_{\mathsf{hsk}}|}, 1 \right).$$

  3. For $i \in [p]$ and $b \in \{0,1\}$ compute $(\mathsf{crs}_{i,b}, c_{i,b}, \mathsf{td}_{i,b}^c) \leftarrow \mathsf{SBCS}.\mathcal{S}^A(1^\lambda, 1^\lambda)$.
  4. Set

  $$\mathsf{pk} := \left(\widetilde{D_{\mathsf{hsk}}}, \{c_{i,b}\}_{i \in [p], b \in \{0,1\}} \right), \qquad \tau := \left(\{\mathsf{lab}_i\}_{i \in [p]}, \{\mathsf{td}_{i,b}^c\}_{i \in [p], b \in \{0,1\}} \right).$$

- $\mathcal{S}_2(\mathsf{crs}, C, \mathsf{pk}, \tau, x)$:
  1. Parse $\mathsf{crs} = \mathsf{hpk}$, $\mathsf{pk} = \left(\widetilde{D_{\mathsf{hsk}}}, \{c_{i,b}\}_{i \in [p], b \in \{0,1\}} \right)$ and $\tau = \big(\{\mathsf{lab}_i\}_{i \in [p]}, \{\mathsf{td}_{i,b}^c\}_{i \in [p], b \in \{0,1\}} \big)$.
  2. Encrypt $\mathsf{ct}_w \leftarrow \mathsf{FHE}.\mathsf{Enc}_{\mathsf{hpk}}(0^k)$, where k is the bit-length of witnesses as determined by C.
  3. Compute homomorphically $\mathsf{ct}_b \leftarrow \mathsf{FHE}.\mathsf{Eval}_{\mathsf{hpk}}(\mathsf{ct}_w, C_x)$, where C_x is the circuit $C_x(\circ) := C(x, \circ)$.
  4. Note that $\mathsf{ct}_b \in \{0,1\}^p$. For $i \in [p]$ let $\widetilde{b}_i$ denote the ith bit of ct_b and compute

  $$d_i \leftarrow \mathsf{SBCS}.\mathcal{S}^B \left(\mathsf{crs}_{i,\widetilde{b}_i}, c_{i,\widetilde{b}_i}, \mathsf{td}_{i,\widetilde{b}_i}^c, \mathsf{lab}_i \right)$$

  5. Output

  $$\pi := \left(\mathsf{ct}_w, \{\mathsf{lab}_i, \ d_i\}_{i \in [p]} \right).$$

We now prove indistinguishability via a sequence of hybrids:

Hybrid $\mathcal{H}_0$. The real Setup, Prove algorithms.

Hybrid $\mathcal{H}_1$. We change the way that the values $\{\mathsf{crs}_{i,b}, c_{i,b}\}_{i \in [p], b \in \{0,1\}}$ and $\{d_{i,\widetilde{b}_i}\}_{i \in [p]}$ are computed in Setup and Prove respectively:

1. In Setup, for $i \in [p]$ and $b \in \{0,1\}$ compute $(\mathsf{crs}_{i,b}, c_{i,b}, \mathsf{td}_{i,b}^c) \leftarrow \mathsf{SBCS}.\mathcal{S}^A(1^\lambda, 1^\lambda)$.
2. In Prove, for $i \in [p]$ compute

$$d_i \leftarrow \mathsf{SBCS}.\mathcal{S}^B \left(\mathsf{crs}_{i,\widetilde{b}_i}, c_{i,\widetilde{b}_i}, \mathsf{td}_{i,\widetilde{b}_i}^c, \mathsf{lab}_{i,\widetilde{b}_i} \right).$$

Hybrids $\mathcal{H}_1$ and $\mathcal{H}_0$ are computationally indistinguishable due to the equivocability of SBCS.

Hybrid $\mathcal{H}_2$. Note that in Hybrid $\mathcal{H}_1$ the values $\{\mathsf{lab}_{i,\tilde{b}_i}\}_{i\in[p]}$ are only used during Prove, and the other p GC labels are never used. In this hybrid we change the way that the values $\widetilde{D_{\mathsf{hsk}}}$ and $\{\mathsf{lab}_{i,\tilde{b}_i}\}_{i\in[p]}$ are computed in Setup and Prove respectively:

1. In Setup, compute

$$\left(\widetilde{D_{\mathsf{hsk}}}, \{\mathsf{lab}_i\}_{i\in[p]}\right) \leftarrow \mathcal{S}_{\mathsf{GC}}\left(1^\lambda, 1^{|D_{\mathsf{hsk}}|}, 1\right).$$

2. In Prove, for $i \in [p]$ set $\mathsf{lab}_{i,\tilde{b}_i} := \mathsf{lab}_i$ and proceed as in the previous hybrid.

Hybrids $\mathcal{H}_2$ and $\mathcal{H}_1$ are computationally indistinguishable due to the security of GC.

Hybrid $\mathcal{H}_3$. Note that in Hybrid $\mathcal{H}_2$ the value hsk is only used when computing the FHE ciphertext ct_w in Prove. In this hybrids we change the way that ct_w is computed: Encrypt $\mathsf{ct}_w \leftarrow \mathsf{FHE.Enc}_{\mathsf{hpk}}(0^k)$, where k is the bit-length of witnesses as determined by C. Hybrids $\mathcal{H}_3$ and $\mathcal{H}_2$ are computationally indistinguishable due to the security of FHE.

Note that this hybrid is identical to the simulators $\mathcal{S}_1, \mathcal{S}_2$. □

Efficiency. Fix λ and note that by the compactness of FHE, there exists some $p = \mathrm{poly}(\lambda)$ such that for all params $= d$ and $(\mathsf{hpk}, \mathsf{hsk}) \leftarrow \mathsf{FHE.Keygen}(1^\lambda, 1^d)$, the size of FHE evaluated-ciphertexts and hsk is at most p. Denote $(\mathsf{crs}, \mathsf{msk}) = (\mathsf{hpk}, \mathsf{hsk})$ and note that the running time of $\mathsf{Setup}_{\mathsf{crs}}(\mathsf{msk})$ is bounded by some $p' = \mathrm{poly}(p, \lambda) = \mathrm{poly}(\lambda)$, i.e. for all params $= d$ and all $(\mathsf{crs}, \mathsf{msk}) \leftarrow \mathsf{GlobalSetup}(1^\lambda, 1^d)$, the complexity of $\mathsf{Setup}_{\mathsf{crs}}(\mathsf{msk})$ is at most p'.

4.2 DP-NIZK from Single-Statement Global-Setup DP-NIZK

Theorem 2. *Assuming the existence of the following building blocks, for every $d \in \mathbb{N}$ there exists a DPNIZK proof system as in Definition 7 for the ensemble $\mathcal{C}_d$ of **NP** relations that are verifiable by circuits C of depth at most d.*

1. *A pseudo-random function PRF $=$ (Setup, Eval) where w.l.o.g. for every $k \leftarrow$ PRF.Setup(1^λ) it holds that $k \in \{0,1\}^\lambda$.*
2. *A single-statement global-setup DPNIZK proof system 1DPNIZK $=$ (GlobalSetup, Setup, Prove, Verify) for $\{\mathcal{C}_d\}_d$, where w.l.o.g. for every $(\mathit{crs}, \mathsf{msk}) \leftarrow$ 1DPNIZK.GlobalSetup($1^\lambda, 1^d$) it holds that the randomness used by 1DPNIZK.Setup$_{\mathit{crs}}$(msk) is of size $\ell = \mathrm{poly}(\lambda)$, the size of msk is some $p = \mathrm{poly}(\lambda)$ and the scheme satisfies $(2^{\lambda-\ell}, \lambda)$-soundness.*
3. *A statistically-binding commitment scheme SBCS $=$ (Gen, Commit, Ver) as in Definition refdef:comm.*

In the rest of this section we prove Theorem 2.

Construction 10 (DP-NIZK from 1-DP-NIZK).

- Setup$(1^\lambda, 1^d)$:
  1. For $i = 0, \ldots, \lambda$ compute $(crs'_i, msk'_i) \leftarrow$ 1DPNIZK.GlobalSetup$(1^\lambda, 1^{d'_i})$ where d'_i is defined in the paragraph bellow.
  2. Sample $r \overset{\$}{\leftarrow} \{0,1\}^\ell$ and for $i \in [\lambda]$ sample $k_i \leftarrow$ PRF.Setup(1^λ).
  3. Compute $crs^* \leftarrow$ SBCS.Gen$(1^\lambda, 1^{p+\lambda})$ and for $i \in [\lambda]$ sample $(c^*_i, d^*_i) \leftarrow$ SBCS.Commit$(crs^*, (msk'_i, k_i))$.
  4. Sample $\left(pk^\emptyset, k^\emptyset_P\right) \leftarrow$ 1DPNIZK.Setup$_{crs'_0}(msk'_0)$.
  5. Output $crs := (\{crs'_i\}_{i=0,\ldots,\lambda}, crs^*, \{c^*_i\}_{i\in[\lambda]}, pk^\emptyset, r)$ and $k_P := \left(\{msk'_i\}_{i=0,\ldots,\lambda}, \{k_i, d^*_i\}_{i\in[\lambda]}, k^\emptyset_P\right)$.

- Prove$_{crs}(C, k_P, x, w)$:
  1. Parse $crs = (\{crs'_i\}_{i=0,\ldots,\lambda}, crs^*, \{c^*_i\}_{i\in[\lambda]}, pk^\emptyset, r)$ and $k_P = \left(\{msk'_i\}_{i=0,\ldots,\lambda}, \{k_i, d^*_i\}_{i\in[\lambda]}, k^\emptyset_P\right)$.
  2. Sample $m \overset{\$}{\leftarrow} \{0,1\}^\lambda$ and for $i \in [\lambda]$ let m^i denote length-i prefix of m (i.e. $m^i = m_1 m_2 \ldots m_i$). In particular denote $m^0 = \emptyset$ and $m^\lambda = m$.
  3. For $i = 0, \ldots, \lambda - 1$ do:
     (a) For $b \in \{0,1\}$ compute

     $$r^{m^i\|b} := r \oplus \text{PRF.Eval}_{k_{i+1}}(m^i\|b)$$

     and sample a 1-DPNIZK instance respective to (crs'_{i+1}, msk'_{i+1}) with $r^{m^i\|b}$ as randomness:

     $$\left(pk^{m^i\|b}, k^{m^i\|b}_P\right) := \text{1DPNIZK.Setup}_{crs'_{i+1}}(msk'_{i+1} \; ; \; r^{m^i\|b}).$$

     (b) Let C'_i be the relation that takes as a statement a pair $(\circ_0, \circ_1)$ and as a witness a 3-tuple $(\bullet_0, \bullet_1, \bullet_2)$, and outputs 1 iff

     $$\text{SBCS.Ver}\left(crs^*, c^*_{i+1}, (\bullet_0, \bullet_1), \bullet_2\right) = accept \quad \wedge$$
     $$\forall b \in \{0,1\}, \quad \circ_b = \text{1DPNIZK.Setup}_{crs'_{i+1}}\left(\bullet_0 \; ; \; r \oplus \text{PRF.Eval}_{\bullet_1}(m^i\|b)\right).$$

     Compute

     $$\pi^{m^i} \leftarrow \text{1DPNIZK.Prove}_{crs'_i}\left(C'_i, (pk^{m^i}, k^{m^i}_P),\right.$$
     $$\left.(pk^{m^i\|0}, pk^{m^i\|1}), (msk'_{i+1}, k_{i+1}, d^*_{i+1})\right).$$

  4. Compute

     $$\pi^m \leftarrow \text{1DPNIZK.Prove}_{crs'_\lambda}\left(C, (pk^m, k^m_P), x, w\right).$$

  5. Output $\pi := \left(m, \{pk^{m^i\|b}\}_{i=0,\ldots,\lambda-1, b\in\{0,1\}}, \{\pi^{m^i}\}_{i=0,\ldots,\lambda}\right).$

- $\text{Verify}_{crs}(C, x, \pi)$:
  1. *Parse* $crs = (\{crs_i'\}_{i=0,\ldots,\lambda}, crs^*, \{c_i^*\}_{i\in[\lambda]}, pk^{\emptyset}, r)$ *and* $\pi = \left(m, \{pk^{m^i\|b}\}_{i=0,\ldots,\lambda-1, b\in\{0,1\}}, \{\pi^{m^i}\}_{i=0,\ldots,\lambda}\right)$.
  2. *For* $i = 0, \ldots, \lambda - 1$ *compute*

  $$\text{1DPNIZK.Verify}_{crs_i'}\left(C_i', pk^{m^i}, (pk^{m^i\|0}, pk^{m^i\|1}), \pi^{m^i}\right)$$

  and if it rejects (outputs 0) then reject (output 0).
  3. *Compute and output*

  $$\text{1DPNIZK.Verify}_{crs_\lambda'}\left(C, pk^m, x, \pi^m\right).$$

Choice of Parameters. Note that by the efficiency of 1DPNIZK there is some fixed polynomial $p = p(\lambda)$ such that for all λ, d and $(crs', msk') \leftarrow \text{1DPNIZK.GlobalSetup}(1^\lambda, 1^d)$ the complexity of $\text{1DPNIZK.Setup}_{crs'}(msk')$ is p. Therefore, there is some fixed polynomial $p' = \text{poly}(\lambda, p) = \text{poly}(\lambda)$ such that for all λ, d and $(crs, k_P) \leftarrow \text{Setup}(1^\lambda, 1^d)$, the complexity of $\{C_i'\}_i$ (the circuits defined in step (b) of $\text{Prove}_{crs}(\cdot, k_P, \cdot, \cdot)$) is at most p'. It follows that there is also some $d'' = \text{poly}(\lambda)$ such that for all λ, d and $(crs, k_P) \leftarrow \text{Setup}(1^\lambda, 1^d)$, the *depth* of $\{C_i'\}_i$ is at most d''. For $i < \lambda$ we set $d_i' := d''$ and for $i = \lambda$ we set $d_\lambda' := d$.

Proof of Completeness. Fix λ, d, C, x, w where C is of depth at most d and $C(x, w) = 1$. Consider $(crs, k_P) \leftarrow \text{Setup}(1^\lambda, 1^d)$ and $\pi \leftarrow \text{Prove}_{crs}(C, k_P, x, w)$. Parse

$$crs = (\{crs_i'\}_{i=0,\ldots,\lambda}, crs^*, \{c_i^*\}_{i\in[\lambda]}, pk^{\emptyset}, r),$$
$$\pi = \left(\{pk^{m^i\|b}\}_{i=0,\ldots,\lambda-1, b\in\{0,1\}}, \{\pi^{m^i}\}_{i=0,\ldots,\lambda}\right).$$

Consider the execution of $\text{Verify}_{crs}(C, x, \pi)$. For $i = 0, \ldots, \lambda - 1$ it holds that

$$C_i'\left((pk^{m^i\|0}, pk^{m^i\|1}), (msk_{i+1}', k_{i+1}, d_{i+1}^*)\right) = 1$$

and therefore $\text{1DPNIZK.Verify}_{crs_i'}\left(C_i', (pk^{m^i\|0}, pk^{m^i\|1}), \pi^{m^i}\right) = 1$.

Moreover, since $C(x, w) = 1$, it holds that $\text{1DPNIZK.Verify}_{crs_\lambda'}(C, x, \pi^m) = 1$. □

Proof of (Statistical) Soundness.
Notation. For any fixed pair $(crs', msk') \leftarrow \text{1DPNIZK.Global.Setup}(1^\lambda, \text{params})$ we divide the space $\{0, 1\}^\ell$ into "good randomness" and "bad' randomness", where a string $s' \in \{0, 1\}^\ell$ is "bad randomness" respective to (crs', msk') if it breaks its soundness, i.e. if

$$\exists(C, x, \pi) : x \notin \mathcal{L}_C \wedge \text{1DPNIZK.Verify}_{crs'}(C, pk', x, \pi) = 1$$

where $pk' \leftarrow \text{1DPNIZK.Setup}_{crs'}(msk' ; s')$, and otherwise s' is "good randomness".

The following lemma follows immediately from the ϵ-soundness of 1DPNIZK if $\epsilon(\lambda) = 2^{-\lambda} \cdot \text{negl}(\lambda)$:

Lemma 2 *For every pair* $(crs', \mathsf{msk}') \leftarrow 1\mathsf{DPNIZK}.\mathsf{Global}.\mathsf{Setup}(1^\lambda, 1^d)$ *and every set* $S \subset \{0,1\}^\ell$ *of size at most* 2^λ,

$$Pr_{r \xleftarrow{\$} \{0,1\}^\ell}[\exists s \in S, \ s \oplus r \ is \ bad \ randomness \ respective \ to \ (crs', \mathsf{msk}')] = \mathsf{negl}(\lambda).$$

We now proceed with the proof of soundness. Fix λ, d and a circuit $C \in \mathcal{C}_d$. Consider the random variable $\mathsf{crs} \leftarrow \mathsf{Setup}(1^\lambda, 1^d)$ and the corresponding circuits $\{C'_i\}_{i=0,\ldots,\lambda-1}$ as described in step (b) of $\mathsf{Prove}_{\mathsf{crs}}$. Parse

$$\mathsf{crs} = (\{\mathsf{crs}'_i\}_{i=0,\ldots,\lambda}, \mathsf{crs}^*, \{c_i^*\}_{i\in[\lambda]}, \mathsf{pk}^\emptyset, r)$$

and recall that crs'_i was computed as $(\mathsf{crs}'_i, \mathsf{msk}'_i) \leftarrow 1\mathsf{DPNIZK}.\mathsf{GlobalSetup}$ $(1^\lambda, 1^{d'_i})$ and $r \xleftarrow{\$} \{0,1\}^\ell$. Moreover, the values $\{c_i^*\}_{i\in[\lambda]}$ were compute as

$$(c_i^*, d_i^*) \leftarrow \mathsf{SBCS}.\mathsf{Commit}(\mathsf{crs}^*, (\mathsf{msk}'_i, k_i))$$

where $\mathsf{crs}^* \leftarrow \mathsf{SBCS}.\mathsf{Gen}(1^\lambda, 1^{p+\lambda})$ and $k_i \leftarrow \mathsf{PRF}.\mathsf{Setup}(1^\lambda)$.

For all $i \in [\lambda]$ consider the set of strings $S^i := \{\mathsf{PRF}.\mathsf{Eval}_{k_i}(m^i)\}_{m^i \in \{0,1\}^i}$. Then due to Lemma 2, it holds that

$$Pr_{r \xleftarrow{\$} \{0,1\}^\ell}[\exists s \in S^i, \ s \oplus r \ is \ bad \ randomness \ respective \ to \ (\mathsf{crs}'_i, \mathsf{msk}'_i)] = \mathsf{negl}(\lambda). \tag{1}$$

Assume that there exist (x, π) such that $x \notin \mathcal{L}_C$ and $\mathsf{Verify}_{\mathsf{crs}}(C, x, \pi) = 1$. Parse

$$\pi = \left(m, \{\mathsf{pk}^{m^i\|b}\}_{i=0,\ldots,\lambda-1, b\in\{0,1\}}, \{\pi^{m^i}\}_{i=0,\ldots,\lambda}\right).$$

- Assume that there exists some $j \in [\lambda]$ such that the value $\mathsf{pk}^{m^{j-1}}$ (as appears in π) was computed "honestly" and the value pk^{m^j} (as appears in π) wasn't computed "honestly", i.e. assume that

$$\mathsf{pk}^{m^{j-1}} = \begin{cases} 1\mathsf{DPNIZK}.\mathsf{Setup}_{\mathsf{crs}'_{j-1}}(\mathsf{msk}'_{j-1}\,;\, r \oplus \mathsf{PRF}.\mathsf{Eval}_{k_{j-1}}(m^{j-1})) & j-1 > 0 \\ 1\mathsf{DPNIZK}.\mathsf{Setup}_{\mathsf{crs}'_0}(\mathsf{msk}'_0\,;\, s \xleftarrow{\$} \{0,1\}^\ell) & j-1 = 0 \end{cases}$$

and

$$\mathsf{pk}^{m^j} \neq 1\mathsf{DPNIZK}.\mathsf{Setup}_{\mathsf{crs}'_j}(\mathsf{msk}'_j\,;\, r \oplus \mathsf{PRF}.\mathsf{Eval}_{k_j}(m^j)).$$

Due to soundness of $1\mathsf{DPNIZK}$ respective to $(\mathsf{crs}'_{j-1}, \mathsf{msk}'_{j-1})$ and $\mathsf{pk}^{m^{j-1}}$ (which holds with all but negl. prob due to Eq. (1)), and since we assume that $\mathsf{Verify}_{\mathsf{crs}}(C, x, \pi) = 1$ and in particular that $1\mathsf{DPNIZK}.\mathsf{Verify}_{\mathsf{crs}'_{j-1}}\left(C'_{j-1}, \mathsf{pk}^{m^{j-1}}, (\mathsf{pk}^{m^{j-1}\|0}, \mathsf{pk}^{m^{j-1}\|1}), \pi^{m^{j-1}}\right) = 1$, with all but negl. prob, there exists a a string $\hat{w}_{j-1}$ such that

$$C'_{j-1}\left((\mathsf{pk}^{m^{j-1}\|0}, \mathsf{pk}^{m^{j-1}\|1}), \hat{w}_{j-1}\right) = 1. \tag{2}$$

Parse $\hat{w}_{j-1} = (\widehat{\mathsf{msk}}_j, \hat{k}_j, \hat{d}_j^*)$, then Eq. (2) in particular means that

$$\mathsf{pk}^{m^j} = \mathsf{1DPNIZK.Setup}_{\mathsf{crs}_j'}(\widehat{\mathsf{msk}}_j \; ; \; r \oplus \mathsf{PRF.Eval}_{\hat{k}_j}(m^j)).$$

Since we assume that pk^{m^j} wasn't generated honestly, i.e. that

$$\mathsf{pk}^{m^j} \neq \mathsf{1DPNIZK.Setup}_{\mathsf{crs}_j'}(\mathsf{msk}_j' \; ; \; r \oplus \mathsf{PRF.Eval}_{k_j}(m^j)),$$

it follows that $(\widehat{\mathsf{msk}}_j, \hat{k}_j) \neq (\mathsf{msk}_j', k_j)$. However, Eq. (2) also implies that

$$\mathsf{SBCS.Ver}\left(\mathsf{crs}^*, c_j^*, (\widehat{\mathsf{msk}}_j, \hat{k}_j), \hat{d}_j^*\right) = accept,$$

and therefore the decommitment $\hat{d}_j^*$ breaks the soundness of SBCS respective to (crs^*, c_j^*) and the pair of messages (msk_j', k_j) and $(\widehat{\mathsf{msk}}_j, \hat{k}_j)$. Since the soundness of SBCS respective to (crs^*, c_j^*) holds with all but negligible probability, it follows that the probability that $\mathsf{pk}^{m^{j-1}}$ was computed "honestly" and pk^{m^j} wasn't computed "honestly" is negligible.

Since for $j - 1 = 0$ the value $\mathsf{pk}^{m^{j-1}}$ is always generated honestly during Setup, an inductive argument implies that with all but negligible probability all of the values $\mathsf{pk}^0, \mathsf{pk}^{m^1}, \ldots, \mathsf{pk}^{m^{\lambda-1}}, \mathsf{pk}^m \in \pi$ were generated honestly.

Lastly, the soundness of 1DPNIZK respective to $(\mathsf{crs}_\lambda', \mathsf{msk}_\lambda')$ and pk^m implies that with all but negligible probability there is no (x, C, π^m) such that

$$x \notin \mathcal{L}_C \wedge \mathsf{1DPNIZK.Verify}_{\mathsf{crs}_\lambda'}(C, \mathsf{pk}^m, x, \pi^m) = 1.$$

$\square$

Proof of (Programmable CRS) Zero-Knowledge. Let $\mathsf{1DPNIZK}.\mathcal{S} = (\mathcal{S}_1, \mathcal{S}_2)$ be the single-statement zero-knowledge simulator of 1DPNIZK and define the zero-knowledge simulator $\mathcal{S} = (\mathcal{S}_1, \mathcal{S}_2)$ as follows:

- $\mathcal{S}_1(1^\lambda)$:
  1. For $i = 0, \ldots, \lambda$ compute $(\mathsf{crs}_i', \mathsf{msk}_i') \leftarrow \mathsf{1DPNIZK.GlobalSetup}(1^\lambda, 1^{d_i'})$.
  2. Sample $r \xleftarrow{\$} \{0,1\}^\ell$.
  3. Compute $\mathsf{crs}^* \leftarrow \mathsf{SBCS.Gen}(1^\lambda, 1^{p+\lambda})$ and for $i \in [\lambda]$ sample $(c_i^*, d_i^*) \leftarrow \mathsf{SBCS.Commit}(\mathsf{crs}^*, 0^{p+\lambda})$.
  4. Compute $(\mathsf{pk}^0, \tau^0) \leftarrow \mathsf{1DPNIZK}.\mathcal{S}_1(\mathsf{crs}_0')$.
  5. Output $\mathsf{crs} := (\{\mathsf{crs}_i'\}_{i=0,\ldots,\lambda}, \mathsf{crs}^*, \{c_i^*\}_{i \in [\lambda]}, \mathsf{pk}^0, r)$ and $\tau := \tau^0$.
- $\mathcal{S}_2(C, \mathsf{crs}, \tau, x)$:
  1. Parse $\mathsf{crs} = (\{\mathsf{crs}_i'\}_{i=0,\ldots,\lambda}, \mathsf{crs}^*, \{c_i^*\}_{i \in [\lambda]}, \mathsf{pk}^0, r)$ and $\tau = \tau^0$.
  2. Compute $m \xleftarrow{\$} \{0,1\}^\lambda$ and for $i \in [\lambda]$ let m^i denote length-i prefix of m (i.e. $m^i = m_1 m_2 \ldots m_i$). In particular denote $m^0 = \emptyset$ and $m^\lambda = m$.
  3. For $i = 0, \ldots, \lambda - 1$ do:

(a) For $b \in \{0,1\}$ compute

$$(\mathsf{pk}^{m^i\|b}, \tau^{m^i\|b}) \leftarrow \mathsf{1DPNIZK}.\mathcal{S}_1(\mathsf{crs}'_{i+1}).$$

(b) Compute

$$\pi^{m^i} \leftarrow \mathsf{1DPNIZK}.\mathcal{S}_2\left(\mathsf{crs}'_i, C'_i, \mathsf{pk}^{m^i}, \tau^{m^i}, (\mathsf{pk}^{m^i\|0}, \mathsf{pk}^{m^i\|1})\right).$$

4. Compute
$$\pi^m \leftarrow \mathsf{1DPNIZK}.\mathcal{S}_2\left(\mathsf{crs}'_\lambda, C, \mathsf{pk}^m, \tau^m, x\right).$$

5. Output $\pi := \left(m, \{\mathsf{pk}^{m^i\|b}\}_{i=0,\dots,\lambda-1, b\in\{0,1\}}, \{\pi^{m^i}\}_{i=0,\dots,\lambda}\right).$

We now prove indistinguishability via a sequence of $2 + 3\lambda$ hybrids:

Hybrid $\mathcal{H}_0$. The real Setup, Prove algorithms.

For $i = 0, \dots, \lambda - 1$ we define the hybrids $\{\mathcal{H}_{i,j}\}_{j\in[3]}$ and consider the sequence

$$\mathcal{H}_0, (\mathcal{H}_{0,1}, \mathcal{H}_{0,2}, \mathcal{H}_{0,3}), (\mathcal{H}_{1,1}, \mathcal{H}_{1,2}, \mathcal{H}_{1,3}), \dots, (\mathcal{H}_{\lambda-1,1}, \mathcal{H}_{\lambda-1,2}, \mathcal{H}_{\lambda-1,3}), \mathcal{H}_\lambda.$$

Hybrid $\mathcal{H}_{i,1}$. Note that in the previous hybrid, 1DPNIZK public-keys respective to crs'_i are sampled with real randomness, and msk'_i is not used elsewhere. We therefore can simulate them and proofs respective to them. Formally, we change the way that values of the form $\mathsf{pk}^{m^{i-1}\|b}$ and π^{m^i} are generated:

– If $i = 0$, change the way that pk^0 is generated during Setup:

$$(\mathsf{pk}^0, \tau^0) \leftarrow \mathsf{1DPNIZK}.\mathcal{S}_1(\mathsf{crs}'_0).$$

If $i > 0$, change the way that $\mathsf{pk}^{m^{i-1}\|b}$ is generated during the $(i-1)$th iteration of Step (3) of Prove:

$$(\mathsf{pk}^{m^{i-1}\|b}, \tau^{m^{i-1}\|b}) \leftarrow \mathsf{1DPNIZK}.\mathcal{S}_1(\mathsf{crs}'_i).$$

– Change the way that π^{m^i} is generated during the ith iteration of Step (3) of Prove:

$$\pi^{m^i} \leftarrow \mathsf{1DPNIZK}.\mathcal{S}_2\left(\mathsf{crs}'_i, C'_i, \mathsf{pk}^{m^i}, \tau^{m^i}, (pk^{m^i\|0}, \mathsf{pk}^{m^i\|1})\right).$$

Hybrids $\mathcal{H}_{i-1,3}$ and $\mathcal{H}_{i,1}$ are indistinguishable due to the single-statement zero-knowledge of 1DPNIZK respective to crs'_i.

Hybrid $\mathcal{H}_{i,2}$. Note that in the previous hybrid, the value d^*_{i+1} is never used. In this hybrid we change the way that the commitment c^*_{i+1} is computed:

$$(c^*_{i+1}, d^*_{i+1}) \leftarrow \mathsf{SBCS}.\mathsf{Commit}(\mathsf{crs}^*, 0^{p+\lambda}).$$

Hybrids $\mathcal{H}_{i,1}$ and $\mathcal{H}_{i,2}$ are indistinguishable due to the hiding of SBCS.

Hybrid $\mathcal{H}_{i,3}$. Note that in the previous hybrid, the value k_{i+1} is only used when computing

$$r^{m^i\|b} := r \oplus \mathsf{PRF}.\mathsf{Eval}_{k_{i+1}}(m^i\|b)$$

during Prove. In this hybrid we sample instead $r^{m^i\|b} \xleftarrow{\$} \{0,1\}^\ell$. Hybrids $\mathcal{H}_{i,2}$ and $\mathcal{H}_{i,3}$ are indistinguishable due to the pseudorandomness of PRF.

Hybrid $\mathcal{H}_\lambda$. Note that in the previous hybrid ($\mathcal{H}_{\lambda-1,3}$), 1DPNIZK public-keys respective to crs'_λ are sampled with real randomness, and msk'_λ is not used elsewhere.

Moreover, the values m which are used by the prover when answering proof queries are sampled uniformly at random from $\{0,1\}^\lambda$. Since the adversary is allowed to make at most a polynomial number of queries, with all but negligible probability the prover does not sample the same m for two different proof queries. In that case, for every pk^m that is sampled respective to crs'_λ, the prover generates at most a single proof.

We therefore can simulate those proofs with the single-statement zero-knowledge simulator of 1DPNIZK. Formally, we change the way that values of the form pk^m and π^m are generated:

- Change the way that pk^m is generated during the $(\lambda-1)$th iteration of Step (3) of Prove:

$$(\mathsf{pk}^m, \tau^m) \leftarrow \mathsf{1DPNIZK}.\mathcal{S}_1(\mathsf{crs}'_\lambda).$$

- Change the way that π^m is generated during Step (4) of Prove:

$$\pi^m \leftarrow \mathsf{1DPNIZK}.\mathcal{S}_2(\mathsf{crs}'_\lambda, C, \mathsf{pk}^m, \tau^m, x).$$

Hybrids $\mathcal{H}_{\lambda-1,3}$ and $\mathcal{H}_\lambda$ are indistinguishable due to the single-statement zero-knowledge of 1DPNIZK respective to crs'_λ. This hybrid is identical to the simulator, which completes the proof. □

References

[BF11a] Boneh, D., Freeman, D.M.: Homomorphic signatures for polynomial functions. In: Paterson, K.G. (ed.) EUROCRYPT 2011. LNCS, vol. 6632, pp. 149–168. Springer, Heidelberg (2011). https://doi.org/10.1007/978-3-642-20465-4_10

[BF11b] Boneh, D., Freeman, D.M.: Linearly homomorphic signatures over binary fields and new tools for lattice-based signatures. In: Catalano, D., Fazio, N., Gennaro, R., Nicolosi, A. (eds.) PKC 2011. LNCS, vol. 6571, pp. 1–16. Springer, Heidelberg (2011). https://doi.org/10.1007/978-3-642-19379-8_1

[BF14] Bellare, M., Fuchsbauer, G.: Policy-based signatures. In: Krawczyk [Kra14], pp. 520–537

[BFKW09] Boneh, D., Freeman, D., Katz, J., Waters, B.: Signing a linear subspace: signature schemes for network coding. In: Jarecki, S., Tsudik, G. (eds.) PKC 2009. LNCS, vol. 5443, pp. 68–87. Springer, Heidelberg (2009). https://doi.org/10.1007/978-3-642-00468-1_5

[BFM88] Blum, M., Feldman, P., Micali, S.: Non-interactive zero-knowledge and its applications (extended abstract). In: Simon, J. (ed.) Proceedings of the 20th Annual ACM Symposium on Theory of Computing, 2–4 May 1988, Chicago, Illinois, USA, pp. 103–112. ACM (1988)

[BGI13] Boyle, E., Goldwasser, S., Ivan, I.: Functional signatures and pseudorandom functions. In: Krawczyk [Kra14], pp. 501–519. IACR ePrint (2013). http://eprint.iacr.org/2013/401

[BV14] Brakerski, Z., Vaikuntanathan, V.: Lattice-based FHE as secure as PKE. In: Naor, M. (ed.) Innovations in Theoretical Computer Science, ITCS 2014, Princeton, NJ, USA, 12–14 January 2014, pp. 1–12. ACM (2014)

[BZ14] Boneh, D., Zhandry, M.: Multiparty key exchange, efficient traitor tracing, and more from indistinguishability obfuscation. In: Garay, J.A., Gennaro, R. (eds.) CRYPTO 2014. LNCS, vol. 8616, pp. 480–499. Springer, Heidelberg (2014). https://doi.org/10.1007/978-3-662-44371-2_27

[CCH+19] Canetti, R., et al.: from practice to theory. In: Charikar, M., Cohen, E. (eds.) Proceedings of the 51st Annual ACM SIGACT Symposium on Theory of Computing, STOC 2019, Phoenix, AZ, USA, 23–26 June 2019, pp. 1082–1090. ACM (2019)

[CJL09] Charles, D.X., Jain, K., Lauter, K.E.: Signatures for network coding. IJICoT **1**(1), 3–14 (2009)

[Dam92] Damgård, I.: Non-interactive circuit based proofs and non-interactive perfect zero-knowledge with preprocessing. In: Rueppel, R.A. (ed.) EUROCRYPT 1992. LNCS, vol. 658, pp. 341–355. Springer, Heidelberg (1993). https://doi.org/10.1007/3-540-47555-9_28

[FLS90] Feige, U., Lapidot, D., Shamir, A.: Multiple non-interactive zero knowledge proofs based on a single random string (extended abstract). In: 31st Annual Symposium on Foundations of Computer Science, St. Louis, Missouri, USA, 22–24 October 1990, vol. I, pp. 308–317. IEEE Computer Society (1990)

[Gen09] Gentry, C.: A fully homomorphic encryption scheme. PhD thesis, Stanford University (2009). crypto.stanford.edu/craig

[GGI+15] Gentry, C., Groth, J., Ishai, Y., Peikert, C., Sahai, A., Smith, A.D.: Using fully homomorphic hybrid encryption to minimize non-interactive zero-knowledge proofs. J. Cryptol. **28**(4), 820–843 (2015)

[GKKR10] Gennaro, R., Katz, J., Krawczyk, H., Rabin, T.: Secure network coding over the integers. In: Nguyen, P.Q., Pointcheval, D. (eds.) PKC 2010. LNCS, vol. 6056, pp. 142–160. Springer, Heidelberg (2010). https://doi.org/10.1007/978-3-642-13013-7_9

[GVW15] Gorbunov, S., Vaikuntanathan, V., Wichs, D.: Leveled fully homomorphic signatures from standard lattices. In: Servedio, R.A., Rubinfeld, R. (eds.) Proceedings of the Forty-Seventh Annual ACM on Symposium on Theory of Computing, STOC 2015, Portland, OR, USA, 14–17 June 2015, pp. 469–477. ACM (2015)

[KNYY19] Katsumata, S., Nishimaki, R., Yamada, S., Yamakawa, T.: Designated verifier/prover and preprocessing NIZKs from Diffie-Hellman assumptions. In: Ishai, Y., Rijmen, V. (eds.) EUROCRYPT 2019. LNCS, vol. 11477, pp. 622–651. Springer, Cham (2019). https://doi.org/10.1007/978-3-030-17656-3_22

[KNYY20] Katsumata, S., Nishimaki, R., Yamada, S., Yamakawa, T.: Compact NIZKs from standard assumptions on bilinear maps. In: Canteaut, A., Ishai, Y. (eds.) EUROCRYPT 2020. LNCS, vol. 12107, pp. 379–409. Springer, Cham (2020). https://doi.org/10.1007/978-3-030-45727-3_13

[KP95] Kilian, J., Petrank, E.: An efficient non-interactive zero-knowledge proof system for NP with general assumptions. Electron. Colloq. Comput. Complex. **2**(38) (1995)

[Kra14] Krawczyk, H. (ed.): PKC 2014. LNCS, vol. 8383. Springer, Heidelberg (2014). https://doi.org/10.1007/978-3-642-54631-0

[KW18] Kim, S., Wu, D.J.: Multi-theorem preprocessing NIZKs from lattices. In: Shacham, H., Boldyreva, A. (eds.) CRYPTO 2018. LNCS, vol. 10992, pp. 733–765. Springer, Cham (2018). https://doi.org/10.1007/978-3-319-96881-0_25

[MPR11] Maji, H.K., Prabhakaran, M., Rosulek, M.: Attribute-based signatures. In: Kiayias, A. (ed.) CT-RSA 2011. LNCS, vol. 6558, pp. 376–392. Springer, Heidelberg (2011). https://doi.org/10.1007/978-3-642-19074-2_24

[PS19] Peikert, C., Shiehian, S.: Noninteractive zero knowledge for NP from (plain) learning with errors. In: Boldyreva, A., Micciancio, D. (eds.) CRYPTO 2019. LNCS, vol. 11692, pp. 89–114. Springer, Cham (2019). https://doi.org/10.1007/978-3-030-26948-7_4

[Reg05] Regev, O.: On lattices, learning with errors, random linear codes, and cryptography. In: Gabow, H.N., Fagin, R. (eds.) STOC, pp. 84–93. ACM (2005). Full version in [?]

[SAH16] Sakai, Y., Attrapadung, N., Hanaoka, G.: Attribute-based signatures for circuits from bilinear map. In: Cheng, C.-M., Chung, K.-M., Persiano, G., Yang, B.-Y. (eds.) PKC 2016. LNCS, vol. 9614, pp. 283–300. Springer, Heidelberg (2016). https://doi.org/10.1007/978-3-662-49384-7_11

[SKAH18] Sakai, Y., Katsumata, S., Attrapadung, N., Hanaoka, G.: Attribute-based signatures for unbounded languages from standard assumptions. In: Peyrin, T., Galbraith, S. (eds.) ASIACRYPT 2018. LNCS, vol. 11273, pp. 493–522. Springer, Cham (2018). https://doi.org/10.1007/978-3-030-03329-3_17

[SMP87] De Santis, A., Micali, S., Persiano, G.: Non-interactive zero-knowledge proof systems. In: Pomerance, C. (ed.) CRYPTO 1987. LNCS, vol. 293, pp. 52–72. Springer, Heidelberg (1988). https://doi.org/10.1007/3-540-48184-2_5

[Tsa17] Tsabary, R.: An equivalence between attribute-based signatures and homomorphic signatures, and new constructions for both. IACR Cryptology ePrint Archive 2017:723 (2017)

Perfect Zero Knowledge: New Upperbounds and Relativized Separations

Peter Dixon[1], Sutanu Gayen[2], A. Pavan[1(✉)], and N. V. Vinodchandran[3]

[1] Iowa State University, Ames, USA
{tooplark,pavan}@iastate.edu, pavan@cs.iastate.edu
[2] National University of Singapore, Singapore, Singapore
sutanugayen@gmail.com
[3] University of Nebraska-Lincoln, Lincoln, USA
vinod@cse.unl.edu

Abstract. We investigate the complexity of problems that admit perfect zero-knowledge interactive protocols and establish new unconditional upper bounds and oracle separation results. We establish our results by investigating certain *distribution testing problems*: computational problems over high-dimensional distributions represented by succinct Boolean circuits. A relatively less-investigated complexity class SBP emerged as significant in this study. The main results we establish are:

(1) A unconditional inclusion that NIPZK ⊆ CoSBP.
(2) Construction of a relativized world in which there is a distribution testing problem that lies in NIPZK but not in SBP, thus giving a relativized separation of NIPZK (and hence PZK) from SBP.
(3) Construction of a relativized world in which there is a distribution testing problem that lies in PZK but not in CoSBP, thus giving a relativized separation of PZK from CoSBP.

Results (1) and (3) imply an oracle separating PZK from NIPZK. Our results refine the landscape of perfect zero-knowledge classes in relation to traditional complexity classes.

1 Introduction

The notion of *zero-knowledge interactive proof* was introduced in the seminal work of Goldwasser, Micali, and Rackoff. Since their introduction, zero-knowledge proofs have played a central role in the development of the foundations of cryptography [18]. Informally, it is a protocol between two parties, a prover and a verifier, where the prover wants to establish possession of certain knowledge without revealing the knowledge itself. Goldwasser, Micali, and Rackoff formalized this intuitive notion using the language of computational complexity theory. It is formalized as follows. A language or a promise problem L admits an interactive proof if there is a computationally unbounded prover P and a

---

Research supported in part by NSF grants 1849053, 1849048, 1934884.

R. Pass and K. Pietrzak (Eds.): TCC 2020, LNCS 12550, pp. 684–704, 2020.
https://doi.org/10.1007/978-3-030-64375-1_24

randomized polynomial-time verifier V such that for a positive instance x, V after interacting with P accepts x with high probability. On the other hand, for a negative instance x for *any* prover P^*, the verifier V after interacting with P^* accepts x with low probability. The protocol is a *statistical zero-knowledge* protocol if for positive instances, the interaction between P and V can be simulated by a randomized polynomial time simulator S so that the output distribution of the simulator is statistically close to the distribution of the interaction. The intuition is that the interaction itself can be simulated efficiently (in randomized polynomial-time) and hence the verifier is not gaining any additional knowledge other than what she can simulate by herself. The class of problems that admit statistical zero-knowledge interactive proofs is denoted by SZK. An important restriction is when the output distribution of the simulator is *identical* to the distribution of the interaction. Such a protocol is called a *perfect* zero-knowledge protocol, and the corresponding class of languages is denoted by PZK [17]. It is also possible to envision a *non-interactive* situation where the only communication in the protocol is from the prover to the verifier. Indeed, Blum, Feldman and Micali [6] and De Santis et al. [7] investigated such non-interactive zero-knowledge proofs and introduced the class NISZK. The corresponding perfect zero-knowledge class NIPZK was first investigated by Malka [21].

Zero-knowledge proofs and corresponding classes have played a key role in bridging computational complexity theory and cryptography. Several computationally hard problems that are not known to be NP-complete, including Graph Isomorphism, Quadratic Residuosity, and certain lattice problems, admit zero-knowledge proofs (some non-interactive and some perfect zero-knowledge) [12–14,23]. Also, several cryptosystems are based on the computational hardness of some of these problems. While these problems are computationally hard in the sense that they lack efficient algorithms, it is interesting that they are unlikely to be NP-complete. Establishing the relationships among zero-knowledge classes and proving traditional complexity class (such as PP and sub-classes of the Polynomial Hierarchy) upper bounds for them continues to be a research focus in complexity theory and cryptography [3,11,22,24]. While there are a few unconditional upper bound results, most of the results establish the hardness of proving upper bounds in the form of oracle results. We briefly discuss them below.

Unconditional Upper Bounds: Two main early upper bound results are that SZK is closed under complement [22,24] and SZK is upper bounded by AM ∩ coAM [3,11,22,24]. The latter result implies that NP-complete problems cannot have statistical zero-knowledge proofs unless it contradicts the widely held belief that the Polynomial Hierarchy is infinite [9]. The relationship between zero-knowledge classes and traditional probabilistic complexity classes has also been explored recently. In particular, Bouland *et al.* show that all problems with perfect zero-knowledge proofs admit unbounded probabilistic polynomial-time algorithms (that is, PZK ⊆ PP) [10].

Relativized Separations: Several significant upper bound questions, including whether various zero-knowledge classes are closed under complement and whether statistical zero-knowledge classes equal the corresponding perfect zero knowledge classes, turned out to be difficult to resolve and led to oracle separation results. Lovett and Zhang showed that the class NISZK is not closed under complement in a relativized world [20]. Bouland et al., in the same paper where they show PZK ⊆ PP, established a comprehensive set of oracle separation results. In particular, they showed that there are relativized worlds where NISZK (and thus SZK) is not in PP, PZK does not equal SZK, and NIPZK and PZK are not closed under complement.

Our Contributions
One of our main contributions is a new unconditional upper bound on the complexity class NIPZK.

Theorem 1. NIPZK ⊆ CoSBP.

The class SBP (Small Bounded-error Probability) was introduced by Böhler, Glaßer, and Meister [8] and is a bounded-error version of PP. Informally, a language is in PP if there is a probabilistic polynomial-time machine for which the ratio between the acceptance and the rejection probabilities is more than 1 for all the positive instances. We obtain the class SBP when we stipulate that this ratio is bounded away from 1, i.e, $(1 + \epsilon)$ for a fixed constant $\epsilon > 0$. This restriction greatly reduces the power of the class. In particular, it is known that SBP is a subset of AM and PP, and contains MA. This class has been studied in other contexts as well, such as in circuit complexity and quantum computation [1, 2, 5, 19]. Even though the relationship between SBP and zero knowledge classes has not been studied earlier, a curious connection exists between them. Watson showed that a certain promise problem regarding the min-entropy of samplable distributions is a complete problem for SBP [25]. Interestingly, the analogous problem where entropy instead of min-entropy is considered was shown to be complete for the class NISZK [16]. Our upper bound result improves the known containments NIPZK ⊆ AM ∩ coAM to NIPZK ⊆ AM ∩ CoSBP and NIPZK ⊆ PP to NIPZK ⊆ CoSBP.

We consider the possibility of establishing other upper bounds for perfect zero-knowledge classes. Since NIPZK is not known to be closed under complement, is it possible to show that NIPZK ⊆ SBP ∩ CoSBP? We also consider whether we can show that PZK itself lies in CoSBP. For these two questions, we prove the following relativized lower bound results.

Theorem 2. *There is an oracle O such that* NIPZK^O *(and thus* PZK^O*) is not in* SBP^O.

This result along with Theorem 1 implies that NIPZK is not closed under complement in a relativized world, a result that was recently established by Bouland et al. [10].

Theorem 3. *There is an oracle O such that* PZK^O *is not in* CoSBP^O.

As Theorem 1 relativizes with respect to any oracle, Theorems 1 and 3 together implies an oracle that separates PZK from NIPZK.

Corollary 1. *There is an oracle O such that* $\text{NIPZK}^O \subsetneq \text{PZK}^O$.

Figure 1 summarizes the known relationships among perfect zero knowledge classes and other complexity classes along with the results established in this work.

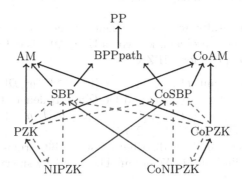

Fig. 1. $A \to B$ indicates that A is a subset of B, $A \dashrightarrow B$ indicates that there is a relativized world where A is not a subset of B. Red and Blue arrows indicate new results. (Color figure online)

Complexity of Distribution Testing Problems. We establish our results by investigating certain *distribution testing problems*: computational problems over high-dimensional distributions represented by succinct Boolean circuits. Interestingly, it turns out that versions of distribution testing problems characterize various zero-knowledge classes. The distribution testing problems are best formalized as *promise problems*. A *promise problem* is a pair of sets $\Pi = (\Pi_{Yes}, \Pi_{No})$ such that $\Pi_{Yes} \cap \Pi_{No} = \emptyset$. Π_{Yes} is called the set of 'yes' instances, and Π_{No} is called the set of 'no' instances. Given a Boolean circuit C mapping from m bits to n bits, the distribution sampled by C is obtained by uniformly choosing $x \in \{0,1\}^m$ and evaluating C on x. We often use C itself to denote the distribution sampled by the circuit C.

STATISTICAL DIFFERENCE (SD): Given two distributions sampled by Boolean circuits C and D, $\Pi_{Yes} = \{\langle C, D \rangle \mid dist(C, D) \leq 1/n\}$ and $\Pi_{No} = \{\langle C, D \rangle \mid dist(C, D) \geq 1 - 1/n\}$.

Here $dist$ denotes the statistical distance between the distributions. When one of the distributions is the uniform distribution, the above problem is called STATISTICAL DIFFERENCE TO UNIFORM (SDU). The seminal work of Sahai and Vadhan showed that SD is complete for the class SZK [24] and Goldreich, Sahai and Vadhan showed that SDU is complete for NISZK [16].

ENTROPY APPROXIMATION (EA): Given a samplable distribution C and an integer k, $\Pi_{Yes} = \{\langle C, k \rangle \mid \mathcal{H}(C) \geq k + 1\}$ and $\Pi_{No} = \{\langle C, k \rangle \mid \mathcal{H}(C) \leq k - 1\}$, where $\mathcal{H}$ is the entropy function.

Goldreich, Sahai and Vadhan showed that ENTROPY APPROXIMATION is complete for NISZK. In the above problem, if the entropy function $\mathcal{H}$ is replaced with the min-entropy function $\mathcal{H}_\infty$, the corresponding problem is known as MIN-ENTROPY APPROXIMATION (MEA). Watson showed that MEA is complete for SBP [25]. It is interesting to note that while ENTROPY APPROXIMATION is NISZK-complete, the analogous MIN-ENTROPY APPROXIMATION problem is complete for SBP.

To establish our results, we study variants of the above distribution testing problems. The following problem, known as UNIFORM, is defined by Malka and was shown to be complete for NIPZK [21].

UNIFORM: Given a circuit $D : \{0,1\}^m \to \{0,1\}^{n+1}$, let $D[1\ldots n]$ denote the distribution of the first n bits of D and let $D[n+1]$ denote the distribution of the last bit of D. $\Pi_{Yes} = \{\langle D \rangle \mid D[1\ldots n] = U_n, \Pr[D[n+1] = 1] \geq 2/3\}$ and $\Pi_{No} = \{\langle D \rangle \mid |sup(D) \cap \{0,1\}^n 1| \leq 2^n/3\}$.

Here U_n denotes the uniform distribution over n-bit strings and $sup(D)$ is the support of the distribution D. We obtain Theorem 1 by showing that UNIFORM is in CoSBP.

Note that we can obtain relativized versions of the distribution testing problems by providing oracle access to the circuits involved. To obtain Theorem 2, we consider a promise problem that is a variant of UNIFORM.

UNIFORM-OR-SMALL: Given a distribution D, $\Pi_{Yes} = \{\langle D \rangle \mid D = U\}$ and $\Pi_{No} = \{\langle D \rangle \mid |sup(D)| \leq 2^{n/2}\}$.

We show that a relativized version of this problem is not in SBP. For Theorem 3, we consider a variant of SD called DISJOINT-OR-IDENTICAL.

DISJOINT-OR-IDENTICAL: Given two samplable distributions C and D, $\Pi_{Yes} = \{\langle C, D \rangle \mid sup(C) \cap sup(D) = \emptyset\}$ and $\Pi_{No} = \{\langle C, D \rangle \mid C = D\}$ (i.e, the distance between C and D is either 1 or 0).

This problem can be shown to be in CoPZK. We construct an oracle relative to which this problem is not in SBP. Theorems 2 and 3 show that there exist relativized worlds where PZK is neither in SBP nor in CoSBP. This suggests that we cannot hope to improve the containment PZK $\subseteq$ PP to either SBP or CoSBP using relativizable techniques.

2 Notation and Definitions

Distributions. All the distributions considered in this paper are over a sample space of the form $\{0,1\}^n$ for some integer n. Given a distribution D, we use $D(x)$ to denote the probability of x with respect to D. We use U_n to denote the uniform distribution over $\{0,1\}^n$. We consider distributions sampled by circuits. Given a circuit C mapping m-bit strings to n-bit strings, the distribution encoded/sampled by the circuit C is the distribution $C(U_m)$. We often use C to denote both the circuit and the distribution sampled by it. Note that given access to the circuit, we can efficiently generate a sample of the distribution by evaluating C on a uniformly chosen m-bit string. For this reason, we call such distributions *efficiently samplable distributions* or just *samplable distributions*. We use $sup(D)$ to denote the set of strings for which $D(x) \neq 0$.

Given two distributions C and D over the same sample space S, the *statistical distance* between them, denoted by $dist(C, D)$, is defined as follows.

$$dist(C, D) = \max_{T \subseteq S}(C(T) - D(T)) = \sum_{C(x) > D(x)} (C(x) - D(x))$$

Complexity Classes. We refer the reader to the textbook by Arora and Barak [4] for definitions of standard complexity classes. For a complexity class $\mathcal{C}$, Co$\mathcal{C}$ denotes the class of complement languages/promise problems from $\mathcal{C}$. The class SBP was introduced in [8] and is defined as follows.

Definition 1. *A promise problem (Π_{Yes}, Π_{No}) is said to belong to the complexity class* SBP *if there exists a constant $\epsilon > 0$, a polynomial $p(\cdot)$, and a probabilistic polynomial-time Turing Machine M such that*

1. *If $x \in \Pi_{Yes}$ then $\Pr[M \text{ accepts}] \geq \frac{1+\epsilon}{2^{p(|x|)}}$*
2. *If $x \in \Pi_{No}$ then $\Pr[M \text{ accepts}] \leq \frac{1}{2^{p(|x|)}}$,*

SBP is sandwiched between MA and AM and is the largest known subclass of AM that is in PP. In fact, it is known that SBP is contained in the class BPP$_{\text{path}}$ which is a subclass of PP.

Theorem 4 ([8]). MA $\subseteq$ SBP $\subseteq$ AM *and* SBP $\subseteq$ BPP$_{\text{path}}$ $\subseteq$ PP.

Although we will not be using explicit definitions of zero-knowledge classes, we give necessary definitions for completeness.

Definition 2 (Non-Interactive protocol). *A **non-interactive protocol** is a pair of functions $\langle P, V \rangle$, the prover and verifier. On input x and random strings r_I, r_P, P sends a message $\pi = P(x, r_P, r_I)$ to V, and V computes $m = V(x, \pi, r_I)$. V accepts x if $m = 1$, and rejects if $m = 0$. The **transcript** of the interaction is the tuple $\langle x, r_I, \pi, m \rangle$.*

Note that the above definition implies that the random string r_I is shared between the prover and the verifier.

Definition 3 (NIPZK [16,21]). *A promise problem $\langle \Pi_{Yes}, \Pi_{No} \rangle$ is in NIPZK (Non-Interactive Perfect Zero Knowledge) if there is a non-interactive protocol $\langle P, V \rangle$ where V runs in polynomial time, and a randomized, polynomial-time computable simulator S, satisfying the following conditions:*

- *(Soundness:) For any function P^* and any $x \in \Pi_{No}$, $\Pr[V \text{ accepts}] \leq 1/3$*
- *(Completeness:) If $x \in \Pi_{Yes}$, $\Pr[V \text{ accepts}] \geq 2/3$*
- *(Zero Knowledge:) For any $x \in \Pi_{Yes}$, the distribution of $S(x)$ is identical to the distribution of the transcript generated by $\langle P, V \rangle$ on input x.*

The class NISZK (Non-Interactive Statistical Zero Knowledge) is defined similarly [16], except that we only require that the statistical distance between the distribution of $S(x)$ and the distribution of the transcript generated by $\langle P, V \rangle(x)$ be less than $1/p(n)$ for every polynomial $p(n)$. Malka [21] showed that the promise problem UNIFORM is complete for the class NIPZK.

Theorem 5 ([21]). *The promise problem* UNIFORM *is complete for* NIPZK.

3   NIPZK $\subseteq$ CoSBP

For a given distribution D, let $CP(D)$ denote the collision probability: $\Pr_{x,y \sim D}(x = y)$. The following lemma is folklore. See [15] for a proof.

Lemma 1. *For a given distribution D over $\{0,1\}^n$, if $dist(D, U_n) \geq \epsilon$, then $CP(D) \geq \frac{1+\epsilon^2}{2^n}$*

Theorem 1. NIPZK $\subseteq$ CoSBP

We show the result by proving that the NIPZK-complete problem UNIFORM is in CoSBP. We start with the following lemma.

Lemma 2. *Let D be a distribution on $n + 1$ bits, and let $T = \{x \in \{0,1\}^n \mid x1 \in sup(D)\}$. Suppose that $|T| \leq 2^n/3$ and $\Pr(D[n+1] = 1) = \frac{1}{3} + \epsilon$ for some $\epsilon \geq 0$. Then $dist(D[1 \ldots n], U_n)$ is at least ϵ.*

Proof. Recall that $dist(D[1 \ldots n], U_n) = \max_{S \subseteq \{0,1\}^n} \left| \Pr_{d \sim D[1 \ldots n]} [d \in S] - \Pr_{u \sim U_n} [u \in S] \right|$

$$\max_{S \subseteq \{0,1\}^n} \left| \Pr_{d \sim D[1 \ldots n]} [d \in S] - \Pr_{u \sim U_n} [u \in S] \right| \geq \left| \Pr_{d \sim D[1 \ldots n]} [d \in T] - \Pr_{u \sim U_n} [u \in T] \right|$$

$$\geq \left| \frac{1}{3} + \epsilon - \Pr_{u \sim U_n} [u \in T] \right|$$

$$= \left| \frac{1}{3} + \epsilon - \frac{|T|}{2^n} \right|$$

$$\geq \frac{1}{3} + \epsilon - \frac{2^n}{3} / 2^n = \epsilon$$

Now we prove Theorem 1 by giving a CoSBP algorithm for UNIFORM.

Proof. Recall the definition of UNIFORM: Given a circuit $D : \{0,1\}^m \to \{0,1\}^{n+1}$, $\Pi_{Yes} = \{D : D[1 \ldots n] = U_n, \Pr[D[n+1] = 1] \geq 2/3\}$ and $\Pi_{No} = \{D : |sup(D) \cap \{0,1\}^n 1| \leq 2^n/3\}$.

Consider the following randomized algorithm: Given D as input, get two samples d_0 and d_1 from D. If the first n bits of both d_0 and d_1 are the same, then *accept*. Else, obtain k additional samples from D, and if the last bit of all these samples is 0, then *accept*, otherwise *reject*.

If D is a 'yes' instance of UNIFORM, then the probability of accepting at the first step is $\frac{1}{2^n}$ and the probability of accepting at the second step is at most $\frac{1}{3^k}$, so the overall accept probability is $\leq \frac{1}{2^n} + \frac{1}{3^k}$. Suppose that D is a 'no' instance of UNIFORM. By Lemma 2, either $D[1\ldots n]$ is at least $\frac{1}{6}$ away from U_n, or $D[n+1]$ is 1 with probability at most $\frac{1}{2}$. Suppose that D is at least $1/6$ away from the uniform distribution, then by Lemma 1, the probability that the first n bits of d_0 and d_1 are the same is at least $\frac{37}{36}\frac{1}{2^n}$. Thus the algorithm accepts with probability at least $\frac{37}{36}\frac{1}{2^n}$. Now suppose that D is less than $1/6$ away from the uniform distribution. This implies that the last bit of D is 1 with probability at most $1/2$. Thus in this case the algorithm accepts with probability $\geq \frac{1}{2^k}$. Thus, a no instance is accepted with probability $\geq \min\left\{\frac{37}{36}\frac{1}{2^n}, \frac{1}{2^k}\right\}$. Choose $k = n - \log(37/36)$, so that a no instance is accepted with probability $\geq \frac{37}{36}\frac{1}{2^n}$ and a yes instance is accepted with probability $\leq \frac{1}{2^n} + \frac{3^{\log(37/36)}}{3^n}$. For large enough n, $\frac{37}{36}\frac{1}{2^n} \geq (1 + \frac{1}{40})(\frac{1}{2^n} + \frac{3^{\log(37/36)}}{3^n})$, so this is a CoSBP algorithm for UNIFORM.

4   Oracle Separations

In this section, we prove Theorems 2 and 3. We first prove a general approach that can be used to construct relativized worlds where promise problems involving circuits are not in SBP.

Lemma 3. *Let $\Pi = \langle \Pi_Y, \Pi_N \rangle$ be a promise problem whose instances are circuits. If there is an oracle circuit family $\{C_n\}_{n\geq 0}$ and a constant $c > 1$ with the following properties:*

- *C_n is a oracle circuit that maps n bits to n bits and makes oracle queries only to strings of length cn.*
- *There exist families of sets $\{A_n\}_{n\geq 0}, \{B_n\}_{n\geq 0} \subseteq \{0,1\}^{cn}$ such that for all n, $C_n^{A_n} \in \Pi_Y$ and $C_n^{B_n} \in \Pi_N$*
- *For every probabilistic polynomial-time Turing Machine M and infinitely many n, for every $D_i \in \{A_i, B_i, \emptyset\}$, $1 \leq i < n$*

$$\frac{\Pr[M^{(\cup_{i=1}^{n-1} D_i)\cup A_n}(C_n^{(\cup_{i=1}^{n-1} D_i)\cup A_n}) accepts]}{\Pr[M^{(\cup_{i=1}^{n-1} D_i)\cup B_n}(C_n^{(\cup_{i=1}^{n-1} D_i)\cup B_n}) accepts]} < 2,$$

then there exists an oracle O such that $\Pi^O \notin \mathrm{SBP}^O$

Proof. We first note that in this definition of SBP, we can choose ϵ to be 1 by using amplification techniques. Thus a promise problem is in SBP if there exists a polynomial $p(\cdot)$ and a probabilistic polynomial-time machine M such that on positive instances M accepts with probability at least $2/2^{p(n)}$ and on negative instances M accepts with probability at most $1/2^{p(n)}$. We call $p(\cdot)$ the *threshold polynomial* for M.

Let $\{M_i\}_{i>0}$ be an enumeration of the probabilistic polynomial-time machines. We consider an enumeration of tuples $\langle M_i, j \rangle_{i>0, j>0}$. In this enumeration considering $\langle M_i, j \rangle$ corresponds to the possibility that M_i is a SBP machine with threshold polynomial n^j. We first start with an empty oracle. Let $O_i = O \cap \{0,1\}^{ci}$. For each i, O_i will be one of $\emptyset$, A_i or B_i. Consider $\langle M_i, j \rangle$ and let n be a length for which O_n is not yet defined and for which the inequality from the lemma holds for the machine M_i. Suppose that M_i makes queries of length $\leq m$. Note that by this, we have defined O_i for all $i < cn$, thus $O \subseteq \{0,1\}^{<cn}$ and for every $i < n$ O_i is either $\emptyset$, A_i or B_i. Suppose that the acceptance probability of $M_i^{O \cup A_n}(C^{A_n})$ is less than $2/2^{n^j}$. We set O at length cn as A_n and for all the lengths from $cn + 1$ to m the oracle O is set to be $\emptyset$. Now C^{A_n} is a positive instance for which M_i cannot be a SBP machine with n^j as the threshold polynomial. Then we set O at length cn as A_n and move to the next tuple in the enumeration. Suppose that $M_i^{O \cup A_n}(C^{A_n})$ accepts with probability at least $2/2^{n^j}$. Now by the inequality from Lemma 3, the acceptance probability of $M_i^{O \cup B_n}(C^{B_n})$ is more than $1/2^{n^j}$. Note that C^{B_n} is a negative instance for which M_i is not a SBP machine with threshold polynomial n^j. Thus we make the oracle O at length cn to be B_n. It is easy to see that Π^O is not in SBP^O: Suppose not, and there exists a probabilistic polynomial-time machine M_i with threshold polynomial n^j. When we considered the tuple $\langle M_i, j \rangle$, we ensured that M_i does not have threshold polynomial n^j on $C^{O_{cn}}$.

4.1   Oracle Separation of NIPZK from SBP

In this section we show that Theorem 2 cannot be improved to show that NIPZK is a subset of SBP using relativizable techniques. For this we show that the oracle version of UNIFORM-OR-SMALL is not in SBP.

Theorem 6. *There exists an oracle O relative to which* UNIFORM-OR-SMALL *is not in* SBP^O.

Malka [21] showed that UNIFORM-OR-SMALL is in NIPZK, and this proof relativizes. Combining this with Theorem 6, we obtain Theorem 2. To prove Theorem 6, it suffices to exhibit sets A_n and B_n that satisfy the conditions of Lemma 3. We construct these sets via a probabilistic argument. We first provide a brief overview of this construction.

Remark: There is a alternate proof of the oracle separation between NIPZK from SBP which we describe here briefly. This was pointed out to us by one of the reviewers of TCC 2020. The proof uses known facts about the well-studied Permutation Testing Problem (PTP). PTP takes as input a truth table of a function $f : [N] \rightarrow [N]$ promised to be either a permutation on $[N]$ or $N/3$ away in Hamming distance from any permutation on $[N]$. The computational goal is to distinguish these two cases. It is known that in the query-complexity setting, there is a NIPZK protocol where the verifier uses public randomness to pick a uniform random element x from $[N]$, which is viewed as an element from the range of the function, and the prover is required to present a preimage of x. Aaronson, in [1] (Theorem 13), gave the construction of an oracle separating SZK from the Quantum version of SBP using degree arguments. The oracle is derived from the PTP problem where the author uses a SZK upper bound for PTP. However, as noted above the upper bound of NIPZK holds for PTP and hence it gives an oracle separation of NIPZK from SBP. Here we provide an oracle separation using elementary arguments.

Overview of the Proof: Consider a non-relativized world with the following restriction on how a probabilistic polynomial-time machine M can access the input circuit C: At the beginning the machine gets to see a sequence S of k independent samples from C. After this the machine ignores C. Note that in this model the underlying machine cannot perform adaptive sampling from C, nor can the machine generate samples that might be correlated. In this model it is easy to see that if C encodes the uniform distribution, the probability that M is presented with a specific sequence S of k samples is precisely $1/2^{nk}$. Thus the probability that the machine M accepts is $\sum_S \left(\frac{1}{2^{nk}} \Pr[M \text{ accepts } S] \right)$, summed over all sequences of size k.

Now given a subset D of $\{0,1\}^n$ of size $2^{n/2}$, let U_D be the uniform distribution over D. Consider the following experiment. Randomly pick D and let C_D be a circuit that samples U_D. Independently draw a sequence of k samples S from U_D and present them as input to M. (In a non-relativized setting, there may not be a small circuit that uniformly samples D, but in the relativized worlds we consider, this is not an issue.) We consider the acceptance probability of M over random choices of D, S and internal coin tosses of M. By a careful analysis we can show that this probability is very close to $\sum_S \left(\frac{1}{2^{nk}} \Pr[M \text{ accepts } S] \right)$. Thus the ratio between the acceptance probabilities of M when given samples from the uniform distributions and samples drawn from U_D (over a random choice of D) is less than $1 + \epsilon$ for any constant ϵ. By a probabilistic argument, there exists a subset D such that the acceptance probability of M on a positive instance (U) and a negative instance (U_D) are the same. Thus M is not a SBP machine.

The crux of the above idea is that when the samples are generated independently and nonadaptively, then it is possible to argue that a SBP machine cannot distinguish between whether they came from the uniform distribution or from a distribution with small support size. Now, we need to argue in the more general model, where a probabilistic machine can do adaptive sampling and generate samples that could be correlated to each other. A first approach to construct the sets A_n and B_n is to encode the uniform distribution in A_n and the distribution U_D in B_n. The set A_n can be defined as $\{\langle i,j \rangle \mid \text{the } i^{th} \text{ bit of the } j^{th} \text{ string of } \Sigma^n \text{ is } 1\}$ (in the standard lexicographical ordering). To define B_n given D, first consider the multiset $\mathbb{D}$ that contains $2^{n/2}$ copies of each elements of D. Thus the cardinality of $\mathbb{D}$ is 2^n. Now, the set B_n can be defined as tuples $\langle \ell, j \rangle$ where the ℓth bit of the jth string of $\mathbb{D}$ is 1. Consider the oracle circuit C which is defined as follows:

Definition 4 (Oracle Circuit). *Let C^O be a fixed linear-size oracle circuit, with n inputs and n outputs, defined as follows: On input $j \in \{1 \ldots 2^n\}$, $C^O(j)$ outputs $O(\langle \ell, j \rangle)$ for all ℓ between 1 and n. In other words, $C^O(j)$ outputs the jth string of O.*

Notice that C^{A_n} is the uniform distribution and C^{B_n} is uniform on D and the goal of the probabilistic machine is to distinguish between the distributions C^{A_n} and C^{B_n}. However, if we allow correlated sampling, a probabilistic machine can easily distinguish C^{A_n} and C^{B_n} by computing $C^O(j)$ and $C^O(j+1)$ for appropriate inputs j and $j+1$ and comparing whether they are equal or not. To guard against such behavior, we apply one more level of randomization - randomize the underlying order of the strings. Thus the tuple $\langle \ell, j \rangle$ will encode the ℓth string in an order that is not necessarily the standard lexicographic order. We argue that when we randomly order $\{0,1\}^n$, then adaptive and correlated sampling does not give significantly more information than independently generated samples. Now, we proceed to give a formal proof.

Detailed Proof: From now on, we fix a length n. We use a probabilistic argument to construct A_n and B_n. For A_n we consider $2^n!$ sets Y_i and define A_n to be one of them (using a probabilistic argument), and similarly for B_n we consider many sets N_{D_i} and define B_n to be one of them.

Definition 5 (Oracle families). *Let* $1 \le i \le 2^n!$ *index the set of all* $2^n!$ *permutations of* $\{0,1\}^n$.

Oracles for Yes instances: $Y_i = \{\langle \ell, j \rangle$: *the* ℓ^{th} *bit of the* j^{th} *string of the* i^{th} *permutation of* $\{0,1\}^n$ *is* $1\}$.

Oracles for No instances: *For each set* D *of size* $d = 2^m$ *(where* $m = n/2$ *) let* $\mathbb{D}$ *be the multiset that contains* 2^{n-m} *copies of each element of* D. *Thus* $|\mathbb{D}| = 2^n$, *and we define* N_{D_i} *as:* $N_{D_i} = \{\langle \ell, j \rangle$: *the* ℓ^{th} *bit of the* j^{th} *string of the* i^{th} *permutation of* $\mathbb{D}$ *is* $1\}$.

For the rest of this section, we will use Y to represent an arbitrary Y_i oracle, N to represent an arbitrary N_{D_i} oracle, and O to represent an arbitrary Y_i or N_{D_i}. Note that for every i, C^{Y_i} is the uniform distribution and $C^{N_{D_i}}$ is the uniform distribution on D and thus has small support.

We first prove the following lemma and show later how to build on it to arrive at the conditions specified in Lemma 3.

Lemma 4. *If* i *is uniformly chosen from* $\{1, \ldots, 2^n!\}$ *and* D *is uniformly chosen from all size* 2^m *subsets of* $\{0,1\}^n$, *then for any constant* $c > 1$ *and every probabilistic polynomial-time algorithm* A, *for large enough* n,

$$\frac{\Pr_{i,r}[A^{Y_i} \text{ accepts } C^{Y_i}]}{\Pr_{i,r,D}[A^{N_{D_i}} \text{ accepts } C^{N_{D_i}}]} \le c$$

where r *is the random choice of* A.

Without loss of generality we can assume that any oracle query that A^O makes can be replaced by evaluating the circuit C^O, by modifying A in the following way: whenever A queries the oracle O for the ith bit of the jth string, it evaluates $C^O(j)$ and it extracts the ith bit. We refer to this as a *circuit query*.

Let k be the number of circuit queries made by A, where k is bounded by a polynomial. We will use $q_1, \ldots q_k$ to denote the circuit queries, and denote the output $C^O(q_i)$ by u_i. We can assume without loss of generality that all q_i are distinct. We use S to denote a typical tuple of answers $\langle u_1, \cdots, u_k \rangle$. We will use A_S to denote the computation of algorithm A when the answers to the circuit queries are exactly S in that order. Notice that the A_S does not involve any oracle queries. Once A has received S, it can complete the computation without any circuit queries. So, the output of A_S is a random variable that depends only on the internal randomness r of A.

Claim. Without loss of generality we can assume that along any random path, A rejects whenever any $u_i = u_j$, $i \neq j$.

Proof. In a Yes instance, C^Y is uniform. Since C has n inputs and n outputs, C^Y is a 1-1 function. By the earlier assumption, u_i will never match any other u_j. In a No instance, C^N will have 2^{n-m} inputs for any output. Rejecting any time $u_i = u_j$ will not affect $\Pr[A$ accepts a Yes instance$]$, and it will reduce $\Pr[A$ accepts a No instance$]$. Thus the ratio of the probability of accepting an Yes instance and the probability of accepting a No instance only increases. We will show that this higher ratio is $< c$.

We will use the following notation.

- "A^O asks $\langle q, i \rangle$" is the event that "the ith circuit query made by A is $C^O(q)$." For simplicity, we write this event as "A^O asks q_i."
- "A^O gets $\langle u, i \rangle$" is the event that "$C^O(q) = u$ where q is the ith query". Again, for simplicity, we write this event as "A^O gets u_i."
- For $S = \langle u_1, \ldots u_k \rangle$, "$A^O$ gets S" is the event that "A^O gets u_1 and A^O gets u_2 and $\ldots A^O$ gets u_k (in that order)".

Lemma 5. *For any probabilistic algorithm A and for any fixed $S = \langle u_1, \ldots u_k \rangle$ where all u_i are distinct,*

$$\Pr_{i,r}[A^{Y_i} \text{ gets } S \text{ and accepts}] = \Pr_r[A_S \text{ accepts}] \prod_{j=0}^{k-1} \frac{1}{(2^n - j)}$$

Proof.

$$\Pr_{i,r}[A^{Y_i} \text{ gets } S \text{ and accepts}] = \Pr_{i,r}[A^{Y_i} \text{ gets } S] \times \Pr_{i,r}[A^{Y_i} \text{ accepts } | A^{Y_i} \text{ gets } S]$$

$$= \Pr_{i,r}[A^{Y_i} \text{ gets } S] \times \Pr_r[A_S \text{ accepts}]$$

The last equality is because A_S is independent of i as discussed before. We will show that $\Pr_{i,r}[A^{Y_i} \text{ gets } S] = \prod_{j=0}^{k-1} \frac{1}{(2^n - j)}$ which will prove the lemma.

$$\Pr_{i,r}[A^{Y_i} \text{ gets } S] = \prod_{j=0}^{k-1} \Pr_{i,r}[A^{Y_i} \text{ gets } u_{j+1} | A^{Y_i} \text{ gets } \langle u_1, u_2, \ldots, u_j \rangle]$$

For any fixed j let E_j denote the event "A^{Y_i} gets $\langle u_1, u_2, \ldots, u_j \rangle$". Then,

$$
\begin{aligned}
\Pr_{i,r}[A^{Y_i} \text{ gets } u_{j+1} | A^{Y_i} \text{ gets } \langle u_1, u_2, \ldots, u_j \rangle] &= \Pr_{i,r}[A^{Y_i} \text{ gets } u_{j+1} | E_j] \\
&= \sum_{q_{j+1}} \Pr_{i,r}[A^{Y_i} \text{ asks } q_{j+1} | E_j] \times \Pr_{i,r}[C^{Y_i}(q_{j+1}) = u_{j+1} | E_j] \\
&= \sum_{q_{j+1}} \Pr_{i,r}[A^{Y_i} \text{ asks } q_{j+1} | E_j] \times \Pr_i[C^{Y_i}(q_{j+1}) = u_{j+1} | E_j] \\
&= \sum_{q_{j+1}} \Pr_{i,r}[A^{Y_i} \text{ asks } q_{j+1} | E_j] \times \frac{1}{(2^n - j)} \\
&= \frac{1}{(2^n - j)} \times \sum_{q_{j+1}} \Pr_{i,r}[A^{Y_i} \text{ asks } q_{j+1} | E_j] \\
&= \frac{1}{(2^n - j)}
\end{aligned}
$$

The third equality is because the output of C is independent of r and the fourth equality follows from the fact that for a random permutation of $\{0, 1\}^n$, once j elements are fixed, there are $2^n - j$ equally likely possibilities for u_{j+1}. The lemma follows.

Lemma 6. *For any algorithm A and any fixed $S = \langle u_1, \ldots u_k \rangle$ where $u_i s$ are distinct,*

$$
\Pr_{i,r,D}[A^{ND_i} \text{ gets } S \text{ and accepts}] = \Pr_r[A_S \text{ accepts}] \times \prod_{j=0}^{k-1} \frac{(2^m - j)2^{n-m}}{(2^n - j)^2}
$$

Proof. The argument is identical to the proof of Lemma 5 except for the probability calculations.

$$
\begin{aligned}
\Pr_{i,r,D}[A^{ND_i} \text{ gets } S \text{ and accepts}] &= \Pr_{i,r,D}[A^{ND_i} \text{ gets } S] \times \Pr_{i,r,D}[A^{ND_i} \text{ accepts } | A^{ND_i} \text{ gets } S] \\
&= \Pr_{i,r,D}[A^{ND_i} \text{ gets } S] \times \Pr_r[A_S \text{ accepts}]
\end{aligned}
$$

The last equality is because A_S is independent of i and D. We will show that $\Pr_{i,r,D}[A^{ND_i} \text{ gets } S] = \prod_{j=0}^{k-1} \frac{(2^m - j)2^{n-m}}{(2^n - j)^2}$ which will prove the lemma.

$$
\Pr_{i,r,D}[A^{ND_i} \text{ gets } S] = \prod_{j=0}^{k-1} \Pr_{i,r}[A^{ND_i} \text{ gets } u_{j+1} | A^{ND_i} \text{ gets } \langle u_1, u_2, \ldots, u_j \rangle]
$$

We will reuse the notation E_j for convenience. For any fixed j, let E_j denote the event "A^{ND_i} gets $\langle u_1, u_2, \ldots, u_j \rangle$" Then,

$$\Pr_{i,r,D}[A^{ND_i} \text{ gets } u_{j+1}|A^{ND_i} \text{ gets } \langle u_1, u_2, \ldots, u_j \rangle] = \Pr_{i,r,D}[A^{ND_i} \text{ gets } u_{j+1}|E_j]$$

$$= \sum_{q_{j+1}} \Pr_{i,r,D}[A^{ND_i} \text{ asks } q_{j+1}|E_j] \times \Pr_{i,r,D}[C^{ND_i}(q_{j+1}) = u_{j+1}|E_j]$$

$$= \sum_{q_{j+1}} \Pr_{i,r,D}[A^{ND_i} \text{ asks } q_{j+1}|E_j] \times \Pr_{i,D}[C^{ND_i}(q_{j+1}) = u_{j+1}|E_j]$$

We will show that for any q, $\Pr_{i,D}[C^{Y_i}(q) = u_{j+1}|E_j] = \frac{(2^m-j)2^{n-m}}{(2^n-j)^2}$.

$$\Pr_{i,D}[C^{ND_i}(q) = u_{j+1}|E_j] = \Pr_{i,D}[u_{j+1} \in D|E_j] \times \Pr_{i,D}[C^{ND_i}(q) = u_{j+1}|u_{j+1} \in D, E_j]$$

$$= \frac{\binom{2^n-j-1}{2^m-j-1}}{\binom{2^n-j}{2^m-j}} \times \frac{2^{n-m}}{2^n - j}$$

$$= \frac{2^m - j}{2^n - j} \times \frac{2^{n-m}}{2^n - j}$$

$$= \frac{(2^m - j)2^{n-m}}{(2^n - j)^2}$$

The second equality is because of the following reasoning. There are $\binom{2^n-j}{2^m-j}$ choices of D where $u_1 \ldots u_j$ are included, and $\binom{2^n-j-1}{2^m-j-1}$ that include u_{j+1} as well. Given that $u_1, \ldots u_{j+1} \in D$, the probability that $C^{ND_i}(q_{j+1}) = u_{j+1}$ is $\frac{2^{n-m}}{2^n-j}$ (since there are 2^{n-m} copies of u_{j+1} remaining, and $2^n - j$ total things remaining).

We need the following claim.

Claim. For any polynomial $k = k(n)$ and any constant $c > 1$, for large enough n,

$$\prod_{j=0}^{k-1} \frac{2^n - j}{2^n - 2^{n/2}j} < c$$

Proof.

$$\prod_{j=0}^{k-1} \frac{2^n - j}{2^n - 2^{n/2}j} \leq \prod_{j=0}^{k-1} \frac{2^n}{2^n - 2^{n/2}j}$$

$$= \prod_{j=0}^{k-1} \frac{2^{n/2}}{2^{n/2} - j}$$

$$\leq \left(\frac{2^{n/2}}{2^{n/2} - k} \right)^k$$

$$= \left(1 + \frac{k}{2^{n/2} - k} \right)^k$$

For any polynomial $k = k(n)$, $\lim_{n \to \infty}(1 + \frac{k(n)}{2^{n/2}-k(n)})^{k(n)} = 1$. Hence the claim.

We can now prove Lemma 4.

Proof (Proof of Lemma 4).
From Lemmas 5 and 6, we have

$$\frac{\Pr_{i,r}[A^{Y_i} \text{ accepts } C^{Y_i}]}{\Pr_{i,r,D}[A^{N_{D_i}} \text{ accepts } C^{N_{D_i}}]} = \frac{\sum_S \Pr_{i,r}[A^{Y_i} \text{ gets } S \text{ and accepts }]}{\sum_S \Pr_{i,r,D}[A^{N_{D_i}} \text{ gets } S \text{ and accepts }]}$$

$$\leq \frac{\displaystyle\sum_{S \text{ distinct}} \Pr_{i,r}[A^{Y_i} \text{ gets } S \text{ and accepts }]}{\displaystyle\sum_{S \text{ distinct}} \Pr_{i,r,D}[A^{N_{D_i}} \text{ gets } S \text{ and accepts }]}$$

$$= \frac{\sum_{S \text{ distinct}} \Pr_r[A_S \text{ accepts}] \times \prod_{j=0}^{k-1} \frac{1}{(2^n - j)}}{\sum_{S \text{ distinct}} \Pr_r[A_S \text{ accepts}] \times \prod_{j=0}^{k-1} \frac{(2^m - j)2^{n-m}}{(2^n - j)^2}} \quad \text{(by lemmas 5 and 6)}$$

$$= \prod_{j=0}^{k-1} \frac{2^n - j}{2^n - 2^{n/2} j} \quad (\text{ substituting } m = n/2)$$

$$< c \text{ (by Claim 4.1)}$$

The second equality follows because when the oracle is Y_i, S is always disjoint (as we never ask the same query twice) and when the oracle is N_{D_i} we assume that the algorithm rejects when S is not distinct.

(Completing the proof of Theorem 6): We will construct an oracle so that conditions of Lemma 3 are met. By a probabilistic argument, there exists an i^* and D^* such that

$$\frac{\Pr[A^{Y_{i*}} \text{ accepts } C^{Y_{i*}}]}{\Pr[A^{N_{D_{i*}^*}} \text{ accepts } C^{N_{D_{i*}^*}}]}] < c$$

for every $c > 1$ (by Lemma 4). Now define A_n as Y_{i*} and B_n as $N_{D_{i*}^*}$. This looks very close to the conditions of Lemma 3 except that we restricted the oracles to be A_n and B_n, However, for Lemma 3, we require that oracles are of the form $(\cup_{i=1}^{n-1} D_i \cup A_n)$ and $(\cup_{i=1}^{n-1} D_i \cup B_n)$. To establish this, we resort to the standard techniques used in oracle constructions. Observe that the sets A_n and B_n can be constructed in double exponential time. Let $n_1 = 2$ and $n_j = 2^{2^{n_{j-1}}}$. We will satisfy the conditions of Lemma 3 at lengths of the form n_j. For every i that is not of the form n_j, we set both A_i and B_i to empty. Now $M^{\cup_{i=1}^{n_{j-1}} D_i \cup A_{n_j}}(C_{n_j}^{\cup_{i=1}^{n_{j-1}} D_i \cup A_{n_j}})$ can be simulated using $M^{A_{n_j}}(C^{A_{n_j}})$. As for queries whose length does not equal $c \cdot n_j$, the machine can find answers to oracle queries without actually making the query.

4.2   Oracle Separation of PZK from CoSBP

In this section we construct an oracle that separates PZK from CoSBP, thus proving Theorem 3. For this we exhibit an oracle where the promise problem DISJOINT-OR-IDENTICAL is not in SBP. This problem is a generalization of graph non-isomorphism (GNI) problem, in the sense that GNI reduces to this problem. Let G_1 and G_2 be two graphs, and let C_i be the distribution obtained by randomly picking a permutation π and outputting $\pi(G_i)$. Observe that if G_1 and G_2 are not isomorphic then the supports of C_1 and C_2 are disjoint, and if G_1 is isomorphic to G_2, then $C_1 = C_2$. Moreover the distributions C_1 and C_2 can be sampled by polynomial-size circuits. The PZK protocol for graph isomorphism can be adapted to show that DISJOINT-OR-IDENTICAL is in CoPZK.

Theorem 7. DISJOINT-OR-IDENTICAL *is in* CoPZK

Theorem 3 follows from the following theorem.

Theorem 8. *There exists an oracle O relative to which* DISJOINT-OR-IDENTICAL *is not in* SBP^O.

Input presentation: In the definition of DISJOINT-OR-IDENTICAL, the input instances are tuples consisting of two circuits. However, we will represent them as just one circuit C in the following manner. Given a circuit C, let C_0 denote the circuit obtained by fixing the first input bit of C to be 0, and the circuit C_1 denote the circuit obtained by fixing the first input bit of C to be 1. An input to DISJOINT-OR-IDENTICAL will be a circuit C and the goal is to distinguish between the cases "the support of distributions C_0 and C_1 are disjoint" or "C_0 and C_1 are identical distributions".

The proof structure of this result is similar to that of Theorem 6 and as in that case, the goal is to construct a circuit family C_n and families of sets A_n and B_n that satisfy the conditions of Lemma 3.

Definition 6 (Oracle families). *Let $i \in \{1 \ldots \binom{2^n}{2^{n-1}}\}$ index the partitions of $\{0,1\}^n$ into two sets S_i^0 and S_i^1 each of size 2^{n-1}. Let $j, k \in \{1 \ldots 2^{n-1}!\}$ index the possible permutations of S_i^0 and S_i^1, respectively.*
Oracles for Yes instances: *Y_{ijk} is an oracle for the set $\{\langle 0, \ell, m \rangle : the\ \ell^{th}\ bit\ of the\ m^{th}\ string\ in\ the\ j^{th}\ permutation\ of\ S_i^0 = 1\} \cup \{\langle 1, \ell, m \rangle : the\ \ell^{th}\ bit\ of\ the m^{th}\ string\ in\ the\ k^{th}\ permutation\ of\ S_i^1 = 1\}$.*
Oracles for No instances: *We construct the No instances similarly, except both 0 and 1 cases query S_i^0. That is, N_{ijk} is an oracle for the set $\{\langle 0, \ell, m \rangle : the\ \ell^{th} bit\ of\ the\ m^{th}\ string\ in\ the\ j^{th}\ permutation\ of\ S_i^0 = 1\} \cup \{\langle 1, \ell, m \rangle : the\ \ell^{th}\ bit of\ the\ m^{th}\ string\ in\ the\ k^{th}\ permutation\ of\ S_i^0 = 1\}$*

An oracle of the above form will be denoted by O which is a disjoint union of sets denoted by O^0 and O^1. Now we define the input circuits that sample the two distributions.

Definition 7 (Oracle circuits). *Let C^O be a fixed linear-size oracle circuit, with $n + 1$ inputs and n outputs, defined as follows: on input $\langle 0, j \rangle$ where $j \in \{1 \ldots 2^n\}$, $C^O(j)$ outputs $O^0(\langle \ell, j \rangle)$ for all ℓ between 1 and n, and on input $\langle 1, j \rangle$ where $j \in \{1 \ldots 2^n\}$, $C^O(j)$ outputs $O^1(\langle \ell, j \rangle)$ for all ℓ between 1 and n. In other words, $C^O(\langle 0, j \rangle)$ outputs the jth string of O^0 and $C^O(\langle 1, j \rangle)$ outputs the jth string of O^1.*

We will establish the following lemma. Then the proof of Theorem 8 follows by arguments identical to that of the previous oracle construction.

Lemma 7. *If i, j, k are uniformly and independently chosen from $\{1 \dots \binom{2^n}{2^{n-1}}\}$, $\{1 \dots 2^{n-1}!\}, \{1 \dots 2^{n-1}!\}$ respectively, then for any probabilistic polynomial-time algorithm A, for any constant $c > 1$, for large enough n,*

$$\frac{\Pr_{i,j,k,r}[A^{Y_{ijk}} \text{ accepts } C^{Y_{ijk}}]}{\Pr_{i,j,k,r}[A^{N_{i,j,k}} \text{ accepts } C^{N_{i,j,k}}]} \leq c$$

We use the same notation and make the most of same simplifications from the previous construction, with the following differences. The first difference is: let h be the (polynomial) maximum number of queries made by an algorithm A for any random choice of i, j, k, r. We will allow A to make $2h$ queries, two at a time, with the restriction that one must begin with 0 and the other must begin with 1. Notationally, $p_1 \dots p_h$ are the queries that begin with 0 and u_i is the result of query p_i. $q_1 \dots q_h$ are the queries that begin with 1 and v_i is the result of query q_i. S is the ordered multiset $\langle u_1, v_1, \dots u_h, v_h \rangle$. Notice that this is without loss of generality as A can simulate the original algorithm by ignoring either q_i or p_i as appropriate. The second difference is that, instead of assuming A rejects if any u_i matches any u_j, we assume A rejects if any u_i matches any v_j.

Lemma 8. *For any probabilistic algorithm A and for any fixed $S = \langle u_1, v_1, \dots u_h, v_h \rangle$ where all elements of S are distinct,*

$$\Pr_{i,j,k,r}[A^{Y_{ijk}} \text{ gets } S \text{ and accepts }] = \Pr_r[A_S \text{ accepts}] \times \prod_{\ell=0}^{h-1} \frac{1}{(2^n - 2\ell)(2^n - 2\ell - 1)}$$

Proof. Note that

$$\Pr_{i,j,k,r}[A^{Y_{ijk}} \text{ gets } S \text{ and accepts }] = \Pr_{i,j,k,r}[A^{Y_{ijk}} \text{ gets } S] \times \Pr_{i,j,k,r}[A^{Y_{ijk}} \text{ accepts } | A^{Y_{ijk}} \text{ gets } S]$$

$$= \Pr_{i,j,k,r}[A^{Y_{ijk}} \text{ gets } S] \times \Pr_r[A_S^{Y_{ijk}} \text{ accepts}]$$

Thus we need to prove that

$$\Pr_{i,j,k,r}[A^{Y_{ijk}} \text{ gets } S] = \prod_{\ell=0}^{h-1} \frac{1}{(2^n - 2\ell)(2^n - 2\ell - 1)}$$

We use E_ℓ to denote the event $A^{Y_{ijk}}$ gets $\langle u_1, v_1, \cdots u_\ell, v_\ell \rangle$. Note that

$$\Pr_{i,j,k,r}[A^{Y_{ijk}} \text{ gets } S] = \prod_{\ell=0}^{h-1} \Pr_{i,j,k,r}[A^{Y_{ijk}} \text{ gets } u_{\ell+1}, v_{\ell+1} \mid E_\ell]$$

and

$$\Pr_{i,j,k,r}[A^{Y_{ijk}} \text{ gets } u_{\ell+1}, v_{\ell+1} \mid E_\ell] = \sum_{p,q} \Pr_{i,j,k,r}[A^{Y_{ijk}} \text{ asks } p_{\ell+1} \text{ and } q_{\ell+1}|E_\ell]$$

$$\times \Pr_{i,j,k,r}[C^{Y_{ijk}}(p) = u_{\ell+1} \text{ and } C^{Y_{ijk}}(q) = v_{\ell+1} \mid A^{Y_{ijk}} \text{ asks } p_{\ell+1} \text{ and } q_{\ell+1}, E_\ell]$$

$$\begin{aligned}
\Pr[A &\text{ gets } u_{\ell+1}, v_{\ell+1}|A \text{ asks } p_{\ell+1}, q_{\ell+1}|E_\ell] \\
&= \Pr_i[u_{\ell+1} \in S_i^0, v_{\ell+1} \in S_i^1|E_\ell] \\
&\quad \times \Pr_j[u_{\ell+1} \text{ is the } p_{\ell+1}^{th} \text{ element of } S_i^0|E_\ell] \\
&\quad \times \Pr_k[v_{\ell+1} \text{ is the } q_{\ell+1}^{th} \text{ element of } S_i^{h+1}|E_\ell] \\
&= \binom{2^n - 2\ell - 2}{2^{n-1} - \ell - 1} \Big/ \binom{2^n - 2\ell}{2^{n-1} - \ell} \frac{1}{2^{n-1} - \ell} \frac{1}{2^{n-1} - \ell} \\
&= \frac{1}{(2^n - 2\ell)(2^n - 2\ell - 1)}
\end{aligned}$$

Thus

$$\Pr_{i,j,k,r}[A^{Y_{ijk}} \text{ gets } u_{\ell+1}, v_{\ell+1} \mid E_\ell] = \sum_{p,q} \Pr_{i,j,k,r}[A^{Y_{ijk}} \text{ asks } p_{\ell+1} \text{ and } q_{\ell+1}|E_\ell]$$

$$\times \Pr_{i,j,k,r}[C^{Y_{ijk}}(p) = u_{\ell+1} \text{ and } C^{Y_{ijk}}(q) = v_{\ell+1} \mid A^{Y_{ijk}} \text{ asks } p_{\ell+1} \text{ and } q_{\ell+1}, E_\ell]$$

$$= \frac{1}{(2^n - 2\ell)(2^n - 2\ell - 1)} \sum_{p,q} \Pr_{i,j,k,r}[A^{Y_{ijk}} \text{ asks } p_{\ell+1} \text{ and } q_{\ell+1}|E_\ell]$$

$$= \frac{1}{(2^n - 2\ell)(2^n - 2\ell - 1)}$$

Since $\Pr_{i,j,k,r}[A^{Y_{ijk}} \text{ gets } S] = \prod_{\ell=0}^{h-1} \Pr_{i,j,k,r}[A^{Y_{ijk}} \text{ gets } u_{\ell+1}, v_{\ell+1} \mid E_\ell]$, using this with the above derived equality we obtain that

$$\Pr_{i,j,k,r}[A^{Y_{ijk}} \text{ gets } S] = \prod_{\ell=0}^{h-1} \frac{1}{(2^n - 2\ell)(2^n - 2\ell - 1)}$$

This completes the proof of the lemma.

Now we turn to the No instances.

Lemma 9. *For any algorithm A, for any fixed $S = \{u_1, v_1, \ldots u_h, v_h\}$ that are all distinct,*

$$\Pr_{i,j,k,r}[A^{N_{ijk}} \text{ gets } S \text{ and accepts}] = \Pr_r[A_S \text{ accepts}] \times \prod_{\ell=0}^{h-1} \frac{(2^n - 2\ell)(2^n - 2\ell - 1)}{(2^{n-1} - 2\ell)(2^{n-1} - 2\ell - 1)} \frac{1}{(2^{n-1} - \ell)^2}$$

Proof. As before,

$$\Pr_{i,j,k,r}[A^{N_{ijk}} \text{ gets } S \text{ and accepts }] = \Pr_{i,j,k,r}[A^{N_{ijk}} \text{ gets } S] \times \Pr_{i,j,k,r}[A^{N_{ijk}} \text{ accepts } \mid A^{N_{ijk}} \text{ gets } S]$$

$$= \Pr_{i,j,k,r}[A^{N_{ijk}} \text{ gets } S] \times \Pr_{r}[A_S^{N_{ijk}} \text{ accepts}]$$

It suffices to show that

$$\Pr_{i,j,k,r}[A^{N_{ijk}} \text{ gets } S] = \prod_{\ell=0}^{h-1} \frac{(2^n - 2\ell)(2^n - 2\ell - 1)}{(2^{n-1} - 2\ell)(2^{n-1} - 2\ell - 1)} \frac{1}{(2^{n-1} - \ell)^2}$$

If E_ℓ denotes the event "$A^{N_{ijk}}$ gets $\langle u_1, v_1, \langle, u_\ell, v_\ell \rangle$", then

$$\Pr_{i,j,k,r}[A^{N_{ijk}} \text{ gets } S] = \prod_{\ell=0}^{h-1} \Pr_{ijkr}[A^{N_{ijk}} \text{ gets } u_{\ell+1}, v_{\ell+1} \mid E_\ell]$$

Now,

$$\Pr_{ijkr}[A^{N_{ijk}} \text{ gets } u_{\ell+1}, v_{\ell+1} \mid E_\ell] = \sum_{p,q} \Pr_{ijkr}[A^{N_{ijk}} \text{ asks } p_{\ell+1} \text{ and } q_{\ell+1} \mid E_\ell]$$

$$\times \Pr_{ijkr}[C^{N_{ijk}}(p) = u_{\ell+1} \text{ and } C^{N_{ijk}}(q) = v_{\ell+1} \mid E_\ell, A^{N_{ijk}} \text{ asks } p_{\ell+1} \text{ and } q_{\ell+1}]$$

Consider the event "$C^{N_{ijk}}(p) = u_{\ell+1}$ and $C^{N_{ijk}}(q) = v_{\ell+1}$", conditioned on E_ℓ and "$A^{N_{ijk}}$ asks $p_{\ell+1}$ and $q_{\ell+1}$". For this event to happen, it must be the case that both $u_{\ell+1}$ and $v_{\ell+1}$ are in S_i^0, and $u_{\ell+1}$ is the $p_{\ell+1}^{th}$ element of S_i^0, and $v_{\ell+1}$ is the $q_{\ell+1}^{th}$ element of S_i^0. The probability that both $u_{\ell+1}$ and $v_{\ell+1}$ are in S_i^0 given that E_ℓ and A asks $p_{\ell+1}$ and $q_{\ell+1}$ is

$$\binom{2^n - 2\ell - 2}{2^{n-1} - 2\ell - 2} \Big/ \binom{2^n - 2\ell}{2^{n-1} - 2\ell} = \frac{(2^{n-1} - 2\ell)(2^{n-1} - 2\ell - 1)}{(2^n - 2\ell)(2^n - 2\ell - 1)}$$

The probability that $u_{\ell+1}$ is the $p_{\ell+1}^{st}$ element given E_ℓ is $1/(2^{n-1} - \ell)$ and similarly, the probability that $v_{\ell+1}$ is the $q_{\ell+1}$st element given E_ℓ is $1/(2^{n-1} - \ell)$. Thus

$$\Pr_{ijkr}[A^{N_{ijk}} gets u_{\ell+1}, v_{\ell+1} \mid E_\ell] = \frac{(2^{n-1} - 2\ell)(2^{n-1} - 2\ell - 1)}{(2^n - 2\ell)(2^n - 2\ell - 1)} \frac{1}{(2^{n-1} - \ell)^2}$$

$$\sum_{p,q} \Pr_{ijkr}[A^{N_{ijk}} \text{ asks } p_{\ell+1} \text{ and } q_{\ell+1} \mid E_\ell]$$

$$= \frac{(2^{n-1} - 2\ell)(2^{n-1} - 2\ell - 1)}{(2^n - 2\ell)(2^{n-1} - 2\ell - 1)} \frac{1}{(2^n - \ell)^2}$$

Thus

$$\Pr_{i,j,k,r}[A^{N_{ijk}} \text{ gets } S] = \prod_{\ell=0}^{h-1} \frac{(2^{n-1} - 2\ell)(2^{n-1} - 2\ell - 1)}{(2^n - 2\ell)(2^n - 2\ell - 1)} \frac{1}{(2^{n-1} - \ell)^2},$$

and the lemma follows.

We need the following claim

Claim. For any polynomial $h = h(n)$ and any constant $c > 1$, for large enough n,

$$\prod_{\ell=0}^{h-1} \frac{(2^{n-1} - \ell)^2}{(2^{n-1} - 2\ell)(2^{n-1} - 2\ell - 1)} < c$$

Proof.

$$\prod_{\ell=0}^{h-1} \frac{(2^{n-1} - \ell)^2}{(2^{n-1} - 2\ell)(2^{n-1} - 2\ell - 1)} \leq \prod_{\ell=0}^{h-1} \frac{(2^{n-1} - \ell)^2}{(2^{n-1} - 2\ell - 1)^2}$$

$$\leq \prod_{\ell=0}^{h-1} \left(1 + \frac{\ell + 1}{2^{n-1} - 2\ell - 1}\right)^2$$

For any polynomial h, the above expression tends to 1 for large enough n.

The rest of the proof of Lemma 7 and that of Theorem 8 is identical to the proofs of Lemma 4 and Theorem 6.

Acknowledgements. We thank the reviewers for their comments and suggestions. In particular, we thank an anonymous reviewer for pointing an alternate proof of Theorem 2 and making us aware of Aaronson's work [1] and also for pointing out Corollary 1.

References

1. Aaronson, S.: Impossibility of succinct quantum proofs for collision-freeness. Quant. Inf. Comput. **12**(1–2), 21–28 (2012)
2. Aaronson, S., Aydinlioglu, B., Buhrman, H., Hitchcock, J.M., van Melkebeek, D.: A note on exponential circuit lower bounds from derandomizing Arthur-Merlin games. Electron. Colloq. Comput. Complex. (ECCC) **17**, 174 (2010)
3. Aiello, W., Hastad, J.: Statistical zero-knowledge languages can be recognized in two rounds. J. Comput. Syst. Sci. **42**(3), 327–345 (1991)
4. Arora, S., Barak, B.: Computational Complexity - A Modern Approach. Cambridge University Press, Cambridge (2009)
5. Aydinlioglu, B., Gutfreund, D., Hitchcock, J.M., Kawachi, A.: Derandomizing Arthur-Merlin games and approximate counting implies exponential-size lower bounds. Comput. Complex. **20**(2), 329–366 (2011)
6. Blum, M., Feldman, P., Micali, S.: Non-interactive zero-knowledge and its applications (extended abstract). In: Simon, J. (ed.) Proceedings of the 20th Annual ACM Symposium on Theory of Computing, 2–4 May 1988, Chicago, Illinois, USA, pp. 103–112. ACM (1988)
7. Blum, M., De Santis, A., Micali, S., Persiano, G.: Noninteractive zero-knowledge. SIAM J. Comput. **20**(6), 1084–1118 (1991)
8. Böhler, E., Glaßer, C., Meister, D.: Error-bounded probabilistic computations between MA and AM. J. Comput. Syst. Sci. **72**(6), 1043–1076 (2006)

9. Boppana, R.B., Håstad, J., Zachos, S.: Does co-NP have short interactive proofs? Inf. Process. Lett. **25**(2), 127–132 (1987)

10. Bouland, A., Chen, L., Holden, D., Thaler, J., Vasudevan, P.N.: On the power of statistical zero knowledge. In: Umans, C. (ed.) 58th IEEE Annual Symposium on Foundations of Computer Science, FOCS 2017, Berkeley, CA, USA, 15–17 October 2017, pp. 708–719. IEEE Computer Society (2017)

11. Fortnow, L.: The complexity of perfect zero-knowledge. In: Proceedings of the Nineteenth Annual ACM Symposium on Theory of Computing, STOC 1987, New York, NY, USA, pp. 204–209. Association for Computing Machinery (1987)

12. Gennaro, R., Micciancio, D., Rabin, T.: An efficient non-interactive statistical zero-knowledge proof system for quasi-safe prime products. In: Gong, L., Reiter, M.K. (eds.) CCS 1998, Proceedings of the 5th ACM Conference on Computer and Communications Security, San Francisco, CA, USA, 3–5 November 1998, pp. 67–72. ACM (1998)

13. Goldreich, O., Goldwasser, S.: On the limits of nonapproximability of lattice problems. J. Comput. Syst. Sci. **60**(3), 540–563 (2000)

14. Goldreich, O., Micali, S., Wigderson, A.: Proofs that yield nothing but their validity for all languages in NP have zero-knowledge proof systems. J. ACM **38**(3), 691–729 (1991)

15. Goldreich, O., Ron, D.: On testing expansion in bounded-degree graphs. Electron. Colloq. Comput. Complex. (ECCC), **7**(20) (2000)

16. Goldreich, O., Sahai, A., Vadhan, S.: Can statistical zero knowledge be made non-interactive? Or on the relationship of SZK and *NISZK*. In: Wiener, M. (ed.) CRYPTO 1999. LNCS, vol. 1666, pp. 467–484. Springer, Heidelberg (1999). https://doi.org/10.1007/3-540-48405-1_30

17. Goldwasser, S., Micali, S., Rackoff, C.: The knowledge complexity of interactive proof-systems. In: Proceedings of the Seventeenth Annual ACM Symposium on Theory of Computing, STOC 1985, New York, NY, USA, pp. 291–304. Association for Computing Machinery (1985)

18. Goldwasser, S., Micali, S., Rackoff, C.: The knowledge complexity of interactive proof systems. SIAM J. Comput. **18**(1), 186–208 (1989)

19. Kuperberg, G.: How hard is it to approximate the jones polynomial? Theory Comput. **11**, 183–219 (2015)

20. Lovett, S., Zhang, J.: On the impossibility of entropy reversal, and its application to zero-knowledge proofs. In: Kalai, Y., Reyzin, L. (eds.) TCC 2017. LNCS, vol. 10677, pp. 31–55. Springer, Cham (2017). https://doi.org/10.1007/978-3-319-70500-2_2

21. Malka, L.: How to achieve perfect simulation and a complete problem for non-interactive perfect zero-knowledge. J. Cryptol. **28**(3), 533–550 (2015)

22. Okamoto, T.: On relationships between statistical zero-knowledge proofs. J. Comput. Syst. Sci. **60**(1), 47–108 (2000)

23. Peikert, C., Vaikuntanathan, V.: Noninteractive statistical zero-knowledge proofs for lattice problems. In: Wagner, D. (ed.) CRYPTO 2008. LNCS, vol. 5157, pp. 536–553. Springer, Heidelberg (2008). https://doi.org/10.1007/978-3-540-85174-5_30

24. Sahai, A., Vadhan, S.P.: A complete problem for statistical zero knowledge. J. ACM **50**(2), 196–249 (2003)

25. Watson, T.: The complexity of estimating min-entropy. Comput. Complex. **25**(1), 153–175 (2014). https://doi.org/10.1007/s00037-014-0091-2

Author Index

Agrawal, Shweta I-117, I-149
Agrikola, Thomas III-639
Alagic, Gorjan III-153
Alon, Bar II-621
Alwen, Joël II-261
Ananth, Prabhanjan I-28, III-123
Applebaum, Benny II-562

Badertscher, Christian III-1
Ball, Marshall II-473
Bartusek, James II-320
Beimel, Amos II-683, III-499
Benhamouda, Fabrice I-260, II-349
Bienstock, Alexander II-198
Bitansky, Nir I-535, I-596
Block, Alexander R. II-168
Blum, Erica I-353
Bootle, Jonathan II-19
Boyle, Elette II-473
Brakerski, Zvika I-1, I-58, I-657
Branco, Pedro I-58
Broadbent, Anne III-92
Bünz, Benedikt II-1

Canetti, Ran II-410, III-1
Cascudo, Ignacio II-652
Cash, David I-457
Chattopadhyay, Eshan III-584
Chawin, Dror III-305
Chia, Nai-Hui III-181
Chiesa, Alessandro II-1, II-19, II-47
Childs, Andrew M. III-153
Choudhuri, Arka Rai I-535
Chung, Kai-Min III-181
Ciampi, Michele II-291
Cohen, Ran II-473, II-621
Coretti, Sandro II-261
Couteau, Geoffroy III-639
Cramer, Ronald III-444

Dachman-Soled, Dana II-595
Dai, Wei III-335
Damgård, Ivan II-229

Devadas, Srinivas I-381, I-412
Dixon, Peter I-684
Dodis, Yevgeniy II-198, III-241
Döttling, Nico I-1, I-58
Drucker, Andrew I-457

Eizenstadt, Noa I-596

Farràs, Oriol III-499
Farshim, Pooya III-241
Fehr, Serge III-470
Fernando, Rex II-379
Fitzi, Matthias I-322

Garay, Juan A. I-291
Garg, Rachit III-550
Garg, Sanjam I-58, I-88, I-657, II-320
Gayen, Sutanu I-684
Gaži, Peter I-322
Gentry, Craig I-260
Gorbunov, Sergey I-260
Goyal, Rishab I-229
Goyal, Vipul II-291
Grilo, Alex B. III-153
Grossman, Ofer III-530
Groth, Jens II-19
Gundersen, Jaron Skovsted II-652

Haagh, Helene II-229
Haitner, Iftach II-683, III-305
Hajiabadi, Mohammad I-88
Halevi, Shai I-260
Hesse, Julia III-1
Holmgren, Justin II-168, III-530
Hong, Matthew M. I-504
Hoover, Alexander I-457
Hubáček, Pavel III-614
Hung, Shih-Han III-153

Ishai, Yuval I-504, III-639
Islam, Rabib III-92

Jaeger, Joseph III-414
Jain, Abhishek I-28, II-291

Jarecki, Stanisław   III-639
Jin, Zhengzhong   I-28
Jost, Daniel   II-261

Kachlon, Eliran   II-562
Kamath, Chethan   III-614
Kaslasi, Inbar   II-139
Katz, Jonathan   I-353, III-390
Khurana, Dakshita   II-532
Kiayias, Aggelos   I-291, I-322
Kitagawa, Fuyuki   I-567
Kohl, Lisa   II-473
Kolobov, Victor I.   I-504
Komargodski, Ilan   II-379
Koppula, Venkata   I-229
Král, Karel   III-614
Krawczyk, Hugo   I-260
Kuykendall, Benjamin   I-627

La Placa, Rolando L.   III-123
Lai, Russell W. F.   I-504
Lanzenberger, David   III-207
Larsen, Kasper Green   I-486
Li, Xin   III-584
Lin, Chengyu   I-260
Lin, Huijia   II-349, II-502
Liu, Tianren   II-502
Liu, Yanyi   II-379
Liu-Zhang, Chen-Da   I-353, II-439
Loss, Julian   I-353, III-390
Lu, George   III-550

Malavolta, Giulio   I-28, I-58
Malkin, Tal   II-473
Masny, Daniel   II-320
Matsuda, Takahiro   I-567
Maurer, Ueli   II-439, III-207
Mazaheri, Sogol   III-241
Mazor, Noam   III-305
Mercer, Rebekah   II-229
Meyer, Pierre   II-473
Mishra, Pratyush   II-1
Moran, Tal   II-473
Mughees, Muhammad Haris   II-532
Mukherjee, Pratyay   II-320
Mularczyk, Marta   II-261

Narayanan, Varun   III-274
Nishimaki, Ryo   I-179

Nissim, Kobbi   II-683
Nitulescu, Anca   II-229

Omri, Eran   II-621
Orlandi, Claudio   II-229
Ostrovsky, Rafail   I-88, II-291

Panagiotakos, Giorgos   I-291
Paneth, Omer   I-596
Patra, Arpita   II-562
Pavan, A.   I-684
Poburinnaya, Oxana   II-410
Prabhakaran, Manoj   III-274
Prabhakaran, Vinod M.   III-274

Rabin, Tal   I-260
Rai Choudhuri, Arka   II-291
Reyzin, Leonid   I-260
Rosen, Alon   II-168
Rösler, Paul   II-198
Rotem, Lior   III-366
Rothblum, Guy N.   II-108, II-139
Rothblum, Ron D.   II-108, II-139, II-168
Russell, Alexander   I-322

Sahai, Amit   III-639
Schul-Ganz, Gili   II-77
Sealfon, Adam   II-139
Segev, Gil   II-77, III-366
Shi, Elaine   I-381, I-412, II-379
Shoup, Victor   III-31
Simkin, Mark   I-486
Slívová, Veronika   III-614
Soni, Pratik   II-168
Spooner, Nicholas   II-1
Stemmer, Uri   II-683
Suad, Tom   II-621

Tackmann, Björn   III-1
Tessaro, Stefano   III-241, III-335, III-414
Tsabary, Rotem   I-657

Vasudevan, Prashant Nalini   II-139
Vinodchandran, N. V.   I-684
Vusirikala, Satyanarayana   I-229

Wan, Jun   I-381, I-412
Waters, Brent   I-229, III-550
Wee, Hoeteck   I-210, II-502
Wichs, Daniel   I-149

Xiao, Hanshen   I-381, I-412
Xing, Chaoping   III-444
Xu, Jiayu   III-390

Yakoubov, Sophia   II-229
Yamada, Shota   I-117, I-149
Yamakawa, Takashi   I-567, III-181

Yeo, Kevin   I-486
Yogev, Eylon   II-47, III-530
Yuan, Chen   III-444, III-470

Zhandry, Mark   I-627, III-61
Zhang, Xihu   III-335
Zikas, Vassilis   III-1

Printed in the United States
By Bookmasters